ROLEX

Presents

The World of
Professional
Golf 2014

ROLEX

Presents

The World of Professional Golf 2014

Founded by
Mark H. McCormack

CARLTON
BOOKS

This book is dedicated to the memory of Bev Norwood (1947-2013)

First published by Carlton Books Ltd 2014
Carlton Publishing Group
20 Mortimer Street
London W1T 3JW

A CIP catalogue record for this book is available from the British Library.

ISBN: 978-1-78097-496-5

Editor: Jan Davis
Contributors: Andy Farrell, Doug Ferguson, Donald (Doc) Giffin, Marino Parascenzo
Designed and produced by Davis Design

Printed and bound by CPI Group (UK) Ltd, Croydon, CR0 4YY

Introduction

Rolex has done so many things over the years that were and are good for golf. Sponsorship of this publication is a prime example. My friends at Rolex, recognizing the historic and research value *The World of Professional Golf* has provided to the game continuously since the middle 1960s, stepped up in 2005 with the support necessary to continue its existence and the service it extends to the world of golf.

I well remember my conversations with my close friend and business manager, the late Mark McCormack, when he outlined his concept of filling a written gap in the game's history with an annual book carrying detailed stories and statistics covering every organized national and international tournament during that particular calendar year. The idea made complete sense to me and I encouraged him to proceed. He did, recruiting a group of talented golf journalists to work with him in producing the first edition that covered the 1966 season worldwide. Its publication has continued and grown in size and scope ever since, keeping pace with the tremendous growth of the game throughout the world.

Mark McCormack passed away in 2003, but his contribution to the historical record of golf did not die. Credit for this goes to IMG executives and others within the organization who considered the book an important continuing tribute to Mark and to the executives at Rolex, whose support has kept the literary chain intact.

Arnold Palmer
Orlando, Florida

Foreword
(Written in 1968)

It has long been my feeling that a sport as compelling as professional golf is deserving of a history, and by history I do not mean an account culled years later from the adjectives and enthusiasms of on-the-spot reports that have then sat in newspaper morgues for decades waiting for some patient drudge to paste them together and call them lore. Such works can be excellent when insight and perspective are added to the research, but this rarely happens. What I am talking about is a running history, a chronology written at the time, which would serve both as a record of the sport and as a commentary upon the sport in any given year—an annual, if you will....

When I embarked on this project two years ago (the first of these annuals was published in Great Britain in 1967), I was repeatedly told that such a compendium of world golf was impossible, that it would be years out of date before it could be assembled and published, that it would be hopelessly expensive to produce and that only the golf fanatic would want a copy anyway. In the last analysis, it was that final stipulation that spurred me on. There must be a lot of golf fanatics, I decided. I can't be the only one. And then one winter day I was sitting in Arnold Palmer's den in Latrobe, Pennsylvania, going through the usual motions of spreading papers around so that Arnold and I could discuss some business project, when Arnold happened to mention that he wanted to collect a copy of each new golf book that was published from now on, in order to build a golf library of his own. "It's really too bad that there isn't a book every year on the pro tour," he said. "Ah," I thought. "Another golf fanatic. That makes two of us." So I decided to do the book. And I have. And I hope you like it. If so, you can join Arnold and me as golf fanatics.

Mark H. McCormack
Cleveland, Ohio
January 1968

Mark H. McCormack
1930 – 2003

In 1960, Mark Hume McCormack shook hands with a young golfer named Arnold Palmer. That historic handshake established a business that would evolve into today's IMG, the world's premier sports and lifestyle marketing and management company —representing hundreds of sports figures, entertainers, models, celebrities, broadcasters, television properties, and prestigious organizations and events around the world. With just a handshake Mark McCormack had invented a global industry.

Sean McManus, President of CBS News and Sports, reflects, "I don't think it's an overstatement to say that like Henry Ford and Bill Gates, Mark McCormack literally created, fostered and led an entirely new worldwide industry. There was no sports marketing before Mark McCormack. Every athlete who's ever appeared in a commercial, or every right holder who sold their rights to anyone, owes a huge debt of gratitude to Mark McCormack."

Mark McCormack's philosophy was simple. "Be the best," he said. "Learn the business and expand by applying what you already know." This philosophy served him well, not only as an entrepreneur and CEO of IMG, but also as an author, a consultant and a confidant to a host of global leaders in the world of business, politics, finance, science, sports and entertainment.

He was among the most-honored entrepreneurs of his time. *Sports Illustrated* recognized him as "The Most Powerful Man in Sports." In 1999, ESPN's Sports Century listed him as one of the century's 10 "Most Influential People in the Business of Sport."

Golf Magazine called McCormack "the most powerful man in golf" and honored him along with Arnold Palmer, Gerald Ford, Dwight D. Eisenhower, Bob Hope and Ben Hogan as one of the 100 all-time "American Heroes of Golf." *Tennis* magazine and *Racquet* magazine named him "the most powerful man in tennis." Tennis legend Billie Jean King believes, "Mark McCormack was the king of sports marketing. He shaped the way all sports are marketed around the world. He was the first in the marketplace, and his influence on the world of sports, particularly his ability to combine athlete representation, property development and television broadcasting, will forever be the standard of the industry."

The London *Sunday Times* listed him as one of the 1000 people who influenced the 20th century. Alastair Cooke on the BBC said simply that "McCormack was the Oracle; the creator of the talent industry, the maker of people famous in their profession famous to the rest of the world and making for them a fortune in the process ... He took on as clients people already famous in their profession as golfer, opera singer, author, footballer, racing car driver, violinist—and from time to time if they needed special help, a prime minister, or even the Pope."

McCormack was honored posthumously by the Golf Writers Association of America with the 2004 William D. Richardson Award, the organization's highest honor, "Given to recognize an individual who has consistently made an outstanding contribution to golf."

Among McCormack's other honors were the 2001 PGA Distinguished Service Award, given to those who have helped perpetuate the values and ideals of the PGA of America. He was also named a Commander of the Royal Order of the Polar Star by the King of Sweden (the highest honor for a person living outside of Sweden) for his contribution to the Nobel Foundation.

Journalist Frank Deford states, "There have been what we love to call dynasties in every sport. IMG has been different. What this one brilliant man, Mark McCormack, created is the only dynasty ever over all sport."

Through IMG, Mark McCormack demonstrated the value of sports and lifestyle activities as effective corporate marketing tools, but more importantly, his lifelong dedication to his vocation—begun with just a simple handshake—brought enjoyment to millions of people worldwide who watch and cheer their heroes and heroines. That is his legacy.

ROLEX

Rolex is delighted to present *The World of Professional Golf*, a retrospective of the highlights and results of the 2013 golf championships and tours worldwide.

We celebrated many exciting moments over the year with the successes of our Testimonees, as well as through our partnerships with the leading institutions and tours in golf. One of the highlights included the return of Tiger Woods to the No. 1 spot in the world rankings after five PGA Tour wins this season, so soon after Rolex welcomed him back to its family of Testimonees the year before.

Rolex was also pleased to congratulate Testimonee Adam Scott on his exciting end to the season and victory at the 2013 Masters. The accomplishment marked two firsts: Scott's first major, as well as the first Masters win for an Australian.

Additionally, Rolex enjoyed more success at a major with another Testimonee, when American Phil Mickelson won The Open Championship, at Muirfield, for the first time in his career. It was a proud moment for Mickelson, who had been trying for the world's oldest major title since his first attempt in 1990.

This year, Rolex invited young American golfer Jordan Spieth to join the Rolex family of Testimonees, during his promising first season as a professional. Spieth, 20, proved his potential and was named the PGA Tour Rookie of the Year.

In team events, the highlights included the American team's victory at the 2013 Presidents Cup, as well as the European women's team's historic victory on U.S. soil at the Solheim Cup. Rolex is a partner of both the Presidents Cup and the Solheim Cup.

Rolex was also proud to support The Evian Championship in its first edition as a major. Rolex has believed in the success of this event since the partnership was forged in 2000 and looks forward to an enduring relationship.

Finally, in November, the European Tour and Rolex announced the extension of their long-standing partnership for a period of 10 years. The extension, which strengthens the brand's position as a leading sponsor in golf, will run until 2022 and includes Rolex's partnership with the Ryder Cup.

Rolex is honoured to be so closely associated with a sport that embodies excellence, performance and prestige – qualities that lie at the heart of the brand.

We hope that you will enjoy the 2014 edition of *The World of Professional Golf*.

Gian Riccardo Marini
Rolex SA
Chief Executive Officer

Rolex and Golf

Rolex is proud to be a major force at play behind the finest events, players and organizations in golf. The company's involvement began with Arnold Palmer in 1967. He, along with fellow Rolex Testimonees Jack Nicklaus and Gary Player — otherwise known as The Big Three — contributed to modernizing golf and giving it a worldwide dimension. Since 1967, the relationship between Rolex and golf has continuously grown and prospered. At present, Rolex is golf's leading supporter and is associated with the most important and prestigious entities governing the sport worldwide, as well as with golf's principal professional tours, competitions and athletes.

David Cannon/Getty Images

Tiger Woods at the Arnold Palmer Invitational

Matteo Manassero

Bernhard Langer

U.S. Open Championship

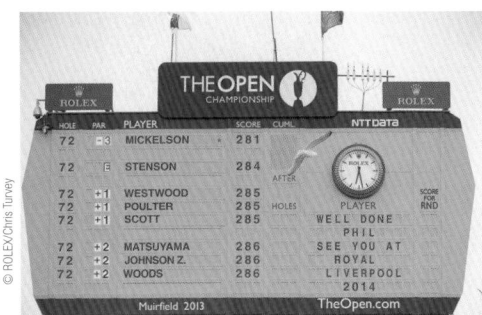

The Open Championship

Fred Couples with the Presidents Cup

The Rolex Rankings Top 10

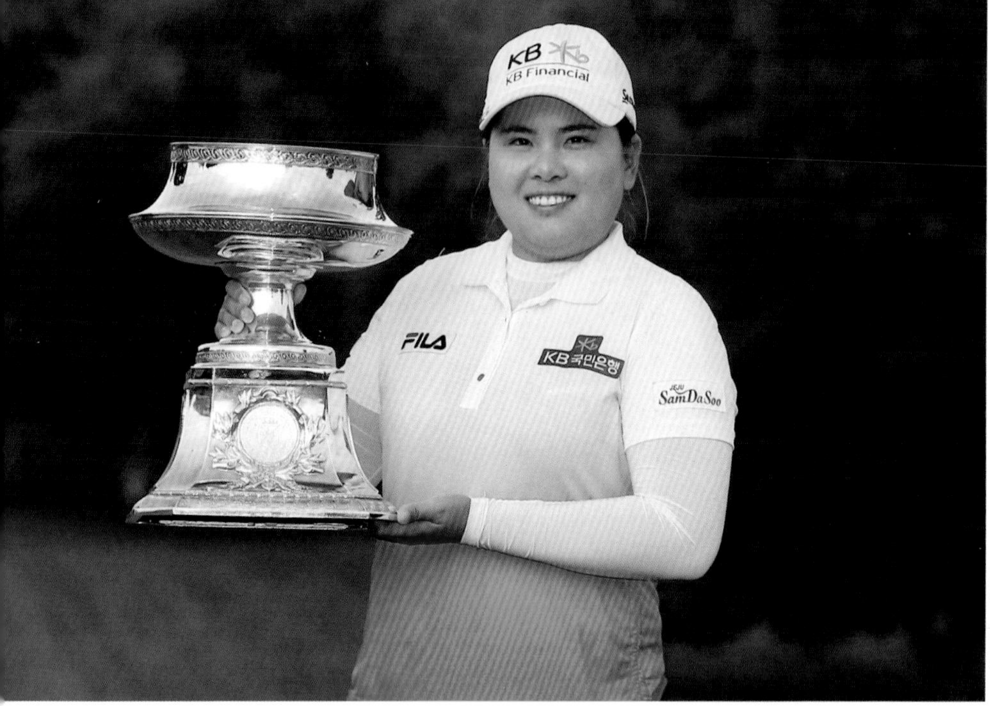

Scott Halleran/Getty Images

1. Inbee Park (Korea) 10.91 points

Richard Heathcote/Getty Images

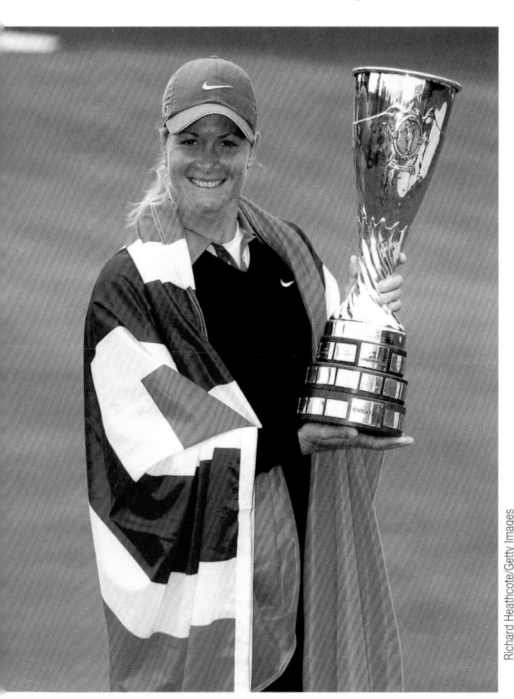

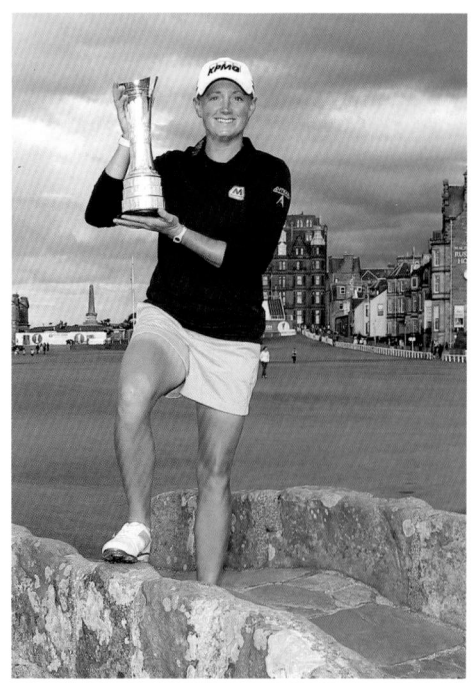

2. Suzann Pettersen (Norway) 10.39 points

David Cannon/Getty Images

3. Stacy Lewis (USA) 9.14 points

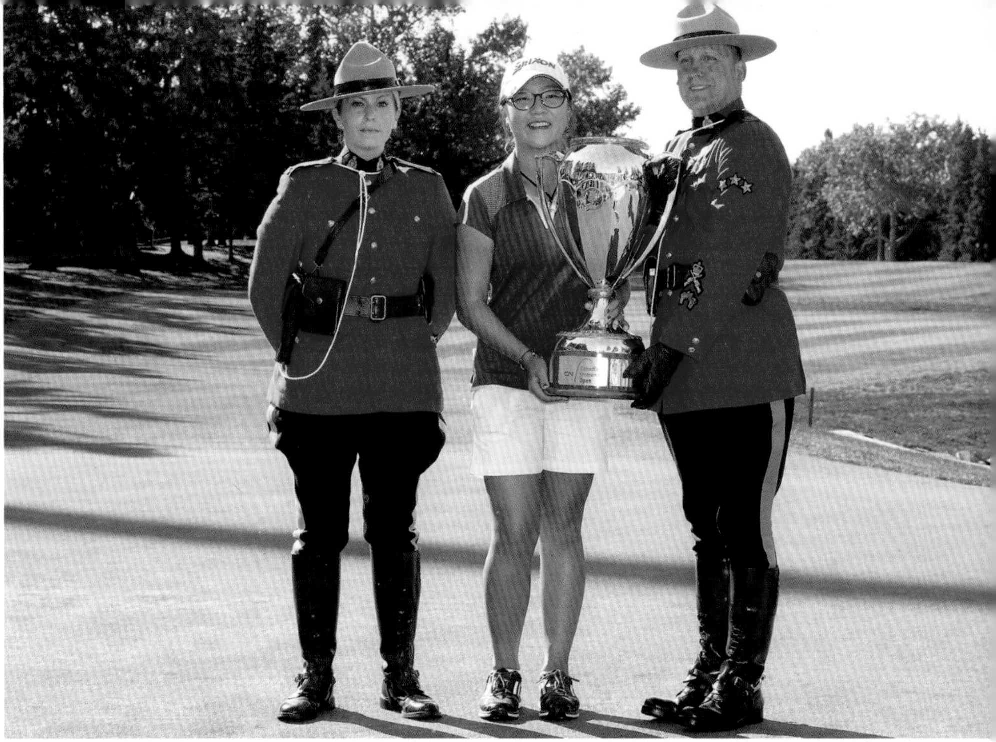

Stephen Dunn/Getty Images

4. Lydia Ko (New Zealand) 7.48 points

Harry How/Getty Images

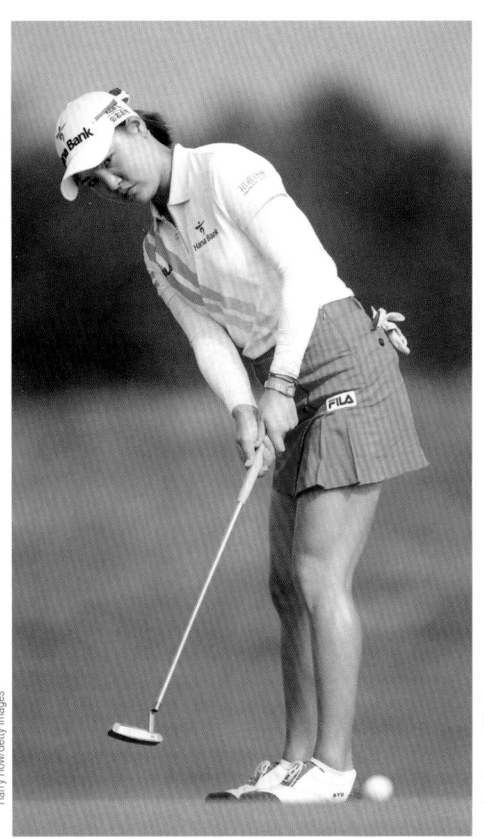

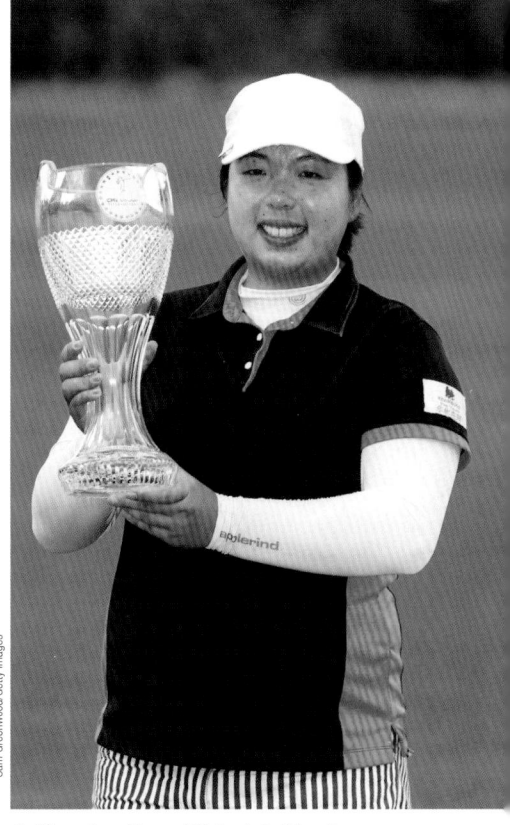

5. So Yeon Ryu (Korea) 6.67 points

Sam Greenwood/Getty Images

6. Shanshan Feng (China) 6.47 points

7. Na Yeon Choi (Korea) 5.75 points

8. Karrie Webb (Australia) 5.16 points

9. Lexi Thompson (USA) 4.91 points

10. I.K. Kim (Korea) 4.63 points

Rolex Rankings

Although Stacy Lewis became the seventh player to top the Rolex Rankings when she won the RR Donnelly Founders Cup in March, there was no disputing the identity of the player who would end 2013 as the world No. 1. Inbee Park had the season of her life, winning three major championships in a row and six tournaments in all on the LPGA circuit. Just weeks before her 25th birthday, Park won the U.S. Women's Open by four strokes to join Babe Zaharias, Mickey Wright and Pat Bradley in winning three majors in the same season.

The South Korean took over at the top of the Rankings shortly after winning the Kraft Nabisco Championship, also by four strokes, before she beat Catriona Matthew in a playoff at the Wegmans LPGA Championship. Park had a points average of 10.91 at the end of the year but was being put under pressure by Suzann Pettersen, who was on 10.39 in second place. Pettersen won the Evian Championship, newly recognized as a major, as well as three other events on the LPGA circuit and one on the Ladies European Tour. Lewis was in third position with an average of 9.14 after winning the Ricoh Women's British Open at St. Andrews for her third victory of the season.

Lydia Ko jumped from 43rd to fourth place on the Rolex Rankings after defending her title at the CN Canadian Open and finishing as runner-up to Pettersen at the Evian, while still an amateur, before turning professional at the age of 16 and winning the Swinging Skirts World Ladies Masters in Taiwan in her second start as a pro. Her average of 7.48 would be better but for the fact she had only played 25 events, 10 fewer than the minimum divisor. Taiwan's Yani Tseng, who was unable to halt a slump that started the previous year, fell from No. 1 on the Rankings at the start of 2013 to 34th place at year's end.

The Rolex Rankings — which was developed at the May 2004 World Congress of Women's Golf — is sanctioned by eight women's professional golf tours: the Ladies Professional Golf Association (LPGA); Ladies European Tour (LET); Ladies Professional Golfers' Association of Japan (JLPGA); Korea Ladies Professional Golf Association (KLPGA); Australian Ladies Professional Golf (ALPG); Symetra Tour; China Ladies Professional Golf Association Tour (CLPGA) and the Ladies European Access Series (LETAS) – as well as the Ladies' Golf Union (LGU) and the United States Golf Association (USGA).

The major golf tours developed the rankings and the protocol that governs the ranking, while R2IT, an independent software development company, was retained to develop the software and to maintain the rankings on a weekly basis. The official events from all of the tours are taken into account and points are awarded according to the strength of the field, with the exception of the five major championships on the LPGA Tour and the Symetra Tour, CLPGA and LETAS events, which have a fixed points distribution. The players' points averages are determined by taking the number of points awarded over a two-year rolling period and dividing that by the number of tournaments played, with a minimum divisor of 35.

The Rolex Rankings are updated and released following the completion of the previous week's tournaments around the world.

Rolex Rankings
(As of December 31, 2013)

Rank	Player	Country	No. of Events	Average Points	Total Points
1	Inbee Park	Korea	63	10.91	687.44
2	Suzann Pettersen	Norway	50	10.39	519.64
3	Stacy Lewis	USA	54	9.14	493.70
4	Lydia Ko	New Zealand	25	7.48	261.70
5	So Yeon Ryu	Korea	56	6.67	373.80
6	Shanshan Feng	China	60	6.47	388.03
7	Na Yeon Choi	Korea	55	5.75	316.15
8	Karrie Webb	Australia	43	5.16	221.71
9	Lexi Thompson	USA	49	4.91	240.78
10	I.K. Kim	Korea	48	4.63	222.12
11	Catriona Matthew	Scotland	45	4.53	203.65
12	Cristie Kerr	USA	46	4.39	202.01
13	Paula Creamer	USA	49	4.38	214.63
14	Ha Na Jang	Korea	34	4.20	146.94
15	Amy Yang	Korea	45	4.08	183.71
16	Jiyai Shin	Korea	55	4.05	222.78
17	Angela Stanford	USA	49	3.88	190.28
18	Hee Young Park	Korea	55	3.80	209.22
19	Beatriz Recari	Spain	55	3.77	207.62
20	Lizette Salas	USA	42	3.76	157.75
21	Ai Miyazato	Japan	48	3.66	175.73
22	Mika Miyazato	Japan	50	3.62	181.05
23	Caroline Hedwall	Sweden	49	3.35	164.08
24	Hyo-Joo Kim	Korea	37	3.13	115.65
25	Karine Icher	France	51	3.11	158.65
26	Anna Nordqvist	Sweden	56	3.09	173.27
27	Sun Ju Ahn	Korea	51	3.04	155.02
28	Chella Choi	Korea	58	2.98	172.69
29	Ariya Jutanugarn	Thailand	13	2.81	98.23
30	Se-Ri Pak	Korea	34	2.80	98.10
31	Azahara Munoz	Spain	55	2.79	153.36
32	Ilhee Lee	Korea	51	2.73	138.99
33	Sei Young Kim	Korea	38	2.71	103.06
34	Yani Tseng	Taipei	49	2.71	132.61
35	Sakura Yokomine	Japan	67	2.66	178.03
36	Pornanong Phatlum	Thailand	55	2.62	144.23
37	Gerina Piller	USA	50	2.61	130.33
38	Rikako Morita	Japan	70	2.57	180.04
39	Carlota Ciganda	Spain	48	2.55	122.29
40	Ha Neul Kim	Korea	46	2.52	115.76
41	Jessica Korda	USA	47	2.50	117.31
42	Bo-Mee Lee	Korea	60	2.49	149.53
43	Hee Kyung Seo	Korea	52	2.45	127.20
44	Miki Saiki	Japan	64	2.37	151.48
45	Sandra Gal	Germany	56	2.34	131.00
46	Brittany Lincicome	USA	49	2.33	114.14
47	Morgan Pressel	USA	50	2.27	113.50
48	Shiho Oyama	Japan	32	2.20	76.88
49	Mi Jeong Jeon	Korea	61	2.18	133.20
50	Mamiko Higa	Japan	51	2.17	110.92

Rank	Player	Country	No. of Events	Average Points	Total Points
51	Sun Young Yoo	Korea	50	2.15	107.73
52	Yumiko Yoshida	Japan	69	2.10	144.98
53	Lee-Anne Pace	South Africa	40	2.09	83.60
54	Jodi Ewart Shadoff	England	48	2.07	99.39
55	Teresa Lu	Taipei	64	2.06	131.98
56	Jennifer Johnson	USA	46	2.05	94.41
57	Haeji Kang	Korea	53	1.97	104.19
58	In Gee Chun	Korea	19	1.96	68.52
59	Soo-Jin Yang	Korea	40	1.93	77.27
60	Caroline Masson	Germany	46	1.86	85.47
61	Michelle Wie	USA	51	1.79	91.27
62	Brittany Lang	USA	53	1.76	93.15
63	Yoo Lim Choi	Korea	37	1.74	64.28
64	MinYoung2 Lee	Korea	40	1.73	69.24
65	Seung Hyun Lee	Korea	35	1.72	60.35
66	Chie Arimura	Japan	49	1.69	82.88
67	Bo Kyung Kim	Korea	36	1.65	59.42
68	Yoon-Kyung Heo	Korea	46	1.61	74.12
69	Jeong Eun5 Lee	Korea	38	1.58	60.19
70	Hee-Kyung Bae	Korea	35	1.57	54.93
71	Jung Min Lee	Korea	34	1.56	54.65
72	Jenny Shin	Korea	54	1.55	83.53
73	Ji Hyun2 Kim	Korea	36	1.54	55.57
74	Meena Lee	Korea	52	1.52	79.22
75	Na-Ri Lee	Korea	67	1.50	100.51
76	Hye-Youn Kim	Korea	40	1.48	59.23
77	Ji-Hee Lee	Korea	58	1.42	82.61
78	Gwladys Nocera	France	46	1.40	64.50
79	Eun-Hee Ji	Korea	54	1.40	75.50
80	Giulia Sergas	Italy	54	1.39	74.80
81	Nicole Castrale	USA	37	1.36	50.40
82	Yuki Ichinose	Japan	62	1.36	84.34
83	Ritsuko Ryu	Japan	71	1.35	96.18
84	Ayako Uehara	Japan	63	1.30	81.64
85	Moriya Jutanugarn	Thailand	28	1.27	44.61
86	Mi Rim Lee	Korea	32	1.26	44.09
87	Yuri Fudoh	Japan	47	1.26	59.03
88	Jane Park	USA	39	1.26	48.97
89	Mo Martin	USA	51	1.23	62.87
90	Candie Kung	Taipei	52	1.22	63.33
91	Char Young2 Kim	Korea	36	1.22	43.80
92	Soo-Yun Kang	Korea	56	1.21	67.95
93	Hiromi Mogi	Japan	51	1.21	61.53
94	Irene Cho	USA	38	1.20	45.53
95	Mina Harigae	USA	52	1.19	61.76
96	Mayu Hattori	Japan	70	1.18	82.56
97	Hyun Soo Kim	Korea	20	1.16	40.61
98	Danielle Kang	USA	45	1.15	51.67
99	Natsuka Hori	Japan	57	1.14	65.14
100	Yukari Baba	Japan	67	1.14	76.46

Rank	Player	Country	No. of Events	Average Points	Total Points
101	Alison Walshe	Ireland	51	1.14	58.16
102	Asako Fujimoto	Japan	69	1.13	78.07
103	Charley Hull	England	21	1.13	39.49
104	Julieta Granada	Paraguay	56	1.12	62.63
105	Junko Omote	Japan	71	1.12	79.30
106	Katherine Hull-Kirk	Australia	55	1.11	60.82
107	Esther Lee	Korea	71	1.10	78.06
108	Rye Jung Lee	Korea	38	1.09	41.34
109	Je-yoon Yang	Korea	32	1.09	38.05
110	Natalie Gulbis	USA	44	1.07	47.07
111	Misuzu Narita	Japan	67	1.05	70.34
112	Seul A Yoon	Korea	37	1.03	38.01
113	Da-Ye Na	Korea	64	1.02	65.12
114	Na Ri Kim	Korea	65	1.01	65.35
115	Stacey Keating	Australia	45	1.01	45.24
116	Kim Dana	New Zealand	31	1.00	34.96
117	Song Yi Ahn	Korea	33	0.99	34.71
118	Pernilla Lindberg	Sweden	60	0.98	58.88
119	Harukyo Nomura	Japan	55	0.98	53.66
120	Hye Jung Choi	Korea	24	0.98	34.13
121	Hae Rym Kim	Korea	33	0.97	33.79
122	Holly Clyburn	England	17	0.95	33.36
123	Thidapa Suwannapura	Thailand	40	0.94	37.69
124	Dewi Claire Schreefel	Netherlands	52	0.92	47.67
125	Mariajo Uribe	Colombia	45	0.91	41.06
126	Jee Young Lee	Korea	38	0.90	34.19
127	Kumiko Kaneda	Japan	68	0.88	59.78
128	Lindsey Wright	Australia	50	0.87	43.68
129	Miki Sakai	Japan	70	0.87	60.85
130	Ayaka Watanabe	Japan	35	0.86	30.20
131	Young Kim	Korea	55	0.86	47.29
132	Diana Luna	Italy	29	0.86	30.01
133	Erika Kikuchi	Japan	69	0.85	58.85
134	Stacy Prammanasudh	USA	29	0.85	29.74
135	Momoko Ueda	Japan	55	0.85	46.62
136	Hyun Min Byun	Korea	28	0.84	29.48
137	Yeon Ju Jung	Korea	33	0.84	29.39
138	Jennifer Rosales	Philippines	34	0.84	29.29
139	Yoon Ji Cho	Korea	36	0.83	29.80
140	Ju Young Park	Korea	28	0.83	28.94
141	Vicky Hurst	USA	53	0.83	43.81
142	Onnarin Sattayabanphot	Thailand	63	0.82	51.74
143	Christel Boeljon	Netherlands	47	0.81	37.99
144	Hannah Burke	England	33	0.79	27.71
145	Mikaela Parmlid	Sweden	28	0.79	27.50
146	Juli Inkster	USA	27	0.78	27.44
147	Hee-Won Han	Korea	48	0.78	37.28
148	Valentine Derrey	France	41	0.77	31.69
149	Ran Hong	Korea	38	0.77	29.32
150	Ji Hee Kim	Korea	38	0.77	29.30

Rank	Player	Country	No. of Events	Average Points	Total Points
151	Eun-Bi Jang	Korea	56	0.77	43.05
152	Sydnee Michaels	USA	43	0.77	32.94
153	Rebecca Artis	Australia	43	0.76	32.89
154	Hee-Won Jung	Korea	39	0.76	29.82
155	Erina Hara	Japan	67	0.76	51.08
156	Mi Jung Hur	Korea	42	0.75	31.67
157	Jacqui Concolino	USA	37	0.75	27.88
158	Cindy LaCrosse	USA	51	0.73	37.21
159	Rui Kitada	Japan	70	0.73	50.97
160	Joanna Klatten	France	39	0.73	28.36
161	Chae-Young Yoon	Korea	32	0.72	25.32
162	Austin Ernst	USA	24	0.72	25.03
163	Hsuan-Yu Yao	Taipei	45	0.71	31.97
164	Yeong Ran Cho	Korea	34	0.70	24.55
165	Maiko Wakabayashi	Japan	70	0.70	48.89
166	Trish Johnson	England	32	0.69	24.27
167	Nontaya Srisawang	Thailand	33	0.69	24.12
168	Lala Anai	Japan	65	0.68	44.09
169	Jin Eui Hong	Korea	33	0.68	23.69
170	Ashleigh Simon	South Africa	31	0.68	23.65
171	Yuki Sakurai	Japan	46	0.68	31.08
172	Belen Mozo	Spain	46	0.67	30.91
173	Akane Iijima	Japan	67	0.67	44.75
174	Megumi Kido	Japan	71	0.66	47.17
175	Kaori Ohe	Japan	71	0.65	46.31
176	Mihoko Iseri	Japan	67	0.63	42.53
177	Karin Sjodin	Sweden	31	0.63	21.99
178	Seung Ji han	Korea	21	0.62	21.78
179	Line Vedel Hansen	Denmark	30	0.61	21.49
180	Florentyna Parker	England	35	0.61	21.18
181	Kyeong Bae	Korea	36	0.60	21.67
182	Soo Hwa Jang	Korea	30	0.60	21.04
183	Hyun-Ji Kim	Korea	30	0.60	20.98
184	Laura Davies	England	60	0.60	35.90
185	Ah-Reum Hwang	Korea	64	0.59	37.81
186	Liz Young	England	38	0.59	22.33
187	Sarah Jane Smith	Australia	47	0.59	27.59
188	Jeong Jang	Korea	32	0.59	20.52
189	Christina Kim	USA	44	0.59	25.76
190	So Yeon Park	Korea	12	0.58	20.38
191	Beth Allen	USA	43	0.58	24.88
192	Xi Yu Lin	China	19	0.57	20.10
193	Hye Jin Jung	Korea	30	0.57	19.82
194	Veronica Zorzi	Italy	32	0.56	19.72
195	Yuko Fukuda	Japan	68	0.56	38.30
196	Kaori Nakamura	Japan	63	0.56	35.15
197	Lisa McCloskey	USA	20	0.56	19.52
198	Katie Futcher	USA	46	0.56	25.57
199	Paola Moreno	Colombia	35	0.56	19.44
200	So-Hee Kim	Korea	64	0.55	35.13

Official World Golf Ranking
(As of December 31, 2013)

Ranking		Player	Country	Points Average	Total Points	No. of Events	2013 Points Lost	2013 Points Gained
1	(3)	Tiger Woods	USA	11.69	479.49	41	-350.08	488.25
2	(5)	Adam Scott	Aus	9.60	393.43	41	-243.02	375.74
3	(53)	Henrik Stenson	Swe	9.16	476.20	52	-117.14	484.60
4	(4)	Justin Rose	Eng	7.16	372.50	52	-301.43	339.06
5	(17)	Phil Mickelson	USA	7.06	345.92	49	-240.47	356.52
6	(1)	Rory McIlroy	NIr	6.50	318.44	49	-462.67	159.81
7	(21)	Matt Kuchar	USA	6.15	319.93	52	-245.86	339.45
8	(18)	Steve Stricker	USA	5.72	228.94	40	-192.80	231.13
9	(25)	Zach Johnson	USA	5.45	283.23	52	-183.64	254.53
10	(16)	Sergio Garcia	Esp	5.31	265.30	50	-207.52	240.82
11	(37)	Jason Day	Aus	5.29	232.65	44	-153.87	259.45
12	(12)	Ian Poulter	Eng	5.24	256.68	49	-193.95	195.73
13	(10)	Brandt Snedeker	USA	5.18	253.89	49	-259.79	241.62
14	(15)	Graeme McDowell	NIr	5.01	260.32	52	-226.31	233.35
15	(9)	Jason Dufner	USA	4.98	258.83	52	-229.07	218.06
16	(23)	Dustin Johnson	USA	4.80	230.55	48	-197.11	218.44
17	(2)	Luke Donald	Eng	4.76	233.48	49	-360.91	154.64
18	(14)	Charl Schwartzel	SAf	4.74	246.50	52	-212.93	206.78
19	(27)	Jim Furyk	USA	4.55	218.20	48	-165.32	184.42
20	(13)	Keegan Bradley	USA	4.31	224.18	52	-231.88	198.43
21	(11)	Webb Simpson	USA	4.30	219.10	51	-238.86	201.59
22	(809)	Jordan Spieth	USA	4.15	166.06	40	-27.52	188.46
23	(127)	Hideki Matsuyama	Jpn	3.88	155.03	40	-54.11	157.47
24	(45)	Thomas Bjorn	Den	3.76	191.95	51	-112.53	185.92
25	(7)	Lee Westwood	Eng	3.69	191.88	52	-276.56	154.91
26	(47)	Jamie Donaldson	Wal	3.66	179.34	49	-109.82	176.75
27	(24)	Ernie Els	SAf	3.55	184.37	52	-185.13	147.38
28	(8)	Bubba Watson	USA	3.45	162.32	47	-218.38	121.27
29	(35)	Bill Haas	USA	3.35	174.21	52	-169.88	180.66
30	(20)	Nick Watney	USA	3.26	169.72	52	-188.72	123.07
31	(26)	Hunter Mahan	USA	3.23	168.15	52	-202.69	170.32
32	(132)	Victor Dubuisson	Fra	3.22	132.20	41	-47.56	130.20
33	(40)	Ryan Moore	USA	3.16	160.96	51	-109.43	137.81
34	(6)	Louis Oosthuizen	SAf	2.96	154.07	52	-249.53	82.89
35	(33)	Gonzalo Fdez-Castano	Esp	2.95	153.59	52	-120.24	141.36
36	(177)	Graham DeLaet	Can	2.86	148.60	52	-48.65	157.01
37	(54)	Miguel A. Jimenez	Esp	2.79	130.96	47	-89.88	108.41
38	(30)	Francesco Molinari	Ita	2.77	144.20	52	-141.63	109.59
39	(28)	Martin Kaymer	Ger	2.71	140.82	52	-164.66	115.51
40	(31)	Rickie Fowler	USA	2.66	133.13	50	-160.00	121.28
41	(312)	Billy Horschel	USA	2.63	136.58	52	-57.88	166.56
42	(74)	Jonas Blixt	Swe	2.62	136.44	52	-77.92	125.73
43	(44)	Matteo Manassero	Ita	2.60	135.32	52	-116.82	117.91
44	(225)	Kevin Streelman	USA	2.58	134.42	52	-73.66	166.62
45	(46)	David Lynn	Eng	2.58	134.13	52	-102.89	121.87
46	(80)	Thongchai Jaidee	Tha	2.57	133.67	52	-82.94	122.79
47	(120)	Jimmy Walker	USA	2.48	128.87	52	-78.54	136.33
48	(19)	Peter Hanson	Swe	2.40	120.12	50	-187.11	66.74
49	(108)	Joost Luiten	Ned	2.35	120.09	51	-78.38	121.92
50	(34)	Branden Grace	SAf	2.34	121.77	52	-139.88	97.27

( ) Ranking in brackets indicates position as of December 31, 2012.

Ranking		Player	Country	Points Average	Total Points	No. of Events	2013 Points Lost	2013 Points Gained
51	(154)	Richard Sterne	SAf	2.29	116.96	51	-58.97	131.23
52	(65)	Bernd Wiesberger	Aut	2.29	118.89	52	-91.29	105.36
53	(140)	Harris English	USA	2.27	117.97	52	-55.26	126.33
54	(299)	Boo Weekley	USA	2.26	117.36	52	-48.92	137.88
55	(41)	Scott Piercy	USA	2.25	116.94	52	-119.39	95.40
56	(152)	Gary Woodland	USA	2.22	113.26	51	-61.90	118.20
57	(22)	Bo Van Pelt	USA	2.15	111.99	52	-178.12	60.59
58	(83)	Brendon de Jonge	Zim	2.12	110.18	52	-81.67	103.44
59	(193)	Kiradech Aphibarnrat	Tha	2.11	109.80	52	-58.32	118.70
60	(115)	Chris Kirk	USA	2.07	107.47	52	-75.31	110.38
61	(148)	D.A. Points	USA	2.06	107.03	52	-80.77	124.24
62	(116)	Hyung-Sung Kim	Kor	2.03	105.54	52	-51.84	90.04
63	(384)	Peter Uihlein	USA	2.02	102.88	51	-24.59	109.61
64	(267)	Angel Cabrera	Arg	2.02	94.74	47	-49.37	114.63
65	(50)	Thorbjorn Olesen	Den	1.99	103.30	52	-109.27	102.09
66	(98)	Stephen Gallacher	Sco	1.99	99.28	50	-80.02	99.08
67	(100)	Koumei Oda	Jpn	1.89	98.43	52	-62.32	80.70
68	(36)	Nicolas Colsaerts	Bel	1.87	97.21	52	-134.82	73.40
69	(91)	Tim Clark	SAf	1.84	84.51	46	-60.03	79.55
70	(281)	Roberto Castro	USA	1.83	95.13	52	-38.72	100.56
71	(94)	Ross Fisher	Eng	1.83	94.95	52	-60.30	80.18
72	(87)	Marc Leishman	Aus	1.82	94.50	52	-81.00	88.31
73	(586)	Patrick Reed	USA	1.79	75.39	42	-17.64	82.88
74	(139)	Chris Wood	Eng	1.77	90.11	51	-65.98	95.91
75	(217)	Brett Rumford	Aus	1.76	87.91	50	-48.59	93.31
76	(52)	Shane Lowry	Ire	1.76	89.65	51	-85.68	67.62
77	(159)	Shingo Katayama	Jpn	1.75	87.71	50	-42.82	78.70
78	(117)	Charles Howell	USA	1.74	90.28	52	-91.46	110.35
79	(86)	Michael Thompson	USA	1.73	89.74	52	-95.66	98.66
80	(39)	Robert Garrigus	USA	1.71	88.99	52	-118.89	60.29
81	(260)	Chris Stroud	USA	1.71	88.95	52	-47.02	99.98
82	(114)	Luke Guthrie	USA	1.69	77.88	46	-48.60	70.98
83	(75)	Ryo Ishikawa	Jpn	1.67	87.02	52	-92.50	68.99
84	(354)	Mikko Ilonen	Fin	1.65	74.10	45	-31.39	86.06
85	(71)	Martin Laird	Sco	1.62	82.76	51	-104.90	87.06
86	(436)	Brooks Koepka	USA	1.62	64.69	40	-19.41	68.61
87	(122)	Paul Casey	Eng	1.60	80.05	50	-64.23	78.98
88	(459)	Matthew Jones	Aus	1.58	79.14	50	-28.04	89.51
89	(131)	Russell Henley	USA	1.58	82.20	52	-57.94	89.16
90	(60)	Marcel Siem	Ger	1.57	81.77	52	-94.34	68.17
91	(228)	John Merrick	USA	1.56	81.31	52	-55.27	97.29
92	(62)	Fredrik Jacobson	Swe	1.56	63.96	41	-101.55	73.39
93	(258)	David Howell	Eng	1.56	81.04	52	-37.66	80.60
94	(186)	Hideto Tanihara	Jpn	1.55	77.57	50	-36.87	64.93
95	(56)	Alexander Noren	Swe	1.55	68.26	44	-98.40	55.87
96	(628)	Sung-Joon Park	Kor	1.55	71.35	46	-13.25	74.82
97	(55)	Marcus Fraser	Aus	1.55	80.65	52	-94.00	64.18
98	(49)	George Coetzee	SAf	1.53	78.09	51	-105.84	63.86
99	(66)	John Huh	USA	1.52	78.98	52	-75.74	75.89
100	(163)	Gregory Bourdy	Fra	1.52	77.35	51	-50.23	70.89

( ) Ranking in brackets indicates position as of December 31, 2012.

Ranking		Player	Country	Points Average	Total Points	No. of Events	2013 Points Lost	2013 Points Gained
101	(85)	Pablo Larrazabal	Esp	1.51	78.75	52	-82.84	70.63
102	(164)	Charley Hoffman	USA	1.51	78.59	52	-59.92	82.03
103	(1492)	Chesson Hadley	USA	1.51	60.36	40	-6.50	66.85
104	(190)	Wen-Chong Liang	Chn	1.48	77.05	52	-35.38	67.10
105	(32)	Carl Pettersson	Swe	1.48	76.85	52	-138.78	42.57
106	(123)	Scott Stallings	USA	1.48	76.74	52	-69.95	77.80
107	(153)	Ken Duke	USA	1.47	76.44	52	-62.24	81.80
108	(38)	John Senden	Aus	1.47	76.22	52	-129.08	59.40
109	(29)	Paul Lawrie	Sco	1.46	70.07	48	-143.69	37.35
110	(220)	Kevin Chappell	USA	1.46	75.80	52	-53.65	86.51
111	(203)	Anirban Lahiri	Ind	1.45	62.39	43	-31.73	59.27
112	(101)	Scott Jamieson	Sco	1.42	74.00	52	-66.84	59.77
113	(126)	Kevin Stadler	USA	1.42	73.92	52	-61.96	68.42
114	(182)	Marc Warren	Sco	1.42	73.88	52	-47.41	69.97
115	(237)	David Lingmerth	Swe	1.41	73.48	52	-49.39	83.03
116	(93)	Danny Willett	Eng	1.41	67.81	48	-66.44	50.31
117	(42)	David Toms	USA	1.39	55.51	40	-101.84	39.26
118	(276)	Tommy Fleetwood	Eng	1.37	71.49	52	-37.59	75.10
119	(364)	Morten Orum Madsen	Den	1.37	67.27	49	-17.11	65.53
120	(119)	Raphael Jacquelin	Fra	1.34	66.90	50	-62.79	58.25
121	(102)	Yuta Ikeda	Jpn	1.33	69.08	52	-58.02	45.83
122	(51)	Geoff Ogilvy	Aus	1.33	62.34	47	-97.24	54.89
123	(262)	Scott Hend	Aus	1.31	65.28	50	-32.42	60.97
124	(150)	Darren Fichardt	SAf	1.31	67.86	52	-49.04	69.40
125	(181)	Hennie Otto	SAf	1.30	67.72	52	-52.07	68.40
126	(118)	Ryan Palmer	USA	1.30	64.91	50	-73.64	68.47
127	(134)	Rory Sabbatini	SAf	1.30	67.36	52	-60.40	63.45
128	(76)	Kyle Stanley	USA	1.29	67.25	52	-100.58	75.01
129	(170)	Ashun Wu	Chn	1.29	64.57	50	-26.58	49.02
130	(188)	Julien Quesne	Fra	1.29	61.91	48	-43.77	59.43
131	(59)	Padraig Harrington	Ire	1.28	66.64	52	-95.69	54.39
132	(124)	Yoshinori Fujimoto	Jpn	1.28	64.04	50	-35.95	47.26
133	(125)	Matthew Every	USA	1.28	66.58	52	-58.15	60.15
134	(48)	K.J. Choi	Kor	1.27	65.90	52	-115.79	62.26
135	(82)	Vijay Singh	Fiji	1.26	65.64	52	-73.12	48.56
136	(57)	Richie Ramsay	Sco	1.25	57.70	46	-87.43	34.09
136	(232)	Daniel Summerhays	USA	1.25	65.23	52	-38.93	63.69
138	(224)	David Hearn	Can	1.25	65.14	52	-43.25	66.66
139	(70)	Sang-Moon Bae	Kor	1.24	64.61	52	-108.74	73.08
140	(58)	Rafael Cabrera Bello	Esp	1.24	64.53	52	-98.88	54.78
141	(73)	Brendan Jones	Aus	1.23	49.16	40	-62.22	25.24
142	(69)	Thaworn Wiratchant	Tha	1.22	63.50	52	-71.30	31.43
143	(278)	Shiv Kapur	Ind	1.20	62.62	52	-31.89	59.61
144	(146)	Jaco Van Zyl	SAf	1.20	62.47	52	-66.63	67.99
145	(43)	Hiroyuki Fujita	Jpn	1.20	62.40	52	-100.76	25.34
146	(284)	Jason Bohn	USA	1.20	62.24	52	-27.10	57.98
147	(344)	John Peterson	USA	1.19	47.60	40	-19.45	46.93
148	(89)	Gaganjeet Bhullar	Ind	1.18	58.92	50	-46.28	37.40
149	(172)	Kyoung-Hoon Lee	Kor	1.15	58.86	51	-31.56	48.90
150	(208)	Alejandro Canizares	Esp	1.14	59.38	52	-39.52	54.23

( ) Ranking in brackets indicates position as of December 31, 2012.

Ranking		Player	Country	Points Average	Total Points	No. of Events	2013 Points Lost	2013 Points Gained
151	(72)	K.T. Kim	Kor	1.14	59.24	52	-86.24	38.06
152	(185)	Eduardo De La Riva	Esp	1.12	50.44	45	-30.62	42.21
153	(136)	Brian Davis	Eng	1.12	58.25	52	-63.50	61.77
154	(1492)	Derek Ernst	USA	1.12	44.71	40	-13.55	58.26
155	(141)	Brad Kennedy	Aus	1.11	52.34	47	-45.53	45.82
156	(61)	Anders Hansen	Den	1.11	46.76	42	-88.90	34.65
157	(555)	Ben Martin	USA	1.11	55.47	50	-16.63	57.91
158	(303)	Brian Gay	USA	1.10	57.26	52	-45.87	73.23
159	(113)	Thomas Aiken	SAf	1.10	57.22	52	-68.39	52.78
160	(288)	Prayad Marksaeng	Tha	1.10	57.18	52	-38.60	61.34
161	(236)	Jason Kokrak	USA	1.09	56.76	52	-39.52	61.25
162	(348)	Scott Brown	USA	1.09	56.70	52	-36.52	67.26
163	(229)	Masanori Kobayashi	Jpn	1.07	55.83	52	-29.20	40.88
164	(242)	Felipe Aguilar	Chi	1.06	55.25	52	-48.05	64.26
165	(319)	Stewart Cink	USA	1.06	49.93	47	-34.57	59.93
166	(206)	Siddikur	Ban	1.05	46.42	44	-31.49	42.05
167	(201)	Josh Teater	USA	1.05	54.77	52	-52.63	62.11
168	(470)	Simon Khan	Eng	1.05	41.83	40	-23.79	49.91
169	(373)	Michael Putnam	USA	1.04	53.17	51	-25.02	57.61
170	(393)	Masahiro Kawamura	Jpn	1.04	49.82	48	-12.54	44.92
171	(63)	Simon Dyson	Eng	1.03	53.80	52	-94.57	43.41
172	(168)	Romain Wattel	Fra	1.03	51.56	50	-45.11	42.81
173	(160)	Brian Harman	USA	1.03	53.49	52	-37.02	48.53
174	(167)	Garth Mulroy	SAf	1.02	53.15	52	-52.73	46.81
175	(247)	Morgan Hoffmann	USA	1.02	42.65	42	-26.33	39.22
176	(95)	Seung-Yul Noh	Kor	1.00	51.80	52	-66.95	36.43
177	(165)	Bob Estes	USA	0.98	43.08	44	-40.64	40.46
178	(238)	Yusaku Miyazato	Jpn	0.97	49.33	51	-29.37	40.07
179	(179)	J.J. Henry	USA	0.97	50.24	52	-45.22	43.05
180	(595)	Paul Waring	Eng	0.96	38.55	40	-11.52	40.08
181	(460)	Brian Stuard	USA	0.96	50.06	52	-26.96	59.27
182	(99)	Jeff Overton	USA	0.96	49.77	52	-72.72	42.47
183	(382)	Andrea Pavan	Ita	0.94	49.01	52	-25.13	52.62
184	(205)	Brendan Steele	USA	0.94	48.80	52	-47.60	51.76
185	(64)	Greg Chalmers	Aus	0.94	48.79	52	-97.05	41.23
186	(606)	Brendon Todd	USA	0.93	48.35	52	-18.08	54.00
187	(196)	William McGirt	USA	0.93	48.23	52	-42.43	43.43
188	(166)	Charlie Beljan	USA	0.92	47.96	52	-39.59	44.37
189	(1492)	Daan Huizing	Ned	0.92	36.83	40	-2.79	39.62
190	(142)	Pat Perez	USA	0.92	46.88	51	-56.56	45.55
191	(78)	Aaron Baddeley	Aus	0.92	46.79	51	-85.71	44.11
192	(88)	Fredrik Andersson Hed	Swe	0.91	44.76	49	-58.66	18.63
193	(361)	Shunsuke Sonoda	Jpn	0.89	38.31	43	-20.27	35.29
194	(414)	Dawie Van der Walt	SAf	0.89	46.32	52	-23.88	50.98
195	(1253)	Stuart Manley	Wal	0.89	35.62	40	-3.57	38.04
196	(290)	Justin Walters	SAf	0.89	46.18	52	-22.93	43.95
197	(209)	Steve Webster	Eng	0.89	45.26	51	-40.31	41.17
198	(169)	Cameron Tringale	USA	0.88	45.66	52	-61.65	52.54
199	(255)	Kazuhiro Yamashita	Jpn	0.88	44.67	51	-24.69	33.41
200	(392)	Marco Crespi	Ita	0.88	36.75	42	-14.55	33.74

( ) Ranking in brackets indicates position as of December 31, 2012.

Age Groups of Current Top 100 World Ranked Players

Under 25	25-28	29-32	33-36	37-40	Over 40
			Scott		
			Rose		
			Kuchar		
			Garcia		
			Snedeker		
			McDowell		
			Dufner		
		D. Johnson	Donald		
		Schwartzel	B. Watson		
		B. Haas	Fdez-Castano		
McIlroy		Watney	Streelman		
Spieth		Mahan	Walker		
Matsuyama		Moore	P. Hanson	Woods	
Dubuisson		Oosthuizen	Piercy	Stenson	
Fowler	Day	DeLaet	de Jonge	Z. Johnson	
Manassero	K. Bradley	F. Molinari	H-S Kim	Poulter	
Grace	W. Simpson	Kaymer	K. Oda	Westwood	
English	Horschel	Blixt	R. Fisher	Donaldson	
Aphibarnrat	Luiten	Sterne	Rumford	Lynn	
Uhlein	Wiesberger	Woodland	Howell	Weekley	Mickelson
Olesen	Kirk	Colsaerts	Garrigus	Van Pelt	Stricker
Reed	Castro	Leishman	Ilonen	Points	Furyk
Guthrie	C. Wood	Stroud	Casey	Gallacher	Bjorn
Ishikawa	Lowry	Laird	M. Jones	T. Clark	Els
Koepka	M. Thompson	Merrick	Siem	Katayama	Jimenez
Henley	S-J Park	Noren	Tanihara	Jacobson	Jaidee
Huh	G. Coetzee	Bourdy	M. Fraser	D. Howell	Cabrera

2013 World Ranking Review

Major Movements

	Upward				Downward		
Name	Net Points Gained	Position 2012	2013	Name	Net Points Lost	Position 2012	2013
Henrik Stenson	358	53	3	Rory McIlroy	303	1	6
Jordan Spieth	161	809	22	Luke Donald	206	2	16
Tiger Woods	138	3	1	Louis Oosthuizen	167	6	34
Adam Scott	133	5	2	Lee Westwood	122	7	25
Phil Mickelson	116	17	5	Peter Hanson	120	19	48
Billy Horschel	109	312	41	Bo Van Pelt	118	22	57
Graham DeLaet	108	117	36	Paul Lawrie	106	29	109
Jason Day	106	37	11	Bubba Watson	97	8	28
Hideki Matsuyama	103	127	23	Carl Pettersson	96	32	105
Matt Kuchar	94	21	7	Hiroyuki Fujita	75	43	145
Kevin Streelman	93	225	44				
Boo Weekley	89	299	54				
Peter Uihlein	85	384	63				
Victor Dubuisson	83	132	32				
Thomas Bjorn	73	45	25				

Highest-Rated Events of 2013

	Event	No. of World Ranked Players Participating					World Rating Points
		Top 5	Top 15	Top 30	Top 50	Top 100	
1	PGA Championship	5	15	29	49	99	841
2	The Open Championship	5	14	29	49	89	806
3	U.S. Open Championship	5	15	30	49	73	763
4	Masters Tournament	5	15	30	49	63	716
5	The Players Championship	5	15	30	46	68	750
6	WGC-Bridgestone Invitational	5	14	28	48	65	697
7	WGC-Cadillac Championship	4	14	29	48	63	692
8	WGC-Accenture Match Play	4	13	28	48	64	694
9	Deutsche Bank Champ.	5	15	27	40	66	683
10	The Barclays	5	14	24	37	65	676
11	BMW Championship	5	15	27	37	56	625
12	Memorial Tournament	5	10	21	32	53	570
13	WGC-HSBC Champions	3	9	20	40	54	530
14	Arnold Palmer Invitational	3	9	20	33	54	513
15	BMW PGA Championship	2	6	9	19	40	341
16	The Tour Championship	4	13	22	26	30	435
17	Northern Trust Open	1	7	18	25	50	427
18	Honda Classic	3	7	14	20	42	399
19	Shell Houston Open	2	7	12	20	39	373
20	DP World Tour Championship	2	5	8	20	39	318
21	Abu Dhabi HSBC Champ.	3	4	9	16	35	330
22	RBC Heritage	1	3	14	22	38	342
23	Turkish Airlines Open	3	3	7	16	36	315
24	Tampa Bay Championship	1	4	11	20	38	329
25	Wells Fargo Championship	1	4	12	18	37	327
26	Waste Mgmt. Phoenix Open	0	4	9	19	44	322
27	BMW Masters	1	4	7	15	34	265
28	Farmers Insurance Open	1	4	8	16	36	286
29	Travelers Championship	1	3	10	18	34	283
30	Commercialbank Qatar Masters	2	3	8	14	28	246
31	CIMB Classic	1	2	8	17	36	270
32	RBC Canadian Open	0	6	9	13	28	256
33	AT&T National	1	2	9	12	36	261
34	N.M. World Challenge	1	9	18	18	18	279
35	Hyundai Tourn. of Champions	0	6	12	17	23	233
36	Crowne Plaza Invitational	0	2	8	15	33	253
37	Nedbank Challenge	2	3	7	19	25	248
38	Alstom Open de France	1	3	5	11	30	222
39	Wyndham Championship	0	1	8	12	28	230
40	Zurich Classic	1	2	7	11	28	230

World Golf Rankings 1968-2013

Year	No. 1	No. 2	No. 3	No. 4	No. 5
1968	Nicklaus	Palmer	Casper	Player	Charles
1969	Nicklaus	Player	Casper	Palmer	Charles
1970	Nicklaus	Player	Casper	Trevino	Charles
1971	Nicklaus	Trevino	Player	Palmer	Casper
1972	Nicklaus	Player	Trevino	Crampton	Palmer
1973	Nicklaus	Weiskopf	Trevino	Player	Crampton
1974	Nicklaus	Miller	Player	Weiskopf	Trevino
1975	Nicklaus	Miller	Weiskopf	Irwin	Player
1976	Nicklaus	Irwin	Miller	Player	Green
1977	Nicklaus	Watson	Green	Irwin	Crenshaw
1978	Watson	Nicklaus	Irwin	Green	Player
1979	Watson	Nicklaus	Irwin	Trevino	Player
1980	Watson	Trevino	Aoki	Crenshaw	Nicklaus
1981	Watson	Rogers	Aoki	Pate	Trevino
1982	Watson	Floyd	Ballesteros	Kite	Stadler
1983	Ballesteros	Watson	Floyd	Norman	Kite
1984	Ballesteros	Watson	Norman	Wadkins	Langer
1985	Ballesteros	Langer	Norman	Watson	Nakajima
1986	Norman	Langer	Ballesteros	Nakajima	Bean
1987	Norman	Ballesteros	Langer	Lyle	Strange
1988	Ballesteros	Norman	Lyle	Faldo	Strange
1989	Norman	Faldo	Ballesteros	Strange	Stewart
1990	Norman	Faldo	Olazabal	Woosnam	Stewart
1991	Woosnam	Faldo	Olazabal	Ballesteros	Norman
1992	Faldo	Couples	Woosnam	Olazabal	Norman
1993	Faldo	Norman	Langer	Price	Couples
1994	Price	Norman	Faldo	Langer	Olazabal
1995	Norman	Price	Langer	Els	Montgomerie
1996	Norman	Lehman	Montgomerie	Els	Couples
1997	Norman	Woods	Price	Els	Love
1998	Woods	O'Meara	Duval	Love	Els
1999	Woods	Duval	Montgomerie	Love	Els
2000	Woods	Els	Duval	Mickelson	Westwood
2001	Woods	Mickelson	Duval	Els	Love
2002	Woods	Mickelson	Els	Garcia	Goosen
2003	Woods	Singh	Els	Love	Furyk
2004	Singh	Woods	Els	Goosen	Mickelson
2005	Woods	Singh	Mickelson	Goosen	Els
2006	Woods	Furyk	Mickelson	Scott	Els
2007	Woods	Mickelson	Furyk	Els	Stricker
2008	Woods	Garcia	Mickelson	Harrington	Singh
2009	Woods	Mickelson	Stricker	Westwood	Harrington
2010	Westwood	Woods	Kaymer	Mickelson	Furyk
2011	Donald	Westwood	McIlroy	Kaymer	Scott
2012	McIlroy	Donald	Woods	Rose	Scott
2013	Woods	Scott	Stenson	Rose	Mickelson

(The World of Professional Golf 1968-1985; World Ranking 1986-2013)

Year	No. 6	No. 7	No. 8	No. 9	No. 10
1968	Boros	Coles	Thomson	Beard	Nagle
1969	Beard	Archer	Trevino	Barber	Sikes
1970	Devlin	Coles	Jacklin	Beard	Huggett
1971	Barber	Crampton	Charles	Devlin	Weiskopf
1972	Jacklin	Weiskopf	Oosterhuis	Heard	Devlin
1973	Miller	Oosterhuis	Wadkins	Heard	Brewer
1974	M. Ozaki	Crampton	Irwin	Green	Heard
1975	Green	Trevino	Casper	Crampton	Watson
1976	Watson	Weiskopf	Marsh	Crenshaw	Geiberger
1977	Marsh	Player	Weiskopf	Floyd	Ballesteros
1978	Crenshaw	Marsh	Ballesteros	Trevino	Aoki
1979	Aoki	Green	Crenshaw	Ballesteros	Wadkins
1980	Pate	Ballesteros	Bean	Irwin	Player
1981	Ballesteros	Graham	Crenshaw	Floyd	Lietzke
1982	Pate	Nicklaus	Rogers	Aoki	Strange
1983	Nicklaus	Nakajima	Stadler	Aoki	Wadkins
1984	Faldo	Nakajima	Stadler	Kite	Peete
1985	Wadkins	O'Meara	Strange	Pavin	Sutton
1986	Tway	Sutton	Strange	Stewart	O'Meara
1987	Woosnam	Stewart	Wadkins	McNulty	Crenshaw
1988	Crenshaw	Woosnam	Frost	Azinger	Calcavecchia
1989	Kite	Olazabal	Calcavecchia	Woosnam	Azinger
1990	Azinger	Ballesteros	Kite	McNulty	Calcavecchia
1991	Couples	Langer	Stewart	Azinger	Davis
1992	Langer	Cook	Price	Azinger	Love
1993	Azinger	Woosnam	Kite	Love	Pavin
1994	Els	Couples	Montgomerie	M. Ozaki	Pavin
1995	Pavin	Faldo	Couples	M. Ozaki	Elkington
1996	Faldo	Mickelson	M. Ozaki	Love	O'Meara
1997	Mickelson	Montgomerie	M. Ozaki	Lehman	O'Meara
1998	Price	Montgomerie	Westwood	Singh	Mickelson
1999	Westwood	Singh	Price	Mickelson	O'Meara
2000	Montgomerie	Love	Sutton	Singh	Lehman
2001	Garcia	Toms	Singh	Clarke	Goosen
2002	Toms	Harrington	Singh	Love	Montgomerie
2003	Weir	Goosen	Harrington	Toms	Perry
2004	Harrington	Garcia	Weir	Love	Cink
2005	Garcia	Furyk	Montgomerie	Scott	DiMarco
2006	Goosen	Singh	Harrington	Donald	Ogilvy
2007	Rose	Scott	Harrington	Choi	Singh
2008	Karlsson	Villegas	Stenson	Els	Westwood
2009	Furyk	Casey	Stenson	McIlroy	Perry
2010	McDowell	Stricker	Casey	Donald	McIlroy
2011	Stricker	D. Johnson	Day	Schwartzel	W. Simpson
2012	Oosthuizen	Westwood	B. Watson	Dufner	Snedeker
2013	McIlroy	Kuchar	Stricker	Z. Johnson	Garcia

World's Winners of 2013

U.S. PGA TOUR

Hyundai Tournament of Champions	Dustin Johnson
Sony Open in Hawaii	Russell Henley
Humana Challenge	Brian Gay
Farmers Insurance Open	Tiger Woods
Waste Management Phoenix Open	Phil Mickelson
AT&T Pebble Beach National Pro-Am	Brandt Snedeker
Northern Trust Open	John Merrick
WGC - Accenture Match Play Championship	Matt Kuchar
Honda Classic	Michael Thompson
WGC - Cadillac Championship	Tiger Woods (2)
Puerto Rico Open	Scott Brown
Tampa Bay Championship	Kevin Streelman
Arnold Palmer Invitational	Tiger Woods (3)
Shell Houston Open	D.A. Points
Valero Texas Open	Martin Laird
Masters Tournament	Adam Scott
RBC Heritage	Graeme McDowell
Zurich Classic of New Orleans	Billy Horschel
Wells Fargo Championship	Derek Ernst
The Players Championship	Tiger Woods (4)
HP Byron Nelson Championship	Sang-Moon Bae
Crowne Plaza Invitational	Boo Weekley
Memorial Tournament	Matt Kuchar (2)
FedEx St. Jude Classic	Harris English
U.S. Open Championship	Justin Rose
Travelers Championship	Ken Duke
AT&T National	Bill Haas
Greenbrier Classic	Jonas Blixt
John Deere Classic	Jordan Spieth
Sanderson Farms Championship	Woody Austin
RBC Canadian Open	Brandt Snedeker (2)
WGC - Bridgestone Invitational	Tiger Woods (5)
Reno-Tahoe Open	Gary Woodland
PGA Championship	Jason Dufner
Wyndham Championship	Patrick Reed

PGA TOUR PLAYOFFS FOR THE FEDEXCUP

The Barclays	Adam Scott (2)
Deutsche Bank Championship	Henrik Stenson
BMW Championship	Zach Johnson
Tour Championship	Henrik Stenson (2)
The Presidents Cup	United States
Frys.com Open	Jimmy Walker
Shriners Hospitals for Children Open	Webb Simpson
McGladrey Classic	Chris Kirk
OHL Classic at Mayakoba	Harris English (2)

SPECIAL EVENTS

Tavistock Cup	Team Albany
CVS Caremark Charity Classic	Steve Stricker/Bo Van Pelt
PGA Grand Slam of Golf	Adam Scott (3)
Callaway Pebble Beach Invitational	Kevin Kisner (2)

Northwestern Mutual World Challenge	Zach Johnson (2)
Franklin Templeton Shootout	Harris English (3)/Matt Kuchar (3)
PNC Father/Son Challenge	Stewart Cink/Conner Cink

WEB.COM TOUR

Panama Claro Championship	Kevin Foley
Colombia Championship	Patrick Cantlay
Chile Classic	Kevin Kisner
Chitimacha Louisiana Open	Edward Loar
Brasil Classic	Benjamin Alvarado
WNB Golf Classic	Alex Aragon
South Georgia Classic	Will Wilcox
Stadion Classic	Brendon Todd
BMW Charity Pro-Am	Mark Anderson
Mexico Championship	Michael Putnam
Mid-Atlantic Championship	Michael Putnam (2)
Air Capital Classic	Scott Parel
Rex Hospital Open	Chesson Hadley
United Leasing Championship	Ben Martin
Utah Championship	Steven Alker
Midwest Classic	Jamie Lovemark
Albertsons Boise Open	Kevin Tway
Mylan Classic	Ben Martin (2)
Price Cutter Charity Championship	Andrew Svoboda
News Sentinel Open	Peter Malnati
Cox Classic	Bronson La'Cassie
Hotel Fitness Championship	Trevor Immelman
Chiquita Classic	Andrew Svoboda (2)
Nationwide Children's Hospital Championship	Seung-Yul Noh
Web.com Tour Championship	Chesson Hadley (2)

PGA TOUR CANADA

Times Colonist Island Savings Open	Stephen Gangluff
Dakota Dunes Open	Wil Collins
Syncrude Boreal Open	Riley Wheeldon
PGA Tour Canada Players Cup	Carlos Sainz, Jr.
ATB Financial Classic	Joe Panzeri
Great Waterway Classic	Hugo Leon
Wildfire Invitational	Mark Hubbard
Cape Breton Celtic Classic	Mackenzie Hughes
Tour Championship of Canada	Max Gilbert

PGA TOUR LATINOAMERICA

Abierto Mexicano de Golf	Ted Purdy
TransAmerican Power Products CRV Open	Manuel Villegas
Abierto OSDE del Centro	Angel Cabrera
Roberto de Vicenzo Invitational Copa NEC	Jose de Jesus Rodriguez
Arturo Calle Colombian Open	Timothy O'Neal
Mundo Maya Open	Jorge Fernandez-Valdes
Dominican Republic Open	Ryan Blaum
Puerto Rico Classic	Ryan Sullivan
Abierto do Brasil	Ryan Blaum (2)
Arturo Calle Colombian Classic	Jose de Jesus Rodriguez (2)
Lexus Peru Open	Julian Etulain
Abierto de Chile	Timothy O'Neal (2)
Personal Classic	Fabian Gomez
Visa Open de Argentina	Marcelo Rozo

EUROPEAN TOUR

Volvo Golf Champions	Louis Oosthuizen
Abu Dhabi HSBC Golf Championship	Jamie Donaldson
Commercial Bank Qatar Masters	Chris Wood
Omega Dubai Desert Classic	Stephen Gallacher
Trophee Hassan II	Marcel Siem
Open de Espana	Raphael Jacquelin
Volvo World Match Play Championship	Graeme McDowell (2)
Madeira Islands Open - Portugal - BPI	Peter Uihlein
BMW PGA Championship	Matteo Manassero
Nordea Masters	Mikko Ilonen
Lyoness Open	Joost Luiten
Najeti Hotels et Golfs Open	Simon Thornton
BMW International Open	Ernie Els
Irish Open	Paul Casey
Alstom Open de France	Graeme McDowell (3)
Aberdeen Asset Management Scottish Open	Phil Mickelson (2)
The Open Championship	Phil Mickelson (3)
M2M Russian Open	Michael Hoey
Johnnie Walker Championship	Tommy Fleetwood
ISPS Handa Wales Open	Gregory Bourdy
Omega European Masters	Thomas Bjorn
KLM Open	Joost Luiten (2)
Open d'Italia Lindt	Julien Quesne
Alfred Dunhill Links Championship	David Howell
Seve Trophy	Continental Europe
Portugal Masters	David Lynn

THE FINAL SERIES

BMW Masters	Gonzalo Fernandez-Castano
Turkish Airlines Open	Victor Dubuisson
DP World Tour Championship	Henrik Stenson (3)

CHALLENGE TOUR

Gujarat Kensville Challenge	Shiv Kapur
Barclays Kenya Open	Jordi Garcia Pinto
Challenge de Madrid	Francois Calmels
Montecchia Golf Open	Brooks Koepka
Telenet Trophy	Daniel Gaunt
Fred Olsen Challenge de Espana	Brooks Koepka (2)
D+D Real Czech Challenge Open	Francois Calmels (2)
Scottish Hydro Challenge	Brooks Koepka (3)
Karnten Golf Open	Dylan Frittelli
Bad Griesbach Challenge	Andrea Pavan
Swiss Challenge	Victor Riu
Mugello Tuscany Open	Marco Crespi
Le Vaudreuil Golf Challenge	Brinson Paolini
Finnish Challenge	Stuart Manley
Norwegian Challenge	Jens Fahrbring
Rolex Trophy	Jens Dantorp
Northern Ireland Open Challenge	Daan Huizing
Open Blue Green Cotes d'Armor Bretagne	Andrea Pavan (2)
Kharkov Superior Cup	Daan Huizing (2)
Kazakhstan Open	Johan Carlsson
Foshan Open	Nacho Elvira
National Bank of Oman Golf Classic	Roope Kakko
Dubai Festival City Challenge Tour Grand Final	Shiv Kapur (2)

ASIAN TOUR

Zaykabar Myanmar Open	Chawalit Plaphol
SAIL-SBI Open	Anirban Lahiri
Avantha Masters	Thomas Aiken
Maybank Malaysian Open	Kiradech Aphibarnrat
Chiangmai Golf Classic	Scott Hend
Panasonic Open India	Wade Ormsby
Solaire Open	Wen-Tang Lin
Ballantine's Championship	Brett Rumford
CIMB Niaga Indonesian Masters	Bernd Wiesberger
Queen's Cup	Prayad Marksaeng (2)
Worldwide Holdings Selangor Masters	Pariya Junhasavasdikul
Yeangder Tournament Players Championship	Thaworn Wiratchant
Mercuries Taiwan Masters	Scott Hend (2)
CJ Invitational	Sung Kang
Venetian Macau Open	Scott Hend (3)
CIMB Classic	Ryan Moore
WGC - HSBC Champions	Dustin Johnson (2)
Hero Indian Open	Siddikur
Resorts World Manila Masters	Wen-Chong Liang
Indonesia Open	Gaganjeet Bhullar
Hong Kong Open	Miguel Angel Jimenez
Thailand Golf Championship	Sergio Garcia

ONEASIA TOUR

Thailand Open	Prayad Marksaeng
Enjoy Jakarta Indonesia PGA Championship	Ho-Sung Choi
Volvo China Open	Brett Rumford (2)
GS Caltex Maekyung Open	Hyun-Woo Ryu
SK Telecom Open	Matthew Griffin
Nanshan China Masters	Charl Schwartzel
Kolon Korea Open	Sung Kang (2)
Dongfeng Nissan Cup	China

JAPAN TOUR

Token Homemate Cup	Yoshinobu Tsukada
Tsuruya Open	Hideki Matsuyama
The Crowns	Michio Matsumura
Japan PGA Championship	Hyung-Sung Kim
Diamond Cup	Hideki Matsuyama (2)
Japan Golf Tour Championship	Satoshi Kodaira
Gateway to the Open Mizuno Open	Brendan Jones
Nagashima Shigeo Invitational	Shunsuke Sonoda
Kansai Open	Brad Kennedy (2)
Vana H Cup KBC Augusta	Sung-Joon Park
Fujisankei Classic	Hideki Matsuyama (3)
ANA Open	Koumei Oda
Asia-Pacific Panasonic Open	Masahiro Kawamura
Coca-Cola Tokai Classic	Shingo Katayama
Toshin Golf Tournament	Yoshinori Fujimoto
Japan Open	Masanori Kobayashi
Bridgestone Open	Daisuke Maruyama
Mynavi ABC Championship	Yuta Ikeda
Heiwa PGM Championship	Ashun Wu
Mitsui Sumitomo Visa Taiheiyo Masters	Hideto Tanihara
Dunlop Phoenix	Luke Donald
Casio World Open	Hideki Matsuyama (4)
Golf Nippon Series JT Cup	Yusaku Miyazato

AUSTRALASIAN TOUR

Turner Plumbing Victorian PGA Championship	David McKenzie
Lexis of Blackburn Heritage Classic	David Bransdon
Coca-Cola Queensland PGA Championship	Brad Kennedy
Victorian Open	Matthew Giles
New Zealand PGA Championship	Michael Hendry
Isuzu Queensland Open	Nick Cullen
South Pacific Open Championship	Andre Stolz
WA Goldfields PGA Championship	Jack Wilson
John Hughes/Nexus Risk Services WA Open	Josh Geary
ISPS Handa Perth International	Jin Jeong
Australian PGA Championship	Adam Scott (4)
Talisker Masters	Adam Scott (5)
ISPS Handa World Cup of Golf	Jason Day
Gloria Jean's NSW Open	Aron Price
Emirates Australian Open	Rory McIlroy

AFRICAN TOURS

Telkom PGA Pro-Am	Oliver Bekker
Joburg Open	Richard Sterne
Africa Open	Darren Fichardt
Dimension Data Pro-Am	Jaco Van Zyl
Tshwane Open	Dawie Van der Walt
Telkom PGA Championship	Jaco Van Zyl (2)
Investec Cup	Jaco Van Zyl (3)
Golden Pilsener Zimbabwe Open	Jake Roos
Investec Royal Swazi Open	James Kingston
Zambia Sugar Open	Adilson Da Silva
Lombard Insurance Classic	Merrick Bremner
Vodacom Origins of Golf - Simola	Jacques Blaauw
Polokwane Classic	Dean Burmester
Vodacom Origins of Golf - Selborne	Jacques Blaauw (2)
Sun City Challenge	Adilson Da Silva (2)
Vodacom Origins of Golf - Euphoria	Heinrich Bruiners
Vodacom Origins of Golf - Langebaan	Jean Hugo
Wild Waves Golf Challenge	Andrew Curlewis
Vodacom Origins of Golf - Parys	Andrew Curlewis (2)
Platinum Classic	Neil Schietekat
Vodacom Origins of Golf Final	J.J. Senekal
BMG Classic	Ulrich van den Berg
Lion of Africa Cape Town Open	Tjaart van der Walt
Nedbank Affinity Cup	Jacques Blaauw (3)
South African Open Championship	Morten Orum Madsen
Alfred Dunhill Championship	Charl Schwartzel (2)
Nedbank Golf Challenge	Thomas Bjorn (2)
Nelson Mandela Championship	Dawie Van der Walt (2)

U.S. LPGA TOUR

Honda LPGA Thailand	Inbee Park
HSBC Women's Champions	Stacy Lewis
RR Donnelley LPGA Founders Cup	Stacy Lewis (2)
Kia Classic	Beatriz Recari
Kraft Nabisco Championship	Inbee Park (2)
LPGA LOTTE Championship	Suzann Pettersen (2)
North Texas LPGA Shootout	Inbee Park (3)
Kingsmill Championship	Cristie Kerr
Mobile Bay LPGA Classic	Jennifer Johnson
Pure Silk-Bahamas LPGA Classic	Ilhee Lee
ShopRite LPGA Classic	Karrie Webb (2)
Wegmans LPGA Championship	Inbee Park (4)
Walmart NW Arkansas Championship	Inbee Park (5)
U.S. Women's Open	Inbee Park (6)
Manulife Financial LPGA Classic	Hee Young Park
Marathon Classic	Beatriz Recari (2)
The Solheim Cup	Europe
CN Canadian Women's Open	*Lydia Ko (2)
Safeway Classic	Suzann Pettersen (3)
Reignwood LPGA Classic	Shanshan Feng
Sime Darby LPGA Malaysia	Lexi Thompson
LPGA KEB - HanaBank Championship	Amy Yang
Sunrise LPGA Taiwan Championship	Suzann Pettersen (5)
Lorena Ochoa Invitational	Lexi Thompson (2)
CME Group Titleholders	Shanshan Feng (2)

LADIES EUROPEAN TOUR

Mission Hills World Ladies Championship	Suzann Pettersen
Lalla Meryem Cup	Ariya Jutanugarn
South African Women's Open	Marianne Skarpnord
Turkish Airlines Ladies Open	Lee-Anne Pace
Deloitte Ladies Open	Holly Clyburn
UniCredit Ladies German Open	Carlota Ciganda
Allianz Ladies Slovak Open	Gwladys Nocera
Open de Espana Femenino	Lee-Anne Pace (2)
ISPS Handa Ladies European Masters	Karrie Webb (3)
Ricoh Women's British Open	Stacy Lewis (3)
Honma Pilsen Golf Masters	Ann-Kathrin Lindner
Aberdeen Asset Management Scottish Open	Catriona Matthew
Helsingborg Open	Rebecca Artis
Evian Championship	Suzann Pettersen (4)
Lacoste Ladies Open de France	Azahara Munoz
Sanya Ladies Open	Lee-Anne Pace (3)
China Suzhou Taihu Open	Gwladys Nocera (2)
Hero Women's Indian Open	Thidapa Suwannapura
Omega Dubai Ladies Masters	Pornanong Phatlum

JAPAN LPGA TOUR

Daikin Orchid Ladies	Rikako Morita
Yokohama Tire PRGR Ladies Cup	Mi-Jeong Jeon
T-Point Ladies	Yuki Ichinose
AXA Ladies	Natsuka Hori
Yamaha Ladies Open	Mamiko Higa
Studio Alice Ladies Open	Na-Ri Kim
Vantelin Ladies Open KKT Cup	Miki Saiki
Fujisankei Ladies Classic	Miki Saiki (2)
Cyber Agent Ladies	Sakura Yokomine
World Ladies Championship Salonpas Cup	Hiromi Mogi

Hoken no Madoguchi Ladies	Onnarin Sattayabanphot
Chukyo TV Bridgestone Ladies Open	Rikako Morita (2)
Resort Trust Ladies	Mamiko Higa (2)
Yonex Ladies	Junko Omote
Suntory Ladies Open	Rikako Morita (3)
Nichirei Ladies	Yumiko Yoshida
Earth Mondahmin Cup	Natsuka Hori (2)
Nichi-Iko Ladies Open	Young Kim
Samantha Thavasa Girls Collection Ladies	Yumiko Yoshida (2)
Meiji Cup	Da-Ye Na
NEC Karuzawa 72	Misuzu Narita
CAT Ladies	Sun-Ju Ahn
Nitori Ladies	Sun-Ju Ahn (2)
Golf 5 Ladies	Yumiko Yoshida (3)
Japan LPGA Championship	Bo-Mee Lee
Munsingwear Ladies Tokai Classic	Sakura Yokomine (2)
Miyagi TV Cup Dunlop Ladies Open	Na-Ri Lee
Japan Women's Open	Mika Miyazato
Stanley Ladies	Soo-Yun Kang
Fujitsu Ladies	Na-Ri Lee (2)
Nobuta Group Masters Golf Club Ladies	Sakura Yokomine (3)
Hisako Higuchi Morinaga Weider Ladies	Bo-Mee Lee (2)
Mizuno Classic	Teresa Lu
Itoen Ladies	Sakura Yokomine (4)
Daio Paper Elleair Ladies Open	Rikako Morita (4)
Japan LPGA Tour Championship Ricoh Cup	Shiho Oyama

AUSTRALIAN LADIES TOUR

Vintage Golf Club Pro-Am	Stacey Keating
Mount Boughton Classic	Caroline Hedwall
Bing Lee Samsung NSW Open	Caroline Hedwall (2)
Volvik RACV Ladies Masters	Karrie Webb
ISPS Handa New Zealand Women's Open	*Lydia Ko
ISPS Handa Women's Australian Open	Jiyai Shin
Women's Victorian Open	Stacey Keating (2)

CHAMPIONS TOUR

Mitsubishi Electric Championship	John Cook
Allianz Championship	Rocco Mediate
ACE Group Classic	Bernhard Langer
Toshiba Classic	David Frost
Mississippi Gulf Resort Classic	Michael Allen
Greater Gwinnett Championship	Bernhard Langer (2)
Liberty Mutual Insurance Legends of Golf	Brad Faxon/Jeff Sluman
Insperity Championship	Esteban Toledo
Senior PGA Championship	Kohki Idoki
Principal Charity Classic	Russ Cochran
Regions Tradition	David Frost (2)
Encompass Championship	Craig Stadler
Constellation Senior Players Championship	Kenny Perry
U.S. Senior Open	Kenny Perry (2)
3M Championship	Tom Pernice, Jr.
Dick's Sporting Goods Open	Bart Bryant
Boeing Classic	John Riegger
Shaw Charity Classic	Rocco Mediate (2)
Montreal Championship	Esteban Toledo (2)
Pacific Links Hawai'i Championship	Mark Wiebe (2)
Nature Valley First Tee Open	Kirk Triplett
SAS Championship	Russ Cochran (2)

Greater Hickory Kia Classic	Michael Allen (2)
AT&T Championship	Kenny Perry (3)
Charles Schwab Cup Championship	Fred Couples

EUROPEAN SENIOR TOUR

ISPS Handa PGA Seniors Championship	Paul Wesselingh
Speedy Services Wales Senior Open	Philip Golding
Bad Ragaz PGA Seniors Open	Paul Wesselingh (2)
The Senior Open Championship	Mark Wiebe
Berenberg Masters	Steen Tinning
SSE Scottish Senior Open	Santiago Luna
Travis Perkins plc Senior Masters	Colin Montgomerie
WINSTONgolf Senior Open	Gordon Brand, Jr.
Russian Open	Simon P. Brown
French Riviera Masters	Peter Fowler
English Senior Open	Steen Tinning (2)
Dutch Senior Open	Simon P. Brown (2)
Australian PGA Seniors Championship	Darryl Purchase
Fubon Senior Open	Paul Wesselingh (3)
MCB Tour Championship	Paul Wesselingh (4)

JAPAN PGA SENIOR TOUR

Kanehide Senior Okinawa Open	Takeshi Sakiyama
ISPS Handa Cup Satsukibare Senior Masters	Boonchu Ruangkit
Kyoraku More Surprise Cup	Kiyoshi Murota
Starts Senior	Tommy Nakajima
ISPS Handa Cup Philanthropy Senior	Satoshi Higashi
Fancl Classic	Yutaka Hagawa
ISPS Handa Cup Akibare-no Senior Masters	Frankie Minoza
Komatsu Open	Kiyoshi Maita
Japan PGA Senior Championship	Tsukasa Watanabe
Japan Senior Open Championship	Kiyoshi Murota (2)
Fuji Film Senior Championship	Seiki Okuda
Iwasaki Shiratsuyu Senior	Kiyoshi Murota (3)

Multiple Winners of 2013

PLAYER	WINS	PLAYER	WINS
Inbee Park	6	Chesson Hadley	2
		Caroline Hedwall	2
Suzann Pettersen	5	Mamiko Higa	2
Adam Scott	5	Natsuka Hori	2
Tiger Woods	5	Daan Huizing	2
		Dustin Johnson	2
Hideki Matsuyama	4	Zach Johnson	2
Rikako Morita	4	Sung Kang	2
Paul Wesselingh	4	Shiv Kapur	2
Sakura Yokomine	4	Stacey Keating	2
		Brad Kennedy	2
Jacques Blaauw	3	Kevin Kisner	2
Harris English	3	*Lydia Ko	2
Scott Hend	3	Bernhard Langer	2
Brooks Koepka	3	Bo-Mee Lee	2
Matt Kuchar	3	Na-Ri Lee	2
Stacy Lewis	3	Joost Luiten	2
Graeme McDowell	3	Prayad Marksaeng	2
Phil Mickelson	3	Ben Martin	2
Kiyoshi Murota	3	Rocco Mediate	2
Lee-Anne Pace	3	Gwladys Nocera	2
Kenny Perry	3	Timothy O'Neal	2
Henrik Stenson	3	Andrea Pavan	2
Jaco Van Zyl	3	Michael Putnam	2
Karrie Webb	3	Beatriz Recari	2
Yumiko Yoshida	3	Jose de Jesus Rodriguez	2
		Brett Rumford	2
Sun-Ju Ahn	2	Miki Saiki	2
Michael Allen	2	Charl Schwartzel	2
Thomas Bjorn	2	Brandt Snedeker	2
Ryan Blaum	2	Andrew Svoboda	2
Simon P. Brown	2	Lexi Thompson	2
Francois Calmels	2	Steen Tinning	2
Russ Cochran	2	Esteban Toledo	2
Andrew Curlewis	2	Dawie Van der Walt	2
Adilson Da Silva	2	Mark Wiebe	2
Shanshan Feng	2		
David Frost	2		

World Money List

This list of the 350 leading money winners in the world of professional golf in 2013 was compiled from the results of men's (excluding seniors) tournaments carried in the Appendixes of this edition. This list includes tournaments with a minimum of 36 holes and four contestants and does not include such competitions as pro-ams and skins or skills contests. It does not include annual performance bonuses such as for the FedExCup (U.S.) and the Race to Dubai (Europe).

In the 48 years during which World Money Lists have been compiled, the earnings of the player in the 200th position have risen from a total of $3,326 in 1966 to $676,248 in 2013. The top 200 players in 1966 earned a total of $4,680,287. In 2013, the comparable total was $381,648,850.

The World Money List includes the official money lists of the U.S. PGA Tour, PGA European Tour, PGA Tour of Japan, Asian Tour, OneAsia Tour, Sunshine Tour, PGA Tour of Australasia, PGA Tour Latinoamerica and PGA Tour Canada, along with winnings in established unofficial tournaments when reliable figures could be obtained. The conversion rates used for 2013 were: Euro = US$1.35; Japanese yen = US$0.01; South African rand = US$0.10; Australian dollar = US$0.98; Canadian dollar = US$0.98.

POS.	PLAYER, COUNTRY	TOTAL MONEY
1	Tiger Woods, USA	$9,490,217
2	Henrik Stenson, Sweden	9,176,583
3	Matt Kuchar, USA	6,847,241
4	Adam Scott, Australia	6,560,459
5	Phil Mickelson, USA	6,456,554
6	Justin Rose, England	6,022,468
7	Brandt Snedeker, USA	5,364,337
8	Zach Johnson, USA	5,154,359
9	Jason Day, Australia	4,987,138
10	Graeme McDowell, N. Ireland	4,945,545
11	Steve Stricker, USA	4,777,532
12	Dustin Johnson, USA	4,601,106
13	Ian Poulter, England	4,599,222
14	Webb Simpson, USA	4,533,999
15	Jordan Spieth, USA	4,125,470
16	Keegan Bradley, USA	4,059,254
17	Thomas Bjorn, Denmark	4,027,860
18	Sergio Garcia, Spain	4,012,762
19	Bill Haas, USA	3,960,163
20	Harris English, USA	3,947,984
21	Billy Horschel, USA	3,923,617
22	Jason Dufner, USA	3,721,193
23	Charl Schwartzel, South Africa	3,638,152
24	Kevin Streelman, USA	3,471,782
25	Jimmy Walker, USA	3,448,070
26	Graham DeLaet, Canada	3,364,567
27	Jim Furyk, USA	3,339,779
28	Jamie Donaldson, Wales	3,262,409
29	Ryan Moore, USA	3,201,165
30	Hunter Mahan, USA	3,160,964

POS.	PLAYER, COUNTRY	TOTAL MONEY
31	Lee Westwood, England	3,062,020
32	Boo Weekley, USA	2,996,554
33	D.A. Points, USA	2,912,073
34	Luke Donald, England	2,888,362
35	Chris Kirk, USA	2,800,924
36	Gary Woodland, USA	2,790,955
37	Rory McIlroy, N. Ireland	2,768,381
38	Gonzalo Fernandez-Castano, Spain	2,737,500
39	Jonas Blixt, Sweden	2,706,023
40	Charles Howell, USA	2,700,463
41	Victor Dubuisson, France	2,636,883
42	Hideki Matsuyama, Japan	2,600,297
43	Nick Watney, USA	2,595,413
44	David Lynn, England	2,422,823
45	Brendon de Jonge, Zimbabwe	2,397,424
46	Thongchai Jaidee, Thailand	2,355,137
47	Chris Stroud, USA	2,320,122
48	Bubba Watson, USA	2,310,609
49	Ernie Els, South Africa	2,280,378
50	Richard Sterne, South Africa	2,224,681
51	Francesco Molinari, Italy	2,221,536
52	Rickie Fowler, USA	2,217,792
53	Roberto Castro, USA	2,189,408
54	Peter Uihlein, USA	2,143,732
55	Russell Henley, USA	2,095,851
56	Matteo Manassero, Italy	2,093,745
57	Tim Clark, South Africa	2,069,835
58	Martin Laird, Scotland	2,055,882
59	John Merrick, USA	2,042,898
60	Joost Luiten, Netherlands	2,034,979
61	Kiradech Aphibarnrat, Thailand	2,012,024
62	Patrick Reed, USA	1,989,519
63	Charley Hoffman, USA	1,974,711
64	Martin Kaymer, Germany	1,937,055
65	Branden Grace, South Africa	1,917,186
66	Scott Piercy, USA	1,916,899
67	Ken Duke, USA	1,862,233
68	Michael Thompson, USA	1,848,647
69	Miguel Angel Jimenez, Spain	1,840,682
70	Angel Cabrera, Argentina	1,823,883
71	Matt Jones, USA	1,788,287
72	Brian Stuard, USA	1,780,228
73	Sang-Moon Bae, Korea	1,776,534
74	Fredrik Jacobson, Sweden	1,767,222
75	David Lingmerth, Sweden	1,762,739
76	Rory Sabbatini, South Africa	1,756,675
77	Brett Rumford, Australia	1,747,722
78	Brian Gay, USA	1,742,134
79	Kevin Chappell, USA	1,688,964
80	Kevin Stadler, USA	1,647,444
81	Scott Brown, USA	1,644,875
82	John Huh, USA	1,641,190
83	Scott Stallings, USA	1,640,850
84	Stephen Gallacher, Scotland	1,637,101

POS.	PLAYER, COUNTRY	TOTAL MONEY
85	Bernd Wiesberger, Austria	1,633,538
86	Jason Bohn, USA	1,598,030
87	Kyle Stanley, USA	1,595,980
88	Thorbjorn Olesen, Denmark	1,581,980
89	Luke Guthrie, USA	1,580,982
90	Ryo Ishikawa, Japan	1,568,033
91	Ross Fisher, England	1,567,825
92	Marc Leishman, Australia	1,565,136
93	Ryan Palmer, USA	1,554,245
94	David Howell, England	1,524,024
95	Louis Oosthuizen, South Africa	1,504,627
96	Jason Kokrak, USA	1,494,477
97	Daniel Summerhays, USA	1,488,110
98	David Hearn, Canada	1,454,885
99	Mikko Ilonen, Finland	1,432,514
100	Stewart Cink, USA	1,422,962
101	Josh Teater, USA	1,421,676
102	Chris Wood, England	1,420,859
103	Matt Every, USA	1,404,340
104	Bo Van Pelt, USA	1,403,225
105	Nicolas Colsaerts, Belgium	1,399,081
106	Derek Ernst, USA	1,387,106
107	Brian Davis, England	1,376,011
108	Gregory Bourdy, France	1,365,237
109	Tommy Fleetwood, England	1,357,053
110	Peter Hanson, Sweden	1,348,008
111	Robert Garrigus, USA	1,339,805
112	Padraig Harrington, Ireland	1,322,789
113	Paul Casey, England	1,310,453
114	Shane Lowry, Ireland	1,280,415
115	Hyung-Sung Kim, Korea	1,242,370
116	Marcel Siem, Germany	1,233,122
117	John Rollins, USA	1,222,690
118	K.J. Choi, Korea	1,220,481
119	Marc Warren, Scotland	1,219,817
120	Pablo Larrazabal, Spain	1,216,101
121	Brian Harman, USA	1,208,190
122	Brendan Steele, USA	1,155,086
123	Hideto Tanihara, Japan	1,150,498
124	Darren Fichardt, South Africa	1,142,529
125	Jeff Overton, USA	1,120,073
126	Jeff Maggert, USA	1,115,502
127	Shingo Katayama, Japan	1,111,504
128	Koumei Oda, Japan	1,108,193
129	Pat Perez, USA	1,083,693
130	Raphael Jacquelin, France	1,078,059
131	George Coetzee, South Africa	1,073,153
132	Thomas Aiken, South Africa	1,066,612
133	Scott Jamieson, Scotland	1,064,884
134	Rafa Cabrera-Bello, Spain	1,063,205
135	Cameron Tringale, USA	1,043,639
136	Justin Hicks, USA	1,021,792
137	Aaron Baddeley, Australia	1,020,824
138	Felipe Aguilar, Chile	1,019,102

POS.	PLAYER, COUNTRY	TOTAL MONEY
139	Marcus Fraser, Australia	1,016,924
140	Jerry Kelly, USA	1,005,607
141	John Senden, Australia	1,003,358
142	Alejandro Canizares, Spain	1,001,276
143	Justin Leonard, USA	993,874
144	Richard Lee, New Zealand	993,506
145	Julien Quesne, France	989,788
146	Nicholas Thompson, USA	987,434
147	J.J. Henry, USA	987,032
148	Brendon Todd, USA	985,378
149	Morgan Hoffmann, USA	984,853
150	Bryce Molder, USA	969,222
151	Geoff Ogilvy, Australia	968,198
152	Wen-Chong Liang, China	966,766
153	James Driscoll, USA	952,181
154	Ashun Wu, China	950,037
155	Carl Pettersson, Sweden	943,836
156	William McGirt, USA	942,444
157	Charlie Beljan, USA	939,939
158	Mark Wilson, USA	927,401
159	Bob Estes, USA	925,717
160	Sung-Joon Park, Korea	920,014
161	D.H. Lee, Korea	893,738
162	Greg Chalmers, Australia	880,953
163	Ted Potter, Jr., USA	872,359
164	Simon Khan, England	871,300
165	James Hahn, USA	867,178
166	Martin Flores, USA	845,467
167	Alexander Noren, Sweden	823,280
168	Ben Crane, USA	820,287
169	Morten Orum Madsen, Denmark	816,942
170	Camilo Villegas, Colombia	813,910
171	Johnson Wagner, USA	813,005
172	Ricardo Santos, Portugal	798,167
173	Lucas Glover, USA	794,662
174	Chesson Hadley, USA	787,982
175	David Horsey, England	786,091
176	Craig Lee, Scotland	782,559
177	Robert Karlsson, Sweden	782,175
178	Danny Willett, England	778,043
179	Yusaku Miyazato, Japan	775,080
180	Yuta Ikeda, Japan	768,853
181	Dawie van der Walt, South Africa	766,053
182	Garth Mulroy, South Africa	760,975
183	Charlie Wi, Korea	757,922
184	Andres Romero, Argentina	733,817
185	George McNeill, USA	727,688
186	Steven Bowditch, Australia	721,543
187	Soren Kjeldsen, Denmark	716,549
188	Masahiro Kawamura, Japan	715,464
189	David Toms, USA	714,086
190	Eduardo De La Riva, Spain	701,950
191	Ricky Barnes, USA	701,635
192	Scott Hend, Australia	700,695

POS.	PLAYER, COUNTRY	TOTAL MONEY
193	Simon Dyson, England	699,299
194	Seung-Yul Noh, Korea	691,899
195	Paul Lawrie, Scotland	690,398
196	Erik Compton, USA	689,208
197	Brooks Koepka, USA	686,446
198	Yoshinori Fujimoto, Japan	685,545
199	Justin Walters, South Africa	680,656
200	John Peterson, USA	676,248
201	Ricardo Gonzalez, Argentina	672,031
202	Fabian Gomez, Argentina	670,152
203	Scott Langley, USA	668,034
204	Retief Goosen, South Africa	663,823
205	Trevor Immelman, South Africa	661,299
206	Robert-Jan Derksen, Netherlands	659,484
207	Maximilian Kieffer, Germany	654,824
208	Satoshi Kodaira, Japan	653,843
209	Chad Campbell, USA	648,522
210	Hennie Otto, South Africa	641,548
211	Stuart Appleby, Australia	635,940
212	Romain Wattel, France	621,887
213	Woody Austin, USA	620,675
214	Prayad Marksaeng, Thailand	620,269
215	Ben Martin, USA	618,912
216	Paul Waring, England	618,514
217	Richie Ramsay, Scotland	617,694
218	Russell Knox, Scotland	614,044
219	Chez Reavie, USA	602,692
220	Gaganjeet Bhullar, India	601,048
221	Kyoung-Hoon Lee, Korea	595,386
222	Jim Herman, USA	590,617
223	Gregory Havret, France	587,351
224	Will MacKenzie, USA	584,361
225	Brad Fritsch, Canada	574,184
226	Masanori Kobayashi, Japan	572,073
227	Tommy Gainey, USA	569,829
228	Michael Putnam, USA	567,599
229	Jorge Campillo, Spain	567,505
230	Siddikur, Bangladesh	564,600
231	Steve Webster, England	563,071
232	Matthew Baldwin, England	557,131
233	K.T. Kim, Korea	556,691
234	Sean O'Hair, USA	550,597
235	Briny Baird, USA	548,375
236	Shunsuke Sonoda, Japan	546,762
237	Graeme Storm, England	545,518
238	Justin Bolli, USA	545,187
239	Kazuhiro Yamashita, Japan	541,372
240	Jaco Van Zyl, South Africa	532,942
241	Troy Matteson, USA	532,890
242	Shawn Stefani, USA	532,334
243	Tomohiro Kondo, Japan	529,764
244	Anirban Lahiri, India	526,135
245	Brad Kennedy, Australia	520,425
246	David Drysdale, Scotland	518,234

POS.	PLAYER, COUNTRY	TOTAL MONEY
247	John Parry, England	517,639
248	S.K. Ho, Korea	511,801
249	Bud Cauley, USA	509,498
250	Shiv Kapur, India	508,742
251	Eddie Pepperell, England	508,440
252	Richard Finch, England	500,265
253	Dicky Pride, USA	499,610
254	Andrew Svoboda, USA	498,976
255	J.B. Hansen, Denmark	493,310
256	Hiroyuki Fujita, Japan	484,801
257	Robert Streb, USA	483,590
258	Tom Lewis, England	473,270
259	Greg Owen, England	471,523
260	Edward Loar, USA	470,439
261	Damien McGrane, Ireland	469,651
262	Sung Kang, Korea	468,703
263	Emiliano Grillo, Argentina	464,082
264	Anders Hansen, Denmark	457,225
265	Yoshinobu Tsukada, Japan	455,857
266	Jonathan Byrd, USA	454,606
267	Robert Rock, England	453,213
268	Tag Ridings, USA	452,789
269	Jbe' Kruger, South Africa	447,090
270	Jin Jeong, Korea	446,589
271	Ben Kohles, USA	445,536
272	Vaughn Taylor, USA	444,061
273	Edoardo Molinari, Italy	441,214
274	Peter Whiteford, Scotland	438,888
275	Casey Wittenberg, USA	438,645
276	Patrick Cantlay, USA	438,516
277	Tim Wilkinson, New Zealand	435,040
278	Michael Hoey, N. Ireland	434,441
279	Y.E. Yang, Korea	433,046
280	Ben Curtis, USA	432,598
281	I.J. Jang, Korea	430,467
282	Alvaro Quiros, Spain	429,515
283	Seve Benson, England	422,899
284	Alexander Levy, France	414,572
285	Gareth Maybin, N. Ireland	413,158
286	Henrik Norlander, Sweden	412,975
287	Kevin Kisner, USA	412,238
288	Stuart Manley, Wales	410,334
289	Michio Matsumura, Japan	406,906
290	Thaworn Wiratchant, Thailand	404,564
291	Davis Love, USA	402,643
292	Nick O'Hern, Australia	395,525
293	Michael Hendry, New Zealand	393,431
294	Lee Slattery, England	390,874
295	Tetsuji Hiratsuka, Japan	386,535
296	Bobby Gates, USA	383,782
297	Seuk-Hyun Baek, Korea	383,118
298	Kevin Na, USA	379,397
299	Magnus A. Carlsson, Sweden	378,209

POS.	PLAYER, COUNTRY	TOTAL MONEY
300	Chris Doak, Scotland	376,922
301	Scott Gardiner, Australia	373,011
302	Darren Clarke, N. Ireland	372,494
303	Mark Foster, England	371,048
304	Prom Meesawat, Thailand	370,719
305	Danny Lee, New Zealand	366,810
306	David Oh, USA	361,493
307	Daisuke Maruyama, Japan	360,404
308	Kunihiro Kamii, Japan	358,596
309	Brendan Jones, Australia	357,089
310	Cameron Percy, Australia	356,096
311	James Kingston, South Africa	351,163
312	Tom Gillis, USA	345,325
313	Mark Tullo, Chile	345,006
314	Yuki Kono, Japan	340,672
315	Steve LeBrun, USA	339,577
316	Doug LaBelle, USA	338,921
317	Andy Sullivan, England	335,910
318	Oliver Fisher, England	328,981
319	Toru Taniguchi, Japan	328,169
320	Matthew Nixon, England	327,671
321	Ho-Sung Choi, Korea	320,932
322	David Higgins, Ireland	320,406
323	Richard Green, Australia	319,640
324	Brandt Jobe, USA	318,230
325	Daisuke Kataoka, Japan	317,715
326	Matthew Griffin, Australia	317,352
327	Cameron Beckman, USA	315,795
328	Toshinori Muto, Japan	309,993
329	Billy Hurley, USA	309,663
330	Mike Weir, Canada	308,670
331	D.J. Trahan, USA	308,199
332	Scott Strange, Australia	306,168
333	S.S.P. Chowrasia, India	305,428
334	Tim Herron, USA	302,570
335	Peter Malnati, USA	300,963
336	Will Claxton, USA	300,387
337	Robert Allenby, Australia	298,943
338	Soren Hansen, Denmark	295,172
339	Chris DiMarco, USA	293,530
340	Andres Gonzales, USA	292,280
341	Han Lee, USA	292,042
342	Jung-Gon Hwang, Korea	291,596
343	Juvic Pagunsan, Philippines	291,519
344	Richard Bland, England	291,178
345	Mathew Goggin, Australia	290,001
346	Bronson La'Cassie, Australia	288,300
347	Paul McGinley, Ireland	288,194
348	Hyun-Woo Ryu, Korea	285,958
349	Kevin Tway, USA	285,766
350	Mikko Korhonen, Finland	284,552

World Money List Leaders

YEAR	PLAYER, COUNTRY	TOTAL MONEY
1966	Jack Nicklaus, USA	$168,088
1967	Jack Nicklaus, USA	276,166
1968	Billy Casper, USA	222,436
1969	Frank Beard, USA	186,993
1970	Jack Nicklaus, USA	222,583
1971	Jack Nicklaus, USA	285,897
1972	Jack Nicklaus, USA	341,792
1973	Tom Weiskopf, USA	349,645
1974	Johnny Miller, USA	400,255
1975	Jack Nicklaus, USA	332,610
1976	Jack Nicklaus, USA	316,086
1977	Tom Watson, USA	358,034
1978	Tom Watson, USA	384,388
1979	Tom Watson, USA	506,912
1980	Tom Watson, USA	651,921
1981	Johnny Miller, USA	704,204
1982	Raymond Floyd, USA	738,699
1983	Seve Ballesteros, Spain	686,088
1984	Seve Ballesteros, Spain	688,047
1985	Bernhard Langer, Germany	860,262
1986	Greg Norman, Australia	1,146,584
1987	Ian Woosnam, Wales	1,793,268
1988	Seve Ballesteros, Spain	1,261,275
1989	David Frost, South Africa	1,650,230
1990	Jose Maria Olazabal, Spain	1,633,640
1991	Bernhard Langer, Germany	2,186,700
1992	Nick Faldo, England	2,748,248
1993	Nick Faldo, England	2,825,280
1994	Ernie Els, South Africa	2,862,854
1995	Corey Pavin, USA	2,746,340
1996	Colin Montgomerie, Scotland	3,071,442
1997	Colin Montgomerie, Scotland	3,366,900
1998	Tiger Woods, USA	2,927,946
1999	Tiger Woods, USA	7,681,625
2000	Tiger Woods, USA	11,034,530
2001	Tiger Woods, USA	7,771,562
2002	Tiger Woods, USA	8,292,188
2003	Vijay Singh, Fiji	8,499,611
2004	Vijay Singh, Fiji	11,638,699
2005	Tiger Woods, USA	12,280,404
2006	Tiger Woods, USA	13,325,949
2007	Tiger Woods, USA	12,902,706
2008	Vijay Singh, Fiji	8,025,128
2009	Tiger Woods, USA	10,998,054
2010	Graeme McDowell, N. Ireland	7,371,586
2011	Luke Donald, England	9,730,870
2012	Rory McIlroy, N. Ireland	11,301,228
2013	Tiger Woods, USA	9,490,217

Career World Money List

Here is a list of the 50 leading money winners for their careers through the 2013 season. It includes players active on both the regular and senior tours of the world. The World Money List from this and the 47 previous editions of the annual and a table prepared for a companion book, *The Wonderful World of Professional Golf* (Atheneum, 1973) form the basis for this compilation. Additional figures were taken from official records of major golf associations. Conversion of foreign currency figures to U.S. dollars is based on average values during the particular years involved.

POS.	PLAYER, COUNTRY	TOTAL MONEY
1	Tiger Woods, USA	$133,094,120
2	Ernie Els, South Africa	85,320,030
3	Vijay Singh, Fiji	82,196,905
4	Phil Mickelson, USA	80,743,656
5	Jim Furyk, USA	67,485,546
6	Davis Love, USA	52,285,948
7	Sergio Garcia, Spain	52,266,952
8	Lee Westwood, England	52,173,329
9	Padraig Harrington, Ireland	50,490,784
10	Retief Goosen, South Africa	50,160,346
11	Luke Donald, England	48,016,370
12	Adam Scott, Australia	46,018,399
13	Bernhard Langer, Germany	43,942,083
14	Steve Stricker, USA	43,635,466
15	David Toms, USA	42,439,697
16	Colin Montgomerie, Scotland	42,105,950
17	Justin Rose, England	40,983,442
18	Kenny Perry, USA	40,746,922
19	Fred Couples, USA	39,488,264
20	Nick Price, Zimbabwe	37,652,760
21	Hale Irwin, USA	37,276,119
22	Ian Poulter, England	37,034,753
23	Justin Leonard, USA	36,296,288
24	Stewart Cink, USA	36,038,607
25	Robert Allenby, Australia	35,994,218
26	Zach Johnson, USA	35,176,921
27	Mark Calcavecchia, USA	34,984,886
28	Tom Lehman, USA	33,947,180
29	K.J. Choi, South Korea	33,895,007
30	Darren Clarke, N. Ireland	33,198,076
31	Graeme McDowell, N. Ireland	33,003,061
32	Fred Funk, USA	32,827,252
33	Jay Haas, USA	32,067,141
34	Rory McIlroy, N. Ireland	31,799,872
35	Stuart Appleby, Australia	31,634,301
36	Matt Kuchar, USA	31,443,457
37	Geoff Ogilvy, Australia	31,164,818
38	Miguel Angel Jimenez, Spain	31,132,046
39	Tom Kite, USA	30,973,720
40	Rory Sabbatini, South Africa	30,475,670

POS.	PLAYER, COUNTRY	TOTAL MONEY
41	Mike Weir, Canada	29,975,964
42	Paul Casey, England	29,352,146
43	Jeff Sluman, USA	29,168,929
44	Scott Verplank, USA	28,778,452
45	Loren Roberts, USA	28,472,854
46	Tom Watson, USA	28,206,552
47	Charles Howell, USA	27,977,705
48	Mark O'Meara, USA	27,749,659
49	Scott Hoch, USA	27,671,900
50	Chris DiMarco, USA	27,430,574

These 50 players have won $2,086,395,097 in their careers.

Women's World Money List

This list includes official earnings on the U.S. LPGA Tour, Ladies European Tour, Japan LPGA Tour and Australian Ladies Tour, along with other winnings in established unofficial events when reliable figures could be obtained.

POS.	PLAYER, COUNTRY	TOTAL MONEY
1	Inbee Park, Korea	$2,508,811
2	Suzann Pettersen, Norway	2,373,236
3	Stacy Lewis, USA	2,005,868
4	Shanshan Feng, China	2,004,949
5	So Yeon Ryu, Korea	1,344,204
6	Lexi Thompson, USA	1,263,609
7	Rikako Morita, Japan	1,258,880
8	Sakura Yokomine, Japan	1,241,179
9	I.K. Kim, Korea	1,141,910
10	Beatriz Recari, Spain	1,106,438
11	Teresa Lu, Taipei	938,457
12	Na Yeon Choi, Korea	929,964
13	Miki Saiki, Japan	916,534
14	Sun-Ju Ahn, Korea	901,986
15	Yumiko Yoshida, Japan	886,138
16	Mamiko Higa, Japan	864,126
17	Hee Young Park, Korea	848,676
18	Paula Creamer, USA	831,918
19	Caroline Hedwall, Sweden	825,012
20	Karrie Webb, Australia	806,440
21	Jiyai Shin, Korea	805,350
22	Bo-Mee Lee, Korea	800,287
23	Angela Stanford, USA	778,234
24	Karine Icher, France	759,537
25	Lizette Salas, USA	759,323
26	Chella Choi, Korea	739,441

POS.	PLAYER, COUNTRY	TOTAL MONEY
27	Amy Yang, Korea	719,481
28	Shiho Oyama, Japan	711,405
29	Cristie Kerr, USA	710,946
30	Anna Nordqvist, Sweden	709,114
31	Pornanong Phatlum, Thailand	700,710
32	Catriona Matthew, Scotland	686,154
33	Natsuka Hori, Japan	645,140
34	Na-Ri Lee, Korea	638,325
35	Mi-Jeong Jeon, Korea	617,736
36	Jessica Korda, USA	606,639
37	Morgan Pressel, USA	603,800
38	Ilhee Lee, Korea	595,800
39	Ai Miyazato, Japan	594,412
40	Gerina Piller, USA	572,690
41	Yuki Ichinose, Japan	559,876
42	Ritsuko Ryu, Japan	542,618
43	Carlota Ciganda, Spain	532,828
44	Asako Fujimoto, Japan	515,459
45	Yukari Baba, Japan	511,136
46	Azahara Munoz, Spain	508,246
47	Jodi Ewart Shadoff, England	493,091
48	Da-Ye Na, Korea	481,235
49	Jennifer Johnson, USA	472,778
50	Onnarin Sattayabanphot, Thailand	469,666
51	Junko Omote, Japan	456,618
52	Erika Kikuchi, Japan	456,388
53	Misuzu Narita, Japan	455,029
54	Brittany Lincicome, USA	449,113
55	Hee Kyung Seo, Korea	446,373
56	Sandra Gal, Germany	445,972
57	Se Ri Pak, Korea	440,162
58	Soo-Yun Kang, Korea	438,244
59	Esther Lee, Korea	431,589
60	Kumiko Kaneda, Japan	427,871
61	Mayu Hattori, Japan	417,929
62	Mika Miyazato, Japan	417,658
63	Haeji Kang, Korea	408,641
64	Yani Tseng, Taipei	405,068
65	Na-Ri Kim, Korea	395,414
66	Ji-Hee Lee, Korea	390,929
67	Ayako Uehara, Japan	384,034
68	Sun Young Yoo, Korea	383,748
69	Hiromi Mogi, Japan	365,149
70	Harukyo Nomura, Japan	356,086
71	Michelle Wie, USA	355,853
72	Brittany Lang, USA	355,809
73	Yuri Fudoh, Japan	352,113
74	Miki Sakai, Japan	350,073
75	Caroline Masson, Germany	339,634
76	Lee-Anne Pace, South Africa	336,243
77	Erina Hara, Japan	332,588
78	Jenny Shin, Korea	332,461
79	Eun-Hee Ji, Korea	332,012

POS.	PLAYER, COUNTRY	TOTAL MONEY
80	Meena Lee, Korea	324,362
81	Mo Martin, USA	319,244
82	Rui Kitada, Japan	314,651
83	Maiko Wakabayashi, Japan	308,363
84	Gwladys Nocera, France	296,526
85	Mina Harigae, USA	293,195
86	Moriya Jutanugarn, Thailand	293,158
87	Giulia Sergas, Italy	283,617
88	Kaori Ohe, Japan	279,572
89	Lala Anai, Japan	276,072
90	Momoko Ueda, Japan	273,917
91	Jane Park, USA	267,757
92	Kaori Nakamura, Japan	259,190
93	Alison Walshe, USA	258,200
94	Irene Cho, USA	257,202
95	Megumi Kido, Japan	253,216
96	Pernilla Lindberg, Sweden	252,074
97	Eun-Bi Jang, Korea	250,155
98	Young Kim, Korea	249,474
99	Yuko Fukuda, Japan	241,564
100	Ah-Reum Hwang, Korea	229,962
101	Candie Kung, Taipei	228,929
102	Julieta Granada, Paraguay	227,097
103	Katherine Hull-Kirk, Australia	223,138
104	Akane Iijima, Japan	221,725
105	Danielle Kang, USA	221,649
106	Phoebe Yao, Taipei	218,728
107	Juli Inkster, USA	211,878
108	Chie Arimura, Japan	211,846
109	Nicole Castrale, USA	209,915
110	Ayaka Watanabe, Japan	205,405
111	Mariajo Uribe, Colombia	197,839
112	Kaori Aoyama, Japan	190,537
113	Yuki Sakurai, Japan	187,496
114	Natalie Gulbis, USA	187,237
115	Dewi Claire Schreefel, Netherlands	186,412
116	Christel Boeljon, Netherlands	186,123
117	Charley Hull, England	182,232
118	Stacy Prammanasudh, USA	181,246
119	Saiki Fujita, Japan	176,472
120	Yun-Jye Wei, Taipei	176,230
121	Jee Young Lee, Korea	172,692
122	Mihoko Iseri, Japan	169,704
123	Ji-Woo Lee, Korea	163,051
124	Christina Kim, USA	156,191
125	Holly Clyburn, England	155,575
126	Jennifer Rosales, Philippines	154,166
127	Jacqui Concolino, USA	150,573
128	Hiroko Azuma, Japan	145,089
129	Hee-Won Han, Korea	143,904
130	Austin Ernst, USA	142,002
131	Cindy Lacrosse, USA	141,734
132	Shiho Toyonaga, Japan	139,943

POS.	PLAYER, COUNTRY	TOTAL MONEY
133	Lindsey Wright, Australia	138,748
134	Thidapa Suwannapura, Thailand	137,554
135	Vicky Hurst, USA	137,069
136	Yayoi Arasaki, Japan	136,658
137	Mami Fukuda, Japan	136,173
138	M.J. Hur, Korea	132,504
139	Valentine Derrey, France	130,899
140	Mikaela Parmlid, Sweden	129,591
141	Satsuki Oshiro, Japan	127,946
142	Sarah Kemp, Australia	126,972
143	Ha-Neul Kim, Korea	125,304
144	Stacey Keating, Australia	125,145
145	Joanna Klatten, France	124,459
146	Lisa McCloskey, USA	123,886
147	Rebecca Artis, Australia	122,703
148	Belen Mozo, Spain	121,352
149	Li-Ying Ye, China	120,585
150	Ashleigh Simon, South Africa	118,714
151	Rebecca Lee-Bentham, Canada	118,441
152	Yuko Saitoh, Japan	114,449
153	Paola Moreno, Colombia	113,151
154	Beth Allen, USA	113,145
155	Katie Burnett, USA	112,066
156	Rie Tsuji, Japan	111,573
157	Sarah Jane Smith, Australia	109,605
158	So-Hee Kim, Korea	109,050
159	Kristy McPherson, USA	108,615
160	Yuko Mitsuka, Japan	108,368
161	Sydnee Michaels, USA	107,365
162	Bo-Bae Song, Korea	106,846
163	Nachiyo Ohtani, Japan	103,267
164	Laura Davies, England	100,636
165	Ryann O'Toole, USA	100,554
166	Mayumi Shimomura, Japan	100,529
167	Sei Young Kim, Korea	100,479
168	Hannah Burke, England	100,425
169	Ariya Jutanugarn, Thailand	99,858
170	Hiroko Fukushima, Japan	98,548
171	Hyun-Ju Shin, Korea	93,184
172	Diana Luna, Italy	91,723
173	Nikki Campbell, Australia	89,716
174	Amelia Lewis, USA	89,582
175	Linda Wessberg, Sweden	88,361

Senior World Money List

This list includes official earnings from the U.S. Champions Tour, European Senior Tour and Japan Senior Tour, along with other winnings in established official and unofficial tournaments when reliable figures could be obtained.

POS.	PLAYER, COUNTRY	TOTAL MONEY
1	Bernhard Langer, Germany	$2,601,104
2	Kenny Perry, USA	2,341,188
3	Fred Couples, USA	2,000,210
4	David Frost, South Africa	1,834,098
5	Russ Cochran, USA	1,477,651
6	Michael Allen, USA	1,454,841
7	Tom Pernice, Jr., USA	1,444,527
8	Kirk Triplett, USA	1,395,679
9	Duffy Waldorf, USA	1,387,224
10	Rocco Mediate, USA	1,341,098
11	John Cook, USA	1,330,929
12	Peter Senior, Australia	1,287,292
13	Esteban Toledo, Mexico	1,271,758
14	Vijay Singh, Fiji	1,151,575
15	Corey Pavin, USA	1,088,648
16	Mark O'Meara, USA	1,086,935
17	Fred Funk, USA	1,079,919
18	Jeff Sluman, USA	1,077,871
19	Jay Haas, USA	1,006,699
20	Bart Bryant, USA	972,961
21	Gene Sauers, USA	893,272
22	Tom Lehman, USA	891,989
23	Mark Calcavecchia, USA	805,681
24	Mark Wiebe, USA	803,025
25	Kiyoshi Murota, Japan	783,286
26	Jay Don Blake, USA	735,614
27	Chien Soon Lu, Taipei	688,749
28	Mike Goodes, USA	677,843
29	Kohki Idoki, Japan	613,526
30	Steve Elkington, Australia	598,957
31	Craig Stadler, USA	573,597
32	John Riegger, USA	567,857
33	Dan Forsman, USA	539,854
34	Colin Montgomerie, Scotland	534,329
35	Rod Spittle, Canada	484,431
36	Brad Faxon, USA	467,416
37	Bill Glasson, USA	459,277
38	Paul Wesselingh, England	459,054
39	Tom Kite, USA	440,813
40	Loren Roberts, USA	425,039
41	Scott Hoch, USA	416,479
42	Steve Pate, USA	393,653
43	Olin Browne, USA	387,063
44	Jeff Hart, USA	380,128
45	John Huston, USA	377,416
46	Anders Forsbrand, Sweden	360,028

POS.	PLAYER, COUNTRY	TOTAL MONEY
47	Willie Wood, USA	341,671
48	Gary Hallberg, USA	341,220
49	Roger Chapman, England	337,433
50	Tom Byrum, USA	336,342
51	Barry Lane, England	336,093
52	Bob Tway, USA	333,026
53	Larry Mize, USA	326,762
54	Seiki Okuda, Japan	319,686
55	Mark McNulty, Zimbabwe	317,366
56	Joe Daley, USA	310,774
57	Sandy Lyle, England	306,428
58	David Eger, USA	293,301
59	Tom Watson, USA	287,849
60	Bobby Clampett, USA	284,476
61	Boonchu Ruangkit, Thailand	284,321
62	Peter Fowler, Australia	283,374
63	Joel Edwards, USA	277,611
64	Jim Rutledge, Canada	271,381
65	Steen Tinning, Denmark	269,974
66	Tsukasa Watanabe, Japan	254,795
67	Larry Nelson, USA	250,285
68	Doug Garwood, USA	249,469
69	Minoru Higashi, Japan	243,732
70	Dick Mast, USA	243,168
71	Brian Henninger, USA	240,787
72	Simon P. Brown, England	237,756
73	Miguel Angel Martin, Spain	237,567
74	Yutaka Hagawa, Japan	236,160
75	Jim Gallagher, Jr., USA	233,612
76	Morris Hatalsky, USA	231,693
77	Brad Bryant, USA	230,516
78	Scott Simpson, USA	223,306
79	Andrew Magee, USA	219,053
80	Mark Brooks, USA	217,100
81	Jeff Freeman, USA	213,896
82	Kiyoshi Maita, Japan	212,776
83	Hale Irwin, USA	210,264
84	Tommy Nakajima, Japan	203,385
85	Philip Golding, England	199,337
86	Andrew Oldcorn, Scotland	192,592
87	Ian Woosnam, Wales	190,106
88	Peter Jacobsen, USA	189,555
89	Hal Sutton, USA	180,168
90	Santiago Luna, Spain	178,423
91	Massy Kuramoto, Japan	176,281
92	Gregory Meyer, USA	175,677
93	Mark Mouland, Wales	168,262
94	Steve Lowery, USA	164,493
95	Angel Franco, Paraguay	161,942
96	Frankie Minoza, Philippines	161,640
97	David J. Russell, England	161,549
98	Steve Jones, USA	153,335
99	Tommy Armour, USA	152,389
100	Gil Morgan, USA	151,544

1. The Year in Retrospect

Rarely have so many players had so much to celebrate in one year of golf. That's what made 2013 so special.

Go back to 1996, about the time Greg Norman was beginning to fade from his best golf and Tiger Woods was just arriving, to find a season that was all about sharing the wealth. It seems only the names changed. There was Nick Faldo winning a sixth major and third green jacket (at the expense of Norman, naturally). Phil Mickelson won four times to signal his emergence. Tom Lehman, a regular in the final group at a major, finally won the big one with his victory at the Open Championship. He also captured the money title in the final week by winning the Tour Championship. Woods turned pro at 20 with hopes of not having to go to qualifying school. He wound up at the Tour Championship, instead, a winner in two of his first seven tournaments. Norman was No. 1 in the world for the entire season. And it might have been an even longer list of players except that one of the game's rising stars, Ernie Els, had a pedestrian year by his standards.

Is that much different from what we saw in 2013?

Phil Mickelson won his fifth major at the Open Championship, the one major hardly anyone thought he could win. Woods had five official victories, the most of any male player in the world. Henrik Stenson played the best golf of anyone the second half of the year when he won twice during the FedExCup to claim the $10 million prize, and the DP World Tour Championship to claim the Race to Dubai. If that wasn't enough, Stenson finished in the top three at the last two majors. Youth was served by Jordan Spieth and Hideki Matsuyama. Spieth, a 20-year-old Texan, started the year with no status and finished it in the Presidents Cup. Matsuyama turned pro in April, not long after he turned 21, and won four times on the Japan Golf Tour, becoming the first rookie to win the money title. And strangely missing from the conversation was Rory McIlroy, the rising star, who began 2013 at No. 1 in the world and didn't win a tournament until December.

To the victors went the spoils, and there was a lot to go around. So if there were comparisons between 1996 and 2013, the same kind of questions surely were raised. After years of dominance by one player (with an occasional party crasher), had golf reached an age of parity? Was the game at a point where the dominant player showed some flaws in his game, just as a new crop of stars were starting to emerge?

Thomas Bjorn was talking about some of the young Americans who had decided to start their careers on the European Tour when he unwittingly gave a defining statement about golf. "The PGA Tour is very hard. It's a hard tour," Bjorn said. Going into 2013, the top 28 players in the World Ranking had PGA Tour membership. There had been talk of a world tour for the last couple of years, and while the PGA Tour is not the model of a world tour that anyone had in mind, it turned into a stage for a heavyweight battle. Yes, it's hard. It's hard to win. And with so much talent, it's hard even to get to the final two hours of a tournament with even a chance to win. Perhaps more than any other time, the game felt very much like a job. Each tournament was a tough day in the office.

"I think it's deeper now than it ever has been," Woods said at the end of the year. "There is more young talent. There are more guys winning golf tournaments for the first time. If you look at the major championships, how long did we go from basically Phil winning and Phil winning?" He was referring to the 13 majors between Mickelson winning the 2010 Masters and the 2013 Open Championship. Eleven of those champions had never won a major. The exceptions were Els and McIlroy. And of those 11 first-time major champions, 10 of them remain in the top 40 of the World Ranking. It's hard out there.

That explains why Woods had so much explaining to do. He won five times, including a pair of World Golf Championships and The Players Championship. No one else in men's golf won more official events (Adam Scott had five wins including the PGA Grand Slam of Golf, a 36-hole exhibition in Bermuda), yet Woods spent the final few months having to justify how he could call it a great year without winning a major. He said it was a "pretty good" year, though he said this with the kind of sarcastic chuckle that suggested it was a little bit better than that.

Woods should be used to playing by a different set of rules. He spent much of the previous decade being compared to his 2000 season. Even now, he is compared mainly to his past, and to quote Roger Maltbie from Woods' 15-shot U.S. Open win at Pebble Beach, it's not a fair fight. Even more unfair is to ask Woods if he would trade his year with anyone else. Sure, he would love to add to his tally of 14 majors, which has been unchanged since that U.S. Open win in 2008 at Torrey Pines. But to swap his season for one major — the U.S. Open by Justin Rose, the PGA Championship won by Jason Dufner — would mean Woods had to give away another PGA Tour money title, another Vardon Trophy for the lowest adjusted scoring average, another vote as PGA Tour Player of the Year. Suffice to say it was a very good year.

But this could not be called the year of the Tiger. Too many other players claimed a rightful share of the glory.

About the only thing Stenson had achieved the first half of the year was a tie for second in the Shell Houston Open. That enabled him to get into the Masters, and ultimately the U.S. Open. The Swede took it from there. His long game was nothing short of spectacular, and he did enough right with the putter that his name seemed to be on the leaderboard every week he played. And not just any leaderboard. He was leading on the last day of the Scottish Open. He was second at the Open Championship. He was second at a World Golf Championship, third at the PGA Championship and won two FedExCup Playoff events. "Obviously, the work was done before. It's not like I woke up in the middle of July and played fantastic," Stenson said.

Woods earned 488.254 World Ranking points in 2013. Stenson had 484.598. The next closest player on that list was more than 100 points down the list. It was the third straight year of a sweep — Luke Donald (2011) and McIlroy (2012) won the money title on the PGA Tour and European Tour. Stenson was the first to sweep the FedExCup and the Race to Dubai. Is there a better definition of "world player of the year" than to claim titles on the two biggest tours?

Scott surely would not trade his season with anyone. In fact, the Australian is not sure whatever he does the rest of his career will match what he achieved in 2013. Sure, he might win more majors. He might someday reached No. 1 in the world. But can any major feel as good as the first one, especially one that made him the first Australian to slip into a green jacket in Butler Cabin? The reactions said it all. After making a 25-foot birdie putt on the 18th hole Sunday, he planted his feet and thrust out his arms — one of them clinging to that long putter — as he screamed with all his might, "C'mon, Aussie!" Then, he won on the second playoff hole over Angel Cabrera with a 10-foot birdie putt in the gloaming. Scott leaned back with his feet firmly planted on the ground and his eyes looking toward heaven. More than that moment alone, Scott also won The Barclays against perhaps the strongest field of the year. And when he finally went home to let a nation see that elusive green jacket, a victory tour took on new meaning. He won the Australian PGA Championship, the Australian Masters, won the team title in the World Cup with Jason Day and nearly made it a clean sweep at the Australian Open until a two-shot swing on the last hole gave McIlroy his first win. A pretty good year? It was way better than that.

Mickelson also was living a dream, even though there were moments when it felt like a nightmare. Already a member of the World Golf Hall of Fame, his place secure as one of the greats in golf, there's always something missing for Lefty. He's the best player to have never been No. 1 in the world since the Official World Golf Ranking began in 1986. He's the best player to have never won a PGA Tour money title, the best to have never won a Vardon Trophy, the best to have never been voted PGA Tour Player of the Year. And while Sam Snead, based on his 82 wins, has to be considered the best to have never won a U.S. Open, Mickelson wins the award for close calls. He now has six silver medals from the U.S. Open after finishing runner-up at Merion. Too bad the USGA doesn't award the Purple Heart as much as Mickelson has been wounded at his national championship. Despite that crushing blow, his season turned spectacular with two weeks in Scotland. First, he won the Scottish Open at Castle Stuart. Then, he closed with a 66 at Muirfield, arguably the best final round of the year, to win the Open Championship. Even as he spoke during his press conference, he never took his hand off the base of that claret jug. It was a special moment. And while it left Mickelson one major shy of the career Grand Slam, winning the right three majors — Augusta National, an American major (PGA Championship) and links golf — showed he was a complete player.

The other majors went to Justin Rose in the U.S. Open at Merion and Jason Dufner in the PGA Championship at Oak Hill. Both were great moments — Rose with his classic swing under pressure with a four iron on the 18th hole, not far from the plaque honoring Ben Hogan's historic one-iron shot in the 1950 U.S. Open; Dufner for his chance at becoming the first player with a 62 in the major. He had a 10-foot birdie putt on the last hole that he left short. Ultimately, he walked off the green with his first major title. Neither of them, however, won another tournament this year.

Matsuyama won't get as much attention as Spieth for what he did this year because his wins were all in Japan, though he outperformed the Texan in the majors. Matsuyama, who didn't play in the Masters, was in the top 20 at the other three majors. He is not as outgoing as Ryo Ishikawa, the Japanese teen idol who preceded him, and he is not as comfortable in front of the camera as Spieth. The young Texan kept resetting his goals until he ended the year as the youngest player in the Presidents Cup at No. 7 in the FedExCup standings.

The other big winner this year would be the Royal & Ancient Golf Club and the U.S. Golf Association, who patiently waited through a 90-day comment period before announcing a new rule that starts in 2016 and will outlaw the anchored method for using long putters. Keegan Bradley was the first player to win a major with an anchored putting stroke (belly putter). He started a trend in which four players with long putters won six majors. Those days will be over in two years.

One reason so many players could claim such a great year was because of Woods. When he was winning six or seven times a year, including a major or more, there wasn't enough wealth to share. Colin Montgomerie used to joke — we think he was joking, anyway — that it was harder than ever to win a major because Woods typically won two of them, another was won by the likes of Mickelson, Els and Vijay Singh, and that left only one for everyone else. That's no longer the case. Woods has played 18 straight majors without winning one; compare that with the start of his career when he won six of the first 18 majors he played. However, he won five times, which is no small task on the PGA Tour these days. It was the 11th time in his career he had won at least five times worldwide in a single season. Five other players won at least three times — Scott, Matsuyama, Graeme McDowell, Mickelson and Stenson.

Might the landscape have looked differently if McIlroy had kept his form? He ended the 2012 season at No. 1 in the world, and it wasn't particularly close. He had won a major in each of the previous two years by eight shots, setting a U.S. Open scoring record (268) at Congressional in 2011 and a PGA Championship record for winning margin (eight shots) at Kiawah Island a year later. McIlroy was trying to join Woods and Mickelson as the only players in the last 30 years to win a major in three successive seasons. But the golf didn't match the hype, and the hype didn't always have to do with his golf. In the worst-kept secret in the industry, McIlroy agreed to a massive deal with Nike in which he switched out his entire line of equipment — driver, fairway metals, irons, putter, golf ball — and only conceded late in the year that it took him until September to find the right driver.

Frustration set in early. A missed cut in the Abu Dhabi HSBC Golf Championship. A first-round loss at the Accenture Match Play Championship. He walked off the course after 26 holes at the Honda Classic and had to face his first serious criticism and his first "mea culpa" before the press. In May, it was revealed that McIlroy was changing management companies (for the second time in two years), a dispute that wound up in an Irish court and likely won't be resolved until it goes to trial right after the Ryder Cup. He finished his long year with a win in Australia and a big sigh of relief when he walked off the 18th green in the final round of the Northwestern Mutual World Challenge. "It's been the first year I had to put up with scrutiny and criticism, and it was trying. You have just to believe in what you're doing and not let it get to you too much," McIlroy said. "I let it get to me a few times."

It was a year to forget for McIlroy, but it is worth remembering because of the Woods factor. They were supposed to be the latest rivalry in golf. McIlroy was No. 1. McIlroy figured to be the favorite in the majors. McIlroy had won five times the previous year, the most of anyone in the world. Would he have the same effect on players' ability to win multiple tournaments the way Woods once did? Stay tuned. That certainly wasn't the case in 2013. Woods was No. 3 in the World Ranking to start 2013. The gap between McIlroy at No. 1 and Woods at No. 3 was comparable to the gap between Woods and Jim Furyk at No. 27.

Woods needed only six tournaments to return to No. 1 in the world. His universe appeared to return to normal when he won the Farmers Insurance Open at Torrey Pines, the seventh time Woods had won the tournament, not including his U.S. Open win in 2008. More telling was that the outcome was inevitable as Woods built an eight-shot lead in the final round, which was completed on Monday because of fog. Only when the pace dragged on did Woods lose patience and stop dropping shots that really didn't matter. He still won by four shots in his PGA Tour debut. He won again at another familiar haunt — the TPC Blue Monster at Doral — after getting a putting tip from Steve Stricker. It turned out to be one of the best putting weeks of his year. Another weather-related finish on Monday, this due to a microburst at Bay Hill that toppled tents, ended with Woods' third win in four stroke-play events. More than his play, there was a sense of peace about him that had been missing the last couple of years. He was comfortable on the golf course and before the media. He announced he was dating Olympic ski champion Lindsey Vonn, and he was having his way with the competition with the Masters right around the corner. That peace was shattered by a perfect shot.

Woods appeared to be in total control when he arrived on the 15th hole Friday at Augusta National, tied for the lead and with a lob wedge in his hand. The shot looked to be perfect — too perfect, as it turned out. It hit the flag and caromed back down the front of the green and into the water. Instead of a short birdie attempt to take the lead, he had to scramble for bogey. Only the next morning was it revealed that Woods had taken an incorrect drop — purposely a few feet behind his divot to avoid hitting the pin — and he was penalized two shots. Woods was not disqualified for signing an incorrect scorecard (his 71 became a 73) because of a committee error. Augusta National said it had information that the drop might have been incorrect but failed to talk to Woods about it before he signed his card. This is covered under Rule 33-7. Woods tied for fourth, four shots out of the lead, though he was not a serious contender on the back nine Sunday. The rest of the weekend was filled with arguments and opinions on how he was not disqualified for signing an incorrect scorecard and that he should have withdrawn. Woods was in the middle of a controversy not of his doing except for going blank when it came to taking the proper drop.

He won The Players Championship for only the second time in his career, and the first time since 2001. He didn't reveal until the U.S. Open that he had an elbow injury at the TPC Sawgrass, and Woods constantly shook his left arm during the U.S. Open at Merion, where he said his elbow was in serious pain. It was serious enough that he withdrew from the AT&T National, which benefits his foundation, and the Greenbrier Classic. He challenged at the Open Championship, and won his fifth tournament of the year at Firestone with a seven-shot victory in the Bridgestone Invitational. It was his 18th title in a World Golf Championship and the sixth time he had won multiple WGCs in one season. A pretty good year, indeed. But his year was equally measured by more than five wins. It was remembered for no majors and three rules violations.

The latter made this a most peculiar year for Woods. He missed the cut in the Abu Dhabi HSBC Golf Championship when he took relief from what he thought was an imbedded ball in vegetation, except that it was considered sand and relief was not allowed. He was docked two shots, taking him outside the cut line. Then came the most memorable ruling at Augusta National, in which Woods said in post-round interviews that he purposely chose not to drop in the same spot. The most perplexing rules violation happened at the BMW Championship at Conway Farms during the FedExCup Playoffs. Early in the second round, Woods went long of the first green and had a small twig in front of his ball that he tried to move. When it appeared the ball began to move, Woods stopped what he was doing. Little did he know that a videographer from PGA Tour Entertainment captured the entire sequence on film because of the scenic nature — all anyone could see beneath the canopy of trees was Woods from the knees down. The videographer shipped the film to headquarters, where an editor thought he detected the ball moved. He notified the tour, which notified the rules officials on site. Video showed the ball moved, if not a fraction of an inch. Woods, however, was insistent than it only oscillated. He was overruled by the rules staff, which assessed him a two-shot penalty.

The timing was only fitting. It was such a strange year on the PGA Tour that while Woods was watching the video replay in a scoring trailer with two officials, Jim Furyk was only a few hundred yards away, knocking in a three-foot birdie putt on his final hole (No. 9) at Conway Farms to become only the sixth player in tour history with a 59. What made this score so unique is that Furyk became the first player to shoot 59 with a bogey! He joined Chip Beck and Paul Goydos as the only players with a 59 who failed to win. Victory that week went to Zach Johnson. The story, as usual, was Woods.

He was celebrated for his five wins on strong courses against the strongest fields. He was criticized for not winning a major. He was under great scrutiny because of the rules violations, even though he was penalized in each case. And the tone turned ugly at the end of the year when Golf Channel analyst Brandel Chamblee, in a column posted to Golf.com, crossed out a grade of "A" and gave Woods an "F" for his season, insinuating that he had cheated. Chamblee ultimately apologized for "going too far" in his analysis, and Woods' agent, Mark Steinberg, suggested a lawsuit might be in order. It ended there. Woods finished out his year by losing a four-shot lead on the back nine of the Northwestern Mutual World Challenge. Zach Johnson holed out from the drop zone in the 18th fairway for par to force a playoff, and Johnson won when Woods missed a short par putt on the first extra hole. These are the kind of things Woods rarely did, if ever.

Stenson's disappearing and reappearing act? Been there, done that. He was at No. 351 in the World Ranking at the start of June in 2004 and then climbed all the way to No. 6 within three years. Injuries contributed plenty to his most recent slide that took him all the way down to No. 230 in the world early in 2012. Perhaps more telling of the slump was that Stenson, who holed the putt that gave Europe outright victory in the 2006 Ryder Cup, was not even close to making the last two teams. He was all but forgotten. History should suggest never to write him off. There were signs of Stenson turning his game around late in 2012 when he had the occasional top-10 (followed by a missed cut), and then won the South African Open to crack the top 100. In the spring, he still needed a late surge just to qualify for the Masters. He got there with a top-10 at the Arnold Palmer Invitational at Bay Hill, and then a 68-66 weekend in the Shell Houston Open to get into the top 50. And he was on his way.

There are various metrics to measure his meteoric rise back to the elite in golf. Stenson earned roughly $2 million in 2012, finishing out of the top 100 on the PGA Tour money list and only No. 40 on the European Tour. He finished 2013 second with just over $9.1 million on the World Money List, second only to the nearly $9.5 million won by Woods. Of course, that doesn't include the $10 million bonus Stenson earned from capturing the FedExCup, or the $1 million bonus from winning the Race to Dubai. He played in only one major in 2012 (the Masters, based on his 2009 victory in The Players Championship). He not only played in all four majors in 2013, he had a chance to win two of them. But perhaps the best measure of progress occurred after the third round of the PGA Championship. After signing his card, a Golf Channel reporter approached and said, "Henrik, can you give us time for a few questions?" To which the droll Swede replied, "Do you have time to show a few of my shots on TV?" He wasn't blaming the reporters, and part of it was tongue-in-cheek. But only part of it. He was annoyed to have the lead on Sunday at the Scottish Open and get what he thought was limited coverage. By the end of the year, golf could not take its eyes off Stenson.

It all started with a tie for third in the Aberdeen Asset Management Scottish Open, and then his runner-up finish in the Open Championship. Two weeks later, he was a side note to Woods winning the Bridgestone Invitational by seven shots at Firestone. Even so, it was another runner-up finish for Stenson, and he followed that with a third-place performance at Oak Hill in the PGA Championship. He had done everything but win. Stenson took care of that, finally, on Labor Day in the Deutsche Bank Championship. Two shots behind Sergio Garcia going into the final round, Stenson closed with a 66 and turned back one final challenge from Stricker by holing out from the bunker on the 17th for a birdie that carried him to a two-shot win. "There's never a bad time to win a golf tournament, I know that much," Stenson said. "I'm just pleased I won here. This was a big goal of mine to win a golf tournament after all those nice finishes." A good year was quickly turning into a great one. And he was just getting warmed up.

For a man at peace with himself, Stenson showed the expectations he has for himself. Two weeks after his big win in Boston, he snapped off the head of his driver in the final round of the BMW Championship, and then smashed up his wooden locker at Conway Farms. The photo of the damaged locker went viral — though not as much as that photo of Stenson playing a shot out of the water at Doral years ago wearing nothing but his white underwear — and Stenson was asked the following week how someone could lose his mind so soon after winning. "I can tell you don't have much experience with Swedes, do you?" Stenson replied, handling criticism with aplomb and his great humor. He apologized and paid for the damage, and later explained he was exhausted from his big stretch and irritated by having to play Monday in Chicago because of rain delays. But the week off reminded him that "the world is in a good place," and so was he.

Stenson at one point had a nine-shot lead in the third round at the Tour Championship, and he only had to hold off a late surge from Spieth on the final day to win the Tour Championship and the FedExCup. Doubling the pleasure, he tied for seventh in the Turkish Airlines Open and then won the season finale in Dubai. And to imagine that only a year earlier, big success for Stenson was winning the South Africa Open. "Obviously, it's been a dream year, a dream summer for me, and the season of my life," he said. "I would be lying if I said I saw all that coming."

For Mickelson, there's never telling what he might do next — or what he might say.

After opening the year with a mediocre performance at the Humana Challenge, he vented to a couple of reporters about the taxes he pays living in California and said there might be drastic changes. *Golf Digest* estimated his earnings the previous year at $45 million, which was a number that resonated more than the percentage he said he paid in taxes from living in San Diego County. It caused a controversy and put Mickelson's vast popularity on the line by going public with a polarizing issue. He tried to blunt the controversy by releasing a statement ahead of his press conference, saying that financial matters are personal and he should have kept his opinions to himself. When he faced the media, which was carried live by Golf Channel, Lefty turned to his self-deprecating humor to put the matter to rest. He drew a parallel to when he blew a chance to win the U.S. Open at Winged Foot in 2006 by hitting a tee shot way left off the corporate tents and then trying to hit three iron around a tree. He made double bogey and lost by one. "So this happened to be way right," he said, a playful reference to his position on higher taxes. "I've made some dumb, dumb mistakes. And obviously, talking about this stuff was one of them."

He made his usual assortment of mistakes on the golf course, too. One exception would be the opening round of the Waste Management Phoenix Open, where Mickelson hardly missed. He was on the cusp of shooting a 59 — finally, a chance to do something Woods never has in an official event — until his 18-foot birdie putt on the 18th hole took a wicked swirl in and out of the cup and he had to settle for a 60. He still went on to a wire-to-wire win, one of three worldwide wins for Mickelson. The biggest blunder on the course, or at least the one that caused the most pain, was at a familiar venue.

Mickelson figured he had prepared so sufficiently at Merion for the U.S. Open that he flew back to California in the days leading to the championship so he could watch his oldest daughter graduate from the eighth grade. He arrived in time for his tee time, and while the pre-tournament days off might not be a good recipe for contending, Mickelson always walks to a different beat. He took a one-shot lead into the final round, and he had the lead when he pitched in for birdie on No. 10. But he came undone on the back with two wedges in his hand. One was at the par-three 13th, where he went long into a bunker and made bogey on a hole that was set up for birdies. The other was on the 15th hole after a magnificent drive. He came up short, on the front of the green, chipped off the putting surface and made bogey. He couldn't make up the strokes to catch Justin Rose. It was yet another runner-up finish at the major he covets.

"Heartbreak. This is tough to swallow after coming so close," he said. "This was my best chance of all. I felt this was as good an opportunity as you could ask for. It really hurts." He later said it took him longer than any other loss to move on. But move on he did.

The Open Championship is the one major where Mickelson has never been much of a threat, except for Royal St. George's in 2011 when he was a runner-up behind Darren Clarke. Mickelson got in some good work ahead of time, however, winning the Scottish Open at Castle Stuart for his first victory in links condition. He playfully — and wrongly, as it turned out — asked the media if they knew the last player to win a major coming off a victory the week before. He was alluding to his 2006 Masters win (after the BellSouth Classic), though he overlooked Woods winning the Bridgestone Invitational and PGA Championship in successive weeks in 2007. Mickelson at least gave himself a reasonable chance, five shots behind Lee Westwood going into the final round at Muirfield. What followed was sheer genius with every club in the bag, from the five iron into the deceptive 13th to start his run of birdies, the consecutive three woods that led to a pivotal birdie on the par-five 17th, and a birdie putt to cap off his remarkable win. Mickelson could not help but look forward to 2014 and a return to Pinehurst No. 2, his next chance at a U.S. Open to complete the career Grand Slam.

That was his last win, however. There was a feeling that three wins, plus a major, would be enough for Mickelson to finally be voted PGA Tour Player of the Year. But he had to settle for an Open Championship and one other U.S. win, not nearly enough to stack up against Woods' five victories, the money title and Vardon Trophy. He finished the year at No. 5 in the World Ranking, up from No. 17 at the start. He celebrated his 42nd birthday. Mickelson still deals with arthritis, though this is one area where he is very much like Woods. When it comes to his health, he is not likely to reveals details. Even so, he picked up his 42nd career win on the PGA Tour as he tries to get to 50. Is time running out on Mickelson? With him, one never knows.

The only mystery with Scott was when he was playing. Stricker nearly walked away from the PGA Tour at the start of the year, instead severely reducing his schedule so he could spend more time with his wife and two daughters in Wisconsin. Scott congratulated him on his "semi-retirement," and then he added with a smile, "Welcome to the club." Scott shifted to a reduced schedule a few years ago, though not for any personal reasons. His record in the majors was woefully lacking. It wasn't so much that he hadn't won a Grand Slam event, he never even came close. There was a tie for third at Medinah in the 2006 PGA Championship, but he was six shots behind Woods. He looked like a winner at Augusta National in 2011 when he made a 10-foot par putt on the 17th hole, only for Charl Schwartzel to close with four straight birdies and reduce Scott to also-ran. So the handsome Australian chose to play less and work more, even if hardly anyone saw him. When he wasn't at a tournament, Scott retreated to what amounts to his "Bat cave" in the Bahamas, where he stuck to a routine in the gym and on the range. He wanted to make sure he was ready when he did tee it up. And for the most part, he was.

In a year filled with a great debate over who had the best year, this might be an even tougher question to ponder: Which player won the more historic major, Scott or Mickelson. The answer depends on whether you're from America, Europe or Australia. Mickelson scores big points for the claret jug, the oldest trophy in golf on a links course that many thought he could never master. And while he's still one major shy of the career Grand Slam, the Open showed he could win on any surface. That showed Mickelson to be a complete player. Scott, however, carried the burdens of an entire nation. Australians have been teased with a green jacket for a half century, with Greg Norman the face behind the frustrations given all his close calls. For Scott to become the first Aussie to win the Masters, to make a 25-foot birdie putt on the final hole of regulation, to win in a playoff with two exquisite shots — the six iron and the 10-foot putt — and to pay tribute to Norman in the midst of his own achievement, it was a major that won't be forgotten. "Sitting there watching Adam, I had a tear in my eye. That's what it was all about. It was Adam doing it for himself, and for the country," Norman said.

It was a Masters victory worthy of a parade, one that was mentioned in the halls of government that Monday morning in the hours after he won. But if a limited schedule required patience, Scott showed he had an abundance of that. Imagine the crowning achievement and then waiting until the end of the year to return home to celebrate. Yet that's exactly what he did. "Yes, it's cause for celebration, but we have a plan in place," Scott said when he showed up again a month later at The Players Championship. "It's hopefully not going to stop with the Masters at the moment. I want to keep focused while I can and try to make this my biggest year yet. I think we can rustle up some celebration when I get home at the end of the year."

He returned to the scene of his unimaginable collapse — the Open Championship — in July and showed he was true to his word. Scott featured all week at Muirfield and briefly had the lead to himself on the back nine Sunday until Mickelson's magical ride over the final two hours. The PGA

Championship ultimately was a two-man show between Dufner and Furyk, though there was that determined Aussie again, tied for the lead after 18 holes, still only three behind going into Sunday until Scott finally faded to a tie for fifth. Next up were the FedExCup Playoffs, and Scott was a big winner again. He played bogey-free on the last day at Liberty National for a 66 and a one-shot victory over Woods and Rose. It moved Scott up to a career-best No. 2 in the world, though he still was a fair distance away from catching Woods. Scott was No. 3 in the FedExCup going into the Playoff finale at the Tour Championship, and he was in the last group with Stenson going into the weekend, four shots behind. Finally, a spell of bad luck. He fell so ill overnight and into the morning that Scott had intravenous fluids administered at East Lake and didn't even show up to the practice range until 25 minutes before his tee time. He shot 40 on the front nine, wound up with a 74 and lost all hope of capturing the FedExCup and its $10 million prize. Not to worry. More bounty awaited Down Under.

The celebration for Australia was worth the wait. Their hero returned, showing off the green jacket, which until then must have seemed like only a myth. Scott was there to play golf, too, and he showed that straight away by winning the Australian PGA Championship, and then the Australian Masters at Royal Melbourne. A week later, he rallied from a poor start and made a run at a third straight title, though he couldn't catch Jason Day. That was okay, for he and Day were teammates and captured the World Cup for Australia at Royal Melbourne. One leg remained in his season at the Australian Open, and Scott looked like a winner. He was on the cusp of the Australian Triple Crown, sweeping the main tournaments, a feat last achieved by Robert Allenby in 2005. Scott had McIlroy beat all day, but a few missed putts down the stretch proved costly. On the 18th hole, with a one-shot lead, Scott went over the green, missing his target by no more than a yard. McIlroy stuffed his shot into about eight feet. Scott made bogey, McIlroy made birdie, and the 24-year-old from Northern Ireland had his first win of the year. McIlroy stopped just short of apologizing for winning and taking the title away from Scott.

No matter. Scott, indeed, had his "biggest year yet." He won the Masters and a FedExCup Playoff event. He won two individual titles in Australia and helped his country win the World Cup on native soil. And he finished the year just 2.09 points behind Woods in the World Ranking. Scott headed into the early part of 2014 with at least a mathematical chance to going to No. 1 before Woods returned from his winter break. Scott didn't think this was possible seven years ago, when Woods looked as though he would never get old, never slow down. He said at the end of 2006, "You can't give up on your hope of being No. 1 in the world. I want to be No. 1, and I believe I can be. But I've got to be realistic. If I play my best golf in the next five years, then I might be No. 1. And it depends on what he does." Maybe his best is yet to come.

Those four — Woods, Mickelson, Scott and Stenson — are the cornerstone of an argument over who had the best year. At least in men's golf. In women's golf, one player rose above the rest with a run through the majors that was remarkable, historic and, at times, confusing. Inbee Park won her first major in the 2008 U.S. Women's Open at Interlachen, the first fruits of the great pioneer Se Ri Pak. Park was a 10-year-old who was woken in the middle of the night by the cheers of her parents, who were watching Pak win the 1998 U.S. Women's Open. Their daughter put a club in her hand the next day, and a decade later, she was a major champion. Park also won the money title on the LPGA Tour last year. But nothing could have braced the women's circuit for what unfolded in 2013.

It started innocently enough with a splash in the pond at the Kraft Nabisco Championship, giving Park the first major of the year. Less than a month later, she ascended to No. 1 in the Rolex Women's World Rankings and picked up her third victory of the year in Texas. In the month before the major season got under way, Park was struggling with her swing. In the Pure Silk-Bahamas LPGA Classic, she missed one par three by some 30 yards. On the next hole, she hit what could only be described as a half-shank into the middle of a pond, and her next tee shot also found the water, some 30 yards short of the flag. She made a nine on the hole. Who could have guessed that this "Silent Assassin" was on the verge of taking aim at the record books. She won the Wegmans LPGA Championship in a playoff over Catriona Matthew, making her the first player since Annika Sorenstam in 2005 to capture the first two majors of the LPGA Tour season. This piqued the interest of everyone from Sorenstam and Pat Bradley, both of whom failed in their bid to win a third straight major. And when Park did what they couldn't — win the U.S. Women's Open for a third straight major — it even got the attention of the great Mickey Wright.

Wright is the only woman to hold all four majors at the same time — the U.S. Women's Open and LPGA Championship in 1961, the Titleholders and Western Open in 1962. She marveled at how composed Park looked in winning her third straight major at Sebonack. Two things stood out to Wright in an interview with The Associated Press. "She certainly is an unflappable young lady. She's probably the best putter I've ever seen, and I've seen some good ones. I'm hoping she can pull it off, and then win the fifth one in France. No one will ever come close to that unless the LPGA adds a sixth major."

A fifth major? Thus the confusion. The LPGA Tour had previously agreed that the Evian Masters in France, which offered one of the richest purses in women's golf and had been a steadfast partner, would be elevated to major championship status in 2013 and changed to the Evian Championship. Just the LPGA's luck. The year it goes to five majors, it has a player with a chance to become the first woman to win the calendar Grand Slam. If nothing else, it allowed for some historical research. On one side of the equation, the argument was the sanctity of only four majors. A Grand Slam had baseball connotations in America, and it scores only four runs. But the Grand Slam didn't enter golf's vernacular until Bobby Jones and the "impregnable quadrilateral" of 1930 when he won the U.S. Open, British Open, U.S. Amateur and British Amateur. Grand Slam was derived from a bridge term of a clean sweep. So in that case, a Grand Slam would have to be all five majors. Then again, no one ever had won four majors in one year.

All the semantics turned into a moot point. Whether it was the internal and external pressure, a strong wind at St. Andrews or a poor week lag-putting, Park never came close. She tied for 42nd, a whopping 14 shots behind Stacy Lewis in the Ricoh Women's British Open. At that point in the LPGA season, she already had six wins, including three majors. The end of her run left her so flat that Park didn't win again the rest of the year. It was reminiscent of the mental hangover suffered by Curtis Strange after his gallant bid for a third straight U.S. Open in 1990.

The LPGA Tour uses a points system to determine its highest honor, the Rolex Player of the Year, and for all that Park had achieved through July, she didn't clinch the award until the second-to-last week of the year. Lewis, who rose to No. 1 briefly at the start of the year, found her form at St. Andrews to win the Women's British Open. Suzann Pettersen came out strong in the late summer, winning the Safeway Classic in Portland and that fifth major, the Evian Championship, a few weeks later. She wound up with five wins this year. Going into the final tournament of the year, the CME Titleholders in Naples, Florida, there was a chance for the women to share the spoils, too. Park was Player of the Year, but Pettersen had an outside shot at the money title and Lewis was leading the Vare Trophy for the lowest scoring average. Lewis held on to win that award, but Pettersen couldn't overtake Park for the money title.

Park summed up her year in a heartfelt speech to receive her Player of the Year award, which drew a long and loud standing ovation when she finished. She conceded that the pressure around her amazing run in the majors was almost too much to bear, even though no one around might have imagined that. Most intriguing was her main goal for the year. She wanted to be happier than she was the year before. "Don't we all want to be happy? Aren't we all doing whatever we do in order to be happy? Unexpectedly, as soon as happiness became my goal, I achieved more things than ever."

Golf was just as busy outside the ropes.

The stage was set at the end of 2012 for a great debate on the method used for long putters. "Anchoring" became as much a part of the golf vernacular as birdies and bogeys when the Royal & Ancient Golf Club and the U.S. Golf Association announced their intentions to create a new rule that banned any stroke in which the club was anchored against the body. That effectively would outlaw broom-handle and belly putters, which had been used by three of the past five major champions (Scott at the Masters made it four of the last six). In a rare move, the ruling bodies allowed for a 90-day comment period before deciding whether to adopt Rule 14-1b. Following a meeting of PGA Tour players in January, commissioner Tim Finchem cranked up the passion over the debate when he stated the PGA Tour's opposition to the proposed rule. "We think if they were to move forward they would be making a mistake," Finchem said. He said the players' opposition stemmed from an absence of data to show there was a competitive advantage from anchoring a putter. PGA of America president Ted Bishop weighed in by suggesting the growth of golf would be hurt by taking away a style of putting that had been allowed for some 40 years. After all the comments, and some rancor, the R&A and USGA approved the new rule in May. It goes into effect on January 1, 2016.

The USGA and R&A were equally busy with video, and Woods helped move the conversation along. The governing bodies two years ago came up with Decision 33-7/4.5 that allowed officials to waive disqualification for an incorrect scorecard if a violation was detected only through the use of high-definition TV. The best example of that was Peter Hanson, who double-hit a chip shot and was not aware until high-def TV was shown in super slow motion. Officials announced in November a new decision effective in 2014. Under Decision 18/4, a player would not necessarily be penalized if his ball moves at rest when the movement can only be detected by enhanced video. The new decision went through several drafts before including the language, "reasonably discernible to the naked eye at the time." This would seem to apply to Woods at the BMW Championship, when video showed his ball moved a fraction of an inch. But the USGA stopped short of saying Woods would have been off the hook in such a situation. An entirely new set of questions would have to be asked, and the USGA chose not to get into a hypothetical situation. Woods' incident in the BMW Championship already was inflammatory enough.

At the heart of this decision was television technology. Over the last decade, the number of cameras in use at a golf tournament has increased substantially. The pictures are clearer. The broadcast is longer. The question is whether this will limit the number of television viewers who call in violations. The governing bodies seemed clear that they welcome any outside help in a sport with such a large arena. That was the case with Woods at the Masters, when rules expert David Eger was the one who noticed his wrong drop. And the use of HD also was raised when Woods' ball moved at Conway Farms. "Our Rules of Golf committees — the USGA and R&A — are always trying to look forward at what they should address. Certainly, HDTV has been on the forefront for the last several years," said Thomas Pagel, the USGA's senior director of rules and competition. "Who knows where we're going to be a year from now?"

Indeed, golf continued to change in so many ways.

The game has been shifting toward a global sport for the last decade or more, and it might be gaining traction. The PGA Tour remains the strongest tour in the world by miles, proof of that in the membership rolls. Of the top 50 players in the world at the end of the year, 42 had PGA Tour membership. Finchem spoke three years ago about the possibility of a world tour, though he had no idea what form it might take. The World Golf Championships began in 1999 to bring together the best from every continent and every tour. Now, the world's best are gathered far more often. The Middle East swing on the European Tour is a hot spot at the start of the year, while Asia is the place where the stars go late in the year. And if golf is to be observed through a truly global lens, ask this question: Who was the best rookie?

Spieth received all the attention, primarily because he was in America. He failed to advance beyond the second stage of qualifying school last year and was content to try to earn a PGA Tour card through the Web.com Tour. But after a strong start on the smaller circuit, he honored a commitment to the Puerto Rico Open and finished second, which sent him on his way. Spieth had enough money for special temporary membership after the Tampa Bay Championship. He had enough money for PGA Tour membership the following year in June, and then he won the John Deere Classic in July. Spieth had to reset his goals four times during the course of an amazing year, which concluded with being the youngest American to ever compete in the Presidents Cup. It was strong stuff from a 20-year-old who only one year earlier had been a sophomore at the University of Texas. And it was arguably the best rookie season since Woods won twice in seven starts after turning pro in 1996.

But what about Matsuyama? He won on the Japan Tour as an amateur, but after turning professional in April at 21, went on to win four times and earn a spot on the Presidents Cup team. Ryo Ishikawa carried the flag of the Rising Sun for so many years, though he never had as strong a performance as Matsuyama. And what set Matsuyama apart from Spieth were the majors. It would be easy to dismiss his four Japan Golf Tour wins as coming against lesser competition. But he had three top 20s in the majors, while Spieth only played in two and was not a factor in either.

The global game showed itself in other ways. Peter Uihlein, the son of Titleist chief Wally Uihlein and the 2010 U.S. Amateur champion, also crashed out of the second stage of qualifying. Uihlein, as a former Amateur champion and with plenty of connections, could easily have taken his allotment of exemptions on the PGA Tour. Instead, he began his professional career in Europe on the Challenge Tour. He broke through for his first victory in Portugal at the Madeira Island Open. He had a putt for 59 in the Dunhill Links Championship, where he wound up losing in a playoff. He had a terrific duel with Gregory Bourdy in the Wales Open at Celtic Manor, losing by one shot. He turned out to be one of the top 15 players on the European Tour. And he had some company. His roommate in Florida is Brooks Koepka, who also started out his career on the Challenge Tour. Koepka went on to win three times to earn an automatic promotion to the European Tour. Not since the days of Payne Stewart in the 1980s have Americans traveled so extensively around the world to round off their games.

There were other reasons for that. The PGA Tour had tournaments in the fall, after the FedExCup, that enabled players to earn money toward finishing in the top 125 on the money list. Those tournaments attracted fields not much stronger than a Web.com Tour event, and there were rumblings the sponsors were no longer interested in being looked upon as second-class citizens. The winners did not get invited to the Masters, for one thing. That led to the PGA Tour to go to a wraparound season for the first time in its history, with the 2013-14 season beginning just three weeks after the FedExCup season ended, and one week after the Presidents Cup. Suddenly, tournaments like the Frys.com Open and the McGladrey Classic were treated equally with the likes of the Arnold Palmer Invitational and the Shell Houston Open.

Because of the new season starting in October, the tour thought it would not make sense for cards to be awarded at qualifying school. Thus, the qualifying tournament was only for Web.com Tour cards. In a unique system, the tour brought together the top 75 players from the Web.com Tour money list and the top 75 players who failed to qualify for the FedExCup Playoffs. They played a series of four straight Web.com Tour events in which the top 50 money earners from those events earned cards (the top 25 from the Web.com Tour regular-season money list already were guaranteed cards). Because a direct route to the PGA Tour from qualifying school was no longer available, Uihlein and Koepka chose Europe. Four Americans earned European Tour cards at qualifying in November. "Looks like I'll have company next year," Uihlein said. Yes, it's a big world of golf out there.

The PGA Tour, meanwhile, began to branch out with its brand. It took over top golf in South America by bringing together a series of loosely run tournaments under the umbrella of the PGA Tour Latinoamerica, in which the top five from the money list earned access to the Web.com Tour. Then, it took over the Canadian tour with the PGA Tour Canada that offered the same perks. And late in the year, Finchem showed up in Shanghai to announce the new PGA Tour China series. "Historically, the elite player comes first, strong growth comes second, and certainly that's been the case in the United States since Arnold Palmer came along in 1960 and it's been 40, 50 years of continuous growth," Finchem said. "So anything we can do to assist the expedition and acceleration of growth is very much in the interest of the professional game, but also golf as a whole."

Is the PGA Tour trying to take over the world? Not yet, maybe not ever. That was still years away. But it was clear that America was setting up smaller circuits that would feed toward the Web.com Tour, and that had become the primary path to the PGA Tour. However it unfolds, it was becoming increasingly evident that golf was producing players from every continent, more countries, and the competition was getting more difficult each year. It showed the strength of Woods that he still won five times. It showed the strength of golf that he was challenged every step of the way — by Scott, by Stenson, by Mickelson and a host of others on the horizon.

2. Masters Tournament

The question came up at Billy Payne's Wednesday "State of the Masters" chat. Someone in the media's crowded interview room asked Payne, chairman of the Masters and of Augusta National Golf Club, whether the Masters would ban "anchoring the putter" against the golfer's body, as the U.S. Golf Association and the R&A were about to do. Their joint ruling would, in effect, ban the long, pendulum putters that were becoming more popular.

"We're not a governing body," Payne said simply. "We're a golf club that puts on a tournament." Then he added: "We hope and believe common ground will be achieved so that one set of rules governs golf."

This exchange reveals Augusta National's role in modern golf. Augusta is a power center of its own.

The first revelation is not in what Payne said, but that someone even asked the question. This underlined what a force Augusta National and the Masters have become in the game. Augusta's strength is in its autonomy. It's a golf club bound only by what it wants to be bound by, and it puts on a tournament that golfers lust to play in. And they will play by whatever standards Augusta chooses to set. Thus it was in recent years that so many in golf were looking to Augusta to establish a one-ball rule in the belief that this would cool the race among manufacturers to produce ever longer balls, which were, in the minds of many — Jack Nicklaus included — distorting the game.

The second revelation in Payne's answer was his call for harmony among players and organizations. Some pros were threatening to ignore the ban, others to sue, and the PGA Tour, for one, had not decided whether or not to follow the lead of the USGA and R&A.

Augusta's role in golf could also be seen in the person of Tianlang Guan, a Chinese amateur who was playing in this Masters, his first. He was 14 — the youngest competitor ever. He got into the field as winner of the Asia-Pacific Amateur, established and run by Augusta and the R&A to help develop golf in Asia. And with a berth in the Masters to the winner as an inducement to play in it.

Payne insists that he is merely following in the footsteps of the chairmen who preceded him. But since he became chairman in 2006, things have gone further and faster in all directions — building, tournament qualifications, and others.

Payne announced another joint initiative for kids' golf, this the Drive, Chip and Putt Championship, in conjunction with the USGA and PGA of America, both of which are involved in other growth programs. It's a nationwide competition for boys and girls that would end up with the finals on the Sunday before the Masters — at Augusta National and carried on the Golf Channel.

And with the rancor of the Martha Burk Flap still rippling through the air, Augusta admitted its first two female members — Condoleezza Rice, former secretary of state, and South Carolina financier Darla Moore. Critics could say they were admitted to silence the uproar against Augusta's male-only policy. If Payne were to talk about members — which he won't — he might only say it was time. And he shuns any attempt to credit him as a heroic pioneer.

"I really don't characterize much of what we've done as change," he said. "What we've done is to do what we're supposed to do, and that is to be a beacon in the world of golf and to do our best to influence others to want to be a part of it."

First Round

No one was surprised to see an Australian atop the board, tied for the lead through the first round. The surprise was, it wasn't Adam Scott or Jason Day up there, but the lesser known Marc Leishman. Leishman, 29, was in his fifth year on the PGA Tour and had one win in the 104 starts of the first four years, and came to the Masters with an underwhelming record for 2013. He also had painful memories of his only Masters, in 2010, when he shot 82-69 and missed the cut, in the grip of the Masters mystique.

"I found myself looking around a bit too much and not concentrating on getting the ball in the hole," he said. He took the mature approach this time. He spotted Augusta National a bogey on No. 1, then made seven birdies from No. 3 the rest of the way, including four straight from the 13th for a six-under-par 66 and a tie for the lead with Spain's ever-young Sergio Garcia, now 33 and in his 14th Masters. Garcia's bogey-free 66 was his best start ever. His outlook had to brighten. Just how much brighter remained to be seen, because Garcia made no secret of his feelings toward Augusta National. "Well, it's obviously not my favorite place," he said. "Let's enjoy it while it lasts."

The 77th Masters opened on an elegant Georgia spring day rather like the start of the Kentucky Derby, with everybody thundering into the first turn. Fully 32 players broke the par of 72.

Obscured in the crowd was Adam Scott, who'd had eight top-10 finishes in the majors but just couldn't bring one in. He started birdie-bogey-birdie and was bogey-free the rest of the way for a 69 that tied him for 10th with Jim Furyk and 2007 champion Zach Johnson. Accuracy was Scott's problem. He hit only nine fairways and 12 greens.

The "other" Johnson, Dustin, missed tying for the lead by bogeying the par-four 17th and took solo third with a scrambling 67. He hit only six of the 14 driving fairways and only 13 greens, but needed just 26 putts. And of course, there was timeless Freddie Couples, 53 now and a star on the Champions Tour, doing his Masters thing again. This time he opened with a 68, one better than in 1992, when he won the tournament, his only major. "I know how to play the course," said Couples, now in his 29th Masters. The problem, he said, is "It's where I'm standing and where the ball goes..."

Tiger Woods, the prohibitive favorite to win his fifth Masters and 15th major (but first since 2008), opened with a 70. It was a good sign. He won three of his four Masters after opening with a 70. But he would have to make his peace with the speed of the greens. "They looked it, but just weren't quite putting it," he said.

Woods is rarely upstaged, but this time he was by a slender 14-year-old amateur who would become known affectionately as "The Chinese Kid" — Tianlang Guan. He was the youngest ever to play in the Masters or in any majors for 148 years. He was in the tournament as winner of the Asia-Pacific Amateur, a joint operation of the Masters and the R&A to further golf in Asia. Guan, the equivalent of an eighth-grader in the United States, opened with a one-over 73, his sharp play with irons and hybrids putting him in the company of Graeme McDowell, Keegan Bradley and others. "Just a little bit nervous on the first tee," Guan said, through an interpreter, "but I hit a great tee shot and after that I just felt comfortable."

"He played like a veteran today," said two-time champion Ben Crenshaw, who played with him and Italian pro Matteo Manassero, the previous "youngest" at 16 in 2010. Guan bogeyed Nos. 1, 7, 9, 11 and 14, and birdied Nos. 3, 10, 13 and 18. Oh — and he brought homework with him and his mom packed him a lunch for the first round.

And Guan didn't lack for ambition. "I want to win a major," he said, "and hopefully I can win the four majors in one year."

Rickie Fowler amazingly recovered from two double bogeys, eagled the par-five 15th and shot 68, his best round in three Masters. "It was actually funny to see them put my name up on the leaderboard when I was on 16 green," Fowler said. "I was like — oh, this is going to be interesting..."

Life wasn't as simple for everyone.

Rory McIlroy, 23, who let the 2011 Masters get away with a final-round blowup, labored to a five-birdie, five-bogey 72. Defending champion Bubba Watson stumbled to four three-putts and shot 75. Said Watson: "I never got the speed right, never got the ball to the hole." Three-time winner Phil Mickelson shot 71 and vowed to attack the course in the second round because of the softness of the greens. "I'm giving this course way too much respect," he said. Also among the 10 at 71 was Argentine Angel Cabrera, who can get up for the big ones. He had only two victories on the PGA Tour — the 2007 U.S. Open and the 2009 Masters. Cabrera turned in an odd 71. He started bogey-birdie, bogeyed the 10th and 11th, then birdied three straight from the 12th.

First-Round Leaders: Marc Leishman 66, Sergio Garcia 66, Dustin Johnson 67, David Lynn 68, Rickie Fowler 68, Gonzalo Fernandez-Castano 68, Trevor Immelman 64, Fred Couples 68, Matt Kuchar 68, Jim Furyk 69, Zach Johnson 69, Adam Scott 69.

Second Round

Rules flaps are nothing new at the Masters, but they may have hit their peak in the second round of the 2013 edition. First, Tianlang Guan, the 14-year-old Chinese amateur, made history again. Not only was he the youngest ever to play in the Masters, he now was the youngest to make the cut, and he was the first known to have been penalized for slow play. The second incident set off reverberations heard around golf. It involved Tiger Woods and didn't fully materialize till late in the day.

Guan, paired with Matteo Manassero and Ben Crenshaw, was timed for much of the back nine, and was informed at the 17th that he would receive a one-stroke penalty. It gave him a 75 and a 148 total. At least it assured him of taking low-amateur honors. He'd made the cut just on the number, and the other five amateurs missed it.

Some said officials were picking on a kid. Others said Guan was a Masters competitor, age 14. Guan took it like a seasoned pro. "I respect the decision," he said.

Woods' case bordered on the unreal. He was five under and seemingly about to take the lead at the par-five 15th. There, his short wedge approach across the pond hit the flagstick and caromed back into the water. He took a penalty drop, wedged to two feet and made bogey. He also bogeyed the 18th for a 71 and was three off the lead. For the moment, that is. A storm was gathering.

Lost in the confusion was the fact that an Australian was atop the leaderboard, but this time it was Jason Day, who took everyone by surprise by threatening in his first Masters, in 2011, then tying for second with fellow-Aussie Adam Scott behind South Africa's Charl Schwartzel. Day shot the day's-best 68 under brisk westerly winds, for a one-stroke lead over another fellow-Aussie, Adam Scott, and the ever-present Fred Couples.

"It's really good to be back here," said Day, referring to having to withdraw in 2012 because of an ankle injury. Day stumbled at two par-threes, the fourth and 12th, and scattered six birdies. Someone again noted that the Masters was never won by an Australian. "I've got to get that out of my mind and plug away," Day said. Leishman lifted to a 73 in the wind but still was tied for second with Couples (71). Couples, at 53, could become the oldest to win the Masters, replacing Jack Nicklaus, who was 46 when he won in 1986. "Am I good enough to play four good rounds in a row on a course like this?" Couples said. "It didn't happen last year." That's when a 75 in the third round cost him a chance to win.

The second round was a tale of gusting winds that shaped this Masters. Some found the calm, some didn't.

Scott, for one, pulled out of a nose dive to stay on the route that would intersect with Cabrera's two days later. Scott bogeyed Nos. 4 and 6, then smoothed out his round with birdies at the seventh, 16th and 18th for a 72 and a share of seventh at 141. Cabrera also turned himself around. He bogeyed the fourth and fifth, then coming home birdied four straight from the 13th and added the 18th for a 69 and tied for fourth at 140. "I like playing with wind," he said. "If it is like this, sunny and windy, it will be perfect."

Phil Mickelson crashed to a 76 and narrowly avoided missing the cut for only the second time in 21 Masters. It started with a bunkered wedge shot at No. 9. "I don't know what happened there," Mickelson said.

Sergio Garcia, first-round co-leader, also was troubled by the wind, watered three shots and made 76, and without a birdie. "It was not only the strength [of the wind] ... but unfortunately it was very, very gusty," he said. Dustin Johnson, who was third after the first round, had edged into the lead through the 13th, then dropped six strokes over the last five holes, including double bogeys at the 15th and 18th. He shot 76 and slipped five strokes off the lead.

The cut, at 148, spared defending champion Bubba Watson, just at that number, and left 61 players for what promised to be a frantic final two rounds. There were 25 players within five strokes of the lead, eight in the top 10 in the World Ranking.

Second-Round Leaders: Jason Day 68-138, Fred Couples 71–139, Marc Leishman 73–139, Angel Cabrera 69–140, Jim Furyk 71–140, Brandt Snedeker 70–140, Adam Scott 72–141, Jason Dufner 69–141, David Lynn 73–141, Lee Westwood 71–141, Justin Rose 71–141, K.J. Choi 71–141, Tiger Woods 71–141.

Third Round

Tiger Woods didn't know it, but he left Augusta National Friday evening with the threat of disqualification hanging over his head. He thought the one-stroke penalty for hitting into the water at the 15th was the end of it. It wasn't. It was just the beginning to possibly the most convoluted rules issue ever at the Masters.

Before Woods had even finished playing Friday, the rules committee had reviewed his drop at the 15th and determined that it was within the rules. The one-stroke penalty was all that applied. Later, a TV viewer called rules officials to say that Woods had taken an improper drop — too far from where he had hit. That called for two more penalty strokes. By this time, Woods had already signed his scorecard — an incorrect card. The penalty for that is disqualification. But the committee had already found the drop to be legal and so it couldn't now, in effect, place him in double jeopardy. The committee then exercised a rule that disqualification could be waived, but did add the additional two-stroke penalty.

The episode had stirred up a furor across the world of golf. Some thought the committee finessed the rules to keep Woods in the tournament. Some thought he should have been disqualified, some that he should have withdrawn. And still others thought that the resolution was fair.

For TV commentators and others calling for him to withdraw, Woods had a brief message: "Under the rules of golf, I can play."

And so Woods, now with a 73 and five strokes off the lead, could play on in search of his fifth Masters and 15th major. His game was on-off in the third round. He was one over after the 11th, then birdied the 12th, 13th and 15th for a 70 and would end the day six off the lead. He had never won a major without holding at least a share of the lead starting the final round. "As we all know," he said, "if you're within six shots starting the back nine, you've still got a shot at this thing."

Apart from the Woods episode, the 2013 Masters took a wry twist. One golfer who did nothing but win majors and one who couldn't win one tied for the third-round lead at seven under. One was Angel Cabrera, who won twice on the PGA Tour — the U.S. Open and the Masters — shot 69, matching Brandt Snedeker, who's looking for his first major.

"I've spent 32 years of my life getting ready for tomorrow," Snedeker said, "and it's all been a learning process, and I am completely 100 percent sure that I'm ready to handle no matter what happens tomorrow. I'm going to be disappointed if I don't win, period." Snedeker, troubled by injuries after a good start to the season, parred the first 12 holes and had some stressful up-and-downs at the third, fourth and 12th. He parred Nos. 13, 15 and 16 coming in.

Cabrera, one under coming in, made two late birdies for his tying 69. He hit an eight iron to seven feet at the par-three 16th and rifled a five iron to 12 feet at the 18th. "I think it's definition time," Cabrera said. "Tomorrow it's more about execution and about patience." And as to experience? "I don't think it's a big advantage that I've won before," he said. "It's more about patience."

The chances of an Australian finally winning the Masters increased exponentially when the scoreboard showed three Aussies in the top five — Adam Scott shot 69 and finished third, one off the lead, and Marc Leishman (72) and Jason Day (73) tied for fourth, two behind. Day was the leading candidate until he bogeyed the last two holes. "It's a great opportunity for all of us to be first," Day said, and then he tried to calm the speculation. "If it happens tomorrow, that's great," he said. "If it doesn't, then we're going to keep plugging away."

After a birdie-bogey exchange, Scott closed with birdies at the 13th, 15th and 17th for his 69 to get to six under, then was asked what a victory would mean to him as the first Aussie to win the Masters. "It's hard to say exactly what it means," said Scott, and was he tiring of the question? "I'd rather not sit here and wonder so much. I'd rather do that if I win tomorrow."

This Masters was over for a number of marquee names. Among them:

Bubba Watson would need a miracle to repeat as champion. Watson, plagued by three-putts in the first two rounds, shot his best of the week, a 70, but was nine off the lead. "Today I don't think I had a three-putt," he said, "but bad swings at the wrong time."

There was no miracle big enough for Phil Mickelson. He followed his 76 of the second round with a 77 — matching his Masters worst — fuelled by double bogeys at the 11th and 12th. He was 15 behind. "I don't know what's going on," he said. "It's not knowing where it's going to go."

The Rory McIlroy revival came to an end. He blew to a 79, dropping 12 behind. "I was only a few off the lead going into No. 7, and all of a sudden I play 7 through 11 in five over par," he said. He had two sevens on his card — a triple bogey at the 11th and a double bogey at the 15th.

Third-Round Leaders: Brandt Snedeker 69–209, Angel Cabrera 69–209, Adam Scott 69–210, Marc Leishman 72–211, Jason Day 73–211, Matt Kuchar 69–212, Tim Clark 67–213, Tiger Woods 70–213.

Fourth Round

Tianlang Guan had the world rooting for him. The 14-year-old had already made plenty of history — now put a good finish on it, kid. He did, to a standing ovation at the 18th. He parred for a two-birdie 75 and 12-over 300, finishing 58th out of 61. "I think I did a pretty good job this weekend," he said. The world agreed with him, then turned to the Australian Question.

So many Aussies had played the Masters, but no one could crack it, not even the best of them. Not Peter Thomson, David Graham or Steve Elkington. Not Greg Norman, who fell short three times, most famously blowing a six-shot lead in the final round in 1996. So why couldn't Aussies win the Masters?

The question was getting irksome. This 2013 Masters should be Australia's time if ever there was one. The third round had ended Saturday with three Aussies in the top five — Adam Scott third, one off the lead, and Marc Leishman and Jason Day tied for fourth, two behind. "Maybe one of us," said Scott, tired of the question, "should just get it done tomorrow."

And so he did. Scott, age 32, finally spiked the question on his 12th try. Scott came through the heavy traffic of the final round, took the clubhouse lead with a birdie at the final hole, got tied by Argentina's Angel Cabrera, then beat him on the second hole of a playoff.

It was his ninth PGA Tour win, his first major, and it took the pain out of folding down the stretch of the 2012 British Open.

On a day of almost steady rain, Scott closed with a 69, Cabrera a 70 to tie at nine-under 279, ending a frantic scramble in which six players had a shot at the green jacket. It began with Cabrera and Brandt Snedeker tied for the lead. Snedeker's putting broke down, costing him a 75 and a tie for sixth. "It's going to be a tough night, a tough couple of days," Snedeker said. Day exploded into a share of the lead with a birdie-eagle start, and seemed the favorite with three consecutive birdies from No. 13, but then he stumbled to bogeys at the 16th and 17th. "I think the pressure got to me a little bit," he said. Day shot 70 and finished third, two strokes out of the playoff. Leishman shot a two-birdie, two-bogey 72 and tied for fourth, four behind, with Tiger Woods, who couldn't get up enough steam after two early bogeys and shot 70.

Scott bogeyed No. 1, birdied No. 3, then played the last six in three under, birdieing the back-nine par-fives, the 13th and 15th, then the 18th on a 25-foot putt that sent him into a wild outburst that few could expect out of the affable boy-next-door.

The thunder rocked Cabrera, who was down in the 18th fairway, huddled under his umbrella, waiting to hit his second. What did he think when he heard the roar? "I think I better get mine close," he was to say, grinning. This was even better than Sandy Lyle's shot out of the fairway bunker in 1988. Lyle's ball hit well above the hole and trickled back down to set up his birdie and win. Cabrera came out from under the umbrella, and from 163 yards away, slashed a seven iron that hit the front of the green, took a bounce and rolled to a stop about two feet from the hole. He made the birdie, his fourth against two bogeys, for a 70 to tie Scott at nine-under 279.

They parred the first playoff hole, No. 18, and went to the downhill 10th. Cabrera hit an iron off the tee, then an iron to the green, about 18 feet below the cup. Scott hit a three wood down the right side, then a six iron to hole-high, 12 feet. Cabrera's birdie try burned the hole but refused to drop.

"That's golf," Cabrera said. "Golf gives and golf takes."

Scott, taking a read from his caddie, Steve Williams, played a break two cups wide right and made the putt that set off a wild celebration on the other side of the world.

Said Scott: "It's amazing that it's my destiny to be the first Aussie to win."

The Final Leaders: Adam Scott 69–279, Angel Cabrera 70–279, Jason Day 70–281, Marc Leishman 72–283, Tiger Woods 70–283.

3. U.S. Open Championship

When the golf course takes over the story in a U.S. Open Championship, that's history. There was, for example, Oakland Hills in 1951, retooled so severely that it moved the taciturn Ben Hogan almost to eloquence. "I'm glad I brought ...this monster to its knees," he said. Apart from Hale Irwin, the winner, who remembers who won the 1974 Open? It went into history as "The Massacre at Winged Foot." (The course was set up so fiendishly, Irwin survived at seven over par.) The 2013 Open wasn't supposed to be anything like that. Just the opposite, in fact. The seers were predicting it was going to be "The Massacre of Merion."

Elegant Merion Golf Club, outside Philadelphia, was so hopelessly short and outdated, observers clucked, that it had no chance against the modern golfer with his modern equipment. This was going to be embarrassing.

Mike Davis, executive director of the U.S. Golf Association, which conducts the U.S. Open, dissented. "This is going to be a magical week," Davis said. "While Merion may be short on the scorecard, it has stood the test of time. The long holes continue to be long. The challenges the players face are similar to what Hogan, Jones and Trevino faced." (Skeptics might demur, noting that Davis was instrumental in bringing the Open there. Time would soon tell.)

Merion had hosted 18 USGA championships, more than any other course, but wasn't on the informal rota for the U.S. Open. Merion's fame came first as the venue where Bobby Jones completed his Grand Slam with the 1930 U.S. Amateur. Merion would host four U.S. Opens — in 1934, won by Olin Dutra, 1950 (Hogan), 1971 (Lee Trevino) and 1981 (David Graham).

England's Justin Rose won the 2013 U.S. Open, finally getting his first major and at last fulfilling the promise he'd shown as a kid amateur some 15 years earlier. He was a great story, but secondary. Merion had taken over the airways, the newspapers and magazines, to say nothing of blogs, tweets and any other "social media" currently in rage.

The playing quality of the course was never in question. But Merion measured only 6,500 yards for Graham's victory in 1981, and even that was short for its time. Perhaps of equal or greater significance was the fact that little Merion, packed into 120 acres, lacked the space for the highly profitable hospitality tents that have been another hallmark of modern golf. But the USGA, keepers of tradition, returned the U.S. Open to Merion, even though they could have made a reported $10 million more at any number of courses. Some adjustments were needed. Merion was lengthened to nearly 7,000 yards (still short), and some hospitality tents had to be put in neighbors' yards, and galleries were limited to 25,000 a day.

Still, this would be a mockery. Everybody knew it. Except for the golfers. Paul Casey came out of practice rounds noting that various TV commentators were chuckling over the 62s and 63s that were coming. "And we didn't know which golf course [they were] talking about," Casey said, "because we knew this was going to be a brutal test."

True, Merion was short overall, but it contained, for example, par-fours ranging from 430 to 521 yards, and three par-threes in the 250-yard range. The fairways were narrowed and the rough was grown thick and long. So little Merion, it turned out, was an illusion. As Rose demonstrated with his win — at one-over-par 281.

Predictions of the massacre of Merion, it turned out, were grossly, grossly exaggerated.

First Round

Psychologists talk about a thing called "conditioned response." It's the old Pavlov's Dogs thing, where you anticipate something once you've seen a certain signal over and over. One would wonder, then, whether Phil Mickelson cringes at the thought of a U.S. Open, he's been beaten so often by it. Coming to Merion, he'd finished second five times, solo or tied. But he keeps fighting. There is no one in the game who prepares more meticulously. So how did he prepare for the 2013 U.S. Open? Well, he attended his daughter Amanda's graduation from eighth grade. The interesting point was that Amanda was back home in San Diego.

Mickelson left Merion Tuesday afternoon, boarded his private jet and headed for San Diego. He attended Amanda's graduation Wednesday evening, then boarded the jet and headed back to Philadelphia. Along the way, he studied notes he had made during earlier practices. He landed in Philadelphia about 3:30 a.m. Thursday, got an hour's nap, went to the course for his 7:11 tee time. And then shot a three-under-par 67 that held up for the first-round lead, even in play that had to be suspended late Thursday after two rain delays and completed Friday morning.

Rain was the prevailing subject for much of this U.S. Open. Storms had poured more than five inches of rain on the area since the preceding Friday, and so the golfers would be dealing with a heavy, soggy Merion East.

"This was as easy as this course is going to play," said Mickelson. "We had very little wind, soft fairways and greens, and no mud balls." Unlike his wild time at Winged Foot in 2006, he hit 11 of the 14 driving fairways, and 14 greens in regulation and needed 28 putts. One reason for this accuracy was that he had no driver but carried five wedges.

Despite playing on little sleep he had just one bogey, a three-putt from 40 feet at this first hole, No. 11 (because of Merion's configuration, golfers starting on the back nine had to begin with No. 11). Of his four birdies, he put his approach to two feet at No. 7 (his 15th), and at the 237-yard par-three No. 9, hit a five iron to 30 feet and holed the bending putt.

Even if Merion was at its easiest, as Mickelson said, it was proving to be a tough test. Tim Clark and Jerry Kelly were two under late in their rounds and both double-bogeyed and finished with 70. Former Masters champion Charl Schwartzel also shot 70 and stepped forward to disabuse anyone who thought Merion was a cakewalk. Said Schwartzel: "It's a lot tougher than they say it is."

The marquee threesome might well agree. Tiger Woods, who apparently hurt his left arm hitting out of the rough on his first hole, bogeyed three of his first five and was two over on the 11th when play was called. He came back Friday morning and finished at 73. What did he feel with his arm? "Pain," he said. Rory McIlroy, erratic since the start of the year, was even par at the delay and posted a 73. Masters champion Adam Scott had the worst of it. He was three under through the 11th, then came back Friday morning and posted a 72.

Luke Donald was four under through 13 holes, making one last birdie before leaving the course, then dropped two shots in the morning for a 68, one behind Mickelson. For all of the high-ranked golfers in the field, the next three spots were taken by comparative strangers — Australia's Mathew Goggin (68), Scotland's Russell Knox (69) and Belgium's Nicolas Colsaerts (69).

Sergio Garcia, who might be described as the star-crossed Spaniard, posted possibly the most remarkable round of the day — in a way. He drove out of bounds at the 14th (his fourth hole) and double-bogeyed, then after the rain delay, drove out of bounds again at the 15th and fired a bunker shot over the green. When he finally sorted it all out, he had a quadruple-bogey-eight, and had gone six over on two par-fours. And true to his mercurial nature, he pulled himself together and shot 73. Then there was the other end of the spectrum. Two former U.S. Open champions came to grief. Graeme McDowell (2010) shot 76, and Jim Furyk (2003) a 77. Darren Clarke, the 2010 British Open champion, soared to an 80.

And true to the nature of the championship, the day produced U.S. Open-styled oddities. For one, Carl Pettersen, in the fifth fairway, was at the top of his backswing when a ball came from nowhere and hit his ball, knocking it several feet away. It turned out to be a bad hook from No. 2. Pettersen was petrified for a moment, fearing a rules violation. But he was allowed to replace his ball, no penalty, and play on. He shot 72. England's Lee Westwood, who seems unable to get it done in the majors, was done in by Merion's famed tradition, the red wicker basket that replaces the flag on the flagsticks. He was solidly three under playing the par-four 12th when his approach hit the basket and caromed off the green. He double-bogeyed and finished at par 70.

"Good times at Merion for all," Westwood tweeted later. "I can't wait until these baskets come into play on Sunday and everybody freaks out about them."

First-Round Leaders: Phil Mickelson 67, Luke Donald 68, Matthew Goggin 68, Russell Knox 69, Nicolas Colsaerts 69.

Second Round

The rain-delayed first round was completed Friday morning, and the second round found some big names climbing the leaderboard — Steve Stricker, Justin Rose and Hunter Mahan among them. Talent like this wouldn't be held down forever. The bigger names, Tiger Woods and Rory McIlroy, were still trying to get going.

The man who would be the leader was perhaps the harshest victim of Merion. Luke Donald, former No. 1 in the world, still seeking that first major, led much of the way, then came apart on his incoming nine, the front. He surrendered the lead with five bogeys in a six-hole stretch from No. 2 (his 11th) and shot 72 and slipped into a tie at even-par 140. He was disappointed but not beaten.

"U.S. Opens get harder as the week goes on," he said. "You try not to panic in U.S. Opens."

So the top of the second-round leaderboard belonged to Phil Mickelson, who felt he had short-changed himself, and the little-known but emerging Billy Horschel, who stole the show with a display of accuracy not seen in the U.S. Open in some 50 years. Mickelson shot a two-over 72 and Horschel a day's-best 67 to tie for the lead at one-under 139. Horschel, 26, winner of the Zurich Classic in April, hit all 18 greens in regulation, a feat so striking it sent USGA officials tunneling through records. It hadn't been done since Johnny Miller shot his record 63 to win the 1973 Open at Oakmont. Horschel said he wasn't in "the zone," that rare and serene state of mind golfers occasionally drift into, where every shot seems automatic and the hole seems eight inches across. "I was still nervous," Horschel said. He had one bogey, ironically at the easiest hole on the course, the little 115-yard, par-three 13th. He had four birdies, the last on a 15-foot putt at the 18th, and then it dawned on him. "I didn't know I hit every green until I walked off 18," he said.

Mickelson also birdied the 18th, holing a 20-foot putt in fading light, and it was his only birdie. "I got shut out today," he said, miffed at his play. "It was the birdie opportunities that I didn't capitalize on."

After Horschel's 67, there was one 68, by Sweden's Henrik Stenson, and four 69s, by Justin Rose, Hunter Mahan, Steve Stricker and David Hearn.

The cut came in at eight-over 148, and among the victims were former champions Jim Furyk (2003), Michael Campbell (2005), Angel Cabrera (2007), Lucas Glover (2009) and Graeme McDowell (2010).

Anyone looking for a clue on how out of date Merion had become had only to check on two veteran past champions. McDowell made seven double bogeys in his two rounds and shot 76-77–153. Furyk had nine bogeys, three doubles and one triple against only two birdies in a 77-79–156. Said Furyk: "I thought myself around the golf course poorly, I putted poorly, I drove the ball poorly."

The survivors included four amateurs, and two of them were within range of the lead. South Korea's Michael Kim, 19, shot 70, and Taiwan's Cheng-Tsung Pan, 21, went four over on his last five holes for a 72.

Tiger Woods and Rory McIlroy weren't hitting on all cylinders, and they could just about match cards. They each shot 73-70 and were tied at 143, four off the lead. "I played well," said Woods, seeking his fourth

U.S. Open and his 15th major. "You just have to keep grinding. We have a long way to go and these conditions aren't going to get any easier." He birdied both of Merion's par-fives, Nos. 2 and 4, and also the little 13th, but also made three bogeys. McIlroy, a runaway eight-stroke winner in 2011, likewise was encouraged. "I'm right there for the weekend and I'm happy about that," he said.

Justin Rose always seems to get into the chase. This time he had three birdies, at Nos. 1, 2 and 8, and bogeyed Nos. 6 and 15, and liked his chances. "That's the job of the first two rounds — to get you in striking distance," Rose said. "And tomorrow is an important day to hang around and give yourself a chance on Sunday. You can't get ahead of yourself on the tee shot tomorrow. You have to stay focused."

McIlroy turned prognosticator for the finish of this U.S. Open. "There were people talking about 62s and 63s at the start of the week, and I never saw that at all," he said. "I still think that something very little under par is going to win. Or if not that, around even par."

Second-Round Leaders: Billy Horschel 67–139, Phil Mickelson 72–139, Luke Donald 72–140, Steve Stricker 69–140, Justin Rose 69–140, John Senden 71–141, Nicolas Colsaerts 72–141, Charl Schwartzel 71–141, Hunter Mahan 69–141.

Third Round

Merion was no respecter of fame, fortune or status. The world's No. 1, 2, 3 and 4 golfers pretty much went down for the count in the third round. Their chances in this 2013 U.S. Open were purely mathematical. Realistically speaking, this Open was over for them.

No. 1 Tiger Woods shot 76. Were there birdies for you out there? someone asked. "They were at the first hole," he said. Woods birdied only the first and made seven bogeys from there. He blamed his putting. "I just didn't have the speed right, and it certainly showed," he said.

No. 2 Rory McIlroy also birdied the first hole and also made seven bogeys, but he got one other birdie, at the 10th, and shot 75. "I think it's confidence and fluidity," McIlroy said.

No. 3 Adam Scott lurched down the back nine. He bogeyed the 11th and 14th, double-bogeyed the 15th, and bogeyed the 16th and 17th. Five birdies on the front nine let him down somewhat easy. He shot 73.

No. 4 Matt Kuchar came through best of all, with a one-birdie, three-bogey 72, but he had started from further behind.

When the smoke had cleared, McIlroy was at 218, nine off Phil Mickelson's lead. Woods and Kuchar were 10 back, Scott 11.

Sergio Garcia had life through the second round. He was three under on the front nine and getting up steam. But he bogeyed the 12th and 14th, then at the par-four 15th, where he made eight in the first round, he hit three tee shots out of bounds and made 10. Would this damage his confidence? "I think," said Garcia, "that a 10 is just a 10, nothing more than that."

The third round was a scramble of the first order. Seven different players had at least a share of the lead somewhere in the round. And Mickelson emerged from the chase with par 70 that gave him a one-stroke lead at one-under 209 — the only player under par. "It's got the makings of something special," Mickelson said. "But I still have to go out and perform, and play some of my best golf."

There was plenty of talent at his heels. A stroke back were Hunter Mahan (69), Charl Schwartzel (69) and Steve Stricker (70). And two off the lead were Justin Rose (71), Luke Donald (71) and Billy Horschel (72).

Stricker, at age 46, was within range of succeeding Hale Irwin as the oldest Open winner. "It would be unbelievable," he said. He double-bogeyed the par-three ninth out of Cobb's Creek and went two under the rest of the way for a 70, one off the lead.

Mickelson, no stranger to the heat of the chase, felt it early in the third round when he bogeyed the third and fifth and gave up the lead. He bounced back with birdies at the 10th, on a four-foot putt, the 11th from 15 feet, and was one behind Donald going to the 17th, the first of Merion's closing brutes. It's a par-three of 253 yards. He took his four iron and hit it brilliantly. "I just stood and admired it," he said. "It was one of the best shots I've ever hit." He put the ball 10 feet from the flag. He got the birdie, and Donald double-bogeyed the 18th up ahead. He bogeyed the 18th, a par-four of 530 yards, but he was back in the lead. It was the first time that only one player was under par through three rounds at a U.S. Open since 2007 at Oakmont, when no one was under par.

The two closing brutes were molding the U.S. Open.

Jason Day saved a 68 with birdie-bogey finish and was three off the lead. Mahan and Schwartzel were close to bettering the tournament low of 67, but both bogeyed the last two for 69s. Rose also bogeyed Nos. 17 and 18 for a 71 and was two behind, and tied with Donald, who finished bogey-double bogey for a 71.

"If you hit one bad shot on any of those [final] four holes," said Rose, "it generally leads to bogey. They're very unforgiving. So you've got to play nine or 10 clean shots in regulation."

There was little chance an amateur would hold together to win the U.S. Open — the last was John Goodman in 1933 — but Michael Kim would give it a try. He climbed the board with four birdies over six holes from the 10th. Then the closing three got him. He went bogey-double bogey-bogey, shot 71 and was a solo 10th and five behind going into the last round.

The inevitable questions came to Mickelson — would memories of all the near-misses and the bitter disappointments make it any tougher tomorrow?

Said Mickelson: "I don't think I feel any more pressure than anybody else who wants to win ... a major championship, the U.S. Open."

Third-Round Leaders: Phil Mickelson 70–209, Hunter Mahan 69–210, Charl Schwartzel 69–210, Steve Stricker 70–210, Justin Rose 71–211, Luke Donald 71–211, Billy Horschel 72–211, Jason Day 68–212, Rickie Fowler 67–213.

Fourth Round

It is ironic that the 2013 US. Open came down to a tale of two kids who thrilled the golf world, each in his own way, so many years and miles apart.

The English kid was just a few weeks off turning 18, and an amateur, but under the stifling pressure of the Open Championship, at the final hole sitting in an amphitheater of thousands of cheering faithful, he was able to hit a long pitch shot out of the rough so delicately and so controlled that he holed it out. That was unknown Justin Rose, tying for fourth in the 1998 Open Championship.

The other kid was an American with big dimples in an innocent face, a right-hander who played left-handed, and a college kid and amateur, just 20. That was Phil Mickelson, taking the Northern Telecom Open, becoming just the sixth amateur ever to win on the PGA Tour.

Rose was 32, and Mickelson would turn 43 on Sunday, the day of the final round. Their lifelines had intersected in the 113th U.S. Open at Merion. There was room for only one to get through.

Cruelly, Mickelson had rather pronounced sentence on himself when he took the lead in the first round. Responding to a question, he would quickly contemplate his play in 22 previous U.S. Opens — second five times, top-10 nine times, but the coveted victory had eluded him.

Said Mickelson: "...if I never get that win, then it would be a bit heart-breaking."

Would he ever get used to the heartbreak?

The final round was played on a cloudy, warm day, and Merion got busy fast, shedding contenders. Luke Donald and Charl Schwartzel, amazingly, matched cards on the front nine. Each made a birdie, five bogeys and a double bogey and shot 42. Steve Stricker's hopes of becoming the oldest U.S. Open champion disappeared at No. 2, on two balls out of bounds and a triple-bogey-eight. Rickie Fowler stayed in the chase till he bogeyed three of the last four holes.

Mickelson started the final round leading by one over Mahan and Schwartzel, but he double-bogeyed both the third and fifth. Then leave it to Mickelson to find a showpiece in the debris. At the par-four 10th, he pulled his tee shot into the right rough, took one of his five wedges and holed the 75-yard shot for an eagle that got him back to even par.

Rose had an interesting run from No. 3 — bogey-birdie-bogey-birdie-birdie to turn in one under. Then he was bogeying the 11th on three putts when Mickelson made his hole-out eagle behind him. But Rose promptly birdied the 12th with a four-foot putt and the 13th from 20 feet to retake the lead.

"I just went about it in a 'one foot in front of the other' fashion," Rose said, downplaying his poise.

Mickelson, with his great touch and short game, figured to eat the 115-yard par-three 13th alive, but it bedeviled him again. He birdied it just once, and now he made his second bogey on it, hooking a wedge into deep rough. His vaunted short game let him down at the 15th, too, a poor wedge costing him another bogey. He bogeyed again at the 18th for a 74 and a three-over 283, and no U.S. Open.

Rose, playing up ahead, wasn't without problems. He bogeyed the 14th and 16th, but he played the killer 17th and 18th in two pars. And at the 18th, he closed with a flourish. The 18th was where Ben Hogan hit the great one-iron shot at the 72nd hole, setting up the par for a tie with Lloyd Mangrum and George Fazio. Hogan then won in a playoff, this just 16 months after his nearly fatal car-bus crash.

"When I walked over the hill and saw my drive sitting perfectly in the middle of the fairway," said Rose, after a perfect tee shot, "with the sun coming out, it was kind of almost fitting." He two-putted for par, a 70 and a one-over 281, the clubhouse lead.

Jason Day challenged all the way, but three bogeys down the last eight holes stopped him. He had bogeyed the 18th for the fourth straight time, shot 71 and tied for second with Mickelson.

"This was tough to swallow after coming so close," said Mickelson, with his sixth second-place finish in the U.S. Open. "This was my best chance of all. It really hurts. I just keep feeling heartbreak."

When Rose holed his final putt, he blew a kiss and pointed skyward, saluting his father, who died in 2002 at age 57. It was June 16, Father's Day, and Rose finally had his major.

"My dad was the inspiration the whole day," Rose said. "You don't often have the opportunity to dedicate victories to someone you love. Today was about him ... That was my time."

The Final Leaders: Justin Rose 70–281, Jason Day 71–283, Phil Mickelson 74–283, Jason Dufner 67–285, Ernie Els 69–285, Hunter Mahan 75–285, Billy Horschel 74–285.

4. The Open Championship

After once again leaving a U.S. Open with a feeling of utter desolation, Phil Mickelson hardly expected redemption to come at the British seaside. A sixth runner-up finish in his national championship at Merion was a loss that hit the American as hard as any in his career. And yet, at least he had put himself in position to win it again. At the Open Championship, his name on the leaderboard was a rare sight indeed. He finished third at Royal Troon in 2004, the year he made his major breakthrough at Augusta, and was tied for second at Sandwich in 2011. But an 11th-place finish in 2000 was his only other top-18 result and at Royal Lytham in 2012 he missed the cut for the fourth time.

Last time at Sandwich had been a breakthrough, however. He made a thrilling charge on the front nine on the final day to give eventual champion Darren Clarke a fright. At Muirfield it was an even more dramatic charge on the back nine, with four birdies in the last six holes, that gave him possession of the claret jug. His timing was perfect, even if few realized he was still in contention after a bogey at the 10th left him four behind. But the leaders were going nowhere fast. Lee Westwood tangled with the bunkers and could not get any forward momentum. Adam Scott, whose late collapse handed the 2012 title to Ernie Els, made a sudden surge, and an even more precipitous retreat. Henrik Stenson was lurking, Tiger Woods was skulking, Ian Poulter's charge all too fleeting. Mickelson swept past the lot, and by the time they realized the threat, it was all over. He won by three over Stenson and was the only player to finish the week under par.

Baked under continuous Scottish sunshine, Muirfield was at its treacherous best. It played firm and fast, with just enough of a breeze on the last few days to stiffen the challenge but not make it a lottery. Ball-striking had to be precise, course management thought out carefully, but not necessarily cautiously, and the short game handled with the touch of a neurosurgeon. This was the 16th time the East Lothian links had hosted the Open and the winners always tend to be the best players of their generation. Mickelson enhanced an already exception list — of the 14 different winners, only Alf Perry is not a multiple major champion. The recent ones bear repeating: Els, Faldo (twice), Watson, Trevino, Nicklaus, Player.

Yet none of them had won with a final round as low as 66. His coach Butch Harmon, who had tried over a number of years to instill the subtle nuances required for links golf into his charge's game, reckoned this was a finer round than the 64 from another of his clients, Greg Norman, at Sandwich in 1993. "I always thought that Greg's was the best round to win an Open," Harmon said. "But I think this tops it. When you consider the course was playing so tough, so hard and fast, and the circumstances, to go out and suck it up in the way he did was phenomenal."

Mickelson won on the 50th anniversary of the only other victory at the Open by a left-hander, that by Sir Bob Charles at Lytham in 1963, and, at 43, became the fifth oldest champion. He was the third player in his

40s to win, following Clarke and Els, and he matched Clarke's record of winning on his 20th appearance. Clarke grew up playing links golf in Northern Ireland while Mickelson learnt a very different game in southern California. "I always wondered if I would develop the skills needed to win his championship," Mickelson said. "It took me a while to figure it out, but I putted these greens phenomenally, the best I've ever putted. To play the best round of my career, hit some of the best shots I've ever hit and to go out and get it the way I've always tried to do, this is just an amazing feeling to win this great championship. It's a day I'll always cherish."

His victory didn't come quite out of the blue, since he had won the Aberdeen Asset Scottish Open the previous week at Castle Stuart. This was the second time in his career he had won the week before winning a major — in 2006 he won in Atlanta and Augusta — and in terms of gaining the necessary confidence on the greens it was vital. "It was exactly what I needed to propel me into this championship. Castle Stuart was very firm and fast, just like here at Muirfield, and it gave me some great links golf experience. And playing well on the final day in difficult conditions gave me the confidence that I could play some of my best golf in links conditions. Today was as good as I could play."

First Round

Not since Hoylake in 2006 had an Open course looked so brown, and while there was no wind to speak of on opening day, the links appeared to speed up alarmingly throughout the day. Combine those conditions with some borderline pin positions and not all the players enjoyed the experience. "Joy would not be the word I'd use to describe it, no," said Mickelson. The American's 69 left him three behind the first-round leader, Zach Johnson. "The pins were very edgy, on the slopes and what not. Even without any wind it's beyond difficult."

There were some unusual sights on offer, as Woods putted the full length of the 14th green and off over the bank. "It really wasn't that bad a putt," he said after a 69 in his first round since the U.S. Open due to an elbow injury. "I could see how guys were complaining about it. As the golf course dried out, it got quick." Westwood, 72, hit a putt at the 13th which he thought would pull up 10 feet short of the hole but actually ran on 16 feet past. Poulter bogeyed four of the last five holes, to also finish on one over, and tweeted in his usual understated manner that, "the 8th was a joke & the 18th needs a windmill and a clown face."

Mark O'Meara, who scored a 67 to share second place with Rafael Cabrera-Bello, had no truck with those players complaining about the conditions. "I've been out there when I could barely hold onto the club and it's freezing, raining and sleeting and cold and I couldn't put my umbrella up," he said. "To me that's way more miserable than what we had out there. I thought it was tough, challenging, but unfair, no. If they think it's that way, they need to look at the old man and say, how did he do it? Seriously. Guys are good, they should be able to play in these conditions."

O'Meara's was the day's romantic story. "I didn't feel like I was 56 years old out there today," said the 1998 champion, who would have tied for the lead had his putt on the last not lipped out. "I felt like I was 32."

He birdied the first two holes from three and a half and three feet respectively, and holed from 11 feet on the sixth to go with two other birdies at the par-fives. He dropped three shots coming home, all caused by finding sand, but a 35-footer for eagle at the 17th quickly restored his good mood. "That was the highlight of the day because I needed a shot in the arm," he said. "I thought the putt at the last was tracking, but it was a tough two-putt so a birdie would have been a bonus. Can I win?" he added. "I hope my wife thinks I've got a chance of winning because I'm building a new house."

Johnson, like O'Meara and Miguel Angel Jimenez, who scored a 68, went out in 31 and returned in even par for a five-under 66. He enjoyed a stunning sequence of four threes and a two from the third hole. The run included an eagle at the fifth when he rolled in a curling 45-footer. At the third and the seventh he holed from under five feet, and although he got to six under with a 20-footer at the 12th, he dropped a shot at the 14th after finding a bunker.

Johnson had lost a playoff for the John Deere Classic the week before and the winner, 19-year-old Jordan Spieth, also got off to a fine start with a 69. There was a late run up the leaderboard from Shiv Kapur, a qualifier out in the fourth-last group who joined those on 68. The 31-year-old from New Delhi raced to the turn in 30, birdieing six of the first seven holes (parring the short fourth). A double bogey at the 10th stalled his progress, but he only dropped one more shot as the shadows lengthened. "It was the dream start, the best nine holes of my life," he said. "They were probably the fastest greens I've ever played in my life. They weren't green, they were white. I was just trying to get as far under par as I could and then hold onto your hat coming in."

First-Round Leaders: Zach Johnson 66, Rafael Cabrera-Bello 67, Mark O'Meara 67, Miguel Angel Jimenez 68, Dustin Johnson, 68, Brandt Snedeker 68, Tom Lehman 68, Shiv Kapur 68, Todd Hamilton 69, Phil Mickelson 69, Angel Cabrera 69, Jordan Spieth 69, Tiger Woods 69, Francesco Molinari 69.

Second Round

After the greens were hand-watered the night before, there were one or two pitch marks that needed repairing first thing on Friday morning. The watering had the desired effect in that the course did not speed up alarmingly as it had on the first day, but it was still playing quick, and the biggest difference was the breeze switching to out of the east, a direction the players had not seen earlier in the week. Where there had been 20 players under par in the first round, only nine remained in red figures after day two.

In comparison to 14 sub-70 figures on Thursday, Friday saw only four. Westwood and Charl Schwartzel, who were playing together, both scored three-under-par 68s, which took the South African to one over par and the Englishman to two under. Henrik Stenson was the first player to finish at two under, after a second successive 70, and when Westwood and Woods, who had a 71, joined the Swede, there were still four players ahead of them who were either on the course or yet to tee off.

By the end of the day, however, only Dustin Johnson had joined them and only Jimenez, who added a 71 to his earlier 68, had bettered their total at three under par. "I have to say the golf course is in very good shape," Jimenez said, "but to me it is extremely hard. With the wind, some pin positions, the ball cannot stay. It is a little bit too hard for me." He was not the only one. Zach Johnson dropped four shots in the last five holes for a 75 and Cabrera dropped three shots in the last five for a 72. They were both at one under par, along with Cabrera-Bello, after a 74, and Scotland's Martin Laird. O'Meara had a 78 to drop back to three over.

Ryan Moore was at even par for 36 holes, and an interesting pack of players at one over included Spieth, after dropping four strokes in the last four holes; the 2011 champion Clarke, despite an eight at the par-four sixth hole; Poulter, who managed the rare feat of parring the entire back nine, and the last four Masters champions, Scott, Bubba Watson, Schwartzel and Mickelson. In fact, 11 of the last 13 Masters winners were on the leaderboard.

But U.S. Open champion Justin Rose missed the cut after rounds of 75 and 77, as did world No. 2 Rory McIlroy, who claimed he was "brain dead" at times on the course and scored 79-75, and Luke Donald, who improved from an opening 80 to a second round of 72. Paul Lawrie, the last Scottish winner of an Open in 1999, thought he had missed the cut after a fine 69 put him at eight over, but after driving home to Aberdeen, walking the dog, having dinner and regripping some new clubs, he discovered he was in for the weekend and drove all the way back to Muirfield. Thongchai Jaidee had flown down to Heathrow and was awaiting a connection to Bangkok when he realized he needed to return.

Westwood spent the afternoon with his feet up in front of the television, alternating between watching his competitors struggle and England hammering the Australians in the cricket. Taking advantage of the marginally easier conditions early in the morning, Westwood holed from 20 feet and 18 feet on the first two greens and went out in 31, the best half of the day. He got to five under for the championship when he birdied the 12th with a wedge to two feet but then dropped three shots coming home. "I was playing some great stuff and it was just getting harder as the holes progressed," he said. "I love playing in the Open Championship. This is the biggest tournament of the year for me, being a Brit and it being played in Britain. Why not enjoy it out there? It's tough for everybody, so smile your way through."

Woods brought a smile to his face as he holed a 15-footer for birdie at the 18th hole. It was an ominous-looking putt and he accompanied it with a fist pump. "I'm in a good spot," Woods said. "I'm just going to continue plodding along, being patient, putting the ball in the right spots." His playing partner, Graeme McDowell, confirmed how well the world No. 1 was playing. "He was very impressive the last two days," McDowell said. "He will not be far away. He plays the course very conservatively but it is incredible how well he controls his ball flight. He is using his iron play to devastating effect, and combined with some great putting, he's going to be dangerous. I said to him on 18, 'That was a clinic the last two days.'"

McDowell returned a 71 to be four over and by making the cut appeared to have guaranteed he would win. At least, in his last eight starts he had either missed the cut (five times) or won (three times). "Get your money on me now," he laughed. But this was the week his binary streak would end.

The day's trickiest pin position was on the 15th green, where the hole was back right and protected by a ridge. Snedeker four-putted, lipping out twice, on the way to an inward 43 and a round of 79. He still made the cut, but Niclas Colsaerts went home after a nine at the 15th which included five putts, most of them misguided attempts at ramming the ball in the hole. Mickelson survived the 15th, only to four-putt at the 16th for a double bogey, his second of the day. "I missed a couple of short ones and that's going to happen to everyone. Fortunately, I made a heck of a lot more of my share today," he said.

Mickelson, who scored a 74, added: "When I made those comments yesterday I was not being totally fair to the R&A. They've done a lot of things great this championship. The setup is great. For me to single out a few sketchy pin placements and not give them credit for all the good things they've done was not fair of me. I think it is set up where if you're playing well, you can make up ground and separate yourself. Really solidly struck shots are giving you easy pars and potential birdies. And poorly struck shots are making it extremely difficult to salvage par. So it's going to be a good test to be able to separate yourself if you're playing well."

Second-Round Leaders: Miguel Angel Jimenez 71–139, Henrik Stenson 70–140, Lee Westwood 68–140, Tiger Woods 72–140, Martin Laird 71–141, Rafael Cabrera-Bello 74–141, Zach Johnson 75–141, Angel Cabrera 72–141, Ryan Moore 70–142.

Third Round

It was the penultimate pairing in the third round that felt like the significant duel of the day. Westwood and Woods, despite their disparity in major titles (0-14), had a Ryder Cup–style encounter followed by a huge gallery. Westwood stood out not just for the bright orange shirt he was wearing. The Englishman "won" the contest with a 70 to a 72 and, more importantly, at three under took a two-stroke lead in the championship over the world No. 1 and Hunter Mahan, who matched the best round of the day with a 68 to climb from tied 20th to a tie for second. But what was impressive about Westwood was the way he went about his round. His duel with Woods swung one way, then the other.

Early on he went three ahead, only to be caught again by Woods a few holes later. He edged ahead by one at the 14th, but dropped a shot at the 16th. It was the 17th which decided the honors for the day, Westwood playing the par-five conventionally and holing from 15 feet for a birdie but Woods making the cardinal error of finding the cross bunkers for his second shot and taking a bogey-six.

Once again it was his putting that gave Westwood a reassuring air of a player on the verge of a major breakthrough. Too often while compiling his seven top-three finishes in the grand slams, it had been his putting that proved the weak link. Not any more. A tip from former Open champion Ian Baker-Finch had worked wonders and Westwood was holing out with confidence. There was a showy 45-footer from short of the fifth green for an eagle, but the really significant development was the way he holed the ones that mattered down the stretch. After he raced his first putt at the 15th six feet past, he made the one back for par. After missing the green in an awful spot at the 16th, he saved his bogey by holing from 20 feet. And with Woods in trouble at the 17th, Westwood converted his own birdie chance to open up some welcome daylight between him and the rest.

"Those are the sort of things you need to do and the sort of things that have being missing, making that putt at 16 and then backing it up with the birdie at the next hole," he said. Having only taken 81 putts in the first three rounds, five fewer than anyone else, Westwood added: "I figured if I'm going to win this tournament, I was going to have to beat Tiger. This was Westwood's 62nd major and no one in the field had played in more without winning one.

Woods made only two birdies all day as he continued a streak of not scoring in the 60s at the weekend of a major, which he last did at the 2011 Masters. Nor had he done so in the Open since the third round at Carnoustie in 2007. "Lee played solid and made a couple of big putts at 16 and 17," Woods said. "I was trying to grind along and play my own game, regardless of what Lee or anyone else was doing. There's a bunch of guys who have a chance to win this tournament."

In the last 10 pairings of the day, no one bettered Westwood's 70 and only Scott matched it. Half of those players failed to break 75. One of them was the overnight leader Jimenez, who had a 77. There were problems all over the course. Clarke did not make a birdie in his 76 and Laird had an 81, including a nine at the third where he had to take two unplayables in the rough and a penalty at the 10th for not informing his playing partner or a referee when he touched his ball to identify it. Hideki Matsuyama, the 21-year-old Japanese player, was making a fine debut in the Open, until he was penalized a stroke for a second bad time at the 17th hole, where he took two minutes and 12 seconds over a shot from the crowd. Commendably, he did not let it affect him the next day and finished tied for sixth.

Scott had won the Masters since his collapse in the Open at Lytham in 2012, but claiming the claret jug would still be a welcome redemption for the Australian. He arrived early in Scotland and had nine practice rounds which had held him in good stead as he quietly compiled scores of 71, 72 and 70 to lie fourth, three behind Westwood. "I said the other day it would be a fairy tale if it were to happen," he said. "They do occasionally happen, so I'm not counting myself out. It is a good feeling to sit here in this position, completely different to last year. I go out tomorrow not carrying the weight of the lead or not having won a major."

Mickelson scored a 72 and, at two over par, was five behind the leader. He had practiced hard with Harmon in the morning but three bogeys in the last six holes took the gloss off the day. It would be a very different story over those closing holes in the final round.

Third-Round Leaders: Lee Westwood 70–210, Hunter Mahan 68–212, Tiger Woods 72–212, Adam Scott 70–213, Ryan Moore 72–214, Angel Cabrera 73–214, Zach Johnson 73–214, Henrik Stenson 74–214, Phil Mickelson 72–215, Francesco Molinari 72–215.

Fourth Round

During the winter, Westwood had moved his family to Florida and so it was ironic that here, in a British heatwave, he might finally win a major and join the ranks of other recent home successes, such as Andy Murray at Wimbledon and cyclist Chris Froome at the Tour de France. But the only other time Westwood had led a major after 54 holes was at the Masters in 2010 when Mickelson beat him. Lightning was about to strike twice. Mickelson left his hotel room at the Marine in North Berwick telling his wife Amy that he was going out to "bring home the claret jug." Birdies at the two par-fives on the front nine, the fifth and the ninth, put him out in 34, but then came his only dropped shot of the day at the 10th. The focus was still very much on Westwood.

The Englishman dropped a shot when he pulled his tee shot in the rough at the third but recovered the stroke at the fifth and was three clear. Stenson made the best start by birdieing the first and third, but not much happened for the Swede after that. Woods bogeyed three of the first six holes and never offered a convincing challenge. Scott bogeyed two of the first four holes, and it was Poulter who first set the gallery abuzz with a run that started with a birdie at the fifth. He then eagled the ninth from 12 feet and birdied the next three holes. He had a Ryder Cup air about him, but he missed from 12 feet for another birdie at the 13th and his charge was over. A 67 meant Poulter took the clubhouse lead at one over.

Westwood's troubles started at the short seventh. Between clubs at a hole playing its full yardage of 198 yards but downwind, he elected to hit a nine iron and came up short in the front bunker. Worse, he was plugged under the lip and could not escape first time. More bunker trouble led to another bogey at the eighth and only a par at the ninth. He was still at one under, but it felt like three dropped shots in a row. "That halted my momentum a bit," he said.

Scott now made his charge when he birdied the seventh, eighth and ninth and then added a fourth in five holes at the 11th from four feet. At two under, he now led by one over Westwood. But the four bogeys in a row with which he concluded the 2012 Open made a most unwelcome reappearance from the 13th hole, where he missed the green. At the next he putted across the green, and at the 15th he three-putted after getting distracted on his first effort. At the 16th he found a bunker. "I let a great chance slip," he admitted. "I was right there, so it is disappointing. It will just have to go down in the experience book as something to build on."

Woods never got the speed of the greens, and despite birdies at the 12th and 14th holes, he finished with a 74 to tie for sixth place with Matsuyama and Zach Johnson. Scott shared third place with Poulter and Westwood, who came unstuck at the two par-threes on the back nine, the 13th and 16th. He closed with a 75 for his eighth top-three finish in a major. "I'm not too disappointed," he said. "I would like to have won but I didn't really feel like I had my 'A' game this week. I was amazed to be in the lead going into the fourth round because every time I turned into the wind I was really struggling." Stenson birdied the 17th for a 70 to finish on even par, but by then Mickelson had done his thing.

The American's run for glory started with a five iron at the 13th which finished 10 feet from the hole. "It was a putt that was going to make the rest of the round go one way or the other," he said. "I thought if I made it, it would give me some momentum." It did and a 20-footer went in at the 14th and now he was one under. He could have come unstuck at the 16th, where his six-iron tee shot ran up towards the hole and then rolled back down the slope off the front of the green. His chip went seven feet past, but he holed that one back for a vital par.

"Walking up 17 was the moment I had to compose myself," Mickelson recalled. "I hit two of the best three woods I've ever hit and that's exactly why I don't have a driver in the bag. Those two three woods were the best shots of the week, and walking onto the green I realized this championship was very much in my control. I knew I was leading and had a chance to get a two-shot lead if I were to two-putt." He did and then hit a six iron to 12 feet at the last and made the putt, sparking a tumultuous ovation.

No one else had seen his charge coming. "That was a bit sneaky of him," said Stenson. "I thought I was one or two back but all of a sudden I was three back. We know Phil is a world-class player so I don't think it took us by surprise, but all credit to him for finishing the way he did. He's a very worthy champion after that finish."

Scott added: "We know he goes for broke, and if that's how he's feeling, he's got the ability to pull it off. He's gone and won an Open easily, it looks now."

Mickelson left Muirfield's 18th green arm-in-arm with his caddie Jim "Bones" Mackay and soon enjoyed a family hug with his wife and three children. How different a scene to that at Merion. "It's a huge difference in emotions, as you can imagine," he said. "Being so down after the U.S. Open, to come back and use it as motivation, as a springboard, knowing I was playing well, pushed me to work extra hard. You have to be resilient in this game because losing is such a part of it." He now had five majors and three legs of the career grand slam under his belt, only lacking that elusive U.S. Open. "I think that is the sign of a complete great player and I'm a leg away," he said. "It's been a tough leg for me. And yet this championship has been much harder for me to get." It was worth the wait.

The Final Leaders: Phil Mickelson 66–281, Henrik Stenson 70–284, Ian Poulter 67–285, Adam Scott 72–285, Lee Westwood 75–285, Hideki Matsuyama 70–286, Zach Johnson 72–286, Tiger Woods 74–286, Francesco Molinari 72–287, Hunter Mahan 75–287, Brandt Snedeker 72–288, Angel Cabrera 74–288.

5. PGA Championship

Golf has drawn on the language for its rich expressions — birdie, eagle, slice, hook, etc. But it's rare that the language draws on golf for a word. It's also rare, and maybe unprecedented, that the word is one made out of a golfer's name. In 2013, there was such a word — "dufnering."

The word comes from Jason Dufner, an easy-going golfer pretty much unknown until he crashed and gave away the 2011 PGA Championship. He survived that, became successful and famous, and then one day a photographer found him in a classroom, with the teacher telling the kids how to relax. Right there with them was Dufner, unintentionally giving them an object lesson. Relaxing? He looked like a big rag doll the kids had dropped at the foot of the wall.

Fellow golf pros immediately had the word for it: "dufnering."

But Jason Dufner is "dufnering" even when he plays golf, as he showed at the 2013 PGA Championship, sauntering along the wooded fairways of Oak Hill Country Club like a kid strolling down the lane on a summer day. One could never read Dufner's game on his face. He was always the same — hitting daring shots, making birdies, recovering from errors or taking his medicine, always with that same impassive face.

Dufner did let his face slip at least once at the PGA. It was when he tapped in the short putt that give him the championship — the third victory of his brief career, and his first in a major. He gave a little smile, and even a little two-handed fist pump.

After the crash of 2011, he'd said: "I've got a feeling that I'm going to win some majors..."

But the favorites coming to Oak Hill were, of course, the usual suspects, led by Tiger Woods, back in his role, ranked No. 1 in the world. He had won five times already in 2013, and that included a runaway victory the previous week in the Bridgestone Invitational. But his year lacked that which he coveted most, a major. He was stuck on 14 in his quest to break Jack Nicklaus' record of 18. By his own definition, it had been only a good year.

"I think winning one major championship automatically means you had a great year," he said.

Phil Mickelson, just two months earlier, spoke of heartbreak when yet another U.S. Open slipped away, but he was soothed three weeks later, winning his first Open Championship with a brilliant finish. His game was in a high state and his outlook, as usual, was sunny. There was another reason he liked his chances in the PGA — Woods' win in the Bridgestone. "Because," he said, grinning, "I can't remember the last time somebody won the week before a major, then went on and won."

Adam Scott, the first Australian to win the Masters, was among the favorites, and quite hungry. "I'd really love to get myself in there with a chance to kind of bookend the Masters with a PGA Championship," Scott said.

Justin Rose, the first Englishman to win the U.S. Open since Tony Jacklin in 1970 and also high on the list of favorites, arrived at Oak Hill in hopes his game was still simple. "I never played well when I add things," he said. "For me, it's about doing the simple things well."

And so the list went on, including big names still looking for that first major, such as Luke Donald, Lee Westwood and Sergio Garcia. Jason Duffner's name was hard to find. He would add it himself — to the Wanamaker Trophy.

First Round

Jim Furyk was nice and comfortable and dry in the clubhouse when the rest of the field still had to slog around the drenched Oak Hill. He had one other thing they didn't have and might not get — a five-under-par 65 for the early lead. Furyk had got off at 8:45 a.m., and his lead would hold up till late in the day when Adam Scott, the Masters champion, came in with a 65 of his own, and together they led the field by a stroke.

At this early point, what their 65s meant was that Oak Hill was being hit pretty hard, and it might have surprised the designer, the legendary Donald Ross, who put all manner of clever deceits and hard-nosed demands into his creations. But not even Ross could spare a course from being so vulnerable after all that rain. In the 2003 PGA at Oak Tree, only 12 scores under par were shot in the first round. In this first round, 35 players broke par.

Furyk, starting from No. 10, was one stray drive from tying the course record of 64. He missed the fairway to the right on his last tee shot. It cost him his only bogey.

"Usually disappointed with ending the day on a bogey," said Furyk, a former U.S. Open champion. "But you know, 65 — PGA — is not so bad." In fact, a 65 was looking quite good to a player who hadn't won for nearly three years.

And 65 was looking quite good, too, to a player who had won the Masters just five months earlier. Scott, who teed off at 1:45 p.m., was off and running with five consecutive birdies from No. 4. "Probably the best run I've ever had," said Scott. "I just hit really nice shots and didn't leave myself too much work. It was a dream start after kind of a nervous first couple of holes."

Phil Mickelson found his famed resolve tested by a ragged 71. Starting in the afternoon from No. 1, he was in a mess in a hurry. "The first four holes was like a shock to my system," he said. He bogeyed the third and double-bogeyed the fourth. He recovered to birdie Nos. 9, 11, 12 and 14, then double-bogeyed the 18th. "If I hit a low round tomorrow," he said, ever-beaming, "I can get right back in it."

Rory McIlroy, the defending champion, had reason to beam, too, which was tough to do so far in this depressed season. His 69 was encouraging. "To shoot under par was a solid way to get off in any major," McIlroy said. And he wasn't surprised at the low scores coming in. "Soft conditions," he said. "A lot of rain last night. [But] it's not like the guys are so far ahead," he said. "You get off to a good start tomorrow, you are right there."

Tiger Woods, who blistered the field in the Bridgestone Invitational a week before, posted an erratic one-over 71. He hit only nine fairways and nine greens. And it was a matter of timing — the clock, in fact. He was playing with past PGA champions Davis Love and Keegan Bradley, and they were informed at the 10th (No. 1) that they were being timed because of slow play. He'd had two birdies on the front, but wiped them out and then some coming in. He missed a three-foot birdie putt at his 11th (No. 2) and said it was because they were being timed. "I hit some good shots there," he said. "Stuffed it at [No. 2]. Probably should have taken a little big longer, but we were on the clock and had to get going, so ended up blocking the putt down the hill." He bogeyed his 13th (No. 4), then double-bogeyed his last, the par-four, dogleg-right ninth, when his attempt to fade his second around a tree came down short of the green. From there, he hit into a bunker, blasted to 12 feet and two-putted for a six. "I played really well today," Woods said. "The round realistically could have been under par, easily."

Would history repeat itself in a foreign accent? This was the question surrounding Thailand's Kiradech Aphibarnrat, 24, known as Asia's John Daly both for his portly physique and his go-for-broke style of play. He opened his first PGA with a 68 as a wiser golfer. He learned his lesson at the U.S. Open, his first major. "I lost confidence really quickly after I make bogey on the first hole," he said. Would he duplicate Daly's famous grip-it-and-rip-it victory at the 1991 PGA? "This week, don't want to force myself," he said. (It was a fine debut. He would finish tied for 25th.)

Jason Dufner got off to a shaky start. He bogeyed the 10th, his first hole, and after two birdies, he bogeyed the 17th and 18th. He got up-and-down from 100 yards for a par at No. 1 (his 10th), then made three quick birdies from No. 5 (14th). "It was good to finish that way," Dufner said. "I've been doing the opposite lately — getting off to a good start and finishing poorly."

First-Round Leaders: Jim Furyk 65, Adam Scott 65, David Hearn 66, Lee Westwood 66, Robert Garrigus 67, Paul Casey 67, Matt Kuchar 67, Marcus Fraser 67, Scott Piercy 67, Jason Day 67.

Second Round

Webb Simpson knew the thrill of making it into the record book. Moreover, he was also in the company of Ben Hogan. He teed off on a rain-drenched Oak Hill from No. 10 and shot a six-under-par 64. That tied the Oak Hill record Hogan set in 1942, tied by Curtis Strange when he won the 1989 U.S. Open.

"Any time you can put your name near Ben Hogan's, it's a great thing," said Simpson who made the cut for the first time in his three PGAs. Then irony of ironies. Just about five hours later, Simpson's name was still there with Hogan's, but they no longer shared the record. Jason Dufner had come in with a 63. That gave Dufner the Oak Hill record, and it also was the 26th 63 in a major. And Dufner had had a clear and tantalizing chance at breaking that record.

In front of the jammed bleachers at the 18th, Dufner had an uphill 12-foot birdie putt for an unthinkable 62. But he left it just short. He tapped in for a par-four and knew the pain of missing history.

"I knew where I stood, and you couldn't have a better chance at history on the last hole," he said.

Like Miller at Oakmont in 1963, Dufner had caught a hot hand on a course softened by rain that fell Thursday afternoon and Friday morning. Although Oak Hill played longer than its 7,163 yards, it also was vulnerable to anyone who could stay in the fairway and hit the softened greens. Thus 32 players broke the par of 70 on Friday, after 35 did it on Thursday.

The 63 put Dufner at nine-under 131 for a two-stroke lead on Adam Scott, Matt Kuchar and Jim Furyk at the halfway point. Dufner started his historic run at the 401-yard, par-four No. 2, where he holed out a 105-yard wedge shot for an eagle. He then birdied two straight, holing a 35-foot putt at No. 4 and a 12-footer at No. 5. His putter rescued him from a sure bogey at the seventh, where he holed a 40-footer for par after escaping Allen's Creek. Birdies at the 11th, 13th and 16th got him to seven under, where he stayed. He missed a birdie try at the 17th, and for his last chance at 62, he played the 18th beautifully. A good tee shot left him 203 yards from the green and between a five iron and a six iron for his approach. He hit the six and put it 12 feet below the hole — perfect. "If I could do it over," he said, "I guess I would hit the putt harder."

Tiger Woods also wished he could have done things over. The best he could do on the softened course was a 70, and that meant that in all six of his rounds at Oak Hill, including the 2003 PGA, he hadn't broken par. At one-over 141, he was 10 shots off Dufner's lead. "I'm going to have to put together a really good weekend," Woods said.

Rory McIlroy, the defending champion, was playing some of his better golf of his troubled season, but his 71 only had him at par 140, nine off the lead. "I was letting the round get away from me," he said, "but making four birdies on the last eight holes was nice."

Phil Mickelson, playing in the morning rain, shot 72 and was at 142 and 11 off the lead. He was ever cheery. "It's just a little bit off," he said. "I feel like it can turn around in a second." But he was just a stroke above the cut. The numbers told the tale of softened Oak Hill. In five previous majors, only nine golfers finished below par. This time, at the halfway point, 27 were under. The cut came in at 144, claiming, among others, former Masters champions Bubba Watson and Charl Schwartzel, Luke Donald, Billy Horschel and young whiz Jordan Spieth.

Both first-round co-leaders, Jim Furyk and Adam Scott, shot 68 and with Matt Kuchar (66) were tied for second, two behind. Furyk had only one bogey, and Scott made three against his five birdies. Kuchar was bogey-free till the 18th. U.S. Open champion Justin Rose, after a 37 on his first nine (from the 10th), blazed home with six birdies for a 29 and a 66 to get within three of the lead.

Dufner said he knew the history of major championships, but the question was, did he know that of the 25 previous 63s, only five times did the author go on to win.

Dufner left the second round pleased, if a little shaken after his 63. "It's tough when you're chasing history," he said. "I don't think I've been the first to do anything in my life. I wish," he added, drooping with golfer's rue, "I had that putt on the last hole back again."

Second-Round Leaders: Jason Dufner 63–131, Adam Scott 68–133, Matt Kuchar 66–133, Jim Furyk 68–133, Justin Rose 66–134, Henrik Stenson 66–134, Robert Garrigus 68–135, Steve Stricker 67–135.

Third Round

The third round offered the field a new problem from nature — the wind. It was frisky and capricious, and could ruin even the best executed shot.

Dustin Johnson handled it best. He shot a five-under 65 that carried him 51 spots up the leaderboard, to a 208 total, seven off the lead. "I played a lot better than my score was for the first couple days," said Johnson, who in four previous PGAs lost his best chance for a championship in that celebrated bunker episode in 2010. A Swede had never won a PGA, and suddenly two were in contention — Henrik Stenson, two strokes off the third-round lead, and Jonas Blixt, three behind. Stenson, runner-up in the Open Championship three weeks earlier, had four birdies going out, but a birdie and four bogeys coming back for a 69. "I think it shows how tricky it was with the breeze," Stenson said. Blixt, who played American college golf at Florida State University, posted a no-bogey 66 and most of all was nervous in front of the media corps. "Feels like going back to college speech class," he said, to sympathetic chuckles.

The attention soon was focused on Jim Furyk, after a 68, now in a familiar place — leading a major. He had converted the position into a victory only once, in the 2003 U.S. Open, and as always, his many slips came into the conversation.

"I'm on a nice little high," said Furyk, "but y'all are trying to bring me down." But he stayed afloat in the interview room as well as he had on the course. He'd bogeyed the second and third, then got the strokes back on two birdies, on a 10-foot putt at No. 4 and a seven-footer at No. 8. He birdied the 10th and 12th and bogeyed the 15th. He made a heroic birdie at the 17th, hitting a hybrid 244 yards to 18 feet. Then he closed with a ragged par at the 18th. He missed the fairway with his three-wood tee shot, and finally curled in a 15-footer from the fringe for the par-four that kept him in the lead.

Jason Dufner, famed for blowing the 2011 PGA down the homestretch, seemed on the verge of another collapse. This time, however, it was early — at No. 5 in the third round. He drove into the creek, and after much milling about, took his penalty drop from the other side of the creek, hit a great four-iron shot off a tight lie, and ended up with a double-bogey-six. It cost him the lead, but he stayed afloat.

"I could've gone sideways quick there," Dufner said. "Things like that happen at majors. Those are the type of things that can really get you unnerved and unsettled, and all of a sudden you can make two or three bogeys, and all of a sudden you're out of the tournament. I was determined I was going to put it behind me."

He did. After two birdies and a bogey, he battled the 18th for a par, chipping out from a stray drive and finally holing an eight-footer for a 71 — his only round out of the 60s — to stay a stroke behind Furyk.

Tiger Woods shot a one-birdie, four-bogey 73 and was out of it at 11 over the lead. Said Woods: "I didn't start off very good and I didn't finish very good." Phil Mickelson's hopes disappeared under a flood of bogeys — five singles, a double and a triple in a 78.

A strong finish saved Adam Scott a crucial stroke and left him four behind. After two birdies and two bogeys, he made an unthinking double bogey at the 16th — "I bit off more than I could chew," he admitted — then had to make a testing 15-footer to save par at the 17th, salvaging a 72. "It was a great way to hang in there and make a four out of nowhere, really," he said.

Rory McIlroy, even par coming down the back nine, birdied Nos. 13, 17 and 18 for a 67. "It was good to feel the rush again," he said. But he was six behind, tied with Lee Westwood (68), which seemed like too much work at Oak Hill. The PGA looked, at best, like a six-man race to the finish.

Third-Round Leaders: Jim Furyk 68–201, Jason Dufner 71–202, Henrik Stenson 69–203, Jonas Blixt 66–204, Steve Stricker 70–205, Adam Scott 72–205, Rory McIlroy 67–207, Lee Westwood 68–207.

Fourth Round

Early in August 2011, Jason Dufner, then little known, went through what by most standards should have been the most wretched day of his career. He was leading by five strokes coming to the 15th, then staggered to three straight bogeys while Keegan Bradley made two birdies to tie him, and then beat him in a playoff. That kind of crash can destroy a golfer. Dufner showed no emotion.

"I'm not going to let this define my career," Dufner said. "I have a lot of things ahead of me. Looking back 10, 15 years from now, I'll feel disappointment that I let this one get away if I never get another chance. But I've got a feeling that I'm going to win some majors..."

Two years later, Dufner — a shaggy-haired 36 who looks like a kid playing hooky from school — was sitting before the media in a crowded interview room at Oak Hill, and never once did he say, "I told you so."

He had just won the 2013 PGA Championship, beating Jim Furyk by two strokes.

Dufner, by now famous for a calm bordering on seeming disinterest, had at last shown emotion. When he tapped in the final putt that gave him his first major, he actually lifted his hands shoulder-high and gave a little two-handed fist pump.

"It feels great," Dufner said. "Probably hasn't sunk in. Been running around here. Today was a tough day. The golf course, again, played pretty tough. Me and Jim — kind of came down to a two-man race there at the end. He's a great champion and he's played so well in so many majors, and he's been there before."

Indeed the unfortunate Furyk had been there before. He had 16 victories on the PGA Tour, won the 2003 U.S. Open, won some $55 million, but had 25 near-misses — tournaments almost in his hand, but that got away. Earlier in the week, he ticked off the majors that slipped away: A Masters, an Open Championship and three U.S. Opens. To them, add the 2013 PGA Championship.

"I don't know if it makes anything easy or less easy," Furyk said, "but

I don't look at it as I lost the golf tournament. I look at it as I got beat by somebody that played better."

There is that distinction in these matters, and it pretty well applied here. Furyk started the final round leading Dufner by a stroke. Dufner made three birdies on the front nine, the last at No. 8, taking the lead, and he led the rest of the way. He finished with a two-under 68 and a 10-under 270 to Furyk's 71–272.

They had reduced this PGA to a two-man race. Nobody could make a serious move on them. Henrik Stenson, trying to become the first Swede to win the PGA, stirred briefly. He got to within two with a birdie at the 13th, but bogeyed the 14th and finished with a 70 for a solo third place. His countryman, Jonas Blixt did well in his first PGA. He also closed with a 70 and finished fourth.

Beyond them, it was not a week for marquee names.

The slumping Rory McIlroy had one of the better outings of his troubled season. He closed with a 70 and tied for eighth. "I saw a lot of great signs out there today," he said.

Tiger Woods, No. 1 in the world, didn't break par in any round. Including the 2003 PGA, that made eight straight rounds without breaking par at Oak Hill. He shot 70 and tied for 40th. "I didn't hit the ball well enough to be in it," he said.

Phil Mickelson? After the 78 in the third round, he closed with a 72, tied for 72nd out of the 75 finishers, and looked forward to going home. "I'm going to be in the air soon," he said.

While they were struggling, Dufner and Furyk were dueling. Furyk parred the first five holes, and Dufner tied him with a birdie at the fourth and edged ahead with another at the fifth. Furyk tied him with a birdie at the par-three No. 6. Dufner then was ahead to stay with a birdie at No. 8, and was up by two when Furyk bogeyed No. 9. Dufner had one-putted the last six holes on the front.

Then they matched each other, hole for hole, all the way home — six straight pars each, then amazingly, they finished birdie-bogey-bogey. At the 16th, Furyk holed a 12-foot putt for a birdie. Dufner had lofted a wedge to 18 inches and matched him. They bogeyed the 17th, Furyk after a chip shot that didn't reach the green and Dufner by missing a three-foot par putt. At the 18th, both drove into the rough and both missed the green. Furyk chipped 20 feet past and missed the par putt. Dufner chipped about 10 feet short and his par putt missed by inches. He tapped in for the win and gave the little two-handed fist pump.

"There's not much to celebrate from six inches," Dufner said.

Later, he would reflect on his victory. "This is definitely going to change my life," Dufner said. "But I'm determined it's not going to change me."

The Final Leaders: Jason Dufner 68–270, Jim Furyk 71–272, Henrik Stenson 70–273, Jonas Blixt 70–274, Scott Piercy 65–275, Adam Scott 70–275, David Toms 67–276.

6. Women's Major Championships

Kraft Nabisco Championship

In the tradition of sports parents everywhere, Gun Gyu Park wanted to see his daughter play, and better yet, win. He had insisted that if ever Inbee was in contention in the final round of the Kraft Nabisco Championship, he would rush right there to watch her. There were two problems with his fatherly ambition: First, he was at home in South Korea, and the Kraft Nabisco, the LPGA Tour's first major of the season, was at Mission Hills, in Southern California. Second, she didn't want him there. Not that she was the ungrateful daughter. It was just that the pressure would be too much.

"My dad, just on his own, he wanted to come," she said. "He packed his bags and booked a ticket and everything, and he was on his way. I called him and said, just don't come. He was very mad because he really wanted to come. It was really tough stopping him, but he actually listened to me, and I'm glad that I won today."

Gun Gyu had granted the wishes of his 24-year-old daughter. But all was not lost for him. Since dad wouldn't get to make the ceremonial jump into Poppie's Pond, he would get the next best thing — a Poppie's Pond shower. Inbee's fiancé, Gi Hyeob Nam, filled a couple of plastic bottles with pond water she would pour over him when they met in Hawaii the following week.

Gun Gyu, of course, had a pretty good idea he'd be scrambling to make a flight to California when Inbee took the lead in the second round. That was by a stroke. The idea got stronger as she went — up by two in the second, by three in the third, at which time he was heading for the airport. With her putter in exquisite working order, Park rolled to a card of 70-67-67-69 for a 15-under-par 273 total and a four-shot win that was easier and bigger than it looked. Her strongest threat was American Lizette Salas, 23, a second-year member of the tour and seeking her first win. Salas stuck closest to Park, tied with her at 70 in the first round, then holding second place through the next two, although slipping each time. Salas, three behind to start the final round, knocked herself out of the running with a double bogey on the first hole. There went her chance at her best finish in a major.

And Park birdied the first hole, doubling her lead to six. Then she was up by seven, with a birdie at No. 2.

The Kraft Nabisco was over, all except for So Yeon Ryu's show. Ryu, the 2011 U.S. Women's Open champion and Park's good friend, made the Kraft look closer than it was with her final-round dash to a tournament-low 65. But she had started eight strokes behind Park, too far back to make a ripple.

The win was Park's fourth in her last 16 starts, her fifth LPGA title and her ninth worldwide. It moved her up to No. 2 in the Rolex Rankings, the highest of her career, behind Stacy Lewis.

Park opened the tournament two off the lead and largely unnoticed in the stories developing around her. Norway's Suzann Pettersen and Korea's Na Yeon Choi shared the early lead with 68s, joined by England's Jodi Ewart Shadoff in the afternoon when her bid for the outright lead fizzled on a drive into the right rough. She managed a beautifully scrambled par, hitting a punch shot around a tree and over a bunker.

Anna Norqvist and Amy Lang tied at 69, and Stacy Lewis, Rolex World No. 1 and the 2011 Kraft champion, triple-bogeyed the 14th and shot 73. It was the start of a frazzled week for her. She would tie for 32nd. "Coming into the week," she was to say, "my swing didn't feel great and I was hoping I would figure things out ... but I just haven't."

After the first round, it was Inbee Park's tournament. She worked up a masterful 67 in the second round, on a Mission Hills hit by heat and gusting winds. She surged into the lead with three consecutive birdies on the back nine, lofting a 70-yard wedge shot to two feet at the 11th, then adding the next two on nine irons to seven feet. She bogeyed the 14th and parred in. "Putted really good, especially on the back nine," Park said. "The wind kicked up, so it was tough on the back nine. Last four holes, I made all pars. I'm really happy with that."

Park was known chiefly for winning the 2008 U.S. Women's Open, the youngest to do so at the age of 19 years, 11 months and 17 days. She got her fourth career win in the LPGA Thailand in February when Ariya Jutanugarn, 17, fell to teenage nerves at the final hole, squandering a two-stroke lead and the win with a triple bogey. But Park was taking this Kraft Nabisco on her own.

Salas moved into second place, a stroke behind, with a 68. Salas, the lone American in the top 11, resisted the temptation to keep pace with Park and prudently saved par at the par-five 18th. She had driven into the left rough and hit her hybrid second into the right rough. The bold move would be to go for the green from there, but the shot had to carry the water. "It was not a good lie," Salas said, "and I knew if I would go for it, it would probably go in the water." So she pitched back to the fairway and hit a wedge from 88 yards to three feet and saved the par, and sat just a shot out of the lead. "I'm not a long hitter, so I have to make it up some way," Salas said. "I've been working hard, dialing in with my wedges because that's your go-to club. I just trusted it and went with my first instinct."

Two other little-known players tied for third, two back — Italy's Giulia Sergas, with a 69, and Sweden's Caroline Hedwall, a 68. Neither would mount a serious challenge from there.

The putts continued to drop obediently for Park in the third round. Park and Salas matched birdies on the first hole, then Park took over from there. She dropped a 25-footer for birdie at the ninth, another at the 10th, and then a pair of 30-inchers at the 12th and 17th. The birdie at 17, in particular, surely had to be a sign that this major had Park's name all over it. At the 17th, a 168-yard par-three, she didn't catch her seven-iron tee shot flush. It felt like it might get away from her. "It was actually a little bit of a mis-shot," Park said. "I aimed a little more right and slightly pulled it." The pin was cut back-left, and she wanted to avoid the bunker back there, where Salas' tee shot ended up. Park's little mis-shot, on the other hand, tracked right for the pin, landed softly and stopped 30 inches away. From what looked like an error, chalk up another birdie for another 67 and a three-stroke lead. She was now bogey-free for 22 holes.

Salas couldn't keep pace entirely with Park, slipping one more stroke behind, but she was still playing well. She pulled within two with a birdie at the 13th, but Park regained that stroke with the birdie at the 17th. Salas saved par out of the bunker there, then narrowly missed picking up a stroke when her six-foot birdie try at the 18th slid by. "I wasn't hitting the ball as well as the first two days, but I kept putting myself in good positions," she said. "Hit some good shots out of the rough, and hit a great bunker shot on 17 to get up and down for par. Overall, pretty good day, considering I didn't hit the ball well. I've just got to stay patient and just trust my putter and keep it simple."

Others were making their moves, getting into a crowd of six at 210, six off the lead. Angela Stanford, who opened with 70-74, crowded in with a 66. "I've been fighting it all week," she said. "I found a thought that worked the rest of the day." Suzann Pettersen, who turned 32 on Sunday, birdied the final four holes for a 67. "I probably should have had six straight birdies coming in," said Pettersen, a three-time Kraft Nabisco runner-up. She shared the lead with a 68 in the first round, but fell hard with a 75 in the second. Karrie Webb, 38, who won the last of her 38 titles in 2011, shot 67. "If we can get some breeze going tomorrow, I think that'll make it interesting."

If there was any real pressure building on Park going into the final round — except that from her dad, trying to board a flight for California — it didn't show. "I feel really good about my swing and the stroke at the moment," she said. "I feel really comfortable around this course, too. This one would mean a lot. It's just been a tournament I always wanted to win. And with the special ceremony of jumping in the water — everybody wants to do that."

In fact, Park all but had a reservation at the edge of the pond. Her lead doubled from three strokes to six right out of the gate in the final round when she birdied No. 1 and Salas double-bogeyed. "That made my day much easier, that's for sure," Park said. She dropped a 20-footer for the birdie under the eyes of the unfortunate Salas, who was about to two-putt for a double bogey. Salas drove into the left rough, topped her second 15 yards, and her next left her 15 yards short of the green. She chipped to 15 feet, and after watching Park make her birdie, two-putted for a six. She would plunge from there to a 79 and a tie for 25th. "Throughout the day, I was really anxious and hit a lot of pulls," Salas said. "I was just not myself today."

And Park was still herself. She also birdied No. 2 from seven feet. But she drove into the water at No. 6 and made her first bogey in 27 holes, then dropped a 22-foot birdie putt at the eighth. She would bogey two more, the 10th and the 17th, but in between were birdies at the 12th, from 25 feet, and the 13th, from 10, in her closing 69.

"I've seen Inbee do it before," Stacy Lewis had said. "When she rolls it, you can't beat her. She's the best putter on tour."

So Yeon Ryu finished her 65 well ahead of Park and noted: "She looks like she played another golf course."

Throughout the tournament, Park was the model of accuracy. She made only five bogeys for the week and was co-leader both in birdies, with 20, and in hitting greens in regulation, at 79.2 percent.

Park took a moment to reflect on her victory. "I've played five tournaments on the LPGA Tour, and I've won two of them, which is a very good start," she said. "It's the pressure off me for the rest of the season."

She might be surprised, though. The win carried her right into the spotlight, an area she wasn't accustomed to and that perhaps she wasn't comfortable in.

"I like to stay a little quiet and just do my own thing," Park said. "If I win a little more, I think I'll get a little bit more attention."

In fact, she could count on it.

Wegmans LPGA Championship

On winning the Kraft Nabisco Championship in April, Inbee Park had mentioned that she preferred to remain quiet and do her thing. "If I win a little more," she said, "I think I'll get a little bit more attention."

What was that noise in the distance? Thunder, perhaps? Certainly applause. Park was turning 2013 into her year.

The golf world turned to the Wegmans LPGA Championship in June, the second major of the LPGA season, and Park had just beaten Scotland's Catriona Matthew on the third hole of a playoff. It was Park's seventh career victory, her third major championship, but more to the point, her second major of the season. That is, by dropping an 18-foot birdie putt on the third extra hole, Korea's Inbee Park, who won the Kraft Nabisco Championship in April, had just won back-to-back majors. She was only the seventh player in the tour's history to win the first two majors in a season, and the first since Annika Sorenstam won the same two in 2005. It was also, by the way, Park's fourth win of the year, her career seventh, and the sixth in the last 22 starts.

"It's almost a miracle that I won today," Park said. "I think I got lucky there, too. And I really tried to fight off and tried not to give up. That really paid off."

Her victory might have been the second miracle of the week, the first being that the tournament was even played. Heavy storms hit Pittsford, New York, in the Rochester area, dumping tons of course-soaking rain — two and a half inches in about 24 hours and forcing the postponement of play on Thursday before it even began, and forcing a 36-hole final on Sunday.

Play began on schedule, if a day late, on Friday, at 7:15 a.m. But Locust Hill Country Club would be playing far differently from what anyone remembered. The thick rough, soaked by rain, and the soggy fairways made the 6,530-yard, par-72 course play a lot longer than expected. The rough was so thick and deep that marshals sometimes had to mark balls with orange flags. Not surprisingly, pre-tournament talk held that whoever could keep it in the fairway had the best chance to score.

South Korea's Chella Choi put a name to that golfer — her own. She shot a five-under-par 67, a sparkling score at any time but a near-amazing one under the heavy, soaked conditions. "I hit a really good driver today," said Choi. "I hit all 14 fairways. So I'm really happy. My goal is just keep fairway." Choi, 22, a five-year veteran of the LPGA Tour and still seeking that first career win, also hit 15 greens in regulation, and she had to battle rain, first a light drizzle on the front nine, then a steady rain on the back. She got to six under with a birdie at the par-four 10th, which had given up only 12 all day, and made her only bogey at the 13th, then parred in. Her 67 carried her a stroke past Morgan Pressel, who posted a 68 and held the clubhouse lead much of the day.

It was only the second time in the season that Pressel broke 70. "I played pretty well," said Pressel, who birdied her last four holes. "I didn't put myself in any bad trouble, which you can certainly find on this course. I hit a lot of fairways ... I only missed ... two or three, and the couple that I did [miss], I most of the time saved par." Pressel was joined at 68 by Jiyai Shin, who had four birdies and no bogeys.

As for Park — as she did on her way to the Kraft Nabisco Championship, she opened the tournament on a modest note. She shot a par 72, tying with, among others, Yani Tseng, two-time winner of the LPGA Championship, who had a hole-in-one at the par-three 15th. Two other big names struggled. Stacy Lewis, the No. 1 American, had a 74, and Karrie Webb, winner of the ShopRite LPGA Classic the week before, shot 76, as did Michelle Wie.

Pressel was starting to look more like the young whiz kid she was when she won the 2007 Kraft Nabisco, then 18 and the youngest ever to win an LPGA major. She last won in 2008, the Kapalua Classic. "It was a long time ago," Pressel said. "I've been through a lot since then." That included thumb and left wrist injuries in 2012. The wrist wasn't hurting as much any more, Pressel had said, and she showed as much by trudging through rain and goopy turf adding a 70 to her opening 68 for the halfway lead by two over Park (68) and Choi, the first-round leader, who struggled for a one-over 73 to go with her opening 67. Pressel, starting from No. 9, got to seven under with birdies on three of her first six holes. She gave two stroke back with bogeys, then coming in she holed a four-footer for birdie at the par-five No. 8.

"The tournament is only halfway finished," she said, "but I feel good about my approach to playing." There would be the problem of having to play 36 holes on a heavy course the next day. "I run a lot," Pressel said. "I'm in plenty good enough shape to get through 36 holes tomorrow."

It looked like a free-for-all was shaping up. Beyond Park and Choi came Jiyai Shin, Amy Yang and Sarah Jane Smith tied for fourth at three under, and seven others at one under or better.

Park didn't share Pressel's enthusiasm for the 36-hole endurance set for

Sunday. "It's going to be very tough physically," she said. "Especially walking on these wet fairways. There's going to be many holes, but just try not to lose my focus." But she had a bright outlook for it. Winning three times in the first three months — including a major — does wonders for the confidence. "I would be less nervous than at the Kraft," Park said. "That kind of experience really helps going into major championships like this, where you get the situation and you've experienced it before. You feel a lot more comfortable."

Michelle Wie was having her best outing at Locust Valley in years. Her 68 — off five birdies and one bogey, and matching her season's best — was also her low in six starts at Locust Hill. "I'm starting to understand this golf course a little more every year," said Wie. It requires patience, she said, and sometimes is best played with the driver in the bag. "It will nip you in the butt if you get a little greedy," she said. She was at even-par 144, six off the halfway lead and light years ahead of where she was in the 2012 championship. She missed the cut badly in that one, at 12-over 156.

Jiyai Shin didn't say whether she believes in signs, but rain forced the 2012 Women's British Open into a 36-hole finish, and she rallied to beat Park by nine shots. Now, after a 73, she was at 141 and three behind Pressel, and she was thinking about strategy, not signs. She planned to play deliberately in the third round Sunday morning, then aggressively in the afternoon, if necessary. "I just try to keep focused and be patient."

Park putted the Kraft Nabisco into submission, and now her magic putter was heating up again, in the 36-hole finale of the LPGA Championship. Under sunny skies in the third round Sunday morning, she hit just nine fairways and 12 greens, but needed just 26 putts for a 68 to move past Pressel and into a one-stroke lead on the field. "I putted great today, and I got up-and-down from a lot of places," said Park, having a quick lunch near the putting green in the 25 minutes before she had to go out for the fourth round. Park caught fire just in time. Pressel expanded her one-shot lead to four by mid-morning, and Park was trailing by five through the ninth. The picture changed completely over the final nine. Pressel bogeyed the 10th and 12th, and Park birdied her last four holes. "You know, I scrambled out there, but I scrambled well," Pressel said, and that included holing a 30-foot putt to save par at the 18th and stay within a stroke of Park. When the third round was in the books, Park had a 68 and was leading at eight-under 208. Pressel was a stroke behind after a 71 and Shin (69) two back.

Catriona Matthew, an established veteran at 42, can be called the Silent Scot. The four-time tour winner from Edinburgh was unnoticed back in the pack for three rounds and in fact didn't really count herself in the hunt until after she had finished with a 68, her low round of the tournament. Her five-under 283 total suddenly was looking good, while Park and Pressel hooked up in an odd battle down the final stretch.

Park started the final round leading Pressel by a stroke, went up by two with a birdie at No. 5, then quickly bogeyed the sixth and eighth. Pressel hit a stray second shot at No. 8, but recovered and birdied the hole to tie Park at seven under. Then came an even more awkward stretch. Pressel bogeyed the 10th, Park birdied the 11th on a three-footer, and Pressel bogeyed the 12th. Just that abruptly, Park was leading by three with six to play. The Inbee Park of the Kraft Nabisco would have made short work of the rest of the tournament, but oddly, little of that Inbee Park was in evidence. She bogeyed Nos. 14, 16 and 18 for a 75 and a 283 total. Pressel also shot 75 and 284, and tied for third.

"I'm definitely disappointed," said Pressel, "but it's the first time in a long time I've contended."

While they were dueling, Matthew was waiting and watching a chance materialize before her eyes. "The last I looked at the scoreboard, Inbee had a solid lead," Matthew said. "So I was quite surprised when suddenly I looked at the leaderboard on 18, and two putts would get me in a playoff. When I stared today, the last round, I probably didn't realize I could win."

"I could have made one more putt on 17 or 16," Park mused. "So bogeys were bound to come with the way I've been striking the ball today. I was hitting the ball everywhere."

They tied on the first two playoff holes. At the third, the par-four 18th — their 39th and last hole of the day — Matthew drove into the rough, caught more rough along the way, and finally had a 50-foot chip shot for a par. She missed it.

Then once again, Park's putter rescued her. She put her approach to 20 feet and dropped the putt for a birdie and her second major of the season and her third overall.

Said Matthew, with the solo second her best finish ever in the LPGA Championship: "Pretty disappointing. But overall, a pretty good week."

Said Park: "I felt like I ran a marathon today. But just putting my name on the championship trophy means so much to me."

Park now had seven career LPGA Tour victories, six in her last 22 starts, and three majors. She was now only the seventh in LPGA history to win the first two majors of the season.

Park had hoped to do her thing quietly, and maybe get a little attention if she would win more. Her quiet days were pretty much over.

U.S. Women's Open

Inbee Park, meet Babe Didrickson Zaharias.

They were generations apart. Zaharias did it in 1950, Park in 2013. They were worlds apart, the late Zaharias an all-around athlete from Texas, Park a single-minded young lady from South Korea. But now they were sisters in the annals of golf.

On the windswept reaches of Sebonack Golf Club on Long Island, New York, hard by the sea, Park became only the second player in history to win the first three LPGA majors in a season. She completed the set with her victory in the U.S. Women's Open in June, three weeks after she won the LPGA Championship and two months after taking the Kraft Nabisco Championship. Zaharias won all three of the majors of her time in 1950 — the Titleholders Championship, the Women's Western Open and the U.S. Women's Open. Mickey Wright, in 1961, and Pat Bradley, in 1986, also won three majors in a single season, but they weren't consecutive.

"I am very honored to put my name by someone like Babe Zaharias," said Park, who also had won the 2008 U.S. Women's Open. "I don't know what I just did today. It's something very great. It's scary," she added, "to think about what I'm capable of doing."

And that, the world of golf was saying, was win the never-before-won Grand Slam. The Ricoh Women's British Open would be played in August, but ironically — and unfortunately for Park — even winning it would not be the Grand Slam. Starting this year, the LPGA had five majors. The Evian Championship, in France in September, had been designated the fifth.

Grand Slam or not, Park had already had a huge year — three majors and six victories overall.

This time, Gun Gyu Park did not have to rush for a plane to see his daughter win a major, did not have her beg him to stay home and keep the pressure down, did not have to have a kind of substitute Poppie's Pond jump poured over his head later. This time, it was the real thing. This time, Gun Gyu Park and his wife, Sung Kim, were in the crowd at Sebonack to watch their daughter Inbee win a major, the U.S. Women's Open. And they didn't have to fret. Park had to go through a three-hole playoff to win the Wegmans LPGA two weeks before, but now, as in the Kraft Nabisco, she was rarely seriously challenged, leading most of the way and shooting Sebonack, a course beset by a variety of wind, rain and fog, in 67-68-71-74–280 for a four-stroke win on an eight-under total that was stronger than it looked, considering that only two other players could break par for the week. In an all-Korean finish, I.K. Kim finished second at 284, and So Yeon Ryu third in a distant 287.

For a short while in the first round, Park was the marvel of sister Korean Ha-Neul Kim. Park had the clubhouse lead with a 67, posted in the morning. "Wow, how did she shoot that score?" said Kim, through an interpreter. Then Kim, a member of the Korean LPGA Tour and a seven-time winner on it, shot a 66 in the afternoon to take the first-round lead in her first appearance in the Women's Open.

"I'm enjoying myself," Kim said. "I'm just happy to be here and to be playing in this big event. I'm not really thinking about winning, or results, but enjoying the moment." (Unfortunately, the fun wouldn't last. Kim shot 77 in the second round and would go on to finish tied for 25th.)

Tournament officials, concerned by the forecast of bad weather, moved the tees up. This played right into Park's hands and into her aggressive game. "Instead of hitting five irons, we were hitting nine irons, and that was making the course much easier," Park said. Whoever saw her putting performances in the first two majors understood what she was talking about. "I was actually able to go for some pins and give myself a lot of opportunities today," Park said. "I made a lot of putts and didn't leave much out there." She birdied her first hole, No. 10, made the turn at two under, then birdied three of the next four. She bogeyed once, at No. 6 (her 15th), but got the stroke back with a chip and a five-foot birdie at No. 8 (her 17th).

A good international mix were tied at 68 — American Lizette Salas, Swedes Caroline Hedwall and Anna Nordqvist and South Korean I.K. Kim. Hedwall and Kim closed with bogeys, while Nordqvist birdied her last two holes to join them. Natalie Gulbis had a promising start, a 70. Gulbis had missed two tournaments and withdrew from another because of malaria she contracted at the LPGA Thailand in February. Defending champion Na Yeon Choi and Rolex world No. 2 Stacy Lewis were in a crowd at 71. And New Zealand amateur Lydia Ko, 16, youngest to win on the LPGA Tour, had 72. Michelle Wie had a tough time. She took a quadruple-bogey-eight on her first hole and birdied three of her last four for an 80.

Before the second round would run its course, the weather would take over. Heavy fog drifted in, forcing officials to suspend play late in the round. The struggling Wie found herself 11 over par for the tournament with one hole to play the next morning. She withdrew, citing illness.

The fog didn't bother Inbee Park. She couldn't follow her final tee shot beyond about 150 yards, but then she hit her approach to 12 feet and sank the birdie putt. That gave her a 68, a nine-under 135 and a two-stroke lead on countrywoman I.K. Kim. England's Jodi Ewart Shadoff was on the fringe of moving into the picture, sitting five strokes behind with three holes to play. She picked up one the next morning, posted a 69 and was four behind at 139.

Sebonack in the second round was hardly a mirror image of itself in the first. On Thursday, anticipating bad weather, officials had moved up the tees for the first round, in effect giving the golfers an easier course. On Friday, for the second round, pins were tucked in tough spots and the wind picked up. Add the late fog, and the second round turned vexing. Of the 114 who finished, a mere nine were under par. It seemed okay with Park. "With the wind and the fog, it really made me think that's what the U.S. Open is all about," she said.

Park's putting might have been a bit off, but she came through in the clutch, rolling in a 20-footer from the edge for a birdie at No. 13 to catch I.K. Kim. She took the outright lead, then, at the par-five 15th. Her approach kicked off the back fringe and trickled down, leaving her with a tap-in for a birdie. It was, Park said, a strange day. "Everything that was closer was not going in, then everything that was further away was going in," she said. "It was weird."

Kim shot 69 in the morning and was very pleased and relieved at the result. "Anything under par I thought was going to be a great score," she said. It put her second and it was a sign of an affinity for perhaps the toughest tournament on the schedule. She sported one of the strongest records by a player who hadn't won the championship — tied for third in 2008 and 2009, solo fourth in 2010 and a tie for 10th in 2011. She missed an outright win in the 2012 Kraft Nabisco when she lipped out a short putt at the last hole and then lost in the playoff. "Everyone has ups and downs," Kim said. "Definitely finishing top five in the U.S. Open is not a bad thing. I just have a faith — if you do your best, everything is going to be okay."

The second round saw a fascinating story emerge — that of the Korda sisters, only the seventh set of sisters to play in the U.S. Women's Open. These would be Jessica, 20, a former standout amateur now on the LPGA Tour, and Nelly, an amateur of 14. Was she scared? "It was nice — I didn't get nervous on the first hole," Nelly said. "Which was a big surprise." She showed pro poise in shaking off a double bogey on her 16th hole and finishing birdie-birdie for a 73. (As her big sister did as an amateur in 2008 and 2009, Nelly would make the cut. She finished at 22 over, tied for 64th.)

The tournament would not be so nice for others. Stacy Lewis, for example, shot a 76 from which she would not recover. (She would go on to tie for 42nd.) Things were worse for others. The halfway cut came in at six-over 150 and claimed some surprise victims — Jiyai Shin, Suzann Pettersen, five-time major champion Yani Tseng and seven-time major champ Juli Inkster.

The third round came on a day with the wind whipping off the sea. Park shot a one-under 71. It didn't look dazzling, but she was the only one in the field to break par for the round. It gave her a commanding four-stroke lead, which she got while being in a snit at herself. Park had just bogeyed three straight. She all but granted the bogeys at the par-four 11th and par-three 12th. They were demanding holes. But the 13th was a par-five of only 504 yards — a birdie hole. But her chip got away and rolled into a bunker. "That bogey was a bad bogey," Park said. Never mind that she still led by three. So she bore down. She came back with birdies at 14 and 15, and birdied the last for good measure.

Some still had a glimmer of a chance. Ewart Shadoff, for one, playing with Park, could have made up ground when Park bogeyed the 12th. But she not only missed her birdie putt, she missed the par, so instead of closing to within two, she was stuck at four behind. Then she bogeyed two of the last three holes. I.K. Kim hurt herself early, making a double bogey a No. 3, and couldn't make up ground and shot 73. She was still second, but four behind Park going into the final round. She was still game. "She is playing great, but you never know — I might have a great day tomorrow," Kim said.

"I'm just going to think that I.K. and I am tied in tomorrow's play," Park said. "Four shots — it could be nothing around this golf course. I'm just going to try my best. A lot of thinking going on, a lot of pressure."

Playing conditions were tough for the fourth round, and Sebonack was still tough, so someone would have to shoot a low score to head off Park. But nobody could. Park made her history with a two-over-par 74 in the closing round. Unimpressive on paper, but, it turned out, insurmountable on the course. Only 17 players did better than 74 — the best a 70 — but no one who was anywhere near being a threat.

"Believe it or not, I was very calm out there," Park said. "It was weird. I didn't feel much pressure when I was on the course. I was nervous last night, but on the golf course, somehow, I felt very calm."

Park bogeyed Nos. 6 and 7, birdied 9 and 10 and bogeyed 14 and 15 for her 74 and the four-stroke win. Kim took second with a one-birdie 74, and So Yeon Ryu third with a three-birdie, three-bogey 72. And so speculation bloomed immediately on four majors in a row, and even a Grand Slam.

Whatever the near future held for her, Park was in no great hurry to get to it. "I've just done three majors in a row now," she said. "I think it's too early to think about the next one. I think I really want to enjoy the moment as it is in the moment."

Ricoh Women's British Open

History is always created at the Old Course in St. Andrews and Stacy Lewis added her own special piece by birdieing the last two holes to win the Ricoh Women's British Open. Her approach shot to the fearsome 17th hole will live long in the memory, a blow destined to win a grand prize at the Home of Golf. It was a moment to savor for any golfer, let alone one whose potential career was in doubt while her teenage years were spent correcting the effects on her spine of scoliosis.

Her story of triumph over adversity is an inspiring one, but Lewis was hardly the center of attention at the start of the week. Instead, all eyes were on Inbee Park, who was attempting to become the first professional to win four major championships in the same season. Both Mickey Wright and Tiger Woods had won four in a row over two years, but having won the Kraft Nabisco, the LPGA Championship and the U.S. Open, Park was looking to create a modern equivalent of Bobby Jones' Grand Slam from 1930. Jones started his quest at St. Andrews by winning the British Amateur Championship and now here at the Home of Golf, Park was trying to make it four out of four. It was the only topic of conversation. "For women's golf, if she won it would be an amazing story," said Catriona

Matthew, who lost to the Korean in a playoff at the LPGA Championship. "Obviously, we are going to be out there trying to stop her. She's the one to beat."

Teeing off at 7:03 on Thursday morning, Park could not have made a better start. She was six under after 10 holes and her putter was once more working efficiently. A 15-footer went in at the first, a 30-footer at the third, an 18-footer at the fourth, a 35-footer at the sixth, a 15-footer at the short eighth, a five-footer at the 10th, and she added a decent par-save at the 12th. "It was funny," Lewis said, "Karrie [Webb] and I were on the 10th green and saw a leaderboard for the first time and I think Inbee was five under through eight, and we just sort of looked at the board at the same time and both looked at each other and shook our heads. We knew she was going to be there, but it's like she keeps doing it over and over again."

It would turn out to be the high point of the round, and the week, for Park. A poor drive at the 13th led to her first bogey and another required a fine up-and-down to save par at the 15th. But then she three-putted not once, but twice, at the 16th and 17th holes. At least she birdied the 18th for a 69. "It felt like a roller coaster," she said. "I played good on the front nine and then I was a bit shaky on he back nine. It was a little disappointing, but I'm glad I did it in the first round instead of the final round."

At three under, Park was three behind the leaders, Morgan Pressel and Camilla Lennarth, a Swede playing in the championship for the first time after qualifying earlier in the week. With little wind, it was a day to take advantage of the soft conditions and at 67 were Americans Lewis, Nicole Castrale, Ryann O'Toole and Sydnee Michaels, plus Koreans Na Yeon Choi, Mi-Jeong Jeon and Eun Hee Ji. Scotland's Matthew birdied the last two holes for a 68, as did 17-year-old British Amateur champion Georgia Hall, while Paula Creamer was also on four under. New Zealand's teenage sensation Lydia Ko was another to finish three-three for a 69.

Lewis, the world No. 2, came home in 31 to continue her love affair with the Old Course, which began when she won all five of her matches in the 2008 Curtis Cup. "More than anything I was just looking forward to playing this course," she said. "I love it. It's a much different feeling to any other British Open I've ever played just because I know the golf course and feel good shots get rewarded here."

Pressel had exactly the opposite first impression of the Old Course after she missed the cut in the 2007 British Open with scores of 80 and 76. Six years ago the Floridian felt she did not understand the course. Now she was prepared to hit "high shots, low shots, bump it, putt it from 40 yards off the green, do whatever it takes." An example came at the par-five fifth, where Pressel was just on the front of the green in two but still had 75 yards to the hole. She pitched to two feet and tapped in for a four but only had the confidence to play the high shot after trying it in a practice round. She came home in 32 and realized she did feel at home — not least since she went to a school named after St. Andrew and plays her golf at St. Andrews Country Club in Boca Raton.

Out early on the second day, Pressel added a 70 which was better than it appeared as she made two birdies and 16 pars. After a heavy rain squall early on the back nine, the wind really got up, so while Suzann Pettersen went out in 31, parring the entire back nine was equally meritorious. Japan's Miki Saiki actually went out in 30 for a 66, but her round was helped by holing out for eagles twice, with an eight iron from 126 yards on the fourth and from 108 yards with a sand wedge at the seventh.

It was Choi who produced the round of the day with a second successive 67, but it was recorded in the afternoon when the wind was up throughout. "My focus was very good," she said. "I don't think that I could have shot any lower." Five practice rounds helped, as did an exercise on the previous Sunday, when the Old Course is closed, and she walked the course with both her own caddie and a local one in reverse, staring at the 18th green and ending up at the first tee.

At 10 under par, Choi led by one over Saiki and by two over Pressel. Pettersen was at seven under alongside Jee Young Lee and Castrale. Lewis and Creamer were at five under and four under respectively after 72s. But a 73 from Inbee Park left the world No. 1 at two under and eight strokes behind. There were four bogeys and only three birdies, one of them at the last hole. Among those who missed the cut, which fell at one over par, equaling the lowest for the championship, were former winner Yani Tseng at two over, and at four over Laura Davies, Charley Hull, Ai Miyazato, who had a nine at the 13th on Friday, and Lennarth, who followed her opening 66 with an 82.

Park made a good start to her third round in windy conditions on Saturday when she birdied the third hole, but a gust of over 40 mph moved her ball on the fifth green. With officials receiving reports of at least five balls moving on the fifth, ninth and 10th greens, play was suspended. The wind only got stronger, with gusts of over 50 mph recorded, and play was called off for the day with only nine players having completed their rounds. The 75s of Ko and Cristie Kerr were the best scores posted, while Anna Nordqvist was one under for 15 holes.

Play resumed at 6:15 on Sunday morning in much calmer conditions. But not for Park, who slumped to a 74, not recording a birdie in the 14 holes she completed, though she lipped out for a three at the last. She admitted that she had struggled to get to grips with the slower greens and that her quest for a fourth successive major was over.

Matthew raised the hopes of the home gallery when she holed a lob wedge from 67 yards for an eagle-two at the 18th, following a birdie at the 17th. Her 68 had started with two bogeys in the wind on Saturday before play was suspended, while Lewis produced the only other round under 70, a 69 that included two late bogeys at the 16th and 17th holes. Pressel, whose drive up the right at the 18th hit Granny Wynd's road and bounded on just short of the green, holed a 20-footer for a birdie and a 71 to take the lead at nine under. Lewis was one stroke back, with Choi taking a 75 to slip back to seven under, along with Saiki, Pettersen and Hee Young Park.

Of the last 42 players on the course in the afternoon, when the wind got up again, Lewis was the only player to match par. No one bettered it. Pressel closed with a 76 to share fourth place with Suzann Pettersen, who had a 74. Second place went to 36-hole leader Choi, who had rounds of 75 and 73 on Sunday, and Hee Young Park, who closed with a 73. Matthew's hopes of a second Open title went with a triple bogey at the fifth hole.

At times in the final round at least four players shared the lead. But when Pressel four-putted at the 12th and Choi holed a long putt at the 10th, the Korean was three ahead. Lewis was still three behind when she bogeyed the 15th, her third dropped shot in five holes, although she also birdied the 14th. After a par at the 16th, Lewis hit a five iron at the notorious 17th to two feet. "One of the best shots of my career," said the 28-year-old from Texas. "It was a shot you see in your mind but then you pull it off exactly as you wanted. It was a low-five, hoping it would turn on the wind and land at the front of the green and roll up. If it had landed on top, it would have run over the back. The wind knocked it down and where it landed was perfect."

Lewis added: "I thought seven under might get in a playoff, but after I made a birdie there, I was going for one more birdie at the last." It came with a putt from just inside 30 feet and left her at eight under and champion by two strokes. "It all happened so fast at the end," Lewis said. "You are fighting for every shot and then you make two birdies and it is all over. I was hanging in there all day. My patience is what won it for me today. After the 15th, that's the most frustrated I was, but I told myself I was still in it."

Choi, who bogeyed three of the last six holes, admitted she had not seen Lewis' charge coming, figuring she was still ahead despite her faltering back nine. "She got birdie on 17 and 18?" Choi questioned. "That's huge on this course. She is playing better than me. I have to accept that."

This was Lewis' third win of the year and her eighth on the LPGA circuit. Her first was her first major championship win, at the Kraft Nabisco Championship in 2011. "The first major was pretty cool but this one is right up there, too," Lewis said. "I love this golf course. I love the history and it is amazing to think of all the great champions who have won here. I felt so comfortable out there, but after the seventh the wind was brutal. I never thought birdieing the last two holes would be possible."

While Lewis claimed a special victory, Inbee Park ended up in 42nd place, her historic attempt at a fourth major win in a row ending in disappointment. Park closed with a 78 to finish on six over par, alongside the two amateurs who shared the Smyth Slaver, Hall and Ko. "I might not have won this week but I've learned a lot," Park said. "I really enjoyed the week, every minute, but I'm relieved it is over. It was tough to be in the center of everything and I feel exhausted. I have never had this many people rooting for me and wanting me to play good. This great experience I had, I will never forget."

Park added: "I've done something amazing this season, winning three in a row. I don't know if I can do that again. That's going to be really tough. It might take a long time to beat that record."

Evian Championship

For the first major championship staged in continental Europe there could not have been a better winner than the continent's finest current player, Suzann Pettersen. It capped a memorable month for both Pettersen and women's golf in Europe. In August, Pettersen helped Europe win the Solheim Cup for the first time on American soil. She then won the Safeway Classic and added the Evian Championship, her second major victory. "This is a dream come true," Pettersen said. "This was by far on my bucket list to win the Evian Championship now that it's become a major. But also, they have been such a great supporter of women's golf. This is my 12th or 13th time I'm here, so this was good timing to win this tournament now."

Since 1994 until 2012, the Evian Masters was played at the Evian Resort Golf Club and from the year 2000 onwards it was sanctioned by the LPGA as well as the Ladies European Tour. It offered one of the richest purses in women's golf and a picturesque setting overlooking Lake Geneva. For 2013, the event was designated as a major championship — a fifth major to follow the Kraft Nabisco, the LPGA Championship, the U.S. Women's Open and the Ricoh Women's British Open. The name was altered and the date shifted from July, where it used to precede the British Open, to September. In the 14 months since the last tournament the course also underwent a multimillion-dollar upgrade. All the greens were re-contoured, adding some severe undulations, 82 bunkers were installed and the layout was rejigged. For example, the 16th hole became a par-three over water and the 18th, previously a reachable par-five, became a long and demanding par-four.

"I was really amazed to see the course change dramatically in one year," said Inbee Park, who won the last Evian Masters in 2012, the first in a run of eight victories, including the first three majors of 2013, that took the Korean to the world No. 1 spot. "I couldn't imagine how much work they have put in to make this work. This course looks great. The layout is great. I think it's really like a true major golf course now."

Having missed out on making history with a fourth major win in a row at the British Open at St. Andrews the previous month, Park still had the opportunity to set a record, since no professional had won four majors in the same year. "I mean four out of five majors is an amazing thing to achieve," Park said. "I would really love to win this week, not because I'm playing for four majors, but because the tournament is really special for me. I just really want to do my best."

Efforts to get the course ready in time for its debut as a major championship venue were hampered by a cold spring, then extreme heat in August and heavy rain leading into the event. With players used to the old layout and better conditions, some got themselves into a negative frame of mind before the tournament even began. Pettersen, notably, did not. "You have to open up for the changes," she said on the eve of the championship. "They kind of grow on you as you get to know this course better. It's kind of hard to say after having only played it a couple of times.

"Obviously a year into a huge project like this, it might take two years for it to settle in. The changes are going to be tough. Probably a much tougher course the way the greens are designed now. It's going to be a tough course to play and compete. I guess that's what really decides a major champion. You have got to be able to excel no matter what the course."

Alas, more heavy rain on Thursday did not help. Due to the newness of the greens and the many undulations, they flooded quickly and there was no chance for them to dry out. Five groups of players teed off but did not get very far and their scores were wiped out when play was called off for the day. Instead, the first round was able to get under way on Friday and Mika Miyazato led the way with a six-under 65. The Japanese player actually got on famously with the greens and took only 25 putts, the longest from 30 feet but most of them from close range thanks to some fine approach play. She only missed one green all day.

Pettersen was only one behind, alongside Se Ri Pak and Sandra Gal. Pettersen, who played late in the day, was lying six under playing the last but three-putted for the second time in the round for a bogey. "That last putt basically just jumped straight offline," she said. "The greens are definitely better in the morning, I would probably assume. They're fairly wet, and with all the footprints and everything, you need to have a few bounces going your way to make a few putts. I played pretty good today. It took forever to play — I'm just happy I maintained my concentration throughout the back nine."

The 32-year-old Norwegian came into the event with six top-10s in her last seven starts and having won her last time out at the Safeway Classic. That was two weeks before, while the previous weekend she had hosted her second Suzann Pro Challenge in Oslo, a 36-hole event attended by a number of LPGA players raising funds for Right to Play, a scheme helping children facing adversity all over the globe. Pettersen went on a trip to Africa with the scheme in 2012 and returned with a new perspective on her career. Explaining how she had been more disciplined about her practice, trying to bring her putting nearer to the level of her quality ball-striking, she added: "I'm just getting too old to waste my energy or time. I'm just really trying to win as many as I can while I'm young."

Gal, a member of the winning European Solheim Cup team in 2011, missed the match in Colorado after spending the early part of the year revamping her swing. The German was pleased to start seeing some positive results and her next goal is to play in the next Solheim in her home country at St. Leon Rot. "It's a huge focus," Gal said. "I hear everybody talk about it already and I think it's going to be so good for German golf just to see all the excitement that's around that tournament. It's the biggest event there is in women's golf and will inspire so many kids in Germany. Being on this team for me is a must. Just say it that way: I have to be on it."

With the addition of a new major, suddenly Pak, the trailblazer for Korean women's golf, was two away from a career grand slam. She now needed to win the Evian as well as the Kraft Nabisco, while Karrie Webb, the only player to win the old Du Maurier Classic as well as the other four majors, had a chance to win a sixth different major. The Australian opened with a

68, one behind Christina Kim, and alongside Michelle Wie, Lindsey Wright and Lydia Ko. The 16-year-old amateur from New Zealand was playing for the first time since winning the Canadian Open for the second year running, her fourth win in a professional event. "My confidence is a little higher after Canada," she said. "I haven't played very well in the majors so far this year, so I really want to be there."

Park opened with a three-over 74 and never got her challenge for the title going. She added a 71 on the second day and closed with a 76 to finish on eight over par. History would have to wait for another year.

In the second round, Miyazato started with back-to-back bogeys but rallied strongly and a birdie at the last gave her a 69. At eight under par, she led by a shot over Pettersen and Ko. The 23-year-old from Okinawa is no relation of the two-time Evian Masters winner Ai Miyazato, but she was hoping to be inspired by her friend and namesake. So Yeon Ryu had the best score of the day with a 66, while Ko, Lewis and Chella Choi all enjoyed 67s. Lewis was two behind the leader in fourth place and aiming for a second successive major win after her triumph at the British Open, while Choi and Ryu shared fifth place with Pak, who returned an even-par 71. At the other end of the scoreboard, Laura Davies missed the cut at five over, Cristie Kerr at six over, and Yani Tseng and Charley Hull on seven over.

Ko, already the youngest ever winner on both the Ladies European Tour and the LPGA, was attempting to become the youngest ever winner of a major and the third amateur to win one. The two who had done it before were Pat O'Sullivan, who won the Titleholders Championship in 1951, and Catherine Lacoste, who won the U.S. Women's Open in 1967. "I've never been really in kind of contention with the leaders at a major before," said Ko after birdieing the last two holes to get into the final threesome for the third round. "Hopefully, it will be a good day tomorrow. But, you know, I can't hit it as good as I did today every single day."

With more rain forecast for late Saturday into Sunday, and still more on the Monday and Tuesday, and beyond, the following week, the decision had been taken to reduce the event to 54 holes. The only previous major played over a reduced distance was the LPGA Championship in 1996 won by Laura Davies. But at least everyone knew they were playing in the final round as they set out on Sunday. Play had been delayed by an hour and a half, but without the precaution of covering all 18 greens with tarpaulins there might not have been any play at all. As it turned out, the rain relented, the sun came out and play was concluded on time.

Miyazato bogeyed the first hole and slipped out of contention with a 79 that dropped her to a tie for 19th place. Lewis had a 73 and dropped down to sixth, while Lexi Thompson came through the field with a 68 to take third place on six under, one ahead of Pak and Ryu. So from fairly early on in the round, it became a duel between the experienced Pettersen, who had finished runner-up four times since her first major win at the 2007 LPGA Championship, and the young New Zealand prodigy half her age.

Ko birdied the first hole, but Pettersen went ahead by birding the next two. The Norwegian dropped a shot at the sixth but recovered it at the next hole. Her lead doubled when Ko dropped a shot at the par-five 13th, and after they both birdied the 15th, Ko missed a good chance after a wonderful tee shot at the short 16th. At the 18th, Ko hit over the green with a three wood and Pettersen dismissed any suggestion of laying up and hit a superb hybrid shot to the heart of the green. She two-putted for a round of 68 and a 10-under-par total of 203, two ahead of Ko, who closed with a 70.

Ko missed out on the second prize of $297,994, which went to Thompson instead, and immediately fueled suggestions that she would soon be turning professional. "The next time you see me I may be a pro," Ko said, and she did indeed end her amateur career before playing in the LPGA's season-ending Titleholders event and then winning her second start as a professional in Taiwan. About her finish at the Evian, she said: "I was pretty happy with my round today. Like yesterday I gave myself a lot of chances to make birdies, so I hit it much closer to the pins. I don't expect myself to make everything, but it was really good to know that I could come so close to the winner at a major."

Pettersen said: "Lydia is a star of the future. She's good enough to win majors at 16." For herself, it was a third LPGA win of the season, her fourth in all, and the second time within a year she had won in successive starts. "It's been such a great month, starting off with the Solheim," she said. "I mean, the feelings during the Solheim never really get old. We had a fantastic team. It was kind of a great kick-start for what became probably the month of my career."

7. American Tours

As the song goes, it was a very good year. Adam Scott became the first Australian to win the Masters; Justin Rose the first Englishman to win the U.S. Open since 1970; Phil Mickelson finally won the Open Championship, with a Fourth of July fireworks finish, and Jason Dufner redeemed himself in the PGA Championship and gave the language a new word in the process.

Even so, 2013 was Tiger Woods' year, and by any standard, it was a great year and his best since the six wins in 2009. At age 37, he won five times, topped the money list at $8.5 million and returned to No. 1 in the world. How would he describe 2013?

Said Woods: "...a very good year." He'd said many times that a year without a major is not a great year, and he was shut out again for the fifth straight season, since the 2008 U.S. Open. He tied for fourth in the Masters, for 32nd in the U.S. Open, for sixth in the Open Championship and for 40th in the PGA Championship, and so he remained on hold at 14 majors in his pursuit of Jack Nicklaus' record 18. But he was up to 79 PGA Tour wins, just three short of Sam Snead's record 82.

Woods' dazzling year was dimmed by controversy. He had four rules problems — one, in Dubai, was a routine one, but three on the PGA Tour that were anything but. A columnist wrote in October that Woods was "cavalier" in his approach to the rules and came close to labeling him a cheater. This drew outrage from the Woods camp and worldwide coverage. But things eventually calmed down.

For all of his success, Woods' game seemed suspect at times. For example, he missed the cut in his first outing at Abu Dhabi on the European Tour, then the next week won his American debut, the Farmers Insurance Open, by four strokes. But that was after leading by eight with five holes to play. "It got a little ugly toward the end," he explained. His season was marked by missed short putts and more stray shots than one used to see from the vintage Tiger Woods.

Then there was the mystery of Rory McIlroy, the Northern Irish whiz, who turned sour for 2013. Like Woods, he missed the cut at Dubai. But unlike Woods, he didn't improve down the year. He started 2013 as No. 1 in the world and sank to No. 6, and saved himself from a shutout in his last tournament of the year in December by winning the Emirates Australian Open on the last hole. It had been a strange year. He had walked off the course at the Honda Classic in the second round, telling reporters he was "not in a good place, mentally," and then his agents put out a statement later saying his poor play was due to the distraction of a painful wisdom tooth. He denied that his erratic play through the year was because of the Nike equipment he switched to for an estimated $20 million per year.

It seems there's always someone waiting in the wings to take the spotlight, and this time it was Jordan Spieth, a whiz kid who left the University of Texas as a sophomore, turned pro, played mostly on sponsor's exemptions, and gained full status on the PGA Tour when he won the John Deere Classic at age 19, the youngest tour winner in 82 years.

Sweden's Henrik Stenson was a different kind of surprise. Stenson, 37, had all but disappeared with a tattered game, but fought his way back and capped a sizzling season with wins in the Deutsche Bank Championship and the Tour Championship, finishing second on the tour money list with $6.3 million, plus a $10 million bonus from winning the FedExCup Playoffs.

• Masters Tournament: Adam Scott led off the season of "firsts" by beating Argentina's Angel Cabrera on the second hole of a playoff. Scott thus won his first major and also was the first Australian to win the Masters. The win moved him up from No. 7 to No. 3 in the World Ranking.

• U.S. Open Championship: Justin Rose also won his first major, at Merion, becoming the second Englishman to win it since Tony Jacklin in 1970. Rose closed with a 70 for a one-over 281, two better than Jason Day and Phil Mickelson.

• The Open Championship: Phil Mickelson, agonizing after falling short at the U.S. Open, rebounded with a brilliant finish to win his first Open Championship. Mickelson birdied four of the final six holes to beat Stenson by three.

• PGA Championship: Jason Dufner made it four first-timers for 2013 when he took the PGA Championship at Oak Hill, coming from behind in the final round to edge Jim Furyk by two. The win eased, if not erased, the pain of blowing up down the final stretch of the 2011 PGA. Dufner also introduced "dufnering" to the language. To oversimplify, it's the art of slouching.

• It was a very good year for PGA Tour Commissioner Tim Finchem. The tour had taken over two troubled circuits and launched them in 2013 under new names — the PGA Tour Canada and PGA Tour Latinoamerica. Then he established the PGA Tour in Asia for the first time, forming a partnership with the China Golf Association to establish the PGA Tour China, to start in 2014. It's a 12-event developmental tour with the goal of producing world-caliber Chinese players.

Finchem also introduced the "wrap-around" season. Beginning with 2013-14, the season will run from October to the next September.

• Chinese amateur Tianlang Guan, at 14 years, five months, became the youngest ever to play in the Masters and youngest to make the cut. He finished 58th with a 12-over 300 that included a one-stroke slow-play penalty.

U.S. PGA Tour

Hyundai Tournament of Champions
Maui, Hawaii
Winner: Dustin Johnson

As one wit observed, some think the PGA Tour season never ends, but the 2013 edition couldn't get started. The gentle January breezes that usually kiss the Hawaiian Islands this time got their huff up and nearly blew the season-opening Hyundai Tournament of Champions right off the schedule. The 30 winners-only field from 2012 was battered relentlessly by heavy winds that gusted to 40 mph and more. Consider that Ian Poulter couldn't reach the green with a four iron from 138 yards. Ben Curtis' 40-foot birdie putt got blown off the green. Charlie Beljan needed an eight iron from just 102 yards. Play was scrubbed on Friday and never got started on Saturday and Sunday, and finally the tournament was cut to 54 holes — 36 on Monday, 18 on Tuesday.

Whereupon Dustin Johnson became the instant favorite. If Al Geiberger can be known as "Mr. 59" for his record-setting score in 1977, then Johnson could be Mr. 54. He now has seven PGA Tour wins, and three have come in tournaments shortened to three rounds, the previous two being the 2009 AT&T Pebble Beach National Pro-Am and the 2011 Barclays.

This was the newly healthy Johnson, and when play finally got under way, he announced his intentions for 2013 with five birdies over the last 10 holes for a four-under 69 and a tie for the first-round lead. He kept barreling along in the second, with six more birdies through the 16th. He bogeyed the 17th — his first slip in 27 holes — then eagled the 18th for a 66, an 11-under 135 and a three-stroke lead. He brushed off the notion that a 54-hole tournament was his meat.

"I just happened to win those two events," Johnson said. "It wouldn't matter if it was 72 holes or 54. Tomorrow is still the last round." But he had already dominated the course. In a 26-hole stretch over the first two rounds, he had 11 birdies and no bogeys. The bogey at the 17th interrupted the streak, and the eagle at the 18th started another. He was hot and cool through the final round Tuesday. He birdied Nos. 3, 6 and 7, and after a bogey at the ninth, he birdied the 12th, but at the 13th, a crisis. A poor drive cost him a double bogey that cut his lead to one.

After that stumble, Steve Stricker was surprised that Johnson wasn't more cautious at the 14th. "Most guys would have been pulling out an iron or some utility club," Stricker said. But Johnson hit driver, and that, Stricker said, was the deciding shot of the tournament.

Johnson ripped it, then chipped in for eagle and was on his way. He birdied the 15th and 18th, wrapping up a card of 69-66-68–203, 16 under, to win by four.

"I think for sure that I'm due for a big year," Johnson said. "I haven't played to my full potential yet. So you know, maybe it will happen this year."

Sony Open in Hawaii
Honolulu, Hawaii
Winner: Russell Henley

Listening in on Russell Henley at the Sony Open in Hawaii, on the occasion of a rookie not only making his first start on the PGA Tour, but winning it, as well:

• "That's the most nervous I've ever been. I couldn't feel my legs or my arms. They were just numb and just moving fast and I felt like I couldn't control them."

• "I was adding up my scorecard, and I was like, oh, wait, I shot 29 on the back. I didn't even know I did."

• Everything I thought about on the range and working on my swing just kind of went away. I couldn't do it anymore. It didn't work. So I had to re-find, redo everything, and the feelings I had in my swing, because they were all so different than what I'm used to when there's no pressure on me."

From the start, the setting was not promising for a 23-year-old rookie making his debut. Henley, a former University of Georgia standout, was fresh from the 2012 Web.com Tour, where he won twice and finished third on the money list. The Sony was the first full-field event of 2013, meaning that although Rory McIlroy, Tiger Woods and Phil Mickelson had skipped the event, Henley still had to contend with such forces as Dustin Johnson and Keegan Bradley, among others. But this wasn't one of those stranger-in-paradise tales, where the rookie hangs on to win. Henley's performance would have left a veteran dancing. He broke records all over the place at Waialae Country Club and outran the field. He held or shared the lead after the first round, shooting 63-63-67-63–256, 24 under, and won by three. He went 50 holes without a bogey and had only two for the entire tournament. His second 63, in the second round, gave him the Sony record for 36 holes, a 14-under 126 and a two-stroke lead. A 67 in the third round gave him a share of the 54-hole record at 17-under 193 with Scott Langley, his good pal and fellow rookie. ("Win this tournament or not," Henley said, "it's already been a very successful week.") And his closing 63 was the record final round by a champion.

Henley's play was decidedly non-rookie-like, especially in the final round. After a bogey at No. 11, his second and last of the tournament, he saved par brilliantly at the 12th — pulling his tee shot, missing the green long, pitching downhill to 10 feet and holing the putt. Then he birdied the last five holes — the 14th from 45 feet; the 16th from 12 after an approach over trees; the 17th from 18 feet, and the 18th with his shortest putt of the bunch, an eight-footer.

Tim Clark, the runner-up, could only laugh. He birdied seven of his last 11 holes and picked up only a shot.

Henley finally showed his true colors as a rookie when it was over. "I don't really know what happened," he said.

Humana Challenge
La Quinta, California
Winner: Brian Gay

It was a birdie bash like few others, when scores in the low 60s showered down like the snows in the mountains; when one player went the first 60 holes without a bogey and lost; when Phil Mickelson made his season debut, shot 17 under and never sniffed the leaderboard, and where the winner, Brian Gay, didn't have the solo lead until the absolute end, and then only by playoff.

It was the Humana Challenge, the third stop on the 2013 PGA Tour, the start of the western swing, played over three user-friendly courses in fine weather — the Palmer, the Nicklaus and La Quinta Country Club, all par 72s. It was such a feast that whoever was at nine-under 207 for three rounds missed the 54-hole cut.

It has to be tough to shoot 25 under par and lose, but that was the fate of Charles Howell, a two-time winner who hadn't won since 2007, and Swedish rookie David Lingmerth. Howell closed with a 64, Lingmerth a 62.

Brian Gay, a 41-year-old journeyman, began the final round six strokes off the lead, shot 63 and also tied at 263, 25 under, and proceeded to win on the second hole of a playoff. Gay and Howell both birdied the first extra hole, and Lingmerth departed with a bogey. On the second, the Palmer course's par-four 10th, Howell drove into the rough, bunkered his approach, and came out and two-putted for a bogey. Gay had split the fairway, hit his nine-iron second to inside six feet and holed the birdie putt.

Gay had shot 67-66-67-63 and trailed by four in the first round, three in the second and six through the third.

"I'm still in a little bit of shock," Gay said. "It happened so fast there at the end, the way things went down."

Said Howell: "Anybody that says that golf is fun or whatever, has really not done it for a living. I would never characterize this as fun. It's different from that. It's awfully challenging, mentally."

But Howell had a cakewalk compared to Scott Stallings. Stallings was the only player to go without a bogey through the first three rounds, or 60 holes, actually. After three straight birdies from No. 2, he took his first bogey on No. 7, then bogeyed the 15th and the 18th. That last one was fatal. He shot 70 and 24-under 264, missed the playoff by a stroke and tied for fourth with James Hahn, who shared the first-round lead on 63 then closed with a 62.

"I felt great," Stallings said. "There wasn't any nerves or anything like that. Just hit a bad shot."

Mickelson closed with a pair of 66s and finished at 17-under 271, tied for 37th and was not really unhappy. "I was rusty starting the year," Mickelson said. "I had a great four days here where I can work on my game with perfect weather..."

Farmers Insurance Open
La Jolla, California
Winner: Tiger Woods

If Tiger Woods stamped himself with a big question mark by missing the cut at Abu Dhabi on the European Tour in his first outing of 2013, he sure erased it a week later in his first PGA Tour start, the Farmers Insurance Open. He won it by only four shots — "only" being a fair assessment considering that he was leading, well, by eight with five holes to play.

But it was just another Folic by the Pacific for Woods. It was his eighth win at Torrey Pines — seven in this tournament and one U.S. Open.

"It got a little ugly toward the end," said Woods. "I started losing patience a little with slow play. I lost my concentration a little bit."

Ugly it was: He bogeyed the 14th out of a bunker, double-bogeyed the 15th out of the rubbery ice plant, and bogeyed the 17th off a pop-up drive. So he was leading by only four coming to the 18th. There, he made a tidy two-putt par to wrap up a card of 68-65-69-72 for a 14-under 274 and the four-stroke win over Brandt Snedeker and Josh Teater. Snedeker shared the first-round lead with K.J. Choi on 65, then Woods took over and led the rest of the way for his 75th tour victory.

"I think he wanted to send a message," said Hunter Mahan, referring to world No. 1 Rory McIlroy, newly signed with Nike, Woods' long-time endorsee.

The field alternated for the first two rounds across Torrey Pines' two courses, the famed South, at 7,668 yards, and the easier North, some 600 yards shorter, both par 72s, then finished on the South. Snedeker shot his opening 65 on the North, and Choi tied him on the South. Woods, starting on the South, three-putted for a double bogey at the fourth, then exploded for three birdies and an eagle through the ninth.

By the end of the second round, Woods was feeling really good. "I'm leading the tournament," he said. Starting on the back nine, he authored a scorching four-hole streak around the turn in his one-bogey 65 on the North. He holed a 25-foot birdie putt at the 17th (his eighth), eagled the 18th on a five iron to five feet from the pin, two-putted for a birdie at the par-five first (his 10th) and birdied from four feet at the second.

The tournament was forced to a Monday finish after a heavy fog on Saturday. Woods led by four after the third round, and all but locked up the title in his 25 holes on Sunday, when he expanded his lead from two to six with 11 holes to play. He upped it to eight with a two-putt birdie at No. 13 on Monday, then came the shaky finish, starting at the 14th. But it couldn't dull his overall brilliant play.

Woods said: "I'm excited about this year."

Waste Management Phoenix Open
Scottsdale, Arizona
Winner: Phil Mickelson

Phil Mickelson didn't leave much suspense to the Waste Management Phoenix Open. What little there was, was confined to the end of the first round and the 25-foot putt he faced for birdie at this final hole. This is when all eyes were on him.

Mickelson put that silky stroke on the ball, and then he was walking toward the hole, pointing with the putter — the sign of a golfer chasing a birdie putt into the cup, with the gallery roaring and playing companions Jason Dufner and Rickie Fowler rooting it on.

Mickelson recapped the moment: "Six feet to go, it was in the center. Three feet to go, it was in the center. A foot to go, it was in the center. And even as it's approaching the hole, I couldn't envision which side of the hole it could possibly miss on."

If this ball drops, Mickelson has shot 59.

But somehow, the putt did miss. At the last instant, the ball caught the right edge of the hole and did one of those maddening 180-degree swings around to the other side. And so Mickelson did not join the five who have shot 59 in official PGA Tour tournaments. But he did shoot an 11-under-par 60, launching a wire-to-wire romp at TPC Scottsdale, adding rounds of 65-64-67 for a 28-under-par 256 and a four-stroke win.

"It's an important one for me because it's been awhile since I won, been awhile since I've been in contention," said Mickelson, who led by six through the third round. "I was certainly nervous heading into today."

A baseball pitcher doesn't dare think of the no-hitter he's working on, but Mickelson feared no jinx. He was thinking of a 59, even a 58.

"I thought of both of them right after 18 [his ninth]," he said after a birdie had him out in 29. He then birdied No. 1, and after birdies at the third and fourth, he was more than bold. "Done deal," he told himself. "I'm going to get this done." A birdie at his 16th (No. 7) got him to 11 under. But at the par-four No. 8, his 18-foot birdie putt stopped one roll short, and then came the lip-out at the last, and there went his 59.

"Well, 60 is awesome," Mickelson said. "But there's a big barrier, a Berlin Wall barrier, between 59 and 60."

He dominated the tournament. In the second round, he played an 11-hole stretch from No. 7 in eight under, and he played the first 35 holes in 19 under without a bogey, then stumbled to a double bogey at No. 18. After that, a bogey at No. 2 in the final round was the only other blot on his card.

Said runner-up Brandt Snedeker, who made a great try but couldn't close the gap: "Sometimes you have to tip your hat and say, 'Phil played unbelievable' ... That's what this week was all about."

AT&T Pebble Beach National Pro-Am
Pebble Beach, California
Winner: Brandt Snedeker

The view from the 18th tee at Pebble Beach can be as daunting as it is beautiful — the sweeping dogleg-left, all that water farther to the left, known as the Pacific Ocean, and that little green at the far end. It's especially daunting if you have a victory at your fingertips. Brandt Snedeker, after just grabbing the lead with a birdie at the 17th, took one last look and fired away. He had to nurse that tiny margin home. And this he did with a tap-in par for a closing seven-under-par 65 and a two-stroke victory over Chris Kirk in the AT&T Pebble Beach National Pro-Am. It was a scary finish, but an inspired one.

"Feels great to finish one," said Snedeker, recently thwarted by Tiger Woods and Phil Mickelson. "The last two weeks, playing great but running into two Hall-of-Famers really motivated me to go out and prove that I can handle the lead." Snedeker, who won twice in 2012 (including $11.4 million in the Tour Championship FedExCup), started 2013 with a third place in the season-opening Hyundai, then tied for second behind Woods in the Farmers Insurance Open and was a solo second behind Mickelson at the Waste Management Phoenix Open. Woods wasn't in this field and Mickelson was off his game, but it didn't matter. Snedeker was busy turning in a tournament-record, 19-under-par 267, shooting 66-68-68-65.

Mickelson, seeking a fifth win in the tournament, saw his hopes die when he hit into the Pacific and triple-bogeyed. He tied for 60th.

The tournament, the old Crosby Clambake, was played over three courses. Snedeker trailed by two with his opening 66 at Monterey Peninsula. He tied for the halfway lead at Spyglass Hill with a flawless four-birdie 68 that included two spectacular eight-iron shots — to three feet at the par-three 12th, and to five feet at No. 8 (his 17th). In the third round, he birdied four straight at Pebble for another 68, including a stunning seven iron over the corner of the ocean to five feet at No. 8, then an eight-iron to four feet at No. 9.

Snedeker broke the tie with James Hahn in a hurry in the final round, playing the first seven holes in five under, sparked by an eagle from four feet at the par-five second. Hahn couldn't keep pace, but Kirk, the 2011 Viking Classic champion, starting one shot off the lead, birdied four of the first eight holes. But against Snedeker's grit, he couldn't overcome bogeys at Nos. 9 and 10, not even with four late birdies. Snedeker birdied the 10th from 25 feet, the 11th from 15, and then the 17th from 10, and had one regret — making only a par at the 18th. The win, his career fifth, lifted him to No. 4 in the world, his highest ranking ever.

Said Snedeker: "Kind of crazy, to think what's happened."

Northern Trust Open
Pacific Palisades, California
Winner: John Merrick

Riviera Country Club was John Merrick's field of dreams. The storied Los Angeles course is known as Hogan's Alley, for all of the success Ben Hogan had there — winning three Los Angeles Opens and the 1948 U.S. Open. Steve Elkington added to the history, taking the 1995 PGA Championship. All this was not lost on Merrick, a native of nearby Long Beach, who played Riviera many times as a standout golfer at UCLA, and wanted to play it in the Northern Trust Open.

"You know, as a kid, you dream about playing that tournament one day," Merrick said. "But to win it?"

Both dreams came true in February when he beat Charlie Beljan in a playoff for his first PGA Tour victory in his 169th start. It must have been in the cards. How else to explain the rash of stumbles that knocked so many contenders out of his path?

Merrick stuck close but never led till the end, shooting the par-71 course in 68-66-70-69 to tie Beljan (67-71-68-67) at 11-under-par 273. Merrick won with a par on the second extra hole. But only after the contenders had fallen left and right.

Two crashed in the third round. Lee Westwood and South Korea's Sang-Moon Bae both made two bogeys and a double bogey down the final stretch. Then came the final round. Bill Haas, leading by three to start, staggered to five bogeys over a seven-hole stretch from No. 7. Sweden's Fredrik Jacobson, co-leader in the second round, needed a par at the 18th to join the playoff. He missed from four feet. Hunter Mahan birdied the 14th to tie for the lead, then dropped four strokes over the last four holes. Charl Schwartzel, former Masters champion, missed a birdie try at the 16th and three-putted the 17th.

Merrick first led when he birdied the difficult par-four 10th, a mere 312 yards but loaded with trouble. He holed a 13-footer to tie Haas, who was back in the fairway. Merrick then took the lead with a birdie at the par-five 11th, two-putting from 23 feet. The tournament was such a scramble that Merrick was tied by three different golfers at three different times — Mahan at the 11th, Jacobson at the 16th, and then Beljan at the 18th, with a birdie from 18 feet to send the tournament into the playoff. They tied on the first extra hole, with pars at the 18th. Next came the devilish 10th. In regulation, Merrick had played it in two pars and two birdies, Beljan in two birdies and two bogeys. Now Merrick was cautious, hitting a three iron off the tee, then a wedge to 18 feet. Beljan drove into the rough, then hit his approach on the fringe, and finally missed his par try from five feet. Merrick two-putted for a par and the win.

"I've been to this tournament more than any other tournament growing up, and this is my first win," Merrick said. "I can't even put it into words."

WGC - Accenture Match Play Championship
Marana, Arizona
Winner: Matt Kuchar

True to the wisdom of marquee billings, World Golf Championships - Accenture Match Play organizers put their top stars in separate brackets — world No. 1 Rory McIlroy, the No. 1 seed, into one and world No. 2 Tiger Woods, No. 2 seed, into another, then sat back to await the irresistible dream championship match. But a funny thing happened on the way to the boffo finish. McIlroy and Woods never got out of the starting gate. McIlroy was knocked out by 64th-seeded Shane Lowry, and Woods by 63rd-seeded Charles Howell.

A day later, Bubba Watson (8) was the only one of the top 10 seeds still in the running.

If the departure of the top stars is one of the dangers of match play, it is also one of its charms. The door is wide open. This time, it came down to a couple of middle-of-the-road seedings in the final, with Matt Kuchar (21) beating Hunter Mahan (23), the defending champion, 2 and 1.

It was a fitting end to an odd February week in the Arizona desert at Dove Mountain that found kids making snowballs and the golfers pulling winter caps down over their ears.

"So much fun to play and so much pressure," said Kuchar, who ironically was knocked out by Mahan in the quarter-finals in 2012.

Kuchar made his way through his bracket with authority, though not totally in a romp. He erased, in order, Hiroyuki Fujita, Sergio Garcia, Nicolas Colsaerts, Robert Garrigus and Jason Day. His biggest wins were by 4 and 3 over Colsaerts and Day. Mahan had a somewhat easier time of it in beating Matteo Manassero, Richard Sterne, Martin Kaymer, Webb Simpson and Ian Poulter. His easiest wins were by 5 and 4 over Manassero and Kaymer.

Kuchar never played the 18th all week, and for a while in the final it seemed things would end long before that. Mahan made four straight bogeys early on, leaving Kuchar three up through No. 6. Kuchar went four up with a three-foot birdie putt at the eighth and held that huge edge through the turn. Then Mahan found his game and cut his deficit to two down with a par at the 10th and a birdie at the 11th. Kuchar cooled him at the par-three 12th, making birdie from 15 feet to offset Mahan's from 10.

After a brief exchange, the match seemed headed to the 18th when Mahan took the 16th with a two-putt par. But things changed abruptly at the 17th. Both drove into a fairway bunker, but Mahan's ball was in an awkward lie. He hit it out, but through the desert and into a bush. It took him two more shots to reach the green, where Kuchar was five feet from a birdie. Mahan conceded, and Kuchar had a 2-and-1 victory, his fifth PGA Tour win.

Said Kuchar: "To come out on top after six matches of playing guys, the top 64 guys in the world, it's an incredible feeling."

Honda Classic
Palm Beach Gardens, Florida
Winner: Michael Thompson

The 2013 Honda Classic was supposed to be another showdown between the two reigning lions of the game, Rory McIlroy and Tiger Woods. Instead, it went into the books as "The time Rory McIlroy walked off the course."

Michael Thompson, 27, out of Birmingham, Alabama, in his second year on the PGA Tour and making his 61st start, would rather the Honda be known as his shining moment. "This week was magical," said Thompson, savoring his first tour victory. "Just had a groove and kept feeling it."

History, however, will put an asterisk on Thompson's big moment because back in the second round things went askew for McIlroy in this strange start to the new season. There was a mix of factors. First came McIlroy, after a sensational 2012, changing equipment and signing with Nike for a reported $20 million a year. Changing equipment is always risky. It didn't help that McIlroy fell flat in his first two starts, missing the cut in the European Tour opener at Abu Dhabi and getting knocked out in the first round of the Accenture Match Play. Then in the Honda, with February turning into March at PGA National, McIlroy couldn't find his way.

McIlroy opened with a par 70, tying Woods six shots behind Camilo Villegas. Then in the second round, he rocketed seven over through his first eight holes and walked off. First, he told reporters in the parking lot that "I'm not in a good place, mentally." Soon after, his management team compounded the problem by having him say that he couldn't concentrate because of a sore tooth. Things grew awkward and embarrassing after that.

Woods himself was struggling and made the cut on the number with three desperate par saves — from six feet at the 16th, a bunker at the 17th and the grandstand at the 18th. Luke Guthrie took the halfway lead with a 63, with Thompson (65) a stroke behind. Thompson (70) and Guthrie (71) ended up co-leaders through the third round at eight under, which found 11 players separated by four strokes going into the final round.

Thompson leaped into the lead in the final round at No. 3, holing a 50-foot putt for eagle, then rode a strong short game through the toughest stretch of the course and went up by four. His dream for that first win was to mosey up the final fairway with a big lead and no stress. Instead, he was in a crisis. He stood in the 18th fairway leading by a stroke and 240 yards from the flag with a big lake in front of him. Instead of laying up, he powered a five wood into a greenside bunker, came out tight and got the birdie for a 69, a nine-under 271 and a two-shot win over Geoff Ogilvy. That shot to the 18th sweetened the dream.

Said Thompson: "It allowed me to walk up the fairway and enjoy the experience, see the crowd and finish strong."

WGC - Cadillac Championship
Miami, Florida
Winner: Tiger Woods

Graeme McDowell, the gritty Northern Irishman, found himself four shots behind Tiger Woods heading into the final round of the WGC - Cadillac Championship and was assessing his chances. With the forecast calling for strong winds, "Hopefully, we'll have a chance," McDowell said.

Well, not really. With the Farmers Insurance Open from January already in his bag, Woods seemed to be gathering steam, and so the closest anyone would get to him in this outing was five-way logjam tie for the lead in the first round. After that, win No. 2 for 2013, though robustly contested, was pretty much a formality. Woods tamed the par-72 Doral Blue Monster with a card of 66-65-67-71 for a 19-under 269 total, outrunning McDowell and finishing with a two-stroke win over Steve Stricker. Who, incidentally, was his own worst enemy. On the eve of the tournament, Stricker had spent 45 minutes helping Woods correct his putting.

Accordingly, Woods averaged just 25 putts per round for the tournament and birdied almost half of his holes through the first two rounds (17 of 36).

Said Woods: "Thank you to Steve for the putting lesson."

There are degrees of domination. This one could be called "low-end" domination, unlike in his first win of the year, the Farmers Insurance Open in January, when he ran away from everybody. But here, after pulling free of the five-way tie in the first round, Woods didn't crush the field but he did keep them well off his heels the rest of the way.

Woods needed a key to his game in the second round, that "one shot," he said, that told him he was in sync. It proved to be a brilliant four iron at the par-three fourth that hit the left edge of the green and rolled to within four feet. It triggered a run of six birdies in an eight-hole stretch around the turn and carried him to a 65 and a two-stroke lead over the frustrated McDowell, who finished birdie-birdie and said that the third round was not about winning but all about "maintaining position." But the third round went even worse for him. Woods led him by six with three holes to play, and McDowell merely got some hope when he chipped in for eagle at the 16th and Woods bogeyed the 17th after an unplayable lie stuck in a palm tree. Then Woods birdied the 18th and led McDowell by four going into the finale.

In the last round, Woods was up by three going into the 18th, made a harmless bogey and won by two over Stricker, taking his 17th WGC and winning at Doral for the fourth time. McDowell (72) tied for third with Sergio Garcia (69), Adam Scott (64) and Phil Mickelson (71).

True, the matter became purely academic and ironic, but did Stricker fall two shots short of tying Woods, or three short of beating him, because of the putting lessons?

Stricker chuckled. "At times," he said, "you kick yourself."

Puerto Rico Open
Rio Grande, Puerto Rico
Winner: Scott Brown

You will understand if Scott Brown has a warm spot in his heart for the Puerto Rico Open. After all, it's been a career-saver for him. As a rookie on the PGA Tour in 2012, he missed the cut in his first six events, then tied for fifth in the Puerto Rico Open. That and another fifth-place finish helped him win enough money to gain conditional status for 2013, which offers some playing chances. Then came the 2013 Puerto Rico Open in March, and Brown came from behind to score his first win and gain fully exempt status — no Monday qualifying for two years.

"I have an eye for these greens a little bit," Brown said, trying to understand his affinity for Trump International. "I putted really well here last year. I putted really good this year. I just see the breaks really well here." He led the field in putting with an average of just 25.2 putts per round. And his control of the four par-fives helped. Brown played them in 12 under par, with 10 birdies, an eagle and no bogeys in shooting 68-63-67-70 for a 20-under 268 and a one-stroke victory over Argentina's Fabian Gomez (71), his co-leader after the third round, and 19-year-old whiz-kid Jordan Spieth (67), who was playing on a sponsor's exemption.

Argentina's Andres Romero, the 2008 Zurich Classic winner, seemed on his way when he opened with a pair of 65s, tied with Cameron Percy in the first round, and in the second held to a one-stroke lead by Brown's sizzling 63. Brown eagled the par-four seventh with a seven-iron hole-out from 170 yards, and among his eight birdies were a 50-foot putt at No. 8 and a tap-in at No. 9.

The tournament, played opposite the WGC - Cadillac Championship, had the makings of a shootout when Brown and Gomez tied in the third round. Gomez raced off to six birdies on the front nine and shot 65, and Brown birdied four times on the back for a 67, tied at a tournament-record 18-under 198 for 54 holes.

The final round was a drama. Gomez shot a one-under 71, and it was the bogey at the 18th that did him in. Spieth, who started four behind, birdied five of the first 10, bogeyed the 16th, then birdied the 18th for a 67 to tie Gomez. Brown had a stormy ride. He eagled the par-five second, firing a three iron to 40 feet and holing the putt. He birdied No. 5, then staggered to bogeys at Nos. 8, 9 and 11. A five iron to 20 feet set up a birdie at the 12th, and he came to the par-five 18th trailing by one. Gomez had bogeyed when he missed the green with his three iron. Brown was short in two and chipped to four feet and birdied.

"I was trying to keep my hands from shaking off the putter," Brown said. "I lined up and just said 'knock it in.'"

Tampa Bay Championship
Palm Harbor, Florida
Winner: Kevin Streelman

For Kevin Streelman, age 34 — Duke University graduate and former club-cleaner and caddie — the road to his goal was about 400,000 miles long and he burned out three cars getting there. Okay, this was his odyssey through a variety of mini-tours over the years, learning his craft and chasing his dream, and he finally caught it in mid-March, taking the Tampa Bay Championship. After 153 starts, he finally had his first victory on the PGA Tour.

"This," said Streelman, the fifth first-time winner on the tour this season, "is a lot of fun."

It was also a tournament of some interesting twists and turns. Shawn Stefani, a former Web.com winner, led through the first two rounds before fading. Adam Scott and K.J. Choi challenged before sinking on 76s in the third round. Luke Donald and Sergio Garcia couldn't quite get going. And it came down to two guys best known for something other than winning tournaments. Streelman's claim to fame and money was winning the $1 million bonus from the Kodak Challenge, a promotional program, in 2009. And Weekley was a kind of cult hero best remembered for riding his driver as a hobby horse in the 2008 Ryder Cup.

Weekley, a two-time winner, the last in 2008, was set for his third. He had teed off three hours before the leaders, posted a tournament-best 63 for the clubhouse lead, an eight-under-par 276 at the Copperhead course at Innisbrook. He closed with three straight birdies from inside two feet.

"It was impressive," Weekley conceded. "Even I am still kind of shocked at how good I really hit it." Next came the long wait to see if his score would hold up.

It looked fairly safe until Streelman reached the tough par-three 13th. There, he smacked a five iron to six feet and made the birdie putt and had the lead for good. "Probably the best shot of my life in that situation," he said. "It's just how I envisioned it and I pulled it off." He pretty well locked it up with a 20-foot birdie putt at the par-three 17th. After a choppy first two rounds, with nine bogeys in his 73-69, he played the last two rounds without a bogey in his 65-67 finish for a 10-under 274, beating Weekley by two.

"Ten years ago, I was in a car driving to mini-tours," Streelman said. "Just keep chasing your dreams. You never know what will happen."

Jordan Spieth, 19, the whiz kid creating such a stir, also caught part of his dream. He holed a 50-foot chip shot for birdie at the 17th and saved par with a seven-foot putt at the 18th to tie for seventh. He won $148,892. Before holing that chip, he figured to be $195 short of qualifying for temporary membership on the tour. To have missed by that little? Spieth grinned. "That," he said, "would have been brutal."

Arnold Palmer Invitational
Orlando, Florida
Winner: Tiger Woods

Tiger Woods was looking more like his old self. The power was there, the putting touch was back, and the domination of the par-fives was complete if not unreal. And most familiar of all — he was back being No. 1 in the world, after being gone since October 2010. The re-coronation came with his third win of the young season, in the Arnold Palmer Invitational (his eighth one of those) in March.

"I'm really excited about the rest of the year," said Woods, who was off to a pretty exciting start. He'd already won twice — his first start, the Farmers Insurance Open, late in January, and then the Cadillac Championship, the start before the Palmer. It was also his 77th career win. He had to come from behind, but as in his first two wins, once he got a real grip on things in the final round, nobody got closer to him than two strokes. He once again showed his affinity for Palmer's par-72 Bay Hill Club, breaking par in all four rounds with 69-70-66-70–275, 13 under and two better than Justin Rose, who led the first round and tied with Bill Haas in the second.

For all of his authority, it was an odd outing for Woods. His brilliance was coming in bunches, and so were the blahs. In his opening 69, for example, he birdied three straight from the fourth, birdied the 12th, eagled the 16th, but bogeyed the last two. In the second round, he played the first 13 in five under but bogeyed the last three. The reverse side of that coin was Woods' performance on the four par-fives, which bordered on the manic. He was 14 under par for 16 trips, including a stray bogey at the 16th in the second round. Otherwise, he made nine birdies and three eagles.

Woods took command in the third round, and he could thank Rose for a huge assist. Rose was still three up on Woods off a short birdie putt at the par-five 12th, then he started to slide, making three crucial bogeys. He three-putted the 13th from 60 feet, hit a bad slice at the par-three 14th, and three-putted the island 17th, and slipped two behind Woods, tying with Rickie Fowler and John Huh going into the final round.

One little episode in the last round showed what the whole tournament was all about. Fowler thought he had pulled to within two of Woods when he holed a 40-foot putt for birdie at the 12th. But then Woods followed him in from 25 feet. Fowler did get within two with a birdie at the 14th, but then watered his approach to the par-five 16th, then watered again and triple-bogeyed. Woods birdied the 16th, then made a cautious bogey at the 18th for a 70 and the two-stroke win.

Getting healthy, he said, was the key to his success. "Once I got there," he said, "then my game turned."

Shell Houston Open
Humble, Texas
Winner: D.A. Points

Mrs. Points can kiss that putter goodbye. Little Darren Andrew isn't about to give it back any time soon.

Golfers are always scrounging around for anything they think will save them on the greens, and so it was with D.A. Points, rummaging through the 30 or 40 putters in his garage and finding one he had commandeered from his mom during his college days. He took it to the Shell Houston Open, and it delivered, even to a 13-foot par-saving putt on the final hole for his second victory, a one-shot decision over Henrik Stenson and Billy Horschel.

"To have a putt to win — you want that starting out every week," said Points. "I would have liked," he added, "for it to have been closer."

Well, those were the longest 13 feet of Points' career. But mom's old putter wasn't about to let him down, and he wrapped up a card of 64-71-71-66, for a 16-under-par 272 at Redstone Golf Club to edge Stenson and Horschel, who both also closed with 66s. Points' other victory was in the 2011 AT&T Pebble Beach National Pro-Am.

Points, who had made just two cuts in nine previous starts, opened the tournament with five straight birdies en route to a 64 and a one-stroke lead. Of greater interest at the time was Rory McIlroy (73), struggling with his new clubs and making a double bogey and three singles (he would finish tied for 45th), and Phil Mickelson, who double-bogeyed the fifth and shot 72 (he doubled it again in the second round, and finished in a tie for 16th).

Points' faithful putter turned balky in the second round. He birdied the 12th and parred the rest for a 71. "I made everything yesterday and made nothing today," Points said. "To be one shot back and be right in the mix is huge." He was tied with Jason Kokrak (69) at 135, a stroke behind Steve Wheatcroft, a Monday qualifier who shot a pair of 67s.

Stewart Cink, who won the 2009 Open Championship but nothing in 81 starts since, saw some hope. He saved par out of a bunker at the 18th for a 68 and a share of the third-round lead with Bill Haas (67). Points shot another 71 and shared third a stroke back with Wheatcroft (72), Kokrak (71) and Ben Crane (67).

Points had to endure a three-hour rain delay in the fourth round before he could lock up his bogey-free 66 and the win. He birdied Nos. 2, 3, 8, 10, 12 and 13 — the 13th when his chip shot hit the hole and stopped three feet away. He ground out pars over the last four holes after the delay, and the last was as scary as it was decisive. He missed the green, lobbed a pitch that came up 13 feet short, then saw his putt drop in from the left for the win.

"Maybe I'm an idiot," Points said, "for not having used this putter the whole time."

Valero Texas Open
San Antonio, Texas
Winner: Martin Laird

Martin Laird was struggling along on a limping game, not expecting much but hoping for the best when he showed up for the Valero Texas Open. Then one of golf's magical moments hit him

"I came in here quietly confident, even though my record this year has been poor," he said. "But golf's a funny game. Doesn't matter what you did two weeks ago. It turns around pretty quickly."

Laird barely stayed in sight of the lead with his 70-71-70 start, then everything clicked in the final round. He came from five strokes off the lead with a bogey-free, nine-under-par 63, tying the course record and taking a two-stroke victory over world No. 2 Rory McIlroy, who himself had been limping along but suddenly was looking forward to the Masters the next week. It was his best finish of the year.

"I feel like my game's in really good shape going into next week," McIlroy said. "A round like that gives me a nice bit of confidence. ... Martin just played too well and holed so many putts. It was hard to keep up." As it was for everyone else. Matt Bettencourt and Peter Tomasulo led the first round with 67s, but fell away. The fast-rising Billy Horschel, 26, seeking his first win, led the middle rounds with 68-68 and led by two going into the final, and was five ahead of Laird. A closing 71 would give Horschel a tie for third with Jim Furyk (69) and Charley Hoffman (69) three shots back.

Coming to the Texas Open, Laird had missed four cuts in eight starts and was 161st on the money list. Finding TPC San Antonio to his liking, he finished with a 14-under 274 for his third PGA Tour victory and first since the Arnold Palmer Invitational in 2011.

In the final round, Laird set about immediately to erase that five-shot deficit, soaring up the leaderboard with birdies on five of his first eight holes — Nos. 2, 3, 5, 6 and 8, and the seven-foot putt he dropped at the eighth tied him with Horschel at 10 under. Then McIlroy became his problem. Laird gained a stroke with a birdie at the 12th, but McIlroy closed to within a shot, getting to 11 under with a 13-foot birdie putt at the par-three

16th. Laird responded with a streak of birdies over the last three holes, capping the run with an electrifying up-and-down out of a fairway bunker at the 17th and a 15-foot putt at the par-five 18th. The victory put Laird into next week's Masters, his third straight visit.

As Laird saw things, there was a simple explanation for holding up under McIlroy's pressure. "I know how good Rory is," Laird said, "but it doesn't matter if it's Rory or Jim or Billy — if someone's behind me making birdies like they were, I know I've got to keep making birdies."

Masters Tournament
Augusta, Georgia
Winner: Adam Scott

See Chapter 2.

RBC Heritage
Hilton Head Island, South Carolina
Winner: Graeme McDowell

Graeme McDowell, another of Northern Ireland's contributions to international golf, won the 2010 U.S. Open, authored six victories on the European Tour, scored the winning point in the Ryder Cup. But he didn't figure he'd made it as a golfer — not really made it — until he had won on the PGA Tour.

He filled in that last blank in the RBC Heritage, with a bit of golf's version of a good Irish drama. He trailed all the way, then, caught up in a stormy fourth round, bogeyed the final hole and beat fellow U.S. Open champion Webb Simpson in a playoff. Both had missed the cut at the Masters the previous week.

"The U.S. was a special victory, but I wasn't a PGA Tour member," McDowell said, in something of a sigh of relief. "This is my first PGA Tour victory as a member. I'm going to call it my first defensive win."

McDowell came out to the final round finding himself four shots behind and in the middle of a windstorm running 20-30 mph and gusting higher, blowing debris and challengers here and there around Harbour Town Links. "I guess the weather was what the doctor ordered," McDowell said. "I needed that to get close to the leaders."

The biggest wind victim was third-round leader Charley Hoffman, who started the day two up on Simpson, four on McDowell, but he was gone on a 77. Luke Donald birdied four of his first six holes but just managed a 69 and a tie for third. "Strongest wind I've played in all year," he said.

Simpson was off and running with birdies at the second and third, but damaged himself badly with three bogeys over six holes from the fifth. McDowell seemed untroubled by the wind. On the front nine he logged eight pars and a birdie at No. 5. He tied Simpson and the falling Hoffman for the lead with a 28-foot birdie putt at the 11th. He took the lead at the 16th with an eight-footer and held on when he saved par from the back of the green at the 17th. But at the 18th, he made his first bogey, not only on the windy day but in 32 holes, to slip back into a tie with Simpson. McDowell shot 71-67-68-69, and Simpson 68-71-65-71 to tie at nine-under 275.

It was a one-hole playoff and pretty anticlimactic. McDowell won with a two-putt par from 15 feet. Simpson wasn't unhappy.

"I came in with not too much confidence, but I just stayed true to the process of what we've been working on," Simpson said.

McDowell, on the other hand, became a hero, setting up the house at Nona Blue, a bar back at his headquarters, Lake Nona, at Orlando. "Give my boys a call," McDowell said, punching up his cell phone. "The bar is open. How long the bar stays open," he added, "will depend on how many people are in there."

Zurich Classic of New Orleans
Avondale, Louisiana
Winner: Billy Horschel

Goodness knows, winning is its own reward. But at the TPC Louisiana, a number of golfers had compelling reasons for taking the Zurich Classic of New Orleans. Ricky Barnes, for example. His baby daughter had just arrived and he hadn't yet got her a birthday present. Lucas Glover was trying to pull free of a long slump. Then there was the little-known Billy Horschel, still trying to crash the party.

Barnes was off and running at the start. He birdied six of his last eight holes for a one-stroke lead at eight-under-par 64. "A pretty stress-free round," he said. But he would fade.

Glover, the 2009 U.S. Open champion, scored the last of his three PGA Tour victories in 2011. He trailed Barnes by a stroke in the first round and shot 67-70 to lead the middle two rounds. "I've been hitting it pretty well for a couple of months and finally started making some putts," he said.

Horschel, 26, a former University of Florida standout who turned pro in 2009, was merely the hottest player on the tour not to have won. By late April, he had made the cut in all of his 12 starts and had three straight high finishes coming to the Zurich Classic — ties for second, third and ninth. All he needed to complete this picture was a win, and this he got coming from behind to wrap up a card of 67-71-66-64 for a 20-under total of 268, edging D.A. Points (65) by a stroke.

It was a matter of timing for Horschel. "This whole week I felt like I'm going to get my victory here," he said. "I felt, it's got to be sooner or later, and thank God I finally won."

"When a player goes out and shoots eight under and birdies the last hole to win — hats off," said Points.

Horschel started the final round two behind Glover, warmed up with a birdie at No. 5, then caught fire and birdied six straight from No. 7 on putts from 2, 9, 4, 13½, 6 and 15½ feet.

There was another matter of time for Horschel — two weather delays. Delays bother most players, breaking their concentration and rhythm. Not Horschel. "For some reason, it puts me at ease a little bit," he said. The second delay, in fact, hit at what could have been a ruinous time. It fell after he'd hit his tee shot at the par-five 18th, and it lasted 52 minutes. Keeping in mind that he had bogeyed the 15th and was clinging to the lead with a birdie at the 16th, he would have almost an hour to dwell on what lay ahead.

When Horschel came back out, he hit his second to the green and then was facing a 27-foot birdie putt, with Points sitting just five feet from a birdie of his own.

Said Horschel: "I was thinking, 'If it's my time, this putt needs to go in.'" It was, and the putt did.

Wells Fargo Championship
Charlotte, North Carolina
Winner: Derek Ernst

A powerhouse field had assembled at weather-ripped Quail Hollow for the Wells Fargo Championship. And once the guys had made their peace with patchy greens and chilling May weather, they found themselves at a surprise birthday party thrown by someone named Derek Ernst, in honor of — well, himself.

Ernst, who would turn 23 in just 11 days, was a 2012 graduate of the University of Nevada Las Vegas, where he was a four-time All-American. He won his PGA Tour card through the qualifying tournament, and so far he tied for 59th in his first start, the Sony Open, and tied for 47th in his seventh, the Zurich Classic, and missed five straight cuts in between. He got into the Wells Fargo by a small miracle. He was on his way to a Web.com Tour event in Georgia when he got the phone call telling him that he was in the Wells Fargo as the fourth alternate. Ernst, No. 1,207 in the World Ranking, headed for Quail Hollow, and there he managed to top a strong field with 67-71-72-70 to tie England's David Lynn (71-68-71-70) at eight-under 280 and win in a playoff. Did he think about winning?

"No, really — not ever," said Ernst.

Short-term goals were the key, as he demonstrated at the 18th in the final round when he needed a birdie to tie Lynn in regulation. "I didn't even think about birdieing the hole," Ernst said. "I just thought — hit the drive down the middle of the fairway, and then a nice [second] shot. If you think ahead, you get in your own way."

And so in a cold rain, Ernst hit that good tee shot at the final hole, then hit a six iron from 192 yards to four feet from the cup. He made the birdie putt for a two-under 70 and tied Lynn, the two of them a stroke ahead of a frustrated Phil Mickelson. On the first playoff hole, at No. 18, Lynn drove into the rough and missed the green while Ernst drilled a three-iron second to 15 feet and made the winning par.

"This feeling is unbelievable right now," Ernst said.

Ernst came to everyone's attention in the first round when he shot an eight-birdie 67 to tie for the lead with another unknown, Nate Smith. The marquee players took over from there. Mickelson led the second round, and he and Nick Watney tied through the third. Early in the fourth, the chase was among Mickelson, Watney, Rory McIlroy and Lee Westwood. Mickelson led by one with three holes to play, but bogeyed the 16th and 17th. "I let it slip away," he said. Ernst and Lynn filled the void. Ernst birdied the 11th, 15th and 18th, and Lynn birdied the 14th and 16th and went into the playoff.

Ernst had to change his travel plans, switching from the Web.com Tour to The Players Championship. Would he rent a car?

Said Ernst, now $1.2 million richer: "No — I'll fly this time."

The Players Championship
Ponte Vedra Beach, Florida
Winner: Tiger Woods

Tiger Woods made the 2013 Players Championship his fourth win of the year, and there was nothing surprising about it. The year simply became the 12th since 1997 that he had won four or more times. The bells and whistles went off this time, however, because he had never won four times so quickly. It was only mid-May, and in his seventh start.

This wasn't the old super-dominant Tiger Woods, blowing away the field. In fact, he gambled and won on finessing two closing pars to outlast Sergio Garcia and Swedish rookie David Lingmerth. But it was a solid two-stroke win on a card of 67-67-71-70–275, 13 under par at TPC Sawgrass.

But first came another installment of Tiger Woods-Sergio Garcia Soap Opera. They were hardly famous friends over the years. The quibbling started when they were paired in the second round.

"It sounds like I was the bad guy here," Garcia was to say. "I was the victim."

Said a dismissive Woods: "Not surprising that he's complaining about something."

For all of that, it was still some spirited golf at the classic par-72 Pete Dye course. Little-known Robert Castro tied the course record with a 63 for the first-round lead. Woods and Garcia took center stage in the second. Garcia holed seven straight putts, six of them for birdies, for a 65 that put him one up on Woods, who continued to roll on the par-fives and was eight under on them so far. The script couldn't have been written better. Woods shot 71 in the third round and Garcia 72, and they were tied going into the finale, along with Lingmerth. They would play together in the final round. "I'm not going to lie," Garcia said. "He's not my favorite guy to play with." It didn't matter to Woods. "I'm tied for the lead, so I'm right there," he said.

It was only fitting that a top tournament not go easy, and this one didn't. Woods, three under through the 13th, hooked his tee shot into the water at the 14th and double-bogeyed, falling into a tie with Garcia, Maggert and Lingmerth. Maggert, 49 and fast approaching the Champions Tour, was tied for the lead coming to the island 17th. He watered his tee shot and double-bogeyed.

Woods, in the next-to-last group, played the 17th with the greatest care. He was content to hit to the center of the green and two-putt from 40 feet for his par, as though sensing Garcia, playing behind him, wouldn't resist going after that back-right pin. Garcia did, and watered his first tee shot, then watered his second, and made a double-bogey-seven. "That hole has been good to me for the most part," Garcia said. "Today, it wasn't."

Woods played the 18th for a conservative par-four and Garcia completed his crash there with a double-bogey-six. Lingmerth was the last challenger, and when he three-putted the 18th for a bogey, Woods hugged his caddie and said, "How about that?"

HP Byron Nelson Championship
Irving, Texas
Winner: Sang-Moon Bae

The last time Sang-Moon Bae and Keegan Bradley were nose-to-nose was in 2011. Bradley had become an instant star that year, winning the PGA Championship, and by late November, he was ranked 27th in the world. Bae, a South Korean, had won three times on the Japan Tour and was one notch higher. Irony does some strange work. Two years later, they were one place apart again. This time, Bradley was leading the 2013 HP Byron Nelson Championship going into the final round, and Bae was one shot behind. But not for long...

Bradley, who opened with a sizzling 10-under-par 60 and led through the first three rounds, might be asking — what does a guy have to do to win? In his case, it would be to handle the 18th at the par-70 TPC Four Seasons Resort somewhat better. Bradley bogeyed it three times in four visits and lost by two as Bae scored his first PGA Tour win.

On going into the final round trailing by a stroke and faced with having to catch Bradley, Bae had a simple approach. "Only just play my game," he said.

Bradley was off and running in the first round when heavy rains left golfers playing under the lift-clean-place provision. Starting at the 10th, he birdied five of his first seven holes, took back-to-back bogeys at his ninth and 10th (Nos. 18 and 1), then birdied three of his next four and finished eagle-birdie-birdie for the 60.

Bradley kept the lead through the middle rounds, and Bae hung on with three 66s, trailing by six in the first and three in the second and closed to within one in the third, whereupon he flashed a sense of humor.

What does it say about Korean golf, a writer asked, that you and John Huh are both in the [hunt]?

"Isn't he American?" Bae said. "Just kidding."

In the final round, with battering 25 mph winds — "Feels a little like the British Open without the rain," said Martin Kaymer — Bradley watered his tee shot at No. 3 and bogeyed, and Bae holed a 27-foot putt for birdie. Three straight birdies from the fifth put him four shots ahead, but he lost three shots with a double bogey at the ninth and a bogey at the 10th.

Bradley made three bogeys in the final round, but he tied for the lead when he birdied the 15th on a 17-foot putt and Bae took a two-putt bogey from six feet. Another birdie-bogey exchange decided the tournament. Bae took a one-shot lead, dropping a five-footer for birdie at the par-five 16th. Then Bradley was long with his tee shot at the par-three 17th and bogeyed. Bae parred in for a 69 and the two-stroke win. Bae, in only his second year on the tour, had a little trouble expressing himself.

"I have confidence that my English will get better," he said, "and the more confidence I get then I like speaking."

Nobody could have said it better.

Crowne Plaza Invitational
Fort Worth, Texas
Winner: Boo Weekley

When last seen — by millions on international TV — former cult hero Boo Weekley was happily galloping down the fairway, riding his driver like a kid on a stick horse. This was at the Ryder Cup in 2008, the year of his second and, as it turned out, last victory. Now it was five years later, and as Weekley was about to win the Crowne Plaza Invitational, he had the butterflies — "It feels good to have [them] again" — but it was his caddie who got nervous. Said Weekley, ever the country boy: "He ain't never walked that fast. He looked like a horse runnin' to get a goat."

Weekley trailed until a string of three birdies through the final turn lifted him into the lead, and at the par-three 13th, he lifted his putter as well in celebration as his 22-foot birdie putt dropped and got him to 14 under par.

"That's when I realized, 'Wow, here I go — I need to do something, either hold on to it or make a couple of more birdies,'" Weekley said. Hold on was the best he could do. Colonial Country Club wouldn't allow him any more birdies, so he parred in and added another four-under 66 to his 67-67-66 for a 266 and a one-stroke victory over Matt Kuchar. Ryan Palmer, who breezed to the first-round lead with a 62, tailed off and tied for 14th.

Before Weekley got hot, and with 12 players within three shots of the lead, Kuchar was the man to beat. He was wielding a hot putter. Of putts inside 10 feet, he made 34 straight until he missed an eight-foot birdie try at No. 3 in the third round. Kuchar completed his weather-interrupted second round with a 65, then faltered a bit in the third. Bogeys at the seventh and eighth dropped him two behind Canada's Graham DeLaet before he recovered for a 69 and a one-stroke lead over him and Weekley.

"To not give away a stroke and maintain a one-shot lead is a good position to be in," said Kuchar, who won the Accenture Match Play in February. "Everybody has got to come get me."

Weekley, playing well despite a strange twitch of his left eye, accepted the invitation. He started with a two-putt birdie at No. 1 and a chip-in birdie at No. 3. After two bogeys, he dashed to three straight birdies around the turn, hitting a six iron to four feet at the par-three eighth, holing an 18-footer at the ninth, then a short putt at the 10th. The 13th really woke him up. That's when he glanced up and saw his name atop the leaderboard.

Weekley had command of his game all the way. He hit 71 percent of the fairways and racked up 24 birdies against eight bogeys, then enjoyed the thought of his name going up on Colonial's Wall of Champions.

Said the country boy: "It don't get no better 'n 'at."

Memorial Tournament
Dublin, Ohio
Winner: Matt Kuchar

Matt Kuchar, still boyish at 34 — allowing for a scraggly beard and a shiny scalp not visible until he removes his cap — was halfway through his ambitions for 2013. One was to become a multiple winner in a season. With the Accenture Match Play already in his bag, he accomplished that goal with his sturdy victory in Jack Nicklaus' Memorial Tournament, only the second multiple winner this season so far, after Tiger Woods and his four. Kuchar's other goal was to win a major, and his next chance would come in two weeks at the U.S. Open. Oozing confidence, he was looking forward to it.

"Great golf breeds more great golf, winning tournaments breeds winning more tournaments," Kuchar said, and his recent play, and especially his two-shot win in the Memorial, made him someone to reckon with. Merion would be a shortish but demanding test, and in the Memorial's tense fourth round, he missed only one fairway, the 17th. But he made a clutch four-foot par putt to cool off Kevin Chappell, who was charging in a bid for his first win. Earlier, Kuchar turned away the only other real final threat, Kyle Stanley, with a birdie-bogey exchange at the 11th.

The final round was a three-man race. Kuchar shot 68-70-70-68–276, 12 under, for the two-stroke win. Chappell, the only other player to score under par in all four rounds, closed with a 68–278. Stanley (71) was a distant third at 281. Charl Schwartzel, the first-round leader with a 65, tied for eighth, and halfway leader Bill Haas tied for fourth.

It's a rare Memorial that goes without super stardom, but this was one. Tiger Woods, No. 1 in the world, had one of his career-worst rounds, a 79 in the third, and tied for 65th in the field of 73. No. 2 Rory McIlroy barely made the cut after an opening 78 and tied for 57th.

Kuchar led by two going into the final round and stayed ahead all the way. Stanley, after a hot front nine, fell out at the par-five 11th. He bunkered his tee shot, missed the green and bogeyed while Kuchar was making a clinical birdie — good tee shot, layup, wedge to 14 feet, one putt. And just when it seemed the tournament was in Kuchar's hands, Chappell — after parring his first 12 holes — birdied four of his last six and three of the last four. Kuchar's clutch four-footer at the 17th left Chappell two behind going to the 18th. There, Chappell's approach was rolling toward the hole. Kuchar's reaction? "Please don't go in," he said, laughing. It stopped two feet away. And Kuchar himself hit to 20 feet. Then, putting first, he rolled it in for his 68 to lock up the win.

Kuchar would arrive at the U.S. Open with a ton of confidence, but without the beard.

"My wife thought it looked good," Kuchar said, with that famous grin. "But it's itchy and scratchy. It's coming off."

FedEx St. Jude Classic
Memphis, Tennessee
Winner: Harris English

With his first PGA Tour victory at his fingertips, it was all about feelings for Harris English at the final hole of the FedEx St. Jude Classic. He ran the gamut at the 18th, from that quivery energy on the tee to a scary sensation at the green — actually, no sensation at all.

English, 23, in his second year on the tour, was first known for winning as an amateur on the then-Nationwide Tour, and he had good reason to be nervous at the TPC Southwind's 18th. It was the end of a Jekyll-Hyde final round that he was barely surviving. One more hole would do it, and that first win would be his.

"It's probably one of the best feelings when you play competitive golf," English said, thinking back to the 18th tee. "To have those butterflies, have that feeling ... I love it and I thrive on it."

But then he found himself at the 18th green with a different feeling. He was facing a two-foot par putt to lock up a two-stroke win over Phil Mickelson and Scott Stallings. "I was glad I had a two-shot lead because my hands were shaking," English said. "I couldn't feel them, and I was just hoping that ball goes in the hole."

English had opened in a traffic-jam tie with Davis Love, recovering from back surgery, and four others at 66. He exchanged the lead with 64-69 in the middle rounds with Shawn Stefani, a rookie chasing a first win of his own. And with that last two-foot par putt, English had a one-under 69 for a 12-under 268 and the two-shot win.

It was a ragged 69. It was actually two different nine-hole rounds. English started the final round one behind Stefani and lurched to a four-bogey, two-birdie 37 front nine. Things were turning really sour when he bogeyed Nos. 5, 8 and 9.

"I really didn't think I'd be in this seat, coming off nine," English said. "I thought I made some really dumb bogeys on eight, nine, and shot myself out of the tournament." But he pulled himself together in a hurry. He birdied the 10th, holing a 14-foot putt, and stuck his tee shot at the par-three 11th to five feet and birdied again. A bogey at the 13th, his fifth of the day, slowed him. Then he birdied the par-five 16th from five feet, and at the par-four 17th, just trying to get his par, instead rolled in a 17-footer for birdie.

Up ahead, Stallings had birdied the 16th, missed a birdie at the 17th, and bogeyed the 18th off a wide tee shot. Mickelson birdied the 13th and 16th, just missed at the 17th, and birdied the 18th after just missing a hole-out eagle from 151 yards for a 67.

Said English, all but mopping his brow: "I knew if I kept it together on the back nine, I could make a run at the thing."

U.S. Open Championship
Ardmore, Pennsylvania
Winner: Justin Rose

See Chapter 3.

Travelers Championship
Cromwell, Connecticut
Winner: Ken Duke

One must keep the faith, Ken Duke, age 44, explained, on finally breaking through in his 187th start on the PGA Tour. But even he might concede that an occasional smile from the golf fates would come in handy. Such as a ball ricocheting off a tree and settling in at comfortable birdie range, and a couple of putts that ordinarily had little chance of going in, along with some timely misplays by challengers.

The Travelers Championship unfolded with Duke in his customary place most of the way — back in the pack — what with Charley Hoffman opening with a nine-under 61 at TPC River Highlands and Hunter Mahan right behind at 62. Duke was eight behind in the first round, then seven after the second, where former Masters champion Bubba Watson took over with a 67–130.

"You gotta believe in yourself, in everything you do," Duke was to say, in his first winner's interview after beating Chris Stroud in a playoff. "That's why those guys at the top are winning week in, week out. Because they believe they can do it."

Duke turned pro in 1994 and has had a lot of practice in believing. "Yeah, it's been a long time," he said. "I've been on the Canadian Tour, the mini tours, Asian Tour, South American tour, Web.com Tour — all of them."

But it was looking like business as usual for him as the Travelers unfolded. He opened with 69-68, only three under at the halfway point. A 65 in the third round, which tied his low for the season to date, carried him up the leaderboard to within two of Hoffman, Watson and Graham DeLaet, all tied for the lead. Watson was the first of the marquee names to fray. He was leading by four through No. 6, then bogeyed three times off stray drives and dropped back into a tie. The slippage ruined him in the final round.

Duke was having a magical stretch, battling Watson. He birdied the 10th after his ball caromed off a tree and ended up five feet from the cup. He dropped a 17-foot putt for birdie at the 11th, and at the 13th his 45-footer took a quick turn and dropped for another. He bogeyed the 14th and birdied the 15th. Then Watson watered his tee shot and triple-bogeyed the par-three 16th and was gone. Duke scrambled for a par at the 18th for his 66–268. He looked like a winner when Stroud's approach bounced off the back of the 18th. But Stroud chipped in from 51 feet for a birdie and a 67 to tie.

At the second playoff hole, again at the 18th, Duke stuck his approach to about 30 inches. He needed that for a birdie and the win.

"I told myself it's my turn," Duke said. "There's no reason why you can't just knock this in. Just slow down just a little bit and knock it in. And that's what I did."

AT&T National
Bethesda, Maryland
Winner: Bill Haas

Happiness is having a three-footer at the last hole to win, and three putts to do it in. But first you have to know it, and Bill Haas didn't. He led the AT&T National by at least two strokes down the final nine, but he was fixed on taking it one shot at a time, and he wasn't happy. He wasn't thinking about the win. He was thinking about the ones that got away and how badly he didn't want it to happen again.

"I could say I blanked all that out and I was so focused and that's the reason I won," Haas said. Not so. "As many times as I've choked and hit bad shots, and I've been nervous and it hasn't worked out," he added, "I was feeling all of those things."

Well, Haas worked his way through it all for his fifth career victory, covering Congressional Country Club in 70-68-68-66–272, 12 under, for a three-stroke decision over Roberto Castro. But he had to survive a carnival third round to do it. Four came out of it tied for the lead, and three defied reason getting there. Castro bogeyed No. 2 and double-bogeyed No. 3, falling from a tie for the lead to five strokes behind in three holes. Then at the 18th, he missed the green with his third, but chipped in for his par four. "Wild day," Castro said. James Driscoll shot a quiet 68. Haas birdied nine of the first 15 holes, but also had three bogeys and a double bogey, all for a 68. Said Haas: "It could have been a six-, seven-, eight-under day. But it could also have been a four-, five-, six-over day."

The final round was a footrace, with six players having a share of the lead here and there until Haas broke away for three straight birdies through the turn — on a 10-foot putt at the eighth, then a 12-footer, and another 10-footer at No. 10. He outran those dark memories coming in. He saved par out of a bunker at the 13th and converted a good break into a birdie at the 14th, where his wide approach kicked over from a mound and left him a 10-footer. He got his last birdie the easy way — a wedge to a foot at the par-five 16th. Finally, that three-footer at the 18th eased the memory of the most recent pains — shooting 76 in the third round of the Memorial Tournament after taking the halfway lead, and worse, blowing to five bogeys over seven holes after leading the Northern Trust Open in the final round.

It gave Haas the comfort of a huge cushion when Castro didn't birdie the 18th.

"When Roberto missed his putt, I knew I had three putts to win from three feet, and I still was ... I mean, I was shaking over that last putt," Haas said. "But today, unbelievably special day. I can't even tell you how good it feels.

Greenbrier Classic
White Sulphur Springs, West Virginia
Winner: Jonas Blixt

Jonas Blixt missed the rainbow.

A rainbow soared briefly after a three-hour storm delay as he was finishing, but he wasn't nature-hunting at that point in the Greenbrier Classic. "Okay, I'll be honest," Blixt said. "I was quite nervous today because I didn't feel too great about my game, but I saw it on 17 when I was walking up to my third shot, but after that I was just kind of, you call it 'in the zone.' I didn't see too many things."

There were more jitters a little while later, but no real need for them. Happiness is sitting in the clubhouse with a two-shot lead while the only two players who can catch you need a hole-in-one on the final hole. Blixt didn't compute the odds against aces, but he didn't start breathing again until after Johnson Wagner and Jimmy Walker teed off at the par-three 18th. They both hit the green — but not the hole. And Blixt, 29, a Swede in his second year on the PGA Tour, had his second victory.

He didn't see it coming, however. Posting 66-67-67, he spent the first three rounds chasing the leaders around the par-70 Old White TPC in the mountain resort. Worse, he was four strokes off the lead going into the final round and nursing a game that had cost him seven missed cuts in his 15 previous starts. He finished with a 13-under 267 and won by two over Wagner (73), Walker (71), and Australians Steven Bowditch (68) and Matt Jones (68).

"It's just been a hard year," Blixt said. "I just haven't played that well and it just feels really weird, missing the cut last week, and I felt like the ball was going everywhere..."

Things might have been easier for Blixt if he had found the secret to No. 13, a hefty 490-yard, dogleg-right par-four. He wasted five shots there, playing it 4-6-6-5.

Wagner was the most frustrated man of the week. He opened with an eight-under 62, tying for the lead with Tommy Gainey, then trailed Matt Every by one at the halfway point, and regained the lead with a 64 in the third and was two ahead of Walker going into the final round. It was a scramble from there.

Wagner stumbled down the back, making three bogeys in a five-hole stretch. "The swing just left," he said. Walker could manage just one birdie against two bogeys. Bowditch was three under for the round, then bogeyed the 13th, and Jones, after an early bogey, got to three under.

Blixt birdied Nos. 5, 9, 10 and 12, and bogeyed the 11th and 13th, and was tied going to the par-four 16th, and facing a nine-foot birdie putt.

"I looked at the scoreboard ... before I hit that putt, and I saw I was tied," Blixt said. "Didn't do anything to me emotionally." But when the putt dropped for the birdie, he suddenly was leading by two — the two he won by.

John Deere Classic
Silvis, Illinois
Winner: Jordan Spieth

Someone noted to Jordan Spieth that Tiger Woods, Phil Mickelson and Rory McIlroy scored their first PGA Tour wins after they had turned 20, but Spieth had just won his, the John Deere Classic, while he was still 19. And what did he make of that?

"I don't think of my age as my age," said Spieth, sounding a lot wiser than 19. "I just think of playing and competing with these guys as my peers." Spieth came to prominence as a high school player in Dallas, and left the University of Texas halfway through his sophomore year in 2012, turned pro, and had the sobering experience of not making it out of the second round of the PGA Tour's qualifying tournament. He got into 15 events before the John Deere, missed three cuts, and his best finish was a tie for second in the Puerto Rico Open.

Spieth was about two weeks from turning 20 when he came away from the John Deere with veteran credentials. He shot the par-71 TPC Deere Run in 70-65-65-65, tying David Hearn and former Masters champion Zach Johnson at 19-under 265, then beat them in a grinding, five-hole playoff. He had came from six strokes off the lead going into the final round and punctuated his superlative performance with a stunning, life-saving shot at the final hole. It seemed his rally fizzled when he bunkered his approach at the 18th. But he settled himself and blasted out, and...

"...the luckiest shot I've ever hit in my life," Spieth said. "It was going a good six, seven feet past ... but the fact that it bounced right and hit the pin and dropped down in the cup, it's just extremely fortunate."

Johnson, who was among the leaders from the start, bogeyed the last hole for a 68, and Hearn, a former Canadian Tour rookie of the year, shot 69. The playoff went back to the 18th. They parred it on the first two trips, then parred the par-three 16th and the par-five 17th. It was back to the 18th for the fifth playoff hole. All three drove into the right rough, and into tree trouble. Hearn punched out, about 60 yards short of the green. Johnson, trying to hook around a tree, hit into the water. Spieth's approach hit the green and rolled to the back edge. Hearn had pitched on, then missed his par putt, leaving Spieth with two putts to win.

"I never had a putt to win a [pro] tournament before," Spieth said. "Even the two-footer to tap it in. I didn't know if I'd get my putter to the ball." But he calmed himself enough to get the ball down for his first victory. Which just strengthened predictions that he would be the next big player in the game.

"My goal is to become the best player in the game," Spieth said, "and I still have a very, very long way to go."

The Open Championship
Gullane, East Lothian, Scotland
Winner: Phil Mickelson

See Chapter 4.

Sanderson Farms Championship
Madison, Mississippi
Winner: Woody Austin

Woody Austin worked his way up from back in the pack and, having found the touch with his irons, took the Sanderson Farms Championship in a three-way playoff and stepped right into a matter of perspectives. The general view would be that the popular Austin had just made a nice run-up to the Champions Tour, six months away. Austin himself, however, saw it differently. "It's been a long road and a long time," Austin said. "This is only my fourth event, so I'm really ecstatic. Now I have a job again."

If the rest of the world saw Austin, age 49, heading for the 50-and-over Champions Tour, Austin did not. Having a "job" again meant he now had a two-year exemption on the PGA Tour — a guaranteed place to play. His previous win was in 2007, and after that exemption ran, he didn't have the automatic spot that this win provided him. But he wasn't ready to move on anyway.

"I've told everybody I want to play out here," Austin said. "I don't like the idea that people say, 'Oh, you're 50 years old, you're not good enough to play anymore and need to go play with the old guys.'"

The Sanderson — previously the True South Classic and the Viking before that — played at Annandale Country Club opposite The Open Championship in July, was just the fourth tournament of the season for non-exempt Austin. And he had missed the cut in the previous three. Things were more promising this time. He started 69-65 and was in the running at the halfway point. Another 65 in the third round left him just two behind Nicholas Thompson, who was pulling for his kid sister Lexi in the Marathon Classic on the LPGA Tour. If both would win, they would become the third brother-sister combination to win in the same week.

But the cast changed abruptly in the final round. Thompson fell behind with a double bogey at No. 5 and finished a solo fourth, and it became a running battle among Austin, Cameron Beckman and Daniel Summerhays the rest of the way. Austin bogeyed the second, but got into the chase with an eagle-birdie-birdie sprint from the fifth. Summerhays took the lead with a birdie at the ninth; Beckman birdied the 11th and 13th, and Austin also birdied the 13th to take a share of the lead. Down the final stretch, Austin birdied the 15th and parred in for a 67, tying with Beckman (67) and Summerhays (69) at 20-under 268. Then Austin dropped an eight-foot birdie putt on the first playoff hole for his career-fourth victory.

"Congrats," said Summerhays. "Forty-nine years old and kicking all of our butts."

Said Austin: "Probably stupidly, I still want to play a couple more majors on the regular tour, and I want one more shot at a Ryder Cup or Presidents Cup."

RBC Canadian Open
Oakville, Ontario, Canada
Winner: Brandt Snedeker

If it wasn't the strangest thank you in the history of the game, it would do for a start.

This was Brandt Snedeker, after winning the RBC Canadian Open: "I can't thank Kandi enough for going into labor early." He was speaking of Kandi Mahan, wife of Hunter Mahan, on the arrival of their first child, Zoe Olivia.

Back on Saturday, Mahan was on the Glen Abbey practice tee warming up for the third round when the phone call came that Kandi had gone into labor. Mahan was leading by two shots going into the final round and he hadn't won yet this season, but he abruptly left the tee to fly home to Dallas. Snedeker, who had started the third round eight shots behind Mahan, reached No. 7 and noticed that Mahan's name was no longer on the leaderboard. "I looked at my caddie, and I go, 'What's going on?'" Snedeker said. Mahan had withdrawn, the caddie said. Snedeker was already four under for the round and had slashed his deficit to four. He rolled on to a bogey-free 63 and a one-shot lead over Sweden's David Lingmerth (65). Matt Kuchar (64) and Jason Bohn (66) were two back.

Early on, Snedeker's prospects weren't that promising. Opening with 70-69, he trailed by five in the first round, and by eight in the second where Mahan took the lead with a 64 and John Merrick came crashing through with a 10-under-par 62 for a solid second place. Then everything changed in the third round when Mahan withdrew. Snedeker vaulted to the top with a 63.

"Kind of left the tournament wide open," Snedeker said. "Hunter was going to be hard to catch." Inspired, relieved or simply focused, Snedeker picked up where he left off and birdied Nos. 8, 9, 11, 13 and 16 for the bogey-free 63 and was one ahead of Sweden's David Lingmerth and two up on Matt Kuchar and Jason Bohn. So Snedeker didn't lack for pressure in the final round. "I know what to expect tomorrow," Snedeker said.

Snedeker closed with a two-under 70. He birdied the second and seventh and bogeyed the sixth to keep the pursuit at bay. A birdie at the 10th got him to 16 under. He bogeyed the 12th, but recovered with a birdie at the 16th and parred in for a 16-under 272 and a three-stroke win over Dustin Johnson, William McGirt, Kuchar and Bohn. Johnson was his biggest threat, tying him for the lead, but he drove out of bounds at the 17th and triple-bogeyed.

"It felt great to get a win, to validate all the hard work over the past three months, where I haven't played my best," Snedeker said. Then Snedeker made the most important announcement: "Zoe will be getting a very nice baby gift from me."

P.S. Zoe Olivia Mahan arrived at 3:26 a.m., Sunday, July 28, 2013. Mother and daughter "doing great," Mahan tweeted. "What a whirlwind of a day."

WGC - Bridgestone Invitational
Akron, Ohio
Winner: Tiger Woods

It's an article of faith in golf that you can't win a tournament in the first round, so Tiger Woods waited till the second.

Woods started the second round birdie-eagle-birdie — quite an announcement — and rolled from there to a nine-under-par 61 and a seven-shot lead. From there, it was pretty much business as usual at one of his favorite stomping grounds, Firestone Country Club, where — ho-hum — he tacked up another World Golf Championships - Bridgestone Invitational, No. 8. It was also his fifth win of 2013. He won it by seven shots. (Woods, by the way, reached his nine under through the first 13 holes and parred in. And he had no bogeys).

Woods may not have eased off completely after that 61, but he didn't press the point, either, in beating the long, rolling course with 66-61-68-70–265, 15 under par. No one got within six shots of him on the final day, and to the formal question of who finished second, the answer was, defending champion Keegan Bradley (67) and Henrik Stenson (70), tied at 272.

"He kind of punctured this tournament on Friday," said Stenson.

The 61 was the fourth of Woods' career and second at Firestone.

"You know, I hate to go on and on about how good he is," Bradley said. "But he's just ... this week, he's playing really well."

As for Woods himself, he put it into the big picture. "The total body of work is pretty good," he said. "One of the things I'm proud of is how many times I've won, plus won World Golf Championships, and how many years I've won five or more tournaments in a season. What is it — like eight or nine times? Ten? That's not bad, either."

The only other player on the stage was Webb Simpson, and that was only briefly, with the first-round lead at 64. It included a run of six birdies in an eight-hole stretch. Woods swept him and everybody else off the stage in the second round.

Woods started by knocking his approach to three feet at No. 1 for his first birdie. He surprised no one by making eagle at everybody's favorite birdie hole, the par-five No. 2. He dropped a 20-footer there. Another birdie at No. 3 had him four under already. When he got another birdie at the par-three seventh, his already big gallery began to swell. Then it approached a gridlock swarm as he headed home with four straight birdies from the 10th, getting to nine under. There was a whiff of a 59 in the air. He needed to go only two under over the last five holes. His best chances came at the 15th and 17th, but he missed birdie putts from inside 10 feet. Then he had to scramble to preserve his round when he drove into the trees at the 18th. He holed a 25-footer for his par and the 61. Disappointed?

"Absolutely not — nope," Woods said. "Sixty-one is pretty good. I'm not bummed."

Reno-Tahoe Open
Reno, Nevada
Winner: Gary Woodland

When Gary Woodland won the Transitions Championship in 2011, he did it the old-fashioned way — with more birdies and fewer bogeys than anyone else, and the lowest score won. When he arrived at the Reno-Tahoe Open, he and the others weren't sure what to make of this modified-Stableford scoring system, except that it was all about points, and the highest score won. This was the system used at the former International tournament.

"I know you'll have to make a lot of birdies, and hopefully we're on top at the end," Woodland said, and that had to be the sentiment of the entire field in this early August event playing opposite the WGC - Bridgestone Invitational. Woodland had it right — he was on top at the end, and he found it a pleasant change from the grind of a regular event.

The scoring system gave no points for pars, two for a birdie, five for an eagle and eight for a double eagle. But it cost a player one point for a bogey and three for a double bogey or worse. If nothing else, it generally means that players will be more aggressive and fire at more flags.

"You're going to have to make birdies," Woodland said. "Anytime somebody can make an eagle or double eagle real quick, the scores change quickly."

They surely did at Montreux Golf and Country Club, sitting in the thin air of the high desert and buffeted by brisk August winds off the Sierra Nevada, which left golfers guessing on shots. As Josh Teater, looking for his first win, discovered. He had an eagle and six birdies against two bogeys and found himself the leader with 15 points. "It was kind of a funny day out there," he said. Woodland, a big hitter, was tied for second with 14. He birdied his first five holes, and he covered the 616-yard, par-five 18th with a 370-yard drive, a 266-yard five iron to eight feet and two putts for birdie.

Woodland broke out with fireworks in the third round. He holed a 50-foot bunker shot for an eagle at No. 2, chipped in from 50 feet for birdie at the par-three No. 7, and stuck his approach to two inches at No. 15, soaring to a 37-30 lead over Brandon Steele. How safe was that seven-point lead?

"It's tough to tell in this format," Woodland said. "Somebody can hole out on a par-five, and all of a sudden a seven-point lead vanishes."

Woodland was very nearly right in the final round. Jonathan Byrd set a single-day record with 18 points and would tie for second while Woodland struggled. He saved par five times but made four birdies, one of them on a 58-foot chip-in at the 14th. He then birdied the par-five 18th, chipping to two feet, for his second tour win. He shot, in this case, 14-7-16-7 for 44 points to beat Byrd and Romero by nine.

Said Woodward: "I felt like it was meant to be this week."

PGA Championship
Rochester, New York
Winner: Jason Dufner

See Chapter 5.

Wyndham Championship
Greensboro, North Carolina
Winner: Patrick Reed

It's been said that caddies get 10 percent of their golfers' winnings. That wasn't the case for this particular caddie.

"I get it all," she said, beaming.

This was Justine Reed, caddie for rookie Patrick Reed — her husband — in the Wyndham Championship, which ended the PGA Tour's regular 2013 season in mid-August. For toting the bag for 72 holes plus two playoff holes and for her husband's first victory, she picked up a check for $954,000. The playoff victory over rookie sensation Jordan Spieth was a crowning moment. Reed seemed to be working up to something good. True, he had missed nine cuts in 23 starts, but he had four top-10 finishes, and two of them came just before the Wyndham.

The win didn't come easily, but except for a shaky third round, Reed played with the air of a veteran. In shooting the par-70 Sedgefield Country Club in 65-64-71-66–266, 14 under, he went a 36-hole stretch without a bogey. He trailed by one in the first round, led by one in the second over John Huh, who shot a 62, and tied Huh in the third. The fourth was a chase.

There were eight players within two strokes of the lead at the start. Reed raced off to four birdies over five holes from No. 5, then saw a three-shot lead melt away on the back nine. Huh had birdied the 15th, and as Reed was bogeying the 16th — his only slip of the round — Spieth, 20, birdied the 17th to tie at 14 under and set up a chance to become the youngest two-time winner in the PGA Tour's modern era. Huh bowed out with bogeys at the last two holes. Reed and Spieth both parred in to tie.

On the first playoff hole, at the par-four 18th, Spieth recovered from a poor drive by holing a 25-foot putt for his par. Reed's chance to win died when he sent his seven-foot birdie putt wide. He got his par. At the second playoff hole, the par-four 10th, Reed knocked his drive into the trees, almost out of bounds. With his ball sitting on pine needles on an uphill lie, Reed hit a seven iron like a baseball swing under a tree branch and put the ball seven feet from the pin.

"It was the best shot of my life, that's for sure," Reed said. And Spieth praised it as "one of the best shots I've ever witnessed."

Spieth missed his 10-foot birdie putt, and Reed dropped his seven-footer for the first victory of Team Reed. The secret to the team?

"I'm usually the composed one," Justine said. "I feel like the less reaction he gets out of me the better. It creates a good balance."

Said Patrick: "I don't ever want anyone else on the bag. As long as I'm playing, I want her caddying for me. I can't imagine winning without sharing it with her on the bag. I couldn't have won without her."

PGA Tour Playoffs for the FedExCup

The Barclays
Jersey City, New Jersey
Winner: Adam Scott

Adam Scott was all packed up and ready to go. There was no point in waiting around. He'd had a good day, a five-under-par 66, and he had the clubhouse lead at 11-under-par 273, but it surely wouldn't be enough, not with so many challengers out on the course and an hour and a half to go. Still — one never knows. So Scott decided to play it safe and wait. Next thing you know, he was unpacking the clubs and heading to the practice range to warm up for a playoff. The next thing after that, Scott, the reigning Masters champion, could pack up the clubs again — along with The Barclays, the first leg of the four-tournament FedExCup Playoffs.

"I'm pretty shocked," Scott said. "There were so many guys out there with a chance, and I really didn't think I had much of a chance. You know, if you hang around the lead long enough, you're going to win some, you're going to lose some, and this one went my way."

But it took its time. Some 12 players were within five strokes of each other heading into the final round of the storm-battered tournament. Matt Kuchar finished his second-round 65 on Saturday morning and shot 70 in the third round in the afternoon to tie Gary Woodland (68) for the lead. They were a stroke up on Kevin Chappell, who set the course record with a bogey-free 62. Scott, who opened with 69-66, dampened his chances with a one-over 72. He started the final round a less-than-encouraging six strokes behind the leaders and nine groups ahead of them.

But in this playoff derby, a good finish could be crucial, so he got to work. After opening with four straight pars, he birdied three in a row from the fifth, then moved into a share of the lead with birdies at the 14th and 16th. He finished with a five-under, bogey-free 66 and the clubhouse lead. But to win, he would need an incredible amount of help. And as he watched and waited, he got it.

Justin Rose had a 25-foot putt at the 18th for a birdie and the lead. He knocked that first putt five feet past and, coming back, missed the par that would have tied him with Scott, and bogeyed. Tiger Woods bogeyed the 10th, 13th and 15th, then needed a 25-footer from off the green for a birdie to tie. He was a tad short. Woodland shot 73, and Kuchar stumbled to five bogeys, a triple bogey and one birdie for a 78. Kevin Chappell, fresh from a 62 in the third round, birdied Nos. 8 and 10, then played the last eight holes in seven over for a 76. All this took place as Scott sat and waited. It must have been tough, someone wondered.

"Not too tough," Scott said. "I didn't have to go out and hit another shot. I didn't mind waiting at all."

Deutsche Bank Championship
Norton, Massachusetts
Winner: Henrik Stenson

Call it the Amazing Summer of Henrik Stenson. At 37, Stenson, the personable Swede, had known the peaks. He won the 2007 WGC - Accenture Match Play and the 2009 Players Championship. Then came a deep valley. In fact, he had dropped out of the top 200 in the World Ranking. And then came the magic of 2013. How else to explain a game that suddenly reversed itself and headed for the heights? In 15 starts coming into the Deutsche Bank Championship in early September, Stenson finished second in the Open Championship and tied for third in the PGA Championship, and had four other top-eight finishes. He capped off the run by winning the Deutsche Bank, the second stop on the FedExCup trail, shooting the TPC Boston in 67-63-65-66 for a 22-under 262 and a two-stroke win over Steve Stricker. It was a command performance. He made only three bogeys in the entire tournament and went a 44-hole stretch without one.

Maybe Stenson could sense it was his time the way the front-runners fell away. First, Phil Mickelson. After leading the first round with a 63, he shot a par 71 that could only be called an adventure. "I was playing terrible, and I shot even par," Mickelson marveled. It was a mish-mash of stray shots — a hazard on the left at the ninth hole, one on the right at the 10th, a tree at the 11th, the gallery at the 12th and 13th, first left, then right. He made two bogeys, a double bogey and saved par five times. But he was out of the chase. Two more 71s dropped him to a tie for 41st. Sergio Garcia was making a good run at it. He led through the middle rounds. Five birdies in seven holes and a closing eagle gave him a 64 in the second round. He shot 65 in the third, built on five birdies coming home, tying the tournament record 19-under 194 for 54 holes. He led Stenson by two starting the final round, then three-putted the par-five No. 2 for a bogey, and was on his way to a 73.

Stenson himself started shaky, bunkering his second and bogeying No. 2. But he got that back and more with three straight birdies from No. 4 that carried him past a faltering Garcia. He strengthened his hold with birdies at the eighth and 11th. Next came Steve Stricker, who had moved to within two. Stenson bunkered his approach at the 17th, while up ahead at the 18th, Stricker had a long putt for eagle. Stricker missed the eagle and birdied, but his hopes were smashed when Stenson holed out his bunker shot for a birdie at the 17th. He came to the 18th still up by two, his winning margin.

BMW Championship
Lake Forest, Illinois
Winner: Zach Johnson

Zach Johnson was barely noticed at the BMW Championship, the next-to-last tournament of the season, and it wasn't surprising. Other things were getting all the attention. Tiger Woods, for example, got hit with a controversial penalty. Sensational young rookie Jordan Spieth was contending again, and veteran Jim Furyk worked his loopy swing for a 59 — with a bogey. Along with this, Brandt Snedeker was making a run, then Furyk moved in, and then Steve Stricker. As for Johnson, he was tagging along in the rain-delayed event until with a closing kick he zipped past a faltering Furyk with hot putting down the stretch for the win.

"It's hard to grasp the last two weeks of golf," said Johnson, going back to the Deutsche Bank Championship the week before, when a long clutch birdie putt on his last hole tied him for 27th and got him the 10th and final spot on the Presidents Cup team. He was on a hot streak — playoff runner-up to Spieth in the John Deere Classic and four more top-eight finishes. Then came the BMW, his first win since July 2012, and it paved his way into the following week's Tour Championship.

Johnson was in the hunt through the first three rounds with his 64-70-69. He was one behind Snedeker in the first round. The second round was pure theater. Furyk became the sixth player in PGA Tour history to shoot a 59. Starting on the back nine, he birdied the first three holes, went birdie-eagle from the 14th and birdied 17 and 18. Coming in, he birdied Nos. 2, 3 and 4, bogeyed No. 5, and birdied 7 and 9.

"It really was a mental battle and a mental grind," said Furyk. He tied Snedeker for the halfway lead, and Johnson was three back.

But Furyk had to share the spotlight with Woods, and not the kind of spotlight Woods wanted. He was assessed a two-stroke penalty when his ball moved, ever so slightly, as he was removing a twig near the first green. The movement was detected by someone editing video for the PGA Tour. Woods argued that the ball had oscillated and returned to its original position, but officials said that it moved. The penalty gave him an eight on the hole and a 72, and left him seven off the lead. It was his second rules flap of the year, following the incident at the Masters.

Stricker closed to within one of Furyk in the third round, and Johnson was three back. Then the unfortunate Furyk went frustrated again in the final round. He birdied the 10th for a two-stroke lead, but he bogeyed the 14th and they were tied. Furyk had two bogeys and a birdie the rest of the way, while Johnson birdied the 16th from 18 feet and the 17th from 12 for a 65, a 16-under 268 and a two-stroke win over Nick Watney. Furyk slipped to third.

Said Johnson: "A great week ... a week of perseverance and patience."

Tour Championship
Atlanta, Georgia
Winner: Henrik Stenson

Henrik Stenson knows what it's like to fall off the radar. How could he forget? It was only early in 2012 that he was ranked 222nd in the world. He was best known, if at all, as the Swede who once stripped down to his shorts to hit a shot out of a water hazard. Next he was wrapping up a breathtaking 2013 season with the Tour Championship, the FedExCup and $11.44 million — for the week.

"It shows I never give up," said Stenson. "I'm just really happy with the way I stuck in there because it didn't feel the best today by far."

He led from the start, shooting East Lake Country Club, home course of the immortal Bobby Jones, in 64-66-69-68, 13-under 267, for a three-stroke victory that had threatened to be a runaway.

Stenson began his amazing season with a tie for third in the Scottish Open in July, followed by seconds at the Open Championship and the WGC - Bridgestone Invitational, a third at the PGA Championship, and then a win at the Deutsche Bank Championship.

Stenson wasted no time at the Tour Championship. He launched his opening 64 with a birdie at No. 2, then four straight from No. 4, and he was on his way to a performance that threatened to swamp the other 29 golfers in the no-cut season finale. He got his lead up to a ridiculous nine strokes halfway through the third round. It took a heavy storm on the back nine plus hot final rounds by Jordan Spieth and Steve Stricker to hold Stenson to a three-stroke win.

A four-birdie front nine sent him on to a 66 and put him at 10 under at the halfway point and a four-stroke lead on Scott. Stenson was still running hot in the third round. He birdied four holes on the front nine, running his lead to nine shots over the challenger of the moment, Dustin Johnson. The Tour Championship was looking like a one-man lark. Then the storm rolled in. Stenson limited the damage. He saved bogey at the 14th with a 12-foot putt and saved par at the 17th with another. But he did make four bogeys coming in, posted a 69 and led by four heading into the final round.

"Henrik was playing phenomenal golf," said Spieth, the 20-year-old rookie wonder. "I felt like once a few putts started falling, we had a shot at it." His reasoning was sound, but Stenson didn't really budge. Spieth got to within one when he rang up four straight birdies from the 13th and Stenson bogeyed the 14th. But that was it. Spieth shot 64, and Stricker, who capped his charge with an eagle at the 15th, shot 65, and they tied for second place, three back.

"It's just been a great summer," said Stenson. "I mean, way beyond what I could imagine. The play that I performed since mid-July has been incredible."

The Presidents Cup
Dublin, Ohio
Winners: United States

Except for some outstanding individual performances and the Internationals' rally in singles, it was business as usual in the Presidents Cup at Muirfield Village Golf Club. The Americans breezed to an 18½-15½ victory, running their record to 8-1-1. As International captain Nick Price warned, without changes, the Presidents Cup might suffer a loss of public interest, much like the Ryder Cup until it adjusted from Great Britain-Ireland to include all of Europe. The most popular suggestion: reduce the Presidents Cup from 34 matches to 28, like the Ryder Cup, to offset the depth of the American side.

"The fewer matches, the more up in the air things will be," said Australian Adam Scott, who went 2-2-1. "The more matches, the more it favors the stronger team." In terms of experience, the U.S. was stronger, with four first-time players to seven for the Internationals.

Rain delays plagued the event, and after the first round Thursday, each day's play was bumped into the next. Except for the 3-3 tie in Friday's foursomes, the U.S. dominated the foursomes (alternate shot) and four-ball (better ball) team matches, and took a huge 14-8 lead into the 12 singles. Then the Internationals turned it into one of the most exciting Presidents Cups, taking the singles, 7½ to 4½. But they had just too much ground to make up.

The matches had their share of highlights and heroes:

• Jordan Spieth, at 20, was the first PGA Tour rookie to make the team, the youngest, and a surprise. Captain Fred Couples made Spieth, so recently a college student, a captain's pick over a number of veterans. Spieth went 2-2, and in the opening four-ball birdied five out of six holes to spike Zimbabwean Brendan de Jonge's eight-birdie effort.

• Japan's Hideki Matsuyama (1-3-1), 21, paired with Adam Scott, fired a spectacular eight iron from a poor lie to two feet at the 18th to earn a four-ball half against Bill Haas and Webb Simpson.

• Canadian rookie Graham DeLaet was the surprise of the Internationals. He and Australia's Jason Day, paired in all four team matches, led the Internationals in points at 3-1-1. DeLaet birdied the tough 18th twice on Sunday. He chipped in from 30 feet to tie a foursomes match in the morning, then holed out a bunker shot to nip Spieth in the singles.

• Tiger Woods got the 18th and winning point with a two-putt par for a 1-up victory over South Africa's Richard Sterne, the third straight time he has scored the clinching point in the Presidents Cup. He led the U.S. with a 4-1 record against one of the Internationals' greatest efforts.

"These guys gave their hearts and souls this week," said Price. "I am proud and honored to be the captain of this team."

Said Couples: "...the matches were all close. At no given time was I a nervous wreck. But it was nice when Tiger two-putted that last green to get the 18th point."

Frys.com Open
San Martin, California
Winner: Jimmy Walker

Some trophies come filled with champagne, some with beer. Jimmy Walker's, on the other hand, came with a yellow flag in it. The message: "Masters 2014." If victory was sweet, how much sweeter was it with a ticket to Augusta National tacked on? For Walker, 34, winning the Frys.com Open was a double dream come true. After nine years and 188 starts, finally his first victory and a Masters berth to go with it.

"There's always this big pressure to get into Augusta," Walker said. "I would press here, press there." He got there thanks to his own sizzling 62 in the third round and then the final-round crash of the globe-trotting hopeful Brian Koepka, a 23-year-old Floridian, who led since the second round and who was looking like a surprising success story about to blossom.

Walker was eight behind Koepka entering the third round and started making up ground in a hurry. Walker birdied the first three holes, then after a bogey at No. 6, he played the remaining 11 holes in seven under, with seven birdies, for a nine-under 62. Koepka added a 67 for a 15-under 198 total, and led by two over George McNeil (71) and Jason Kokrak (68), and Walker's spurt carried him to within three.

Koepka, who didn't get through the PGA Tour qualifying tournament, had no status on the tour and had gone off to play elsewhere. He won his European Tour card with three wins on its Challenge Tour and was playing in Kenya, Kazakhstan, Switzerland and South Africa. "It's a good experience playing overseas," Koepka said. He was in the Frys.com on a sponsor's exemption and was making the most of it until he ran into a bad patch in the final round. He was leading by four with 11 holes to play, then missed a three-footer for par at No. 9. He two-putted the 11th for a bogey, and remained tied with a birdie at the 12th on a three-footer, and saved par on a six-footer at the 14th. He missed a birdie from six feet at the 15th, bogeyed the 16th off a pulled tee shot, and bogeyed the 17th out of the water. His 72 dropped him to a tie for third, and Vijay Singh shot 68 and finished second. "I know I'll be criticized," Koepka said. "It happens to the best of them."

Walker grabbed the lead at the par-five 15th with a birdie from six feet, and parred in, completing a card of 70-69-62-66 for a two-stroke win over Singh. The richest part of Walker's 17-under 267 total came on three of the par-fives. He played them in seven birdies and no bogeys, and they helped put him not only into the Masters but also the Tournament of Champions and the PGA Championship.

"I felt like I was good enough to be in them," Walker said. "You want to be playing in the big stuff."

Shriners Hospitals for Children Open
Las Vegas, Nevada
Winner: Webb Simpson

Webb Simpson got the hint that this was going to be one of those weeks when he went through the first round with seven birdies, no bogeys, shot a 64, a mere stroke off his career low, and found himself four shots off the lead in the Shriners Hospitals For Children Open. But he was hardly one to dwell on the point. From there, Simpson, the 2012 U.S. Open champion, was in that state golfers envy. He was pretty much playing alone, focusing only on what he was doing. In fact, after he had hit his shot to the 17th in the final round, he wasn't sure where he stood. He turned to his caddie. "I asked if I needed to know anything," Simpson said, "and he said, no, we're in control. Just keep hitting shots."

As Simpson would soon learn, the expression "in control" meant that he was in the lap of luxury. Winning by six strokes will put a fellow into that category.

Right from the start, the field turned the TPC Summerlin into a shooting gallery. J.J. Henry, a two-time winner on the PGA Tour, set the course record with his opening 11-under-par 60. "I finally made some putts," said Henry. He also holed a 50-foot chip shot for an eagle on his last hole. His touch wasn't quite the same in the second round. He went up to a 71, on his way to a tie for 15th. Argentina's Andres Romero suffered a wilder swing. He opened with a 61, then blew to an 81 and missed the cut.

Simpson, making his single-minded way, took over in the second round. Taking advantage of excellent conditions, he posted nine birdies and only one bogey for a 63, getting to 15 under and a four-stroke lead. "There's no wind, no clouds in the sky and it's really quiet, so it's easy to kind of daydream," he said. "You've got to really focus on what you're doing." He was four up on Henry, John Senden, Jeff Overton, Chesson Hadley and Jason Bohn. No one would get closer the rest of the way.

"I knew guys were shooting low numbers," Simpson said. "I felt like I was playing well enough. I just was shooting pretty bad — parred No. 9, dropped the shot at 11. My caddie told me to stay patient and let the birdies come." Which they did. He made four down the last seven holes — at 12 and 13, and 15 and 16 — for a 67 and a 19-under 194. He was content to let the field chase him after he got off to a quick start in the final round. So ended his lark. In his tour of 64-63-67-66, a 24-under total of 260, Simpson made 28 birdies and only four bogeys for his fourth career win, his first in 18 months.

"Never thinking I can't win again," Simpson said. "I knew I was getting better. I knew I just had to stay patient."

CIMB Classic
Kuala Lumpur, Malaysia
Winner: Ryan Moore

See Asia/Japan Tours chapter.

WGC - HSBC Champions
Shanghai, China
Winner: Dustin Johnson

See Asia/Japan Tours chapter.

McGladrey Classic
St. Simons Island, Georgia
Winner: Chris Kirk

Sometimes, winning can hurt.

"Obviously, I wanted to win," Chris Kirk was saying, after making the McGladrey Classic his second career victory, "but you hate to see it happen that way, you know? I had some pretty grand plans of hitting it to a foot and making a birdie on the last hole, but that all changed there at the end."

But it hurt Briny Baird a lot worse than it did Kirk. Baird had a good chance to win, but things went badly, and suddenly there he was, 0-for-365 on the PGA Tour.

"It hurt to do what I did on the last hole," Baird said.

They had been dueling down the final round and were headed for a playoff. Kirk was sure he would need a heroic birdie finish, but the unfortunate Baird resolved things himself at the final hole — stumbling out of a fairway bunker to a bogey and a 67, falling to a tie for second with Tim Clark (62), who started the day five off the lead. But he ran afoul of Sea Island's par-four 14th again, a bogey this time after a double bogey in the third.

Kirk had the comfort of playing for a safe par for a one-stroke victory, his first win since the 2011 Viking Classic (now the Sanderson Farms Championship).

Kirk — he shot 66-66-68-66–266, 14 under — was in the mix with Baird from the fog-delayed start. Baird shared the opening lead with a 63 until George McNeil completed the first round the next morning for a flawless eight-under 62. (A second-round 76 ruined that promising start for McNeil.) Kirk took a one-stroke lead in the cold and blustery second round with a second 66 that included one of the finest shots of the week. At the par-five 15th, his approach was blocked by a tree. "I had to effectively hit a 30-, 35-yard hook just to get it around the tree and fight the wind," Kirk said. And he put it to 10 feet and two-putted for birdie. Baird shot 70 and was a stroke behind. In the third round, at the 18th, Kirk dropped a 25-foot putt for birdie and a 68, and Baird matched him from eight feet for a 67, and they shared a one-stroke lead going into the final round.

Baird leaped ahead with birdies at Nos. 2 and 4, and Kirk tied him with birdies at the seventh and ninth. Kirk added birdies at the 11th and 12th and was two ahead, but fell a stroke behind when he bogeyed the 14th and Baird birdied the 13th and 14th. Baird held that narrow lead until Kirk caught him with a 15-foot birdie putt at the 17th. At the fateful par-four 18th, Baird drove into a fairway bunker and, from an awkward lie, topped his four iron just 90 yards into a hazard and lost with a bogey.

Said Baird: "It's not all about winning. I've said that. But this hurts. This really does."

OHL Classic at Mayakoba
Playa del Carmen, Mexico
Winner: Harris English

It can be the latest high-tech beauty fresh off the top shelf or a $5 scruffy center-shafted thing from the barrel at the local muni, but whatever form it takes, sooner or later every golfer will switch putters like a guy grasping at straws. For Harris English, who had fallen on hard putting times since winning the FedEx St. Jude Classic in June, it was an old pal from his college days a few years ago. "What did I have to lose?" English said. More to the point, what did he have to win?

The answer was: The OHL Classic at Mayakoba Resort in Mexico, in mid-November. On a par-71 El Camaleon course soggy after four and a half inches of rain in two days, English was soaring with his putter. "I felt if I could get it on the green somewhere 30 feet or in," he admitted, after winning, "I had a really good chance of making it." As he demonstrated in the final round. From the seventh, he had six one-putt greens in seven holes. All told, after a bogey at No. 2, he made seven birdies from No. 3 to wrap up a card of 68-62-68-65, for a 21-under 263 total and a four-stroke victory over Brian Stuard, who made four birdies over seven holes for a 67, but more noticeably, by six over Sweden's Robert Karlsson, the leader who crashed coming home.

The OHL turned on a tight stretch down the final nine. In four holes from the 10th, English went birdie-birdie-par-birdie. Karlsson self-destructed over three holes from the 12th, going bogey-bogey-double bogey. "That was it," said Karlsson. He shot 72 and tied for sixth.

The weather made for tough conditions and brought on preferred lies for the first two rounds. Only 15 players could complete the first round on Thursday, and from there, things backed up for everybody. Karlsson, 44, had to play the first two rounds on Friday. He led the first with a 63, five ahead of English, who had three penalty strokes in his 68. English rebounded with a bogey-free 62 to tie Karlsson (67) for the halfway lead at 130. The third round was postponed by darkness, and in a Sunday morning finish, Karlsson (67) emerged leading English (68) by one going into the final round.

Karlsson, seeking his first PGA Tour win, got the final round off to an encouraging start, with an eagle at No. 5 and a birdie at No. 8. He fell quiet after that. English also built up steam fast on the front. He bogeyed No. 2, then birdied Nos. 3, 5, 7 and 8. Then came his burst of birdies from the 10th against Karlsson's three-hole crash and Brian Stuard's sprint to second place.

English said he owed his success to his mother, who told him to control his emotions on the course — or else. And, of course, to an old pal of a putter.

Special Events

Tavistock Cup
Windemere, Florida
Winner: Team Albany

The 10th edition of the Tavistock Cup, played at Isleworth Golf & Country Club, would go into the archives as not only the one that ended Team Lake Nona's four-year run, but also as the first to go only one round.

Heavy March rains hit in the Orlando area Sunday, forcing the Arnold Palmer Invitational at Bay Hill to finish on Monday, which was the scheduled opening of the two-day Tavistock, which in turn had to be cut to one round of stroke play on Tuesday for the four-man teams from six clubs. Team Albany (Ian Poulter, Tim Clark, Tiger Woods and Justin Rose) tied at 295, seven over par, with Lake Nona (Graeme McDowell, Ross Fisher, Henrik Stenson and Peter Hanson).

Poulter birdied the first extra hole to give Albany the win and end Lake Nona's reign. Primland finished third at 296, followed by Isleworth (297), Oak Tree National (300) and Queenwood (308).

Primland's Webb Simpson was the low individual at two-under 70.

CVS Caremark Charity Classic
Barrington, Rhode Island
Winners: Steve Stricker and Bo Van Pelt

The huge roar just behind them could only be bad news for Billy Andrade and Bill Haas. They had crept up the scoreboard and were just a stroke behind, preparing to tee off at Barrington Country Club's par-three 17th when the roar hit. Steve Stricker had just holed out a 121-yard wedge shot back at the 16th, all but locking up the better-ball CVS Caremark Charity Classic for himself and Bo Van Pelt. They parred the last two holes to win with a tournament record 25-under-par 117.

"When Steve dumped the eagle on 16, we knew it was over," Andrade said.

Stricker and Van Pelt led the first round with a 12-under 59 on Monday, then started the second with six straight birdies. Stricker eagled the eighth on a 30-foot putt, they birdied three straight from the 12th, and Stricker added his second eagle of the day with the hole-out at the 16th.

"This is the first time Bo and I have teamed up on anything, and I thought we just carried each other when we needed to," said Stricker. "We had a good feeling for the course."

Andrade — co-host with Brad Faxon — and Haas finished second by four strokes in the 10-twosome field. Faxon and Jeff Sluman tied for fifth. In a rare playing appearance, retired LPGA star Annika Sorenstam teamed with Billy Horschel and finished 10th and last.

PGA Grand Slam of Golf
Southampton Parrish, Bermuda
Winner: Adam Scott

"Standing on the 11th tee," Adam Scott was saying, "it didn't look like a score like that was going to be possible." Actually, it was not only possible, but Scott shot it, coming from behind to win the Grand Slam of Golf, the PGA of America's annual 36-hole shootout among the winners of the season's four majors. Scott, who opened with a 70, was talking about his second-round seven-under 64, the Port Royal course record, that carried him from three shots behind U.S. Open champ Justin Rose to a two-stroke victory at eight-under 134. The clincher came with a tap-in eagle at the par-five 17th, which Scott reached with a soaring six-iron second from 190 yards that almost holed out.

Rose, the first-round leader, shot 67-69–136. PGA Champion Jason Dufner was third with 69-70–139, and Padraig Harrington, filling in for Open Championship winner Phil Mickelson, was last at 74-71–145.

Rose looked like a runaway winner in the second round, running off four straight birdies from No. 4. Then he bogeyed No. 9. Scott had five birdies, the last on a 25-foot putt at the 15th, and they were tied when Rose bogeyed the 16th out of a hazard, setting the stage for Scott's eagle at 17. "When somebody finishes like that," said Rose, "you have to tip your hat."

Callaway Pebble Beach Invitational
Pebble Beach, California
Winner: Kevin Kisner

For Kevin Kisner, the Callaway Pebble Beach Invitational in late November proved to be a hearty farewell to the Web.com Tour and a cheery hello to the 2014 PGA Tour. Kisner, who spent 2013 on the Web.com and won a return berth to the PGA Tour, dropped a 15-foot putt for par on the final hole to win by a stroke over Chesson Hadley.

This was the 42nd annual Callaway. The 80-player field drew pros from the PGA, Champions, LPGA and Web.com Tours playing Pebble Beach, Del Monte, Spyglass Hill and finishing at Pebble. Kisner, playing them in that order, shot 70-67-64-74–275, 13 under par.

Kisner, 29, thought that winning the 2013 Chile Classic was his biggest thrill, but no longer. "I think winning here probably beats that," he said. "It's something else walking up the 18th green here, with the ocean and all. I look forward to coming back in a few months for the AT&T Pro-Am."

Kisner eagled the par-five No. 6 and made the turn at 17 under and seemed to be coasting. Hadley, who finished No. 1 on the Web.com Tour, birdied the fifth but double-bogeyed the eighth. Still, his prospects brightened when he birdied the 13th and Kisner double-bogeyed the 14th. Then the par-three 17th looked pivotal, but Hadley missed a seven-foot birdie try while Kisner bogeyed. Hadley didn't get another chance. Both parred the 18th, with Kisner holing the clutch 15-footer.

"We were feeling the heat the whole back nine," Kisner said. "That always seems to happen when you're in position for a win. To make that putt on 18 to win it, that's all you can ask for."

Northwestern Mutual World Challenge
Thousand Oaks, California
Winner: Zach Johnson

Tiger Woods had his sixth Northwestern Mutual World Challenge all wrapped up, taking a four-stroke lead with eight holes to play when Zach Johnson bogeyed the 10th. Woods does not lose with a plum like that in hand.

Ooops. Add the Northwestern to Johnson's growing reputation as a gritty finisher. Johnson holed a long putt at final hole to lock up the 2007 Masters, more recently birdied the final hole of the Deutsche Bank Championship to grab the final automatic spot on the Presidents Cup team, and this time birdied Sherwood Country Club's 11th, 12th, 16th and 17th holes in the final round, and holed a cross-water pitch to par the 18th and tie Woods. On the first playoff hole, Woods missed a four-foot par putt and bogeyed, and Johnson parred for the win. But that was anti-climax. It was the final hole that was the star of the show. Johnson, after making up those four strokes, amazingly was short and in the fronting pond with his approach. He was looking at bogey or worse with the penalty stroke, then dropped and holed the next for the par to tie Woods.

"A little bit too dramatic for me," he said. "I'm lucky it went in."

Johnson shot a bright 67-68-72-68–275, 13 under at Sherwood, that proved to be tricky for some big names in the 18-man field. Hunter Mahan had an 80, Rory McIlroy 77, and Matt Kuchar, Ian Poulter and Jason Day 76s.

Said Woods: "I had a two-shot lead starting out the day. Zach — it was pretty impressive on 16, 17, and 18. He got me."

Franklin Templeton Shootout
Naples, Florida
Winners: Harris English and Matt Kuchar

"It was a fun week," Matt Kuchar said, summing up the Franklin Templeton Shootout.

His partner, Harris English, was a bit more expansive. "It's such a relaxing event," Harris said. "It's really cool being part of this event."

It was, as the saying goes, easy for them to say. With a 14-under-par 58 in the final-round scramble, they simply raced away from the other 11 teams, finishing at 34-under 182 for a seven-stroke victory over Retief Goosen and Fredrik Jacobson at the par-72 Tiburon Golf Club. That margin tied the record set in 1989 in the first tournament by Curtis Strange and Mark O'Meara.

Kuchar and English opened with a 64 in modified alternate shot on Friday, and shot 60 in better ball on Saturday. They averaged nearly a birdie per hole for one stretch, shooting their last 28 holes in 25 under. Nothing showed their domination more than the last 11 holes in the second round

Saturday. They were just one under through No. 7, then they exploded. Kuchar birdied No. 8 from 20 feet, triggering a run of six straight, then made an eagle and three more birdies. They had played 10 of the last 11 holes in 11 under.

Jacobson was talking about the final round, but he might well have been speaking for everyone and the entire tournament. "It was unbelievable, quite an exhibition," Jacobson said. "...we knew we had to pick up the pace. But they played so well, there's not much you can do about it."

PNC Father/Son Challenge
Orlando, Florida
Winners: Stewart and Connor Cink

For a college freshman engineering student and former kid hockey player who doesn't play golf, Conner Cink did a pretty fair imitation of his dad Stewart at the PNC Father/Son Challenge. The Cinks retook the lead in the second and final round when Conner holed a 30-foot putt for eagle at the 14th hole. Dad took over for birdies at the next two, then got an eagle of his own on a 20-footer at the par-five 18th for a three-stroke victory in a field of 20 twosomes playing a scramble format. They shot 61-61, for a 22-under-par 122 at the par-72 Ritz-Carlton Golf Club. Steve and Sam Elkington and Vijay and Qass Singh tied for second at 125 in the 16th playing of the event.

"I think it's pretty monumental," said Stewart Cink, teaming with his son for the first time. "Connor doesn't play golf. We're not talking about a kid who plays in college or has played on various tours. He hasn't played 30 rounds since he was 14 years old. He doesn't play golf, but he's very talented in a lot of his sports." The Cinks played the final nine in nine consecutive threes for a 27, and needed just nine putts.

"Who would have picked the Cinks to win the tournament?" said Elkington, who was leading, with son Sam, until Connor made that eagle. "And here they did it. They did it easy." The Cinks had made a strong statement with that opening 11-under 61 for the first-round lead, by one over the Elkingtons.

"After this week," Connor said, "I might try to hit the links a little bit more often."

Web.com Tour

In the Web.com Tour's complex new process for advancing to the PGA Tour, Chesson Hadley produced the gee-whiz story of the season. He finally found his first career victory in the place where it all began — and that's literally.

Hadley, nearing his 26th birthday, won the Rex Hospital Open, namesake for the hospital where he was born in Raleigh, North Carolina. Hadley made a putting adjustment during a rain delay halfway through the final round and something clicked. After making yards of putts coming in, Hadley wedged to a foot on the final hole for a seven-under 64 and a one-stroke win over third-round leader Danny Lee. It was his first win on the Web.com Tour.

"Honestly I can't believe I won this," said Hadley. "I never thought about winning this tournament. I didn't think I had a chance. I just wanted to hold things together and take a step closer to the big goal, which is playing on the PGA Tour."

Hadley got his wish and more with a victory in the season-ending Web.com Tour Championship at TPC Sawgrass Valley, which also seemed to surprise him. "This is incredible," he said, after coming from behind with a 69. "I was just trying to not puke on myself on the way in."

Hadley, who led the final money list with $535,432, was one of four double-winners — with Michael Putnam, Ben Martin and Andrew Svoboda — among those advancing to the PGA Tour.

Putnam, with the two wins, a second and a third, was voted Player of the Year by the players.

In all, 50 players gained their PGA Tour cards for the 2013-14 seasons. For the first time, cards went to the top 25 on the regular-season money list, and the other 25 from the Finals Series.

Putnam blitzed the tour with the two quick wins. First was the Mexico Championship at El Bosque Country Club in Leon, with some late heroics. Putnam faced a clutch 220-yard approach over water with the wind kicking up. "I was definitely holding my breath because I didn't know if it would get over," he said. "I knew if it got over it would go in the bunker." It did find the bunker. He splashed out to five feet, made the birdie putt for a six-under 66 and a two-stroke win over Alex Prugh, Wes Roach and Whee Kim. "I came to Mexico to win," he said. "I came here this week because I wanted to win the golf tournament."

The following week found him in Potomac, Maryland, for the Mid-Atlantic Championship at TPC Potomac, where he turned 30. The co-leader through three rounds, he opened the fourth with three birdies over the first six holes and was on his way to a two-under 68 and a two-stroke win over Hadley. "It's the second week in a row, and I can't get used to it enough," Putnam said.

Ben Martin, a third-year pro, took the United Leasing Championship — his career first — at Victoria National at Newburgh, Indiana, and the Mylan Classic at Southpointe in suburban Pittsburgh.

Martin won the United Leasing with a two-putt par on the first playoff hole of a four-way playoff on Monday morning after a rain delay didn't leave enough daylight on Sunday. Martin, Joe Affrunti, Ashley Hall and Billy Hurley, tying the tour record for a playoff, were deadlocked at 11-under 277.

Martin was relieved to draw No. 1 and hit first in the playoff. It was at the demanding par-four 18th, with water on the right and heavy rough and a bunker on the left. Martin drove into the fairway. "I was happy to get it out of the way, and that probably put a little pressure on them," he said. Affrunti drove into the rough, and Hurley and Hall drove into the water. Martin hit a six-iron approach to 20 feet and two-putted for his winning par.

At the Mylan Classic, Martin closed with a four-under 67 and won by five strokes. That made him the hottest player on the tour, with five top-six finishes in his last six starts, and 13 top-30s in 17 starts.

"At the start of the year consistency is one of the things I wanted to work on," said Martin. "This is the most consistent I've ever played."

Andrew Svoboda, 33, who made only four cuts in 17 starts on the PGA Tour and was thinking of giving up golf, took his first Web.com title at the Price Cutter Charity Classic in August, then added the Chiquita Classic in September. "This really came out of nowhere," said Svoboda, after his closing 64 won by three at the Price Cutter at Highland Springs, at Springfield, Missouri. "It's a crazy game." In the Chiquita, at Davidson, North Carolina, second of the four Web.com Tour Finals, Svoboda tied Will MacKenzie with a 70, then beat him with a par on the first playoff hole.

Two players shot 59s — the fourth and fifth in tour history — within two weeks of each other in July. Will Wilcox got his in the final round of the Utah Championship and tied for third, and Russell Knox got his in the second round of the Albertsons Boise Open and tied for 12th.

Hadley wasn't the only winner at the Web.com Championship. There was Lee Williams at the final hole, 55 feet from the flag and needing a birdie to have a chance at his PGA Tour card. Williams rapped it up over the ridge and down into the cup. His next break came when playing partner Andres Gonzales, after high-fiving him, missed a 12-foot birdie putt that would have knocked him out of the top 25.

Rookie Patrick Cantlay scored his first win in the Colombia Championship with a tournament-record 18-under 266. He also became the second-youngest winner, at 20 years, 11 months, 15 days. The youngest was Jason Day, at 19 years, seven months, 26 days in 2007.

PGA Tour Canada

The PGA Tour Canada — the former Canadian Tour now under the PGA Tour umbrella — made its debut in 2013 and was amazing for the evenness of the competition. It was tight all the way, and ended up with no multiple winners — nine events, nine winners, with three decided by two strokes, the other six by one.

There was no dominating player, but one did stand out both for topping the money list and for the appeal of his hometown-boy-makes-good story. Mackenzie Hughes, 23, a Canadian who played college golf at Kent State University in the United States, won the 2011 and 2012 Canadian Amateur. He entered the PGA Tour Canada with no playing status. It took him awhile to warm up, but when he did, he broke through like a veteran pro.

It was in the eighth of the nine events, the Cape Breton Celtic Classic in September. In the final round, he birdied five of his first six holes and four of his last five for a six-under 66 and a one-stroke victory over Ryan Williams, a pro out of Vancouver, British Columbia. "To win here on PGA Tour Canada means so much. It's been a crazy year," said Hughes. "If you told me at the start of the year after I missed those first few cuts that I'd be No. 1 on the Order of Merit heading to the Tour Championship, I'd say 'Stop messing with me.'"

The win and three other top-10 finishes put Hughes atop the money list with C$52,114. He also gained his playing card for 2014 on the Web.com Tour, as did the next four on the list. In both the PGA Tour Canada and the new PGA Tour Latinoamerica, the top five from the money list would win berths on the Web.com.

Riley Wheeldon became the first Canadian to win on the new tour when he took the third event, the Syncrude Boreal Open in July at Fort McMurray Golf Club. Wheeldon came out of the pack on the final nine, birdieing three of the first five holes, then parred in for a 66 and a 13-under total, edging Brazil's Lucas Lee by one. The victory and two other top-10s put him second on the money list with C$45,322.

Mark Hubbard, a 24-year-old American from Colorado, pretty well summed up the PGA Tour's new qualifying system after scoring his first victory in the Wildfire Invitational. "Between playing down in Latinoamerica [the new PGA Tour Latinoamerica], up here and in [qualifying] school, the guys have three chances to get to the Web.com Tour," he said. "But you can't really think about stuff when you're playing. You just have to go out and play and that's what I feel like I did the best this week." Hubbard holed a clutch 15-foot putt birdie at the 16th in the final round for a three-stroke lead, then parred the last two for a 66 and a two-shot win over Hughes and Kyle Stough. The win, plus two other top-10s, put him third on the money list with C$40,696.

Chile's Hugo Leon was fourth with C$39,897 off winning the Great Waterway Classic in August plus one other top-10. "I'm feeling great — I'm still floating right now," said Leon. "I knew if I got to 17 within striking distance I was going to have a shot. I trusted that my game was going to come through for me." Leon checked the leaderboard at the 14th in the final round and saw that Brandon Harkins had blistered the course with a 62 and was in at 21 under. "It's nice to know there's a number you have to match," Leon said. He birdied the 16th and 17th with 10-foot putts, then parred the 18th for a 67 and a one-shot win over Harkins.

The fifth Web.com card was snatched up by Wil Collins of the United States, with C$39,708 from his win in the second stop, the Dakota Dunes Open, and two other top-10s. Collins, 34, was tied with John Ellis coming to the final hole. Ellis was short with his approach, and Collins hit the green and two-putted for a par and a 66 that held up for a one-stroke victory. Said Collins: "I've been playing out here since 2006 and I've never got a win. This win couldn't have come at a better time." It was on to the Web.com Tour for him.

The next five on the money list earned an exemption into the final stage of the Web.com Tour qualifying tournament. Two other winners got the exemptions — Joe Panzeri, the ATB Financial Classic, and Carlos Sainz Jr., the Players Cup. The other three spots were taken by players who piled up enough money in high finishes — Nick Taylor, Chris Epperson and Kyle Stough.

The other two winners — American Stephen Gangluff, in the Times Colonist Island Savings Open, and Canada's Max Gilbert, in the Tour Championship of Canada — were in the group 11 through 20, earning an exemption into the second stage of the qualifying school.

PGA Tour Latinoamerica

"Los Cinco" was the byword as a new day dawned in Latin American golf in 2013.

"Los Cinco" is Spanish for "The Five," and that was the goal of the golfers with the arrival of NEC Series — PGA Tour Latinoamerica, making its debut. A number of attempts at staging a pro tour in Latin America had met with little or shaky success. Now this was the new organization for pro golf throughout the Central and South Americas region. It had the organizational skills and wherewithal of the PGA Tour behind it. As with its northern neighbor, the PGA Tour Canada, it was now under the umbrella of the PGA Tour, but it also had a title sponsor, NEC, the electronics giant. The tour consisted of 14 tournaments, each with a $150,000 purse, scattered from Mexico south to Uruguay, Argentina and Chile.

"The Five" would be the top five players on the final money-winning list, who would graduate directly to the Web.com Tour for 2014, now the qualifying path to the PGA Tour. And the first Los Cinco were:

1. Ryan Blaum, USA, $99,135
2. Jose de Jesus Rodriguez, Mexico, $98,383
3. Timothy O'Neal, USA, $90,015
4. Jorge Fernandez-Valdes, Argentina, $65,178
5. Manuel Villegas, Colombia, $60,671

Less direct paths were open to the next five and others.

There were three multiple winners over the 14-tournament schedule, and not surprisingly, the top three money winners — Blaum, Rodriguez and O'Neal, in that order.

Blaum won the Dominican Republic Open, the final event of the first half of the season in June, coming from four behind in the final round with a 68 for a two-stroke win over Argentine Maximiliano Godoy, who bogeyed three holes down the stretch to give the title away. "I put my head down all day, and it seemed to work," Blaum said. Then Blaum became the first two-time winner of the season, beating Argentine Alan Wagner on the first playoff hole in the 60th Brazil Open. Said Blaum: "I did what was necessary, and I was able to get lucky in the playoff."

Rodriguez, all 5-feet-8 of him, answers to the nickname "El Camaron" — "The Shrimp" — but he turned giant in the tour's maiden voyage. Rodriguez scored both of his wins in playoffs. He won the Roberto de Vicenzo Invitational on the second hole of a three-way playoff over O'Neal and Sebastian Saavedra. Thanks, he said, to his caddie for reading the winning putt. "Without him, I would not have done this," Rodriguez said. Then he took the Arturo Calle Colombian Classic in a two-hole playoff over Manuel Villegas, after he had a talk with himself. "I said to myself," Rodriguez said, "'This is your time and you have to take advantage of it.'"

O'Neal shook off his loss of a week earlier and won the Arturo Calle Colombian Open with a closing 66 fuelled by three birdies over four holes from the 14th. In October, he won the 87th Chile Open in a sudden hurry. He ended a three-way playoff with Blaum and Saavedra with an eagle on the first extra hole, off a four-iron approach to six feet. It was a win loaded with hope. Said O'Neal: "This second win should definitely lock me up one of those spots in the top five."

Argentina's Angel Cabrera had just lost to Adam Scott in a playoff at the Masters, and if that bruising experience crushed him, it sure didn't show at the OSDE del Centro Open the following week. He gave the homefolks something to cheer about with a spectacular win, coming from behind in the last round and holing out for eagle at the par-four final hole, forcing former leader Rafael Gomez to birdie it to tie. Then Cabrera beat him with a birdie on the first playoff hole. He thanked his good fortune for his closing eagle. "I was lucky that the ball stopped there," Cabrera said, "and I could make one of my best chips in recent times."

Colombia's Manuel Villegas — younger brother of PGA Tour member Camilo — put on some fireworks of his own in the TransAmerican Power Products CRV Open. Trailing by two strokes with four holes to play, he holed out for eagle at the par-five 15th and birdied the 18th to nip Rodriguez by a shot. The eagle, he said, "...gave me the encouragement to know that I could close well."

Argentina's Jorge Fernandez Valdes was young and old at the same time. Old in that he felt he'd waited a long time for his first win as a pro. Valdes built a two-stroke lead to five, then started tailing off down the back nine but held on to win by one in the Mundo Maya Open. As for young: At 20 years, nine months and 13 days of age, he was the youngest-ever Latin tour winner.

Ted Purdy, 39, a journeyman pro from Arizona with wins on both the PGA Tour and the Web.com Tour, got the PGA Tour Latinoamerica debut off and running with a win in the 55th Mexico Open in March. He took the lead with a birdie on the 17th hole to nip Colombia's David Vanegas by a stroke. "This is my first win since 2005," Purdy said, "so I'm very excited." Then Marcelo Rozo wrapped up the season in December when he coasted from a seven-stroke lead to a two-stroke win in the 108th Argentina Open. He was the first Colombian to win the oldest tournament in Latin America. Said Rozo: "I feel very happy, very satisfied because the hard work has paid off."

8. European Tours

Since the start of the Race to Dubai in 2009, the winners have all been ranked as the world No. 1 at some point. Whether Henrik Stenson will reach that lofty perch remains to be seen, but the excellence of the golf that the 37-year-old Swede produced in 2013 certainly put him up alongside his predecessors, Lee Westwood, Martin Kaymer, Luke Donald and Rory McIlroy. Though he rose to a career-high of third on the World Ranking, behind Tiger Woods and Adam Scott, Stenson was undisputedly the hottest golfer of the second half of the year, and should he maintain that form into 2014, then Woods and Scott will need to be on their toes.

From the middle of July, Stenson was in another league. By winning the DP World Tour Championship, by no less than six strokes over his nearest rival, Ian Poulter, Stenson won the Race to Dubai ranking. He had also created history in being the first player to win both the FedExCup on the PGA Tour and the Race to Dubai — Donald in 2011 and McIlroy in 2012 had claimed the transatlantic money list double, but this was a step up. And Stenson was also the first player to win the Tour Championship on the PGA Tour and the DP World Tour Championship on the European Tour (or its equivalent season-ending event, bearing in mind that for many years in the past the two seasons climaxed on the same week).

Stenson's run started with a third-place finish at the Aberdeen Asset Management Scottish Open. The event was noteworthy for being the first regular European Tour event to be broadcast on national television in America, with NBC taking the Golf Channel feed, and for Phil Mickelson winning his first regular tour event in Europe — the American had won the Tournoi Perrier on the Challenge Tour 20 years earlier. The following week, Stenson was runner-up to Mickelson at the Open Championship and he was joint runner-up to Woods at the WGC - Bridgestone Invitational and third at the U.S. PGA Championship at Oak Hill.

During the FedExCup Playoffs, Stenson won the Deutsche Bank Championship before winning again at the PGA Tour finale at East Lake. He then switched to the inaugural Final Series on the European Tour, a four-tournament culmination to the season offering over $35 million in prize money. Although Stenson was worried by a wrist injury, he played in all four, while others raised doubts about the hectic schedule and some criticized the requirement to play in two of the first three in order to qualify for Dubai. Ernie Els, Sergio Garcia and Charl Schwartzel fell foul of the regulation, and with the Race to Dubai extended to 2017, the European Tour promised tweaks to the fine print.

After two lackluster tournaments, during which Poulter and Rose made a dent in his large points lead, Stenson gritted out a seventh-place finish in the inaugural Turkish Airlines Open. There he was helped by Poulter, who was ranked second when defending his WGC - HSBC Champions title, falling to fifth place after pushing eventual winner Victor Dubuisson early in the final round.

At the DP World Tour Championship, Stenson was in superb form, missing only one green in regulation each day and amassing a tournament record of 25 under par thanks to two rounds of 64, the second of them when it mattered most on the closing day of the season. Poulter had pushed him all the way. To liven up what might have been a Race to Dubai formality, the Englishman had challenged the Swede to a bet at the start of the Final Series. It was for $100 at odds of 10-1, but more importantly the loser would have to pour the drinks for the winner on a night out. When Stenson walked off the 18th green in Dubai, Poulter was there with a white towel over his arm, in waiter pose, and Stenson took advantage by asking the Englishman to wipe his sizzling brow.

"To get the double-double, winning the Tour Championship on both the tours, that's going to take some beating in the future," Stenson said. "It's been a dream year, a dream summer for me, and the season of my life."

It was a remarkable recovery for Stenson. Some 18 months or so earlier he was ranked 230th in the world, the second time in his career he had suffered a severe slump in form, the latest not helped by injury, illness and the fallout from the Allen Stanford banking fraud in which the Swede lost around $5 million. Tellingly, Stenson's rivals were genuinely delighted for a popular colleague. "I have to take my hat off to him, unbelievable," Poulter said. "I have thrown a lot at him and given him so much stick, but he is the best player on the planet right now."

Rose said: "It's an emphatic way for him to finish the season and exactly like he did in the FedExCup. It's been a very impressive year. It was going to take a great performance to get past Henrik. He's done well to hold off all challengers this week."

"I don't think there's been a better player in golf the last six months, and Henrik looks in total control," Donald said. "He's making golf look easy, and believe me, it's not that easy. Hats off to him and he deserves everything he's getting."

It was Rose who provided the defining achievement from the major championships by winning the U.S. Open at Merion. Rose defeated Mickelson and Jason Day by two strokes and hit a wondrous four iron at the last hole from near the plague commemorating Ben Hogan's famous one iron from the 1951 U.S. Open. On Father's Day, he holed out and gave a nod to the heavens, his victory coming 11 years after the death of his dad, and first coach, Ken.

Rose was the first Englishman to win the U.S. Open since Tony Jacklin in 1970 and the first to win any major since Sir Nick Faldo at the 1996 Masters. It was Scott's victory at Augusta in 2013 that helped inspire Rose. When he texted Scott his congratulations, the Australian replied that Rose was next: "This is our time," he wrote.

If Rose, at 32, was in his prime, there were plenty of impressive young players on display, especially Matteo Manassero. Not only did he become the first 20-year-old to record his fourth career win on the European Tour, he became the youngest-ever winner of the BMW PGA Championship at Wentworth, erasing Bernard Gallacher's name from the record books from 1969. England's Chris Wood won the Qatar Masters with an eagle on the final hole, and Dubuisson, of France, broke through in startling fashion by holding off a stellar field that included Woods, Rose, Poulter and Stenson to win in Turkey. He followed that up with a highly creditable third-place finish at the DP World Tour Championship to finish sixth on the Race to Dubai.

Joost Luiten, from the Netherlands, emerged as another fine prospect with two wins, in Austria and on home soil at the KLM Open. As a two-time winner he joined Mickelson, Woods, who claimed two of the WGC titles, Brett Rumford, who won back-to-back in Korea and China, and Graeme McDowell. The Northern Irishman claimed two big titles with the Volvo World Match Play, which provided Bulgaria's debut on the European Tour, and the French Open, to go with his Heritage win on the PGA Tour. Meanwhile America's Peter Uihlein, who started the season on the Challenge Tour, won the Madeira Islands Open and then produced a string of impressive performances to be voted the Sir Henry Cotton Rookie of the Year.

However, with Stenson leading the way, comebacks were the theme of the year, and Paul Casey, plagued with injuries over recent times, won for the first time in two and a half years at the Irish Open at Carton House, just two weeks after seeing his friend Rose win the U.S. Open. An even more sentimental victory came at the Alfred Dunhill Links Championship when David Howell won for the first time in seven years.

There was time for one last great story when in December Miguel Angel Jimenez won the Hong Kong Open, an event on the 2014 schedule. It was the fourth time the Spaniard had won the title and the second year in a row, and it extended his record as the oldest winner on the European Tour by a year, to 49 years and 337 days. And it came after he started the year with a broken leg suffered while skiing. His return to the game in the spring, as he passed 600 appearances on the European Tour, was remarkable enough, but he finished the year not looking forward to action on the Champions or European Seniors Tour but with a chance of playing in another Ryder Cup. "I worked very hard to come back from that. I work very hard in the gym every day with stretching and cardio," he explained. "And the main thing is my head. The head is still very competitive."

Volvo Golf Champions
Durban, South Africa
Winner: Louis Oosthuizen

Just as in 2012 when he won the Africa Open, Louis Oosthuizen claimed victory in his first tournament of 2013. Where his friend Charl Schwartzel ended 2012 by winning the last event of the year in South Africa at the Alfred Dunhill Championship, Oosthuizen picked up the baton by winning the Volvo Golf Champions, an event for winners from the previous year on the European Tour and not counting on the Sunshine Tour. The 30-year-old South African won by one stroke over Scott Jamieson, but the victory was not confirmed until Jamieson's chip for eagle to tie at the last just missed and just two inches away.

This was the sixth time a European Tour event was played at the Durban Country Club and Oosthuizen followed Wayne Westner, Ernie Els and Tim

Clark (the last two twice each) by providing a home victory. After an opening 68, the 2010 Open champion returned a 64 in the second round to take a one-shot lead over Jamieson and first-round leader Thongchai Jaidee. It was a timely round since Friday's round was played with a pro-am format, and Oosthuizen won a Volvo Compact Excavator EC55. The prize had been promised to him instead of a car if his team, including Jaidee and two-handicapper Colin Ledwith, won, which they did after Oosthuizen and Ledwith both birdied the last. "It's a very nice gift for my farm," Oosthuizen said. "That's going to be a lot of fun next week, playing around with it."

A 74 in the third round still kept him in second place, alongside Jaidee and Julien Quesne, but five strokes behind Jamieson, who followed a second-round 64 with a 68. But two early birdies from Jamieson were wiped out by a double bogey at the fifth, and with six birdies in the first 11 holes, Oosthuizen took the lead. His cushion was two with a seventh birdie at the 14th, but he missed a short putt to bogey the 16th, only for Jamieson also to drop a shot there before almost chipping in at the short par-four 18th.

"When I finished everybody was congratulating me," said Oosthuizen, "but I saw Scott still had a chip to force a playoff. That was an unbelievable chip. I thought he'd holed it, so I was pretty relieved when it didn't drop. He played great all week, but today was my day. It's a great start to the year." Jaidee took third place, two behind the winner, with Padraig Harrington in fourth ahead of Quesne and Danny Willett.

Abu Dhabi HSBC Golf Championship
Abu Dhabi, United Arab Emirates
Winner: Jamie Donaldson

After waiting 255 starts on the European Tour for his maiden victory, Jamie Donaldson claimed his second title only 13 events later and achieved it against a high-quality field at the Abu Dhabi HSBC Golf Championship. The winner of the 2012 Irish Open survived a three-putt bogey at the final hole to beat Justin Rose and Thorbjorn Olesen by one stroke, and Ricardo Santos by three. Donaldson also came out ahead of Martin Kaymer, the three-time former winner who tied for sixth place, and the world's No. 1 and No. 2 players, Rory McIlroy and Tiger Woods.

At the start of the week McIlroy was introduced as the latest highly rewarded client of Nike and he had changed every club in the bag. However, the Northern Irishman struggled with his new equipment, even switching back to his old putter for the second day. He missed the cut at six over par after rounds of 75 and 75. Tiger Woods also struggled but thought he had made the cut at one over par until chief referee Andy McFee confirmed a two-shot penalty applied at the fifth hole in the second round. Woods had taken a free drop for an embedded ball in an area covered by creeping vegetation. However, underneath it was a sandy area, so the embedded ball rule did not apply. Woods had checked with playing partner Kaymer but not a referee. He conferred with McFee at the scorer's hut and his 73 became a 75 and at three over he also missed the cut. It was the only time

Woods had missed the cut in a regular European Tour event and only the fifth time ever the world's top two players had failed to qualify.

In the pro-am, Donaldson had thought the Abu Dhabi course so difficult a top-10 finish would be a miracle. "To be here with the trophy is mad," he said. His opening 67 was matched by Rose, who was playing in the windier afternoon, but then Donaldson dropped a shot behind Rose on Friday and two behind on Saturday. Olesen was the first to challenge Rose on the final day before a double bogey at the sixth hole, and then David Howell took the lead with five birdies in the first 10 holes but then had four putts from four feet for a triple bogey at the 13th.

Birdies at the first, ninth, 11th, 14th and 15th holes took Donaldson two ahead, but he three-putted the last, missing from five feet for his par. His 68 left him at 14 under with a total of 274, but he had now given Rose, who had bogeyed the 16th, and Olesen the chance to tie with a birdie. Both had putts for a four, with Rose's lipping out. "The putt was just like against Mickelson at the 18th in the Ryder Cup," Rose said. "Would I swap them? No."

Donaldson, the 37-year-old Welshman who lives in Macclesfield, England, said: "It's a bit like buses, isn't it? I had to wait so long for my first win in Portrush last year and then the second has come along just like that."

Commercial Bank Qatar Masters
Doha, Qatar
Winner: Chris Wood

When his maiden victory on the European Tour finally arrived, Chris Wood did it in style. An eagle at the closing hole took him from one behind Sergio Garcia and George Coetzee and requiring a birdie to get into a playoff, to a one-stroke win without the need for extra time. After a fine drive and regardless of the water down the left-hand side of the fairway, Wood hit a six iron from 202 yards to 10 feet and holed the putt. "Chris hit a great drive and a great six iron and then a wonderful putt," marveled Garcia. "Obviously he's been trying for a while and he deserves it."

Wood, 25, claimed his first victory as a professional at the Thailand Open on the OneAsia circuit in 2012 but had been a runner-up three times on the European Tour. "There's an enormous weight lifted off my shoulders today," Wood, the six-foot, five-inch golfer from Bristol, said. "I feel like I can go on and win more. I've seen a few mates picking up trophies and I've been waiting patiently for my time."

Twice before Wood had held the lead after 54 holes on the European Tour and then shot in the high 70s to let the opportunity slip. This time it was a round of 64, with an eagle, seven birdies and a bogey, that put him three clear of the field in the third round. There had been four co-leaders at the halfway stage and they all fell back, including Garcia and Martin Kaymer with rounds of 70 and 72 respectively.

Garcia, who was aiming to start his new season the way he had ended the last one, with a victory, rebounded with a closing 66, while Coetzee came from even further back with a 65. Wood did not have a confident start, missing a short birdie putt at the second and then taking a double bogey at the third, but rallied and holed from 15 feet for an important birdie at the 14th. Coetzee, who himself keeps knocking on the door for a first European Tour win, birdied the 16th and 18th holes to set the clubhouse target at 17 under par. Garcia matched him with birdies at the last two holes, which set up Wood to eagle the last for a 69 and an 18-under total of 270.

"I didn't know the situation when I was on the 18th fairway," Wood said, "but luckily I'd hit a great drive and I had the perfect yardage for a six iron. I knew I had to just let my swing go and trust it. It's up there as one of the best shots I've ever played, because it was to win a tournament."

Omega Dubai Desert Classic
Dubai, United Arab Emirates
Winner: Stephen Gallacher

Stephen Gallacher produced a succession of special shots to claim his first victory in more than eight years at the Omega Dubai Desert Classic. The 38-year-old Scot was expected to kick on after winning his maiden title at the Alfred Dunhill Links Championship in 2004, but his long wait for his second win — including a runner-up finish at the Emirates in 2012 — finally came to an end with a three-stroke victory over Richard Sterne.

Gallacher, who had started the last round with a three-shot advantage but only edged in front by a stroke when Sterne bogeyed the par-three 15th, effectively ended the contest when he holed his second shot from just off the fairway at the 16th with a sand wedge from 115 yards for an eagle-two. "Great shot," Sterne told the Scot as they walked up the fairway. "I don't like it, but great shot." Sterne bogeyed to fall four behind and that was that. The South African birdied the 17th to match Gallacher's closing 71 but was no match for the winner's 22-under-par winning total of 286 that equaled Thomas Bjorn's record total from 2001.

"These days you need to do something special to win an event, and I had the perfect distance for that wedge and it came out perfectly," Gallacher said of his holed shot at the 16th. "I knew if it wasn't in it would be very close. It's been eight years since I last won. I'm maturing with age hopefully. I've come close a number of times over the years, but there has always been someone else who's gone one better."

Gallacher had five eagles during the week, including two on both Thursday and Saturday. In the first round he holed from the fairway for a two at the sixth and then got a three at the par-five 13th. His 63 put him one off Sterne's first-round lead. The South African's 62 was one outside Ernie Els' course record from 1994. Sterne still led by one at the halfway stage but was overtaken by Gallacher's 62 on Saturday. The Scot hit the pin with an eight iron at the 13th and tapped in for eagle and then holed out of the back bunker for yet another eagle at the 18th. His 54-hole total of 195, 21 under par, was a new record, one better than Tiger Woods' effort from 2001. Thorbjorn Olesen and Felipe Aguilar shared third place, while Lee Westwood tied for fifth place in his season's debut.

Joburg Open
Johannesburg, South Africa
Winner: Richard Sterne

See African Tours chapter.

Africa Open
Eastern Cape, South Africa
Winner: Darren Fichardt

See African Tours chapter.

Tshwane Open
Centurion, South Africa
Winner: Dawie Van der Walt

See African Tours chapter.

Avantha Masters
Noida, India
Winner: Thomas Aiken

See Asia/Japan Tours chapter.

Maybank Malaysian Open
Kuala Lumpur, Malaysia
Winner: Kiradech Aphibarnrat

See Asia/Japan Tours chapter.

Trophee Hassan II
Agadir, Morocco
Winner: Marcel Siem

It helps if you have a double former Masters champion on speed dial. Marcel Siem gave his countryman Bernhard Langer a call on Saturday night and in less than 24 hours was celebrating victory at the Trophee Hassan II. The German had to wait a few more hours to find out if he would be joining Langer at the Masters a fortnight later, but after the conclusion of the Shell Houston Open, when the top 50 in the World Ranking earned invitations to Augusta National, Siem, who started the week in 72nd place, had come up one spot shy in 51st place.

But Siem could still look back on a job well done. He led from wire-to-wire and converted a four-stroke lead after 54 holes into a three-stroke victory over Mikko Ilonen and David Horsey. However, a third European Tour victory, and a second in under a year following his win at the French Open in 2012, was not straightforward for the 32-year-old. A bogey at the second and three birdies in the first four holes from Ilonen meant the pair was tied. Siem managed to edge ahead at the fifth, and a double bogey at the 12th from Ilonen gave Siem breathing space again.

Siem had opened with a 64 and added rounds of 68, 69 and 70 for a 271 total, 17 under par. Ilonen and Horsey both closed with 69s and Pablo Larrazabal a 71 to take fourth place at 12 under. "I am so happy right now," said Siem, after being presented with a jewel encrusted gold dagger by His Royal Highness Prince Moulay Rachid, the Crown Prince of Morocco. The event was again played on the Golf du Palais Royal within the monarchy's estate in Agadir. It was also played simultaneously with the Lalla Meryem Cup on the Ladies European Tour at nearby Golf de l'Ocean and the winner of that event, Ariya Jutanugarn, joined Siem at the presentation.

"It was a big day for me and there was a lot of pressure out there," added Siem. "The guys really came at me. I spoke to Bernhard last night because I have never been in the situation of going into the final round with a big lead and I just wanted to know if he had any advice on how to cope with that.

"I wasn't sure if I should play defensive or aggressive, but he said just play your game and play the way you have been for the last three rounds, you shouldn't change anything or have any fear."

Open de Espana
Valencia, Spain
Winner: Raphael Jacquelin

It took nine holes, equaling the longest playoff in the history of the European Tour, and over two hours before Raphael Jacquelin claimed victory in the Open de Espana at El Saler. All the overtime was worth it for the 38-year-old Frenchman as he won for the fourth time in his career and for the first time since the 2011 Sicilian Open. Rounds of 73, 66, 73 and 71 left Jacquelin at five under par with a total of 283 and tied with Felipe Aguilar, who closed with a 70, and Maximillian Kiefer, who matched Jacquelin's closing 71.

Nine more times Jacquelin and Kiefer played the 18th hole. Aguilar dropped out on the third extra hole when he failed to match the birdies from the Frenchman and the German. Jacquelin thought he might have won when he put his approach to two feet, but then Kiefer holed his putt from 30 feet to stay alive. Jacquelin had birdied the hole in regulation and finally did so for the third time in 10 attempts when he hit a wedge to five feet and made the winning putt. In the only previous playoff of such a length in Europe, Jose Maria Olazabal beat Ronan Rafferty and Roger Chapman at the 1989 Dutch Open.

Jacquelin said: "It's difficult to describe how I feel, a little bit tired at the moment after nine holes of playoff, but I'm really happy. At the ninth time of asking makes it even better — after the win. It would have been really disappointing if I had lost this tournament, but it was a real fight, and very hard to put the ball in the hole, but I managed in the end."

Kiefer said: "It's been a very long day. When I got into the playoff I said to myself: 'I have played very well today, I'll do my best and let's see what happens.' I was proud of being up there. But after playing nine times, then it's a bit disappointing to lose."

Earlier, Marc Warren, the third-round leader, was still on course for victory until he finished with four bogeys in the last five holes, plus a birdie at the 16th. He three-putted at both the last two holes to miss the playoff by one stroke, tying for fourth place with Magnus Carlsson, David Horsey and Paul Waring.

Ballantine's Championship
Seoul, South Korea
Winner: Brett Rumford

See Asia/Japan Tours chapter.

Volvo China Open
Tianjin, China
Winner: Brett Rumford

See Asia/Japan Tours chapter.

Volvo World Match Play Championship
Kavarna, Bulgaria
Winner: Graeme McDowell

Graeme McDowell became the first Irishman to win the Volvo World Match Play Championship, an event that dates back to 1964. McDowell was the first No. 1 seed to win since Ernie Els in 2004 and in the process he avenged his defeat in the final a year before.

Padraig Harrington and Paul McGinley were both defeated in finals at the World Match Play, as McDowell was by Nicolas Colsaerts in 2012 at Finca Cortesin. The new venue of Thracian Cliffs in the Black Sea resort of Kavarna in Bulgaria, the first time a European Tour event had been played in that country, proved to the Northern Irishman's liking. He topped his group by beating Chris Wood 5 and 3 and then Stephen Gallacher 4 and 3. In the last 16, McDowell beat America's Bo Van Pelt at the 18th before defeating Colsaerts 2 and 1 in the quarter-finals. The match included an amusing incident when the Belgian had to take relief from a hazard by dropping in a stone-built toilet, before taking further relief away from the convenience — and then getting up and down for a par.

But the defending champion finished as a busted flush, and McDowell beat Branden Grace in the semi-finals to stay on course to match Bob Charles (1968-69), Sandy Lyle (1987-88), Nick Faldo (1988-89) and Ian Woosnam (1989-90) as a losing finalist who returned the following year to win. He did just that by beating Thailand's Thongchai Jaidee 2 and 1.

On the last day, McDowell did not drop a shot and was eight under in beating Grace, who was five under par himself, in the best match of the week, before rallying from two down after four holes against Jaidee. It was the first time he had trailed all week, and a series of par saves at the fifth, ninth and 10th holes kept him in it, as birdies at the seventh and 12th, a dropped shot by Jaidee at the 14th before another birdie by McDowell at the 15th gave him victory against the 43-year-old former paratrooper.

McDowell, 33, won the week after missing the cut at The Players, as he did at the Heritage at Hilton Head the week after missing the cut at the Masters. Following in the footsteps of great former winners such as Ballesteros, Els, Faldo, Player and Palmer, McDowell said: "These guys are legends of the European Tour and legends of golf, so to have your name on a trophy this cool is pretty special. This is a special moment in my career, no doubt about it."

Madeira Islands Open - Portugal - BPI
Madeira, Portugal
Winner: Peter Uihlein

As a former U.S. Amateur champion from 2010 and a winning Walker Cup player in 2009, Peter Uihlein might never have guessed where his maiden professional title might come. It arrived at the Madeira Islands Open - Portugal - BPI, high on the mountain overlooking the Atlantic Ocean at Santo da Serra. The 23-year-old American turned professional late in 2011 and in 2012 played mainly on the European Challenge Tour. He failed to get a full card for the European Tour so was mixing starts on the main circuit and the Challenge Tour in 2013 until he won this double-badge event that counts on both. It meant he was fully exempt for the European Tour until the end of 2014.

Uihlein, who is the son of Acushnet CEO Wally, was on course for a potential 59 on Friday before a couple of late bogeys meant settling for a 64. He had opened with a 72 and had a 69 on Saturday to lie one behind Mark Tullo, but on Sunday showed he had saved a sparkling finish for the right moment as he came home with four birdies, including three in a row from the 11th. A closing 68 gave him a total of 273, 15 under par. He won by two over Tullo and Morten Orum Madsen. Tullo, for the 13th time in his career, had a hole-in-one with an eight iron, from 201 yards, at the fifth hole, but with bogeys immediately before and after, the magic moment failed to propel the man from Santiago to victory. He closed with a 71, while Madsen made a fine charge with a 67 but had a double bogey at the 18th to give Uihlein a two-shot cushion playing the last.

"I'm just thrilled," said Uihlein. "To do it playing well on the back nine, coming down the stretch, is sweet. I know Morten played a heck of a round and Mark played really well, so it was nice to come out on top."

After such a stunning amateur career, Uihlein had a lean start as a professional, which forced him to travel overseas. "I've learned a lot over the last year," he said. "When you're struggling, it's one of those things, you hate it when it happens, but it's almost the best thing that could happen to you. It definitely was for me and I'm pretty happy with how things turned out. You grow up quick out here and that was the main reason I came over. It's been a good process so far and hopefully I can keep going."

BMW PGA Championship
Virginia Water, Surrey, England
Winner: Matteo Manassero

At the age of 20 Matteo Manassero has not finished claiming new records for youthful achievement, but his victory at the BMW PGA Championship marked the boy wonder's blossoming into a contender for the game's biggest titles. The Italian's four-hole playoff win at Wentworth was the fourth and biggest victory of his career to date. The only teenager to win three times on the European Tour, he claimed the circuit's flagship event at an age when he was still a couple of months younger than Bernard Gallacher when the Scot won the PGA in 1969.

Manassero was wearing green trousers on the final day, as he does occasionally in honor of his idol Seve Ballesteros, and the Italian was delighted to win at a venue where Seve had so much success and was loved so dearly by the gallery. This was Manassero's second playoff success and came against Simon Khan and Marc Warren. With the par-five 18th hole played each time, Warren went out on the first extra hole when he drove into bushes on the right and had to take an unplayable. He was forced back to the tee and then found the water with his fourth shot.

Manassero and Khan halved the hole in birdies, then pars and then birdies again. On the fourth extra hole Manassero switched to a driver, rather than a three wood off the tee, and hit a superb shot. Although Khan was much farther back, he was forced to go for the green and his three wood did not carry the stream. Manassero found the green with a three-hybrid and two-putted for the victory.

Khan won the PGA in 2010, when he started the final round seven shots behind. Here he was five back and closed with a superb 66 to set the clubhouse target at 10 under par. Alejandro Canizares was the overnight leader and tied for fourth place with Miguel Angel Jimenez, who was playing his 600th event but only his second since breaking his leg while skiing. With Luke Donald, the two-time defending champion, Rory McIlroy, Graeme McDowell and Ian Poulter all missing the cut, Lee Westwood was the best-placed member of Europe's 2012 Ryder Cup team to take the title. A stroke adrift overnight, birdies at the second, third and fourth holes put him two clear of the field. But he bogeyed the sixth and seventh holes, and hooked drives at the 11th and 12th holes cost him three shots in all. He finished tied for ninth after a 73.

Warren made four birdies in a row from the 10th to take the lead. Having hit the lip of a fairway bunker at the 13th, he holed a full wedge shot for his three, but his playing partner, Manassero, who had earlier holed from a greenside bunker at the ninth, kept in touch by birdieing the hole himself. Warren dropped a shot at the 15th as he and Manassero both parred in for rounds of 69 to tie with Khan.

"It's been an amazing week," said Manassero, the 2009 Amateur champion. "I've always felt something really special about this place and this tournament. Everything has come together this week, and I managed to play well and stay in contention after a tough day on Friday, and pull it off in this playoff. I'm really excited. Besides this victory, you get all of these achievements that are amazing, but right now, I'm just thinking of winning the BMW PGA Championship."

Nordea Masters
Stockholm, Sweden
Winner: Mikko Ilonen

Mikko Ilonen capitalized on a fine run of form which had seen him finish as a runner-up twice in his previous four events to win the Nordea Masters at Bro Hof Slott. It was the second time the 33-year-old Finn had won the title but his first win since doing so in 2007, the year of his only two victories on the European Tour. With Matteo Manassero looking to continue his winning form from Wentworth for the first two days, it was in the third round that Ilonen took control of the event and never looked back. Manassero opened with rounds of 66 and 65 to take a two-stroke lead over Ilonen, who followed a 70 with a 63. He then added a 65 on Saturday to take over at the top of the leaderboard. Two behind was Alexander Noren, the 2011 winner, while Manassero dropped to four back after a double bogey at the 18th.

On Sunday Manassero's approach at the ninth flew into the cup and bounced out again into rough next to the green. He saved par, but a rally for back-to-back victories did not occur. Instead, Ilonen's two-shot advantage was never narrowed. He birdied the second from three feet and the third from six feet. Another birdie on the 11th was followed by his only mistake of the round, a three-putt bogey at the 12th, but he chipped close at the 13th for another birdie. He closed with a 69 for a 21-under-par total of 267 and finished three ahead of Sweden's Jonas Blixt. A winner on the PGA Tour, Blixt had a rollercoaster back nine including four birdies, two bogeys and a double bogey as he finished with a 68. Bernd Wiesberger closed with a 66, after a third round of 64, to take third place, and Manassero shared fourth place with Noren, who had a 72, Thomas Bjorn and Rikard Karlberg. "It's pretty special," Ilonen said. "I felt a lot of support from Finland. It's been a long time since I last won, but I haven't forgotten how it felt."

Andrew Dodt became the first player on the modern European Tour to have two holes-in-one in the same round. The Australian started the second round at the 10th and then holed a six iron at the 175-yard 11th before making his second ace with an eight iron at the 208-yard seventh hole. After an opening 77, he still needed a birdie at the ninth for a 65 to make the cut. He received a box of champagne from the sponsors.

Lyoness Open
Atzenbrugg, Austria
Winner: Joost Luiten

Not even a hour's delay due to thunderstorms on the back nine of the final round could prevent Joost Luiten from collecting his second European Tour title at the Lyoness Open. The suspension came with Luiten on the 14th tee, but rather than put him off, it gave the 27-year-old Dutchman a chance to regroup. Upon the resumption, Luiten, dressed in his national colors of orange, picked up a birdie at the 16th hole and held on to win by two strokes over Thomas Bjorn at Diamond Country Club in Atzenbrugg, Austria.

Bjorn put in a fine charge on the final day as he closed with a 68, but after starting five back he could not get in front of Luiten. An opening 65 put Luiten in second place, two behind the nine-under 63 of England's Tom Lewis. Luiten then had a 68 to take a one-shot lead at the halfway stage, and after a poor start to his third round, he came home with five birdies on Saturday to lead by three going into the final day.

Despite two bogeys, both caused by three-putting, Luiten played steadily to close with a 71 for a 17-under-par total of 271. Romain Wattel, who had birdied four of the first six holes, and Wen-Chong Liang shared third place, one behind Bjorn, with Jorge Campillo and Paul Waring tying for fifth place.

"It's a great feeling and it's been a great week," said Luiten, whose first win came in the 2011 Iskandar Johor Open. "It was a long day and I started with a three-putt for bogey. But I was hitting the ball really nicely and I was just trying to hit the greens and two-putt and let the others chase me. I made a few mistakes on the greens, but after the birdie at the 16th I had a cushion and it was nice to finish with two pars to get the trophy. The break came at a good time because I wasn't playing that well. I had some food and tried to refocus, and then went back out to try to make par and sneak in a couple of birdies, and that's what I did."

Najeti Hotels et Golfs Open
St. Omer, France
Winner: Simon Thornton

Simon Thornton finally completed a journey that first saw him depart Bradford, England, for Northern Ireland with a seven handicap to eventually become a European Tour winner at the Najeti Hotels et Golfs Open. The 36-year-old, who is now an Irish passport-holder, beat South African Tjaart van der Walt at the first extra hole of a playoff at the Aa St. Omer Golf Club.

It was a weekend of firsts for Thornton, who had his first hole-in-one as a professional with a seven iron from 206 yards at the 11th hole on Saturday. Two holes earlier he had had an eagle and in high winds his third round of 65 moved him into a tie for the lead with van de Walt and Baptiste Chapellan. It was a remarkable turnaround for the former assistant professional at Royal County Down as after 27 holes he had been seven over par. On the final day, he and van der Walt closed with rounds of 70 to tie at 279, five under par, but Thornton was forced to hole from 10 feet at the last to join the South African in the playoff.

Back at the 18th in the playoff, van der Walt found a greenside bunker, but Thornton left his 30-foot birdie putt stone dead. After van der Walt missed from 12 feet for his par, Thornton tapped in for a victory with which to celebrate Father's Day. It was a bittersweet moment, however.

"It's so big for me," said Thornton. "On Father's Day, too, he passed away three years ago and it still hurts, but they are happy tears today. This is dedicated to him.

"I didn't play particularly well today in perfect conditions, but I got up and down when I had to and holed good putts. On the last putt in regulation, I had been saying to myself all day, if I'm going to make it easy for myself, I need to try on every putt and make sure it goes where you want to hit it. So I just picked a line and willed it in and it dropped."

BMW International Open
Munich, Germany
Winner: Ernie Els

On the 25th playing of the BMW International Open, Ernie Els replicated a feat achieved by the inaugural winner, David Feherty, in 1989. Along with Sandy Lyle in 1991, the trio have all won the event wire-to-wire. Els opened up with a 63 at Golfclub Munchen Eichenried to lead by one over a group of four players who included Martin Kaymer and Alexander Noren. Conditions were perfect for scoring, belying the tougher course the players returned to after the tournament moved to Cologne for one year in 2012.

Els completed the week with three rounds of 69 for an 18-under-par total of 270. After the second round the 43-year-old South African still led by one over Matthew Baldwin and Alexander Levy, but by the end of round three, which was delayed by torrential overnight and morning rain, he had been caught by Noren and Levy.

Levy, a French rookie, closed with a 71 and Noren a 72, but Els' biggest threat became two-time former winner Thomas Bjorn. The Dane birdied three holes in a row from the third to briefly take the lead, but Els responded with birdies himself at the fifth, sixth and eighth holes. Both men bogeyed the 11th, but while Els parred his way to the 18th, where he closed out the win with a two-putt birdie, Bjorn had three birdies and a double bogey at the 14th to finish second, one behind. Levy took third place, one ahead of Kaymer, Noren and Bernd Wiesberger, who all shared fourth place.

This was Els' first win in the tournament in six appearances, his 28th on the European Tour, but only his second in continental Europe after the 2003 European Masters. It was the seventh time in his career he had led from start to finish. Coming four weeks prior to the defense of his Open crown, Els said: "I've got to just start off with saying again, thank you to BMW for their continued support of golf in Europe, especially here in Munich. It's wonderful to have sponsors like that around the world, and especially on the European Tour.

"Obviously my play this week has been great, as we talked about how much tougher the course is, but I just felt good this week. I just felt my game was there and lucky enough it was one shot good enough. As always, when you get to my age, to get a win, it's a wonderful feeling."

Irish Open
Maynooth, Co. Kildare, Republic of Ireland
Winner: Paul Casey

Inspired by Justin Rose winning the U.S. Open two weeks earlier, Paul Casey claimed his 12th victory on the European Tour at the Irish Open on the Montgomerie course at Carton House. It was his first European title for two and a half years since the Volvo Champions early in 2011 but also only his second since the BMW PGA Championship in 2009. At that point Casey was ranked third in the world and in the opinion of many would be the next Englishman to win a major championship. However his career stalled due to a sequence of injuries including issues with a rib and then his big toe. He was divorced in 2011 and then missed much of the 2012 season due to a broken collarbone while snowboarding.

When he returned to action a weak shoulder hampered his swing, and having returned from America to play full time on the European Tour, he entered the Irish Open ranked 169th in the world. Rounds of 68, 73 and 67 left him four behind overnight leader Joost Luiten, who had won the Lyoness Open three weeks earlier. The final day featured howling winds, squally showers and sunshine, but Luiten collected his only birdie of the day at the last as he closed with a 74. Pablo Larrazabal, who was one behind Luiten, had a 75 to finish fourth, while Jose Maria Olazabal challenged early before falling into a tie for fifth. An exciting climax was in order after the four Irish major winners — Padraig Harrington, Rory McIlroy, Graeme McDowell and Darren Clarke — all missed the cut

Casey displayed the sort of explosive golf of old when he birdied four holes in a row from the eighth and made it five in six with another at the 13th. He dropped shots at the 15th and 16th holes but accepted that sort of misfortune would be common on such a day. At the 18th his drive leaked into the right rough almost behind a tree, but he had a clear swing and a good lie to belt a three iron onto the green, a marvelous stroke. He then finished in style by holing from over 60 feet for an eagle. His closing 67 gave him a total of 274, 14 under par, and a three-stroke win over Luiten and Robert Rock, runner-up in the event for the second time.

"I have always wanted a grandstand finish but never holed a putt like that to win a tournament," Casey said. "It feels like a first win again. I have struggled with the confidence, and this is a huge relief. Justin's victory was phenomenal. He's a good friend and I was so proud of what he did."

Alstom Open de France
Paris, France
Winner: Graeme McDowell

Graeme McDowell continued his run of "binary golf" while winning the Alstom Open de France at Golf National in Paris. It was his third win in a run of eight events dating back to the Masters in which he has also missed the cut five times: 0 1 0 1 0 0 0 1. He won the Heritage in America the week after the Masters, missed the cut at the Players but won the Volvo World Match Play Championship the next week. Before claiming his ninth European Tour win in Paris he had played only 36 holes at the BMW PGA, the U.S. Open and the Irish Open.

"Yes, it has been binary golf," said the 33-year-old Northern Irishman. "The three wins have been fantastic but the missed cuts have been important, too, because they have been my motivation. They have made me work harder and made me more hungry when I get in position to win. It's been an inconsistent season, but my good has been really good."

McDowell won by four strokes over South Africa's Richard Sterne, but the pair enjoyed a fine duel throughout the final round. The pair shared the lead overnight, but Sterne, who was out in three under helped by holing a putt from off the green and down a bank at the fifth, went to the turn one ahead thanks to McDowell's bogey at the seventh.

It was the Ulsterman who thrived on the back nine, however, with a birdie at the 10th to put him back even, while Sterne bogeyed the 12th and only just saved par at the 13th after going in the water. Dropped shots at the 16th and 17th holes, where McDowell picked up his second shot of the back nine, ultimately stalled Sterne's challenge, although McDowell had been relieved when his par putts at the 15th and 16th both dropped in the side door when he thought he had missed. "The crowd must have sucked the ball into the hole each time," he said.

With fierce rough, the National course was in superb condition, but scoring was only possible by driving the ball in the fairway as McDowell did all week with his trusty three wood. His rounds of 69, 69, 70 and 67 left him on a total of 275, nine under par. Sterne closed with a 71 to take second place by one over Graeme Storm and Eduardo De La Riva. Luke Donald finished at six over par after twice taking triple bogeys at the 18th, and Matt Kuchar, seeing the 2018 Ryder cup venue for the first time, at seven over.

Aberdeen Asset Management Scottish Open
Inverness, Scotland
Winner: Phil Mickelson

Phil Mickelson almost got out-Mickelsoned at the Aberdeen Asset Management Scottish Open, but the American hung on to win in exciting fashion at Castle Stuart. At the start of the final round, Denmark's J.B. Hansen had a quadruple-bogey-nine at the second hole after twice hitting into the gorse and taking penalty shots. He bounced back with five birdies in a row and six in seven holes, but a string of late bogeys dropped the youngster back to joint third place with Henrik Stenson.

Mickelson, meanwhile, started the final day two behind Stenson and had a double bogey at the first hole. Nevertheless, the 43-year-old was out in 33, and three birdies on the back nine put him in front of Branden Grace, who had four birdies coming home to set the clubhouse target at 17 under par. Yet Mickelson three-putted the 18th, and a late evening in the Highlands — for the benefit of NBC viewers of the first regular European Tour event to be screened live on American network television — got even later. "Nobody likes a movie that's predictable," Mickelson said. Both the playoff combatants closed with rounds of 69 for a total of 271.

Playing the par-five 18th again, Grace left his third shot 30 feet away while Mickelson produced a moment of pure magic with a chip from a bare lie to tap-in range. The birdie sealed the win after Grace missed his long attempt to force another hole.

"It's very special for me to have some success over here, in the Home of Golf," said Mickelson, whose only other success in Scotland was at the Dunhill Cup as part of an American team in 1996. In fact, while this was Mickelson's eighth European Tour victory, it was his first in Europe. His only other win on the continent was at the Perrier tournament at Disneyland Europe on the Challenge Tour in 1993.

"It's been the biggest challenges of my career, adapting to links style golf, and this was a great challenge for me this final round in some difficult conditions on firm ground. I played some good golf to come out on top, and this is really fulfilling and special.

"I don't think there's a better way to get ready for the Open Championship than playing well the week before and getting into contention, and coming out on top just gives me more confidence."

The Open Championship
East Lothian, Scotland
Winner: Phil Mickelson

See Chapter 4.

M2M Russian Open
Moscow, Russia
Winner: Michael Hoey

Michael Hoey produced a superb third round of 65 on the way to winning the M2M Russian Open at the Tseleevo Golf and Polo Club outside Moscow. An eagle, six birdies and just one bogey took the 34-year-old Northern Irishman from two behind the leader to five in front, and a 70 on the closing day was good enough to wrap up a four-stroke victory over Alexandre Kaleka, who scored a 68, and Matthew Nixon, who closed with a 69. Hoey finished at 16 under par on a total of 272 for his fifth victory on the European Tour. It also meant he had won in four of his last five years on the circuit.

"It's pretty amazing to think that I have won five European Tour titles," Hoey said. "It is a great feeling to win and every time you do it you just want more and more. Hopefully I can get at least another one before the end of the season. It has given me a great boost. I am not the most consistent player in the world, but when I get into these positions I usually do okay. But the next aim for me has to be to become a bit more consistent, because that is the only way I will be able to get back among the best players in the world and stay there."

Hoey's last win was at the Hassan Trophy in 2012, but so far in 2013 he had not been better than 25th and he had missed the cut in seven of his previous 10 tournaments. But he took a liking to the course in Russia. "I have absolutely loved the golf course this week," said Hoey. "It is a great Nicklaus design and one of the best we will play on tour for the whole year. The greens are just so pure, and when you have surfaces like that to putt on, then you can make a lot of putts.

"The putting was the key for me this week. I have been working hard on that a lot recently and the improvement is really showing because I'm making a lot of birdies. That is the main difference at this level — you have to be able to make a lot of putts, because the standard is so high these days that it usually comes down to who makes the most putts."

Johnnie Walker Championship
Perthshire, Scotland
Winner: Tommy Fleetwood

Two years after becoming the youngest player to win the Challenge Tour rankings, Tommy Fleetwood completed the journey to maiden winner on the European Tour with victory at the Johnnie Walker Championship. Played on the PGA Centenary course at Gleneagles which will host the Ryder Cup in 2014, Fleetwood, 22 from Southport, triumphed in a playoff against home favorite Stephen Gallacher and Argentina's Ricardo Gonzalez, who led or shared the lead for the first three rounds. Fleetwood and Gonzalez were the co-leaders after 54 holes and both closed with rounds of 70 to join Gallacher on a total of 270, 18 under par.

Gallacher, with a 67, had the most amazing final round with a bogey, a triple bogey at the 11th, five birdies and two eagles, including at the 18th where he holed from 15 feet. Moments earlier compatriot Scott Hendry had also eagled the last as he shared fourth place with Bernd Weisberger. Gallacher's three at the 18th had the spectators on the their feet, but Fleetwood, who had eagled the 16th, birdied the hole, as did Gonzalez, having very nearly holed his bunker shot for a three.

In the playoff at the 18th, Gallacher could not get up and down from a bunker, while Gonzalez three-putted from the back of the green. Fleetwood knocked in a four-footer for his birdie and the victory that was celebrated alongside his parents and Maisy, the family dog. Fleetwood, who had earlier returned scores of 68, 65 and 67 for the first three rounds, had struggled in his debut season on tour but settled in better in 2013 and had two top-10 finishes before his breakthrough victory.

"It is unbelievable," he said. "I've been out here on tour awhile and I haven't even had a top five the last two years. And then all of a sudden you come out with a win. I don't know how it happened, but it just seemed to come a bit easier this week. I was nervous as hell on the first green today, and after that, I felt pretty calm and I felt fine within myself. It was so tight, you couldn't really do much. It was a bit claustrophobic on the leaderboard. To win is just absolutely amazing. You look at all the winners on tour, and I'll admit I'm so jealous when somebody wins, but finally it's my turn."

ISPS Handa Wales Open
City of Newport, Wales
Winner: Gregory Bourdy

In a finish that would have been worthy of the climax to a Ryder Cup, Gregory Bourdy stole the ISPS Handa Wales Open away from Peter Uihlein with a trio of amazing putts on the final three holes of the Twenty Ten course at Celtic Manor. The venue for the 2010 Ryder Cup got another electrifying Europe versus America moment as the 31-year-old Frenchman overhauled the 24-year-old Uihlein, who started the season on the Challenge Tour before winning the Madeira Islands Open in May. Rounds of 69, 70 and 67 put Uihlein three clear of Bourdy, who had scores of 67, 72 and 70, and another Frenchman, Thomas Levet. Although Soren Kjeldsen also got into contention, finishing in third place in the end after a best-of-the-day 66, Uihlein birdied the 15th to lead Bourdy by one.

Then Bourdy started unleashing his putting magic. He holed from 50 feet from just off the back of the 16th green, made a 15-footer at the 17th and recorded his third birdie in a row with a 30-foot putt at the par-five 18th. A 67 put him on eight under par with a total of 276. Uihlein also birdied the 17th but needed to make a four at the last to tie. He had a 20-footer for his birdie, but rushed it past and missed the one back, so fell two behind the winner after a closing 72. "I put myself in with a chance with the birdies at 15 and 17," said Uihlein. "I didn't expect Gregory to birdie the last three holes. That's just great golf, so hats off to him."

It was Bourdy's fourth win on the European Tour but his first for almost five years. His timing was good with the qualifying starting for the European team for the 2014 Ryder Cup at Gleneagles.

"It was an amazing round," Bourdy said. "I started great with an eagle on the second, which gave me a lot of confidence for the rest of the round. Unfortunately I made two bogeys on 13 and 14, so I knew I needed some birdies and to finish with three in a row was amazing. I'm going to remember this finish for a long time. A lot of great moments have taken place here during the Ryder Cup, and I was thinking about that on the 18th hole when I was walking up the fairway. So I'm very proud to win this trophy at Celtic Manor."

Omega European Masters
Crans Montana, Switzerland
Winner: Thomas Bjorn

After a few weeks when his game had not been as he would have wished, and his frustration level was high, Thomas Bjorn could not have come to a better place than one of his favorite courses high in the Alps at Crans-sur-Sierre. Determined to smile through whatever happened, the 42-year-old Dane was left with a broad grin when he won the Omega European Masters for the second time in three years. Ultimately, patience won the day as he beat Scotland's Craig Lee at the first playoff hole with a birdie from 12 feet.

When he won in 2011, Bjorn was five under for the last five holes. This time it was on the front nine that he did the damage, making five birdies in an outward 31. He added one more birdie at the 15th to post 20 under par. He only dropped two shots all week and scores of 66, 66, 67 and 65 gave him a total of 264. On a rainy, misty day in the mountains, the clouds descended enough to cause play to be delayed for half an hour with the players still to play the final hole, but the interruption did not faze Bjorn.

"I came into this not feeling particularly great about my golf," he said. "But I've got a long-standing love relationship with this course. I've finished runner-up here twice and now won twice. It is a golf course that suits me. The one good thing about my game was my wedge game and you need that this week. I never really let myself down this week. I had that bit between my teeth that made me go that little bit extra."

Lee was the overnight leader by two strokes after a career-best round of 10-under 61 on Saturday. It was 10 strokes better than an opening 71 which had him sweating on making the cut, which came at one under. He made it comfortably with a 65 and then had a magical start to his round on Saturday with nine birdies in the first 10 holes (only making a par at the seventh). A bogey at the 12th stalled hopes of a 59, but he birdied the 13th and 14th holes before parring in. "It was pretty surreal to see all these good golf shots coming out in the same day," Lee said.

In the final round, Lee made four birdies in a 67, but his birdie chance at the last that would have given him the win lipped out. Having started the week at 108th on the money list, at least his card was assured for 2014.

KLM Open
Zandvoort, The Netherlands
Winner: Joost Luiten

Joost Luiten sparked some wild scenes of celebrations at the seaside links of Kennemer when he became only the second Dutchman to win the KLM Open. Ten years after Martin Lafeber's victory in his national championship, Luiten repeated the feat by beating Miguel Angel Jimenez in a playoff. It was a historic day for Dutch golf as Luiten's compatriot won the Kharkov Superior Cup on the Challenge Tour on the same day.

Jimenez, 49, was attempting to extend his record as the oldest winner on the European Tour and prove his broken leg, suffered while skiing during the winter, could not interrupt his success. He led after an opening 64, shared the lead on day two with fellow Spaniard Pablo Larrazabal, and only fell one stroke behind Luiten when the Dutchman added a 66 to his earlier efforts of 69 and 65. But four birdies in an outward 32 on the final day put Jimenez in front again until a bogey at the 15th. Both men bogeyed the 17th and Luiten settled for a 68 and Jimenez a 67 as they tied on 12-under 268.

Returning to the 18th for the playoff, Jimenez required a wood for his second and came up right at the front of the green. His long birdie putt came up six feet short and he missed the par effort to hand victory to

Luiten, who two-putted for a tidy par. "I was very solid all day but made a couple of mistakes in the playoff and got punished," Jimenez said. "But Joost played very well, he's a deserving winner. I gave it my best shot — and I'm still alive!"

"I'll never forget this day," said Luiten. "I came second here in 2007, which was a pretty special week. But this has topped that by quite a way. To win your national Open is an unbelievable feeling, I'm so proud.

"There were a lot of nerves jangling inside. I tried to stay calm and focus on my game, though it was very tough in the wind. I have to say the crowd were unbelievable all week. Even when it rained all day yesterday, they still came out to support me, and I'll never forget that. It makes it so much more enjoyable when you're playing in front of large crowds, because you know it means something and you want to do well for them. I'm just so pleased I was able to give them this win."

Open d'Italia Lindt
Turin, Italy
Winner: Julien Quesne

It was a special week for Francesco Molinari playing in the 70th Open d'Italia Lindt at Torino, the club where he first played golf at the age of eight. He put himself right in contention by sharing the lead at the halfway stage with rounds of 68 and 67, using all his local knowledge to good effect.

"Playing your national Open where you learned the game might only happen once in your lifetime, so I am trying to make the most of it," said Molinari, who won the title in Milan in 2006. His presence on the leaderboard helped to bring out huge crowds over the weekend, but Molinari perhaps put too much pressure on himself as the putts refused to drop. He closed with rounds of 71 and 75 to tie for 16th place but did excite the gallery on Sunday by holing a bunker shot at the eighth and making another birdie at the ninth. But he came home in 39 as third-round leader Marcus Fraser continued to head a packed leaderboard.

Fraser birdied the 13th hole to get to 12 under and take a two-stroke lead, but the Australian struggled over the closing holes as Julien Quesne made a superb charge to take victory. Quesne started four behind at the start of the day and it got worse after a double-bogey-six at the second hole. However, he got those shots back by the turn and then came home in 31 with birdies at the 10th and 11th as well as three of the last four holes. He made a birdie-four at the 15th and then holed a good putt to save par at the 16th. Just off the fringe at the front of the green at the 17th, the Frenchman chipped up the length of the putting surface and into the hole before hitting his approach to six feet at the last and making what would turn out to be the winning putt.

It got the 33-year-old to 12 under par and, after rounds of 70, 68, 71 and 67, left him on a total of 276. He was one clear of the earlier clubhouse leaders, David Higgins and former winner Steve Webster; moments later Fraser three-putted the 15th to give Quesne sole possession of the lead. As Quesne, who won the Open de Andulcia in 2012, cuddled his young child in the players' lounge, Fraser also bogeyed the 16th and 17th holes to finish tied for eighth after a 74.

"I am very proud of this back nine," Quesne said. "My attitude was very good this week and I think this is the key. After my double bogey I just kept calm. I thought, 'just keep working and we will see what happens.'"

Alfred Dunhill Links Championship
St. Andrews & Fife, Scotland
Winner: David Howell

In 2006 David Howell won his biggest of his then-four European Tour titles at the BMW PGA Championship and was ranked in the top 10 in the world. The wait for his fifth title lasted seven years during which the 38-year-old Englishman admitted to desperation both on and off the course. He slumped outside the world's top 500, but after marriage to Emily and the arrival of a son, with twins on the way, his form slowly improved after he rededicated himself to the game. It is fair to say that when he finally won again, at the Alfred Dunhill Links Championship at St. Andrews, it was a universally popular result, even with the man he defeated in a playoff, Peter Uihlein.

Uihlein, the 24-year-old American looking for a second title of the season, had a remarkable week. After an opening 71 at Carnoustie, Uihlein scored a 60 at Kingsbarns, his 25-footer for eagle at the last only just missing for the first-ever 59 on the European Tour. A day later he holed his second shot at the 18th of the Old Course for a 65 that put him two strokes ahead of a group of players which included Howell, Ernie Els, Shane Lowry and Martin Kaymer.

Howell opened with a 67 at Carnoustie, added a 68 at Kingsbarns and then a 63 on the Old Course. Five birdies back on the Old Course in the final round put him out in 31, and a 67 put him one ahead of Lowry, after a 68, and Tom Lewis, who closed with a 64 to save his card for the 2014 season. Howell was in the clubhouse at 23 under par with a total of 265, and Uihlein matched it with a closing 69 despite bogeying the first hole. Out in 34, the American birdied the 12th and then parred in to force the playoff. After both parred the first hole, Uihlein missed a chance from 15 feet on the 18th green only to see Howell hole from 10 feet for an emotional victory.

"It's been an interesting seven years," Howell said. "A lot of the ups and downs, and the downs were really pretty low. I lost my way in life and on the course, as well, but obviously it's a really sweet moment and life off the course life has never been better. To finally win a massive championship really seals things for me. I'm in a very happy place now — it really doesn't get much better than winning the Alfred Dunhill Links Championship at the Home of Golf."

Howell was partnered by British actor Hugh Grant in the team competition, which was won by Thomas Levet and his amateur partner David Sayer on 40 under par.

Seve Trophy
Paris, France
Winners: Continental Europe

A lengthy list of players from the winning 2012 European Ryder Cup team at Medinah, including Rory McIlroy, Ian Poulter, Luke Donald, Sergio Garcia and Martin Kaymer, were unavailable for the eighth playing of the Seve Trophy at Saint-Nom-la-Breteche. If the absence of some of the stars of the European game was the story leading into the match between Great Britain and Ireland, and Continental Europe, Nicolas Colsaerts and Francesco Molinari put their experience from a year earlier to good effect in Paris.

Molinari was in the last singles match at Medinah and earned a half point against Tiger Woods that ensured Europe won the Ryder Cup rather than just retained it. Molinari was again in the last singles and by holing a six-foot birdie putt at the 16th hole he defeated Chris Wood 3 and 2 and ended GB&I's six-match winning streak. Continental Europe won 15-13 for only their second victory, the first coming in the inaugural match at Sunningdale in 2000 when they were led by the man the event was named for, Seve Ballesteros.

Jose Maria Olazabal was the other link from Medinah, the winning captain then as now. "Obviously, I'm very emotional right now because this has been a tough day with everything going to the last match," Olazabal said. "But the boys played really well and I'm very, very happy to have won the Seve Trophy again after 13 years."

Olazabal's team got off to a great start by winning the first day's fourballs 3½-1½. Two tight sessions followed before GB&I, led by another former winning Ryder Cup captain in Sam Torrance, won the Saturday afternoon foursomes 3-1 and evened the contest at 9-9 going into the singles. France's Gregory Bourdy, enjoying his debut on home soil, and Dutchman Joost Luiten won all four of their matches together, with Bourdy going on to beat Scott Jamieson 4 and 3 in the singles to become the first player to win five matches out of five in the Seve Trophy. Luiten lost his singles to English youngster Tommy Fleetwood.

Simon Khan was forced to withdraw due to a back injury on the final day and Thomas Bjorn sat out as well having put himself "in the envelope" to allow his younger teammates to play instead. Colsaerts holed a five-footer at the last to win an important point against Paul Casey, while Gonzalo Fernandez-Castano claimed a half against Jaime Donaldson in the top match. When Marc Warren beat Thorbjorn Olesen 4 and 3, the match was still tied at 12-12.

However, Continental Europe led in three of the final four matches. Matteo Manassero duly beat Stephen Gallacher 3 and 2, and Miguel Angel Jimenez, after four birdies in the first six holes, beat an unwell David Lynn 6 and 4. Paul Lawrie, GB&I's only Medinah representative, beat Mikko Ilonen 2 and 1, to leave Wood, who replaced Khan in the anchor match, with an uphill battle against Molinari.

"This feels great for us," said Molinari. "I played the last two before this, and it's never good to finish on the losing side, so we tried really hard. It was funny yesterday when Olazabal was reading the list, I kind of knew I was going to be last, but I was waiting every name, hoping to hear mine, and I didn't until the 10th spot.

"I tried to stay away from the leaderboards as much as possible today, but then obviously you see everyone coming up to your match and watching you. I tried not to do the maths, but I realized that I needed a half a point, so I wasn't going to hit my putt too firm obviously on the 16th. But it's good to finish in style."

Portugal Masters
Algarve, Portugal
Winner: David Lynn

Having spent the 2013 season mainly in America following his runner-up finish at the 2012 U.S. PGA Championship, David Lynn took advantage of a late-season start on the European Tour to win for the first time in nine years. Lynn last savored victory at the KLM Open in 2004 but claimed his second title on his home circuit by taking the Portugal Masters at Oceanico Victoria. After opening with two rounds of 65, Lynn stumbled to a 73 in the third round to lie six strokes behind 54-hole leader Paul Waring. But a closing 63, 10 strokes better than the previous day, gave the Englishman victory by one stroke over South African Justin Walters.

Lynn, whose approach at the last cleared a water hazard by two feet, finished at 18 under par with a total of 266 that could not be beaten by those finishing behind him. Lynn began with two birdies and added three more in an outward half of 30. Although he dropped a shot at the 10th, four more birdies at the 11th, 14th, 15th and 17th left him in an unassailable position. A week before he had suffered from a virus while being hammered 6 and 4 by Miguel Angel Jimenez at the Seve Trophy, but this victory proved an early celebration of his 40th birthday a week later.

"I was really disappointed when I walked off the course yesterday and thought maybe I had played myself out of it," Lynn said. "Today was just a case of I've got to make as many birdies as I can. I really caught fire on the front nine, I was making everything I looked at."

Walters, who started the week in 126th place on the Race to Dubai, was highly emotional after finishing with four birdies in a row from the 14th and then parring the last with a putt of over 40 feet. He had lost his mother just two weeks before and his closing 66 ensured his card for 2014. "I just wanted to play and honor my mum and make her proud," Walters said. "The putts kept dropping and I kept hitting some decent shots, and the last one at the end, she made it for sure."

Overnight leader Waring finished tied for third place alongside Stephen Gallacher and Bernd Weisberger. Scott Jamieson, who was joint second at the start of the last round, dropped to a tie for 13th after a 72 that followed his 60 on Saturday, the 18th such round on the European Tour. For the second time in two weeks a player had a chance to score the circuit's first 59 after Jamieson went out in 29, collected seven birdies in eight holes and saw his chip at the 18th catch the hole but lip out.

ISPS Handa Perth International
Perth, Western Australia
Winner: Jin Jeong

See Australasian Tour chapter.

The Final Series

BMW Masters
Shanghai, China
Winner: Gonzalo Fernandez-Castano

Gonzalo Fernandez-Castano got his timing spot on, not only with his final-round charge to victory at the BMW Masters but in claiming the first event of the European Tour's Final Series. The four-event series added the BMW Masters, the WGC - HSBC Champions and the Turkish Airways Open as precursors to the DP World Tour Championship. Participation in two of the first three events was essential to play in the season-ending event in Dubai — Joost Luiten withdrew with injury after his opening tee shot, so it counted as an event played — while playing in all three would mean a 20 percent bonus in points gained from those events being added to their Race to Dubai tally prior to the final event. Victory at Lake Malaren not only gave Fernandez-Castano the huge first prize of £719,058 but meant he could play in the HSBC Champions the following week, also in Shanghai, when he was not otherwise qualified. "There's never a bad time for a victory, but this has been just perfect," said the 33-year-old Spaniard, who also gave his Ryder Cup qualification a boost in the right direction.

Young American Luke Guthrie, who was playing on an invitation, was the surprise leader for the first three days, a 65 in the first round giving him a three-shot advantage over John Daly, another playing on an invitation and just returned from elbow surgery. Guthrie went four ahead at the halfway stage but was caught by Rafael Cabrera-Bello on day three. Neither of the leaders fared well on Sunday, but Guthrie hung on to fourth place with a 71.

Fernandez-Castano was one behind at the start of the last round and followed up a third-round 67 with a 68 to win on 11-under 277. Francesco Molinari produced a brilliant charge with an eagle at the 13th followed by four birdies in a row for a 64 that put the Italian on 10 under alongside Thongchai Jaidee, who closed with a 66. Fernandez-Castano was level with Molinari until he made birdies at the 13th, 15th and 17th holes, chipping in for the last of those. He was three ahead playing the 18th but then drove into a bunker at the last and found more sand with his third shot. He eventually signed for a double bogey which kept him one in front. It was his seventh win on the European Tour, and his third in a tournament sponsored by BMW, having won the Asian Open in 2006 and the Italian Open, his last on the circuit, in 2012.

"I knew it wasn't going to be an easy round, especially the way I started. I started hitting the ball pretty bad," Fernandez-Castano said. "But my caddie kept me cool and told me how good I had been hitting the ball through the week, and I played fantastic after that. On the last I played too conservative and it was a fighting six at the end for sure."

WGC - HSBC Champions
Shanghai, China
Winner: Dustin Johnson

See Asia/Japan Tours chapter.

Turkish Airlines Open
Anatalya, Turkey
Winner: Victor Dubuisson

Even with a five-stroke lead going into the final round there would have been mitigating circumstances had Victor Dubuisson not gone on to win the inaugural Turkish Airlines Open. The 23-year-old Frenchman was looking for his maiden victory at a tournament offering a first prize of £725,962, with some of the greatest players in the game attempting to chase him down and with potential benefits including a huge jump up the Race to Dubai standings and even an invitation to the 2014 Masters by breaking into the world's top 50. Lesser characters might have crumbled, even before an outward half of nine successive pars that saw his lead cut to two strokes.

But Dubuisson held firm despite his lead disappearing totally when he dropped his only shot of the day at the 14th at the same time as Jamie Donaldson holed in one at the 16th, earning a million Turkish Airlines air miles, and Justin Rose, who like his playing partner had started eight behind, birdied the same hole. Dubuisson responded with three birdies in the final four holes to claim a two-stroke win over Donaldson, who closed with a 63. Donaldson missed a 20-footer for eagle at the last which would have put even more pressure on the leader, while Rose bogeyed the last for a 65 to finish four behind in a tie for third place with Tiger Woods, whose challenge stumbled with a couple of bogeys around the turn before he birdied four of the last six holes for a 67. Ian Poulter, the nearest challenger overnight, birdied four of the first 11 holes to get within two of the leader but faded for a 69 and joint fifth place with Raphael Jacquelin. Henrik Stenson finished tied for seventh place to retain his lead at the top of the Race to Dubai, while Rose slipped into second place.

Playing with Poulter and Dubuisson on the final day, Jacquelin could not have been happier for his young compatriot. On Saturday, he set a new course record of 62 at the Montgomerie Maxx Royal, but it was a 63, with nine birdies, on the same day that vaulted Dubuisson so far out in front. The former world No. 1 amateur, who turned professional in 2010, holed from 25 feet for a birdie at the 17th on the final day and then got up and down for a birdie-four at the last for a 69 and a 24-under-par total of 264.

"It hasn't sunk in that I just won such a big tournament," he said. "Tiger, Henrik Stenson, Justin Rose, they were all in contention with me today. So it's a really great feeling, and I'm really proud of what I did because it was the toughest golf day of my life. I played great on the front nine but I was struggling on the greens. On this course, level par is a good score, but with this level of players, you cannot win a tournament with a level-par score, even with a five-shot lead."

DP World Tour Championship
Dubai, United Arab Emirates
Winner: Henrik Stenson

Sheer brilliance from Henrik Stenson left the 37-year-old Swede as the undisputed No. 1 golfer on the European Tour. Victory by six shots in the DP World Tour Championship on the Earth course at Jumeirah Golf Estates in Dubai sealed his victory in the Race to Dubai, ahead of the man who pushed him all the way, Ian Poulter, who finished second in both the tournament and the ranking. Stenson created history by becoming the first player to win the FedExCup in America as well as the Race to Dubai. In the previous two years Luke Donald and Rory McIlroy had both topped the money list on the PGA Tour without winning the FedExCup before claiming the No. 1 spot on the European Tour. Stenson also became the first player to win the Tour Championship on the PGA Tour and the equivalent season-ending event on the European Tour (though for many years they were held in the same week).

It was all the more remarkable that Stenson was suffering from a wrist injury that badly needed rest but forged ahead despite playing in all four of the new Final Series events. After an opening 68, the Swede hit the front with an eight-under 64 in the second round and stayed at the top of the leaderboard with a 67 in the third round. His second 64 of the week wrapped up the title. He had four birdies going out, including an approach at the fifth to three feet, and then birdied the 12th and 14th holes. His approach at the 12th, a five iron from 190 yards up the hill and into the wind to 18 inches was only one of the shots of the day. He finished with an even better one, a three wood from 260 yards to a foot, for an eagle that put the exclamation point on an amazing sequence of results. Since he finished third at the Scottish Open in July, he had won three times — this was the only win on the European Tour — and finished in the top-three seven times, including at both the Open Championship and the U.S. PGA.

In Dubai, he missed only one green in regulation each day and his 25-under-par total of 263 was two shots lower than the previous tournament record set by Lee Westwood and matched by McIlroy. Poulter finished with back-to-back 66s to finish two ahead of Victor Dubuisson, the previous week's winner, with Joost Luiten fourth and Donald, McIlroy and Westwood tying for fifth place.

"I'm just very, very pleased with the way I played," Stenson said. "I knew it was going to be a tough week and I knew the guys were going to keep on charging and trying to catch me. Being in the lead, you want to play solidly and not make any silly mistakes. I had a couple of really good iron shots early in the round to set up three birdies in the first five holes. It was blowing pretty hard with a lot of sand in the air on the back nine. I was just trying to hit fairways and greens and make pars coming in."

South African Open Championship
Ekurhuleni, Gauteng, South Africa
Winner: Morten Orum Madsen

See African Tours chapter.

Alfred Dunhill Championship
Mpumalanga, South Africa
Winner: Charl Schwartzel

See African Tours chapter.

Nedbank Golf Challenge
Sun City, South Africa
Winner: Thomas Bjorn

See African Tours chapter.

Hong Kong Open
Fanling, Hong Kong
Winner: Miguel Angel Jimenez

See Asia/Japan Tours chapter.

Nelson Mandela Championship
Durban, South Africa
Winner: Dawie Van der Walt

See African Tours chapter.

Challenge Tour

For all the talented young American players who waltz straight onto the PGA Tour after turning professional, or get through via a year on the Web.com Tour, there were always others who got experience around the globe before making it big at home. Tom Lehman and John Daly were two good examples. But for the first time, some of the latest young Americans have decided to complete their golfing education on the European Challenge Tour, and the success of Peter Uihlein and Brooks Koepka will surely mean that more follow in their footsteps, especially with the qualifying tournament in America now only offering spots on the secondary circuit rather than direct access to the PGA Tour.

For Uihlein, a former U.S. Amateur champion, the chance to gain experience playing in different conditions about the world had an appeal, but it did not go as smoothly as he had expected. He went to the European qualifying school in both 2011 and 2012 and neither time gained his card for the full European Tour, and his season on the Challenge Tour in 2012 led to a 26th-place finish on the Ranking which meant a second season on a feeder circuit that is equally as far-flung as its more senior counterpart but with rather less glamour.

Still, the experience held the young American in good stead, and when he won the Madeira Islands Open, one of the two "double-badge" events, it meant an immediate exemption for the full tour — Ireland's Simon Thornton made the same journey by winning the Najeti Hotels Open. Uihlein admitted his experience had been an eye-opener. "When you're struggling, it's one of those things, you hate it when it happens but it's almost the best thing that could happen to you," he said. "It definitely was for me and I'm pretty happy with how things turned out. You grow up quick out here and that was the main reason I came over. It's been a good process so far and hopefully I can keep going." He did. He was second at the Wales Open and lost in a playoff at the Alfred Dunhill Links, during which he scored a 60 at Kingsbarns. The 24-year-old finished 14th on the Race to Dubai and was named the Sir Henry Cotton Rookie of the Year.

Koepka had little pedigree in the amateur or college game when he followed his close friend Uihlein onto the Challenge Tour after turning professional in July 2012. Within 11 months he, too, was on the main European Tour. He won once late in 2012, but three wins in seven events in May and June 2013 saw him earn a "battlefield promotion." The 23-year-old from West Palm Beach won the Montecchia Open in Italy, the Fred Olsen Challenge de Espana in the Canary Islands and then the Scottish Hydro Challenge, posting a course-record 62 at Macdonald Spey Valley in the process. "It was a big change for me, coming over here," he said. "I didn't know what to expect when I came, but I know what to expect now. I've learned so much in less than a year, more than I learned in college golf. It's been really good as a golfer and as a person too. I grew up in Florida where as soon as there is a drop of rain you are out of there, so you never play in bad weather. I used to be unable to stand playing in rain gear, but playing on the Challenge Tour I've now gotten used to it. It makes you a more complete player."

Italy's Andrea Pavan, who was second overall in 2011, led the Challenge Tour Ranking after wins at the Bad Griesbach Challenge and Open Blue Green Cotes d'Armor Bretagne. He clinched the top spot with a fourth place at the final event to return to the European Tour, where he lost his card after his rookie season in 2012. He was naturally delighted to jump right back up at the first opportunity. "It's a great accomplishment," said Pavan. "I'm so happy with how things turned out this year and I'm really looking forward to next year. I was proud to make such a good comeback. It's not easy to get back up and I showed that I can do it. It gives me a lot of confidence, especially because I do get down on myself sometimes, so I need to believe in myself a bit more."

Shiv Kapur, drawing on seven years of previous experience on the main circuit, became the first Indian to gain his European Tour card from the Challenge Tour after winning the first event of the year, the Gujarat Kensville Challenge, and the last, the Dubai Festival City Challenge Tour Grand Final. Four behind Pavan after eight holes of the third round, he led by four by the end of the day and kept that advantage the following day. "It was a tough week and I had to battle away," he said after graduating from only nine events. "I made it a little hard on myself this year not playing as many tournaments as some other players on the Challenge Tour, but I backed myself and told myself that if I played well enough I would make it back onto the European Tour. I have had five or six professional wins, but given the circumstances and everything leading up to the week, this one is right up there with the best of them."

Kapur jumped from 20th to fourth on the Ranking with his win, while Scotland's Jamie McLeary, who tied for second with Jose Lima, did just enough to grab the 15th, and last, card. "I worried that I would never make it to the European Tour, that I was one of those guys that was really consistent but without the big finishes at the big events that I needed," said the 32-year-old. "It has taken a lot longer than I thought it would, and the older you get the more nervous you get, but I've got my chance and I'm confident I'll take it."

The other players to earn their cards were Lima, who was second behind Pavan, Daan Huizing, a two-time winner, Johan Carlsson, Adrian Otaegui, Roope Kakko, Sihwan Kim, Tyrrell Hatton, Victor Riu, Robert Dinwiddie, Francois Camels and Nacho Elvira, who took the 14th spot after a final round of 66 at the Grand Final.

9. Asia/Japan Tours

Of all the promising young talents to emerge from Asia, Thailand's Kira-dech Aphibarnrat — perhaps to the surprise of some — stamped himself "Most Likely to Succeed" with a strong 2013 in which he won once and had enough other high finishes to top the Asian Tour's Order of Merit.

Aphibarnrat, 24, who turned pro in 2008, held on to take the Maybank Malaysian Open, shortened to three rounds by rain, by a stroke over Italy's Edoardo Molinari. The co-sanctioned event became his first win on the European Tour and his second on the Asian Tour, after the 2011 SAIL Open. Aphibarnrat also had two thirds, two fourths and two fifths, piling up $1.1 million to top the money list by almost double over second-place Scott Hend.

If nothing else, Aphibarnrat will go down as the heftiest young talent, at 5-feet-9 and some 225 pounds. "I don't work out a lot," he said. "I just try to play good golf. You don't have to have a good body for that." He's known as Asia's John Daly. He's portly and he has a bold game.

Australia's Scott Hend did everything but take the Order of Merit. He was the only multiple winner for the season, winning three tournaments to finish a solid second on the Order of Merit with $571,400. At the inaugural Changmai Golf Classic, Hend was saying he had no chance to win. "I was just hoping for a solid top-five finish," he said. But he came from six behind in the final round to win by three. He won by four in the Mercuries Taiwan Masters, battling 55 mph gusts in the final round. Then Hend, known for his big hitting, turned to his putter — averaging only 26.5 putts per round — to win the Venetian Macau Open by three shots. Said Hend: "Three wins in a year is definitely the best golf of my career."

Asian Tour players made progress on the Official World Golf Ranking, with 13 of them in the top 200. Thailand's Thongchai Jaidee went from 80th to 46th at the end of 2013. Finishing in the top 50 for the year won him his third berth in the Masters. Aphibarnrat finished 59th.

The real world left its mark on golf late in April when Americans Dustin Johnson and Zach Johnson (not related) and Spain's Alvaro Quiros skipped the Asian Tour's Ballantine's Championship at Seoul, South Korea, with North Korean leader Kim Jong Un threatening to launch nuclear missiles at South Korea, Japan and the United States. The tournament played on, though with a nervous field, and Australia's Brett Mumford ended a six-year victory drought with an eagle in a playoff.

On the OneAsia Tour, Australia's Matthew Griffin, a natural left-hander who plays right-handed, rode his victory in the SK Telecom Open to the top of the Order of Merit, with winnings of $257,480 on the nine-event schedule.

"I always try to set myself goals and this year was to win the OneAsia Order of Merit," Griffin said. "My main goal for next year is to try to do well in the [European and Japan Tour] co-sanctioned events and try to get some status there as well."

The OneAsia Tour had an awkward moment. The tour had scheduled a grand finale, the OneAsia Championship, a $2 million event at Mission Hills, near Shenzhen, China, early in December. But officials called it off late in November. Said the tour's announcement: "Unfortunately several of the targeted players already had commitments, so the first edition has been postponed until next year [2014]."

South Africa's Charl Schwartzel, the 2011 Masters champion, added another to his bag with his victory in the Nanshan China Masters. With Darren Clarke playing well, Schwartzel seemed to have no chance — until the final nine. Clarke slipped a bit and Schwartzel finished strong for a one-stroke win. Said Schwartzel, who didn't lead until Clarke's bogey at the 17th: "I never thought I was out of it, for any second."

Brett Rumford doubled up, adding the OneAsia's Volvo China Open to his Asian Tour Ballantine's. And reigning Masters champ Adam Scott returned home to take the Australian PGA Championship.

The Japan Tour season was almost all about Hideki Matsuyama, the now 21-year-old who gained international acclaim when he won the new Asian Amateur to qualify for and finish low amateur in the Masters in 2011 and 2012. The only player with more than one victory, Matsuyama rode four wins and impressive showings in three of golf's four major championships to an overwhelming capture of the Japan Tour money list in his rookie season.

Just the third man to top the ¥200 million mark in tour history, Matsuyama did it despite playing in only 13 of the season's 25 official events, although top-10s in the U.S. and British Opens and a tie for 19th in the PGA Championship embellished the total. He finished second by a stroke twice and was out of the top 10 just three times in those 13 starts.

South Korea's Hyung-Sung Kim, who won the Japan PGA Championship, was a distant second on the money list and one of only seven non-Japanese winners all year, two of them in the co-sponsored tournaments in March in Thailand and Indonesia. The other foreign victors in Japan were veteran Australians Brendan Jones and Brad Kennedy, China's Ashan Wu and international star Luke Donald, who ran away with the rich Dunlop Phoenix as defending champion. The other Japanese majors went to Masanori Kobayashi (Open) and Satoshi Kodairi (Tour Championship).

Shingo Katayama, the colorful, five-time money leader, scored his first victory since 2008 and finished third in the final standings, but Toru Taniguchi went winless for the first time since 2008.

The popular young Ryo Ishikawa, a regular on the U.S. PGA Tour, played in just four events in Japan during his winless season.

Asian Tour

Zaykabar Myanmar Open
Yangon, Myanmar
Winner: Chawalit Plaphol

The Asian Tour opened its 2013 season with the Zaykabar Myanmar Open late in February and, fittingly, hopes were blossoming all over Royal Mingalardon Golf and Country Club. There was, for example, Thailand's Kiradech Aphibarnrat, seeking to soothe the memory of a playoff loss a year ago and also his second tour victory. Joonas Granberg, one of three Finns in the field, was looking to bounce back after his struggle with personal problems in 2012. And a budding show-stopper, Mithun Perera, age 26, was hoping to make history as the first Sri Lankan to win on the tour. But then there was Thailand's Chawalit Plaphol, age 38, killing all dreams, and especially Perera's, with birdies on the last two holes to take his fourth tour title.

Plaphol took the lead in the third round and was leading much of the fourth until Perera, playing up ahead, charged to the front from five behind with five birdies over the last seven holes, closing with a seven-under-par 65. Plaphol tied him at the 17th, holing a 15-foot birdie putt, then hit a beautiful approach to three feet at the par-five 18th, setting up another birdie to tack a three-under-par 69 onto his card of 67-66-68 for an 18-under 270 to edge Perera by one.

"It wasn't smooth for me during the front nine because I was forcing myself to play it safe," said Plaphol. "I gave myself a bit of pressure and it felt better on the back."

Aphibarnrat, frustrated by a cold putter, shot 70 and finished third, two behind.

Said the disappointed Perera, who was 50th on the 2012 Order of Merit: "All you need is one good week to turn your life around. I think the win is not far away for me."

SAIL-SBI Open
New Delhi, India
Winner: Anirban Lahiri

The old axiom says there are courses for horses, but India's Anirban Lahiri was turning it into a real laugher. His victory in the SAIL-SBI Open was his third on the Asian Tour, and all three came on Delhi Golf Club, and all by playoffs. And on a course he used to hate. Now?

Said Lahiri, with a big grin: "I feel great winning here again."

This time it was looking like a youth parade until Lahiri, himself only 25, made a clutch 10-foot birdie putt at the final hole in regulation to tie fellow Indian Rashid Khan, 22, the clubhouse leader, then beat him with a birdie on the first playoff hole.

"I'm still in disbelief that I made the putt in regulation and got into the playoff," Lahiri said. "After that, in the next 15 minutes, I didn't know what happened." The final birdie capped rounds of 71-68-66-68 and tied Khan at 273, 15 under par.

Said Khan, a third-year player seeking his first win: "I knew it was going to be a playoff. I was prepared for it. But it didn't work out."

Lahiri came from five behind in the first round, climbed over Bangladesh's Siddikur in the fourth and dueled Khan down the final stretch, to the final birdie. Then came his third victory at Delhi — following the 2011 Panasonic India Open and the 2012 SAIL.

Delhi had become a course a guy could love. But why did Lahiri detest it at first? Because he had trouble keeping it on the course. Things changed once he took the hint and cut back on using the driver. "The key is to stay out of the bushes and hit it into the fairway," Lahiri said, echoing another old golf saying.

Avantha Masters
Noida, India
Winner: Thomas Aiken

Thomas Aiken figured the Avantha Masters had turned into a game of fox-and-hounds — with him starring as the fox.

"These guys just kept coming at me today," said Aiken. But he kept his head, and it helped that the pressure came from here, then there, and no one guy could get up enough steam to chase him down. So after smashing his way into the lead in the third round, he came rolling home with a comfortable three-stroke victory at the Jaypee Greens golf course in the Asian-European co-sanctioned event.

Aiken started with 67-69, then erupted with a 10-under-par 62 for the third-round lead. His strategy was simple. "I wasn't thinking about my score at all today," he said. He also largely ignored his driver, preferring to avoid fairway bunkers. Result: Eight birdies, an eagle and a seven-stroke leap into a three-stroke lead.

Aiken was six off in the first round, behind Thailand's Chinnarat Phadungsil (61), then four off at the halfway point, behind Thailand's Chapchai Nirat and Chinese standout Wen-Chong Liang, both with 66s. Then Aiken took over in the third round with his 62, but not without a fight. Liang got within three with a 69. "Anything can happen in golf," Liang said. As he proved in the final round. After three birdies in the first five holes, he double-bogeyed No. 6, then got the strokes back with a hole-in-one at No. 7, but didn't gain ground. India's Gangajeet Bhullar jumped in. Six shots back to start the last round, he got three birdies and an eagle in the first five holes, shot 64 and clinched a solo second place after Aiken closed with a flawless 67 and a 23-under 265.

"Nobody remembers the second-place guy," said Bhullar.

Said Aiken, of his three-shot win: "It was by no means a walk in the park."

Maybank Malaysian Open
Kuala Lumpur, Malaysia
Winner: Kiradech Aphibarnrat

"I couldn't eat anything," Thailand's Kiradech Aphibarnrat was saying. "When I walked out, everything was shaking, even my voice."

And it wasn't even his wedding day.

This was the portly Aphibarnrat, age 23, all 5-foot-8, 230 pounds of him. There had been another storm delay in the Maybank Malaysian Open, and now he had to come back out and face a chance to win. The situation couldn't be iffier for Aphibarnrat, known as Asia's John Daly, both for his style of play and his physique. He was not only nervous, and also tired from a thyroid problem, but he was troubled by the intense heat. And he would have to hold off some real threats in the Asian-European Tour co-sanctioned tournament, in a field top-heavy with Europeans. Coming down the closing holes, his biggest problem was Italian Ryder Cupper Edoardo Molinari, with Anders Hansen, Charl Schwartzel and others close behind.

The weather-battered tournament had been reduced to three rounds, and Aphibarnrat, who led through the first two, was leading by one through the 15th when play was suspended again.

He bumped his lead to two at the 16th on a birdie putt from four feet. He saved par at the 17th, holing a 15-foot putt after a weak chip. At the 18th, the win almost in hand, he played safe and hit an iron off the tee and bogeyed, but he could afford it, filling out a card of 65-68-70–203, 13 under, nipping Molinari by one for his second Asian win and first on the European Tour. That's when his words in the opening round came echoing back.

"I didn't set any goals," Aphibarnrat had said. "I didn't tell myself that I should finish in the top five or win this event. I want to take it shot by shot."

Chiangmai Golf Classic
Chiangmai, Thailand
Winner: Scott Hend

"To be honest, I didn't think I had a chance to win," Scott Hend was saying. "I was just hoping for a solid top-five finish."

Hend's game had two weaknesses: First, he underestimated himself, and second, he'd stay too close to the leaders. Give him some breathing room, and no telling where he might end up. Winning, for example.

Consider that the big-hitting Australian, age 40, had won twice on the Asian Tour, coming from behind in the final round each time — from five shots in the 2008 Indonesian Presidents and four in the 2012 ISPS Handa Singapore Classic. This time, he trailed through the first three rounds, shooting the Alpine Resort in 68-69-67, and was six behind entering the fourth. And here he came again, rocketing to an eight-under-par 64 for a 20-under 268 to win by three over South Africa's Bryce Easton.

"Obviously, it all fell together," Hend said. "Unfortunately for the other guys, they didn't quite keep pace." The most unfortunate was Thai veteran Prayad Marksaeng, who led from the start and was five up on countryman

Thongchai Jaidee and Aussie Matthew Steiger going into the final round. Then he shot 74 and finished third. Ernie Els tried the short putter for the first three rounds, then went back to the belly variety, but neither mattered. He tied for 14th.

Hend hurt his chances for that solid finish with a bogey on No. 3. Then off he went. He eagled No. 4, holing a 30-foot putt, then birdied four of the next five holes and outran the field. But some players are never contented.

"I never had the chance to lead from the front," Hend said. "I would love to lead into the last round by three and see if I can hold the guys off."

Panasonic Open India
New Delhi, India
Winner: Wade Ormsby

Wade Ormsby is a speed freak. But no hot car could provide the heart-in-the-mouth thrills he gave himself in the third round of the Panasonic Open India. How about expanding his lead to three shots with a birdie on the first hole, then blowing it all with four bogeys over the next eight? But the gritty Aussie held himself together and shrugged off a triple bogey in the final round to score his first pro victory in a wire-to-wire performance that nipped, of all people, Thai veteran Boonchu Ruangkit.

Ruangkit had come from three behind in the final round and, at 56, was verging on becoming the oldest Asian Tour winner ever. "I've shown that I still have what it takes to compete against the younger boys, but I just ran out of steam," said Ruangkit, second by a stroke after a closing 69.

Ormsby shared the first-round lead on a five-under-par 67, then led the rest of the way with rounds of 67-74-71, for a nine-under 279 total at Delhi Golf Club. It was his first win since turning professional in 2001.

"I've played tournaments worldwide, but to finally get a win in Asia is fantastic," said Ormsby, veteran of the Australasian Tour and the then-Nationwide Tour. "It means so much." Ormsby survived that four-bogey front nine in the third round and retook the lead with a birdie at the 18th after Singapore's Lam Chih Bing suffered a four-bogey collapse down the stretch. In the last round, Ormsby birdied the second but triple-bogeyed the third. Then he rebounded with birdies at Nos. 5, 7 and 8, and finally locked it up on an 18-foot birdie putt at the 17th.

"I knew there was a win here for me," Ormsby said. "I'm glad I came here."

Solaire Open
Manila, Philippines
Winner: Wen-Tang Lin

Taiwan's Wen-Tang Lin was playing well, doing the right things — good tee shots, good approaches, good putts. But just in case she should desert him, he went the extra step and paid tribute to the one friend every golfer courts feverishly. "I think," Lin said, "that Lady Luck is really on my side to let me win this tournament."

Lin had a point. It seems the Grand Dame showed up at the inaugural Solaire Open when he needed her most. He had shared the lead in the second round and held the solo lead through the third, but late in the fourth, the tournament was slipping away. Heading to the 17th at windy Wack Wack, he was trailing Thailand's Thammanoon Sriroj. He proceeded to hit his tee shot into the trees. But he managed to punch a nine iron to the green, setting up only his second birdie of the round. Lady Luck beamed on him again at the 18th. This time he hit a branch with his second shot, but again hit a low punch shot that ended up 15 feet from the flag. He holed that putt, too, for the par that gave him a one-stroke win over Sriroj and Canadian rookie Richard Lee. It was his sixth Asian Tour victory, the first since 2009.

Lin played Wack Wack in 69-73-70-73, tying for the lead in the second round after American rookie Dodge Kemmer awkwardly went 66-79. Lin led by one in the third, then settled into a struggle with Sriroj and Lee, winning on a three-under 285 total, again tipping his cap to Lady Luck for that clinching putt. Said Lee: "Second or third place are the same. The only difference, if you are the champion."

Ballantine's Championship
Seoul, South Korea
Winner: Brett Rumford

Brett Rumford called it a "rollercoaster day," and so it was — right out of Disney World. Make that a rollercoaster two days. How about running off 11 birdies in a stretch of 14 holes from the third round into the fourth, squandering a two-stroke lead with a double bogey with two to play, scrambling to tie, then winning with an eagle in the playoff?

Five straight birdies to close the third round and six birdies over the front nine in the fourth had him on his way to his first win in nearly six years, his fourth overall. But first, trouble.

"I seemingly had everything under control, and I was thinking, it's just two good drives coming home...," Rumford said. But it wasn't that simple, and so the drama was on in the co-sanctioned Asian-European Tour Ballantine's Championship at Blackstone. "I battled today with my driver, leaking a few drives," he said. The worst came at the 17th — a bush, an unplayable lie and a double bogey that erased his two-shot lead. He missed the fairway at the par-five 18th as well and had to make a 10-foot putt to save par. He shot Blackstone in 73-67-69-68 to tie Marcus Fraser (68) and Peter Whiteford (69) at 11-under 277.

The playoff went back to the 18th and was brief. Fraser and Whiteford both missed the green, and Rumford fired a sensational second to six feet. He dropped the putt for an eagle and the victory.

And Rumford thanked his coach, Pete Cowen, who was watching on TV in the United Kingdom. He gave Cowen a quick call before the playoff. "Just to say, hey, Pete, just give me a one-minute lesson, mate, before I go on," Rumford said. The tip worked. Rumford hit the fairway.

CIMB Niaga Indonesian Masters
Jakarta, Indonesia
Winner: Bernd Wiesberger

It must have been like one of those nightmares for Bernd Wiesberger, the kind where you can't get away.

There was Wiesberger, coming down the final stretch with his second Asian Tour victory almost in hand, and just when he thought he was pulling away with the eagle at the 12th, along came the monster who was chasing him — in this case, the formidable Ernie Els, his playing partner — making an eagle of his own at the same hole. The hot breath of the devil was still on his neck. But it turned into a sweet dream for the tall Austrian, with just enough spice at the end to quicken one's pulse.

"It was good to hole the eagle," Wiesberger said, "and it was nice that Ernie stayed in touch. He wouldn't let go, and that's why he is such a great champion." Wiesberger pulled two ahead with a birdie at the 16th and went on to wrap up Royale Jakarta Golf Club in 67-72-67-67–273, 15 under. Els got within a stroke with a birdie at 18.

"I played with Bernd for three rounds and I think he played better than all of us," Els said. "I think he deserves to win."

Wiesberger and Els both had to come from back in the pack. They entered the final round a stroke behind Japan's Daisuke Kataoka, who reminded himself — fatally, perhaps — "This is the first time I'm leading a tournament." He managed to gather himself to finish third, his best finish since turning pro in 2007. Wiesberger launched his final round with a birdie, but bogeyed the fourth and got tied by Els' birdie at the sixth. Wiesberger moved ahead with birdies at the eighth and ninth, then arrived at his moment of truth at the 12th.

Queen's Cup
Samui, Thailand
Winner: Prayad Marksaeng

It had to be in the cards. This was Prayad Marksaeng's week. The big clue was the third round. If he could survive that, then the fates had something special in mind for him — his seventh Asian Tour win, and his first since 2007, and that was a long time for such a talent.

But the fates made him earn it in the final round, and he responded with two eagles, shooting Santiburi Samui Country Club in 71-64-68-67–270, 14 under, and a three-stroke victory that wasn't as cushy as it looked.

"I've come close to winning here, but couldn't finish the job previously," said Marksaeng, an elder statesman at 47. He'd had three top-three finishes and all the frustration that went with them. This edition was looking like more of the same. Marksaeng didn't lead until he won it. It was a strange outing, especially the third round. "It was a rollercoaster day, and on the 14th I misjudged my shots and made a real mess of it," he said. Consider that he birdied the first three holes, then bogeyed the next two. And so it went. It all climaxed at the 14th, which he chopped up for a triple bogey.

Marksaeng's final round also was hardly routine. He made two birdies and two bogeys and was at even par through the seventh. Next, he eagled the par-five eighth, ran off nine pars, then eagled the par-five 18th as well for the 67 and the comfortable-looking win. In the process, he raced over Bangladesh's Siddikur, the third-round leader, fading fast to a 77, and his toughest foe, fellow Thai Arnond Vongvanij (69).

"When Arnond bogeyed the 12th, I had a feeling that this would be my week," Marksaeng said.

Wasn't it already in the cards?

Worldwide Holdings Selangor Masters
Petaling Jaya, Selangor, Malaysia
Winner: Pariya Junhasavasdikul

Thailand's Pariya Junhasavasdikul ran the full gamut of the champion — from tossing and turning all night to a case of the shakes. But he got it all sorted out in time to hoist the trophy of the Worldwide Holdings Selangor Masters.

"I'm still shaking right now," said Junhasavasdikul, who noted the same reaction when he scored his other Asian Tour win in 2010. "Walking down the last three holes, there was tremendous pressure." The pressure came mainly from India's Anirban Lahiri, who finished ahead of him with a 68 and the clubhouse lead of eight-under-par 276.

South Korea's Seuk-Hyun Baek dogged his good friend across Seri Selangor Golf Club shot-for-shot until the pressure got him down the final stretch, leaving Lahiri the last real challenger. Finally, it came down to Junhasavasdikul needing a par at the last hole, and for that, he had to get up and down after missing the green. He got up okay. Next, the putt. The answer came from watching the putts of his playing partners, Baek and Malaysian amateur Gavin Green, and so something of a calm came over him.

"I didn't feel any pressure then," Junhasavasdikul said. "I kept to the routine and got it over with."

Junhasavasdikul went coast-to-coast, shooting 66-68-71-70, leading Baek by a stroke for the first three rounds, then edging Lahiri by one on his nine-under 275 total. That 68 in the second round included two eagles, the first at No. 6 on a 12-foot putt, the second at No. 13 from eight.

About the sleepless night: "I started thinking what would happen if I won," Junhasavasdikul said. "And then it hits me that I've not won it yet. I reminded myself that I still had to play 18 holes and it took the pressure off a bit."

Omega European Masters
Crans Montana, Switzerland
Winner: Thomas Bjorn

See European Tours chapter.

Yeangder Tournament Players Championship
Chinese Taipei
Winner: Thaworn Wiratchant

The state of Thaworn Wiratchant's approach game at the Yeangder Tournament Players Championship was such that he thought he was wasting his time. In the second round alone, he hit just four greens. "I was really struggling with my irons," the veteran Thai said. "I honestly didn't think that I could win."

Maybe change the adage to "Beware the golfer with the sick irons." Wiratchant, 46, resigned himself to chipping and putting his way around Linkou International. When he finally looked up, to his surprise, he had his Asian Tour record 16th win. He won by a stroke over Korean-American Chan Kim, 23, who taught himself an expensive lesson. The big-hitting rookie took the lead with a four-under-par 68 in the third round. "I just told myself to stay patient and keep grinding," he said. But he ignored himself down the final stretch. "I got a little greedy," he admitted. "I tried to get myself a shorter club into the green." He bogeyed three straight from the 15th, shot 70, and cost himself his first win. The Philippines' Angelo Que, with only 21 putts in a 66, finished third.

Wiratchant's irons were shaky from the start in his 69-67-71-68—275 tour of Linkou. He led only once, by a stroke after the second round. He trailed Kim by one going into the fourth, made two birdies and a bogey against Kim's eagle and birdie and was three behind through No. 4. Wiratchant came back from a rain delay with birdies at Nos. 5, 6 and 13. Kim birdied the 10th, then "got a little greedy."

Said a surprised Wiratchant: "I didn't think I could have won, but he started to drop shots and all of a sudden I was in the lead and I won."

Asia-Pacific Panasonic Open
Osaka, Japan
Winner: Masahiro Kawamura

See Japan Tour section.

Mercuries Taiwan Masters
Chinese Taipei
Winner: Scott Hend

It isn't often a golfer can shoot a two-over-par finish and win. Maybe more to the point, it isn't often that a player can post five over and finish second. But that was one way to measure the wind — and who could handle it — at the Mercuries Taiwan Masters.

It was Australian veteran Scott Hend, 40, fresh from playing in breezy Scotland, who managed the treacherous elements best as Typhoon Fitow approached Taiwan Golf and Country Club early in October.

"I wanted it to blow, but I didn't want it to blow that hard," Hend said, chuckling. "I thought, if the wind blows, it'll be hard for somebody to shoot in the low 60s and try to catch me. The only problem was for me not to shoot high 70s."

Hend shot 69-72-70 under less blustery conditions earlier. Said Hend, after taking the first-round lead: "It's only Day One. I wouldn't want to talk about my chances now, but let's see how it goes once we get to Sunday."

Came Sunday, and it was as though Hend scripted the final round. He entered leading American Sam Cyr by one, and battled gusts that hit 55 mph for a superb two-over 74 and a three-under 285 total. Cyr ballooned to a 77, but under the circumstances that was good for second place, if four shots back. Thailand's Thaworn Wiratchant, with a 71, was the only one of the 53 finishers to break par, and no one matched it. There were two 73s and five 74s — one of them Hend's.

It was Hend's fourth Asian Tour victory, and it had a certain luxury about it. In the first three, he had to rally. Not this time. "It's nice to win from the front instead of always coming from behind," Hend said.

CJ Invitational
Seoul, South Korea
Winner: Sung Kang

Sung Kang enjoyed fellow Korean K.J. Choi's hospitality when he played on the PGA Tour in the United States, then he absolutely embraced it back home in Korea at the CJ Invitational hosted by K.J. Choi. Which is to say, Kang, 26, ran away with his second Asian Tour victory.

"Maybe I'll wake up tomorrow and the winning feeling will sink in," said Kang, after breezing through Nine Bridges Golf Club for a five-shot win. And why did it mean so much? Kang thought back to his days as a Korean kid in the U.S., trying to find his way in golf. "I lived very near to K.J.," he said. "We had dinners together and he would give me a lot of advice."

In a tournament with rounds suspended by weather and carried over, Kang came to the top in the fragmented third. Sweden's Richard Karlberg, looking for his third tour win, finished in failing light and was the club-house leader at eight under, while Kang was 11 under through the 16th when he left the course. He finished his round the next morning and held a two-stroke lead, and then it was all but over a short while later, early in the final round. Kang birdied four straight from No. 3, then made his way home carefully.

"I felt comfortable after nine holes," Kang said. "I saw I had a big lead, so I was able to play it safe." He wrapped up a card of 68-69-69-70–276, 12 under and five ahead of Korea's Tae-Hoon Kim and India's Jyoti Randhawa.

As to the host — Choi, who won the first two CJ Invitationals, was off his game, never challenged in this one and tied for 21st.

Venetian Macau Open
Macau
Winner: Scott Hend

Once big-hitting Aussie Scott Hend got his putter working, no one was going to turn him off in the Venetian Macau Open — not even Big Easy Ernie Els. So ring up victory No. 3 of the season.

"Thursday was a difficult day, mentally and physically," said Hend. "Then on Friday and Saturday, I started holing putts, which I haven't done the whole year, even when I won a couple of weeks ago."

Hend, who didn't even seem to be in contention through the first two rounds, was in command the rest of the way and averaged only 26.5 putts while shooting the Macau Golf and Country Club in 74-64-63-67–268, 16 under par, for a three-stroke win over India's Anirban Lahiri. Lahiri leaped over Els (67) and the Philippines' Elmer Salvador (66) with a closing 62, tying the course record.

Els, arriving less than 24 hours from the tournament start, was four over on his first seven holes, then birdied four of his last 10 for a par 71. "It was a tough start," Els said. He was three out of a three-way tie for the lead, and Hend, with a shaky 74, was six behind. Hend didn't seem like the same player who won the Mercuries Taiwan Masters by four shots just two weeks ago, and the Changmai Classic by three back in March. He took the lead by four with the 63 in the third round. "Just played a little bit better today," he said.

Els didn't go quietly. Two quick birdies in the final round pulled him to within two until Hend birdied the fifth and seventh. Then he birdied the ninth against Els' bogey, and was on his way.

"Three wins in a year is definitely the best golf of my career," Hend said. "The year hasn't finished yet."

CIMB Classic
Kuala Lumpur, Malaysia
Winner: Ryan Moore

The CIMB Classic, an Asian Tour tournament but now also the first official PGA Tour event in Asia, left Ryan Moore feeling like a million bucks — actually, $1.26 million — and Phil Mickelson feeling like a weekend golfer.

First Mickelson: "I'm swinging awful," he said, after an opening one-under-par 71 at Kuala Lumpur Country Club that included wild drives and two double bogeys. "I would go hit balls, but I don't know what to try to fix," he said. He wasn't the only big name in distress, what with the WGC - HSBC Champions coming up in Shanghai the following week. Most prominently, Nick Watney shot 74, Ernie Els 76 and Bubba Watson 78.

Moore, on the other hand, crafted a nine-under 63 to lead the first round by two, and from there played tag with such as Keegan Bradley and Sergio Garcia, with rounds of 72-69-70, and ended up in the final hunt with Gary Woodland and Kiradech Aphibarnrat, the latter bidding to become the first Thai to win on the PGA Tour.

In a final round hampered by rain and weather delays, Moore and Chris Stroud started out sharing a one-stroke lead over Woodland and Kiradech. A double bogey at No. 9 sank Stroud. He would tie for third with Kiradech, who could only par in after bogeying the 10th. Woodland led with three early birdies, and Moore caught him at the turn. Both had two birdies and a bogey down the stretch, Moore shooting 70, Woodland 69, to tie at 14-under 274. In the playoff, forced by darkness into Monday, Moore holed a five-foot putt for a birdie and the win, his third on the tour and first since 2012.

Said Moore: "Playing in a playoff against Gary, I know I don't want it to last too long."

WGC - HSBC Champions
Shanghai, China
Winner: Dustin Johnson

It wasn't long after Dustin Johnson won the World Golf Championships - HSBC Champions at Shanghai, the biggest win of his career to date, that the subject of winning a major came up. "You know what?" Johnson said. "If I play like I did this week, I'm going to win one, for sure."

Johnson didn't have a major yet, but if he played like that, he would probably win a bunch of them. Question: How does one shoot 66 with two double bogeys? Answer: By making lots and lots of birdies. And he certainly did that. The growing golf cognoscenti in China witnessed a display at Sheshan International that ranged from brilliant to baffling, with Johnson shooting 69-63-66-66 for a 24-under 264 total and a three-stroke win over Ian Poulter that was in question until the final six holes.

"Those guys put a lot of pressure on me," said Johnson, including Graeme McDowell in the final mix. "I'm really proud of the way I handled myself."

Johnson did it well. The tournament nearly got away from him in the final round after streaks of brilliance: In the first round, an eagle and two birdies on the front nine, then a double bogey at the 13th. In the second, six birdies through the first seven holes, then four birdies coming home for a 63. In the third, a birdie at No. 3, then five straight from No. 5, then four straight from the 13th bracketed by double bogeys at the 10th and 18th.

Johnson broke away from Poulter and McDowell in the final round with birdies at the 13th and 14th, an eagle at the 16th, and a birdie at the 17th to lock up the win.

"Hopefully," Johnson said, "there's just better things to come."

Hero Indian Open
New Delhi, India
Winner: Siddikur

Bangladesh's Siddikur was paired with Americans Keegan Bradley and Bubba Watson — not exactly timid golfers — in the recent CIMB Classic in Malaysia, and came away a changed man.

"They played very aggressively," Siddikur said. "Most players can hit the ball, but not all of them can play like them. Since then, I've been trying to play more aggressively, and the results seem to be showing." That was Siddikur's revelation after tying with five others at 66 for the first-round lead in the Hero Indian Open. India's Rahil Gangjee, in that mix, was taken by surprise. "I had no idea that Siddikur was on six under," he said.

Siddikur was showing everyone he could go low. He pulled away with 66-67 in the middle rounds and was leading by four going into the fourth. There, he survived a shaky finish and a 75 for a 14-under 274 and a one-stroke win over Anirban Lahiri, seeking his fourth win, and S.S.P. Chowrasia, his third. It was Siddikur's second career win, after the 2010 Brunei Open.

Siddikur didn't try to protect his four-shot lead in the final round, and perhaps it cost him. He birdied Nos. 2 and 5, but bogeyed four out of six holes around the turn. Birdies at the 13th and 14th looked good, but then he triple-bogeyed the 15th and bogeyed the 16th. He finally retook the lead with a 15-foot birdie putt at the par-three 17th, and that got him his winning margin. The shaky stretch wasn't nerves, he said, but playing aggressively to hold off the pursuit. Anyway, he had a new outlook. He said he was playing for money and trying to save his card back when he won in 2010.

"But now I am not playing for money," Siddikur said. "I am playing to achieve something."

Resorts World Manila Masters
Manila, Philippines
Winner: Wen-Chong Liang

China's Wen-Chong Liang faced that old argument — to keep the pressure on or turn conservative and protect the lead? There's no one simple answer. Liang picked conservative this time, and it nearly cost him the Resorts World Manila Masters as the 2013 Asian Tour was winding down.

Liang, returning to the Philippines after a five-year absence, shot the par-72 Southwoods in 67-69-67 and led by a stroke. In the final round, birdies at the third and fourth holes upped that margin, and he was feeling more secure. But he bogeyed the par-three fifth, and trouble really hit when he double-bogeyed the par-four ninth. It was a sobering experience. He went back to his aggressive play, and coming in flashed the game that made him China's top golfer. He ran off birdies at Nos. 11, 13, 15 and 18, and tied Thailand's Prom Meesawat, who had finished.

Meesawat trailed Liang by four entering the final round, and charged to a flawless 65 and the clubhouse lead at 16-under 272. He'd have had his second Asian Tour win if his 10-footer at the 18th had just dropped. But it burned the hole and stayed out. Liang stepped through that open door. He needed that birdie at the 18th to tie, and he got it on a seven-foot putt for a 69 and a matching 272.

The playoff, at the par-five, 554-yard 18th, went one hole. Liang put his approach just beyond the fringe. Meesawat put his into a bunker, 40 yards short of the green. He blasted out and chipped to 12 feet. Liang, using his wedge, putted to within a foot and tapped in for his winning birdie.

In a touching gesture, Liang pledged half of his winnings to victims of Typhoon Haiyan, which had devastated parts of the southern Philippines about two weeks earlier.

Indonesia Open
Jakarta, Indonesia
Winner: Gaganjeet Bhullar

India's Gaganjeet Bhullar, clearly having shaken his recent problems, was on his way to a wire-to-wire victory in the Indonesia Open. But it took a little heat to get him out of a par rut and let him roll to his first win since late in 2012 and his fifth on the Asian Tour.

Bhullar had opened the final round tied for the lead with Thailand's Jazz Janewattananond, newly 18, and when Jazz began to falter, Bhullar settled into par golf. He ran off 10 pars in a row, and suddenly there was pressure. Malaysia's Nicholas Fung, 23, and Thai veteran Chapchai Nirat were closing fast.

Bhullar, who opened with 64-67-69, got cracking after that string of pars and birdied Nos. 11, 13 and 14 for a bogey-free 68 and a 16-under total of 268 at Damai Golf. He won by three over Fung and Nirat. Fung started the day five off the lead and was out in 32. He made only one bogey and birdied the 17th under great pressure, blasting a 30-yard bunker shot to two feet, and shot 66. He tied at 271 with Nirat, who started four off the lead and charged down the stretch, making eagle at the 13th and 17th, both par-fives, but bogeying the 15th. He also shot 66. Jazz, another of the promising young Asians, wobbled in the rain-interrupted final round. A bogey at No. 7 and a double bogey at No. 9 knocked him out of the running. He closed with a 74 and tied for sixth.

"I haven't had much success this season," Bhullar said, "but I know my game was up there, and winning is just a matter of time. I waited so long for my fifth win..."

Hong Kong Open
Hong Kong
Winner: Miguel Angel Jimenez

With apologies to Omar: "A good cigar, a jug of wine and thou..."

The "thou" in this case was the Hong Kong Open, and the cigar and the wine surely tasted all the sweeter that Sunday night to Spain's Miguel Angel Jimenez, connoisseur of both, after he came from back in the pack and took his second straight Hong Kong Open and fourth overall, and in a playoff. And in the process, he became — at the age of 49 years and 337 days — the oldest winner on the European Tour and the second oldest on the Asian Tour in the co-sanctioned event. It was also his career 20th win.

"It just gets better and better," said Jimenez. "I love Hong Kong and this course. This is my fourth, and it was my hardest."

It was an uphill fight all the way for the jovial Spaniard. With 70-67-65, he trailed David Higgins by six in the first round, Jbe' Kruger by four in the second, and Stuart Manley by two in the third. The final was a scramble.

Jimenez ended up chasing Thailand's Prom Meesawat, who had two eagles and two birdies and would have won except a bogey at the 14th cost him the decisive stroke. He finished with 65–268, 12 under at Hong Kong Golf Club. Jimenez rang up five birdies but a bogey at the 15th gave him a 66, which tied Meesawat. Manley joined them with a wild six-birdie, four-bogey 68. Then Jimenez made short work of the playoff. On the first extra hole, Meesawat's approach reached only the edge of the green and Manley bounced his off a hospitality tent. Jimenez put his second 15 feet from the cup and holed the birdie putt for the win.

Said Jimenez: "My experience paid off."

Thailand Golf Championship
Chonburi, Thailand
Winner: Sergio Garcia

Free-spirited Sergio Garcia knew how it felt to be shut out for a season and he didn't want to go through it again. But here he was, in mid-December, with one last chance in 2013 at the Asian Tour's Thailand Golf Championship. And down the final round, his last real challenger was Henrik Stenson, the surprise world golfer of the year but now, as he said, running on fumes.

Garcia, maybe still a bit skittish since May, after blowing The Players Championship on the last two holes, thought for a while he was in trouble when he really wasn't. "I made three very important birdies on the first three on the back nine and gave myself a little bit of a cushion," Garcia said. Actually, when he bogeyed the seventh after Stenson birdied the fifth, he still was leading by two. Then the burst of three straight birdies from No. 10 boosted him to a four-stroke lead. He wrapped up the win — his fourth on the Asian Tour — shooting Amata Spring Country Club in 68-65-65-68 for a 22-under 266 total and a four-shot win over Stenson. "I've had a great year," said Stenson, the first to win both the FedExCup and the Race to Dubai, "but came here really on the fumes left in the tank, not much going for me."

Garcia surfaced in the second round with a 65, sparked by hole-in-one at the par-three No. 8, to tie Justin Rose for the halfway lead. Then he took a grip on the tournament with a one-bogey 65 in the third round for the four-shot lead.

"I'm very, very happy," Garcia said. "I can't wait to go back home to Switzerland and kind of sleep on it a little bit."

OneAsia Tour

Thailand Open
Bangkok, Thailand
Winner: Prayad Marksaeng

Native son Prayad Marksaeng, the very epitome of the streaky golfer, kicked off the OneAsia Tour's 2013 season by turning the Thailand Open into a national holiday.

After trailing most of the way, Marksaeng put on a rousing finish to become only the third Thai and the first since 2004 to win Thailand's national championship. It was also his career sixth victory, but first since 2008. It left him in tears.

"This means so much to me," Marksaeng said. "Yes, I cried a bit. I am happy the King's Trophy will stay in Thailand." It wasn't a cakewalk, however. Australia's Scott Strange, strong all the way, bogeyed the last to finish two behind. Marksaeng's finish did the trick. He stuck close with 68-67-65 through the first three rounds, and he started the final round two off the lead and closed with a 64 for a 24-under-par 264 total and the two-shot victory. Marksaeng streaked his way to this one. He came to everybody's attention when he opened the third round with five straight birdies, shot 65, and tied for sixth, two off the lead going into the final round. He started humming again in the final round, starting with three straight birdies. He stumbled to a bogey at the easy par-five fifth, then ran off four more birdies around the turn. He all but locked up the win with a chip-in birdie at the 16th. Then his chasers obliged by falling short.

"I have waited so long for this," Marksaeng said. "It is something I have dreamed about, but I have tried so many times and failed. This time, it was my turn."

Then Marksaeng did what any loyal son of Thailand would do to mark the great moment. After the prize presentation at the 18th green, he jumped into the lake.

Enjoy Jakarta Indonesia PGA Championship
Jakarta, Indonesia
Winner: Ho-Sung Choi

Korea's Ho-Sung Choi entered the final round of the Enjoy Jakarta Indonesia PGA Championship trailing by a shot, but with the next best thing to a lock on the title. The leader, it developed, had already written himself off.

Japan's Kaname Yokoo birdied the last hole in the third round and much to his dismay found himself with the lead, whereupon he announced: "I have no pressure and I'm not nervous because I don't think I will be able to win this tournament." Bunched just a shot right behind him were six players delighted to hear the news, but it was Choi who would weather a three-hour storm delay in the final round and come back out and birdie the 18th to win.

"I can't believe it," said Choi, 40. "I thought we might not be able to finish. I really didn't want to have to do it all over again tomorrow." He guaranteed it with his gutsy finish, upping his one-stroke lead to a two-stroke victory with the clutch birdie that ended a week of stifling March heat and humidity at Emeralda Golf Club. On a card of 67-70-65-67, a 19-under 269 total, Choi trailed three different leaders through the first three rounds, and by as much as six shots in the second.

Choi leapfrogged into the lead in the fourth round with an eagle at No. 1. But an hour ahead of him, the Philippines' Juvic Pagunsan birdied the last two holes to give Choi a 66 to look at. Choi birdied the 12th and 13th, slipped behind with a bogey at the 15th, but birdied the 17th before the storm hit. Three hours later, he was dropping an eight-foot birdie putt at the last for the comfy win over Pagunsan, Korea's Young-Han Song and, sure enough, the doomsayer, Yokoo.

Volvo China Open
Tianjin, China
Winner: Brett Rumford

For caddie John "Ronnie" Roberts, it was a birthday present that kept on giving. That takes some explaining:

Roberts signed on with Australia's Brett Mumford for 2013, and the mix worked beautifully. Rumford won the Ballantine's Championship, his first victory in nearly six years. The following week, Roberts' birthday fell on the second round of the OneAsia-European Tour co-sanctioned Volvo China Open at Tianjin Binhai Lake Golf Club early in May. "It was in my mind," said Rumford, "that it would be nice to shoot 67 on Ronnie's 67th birthday." And so he did. The 67, accompanied by a bottle of 17-year-old scotch, worked magic. Two rounds later, Rumford had his second victory in two weeks, this one by a comfy four shots. The two victories lifted him from a remote 253rd to 76th in the World Ranking.

Rumford trailed through the first two rounds and led the rest of the way in a solid performance marked by bursts of brilliance — five straight birdies in the second round, three in the third, three in the fourth. He was bogey-free in two rounds and had just two each in the other two, shooting 68-67-69-68–272, 16 under.

"It's surreal," said Rumford. "I'm more than pleased, but it's not my doing completely. I have a great team around me."

Meanwhile, the Chinese youth movement, paced by Tianlang Guan, 14, the youngest to play in and also make the cut in the Masters, marched on. Ze-Cheng Dou, 16, became the youngest to make the cut in the China Open, tying for 34th. And Wechong Ye, 12, became the youngest ever to play in a OneAsia or European Tour event. He missed the cut with 79-79–158, tying for 149th out of 155.

GS Caltex Maekyung Open
Seoul, South Korea
Winner: Hyun-Woo Ryu

Golfers like to say you can't win a tournament in the first round, but you sure can lose it there. Precisely what Hyun-Woo Ryu was afraid of. But he was in for a shock at the GS Caltex Maekyung Open. He did win.

"I am really pleased," said Ryu, with his second victory as a pro. "I didn't think I had a chance after starting with a 72." That was a par 72 that left him feeling rather alone in a crowd in the first round. Korea's Min-Gyu Cho and Australia's Terry Pilkadaris shared the lead at 64, and 59 others who caught Nam Seoul Country Club under ideal May conditions stood between them and Ryu and his fellow par-shooters.

Ryu soon enough enjoyed a more encouraging lonely feeling. A 65 in the second round lifted him to within three of Hyung-Sung Kim's halfway lead, and a 67 put him atop the pile by one in the third. In a late skirmish in the final round, Ryu had the experience of his first victory — on the Japan Tour the previous year — to bring him through the crunch.

In an all-Korean finish, Ryu, Do-Hoon Kim and Hyung-Sung Kim were tied for the lead coming to the par-three 17th. The two Kims missed the green and Ryu flushed a six iron to within five feet — bogey-bogey-birdie. And Ryu had a two-shot lead with one to play. The extra stroke came in handy. Ryu bogeyed the 18th, shot 14-under 274 and beat them by one.

Meanwhile, China's Minghao Wang was giving himself a nifty graduation gift. Wang graduated from Georgia Tech just the week before, turned pro, and not only made the cut in his debut, he tied for 46th.

SK Telecom Open
Jeju-do, South Korea
Winner: Matthew Griffin

If Australia's Matthew Griffin ever retires from golf, he might want to take up reading the future for fun and profit. He was dead on at the SK Telecom Open.

This was Griffin after a dazzling par-save at the final hole in the third round: "That was huge ... that could be the difference at the end of the tournament."

How right he was. "Big" wasn't the word. As things developed, that was the end of the tournament. The next day, a dense May fog enveloped Pinx Golf Club and wiped out the final round, leaving Griffin with his second OneAsia Tour title within a year. The headliner, native son K.J. Choi, a standout on the U.S. PGA Tour, was in the chase until he triple-bogeyed No. 7.

"It's unfortunate to finish like this, but I'll take it," said Griffin, 29, who won his first in the Charity High 1 Open the previous September. The 2011 Telecom also was ended by fog. Griffin didn't luck into this one. Shooting the par-72 Pinx in 64-67-72–203, he led Wook-Soon Kang by one in the first round, trailed Chang-Yoon Kim by one in the second, and outlasted Kang by one for the win after his amazing save at what proved to be the final hole. In the stiff winds of the third round, when only 10 players could break par, Griffin started bogey-bogey but got the strokes back with a chip-in eagle from 40 yards at the par-five No. 9. He parred in from there, ending with his spectacular finish.

At the tough par-four 18th, the wind carried his approach off the back edge of the green, 40 feet from the flag. Then he holed the putt. It was a par one day, the winner the next.

Nanshan China Masters
Nanshan, China
Winner: Charl Schwartzel

South Africa's Charl Schwartzel wrote a certain irony into a week early in October. Schwartzel came from behind to win the 2011 Masters — his only win on the PGA Tour — and two years later, he came from behind to win another Masters, the 2013 Nanshan China Masters.

Schwartzel played Nanshan International handily in the third round and was still three back. "At least I'm not far behind," he said, "so hopefully I can find something ... and at least give Darren a run."

But going down the final round, Schwartzel was running out of time, holes and hope. He had mentioned one other thing. "We all know the game, and sometimes it changes overnight," Schwartzel had said. This time, it changed over a few holes. Northern Ireland's Darren Clarke, who hadn't won since taking the 2011 Open Championship, had surged into a tie for the third-round lead with China's Wen-Chong Liang, with Schwartzel tied for sixth.

Clarke looked solid with the finish line just on the horizon. Then trouble hit. First, he missed a three-footer for par and bogeyed the 13th while Schwartzel was coming on. After an early birdie-bogey exchange, Schwartzel shot the last 10 holes in four under, with birdies at the ninth, 12th, 15th and 16th. The difference-maker came at the par-three 17th, where Clarke had to chop his tee shot out of heavy rough and bogeyed.

Schwartzel, now one ahead, parred the last two holes for a nine-under 209 on rounds of 71-72-68-68 for a one-stroke win over Clarke and Liang. Both closed with 72s.

Said Clarke, who needed 66 putts over the first two rounds: "I couldn't buy a putt from anywhere."

Said Schwartzel, who didn't lead until Clarke's bogey at the 17th: "I never thought I was out of it, for any second."

Kolon Korea Open
Cheonan, South Korea
Winner: Sung Kang

A win is a win, philosophers like to say. But no amount of logic could make this one feel completely good for Sung Kang in the Kolon Korea Open. That's because his old friend, Hyung-Tae Kim, was about to win until, with two holes to play, he was informed that he had incurred a two-stroke penalty for grounding his club in a hazard earlier. The penalty knocked

Kim a shot behind, into a tie for second, and Kang, who started the final round seven shots off the lead, had his second victory in two weeks. He won the CJ Invitational on the Asian Tour the week before.

"I'm a really good friend of his," Kang said, "so at the moment it doesn't feel great. Even though I won, I just feel really sorry for him."

Kim and playing partner Soon-Sang Hong were on the 17th tee when a rules official informed them they had been penalized two strokes for grounding their clubs back at the 13th.

Kang did his part. After shooting Woo Jeong Hills in 68-70-73 in the first three rounds, he entered the final round a discouraging seven shots off the lead. He rallied, then birdied four holes down his final nine, including the one at the 18th for a 69 and a 280 total for a one-stroke edge over, among others, his pal, Kim (77) and the tournament headliner, world No. 6 Rory McIlroy (67).

"I could have shot anything, absolutely anything," said McIlroy, who rallied in the final round after struggling from the start. "I only missed two greens and had so many chances."

The tournament closed with an ironic twist. Kang signed for his 69, then went out to congratulate his pal, Kim, and ended up with the trophy. "I don't know what to say," Kang said.

Australian PGA Championship
Gold Coast, Queensland
Winner: Adam Scott

See Australasian Tour chapter.

Emirates Australian Open
Sydney, New South Wales
Winner: Rory McIlroy

See Australasian Tour chapter.

Dongfeng Nissan Cup
Shenzhen, China
Winner: China

China's vice captain Jun Cheng said it as well any anyone after the first round of the Dongfeng Nissan Cup. "I felt," he said, "we were like high school players up against college students." That was after the Asia-Pacific Select side breezed past China, 4½-1½ in the opening fourballs of the Ryder Cup-like competition. He was merely echoing the prevailing assessment of Chinese golfers. China had lost the first two Dongfengs, and although they were coming fast, they didn't seem ready yet for the world stage. Three days later, Peter Thomson, five-time British Open champion and captain of the Asia-Pacific side, was offering a different view. "I am very impressed with the progress they have made," Thomson said. "They are ready to take on anyone."

Compliments don't get much rosier. What triggered this one was China's rousing comeback to take their first victory in the young competition. The Chinese rallied in the second-round foursomes to cut their deficit to one point, then surged in the final-round singles for a dramatic one-point win, 12½-11½. The Chinese won on the last hole of the last match on the course. Dong Su, playing in summery shirt sleeves despite the chilling rain, missed winning the cup when his four-foot putt at the 17th slipped by, keeping Scott Laycock alive. But at the 18th, after Laycock missed his 20-foot birdie try, Su holed a four-footer for a half and the win, touching off a wild celebration in his teammates.

One match drew particular attention. In what could be a preview of what's to come from China, Zecheng Dou, a 16-year-old amateur, walloped the Thai veteran Thaworn Wiratchant, 4 and 3.

"I said last week that when it comes to golf, China has been asleep for 40 years," Thomson said, "but they have certainly woken up now."

Japan Tour

Thailand Open
Bangkok, Thailand
Winner: Prayad Marksaeng

See OneAsia Tour section.

Enjoy Jakarta Indonesia PGA Championship
Jakarta, Indonesia
Winner: Ho-Sung Choi

See OneAsia Tour section.

Token Homemate Cup
Nagoya, Mie
Winner: Yoshinobu Tsukada

After two decades as a golf professional and 12 seasons on the Japan Tour, persistence finally paid off for Yoshinobu Tsukada in the Token Homemate Cup, the circuit's homeland opener following its earlier joint events in Thailand and Indonesia.

"This is a new start for me," exclaimed the 43-year-old player after he had finally broken the victory ice with an impressive, four-stroke victory at Token Tado Country Club in Nagoya.

The week didn't begin particularly well for Tsukada. His opening, one-over-par 72 left him in a tie for 77th place, but just six off the lead. When conditions toughened Friday, his even-par 71 jumped him into a tie for 12th and he raced within a stroke of third-round leader Kunihiro Kamii with a sparkling, 21-putt 63 for 206. Aided by an albatross-deuce on the par-five 17th, Kamii shot 62 when, like Thursday, low scores were a dime a dozen.

It turned windy Sunday, but Tsukada handled the pressure of going for the long-sought first win well with a solid 69 for 275. It was a four-shot victory over Kamii, who slipped to 74, and Koumei Oda, the first-round co-leader with Atomu Shigenaga and Steven Conran, who shot 71 for his 279.

Tsuruya Open
Kawanishi, Hyogo
Winner: Hideki Matsuyama

Hideki Matsuyama took a further step at home in stealing some of Ryo Ishikawa's thunder as Japan's No. 1 young star while the current shining light of the country's golfers campaigned primarily in America. Also just 21, Matsuyama picked off a victory in only his second start as a professional on the Japan Tour, a one-stroke triumph in the Tsuruya Open.

The win embellished Matsuyama's brilliant amateur record that includes a Japan Tour victory in the 2011 Taiheiyo Masters and wins in the first two Asian Amateurs that led to a pair of impressive low-amateur performances in the U.S. Masters Tournament in 2011 and 2012.

Before Matsuyama rocketed into contention in the Tsuruya Open with a Friday 63 at Yamanohara Golf Club, the stage belonged to 66-year-old World Golf Hall-of-Famer Masashi (Jumbo) Ozaki, who shot an amazing 62 — an eagle, nine birdies and two bogeys — and led the opening round by three strokes before eventually fading to a 51st-place finish.

South Korean Tae-Hee Lee, a 28-year-old newcomer to the tour, shot rounds of 65 and 67 Friday and Saturday for 198 and led by two over Matsuyama, Kodai Ichihara and Juvic Pagunsan after 54 holes. But Matsuyama showed his mettle Sunday when he birdied the final four holes for 66 and the winning, 18-under-par 266, two better than American David Oh, who also closed with 66 to nab second place.

The Crowns
Togo, Aichi
Winner: Michio Matsumura

The biggest questions as The Crowns tournament entered its final round focused on Hideki Matsuyama and Shingo Katayama. Would Matsuyama, the new young sensation, make it two wins in his first three pro starts on the Japan Tour? Or would Katayama, five times the circuit's leading money winner, end a victory drought dating back to 2008? Michio Matsumura made both answers "no" by matching Matsuyama's closing 67 and snatching his third career win by a stroke with his two-under-par 278.

Matsuyama (72-67–139) had the lead at the halfway mark and Katayama (72-68-69–209) took it away from him after 54 holes. Meanwhile, Matsumura stayed in the thick of contention two behind Katayama after rounds of 71-71-69. Matsuyama and Australia's Steven Conran were another shot back.

The 29-year-old Matsumura gained the upper hand early in Sunday's round. Matsumura, whose first two wins in lucrative 2010 tournaments helped him finish fifth on the money list, birdied four of the first seven holes. Conran made five on the front nine, but stumbled badly coming in. He shot 70 and tied for third with Katayama, who slipped to a disappointing 73. Matsuyama's 67 gave him second place, his third top-10 and strengthened his position as leading money winner.

Japan PGA Championship
Sobu, Chiba
Winner: Hyung-Sung Kim

Going into the final round nine strokes behind Hideki Matsuyama, the sensational rookie who already had a victory and a runner-up finish early in his first pro season on the Japan Tour, Hyung-Sung Kim seemed to be in a hopeless position insofar as winning the Japan PGA Championship was concerned.

In a classic example of the principle of "it's never over until it's over," Kim shot a closing, front-nine 29, a final five-under-par 65, posted 279 and waited in the clubhouse an hour for Matsuyama and the other contenders to finish. Matsuyama, who carried a four-stroke lead into the final round with his eight-under-par 205, surprisingly slumped Sunday with a 75 and fell a shot short of Kim when he bogeyed the final hole. That dropped Matsuyama into a three-way tie for second at 280 with Yoshinori Fujimoto (68) and Hiroyuki Fujita (69), the 2012 money leader.

It was the second Japan Tour victory for Kim, who seemed to have blown his victory chances with a third-round 75 before his blistering comeback Sunday at Sobu Country Club in Chiba Prefecture. The South Korean's only other win in Japan was in the 2012 Vana H Cup KBC Augusta in a season when he had three runner-up finishes and placed eighth on the money list.

Diamond Cup
Oarai, Ibaraki
Winner: Hideki Matsuyama

The elder statesmen of the Japan Tour gave notice that they were still viable contenders, but youth was again served in the Diamond Cup tournament as 21-year-old Hideki Matsuyama continued the remarkable start of his professional career with his third circuit win and second of the 2013 season.

Before Matsuyama wrapped up the victory and embellished his astonishing debut-season record to two victories, two seconds and a 10th in his first five starts, he had to fend off, among others, three of the aging all-time top five money winners on the circuit — No. 2 Shingo Katayama, 40; No. 3 Tsuneyuki (Tommy) Nakajima, 58, and No. 5 Toru Taniguchi, 45.

Just a few weeks after 66-year-old No. 1 Masashi (Jumbo) Ozaki startled the golf world with a 62 opening round in the Tsuruya Open, Nakajima, his long-time rival in earlier seasons, mounted the best challenge against the brilliant young Matsuyama at Oarai Golf Club. He linked 68-66 middle rounds to jump into a first-place tie with Matsuyama at 208, and after eight holes Sunday, the 48-tournament winner led Matsuyama by a stroke. However, a double bogey at the ninth dropped him a shot behind.

Matsuyama then birdied the 10th and finished with seven pars and a bogey for 71–279, seven under par, and a two-stroke victory over Australian Brad Kennedy and South Koreans Sung-Joon Park and Hyung-Sung Kim, who had nipped him two weeks earlier in the Japan PGA Championship. Nakajima bogeyed three of the last four holes for 75 and sixth-place finish with Katayama, a shot behind Taniguchi at 212.

Japan Golf Tour Championship
Kasama, Ibaraki
Winner: Satoshi Kodaira

Satoshi Kodaira sent out signals that something special might be on the horizon in the weeks before the Japan Golf Tour Championship, the season's second major event. Finishes of fifth and sixth place in his two previous starts primed the 23-year-old for the lucrative, one-stroke victory, the first of his three-season career.

The key to the win that vaulted Kodaira to second on the money list was his eight-under-par 64 in the second round. It carried him from 25th place into the runner-up slot, a stroke behind South Korea's Eun-Shin Park and his 69-64–133. Scoring went up on a rainy Saturday that brought a thunderstorm-induced two-hour, 35-minute suspension of play, and Kodaira slipped a shot in front with his 70–204. Trailing by one were Thailand's Kiradech Aphibarnrat, South Korea's S.K. Ho and Hiroyuki Fujita, the 2012 money leader and 15-time career winner.

Surprisingly, it was Ho and Aphibarnrat rather than Fujita who mustered the biggest threats to Kodaira in the final round. Kodaira got off to a fast start with four birdies on the first six holes, but after 11 holes found himself in a three-way tie with Ho and Aphibarnrat. Aphibarnrat fell back when he bogeyed the 13th and 15th holes, and Ho dropped a shot at the 17th as Kodaira parred in for the one-shot win. Fujita gave up five strokes on the last three holes and, with 77, dropped to 22nd place in the final standings.

Gateway to the Open Mizuno Open
Kasaoka, Okayama
Winner: Brendan Jones

There was nothing unlucky about Brendan Jones' 13th victory on the Japan Tour. The win not only ended his somewhat drab showing that far into the 2013 season with his first triumph in Japan in a year, but also gave him a spot in the year's Open Championship at Muirfield.

The 38-year-old Australian, one of the most successful overseas players over the years in Japan since he first won in 2002, was spot on all the way at JFE Setonaikai Golf Club at Kasaoka, Okayama Prefecture. Just a shot off the lead behind Yasuharu Imano after the first round, Jones duplicated Imano's opening 66 on Friday, edged into the lead by a stroke and marched to a 19-under-par 269, three in front of runner-up South Korean K.T. Kim, the No. 1 player in 2010.

Jones continued his run of sub-70 rounds with a 68 Saturday, sitting two ahead of Kim, who birdied three of his final four holes for 67–203. The key shot in Jones' 68 finish Sunday came when he holed a bunker shot for eagle on the par-five sixth hole to extend his lead to the three-shot margin he carried to his second Mizuno victory.

"I felt like I was in control of the tournament all weekend," said the Aussie afterward. "That doesn't happen very often."

Nagashima Shigeo Invitational
Chitose, Hokkaido
Winner: Shunsuke Sonoda

Shunsuke Sonoda had no reason to feel optimistic when he teed off in the Nagashima Shigeo Invitational SEGA Sammy Cup in Hokkaido. January surgery on his left knee had kept him on the shelf until the end of May, and in his four starts since then Sonoda missed three cuts and tied for 31st in the other one. He sat 149th on the money list, a far cry from his rookie 2010 season when he won his only tournament and finished in the No. 10 spot. On the other hand, Sonoda had tied for first and lost in a playoff that year on the same North Country Golf Club course.

No overtime in 2013. Sonoda produced a stunning, 11-under-par 61 in the third round and went on to a three-stroke victory, 20 under par at 268. The ¥30 million prize, largest of the season at that point, lifted him all the way to fifth place on the money list.

Hiroyuki Fujita, 44, No. 1 in 2012 and 15 times a winner but erratic earlier in the season, started fast. He led by one at the midpoint after rounds of 64 and 71. Sonoda was five back at 69-71–140, then caught fire. On Saturday, he birdied five of the first seven holes and polished off the 21-putt round with birdies on the final six holes. At 201, he led Fujita (68) by two, then fashioned a solid outgoing 32 Sunday afternoon and breezed to 67 and the three-shot win over Tomohiro Kondo (65) and Yuki Kono (66).

Kansai Open
Hyogo
Winner: Brad Kennedy

Brad Kennedy had a choice: Go for a Queensland double or return to Japan for the Kansai Open when the Japan Tour resumed play after a six-week hiatus. The 39-year-old Aussie had won his home-state PGA Championship earlier in the year and would have had a good shot in the Queensland Open. Instead, he opted for the Kansai Open, the tournament with the smallest purse of the year in Japan.

He must have known something. He picked up his second win in Japan and only had to go 54 holes at Olympic Golf Club in Hyogo Prefecture to do it. Bad weather forced cancellation of the final round and Kennedy, the 54-hole leader, was declared the winner. His 10-under-par 206 gave him a one-stroke victory over South Korea's Sung-Joon Park.

Park and three others — Kaname Yokoo, Yasuharu Imano and Byung-Jun Kim — led the first day at 68, with Kennedy in an eight-man jam at 69. In a surprising turn of events, amateur Yujiro Ohori, one of the other 69 shooters, jumped in front with 68-137. Yuta Ikeda (70-68) trailed by one with Kennedy (69-70), Park (68-71) and three others another shot back. Kennedy's 67 Saturday proved the winner as Park shot 68 and Azumo Yano, who was in 110th place after a first-round 76, finished third with follow-up scores of 65 and 67. Ohori shot 74 and tied for ninth.

Vana H Cup KBC Augusta
Shima, Fukuoka
Winner: Sung-Joon Park

Wet weather continued to plague the Japan Tour in late August. For the second straight week, officials were forced to shorten a tournament to 54 holes as the fringes of a typhoon stretched the second round of the Vana H Cup KBC Augusta over two days and allowed only a single round Sunday.

The beneficiary was South Korea's Sung-Joon Park, coming off a runner-up finish the previous Sunday in the Kansai Open and sporting second- and fourth-place showings earlier in the season. The 27-year-old Park, co-leader after the first two rounds, polished off his initial victory in Japan with a final-round, three-under-par 69 at Keya Golf Club. His 204 gave him a two-stroke win over fellow countryman Jung-Gon Hwang.

Before the rains came, Park shot 67 Thursday and shared the lead with Yuki Inamori. His second-round 68-135 kept him on top, tied with Yoshinori Fujimoto and Satoshi Tomiyama (67s). While Park was racking up four birdies and a bogey for the victory, Fujimoto slipped into a third-place tie with a 72 and Tomiyama fell to seventh with a 74. The win jumped Park to third place on the money list.

Fujisankei Classic
Fujikawaguchiko, Yamanashi
Winner: Hideki Matsuyama

He made it exciting at the end, but Hideki Matsuyama won for a third time in his sensational rookie season when he returned from abroad for the Fujisankei Classic. The 21-year-old phenom, playing in just his ninth tournament of the year on the Japan Tour, shook off a faulty final-round finish and captured the title with a birdie on the second hole of a playoff.

Matsuyama, who had also fared so well in international competition that he qualified for and played impressively in the Presidents Cup in America, moved into a first-place tie the second day with 66-70–136 with Hyung-Joon Lee (68-68), Kaname Yokoo (67-69), and Hideto Tanihara (66-70), the 2007 Fujisankei champion.

Matsuyama appeared headed for an easy victory Sunday when he posted another bogey-free 66 Saturday for 11-under-par 202 to take a four-stroke lead over five players — Lee, Yokoo and Tanihara (all 70s), Shingo Katayama (69) and Sung-Joon Park (68), coming off second-win showings the past two weeks.

Matsuyama had things in hand Sunday until he double-bogeyed the 16th hole at Fujizakura Country Club and bogeyed the 18th for 73, dropping into a deadlock with Tanihara and Park, who closed with 69s for their nine-under-par 275s. After all three parred the first playoff hole, Matsuyama recovered brilliantly from a fairway bunker the next time around and holed the winning birdie putt.

With the three victories and a pair of seconds, Matsuyama had a huge lead over runner-up Park in the money race. He remained the only multiple winner of the season.

ANA Open
Kitahiroshima, Hokkaido
Winner: Koumei Oda

Confidence always helps and Koumei Oda had a plentiful supply of it when he teed off in the final round of the ANA Open, even though he led by just a stroke.

"Today was not the most nerve-wracking day," assessed Oda after scoring his sixth career victory on the Japan Tour by four shots, 15 under par with a 273. "From the time I began my practice, I was thinking I was going to win."

After making three birdies on the front nine of the Wattsu course of Sapporo Golf Club, Oda iced the cake by holing an 80-foot monster on the 11th green for another. "Then, I felt it was going to happen."

The distant second-place finishers were South Korean Kyoung-Hoon Lee and Shingo Katayama, the long-time Japanese star winless since 2008. It was the 40-year-old Katayama's fourth top-four finish of the season. He was the first-round leader with 65, dropped a stroke behind Oda (66-68–134) Friday, then crippled his hopes with a third-round 73 as Oda shot 71–205 to set up his self-comfortable one-shot lead over Hiroyuki Fujita, which he converted into his first win in two seasons Sunday.

Asia-Pacific Panasonic Open
Ibaraki, Osaka
Winner: Masahiro Kawamura

Masahiro Kawamura glowed over the turn in his season that came when he pulled out a one-stroke victory in the Asia-Pacific Panasonic Open. Nursing a thumb injury earlier in the season, the 20-year-old Kawamura had missed seven cuts before starting to show his true colors in August and September.

After the Panasonic victory on the West course of Ibaraki Country Club, Kawamura realized: "This win is obviously the biggest thing in my career. Now I get to play in Japan and on the Asian Tour as well." The annual tournament is jointly sponsored by the Japan and Asian Tours.

The tournament also saw another strong performance from the red hot Sung-Joon Park — a win and three seconds in his last five starts — and another disappointment for Shingo Katayama, who was the first-round leader for a second straight week with a nine-under-par 63 but plummeted to 27th place by week's end.

As Katayama started to fall with 73, Thailand's Pariya Junhasavasdikul took the second-round lead with 65-70–135. Kawamura sat in third place at 69-68–137 with veteran Tetsuji Hiratsuka. Park shot 68–206 Saturday to climb into the lead by two shots over Kawamura (71) and international standout Y.E. Yang (69), a former winner of the U.S. PGA Championship.

The final holes told the story Sunday. A triple bogey at the 11th eliminated Yang, and Park was in command until he bogeyed the 16th and 17th holes and Kawamura birdied the 17th and 18th, claiming the one-stroke victory when Park missed a tying 10-footer on the 18th green.

Coca-Cola Tokai Classic
Miyoshi, Aichi
Winner: Shingo Katayama

It had not been a matter of "if" but rather of "when." Nobody in the know thought Shingo Katayama was beyond his winning days, even though he hadn't won a tournament on the Japan Tour in almost five years. Time and again Katayama had made serious passes at victory. Five times earlier in the 2013 season he finished sixth or better, and in 2012 when he played in the Coca-Cola Tokai Classic, he lost unexpectedly in a playoff.

The drought ended in the return engagement and with a Katayama flair. Katayama, the star bridge between the earlier era's Jumbo Ozaki and Tommy Nakajima and current headliners Ryo Ishikawa and Hideki Matsuyama, stormed from a four-stroke deficit in the final round at Miyoshi Country Club into a three-way playoff and this time was the winner for a 27th time. It jumped the five-time leading money winner into second place on the money list behind Matsuyama.

Victory certainly seemed unlikely as Katayama started 74-76 and was tied for 49th place, 10 strokes behind leader Yusaku Miyazato. Even after an eight-under-par 64 in Saturday's third round, Katayama was in a seventh-place tie as Toshinori Muto took over the lead with 69–210. As Muto faded to a 76 Sunday, Katayama and Hidemasa Hoshino with 67s and Satoshi Tomiyama with 69 deadlocked at 281. Katayama won on the first extra hole.

Toshin Golf Tournament
Gifu
Winner: Yoshinori Fujimoto

A peculiar Japan Tour season continued when Yoshinori Fujimoto won the Toshin Golf Tournament in mid-October. The 23-year-old was the 15th different winner in the year's first 17 events. Only money leader Hideki Matsuyama, with three wins, had scored multiple victories.

Fujimoto, who nailed his first win in the 2012 Japan Tour Championship, was in total command of his game all week on the Central course of Toshin Golf Club. Even though he opened with a nine-under-par 63, he trailed China's Ashun Wu, the defending champion, by a stroke on a day of very low scoring. When Fujimoto followed with 64 for 127 Friday, though, he moved into a two-stroke lead over Koumei Oda (64-65).

The two players then matched 70s Saturday before Fujimoto pulled away to a four-stroke triumph with a 67 Sunday. Oda moved within a stroke with an eagle at the ninth hole, but Fujimoto was undaunted, rolling to 67–264 and a four-shot victory with his overpowering, 24-under-par 264. Wu crafted a closing 63 to tie for third place with Yosuke Tsukada.

Japan Open
Tesukubamirai, Ibaraki
Winner: Masanori Kobayashi

Experience is paying off for Masanori Kobayashi. The veteran was 35 when in 2011 he won his first tournament on the Japan Tour. He followed with a second victory in 2012, then topped it off by capturing the 2013 Japan Open. Kobayashi's three-stroke triumph at Ibaraki Golf Club came at the expense of 35-year-old Koumei Oda, another long-time campaigner who seemed primed to nail his first major.

Already a 2013 winner (ANA Open) and coming off his second runner-up finish of the season the preceding Sunday, Oda had staked himself to a three-shot lead — 69-68-67–204 — over Kobayashi — three 69s — after Saturday's round. He had to sit on that lead an extra 24 hours when violent weather washed out play on Sunday, forcing the Monday finale.

In contrast, Kobayashi came to Ibaraki's East course with just one top-10 finish and was 67th on the money list.

As Oda struggled with two bogeys, Kobayashi overtook him with three birdies and a pair of bogeys of his own through eight holes. Another birdie at the 10th gave Kobayashi the lead for keeps. He matched Oda's lone birdie at the 15th, went two ahead when Oda bogeyed the 17th, and capped it with a final birdie at the 18th for 67 and a 10-under-par 274.

Shingo Katayama, a two-time Japan Open champion, had a shot at his third win, opening the tournament in a three-way tie for the lead with Hyung-Sung Kim and Shintaro Kai at 66. He remained in contention into the final round before closing with 70–279 in a tie for third with Hung-Sung and K.T. Kim and Juvic Pagunsan of the Philippines.

Bridgestone Open
Chiba
Winner: Daisuke Maruyama

Daisuke Maruyama was equal to the challenge he faced going into the final round of the Bridgestone Open. Without a victory on the Japan Tour in four years and only one before that, the 42-year-old pro was up against Toru Taniguchi, one of Japan's brightest stars for decades, who was going after a rare third consecutive Bridgestone Open title and his 19th career victory.

After 36 holes the two veterans were tied for the lead at Sodegaura Country Club at 135 with little-known Eun-Shin Park, who at 74th on the money list was six spots behind Maruyama. The tension tightened when the bad weather that had been plaguing much of Japan for weeks brought cancellation of the Saturday round and dictated a 54-hole finish Sunday.

As things turned out, neither Taniguchi nor Park threatened Maruyama the last day. "I was able to keep up with Taniguchi on the front nine and things began going my way after the turn," recalled Maruyama after he polished off his three-under-par 68 and victorious 203 total. He won by three strokes over I.J. Jang, who closed with 66. Jang edged four others by a stroke for the No. 2 slot. Taniguchi slipped to 73 and Park to 75.

"I had thought I wouldn't win again," Maruyama said. "So, to earn my first win in four years here in Chiba, where I'm from, makes me really happy."

Mynavi ABC Championship
Kato, Hyogo
Winner: Yuta Ikeda

Yuta Ikeda had been relatively quiet in the current Japan Tour season for a man who in 2012 became at age 26 the youngest man ever to have won 10 tournaments on the circuit, those coming primarily in his first two full seasons of 2009 and 2010 when he copped four each year and placed second and fourth, respectively, on the final money list. Even with an October spurt, Ikeda sat in the 42nd slot in the current standings when he teed off in the Mynavi ABC Championship at Kato's ABC Golf Club at the end of the month.

He promptly flashed his earlier form with a sizzling, eight-under-par 63 in the opening round, fell out of the lead only once the rest of the way and fought off a depressing finish with a playoff victory over 30-year-old South Korean S.K. Ho, an eight-time winner in Japan but without a title since 2008.

Ikeda followed the 63 with 69, then leading Keiichiro Fukabori (64-69), Yoshinori Fujimoto (69-64), Hiroo Kawai (67-66) and Ho (also 67-66) by a shot. Ho slipped in front by a stroke with a 68 to Ikeda's 70 Saturday, but dropped back quickly Sunday when he bogeyed the first two holes. The Korean rallied after Ikeda had built a four-shot lead and wound up tied (68–269) when Ikeda bogeyed the last two holes for 67 and his 269.

Ikeda bounced back immediately in the playoff with a birdie, hitting the green on the par-five extra hole in two and just missing the eagle putt as Ho drove into a bunker and took four strokes to reach the green.

Heiwa PGM Championship
Kasumigaura, Ibaraki
Winner: Ashun Wu

When Ashun Wu became China's first winner of the Japan Tour in 2012, it came via a weird, four-hole playoff in near darkness. Another playoff seemed in the offing for him in the new Heiwa PGM Championship when, on the 17th hole, Wu blew the last two strokes of the four-shot lead he carried into the final round with a double bogey. Unexpectedly, though, Hyung-Sung Kim, the reigning PGA champion, who was then tied with him, bogeyed the 18th, and Wu's par for a four-over-par 75 gave him his second victory in Japan.

The 28-year-old Chinese pro had established his four-stroke advantage over Kim and Koumei Oda with a six-under-par 65 Saturday after sharing the lead with Katsunori Kuwabara at the midpoint as both shot 67-66s.

Heavy winds battered the Miho Golf Club course Sunday, sending the scores soaring. Only six players broke par. Wu's margin slipped as he took four bogeys and made just two birdies before the double bogey at the 17th hole. Kim was at even par through the 17th before suffering the fatal bogey on the final green as Wu dropped a four-footer for the winning par and 273.

A bright spot for Kim, though, was his jump into second place on the money list with ¥20 million from the runner-up finish, although leader Hideki Matsuyama, who hadn't played in Japan for seven weeks, still had a huge margin, thanks to his lucrative international play in major championships.

Mitsui Sumitomo Visa Taiheiyo Masters
Gotemba, Shizuoka
Winner: Hideto Tanihara

A windy Sunday both hindered and helped Hideto Tanihara as he eked out a one-stroke victory in the Mitsui Sumitomo Visa Taiheiyo Masters with a one-over-par 73 on the Taiheiyo Club's Gotemba course. He made only one birdie and bogeyed twice, but the rough weather also prevented any of the serious challengers from overtaking him.

"The reason I won is because the other players weren't improving their scores," the 35-year-old noted after wrapping up his 10th career victory with a 13-under-par 275. That gave him the one-shot margin over Tomohiro Kondo, Masahiro Kawamura and Ryo Ishikawa, the defending champion back home from his season in America.

Tanihara, who hadn't won since 2010, was a constant contender all week in the venerable tournament which used to attract a sprinkling of international stars. His first-round 66 put him in a five-way tie for the lead with Kondo, Kawamura, Koumei Oda and S.K. Ho. He slipped two behind Oda (67–133) with a 69 Friday, then jumped two ahead of Kawamura Saturday, starting fast with five birdies on the first seven holes and shooting 67–202.

Money leader Hideki Matsuyama, playing in Japan for the first time since mid-September, shot a mediocre 285 and tied for 28th place.

Dunlop Phoenix
Miyazaki
Winner: Luke Donald

The Dunlop Phoenix tournament came up on Luke Donald's schedule at the right time. The No. 1 player in the world in 2011 and No. 2 in 2012 had gone through a winless season and drifted well down the rankings when it came time for him to defend one of his 2012 victories in one of the Japan Tour's premier events.

Defend it he did, with a flourish! After a slow start, the 35-year-old Englishman, one of a half dozen international players in Japan for the tournament, pieced together three fiery rounds and rolled to a six-stroke victory, the biggest winning margin of the season. It was the third time American pros won the Dunlop Phoenix in successive years. Tiger Woods did it in 2004 and 2005, Larry Mize in 1989 and 1990. Jumbo Ozaki posted three consecutive Dunlop Phoenix wins in 1995-96-97.

Donald was tied for 35th place when he opened with 73 at Phoenix Country Club, but vaulted all the way into a first-place tie with Hyung-Sung Kim, Yoshinobu Tsukada and Sung-Joon Park when he shot 66 Friday for 139. His 65–204 Saturday staked him to a two-stroke lead over Kim, the second-place contender on the money list who shot 67. Donald racked up seven birdies Sunday as he shot another 66 for his final 18-under-par 270 and the six-shot margin over Kim.

Casio World Open
Geisel, Kochi
Winner: Hideki Matsuyama

Hideki Matsuyama returned home from his international forays in mid-November to take care of unfinished business. He wrapped it up in his third week back. His narrow victory in the Casio World Open clinched his hold on the No. 1 spot on the Japan Tour's money list that he never relinquished after winning his first of four 2013 victories in the fourth tournament of his rookie season.

The significant one-stroke victory appropriately came on the Koichi Kuroshio Country Club course in Kochi Prefecture that was the 21-year-old's training ground growing up. "To win a championship and clinch the money title at a course I practiced at in middle school and high school makes me really happy," he reflected afterward.

Matsuyama started slowly with a par round, then surged into a first-place tie with Koumei Oda the second day when both 72-shooters followed with 66s. Matsuyama stood alone at the top after posting 68–206 in the third round, two in front of Oda (70) and Yuta Ikeda (68).

Ikeda gave Matsuyama a run for his money Sunday. He birdied six of the first 10 holes, but three bogeys on the back nine brought him up a stroke short with 69 as Matsuyama parlayed four birdies and two bogeys into the winning 70–276. Oda, with 71–279, finished third.

Golf Nippon Series JT Cup
Tokyo
Winner: Yusaku Miyazato

Yusaku Miyazato made it a complete family of winners as the 2013 Japan Tour season ended with the Golf Nippon Series JT Cup in Tokyo. While younger sister Ai was establishing herself as an international star in women's golf, Yusaku and older brother Kiyoshi were laboring for success on the Japan Tour. Kiyoshi broke through with his first and only victory at the end of the 2004 season before, almost 10 years later, Yusaku nailed the JT Cup, preserving a three-stroke lead in the final round at Tokyo's Yomiuri Country Club with a one-over-par 71 for the winning 267.

The 33-year-old Miyazato got into the field by the skin of his teeth. A seventh-place finish with closing rounds of 69-68 the week before in the Casio World Open elevated him to 24th place on the money list, barely enough to qualify him for the limited-field season finale that takes only the year's winners and the top 25 on the money list after the Casio.

The momentum carried over to the Nippon Series for Miyazato, who shot rounds of 66, 66 and 64 the first three days. He was tied for the lead with Yoshinori Fujimoto and Tomohiro Kondo after the first round, a shot behind South Korean Kyoung-Hoon Lee at the midpoint, and three strokes in front of Hideto Tanihara and Kazuhiro Yamashita going into the final round. Miyazato offset five bogeys with four birdies for the 71 Sunday and, with the scoring generally high, was not seriously challenged. China's Ashun Wu, six back starting the day, shot 68 to pick off second place.

Hideki Matsuyama, nursing a bad thumb, did not play, so his ¥201,076,781 was his final total as the 2013 money-winning champion. He was just the third player in history to top the ¥200 million mark and was the only man to win more than once during the entire 2013 season, a rare circumstance.

10. Australasian Tour

Something was always missing from Greg Norman's wardrobe. A green jacket would have fitted the Shark nicely, and he had plenty of chances, but his losses at Augusta were felt not just by the golfer himself but an entire nation. Winning the Masters was not just the only thing in golf that an Australian had not done. It was just about the only thing in sport where someone from Down Under had not come out on top. Monday mornings on the other side of the world were painful as Norman failed to beat Jack Nicklaus in 1986, lost a playoff to a miraculous chip-in by Larry Mize the following year and got turned over by Nick Faldo, from six ahead to five behind, in 1996. There were other times as well, and other Australians had also got close without a cigar or a green jacket. In 2011 there was double the disappointment as Adam Scott and Jason Day shared second place behind Charl Schwartzel and the South African's four-birdie finish.

Scott, however, had a plan to make sure he contended regularly in the majors. He cut down his schedule, revamped his practice regime, turned to the long putter and almost won the Open Championship at Royal Lytham in 2012. He should have won but bogeyed the last four holes to lose to Ernie Els' birdie at the last. A lesser man might have been crushed by the collapse. "Next time, I'll do a little better," he said. The next time came at Augusta National in 2013 and he did more than a little better.

This time there were three Aussies to share the burden of breaking their Masters hoodoo. Scott started the final round one behind Angel Cabrera and Brandt Snedeker, with Day and Marc Leishman a further shot back. Scott bogeyed the first and then had four birdies, the last of them on the 18th green and celebrated with a huge roar of "C'mon Aussie." To the side of the green, Leishman, his own chances of winning having fallen away, gave a fist pump in support of his compatriot. For a moment, Scott, and everyone, thought he had won, but Cabrera also birdied the last to set up a playoff. At the second extra hole, on the 10th green, in fading light and thanks to a read from his caddie, Kiwi Steve Williams, Scott holed a 15-footer and Australia had its first Masters champion.

"We are a proud sporting country and like to think we are the best at everything," Scott said. "We have a long list of great golfers but this was the one thing we had not been able to win. I am a proud Australian and I hope this sits well at home and even in New Zealand — we were a trans-Tasman combo with Steve on the bag."

Scott added: "Part of this belongs to Greg. He inspired a nation of golfers. He was the best player in the world and was an icon in Australia. He has devoted so much time to myself and other Australian players who have come after him. He has given me so much inspiration and belief."

Now a generation will be inspired by Scott. When he returned home in November, huge crowds turned out to see the new U.S. Masters champion, many wearing green in his honor. Photos with Scott in his new jacket became prized possessions. He was handed the keys to the city of the Gold Coast, where he grew up, and was awarded Australia's highest sporting honor, The Don, named after cricket legend Don Bradman. His golf did not disappoint either. He won the Australian PGA Championship at Royal Pines and then defended his title at the Talisker Masters at Royal Melbourne. A quintuple-bogey-nine on the first day of the World Cup of Golf scuppered his chances of the "Scotty Slam" but Day took the individual honors — an emotional victory just a week after eight members of his family died in the Philippines typhoon — and Day and Scott won the team event for Australia by 10 strokes over America.

Scott's bid to match Robert Allenby from 2005 as a winner of the Australian Triple Crown started in the perfect fashion with a course-record 62 at Royal Sydney. But there was a sting in the tail at the climax to Australia's "Summer of Golf" as Rory McIlroy won the Australian Open with a birdie on the last to Scott's bogey. McIlroy, relieved to end a disappointing year on a positive note, nonetheless had mixed feelings about the result. "I am really pleased I was able to take on one of the best players in the world down the stretch and come out on top," said McIlroy. "He's a phenomenal golfer, a great competitor and probably an even better guy. I feel a bit sorry that I'm the one to ruin the Triple Crown for him, but I'm happy for myself."

Scott said: "It's been a great year but obviously I didn't want to finish like that. If I didn't play any good the first few days and played great today and finished second, I'd be pretty chuffed going into Christmas, so that's how I should look at it. I'll get over this tonight and look forward to a few weeks' rest and get ready to go next year."

The impact Scott made in 2013 cannot be overemphasized. Mike Clayton, golfer-turned-writer stated: "Scott, as is his way, took the loss with grace and he will steal off into the night with the knowledge he has made the summer of golf in Australia. For a month he has signed autographs, spoken at dinners arranged in his honor, had hundreds if not thousands of photographs taken with green-jacketed arm around adoring fans, and all the way he was shooting even 67s.

"What is more impressive is he looked like he enjoyed every step of the four-week journey through Queensland, down to Melbourne and then up to Sydney. Nothing was a problem or a drama. He never once looked like he was doing us a favor by being here when he could have been sunning himself in Bermuda. Australians have always loved the self-deprecating and modest sportsman. Scott is a throwback to the generation of Thomson and Nagle, outwardly modest men who understood their golf scores were not the most important things in the world, and he surely will win a lot more."

Behind Scott, there were many other successes for Australian golfers in 2013. Brett Rumford won twice on the European Tour in successive weeks in Korea and China, Scott Hend won three times on the Asian Tour, Matt Griffin won on the OneAsia Tour and claimed that circuit's Order of Merit title. In Japan, there were wins for Brad Kennedy and Brendan Jones, while at home Jack Wilson emerged as a young player to watch and former British Amateur champion Jin Jeong claimed his maiden professional win at the Perth International.

Turner Plumbing Victorian PGA Championship
Creswick, Victoria
Winner: David McKenzie

Almost two decades after a missed short putt cost David McKenzie the title, the 45-year-old finally claimed the Turner Plumbing Victorian PGA Championship at Forest Resort in Creswick. McKenzie won by two strokes over Scott Laycock and by five over Stephen Dartnall. He had taken a four-shot lead after the third round after matching Dartnall's course record of the previous day with a seven-under 65. On the last day McKenzie started with back-to-back bogeys but then posted the first of three eagles at the fourth. He also had two double bogeys, at the 10th hole and also at the 18th. A closing 70 left him on a total of 275, 13 under par, while Laycock closed with a 68 that included four eagles.

McKenzie, who won on the then-Nationwide Tour in 2005, claimed his first title since joining the Australasian Tour in 1990. "It's been hard work for a while. It's been a long time coming," he said. "Words are eluding me now. I actually lost a Victorian PGA by missing a short putt about 20 years ago, so it's nice to actually win."

McKenzie paid tribute to his late friend Ramsay McMaster, a golf physiotherapist. "Ramsay was one of my biggest supporters," said McKenzie. "He'd call at three in the morning just to give me a rev up and just to say to keep going in only a way that Ramsay knows how. It has and will take me a long time to get over it."

Lexus of Blackburn Heritage Classic
Chirnside Park, Victoria
Winner: David Bransdon

David Bransdon opened the inaugural Lexus of Blackburn Heritage Classic with a course-record 64 at the Jack Nicklaus-signature Heritage course. But it took a playoff for the 37-year-old Victorian to win his third title on the Australasian PGA Tour. A birdie at the 18th hole in the playoff, when he hit his approach to three feet and holed the putt, gave Bransdon the victory ahead of Max McCardle, who could only par the hole, and amateur Lucas Herbert, who bogeyed. The trio tied at 14 under par on a total of 274, McCardle closing with a 67, Herbert with 68 and Bransdon with 71. Bransdon had led for the first two rounds, but Kiwi Michael Hendry equaled his 64 in the third round to top the leaderboard but closed with a 73 to fall one outside the playoff after a bogey at the 16th.

Bransdon had bogeyed four of the last 10 holes, but once he got to the playoff his confidence returned. "I was actually more relaxed in the playoff than I was in regulation playing the 18th. It was just a bizarre thing," Bransdon said. "I thought I had put myself in a good position to win, so I just went out and hit the shots. I had hit good shots all day, so I just trusted what I was doing and pulled it off."

Coca-Cola Queensland PGA Championship
Toowoomba, Queensland
Winner: Brad Kennedy

Brad Kennedy took advantage of the long off-season break on the Japan Tour to claim his native state PGA title for the first time at the Coca-Cola Queensland PGA Championship. Kennedy, who won the 2012 Mizuno Open in Japan, claimed his third Australasian Tour title with a birdie at the final hole at City Golf Club in Toowoomba to win by two strokes over Michael Hendry, who bogeyed the last hole. On the par-68 layout, Kennedy had rounds of 64, 62, 65 and 63 for an 18-under-par total of 254. Hendry, who led by one over Kennedy with a round to play, closed with a 66 to finish two ahead of Anthony Summers, with amateur Cameron Smith taking fourth place.

One over for the day after six holes and trailing by three, Kennedy made six birdies over the last 12 holes, and a fine six iron at the last set up the winning three. "I have been a pro for nearly 16 years now, I did my traineeship, have been a club pro and done all that, so to win a Queensland PGA is great," Kennedy said. "I came close five or six years ago, so it's great to get another trophy in the cabinet."

Jason Norris, the first-round leader who needed a par at the last for a 59 but bogeyed instead, was still a co-leader at the halfway stage before withdrawing after a 72 in the third round and then heading to the hospital with suspected meningitis.

Victorian Open
Barwon Heads, Victoria
Winner: Matthew Giles

After losing his card on the Web.com Tour in America at the end of 2012, during a turbulent season in which he spent a night in jail in Arizona after crashing his car while allegedly under the influence of alcohol, Matthew Giles got his career back on track with his maiden professional victory at the Victorian Open. The 23-year-old birdied the 18th hole at 13th Beach Golf Links, one of four on the back nine, to win by one stroke over Ryan Lynch and amateur Nathan Holman. Giles scored rounds of 69, 71, 68 and 67 for a 13-under total of 275.

Giles had started the last round two behind third-round leader Holman, who had also led early in the Victorian PGA. Holman closed with a 70 as a birdie chance at the 18th slipped by, while Lynch, whose father Dale, the renowned golf coach, was caddieing for him, finished with a 68 after his 10-footer at the last also lipped out.

"I was one under at the turn, should have been three or four under, and gave myself a good talking to at the 10th and the birdie there kicked things off," Giles said. "I didn't have the greatest 2012, but this does a lot for my confidence."

Large galleries attended with the women's tournament played alongside the men's. "It was a good week out here, it's great to see the support this event has had this week with the men and women together, it's been fantastic," said Giles. "That made it a lot of fun out there playing, especially over the weekend with the crowds."

New Zealand PGA Championship
Queenstown, New Zealand
Winner: Michael Hendry

Michael Hendry went into the New Zealand PGA Championship with the attitude of not wanting to give away the trophy, and at the end of a playoff with Scott Strange he had successfully defended the title. Hendry became the first back-to-back winner since compatriot Frank Nobilo won in 1985 and 1987 (there was no tournament in 1986).

The pair tied on 269, 19 under par, to finish four ahead of Gareth Paddison and Josh Geary. Paddison birdied seven of the first 11 holes at The Hills in Queenstown as the spectacular scenery was matched by some inspired spurts of action. Hendry birdied the first three holes on his way to a 67, while Strange had five birdies in a row from the ninth as the Australian closed with a 66. In the pro-am event that ran over the weekend, Strange was partnered with former England cricketer Sir Ian Botham, while prime minister John Key and 15-year-old amateur sensation Lydia Ko also took part.

In the playoff at the 18th hole, Strange found a bunker with his approach, but Hendry hit his second to 10 feet and holed the putt for a winning birdie that was greeted with loud applause. "I've actually won every playoff I've ever been in, which is obviously a good record — not that I thought about that prior to going out," said Hendry. "I felt pretty comfortable on the tee — I just said you've done the hard work, now just finish it off.

"To get across the line and for it to be at home and with the retention of the trophy, it's just magic. You come into the week thinking this is my trophy, I'm not going to give it to anyone else. I had that attitude all week, so to retain it is unbelievable."

Isuzu Queensland Open
Ipswich, Queensland
Winner: Nick Cullen

Nick Cullen was expecting a strong challenge from 48-year-old Peter O'Malley and for much of the final round of the Isuzu Queensland Open that is what he got. Ultimately, Cullen recorded a five-stroke victory, but the duel was still on until a two-shot swing at the 12th hole. O'Malley failed to get up and down from a bunker while Cullen holed from seven feet for a birdie to go three strokes clear. He closed the round as he had started, with a birdie, for a closing round of 69 to go with earlier efforts of 73, 72 and 65. His third round was a new course record for the Brookwater course at Ipswich, west of Brisbane, and catapulted the 29-year-old South Australian to the top of the leaderboard. Starting the final round with a one-stroke advantage, he birdied two of the first three holes and never looked back. He finished on a nine-under-par total of 279, with O'Malley holding on to second place on four under after a 73. David McKenzie, at two under, and Jake Higginbottom, one stroke further back, were the only other players to finish under par for the week.

This was Cullen's first win on the PGA Tour of Australasia, adding to his victory at the 2012 Indonesian Open on the OneAsia circuit. "It was really great to get off to a good start, because around a course like Brookwater, if you get off to a bad start it's hard to recover," he said. "The whole time I was wary that Pom was really close, he was only two, three, even one shot behind me for a lot of the day. This course can really eat you up on every hole, so two shots is nothing; honestly, until I was 15 feet away on the last I wasn't ready to relax."

South Pacific Open Championship
Noumea, South Caledonia
Winner: Andre Stolz

Michael Wright started the South Pacific Open Championship by claiming a share of the course record at Tina Golf Club in Noumea, South Caledonia, but after five holes of a playoff he had to relinquish his hopes of winning the title. Playing the par-four 18th for the fifth successive time, Stolz made his fifth par in a row to win his fifth title on the PGA Tour of Australasia. Wright pulled his tee shot into the water on the left and could not keep the tournament going. He had opened with a nine-under 62 to match Theo Coroneo for the first-round lead and was one ahead of the field going into the last round. He closed with a 69 and tied on 16-under 268 with Stolz, who came from three behind with a 66 on the last day after earlier rounds of 67, 66 and 69.

"I had been stripping my three iron all day as well as four times in a row in the playoff," said Wright. "But on the fifth tee shot I had a bad swing, turned it over a little, and the ball kicked left into the hazard. I'm quite disappointed at the moment. Especially after going through five holes of the playoff. But I will look back on this as a great week and a great learning experience."

Stolz, who won on the PGA Tour in the States in 2004 prior to suffering a wrist injury, collected his first win since the 2011 Thailand Open. "I am relieved more than anything," said Stolz. "I have had some good opportunities to win tournaments this year and have just been messing them up."

Western Australia Goldfields PGA Championship
Kalgoorlie, Western Australia
Winner: Jack Wilson

Jack Wilson created history at the Western Australia Goldfields PGA Championship at Kalgoorlie by becoming the first PGA trainee to win on the PGA Tour of Australasia. Wilson birdied his first three holes of the tournament and led from the start almost to the very end but needed a playoff to claim his maiden victory. He defeated New Zealand's Nick Gillespie at the first extra hole after the pair tied on 278, 10 under par.

Wilson, 22, a former Australian PGA trainee of the year, is in his third and final year as a trainee based at Kingwood in Melbourne, and was playing in only his second event of the year. He recorded scores of 67, 68 and 71 to build a three-stroke advantage and was comfortably in front for much of his final round of 72. However, a double bogey at the 15th dropped him back into a tie with Gillespie, who closed with a 69. James Nitties and Adam Bland shared third place one stroke behind.

"It's a goal that I really wanted to achieve," said Wilson. "I always want to be the first to do things and hopefully this is just the start. I'm so pumped to have the opportunity to play the Perth International, Australian PGA and Australian Open. I was looking for invites, but now there's no need. The money is great, but it's playing these events and having these opportunities that's really huge for me."

John Hughes/Nexus Risk Services WA Open
Perth, Western Australia
Winner: Josh Geary

Josh Geary proved his runaway win at a minor tour event in New Zealand was no fluke when he did something similar at a higher level with his first victory on the PGA Tour of Australasia. Geary won the Tauranga Open on the Charles Tour by eight strokes and took that confidence into a top-20 finish at the Western Australia PGA before winning the John Hughes/Nexus Risk Services Western Australia Open by five strokes. The 28-year-old New Zealander became increasingly at home on the Mt. Lawley course in Perth, and after opening with a 73, he added scores of 68, 67 and 65 for a 15-under-par total of 273.

Geary started the final round one behind 23-year-old Victorian Kris Mueck, who opened the door for his rival with bogeys at the second and third holes. Mueck recovered to a 71 to finish at 10 under, one ahead of Nathan Holman, who took third place in only his second event as a professional. But Geary was long since gone with four birdies in a row from the second and another at the ninth for an outward 31. There was a bogey at the 12th, but birdies at the next two holes and another at the 17th.

"I set out there with high hopes and played great all day. I kept within myself and managed to finish it off quite nicely," said Geary. "I was pretty relaxed, I tried to stay calm and not let the outside influences affect what I was doing. It has been six or seven years now that I have been trying for a win. The highest hurdle is the first one. Now I have broken through I should be good for the near future."

ISPS Handa Perth International
Perth, Western Australia
Winner: Jin Jeong

There can be no less encouraging start to a final round of a tournament than four-putting for a double bogey on the first hole. Jin Jeong was only one stroke behind Brody Ninyette when he teed off on the last day of the ISPS Handa Perth International but soon dropped further behind. Yet the 23-year from South Korea, who has been based in Australia for a number of years, rallied superbly to claim his maiden victory on both the PGA Tour of Australasia and the European Tour at Lake Karrinyup. Jeong beat Ross Fisher in a playoff at the first extra hole after the pair tied on a 10-under-par total of 278.

Local favorite Ninyette closed with a 72 and dropped out of contention with three bogeys in the last six holes as he shared third place with Dimitrios Papadatos and Danny Willett on eight under. Jeong was flawless for the remainder of his round, and birdies at the fourth and fifth settled him down before scalps at the 11th, 12th and 15th took him to the top of the leaderboard. Fisher hit his tee shot at the 17th to a foot as he came in with a 68, while Jeong holed good par putts at both the 16th and 17th to sign for a 69. Playing the 18th in the playoff, Fisher dragged his drive into the left semi-rough and from there saw his second skip through the green. While Jeong hit a fine approach to 35 feet, Fisher's chip came up eight feet short and he missed the par putt, leaving Jeong to hole out from three feet for the victory.

It was the third time in three attempts that Fisher had lost a playoff on the European Tour, but the runner-up's finish probably ensured he would qualify for the DP World Tour Championship in Dubai from the top 60 on the money list. Peter Lawrie's 18th-place finish meant he kept his card for 2014 from the top 110 on the money list, which was finalized after this event. Those outside that mark prior to the new Final Four series had to return to the qualifying tournament.

Jeong, who won the British Amateur Championship at Muirfield in 2010, had got through the first stage of qualifying for the European Tour but now earned a two-year exemption thanks to his win.

"I was nervous, I was shaking, but I controlled myself pretty well all day I thought," said Jeong. "I don't know what I've done, to be honest. I was struggling quite a bit when I was turning pro, but it was going to happen in the learning circuit I guess. I had played playoffs in mini-tour events, but playing with Ross Fisher, he's one of my heroes. Playing with him in the playoff, it was unbelievable."

Australian PGA Championship
Gold Coast, Queensland
Winner: Adam Scott

Masters champion Adam Scott made a triumphant return home to win the Australian PGA Championship at the RACV Royal Pines Resort on the Gold

Coast. It was Scott's first visit to his homeland since winning at Augusta National and the celebrations included the 33-year-old being presented with the keys to the city of the Gold Coast, where he spent much of his childhood, and a "Wear Green for Adam Scott Day" on the Friday of the tournament. After Rickie Fowler led with an opening 63, Scott took over the lead in the second round and extended his lead from two to three on Saturday.

Huge crowds came out to see Scott and he got a thunderous ovation as he teed off last on the final day. An even-par front nine meant Fowler and WA PGA champion Jack Wilson got within one shot when a thunderstorm delayed play for almost two hours. Scott's first shot after returning to the course was to hit a four iron from 264 yards at the 12th hole and the ball almost went in for an albatross before finishing four inches away. "When I came out, I knew I had to do something great — that's what happens at these tournaments, someone always does something great," Scott said. "I came out and hit some great shots and that four iron was just perfect — I mean, I just flushed it!"

Scott added two more birdies to finish on 270, 14 under par after rounds of 65, 67, 71 and 67, to win by four over Fowler and by six over Wilson, who had a double bogey at the short 14th hole when he returned to the course.

"This is the one I wanted desperately, and it's kind of the icing on the cake for me," Scott said. "This one is for my folks — especially for my dad, who is a PGA member. I hope he's feeling proud at the moment."

Talisker Masters
Melbourne, Victoria
Winner: Adam Scott

Adam Scott won for the second time in two weeks and became the first player to successfully defend at the Talisker Masters since Greg Norman in 1990. After defeating Rickie Fowler at the Australian PGA, at Royal Melbourne Scott dueled another American, Matt Kuchar, before winning by two strokes. Scott started the final round with a four-stroke lead, but Kuchar came from five behind with a run of seven birdies between the third and 15th holes. With Scott taking a double bogey from a deep bunker at the 14th, the American led by two. However, Scott birdied the 15th as Kuchar bogeyed the 16th, so they were tied approaching the 18th hole. Kuchar, in the group ahead, found a tricky spot in a greenside bunker and took two to get out on the way to a double bogey. Scott got his par to post a 14-under-par total of 270 after rounds of 67, 66, 66 and 71. Kuchar closed with a 68 to finish two ahead of Vijay Singh.

"I've never won back-to-back weeks, so this is a first and something that I like," said Scott. "I think it's very hard to win two tournaments full stop, let alone back to back, so I'm quite pleased with myself this week. Sometimes you win a little bit ugly. All the good stuff I had done in the first three rounds counted for a lot, even though it wasn't the prettiest golf today."

There was an emotional start to the tournament when Jarrod Lyle returned to action after 21 months out fighting leukemia for the second time. "It was nice to get out there and see everybody that I love standing around the tee and even people I have never met before. The crowd on the first tee was something I was not expecting," said Lyle. "I hit that first tee shot with tears all through my eyes. I was happy when I saw it going in the air down the fairway." He scored a 72 and went on to complete his aim of making the cut.

ISPS Handa World Cup of Golf
Melbourne, Victoria
Winner: Jason Day

Australia's "Summer of Golf" got better and better as Jason Day won the individual prize at the ISPS Handa World Cup of Golf and combined with Adam Scott to land Australia the title for the fifth time and the first since 1989. It was a highly emotional win for Day, his second as a professional after claiming the 2010 Byron Nelson title and his first on home soil, after eight members of his mother's family were killed in Typhoon Haiyan in the Philippines the week before. His mother, Denning, was in the gallery as Day won by two strokes over Thomas Bjorn.

"It would have been the easiest thing for me to just go ahead and pull out of the tournament with what has been going on over the last week," said Day. "But I really wanted to come down here and play with Adam and really try and win the World Cup, and we achieved that, which is great. This is really special to me and my family."

The revamped competition featured both an individual 72-hole stroke-play competition with Official World Ranking points on offer as well as the two-man aggregate team event. Australia, on 17 under par, won the latter by 10 strokes over America's pairing of Matt Kuchar and Kevin Streelman, with Denmark (Bjorn and Thorbjorn Olesen) in third place. The event was staged at Royal Melbourne, the same track as for the previous week's Talisker Masters. Scott, going for three wins in a row, was derailed by a nine at the par-four 12th on the first day but finished strongly with a 66 in the team cause. He finished third in the individual event, one ahead of Kuchar.

Day led by one over Bjorn entering the final round and holed out with his second shot at the sixth as he established a four-shot lead when Bjorn had his second bogey in a row at the seventh. But Day had a double bogey at the 10th, and two birdies from Bjorn meant they were tied after 13. Both birdied the 15th, but Bjorn bogeyed the 16th and 18th holes to slip back into second place after a closing 71. Day had rounds of 68, 70, 66 and 70 for a 10-under-par total of 274. "It's taken me awhile to get my second win and it couldn't be more fitting with Scotty by my side winning the World Cup," said Day. "It was a complete honor to win here at Royal Melbourne. To win in front of the Melbourne fans who are so passionate about their sport was an amazing feeling."

Stuart Manley, of Wales, had an amazing start to his third round. He birdied the first two holes then had a hole-in-one at the third. He went over

to pat the Mercedes behind the tee but was told when he got to the green
that the car was only on offer for the final round. Then at the fourth hole,
he had an 11. He was in a greenside bunker for three, over the green for
four, chipped back down in front of the green for five, took three more
chips to find the green and then three-putted. "It's the highest high and
then the lowest low I've ever experienced on a golf course," he said.

Gloria Jean's NSW Open
Sydney, New South Wales
Winner: Aron Price

Aron Price, a former winner on the Web.com Tour in America, claimed
his first professional win on home soil by taking the Gloria Jean's New
South Wales Open at Castle Hill. Price won by four strokes after the player
he was tied with after three rounds, Steven Bowditch, slipped to a 76, 12
strokes higher than the previous round, and finished tied for seventh. Price
had scores of 66, 66, 67 and 70 for a 19-under-par total of 269. Adam
Bland, after a 67, Aaron Townsend and Jack Wilson, who both had 68s,
shared second place.

Price had only one bogey all week, at the second hole on the second day,
and had to play 27 holes on the final day due to thunderstorms earlier in
the week. He was steady in the final round, with birdies at the first and
15th his only non-pars. "I didn't have too many challenges; I saw Adam
coming and Steve had his ups and downs, so I was just trying to play my
own game," said Price. "A couple of times when I did get in trouble I
made some great pars, like on the 10th. Obviously I made four, if I had
made a five it could have spiraled into anything."

The win gave Price an exemption into the Australian Open and meant he
avoided having to qualify. "It's just like that song, I don't like Mondays.
Monday qualifying stinks, it was going to be 80 guys for three spots. I was
pretty confident that I could play well, but you never know in qualifiers."

Emirates Australian Open
Sydney, New South Wales
Winner: Rory McIlroy

Seeking to become only the second player after Robert Allenby in 2005 to
win the Triple Crown of Australian golf — the PGA and Masters titles as
well as the Emirates Australian Open — in the same season, Adam Scott
made the perfect start with a course record of 62 in the opening round at
Royal Sydney. Starting at the 10th, Scott birdied the first six holes and then
his last four holes — so on the card it appeared as if he had birdied 10 in
a row from the sixth. He led by three strokes that night, by two after the
second day and by four over Rory McIlroy with a round to play. Again
in front of huge crowds hoping to see the U.S. Masters champion create
more history, Scott made a poor start with a bogey at the first, though he
recovered the shot at the next hole.

McIlroy then birdied the fifth, eagled the seventh and birdied the eighth to draw even, only for Scott to birdie the ninth to edge in front again. Both birdied the 13th but parred every other hole until the 18th. While McIlroy hit his approach to 12 feet, Scott went over the green and chipped back 40 feet past the hole. He two-putted for a bogey but had opened the door for McIlroy to get ahead for the first and only time. He holed the putt and then said: "I'm a bit sorry that I'm the one to ruin the Triple Crown for Adam."

McIlroy had rounds of 69, 65, 70 and 66 for an 18-under-par total of 270, while Scott followed his 62 with scores of 70, 68 and 71 to finish one behind. Scott said: "I'm gutted. I felt like I never had a better chance to win the Aussie Open, but it was tight the whole back nine." John Senden was third, six shots further back, and scooped a qualifying place for the 2014 Open Championship along with Rhein Gibson and Bryden Macpherson.

For McIlroy, it was a good way to end a disappointing year, which he started as the world No. 1 only to lose form and confidence while adjusting to new equipment and dealing with off-course issues with his management company. "Since the end of September I've just felt in a better place, a better place mentally with some things off the course," said McIlroy. "Golf's a long career and I'm 24 years old. I get a little impatient at times, and if I actually just took a step back and looked at the bigger picture, it hasn't been too bad a year. I am really pleased I was able to take on one of the best players in the world down the stretch and come out on top."

11. African Tours

For the first time in four years, no South African won a major championship. Louis Oosthuizen won the Open Championship in 2010, Charl Schwartzel won the Masters in 2011 and Ernie Els won the Open at Lytham in 2012. In 2013, Els produced the best result in the majors, finishing fourth at the U.S. Open at Merion, which was won by Justin Rose, who happened to be born in South Africa of English parents and grew up in England.

For all South Africans, the year of 2013 will be remembered for the death of Nelson Mandela. The former president died at the age of 95 on the evening after the first round of the Nedbank Golf Challenge at Sun City. Els, who met Mandela for the first time when the South African PGA Championship was played at Houghton in 1994 and who received a phone call from Mandela each time he won thereafter, said: "It is a very sad day. A very sad day for South Africa and the world really. We have lost one of the iconic leaders of our time. You cannot say anything bad about the man. He fought for what he believed in, went to prison for so many years and came out to lead our country up until now. He was the father of our country and our continent. It's just very sad that he had to go. He was 95 and led a full life, but a lot of that wasn't spent on what he was so good at because he was away for so many years."

Thomas Bjorn won the Nedbank Challenge, with two eagles on the back nine in the final round. The presentation ceremony at the end of the tournament was opened with the national anthem and the grandstands at the 18th green awash with South African flags. "If everyone could live their lives just a little bit like Nelson Mandela, the world would be a better place," Bjorn said.

The following week, the last event of the season was the Nelson Mandela Championship, in aid of the Mandela Children's Charity. It was moved forward a day to avoid a clash with Mandela's funeral on the Sunday and a two-stroke victory for Dawie Van der Walt proved highly emotional. He received the unique trophy, which depicts Mandela surrounded by children, and a portrait of Mandela by Harold Riley and signed by the former president. "This is so small compared to what Nelson Mandela did," Van der Walt said of his victory. "But it makes it a little more special. You can always win the Nelson Mandela Championship in 10 years' time, but this one will always be a special one."

Van der Walt won twice in events co-sanctioned by the European Tour, first at the Tshwane Open and then at the Mandela event. Between those victories, his campaign in Europe was plagued by injury and loss of form, so to return home and end the year victorious was not just a boost for his confidence. He also won the Sunshine Tour Order of Merit for 2013, going ahead of Darren Fichardt, who won the Africa Open early in the year. "I haven't been in that good form, I've been struggling with an injury, so this is almost overwhelming," said Van der Walt. "To win the last event of the year is going to make Christmas a lot more fun."

South Africa's reputation as a breeding ground for new stars was backed up by the fact that no less than eight events played in the country during 2013 counted on the European Tour, four early in the year on the 2013 schedule and four at the end of the year that count towards the 2014 European Tour season. America, with three majors and three World Golf Championships, was next with six, while China provided four events and the United Arab Emirates three.

Van der Walt and Fichardt were not the only home players to take advantage of being able to compete in familiar surroundings but on the international stage at the same time. Oosthuizen won the Volvo Champions, though later suffered from injury which only just relented in time for him to play in the Presidents Cup; Richard Sterne won the Joberg Open, and Schwartzel won the Alfred Dunhill Championship at Leopard Creek for the third time. As well as Bjorn taking the Nedbank Challenge, which featured on the European Tour for the first time, his young compatriot and protégé Morten Orum Madsen won the South African Open.

On the Sunshine Tour alone, there were three wins for Jaco Van Zyl, including at the Telkom PGA, and Jacques Blaauw, while Adilson Da Silva and Andrew Curlewis each won twice.

Nick Price took over from his friend Greg Norman as captain of the International team at the Presidents Cup, but there was no change in luck for the visitors at Muirfield Village as America won for the eighth time in 10 matches. Zimbabwe's Brendon de Jonge made his debut alongside regulars Els, Oosthuizen and Schwartzel, but the hosts ran out winners 18½-15½.

Telkom PGA Pro-Am
Tshwane, South Africa
Winner: Oliver Bekker

After a best-ever finish of 10th on the Sunshine Tour Order of Merit in 2012, Oliver Bekker opened 2013 in perfect fashion by winning the Telkom PGA Pro-Am at Century Country Club. The 28-year-old from Stellenbosch won by two strokes over P.H. McIntyre and Ryan Strauss after rounds of 66, 64 and 66 for a 20-under total of 196. Birdies at the 16th and 17ht holes, which he birdied all three days, sealed the victory after he started the final round tied for the lead with McIntyre. While McIntyre could not keep pace and closed with a 68, there was a late charge from Strauss, whose 64 came just two weeks after gaining his card at the qualifying tournament.

It was a third win on the Sunshine Tour in as many years for Bekker, after he claimed the Northern Cape Classic in 2011 and the Dimension Data Pro-Am in 2012. "I couldn't have asked for anything better than this. It's the first time I'm starting out a year with a win, so it's an awesome feeling and I'm very happy at the moment," he said. "I played a solid round of golf today. It was probably my best ball-striking of the week, and under the pressure I'd say I did very well for myself."

Joburg Open
Johannesburg, South Africa
Winner: Richard Sterne

Charl Schwartzel won his last two tournaments of 2012 by a combined 23 strokes at the Thailand Championship and the Alfred Dunhill Championship but suffered some of his own medicine in his first event of 2013 as the former Masters champion finished runner-up by seven strokes to Richard Sterne. After his just missing out to Stephen Gallacher in Dubai the previous week, Sterne continued his fine form and low scoring to win the Joburg Open at Royal Johannesburg and Kensington.

Sterne won the event early in 2008, but this was his first victory since his back-to-back wins at the Alfred Dunhill Championship and the South African Open at the end of that year. The 31-year-old may have fallen behind the likes of Schwartzel, Louis Oosthuizen and Branden Grace after playing less than a dozen times in 2010 and 2011 due to an arthritic back problem, but his sixth victory on the European Tour showed he was back to his best.

After an opening 63 on the par-71 West course, Sterne added rounds of 65, 68 and 64 on the par-72 East course for a 27-under-par total of 260. He shared the first-round lead with Max Kieffer and on days two and three was tied with Trevor Fisher, Jr., who had a 62 in the second round. The pair were five clear of the field going into the final round, but Fisher could not keep pace with Sterne and slipped to a 73 to tie for sixth place. Schwartzel, who started the final day six behind, charged into the runner-up spot with a 66 to finish one ahead of Felipe Aguilar, George Coetzee and Ricardo Santos.

Sterne made five birdies in the first eight holes to be out in 32 and added three more coming home, including at the last two holes. "It was a pretty special day," said Sterne. "I played really good golf today and the whole week really. It's quite tough coming from a good week into another week; you kind of do expect to play well. But I got off to such a good start on the West course and felt comfortable. Having won here before I do enjoy the place and that's why I keep coming back."

Africa Open
Eastern Cape, South Africa
Winner: Darren Fichardt

In the end his four-stroke advantage after notching up his fourth birdie of the final day at the 13th hole proved to be enough for Darren Fichardt, but in a healthy wind at East London nothing is to be taken for granted. Fichardt bogeyed three of the next four holes but held his nerve at the last to win the Africa Open by two strokes over Jaco Van Zyl and Gregory Bourdy. Garth Mulroy finished a stroke further back in fourth place.

Fichardt followed Charl Schwartzel and two-time winner Louis Oosthuizen as the fourth home winner in the event's four-year history. As often in the Eastern Cape, wind was a factor all week, and the first day's play was interrupted as the gales got too strong. Adilson Da Silva returned on Friday to play 28 holes in which he completed a 62, one outside Richard Sterne's course record, which gave him a four-stroke first-round lead, and a 68 for a three-shot halfway advantage. But Da Silva fell back with scores of 73 and 76 over the weekend, as Fichardt, with a 65 in the third round after scores of 69 and 67, tied Van Zyl at the top of the leaderboard heading into the final round.

Birdies at the first, third and seventh holes edged Fichardt one ahead of Van Zyl, who bogeyed the ninth and 12th to fall behind. But with one in it at the 18th, Fichardt made a safe par while Van Zyl failed to get up and down from just off the green. Fichardt closed with a 72 for a 272 total of 16 under par while Van Zyl finished with a 73 and was caught for outright second by Bourdy's 70.

It was Fichardt's fourth win on the European Tour, including the St. Omer Open in 2012, and in all four he was leading or sharing the lead with a round to play. It was also his 13th win on the Sunshine Tour. Fichardt said: "I started losing focus after my birdie putt on the 13th. I was four shots clear at that point and I probably took the win for granted, but you can't afford to do that. I missed a short one on the 14th and then made two more bogeys, and all of a sudden I was struggling a little bit. The last few holes here are really tough, especially in the conditions, so I was just pleased to get the job done in the end.

"I always seem to play well in the wind, and I just love playing this course. You don't play too many courses like this overseas, where there are lots of options and you really have to think about what shot you're going to play. So I always enjoy coming here, and obviously winning the tournament makes the week especially enjoyable."

Dimension Data Pro-Am
George, South Africa
Winner: Jaco Van Zyl

It was third time lucky for Jaco Van Zyl as he turned a third successive appearance in the final grouping on the final day into victory at the Dimension Data Pro-Am at Fancourt. "You kind of feel you need to close at least one of them off," said Van Zyl, "so I definitely felt a lot of pressure coming up the stretch." The 34-year-old birdied two of the last three holes to win by a stroke over England's Daniel Brooks with Hennie Otto, Dean Burmester, Wallie Coetzee and Trevor Fisher, Jr. all two strokes further back.

After missing out at the Joburg and Africa Opens, Van Zyl claimed his 11th Sunshine Tour victory over three courses at Fancourt. He opened with a 68 on the Outeniqua course, then equaled the course record with a 64 on the famous Links circuit, before finishing with twin rounds of 70 on the Montagu course over the weekend. He finished on a 17-under-par total of 272.

The event came in a run of three co-sanctioned events in four weeks. Van Zyl said: "I've been getting better every week, and I'm looking forward to the European Tour co-sanctioned event in Tshwane."

Tshwane Open
Centurion, South Africa
Winner: Dawie Van de Walt

Dawie Van der Walt overcame the in-form Darren Fichardt to claim his first title on the Sunshine and European Tours. The only other wins for the 30-year-old in his professional career had come on mini-tours in America, where he now lives, and the first prize of R2.7 million was over R600,000 more than his previous career earnings on the Sunshine Tour.

Van der Walt beat Fichardt by two strokes after rounds of 68, 65, 67 and 67 for a 21-under-par total of 267 at the Els Club Copperleaf. The pair had started the final round tied for the lead alongside compatriot Charl Coetzee and Chile's Mark Tullo. Fichardt closed with a 69 to pip local professional Louis de Jager by one, with former world No. 1 amateur Peter Uihlein in fourth. Coetzee, who was penalized a shot for slow play, dropped to a share of fifth place, while Tullo came home in 42 to plummet to a share of 27th place.

Fichardt birdied three of the first five holes to claim the lead but parred the last 13 holes as he stuck at 19 under. Van der Walt hit a superb shot at the fourth hole, at 685 yards the longest ever on the European Tour, and tapped in for an eagle before birdies at the sixth and seventh holes took him out in 32. His only bogey of the week came at the 11th, but he settled himself by birdieing the 12th to go ahead again and made it a two-shot cushion with another at the 15th. Although he raced his first putt at the 18th past the hole, opening the possibility of Fichardt claiming a tie, Van der Walt saw his opponent miss yet another chance before safely making his par putt.

"You can only imagine what it's like to win such a big one," said Van der Walt. "I'm just really happy that I played well and won, because you can play well and not win. You start doubting yourself and at 30 years old you start to wonder if you're good enough and this shows me that I am. I would have liked to win before 30, but I'll definitely take this. Golf is a game where you don't get a lot of chances to win, and to do it is fantastic.

"I don't know what I'll do yet. The purses are a lot bigger in the European Tour, so I'll have to rethink some things. You can make your own schedule, which is important. I hit the ball really good and I never really had to chip, which is not my strength. If you hit a lot of greens and don't three-putt, then you're going to do well."

Telkom PGA Championship
Johannesburg, South Africa
Winner: Jaco Van Zyl

Jaco Van Zyl continued his good form from winning the Dimension Data Pro-Am and claimed one of the biggest events on the summer schedule of the Sunshine Tour with victory at the Telkom PGA Championship. It was the second time the 34-year had won the title after also winning in 2009. "I won often in the smaller events, so winning the Dimension Data Pro-Am and then backing it up with this one definitely helps with the confidence," he said after his 12th career victory.

Van Zyl had to hold steady over the last nine holes at Country Club Johannesburg as he came back from four-strokes behind at the turn. He had shared the lead with Chris Swanepoel, who had a third-round 63, but only went to the turn in even par while Swanepoel was out in 32. But Swanepoel self-imploded on the back nine, bogeying four of the last five holes while Van Zyl came home in three under. His closing 69, after rounds of 67, 65 and 67, gave him a 20-under total of 268 and a one-stroke victory over Dylan Frittelli, who closed with a 67, with Swanepoel taking third place after a 71.

"After Chris followed my birdie on 13 with his own, I asked him as we walked to the next tee how he expected me to catch him," admitted Van Zyl. "After nine holes, I thought it was pretty much done, but my caddie kept me motivated and reminded me it boils down to the last nine holes on Sunday. Things swung a little bit when I chipped in on 12 and the nice putt on 13, and then Chris started making a couple of unfortunate bogeys."

Investec Cup
Sun City, South Africa
Winner: Jaco Van Zyl

Jaco Van Zyl completed a superb summer on the Sunshine Tour by winning his third title at the Investec Cup and claiming the inaugural Chase for the Investec Cup Bonus Pool worth R2 million. The event for the top 30 on the points list compiled over the summer season were eligible to play on the Millvale Private Retreat course, the Rustenburg Golf Club and the Lost City Golf Club at Sun City, where the final 36 holes were played. Van Zyl continued his sparkling form after winning the previous week to take the lead with rounds of 66, 64 and 69.

But Hennie Otto, who started the last day six behind, produced a characteristically brilliant charge to close with a 62, with matching halves of 31. He birdied the last three holes and that meant Van Zyl, who was out in even par, had to conjure a fourth inward birdie at the 18th to tie. His 68 joined Otto on 267, 21 under par, with Justin Walters two behind in third place.

In the playoff Van Zyl could only match a par-five at the 18th, but Otto's brilliance suddenly disappeared. His chip stopped in the thick rough by the fringe and he then saw his par putt from two and a half feet lip out.

"It's not good to win like that," admitted Van Zyl, while of his bonus pool prize he added: "I was always told if I play good golf, the money will take care of itself. I've got a wife and two boys who will take care of the money — I've got a career to worry about."

Golden Pilsener Zimbabwe Open
Harare, Zimbabwe
Winner: Jake Roos

When Darren Fichardt's long putt from the back of the green hit the hole, bounced into the air and stopped inches away, and Francesco Laporta's more makeable birdie putt just slipped by on the 18th green, Jake Roos had achieved something for the first time at the Golden Pilsener Zimbabwe Open. All his previous five victories on the Sunshine Tour came after a playoff, but this time at Royal Harare the 32-year-old South African managed to avoid going to extra time. A closing 67, after rounds of 69, 67 and 71, gave Roos a total of 274, 14 under par, and a one-stroke win over the two third-round leaders, Fichardt and Italy's Laporta, who both closed with even-par 72s.

Roos had started the final round four strokes behind but finished strongly with birdies at the 13th, 15th and 16th holes. The leaders never got momentum on the final day, Fichardt having six bogeys to match his six birdies, while Laporta, who had a 63 on Saturday, had to recover from a triple bogey at the third hole.

"At the beginning of the back nine, I saw that no one was really pulling away, so I knew I still had a great chance, and, from there on, things started to happen for me," said Roos. "I'm glad I didn't have to play extra holes," said Roos, "but you can't count out the other guys until the last hole is done."

Investec Royal Swazi Open
Mbabane, Swaziland
Winner: James Kingston

Eleven years after his first victory in the Investec Royal Swazi Open James Kingston took the title again after beating Ruan de Smidt in a playoff. Kingston holed a 12-footer on the 18th green to win after the paired tied on 45 points at the Royal Swazi Sun Country Club.

Under the modified-Stableford points system, eight points were awarded for an albatross, five for an eagle, two for a birdie, with one point deducted for a bogey and three for a double bogey or worse. Kingston had daily point scores of 10, 9, 17 and 9 and made 21 birdies and two eagles over the 72 holes of regulation play. De Smidt had scores of 14, 7, 13 and 11, with four birdies coming in his last seven holes. The pair finished one point ahead of Mark Williams and Darryn Lloyd. Williams lipped out with a chip at the 18th that would have given him victory but then missed his short par putt.

"Every win is a big win and they're all gratifying," said the 47-year-old Kingston, who claimed his 12th Sunshine Tour victory. "I haven't won in awhile, and I've grinded over the last few months, so coming away with a win just makes it all worth it. Deep inside I knew I was playing well, and the fact that I've won before in Swaziland helped. It was a tough pin to attack today, but I had to take it on, because I went out to win."

Zambia Sugar Open
Lusaka, Zambia
Winner: Adilson Da Silva

Adilson Da Silva won the Zambia Sugar Open for the second time by one stroke over Martin du Toit and Alex Haindl. In blustery conditions on the final day, the 41-year-old Brazilian used all his experience in the closing stages to return a even-par 73, after rounds of 67, 72 and 69 at Lusaka Golf Club, to finish on an 11-under-par total of 281. Halfway leader du Toit, who had fallen back with a third round of 74, made a swift start on the final day with four birdies in the first five holes but could not sustain the challenge as he closed with a 72, while Haindl hauled himself up the leaderboard with a 70. Doug McGuigan, the 2011 winner, was lying joint second after 54 holes but dropped down with a 74 to tie for fourth place.

"It's always nice to come back to Zambia, and to win twice is great. I have a good feeling about this place and to win here again is a big thing for me," said Da Silva, the 2010 winner, after his 11th Sunshine Tour victory. "It's absolutely great to seal the win. Mentally it was a big thing to stay calm today and focus. I've been in this situation a couple of times, and I'm learning how to handle it."

Lombard Insurance Classic
Mbabane, Swaziland
Winner: Merrick Bremner

Merrick Bremner went wire-to-wire to claim his first win in five years back at the scene of his first victory. Bremner won the Lombard Insurance Classic at the Royal Swazi Sun Country Club in 2008. He claimed a second victory that season but had to wait until now to repeat the feat. It came a week after undergoing Lasik eye surgery which helped him read the greens much better and after vowing to concentrate fully over every shot. It was a stunning turn for the 27-year-old from Kempton Park who led by two strokes after an opening 63 with nine birdies, an eagle and two bogeys. He doubled his advantage with a bogey-free 65 in the second round but opened with two bogeys in the final round to give his opponents a chance.

Bremner got one of those dropped shots back before the turn, but it was his two birdies in the last four holes for a 71 that left him at 17 under par with a 199 total and a two-shot win. A 67 from P.H. McIntyre secured second place, two ahead of Jean Hugo, with Justin Harding in fourth place.

"It's been five years since I've been in the winner's circle, so the win is great," Bremner said. "I've been close a couple of times over the last few years and thankfully I managed to pull it off today."

Vodacom Origins of Golf - Simola
Eastern Cape, South Africa
Winner: Jacques Blaauw

A moment that Jacques Blaauw described as a "fluke" nevertheless won him a maiden title on the Sunshine Tour at the Vodacom Origins of Golf tournament at Simola. Blaauw made an eagle-two at the 16th hole and it proved the crucial strike that gave the 27-year-old South African a one-shot win over Danie van Tonder, P.H. McIntyre and Neil Schietekat. Five years after turning professional, Blaauw initially did not respond well after holding a one-stroke lead going into the final round and missed a putt from a foot and a half at the fourth as he went out in 38.

Having fallen behind a large pack of contenders, Blaauw then responded with a superb run on the back nine. He birdied the 11th, 14th and 15th holes before going ahead for good with an eagle at the 442-yard 16th. "I had 147 yards to the flag on 16," said Blaauw. "It was a bit long for me, so I had to hit quite a hard wedge, and luckily for me, it pitched, spun back about five meters and went in the hole. A fluke, really, but I'll take it. I was really tense at the start and I knew I needed to go deep on the back nine. I'm just so chuffed." Blaauw recorded scores of 68, 67 and 69 for a 12-under-par total of 204.

Polokwane Classic
Limpopo, South Africa
Winner: Dean Burmester

From four behind going into the final round, Dean Burmester may not have started the day thinking about winning his maiden title at the Polokwane Classic, but that is exactly as it turned out. Indeed, it was quite a turnaround as Burmester eventually won by four strokes over Merrick Bremner and Justin Harding. A consistent week was the key for the 24-year-old, in his third year on tour, as he returned rounds of 69, 67 and 68 for a 12-under-par total of 204. Bremner closed with a 67 and Harding a 72.

Titch Moore was the second-round leader, but he started the last day with a couple of bogeys and slipped to fourth place after a closing 77. Burmester, meanwhile, went out in 34 and birdied the 13th and 15th holes to go four ahead. At the latter he hit his approach from the rough to a foot for a tap-in birdie.

"I saw Titch was a little jittery after his start," said Burmester. "I just kept telling myself that with the wind blowing like it was, I just needed to focus on my pars and the birdies would come on their own. I think 15 was big. My caddie said to play it 77 meters and I pitched it 77, so I couldn't have hit a better one. It stopped a foot from the pin and after that I was four shots ahead."

Vodacom Origins of Golf - Selborne
KwaZulu-Natal, South Africa
Winner: Jacques Blaauw

One moment of brilliance late in the day helped Jacques Blaauw to his maiden title three weeks earlier, but it was a sustained assault on the front nine at Selborne Park that helped the 27-year-old to his second Vodacom Origins of Golf title. Six birdies in an outward nine of 30 put Blaauw in contention after he started the final round three strokes behind Merrick Bremner.

Bremner had opened with a 63, but it was the 64 of Blaauw on the last day that gave him victory at 18 under par. Two earlier rounds of 67 helped him to a total of 198, but on the back nine he still had plenty of work to do. Not dropping a shot all day was key, though after a birdie at the 12th he still needed another at the last to ensure a one-stroke win over defending champion Adilson Da Silva and Danie van Tonder, who both closed with 66s. Bremner finished with a 70 to finish three behind in fourth place. Blaauw said he "thinned" his drive at the 292-yard 18th onto the green and then two-putted for the winning birdie, while Da Silva missed from 15 feet to force a playoff.

"I had to have a fast start," Blaauw said, "because Merrick Bremner was three shots ahead of me. I knew I had to get up to his score pretty quickly and put some pressure on him. The front nine was amazing golf, the best golf I've played this year — and maybe the best of my career."

Sun City Challenge
Sun City, South Africa
Winner: Adilson Da Silva

Even a veteran winner like Adilson Da Silva can suffer from nerves down the stretch in a tournament, and what looked like being a comfortable victory at the Sun City Challenge suddenly became a test of the 41-year-old Brazilian's mettle. Both the windy conditions and a late charge challenged Da Silva. Big-hitting Jared Harvey, who has won twice on the Big Easy circuit but not yet on the Sunshine Tour, came home in 31 with an eagle and three birdies to set the clubhouse target at eight under par. After Da Silva had his second bogey in three holes at the 14th, Harvey birdied the 15th to get within one and then the par-five 18th to go even.

When Da Silva himself came to the last he faced a second shot with the wind off the left and water on the right but hit a four iron onto the green. His first putt from 30 feet ran two feet past and he knocked that one in for a one-stroke win. "That was maybe the best shot I played all week," he said. "I choked down on a four iron, and I aimed left because of the threat of the water on the right. With the wind coming from the left, it came off the club perfectly. I know my swing is good, but I've been working on the mental game and that helped today."

Da Silva secured his 12th Sunshine Tour win with rounds of 67, 70 and 70 for a 207 total of nine under par. Harvey closed with a 67 to finish four ahead of Merrick Bremner and Vaughn Groenewald.

Vodacom Origins of Golf - Euphoria
Naboomspruit, Limpopo, South Africa
Winner: Heinrich Bruiners

With the tournament finishing on National Women's Day, it was appropri-
ate that for the first time the Sunshine Tour staged an event on a course
designed by a woman. Not just any woman, however, but former world
No. 1 Annika Sorenstam whose course at Euphoria Golf Estates opened in
2008. Sorenstam said she made sure players would have to think on every
shot and the tough layout won praise from the competitors at the Vodacom
Origins of Golf event, but no one liked it better than Heinrich Bruiners.
The 25-year-old from George, who had to miss the entire 2011 season after
breaking his femur in a car accident, claimed his maiden victory by five
strokes. In the process he became the first qualifier to win an event on the
Sunshine Tour since Tim Clark in 2002.

Bruiners scored a four-under 68 to lead the qualifying by two strokes and
another 68 the next day put him two clear at the end of the first round.
A 69 in the second round gave Bruiners a four-stroke lead and put him in
the final group on the final day for the first time in his career. Two early
bogeys at the third and fourth holes did not bode well, but a birdie at the
ninth settled him down, and he eagled the 12th hole, with two three irons
to 20 feet, and birdied the 13th to stretch his lead again. He closed with a
71 for an eight-under total of 208. Jake Roos and Adilson Da Silva shared
second place on three under, with Allan Versfeld and Desvonde Botes sharing fourth place.

"It's a lot like the course I learned my golf on at Fancourt," said Bruiners. "You have to be straight off the tees and good off the fairways, and
I certainly felt comfortable with those aspects of my play all week."

Vodacom Origins of Golf - Langebaan
Western Cape, South Africa
Winner: Jean Hugo

Jean Hugo cruised to a record eighth victory in the Vodacom Origins of
Golf series, and his 15th in all on the Sunshine Tour, by finishing seven
strokes clear at Langebaan. After an opening 72, a nine-birdie 63 in the
second round had only put the 37-year-old one clear of the field, but his
67 on the last day spread-eagled the field in tricky conditions. Three birdies
on the front nine put him well in front, and he responded to a bogey at
the 11th, only his third of the week, with birdies at the next two holes and
another for good measure at the 18th. He finished on 202, 14 under par,
with Merrick Bremner, Jbe' Kruger and Andrew Curlewis all sharing second
place on seven under. Bremner had scores of 66 and 67 in the last two
rounds, but the damage was done with two triple bogeys in his opening 76.

"You feel it building," Hugo said of his ever-increasing lead, "and you
just have to stay within yourself. It's easy to just run away in your head
and think you've won the tournament after nine holes. That's obviously
what happened on 11. I had a three-putt for bogey, and I told myself the

closing holes were quite tough into the wind, and anything can happen. So I just knuckled down and made two more birdies on 12 and 13 which really gave me a nice cushion. And when I saw a leaderboard again, I was six shots clear. From then on, I just tried to protect that lead, and the birdie on 18 was a bonus."

Wild Waves Golf Challenge
KwaZulu-Natal, South Africa
Winner: Andrew Curlewis

Having finished runner-up the previous week for his fourth top-10 finish of the season, Andrew Curlewis capitalized on his good run of form with his first win in six years at the Wild Waves Golf Challenge at the Wild Coast Sun Country Club. Curlewis picked up his second victory after a lengthy wait by edging out Titch Moore and Desvonde Botes by a single stroke in a fascinating battle over the final round.

With the three leaders playing together, Moore started the day with a one-shot advantage over Curlewis and two over Botes, but it was the last who broke clear with a birdie at the 14th hole. But at the 15th he bogeyed and Curlewis birdied to jump into the lead. He went two up with a birdie at the 16th, but then Moore birdied the last two holes and Botes holed a 30-footer for a birdie at the last, meaning Curlewis had to make sure of his par for the win. He tapped in for a closing 65, after rounds of 66 and 63, to finish on a 16-under total of 194, having dropped just one shot all week. Christiaan Basson and Ulrich van den Berg shared fourth place, four strokes behind the runners-up.

"It was tough to keep the belief over the last few years," said Curlewis. "There have been lots of downs, and some ups, but my mom and dad, my girlfriend Tammy, other friends — they have kept me going. It's been a few long years, so to give myself a chance and then hold the others off coming down the last three holes feels very special."

Vodacom Origins of Golf - Parys
Parys, South Africa
Winner: Andrew Curlewis

Having gone six years between his first and second wins on the Sunshine Tour, Andrew Curlewis left it no longer than a fortnight to claim his third by winning his very next event at the Vodacom Origins of Golf tournament at Parys. Curlewis was four behind going into the final round, but in the windy conditions his 68 was the best score of the day. With earlier rounds of 72 and 69, he set the clubhouse target at seven under with a total of 209. He had two bogeys and two birdies in his first four holes, but the 30-year-old eagled the ninth and birdied the 10th and 13th holes to put himself in a good position, albeit he thought one too many. But overnight leader Lyle Rowe, after a second round of 65, could only manage a 72 and missed the green with his second at the par-five 18th and could only make a par to tie.

In the playoff at the 18th, Curlewis hit a fine second shot inside 10 feet and two putts were enough to beat Rowe, who had tangled with reeds on the bank of the Vaal River to the right of the 18th green.

"I feel for Lyle," said Curlewis. "I have never lost in a playoff, so I can't say I know what it feels like, but it can't be great. His time will come. He had a great second round, and he will close the deal sometime soon now. Once I was in the playoff, I was fairly relaxed. After all, the worst you can do is come second! And I hit two great shots to set myself up."

Platinum Classic
Rustenburg, South Africa
Winner: Neil Schietekat

Neil Schietekat was inspired by a loss earlier in the winter swing of the Sunshine Tour to finally record his maiden title at the Platinum Classic, where each round is played over two loops of the nine-hole Mooinooi course. The 29-year-old from Johannesburg won by three strokes over Jaco Ahlers and by four over James Kamte.

"Not winning never really bothered me," said Schietekat, "until I came second at the Vodacom Origins of Golf tournament at Simola. I told myself I should have won that one, and I started to take steps to fix things. I've been working hard on the mental side of things, and that makes a big difference. I won't tell you what goes on in my head, but it's some strange stuff, I can tell you."

Schietekat started the day one behind rookie Jacques Kruyswijk, who fell away with a 75, and played his first nine holes in 31 with an eagle at the third and birdies at the seventh, eighth and ninth holes. Now comfortably in front of the field, he played conservatively and parred in until a sloppy bogey at the last which was of no account. He recorded scores of 65, 68 and 68 for a 15-under total of 201. "Maybe the floodgates will open now," he added.

Vodacom Origins of Golf Final
Eastern Cape, South Africa
Winner: J.J. Senekal

Inspired by other first-time winners on the Sunshine Tour, J.J. Senekal, a 25-year-old from Somerset West, claimed his maiden victory at the Vodacom Origins of Golf Final at St. Francis Links. Senekal looked out of contention when he dropped three behind local favorite and former winner Titch Moore with two to play after three bogeys in a row and a birdie from Moore at the 16th. But Senekal rallied to win a playoff at the second extra hole as Moore suffered in the sand at the 18th.

Senekal birdied the 17th from 12 feet and then rolled in a 25-footer from the front of the 18th green to record scores of 70, 70 and 72 for a four-under total of 212. Moore, who teed off at the last with a two-shot lead, had found the back bunker and failed to get up and down, missing from 20 feet for victory. He closed with a 72 as the playoff pair finished two ahead of Lyle Rowe and three ahead of Charl Coetzee, Jean Hugo and Riekus Nortje, who led Senekal and Moore by one stroke with a round to play.

At the first playoff hole, Senekal got up and down to match Moore's par, but at the 18th again Moore's approach plugged under the lip of the front greenside bunker. He failed to recover with his first two attempts, so Senekal's two-putt par took the honors.

"I've dreamt of winning for a long time and now I've finally done it," Senekal said. "Some of the maiden winners from this year have inspired me, like Neil Schietekat at the Platinum Classic and Heinrich Bruiners at Euphoria. They've shown me that any of us can win, and today is a result of that."

BMG Classic
Johannesburg, South Africa
Winner: Ulrich van den Berg

With Glendower in Johannesburg hosting the South African Open in little more than a month after also staging the BMG Classic, Ulrich van den Berg made a timely return to the winner's circle. The 38-year-old won for the first time on the Sunshine Tour in three years to take his seventh title with a five-stroke victory over Hennie Otto and Titch Moore. Otto and van den Berg shared the first-round lead on 65, then Otto added a 68 to nudge one in front. But while van den Berg produced seven birdies and two bogeys for a closing 65 and a 15-under total of 201, Otto mixed an eagle and only two birdies with three bogeys and a double bogey.

Van den Berg saw a six-footer for par lip out at the fifth, which put Otto three ahead, but then responded with four birdies in a row from the ninth. Otto eagled the eighth as the pair both turned on 13 under, but then he had a double bogey at the 10th and came home in 39. Van den Berg drew away from his opponent with birdies at the 13th, 14th and 16th holes before dropping only his third shot of the tournament at the 17th. Moore closed with a 70 to tie for second with Otto, while Colin Nel and Merrick Bremner shared fourth place.

"Hennie is one of the hardest competitors we have," said van den Berg. "He never quits and to beat him is a real feather in my cap, especially to do it on the stretch. I knew I was in the lead, but I didn't know I had won it until I made the putt at 16. Glendower is our gem in Joburg. This is my favorite course up here and I'm looking forward to the SA Open, especially after this win!"

Lion of Africa Cape Town Open
Western Cape, South Africa
Winner: Tjaart van der Walt

After a lucky 13th runner-up finish earlier in the year, Tjaart van der Walt finally stepped into the winner's enclosure at the Lion of Africa Cape Town Open. The 39-year-old, who turned professional in 1996, was second at the Najeti Hotels Open at St. Omer in July, his second runner-up spot on the European Tour to go with five on the Sunshine Tour, three on the Web.com Tour and one each on the PGA Tour and the Asian Tour. But at Royal Cape Town, he took the lead with a third round of 65, including eight birdies in the first 12 holes, and did not relinquish it on the final day when a closing 71 left him at 274, 14 under par. Hennie Otto, who led at the halfway stage and was two behind overnight, slipped back to third place with a 76, while Michael Hollick had a best-of-the-day 68 to take second place, six behind the winner. Van der Walt bogeyed the first but recovered with birdies at the sixth and eighth holes before coming home with a steady, even-par back nine.

"After so many seconds you start to wonder if it's going to come through," said van der Walt, whose wife Vicki was caddieing for him. "It happened this week, so I'm over the moon. You have to just back yourself and go for it. If you pack in and stop playing, you will never know. I am living proof that you should never, never give up."

Nedbank Affinity Cup
Sun City, South Africa
Winner: Jacques Blaauw

There is never a good time for an interruption of play for dangerous weather, but when you need a birdie at the last hole to win and are faced with a greenside bunker shot, the timing is unfortunate. But Jacques Blaauw returned an hour later and got up and down to win the Nedbank Affinity Cup at the Lost City course at Sun City. Blaauw led from wire-to-wire after rounds of 64, 69 and 68 for a 15-under-par total of 201, but at the par-five last he was only tied with Ulrich van den Berg, who closed with a 67 that included an inward 32, and England Steve Surry, who had birdied three of the first four holes in his closing 68. Ross Wellington took fourth place after a final round of 65.

Blaauw broke through with two wins on the Vodacom Origins of Golf circuit and now added a third victory after birdieing the 14th from eight feet and hitting a wedge to two feet at the 16th. But he still needed that final birdie at the last. "That was the best bunker shot I have played," said the 27-year-old, "especially with everything on the line. I was very nervous, so I'm ecstatic with the chip and putt there. It's been five years and all the hard work is paying off and it's a great feeling to win again before the big summer events."

South African Open Championship
Ekurhuleni, Gauteng, South Africa
Winner: Morten Orum Madsen

On the same day that Thomas Bjorn almost won the individual section of the World Cup of Golf, finishing runner-up to Jason Day, a member of the same golf club, Silkeborg in Denmark, earned his maiden victory on the European Tour. Morten Orum Madsen claimed the South African Open Championship, the opening event on the 2014 European Tour season, by two strokes over Jbe' Kruger and Hennie Otto. The 25-year-old became only the third winner from continental Europe at one of the world's oldest championships and in his second season on the European Tour applied much of what he had learnt from studying the career of Bjorn. "He has always been my idol," he said of Bjorn. "Being from the same club and all the success he has had on the European Tour, everything about how he approaches the game and how he works and how he prepares for tournaments — I've always been very inspired by him, so I try and emulate some of those things and apply them to my game."

For much of the week at Glendower, there was a distinct possibility there would be a home winner as Charl Schwartzel shared the lead at the halfway stage and then went ahead on his own after the third round, with Madsen and Marco Crespi trailing by one. Schwartzel went three clear after three birdies in a row from the second but then collapsed with a triple bogey at the sixth and a double bogey at the 10th. Three birdies on the way home pulled him up into a tie for fourth place with Crespi, but it was Otto who appeared to have inherited the title. The former winner was four in front with four holes to play but bogeyed the 15th and had a double bogey at the 16th after his second shot finished just off the back of the green. He chipped on and three-putted.

Madsen, who picked up a shot on Otto by birdieing the 13th, then birdied each of the 15th and 16th holes to take the title. The Dane had rounds of 67, 66, 69 and 67 for a 19-under-par total of 269. Kruger posted a final round of 65, including seven birdies and an eagle, earlier in the day, while Otto closed with a 68 and Schwartzel with a 71. Madsen did not drop a shot on the final day and kept his nerve when he suddenly found himself in front.

"It's been an amazing day," he said. "Coming down here, I expected to play well but I didn't expect to stand here right now, that's for sure. I love the golf course. It's pretty similar to my home course. It's tree-lined and has really good greens."

Alfred Dunhill Championship
Mpumalanga, South Africa
Winner: Charl Schwartzel

After letting a chance to win the South African Open slip the previous week, Charl Schwartzel did not make the same mistake again when he returned to his happy hunting ground of Leopard Creek, on the edge of the Kruger National Park. Schwartzel won the Alfred Dunhill Championship for the third time, having previously triumphed at the co-sanctioned event in 2005, which was his first win on the European Tour, and in 2008. The 29-year-old never looked back after a double bogey at his 10th hole (actually the first hole) in his first round, not dropping a shot in the remaining 62 holes. Ultimately, he won by four strokes over Richard Finch, who finished three in front of Ross Fisher, Simon Dyson and Romain Wattel.

Morten Orum Madsen continued his fine form from the previous week, when he won the South African Open, by leading for the first two rounds before fading from contention. Schwartzel had rounds of 68, 68 and 67 to take a two-shot lead after three rounds, but Finch birdied two of the first three holes on the final day to draw even. While Finch went out in 31, Schwartzel had three birdies going out to stay one ahead before Finch bogeyed the 11th and had a double bogey at the 14th.

Schwartzel birdied the 13th to complete a 68 and finish on 271, 17 under par. Finch, who closed with a 70, had the satisfaction of knowing the result would go a long way to regaining his European Tour card, which he lost after the 2013 season and failed to recapture at the qualifying tournament. Dyson, with a disciplinary hearing for tapping down a spike mark at the BMW Masters hanging over him with a fine and an 18-month suspended ban handed down the following week, finished strongly with a 69, while Fisher had a 69 and Wattel a 71.

"I had that hiccup in the first round and after that pretty much flawless with no bogeys from there on in," said Schwartzel, whose only other win in 2013 was at the China Masters on the OneAsia Tour. "Most of the time if you play 60 holes or whatever it may be without bogey, then hopefully you'll win. It's always nice to get a win and get some confidence up. It's been one of those years where I have played well and just didn't get the wins. Whenever you win and you're playing well is great, whichever time of the year it happens."

Nedbank Golf Challenge
Sun City, South Africa
Winner: Thomas Bjorn

After the death of Nelson Mandela, the first black president of South Africa, at the age of 95 on the first evening of the Nedbank Golf Challenge, it was perhaps expecting too much for a home player to triumph as their nation mourned. Instead, one of the game's elder statesman not only produced a thrilling finale with two eagles on the back nine but delivered an eloquent tribute to the fallen Mandela at the presentation ceremony. "If everyone could live their lives just a little bit like Nelson Mandela, the world would be a better place," he said.

Bjorn, who added a closing 65 to earlier rounds of 67, 70 and 66, finished on a 20-under-par total of 268 at the Gary Player Country Club at Sun City and won by two strokes over Jamie Donaldson and Sergio Garcia, with Henrik Stenson taking fourth place. It was a 15th European Tour victory for Bjorn at the age of 42, following his win at the European Masters in the 2013 season in September. For the first time, the event was co-sanctioned by the European Tour.

Donaldson was ahead by three strokes after both the second and third rounds, having posted scores of 67, 66 and 67, and made two early birdies in the final round before a bogey at the ninth. However, he was caught by Garcia, who raced to the turn in 30. Although Donaldson completed a 70 and Garcia confirmed a 65, neither could keep pace with Bjorn, who went to the turn in 33 and then hit a superb five iron onto the green at the 10th and holed the putt for an eagle. At the 14th, he was slightly luckier that his approach ran through a bunker and skipped onto the green, but he again converted for his second eagle in five holes. He birdied the 15th to remove any doubt over the result and a bogey at the last was of no consequence.

"This is right up there with the best days of my career," said Bjorn, who took home the biggest check of his career worth $1.25 million. "You never forget your first victory, and then my win against Tiger in Dubai when I went toe-to-toe with him for four days and came out top was special, but winning here in the way that I did against a field of this quality is up there. It's not often you make two eagles on the back nine on a Sunday when you are in contention, and it was just one of those days when it was my day."

Nelson Mandela Championship
Durban, South Africa
Winner: Dawie Van der Walt

So it was that the tournament named after the former president of South Africa, the Nelson Mandela Championship, should take place during the official mourning period for the death of Mandela at the age of 95. With the funeral taking place on the Sunday that the tournament was due to finish, it was brought forward by a day to start on the Wednesday. Heavy rain, however, which left some fairways waterlogged, meant the first round took two and a half days to complete, the Mount Edgecombe course near Durban having been reduced to a par 70. While the inaugural event in 2012 at Royal Durban had to be shortened to 36 holes, this time the event finally got into its stride and England's Daniel Brooks led by three strokes after 36 holes without having dropped a stroke. Friday's second-round action also provided two players scoring 59s, Colin Nel, of South Africa, and Jorge Campillo, of Spain. Neither counted as the first sub-60 round on the European Tour as they were playing preferred lies.

Brooks' card was littered with bogeys in the third and final round as he slumped to a 76, and it was Dawie Van der Walt who took advantage. Having added a 62 in the second round to an opening 67, he was three behind Brooks at the start of the round, and a closing 66 gave the 30-year-old a two-stroke win over Campillo and Matthew Baldwin, who both scored 68s. Van der Walt holed from 30 feet for an eagle at the 12th and then birdied the 13th and 15th holes to seal his second victory on the European Tour. The first also came on home soil at the Tshwane Open, but in between he suffered injury and loss of form, meaning in the European Tour events the 30-year-old played in the summer he only made one cut.

His victory meant Van der Walt won the Sunshine Tour Order of Merit, but it was special for very different reasons. "It's obviously really special, making you a part of history," said Van der Walt. "Winning The Nelson Mandela at this time, when it's sad for everyone, everyone is mourning and tomorrow's the big day, it means a lot and it's something I can keep close to my heart for ever."

12. Women's Tours

Inbee Park is a young Korean golfer who enjoys peace and quiet and who was content to let attention come in its own good time, when it was ready and earned. She had no idea what she was in for. When attention came, in came in an avalanche.

Winning three majors in a row, and six tournaments overall, will tend to attraction attention. But through it all, she had a different goal. "I am most proud that I kept my eye on the higher goal — happiness," Park said. "I found it."

In the process of finding happiness, Park also triggered talk about winning the Grand Slam and made 2013 her year, and she became the first South Korean to win the Rolex Player of the Year Award. "I am especially proud to be the first player from South Korea to win this award," she said. "My hope is that my achievement will inspire a new generation of young girls … to pick up a set of golf clubs and follow their dreams."

Park capped off her huge year with the season-ending money title with $2,456,619.

Park already had one major to her credit, the 2008 U.S. Women's Open. This time she won, in order, the Kraft Nabisco Championship, the Wegmans LPGA Championship and the U.S. Women's Open. But the fourth major, if she had won it — the Ricoh Women's British Open — would not have constituted the Grand Slam because the Evian Championship had been designated the fifth major, beginning in 2013. Still, as someone noted, three out of five isn't bad.

Park won the season's first major, the Kraft Nabisco Championship, by four shots. In the Wegmans LPGA Championship, she blew a three-shot lead, birdied three of the last five holes to tie Catriona Matthew, then beat her with a birdie on the third hole of a playoff. Then she took the U.S. Women's Open, her second, by four strokes, becoming the first woman since Babe Zaharias in 1950 to win the first three majors of a year. To the Honda LPGA Thailand she added the North Texas LPGA Shootout and the Walmart NW Arkansas Championship for her six-win season.

In the other two majors: Stacy Lewis birdied the last two holes to win the Ricoh Women's British Open, taking her career-second major and stopping Park's bid for a fourth of the season. Norway's Suzann Pettersen took the Evian Championship in its debut as a major. It was her career-second major. Pettersen posted four wins for the season, Lewis three, and Shanshan Feng, Beatriz Recari and Lexi Thompson two each.

The year was a big time for youth. First, Park, only 24 during her wins, got the first one as a gift when Thailand rookie pro Ariya Jutanugarn, 17, suffered the pangs of inexperience and blew a two-stroke lead with a triple bogey on the final hole of the Honda LPGA Thailand. Lexi Thompson's distinction as the youngest ever to win on the LPGA Tour (the 2011 Navistar LPGA Classic at 16) lasted only 11 months, until New Zealand amateur Lydia Ko won the 2012 CN Canadian Women's Open at 15. Ko won it again in 2013, still an amateur. Then in October, the LPGA waived the age 18 requirement and admitted her as a professional. She won her first pro event in December, the Swinging Skirts World Ladies Masters, an event co-sanctioned by the Taiwan and Korea LPGAs.

Lewis took the Vare Trophy, for the lowest stroke average of the season, becoming the first American since Beth Daniel in 1994 to win it. Lewis posted a 69.484 average, edging Pettersen (69.696) and Park (69.869). It was the first time in LPGA history that three players averaged under 70 for a season.

Thailand's Moriya Jutanugarn, 19, older sister of Ariya, won the Rolex Rookie of the Year Award. She finished 47th on the money list with $293,158.

The year was busy with all kinds of stories, but none more intriguing than the chase for No. 1 in the Rolex Rankings. Time was when the occupant was fairly fixed for a while. Taiwan's Yani Tseng, for example, spent 109 weeks at the top. She slipped to 34th for 2013, and for the first time in six years on the tour, she failed to win, and for the first time in her career she slipped under $1 million in winnings, finishing with $405,068. Lewis took over for a while, and then Park, and along the way Suzann Pettersen challenged for it.

In the Solheim Cup at Colorado Country Club, a stunning sweep in the Saturday afternoon four-balls launched the Europeans to a historic 18-10 victory. It was Europe's second win in a row over the Americans and their first victory on American soil.

On the Japan LPGA Tour, a playoff in the first tournament foretold the way the year would end. Rikako Morita defeated Sakura Yokomine to win that Daikin Orchid overtime event and, eight months later, nosed her out in the race for the money-winning title.

Morita, 23, who won twice early in the 36-tournament season, was No. 1 most of the year, but Yokomine, a dominant figure on the circuit for nearly a decade, made a run at her in the fall. When she won her fourth of the year and 22nd of her career in mid-November, Yokomine jumped ahead, but Morita came back with a fourth victory of her own in the next-to-last event and held on in the finale to win the title by just over ¥1 million. It was the third second-place money finish for Yokomine, who was No. 1 in 2009 and fourth or better every year since 2005 except in 2012.

Multiple winners abounded behind Morita and Yokomine. Yumiko Yoshida won three times and Miki Saiki, Mamiko Higa, Natsuka Hori, Sun-Ju Ahn, Na-Ri Lee and Bo-Mee Lee twice each. Mika Miyazato came off the U.S. LPGA Tour to take the Japan Women's Open, Bo-Mee Lee took the Japan LPGA Championship and Shiho Oyama the season-ending Japan Tour Championship.

U.S. LPGA Tour

ISPS Handa Women's Australian Open
Canberra, ACT
Winner: Jiyai Shin

See Australian Ladies Tour section.

Honda LPGA Thailand
Chonburi, Thailand
Winner: Inbee Park

Inbee Park could see her victory emerging, one shot at a time. Only they weren't her shots. She had already finished, and she was watching Thailand's Ariya Jutanugarn, the latest of the young phenomenons, coming apart a little at a time on the final hole of the Honda LPGA Thailand.

Park, shooting Siam Country Club in 67-71-71-67, hadn't really challenged. She trailed Stacy Lewis by four in the first round, six through the second, and was four behind Jutanugarn after the third. Park finished at 12-under 276 and so was resigned to a high finish.

This was late February, only the second tournament, and the kids were already putting their stamp on the year. New Zealand amateur Lydia Ko, 15, nearly won the opener, the Women's Australian Open. Now Jutanugarn, 17, a rookie pro, was only one hole from winning, and against the class of the LPGA. Stacy Lewis, 2012 Player of the Year, opened with a 63, led by three through 36 holes, then blew to a 76. Rolex No. 1 Yani Tseng opened with a 75, then closed with a 63, joining Lewis in a group at third place.

Jutanugarn, playing on a sponsor's invitation, leaped to a three-stroke lead with a 70 in the third round. In the fourth, Park, playing ahead of her, was dazzling with six birdies through the 11th and took the lead when Jutanugarn bogeyed the eighth. Jutanugarn took it right back with a hole-in-one at the par-three 12th. A bogey at the 14th left her with the luxury of a two-stroke lead at the par-five 18th, and there, the rookie took over. She went for the green in two — "I was crazy to do that," she would say — bunkered the approach, took an unplayable lie drop, blasted over the green and ended up three-putting for a triple-bogey-eight that cost her the win.

And Park ended up with the easiest of her four tour victories. "This win just felt like it was not as much work," Park said. Well, wasn't it the unfortunate Jutanugarn who did most of the work?

HSBC Women's Champions
Singapore
Winner: Stacy Lewis

Stacy Lewis, 2012 Player of the Year, was battling three demons in the HSBC Women's Champions — her own nerves, Korean standout Na Yeon Choi and Sentosa Golf Club's 15th hole. Dealing with just one might not do it. She pretty much had to go 3-for-3. And she did, coming away with her sixth career LPGA victory.

Lewis and Choi chased Azahara Munoz through the first round, then turned the tournament into their personal shootout. They started the final round sharing a two-stroke lead over Paula Creamer. Lewis shook off an early birdie-bogey exchange and enjoyed a smashing finish to the front nine. She had a tap-in eagle at the par-five seventh off a 200-yard approach. "It was probably one of the best shots I've ever hit," Lewis said. It put her one up on Choi, two on Paula Creamer. She added a birdie on the ninth. Then came a jittery back nine.

"The last four or five holes, I was pretty nervous," Lewis admitted. "I just played hard and put my head down and tried to make as many putts as I could."

The par-four 15th tripped her again. She was leading by two coming to it, watered her tee shot again, bogeyed, letting Choi within a stroke. "I hit the fairway [at 15] in the practice rounds, but I didn't hit it on any tournament day," said a frustrated Lewis, who played it 5-4-3-5. "I had two in the water and two in the bunker. Today, I was just glad to get out of there with a bogey."

At the 17th, she bunkered her tee shot and bogeyed again, giving Choi one last chance. Choi's desperation birdie try at the 18th just missed wide, leaving her with a 72. Lewis holed her par putt, wrapping up a card of 67-66-69-71–273, 15 under, for the one-stroke win. Creamer was third, another stroke back.

"It's not the way I would have liked it, coming up 18," Lewis said, "but it was nice to have just the little tap-in to win."

RR Donnelley LPGA Founders Cup
Phoenix, Arizona
Winner: Stacy Lewis

Stacy Lewis, who found a golf career on an operating table, was groping for a word that wouldn't come — maybe "fate" would do — right after she won the RR Donnelley LPGA Founders Cup, her second straight victory, lifting her to No. 1 in the Rolex Rankings, ending Yani Tseng's reign at 109 weeks.

This was the young lady who spent years wearing a brace to correct her scoliosis, a curvature of the spine, and finally having a metal rod inserted in her back with screws.

"That was just 10 years ago," Lewis said. "That's not normal. That's not supposed to happen. I'm really not supposed to be here. People with metal in their back — how do you play golf? I don't know. I don't know why I'm here. I know that there's a reason and I know that everything happens for a reason."

Would Japan's Ai Miyazato feel the same way? A third-round 67 sent her into the final round with a four-stroke lead over South Korea's Jee Young Lee (72) and Lewis, who shot 66 but got a 68 on a freak two-stroke penalty when it was ruled that her caddie, Travis Wilson, had tested the sand when he stepped into a bunker at the 16th. Miyazato, looking for her 10th win, was leading Lewis by three with six holes to play. Then Miyazato's lead was down to one at the 16th, the hole where Lewis drew the penalty the day before. This time, Lewis drove into a fairway bunker, then hit a wedge from 123 yards to 18 feet and dropped the birdie putt. Miyazato hit her wedge into scrub bush, took an unplayable lie, and double-bogeyed.

Lewis, after shooting 68-65-68, made a spectacular charge to an eight-under 64 in the final round, with nine birdies — four over five holes from the 13th — and one bogey. She shot a 23-under 265 and won by three over Miyazato.

Said Lewis: "I couldn't have dreamed the kid growing up wearing a back brace 18 hours a day is the No. 1 player in the world."

Kia Classic
Carlsbad, California
Winner: Beatriz Recari

Caddies help their golfers in many ways — club selection, reading the greens, a pat on the back at the right time, etc. Trickery doesn't figure to be one of them. But it worked on Spain's Beatriz Recari in the Kia Classic, and she came away with her second LPGA Tour victory.

It happened on the second hole of a playoff with I.K. Kim, the 18th at Aviara Golf Club. She had already bogeyed it twice, three-putting it in the final hole of regulation and again on the first extra hole. What saved her is that Kim also three-putted it both times. Recari's caddie was ready for her on the second extra hole.

"I think my caddie tricked me a little bit," Recari said. "I think he put me more toward the right, more toward the pin." This time her aim was right and her six iron came down 18 feet from the cup, just on the fringe. Kim putted first, from 30 feet. She missed, and Recari was already celebrating before her 18-footer dropped.

The tournament was Kim's to win when she got hot in the final round and Recari wobbled a bit. Kim birdied three of her first seven holes and gave all the strokes back with three straight bogeys from the 11th. After two more birdies, she three-putted the 18th for a bogey and a 71. Recari was solid with 69-67-69 in the first three rounds, then was so-so in the final. She made her first bogey of the tournament at No. 6 — her 60th hole — then bogeyed the 11th. A birdie at the 16th set her up for the win, but she three-putted the 18th for a 74 and tied Kim at nine-under 279.

Recari staked her claim to the tournament at the 285-yard par-four 16th in the third round, where she fired her tee shot to four feet and got the eagle. It carried her to a two-stroke lead going into the final round.

The tournament opened on an odd note. Defending champion Yani Tseng was dropped from the field after missing the Wednesday pro-am.

Kraft Nabisco Championship
Rancho Mirage, California
Winner: Inbee Park

See Chapter 6.

LPGA LOTTE Championship
Kapolei, Hawaii
Winner: Suzann Pettersen

Suzann Pettersen was talking about the way she plays. Strictly pedal to the metal. But a quick glance in her rearview mirror, and the next words out of her mouth were: "I'm like, 'Oh my God! Where did she start this day?'"

Here came Lizette Salas, a second-year player of little accomplishment, who started the final round five off the lead in the LPGA LOTTE Championship. But suddenly, she was tearing up Ko Olina. Pettersen, the outstanding Norwegian, led through the middle rounds, and given her talent there was every reason to believe she could wrap up the win. But Salas didn't agree. After two early birdies and a bogey, she sprinted the rest of the way — birdies at the eighth and ninth, and a hole-out six iron from 169 yards for an eagle at the 10th, followed by five straight birdies from the 12th for a 10-under 62.

That's what caught Pettersen's attention. Suddenly, she was in a real fight. That triggered memories of her statement of just a day earlier, after she came out of the third round leading by one at 14 under. "I thought 20 [under] was going to do it," said Pettersen, aiming for a six-under 66 in the final round. "That would take a fantastic round from anyone behind me." That's what Salas delivered — a fantastic 62. Pettersen wasn't exactly slouching along. She birdied three out of six on the front nine, then birdied Nos. 14, 15 and 17, and it was a bogey at the 18th, where she missed the green, that cost her the outright win. After shooting 65-69-68-67–269, 19 under, Pettersen found herself in a playoff.

It was short. On the first playoff hole, Salas chunked her approach into the water and Pettersen had her career 11th win with a routine par. Salas wasn't crushed. She had the best finish of her two-year career, and thought of her collapse in the recent Kraft Nabisco. "I feel so proud of myself to put that 79 in the back of my mind," Salas said.

North Texas LPGA Shootout
Irving, Texas
Winner: Inbee Park

For Inbee Park, the inaugural North Texas LPGA Shootout started on the back nine of the final round. Put another way, that's where it ended for Carlota Ciganda.

Park, who trailed from the start, was playing excellent golf but just couldn't catch up. Spain's Ciganda, 22, the top rookie on the Ladies European Tour in 2012, was easily keeping Park at arm's length — until she stumbled in the back stretch. And so Park, Rolex No. 1 and the hottest player on the LPGA Tour, picked up her third victory in just the eighth event on the 2013 tour, and the fifth in her last 18 starts. She shot Los Colinas in 67-70-67-67–271, 13 under, and won by a stroke. And it was a surprise win.

"Coming into the final round, I was two shots back and I didn't really think about winning so much," Park said. "Carlota was playing really almost perfect. ... And until No. 13, I thought I wouldn't have a chance."

Park birdied the first and eighth but couldn't gain ground. Ciganda shook off an early bogey and kept her two-stroke lead with birdies at Nos. 3, 6 and 8. They matched birdies at the 10th. Then came Ciganda's fatal stumbles. She bogeyed the par-four 14th from the right rough, then double-bogeyed the par-four 15th after watering her approach. Park parred both and emerged with a one-stroke lead. It held up for the win in a dramatic finish at the par-five 18th. Ciganda holed a 15-foot putt for birdie and a 70 to tie Park, but briefly. Park dropped her own four-footer for the one-stroke win.

Ciganda got into contention with a game that was interesting, to say the least. She trailed Germany's Caroline Masson through the first two rounds with 66-70, hitting just four fairways in the first and needing only 26 putts, then hitting four fairways and needing 32 putts. She grabbed the lead in the third round with the help of a Ballesteros-like birdie, knocking a half-submerged ball out of a concrete drainage ditch to 10 feet. "I didn't think much," she said.

Kingsmill Championship
Williamsburg, Virginia
Winner: Cristie Kerr

The fact of the matter was that Michael Kerr was hitting the 19th hole before his daughter Cristie got to the 18th in the Kingsmill Championship.

"I rarely get nervous when she plays," Michael Kerr said. "This was the most nervous I have been. It wasn't the playoff. It was the last three holes. Honestly, I was in the bar, drinking, which I don't normally do."

Well, when a guy's daughter fights from behind, then ties, then has to go through a playoff to win — well, maybe a guy needs to settle himself.

"Where's my dad?" Cristie yelled, when the celebration erupted on the 18th green after she beat Suzann Pettersen on the second hole of their playoff. And her dad was already on his way, and hugs followed.

It was a long fight. Thailand's Ariya Jutanugarn, 17 — a rookie on the Ladies European Tour though not a member of the LPGA Tour — took command with 64-71–135 on the Kingsmill Rivers course and a one-stroke lead at the halfway point. Kerr (66-71) and Suzann Pettersen (68-69) were in a tie for fourth, two behind. Then Kerr moved in front with a six-birdie 66 in the third round, and was reminded that she was a two-time winner of the tournament.

"There's definitely no chickens to be counted," said Kerr, psyching herself out. "I've got to look at it like I'm two back tomorrow because that's when I play my best golf."

Pettersen was likewise not conceding anything. "Cristie's two ahead," she said. "I don't think that's a massive advantage." Ironically, she had just set the stage for the closing drama. Kerr led most of the final round, but a bogey at the 14th dropped her into a four-way tie for second and Pettersen took the lead with a birdie. Kerr caught her with a birdie at the 16th and they parred in, Kerr shooting 69, Pettersen 67 to tie at 12-under 272. Kerr got her 16th win with a par on the second extra hole.

"I wasn't going to lose — not today, not with my dad here," Kerr said.

Mobile Bay LPGA Classic
Mobile, Alabama
Winner: Jennifer Johnson

It might not be out of order to add a name under Jennifer Johnson's on the Mobile Bay LPGA Classic trophy, that of Chris Cunningham, who also might be a great guy to have at one's side at the pari mutuel window. Cunningham, a business executive, played with Johnson in the Wednesday pro-am. "When we shook hands on 18 he told me that everyone he's played with ends up winning the tournament that year," said Johnson. "He tells everyone he's the luckiest man in the world. But I didn't really think much about it."

Johnson, 21, a third-year pro looking for her first win, opened nicely if unimpressively with 67-70, joining a big crowd back in the pack at The Crossings, a par-72 in the Robert Trent Jones Trail. Then everything she had worked for and dreamed of clicked. A hard-fought 65-65 finish, an uncommon piece of work for such a young golfer, lifted her to a one-shot victory. In both rounds, after an early birdie-bogey exchange, she ran the table, going seven under for a 10-hole stretch in the third round, and seven under in a 12-hole run in the fourth. And the victory came as a surprise to her.

"It was fun," said Stacy Lewis, her playing partner. "I don't think she realized what she was doing. I told her when I hugged her, 'I think you just won yourself a golf tournament.'"

Johnson drew on veterans' nerves at the 17th. She faced a 15-foot birdie putt while Thailand's Pornanong Phatlum was tied with her at 20 under par. "I didn't want a playoff," Johnson told herself, "so I said, I'm going to make this thing." And she did, for a tournament record 21-under 267.

"I'm a little shocked," Johnson said. "I didn't even realize I shot 65.

The whole back nine, I didn't even know what was happening. The birdie putt on 17 — that's when I started thinking about winning."

Then she went looking for the prescient Chris Cunningham. "I almost feel like I owe the win to him," she said.

Pure Silk-Bahamas LPGA Classic
Paradise Island, Bahamas
Winner: Ilhee Lee

The brand-new Pure Silk-Bahamas LPGA Classic debuted in May and immediately earned the biggest asterisk in golf. The note would read: "Most discombobulated tournament in LPGA history." And not because Korea's Ilhee Lee scored her breakthrough victory. When a foot of rain hits a course in a five-hour stretch on Tuesday night of tournament week, it's clear things won't be combobulated.

The incredible storm flooded and damaged much of the Ocean Club course. The LPGA had to make some radical and probably unprecedented adjustments. There were two principal changes. First, the tournament was cut from 72 to 36 holes, the minimum required to make it official. But the 36 holes would be three rounds of 12, on a course cobbled together from playable holes, which led to baffling routing. The first round played like this: 10, 6, 7, 4, 5, 11, 12, 13, 14, 2, 3, 8. With changes through the tournament, par was 45-45-47. Just navigating the course was an adventure.

Cracked Laura Davies: "I just hope I don't get disqualified if I can't find my way to the next tee. I'll just walk slow and follow everybody else." Lindsey Wright made six straight threes but didn't know where. "I didn't know what was going on," she said. "I just play."

This was the stage for Lee, 24, who turned pro in 2006, joined the tour in 2010, and had a best finish of a tie for third at Kingsmill two weeks earlier. Lee came from behind, shooting 41-43-42–126, 11 under par, winning by two over Irene Cho. Like the tournament itself, Lee's finish was one for the books. In a howling wind, she holed a clutch par putt on the next-to-last hole, then birdied the last off a fairway wood out of light rough in a downpour.

Lee was in her element in the Bahamas, with the ocean and casinos nearby. "This week, I was very happy," she said. "I can play golf. I can swim. I can gamble. This is the best job in the world."

ShopRite LPGA Classic
Galloway Township, New Jersey
Winner: Karrie Webb

Karrie Webb was faced with the kind of choice no one should ever have to make. Should she follow her heart and race home to Australia to be with her dying grandmother, or listen to grandma and stay at the tournament and win it for her?

"She talked to me on the phone and said she didn't want me to come home, and that I had to win one for her," said Webb, through the tears. She listened to grandma. But spirit wouldn't be enough for a happy ending to the story. First off, Webb, a Hall-of-Famer, hadn't won in two years. Second, the Bay course at the Stockton Seaview Hotel had been tough on her.

"I've never really even had a shot to win here," Webb said. "So when I got off to that start, I thought, 'Oh, my God.' Well, when she started to make a turn for the better, my dad said, 'Look, she's going to make it, so the pressure is off.' ... I thought, 'Wow, I might actually be able to do this for her.'"

After opening with a one-over 72, Webb did it with two outstanding rounds — 69-68 — in heavy winds that sent scores sailing. Rolex No. 2 Stacy Lewis shot 80 in the second round and tied for 58th. No. 1 Inbee Park never challenged and tied for 38th, and Yani Tseng shot 80 in the third round and tied for 69th.

Webb came from five behind in the final round, and the start that inspired her was a birdie at No. 2, off a 25-foot putt, and an eagle at No. 3 on a six-footer. She added a birdie from five feet at the 18th, and also had made a remarkable six par-saving putts from five to six feet. She won by two over second-round leader Shanshan Feng with a four-under 209 total. That tied the highest winning score at the Bay course, and it gave Webb her career 39th win.

"It never gets old," Webb said. "It never gets any easier, either."

Wegmans LPGA Championship
Pittsford, New York
Winner: Inbee Park

See Chapter 6.

Walmart NW Arkansas Championship
Rogers, Arkansas
Winner: Inbee Park

Inbee Park and So Yeon Ryu are fellow South Koreans, the best of friends and practice partners. But in the Walmart NW Arkansas Championship at Pinnacle Country Club, Ryu committed a fatal error and went into the books as just another runner-up to the hottest player on the LPGA Tour.

Park capitalized on Ryu's double bogey in the final round and went on to beat her in a playoff, notching her second win in a row — after the LPGA Championship — and fifth of the season.

"I've won a lot of times this year, but I still feel the pressure coming into the final round every time," Park said. "I think that's going to happen no matter how many times I win."

Park came from behind in this one, trailing Mika Miyazato by four in the first round and Ryu and three others by two in the second. It was a shootout in the final round. Park fell three back when Ryu, playing behind her, birdied No. 2. Then Park roared into the hunt with three straight birdies from the sixth, and Ryu birdied the seventh. A crisis lurked just around the corner.

After Park bogeyed the 11th, Ryu nearly self-destructed. At the par-four 13th, Ryu reached the green in two, then suffered a golfer's nightmare. She four-putted for a double bogey. They each birdied again, and the tournament came down to the last hole. Park hit the green of the par-five in three and dropped her eight-foot putt for a birdie and the lead. Ryu, coming behind, had to match her. She did, with a 10-footer. Park shot 69-65-67, Ryu 66-66-69, and they tied at 12-under 201.

The playoff went back to the 18th. Park drove into the fairway, just missed the green and pitched to four feet. Ryu missed the fairway, had to lay up, then missed the green. She missed her birdie chip, and Park dropped her four-footer for her fifth win of the year, and it was only June.

Nerves, pressure and all — "It gets more exciting and more exciting," Park said. "That's for sure."

U.S. Women's Open
Southampton, New York
Winner: Inbee Park

See Chapter 6.

Manulife Financial LPGA Classic
Waterloo, Ontario, Canada
Winner: Hee Young Park

Inbee Park, going for her fourth straight victory, couldn't find the touch and tied for 14th in the Manulife Financial LPGA Classic. Meanwhile, another Park — Hee Young — didn't know it at the time, but when she birdied No. 1 in the third round, she had just entered into golf's mysterious sanctum, the zone. When she came out the other side that day, she had a flawless 10-under-par 61 and a one-shot lead.

"I didn't realize it," said Park, 26. Her only explanation: "My long putting was pretty awesome. I just tried to trust it."

The 61 — she was the 11th player in tour history to get one — was the big step that carried her to her second victory, but she had to go three extra holes to beat Angela Stanford the next day to get it.

Park opened her 61 modestly, with the birdie at the first. She eagled the par-five sixth, and that was it on the front nine. Then, riding the hot putter, she sprinted home with birdies at Nos. 10, 11, 13, 15, 17 and 18, reaching a 20-under 193. Stanford, who tied for the first-round lead, got to within one of Park with a 64 in the third. "When you see everybody going low, you have to go with them or you're going to be left behind," Stanford said. For Park, the question was getting that second victory. "It's going to be hard," she said. "Everybody can hit 10 under, nine under, any time, so I cannot breathe."

The finish was breathtaking. Park and Stanford fell behind Catriona Matthew down the stretch, but pulled ahead when she stumbled. Park scored five birdies down the back nine for her 65, and Stanford four for a 64, to tie. In the playoff at the par-five 18th, they matched birdies on the first two visits. On the third, Stanford bunkered her approach and Park ended it with a two-putt birdie.

Said Park: "I just kept reminding [myself], this is just another round. Keep it simple and just think about [hitting] my target."

Marathon Classic
Sylvania, Ohio
Winner: Beatriz Recari

Here were Paula Creamer and Spain's Beatriz Recari slugging it out, toe-to-toe, shot-for-shot, like a scene in the singles of the Solheim Cup. But this was the final round of the Marathon Classic, a stroke-play tournament in mid-July.

"Back and forth, back and forth," Recari said. "It felt like the Solheim Cup."

In a thrilling finish, Recari moved ahead down the back stretch and held on to win. They nearly matched each other over the four rounds. Recari shot the par-71 Highland Meadows in 69-65-67-66, a 17-under 267 total, to Creamer's 66-68-67-67–268.

They shared the lead with Allison Walshe in the second round, then moved three shots clear in the third, making it their own battle. It was this tight — both went the last 43 holes without a bogey.

"I still can't believe it, because I was so focused for the last two rounds," said Recari. "To just keep cool and just focus on my game."

Creamer, winless for three years, took the lead with a birdie at the third hole. Recari birdied the fourth to tie. Creamer edged ahead with a birdie at the fifth, Recari answered at the sixth. Both birdied the seventh. Recari's move came at the 181-yard, par-three 14th. She hit her hybrid tee shot to 12 feet, and Creamer put hers 25 feet away. Creamer missed her birdie try, and Recari dropped hers for the lead. They matched birdies at the par-four 16th, where Recari holed an uphill 25-footer and Creamer had stuck her wedge to three feet. Both narrowly missed birdies at the par-five 17th, and at the par-five 18th, Creamer recovered from the trees and missed a birdie try from 20 feet. Recari missed the green but saved par with a chip to five feet for her second win of the year.

"In all that golf out there," said Creamer, who last won in the 2010 U.S. Women's Open, "it's funny how it all comes down to the wire."

Said Recari: "I was definitely shaky on the last putt. I knew I had to make it and win and avoid a playoff."

Ricoh Women's British Open
St. Andrews, Fife, Scotland
Winner: Stacy Lewis

See Chapter 6.

The Solheim Cup
Parker, Colorado
Winners: Europe

The Solheim Cup, like the Ryder Cup of decades ago, used to be a nice vacation for the Americans. No longer. The Europeans? No more Ms. Nice Girls.

The 2013 Solheim, at Colorado Golf Club, echoed the 1987 Ryder Cup — the first European victory on U.S. soil. More to the point, it was not only the Europeans' second straight win, it was an 18-10 blowout, and cut the American superiority to an 8-5 edge in the biennial matches. If it was a sign of maturity for the Europeans, it was a strange kind of maturity. Six of the 12 were rookies, and one of them, a mere 17-year-old named Charley Hull, not only had a winning record, 2-1-0, she routed American star Paula Creamer, 5 and 4, in singles. And then asked Creamer for her autograph. The six European rookies went a collective 12-5-2 compared to the 2-7-4 of the four American rookies.

"They all just played so great this week," said European captain Liselotte Neumann. "We just came together as a great team ... and we're all just extremely proud and happy." But it was more than team spirit. Neumann credited her team with spending so much extra time studying the fast greens.

Said U.S. captain Meg Mallon: "I said ... in the beginning of the week [Europe] was such a young team, with nothing to lose. It just seemed like they were a little bit looser, they were making more putts, and we were not."

The turning point came in the Saturday afternoon four-balls. The Europeans were leading by a point coming into them, then swept all four matches and went into the Sunday singles with a commanding five-point lead. They completed their romp with a 7½-4½ win in the singles for the 18-10 victory.

Led by Sweden's Caroline Hedwall, the only golfer ever to win five points in the Solheim Cup, the Europeans went nine deep with winning records. The Americans had one, Brittany Lang (3-1-0). Michelle Wie was next at 2-2-0. The other 10 had losing records.

Said Hedwall, surely speaking for her teammates: "I don't know what to say right now. I'm just shaking. It's unbelievable."

CN Canadian Women's Open
Edmonton, Alberta, Canada
Winner: Lydia Ko

It was the 2013 CN Canadian Women's Open, and here came the defending champion, Lydia Ko, a year older and a year wiser, now all of 16, still an amateur kid taking on the best women golfers in the world. A year earlier, at age 15 years, four months, she became the youngest ever to win an LPGA Tour event. Now she came to Royal Mayfair as a teenager to be reckoned with.

"Because you're the defending champion, people are going to expect more," said Ko, a Korean-born New Zealander. "I called my dad a couple of days ago and he just said, 'Relax, you can't control everything. Just play the game that you want to play.'"

Ko took the fatherly advice, and after trailing only in the middle two rounds, posted a card of 65-69-67-64 for a five-stroke victory at 15-under 265. That opening 65 put her perfectly in her setting. She was tied for the lead with American Angela Stanford, 35, five-time winner on the LPGA Tour, and Christel Boeljon, 26, three-time winner on the Ladies European Tour — a girl among women, despite her record. This was her fourth victory in a professional event, and she had played in 14 LPGA events over two years and never missed a cut.

Ko trailed through the middle rounds, by two shots in the second and one in the third, then ran away from the field in the fourth. France's Karine Icher closed with a 67 to finish second and got the $300,000 first-place prize Ko couldn't take as an amateur.

Ko birdied five of the first eight holes and went to 15 under with another at the 12th. After a bogey at the 13th and four straight pars, she birdied the 18th, sinking a 15-foot putt for her five-shot win and another chapter in golf history.

"I never really thought about making history and all that," Ko said. "History is — I don't know where it starts. So, yeah, it's awesome to be a part of history."

Said Icher: "As an amateur, and so young — it's great for women's golf, but not so great for us."

Safeway Classic
Portland, Oregon
Winner: Suzann Pettersen

It's some 4,700 miles from Norway, but Portland, Oregon, still feels like home to Suzann Pettersen. Chalk up another Safeway Classic, the second in three years for the Norwegian ace.

"Seems like Portland is a good stop for me," said Pettersen, after shooting Columbia Edgewater in 68-63-70-67–268, 20 under par, for a two-stroke victory over Stacy Lewis. "Seems like I always play well here."

Pettersen, in the mix from the start, had to come from behind in the final round, and even then she might not have made it without Yani Tseng's monumental collapse. Tseng, the former Rolex World No. 1, who has fallen on erratic times, led by three going into the fourth round, then came apart completely. She made two birdies, but scattered a double bogey and six bogeys across 15 holes for a 78.

That's when Pettersen, playing with Tseng and trailing her by three, jumped in. But first came a rocky start. A poor eight-iron tee shot at the par-three No. 2 sent her to a double bogey. "I felt like an amateur," she said. Then while Tseng was coming undone, Pettersen was chasing Lewis and caught fire. She scorched Columbia Edgewater with eight birdies across the next 11 holes. She tied Lewis at the par-three eighth, dropping an 18-foot birdie putt. She added a five-footer at the 10th and a 25-footer at the 11th, and got her lead to four with an eight-footer at the par-three 13th. Finally, a bogey at the 16th marred the finish, but Pettersen had her second win of the year and the 12th of her career.

"Once I got going, I felt like I made a lot of clutch putts," Pettersen said. "The putter was a good friend of mine."

She was still smarting from her showing of a week earlier at the Canadian Women's Open, when she started the final round trailing by one and ended up eight behind the winner, Lydia Ko.

Said Pettersen: "I felt this was like a good bounce back."

Evian Championship
Evians-les-Bains, France
Winner: Suzann Pettersen

See Chapter 6.

Reignwood LPGA Classic
Beijing, China
Winner: Shanshan Feng

The LPGA appeared in China for the first time with the playing of the Reignwood Classic, and the debut was both auspicious and inauspicious. Shanshan Feng made it a point of national pride that a native daughter should win the inaugural event, and in a stunning conclusion. On the other hand, Beijing's notorious air pollution drew worldwide attention. Some golfers played wearing surgical masks, and while rain and lightning delays are common in golf, the Reignwood is believed to be the first tournament to have smog delays.

With Jessica Korda fading from the lead through the first two rounds, and with Rolex No. 1 Inbee Park a bit off her game, the tournament became a battle between Feng, China's first major winner, with the 2012 Wegman's LPGA Championship, and Stacy Lewis. They came out of the second round deadlocked at two-under 134, Feng off 70-64 and Lewis, 68-66. Feng inched ahead in the third round, a 64 to Lewis' 65. Both birdied the last two holes, and Feng expected the same kind of battle in the final round. "I've played Stacy many times," Feng said. "I know she's a very aggressive player. A one-stroke lead is very small."

Aggressive was right. Lewis birdied No. 1, then three straight from No. 4 to inch ahead of Feng, and she led for most of the round. The golf was of top quality. When both bogeyed the 14th, it was Lewis' only bogey of the tournament, and Feng's was her first for 50 holes and only her third of the tournament.

The difference came at the end. Lewis was one hole away from her fourth win of the year, coming to the par-five 18th. Feng said she knew Lewis would go for the green, so she had to go after it, too.

"Suddenly I heard the noise, and the crowd was excited," Feng said. "So I thought it must be good."

Her ball had hit the flagstick and stopped a few feet away. She dropped the eagle putt over Lewis' par for a matching 68 and a one-shot win at 26-under 266.

Sime Darby LPGA Malaysia
Kuala Lumpur, Malaysia
Winner: Lexi Thompson

It had been two years, almost to the week, since Lexi Thompson won her first tournament, and much was expected of her after that. So it surprised some that it was two years before she won her second, the 2013 Sime Darby LPGA Malaysia in mid-October. Expectations sometimes weigh very heavy. Forgotten in this situation was that Thompson was only 16 when she won the Navistar, and now was 18 in winning the Sime Darby at Kuala Lumpur Golf and Country Club.

"I mean, it took a little longer than I thought," Thompson said. "But it's the top players in the world here ... Every tournament, you have to shoot super low and you have to have your 'A' game, and that's what I had this week."

Thompson made her big move in the second round, challenging Ilhee Lee with a sizzling charge, birdieing Nos. 5, 6, 12 and 13, holing out for an eagle at the par-four 14th, then adding birdies at the 15th and 16th for an eight-under 63 to close within a stroke heading into the third round. Thompson went on another spree in the third, notching five birdies from the fourth through the 13th, and with her bogey-free 66 she vaulted to a three-stroke lead on Lee going into the final round. Suzann Pettersen, six behind, still had hopes. "Lexi is playing great, so there's definitely a low one needed tomorrow," she said. But she wouldn't be the one to get it. That would be Shanshan Feng, Reignwood winner last week, but she wouldn't get low enough.

Thompson started par-bogey in the final round, then went on another tear. She birdied the 10th on a wedge to four feet, the 11th on a 35-foot putt, and added another birdie at the 12th. She went birdie-bogey from the 16th and then headed for home. She closed with a 69, a tournament-record 19-under 265 and a four-stroke win over Feng. "I was feeling very good coming up to the 18th green," she said, not sounding like a teenager.

Said Feng, all of 24: "I think she's making us look old."

LPGA KEB - HanaBank Championship
Incheon, South Korea
Winner: Amy Yang

If Amy Yang ever writes a book, she might want to call it, "How To Succeed in Golf Without Trying So Hard."

Yang, 24, who took up the game at age 10, won three times on the Ladies European Tour and once on her home KLPGA Tour, but on the U.S.

LPGA Tour she had been banging her head against the wall for years. She admitted she even thought about quitting.

"I used to go all out in practice, hitting shots until dusk without taking breaks," Yang said. "But I decided to step back and look at the world around me. I also took some time off, and I gradually got better."

For 118 starts, her best finish was a playoff runner-up in 2011. Finally, in her 119th, Yang got that coveted first win in the LPGA KEB - HanaBank Championship, at home in South Korea, beating countrywoman Hee Kyung Seo in a playoff.

Yang, shooting Sky 72 Golf Club in 67-71-69–207, shared the first-round lead off a run of five birdies from the fourth hole, but in the second, three bogeys in five holes from the 10th made it look like more of the same old thing. She slipped a stroke behind Anna Nordqvist and Katherine Hull-Kirk and was tied with defending champion Suzann Pettersen, quiet since winning her third of the season early in September.

First, a path opened up in the final round. Nordqvist struggled to a 75 and Hull-Kirk collapsed with an 80. Yang birdied the eighth, took her only bogey at the 11th, then holed out for an eagle at the par-four 15th and birdied the last. Seo also had a hole-out eagle, hers at the par-four 11th, and she also birdied the last, tying Yang with a 68.

In the playoff at the par-five 18th, both drove into the rough, both chopped out and both hit the green. Seo missed her birdie try from 25 feet, but Yang nailed hers from 16 and had that first win.

"I don't think I will be able to sleep tonight," Yang said.

Sunrise LPGA Taiwan Championship
Yang Mei, Taiwan
Winner: Suzann Pettersen

When a golfer calls the shot on a hole-in-one and pulls it off, it's time for the rest of the field to start thinking about second place.

Suzann Pettersen, the defending champion, came to Sunrise Golf and Country Club's 133-yard second, tested the wind, then reached for her pitching wedge. "I called the shot," the Norwegian said. "I hit it exactly how I wanted and was fortunate enough that I had a good break."

It was a big help. It gave her some breathing room in a five-stroke win that wasn't nearly as comfortable as it looked in the nine-under-par 279 performance (68-69-73-69) that made the Sunrise LPGA Taiwan Championship her fourth win of the year and 14th of her career. Pettersen led all the way, but her plush-looking win was as much about the sluggishness of challengers as it was about her own play. Four shots was her narrowest lead, and a three-under 69 was the lowest any challenger could throw at her.

But she did get a good scare in the final round. Spain's Azahara Munoz, four behind starting the round, charged to three birdies in five holes from the fourth, and came to within one when Pettersen bogeyed the ninth. Munoz, seeking her second win, also birdied the 12th, but bogeys at 13 and 16 ruined her bid, and Pettersen pulled safely away with birdies at 13,

14 and 18. As Pettersen already had said after the third round, "I could easily have lost it out there."

The surprise of the tournament was Taiwanese star Yani Tseng, if surprise was the right word. Even playing before the homefolks couldn't revive her considerable game. Tseng, the 2011 Sunrise winner, opened with 76-78 and finished 19 shots off the lead. The tour's dominant player not long ago, she was now winless in 42 starts, and had dropped from No. 1 to No. 25 in the Rolex World Rankings in seven months.

P.S. on Pettersen's ace: "It's nice to get a hole-in-one," she observed, "when you actually call the shot and then pull the trigger."

That's called understatement.

Mizuno Classic
Shima, Mie
Winner: Teresa Lu

See Japan LPGA Tour section.

Lorena Ochoa Invitational
Guadalajara, Mexico
Winner: Lexi Thompson

The excitement around the wondrous Lydia Ko, all of 16, was such that one might think there were no other kids playing serious golf. Lexi Thompson disabused everybody of such a notion with a come-from-behind win in the Lorena Ochoa Invitational, the next-to-last tournament of the season, a fund-raiser for the retired star's youth golf foundation.

Thompson, a grizzled veteran of 18 now, had to come through in the absolute clutch, with a birdie on the final hole, to edge Stacy Lewis with a 16-under 272 total at Guadalajara Country Club. It was her second win of the season, after the Sime Darby in Malaysia a month earlier, which broke a two-year dry spell since her first win at age 16, in 2011. Thompson trailed by six in the first round and one in the second on her 72-64 start, then took the lead with a 67-69 finish, but played like a seasoned veteran and not a teenager going head-to-head with Lewis down the stretch.

Thompson had to share the spotlight with Inbee Park, who clinched the Rolex Player of the Year award with her fourth-place finish. She was the first South Korean to win the award.

Going down the final nine, Lewis fell three behind with a bogey at the 11th, then birdied three straight from the 12th and was up by one over Thompson, leading for the first time in the tournament. They were tied again when Lewis bogeyed the par-three 17th, and the stage was set for Thompson's dramatic win.

Lewis' chances died when she lipped out a short birdie putt at the 18th just after Thompson birdied from five feet. "I gave that one to her," Lewis said. "I had that one in my hands, and just didn't get it done."

Thompson had reached the par-five 18th, but was some 50 feet from the flag. She got her first putt up to five feet. "On the second putt, that's what it all came down to — thinking I can make it," she said. "And I went up to it confidently. Just knock it in." And so she did.

CME Group Titleholders
Naples, Florida
Winner: Shanshan Feng

There was a lot at stake in the CME Group Titleholders, the LPGA Tour's season finale — the money-winning title, the Vare Trophy, for the lowest scoring average, one last chance for a victory, and to complete the picture, the Rookie of the Year award.

China's Shanshan Feng was only in the running for a chance for a win, but wasn't hugely confident. "Before I started, I never thought I was going to win," Feng said, after the final round. "I knew I was only two behind. But I thought all the people in the last group were really strong competitors." They indeed were, but they slipped while Feng was getting up steam, and then she walked off Tiburon Golf Club's last green with her second win of the year, after the Reignwood LPGA Classic early in October, and the third of her young career.

Natalie Gulbis suffered the cruelest fall of all. She raced into a tie for the third-round lead with a 65 and had at least a chance at the second win of her career. Then she soared to an 82 in the final round. Her third-round co-leaders also fell short. Gerina Piller needed a birdie at the last to tie Feng, but her 10-foot putt just missed. Thailand's Pornanong Phatlum couldn't get going, shot 70 and finished third.

Feng went the last 31 holes without a bogey. She erased her final-round deficit in a hurry, with four birdies in six holes, jumped into the lead and stayed there, posting a card of 66-74-67-66–273, 15 under, and won the richest prize of the season, $700,000. What did it mean?

"Maybe it means I can take more time off in the off-season," said Feng.

In the final races: Inbee Park, who clinched the Player of the Year award the previous week, added the money-winning title. She finished a solo fifth, won $63,106, and took the money title with $2,456,619. Stacy Lewis tied for sixth and won the Vare Trophy with an average of 69.48. Thailand's Moriya Jutanugarn tied for 33rd to win the Rolex Rookie of the Year award.

Ladies European Tour

Volvik RACV Ladies Masters
Ashmore, Queensland
Winner: Karrie Webb

See Australian Ladies Tour section.

ISPS Handa New Zealand Women's Open
Christchurch, New Zealand
Winner: Lydia Ko

See Australian Ladies Tour section.

ISPS Handa Women's Australian Open
Canberra, ACT
Winner: Jiyai Shin

See Australian Ladies Tour section.

Mission Hills World Ladies Championship
Haikou, Hainan, China
Winner: Suzann Pettersen

Suzann Pettersen extended her trip to Asia after playing two LPGA events in the previous fortnight and was thankful she did after beating Inbee Park, winner of the Honda LPGA Thailand two weeks earlier, at the Mission Hills World Ladies Championship.

Park, who led after the second and third rounds, was two ahead of Pettersen at the start of the final day, and the 31-year-old Norwegian knew she had to produce her best golf of the week to win. She closed with a bogey-free 66, following rounds of 70, 67 and 67, to finish on an 18-under-par total of 270. Park birdied the last hole to finish only one stroke back, but twin weekend rounds of 69 could not match her earlier efforts of 68 and 65. Defending champion Shanshan Feng took third place, six strokes behind the runner-up. Carlota Ciganda set a new course record of 63 at the Sandbelt Trails course but slipped to a tie for eighth on the weekend.

"I felt like there was a 64 out there today, and I got off to a good start," said Pettersen, who birdied the second, third and fourth holes. "My goal was to get it to 20 under par. I know Inbee is in there and if she just gets one look at a putt, it's in, so I had to bring my best and the putter was hot today. This sets me up for a good start to the year."

It was a sixth LET win for Pettersen and the 16th of her career. Korea won the team event with Park and Ha-Neul Kim finishing on 16 under par and five ahead of Pettersen and Marianne Skarpnord for Norway, with Thailand third and England fourth.

Lalla Meryem Cup
Agadir, Morocco
Winner: Ariya Jutanugarn

Ariya Jutanugarn won her maiden professional title in only her fourth start on the Ladies European Tour at the Lalla Meryem Cup at Golf de l'Ocean in Agadir. The 17-year-old Jutanugarn had enjoyed a precocious opening to her pro career after winning the LET qualifying tournament in Morocco in December. The Thai returned to the country for a three-stroke victory after twice finishing runner-up in the intervening three months. She was second to Karrie Webb at the Volvik Masters in Australia and then appeared about to win in her home country at the Thailand LPGA until she had a triple bogey at the final hole.

A double bogey at the 15th hole of the final round was a late worry for Jutanugarn, but she birdied the 17th, and although Beth Allen had briefly closed within one, Allen shared second place with England's Charley Hull. Just 17 herself, and only having earned conditional status at the qualifying tournament, Hull had overtaken Jutanugarn's lead with a third-round seven-under 64. Leading the Thai by one overnight, there was a two-shot swing at the first hole when Hull's ball finished in a hole over the green, but with no evidence of a burrowing animal there was no relief. She eventually holed from 15 feet for a bogey.

Jutanugarn closed with a third successive 67, after an opening 69, for a 14-under-par total of 270. Allen finished off with a 68, while Hull had a 71. Katie Burnett finished fourth, with Mel Reid and Laura Davies among those sharing eighth place.

After winning €48,750, Jutanugarn said: "It's all for my dad! I'm going to keep playing on the European Tour and I hope to win some more."

South African Women's Open
Hibiscus Coast, South Africa
Winner: Marianne Skarpnord

On the opening day of the South African Women's Open at Southbroom, Norway's Marianne Skarpnord scored a three-under-par 69 and it turned out that round was good enough for victory. The second day's play was washed out by torrential rain and the event was cut to 36 holes. However, on Sunday, the scheduled third and final day, there was only time for a few more holes to be played before both rain and then gale force winds, gusting over 65 mph, interrupted play again. With similar weather forecast for the following day, the decision was taken to reduce the event further to 18 holes.

Skarpnord therefore won by one stroke over Ashleigh Simon, Stacy Lee Bregman, Camilla Lennarth, Minea Blomqvist, Charley Hull, Katie Burnett and Nina Holleder. It was Skarpnord's third win on the LET, following two in 2009, although the 27-year-old had won on the LET Access Series in 2012.

"It's not the way we all would have liked to end the tournament, but we all understand how difficult the weather was. It was a very challenging week for everybody," said Skarpnord.

Turkish Airlines Ladies Open
Belek, Antalya, Turkey
Winner: Lee-Anne Pace

On one of the toughest courses on the circuit, Lee-Anne Pace secured her first win in three years. In 2010 the 32-year-old South African claimed the Order of Merit title and won five times around the world. Her wait for another victory ended at the Turkish Airlines Ladies Open with a one-stroke victory over Carlota Ciganda, Charley Hull and Minea Blomqvist. Christel Boeljon finished in fifth place, two strokes behind. It was the Belgian's worst finish in the tournament after back-to-back victories in 2011 and 2012 and a runner-up finish in 2010 at the National Club in Belek.

Pace came from two behind third-round leaders Ciganda and Hull, with a closing round of 72. She had two rounds of 70, as well as a 77 in the second round, for an overall total of three-under-par 289. Birdies at the second and fourth holes gave her a one-shot lead at the turn, and a run of bogey-birdie-par-bogey from the 11th meant she set the clubhouse target. Ciganda, Hull and Boeljon all had the chance to tie with a birdie. Boeljon faltered when she bunkered her drive and took a bogey, while Ciganda lipped out from 25 feet, and Hull's birdie effort just slipped. For the 17-year-old Englishwoman, it was a third runner-up finish in three events this year.

"It's so nice to win again. It's been awhile and to do it again is fantastic," Pace said. "My heart stopped for a beat with those putts at the end, I was trying not to look. It is a tight course and the greens got harder by the end of the week, definitely one of the toughest courses we play."

Deloitte Ladies Open
Amsterdam, Netherlands
Winner: Holly Clyburn

Holly Clyburn won the battle of the 2012 Curtis Cup-winning teammates as the 22-year-old from Cleethorpes beat Charley Hull by three strokes to win the Deloitte Ladies Open. Hull maintained her position as the player to beat on the tour in 2013 with a brilliant last-round charge, but Clyburn held firm to claim her maiden title on the circuit. A winner on the LET Access Series just days after turning professional in October, Clyburn was playing in only her fourth event of the season but compiled rounds of 71, 69 and 71 to finish on an eight-under-par total of 211.

It was seasonably cold on the opening two days at The International, a new course next to Schiphol Airport in Amsterdam, and though it warmed up marginally for the final round, the wind was gusting to over 20 mph. Clyburn started the last day one behind Camilla Lennarth, the leader for the first two days who closed with a 77 to tie for fourth place alongside defending champion Carlota Ciganda and Bree Arthur, while Carin Koch took third place.

Hull had six birdies in nine holes from the third, but two late bogeys meant a last round of 69 as she set the clubhouse target at five under. It was good enough for a fourth successive runner-up finish and top spot on the Order of Merit. But after a bogey at the fourth, Clyburn birdied the fifth and sixth holes and holed from 15 feet at the 12th for another. She then parred in for an impressive victory.

"I'm flabbergasted," said Clyburn. "I played great golf all week pretty much. It proves that I can win, makes me believe in myself and makes me think that I can go on to win bigger things."

UniCredit Ladies German Open
Munich, Germany
Winner: Carlota Ciganda

Amid torrential rain and flooding that caused problems across Germany and the Czech Republic, Spain's Carlota Ciganda celebrated her 23rd birthday with a playoff victory over England's Charley Hull. Amazingly, it was a fifth successive runner-up finish for the 17-year-old Hull as she came agonizingly close to victory before Ciganda, who won the Order of Merit as a rookie in 2012, claimed her third title. After a first round in which Hull was one of five co-leaders after a 67 and Ciganda had a 68, the second day's play was entirely washed out. On the third day, the second round was played over only nine holes, three from the front nine and the first six from the back nine.

More rain, at times torrential, meant the leaders had to return to the course late in the evening to complete their last few holes. Hull had taken a two-shot lead, but Ciganda birdied the 14th, the penultimate hole, while Hull came up short at the same hole and did not get up and down. They tied at six under par with a total of 101 strokes, Hull after a 34, Ciganda with a two-under 33, and finished one ahead of Rebecca Hudson. Nontaya Srisawang, Stefanie Michl, Linda Wessberg and Marjet van der Graff were all a further stroke back.

No play was possible on Sunday, or would be on Monday due to the forecast, so there was a playoff at the par-three 15th. Ciganda, who had been practicing with a seven iron on the range, hit the club to six feet, and then Hull hit a three-quarter six iron to 20 feet. Hull's birdie putt came up just an inch in front of the hole while Ciganda holed hers for the win. "I hit a great shot, but I'm very lucky to make that putt because the greens were slow," Ciganda said. "I hit a good putt and won, so I'm very happy!"

Hull turned to her father, Dave, afterwards and asked: "When am I going to win?"

Allianz Ladies Slovak Open
Brezno, Tale, Slovakia
Winner: Gwladys Nocera

Charley Hull's run of second-place finishes came to an end at the Allianz Ladies Slovak Open, but not in the way she wanted. Instead of the victory, Hull was out of the running all week and finished in a tie for 40th place. If a win was overdue, however, it was for Gwladys Nocera who had not won for five years. In 2008 the 38-year-old from France won three times and topped the Order of Merit. Since then she had slipped down the rankings, but at Golf Resort Tale, in Brezno, Nocera earned her 11th win on the tour with a four-stroke victory.

Nocera led after the second and third rounds but had to duel with another former tour No. 1 in Lee-Anne Pace. The South African started the final round two shots behind and caught Nocera at the sixth, only to take a double bogey at the short seventh. Nocera went three ahead at the eighth, then bogeyed the ninth, but a two-shot swing at the 14th, with a birdie to a bogey, put Nocera four in front. A 45-minute delay for a threat of lightning in the valley near the course did not affect the Frenchwoman, and she finished at nine under par after rounds of 70, 68, 71 and 70 for a total of 279. Australian rookie Whitney Hillier claimed her best-ever finish with third place, one stroke behind Pace.

"I'm very happy and pretty emotional," said Nocera. "It's been awhile since I lifted a trophy. It was hard again today. I don't feel like I'm hitting the ball like I should, but I tried to stay patient and draw on my experience. I made probably the best putt of the week to save par on the 16th, so it made things easier for the last two holes."

Open de Espana Femenino
Madrid, Spain
Winner: Lee-Anne Pace

Lee-Anne Pace survived a late scare to win the Open de Espana Femenino at Club de Campo in Madrid. Although ahead by as many as four strokes earlier in the round, a double bogey at the par-three 17th meant she was only one ahead of Sweden's Mikaela Parmlid. The 32-year-old South African then did what she does best. "I thought, 're-group, recover, you've been hitting it well all week, so smash it down the middle.'" She did just that and a par at the 18th was enough to secure a one-stroke victory.

It was Pace's second win of the season, after she claimed victory in Turkey two months earlier, and a seventh on the LET for the 2010 Order of Merit winner. This victory took her to the top of the 2013 money list and arrived with rounds of 67, 68, 68 and 71 for a 13-under total of 275. Parmlid closed with a 70 to take second place, with Joanna Klatten taking third, three behind Parmlid, and Celine Herbin fourth after a 76.

Pace and Herbin were tied for the lead after 54 holes, but Pace made a great start with four birdies in the first seven holes. Three ahead at the short 17th, she bunkered her tee shot and then flew her recovery over the green. Her next chip finished 15 feet away and she two-putted for a five.

"On 17 I went straight at the pin and a mental error cost me two shots, but I'm really happy I won," Pace said. "The bunker was actually quite hard when I thought it was going to be softer. It flew over. I think it hit somebody over the green, so thank you to the guy who stopped my ball!"

ISPS Handa Ladies European Masters
Denham, Buckinghamshire, England
Winner: Karrie Webb

Karrie Webb, the world No. 7, justified her billing as the best player in the field at the ISPS Handa Ladies European Masters by taking victory with a stunning final round of 65. Hoping for a good week in preparation for the Ricoh Women's British Open at St. Andrews, Webb got better and better over a parkland course baked hard and fast by a mini heatwave at Buckinghamshire. Rounds of 68 and 67 put the Australian three behind Ashleigh Simon, Caroline Masson and Klara Spilkova.

Simon and Masson had opened with nine-under 63s, but in the final round their 69 and 70 meant taking second and third places as Webb roared through the field with the closing 65 for a 16-under total of 200. Webb birdied four of the first seven holes and then added two eagles at the ninth and 14th. She dropped a shot at the 16th, but it did not matter after Masson, who hit the flag with her bunker shot at the last, ended with a bogey and Simon's birdie putt came up short.

"I came over here to get some tournament rounds under my belt, get some confidence going, get into the time zone and British conditions," Webb said. "To win is just the icing on the cake. I'm very happy with how I played this week and I got more and more confident on the course as the week went on. I hadn't played the par-fives particularly well this week, but today I played them well with two eagles. It's a great boost when conditions are tough."

Webb's playing partner, Christina Kim, holed in one at the 18th to take fourth place alongside Sandra Gal.

Ricoh Women's British Open
St. Andrews, Fife, Scotland
Winner: Stacy Lewis

See Chapter 6.

Honma Pilsen Golf Masters
Prague, Czech Republic
Winner: Ann-Kathrin Lindner

Germany's Ann-Kathrin Lindner won for the first time as a professional in only her seventh start on the Ladies European Tour at the Honma Pilsen

Golf Masters at Golf Park Plzen in the Czech Republic. Lindner worked in the office at St. Leon-Rot for two and a half years while she was on the German national team and practiced there in the evenings. Her aim is to be on the European team when the Solheim Cup is played there in 2015, but for now it was enough that a number of friends from the club were on hand to celebrate her maiden victory.

Lindner, who started the last round two behind overnight leader Anais Maggetti, followed rounds of 66 and 67 with a closing 68 for a 12-under-par total of 201. The 25-year-old from Hanover won by one stroke over Italy's Diana Luna, who posted an eighth runner-up finish to go with her five victories, and France's Alexandra Vilatte, who closed with a 63. Lindner holed a short par putt at the 18th to finish in front of both Luna and Vilatte and could start celebrating once it was obvious the leaders would not catch her, Maggetti having fallen back with a 77.

At the European Masters, Lindner had played alongside Christina Kim and winner Karrie Webb on the last day, and although she dropped out of contention with an 80, she said the experience had helped her enormously. "Two weeks ago I was in the same situation and I played with Webbie and Christina, but it was a bit too early to play with those players and I learned a lot. I learned to be by myself, play my game and play shot by shot, and I think that's the key," Lindner said.

The Solheim Cup
Parker, Colorado
Winners: Europe

See LPGA Tour section.

Aberdeen Asset Management Scottish Ladies Open
East Lothian, Scotland
Winner: Catriona Matthew

For the second time in two years Catriona Matthew won at the course where she is an honorary member, Archerfield Links, just a few minutes drive down the road from her home in North Berwick. The 44-year-old Scot won the Aberdeen Asset Management Scottish Ladies Open by two strokes over England's Hannah Burke just two weeks after securing a half in the singles that ensured Europe would win the Solheim Cup on American soil for the first time.

Matthew opened with a 71 and then added a 67 in the second round which put her into the lead by three strokes. In foul weather on the final day, cold, wet and windy, there were only four sub-par rounds and one of them came from Matthew with a 70, to finish on 208, eight under par. Also shooting under par were Burke with a 68 and Holly Clyburn with a 71 to finish third, eight strokes adrift of Burke. Scots Pamela Pretswell and Carly Booth shared fourth place.

With early birdies Matthew went six clear of Burke after eight holes, before a bogey at the ninth. Three more birdies on the back nine followed, though her winning margin would have been bigger but for a double bogey at the 16th.

"It's great to win at home," said Matthew, who had husband Graeme on caddie duties and was congratulated by daughters Katie and Sophie on the 18th green. "It's always nice play at home in front of your family and makes it special. I saw the leaderboard after 15 and I thought I'd be a few more ahead than I was. It was an amazing score by Hannah and made it a little tense coming down the last few holes."

Helsingborg Open
Helsingborg, Skane, Sweden
Winner: Rebecca Artis

With Caroline Hedwall four strokes clear with one round to go, it looked like the Helsingborg Open was going to be a fitting homecoming for the Solheim Cup heroine who became the first person to win all five of her matches during Europe's victory in Colorado. Hedwall's family home is only 15 minutes from the Vasatorp course and a third round of 67 put her in a commanding position. But in contrast to her match-play form the previous month, Hedwall struggled with her putting on the final day. A double bogey at the fifth was followed by two bogeys early on the back nine, and although she made a solitary birdie for the day at the 17th, her 75 was not enough to beat Australia's Rebecca Artis. The 24-year-old had been showing improving form all summer, and despite starting the final day five strokes behind Hedwall, she pinched the victory by one stroke.

It was a burst of five birdies in six holes from the seventh which put Artis into contention, and she did not seem to be worried by the windy conditions. Her only scare came at the last where she three-putted from only 12 feet, but it was still good enough to pip the local heroine. Artis had scores of 69, 71, 71 and 69 for an eight-under-par total of 280. Hedwall finished on seven under, with France's Valentine Derrey taking third on five under. Lee-Anne Pace was fourth and Laura Davies fifth.

"I like playing in the wind, and grinding it out," Artis said. "I put myself into contention going into the back nine and knew that if the conditions were like they were the first three days and windy, that anything could happen. It's not an easy golf course when the wind's up like that."

Evian Championship
Evians-les-Bains, France
Winner: Suzann Pettersen

See Chapter 6.

Lacoste Ladies Open de France
Saint-Jean-de-Luz, Aquitaine, France
Winner: Azahara Munoz

Spain's Azahara Munoz nipped over the border and stole the Lacoste Ladies Open de France from a trio of home players. Gwladys Nocera, Joanna Klatten and Valentine Derrey shared the lead with a round to play, but it was Munoz, who started one stroke behind, who claimed victory at Chantaco. It was her second win on the Ladies European Tour — her first coming on her professional debut at the 2009 Madrid Masters — and her third in all after winning the Sybase Match Play Championship on the LPGA circuit in 2012. She was also the third member of the European team which won the Solheim Cup to win since the match in Colorado, following Catriona Matthew at the Scottish Open and Suzann Pettersen at the Evian Championship.

After rounds of 68, 65 and 68, Munoz was in fine form on the front nine of the final round with five birdies, many from no more than tap-in range. The 25-year-old from Malaga also birdied the 15th and dropped a shot at the 17th, but the more tricky back nine caused problems for everyone. Nocera, who had been disappointed to three-putt the 18th on Saturday, bogeyed the 11th and 16th holes, with her only birdie coming in at the 15th, while Derrey bogeyed the 13th and 14th. Munoz, who got up and down from the back of the green at the last, closed with a 65 to finish on a 14-under total of 266, one ahead of Nocera and Derrey, who both had 67s, and two ahead of Klatten. Karine Icher and Lee-Anne Pace shared fifth place.

"It's been a long year and I've been playing really bad, but since Solheim it's got much better and I'm just really happy to have won here," Munoz said. "Lacoste is one of my best sponsors, so I'm really happy to be here and holding the trophy."

Sanya Ladies Open
Sanya, China
Winner: Lee-Anne Pace

Lee-Anne Pace won the Sanya Ladies Open for the second time when she defeated Yu Yang Zhang at the first extra hole. The 32-year-old South African won the inaugural event in 2010 and returned to Yalong Bay in Sanya on Hainan Island in China to collect her third title of the season and eighth in all on the Ladies European Tour. Pace overcame a one-shot deficit to Korea's Ye Na Chung in the final round but could not squeeze past Zhang in regulation. The 22-year-old Chinese rookie closed with a 65, containing nine birdies and including four in a row from the sixth, to post the clubhouse target at 203, 13 under par.

Pace, who was out in one under, birdied the 15th and 16th holes to go one in front, only to three-putt the 17th and miss a winning chance at the last from 12 feet. But in the playoff at the 18th, Pace sealed the victory by holing a superb birdie putt from 20 feet. Zhang had a chance to match her from 15 feet but could not follow in her opponent.

"I love it here," Pace said. "It's a really nice feeling to come back and win here again. I started to get really pumped up towards the end and all the feelings came back from 2010 when I won here."

Chung took third place after a closing 72, while Yu Ting Shi, a 15-year-old local amateur, tied for fourth with Linda Wessberg, and Xi Yu Lin, a 17-year-old LET rookie, tied for sixth place, her fourth top-10 finish in the four stagings of the event.

China Suzhou Taihu Open
Suzhou, China
Winner: Gwladys Nocera

On a day when a 17-year-old Chinese amateur, Jing Yan, led after 14 holes and created quite a stir at the Suzhou Taihu International Golf Club, it was the experience of Gwladys Nocera which won out in the end, thanks to five birdies in the last six holes, including all of the last three. The 38-year-old Frenchwoman won for the second time in the season and for the 12th time in all by two strokes over defending champion Carlota Ciganda and by three over Yan, who started the back nine with four birdies in five holes before her challenge stalled with a bogey at the 15th. Nocera posted rounds of 69, 67 and 65 to finish on a 15-under total of 201 after coming from three behind overnight leader Veronica Zorzi, who dropped to ninth with a 75. Ciganda had six birdies in her 68, but her eagle attempt at the last to force a playoff led only to a par.

Nocera had lost the 2009 version of the Suzhou Taihu Open by a shot after being penalized two strokes for being late on the tee. "It took me a while, but I have my revenge and it's nice," said Nocera, who arrived at the prize ceremony in local Chinese dress and carried on a chariot by four men dressed as Chinese warriors. "I played really well today and made all the putts. I've been struggling for many years with my putting and it's coming back. It's a really good feeling."

Hero Women's Indian Open
New Delhi, India
Winner: Thidapa Suwannapura

Thidapa Suwannapura continued the Thai dominance of the Hero Women's Indian Open by claiming a three-stroke victory at the Delhi Golf Club. The 21-year-old from Bangkok, whose only previous win came on the Symetra Tour in America in 2012, shared the lead with Valentine Derrey after an opening 66, and despite a 74 the next day she went a shot clear of the field. A bogey-free 68 on the final day, with birdies at the first, ninth (where she holed a tricky, downhill 18-footer), 13th and 14th holes, left her at eight under par on a total of 208.

Derrey, who twice drew level on the last day on the front nine but came home with nine pars, claimed second place after a 70, one ahead of Hannah Burke and another Thai, Saraporn Chamchoi, with Charley Hull, who was only one behind after seven holes, tying for fifth place.

Suwannapura, a member of the Ladies Asian Tour, one of the co-sanctioning bodies for event, said: "Today I was concentrating on my game all day and was not looking at anyone else. I didn't see them at all. All my mind was concentrating on golf. I played my game and tried to make it good, play my best. I knew that I was leading, but I didn't know by how much."

Omega Dubai Ladies Masters
Dubai, United Arab Emirates
Winner: Pornanong Phatlum

Pornanong Phatlum only got her nose in front at the Omega Dubai Ladies Masters for one hole, but since it was the 72nd of the tournament, the 24-year-old Thai got her timing exactly right. She birdied four of the last six holes, including the last two, to beat world No. 3 Stacy Lewis by one stroke at the Emirates Golf Club. Lewis led after the second and third rounds, and for much of the final round was two or three shots ahead. The American was four under for the day when she birdied the 10th and appeared to be cruising to victory until Phatlum birdied the 13th and 14th to get within one. Both players bogeyed the par-three 13th and parred the 16th, but then the 17th was a shock to the leader. While Lewis hit her approach to six feet, Phatlum got inside her. Lewis missed, Phatlum holed from three feet, and they went to the 18th tied.

Both missed the fairway and had to lay up, but while Lewis played her third from more rough and only got her approach to 40 feet, Phatlum hit a beauty to two feet, the ball almost going in after the first bounce and again when it spun back past the hole. Phatlum tapped in to finish on 273, 15 under par, after rounds of 68, 70, 69 and 66, while Lewis, who posted a 65 in the second round, closed with a 69 for 14 under. Carlota Ciganda finished in third place but seven strokes behind Lewis. It was a second win on the Ladies European Tour for Phatlum, who also claimed the 2012 Indian Open. She is recognizable on the course due to her multicolored outfits which are always coordinated with those of her brother, who caddies for her.

"I am very excited. I just played my own game and stayed calm under pressure," said Phatlum. "I have learned how to stay focused through meditation which I practice with my brother. When I'm on the course I just play my game and I didn't think about the win, or like, I don't want to pressure myself."

The season-ending tournament saw 17-year-old Solheim Cup player Charley Hull collect her 10th top-10 of the season, in 15 appearances, to finish sixth on the Order of Merit and take the Rookie of the Year Award ahead of Holly Clyburn. Two-time winner Suzann Pettersen, the Evian champion, won the ISPS Handa Order of Merit, while Lee-Anne Pace, the only three-time winner on the circuit, was voted as the Players' Player of the Year.

Japan LPGA Tour

Daikin Orchid Ladies
Nanjo, Okinawa
Winner: Rikako Morita

Rikako Morita got the new season off to a fast start in the traditional Daikin Orchid opener, but for Sakura Yokomine it was a continuation of nearly two years dotted with nothing better than near-misses. Morita picked up her third win in her fifth season on the Japan LPGA Tour when she defeated a frustrated Yokomine on the first hole of a playoff at Ryukyu Golf Club in Okinawa.

Yokomine, the 27-year-old claimant to the money title in 2009 and 18 victories in her eight-season career, but none since early 2011, went head to head with Morita in the final round. They trailed Megumi Kido, the second-round leader at 68-66–134, Morita by one (68-67) and Yokomine by three (70-67).

Yokomine ran off four birdies on the first five holes Sunday and forced the overtime when she birdied the final hole for 66–203, 13 under par. Morita, who had a bogey-free round and birdied the 17th to lead by one, missed her birdie try at the 18th and posted 68 for her 203. She then ran in a 12-foot birdie putt on the first extra hole for the win. Kido shot 72 and tied for third at 206 with Thailand's Onnarin Sattayabanphot, Junko Omote, Ritsuko Ryu and Soo-Yun Kang of South Korea.

Yokohama Tire PRGR Ladies Cup
Kanan, Kochi
Winner: Mi-Jeong Jeon

The Japan LPGA Tour had a look-alike similarity to the 2012 season in the early going. Again the first two titles were determined by playoffs and Mi-Jeong Jeon, the leading money winner in 2012 with four of her now career 22 victories, carried over her success with the overtime victory over South Korean compatriot Young Kim in the Yokohama Tire PRGR Ladies Cup.

Jeon was right on the heels of the leaders the first two days at Tosa Country Club. Asako Fujimoto, a winner at age 21 in 2011, topped the first-round leaderboard with a six-under-par 66. When she fell back Saturday, Esther Lee went in front with 69-67–136, only to suffer the same fate Sunday.

Rounds of 68-70 placed Jeon two shots off the lead, equaled by Kim, who bounced back from an opening 73 with a 65 Saturday.

The two South Koreans matched strokes and scores Sunday with five birdies and two bogeys each for 69s and 207, one better than Rikako Morita, just missing a rare two-win start to the season. Jeon ended the playoff quickly with a birdie on the first overtime hole.

T-Point Ladies
Kamo, Kagoshima
Winner: Yuki Ichinose

Talk about pressure. Winless in her sixth season on the tour, Yuki Ichinose played the final 18 holes of the T-Point Ladies tournament with Rikako Morita and Mi-Jeong Jeon, the winners of the two previous tournaments, in close pursuit and waiting to pounce. Thanks to a three-stroke cushion, though, Ichinose prevailed — by a single stroke — to land that precious first victory at Kagoshima Takamaki Country Club.

Ichinose seized the three-shot lead the second day with an eight-under-par 64 for 132, replacing Erina Kikuchi, another winless player, and Yukari Baba, who opened the tournament with 66s. Morita, with a win and a third-place finish the first two weeks, entered the final round in second place with 69-66–135 and Jeon was third at 137.

Ichinose squeezed out a two-under 70 Sunday for 202, edging Morita (68) by a shot and Jeon (67) by two strokes. Five others, including first-round leaders Baba and Kikuchi, finished at 206.

AXA Ladies
Miyazaki
Winner: Natsuka Hori

The season's second consecutive first-time winner didn't come completely out of the blue, but Natsuka Hori, in her third year on the Japan LPGA Tour at age 20, had never finished better than 15th (in the 2012 Resort Trust) before grabbing the title in the AXA Ladies, which returned to the circuit after a three-year absence.

A sensational, second-round 64 paved the way for Hori's 14-under-par 202 and three-stroke victory. Two shots behind first-round tri-leaders Megumi Kido, Shiho Oyama and Thailand's Onnarin Sattayabanphot at 67, Hori exploded a front-nine, seven-birdie 29 on the field Saturday and went on with three more birdies and two bogeys to a 64–133 and a three-stroke lead over Oyama (69).

Hori maintained her cool and that margin with a solid 69 Sunday. Haru-kyo Nomura shot 68 to take second place, while Oyama, with 70, tied for third with the impressively consistent Rikako Morita, whose record for the first four events of the year sported a win, a second and two thirds.

Yamaha Ladies Open
Fukuroi, Shizuoka
Winner: Mamiko Higa

The non-winners on tour continued, at least for the time being, to push the older name players aside as Mamiko Higa became the third straight new champion and the youngest of the trio at age 19. Following on the heels of wins by 20-year-old Natsuka Hori and slightly older Yuki Ichinose, Higa landed the Yamaha Ladies Open in the third playoff in the fifth week of the season.

Sunday was a free-for-all at Katsuragi Golf Club in Shizuoka Prefecture. Bo-Mee Lee, the leader by two after the third round (68-70-71), came apart early Sunday, surrendering her two-stroke lead as a host of players got into the act. Higa was one of the more surprising ones, since she had missed two cuts and finished 24th and 47th in her other two 2013 starts. Five back after rounds of 69-74-71, she lost two strokes to par early, but put up three birdies over the final 13 holes for 71 and 284.

Of all the others in contention, Kaori Ohe and Teresa Lu were the only ones to match Higa's 284. Five under after the 13th hole, Ohe had to birdie the last hole to reach the playoff. On the other hand, Lu had her first tour victory in hand before she bogeyed the 72nd hole.

All three players parred the first extra hole, then Higa dropped a birdie putt at the second for the win.

Studio Alice Ladies Open
Miki, Hyogo
Winner: Na-Ri Kim

Na-Ri Kim was pleased but not particularly satisfied with her first victory in more than two years on the Japan LPGA Tour. "My goal is to win three tournaments this year," Kim emphasized after her one-stroke win in the Studio Alice Open in mid-April. She emerged from a cluster of contenders with a final-round 70 for a wind-blown 212, four under par for the route at the Yokawa course of Hanayashiki Golf Club in Hyogo Prefecture.

The 27-year-old South Korean, whose only previous win was in the Daio Paper Elleair tournament at the end of the 2010 season, was in the hunt all the way. She and Kaori Nakamura shared the first-round lead, then yielded it to 21-year-old Miki Sakai (74-67) and Ah-Reum Hwang (73-68) Saturday. Kim shot 72, and with Mayu Hattori, Nozomi Uetake, Nakamura and Natsuka Hori, the AXA Ladies winner two weeks earlier, sat just a shot off the pace after 36 holes.

The leaders fell back early on Sunday and so, it appeared, did Kim when she double-bogeyed the third hole. But she was flawless the rest of the way, racking up four birdies for the 70 that brought her the victory. Yuki Sakurai also shot 70, jumping from a tie for eighth into the runner-up slot.

Vantelin Ladies Open KKT Cup
Kikuyo, Kumamoto
Winner: Miki Saiki

Miki Saiki put her sixth victory on the Japan LPGA Tour into the books at the Vantelin Ladies Open, embellishing a seven-year record that is most impressive with its consistency. In her previous six full seasons, the 28-year-old Saiki never finished outside the top 20 on the money list and was off and running again in 2013 with top-20 finishes in five of the previous six events before her clutch, one-stroke victory at Kumamoto Kuko Country Club.

What's more, Saiki was coming off neck surgery in December and was surprised about the fast start. "I didn't think I would be able to get back to my best so quickly."

Saiki opened with a one-over-par 73, four shots behind leader Esther Lee, then vaulted into the lead with a 68–141 Saturday on a day when only one other player broke 70. Yuki Ichinose, the T-Point Ladies victor, then trailed by one shot, Sakura Yokomine by two.

Sunday proved a battle royal as a handful of players had shots at the title. In fact, playing in the group behind her, Saiki watched Ritsuko Ryu birdie the last two holes for 70–213 and a one-stroke lead, then birdied them herself for 71–212 and the victory. Not to be confused with the winner, 21-year-old Miki Sakai finished a frustrating third at 71–214 with a lone birdie and 17 pars.

Fujisankei Ladies Classic
Ito, Shizuoka
Winner: Miki Saiki

Talk about momentum! Miki Saiki never slowed down as she followed up her strong overall start and victory in the Vantelin Open with a decisive second win in the Fujisankei Classic. It carried her into first place on the money list.

The victory, Saiki's career seventh and second in the Fujisankei event (2007), came to the 28-year-old much more easily than the one the previous Sunday, when she had to birdie the final two holes to win by a stroke. Saiki led by a stroke entering the last round, shot a solid 67 Sunday for a 14-under-par 202 and left Sakura Yokomine three strokes behind, a frustrated runner-up for the second time in 2013. It was just the second tournament of the young season that wasn't decided by a playoff or a single stroke.

Soo-Yun Kang, the South Korean who finished third, a shot behind Yokomine, shared the first-round lead at the Kawana Hotel Golf Club with Na-Ri Lee, Teresa Lu and Young Kim at 68. One back at 69, Saiki surged ahead Saturday, putting together an eagle and four birdies in a bogey-free round of 66 for 135. That positioned her a stroke in front of Lu and young Miki Sakai.

Saiki took the drama out of Sunday's round early with four birdies on the first seven holes and cushioned her lead with two more on the back nine before taking her only bogey for the 67.

Cyber Agent Ladies
Ichihara, Chiba
Winner: Sakura Yokomine

It had seemed just a matter of time before Sakura Yokomine would break through with another victory and that time came at the Cyber Agent Ladies.

Since winning the Resort Trust early in the 2011 season, Yokomine, the 2009 money-winning champion, had finished second six times, including the previous week's Fujisankei Classic, and third in four other events before stashing away a two-stroke victory at Tsurumai Country Club the first week of May.

"The victory I had been waiting so long for was staring me in the face," enthused Yokomine, who took advantage of Mi-Jeong Jeon's final-round skid to score her 19th win, posting a final-round 70 for 10-under-par 206, two ahead of Jeon, Natsuka Hori, Yuki Sakurai and Maiko Wakabayashi. Adding to the glow of victory, she set a new tour record of 92 consecutive starts without missing a cut.

Yokomine shared the first-round lead at 68 with Sakurai and Erina Hara. She and Hara repeated the 68s Saturday, but slipped two off the pace when Jeon, the 2012 money leader, shot 65 for 134. Yokomine and Jeon were tied after 10 holes in the final round before Yokomine jumped in front to stay. She birdied the 13th, got a cushion when Jeon double-bogeyed the 14th, and coasted home. Oddly, Miki Saiki, winner of the previous two tournaments, took the week off.

World Ladies Championship Salonpas Cup
Tsukubamiral, Ibaraki
Winner: Hiromi Mogi

It wouldn't be fair to label Hiromi Mogi a surprise winner of the major World Ladies Championship Salonpas Cup. Although Mogi emerged from a cluster of players then dominating the game, she called upon her experience as a five-time winner over the previous 10 years on tour to walk off with a two-stroke victory.

Mogi entered the final round on the West course of Ibaraki Golf Club in a second-place tie at 211 (71-70-70) with leading money winner Miki Saiki, who was gunning for her third straight victory after taking a week off. Both were two strokes behind the hottest player overall in 2013, Rikako Morita, who had yielded the money lead to Saiki two weeks earlier. With a 68–209 Saturday, Morita supplanted Saiki Fujita, who led the first two rounds. Even Lydia Ko, New Zealand's 16-year-old amateur sensation, and Sakura Yokomine, coming off her 19th win, were within range.

Mogi simply outplayed them all Sunday. She took over first place with a three-under-par 33 on the front nine and added two birdies on the next seven holes to build a lead that easily survived a late bid of Miki Saiki, who made up three shots on the final two holes. Mogi finished with 68 for a nine-under-par 279 total. Saiki padded her money lead with her 70–281 finish. Morita, who stumbled with three early bogeys, birdied three of the last seven holes, shot 73 and finished third.

Hoken no Madoguchi Ladies
Asakura, Fukuoka
Winner: Onnarin Sattayabanphot

Now Thailand, with winners on virtually all of the other world tours, has one on the Japan LPGA Tour. Onnarin Sattayabanphot, sometimes referred to simply as O. Sattaya, eked out a one-stroke victory in the Hoken no Madoguchi Ladies despite two late bogeys in Sunday's final round at Fukuoka Country Club.

With a front-nine 31 in Saturday's second round, Sattayabanphot seemed to be paving the way for a decisive maiden victory, but wound up carrying just a one-shot lead to the final 18 holes when she went 37–68 coming home. Ritsuko Ryu, Maiko Wakabayashi and Yuki Ichinose, all winners the previous year, were one behind, and four others, including Kumiko Kaneda, trailed by just two strokes.

But the title joust settled into a duel between Sattayabanphot and Kaneda over the final holes Sunday. Starting at the 15th, though, the two traded bogeys, Kaneda at the 15th and 17th, Sattayabanphot at the 16th and 18th. The Thai golfer wound up with a 72 and 210, one better than Kaneda (71) and Wakabayashi (72) on a day when only Phoebe Yao (69) broke 70. Sattayabanphot was the fourth first-time winner of the 2013 season.

Chukyo TV Bridgestone Ladies Open
Toyota, Aichi
Winner: Rikako Morita

The setup seemed perfect, going into the final round of the Chukyo TV Bridgestone Open, for a tense duel between Rikako Morita, the new young star, and veteran Shiho Oyama, a former money-winning champion striving for her first victory in nearly two years and 13th of her career.

Morita, 23, who won the season-opening Daikin Orchid tournament, had just wrested the lead from Oyama with her second straight 67 for 134, as Oyama followed her opening 66 with a two-under-par 70 on the Ishino course of Chukyo Golf Club. Another 23-year-old, winless Shiho Toyonaga, was third, three strokes behind Oyama, who salvaged her round with four birdies on the last six holes Saturday.

Things didn't work out as expected. Neither player fared well in the early going Sunday, opening the door to South Korean powerhouse Mi-Jeong Jeon, shooting for her 23rd win and second of the season. Jeon's fourth birdie at the 12th hole narrowed Morita's lead to one. Two over par at that point, Morita steadied her game and matched pars with Jeon to win by a stroke with her 74 and eight-under 208. Oyama shot 75 and slipped to a fourth-place tie with Momoku Ueda, a shot behind Natsuka Hori.

The victory enabled Morita to regain the No. 1 position on the money list as Miki Saiki tied for 19th.

Resort Trust Ladies
Miki, Hyogo
Winner: Mamiko Higa

For a 19-year-old less than a year into her career on the Japan LPGA Tour, Mamiko Higa has shown an ability to handle pressure in her first two victories.

Less than two months after prevailing in a three-woman playoff in the Yamaha Ladies for her maiden win, Higa staved off the challenge of experienced Mayu Hattori and eked out a one-stroke victory in the Resort Trust Ladies in early June.

After South Korean star Bo-Mee Lee and Japan's Maiko Wakabayashi opened the tournament at Miki's Kansai Country Club with leading, six-under-par 66s, Higa forged into a first-place tie Saturday, shooting 67–137 to match Megumi Kido's 69–137.

Higa remained in front Sunday until she bogeyed the ninth hole and lost the lead temporarily to Hattori, playing three holes ahead of her. Higa bounced right back with birdies at the 10th and 12th holes to regain first place. The par-four 15th proved the deciding hole, though. Both players birdied it and Higa then parred in for 70–207, a shot in front of Hattori and her 68–208. Money leader Rikako Morita closed with 70–210 to take third place and widen her margin over Miki Saiki in the standings.

Yonex Ladies
Nagaoka, Niigata
Winner: Junko Omote

Many seasons had passed since Junko Omote was a prominent player on the Japan LPGA Tour, but, when the opportunity presented itself in the Yonex Ladies tournament in early June, she made the most of it. In clearly one of her career-best showings over 17 seasons, Omote cruised to a wire-to-wire victory. She finished with a 70 and a 10-under-par 206, fending off a spirited challenge from Rikako Morita, the year's most dominant player.

Omote began her run at her third tour title with a first-round 67 and a one-stroke lead over five ladies, including Miki Saiki, already a two-time winner in 2013 and second on the money list behind Morita. Omote made her only bogey of the week that day, following up Saturday with 69–136 that left her in a four-way tie for the lead with Li-Ying Ye of South Korea, Tamie Durdin of Australia and compatriot Yuko Fukuda.

The 39-year-old Omote broke from the contenders with birdies at the third and fourth holes in tough playing conditions Sunday at Yonex Country Club and produced an unbroken string of pars the rest of the way for a two-stroke victory over Morita, who charged up the leaderboard with a 65 to pick off second place and enhance her position atop the money list. Ye tumbled to 75 and Durdin and Fukuda to 77s Sunday.

Suntory Ladies Open
Kobe, Hyogo
Winner: Rikako Morita

Rikako Morita's remarkable run of exceptional golf continued at the Suntory Ladies Open. She capped a four-week span of excellence that in sequence went win, third place, second place with her third victory of the season, a triumph that didn't come easily.

The 23-year-old Morita emerged from a cluster of contenders Sunday with birdies on the final two holes at Rokko Kokusai Golf Club in Kobe, completing a back-nine 31 for 67 and a one-stroke victory at 10-under-par 288 over Kumiko Kaneda, Yumiko Yoshida and Mamiko Higa, the two-time, teenaged winner earlier in her rookie season.

Morita got off to a rocky start, seven strokes off the pace with a 73, but made up ground rapidly with a second-round 66 that pulled her within two strokes of leaders Esther Lee (66-71) and Akane Iijima (69-68). Kaneda, seeking her second career win, came up with a 69–218 Saturday that put her a shot ahead of Lee (72) and two ahead of three others.

Morita's 72 left her three off the pace and an early bogey Sunday dampened her chances. Birdies at the fifth, 10th and 11th moved her into contention, though. At one point on the back nine she was tied for the lead with Kaneda, Higa and Yuri Fudoh before putting on her finishing spurt.

Nichirei Ladies
Chiba
Winner: Yumiko Yoshida

Victory came much more easily for Yumiko Yoshida the second time around. Yoshida had to go six extra holes in a 2012 playoff before scoring her maiden win on the Japan LPGA Tour in the NEC Karuizawa 72 tournament. A year later, the 26-year-old pro rode a second-round lead to a much more comfortable two-stroke victory in the Nichirei Ladies event in hanging up No. 2.

Starting just a shot off the lead with her opening 68 — Kumiko Kaneda led with 67 — Yoshida followed with a 67 of her own Saturday at Sodegaura Country Club and moved a stroke in front of Na-Ri Lee with her 135. Yun-Jye Wei and Phoebe Yao were at 137.

Nobody really threatened Yumiko Sunday, particularly after she posted her only birdies at the sixth and seventh holes. She made the two-stroke margin stand up with 11 solid pars for 70 and the winning, 11-under-par 205.

Lee shot 71 for 207, sharing the runner-up slot with Kaori Aoyama and Kaori Ohe, who both closed with 68s. Rikako Morita had a rare off-form week, barely making the cut and finishing in a tie for 47th position.

Earth Mondahmin Cup
Sodegaura, Chiba
Winner: Natsuka Hori

Perhaps Natsuka Hori should adopt 64 as her lucky number. The score, which propelled Hori to her first victory on the Japan LPGA Tour in the AXA Ladies tournament in March, produced another 64 three months later in the third round of the Earth Mondahmin Cup, where she rode it to an eight-stroke win, the biggest victory margin by far at that point in the season.

Hori's 64 was the third of the week at Camellia Hills Country Club, Chiba Prefecture. Nineteen-year-old Mamiko Higa opened with that score in her bid for a third 2013 victory, but fizzled out the rest of the way. Next came veteran star Mi-Jeong Jeon, gunning for her 23rd tour win. Her 64 lifted her into a three-stroke lead at 132 over Teresa Lu as Hori took a share of third place with 69-67–136. Hori, just a week shy of her 21st birthday, then took command, her 64 jumping her three shots ahead of Jeon (70).

Hori gained a shot on Jeon on the front nine Sunday, then had smooth sailing going home after the challenger bogeyed the first two holes on the back nine. Just to make sure, Hori eagled the 14th on the way in with a final 67 and a 21-under-par 267. She didn't have a bogey in the last two rounds. Jeon shot 73, but still finished second.

Nichi-Iko Ladies Open
Toyama
Winner: Young Kim

Young Kim's decision to switch from the U.S. LPGA Tour, where she once was a winner, to the Japan LPGA circuit paid off in the Nichi-Iko Open in her 15th start of the season. The 33-year-old South Korean made it a wire-to-wire victory when she endured three rain delays during Sunday's final round, shot 69–203 and edged Mayumi Shimomura by a stroke.

Kim, who played in America for seven years, shared the first-round lead at five-under-par 67 with Megumi Kido and Ji-Woo Lee, then edged a stroke in front Saturday with another 67. The ever-present Mi-Jeong Jeon, South Korea's brightest star in Japan who won her 22nd title in March (Yokohama Tire), shot 66 for 135, but the defending champion could only manage a 71 Sunday and dropped into a tie for fifth place.

Kim clung to a one-stroke lead Sunday until she took her only bogey at the 13th to drop into a tie with Shimomura. However, she immediately regained the top spot with a birdie at the 14th, then both players birdied the 15th and parred home as Shimomura's winless record over 10 seasons continued. Kim's victory was the third of the season for South Koreans and the first since March.

Samantha Thavasa Girls Collection Ladies
Ami, Ibaraki
Winner: Yumiko Yoshida

Yumiko Yoshida was so proud of what she had just done that "I want to give myself a pat on the back." The inspiration came from her playoff victory in the Samantha Thavasa Girls Collection Ladies tournament, Yoshida's second triumph of the season. She became the year's fifth multiple winner.

Yoshida's victory came at the expense of veteran Junko Omote, who appeared headed for her second win of the season after opening with a nine-under-par 63 at Eagle Point Golf Club and widening her lead to five strokes when she followed with a 65 Saturday. Yoshida sat alone in second place after rounds of 66 and 67.

The 26-year-old Yoshida closed the gap Sunday with five birdies on the first 13 holes and took the lead when Omote, a three-time winner during her 15-year career on tour, bogeyed the 12th and 13th after taking just one prior bogey in the tournament. Omote bounced back with a birdie on the par-five 15th and matched pars with Yoshida on the remaining three holes, shooting 72 to Yoshida's 67 for the playoff-forcing, 16-under-par 200s. Yoshida then birdied the second extra hole to pick up the third title of her seven-year pro career.

Meiji Cup
Kitahiroshima, Hokkaido
Winner: Da-Ye Na

Da-Ye Na generated no great excitement when she shot a five-under-par 67 in the first round and led the field in the Meiji Cup tournament. After all, the 25-year-old South Korean had never won during her four years on the Japan LPGA Tour and was coming off missed cuts in the previous two events. Two days later, after a remarkable turnaround, Na was accepting plaudits as the champion, having never yielded the lead at Sapporo International Country Club.

Na followed the opening 67 with a 70, allowing Harukyo Nomura to overtake her at 137 with her 70-67–137, but she came back Sunday with another 67 and a one-stroke victory over Yuki Ichinose with her 12-under-par 204, becoming the sixth first-time winner of the year.

Nomura faded to 75 the last day as Ichinose and Shanshan Feng, China's No. 1 player, mounted the biggest challenges to the South Korean. Ichinose, who picked up her first title in March's T-Point Ladies, produced seven birdies and a 65 Sunday, falling a stroke short of Na, who had six birdies and a bogey in the final round. Feng, the Meiji winner in 2011 and 2012, closed with 67 for 206.

NEC Karuizawa 72
Karuizawa, Nagano
Winner: Misuzu Narita

Esther Lee made a good living and popped into contention from time to time during her first six seasons on tour, once even finishing second in the major Japan Women's Open, but she always came up short of victory. Finally, in her seventh year at the NEC Karuizawa 72 tournament in mid-August, the 27-year-old South Korean seemed ready to break through.

After 36 holes and a blazing, second-round 64 for 131, Lee had staked herself to a three-stroke lead, albeit the runner-up happened to be Japan's winningest (50) active player, Yuri Fudoh. But it wasn't to be nor was it Fudoh who kept Lee winless. It was Misuzu Narita, another of the bright young stars on the circuit.

Six strokes behind Lee after a second-round 65, the 20-year-old Narita, a first-time winner in 2012, repeated the 65 Sunday, and her 14-under-par 202 lifted her into a tie with Lee, who managed only a 71 in the final round. Then, in the playoff, Narita birded the second extra hole to nab the title and frustrate Lee again. Fudoh shot 70–204, finishing fourth, a shot behind Ritsuko Ryu.

CAT Ladies
Hakone, Kanagawa
Winner: Sun-Ju Ahn

It wasn't that Sun-Ju Ahn had disappeared from view, but the South Korean's performances over the first six months certainly hadn't lived up to the high standards she had set during the previous three seasons. The player who led the money list in 2010 and 2011 and placed fourth in 2012 while winning 11 tournaments had not finished better than third and was 24th on the current standings when she teed it up in the CAT Ladies in late August.

The 25-year-old Ahn showed her old form that week at Daihakone Country Club in Kanagawa Prefecture, carving out a closing, seven-under-par 66 for 204 that not only gave her a 12th victory but set a new tournament record. It was the day's best score by three strokes and one of just three rounds in the 60s Sunday. Ahn finished three strokes in front of Ritsuko Ryu, with whom she had shared fourth place entering the final round, three back of co-leaders Na-Ri Kim, the Studio Alice winner, and Miki Saiki, a two-time victor early in the season.

Saiki opened with 66, tied for first with Da-Ye Na, the Meiji Cup winner two weeks earlier, and remained on top Saturday, then sharing the lead with Kim at 135. Both players collapsed in the final round, Kim soaring to 77 and Saiki to 79, as Ahn breezed to victory.

Nitori Ladies
Tomokai, Hokkaido
Winner: Sun-Ju Ahn

Her confidence restored the previous week by her first win of the season and playing as the defending champion, Sun-Ju Ahn celebrated her 26th birthday a day late with a back-to-back victory in the Nitori Ladies tournament when the scene shifted to Hokkaido.

The two-time leading money winner on the Japan LPGA Tour produced a powerful, bogey-free round of 65 Sunday at Katsura Golf Club, coming from two strokes off the lead to post a two-shot victory, her 13th in Japan. Ahn finished at 11-under-par 205, two strokes in front of Taiwan's Teresa Lu, who also mustered a 65 Sunday.

Lala Anai, seeking her first tour victory, put herself in position, leading the first two days with rounds of 66 and 72. Her 138 set her two in front of Ahn, Bo-Mee Lee and Esther Lee, but she slipped to a seventh-place finish with a 74. The victory lifted Ahn to a familiar area of the money list — sixth — but still far behind leader Rikako Morita.

Golf 5 Ladies
Hokkaido
Winner: Yumiko Yoshida

Still flying high after victories the previous two weeks, Sun-Ju Ahn had her sights set on three in a row, something that hadn't happened on the tour in six years, when she teed off as defending champion in the Golf 5 Ladies tournament. She nearly did it, falling two strokes short of joining a playoff between Yumiko Yoshida and Miki Saiki, two other multiple 2013 winners. Those two went four extra holes before a Saiki bogey gave Yoshida her third win of the year and fourth career victory in Japan.

Those who relish tight battles got their money's worth at Alpen Golf Club.

The tournament began with five players — Yun-Jye Wei, Phoebe Yao, Na-Ri Lee, Saiki and Ahn — tied for the lead at 67. Then, on Saturday, Yoshida (69-68) caught up to Saiki and Ahn, who posted 70s for their 137s. Three others, including Shiho Oyama, a 12-time winner, trailed by one.

It remained close between that quartet through the front nine of the Bibai course Sunday. Ahn ran out of birdies after the 11th hole, and a bogey at the 16th hurt Oyama's chances. Saiki birdied that hole to overtake Yoshida at 12 under par and the two parred in.

Japan LPGA Championship
Eniwa, Hokkaido
Winner: Bo-Mee Lee

After the third round of the Japan LPGA Championship, the stage was set for a final-round duel for the Konica Minolta Cup between South Korea's

Bo-Mee Lee and Mamiko Higa, the talented Japanese 19-year-old who already had scored two victories in her rookie season. They led the field by four strokes after 54 holes with 11-under-par 205s.

The head-to-head battle did take place, but not as expected. Heavy rains inundated Eniwa Country Club early Sunday, forcing cancellation of the scheduled round, but enough of a window amid the thunderstorms existed for Lee and Higa to play off for the important title. Ironically, after five matching holes, the duel came to a wet ending at the sixth when Higa fell victim to a water hazard.

The victory was the 25-year-old Lee's fourth in Japan and her second major. She won the year-ending Japan LPGA Tour Championship in 2012.

Lee and Higa headed the field from the second round on after Miki Sakai led the first day with 66. Lee shot 68-69, Higa 69-68, then both had 68s Saturday to establish the four-stroke margin over storied Yuri Fudoh, 36, who counts two PGA Championships among her 50 victories in Japan.

Munsingwear Ladies Tokai Classic
Minami, Aichi
Winner: Sakura Yokomine

Sakura Yokomine, absent from the winning ranks of the tour since early 2011, regained her winning touch in 2013. Following a win and two seconds early in the year, Yokomine latched onto her 20th career victory in the Munsingwear Ladies Tokai Classic in late September and climbed into the runner-up position on the money list.

The 27-year-old, No. 1 in 2009 and second the following year, fended off several challenges late in the final round at Shin Minami Aichi Country Club, chalked up a five-under-par 67 and finished two strokes ahead of three of those contenders with her 15-under-par 201.

A second-round 66 pulled Yokomine into a first-place tie with Erika Kikuchi (69-65) at 134 as the two moved a stroke in front of Na-Ri Lee, the first-round leader with 65; Asako Fujimoto, and Da-Ye Na, the Meiji Cup victor. Yokomine's fast start Sunday made the difference. Out in 31, she managed just a par 36 on the incoming nine, more than enough for the triumph. Ji-Hee Lee (65) and Fujimoto (68) made serious runs at the lead and wound up in second place with Na (68).

Miyagi TV Cup Dunlop Ladies Open
Rifu, Miyagi
Winner: Na-Ri Lee

Na-Ri Lee willingly played the role of spoiler at the Miyagi TV Cup Dunlop Ladies Open. Until she posted her final-round 70 and won the tournament, the story of the week was the first appearance of the year and the play of Ai Miyazato, Japan's greatest female player of the current era.

Miyazato, who won her first of 15 Japan LPGA Tour titles in the Miyagi Dunlop 10 years earlier as an 18-year-old high school senior, has played successfully and almost exclusively on the U.S. LPGA Tour in recent years, even heading the Rolex World Rankings for a short time.

She didn't disappoint her fans at Rifu Golf Club, shooting an opening-round, three-under-par 69 to share the lead with Taiwan's Teresa Lu. Two strokes back amid five others was Na-Ri Lee. When Miyazato skidded to 75 Saturday, the South Korean shot 70 and moved into a first-place tie at 141 with Lu (72).

Miyazato caught fire Sunday. She birdied seven of her first 14 holes to surge three strokes ahead of Lee, only to collapse in the stretch. The South Korean caught up immediately when she birdied the 15th hole while Miyazato was taking a double bogey. Then, as Lee was parring in, Miyazato bogeyed the 17th to fall a shot behind, finishing with 68–212, deadlocked with Lu, who closed with a 71.

Na was the seventh first-time winner of the season.

Japan Women's Open
Sagamihara, Kanagawa
Winner: Mika Miyazato

Like the other Miyazato, Mika Miyazato has devoted most of her playing time in recent years with moderate success to the U.S. LPGA Tour, making only rare appearances on the home circuit in Japan. Unlike the other Miyazato, who blew a homecoming victory the previous week, Mika held on at the end and pulled off a victory when she returned for the major Japan Women's Open in early October.

Rolling into the final round on the demanding Sagamihara Golf Club's East course with a five-stroke lead, Miyazato had to birdie the 72nd hole to shoot 75 and win the Women's Open for the second time by a single stroke with even-par 288. Those two victories are her only ones on the Japan LPGA Tour. Interestingly, the year before the first win in 2010 she blew a four-stroke lead in the final round of that season's Women's Open.

Surely that came to her mind in 2013 as her lead dissolved in Sunday's final round. Miyazato had at least a piece of the lead after each of the first three rounds. After sharing a four-way tie at 70 the first day, she jumped to a three-stroke lead over Shiho Oyama with another 70 Friday, and widened the gap to five over Erika Kikuchi Saturday with 73–213 despite bogeys on two of her last four holes.

Miyazato slid back to the field with a no-birdies 40 on the front nine Sunday, treaded water for the next few holes, and then fell a stroke behind Kikuchi with a bogey at the 15th hole. Meanwhile, Miki Saiki, already a two-time winner in 2013, finished with 69–289 for the clubhouse lead. Bogeys at the 16th and 17th dropped Kikuchi a stroke behind Miyazato, who finished par-par-birdie for the victory. With 71, Kikuchi tied Saiki for second place.

Stanley Ladies
Susano, Shizuoka
Winner: Soo-Yun Kang

The first-time winners kept coming. Soo-Yun Kang of South Korea was the ninth of the year, finishing strongly to score a three-stroke victory in the Stanley Ladies tournament in Susano, Shizuoka Prefecture.

Mayu Hattori showed the way at Tomei Country Club. She got off to a great start with a seven-under-par 65, snagging birdies on the last four holes and six in all on the back nine, yet she led Satsuki Oshiro by only one shot. Hattori maintained that margin Saturday with 71–136 as Sakura Yokomine, seeking her third win of the season, posted 69-68–137. Kang, Harukyo Nomura and three others were at 138.

Those two 138-shooters edged in front on the outgoing nine Sunday, Kang with four birdies and Nomura with an eagle and a birdie. They both birdied the 11th, but the South Korean gained the upper hand at the next hole with a birdie to Nomura's bogey. Nomura still trailed by a stroke after Kang bogeyed the 17th, but Kang salted it away with a birdie on the final green for 66–204. Nomura bogeyed there for 69–207, dropping into a second-place tie with Yokomine. Hattori managed only a par round and finished in a three-way tie for fourth at 208 with Ah-Reum Hwang and money leader Rikako Morita, making her best showing in 11 tournaments since July.

Fujitsu Ladies
Chiba
Winner: Na-Ri Lee

Na-Ri Lee picked up her second victory of the season at a tournament that might never have been played. Had powerful Typhoon Wipha deviated its path ever so slightly as it battered nearby parts of Japan, it could have wreaked such havoc on the Tokyu 700 Club that the Fujitsu Ladies tournament probably would have had to be cancelled. As it was, heavy rains at week's end washed out the Sunday round, and Lee, the second-round leader, was awarded the victory with her 36-hole score of six-under-par 138.

Lee, who scored her first triumph in Japan just three weeks earlier with a brilliant late surge that overcame Ai Miyazato, started the Fujitsu tournament with a 71, four strokes off the lead in a tie for 11th place. The frontrunners were Yukari Baba and Mihoko Iseri, who matched seven-birdie, five-under-par 67s.

The deck shuffled Saturday. Baba (74), Iseri (76) and the other close contenders fell back, as Lee came up with five birdies on the first six holes of the back nine and a 67 of her own. That vaulted her that decisive shot ahead of 20-year-old Ayaka Watanabe (69) and two in front of young Miki Sakai, Esther Lee, Teresa Lu and amateur Megumi Takahashi.

Nobuta Group Masters Golf Club Ladies
Miki, Hyogo
Winner: Sakura Yokomine

By the end of October, what once looked like a runaway in the race to win the 2013 money list seemed more likely to be settled with a photo finish. Sakura Yokomine, exhibiting the talent she showed best a few years earlier, all but wiped out the huge early-season lead of Rikako Morita when she won her third tournament of the year and 21st of her career.

Interestingly, Morita, whose game had tailed off in mid-season, struck first at the Nobuta Group Masters Golf Club tournament, leading by a stroke with a four-under-par 68 the first day. The persistently bad weather trailing the tour hit Friday, wiping out the round. Then, Yokomine took over, firing a dazzling 63 Saturday to spurt into a five-stroke lead with 133 as Morita headed downhill with 72 and eventually ended in 21st place. Yokomine had nine birdies, including four on her last five holes.

None of her closest pursuers — runners-up Su-Ju Ahn, Shanshan Feng and Phoebe Yao — seriously challenged Yokomine Sunday. Pairs of birdies on both nines offset three bogeys as Yokomine chalked up a 71 for 204 total, three shots ahead of Ahn, who followed Yokomine (2009) as leading money winner in 2010 and 2011. Ahn had three 69s and moved to fifth in the standings.

Hisako Higuchi Morinaga Weider Ladies
Ichihara, Chiba
Winner: Bo-Mee Lee

Bo-Mee Lee injected herself into the late-season scramble for the money title on the Japan LPGA Tour with a resounding victory in the Hisako Higuchi Morinaga Weider tournament the first weekend of November. She did it with a flourish, firing a course-record, seven-under-par 65 at Morinaga Takataki Country Club and romping to a five-stroke triumph.

With the win, her second of the year and fifth in Japan, the 25-year-old South Korean moved to sixth on the money list as she and four others tightened the pursuit of Rikako Morita, who had held the No. 1 spot almost the entire season. Lee finished second to compatriot Mi-Jeong Jeon in the 2012 money race.

She turned on the juice in Saturday's second round at Ichihara after Yuki Sakurai, struggling to keep her tour card, opened on top with 66. Lee matched that, and her 70-66–136 gave her a one-stroke lead over Sun-Ju Ahn and Mayu Hattori, as Sakurai tumbled from contention with 79. There was no stopping Lee Sunday as she ran off a four-birdie stretch on the front nine and added three more coming in to finish five ahead of Ahn with her 15-under-par 201. Ahn shot 69–206 to edge China's Shanshan Feng by a stroke for second place.

Mizuno Classic
Shima, Mie
Winner: Teresa Lu

Teresa Lu resolved not to let another opportunity to land her first professional title get away from her as the Mizuno Classic reached its climax. Titles had eluded her during the eight years she played first in the U.S., then since 2010 on the Japan LPGA Tour. Three times in 2013 the 25-year-old Taiwanese player had to settle for runner-up finishes, once in a playoff. Not this time.

Trailing by two strokes going into the final round on a wet and windy Sunday at Kintetsu Kashikojima Country Club and three behind Chella Choi at the turn, Lu overhauled the leader on the strength of four birdies and broke from a tie with Choi with birdies on the final two holes for an incoming 30, an eight-under-par 64 and the two-stroke victory at 202.

"I've been waiting for this day for so long," said the overjoyed Lu.

Shiho Oyama, nursing a sore neck, led the first day with a six-birdie 68 and, with another 68 Saturday, shared first place at 136 with compatriots Mamiko Higa and Yuki Ichinose, who both shot 66. Lu and Choi were at 138, a stroke behind Asako Fujimoto and Brittany Lincicome, the only "name" player from America to seriously contend in the jointly sanctioned tournament, and she faded badly with a 77 Sunday.

After the long wait, Lu became the 10th first-time winner of the season.

Itoen Ladies
Chonan, Chiba
Winner: Sakura Yokomine

Sakura Yokomine maintained the momentum that was producing her finest season in four years by snatching her fourth victory on the 2013 LPGA Tour in the Itoen Ladies tournament. It propelled her to the top of the money list ahead of Rikako Morita, who had held the No. 1 spot for the last six months and all but a few weeks of the entire season. With just two tournaments remaining, the 27-year-old Yokomine had her sights set on a second money title to go with the one she won in her six-victory season in 2009. She led Morita by ¥12 million.

The Itoen triumph, her 22nd, was a bit of a nail-biter for Yokomine, who birdied four of the first 10 holes to get to 10 under, then parred the final eight holes at Great Island Club in Chonan, Chiba Prefecture, for 68–206. That was just good enough. Da-Ye Na, Yumiko Yoshida and Shiho Oyama all had their chances but faltered on the final holes. Yokomine won by a stroke over Yoshida (68) and two over Na (65), Oyama (71), Na-Ri Kim (70) and Mayu Hattori (69).

Yokomine, with 70-68, had entered the final round tied with Kim and 21-year-old newcomer Akane Yoshino, the first-round leader with 65, a stroke off the pace of two-time winner Miki Saiki, Ayaka Watanabe and Oyama at 137. Morita reached eight under through 12 holes Sunday, but three back-nine bogeys dropped her into a tie for 10th place.

Daio Paper Elleair Ladies Open
Matsuyama, Ehime
Winner: Rikako Morita

And then there were two — Rikako Morita and Sakura Yokomine.

Dislodged from the top of the money list by Yokomine after owning the position for nearly all of the season, Morita counterpunched immediately with her fourth win of the year in the Daio Paper Elleair Ladies Open. With that, she regained the No. 1 spot by less than ¥2 million going into the Tour Championship Ricoh Cup, the final event of 2013, and eliminated everybody else from the chase.

Trailing Yukari Baba by four strokes after starting with a pair of 70s, the 23-year-old Morita struck pay dirt in the third round at Elleair Golf Club. With a sizzling, nine-birdie round of 64, she jumped two strokes in front of Momoko Ueda with her 12-under-par 204 and held on amid a wild Sunday round of 69. She ranged from an eagle to a double bogey as her 273 gave her a one-stroke victory over Asako Fujimoto, who closed with a 66.

Yokomine, also a four-time winner in 2013, never fully recovered from a 73 start and finished seventh, four strokes behind Morita.

Japan LPGA Tour Championship Ricoh Cup
Miyazaki
Winner: Shiho Oyama

Plagued by elbow injuries since her banner years in the first decade of the 2000s when she won 11 of her 13 victories and led the money list in 2006, Shiho Oyama wound up the 2013 season on a high note with her second Japan LPGA Tour Championship, an impressive, four-stroke victory in the year's final major. It was the 36-year-old's first win in two years and just her second since 2008.

Sharing the excitement with Oyama's Ricoh Cup triumph was the battle for the season's money title. Despite a so-so week during which she never broke par, Rikako Morita, the 23-year-old, four-time 2013 winner who led the list most of the season, hung on to first place by just a little over ¥1 million with her earnings of ¥126,675,049. Sakura Yokomine, her only challenger, got off to a 74-76 start and, although she rallied to finish a stroke ahead of Morita, in her bid for a second money title she failed to overtake her.

Oyama, who played in just 22 tournaments on the Japan circuit in 2013, had only one slip in her run to her second Ricoh Cup victory. After opening rounds of 69 and a 71 that included a closing double bogey gave her a one-stroke lead at Miyazaki Country Club, Oyama slipped a stroke off the pace behind Teresa Lu and Bo-Mee Lee with a one-over-par 73 Saturday.

She dropped two behind Lu Sunday when she bogeyed the fourth hole, but then put on a dazzling performance with five birdies and an eagle in a seven-hole stretch starting at the sixth, finished with a 66 for 279 and the four-shot margin over Lu, who edged Sun-Ju Ahn for third place on the final money list.

Australian Ladies Tour

Bing Lee Samsung NSW Open
Sydney, New South Wales
Winner: Caroline Hedwall

Caroline Hedwall, who won her first tournament as a professional at Oatlands in 2011, returned two years later to reclaim the Bing Lee Samsung New South Wales Open. To do so, the 23-year-old Swede again beat the same opponent, New Zealand amateur Lydia Ko, who won the tournament as a 14-year-old in 2012. Ko overcame bogeys at the first two holes with an eagle and four birdies to share the lead with Hedwall for much of the back nine until she drove into the trees at the 17th and made a bogey. Hedwall birdied the 18th for a two-stroke victory after rounds of 66, 69 and 68 for a 13-under-par total of 203. Ko closed with a 69, while Australian Amateur champion Minjee Lee, 16, who tied Hedwall going into the last round, took third place with a 71.

"It's always good when young players come up and battle with the older ones and I think it's fun," said Hedwall, who warmed up for the event by winning the 36-hole Mount Broughton Classic the previous week. "I actually thought about the last time I was here two years ago, and Lydia was one up going into the last hole. This time I hit a great tee shot and set up for a nice birdie putt and took a lot of pressure off. I really enjoy those situations, I love being under pressure and that's what I practice for."

Volvik RACV Ladies Masters
Ashmore, Queensland
Winner: Karrie Webb

They call it "Karrie Pines" and only partly in jest as Karrie Webb showed again by winning the Volvik RACV Ladies Masters for a historic eighth time at the RACV Royal Pines Resort on the Gold Coast. The Queensland native matched the achievement of Sam Snead who also won the Greater Greensboro Open eight times, while the victory came just a week after Tiger Woods won for an eighth time at Torrey Pines, seven times in the regular PGA Tour event there plus the 2008 U.S. Open. Webb won this tournament four times in a row from 1998 and also claimed the title in 2005, 2007 and 2010. "I am very happy, it never gets old when you get a win, what a way to start the year!" she said.

Webb, now 39 and with 38 wins on the LPGA circuit in America behind her, started the final round two strokes behind co-leaders Su-Hyun Oh, a 16-year-old Australian amateur who posted an impressive 64 in the second round, and Ariya Jutanugarn, a 17-year-old from Thailand in her first event as a professional on the Ladies European Tour. Webb had opened with rounds of 70 and 66, but it was a closing 67 that proved crucial in reaching a 13-under-par total of 203 and gave her a two-stroke win over Oh, Jutanugarn and South Korean Chella Choi.

Webb made only one birdie on the front nine and admitted her experience helped her grind out the round before an important up-and-down to save par at the 10th. A four at the par-five 12th put her into a share of the lead once Jutanugarn had bogeyed the hole and Oh had a taken a double bogey. Webb then chipped in from over the green at the short 14th for a birdie and added two more at the 15th and 17th holes to pull well clear.

ISPS Handa New Zealand Women's Open
Christchurch, New Zealand
Winner: Lydia Ko

Faintly embarrassed when she first saw the billboards for the tournament around the Clearwater course in Christchurch, Lydia Ko nevertheless lived up to top billing by becoming the first home player to win the ISPS Handa New Zealand Women's Open. The remarkable 15-year-old amateur claimed her third professional title in only 12 tournaments with a one-stroke victory after displaying her trademark golf maturity. But once it was over the Kiwi schoolgirl showed her true emotions to the largest gallery ever to watch women's golf in New Zealand by leaving the 18th green in tears of joy. "I didn't cry at the Canadian Open so I don't know why I cried here," Ko said later. "I guess it meant more. It is our national Open, so to win means a lot. I am not the person who shows expression of feeling, but I guess the tears showed it."

At 15 years, eight months and 17 days, Ko became the youngest ever winner on the Ladies European Tour. The previous record holder was 16-year-old Amy Yang at the 2006 ANZ Ladies Masters, and Ko joined Yang and Gillian Stewart as the only amateurs to win on the LET. She had already become the youngest winner on the LPGA with her Canadian Open victory in 2012 and the youngest ever on a major women's circuit at the 2012 New South Wales Open when she was still 14. But this was her best victory, Ko said: "It is the national Open and I came so close in the last three years. This topped it off. The New South Wales Open and the Canadian Open were obviously great wins as well."

Ko was the joint second-round leader after rounds of 70 and 68 and another 68 left her on 206, 10 under par. It was America's Amelia Lewis who made the biggest charge on the final day, with six birdies and an eagle in the first 13 holes. But Ko crept back into a tie with a birdie at the 15th, and after Lewis three-putted at the 18th for a bogey, Ko made sure she did not make the same mistake.

ISPS Handa Women's Australian Open
Canberra, ACT
Winner: Jiyai Shin

Jiyai Shin overcame both world No. 1 Yani Tseng and the game's newest sensation, Lydia Ko, to win the ISPS Handa Women's Australian Open. After twice being a runner-up in the event, Shin became the first South Korean to win the Open, which was played at Royal Canberra as part of the centenary celebrations of Australia's capital city.

Shin, who recovered from hand surgery in 2012 to win the Ricoh Women's British Open for the second time at Hoylake, made the perfect start to the LPGA season, in an event co-sanctioned by the Ladies European Tour as well as home circuit ALPG. It was the 24-year-old Shin's 11th LPGA victory. "Lydia asked me when we finished how many times I win on LPGA and I said 11, but you are a lot younger than me so you have lots more chances to win."

Ko, the 15-year-old amateur who played with Shin on the final day, had stolen the limelight by winning the New Zealand Open the previous week and then opening with a 10-under-par 63 here. It was five strokes better than one of her playing partners, Tseng, and 11 better than the other, Michelle Wie. Ko had only 21 putts the first day to lead by one over Mariajo Uribe and by two over Tseng. Uribe led at the halfway stage, but after the third round Ko and Shin went six clear of Beatriz Recari and eight clear of Tseng.

A final-round duel between Ko and Shin appeared to fade when Ko started with a double bogey and a bogey to fall four behind, while Tseng, a two-time winner of the tournament, put in a mighty charge. Stung by a bogey at the first, Tseng collected six birdies and an eagle in a 66 to set the target at 16 under par. Shin failed to capitalize on Ko's nervy start, and after a birdie at the first, she bogeyed the fifth and the 12th holes. With a birdie at the latter for a two-shot swing, Ko was back on even terms, but then there was a two-shot swing the other way at the 14th. While Ko failed to get up and down from sand, Shin holed a 15-yard chip shot from thick rough beside the green.

"This chip was very important for the tournament," Shin said. "It was great for me and I got more in the legs and enjoyed the last few holes. Finally, I win in Australia, so I am really happy about that." She birdied the 15th to close with a 72 and finish on 274, 18 under par, to win by two shots over Tseng and by four over Ko, who dropped a shot at the 17th for a closing 76.

"I had a few struggles with my drives, but I mean I can't play good every single round," Ko said. "I came third? Third in a professional tournament is a pretty good result. I can't say I'm not fully pleased."

Women's Victorian Open
Bellarine Peninsula, Victoria
Winner: Stacey Keating

Stacey Keating, who made a breakthrough with two wins on the Ladies European Tour in 2012, won for the first time in Australia and in front of many friends and family at the Women's Victorian Open. Large crowds watched at the 13th Beach Golf Links as the men's and women's tournaments were played alongside each other. Despite the presence of the likes of Laura Davies and Sophie Gustafson, the 26-year-old from nearby Cressy was the center of attention as she won by two strokes over England's Hannah Burke and Western Australian Kristie Smith. Keating had rounds of 71 and 68 over the Creek course before the women switched to the Beach course over the weekend when the men and women played in alternate groups.

Keating opened up a four-stroke lead with a third round of six-under 68 and then closed with a 71 for an 18-under-par total of 278. A poor start to the final round was eased with an eagle at the ninth, while a run of three birdies in four holes on the back nine was helped by her tee shot at the short 12th hitting a spectator and rebounding to six feet.

"It means everything this win, it is the best," Keating said. "I was over par and had just missed a short putt on the eighth, then the eagle got me from over par to under par, which made me feel better going into the back nine." Keating's victory also secured the Club Car Series title for 2013.

13. Senior Tours

Kenny Perry finally bagged a couple of those big ones that used to get away.

Perry made a smashing success of 2013 by winning the Constellation Senior Players Championship and the U.S. Senior Open, his first two career majors, in back-to-back starts. And while they may not completely heal the wounds from the 1996 PGA Championship and the 2009 Masters slipping from his hands, they would help.

In the Players, Perry shot the last three rounds in the low 60s to beat Fred Couples and Duffy Waldorf, and was relieved that he could hold on this time. "I thought I was snake-bit," he said. "I just seemed to mess up down the homestretch. I had so much heartache and so many losses." In the Senior Open, he roared from 10 back after 36 holes to a 64-63 finish to win by five for his second major.

"Now I have a USGA title," Perry said. "Even though it's a Senior Open, I still regard it as a very high honor." But he wasn't finished yet. Perry settled his season-long battle for supremacy with Langer in the AT&T Championship in October with a birdie on the first playoff hole for his third win of the year (tour fifth). He had 12 top-10s and three seconds to lock up the Player of the Year Award. But his $2.1 million left him second on the money list.

The attention-getters for 2013:

Leading Money-Winner: Bernhard Langer had two victories, five seconds and 10 other top-10 finishes to top the money list with $2.4 million. In the ACE Group Classic, he blew a late lead and ended up two-putting the final hole from 50 feet for a par and the win. Then he took the Greater Gwinnett Championship by three. Someone wondered whether it was getting easier for him. "When things look easier," Langer said, "it's when you do things very well."

Rookie of the Year: Rocco Mediate lived every rookie's dream, winning in his debut, taking the Allianz Championship in February. His 17-under-par total included a course-record 61 in the second round. He was the 16th player to win his tour debut, a group that included Arnold Palmer, Jack Nicklaus and Gary Player. "I don't belong with those guys," Mediate said. In the Shaw Charity Classic, he eagled two of the last four holes for a first-round 63, went on to his second win, and finished ninth on the money list with $1.3 million.

Feel-Good Player of the Year: Esteban Toledo, also a rookie, was winless on the PGA Tour and a one-time winner on the Web.com Tour, but broke through for two victories on the Champions Tour, both in playoffs. He beat Mike Goodes and Gene Sauers in the Insperity Championship, then chipped in to beat Perry in the Montreal Championship and delivered an odd fist pump. Said Toledo, a former pro boxer: "I always celebrate with a left hook." He earned $1.2 million, 12th on the money list.

Surprise of the Year: Kohki Idoki, a Japan Golf Tour veteran, was on his first visit to the United States. Next thing he knew, he was winning the Senior PGA Championship. Idoki raced from five behind in the final round, shot 65, and won by two. He was the 17th to win his debut. Said Idoki: "I can't believe I am the champion."

All told, there were 18 different winners in 2013, one three-time winner (Perry) and seven who won twice: Langer, Mediate, Toledo, David Frost, Michael Allen, Russ Cochran and Mark Wiebe.

Elsewhere on the tour:

• In one of the wildest finishes ever in the Senior British Open, Wiebe beat Langer on the fifth extra hole for his first major. Langer had it won until he double-bogeyed the final hole to slip into a tie with Wiebe. They tied the first two holes of the playoff before darkness halted play, then resumed on Monday. Wiebe won it with a par at the fifth extra hole.

• Frost posted his first major in the Regions Tradition, beating Couples by a stroke. It was Frost's second win in his last seven starts.

• Couples was in danger of being shut out for 2013 until he caught fire in the season-ending Charles Schwab Cup. He shot four rounds in the 60s and won by six shots for his ninth tour victory. Said Couples: "Just winning — even if it's a club championship, you're thrilled."

• John Cook played all 54 holes in regulation without a bogey, then sank a 12-foot birdie putt on the second playoff hole to beat Frost and win the Mitsubishi Electric Championship at Hualalai for the second time in the last three years.

Both the European and Japan Senior Tours had a dominant performer in 2013, each with a decidedly different background.

England's Paul Wesselingh, 51, joined the thin ranks of club pros who have made it big in senior golf when he pulled away late in the season and landed the European Senior Tour's Order of Merit title in just his second year. Wesselingh, who won the Senior PGA and another tournament early in the season, ran away with the honors by winning the final two events, lastly the MCB Tour Championship.

The old guard took a back seat all year. The only other multiple winners and challengers were Steen Tinning of Denmark and Simon P. Brown of England, tour newcomers, who each won twice. Colin Montgomerie also made his senior tour debut with a victory in the Travis Perkins Masters.

A solid veteran ruled the roost on the Japan Senior Tour. A six-time winner on the Japan Tour in his younger days, Kiyoshi Murota, 58, bagged the Japan Senior Open and two other titles in the 12-tournament season, running his career senior total to 11 victories. He more than doubled the earnings of runner-up Seiki Okuda with ¥62 million.

Champions Tour

Mitsubishi Electric Championship
Ka'upulehu-Kona, Hawaii
Winner: John Cook

The Champions Tour opened the 2013 season with its rousing Hawaiian luau, the Mitsubishi Electric Championship, and John Cook was the one who came away with the party hat. That wasn't poi he was feasting on, it was Hualalai Golf Club's par-fives. He birdied them 10 times in his 12 regular visits, including all four times in the final round, and in the process ran down David Frost and beat him in a playoff for his ninth tour victory.

"It was kind of a survival day," said Cook, all but mopping his brow after the final round, "until it got down to the nitty-gritty and you knew what you had to do." And that was to hang on while Frost was threatening to run away with the tournament.

Cook could thank some great luck in the second round for keeping Frost in sight. Frost erupted down the back nine, birdieing five of the first six holes to open a four-stroke lead. Cook then abruptly cut that in half when his 114-yard wedge approach at the 18th found the hole for an eagle and his second 66 to Frost's pair of 65s. Cook still had to dog Frost through the final round, and didn't catch him till the last hole, dropping a 16-foot birdie putt, wrapping up a card of 66-66-67–199, 17 under par. Frost's last chance was a 15-footer for birdie at the last, and he just missed, finishing with 65-65-69. They tied on the first playoff hole, the par-four 18th, with birdies from inside 10 feet. At the second, the par-three 17th, Cook put his tee shot 12 feet from the hole, inside Frost's. Frost missed the birdie try, but Cook didn't.

It had been a remarkable show. Cook went the entire way without a bogey, and Frost had just one.

Bernhard Langer gave it a great run but fell a shot short of joining the playoff and took solo third. He started the final round six off the lead, then birdied 10 of the last 15 holes for a 64.

Allianz Championship
Boca Raton, Florida
Winner: Rocco Mediate

It didn't take Rocco Mediate long to make himself right at home on the Champions Tour. On the PGA Tour, it took him six years to win the first of his six titles, but he was a shameless party-crasher on the Champions. He did it in just three days. Mediate, who turned 50 two months earlier, was debuting on the senior circuit early in February in the Allianz Championship, the first full-field event of 2013. He announced his presence with an 11-under-par blitz of Broken Sound in the second round.

The talkative Mediate was almost speechless. "I'm ecstatic," he said. Then he added: "I've been saying all week it's never easy — it shouldn't be easy." And it wasn't. He turned in a powerful 67-61-71 performance, but he had to battle down the final stretch for his 17-under-par 199 total and a two-stroke win over the Tom Pernice, Jr. and the ubiquitous Bernhard Langer.

Mediate started the third and final round with a three-shot lead over Pernice and birdied the fourth, eighth and ninth going out. But he slipped into a tie with Pernice at the par-three 14th when he missed the green and bogeyed.

"That made me really mad," said Mediate, best known for a thrilling 18-hole playoff loss to Tiger Woods in the 2008 U.S. Open. The Allianz was decided at the par-four 17th. Mediate parred and retook the lead when Langer and Pernice both bogeyed. He locked up the win at the par-five 18th, where he tapped in from two feet for his birdie after missing the green long. Pernice shot 70, Langer 68.

Mediate's 61, a course record and career-low, was the bulk of a 30-hole stretch without a bogey. It began with five straight birdies from No. 3. Coming in, he birdied Nos. 10, 11, 12 and 17, and eagled the par-five 18th from 10 feet, and went on to become the 16th to win his Champions Tour debut. That put him in a group that includes Arnold Palmer, Jack Nicklaus and Gary Player.

"I don't belong with those guys," Mediate said.

ACE Group Classic
Naples, Florida
Winner: Bernhard Langer

Bernhard Langer was looking great at the ACE Group Classic. He was 10 under par in the first round, 12 under after the second and flying high. It was the landing that nearly killed him.

Langer was leading by three shots going into the third and final round when suddenly he went staggering and stumbling all over TwinEagles. But he pulled himself together just in time to slip past Jay Don Blake by a stroke for his first victory of the year and 17th on the Champions Tour.

"It was definitely a grind," a baffled Langer said. "I was hoping to come down to the last hole with, whatever, a three-shot lead or something. Make it easy." The easy part was the first two rounds. He opened with a dazzling 10-under-par 62. First, birdies at the fifth, sixth and eighth. Then a stunning eagle at the par-four 10th, on a nine iron from 141 yards that plummeted right into the cup, and he followed that with a birdie at the 11th and four straight from the 13th.

Langer turned in a strong no-bogey 70 in blustery winds in the second round and kept his lead at three, this time over Chien Soon Lu (68). Blake was five back. It looked like it was all over when Langer open the final round with birdies at the first and third. He had gone 39 holes without a bogey. And then the staggers set in.

Langer double-bogeyed the fourth, birdied the sixth and bogeyed the ninth and 10th. Blake, playing just ahead, two-putted for birdie at the 13th to take the lead briefly. Langer came along and birdied the 13th and 14th to retake the lead. Blake bogeyed the 16th, missing his par from three feet, and Langer bogeyed the 15th, but brilliantly. He lobbed a wedge to five feet after watering his approach from the fairway. He still led by one. Blake's final chance came at the 18th, a 19-footer for birdie. But he missed. Then Langer sealed the win with a par, but an unlikely one — two-putting from 50 feet.

Said Langer: "I'm certainly relieved."

Toshiba Classic
Newport Beach, California
Winner: David Frost

If there was a turning point in the Toshiba Classic, it came at the final hole of the first round. That's when David Frost, who has been living under par in this young Champions Tour season, tapped in at the par-five 18th for his eighth birdie, a flawless 63 and a one-stroke lead over Fred Couples. Frost led the rest of the way and won by five, his first of the season and fourth of his career.

"I really enjoyed the tussle with Freddie out there," said Frost, who shot 63-66-65 at Newport Beach Country Club in mid-March, tying the tournament record of 19-under-par 194. Couples probably didn't really share the enthusiasm after his bad back kicked up again. "I hit a lot of bad wedges," Couples said, after the final round.

Frost broke par for the eighth time in 10 tour rounds with that opening 63, the result of digging into the modern mysteries of the golf swing. "I've really enjoyed the biomechanical part of the game," he said. "It's given me a lot more flow to the game." That's guru talk, but Frost's translation included four birdies on his first five holes, and three of them when his approach shots stopped within a foot of the hole. Couples was in only his second tour event and his putter was working. He made six putts from 15 feet or more, including a 50-footer for birdie at the seventh. "I made a mile of putts," Couples said. "I just happened to make more putts than I expected to."

If Frost's birdie at 18 in the first round was the turning point, what was the eagle at the 18th in the second? Frost dropped an 18-footer while Couples two-putted from 35 feet for a 66 and remained a shot behind and facing a big job the next day. "I have to shoot something very, very good," Couples said.

Couples did tie Frost with a birdie at No. 1 in the final round, but Frost birdied the next two and was on his way.

Mississippi Gulf Resort Classic
Biloxi, Mississippi
Winner: Michael Allen

It was a case of good news-bad news-and-really bad news for Michael Allen in the wind-battered Mississippi Gulf Resort Classic. The good news was that Allen came from behind in the final round to take the clubhouse lead. The bad news was that he blew a short par putt on the final hole, costing himself an insurance stroke, a little more cushion for his tenuous lead. The really bad news was Bernhard Langer was out at the 15th, needing a mere stroke to tie, and he hadn't met the four-hole stretch that could shut him out. So Allen fretted quietly and warmed up for a possible playoff. Finally, blessed silence.

"It was nice to hear no big roar," Allen said.

Langer, chasing that stroke, birdied the 13th, but ran afoul of the winds at the 16th, where he couldn't get home despite switching from an eight iron to a five iron for his approach and ended up in a bunker. "That was a big blow, because I had no shot," Langer said. It cost him a bogey and knocked him a stroke behind. His last chance to tie was at the 18th, and he just missed holing out a chip from the rough. He finished with a 70–206, second by a stroke.

Allen, shooting the par-72 Fallen Oak in 70-68-67 for an 11-under 205 total and his fourth Champions Tour win, stayed close all the way, but never seemed to be a serious threat. Hal Sutton, coming back from hip surgery, shared the first-round lead at 69. Corey Pavin caught fire in the second round, birdieing his first six holes and shooting a 67 to tie for the 36-hole lead.

Allen opened the final round two off the lead and erased that deficit in nothing flat, with five straight birdies from No. 3. He played the back nine in three birdies and three bogeys, the last that four-footer at the final hole.

"That was a very, very empty feeling," said Allen. But before long, he was breathing easier.

Greater Gwinnett Championship
Duluth, Georgia
Winner: Bernhard Langer

Bernhard Langer was saying he's wiser now. Wiser? He hadn't exactly shown any signs of being short on wisdom. Still, after taking the Champion Tour's inaugural Greater Gwinnett Championship, that's what he said: "I have a lot more wisdom."

"Easier" was another word he tossed out. "I'm trying to make it easier," he said. "When things look easier, it's when you do things very well."

Well, then we can take his words for it — the birdie at TPC Sugarloaf's par-five 10th in the final round, which set up his win, was wise, but if it looked easy, someone wasn't paying attention.

Coming to the 10th, Langer was a shot up on playing partner Esteban Toledo, whose chances for that first win had brightened. Langer had scrambled to save par at the eighth and ninth, and then drove into a bunker at the 10th and topped his shot coming out. But Toledo's big chance evaporated when his two-iron approach from 240 yards bounced 30 yards over the green and he was short coming back. Langer's third was just over, and hitting first, he chipped in for birdie from 40 feet. Esteban then missed his birdie chip.

"It looked like a one- or two-shot swing [for Toledo]," Langer said. "You never know."

Toledo started his plunge to a 75 and a tie for seventh with double bogeys on the next two holes. Tom Pernice, Jr., playing just ahead, finished strong for a 70 after a double bogey at the 12th and tied for second with Tom Lehman, who closed with a bogey-free 67.

Langer missed the fairway at the par-five 18th but still birdied, completing a card of 73-66-67–206, for a three-stroke victory. It was his second win of the young year, his fifth top-three finish in the six events, and his 18th win on the tour.

"He doesn't get ruffled," said Lehman.

Said Roger Chapman (75), who slipped to a tie for 13th: "I just thought, can you ever stop this guy?"

"It's gratifying," Langer said, "to see all the hard work pay off."

Liberty Mutual Insurance Legends of Golf
Savannah, Georgia
Winners: Brad Faxon and Jeff Sluman

They slapped the responsibility back and forth like a tennis ball. Jeff Sluman said that Brad Faxon was his horse. "I felt like I rode Secretariat all day," Sluman said, beaming. And said Faxon: "I always have this dream I'm going to play 54 holes with Jeff and never help him." The truth was somewhere in the middle, and it all worked out beautifully.

This was a marriage — Faxon's word for it — made on the scoreboard. Sluman loved Stads — Craig Stadler — but they weren't getting anywhere in the Liberty. So two years ago, Sluman called Faxon and said, wanna pair up? And they held together through the tough going at the Club at Savannah Harbor for a one-stroke win in the 33-team better-ball event.

The Jeff and Brad Show led by a shot in the first round, trailed by a shot in the second, then barged ahead down the backstretch, wrapping up a card of 62-66-65–193 to edge Fred Funk and Mike Goodes, and Kenny Perry and Gene Sauers. Faxon is the celebrated putter, but Sluman led the charge, running off five birdie putts, including the 35-footer at the 12th. He dropped an eight-footer at the 14th that put them into the lead for good.

"This is a perfect marriage because it's not like we're going to get mad at each other if either one doesn't play well," Faxon said. Sounds reasonable enough. But through 54 holes of the Liberty, it was a theory that didn't get tested. For that test, at least one of them had to play badly.

Insperity Championship
The Woodlands, Texas
Winner: Esteban Toledo

Esteban Toledo's timing was impeccable, and he wasn't bad when it came to high drama, either, in the Insperity Championship. He started the final round seven shots off the lead, then caught the leaders and won in a playoff, scoring his first victory on the Champions Tour and becoming the first Mexican to win on the tour, and also doing it on May 5 — Cinco de Mayo, the date of a Mexican military victory.

"It's a special day for me," said Toledo, 50. "We don't celebrate in Mexico as much as in the U.S. It's more Americanized. Just winning on that day is the most incredible thing I've ever done."

Toledo's only previous victory was on the Web.com Tour in 2005. A Champions Tour rookie now, his best finish in eight previous starts was a tie for sixth in the Toshiba Classic in March. But prospects weren't promising in the Insperity, in blustery weather at The Woodlands. Only seven players in the 81-man field broke the par 216 for the tournament, the fewest since the five in the 2007 Outback Steakhouse Pro-Am. And the tournament had turned into a Mike Goodes-Gene Sauers battle.

Goodes and Sauers traded the lead through the first two rounds, Goodes up by one with a 69, then Sauers by two with a 66–136. Toledo started 72-71–143, seven shots behind.

Then he announced his entrance into the fray with an eagle at the par-four No. 1 — a drive and a hole-out wedge from 25 yards. He birdied four of the last 13, from the sixth, holing an eight-footer at the 13th and two-putting the 15th from 20 feet. He closed with a 67 to tie Sauers and Goodes. In the playoff, Sauers dropped out with a bogey at the second extra hole. At the third, No. 17, Goodes missed a five-foot par putt and Toledo tapped in for his par and his precious first victory.

"I have dreams and goals," Toledo said. "I believe in myself, that I can go up there and win again and again and again."

Senior PGA Championship
St. Louis, Missouri
Winner: Kohki Idoki

No matter how you slice it, the 2013 Senior PGA Championship, at Bellerive Country Club, will not go into the books as being won by Kohki Idoki, an unknown Japanese making his first trip to the United States. It will be known as yet another major that Kenny Perry, nice guy from Kentucky, let slip through his fingers.

Perry had downplayed the thought back when he finished the third round with a two-shot lead. If it didn't hold up, he said, "It's not going to be the end of the world."

When it happened though, it certainly had to feel like the next worst thing. Perry, famed for letting the 1996 PGA Championship and the 2009 Masters get away, had blown another.

But while Perry was slipping in the final round, Idoki was putting on a show. The diminutive Japanese, 51, a mere 5-foot-5 and 136 pounds, came tearing from five strokes behind with birdies at Nos. 2, 3, 7 and 8. Still, the race didn't get hot until Perry and Haas began staggering. Perry got to 12 under with three quick birdies and was leading by two going to the 13th. There, with his ball on the fringe, nudging the rough, he knocked his bogey try three feet past and holed that for a double. Then he bogeyed the 16th and 17th. Haas also buckled, bogeying the 11th, 14th and 16th. Both would birdie the 18th, but it was far too late. Idoki birdied the 14th and 17th, wrapping up a card of 71-69-68-65–273, 11 under, to beat Perry (72) and Haas (70) by two.

Afterward, Perry spoke of having pain walking the course, left over from knee surgery in February. "I struggled with my knee all week," Perry said, and added, "This one doesn't hurt nearly as bad as the Masters or the PGA did."

Said Idoki, through an interpreter: "It is one of the greatest things to win in this game. I can't believe I am the champion."

Would he defend? Said Idoki: "I prefer to just stay in Japan."

Principal Charity Classic
Des Moines, Iowa
Winner: Russ Cochran

Russ Cochran preferred to sit this one out in the locker room. Well, pacing there, anyway, like an expectant father, and not watch. He had finished with the clubhouse lead in the Principal Charity Classic, but outside, on the 18th green, was a guy who could spoil it all. Jay Don Blake was looking at a 10-foot birdie putt that would tie him and force a playoff.

But Blake missed, and Cochran, who spent much of his four years on the Champions Tour fighting injuries, had his fourth victory, but first since 2011.

"I didn't really expect to win," said Cochran, who trailed all the way, shooting the Wakonda Club in 71-67-67–205, 11 under. "But I knew I could compete and get in contention. When you do that, sometime good things happen."

Blake was kicking himself for letting his fourth win get away. Two early bogeys were bad enough, but after six birdies came two more mistakes. At the par-three 17th, only 174 yards long, he left his tee shot about 50 feet short and three-putted for a bogey. Then came the 18th — a 10-footer is no cinch, but he missed this one badly. "I quit on the stroke and left it out there to the right," Blake said.

Cochran began to move up with the 67 in the second round, finishing two behind of Duffy Waldorf, a rookie looking not only for his first Champions win but his first in 13 years, and one behind Blake and Bart Bryant.

Blake stumbled to two early bogeys, but Cochran was off and running in the final round. He birdied three of the first five, then added at the 11th, 13th and 15th, the last giving him a one-stroke lead. But he missed a four-foot par putt at the 16th and slipped back into a tie with Blake.

Playing behind him, Blake then three-putted the 17th, opening the door to Cochran, who ended up in the locker room.

"I really didn't want to watch Jay Don," Cochran said. "He's really a good friend. I felt like he was going to make that putt."

Regions Tradition
Shoal Creek, Alabama
Winner: David Frost

The Regions Tradition, the second major of the Champions Tour season — and the return of big-time golf to Shoal Creek for the first time since the 1990 PGA Championship — had the two chief contenders talking to themselves. About each other, that is.

Said David Frost, seeking that coveted first major, "I said to myself, 'It's not going to be easy. Freddy's going to fire at the pins. I've just got to be up to the challenge.'"

Fred Couples, a two-time major winner, was equally complimentary. "I gave him everything I had," Couples said later. "He was just better the whole day."

Couples was a challenger from the start. His opening 66-71 had him one behind in the first round, two behind in the second. Frost started 68-70 and trailed by three in both rounds. Then Frost made his move in the third. He birdied four of the last eight and took the lead with 66–204 over Couples' 68–205.

In the final round, John Cook birdied five of the first eight, shot 66 and was in the clubhouse at 13 under, but Frost and Couples were too preoccupied to notice.

The shootout started immediately. Frost birdied No. 1 and upped his lead to two. Couples birdied No. 3, but bogeyed the next, and tied Frost with birdies at the sixth and seventh. Frost nosed in front on a birdie at the par-three eighth, then was up by two on Couples' bogey at the ninth. They matched birdies at the par-five 11th, then Frost also birdied the 12th to go ahead by three. A bogey at the 13th dropped him back, and the Couples got to within a shot with a birdie at the 15th. Then the weather delay hit.

Both came back out and birdied the 16th, then battled to hard-fought pars the rest of the way for 68s. Frost finished at 16-under 272 for his second win of the season, his fifth on the tour and his first major in 17 tries.

"I am delighted...," Frost said. "I didn't ever think it would be easy, and it wasn't easy."

Encompass Championship
Glenview, Illinois
Winner: Craig Stadler

The Encompass Championship was brand new on the Champions Tour, but it seemed like old times to Craig Stadler — literally. Right down to the putt he was facing on the last hole.

It was a 12-footer for par with the championship hanging in the balance and Fred Couples pressing the issue. Stadler, 60, the Walrus himself, hadn't won in eight years and nine months — the longest dry stretch in tour history — and 170 starts. ("It was getting embarrassing," Stadler said.) He led by as much as five strokes with 10 holes to play. But it ultimately came down to one putt on the final hole.

"It looked really similar to the putt I made a billion years ago at Akron," said Stadler. That was in the 1992 World Series of Golf at Firestone, which he rolled in to beat Corey Pavin by a stroke. Said Stadler: "I just talked to myself ... 'You made that one, make this one. What the heck.'" And so he did, for his ninth tour victory, ending the long drought with a 67-65-71 performance, a 13-under 203 total at North Shore Country Club.

The Encompass was barely under way when Stadler showed that his game was back — at least for the moment. He birdied five of his first 11 holes and tied for the lead at 67. He would go 35 holes before making a bogey, that at the 18th in the second round after making birdie at eight of the first 16 holes. All told, he birdied 13 of the first 35 holes. He was turning the tournament into a runaway in the final round, with four birdies over the first six holes and taking a five-stroke lead through the eighth.

Then the trouble started. He missed the green and bogeyed No. 9, birdied No. 11, then bogeyed 12, 14 and 15, missing all three fairways. He parred in from there and got the margin he needed when Couples missed the 18th green and bogeyed for a 66.

"Golf," said a relieved Stadler, "hasn't been fun in a long time."

Constellation Senior Players Championship
Pittsburgh, Pennsylvania
Winner: Kenny Perry

Kenny Perry was beginning to wonder whether he had the stuff to pull in a major. He was stamped by the two he folded in, the 1996 PGA Championship and the 2009 Masters. And now on the Champions Tour, he collapsed again at the Senior PGA Championship late in May.

A month later, he finally broke through. He was spectacular in the Constellation Senior Players Championship, coming from behind in the final round to beat Fred Couples and Duffy Waldorf by two shots. What a relief.

"I thought I was snake-bit," Perry said. "I just seemed to mess up down the homestretch. I had so much heartache and so many losses."

Not this time. Perry opened with a 71, one over par on a Fox Chapel Golf Club so softened by torrential rains that all four rounds were played under the lift-clean-place provision. He added a pair of 63s — the 126 total broke Jack Nicklaus' record for 36 holes — and closed with a 64 for a 19-under 261 to win by two over Couples (68) and Waldorf, whose 64 included a front-nine 29. New Hall-of-Famer Colin Montgomerie made his tour debut and tied for ninth.

Perry, nearly desperate, had tried a new strategy. "Today, I went the other direction," he said. "I wasn't trying to hang on. Instead of trying to make pars, I was trying to make birdies."

"They played great, and Kenny didn't make any mistakes, but I sure did," said Couples, who took the lead with a 62 in the second round. But the top putter on the tour was betrayed by his putter in the fourth round. He three-putted the drivable No. 7 from 20 feet for par, and the 15th from eight feet for bogey. Waldorf also bogeyed, and Perry sealed his win with two birdies — a wedge stiff to the 16th and a six iron to two feet at the par-three 17th. He had his first major.

Through it all, one thing was uppermost in his mind. Said Perry: "I was just thinking — you know what? I'm tired of worrying about it. I really was."

U.S. Senior Open
Omaha, Nebraska
Winner: Kenny Perry

It seems that Kenny Perry had finally figured out how it's done in the majors. Now everyone's wondering how to turn him off.

The guy best known for folding in majors suddenly had his second, the U.S. Senior Open, and in back-to-back starts. No folding this time. He came from behind and ran away and hid.

This was great news for Perry fans, who are many, and especially for Perry himself, a Mr. Nice Guy best known for blowing majors — the 1996 PGA Championship, the 2009 Masters, and then the Senior PGA, just in May. Now fans could think about the ones that didn't get away, this one and the Constellation Senior Players Championship just three weeks earlier.

"This is by far the biggest tournament I ever won," said Perry, now with his fourth Champions Tour victory. "Now I have a USGA title. It's an Open, it's our Open — it's what the players play for. To finally get it, even though it's a Senior Open, I still regard it as a very high honor."

Perry was not in the running till late in shooting the par-70 Omaha Country Club in 67-73-64-63–267, 13 under. That 64-63 finish is what carried him past the field.

Said Fred Funk, runner-up by five shots: "He just smoked the field on the weekend."

Perry was in a crowd tied for the lead at 67 in the first round, then was 10 behind Michael Allen (63) in the second. The 64 brought him to within two of Allen through the third. "I birdied the first two holes right out of the gate, and it was foot to the floor," Perry said. "I was trying to birdie every hole out there."

He was still trying in the final round. He went out in six birdies for a one-bogey 30. And he battered the three par-fives, with six birdies and an eagle, going eight under in 12 visits.

"Why, after all these years?" said Perry, happy, relieved and baffled. "Here I am, [almost] 53 years old, and it finally came together for me."

The Senior Open Championship presented by Rolex
Southport, Merseyside, England
Winner: Mark Wiebe

See European Senior Tour section.

3M Championship
Blaine, Minnesota
Winner: Tom Pernice, Jr.

Tom Pernice, Jr. found the secret to happiness in golf — make a couple of 40-footers and pretend the guy up ahead isn't really shooting 62.

With these truths in hand, Pernice took the 3M Championship, his second on the Champions Tour after an 0-for-50 drought dating to his debut in the 2009 SAS Championship.

That was Jeff Sluman, coming from seven shots behind in the final round, torching the TPC Twin Cities for a 10-under-par 62, not exactly an encouraging show for Pernice, an hour behind.

"I just tried to tell myself to stay patient, stay relaxed, and I did," said Pernice, after shooting 66-65-68–199, 17 under, to win by one. "I feel fortunate enough to escape with a victory."

Escape was the right word. Pernice had to come from behind twice. But it had already been a battle, starting with Mark Wiebe taking the first-round lead with a 64 despite being badly jet-lagged in a late arrival after a playoff victory over Bernhard Langer in the Senior British Open. "Maybe I need to be exhausted to play this course," Wiebe said.

Pernice took the lead in the second round with a one-bogey 65, and what a bogey it was. After six birdies over the first 12 holes, he was 40 feet from the pin at the 14th — very likely a two-putt double bogey. But he rolled in the 40-footer to save a bogey and his round, and was leading Tom Kite (65) by two.

Kite slipped, but Sluman, after a 69-69 start, caught fire in the final round. He birdied the first seven holes for a tournament-record 28 for nine holes. Two back-nine birdies gave him a flawless 62.

Pernice, two under for the day, was a shot behind Sluman and 40 feet from the pin at the par-three 17th. And he rolled it in for a birdie. At the par-five 18th, he fired his 200-yard approach to eight feet and two-putted for the win.

"I'm just thrilled to finally get the victory," Pernice said. "It's been a long, long spell."

Dick's Sporting Goods Open
Endicott, New York
Winner: Bart Bryant

Bart Bryant, a rookie on the Champions Tour, did more than score his first victory in the Dick's Sporting Goods Open at En-Joie Golf Course. He was part of history. In the trophy presentation, that wasn't a CEO doing the honors. It was Don January, a famous name from another era of the game. January, now 83, won the tour's first event, the 1980 Atlantic City Senior Invitational, and now 33 years later, he was presenting the trophy to Bryant, on winning the 1,000th.

"When we first started out, we had no idea ... whether it would even be successful," January said. "I never thought ... of a thousand tournaments. My God, that's forever. It's come a long way."

Bryant seemed as much relieved as honored. He won with a hot-and-cool performance that bothered him. After opening 66-62 and taking a four-stroke lead into the final round, he battled a shaky game for a par 72 to win by one over Corey Pavin (69) and Russ Cochran (67). "I just never really felt settled," he said. "I really didn't play great. Somehow, I managed to get it in."

In his second-round 62, he birdied six of his first seven holes, holing putts from everywhere, including a 20-footer at the second, 30-footers at the sixth and seventh, and an 18-footer at the 11th. He hit 10 of the 14 driving fairways in each of the first two rounds, missed only two greens in regulation and was bogey-free for the first 39 holes.

His finish, a deceptive two-birdie, two-bogey par 72, was the reverse. He struggled over the first seven holes and bogeyed No. 4. After birdies at the eighth and ninth, he ground out eight straight pars coming in, then bogeyed No. 18, cutting his margin to one stroke. But it was a relief. Bryant had been sidelined for nearly three years after two surgeries on his left wrist. Would he ever play again, never mind win?

"I dreamed about it," Bryant said. "I don't know if I believed it would ever happen."

Boeing Classic
Snoqualmie, Washington
Winner: John Riegger

Things were not looking good for John Riegger, unaccustomed as he was to his position. After years of hunting, suddenly he was the hunted. Riegger, 50, in just his fifth start on the Champions Tour, had taken the lead in the Boeing Classic, and the chase was on. It could not have been comfortable knowing that Tom Lehman, Bernhard Langer, Fred Couples and the like were at his heels.

"I don't look at the board," said Riegger, the fifth rookie to win this season. "The only person to put pressure on you is yourself." The trick, he said, was stick to your own game. He trailed Bart Bryant, himself a new winner, in the first round, and led from there, shooting TPC Snoqualmie Ridge in 69-64-68–201, 15 under par, for not only his first Champions victory but his third overall, after two wins on the Web.com Tour.

But he did it in real style. He birdied three of the last four holes for a two-stroke victory over John Cook, who put the pressure on with a 66. "For him to come out and not have that much experience, to do what he did down the stretch, is very commendable," said Cook.

Riegger finished strong in all three rounds. He birdied the 16th and eagled the par-five 18th for a three-under 69 in the first round, three behind Bryant. He took the lead in the second with a one-bogey 64 that included an eagle at the par-five 15th. "It wasn't anything fancy," he said. "It was just a straight-forward pitch. It landed just on the green and rolled in just like a putt." He added a birdie at the 16th and led Lehman, Langer, Kirk Triplett and Bobby Clampett by three. He capped his rousing finish with a 20-foot birdie putt at the 18th for his two-shot win.

"It's been a long, crazy career," Riegger said. "I've been around the world and had a little success on the PGA Tour, European Tour, Web.com, but my game has actually gotten better ... I was just trying to play my game."

Shaw Charity Classic
Calgary, Alberta, Canada
Winner: Rocco Mediate

Rocco Mediate, possibly the chattiest player in professional golf, was making a statement in the first round, and that statement was: "This one is mine!"

He eagled two of the last four holes, played the final five in six under, shot 63 in the first round and rolled from there to a seven-stroke victory in the inaugural Shaw Charity Classic.

Mediate, scoring the second win of his Champions Tour rookie year, tore through the par-71, tree-lined Canyon Meadows in 63-64-64 for a 22-under-par 191, tying the tour record for a 54-hole event. "I liked it when I saw it," Mediate said, and apparently so did everyone else. It was a time for shrinking scoring averages. Of the top 14 finishers (through a tie for 10th), there were only four rounds in the 70s, and only one of them over par, a 72. Out of 81 finishers, only 11 didn't break par for 54 holes. "It's just that you've got to drive real straight," Mediate said. "You can't do anything if you don't drive straight."

Mediate clearly got laser straight coming home in the first round. After a one-birdie 34 going out and a birdie at the 10th, he went birdie-eagle-par-birdie-eagle from the 14th for a 29, a 63 and a one-stroke lead. Thanks, he said, to a putting tip from his caddie. "Just had Martin [Courtois] line me up," Mediate said. "We'll stick with that for awhile."

He shot the back in 29 under again in the second round for a 64–127, expanding his lead to two on an uncertain Bobby Clampett, who shot 65 while "just trying to hang in there."

Mediate was on one final spree in the last round, moving Fred Couples, who tied for 10th, to note, "If you could just tone down Rocco, you'd have a hell of a tournament out there." But Mediate ran away from the field with another 64.

He said he'd thought: "'It'd be really nice if it was a nice, fun, easy back nine. Maybe one time that could happen.' And it did."

Montreal Championship
Sainte-Julie, Quebec, Canada
Winner: Esteban Toledo

Esteban Toledo went the traditional fist pump one better. He came off the final green swinging. In a manner of speaking, of course. Said Toledo, a former boxer: "I always celebrate with a left hook."

Toledo had something to swing about. He had just chipped in for birdie on the third playoff hole to beat Kenny Perry in the Montreal Championship, his second win in his rookie season on the Champions Tour. Ironically, the first, the Insperity Championship in May, also came in a playoff and on the third hole, where he beat Mike Goodes with a par. The Insperity victory made him the first Mexican to win on the Champions Tour.

At the Montreal Championship, Toledo was back in the pack for the first two rounds, shooting La Vallee du Richelieu Rouville in 73-69. He trailed Dick Mast by four in the first round and Bernhard Langer by four in the second. He didn't warm up in the third until after a bogey at No. 2. Then he birdied Nos. 4, 10, 14 and 16 for another 69 to catch Perry at five-under-par 211, while Perry was shooting a painful 70. A sore back and heel left him using a golf cart for the final round.

"I was just trying to finish," Perry said. "I drove the ball beautifully. I drove it better today than I've driven it all week. There is something to be said about the wounded guy." He posted four birdies but also took two bogeys, the last at the 17th, which dropped him back into the tie. They parred the first two playoff holes, both at the par-four 18th. Then at the par-three 10th, Toledo missed the green but chipped in for birdie and Perry hit the green, but missed his birdie try.

"I was shocked, really," Toledo said. "I know it was a 20-footer, but it was makeable to tie me."

Langer led by three going into the final round, but double-bogeyed the fourth and 16th and had just one birdie for a 75 that dropped him into a tie for fourth.

Pacific Links Hawai'i Championship
Kapolei, Hawaii
Winner: Mark Wiebe

At first glance, Mark Wiebe's 2013 record wasn't looking very good — just two top-10 finishes in 21 starts. At second glance, it was looking very good. Those two top-10s? Both victories.

Wiebe added No. 2 in September in the Pacific Links Hawai'i Championship, which started with a trail of birdies across the first round and ended on the second hole of a playoff over Corey Pavin. His first win was in July at the Senior Open Championship in Britain, and ironically, that was also in a playoff, a five-hole grind with Bernhard Langer.

Wiebe launched his Pacific bid with a rampage on the windy, par-72 Kapolei Golf Course, ringing up nine birdies over a 12-hole stretch. The round was marred only by a bogey at the 18th, which left him with an eight-under-par 64 and a two-stroke lead on Mark Calcavecchia and John Cook. Hall-of-Famer Vijay Singh, who turned 50 in February and left the golf world wondering whether he'd play the Champions Tour, made his debut and shot 69.

Singh left a stronger impression in the second round with a six-birdie, bogey-free 66 that lifted him to within two of Wiebe's 69–133. Pavin, after a second 68, would enter the final round three behind Wiebe, and they would be the two finalists. Pavin closed with a flawless three-birdie 69. Wiebe came to the 18th facing an eight-foot birdie putt to tie Pavin. He dropped it, completing an erratic four-birdie, four-bogey 72 for the 11-under 205.

At the second playoff hole, Wiebe rolled in a 20-foot birdie putt that was the winner when Pavin's 10-footer pulled up just short.

"I didn't play as well as I did the first two days," Wiebe said. "But I played my butt off."

Singh, who had made just one bogey in his first 48 holes, made a double bogey and two single bogeys down the last six holes, closed with a 73 and tied for sixth. As to his future on the tour: "I'll need to decide soon," Singh said. "Maybe I'll go back and forth between the Champions Tour and the PGA Tour."

Nature Valley First Tee Open
Monterey Peninsula, California
Winner: Kirk Triplett

Maybe Kirk Triplett has found a home on the Champions Tour. Mailing address: Pebble Beach.

The man in the big hat eased onto the tour in 2012 and marked his coming of age (50) with a victory in the Nature Valley First Tee Open. He came back a year later, in September, trailed Bernhard Langer by four strokes in the first round, trailed Tom Lehman by three in the second, then took over in the third for a repeat victory, his second on the tour.

"I played 20 AT&T and 20 Callaway events and a couple of U.S. Opens at Pebble Beach," Triplett said, "I knew it would be a dogfight. But I just have an affinity for the place."

Triplett opened with a 67 at Del Monte, where Langer posted a nine-birdie, bogey-free 63. Langer stumbled to a 74 at Pebble in the second round, and Lehman took over the lead, holing a 20-foot birdie putt at the 18th there for his second 67 and a one-shot edge. "It's too early to talk about winning," Lehman noted. And then he finished with a 74.

Triplett's battle came with the veteran Dan Forsman and rookie Doug Garwood, 50, making his fourth start. And he turned in a sparkling report card. He led the field on the greens, needing just 78 putts, including 30 one-putts, and needed just nine on his final nine. Both shot 69, two behind Triplett.

But Triplett had to scramble late. He led Lehman, Forsman and Garwood by two with three holes to play, then ran into trouble. He drove into the rough at the par-four 16th, but chipped to two feet to save his par. At the famed and treacherous par-three 17th, he bunkered his tee shot, but saved again.

An affinity for the place? Triplett made just three bogeys for the tournament and was the only player in the 81-man field to go bogey-free in the final round. And he made hay on the par-fives for the week. He birdied seven of the eight, and played them in a total of nine under.

SAS Championship
Cary, North Carolina
Winner: Russ Cochran

When Russ Cochran won the Principal Charity Classic back in June, he sweated out the final minutes, leader in the clubhouse. In the SAS Championship in October, it was all unfolding right in front of him.

That was David Frost in the group just ahead in the final round, wrapping up a charge that was about to snatch away a title Cochran had at his fingertips all the way. Frost had edged into the lead, then birdied the 16th to get to 16 under par. Cochran needed birdies. He got them — at 15, 16, 17 (tying Frost). He needed one more, at the final hole, and it was in that scary makeable-missable range, eight feet. Cochran holed it and had his second win of the year and fifth on the Champions Tour.

"It's not often you get in that groove where you know something good's going to happen," Cochran said. "And you've got to shoot low to win."

Cochran, a left-hander who battled rib and wrist injuries for years, shared the lead in the first round and led the rest of the way in his 66-66-67–199, 17 under, and in all three rounds he was making birdies by the bunches. He started in the first round. On the back nine, in fact. He spotted Prestonwood Country Club a bogey at the ninth, then played the par-37 back nine in seven under — an eagle at the par-four 10th, birdies at the 12th and 14th, and three more from the 16th to tie for the lead at 66 with Mark Mouland and Larry Nelson. He birdied Nos. 1, 2, 4, 5, 6 to start a 66 in the second round. "They were going in from everywhere," he said, and he led Bernhard Langer by two. In the third, he bogeyed No. 1, then birdied 6, 7 and 9, then made only his fourth bogey of the tournament at the 13th before launching his closing run of four.

"David played a great round," Cochran said. "I was hoping to hang around there and catch fire. And it took every hole to do that."

Greater Hickory Kia Classic
Conover, North Carolina
Winner: Michael Allen

Michael Allen was looking over his shoulder at Bernhard Langer. He should have kept an eye on Olin Browne.

The Greater Hickory Kia Classic was heading down the homestretch, and Allen was paired with Langer, who had run into a rough patch after leading through the first two rounds. Allen had taken the lead, but knowing Langer, he was far from comfortable. Already this season, Langer had two wins, three seconds and 10 other top-10 finishes.

"All of a sudden, here comes Olin," Allen said. "I thought I was going to be battling Bernhard, but it wasn't until I got to 16 or 17 that I knew he [Browne] was leading. So I had to be more aggressive on my putts."

Allen was one of the surprise success stories of the Champions Tour — on coming of age, making his debut with an invitation to the 2009 Senior PGA Championship, and then winning it. He became a regular and won three more events, most recently the Mississippi Gulf Resort Classic in March, beating Langer by a shot. Now Langer was his point of focus but Browne was his problem.

"I got off to a little bit of a slow start," said Browne, who closed with a 64. "But I had that great run, and gave myself a chance. One more putt here or there, and I would have had no worries."

Browne began the final round three shots off the lead, bogeyed the third, then made seven birdies over a nine-hole stretch from the sixth, including five straight from the 10th. That got Allen's attention.

Allen stayed close with a birdie at the 16th, then birdied the 18th for a 65, tying Browne at 13-under 197. Allen shot 67-65-65, and Browne 65-68-64.

In the playoff at the par-five 18th, Browne missed the green with his approach, chipped on to 40 feet and two-putted for par. Allen put his second to 10 feet and two-putted for the winning birdie. Langer shot 69 and finished third, a stroke out of the playoff, and now had his 16th top-10 of the season.

AT&T Championship
San Antonio, Texas
Winner: Kenny Perry

Kenny Perry sounded as though he was being chased by one of those childhood dream monsters. "I can't shake that guy," Perry was saying. "He's had a chance to win on Sunday the last 10 weeks. He's been there just inching away at me, picking on me. I need to find a way to get it done this weekend."

That was no monster. That was just the ubiquitous and durable Bernhard Langer, without whom no leaderboard is complete. And there he was again, at the AT&T Championship in October, the Champions Tour's regular season finale. The AT&T would settle the field of the top 30 money winners for the season-ending Charles Schwab Cup Championship the following week.

Perry found himself tied with Langer for the lead going into the AT&T's final round — along with Mike Goodes, Colin Montgomerie and Anders Forsbrand, all at eight-under-par 136. It was leapfrog down the final round. Goodes, after a 63 in the second round, fell out with a 75. Forsbrand, one of the first Swedes to reach the international stage, slipped with a 71. Monty birdied five of the first six and had taken the lead, but four late bogeys would keep him winless in the U.S. after 147 PGA and Champions Tour starts.

In their personal duel, Perry went birdie-bogey from the third and fell two behind on Langer's birdies at the second and fourth. Perry got to 10 under on a birdie at the seventh, and when Langer bogeyed the ninth, they were tied the rest of the way. Perry birdied Nos. 9, 11 and 12, and was 13 under. Langer, after birdies at 11 and 12, needed one more to tie Perry. He got it at the 17th. Langer shot 67-69-67, and Perry 65-71-67 and tied at 13-under 203.

Back to the 18th for the playoff: Both drove into the fairway. Perry put his second to nine feet. Langer missed the green and chipped to eight. Perry dropped his birdie putt. Langer missed. So Perry, with his third win of the season, had calmed his nightmare. For a week, at least.

Charles Schwab Cup Championship
San Francisco, California
Winner: Fred Couples

Time also flies when you're not having fun, Fred Couples observed. "It seems like four years ago," Couples said, on winning the Champions Tour's season-ending Charles Schwab Cup in November. Meaning since he last won. Actually, it had been only some 16 months since he won the 2012 Senior British Open. It was the sentiment that counted. The Schwab was his ninth victory in his four years on the tour, but he had gone 16 tournaments without one.

"This year," Couples said of 2013, "I wouldn't call it a waste, but it was a waste as far as not winning [is concerned]." Before the Schwab win, he had nine top-10 finishes in 14 starts, including four seconds and a third.

He was never in real trouble in the Schwab Cup. Shooting the classic Harding Park in 65-65-68-69, he trailed only in the first round, behind Peter Senior's eight-under 63, then went two ahead of him in the second, and five up on Mark O'Meara in the third before winning by a runaway six at 17-under 267 over a three-way tie for second among Senior, O'Meara and Bernhard Langer in the 30-man, no-cut event.

"I didn't miss many shots," Couples said. "I got the lead and I kept it. Just winning — even if it's a club championship, you're thrilled."

"He did what he had to do," O'Meara said. "It's not easy with the lead."

Kenny Perry tied for fifth and topped the season-long points chase to win a $1 million annuity. He won three times in 2013, including his first two majors, the Senior Players Championship and the U.S. Senior Open.

Couples had a remarkable start. After a bogey at No. 2, he tore through the next 12 holes in nine birdies — a streak interrupted by a double bogey at the par-three No. 8. Apart from that double, Couples had only three bogeys, and 22 birdies. For the man with a sore back, it was quite a finish to the year.

"I'm done for two months," Couples said, "and I'm looking forward to next year."

Major Champions

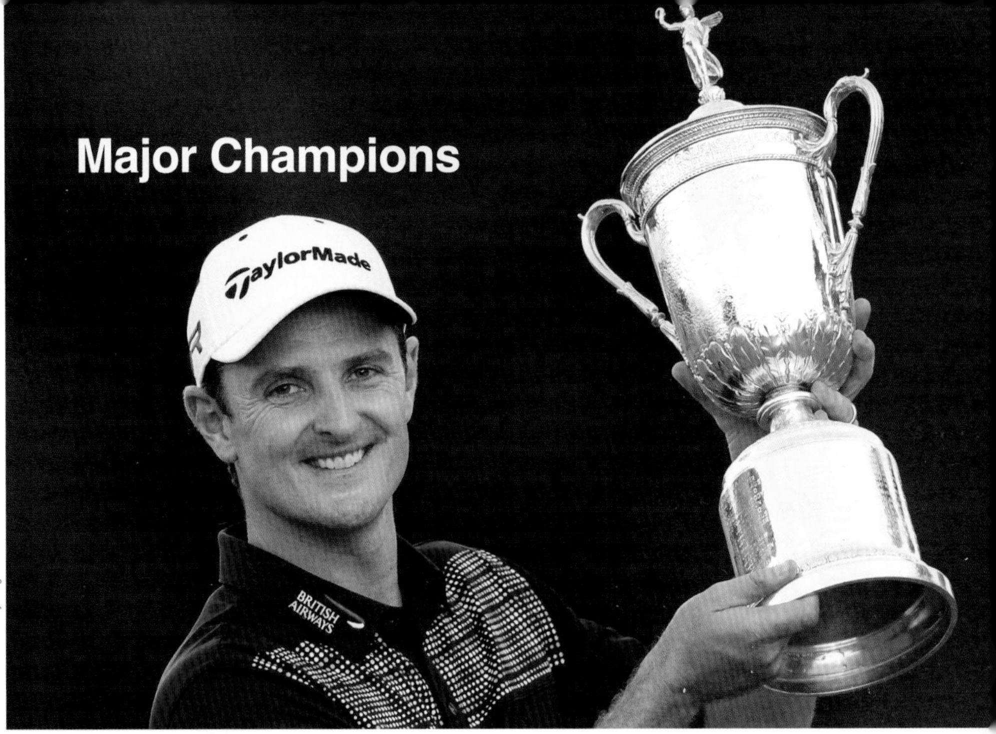

David Cannon/Getty Images

Justin Rose was the first Englishman for 43 years to win the U.S. Open Championship.

Rob Carr/Getty Images

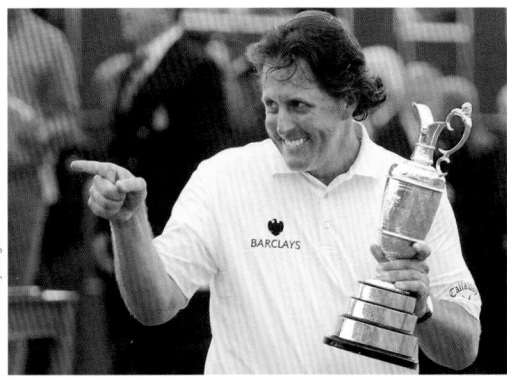

Phil Mickelson, Open Championship

Stuart Franklin/Getty Images

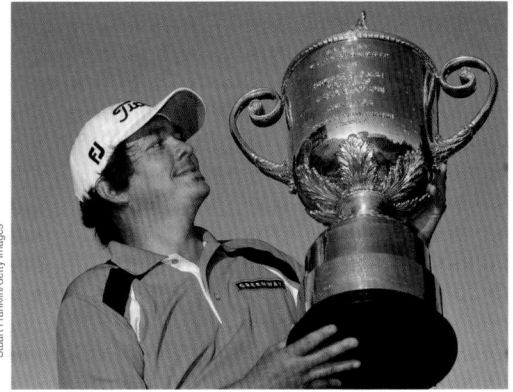

Jason Dufner, PGA Championship

Ross Kinnaird/Getty Images

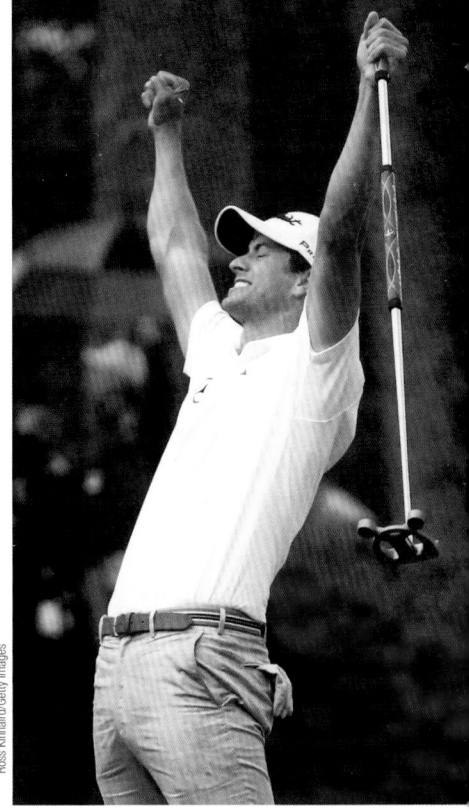

Adam Scott, Masters Tournament

Masters Tournament

With his playoff win, Adam Scott became the first Australian to claim the green jacket.

Angel Cabrera lost at the second extra hole.

Marc Leishman made three Aussies in the top five.

Jason Day, also from Down Under, took third.

Tiger Woods tied for fourth place.

On Father's Day, Justin Rose showed off the trophy for his late father, Ken.

Jason Day finished two behind Rose.

Phil Mickelson was a runner-up for the sixth time.

Ernie Els claimed a share of fourth place.

Jason Dufner closed with 67 despite a triple bogey.

The Open Championship

With four birdies in the last six holes, Phil Mickelson won at the 20th attempt.

Andrew Redington/Getty Images

As in 2012, Adam Scott had four bogeys in a row.

David Cannon/Getty Images

Ian Poulter closed with 67 to tie for third.

Ian Walton/R & A

Lee Westwood could not hang on to the lead.

Rob Carr/Getty Images

Henrik Stenson birdied the 17th to finish second.

PGA Championship

Jason Dufner became the sixth player to score 63 in a major and go on to victory.

Henrik Stenson was well-placed again in third.

Adam Scott opened with a 65.

Scott Piercy closed with a 65.

Jim Furyk saw his third-round lead slip away.

Jonas Blixt, fourth in only his second major.

Presidents Cup

Andy Lyons/Getty Images

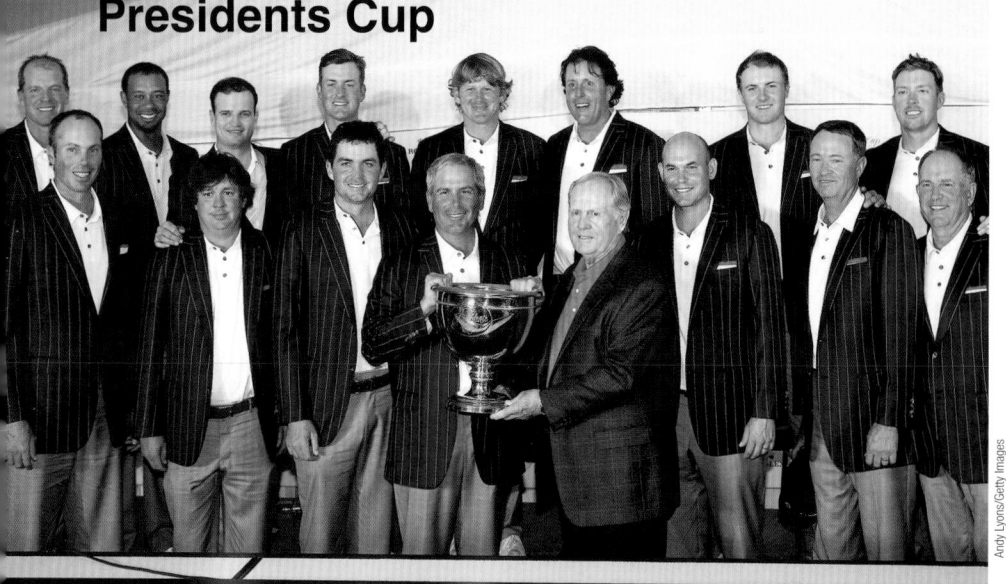

Team USA won the Presidents Cup for the eighth time in 10 matches at Muirfield Village.

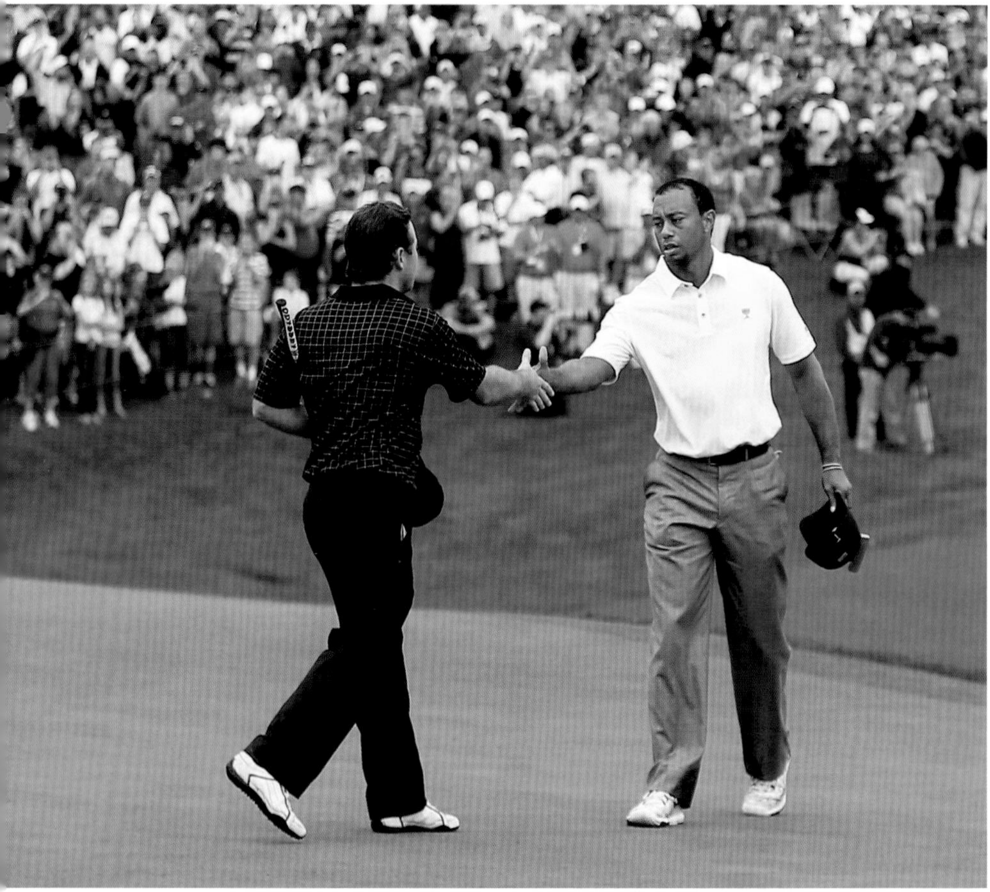

David Cannon/Getty Images

Tiger Woods beat Richard Sterne 1 up for his fourth win out of five matches.

Graham DeLaet claimed a singles win on debut.

Ernie Els, Nick Price and Brendon de Jonge.

Els made his eighth appearance in the event.

Jason Day won three and a half points.

Fred Couples held the trophy for the third time.

Around The World

Henrik Stenson became the first player to win the FedExCup (above) and the Race to Dubai.

Tiger Woods won five times.

Adam Scott claimed the Barclays trophy.

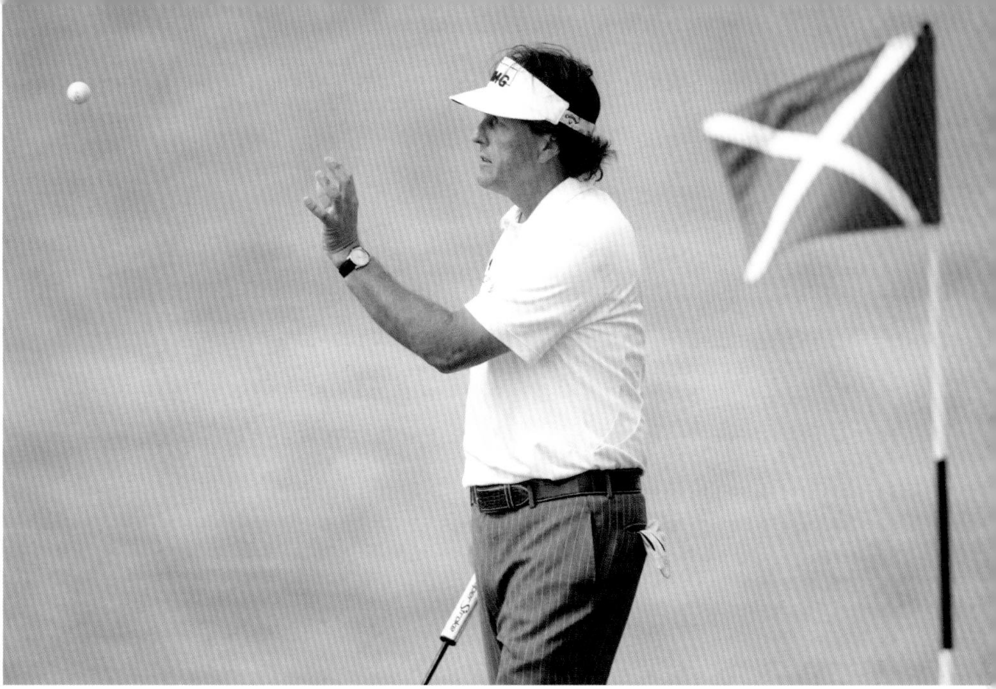

Warren Little/Getty Images

Phil Mickelson had back-to-back wins in Scotland at Castle Stuart and Muirfield.

Michael Cohen/Getty Images

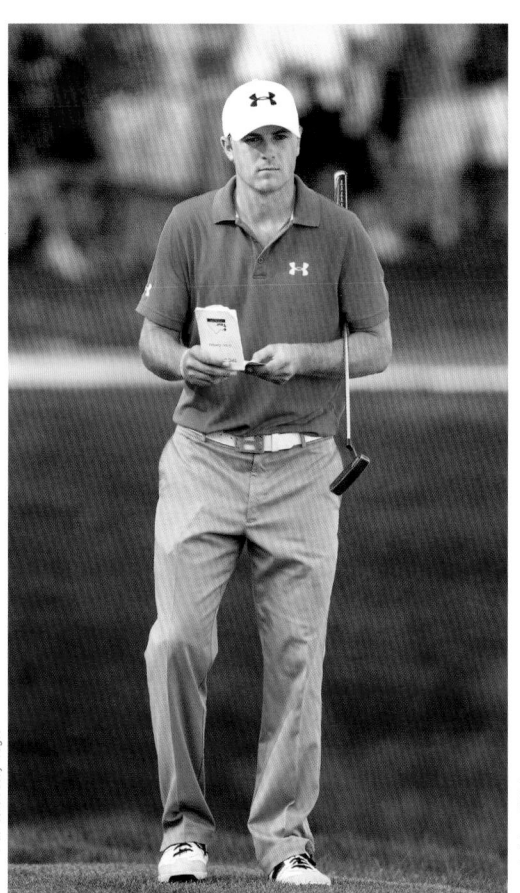

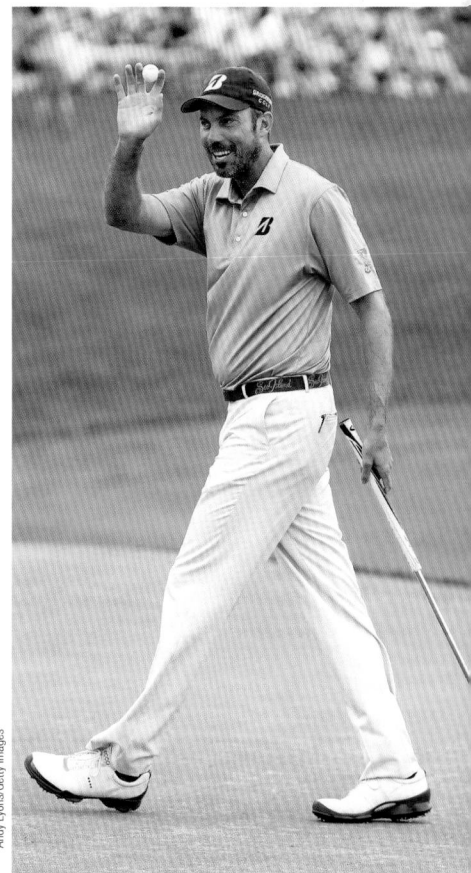

Jordan Spieth won the John Deere Classic aged 19.

Andy Lyons/Getty Images

Matt Kuchar won three events.

Brandt Snedeker shone at Pebble Beach.

Justin Rose claimed his first major at Merion.

Steve Stricker had eight top-10s in 13 events.

Zach Johnson won the BMW Championship.

Rookie Hideki Matsuyama won four times.

Three wins for Graeme McDowell.

Ian Poulter finished second on the Race to Dubai.

Luke Donald retained his Dunlop Phoenix title.

Andrew Redington/Getty Images

Paul Casey won for the first time in two and a half years at the Irish Open.

Warren Little/Getty Images

Matteo Manassero, BMW PGA champion.

Rob Carr/Getty Images

Bill Haas claimed the AT&T National title.

Ian Walton/Getty Images

Wen-Chong Liang won in Manila.

Ross Kinnaird/Getty Images

Jamie Donaldson triumphed in Abu Dhabi.

European Senior Tour

U.S. Senior PGA Championship
St. Louis, Missouri
Winner: Kohki Idoki

See Champions Tour section.

ISPS Handa PGA Seniors Championship
Cheshire, England
Winner: Paul Wesselingh

Paul Wesselingh was in a state of astonishment after he blitzed the field in the final round and rolled to a four-stroke repeat victory in the ISPS Handa PGA Seniors Championship.

"I couldn't believe I'd done it last year, and I can't believe I've done it again this year," said the 51-year-old former club pro after his closing, nine-under-par 64 at De Vere Mottram Hall outdistanced runner-up Angel Franco by that margin. The 2012 PGA Seniors victory, a weather-shortened 54-hole event, came in just his fourth start on the European Senior Tour.

Wesselingh was never more than two strokes off the pace all week in the 2013 season-opening tournament in early June. He was just a shot behind Gordon J. Brand, the first-round leader at 67, and two back of Des Smyth (67-69) with his following 70 the second day.

After moving a shot in front of Smyth (73), D.J. Russell (71) and Mike Cunning (70) Saturday with another 70, Wesselingh came out firing in the final round. He racked up five birdies on the first 10 holes and added four more coming home with the bogey-free 64 for his 20-under-par 272 and the four-shot margin over Paraguay's Franco (66). Ian Woosnam grabbed third with 65–277.

Speedy Services Wales Senior Open
Bridgend, Wales
Winner: Philip Golding

Philip Golding got his senior career off to a fast start in 2012, one of his two second-place finishes coming in the Speedy Services Wales Senior Open in late August. He remedied the near-miss in Wales 10 months later with a brilliant final round and two-stroke victory in extremely adverse conditions at Royal Porthcawl Golf Club.

"I kind of spoiled Woosie's party," said the second consecutive English winner on the European Senior Tour after his closing, five-under-par 66 carried him past Ian Woosnam, the golfing hero of Wales, who led the way for two days before fading to a third-place finish Sunday.

Woosnam opened with a 65, a shot in front of Golding and Scotland's Andrew Oldcorn, and kept the lead Saturday as the weather turned sour with 40 mph winds, preventing anybody in the field from breaking par. Woosnam's 18th-hole birdie and 74–139 were good enough for him to stay a shot in front of Mark James (71) and Denis O'Sullivan (72), as Golding seemed to have ruined his hopes with 79–145.

With five birdies on the first 11 holes Sunday, though, Golding came roaring back and went in front to stay as Woosnam lost his ball and double-bogeyed No. 9. Golding birdied again at the 15th and his margin climbed to four when Woosnam double-bogeyed again at the 13th. Golding played the final three holes in one over for the splendid 66–211, two ahead of David J. Russell (71).

Bad Ragaz PGA Seniors Open
Bad Ragaz, Switzerland
Winner: Paul Wesselingh

Paul Wesselingh missed his mark by a hair, but still captured his second title of the season in a three-hole playoff in the Swiss mountains. Five strokes off the pace going into the final round of the Bad Ragaz PGA Seniors Open, Wesselingh "set myself a target of 10 under to win." He proceeded to shoot a blazing six-under-par 64 for a nine-under 201 that put him into a first-place tie with fellow Englishman Kevin Spurgeon, who also finished strongly with a 65, then Wesselingh won the playoff with a 25-foot birdie putt on the third extra hole.

The 51-year-old Wesselingh, landing his third senior title in just 19 starts, put himself in an early hole when he started the tournament with a one-over 71 and trailed co-leaders Gary Wolstenholme and Spanish newcomer Santiago Luna by seven strokes. He was five back after a Saturday 66–137 as Wolstenholme and Luna remained on top with matching 68s for their 132.

Wesselingh surged in front when he spurted to five under on the first six holes of Sunday's round and was in command until he bogeyed the 14th and 15th holes, his first of the round. Another bogey at the 18th dropped him into the deadlock with Spurgeon, who birdied three of the last four holes. Carl Mason, the circuit's all-time winner, and Spain's Pedro Linhart finished in a third-place tie at 204 as Wolstenholme shot 73 and Luna 74.

U.S. Senior Open
Omaha, Nebraska
Winner: Kenny Perry

See Champions Tour section.

The Senior Open Championship presented by Rolex
Southport, Merseyside, England
Winner: Mark Wiebe

Mark Wiebe landed his first major title in a playoff that wasn't likely to happen and that, stretched over two days, lasted longer than any other in the history of the Senior Open Championship.

Despite a solid 66 Sunday in the rain-delayed final round at Royal Birkdale Golf Club, Wiebe was destined for a second-place finish at 271 as Hall-of-Famer Bernhard Langer teed off at the last hole leading by two strokes. Instead, Langer left his third shot in a greenside bunker and two-putted for a double bogey that brought on the overtime in the fading light of dusk at Southport, England.

The two 55-year-olds played two extra holes all-square before play was suspended, then matched scores the next two trips on the 18th the next morning before the American put up another par and Langer missed his matching effort from 15 feet to end the match.

Wiebe (70-65), who had been troubled most of the earlier season with elbow and back ailments and hadn't had a top-10 finish all year, and Langer (68-67), gunning for his second Open Championship and 19th senior title, shared the second-round lead at five-under-par 135 before Langer produced a 66 Saturday and forged three strokes ahead of David Frost and four in front of Wiebe. The victory was Wiebe's fourth on the Champions Tour and sixth of his career.

Berenberg Masters
Cologne, Refrath, Germany
Winner: Steen Tinning

The stage was set for a storybook finish to the Berenberg Masters in Cologne. Coming off a playoff loss the previous week in the Senior Open Championship, Bernhard Langer was in good position to add another victory to his outstanding career record in what would have been a popular one in the European Senior Tour's lone event in his home country.

Germany's greatest golfer (by far) sat just two strokes off the pace entering Berenberg's final round. Langer made his run Sunday with a 68, but fell a stroke short of tour rookie Steen Tinning of Denmark, whose solid 69 and nine-under-par 207 brought him his first senior title in just his sixth start in over-50 company.

In reality, Langer spoiled his chances with his second-round 73 as Tinning and England's Nick Job took over first place at Golf-und Land-Club. Langer had opened strongly with 67, tied with 2011 champion Ian Woosnam and Barry Lane two strokes behind New Zealand's Greg Turner, another senior rookie. But Langer's 73 Saturday left him two back of Tinning (68-70) and Job (69-69) as Turner managed just 74–139.

Tinning, playing just behind the German ace Sunday, watched him fail to birdie the par-five 18th from a greenside bunker, then fashioned a regulation par for the victory. Job finished third with 71–209.

SSE Scottish Senior Open
St. Andrews, Fife, Scotland
Winner: Santiago Luna

It had been a long time between victories for Spaniard Santiago Luna, but things happened quickly in a new atmosphere. Luna, whose only title on the regular European Tour was the 1995 Madeira Islands Open, eked out a one-stroke victory on the Fairmont St. Andrews course in the SSE Scottish Senior Open in just his sixth start on the European Senior Tour.

"Now I'm back with my generation and it is great to win," said Luna, whose final-round, one-under-par 71 enabled him to hold off the late charge of the esteemed Sam Torrance, an 11-time winner of the over-50 circuit who designed the course. Torrance's 70 fell a shot short of Luna's five-under-par 211. Irishman Denis O'Sullivan, with 72, shared the runner-up spot, failing at age 65 to become the second oldest (behind Neil Coles) winner in Senior Tour history.

Luna sat a shot off the lead the first two days with rounds of 69 and 71 in the town where he beat Tiger Woods 15 years earlier in a Dunhill Cup match. English rookie Jamie Spence led the first day with 68 and Peter Fowler Saturday with 73-66—139.

O'Sullivan had the lead in the early going Sunday, but two late bogeys proved too costly as Luna birdied twice at the start of the back nine and never relinquished first place as he played the final six holes in even par. That was enough to edge Torrance and O'Sullivan, who both birdied the final hole.

Travis Perkins plc Senior Masters
Woburn, England
Winner: Colin Montgomerie

It didn't take Colin Montgomerie long. Nor was it extraordinary when he rolled to a six-stroke victory in the Travis Perkins plc Senior Masters in his third start on the European Senior Tour, even though he hadn't won a tournament in six years. After all, the Scot sported a brilliant record of 40 professional victories and eight Order of Merit titles when he teed off on the Duke's course at Woburn Golf Club.

Only 70 days beyond his 50th birthday, Montgomerie took command of the tournament the second day. A shot off the opening-day pace of Argentina's Luis Carbonetti, Monty put up his second straight, four-under-par 68 to move into first place, three strokes in front of Carl Mason (70-69), holder of the tour's record 25 wins, including a pair of Travis Perkins titles. Six consecutive birdies in the middle of his round did the trick for Montgomerie.

The Scot needed only a 70 Sunday to expand his victory margin to six strokes at 206, and he made it easy when he birdied the par-five first hole and eagled the par-five fifth from just six feet. Mason slipped back to fourth place with a 74, as Spain's Miguel Angel Martin with 71 and two-time 2013 winner Paul Wesselingh with the week's best 66 tied for second at 212.

"It is like a new lease of life turning 50 in golf," observed Montgomerie.

WINSTONgolf Senior Open
Vorbeck, Germany
Winner: Gordon Brand, Jr.

Pickings had been slim for Gordon Brand, Jr. on the European Senior Tour. The Scot's only victory in his five seasons was three years behind him and, in his own words, "I've been playing awfully for the last year and a half. My coach told me that I'm the best player on the range and the worst player on the course."

Brand was the best player on the course in the WINSTONgolf Senior Open, though, ringing up three consecutive 68s and picking off a one-stroke victory on a stirring closing day. Fellow Scot Andrew Oldcorn provided most of the excitement. Off in the round's first group, Oldcorn ran off 11 birdies on the first 15 holes and parred in for 61, matching the tour's all-time record low score.

After waiting for hours for the contenders to finish, Oldcorn saw Angel Franco of Paraguay and David J. Russell equal his 205 and Brand par the water-fronted, par-four 18th hole to edge the three men by a stroke.

Englishman Bob Cameron had the hot hand Saturday. Winless for nearly a decade, Cameron shot 63 for 134 and a two-shot lead over Brand, Franco and Canada's Phil Jonas, who had shared the first-round lead with Ian Woosnam, the great Welsh player, at seven-under-par 65. Cameron fell back early Sunday, shot 73 and tied for ninth place.

Russian Open
Moscow, Russia
Winner: Simon P. Brown

The parade of first-time winners resumed when the circuit visited Moscow in mid-September. Englishman Simon P. Brown, little known in tournament circles, having spent most of his career as a club professional in Germany, became the seventh player of the season to score a maiden victory when he survived an erratic run to the wire on a rain-drenched Moscow Country Club course Sunday and nailed a two-stroke triumph.

The fifth first-time winner in six tournaments, Brown, a 50-year-old rookie who finished fourth when he played in the Moscow Open when it was a Challenge Tour event 17 years ago, never trailed this time around. He opened with a six-under-par 66, tied for the lead with Spain's Miguel Angel Martin, and moved in front to stay Saturday. Remaining bogey-free, Simon shot 68, his 134 one better than Denmark's Steen Tinning (68), the Berenberg Masters winner in August, and Martin, who led by three shots before settling for 69–135.

Brown was in good shape Sunday until he lost his ball on an errant drive on the 14th hole. Meanwhile, Carl Mason, the tour's top career winner, and Australia's Mike Harwood were finishing with 68s, matching Brown's 10-under score through 16 holes. But Brown finished with a flurry, holing a 25-foot birdie putt at the 17th and firing a seven-iron approach to tap-in range at the 18th for 70 and the winning 204.

French Riviera Masters
Provence, France
Winner: Peter Fowler

Andrew Oldcorn might have known it would happen. Though Peter Fowler was four strokes behind him going into the final round of the French Riviera Masters, Oldcorn could have thought about the past.

Fowler had won twice on the European Senior Tour and both times Oldcorn finished second to him.

"I'm sick of the sight of Peter," quipped the Scot after Fowler raced from that deficit to a three-stroke victory in an unexpected turn of events at the Terre Blanche Golf Resort. His six-under-par 66 and 205 total left Oldcorn and Spain's Santiago Luna in the runner-up position.

Oldcorn, riding a streak of five straight sub-par rounds, including his brilliant 61 in the WINSTONgolf Senior, rode in front the first two days. He shared the lead with Argentine Luis Carbonetti at 67 Friday, and moved into his four-stroke lead over Australian Fowler and South African Chris Williams Saturday for 135 as closest contenders Carbonetti and Philip Golding both faltered in the stretch.

Things turned around early Sunday. Oldcorn absorbed three bogeys on the first five holes as Fowler, winless and hurting for more than two years, posted a birdie and four pars and overtook him. Fowler then completed an eight-shot swing with birdies at the seventh and eighth to go four ahead when Oldcorn double-bogeyed the eighth. Two more birdies and a seven-under-par finish wrapped up the win. Oldcorn shot 73 for his third second-place finish to Fowler, tied with Luna, who matched Fowler's 66 for his 208.

English Senior Open
County Durham, England
Winner: Steen Tinning

Steen Tinning, an ironman fitness aficionado, needed all of his physical endurance and mental toughness to stand off the determined challenge of fellow European Senior Tour rookie Santiago Luna and capture his second victory of the season in the revived English Senior Open.

Trailing Luna by two strokes with three holes to play at Rockliffe Hall, Tinning finished birdie-birdie-par for 67–199, 17 under par, and won by a shot as Luna, also a winner in his first season on the circuit, went one over on those holes with a bogey at the 17th. The victory moved the Dane to the top of the Order of Merit past Paul Wesselingh, the only other double winner of 2013.

Tinning seized the lead from Englishman Peter Mitchell (66 on Friday) with a blistering, nine-under-par 63 in the second round.

At 132, Steen had three Spaniards as his nearest pursuers — Luna at 134 after a pair of 67s, and Miguel Angel Martin (70-66) and Jose Manuel Carriles (67-69) at 136.

Tinning and Luna staged a back-and-forth battle in Sunday's final round, the Spaniard eventually taking a two-stroke lead when the Copenhagen native bogeyed the 14th hole and he birdied the 15th, setting the stage for the pressure-packed finish.

Dutch Senior Open
Amsterdam, The Netherlands
Winner: Simon P. Brown

Drenching weather made a mess of the Dutch Senior Open, but at the end, Simon P. Brown had no complaints. When the nearly incessant rains made the respected International course beside Amsterdam's main airport unplayable by Sunday, the tournament was declared over after 36 mushy holes and Brown was awarded the title.

The 50-year-old Englishman, who led after the two rounds that were barely squeezed in amid the downpours with 72-71–143, became the second rookie with a pair of wins in 2013, establishing a challenge to Denmark's Steen Tinning for Rookie of the Year and Order of Merit honors. Tinning picked up his second title of the season the previous Sunday in the English Senior Open.

The weather was so wet and cold Friday that Brown, France's Marc Farry and English veteran Nick Job led the field with one-under-par 72s, the highest opening-round leaders of the season. The skies cleared long enough to get in the finish of the first round and the full second round Saturday.

Still, Brown took his decisive lead with just a two-under, three-birdie 71 for 143, two better than Scotland's Ross Drummond, whose 69–145 edged Paul Eales, Jose Manuel Carriles and Farry by a stroke for the runner-up spot after heavy overnight rains forced the final cancellation.

Australian PGA Seniors Championship
Richmond, New South Wales
Winner: Darryl Purchase

Darryl Purchase's decision to turn professional and play senior tour golf paid off in early November when he scored his first career victory in the Australian PGA Seniors Championship.

Purchase came from five strokes off the pace in the final round with three back-nine birdies and a three-under-par 67, the low round of the week at Richmond Golf Club in New South Wales, to land the title. His even-par 210 gave him a two-stroke victory over Kym Olsen, the second-round leader.

The winner had skidded down the standings with his second-round 74–143 after sharing the first-day lead at 69 with Wayne Grady, Michael Clayton and Norman Wall. Olsen (70-68–138), who led Clayton (69-70) by a stroke after two rounds, had a 74 of his own Sunday, but held on to the runner-up spot, a shot ahead of David Merriman and Russell Swanson. His hopes for a tying birdie at the last hole disappeared with a bad drive.

Fubon Senior Open
Taipei, Taiwan
Winner: Paul Wesselingh

Paul Wesselingh, the European Senior Tour's Rookie of the Year in 2012, became the man to beat for the John Jacobs Trophy as Order of Merit champion a year later when he won the Fubon Senior Open in Taiwan in mid-November.

Wesselingh swished past Denmark's Steen Tinning to the top of the standings when he edged Wen-Teh Lu by a stroke in the circuit's next-to-last event after trailing the Taiwan favorite by a shot after 36 holes at Miramar Golf and Country Club. The Englishman shot a two-under-par 70 to Lu's 72 Sunday, finishing at 207.

Wesselingh was in contention from the start, sharing second place after the first round with Bob Cameron at 69, a stroke behind leader Andre Bossert of Switzerland. He was alone at 137 behind Lu (70-66) after the second round, then started and finished well on a gusty Sunday with birdies at the first two holes, the 16th and the 18th around a pair of bogeys on the front nine. He sank a four-footer at the last hole for the win, his third of the season and fourth overall.

MCB Tour Championship
Poste de Flacq, Mauritius
Winner: Paul Wesselingh

Paul Wesselingh left no question about who was the best player on the European Senior Tour in 2013 when he put a bold exclamation point on his season with a runaway victory in the wind-up MCB Tour Championship.

Undaunted by the challenging presence of the formidable Colin Montgomerie as his final-round playing companion, Wesselingh rolled to his fourth victory of the year, winning the finale by five strokes with his 14-under-par 202 at Constance Belle Mare Plage in Mauritius.

In 12 months, the 51-year-old Englishman went from the tour's Rookie of the Year to the holder of the John Jacobs Trophy as No. 1 on the final Order of Merit standings, more than €100,000 ahead of runner-up Steen Tinning.

Wesselingh opened the Tour Championship strongly with 67, a shot behind Spaniard Miguel Angel Martin, the eventual runner-up at 207 with David Frost, the 2012 winner at Mauritius. When Wesselingh followed with 66–133, he moved in front, three strokes ahead of Montgomerie, who also shot 66 and figured to be a serious threat on Sunday.

It didn't turn out that way. Montgomerie, with an early bogey and double bogey, faded from contention, while Wesselingh, with four birdies on the first 10 holes, skied to a seven-shot lead before coasting to a 69 and the winning 202. Montgomerie shot 74, finishing sixth.

"It's hard to believe what I've done this year, really," proclaimed the long-time club pro and Liverpool native. "To win four times and to win the Order of Merit is an incredible achievement."

Japan PGA Senior Tour

Kanehide Senior Okinawa Open
Okinawa
Winner: Takeshi Sakiyama

The Japan Senior Tour opened its season in mid-April with the first of two 36-hole events and came up with a first-time winner. Takeshi Sakiyama, a shot off the lead after an opening-round 66 in the Kanehide Senior Okinawa Open at Okinawa's Kise Country Club, shot a two-under-par 70 the second day to land victory by three strokes.

Surprisingly, the man who led the first day with 65 and couldn't finish it off in the second round was Katsunari Takahashi, the circuit's all-time title winner with 12 victories, the last one in 2007. His follow-up 74 dropped him into a three-way tie for second at 136 with Akihiro Ito (69-70) and Kohki Idoki (68-71).

ISPS Handa Cup Satsukibare Senior Masters
Hukuoka
Winner: Boonchu Ruangkit

Already well established as a fine player on the international level, Boonchu Ruangkit made his first mark on the Japan Senior Tour with a playoff victory in the ISPS Handa Cup Satsukibare Senior Masters at the end of May.

The Thailand standout, a five-time winner on the European Senior Tour and its Order of Merit champion in 2011, birdied the first extra hole to defeat Kiyoshi Maita after the two players tied at the end of regulation at Hukuoka's Kyusyu Golf Club with three-under-par 141s — Ruangkit with 70-71 and Maita with 71-70.

Again, veteran winner Katsunari Takahashi took the first-round lead and fell back badly the second day. His 67 led Kohki Idoki by a shot and Seiki Okuda, Tatsuya Shiraishi and Thailand's Jamnian Chitprasong by two. Okuda, with 73, and Masami Ito, with 70-72–142, missed the playoff by a stroke, but Takahashi skied to 78.

Kyoraku More Surprise Cup
Mie
Winner: Kiyoshi Murota

Age isn't slowing down Kiyoshi Murota. The 58-year-old Japanese veteran, a six-time winner in his years on the regular Japan Tour, chalked up his ninth on the Japan Senior Tour in the Kyoraku More Surprise Cup tournament, this time in a playoff over Seiki Okuda.

Murota, who counts three Senior PGA Championships among his victories, never trailed at Ryosen Golf Club in Mie Prefecture. He shared the first-round lead at five-under-par 67 with Australia's Gregory Meyer and Minoru Hatsumi, then moved three strokes ahead of Meyer the second day with 66—133.

Okuda made his run in the third round with a 65 for a 204 and reached the playoff when Murota shot 71 for the tie. Murota birdied the first extra hole for the win.

Starts Senior
Ibaraki
Winner: Tommy Nakajima

Tommy (Tsuneyuki) Nakajima brought back memories of his glory days on the Japan Tour with his fifth Senior Tour victory in the Starts Senior in mid-June. Five seasons beyond No. 4, the 59-year-old Nakajima, the third-ranking all-time money winner on the Japan Tour with 48 victories, lashed together rounds of 65 and 64 the last two days for an 18-under-par 198 and a one-stroke triumph.

Opening day, though, belonged to Kohki Idoki, who had startled the international senior world when he came out of nowhere to win the Senior PGA Championship in America just three weeks earlier. Idoki tore up the Starts Kasama Golf Club course with an 11-under-par 61 to lead by four strokes over Satoshi Higashi and eight over Nakajima.

Idoki came back to earth with 71 Saturday, though. He still led by a shot over Higashi (68), but only by two over Nakajima (69-65), Katsunari Taka-hashi (70-64) and Kiyoshi Murota (66-68), who had won his ninth senior title the previous week. Sunday turned into a duel between Nakajima and Murota as Idoki faltered with 73 and tied for 10th. Taking the lead with his outgoing 31, Nakajima put together the 64 that edged Murota (65) by a shot.

ISPS Handa Cup Philanthropy Senior
Kanagawa
Winner: Satoshi Higashi

It had been an 18-year victory drought for Satoshi Higashi since his brilliant 1995 season when he nearly dethroned the great Masashi (Jumbo) Ozaki as No. 1 on the Japan Tour money list. The four wins he racked up that year were Higashi's last until he captured the 36-hole ISPS Handa Cup Philanthropy tournament in mid-July in his second season on the Japan Senior Tour.

A pair of six-under-par 65s gave him a three-stroke victory over Nobumitsu Yuhara, who also closed with 65 for his 133. Higashi and David Ishii, the 58-year-old Hawaiian who led the money list in 1987 with six victories, trailed Toshiaki Nakagawa by a shot and led Australian Gregory Meyer and Minoru Hatsumi by one after the first round at Hokone Kohan Golf

Course. Only Higashi maintained the pace the second day. Yoichi Sugawara came up with a 63 and tied for third at 135 with Kuzuhiro Takami.

Fancl Classic
Susono, Shizuoka
Winner: Yutaka Hagawa

Talk about coming from nowhere. Yutaka Hagawa conjured up an almost unbelievable rally when he won the Fancl Classic, the long-standing Japan Senior Tour event, in mid-August.

After 36 holes and a pair of 73s, the 56-year-old Hagawa seemed hopelessly out of contention, nine strokes behind co-leaders Gregory Meyer of Australia (67-70) and Jong-Duck Kim of South Korea (71-66) going into the final round. Hagawa's chances didn't seem that much better after an unexciting 34 on the outgoing nine of Susono Country Club. Then he caught fire, rocketed home in 28 strokes for 10-under-par 62 for 208 total, which, after a long wait, pitted him in a playoff against Kohki Idoki (68–208), as Meyer and Kim shot 72 and 74, respectively.

Hagawa had another birdie left in the bag and that won the playoff for him on the first extra hole. It was the second victory on the Senior Tour for Hagawa, who was a five-time winner on the regular circuit in the late 1990s.

ISPS Handa Cup Akibare-no Senior Masters
Hokkaido
Winner: Frankie Minoza

Frankie Minoza, the leading Philippines pro for many years on the international scene, put a win in the Japan Senior Tour records book for a third straight year, posting a one-stroke victory in the 36-hole ISPS Handa Cup Akibare-no Senior Masters at the end of August.

The first-round leaders at 68 were Takeshi Sakiyama and 64-year-old Seiji Ebihara, 11 years beyond his great 2002 season, when he was No. 1 on the European Senior Tour and won his third and most recent victory on the Japan Senior Tour. Minoza, Taiwan's T.C. Chen and Masami Ito had 69s.

Minoza followed with 70 for 139 to edge Ikuo Shirhama, was had his second 70 at Hokkaido Brooks Country Club. Ebihara slipped to 74 and finished third.

Komatsu Open
Komatsu, Ishikawa
Winner: Kiyoshi Maita

Kiyoshi Maita made up for two earlier near-misses during the season with a September victory in the Komatsu Open. Maita, who lost in a playoff

332 / SENIOR TOURS

against Boonchu Ruangkit in the Satsukibare Masters and tied for third in the Kyoraku More Surprise Cup, put up three rounds in the 60s and won by a stroke with his 12-under-par 204.

Maita began with a 67, tied with Yutaka Hagawa a stroke behind co-leaders Yoshinori Mizumaki, Yoichi Shimizu and Ikuo Shirahama, who was coming off a runner-up finish in the Akabare tournament. A second-round 69 moved Maita into a three-way tie for first with Mizumaki (70) and Seiki Okuda (71-65), and his 68 the last day gave him the one-stroke margin over Okuda (69) and Kazuhiro Takami (68). It was his second victory on the circuit.

Japan PGA Senior Championship
Ibaraki
Winner: Tsukasa Watanabe

Tsukasa Watanabe, who won just twice in run-of-the-mill tournaments during his Japan Tour career, has made a much bigger impact on the Japan Senior Tour as an amasser of majors. Three of his four victories on the over-50 circuit came in one or the other of the tour's two major championships — in the 2013 season the Japan PGA Senior Championship to go with his earlier PGA in 2008 and the Senior Open the following year.

The 56-year-old pro appeared to have things well in hand in the October event at Summit Golf Club when he took a five-stroke lead into the final round, but he wound up needing a birdie in a playoff to clinch the title. Watanabe laced a 64 to go in front by two over first-round leader Katsumi Nanjo (66-70) with 134, then widened the margin to five over Gregory Meyer Saturday with 70–204.

Eight strokes back in sixth place at that point, Kiyoshi Murota, who had won his ninth senior title earlier in the season in the Surprise Cup, raced up the leaderboard Sunday as Watanabe treaded water. The two men eventually finished in a tie at 277, 11 under par, as Watanabe shot 73 to Murota's 65. Watanabe nabbed the victory with the birdie on the first extra hole.

Japan Senior Open Championship
Fukuoka
Winner: Kiyoshi Murota

Kiyoshi Murota relishes major championships. Three weeks after being denied a fourth Japan PGA Senior title in a playoff loss, the 58-year-old added a second Japan Senior Open Championship to his gaudy record on the Japan Senior Tour. The three-stroke victory at Aso Iizuka Golf Club, his 10th since joining the circuit in 2005, boosted his season earnings to more than ¥45 million, virtually assuring him of the year's Order of Merit money title.

Murota had at least a share of the lead most of the way on Aso Iizuka's Green course. He began with a six-under-par 66, tied for first with Yoshinori Mizumaki before they yielded the lead to visiting Englishman Paul

Wesselingh, one of the leading players on the European Senior Tour. Wesselingh shot 67–138 to their 73–139s Friday.

Murota had first place to himself after his 67–206 Saturday as Mizumaki remained close with 69–208 and Wesselingh tumbled from contention with 74–212. Murota wasn't particularly sharp Sunday, but an eagle helped him counter four bogeys and nobody challenged him. Mizumaki faded with 75, and Murota's 73–279 gave him the three-stroke final margin over Satoshi Higashi, who closed with 67–282.

Fuji Film Senior Championship
Chiba
Winner: Seiki Okuda

Seiki Okuda experienced the joy of winning for the first time in nearly two decades with his victory in the Fuji Film Senior Championship. This came after two near-misses earlier in the season and 18 years after Okuda landed his sixth and last win on the regular tour.

He did it wire-to-wire with two-stroke margins after each round. His first-day 67 led four 69-shooters — Ahmad Bateman, Yutaka Hagawa, Masahiro Kuramoto and Yuji Takagi. He followed with 69–136 as Nobuo Serizawa moved into the runner-up slot with 70-68–138.

Kiyoshi Murota, who defeated Okuda for his first of two wins earlier in his fine season, staged the strongest challenge to Okuda Sunday. Murota came up with a 67 for 206, two shots short of Okuda and his 68–204. Serizawa, the Fuji Film winner in 2011, finished third with 69–207.

Iwasaki Shiratsuyu Senior
Kagoshima
Winner: Kiyoshi Murota

Kiyoshi Murota put the finishing touches on one of the finest seasons in Japan Senior Tour history with his third victory of the year in the Iwasaki Shiratsuyu Senior finale.

Winning more than twice as much money — ¥62 million — as any other player while playing in just nine of the 12 events, Murota ran his Senior Tour victory total to 11, just one shy of career leader Katsunari Takahashi. Besides the three wins, one of which was the Japan Senior Open, Murota lost a playoff in the Japan Senior PGA, was second in two other tournaments and never finished higher than 16th place all year.

Murota never trailed at Iburuki Golf Club in the late November tournament. He opened with a five-under-par 67, leading Kohki Idoki and Nobuo Serizawa by a shot and Tsukase Watanabe by two. Watanabe (66) and Idoki (67) joined Murota at the top Saturday as he shot 68 for his 135. He then pulled away with his best round — 65 — Sunday for 200. Watanabe took second place with 67–202.

APPENDIXES

American Tours

Hyundai Tournament of Champions

Kapalua Resort, Plantation Course, Maui, Hawaii
Par 36-37–73; 7,411 yards
(Event shortened to 54 holes and completed on Tuesday—wind.)

January 4-8
purse, $5,700,000

	SCORES			TOTAL	MONEY
Dustin Johnson	69	66	68	203	$1,140,000
Steve Stricker	71	67	69	207	665,000
Brandt Snedeker	70	70	69	209	432,000
Bubba Watson	70	69	71	210	304,000
Keegan Bradley	71	69	70	210	304,000
Rickie Fowler	70	74	67	211	212,500
Tommy Gainey	72	69	70	211	212,500
Carl Pettersson	70	72	70	212	190,000
Ian Poulter	71	74	69	214	175,000
Matt Kuchar	74	71	69	214	175,000
Mark Wilson	69	76	70	215	155,000
Webb Simpson	72	72	71	215	155,000
J.J. Henry	71	74	71	216	120,400
Johnson Wagner	72	72	72	216	120,400
Scott Stallings	72	74	70	216	120,400
Scott Piercy	72	71	73	216	120,400
Nick Watney	69	73	74	216	120,400
Jonas Blixt	72	74	72	218	87,600
Ben Curtis	70	76	72	218	87,600
John Huh	73	71	74	218	87,600
Zach Johnson	74	72	72	218	87,600
Jason Dufner	72	77	69	218	87,600
Charlie Beljan	71	75	75	221	73,000
Bill Haas	71	75	75	221	73,000
Marc Leishman	75	75	71	221	73,000
Hunter Mahan	72	77	74	223	67,000
Ted Potter, Jr.	75	75	73	223	67,000
Ryan Moore	72	77	76	225	63,000
George McNeill	79	73	73	225	63,000
Kyle Stanley	78	80	72	230	61,000

Sony Open in Hawaii

Waialae Country Club, Honolulu, Hawaii
Par 35-35–70; 7,068 yards

January 10-13
purse, $5,600,000

	SCORES				TOTAL	MONEY
Russell Henley	63	63	67	63	256	$1,008,000
Tim Clark	64	66	66	63	259	604,800
Charles Howell	66	64	67	66	263	324,800
Scott Langley	62	66	65	70	263	324,800
Chris Kirk	68	62	68	66	264	204,400
Matt Kuchar	66	63	70	65	264	204,400
Brian Stuard	66	68	65	65	264	204,400
Jeff Overton	65	68	67	65	265	173,600
Harris English	69	69	62	66	266	145,600
Marc Leishman	67	68	64	67	266	145,600

	SCORES				TOTAL	MONEY
Pat Perez	68	63	67	68	266	145,600
Dicky Pride	68	67	64	67	266	145,600
Shane Bertsch	69	67	65	66	267	112,000
Danny Lee	66	66	66	69	267	112,000
Scott Gardiner	68	64	65	71	268	89,600
Justin Hicks	69	68	64	67	268	89,600
Matt Jones	66	68	64	70	268	89,600
Scott Piercy	64	64	72	68	268	89,600
Josh Teater	70	68	65	65	268	89,600
Stephen Ames	65	67	70	67	269	60,666.67
John Rollins	68	66	70	65	269	60,666.67
Webb Simpson	66	69	68	66	269	60,666.67
Vijay Singh	67	67	68	67	269	60,666.67
Ricky Barnes	70	65	66	68	269	60,666.66
Y.E. Yang	70	68	68	63	269	60,666.66
Tim Herron	66	66	68	70	270	41,440
John Senden	69	66	66	69	270	41,440
Kevin Streelman	71	67	66	66	270	41,440
Jimmy Walker	69	69	68	64	270	41,440
Charlie Wi	67	69	69	65	270	41,440
Erik Compton	67	68	67	69	271	33,208
Brian Gay	70	68	66	67	271	33,208
David Hearn	70	70	66	68	271	33,208
John Huh	71	63	68	69	271	33,208
David Lingmerth	69	68	66	68	271	33,208
Brad Fritsch	67	70	67	68	272	26,376
Tommy Gainey	66	69	65	72	272	26,376
Justin Leonard	70	68	67	67	272	26,376
George McNeill	70	68	69	65	272	26,376
Alistair Presnell	68	66	68	70	272	26,376
Bart Bryant	68	67	71	67	273	19,068
Chad Campbell	69	68	68	68	273	19,068
Russ Cochran	68	68	66	71	273	19,068
Ben Kohles	67	70	68	68	273	19,068
David Mathis	69	66	66	72	273	19,068
Henrik Norlander	70	64	71	68	273	19,068
Nicholas Thompson	69	68	67	69	273	19,068
Peter Tomasulo	68	68	67	70	273	19,068
Keegan Bradley	68	69	66	71	274	13,820.80
Doug LaBelle	71	66	66	71	274	13,820.80
D.H. Lee	68	68	71	67	274	13,820.80
Jeff Maggert	71	67	67	69	274	13,820.80
Lee Williams	69	66	71	68	274	13,820.80
Mark Anderson	73	64	70	68	275	12,824
Brendon de Jonge	69	68	69	69	275	12,824
Billy Horschel	66	70	70	69	275	12,824
Hideto Tanihara	70	65	69	71	275	12,824
Sang-Moon Bae	72	66	68	70	276	12,544
Derek Ernst	71	67	70	69	277	12,096
Steve Marino	69	67	70	71	277	12,096
Cameron Percy	71	67	68	71	277	12,096
Carl Pettersson	68	69	70	70	277	12,096
Rory Sabbatini	69	65	70	73	277	12,096
Shawn Stefani	68	67	72	70	277	12,096
Dean Wilson	69	68	69	71	277	12,096
Ryan Palmer	67	68	73	70	278	11,648
Steven Bowditch	67	69	72	71	279	11,312
Fabian Gomez	69	69	71	70	279	11,312
James Hahn	70	67	75	67	279	11,312
Morgan Hoffmann	66	70	67	76	279	11,312
Kyle Stanley	73	65	68	73	279	11,312
Jason Kokrak	69	69	73	69	280	10,976
Robert Streb	67	71	77	68	283	10,864
John Daly	70	68	79	67	284	10,752

Humana Challenge

PGA West, Palmer Course: Par 36-36–72; 6,950 yards
PGA West, Nicklaus Course: Par 36-36–72; 6,924 yards
La Quinta CC: Par 36-36–72; 7,060 yards
La Quinta, California

January 17-20
purse, $5,600,000

	SCORES				TOTAL	MONEY
Brian Gay	67	66	67	63	263	$1,008,000
Charles Howell	67	65	67	64	263	492,800
David Lingmerth	68	64	69	62	263	492,800
(Gay defeated Lingmerth on first and Howell on second playoff hole.)						
James Hahn	63	67	72	62	264	246,400
Scott Stallings	66	65	63	70	264	246,400
Ryan Palmer	65	69	66	65	265	194,600
Nicholas Thompson	69	66	66	64	265	194,600
Kevin Chappell	68	69	67	62	266	168,000
Jason Kokrak	63	69	69	65	266	168,000
Billy Horschel	67	68	65	67	267	124,133.34
Richard Lee	66	65	70	66	267	124,133.34
Stewart Cink	66	67	66	68	267	124,133.33
Charley Hoffman	65	67	67	68	267	124,133.33
Kevin Streelman	69	65	66	67	267	124,133.33
Brian Stuard	71	67	62	67	267	124,133.33
Ricky Barnes	65	68	69	66	268	78,560
Bob Estes	69	69	67	63	268	78,560
Robert Garrigus	66	67	69	66	268	78,560
Matt Kuchar	70	64	69	65	268	78,560
Bryce Molder	66	68	68	66	268	78,560
John Rollins	70	65	64	69	268	78,560
Robert Streb	67	69	68	64	268	78,560
Zach Johnson	66	66	70	67	269	51,520
Matt Jones	68	68	69	64	269	51,520
Brandt Snedeker	67	68	67	67	269	51,520
Jimmy Walker	66	70	66	67	269	51,520
Aaron Baddeley	64	68	70	68	270	35,728
Sang-Moon Bae	67	69	64	70	270	35,728
Tom Gillis	69	66	69	66	270	35,728
Fabian Gomez	69	67	67	67	270	35,728
Luke Guthrie	73	67	64	66	270	35,728
Geoff Ogilvy	70	65	70	65	270	35,728
Jeff Overton	69	71	66	64	270	35,728
Kevin Stadler	66	66	68	70	270	35,728
Daniel Summerhays	65	68	69	68	270	35,728
Bo Van Pelt	66	68	68	68	270	35,728
Stephen Ames	67	68	68	68	271	22,400
Roberto Castro	63	67	69	72	271	22,400
Bud Cauley	70	63	72	66	271	22,400
Justin Hicks	69	69	65	68	271	22,400
Doug LaBelle	64	70	70	67	271	22,400
Justin Leonard	67	69	67	68	271	22,400
Phil Mickelson	72	67	66	66	271	22,400
Cameron Tringale	65	72	66	68	271	22,400
Johnson Wagner	66	70	67	68	271	22,400
Lee Williams	67	65	68	71	271	22,400
Steven Bowditch	71	65	67	69	272	14,062.23
Carl Pettersson	68	66	69	69	272	14,062.23
Greg Chalmers	64	68	71	69	272	14,062.22
Brendon de Jonge	69	69	66	68	272	14,062.22
Lucas Glover	71	69	65	67	272	14,062.22
Jerry Kelly	65	71	69	67	272	14,062.22
Martin Laird	69	69	66	68	272	14,062.22
Jeff Maggert	65	72	67	68	272	14,062.22

	SCORES				TOTAL	MONEY
Camilo Villegas	71	67	67	67	272	14,062.22
Ross Fisher	74	65	67	67	273	12,432
Russell Henley	64	69	71	69	273	12,432
William McGirt	68	66	70	69	273	12,432
Tag Ridings	67	71	68	67	273	12,432
Brendan Steele	72	70	64	67	273	12,432
Darron Stiles	66	65	72	70	273	12,432
D.J. Trahan	69	68	68	68	273	12,432
Colt Knost	68	67	71	68	274	11,928
D.A. Points	67	69	69	69	274	11,928
Stuart Appleby	67	70	68	70	275	11,424
Graham DeLaet	71	70	65	69	275	11,424
Harris English	67	69	67	72	275	11,424
Brad Fritsch	69	65	71	70	275	11,424
Luke List	70	66	69	70	275	11,424
John Senden	72	66	68	69	275	11,424
Boo Weekley	68	67	71	69	275	11,424
D.H. Lee	70	66	70	70	276	10,808
David Mathis	70	66	70	70	276	10,808
Alistair Presnell	68	70	65	73	276	10,808
Shawn Stefani	68	69	69	70	276	10,808
Jason Bohn	70	69	67	71	277	10,416
Michael Bradley	65	69	72	71	277	10,416
Charlie Wi	72	64	70	71	277	10,416
Ben Kohles	68	68	66	76	278	10,136
David Toms	75	67	64	72	278	10,136
Greg Owen	72	65	68	75	280	9,968

Farmers Insurance Open

Torrey Pines, La Jolla, California
South Course: Par 36-36–72; 7,569 yards
North Course: Par 36-36–72; 6,874 yards
(Event completed on Monday—fog.)

January 24-28
purse, $6,100,000

	SCORES				TOTAL	MONEY
Tiger Woods	68	65	69	72	274	$1,098,000
Brandt Snedeker	65	75	69	69	278	536,800
Josh Teater	66	70	73	69	278	536,800
Jimmy Walker	67	69	72	71	279	268,400
Nick Watney	69	68	71	71	279	268,400
Aaron Baddeley	71	72	68	69	280	204,350
Rickie Fowler	77	65	70	68	280	204,350
Robert Garrigus	72	69	72	67	280	204,350
K.J. Choi	65	73	71	72	281	146,400
Jason Day	73	70	72	66	281	146,400
Graham DeLaet	68	70	72	71	281	146,400
Brad Fritsch	69	67	70	75	281	146,400
Bill Haas	69	69	72	71	281	146,400
Charles Howell	66	72	71	72	281	146,400
Erik Compton	71	65	71	75	282	94,550
Brendon de Jonge	74	66	73	69	282	94,550
Hunter Mahan	69	72	69	72	282	94,550
Steve Marino	68	68	73	73	282	94,550
Tag Ridings	67	70	71	74	282	94,550
Casey Wittenberg	69	67	72	74	282	94,550
Ross Fisher	66	71	73	73	283	61,000
Luke Guthrie	68	69	71	75	283	61,000
Pat Perez	72	67	70	74	283	61,000
Chez Reavie	71	70	74	68	283	61,000

	SCORES				TOTAL	MONEY
Nicholas Thompson	69	70	72	72	283	61,000
Charlie Wi	71	66	75	71	283	61,000
Jerry Kelly	67	71	78	68	284	41,480
Seung-Yul Noh	71	72	72	69	284	41,480
John Senden	69	68	74	73	284	41,480
Vijay Singh	68	73	70	73	284	41,480
Brendan Steele	67	73	71	73	284	41,480
Cameron Tringale	68	72	69	75	284	41,480
Gary Woodland	72	69	69	74	284	41,480
Jonas Blixt	70	72	72	71	285	31,476
Martin Flores	69	69	76	71	285	31,476
Charley Hoffman	70	72	74	69	285	31,476
David Lynn	67	75	73	70	285	31,476
Boo Weekley	74	67	73	71	285	31,476
Lucas Glover	69	73	70	74	286	25,010
J.J. Henry	69	71	75	71	286	25,010
Billy Horschel	66	69	76	75	286	25,010
Patrick Reed	73	69	74	70	286	25,010
Brian Stuard	68	74	73	71	286	25,010
Roberto Castro	71	68	75	73	287	18,003.72
Brian Harman	74	68	72	73	287	18,003.72
John Rollins	70	71	75	71	287	18,003.72
Nicolas Colsaerts	69	74	75	69	287	18,003.71
Jeff Klauk	71	72	72	72	287	18,003.71
Jin Park	72	70	74	71	287	18,003.71
Peter Tomasulo	67	75	75	70	287	18,003.71
Justin Bolli	72	67	74	75	288	14,124.89
Ben Curtis	72	71	73	72	288	14,124.89
James Driscoll	68	75	77	68	288	14,124.89
Jim Herman	69	69	76	74	288	14,124.89
Dustin Johnson	69	72	75	72	288	14,124.89
Hank Kuehne	68	74	76	70	288	14,124.89
Phil Mickelson	72	71	75	70	288	14,124.89
Greg Owen	74	68	71	75	288	14,124.89
Eric Meierdierks	69	74	72	73	288	14,124.88
Matt Every	69	74	73	73	289	12,993
Tom Gillis	69	73	73	74	289	12,993
John Huh	69	71	77	72	289	12,993
Trevor Immelman	72	71	71	75	289	12,993
Doug LaBelle	72	71	75	71	289	12,993
Martin Laird	72	71	73	73	289	12,993
Michael Letzig	68	73	75	73	289	12,993
Jeff Overton	71	69	75	74	289	12,993
Robert Karlsson	69	74	77	70	290	12,200
Luke List	66	75	78	71	290	12,200
Bryce Molder	68	72	78	72	290	12,200
Daniel Summerhays	72	71	74	73	290	12,200
Mike Weir	66	75	73	76	290	12,200
Will Claxton	69	69	79	74	291	11,590
Harris English	68	70	75	78	291	11,590
Scott Gardiner	70	73	74	74	291	11,590
Justin Hicks	67	70	80	74	291	11,590
Colt Knost	69	71	73	78	291	11,590
James Hahn	71	72	70	79	292	10,919
Neal Lancaster	72	71	73	76	292	10,919
Justin Leonard	68	71	77	76	292	10,919
John Mallinger	67	74	77	74	292	10,919
Michael Thompson	71	71	75	75	292	10,919
Bo Van Pelt	67	72	72	81	292	10,919
Steve LeBrun	68	75	74	76	293	10,431
D.H. Lee	68	74	78	73	293	10,431
Sang-Moon Bae	70	72	76	76	294	10,248

Waste Management Phoenix Open

TPC Scottsdale, Scottsdale, Arizona
Par 35-36–71; 7,216 yards

January 31-February 3
purse, $6,200,000

	SCORES				TOTAL	MONEY
Phil Mickelson	60	65	64	67	256	$1,116,000
Brandt Snedeker	64	66	65	65	260	669,600
Scott Piercy	70	66	64	61	261	421,600
Ryan Moore	66	66	65	65	262	297,600
Ryan Palmer	64	73	66	62	265	248,000
Brendon de Jonge	66	67	67	66	266	207,700
Bill Haas	65	64	70	67	266	207,700
Brendan Steele	69	65	65	67	266	207,700
Matt Every	65	67	69	66	267	173,600
Padraig Harrington	64	70	63	70	267	173,600
Ben Crane	67	71	64	66	268	136,400
Robert Garrigus	66	66	69	67	268	136,400
Billy Horschel	69	68	64	67	268	136,400
Kevin Stadler	68	68	69	63	268	136,400
Bubba Watson	67	67	71	64	269	111,600
Roberto Castro	65	68	67	70	270	84,165
James Hahn	71	67	70	62	270	84,165
David Hearn	67	65	73	65	270	84,165
Jeff Klauk	67	68	67	68	270	84,165
Hunter Mahan	67	67	67	69	270	84,165
Troy Matteson	67	65	66	72	270	84,165
Bo Van Pelt	68	67	71	64	270	84,165
Gary Woodland	67	66	67	70	270	84,165
Keegan Bradley	67	63	73	68	271	47,972.50
Bud Cauley	71	67	68	65	271	47,972.50
Kevin Chappell	66	68	71	66	271	47,972.50
Brian Gay	65	66	72	68	271	47,972.50
Chris Kirk	67	69	69	66	271	47,972.50
Bryce Molder	67	67	67	70	271	47,972.50
Ted Potter, Jr.	64	69	68	70	271	47,972.50
John Rollins	66	66	69	70	271	47,972.50
Brian Harman	70	65	68	69	272	35,882.50
Justin Leonard	65	71	66	70	272	35,882.50
John Mallinger	65	69	69	69	272	35,882.50
William McGirt	67	66	69	70	272	35,882.50
K.J. Choi	71	67	67	68	273	27,944.29
Charles Howell	67	68	69	69	273	27,944.29
Kevin Na	69	64	72	68	273	27,944.29
Casey Wittenberg	67	67	70	69	273	27,944.29
Angel Cabrera	66	65	70	72	273	27,944.28
Greg Chalmers	68	68	66	71	273	27,944.28
George McNeill	70	68	68	67	273	27,944.28
Cameron Tringale	69	67	69	69	274	19,881.34
Nick Watney	65	71	68	70	274	19,881.34
Ken Duke	66	69	71	68	274	19,881.33
Colt Knost	71	65	71	67	274	19,881.33
Hank Kuehne	65	71	72	66	274	19,881.33
Carl Pettersson	72	65	69	68	274	19,881.33
Sang-Moon Bae	72	64	72	67	275	15,301.60
Tim Clark	69	68	68	70	275	15,301.60
Jeff Maggert	64	70	71	70	275	15,301.60
Rory Sabbatini	68	66	70	71	275	15,301.60
Charlie Wi	68	63	71	73	275	15,301.60
Lucas Glover	68	70	67	71	276	14,260
David Toms	69	67	71	69	276	14,260
Jimmy Walker	68	69	72	67	276	14,260
Jason Day	70	68	72	67	277	13,764

	SCORES				TOTAL	MONEY
James Driscoll	72	66	69	70	277	13,764
Harris English	67	67	73	70	277	13,764
Martin Flores	65	71	72	69	277	13,764
John Merrick	69	69	70	69	277	13,764
Chris Stroud	71	66	69	72	278	13,392
Richard Lee	68	68	72	71	279	13,206
Boo Weekley	69	66	72	72	279	13,206
Aaron Baddeley	69	67	73	71	280	12,958
Dicky Pride	67	71	73	69	280	12,958
Russell Henley	69	67	74	71	281	12,648
J.J. Henry	70	68	73	70	281	12,648
David Mathis	72	65	70	74	281	12,648
Jeff Overton	66	69	75	72	282	12,338
Scott Verplank	66	72	71	73	282	12,338
Chad Campbell	73	65	71	74	283	12,090
Y.E. Yang	65	73	74	71	283	12,090
Kyle Stanley	67	71	74	72	284	11,904

AT&T Pebble Beach National Pro-Am

Pebble Beach GL: Par 36-36–72; 6,816 yards
Monterey Peninsula CC: Par 36-36–72; 6,838 yards
Spyglass Hill GC: Par 36-36–72; 6,858 yards
Pebble Beach, California

February 7-10
purse, $6,500,000

	SCORES				TOTAL	MONEY
Brandt Snedeker	66	68	68	65	267	$1,170,000
Chris Kirk	71	68	64	66	269	702,000
James Hahn	71	65	66	70	272	338,000
Kevin Stadler	69	69	69	65	272	338,000
Jimmy Walker	68	71	67	66	272	338,000
Jason Day	68	68	70	67	273	234,000
Fredrik Jacobson	71	66	70	67	274	209,625
Patrick Reed	68	69	67	70	274	209,625
Patrick Cantlay	66	70	72	67	275	175,500
James Driscoll	72	67	67	69	275	175,500
Retief Goosen	71	68	67	69	275	175,500
Aaron Baddeley	69	71	69	67	276	131,625
Justin Hicks	71	68	70	67	276	131,625
Richard Lee	68	71	66	71	276	131,625
Bryce Molder	71	72	69	64	276	131,625
Hunter Mahan	66	69	73	69	277	94,250
William McGirt	72	69	67	69	277	94,250
John Merrick	68	67	74	68	277	94,250
Sean O'Hair	70	67	70	70	277	94,250
Ted Potter, Jr.	67	67	73	70	277	94,250
Charlie Wi	70	70	68	69	277	94,250
Robert Garrigus	71	69	66	72	278	65,000
Kevin Na	68	72	68	70	278	65,000
Jordan Spieth	70	70	68	70	278	65,000
Cameron Tringale	71	71	70	66	278	65,000
Luke Guthrie	68	70	69	72	279	51,025
Webb Simpson	71	71	65	72	279	51,025
Billy Horschel	70	71	67	72	280	47,125
Russell Knox	64	73	71	72	280	47,125
Scott Brown	72	68	69	72	281	36,205
Bob Estes	69	71	72	69	281	36,205
Matt Every	67	70	71	73	281	36,205
Jim Furyk	75	69	68	69	281	36,205
Matt Jones	69	72	72	68	281	36,205

	SCORES				TOTAL	MONEY
Doug LaBelle	69	75	69	68	281	36,205
Greg Owen	65	75	73	68	281	36,205
Alistair Presnell	68	72	68	73	281	36,205
Heath Slocum	69	71	71	70	281	36,205
Brian Stuard	69	72	72	68	281	36,205
Jason Bohn	71	70	71	70	282	24,700
Brad Fritsch	69	73	71	69	282	24,700
Ryuji Imada	65	73	73	71	282	24,700
Kelly Kraft	69	71	72	70	282	24,700
Bill Lunde	71	70	68	73	282	24,700
Kevin Streelman	69	69	75	69	282	24,700
Tim Clark	76	67	70	70	283	18,427.50
Brendon de Jonge	67	71	73	72	283	18,427.50
Jeff Maggert	67	73	73	70	283	18,427.50
Lee Westwood	68	70	73	72	283	18,427.50
Ken Duke	71	72	69	72	284	15,184
Scott Gardiner	73	69	68	74	284	15,184
Brian Harman	68	73	70	73	284	15,184
J.B. Holmes	72	70	71	71	284	15,184
Pat Perez	69	69	74	72	284	15,184
Sam Saunders	76	71	66	71	284	15,184
Vijay Singh	72	72	66	74	284	15,184
Josh Teater	70	72	68	74	284	15,184
Peter Tomasulo	71	75	66	72	284	15,184
Mike Weir	75	65	71	73	284	15,184
Phil Mickelson	69	71	73	72	285	14,235
Rod Pampling	71	70	72	72	285	14,235
Stuart Appleby	70	71	71	74	286	13,715
Troy Kelly	73	68	72	73	286	13,715
Scott Langley	65	77	69	75	286	13,715
John Mallinger	68	75	69	74	286	13,715
Cameron Percy	74	68	71	73	286	13,715
Chez Reavie	70	72	68	76	286	13,715
Nick O'Hern	70	66	76	75	287	13,260
J.J. Henry	72	71	70	75	288	13,065
Seung-Yul Noh	67	73	72	76	288	13,065

Northern Trust Open

Riviera Country Club, Pacific Palisades, California
Par 35-36–71; 7,298 yards

February 14-17
purse, $6,600,000

	SCORES				TOTAL	MONEY
John Merrick	68	66	70	69	273	$1,188,000
Charlie Beljan	67	71	68	67	273	712,800
(Merrick defeated Beljan on second playoff hole.)						
Bill Haas	70	67	64	73	274	343,200
Fredrik Jacobson	68	65	72	69	274	343,200
Charl Schwartzel	69	67	68	70	274	343,200
Webb Simpson	70	66	68	71	275	229,350
Josh Teater	70	68	68	69	275	229,350
Sang-Moon Bae	68	65	76	67	276	198,000
Hunter Mahan	70	69	68	69	276	198,000
Greg Chalmers	69	69	73	67	278	165,000
Ted Potter, Jr.	71	67	71	69	278	165,000
Adam Scott	71	67	70	70	278	165,000
Ernie Els	70	68	73	68	279	127,600
Jim Furyk	68	72	69	70	279	127,600
Sergio Garcia	65	73	69	72	279	127,600
Keegan Bradley	71	70	69	70	280	99,000

	SCORES				TOTAL	MONEY
Luke Donald	69	66	70	75	280	99,000
Seung-Yul Noh	70	70	71	69	280	99,000
John Rollins	69	65	77	69	280	99,000
Jimmy Walker	70	70	71	69	280	99,000
Graham DeLaet	72	68	69	72	281	66,000
Luke Guthrie	69	71	71	70	281	66,000
Phil Mickelson	71	67	72	71	281	66,000
Bryce Molder	74	65	74	68	281	66,000
Cameron Tringale	73	69	71	68	281	66,000
Lee Westwood	68	68	74	71	281	66,000
Stewart Cink	71	72	67	72	282	45,870
Brian Davis	70	69	73	70	282	45,870
Bob Estes	68	72	72	70	282	45,870
Ryan Moore	70	67	71	74	282	45,870
Greg Owen	69	71	70	72	282	45,870
Kevin Streelman	73	69	72	68	282	45,870
Angel Cabrera	69	72	71	71	283	35,640
K.J. Choi	71	70	72	70	283	35,640
Chris Kirk	73	68	73	69	283	35,640
George McNeill	71	70	72	70	283	35,640
Charlie Wi	75	66	71	71	283	35,640
Ross Fisher	72	71	68	73	284	29,040
Trevor Immelman	70	69	72	73	284	29,040
Jerry Kelly	71	73	71	69	284	29,040
Matt Kuchar	64	73	74	73	284	29,040
Blayne Barber	69	70	72	74	285	23,760
Justin Leonard	70	73	68	74	285	23,760
Kevin Stadler	72	71	68	74	285	23,760
Jeremiah Wooding	75	66	70	74	285	23,760
Fred Couples	68	72	73	73	286	18,295.20
Martin Flores	74	70	69	73	286	18,295.20
Scott Harrington	73	71	68	74	286	18,295.20
David Lynn	67	74	71	74	286	18,295.20
Brendan Steele	70	71	73	72	286	18,295.20
Harris English	73	67	72	75	287	15,444
Brian Harman	76	67	70	74	287	15,444
Jesper Parnevik	70	70	74	73	287	15,444
Pat Perez	68	73	76	70	287	15,444
Vijay Singh	75	68	73	71	287	15,444
Johnson Wagner	73	71	73	70	287	15,444
Casey Wittenberg	71	73	71	72	287	15,444
Ben Curtis	68	72	72	76	288	14,652
Tim Herron	68	74	70	76	288	14,652
John Mallinger	71	66	78	73	288	14,652
James Hahn	67	74	75	73	289	13,992
J.J. Henry	72	69	76	72	289	13,992
Ryo Ishikawa	71	73	71	74	289	13,992
Brandt Jobe	66	75	74	74	289	13,992
Marc Leishman	69	75	68	77	289	13,992
Scott Piercy	72	71	72	74	289	13,992
Mark Wilson	71	72	70	76	289	13,992
Stuart Appleby	73	69	71	77	290	13,332
Matt Every	70	73	72	75	290	13,332
Charley Hoffman	73	70	72	75	290	13,332
Andres Romero	71	71	74	75	291	13,002
Y.E. Yang	70	72	75	74	291	13,002
Michael Bradley	73	71	73	79	296	12,804
Retief Goosen	71	72	75		218	12,672
Jeff Maggert	72	72	75		219	12,540
Michael Block	69	73	79		221	12,342
David Mathis	71	73	77		221	12,342
Peter Hanson	69	73	80		222	12,144
Jason Kokrak	71	72	81		224	12,012

WGC - Accenture Match Play Championship

The Golf Club at Dove Mountain, Marana, Arizona
Par 36-36–72; 7,849 yards

February 20-24
purse, $8,750,000

FIRST ROUND

Shane Lowry defeated Rory McIlroy, 6 and 5.
Carl Pettersson defeated Rickie Fowler, 19 holes.
Alexander Noren defeated Dustin Johnson, 6 and 4.
Graeme McDowell defeated Padraig Harrington, 2 up.
Bubba Watson defeated Chris Wood, 2 and 1.
Jim Furyk defeated Ryan Moore, 4 and 2.
Russell Henley defeated Charl Schwartzel, 1 up.
Jason Day defeated Zach Johnson, 6 and 5.
Louis Oosthuizen defeated Richie Ramsay, 2 up.
Robert Garrigus defeated Branden Grace, 4 and 3.
Marcus Fraser defeated Keegan Bradley, 1 up.
Fredrik Jacobson defeated Ernie Els, 1 up.
Justin Rose defeated K.J. Choi, 2 and 1.
Nicolas Colsaerts defeated Bill Haas, 5 and 4.
Sergio Garcia defeated Thongchai Jaidee, 20 holes.
Matt Kuchar defeated Hiroyuki Fujita, 3 and 2.
Charles Howell defeated Tiger Woods, 2 and 1.
Gonzalo Fernandez-Castano defeated Francesco Molinari, 2 up.
Webb Simpson defeated David Lynn, 5 and 4.
Peter Hanson defeated Thomas Bjorn, 3 and 2.
Rafa Cabrera-Bello defeated Lee Westwood, 19 holes.
Martin Kaymer defeated George Coetzee, 2 and 1.
Richard Sterne defeated Jason Dufner, 1 up.
Hunter Mahan defeated Matteo Manassero, 5 and 4.
Luke Donald defeated Marcel Siem, 1 up.
Scott Piercy defeated Paul Lawrie, 4 and 3.
Steve Stricker defeated Henrik Stenson, 5 and 4.
Nick Watney defeated David Toms, 5 and 4.
Tim Clark defeated Adam Scott, 2 and 1.
Thorbjorn Olesen defeated Jamie Donaldson, 3 and 2.
Ian Poulter defeated Stephen Gallacher, 2 and 1.
Bo Van Pelt defeated John Senden, 6 and 5.

(Each losing player received $46,000.)

SECOND ROUND

Lowry defeated Pettersson, 6 and 5.
McDowell defeated Noren, 20 holes.
Watson defeated Furyk, 22 holes.
Day defeated Henley, 19 holes.
Garrigus defeated Oosthuizen, 3 and 2.
Jacobson defeated Fraser, 4 and 3.
Colsaerts defeated Rose, 4 and 2.
Kuchar defeated Garcia, 2 and 1.
Fernandez-Castano defeated Howell, 6 and 5.
Simpson defeated Hanson, 1 up.
Kaymer defeated Cabrera-Bello, 2 and 1.
Mahan defeated Sterne, 4 and 3.
Piercy defeated Donald, 7 and 6.
Watney defeated Stricker, 21 holes.
Clark defeated Olesen, 3 and 2.
Poulter defeated Van Pelt, 3 and 1.

(Each losing player received $96,000.)

THIRD ROUND

McDowell defeated Lowry, 3 and 2.
Day defeated Watson, 4 and 3.
Garrigus defeated Jacobson, 3 and 1.
Kuchar defeated Colsaerts, 4 and 3.
Simpson defeated Fernandez-Castano, 2 up.
Mahan defeated Kaymer, 5 and 4.
Stricker defeated Piercy, 1 up.
Poulter defeated Clark, 5 and 3.

(Each losing player received $144,000.)

QUARTER-FINALS

Day defeated McDowell, 1 up.
Kuchar defeated Garrigus, 3 and 2.
Mahan defeated Simpson, 1 up.
Poulter defeated Stricker, 3 and 2.

(Each losing player received $275,000.)

SEMI-FINALS

Kuchar defeated Day, 4 and 3.
Mahan defeated Poulter, 4 and 3.

PLAYOFF FOR THIRD-FOURTH PLACE

Day defeated Poulter, 1 up.

(Day earned $615,000; Poulter earned $500,000.)

FINAL

Kuchar defeated Mahan, 2 and 1.

(Kuchar earned $1,500,000; Mahan earned $875,000.)

Honda Classic

PGA National, Champion Course,
Palm Beach Gardens, Florida
Par 35-35–70; 7,158 yards

February 28-March 3
purse, $6,000,000

	SCORES				TOTAL	MONEY
Michael Thompson	67	65	70	69	271	$1,080,000
Geoff Ogilvy	68	66	70	69	273	648,000
Luke Guthrie	68	63	71	73	275	408,000
Keegan Bradley	68	68	70	71	277	226,200
Erik Compton	69	68	70	70	277	226,200
Lucas Glover	69	66	72	70	277	226,200
David Lynn	72	68	68	69	277	226,200
Justin Rose	68	66	72	71	277	226,200
Graham DeLaet	65	68	73	72	278	156,000
Graeme McDowell	67	68	73	70	278	156,000
Charl Schwartzel	70	68	71	69	278	156,000
Lee Westwood	66	68	70	74	278	156,000
Rickie Fowler	65	71	69	74	279	109,200
Peter Hanson	71	67	68	73	279	109,200
Russell Henley	68	71	70	70	279	109,200
Darron Stiles	71	68	68	72	279	109,200

	SCORES				TOTAL	MONEY
Chris Stroud	67	70	72	70	279	109,200
Matt Jones	67	73	72	68	280	78,240
Sean O'Hair	66	68	74	72	280	78,240
Kyle Stanley	70	69	69	72	280	78,240
Robert Streb	65	70	74	71	280	78,240
Y.E. Yang	67	72	67	74	280	78,240
Bob Estes	69	69	70	73	281	60,000
Nicholas Thompson	69	66	72	74	281	60,000
Tom Gillis	67	68	72	75	282	47,850
Freddie Jacobson	70	69	72	71	282	47,850
Vaughn Taylor	71	68	73	70	282	47,850
Boo Weekley	66	67	74	75	282	47,850
Steven Bowditch	70	69	72	72	283	36,525
Brendon de Jonge	70	68	73	72	283	36,525
James Driscoll	69	68	70	76	283	36,525
Charles Howell	67	67	71	78	283	36,525
Jeff Klauk	67	69	73	74	283	36,525
Matteo Manassero	73	67	71	72	283	36,525
Scott Stallings	74	66	72	71	283	36,525
Brian Stuard	66	69	75	73	283	36,525
Doug LaBelle	66	68	77	73	284	27,600
Jeff Overton	67	71	74	72	284	27,600
Mark Wilson	70	68	71	75	284	27,600
Tiger Woods	70	70	70	74	284	27,600
Stewart Cink	68	71	71	75	285	22,200
Ben Kohles	66	73	69	77	285	22,200
George McNeill	71	68	71	75	285	22,200
Ryan Palmer	69	69	75	72	285	22,200
Kevin Streelman	71	68	73	73	285	22,200
Ernie Els	69	70	75	72	286	16,632
Billy Horschel	66	69	81	70	286	16,632
Trevor Immelman	73	67	71	75	286	16,632
Brandt Jobe	69	71	68	78	286	16,632
Dustin Johnson	66	71	74	75	286	16,632
Greg Chalmers	68	71	73	75	287	14,040
Jason Dufner	69	70	74	74	287	14,040
Brian Gay	67	72	73	75	287	14,040
Martin Kaymer	71	66	76	74	287	14,040
Chris Kirk	68	68	75	76	287	14,040
Hank Kuehne	67	72	75	73	287	14,040
Brendan Steele	72	67	73	75	287	14,040
Jamie Donaldson	73	66	76	73	288	13,200
Marc Leishman	69	69	77	73	288	13,200
Patrick Reed	67	73	75	73	288	13,200
Kevin Stadler	67	71	74	76	288	13,200
Daniel Summerhays	69	67	74	78	288	13,200
Ross Fisher	71	66	77	75	289	12,840
Ben Crane	70	69	72	79	290	12,540
Fabian Gomez	66	72	72	80	290	12,540
Retief Goosen	72	67	71	80	290	12,540
Justin Hicks	71	68	77	74	290	12,540
Nicolas Colsaerts	69	71	72	79	291	12,120
D.A. Points	67	71	77	76	291	12,120
Gary Woodland	68	70	77	76	291	12,120
Jason Bohn	70	69	79	74	292	11,760
Branden Grace	65	71	75	81	292	11,760
Cameron Percy	71	66	77	78	292	11,760
Brad Fritsch	68	72	77	77	294	11,460
Steve Marino	71	69	75	79	294	11,460

WGC - Cadillac Championship

TPC Blue Monster at Doral, Miami, Florida
Par 36-36–72; 7,334 yards

March 7-10
purse, $8,750,000

	SCORES				TOTAL	MONEY
Tiger Woods	66	65	67	71	269	$1,500,000
Steve Stricker	67	67	69	68	271	880,000
Sergio Garcia	66	72	67	69	274	417,500
Graeme McDowell	66	67	69	72	274	417,500
Phil Mickelson	67	67	69	71	274	417,500
Adam Scott	72	70	68	64	274	417,500
Keegan Bradley	68	68	69	71	276	240,000
Peter Hanson	67	71	70	70	278	163,750
Rory McIlroy	73	69	71	65	278	163,750
Justin Rose	68	72	70	68	278	163,750
Michael Thompson	69	69	67	73	278	163,750
Jason Dufner	69	69	69	72	279	113,750
Charles Howell	68	71	69	71	279	113,750
Dustin Johnson	68	69	70	72	279	113,750
Richard Sterne	70	71	71	67	279	113,750
Freddie Jacobson	66	69	71	74	280	98,000
Charl Schwartzel	71	65	69	75	280	98,000
Nicolas Colsaerts	71	71	67	72	281	93,000
Bubba Watson	66	69	71	75	281	93,000
Alexander Noren	69	70	72	71	282	88,000
John Senden	69	69	70	74	282	88,000
Webb Simpson	72	67	71	72	282	88,000
Scott Jamieson	70	69	72	72	283	83,000
Matteo Manassero	71	71	75	66	283	83,000
Hunter Mahan	67	72	71	74	284	79,000
Scott Piercy	70	73	69	72	284	79,000
Lee Westwood	73	69	71	71	284	79,000
Ernie Els	73	69	72	71	285	75,000
Russell Henley	70	72	70	73	285	75,000
John Huh	71	67	71	76	285	75,000
Francesco Molinari	78	66	72	69	285	75,000
Ian Poulter	68	70	72	75	285	75,000
Jason Day	74	66	75	71	286	71,500
Louis Oosthuizen	70	75	69	72	286	71,500
Rickie Fowler	69	69	71	78	287	68,500
Francesco Molinari	78	66	72	69	285	75,000
Jim Furyk	72	70	72	73	287	68,500
Brian Gay	70	76	69	72	287	68,500
Matt Kuchar	72	72	72	71	287	68,500
Padraig Harrington	76	72	68	72	288	64,500
David Lynn	71	70	76	71	288	64,500
Marcel Siem	75	73	70	70	288	64,500
Bo Van Pelt	68	75	71	74	288	64,500
Luke Donald	70	76	71	72	289	60,500
Gonzalo Fernandez-Castano	72	70	73	74	289	60,500
Bill Haas	72	73	72	72	289	60,500
Chris Wood	71	74	71	73	289	60,500
Zach Johnson	71	67	77	75	290	57,500
Geoff Ogilvy	69	74	73	74	290	57,500
Branden Grace	73	74	72	72	291	54,500
Martin Kaymer	76	68	73	74	291	54,500
Carl Pettersson	71	75	71	74	291	54,500
Nick Watney	69	71	77	74	291	54,500
George Coetzee	70	69	73	80	292	50,600
Stephen Gallacher	74	75	69	74	292	50,600
Ryan Moore	73	71	72	76	292	50,600
Thorbjorn Olesen	75	75	70	72	292	50,600

	SCORES				TOTAL	MONEY
Thaworn Wiratchant	69	69	77	77	292	50,600
Michael Hendry	72	66	78	77	293	48,750
Paul Lawrie	78	73	72	70	293	48,750
Tim Clark	72	73	71	79	295	47,500
Marcus Fraser	73	72	77	73	295	47,500
John Merrick	75	72	72	76	295	47,500
Rafa Cabrera-Bello	71	74	76	78	299	46,250
Jamie Donaldson	72	77	76	74	299	46,250
Robert Garrigus	75	75	74	76	300	45,500

Puerto Rico Open

Trump International Golf Club, Rio Grande, Puerto Rico
Par 36-36–72; 7,569 yards

March 7-10
purse, $3,500,000

	SCORES				TOTAL	MONEY
Scott Brown	68	63	67	70	268	$630,000
Fabian Gomez	69	64	65	71	269	308,000
Jordan Spieth	69	66	67	67	269	308,000
Justin Bolli	67	69	68	66	270	154,000
Brian Stuard	67	69	66	68	270	154,000
Andres Romero	65	65	75	66	271	121,625
Peter Uihlein	67	65	72	67	271	121,625
David Hearn	68	67	71	66	272	101,500
D.J. Trahan	72	65	69	66	272	101,500
Boo Weekley	71	67	66	68	272	101,500
Brendon de Jonge	70	69	65	69	273	80,500
Dicky Pride	68	67	72	66	273	80,500
Robert Streb	71	65	70	67	273	80,500
Morgan Hoffmann	67	68	68	71	274	61,250
Matt Jones	71	69	64	70	274	61,250
Cameron Percy	65	70	71	68	274	61,250
Vaughn Taylor	69	68	69	68	274	61,250
Graham DeLaet	70	68	67	70	275	44,100
Luke Guthrie	70	67	69	69	275	44,100
Brian Harman	70	68	71	66	275	44,100
Nick O'Hern	69	69	68	69	275	44,100
Chris Stroud	68	69	70	68	275	44,100
Camilo Villegas	71	69	66	69	275	44,100
Blayne Barber	66	70	66	74	276	28,350
Matt Bettencourt	68	67	72	69	276	28,350
Roberto Castro	69	70	68	69	276	28,350
Erik Compton	69	72	68	67	276	28,350
Jon Curran	66	69	70	71	276	28,350
Steve LeBrun	67	65	70	74	276	28,350
Patrick Reed	73	68	70	66	277	19,911.12
Angel Cabrera	67	68	72	70	277	19,911.11
Patrick Cantlay	70	67	69	71	277	19,911.11
Robert Karlsson	68	73	67	69	277	19,911.11
Bryce Molder	68	71	69	69	277	19,911.11
Rory Sabbatini	70	68	70	69	277	19,911.11
Brendon Todd	68	73	69	67	277	19,911.11
Aaron Watkins	70	67	71	69	277	19,911.11
Y.E. Yang	70	70	70	67	277	19,911.11
Will Claxton	70	71	71	66	278	12,294.55
James Driscoll	68	70	71	69	278	12,294.55
Ben Kohles	69	72	70	67	278	12,294.55
Shawn Stefani	73	65	71	69	278	12,294.55
Henrik Stenson	68	69	73	68	278	12,294.55
Josh Teater	68	69	71	70	278	12,294.55

	SCORES				TOTAL	MONEY
Brad Fritsch	67	70	71	70	278	12,294.54
Jim Herman	69	70	69	70	278	12,294.54
Ryo Ishikawa	70	68	66	74	278	12,294.54
Russell Knox	70	69	68	71	278	12,294.54
Duffy Waldorf	69	68	70	71	278	12,294.54
Michael Bradley	69	70	68	72	279	8,320
John Daly	70	70	70	69	279	8,320
Justin Leonard	72	68	70	69	279	8,320
Luke List	68	71	68	72	279	8,320
Eric Meierdierks	70	68	70	71	279	8,320
Tim Petrovic	71	70	68	70	279	8,320
Heath Slocum	68	68	71	72	279	8,320
K.J. Choi	72	67	71	70	280	7,700
Jeff Gove	73	65	71	71	280	7,700
D.H. Lee	73	66	73	68	280	7,700
George McNeill	71	64	69	76	280	7,700
Henrik Norlander	71	70	70	69	280	7,700
Rod Pampling	72	68	70	70	280	7,700
Sebastian Vazquez	69	69	69	73	280	7,700
Martin Flores	72	64	72	73	281	7,385
Alexandre Rocha	72	68	72	69	281	7,385
Lee Williams	69	71	71	71	282	7,280
Sang-Moon Bae	70	71	66	76	283	7,140
Troy Kelly	69	70	71	73	283	7,140
Colt Knost	68	71	73	71	283	7,140
Doug LaBelle	72	68	75	69	284	6,965
Troy Matteson	70	71	73	70	284	6,965
Kevin Stadler	71	69	71	74	285	6,825
Nicholas Thompson	71	70	72	72	285	6,825
John Mallinger	71	69	72	74	286	6,720
*Jorge Garcia	70	70	73	74	287	
Rafael Campos	67	74	73	74	288	6,650
Paul Casey	70	71	74	76	291	6,580

Tampa Bay Championship

Innisbrook Resort, Copperhead Course, Palm Harbor, Florida
Par 36-35–71; 7,340 yards

March 14-17
purse, $5,500,000

	SCORES				TOTAL	MONEY
Kevin Streelman	73	69	65	67	274	$990,000
Boo Weekley	72	70	71	63	276	594,000
Cameron Tringale	71	70	70	66	277	374,000
Luke Donald	70	72	67	69	278	227,333.34
Greg Chalmers	71	68	69	70	278	227,333.33
Justin Leonard	71	69	67	71	278	227,333.33
Harris English	68	69	73	69	279	148,892.86
Sergio Garcia	71	67	72	69	279	148,892.86
Pat Perez	71	71	70	67	279	148,892.86
Jordan Spieth	72	68	69	70	279	148,892.86
Shawn Stefani	65	70	74	70	279	148,892.86
Jim Furyk	72	69	67	71	279	148,892.85
Ben Kohles	72	67	69	71	279	148,892.85
Stewart Cink	76	68	68	68	280	99,000
Brian Harman	67	70	72	71	280	99,000
Matt Kuchar	72	68	71	69	280	99,000
George Coetzee	71	68	68	74	281	79,750
Graham DeLaet	73	71	70	67	281	79,750
Tag Ridings	68	70	70	73	281	79,750
Webb Simpson	73	69	71	68	281	79,750

	SCORES				TOTAL	MONEY
Roberto Castro	69	73	68	72	282	55,000
K.J. Choi	69	67	76	70	282	55,000
James Driscoll	74	66	72	70	282	55,000
Jason Dufner	71	66	74	71	282	55,000
Jerry Kelly	70	70	73	69	282	55,000
Dicky Pride	69	73	70	70	282	55,000
Scott Brown	70	70	72	71	283	40,700
Justin Hicks	70	71	69	73	283	40,700
Rory Sabbatini	73	71	68	71	283	40,700
Stephen Ames	72	71	69	72	284	31,968.75
Erik Compton	75	65	72	72	284	31,968.75
Scott Langley	72	70	70	72	284	31,968.75
George McNeill	72	72	70	70	284	31,968.75
Bryce Molder	72	69	68	75	284	31,968.75
Ryan Palmer	71	70	72	71	284	31,968.75
Adam Scott	70	66	76	72	284	31,968.75
Jimmy Walker	73	68	70	73	284	31,968.75
Jonas Blixt	75	69	72	69	285	23,650
Lucas Glover	69	74	70	72	285	23,650
Marc Leishman	70	70	75	70	285	23,650
Vijay Singh	69	73	72	71	285	23,650
Charlie Wi	71	72	71	71	285	23,650
Sang-Moon Bae	73	70	71	72	286	16,747.50
Jason Day	70	72	75	69	286	16,747.50
Brendon de Jonge	71	73	72	70	286	16,747.50
Tim Herron	71	71	72	72	286	16,747.50
Jeff Overton	72	72	70	72	286	16,747.50
Brendan Steele	68	75	74	69	286	16,747.50
Brian Stuard	75	68	74	69	286	16,747.50
Nick Watney	70	72	70	74	286	16,747.50
Martin Flores	73	69	73	72	287	13,024
J.J. Henry	70	74	72	71	287	13,024
David Lingmerth	74	70	70	73	287	13,024
Robert Streb	73	70	69	75	287	13,024
Peter Tomasulo	69	68	75	75	287	13,024
Aaron Baddeley	72	71	72	73	288	12,320
Brian Davis	71	69	73	75	288	12,320
Robert Garrigus	72	71	72	73	288	12,320
Billy Horschel	70	73	74	71	288	12,320
John Mallinger	74	70	71	73	288	12,320
Stuart Appleby	74	68	74	73	289	11,935
Geoff Ogilvy	69	72	76	72	289	11,935
Angel Cabrera	74	69	75	72	290	11,495
Trevor Immelman	70	73	75	72	290	11,495
Troy Kelly	72	70	73	75	290	11,495
Chez Reavie	69	75	70	76	290	11,495
Chris Stroud	75	67	74	74	290	11,495
Daniel Summerhays	71	73	74	72	290	11,495
Sean O'Hair	73	68	75	75	291	11,110
Colt Knost	71	72	74	75	292	10,835
Martin Laird	73	71	73	75	292	10,835
Richard Lee	72	72	74	74	292	10,835
John Rollins	76	68	71	77	292	10,835
Jesper Parnevik	72	72	72	77	293	10,560
Charley Hoffman	71	70	77	77	295	10,395
Troy Matteson	71	72	77	75	295	10,395
Josh Teater	74	69	77	77	297	10,230

Arnold Palmer Invitational

Bay Hill Club & Lodge, Orlando, Florida
Par 36-36–72; 7,381 yards
(Event completed on Monday—rain.)

March 21-25
purse, $6,200,000

	SCORES				TOTAL	MONEY
Tiger Woods	69	70	66	70	275	$1,116,000
Justin Rose	65	70	72	70	277	669,600
Keegan Bradley	74	69	66	71	280	297,600
Gonzalo Fernandez-Castano	69	71	68	72	280	297,600
Rickie Fowler	73	67	67	73	280	297,600
Mark Wilson	71	68	70	71	280	297,600
Thorbjorn Olesen	69	73	66	73	281	207,700
Ken Duke	70	68	70	74	282	167,400
Bill Haas	69	66	73	74	282	167,400
William McGirt	74	70	70	68	282	167,400
Henrik Stenson	71	71	69	71	282	167,400
Jimmy Walker	69	69	70	74	282	167,400
Scott Brown	74	71	69	69	283	130,200
Ben Kohles	69	73	70	72	284	114,700
Bubba Watson	74	71	72	67	284	114,700
Erik Compton	72	72	70	71	285	93,000
Chris Kirk	71	72	72	70	285	93,000
John Rollins	68	72	71	74	285	93,000
Brian Stuard	74	69	67	75	285	93,000
Camilo Villegas	71	74	70	70	285	93,000
Ben Curtis	72	70	70	74	286	62,000
Hunter Mahan	71	70	70	75	286	62,000
Carl Pettersson	72	72	71	71	286	62,000
Ian Poulter	72	69	70	75	286	62,000
Kevin Streelman	74	71	70	71	286	62,000
Vaughn Taylor	71	74	70	71	286	62,000
Retief Goosen	73	69	73	72	287	42,160
John Huh	67	69	71	80	287	42,160
John Senden	71	72	70	74	287	42,160
Josh Teater	75	71	70	71	287	42,160
Cameron Tringale	72	73	68	74	287	42,160
Johnson Wagner	76	71	69	71	287	42,160
Gary Woodland	70	73	73	71	287	42,160
Matt Every	72	75	66	75	288	31,310
Brad Fritsch	68	72	70	78	288	31,310
Zach Johnson	70	76	69	73	288	31,310
Martin Laird	74	73	68	73	288	31,310
Francesco Molinari	75	71	70	72	288	31,310
Chris Stroud	72	71	74	71	288	31,310
Sang-Moon Bae	71	69	76	73	289	24,180
Bob Estes	71	69	75	74	289	24,180
Luke Guthrie	73	67	73	76	289	24,180
J.J. Henry	71	67	76	75	289	24,180
Sean O'Hair	69	76	69	75	289	24,180
Jason Day	71	74	68	77	290	18,153.60
David Hearn	75	71	71	73	290	18,153.60
Charles Howell	73	69	73	75	290	18,153.60
Graeme McDowell	72	74	75	69	290	18,153.60
Nick Watney	69	76	72	73	290	18,153.60
Chad Campbell	77	67	75	72	291	14,738.29
Graham DeLaet	76	69	73	73	291	14,738.29
Greg Owen	74	73	71	73	291	14,738.29
Tag Ridings	70	74	73	74	291	14,738.29
Matt Jones	71	70	74	76	291	14,738.28
David Lingmerth	71	74	71	75	291	14,738.28
Pat Perez	71	75	70	75	291	14,738.28

	SCORES				TOTAL	MONEY
George Coetzee	73	74	69	76	292	13,702
Harris English	75	72	73	72	292	13,702
Tommy Gainey	72	73	77	70	292	13,702
Richard Lee	73	70	72	77	292	13,702
Vijay Singh	71	68	75	78	292	13,702
David Toms	74	72	70	76	292	13,702
Stewart Cink	70	73	76	74	293	13,206
Lee Westwood	71	75	72	75	293	13,206
Ben Crane	70	74	71	79	294	12,834
Jim Furyk	71	74	75	74	294	12,834
Justin Hicks	74	71	77	72	294	12,834
Ryo Ishikawa	69	77	72	76	294	12,834
Charlie Beljan	76	71	73	75	295	12,400
Lee Janzen	73	73	71	78	295	12,400
Boo Weekley	72	70	76	77	295	12,400
Robert Allenby	73	74	74	75	296	12,090
Nicholas Thompson	74	72	75	75	296	12,090
Doug LaBelle	73	73	77	74	297	11,904
Billy Horschel	72	73	69	85	299	11,780
Rod Perry	76	71	78	82	307	11,656

Shell Houston Open

Redstone Golf Club, Tournament Course, Humble, Texas   March 28-31
Par 36-36–72; 7,457 yards   purse, $6,200,000

	SCORES				TOTAL	MONEY
D.A. Points	64	71	71	66	272	$1,116,000
Billy Horschel	68	72	67	66	273	545,600
Henrik Stenson	69	70	68	66	273	545,600
Ben Crane	69	70	67	68	274	272,800
Dustin Johnson	69	70	70	65	274	272,800
Kevin Chappell	70	70	67	68	275	207,700
Stewart Cink	71	66	68	70	275	207,700
Brian Davis	67	70	71	67	275	207,700
Jason Kokrak	66	69	71	70	276	179,800
Brendon de Jonge	71	68	72	66	277	137,433.34
Charles Howell	69	72	70	66	277	137,433.34
Keegan Bradley	70	70	67	70	277	137,433.33
Bill Haas	68	70	67	72	277	137,433.33
Louis Oosthuizen	70	72	65	70	277	137,433.33
Lee Westwood	68	72	67	70	277	137,433.33
Angel Cabrera	66	72	69	71	278	96,100
Bud Cauley	68	74	65	71	278	96,100
Phil Mickelson	72	71	67	68	278	96,100
Cameron Tringale	65	73	69	71	278	96,100
Charley Hoffman	68	71	70	70	279	77,500
John Rollins	65	74	71	69	279	77,500
Chris Kirk	71	70	72	67	280	59,520
Doug LaBelle	71	71	72	66	280	59,520
Greg Owen	68	73	68	71	280	59,520
Robert Streb	70	71	71	68	280	59,520
Steve Wheatcroft	67	67	72	74	280	59,520
Jeff Overton	67	73	71	70	281	44,950
Pat Perez	72	71	70	68	281	44,950
Kevin Stadler	70	73	69	69	281	44,950
Nick Watney	71	71	72	67	281	44,950
Aaron Baddeley	70	71	72	69	282	35,162.86
Ross Fisher	73	69	72	68	282	35,162.86
Tim Herron	69	73	69	71	282	35,162.86

	SCORES				TOTAL	MONEY
Jin Park	69	74	69	70	282	35,162.86
Daniel Summerhays	72	71	69	70	282	35,162.86
Graham DeLaet	71	71	68	72	282	35,162.85
Chez Reavie	72	70	68	72	282	35,162.85
Charlie Beljan	71	72	70	70	283	25,420
Bob Estes	71	69	74	69	283	25,420
Matt Jones	68	73	70	72	283	25,420
Brendan Steele	70	71	71	71	283	25,420
Steve Stricker	73	68	71	71	283	25,420
Chris Stroud	71	72	71	69	283	25,420
Josh Teater	74	67	69	73	283	25,420
Russell Henley	72	70	74	68	284	18,153.60
Rory McIlroy	73	70	71	70	284	18,153.60
John Merrick	68	72	69	75	284	18,153.60
Scott Stallings	70	69	73	72	284	18,153.60
Boo Weekley	70	69	75	70	284	18,153.60
Harris English	69	74	73	69	285	14,838.67
Jordan Spieth	72	70	74	69	285	14,838.67
Jimmy Walker	68	71	78	68	285	14,838.67
Gary Woodland	72	70	73	70	285	14,838.67
Kelly Kraft	70	72	72	71	285	14,838.66
Justin Leonard	71	72	70	72	285	14,838.66
Steven Bowditch	73	70	69	74	286	13,950
James Hahn	74	69	68	75	286	13,950
David Lynn	72	70	72	72	286	13,950
Troy Matteson	71	71	73	71	286	13,950
Chad Campbell	72	71	74	70	287	13,392
Brandt Jobe	69	73	70	75	287	13,392
Jerry Kelly	71	72	75	69	287	13,392
D.H. Lee	72	71	68	76	287	13,392
Nicholas Thompson	70	73	71	73	287	13,392
Hunter Haas	69	71	74	74	288	12,834
Henrik Norlander	74	68	73	73	288	12,834
Carl Pettersson	74	69	74	71	288	12,834
Scott Verplank	72	68	70	78	288	12,834
Ricky Barnes	73	68	73	75	289	12,524
George Coetzee	72	71	72	75	290	12,276
Cameron Percy	73	70	71	76	290	12,276
Wes Short, Jr.	71	70	75	74	290	12,276

Valero Texas Open

TPC San Antonio, San Antonio, Texas
Par 36-36–72; 7,522 yards

April 4-7
purse, $6,200,000

	SCORES				TOTAL	MONEY
Martin Laird	70	71	70	63	274	$1,116,000
Rory McIlroy	72	67	71	66	276	669,600
Jim Furyk	69	70	69	69	277	322,400
Charley Hoffman	71	67	70	69	277	322,400
Billy Horschel	68	68	70	71	277	322,400
K.J. Choi	72	67	72	68	279	223,200
Daniel Summerhays	69	69	73	69	280	193,233.34
Bob Estes	72	69	69	70	280	193,233.33
Jeff Overton	69	72	70	69	280	193,233.33
Martin Flores	71	72	70	68	281	155,000
Padraig Harrington	68	73	70	70	281	155,000
Marcel Siem	76	67	69	69	281	155,000
Richard Lee	74	70	69	69	282	130,200
David Lynn	72	70	71	70	283	117,800

	SCORES				TOTAL	MONEY
Aaron Baddeley	74	70	71	69	284	93,000
Kevin Chappell	75	69	72	68	284	93,000
Freddie Jacobson	70	74	71	69	284	93,000
Jason Kokrak	74	68	72	70	284	93,000
Shane Lowry	70	72	72	70	284	93,000
Ryan Palmer	71	71	68	74	284	93,000
D.J. Trahan	70	71	71	72	284	93,000
Brendon de Jonge	70	69	77	69	285	55,888.58
Chris DiMarco	75	69	73	68	285	55,888.57
Peter Hanson	70	71	78	66	285	55,888.57
Brian Harman	72	69	75	69	285	55,888.57
Matt Kuchar	74	70	71	70	285	55,888.57
Bryce Molder	68	74	75	68	285	55,888.57
Charl Schwartzel	72	73	70	70	285	55,888.57
Brian Davis	69	72	75	70	286	43,090
John Mallinger	73	72	70	71	286	43,090
Todd Baek	73	72	72	70	287	35,960
Bud Cauley	71	71	73	72	287	35,960
Ben Curtis	74	71	72	70	287	35,960
Ken Duke	73	68	75	71	287	35,960
Nathan Green	69	72	76	70	287	35,960
Jimmy Walker	71	73	76	67	287	35,960
Greg Chalmers	72	71	77	68	288	25,420
Joe Durant	70	71	76	71	288	25,420
Brad Fritsch	70	73	75	70	288	25,420
Ben Kohles	69	70	76	73	288	25,420
Steve LeBrun	72	69	74	73	288	25,420
Justin Leonard	72	71	74	71	288	25,420
William McGirt	70	72	73	73	288	25,420
Cameron Percy	72	71	77	68	288	25,420
Ian Poulter	70	75	74	69	288	25,420
Stuart Appleby	75	69	73	72	289	16,580.58
Matt Bettencourt	67	73	77	72	289	16,580.57
Jeff Gove	71	73	75	70	289	16,580.57
Luke List	73	71	75	70	289	16,580.57
Seung-Yul Noh	73	71	73	72	289	16,580.57
Joe Ogilvie	71	74	74	70	289	16,580.57
Brendan Steele	72	72	72	73	289	16,580.57
Retief Goosen	70	69	80	71	290	14,089.50
Neal Lancaster	75	70	71	74	290	14,089.50
Troy Matteson	76	69	74	71	290	14,089.50
John Merrick	74	71	73	72	290	14,089.50
Henrik Norlander	74	71	73	72	290	14,089.50
D.A. Points	74	71	74	71	290	14,089.50
Scott Stallings	73	70	75	72	290	14,089.50
Nicholas Thompson	71	73	71	75	290	14,089.50
Charlie Beljan	71	74	71	75	291	13,082
Harris English	68	75	75	73	291	13,082
Brian Gay	71	70	76	74	291	13,082
Lee Janzen	70	69	79	73	291	13,082
Alistair Presnell	69	72	75	75	291	13,082
Andres Romero	69	76	73	73	291	13,082
Brendon Todd	73	72	75	71	291	13,082
Peter Tomasulo	67	73	77	74	291	13,082
Steven Bowditch	69	69	77	77	292	12,462
Russell Knox	73	72	74	73	292	12,462
Scott Langley	73	70	77	73	293	12,276
John Huh	74	69	76	75	294	12,152
Paul Haley	73	70	74	78	295	12,028
John Peterson	70	75	76		221	11,594
Wes Short, Jr.	71	71	79		221	11,594
Johnson Wagner	74	70	77		221	11,594
Gary Woodland	71	74	76		221	11,594

	SCORES			TOTAL	MONEY
Kyle Stanley	74	70	78	222	11,284
Justin Bolli	76	69	78	223	11,098
Matt Every	70	75	78	223	11,098
Joey Snyder	72	73	87	232	10,912

Masters Tournament

Augusta National Golf Club, Augusta, Georgia   April 11-14
Par 36-36–72; 7,445 yards   purse, $8,000,000

	SCORES				TOTAL	MONEY
Adam Scott	69	72	69	69	279	$1,440,000
Angel Cabrera	71	69	69	70	279	864,000
(Scott defeated Cabrera on second playoff hole.)						
Jason Day	70	68	73	70	281	544,000
Marc Leishman	66	73	72	72	283	352,000
Tiger Woods	70	73	70	70	283	352,000
Thorbjorn Olesen	78	70	68	68	284	278,000
Brandt Snedeker	70	70	69	75	284	278,000
Sergio Garcia	66	76	73	70	285	232,000
Matt Kuchar	68	75	69	73	285	232,000
Lee Westwood	70	71	73	71	285	232,000
Tim Clark	70	76	67	73	286	192,000
John Huh	70	77	71	68	286	192,000
Fred Couples	68	71	77	71	287	145,600
Ernie Els	71	74	73	69	287	145,600
Dustin Johnson	67	76	74	70	287	145,600
David Toms	70	74	76	67	287	145,600
Nick Watney	78	69	68	72	287	145,600
Branden Grace	78	70	71	69	288	116,000
Henrik Stenson	75	71	73	69	288	116,000
Jason Dufner	72	69	75	73	289	89,920
Gonzalo Fernandez-Castano	68	74	73	74	289	89,920
Bill Haas	71	72	74	72	289	89,920
Steve Stricker	73	70	71	75	289	89,920
Bo Van Pelt	71	74	70	74	289	89,920
Stewart Cink	75	71	73	71	290	56,040
Luke Donald	71	72	75	72	290	56,040
Jim Furyk	69	71	74	76	290	56,040
Freddie Jacobson	72	73	72	73	290	56,040
Bernhard Langer	71	71	72	76	290	56,040
Rory McIlroy	72	70	79	69	290	56,040
Justin Rose	70	71	75	74	290	56,040
Charl Schwartzel	71	71	75	73	290	56,040
Richard Sterne	73	72	75	70	290	56,040
Michael Thompson	73	71	79	67	290	56,040
Zach Johnson	69	76	71	75	291	41,200
Martin Kaymer	72	75	74	70	291	41,200
John Senden	72	70	75	74	291	41,200
Rickie Fowler	68	76	70	78	292	32,000
Robert Garrigus	76	71	72	73	292	32,000
Brian Gay	72	74	74	72	292	32,000
Ryo Ishikawa	71	77	76	68	292	32,000
Paul Lawrie	76	70	75	71	292	32,000
Ryan Moore	71	72	81	68	292	32,000
D.A. Points	72	75	72	73	292	32,000
Vijay Singh	72	74	74	72	292	32,000
Thomas Bjorn	73	73	76	71	293	23,307
K.J. Choi	70	71	77	75	293	23,307
David Lynn	68	73	80	72	293	23,307

	SCORES				TOTAL	MONEY
Lucas Glover	74	74	73	73	294	20,800
Peter Hanson	72	75	76	72	295	19,480
Trevor Immelman	68	75	78	74	295	19,480
Jose Maria Olazabal	74	72	74	75	295	19,480
Bubba Watson	75	73	70	77	295	19,480
Keegan Bradley	73	73	82	69	297	18,320
Sandy Lyle	73	72	81	71	297	18,320
Phil Mickelson	71	76	77	73	297	18,320
Scott Piercy	75	69	78	75	297	18,320
*Tianlang Guan	73	75	77	75	300	
Kevin Na	70	76	74	81	301	17,920
John Peterson	71	77	74	80	302	17,760
Carl Pettersson	76	70	77	81	304	17,600

Out of Final 36 Holes

George Coetzee	75	74	149	T.J. Vogel	77	75	152
Jamie Donaldson	74	75	149	Michael Weaver	78	74	152
Martin Laird	76	73	149	Thaworn Wiratchant	79	73	152
Matteo Manassero	75	74	149	Padraig Harrington	78	75	153
Graeme McDowell	73	76	149	Russell Henley	72	81	153
Larry Mize	73	76	149	Kevin Streelman	76	77	153
Ted Potter, Jr.	76	73	149	Francesco Molinari	74	81	155
Webb Simpson	73	76	149	Nathan Smith	77	78	155
Y.E. Yang	72	77	149	Steven Fox	76	81	157
Louis Oosthuizen	74	76	150	Tom Watson	79	78	157
Nicolas Colsaerts	74	77	151	Hunter Mahan	76	82	158
Ben Curtis	76	75	151	Craig Stadler	79	79	158
John Merrick	74	77	151	Ian Woosnam	80	78	158
Mark O'Meara	74	77	151	Alan Dunbar	83	77	160
Ian Poulter	76	75	151	Ben Crenshaw	80	84	164
Mike Weir	72	79	151	Hiroyuki Fujita	79	85	164

(Professionals who did not complete 72 holes received $5,000.)

RBC Heritage

Harbour Town Golf Links, Hilton Head Island, South Carolina
Par 36-35–71; 7,101 yards

April 18-21
purse, $5,800,000

	SCORES				TOTAL	MONEY
Graeme McDowell	71	67	68	69	275	$1,044,000
Webb Simpson	68	71	65	71	275	626,400
(McDowell defeated Simpson on first playoff hole.)						
Luke Donald	69	68	71	69	277	336,400
Kevin Streelman	66	70	69	72	277	336,400
Jerry Kelly	69	72	66	71	278	232,000
Russell Henley	73	70	67	69	279	194,300
Charley Hoffman	66	70	66	77	279	194,300
Chris Stroud	70	70	69	70	279	194,300
Trevor Immelman	72	72	66	71	281	125,666.67
Richard Lee	68	71	69	73	281	125,666.67
Marc Leishman	67	71	71	72	281	125,666.67
Rory Sabbatini	69	69	72	71	281	125,666.67
Jordan Spieth	70	69	69	73	281	125,666.67
Mark Wilson	69	75	67	70	281	125,666.67
Brendon de Jonge	70	69	67	75	281	125,666.66
Billy Horschel	71	68	68	74	281	125,666.66
Camilo Villegas	68	71	68	74	281	125,666.66
K.J. Choi	70	71	71	70	282	73,080

	SCORES				TOTAL	MONEY
Ken Duke	70	70	71	71	282	73,080
Justin Hicks	69	70	68	75	282	73,080
Steve LeBrun	68	68	71	75	282	73,080
Pat Perez	68	70	70	74	282	73,080
Johnson Wagner	67	71	71	73	282	73,080
Stewart Cink	70	69	73	71	283	46,980
Tim Clark	68	71	68	76	283	46,980
Robert Garrigus	70	71	70	72	283	46,980
Bill Haas	68	69	70	76	283	46,980
Scott Langley	71	69	72	71	283	46,980
Darron Stiles	70	69	71	73	283	46,980
Brian Davis	65	75	70	74	284	36,018
Jason Day	67	73	71	73	284	36,018
Bob Estes	70	73	71	70	284	36,018
Matt Jones	75	67	68	74	284	36,018
Chris Kirk	73	69	70	72	284	36,018
Justin Bolli	68	72	75	70	285	27,384.29
Jason Dufner	71	69	75	70	285	27,384.29
Matt Kuchar	70	73	72	70	285	27,384.29
Carl Pettersson	68	75	72	70	285	27,384.29
Stuart Appleby	70	68	70	77	285	27,384.28
James Hahn	71	73	66	75	285	27,384.28
Ted Potter, Jr.	68	71	75	71	285	27,384.28
Aaron Baddeley	70	72	69	75	286	19,720
Will Claxton	68	73	69	76	286	19,720
Brad Fritsch	71	69	75	71	286	19,720
Jim Furyk	70	72	66	78	286	19,720
Kevin Stadler	72	71	68	75	286	19,720
Boo Weekley	71	73	70	72	286	19,720
Michael Bradley	73	71	70	73	287	14,417.15
Brandt Jobe	69	75	71	72	287	14,417.15
Sang-Moon Bae	70	71	71	75	287	14,417.14
Ben Crane	70	74	66	77	287	14,417.14
Ryo Ishikawa	68	72	67	80	287	14,417.14
Zach Johnson	72	72	68	75	287	14,417.14
Nicholas Thompson	70	71	70	76	287	14,417.14
Brian Gay	71	71	70	76	288	13,166
Justin Leonard	74	68	73	73	288	13,166
Cameron Percy	70	70	72	76	288	13,166
Chez Reavie	70	71	70	77	288	13,166
Brian Harman	71	73	69	76	289	12,644
Tim Herron	71	70	74	74	289	12,644
Greg Owen	75	69	70	75	289	12,644
Jin Park	73	68	71	77	289	12,644
Brandt Snedeker	73	71	71	74	289	12,644
Scott Brown	72	68	70	80	290	12,238
Ryan Palmer	72	72	69	77	290	12,238
Jason Bohn	72	72	71	78	293	11,890
Jonathan Byrd	71	70	73	79	293	11,890
Martin Kaymer	69	70	76	78	293	11,890
Jeff Maggert	71	72	70	80	293	11,890
Casey Wittenberg	75	69	70	80	294	11,600
Ricky Barnes	70	74	72		216	11,136
Tommy Gainey	70	73	73		216	11,136
Jeff Klauk	72	71	73		216	11,136
Jason Kokrak	76	68	72		216	11,136
Patrick Reed	71	72	73		216	11,136
Josh Teater	71	71	74		216	11,136
Bo Van Pelt	68	73	75		216	11,136
Jonas Blixt	73	70	74		217	10,440
Henrik Norlander	71	69	77		217	10,440
Jesper Parnevik	72	72	73		217	10,440
Lee Williams	69	72	76		217	10,440

	SCORES			TOTAL	MONEY
Gary Woodland	68	73	76	217	10,440
Glen Day	68	75	75	218	9,918
Matt Every	73	71	74	218	9,918
D.H. Lee	70	68	80	218	9,918
Troy Matteson	71	71	76	218	9,918
David Hearn	74	70	75	219	9,628
Nicolas Colsaerts	74	70	76	220	9,396
James Driscoll	74	70	76	220	9,396
William McGirt	70	70	80	220	9,396
Hunter Mahan	68	76	78	222	9,164

Zurich Classic of New Orleans

TPC Louisiana, Avondale, Louisiana
Par 36-36–72; 7,341 yards

April 25-28
purse, $6,600,000

	SCORES				TOTAL	MONEY
Billy Horschel	67	71	66	64	268	$1,188,000
D.A. Points	66	68	70	65	269	712,800
Kyle Stanley	72	67	65	67	271	448,800
Bobby Gates	67	70	70	66	273	290,400
Lucas Glover	65	67	70	71	273	290,400
Harris English	68	70	69	67	274	229,350
Boo Weekley	65	68	73	68	274	229,350
Nicolas Colsaerts	70	68	70	67	275	165,000
Luke Guthrie	67	71	69	68	275	165,000
D.H. Lee	70	70	68	67	275	165,000
John Peterson	71	67	70	67	275	165,000
Kevin Stadler	68	72	65	70	275	165,000
Jimmy Walker	67	71	66	71	275	165,000
Aaron Watkins	71	69	70	65	275	165,000
Ernie Els	67	69	72	68	276	102,300
Henrik Norlander	71	70	65	70	276	102,300
Justin Rose	68	69	70	69	276	102,300
Peter Tomasulo	73	67	68	68	276	102,300
Nick Watney	69	69	69	69	276	102,300
Bubba Watson	73	65	72	66	276	102,300
Ken Duke	70	69	68	70	277	58,740
Retief Goosen	71	70	68	68	277	58,740
David Hearn	71	69	68	69	277	58,740
Morgan Hoffmann	66	69	73	69	277	58,740
Brandt Jobe	70	70	69	68	277	58,740
Chris Kirk	67	72	69	69	277	58,740
Steve LeBrun	70	68	72	67	277	58,740
Richard Lee	70	69	69	69	277	58,740
Ken Looper	73	66	67	71	277	58,740
Joey Snyder	72	67	72	66	277	58,740
Luke List	71	70	68	69	278	42,900
Stephen Ames	67	72	69	71	279	33,528
Brian Davis	68	69	73	69	279	33,528
Matt Every	68	72	71	68	279	33,528
Rickie Fowler	67	73	71	68	279	33,528
Tommy Gainey	68	71	73	67	279	33,528
Fabian Gomez	71	70	68	70	279	33,528
Matt Jones	67	71	73	68	279	33,528
Doug LaBelle	70	67	73	69	279	33,528
Ryan Palmer	70	70	69	70	279	33,528
Brendan Steele	70	71	70	68	279	33,528
Ricky Barnes	64	76	66	74	280	23,100
Scott Brown	69	71	72	68	280	23,100

	SCORES				TOTAL	MONEY
Jason Dufner	70	71	67	72	280	23,100
Jeff Overton	73	68	69	70	280	23,100
Rod Pampling	71	70	67	72	280	23,100
Stuart Appleby	70	70	71	70	281	16,159
Jason Bohn	68	71	73	69	281	16,159
Roberto Castro	71	70	68	72	281	16,159
Graham DeLaet	68	71	74	68	281	16,159
Derek Ernst	73	67	70	71	281	16,159
Hunter Haas	72	69	70	70	281	16,159
Jerry Kelly	70	67	71	73	281	16,159
Michael Letzig	72	68	72	69	281	16,159
George McNeill	74	67	70	70	281	16,159
Sean O'Hair	70	70	70	71	281	16,159
Andrew Svoboda	70	70	69	72	281	16,159
David Toms	72	68	73	68	281	16,159
Chad Campbell	68	71	72	71	282	14,520
Chris DiMarco	68	70	75	69	282	14,520
Jason Kokrak	68	71	73	70	282	14,520
J.J. Henry	68	72	72	71	283	14,256
Jeff Maggert	70	67	73	74	284	14,124
Gary Woodland	68	70	73	74	285	13,992
Steven Bowditch	73	67	71	75	286	13,728
Greg Chalmers	70	71	71	74	286	13,728
Trevor Immelman	68	73	71	74	286	13,728
Lee Williams	70	71	73	73	287	13,464
Colt Knost	72	68	74	74	288	13,332
Jonas Blixt	71	69	74	75	289	13,200
*Guan Tianlang	72	69	77	74	292	

Wells Fargo Championship

Quail Hollow Club, Charlotte, North Carolina
Par 36-36–72; 7,442 yards

May 2-5
purse, $6,700,000

	SCORES				TOTAL	MONEY
Derek Ernst	67	71	72	70	280	$1,206,000
David Lynn	71	68	71	70	280	723,600
(Ernst defeated Lynn on first playoff hole.)						
Phil Mickelson	68	67	73	73	281	455,600
Robert Karlsson	69	72	69	72	282	294,800
Lee Westwood	70	68	72	72	282	294,800
Ryan Moore	67	75	68	73	283	216,912.50
Kyle Stanley	74	68	73	68	283	216,912.50
Kevin Streelman	68	72	71	72	283	216,912.50
Bo Van Pelt	74	70	68	71	283	216,912.50
Ross Fisher	70	71	73	70	284	148,516.67
Charles Howell	72	72	69	71	284	148,516.67
Rory McIlroy	67	71	73	73	284	148,516.67
Vaughn Taylor	70	72	71	71	284	148,516.67
Brian Harman	70	70	71	73	284	148,516.66
Nick Watney	67	70	71	76	284	148,516.66
Sergio Garcia	72	68	72	73	285	97,150
D.H. Lee	72	71	69	73	285	97,150
Luke List	71	75	71	68	285	97,150
George McNeill	69	68	72	76	285	97,150
Henrik Norlander	74	70	69	72	285	97,150
D.A. Points	71	69	71	74	285	97,150
Scott Gardiner	70	67	76	73	286	64,320
John Merrick	74	71	68	73	286	64,320
John Rollins	69	74	72	71	286	64,320

	SCORES				TOTAL	MONEY
John Senden	70	73	67	76	286	64,320
Jimmy Walker	71	72	73	70	286	64,320
Robert Allenby	76	70	71	70	287	47,570
Brian Davis	72	74	69	72	287	47,570
Robert Garrigus	67	72	75	73	287	47,570
Lucas Glover	68	71	73	75	287	47,570
Shawn Stefani	69	73	72	73	287	47,570
Jordan Spieth	69	71	75	73	288	37,073.34
Josh Teater	72	73	71	72	288	37,073.34
Pat Perez	76	69	72	71	288	37,073.33
Ted Potter, Jr.	71	70	75	72	288	37,073.33
Patrick Reed	70	74	73	71	288	37,073.33
Webb Simpson	70	74	71	73	288	37,073.33
Scott Brown	74	71	75	69	289	28,810
Bud Cauley	70	73	73	73	289	28,810
James Driscoll	70	72	73	74	289	28,810
Martin Flores	73	71	72	73	289	28,810
Geoff Ogilvy	74	72	71	72	289	28,810
Brendon de Jonge	74	71	72	73	290	20,904
David Hearn	69	72	75	74	290	20,904
Russell Henley	69	71	73	77	290	20,904
Richard Lee	73	70	72	75	290	20,904
Rod Pampling	69	69	74	78	290	20,904
Daniel Summerhays	67	73	75	75	290	20,904
Lee Williams	73	71	71	75	290	20,904
Stuart Appleby	71	71	75	74	291	15,828.75
Tommy Gainey	74	72	73	72	291	15,828.75
James Hahn	72	74	72	73	291	15,828.75
Ryo Ishikawa	73	73	71	74	291	15,828.75
Chris Kirk	72	71	72	76	291	15,828.75
Jason Kokrak	68	70	73	80	291	15,828.75
Nate Smith	67	74	77	73	291	15,828.75
Peter Tomasulo	71	73	72	75	291	15,828.75
Trevor Immelman	70	72	78	72	292	14,874
Dicky Pride	71	71	75	75	292	14,874
Boo Weekley	68	75	77	72	292	14,874
Steven Bowditch	69	76	73	75	293	14,405
Will Claxton	73	73	73	74	293	14,405
Steve Marino	71	72	73	77	293	14,405
Gary Woodland	70	73	74	76	293	14,405
Roberto Castro	71	73	74	76	294	13,936
Hunter Haas	75	71	73	75	294	13,936
Zach Johnson	68	72	77	77	294	13,936
Brad Fritsch	71	72	77	75	295	13,534
Matteo Manassero	71	75	73	76	295	13,534
Casey Wittenberg	73	71	74	77	295	13,534
Angel Cabrera	73	69	75	80	297	13,266
Luke Guthrie	74	69	75	84	302	13,132
Rickie Fowler	72	72	77		221	12,596
Matt Jones	73	73	75		221	12,596
Doug LaBelle	74	72	75		221	12,596
Hunter Mahan	73	72	76		221	12,596
Kevin Stadler	73	71	77		221	12,596
Kevin Sutherland	73	73	75		221	12,596
Mike Weir	72	73	76		221	12,596
Jonathan Byrd	72	73	77		222	11,926
Kevin Chappell	73	71	78		222	11,926
Chris Stroud	71	75	76		222	11,926
Justin Hicks	74	72	78		224	11,658

The Players Championship

TPC Sawgrass, Ponte Vedra Beach, Florida
Par 36-36–72; 7,215 yards

May 9-12
purse, $9,500,000

	SCORES				TOTAL	MONEY
Tiger Woods	67	67	71	70	275	$1,710,000
Kevin Streelman	69	70	71	67	277	709,333.34
David Lingmerth	68	68	69	72	277	709,333.33
Jeff Maggert	70	71	66	70	277	709,333.33
Martin Laird	71	67	73	67	278	346,750
Ryan Palmer	67	69	70	72	278	346,750
Henrik Stenson	68	67	71	72	278	346,750
Ben Crane	69	71	72	69	281	237,500
Sergio Garcia	68	65	72	76	281	237,500
Marc Leishman	72	66	71	72	281	237,500
Rory McIlroy	66	72	73	70	281	237,500
Brandt Snedeker	71	69	71	70	281	237,500
Lee Westwood	69	66	74	72	281	237,500
Casey Wittenberg	67	69	70	75	281	237,500
Brendon de Jonge	72	69	70	71	282	156,750
Tim Herron	71	69	74	68	282	156,750
Webb Simpson	67	71	74	70	282	156,750
Jimmy Walker	72	71	72	67	282	156,750
Jason Day	69	75	71	68	283	107,214.29
Luke Donald	72	69	73	69	283	107,214.29
Zach Johnson	66	71	76	70	283	107,214.29
Adam Scott	69	68	75	71	283	107,214.29
Roberto Castro	63	78	71	71	283	107,214.28
Hunter Mahan	67	70	71	75	283	107,214.28
Louis Oosthuizen	69	75	67	72	283	107,214.28
Graham DeLaet	71	70	74	69	284	67,450
James Driscoll	75	68	70	71	284	67,450
Matt Every	70	71	71	72	284	67,450
David Hearn	72	71	71	70	284	67,450
David Lynn	72	68	68	76	284	67,450
Jeff Overton	71	70	69	74	284	67,450
Daniel Summerhays	69	74	69	72	284	67,450
Sang-Moon Bae	68	71	75	71	285	52,487.50
Harris English	70	71	73	71	285	52,487.50
Kyle Stanley	75	68	68	74	285	52,487.50
Chris Stroud	73	69	69	74	285	52,487.50
Greg Chalmers	68	73	68	77	286	41,800
Charley Hoffman	70	74	71	71	286	41,800
Jerry Kelly	71	68	73	74	286	41,800
Andres Romero	69	72	71	74	286	41,800
Steve Stricker	67	71	72	76	286	41,800
Bubba Watson	73	70	70	73	286	41,800
Chad Campbell	71	72	74	70	287	31,350
Martin Kaymer	73	69	76	69	287	31,350
William McGirt	70	74	70	73	287	31,350
Sean O'Hair	70	71	69	77	287	31,350
John Senden	73	70	71	73	287	31,350
K.J. Choi	69	73	74	72	288	23,614.29
Freddie Jacobson	72	71	71	74	288	23,614.29
D.A. Points	72	70	77	69	288	23,614.29
Boo Weekley	71	71	73	73	288	23,614.29
Branden Grace	73	71	67	77	288	23,614.28
Matt Kuchar	71	66	75	76	288	23,614.28
Davis Love	70	72	70	76	288	23,614.28
Jason Bohn	68	74	75	72	289	21,280
Angel Cabrera	74	70	69	76	289	21,280
Chris Kirk	70	69	75	75	289	21,280

	SCORES				TOTAL	MONEY
Justin Leonard	70	74	74	71	289	21,280
Charl Schwartzel	72	71	75	71	289	21,280
Michael Thompson	69	75	72	73	289	21,280
Charlie Wi	74	70	75	70	289	21,280
Jason Dufner	71	67	72	80	290	20,235
James Hahn	70	74	73	73	290	20,235
Josh Teater	72	72	76	70	290	20,235
Bo Van Pelt	69	74	79	68	290	20,235
Charles Howell	71	67	77	76	291	19,665
Seung-Yul Noh	70	74	73	74	291	19,665
Kevin Chappell	69	66	78	79	292	19,190
John Huh	70	72	73	77	292	19,190
Carl Pettersson	70	72	75	75	292	19,190
Rory Sabbatini	75	68	76	74	293	18,810
Ricky Barnes	71	71	74	78	294	18,430
Brian Davis	78	66	75	75	294	18,430
Peter Hanson	70	70	72	82	294	18,430
Ben Curtis	69	72	80	74	295	17,955
Padraig Harrington	68	76	75	76	295	17,955
Jonas Blixt	69	75	77	76	297	17,670

HP Byron Nelson Championship

TPC Four Seasons Resort, Irving, Texas
Par 35-35–70; 7,166 yards

May 16-19
purse, $6,700,000

	SCORES				TOTAL	MONEY
Sang-Moon Bae	66	66	66	69	267	$1,206,000
Keegan Bradley	60	69	68	72	269	723,600
Charl Schwartzel	63	70	69	68	270	455,600
Justin Bolli	69	69	68	65	271	321,600
Morgan Hoffmann	69	71	66	66	272	244,550
Martin Kaymer	68	67	69	68	272	244,550
Scott Piercy	66	68	66	72	272	244,550
Charley Hoffman	68	68	70	67	273	201,000
John Huh	69	64	69	71	273	201,000
Graham DeLaet	67	67	70	70	274	174,200
Ryo Ishikawa	71	68	68	67	274	174,200
Ricky Barnes	68	71	70	66	275	131,320
Angel Cabrera	65	69	70	71	275	131,320
Tom Gillis	69	63	67	76	275	131,320
Marc Leishman	66	70	69	70	275	131,320
D.A. Points	69	68	67	71	275	131,320
Harris English	64	70	68	74	276	97,150
Charles Howell	67	69	70	70	276	97,150
Freddie Jacobson	68	69	70	69	276	97,150
Brendon Todd	69	68	72	67	276	97,150
Jason Bohn	71	68	69	69	277	67,000
Justin Hicks	69	70	68	70	277	67,000
Jerry Kelly	69	70	66	72	277	67,000
Colt Knost	68	70	71	68	277	67,000
Chez Reavie	69	67	71	70	277	67,000
John Rollins	74	64	70	69	277	67,000
Will Claxton	66	73	69	70	278	46,565
Jason Day	72	68	66	72	278	46,565
Brian Harman	68	69	70	71	278	46,565
Ted Potter, Jr.	64	70	70	74	278	46,565
Wes Short, Jr.	68	71	71	68	278	46,565
Jimmy Walker	68	68	70	72	278	46,565
Erik Compton	72	63	72	72	279	32,495

	SCORES				TOTAL	MONEY
James Driscoll	67	72	67	73	279	32,495
Jason Dufner	70	70	67	72	279	32,495
Nathan Green	67	68	68	76	279	32,495
Matt Kuchar	69	70	71	69	279	32,495
Jeff Overton	68	70	70	71	279	32,495
Ryan Palmer	65	68	73	73	279	32,495
Kenny Perry	71	69	69	70	279	32,495
Marcel Siem	68	68	68	75	279	32,495
Mike Weir	68	68	73	70	279	32,495
Charlie Beljan	70	69	72	69	280	22,110
Martin Flores	67	68	71	74	280	22,110
D.H. Lee	68	69	69	74	280	22,110
Justin Leonard	70	70	70	70	280	22,110
Rory Sabbatini	69	71	68	72	280	22,110
Stephen Ames	67	68	71	75	281	16,362.89
Matt Bettencourt	73	64	72	72	281	16,362.89
Padraig Harrington	70	70	71	70	281	16,362.89
Steve Marino	68	69	70	74	281	16,362.89
William McGirt	68	69	69	75	281	16,362.89
Joe Ogilvie	68	69	70	74	281	16,362.89
Camilo Villegas	65	70	71	75	281	16,362.89
Duffy Waldorf	68	67	73	73	281	16,362.89
Gary Woodland	69	65	68	79	281	16,362.88
Stuart Appleby	69	70	68	75	282	14,807
Ben Crane	67	69	73	73	282	14,807
Henrik Norlander	71	67	70	74	282	14,807
Cameron Percy	68	68	69	77	282	14,807
Tag Ridings	68	70	71	73	282	14,807
Andrew Svoboda	69	70	70	73	282	14,807
Gary Christian	69	69	70	75	283	14,204
Scott Langley	71	69	70	73	283	14,204
David Mathis	70	67	73	73	283	14,204
John Daly	71	66	70	77	284	13,869
Alexandre Rocha	67	68	75	74	284	13,869
Zack Fischer	73	65	71	76	285	13,601
Jordan Spieth	69	68	73	75	285	13,601
Seung-Yul Noh	68	71	72	78	289	13,400
Chad Campbell	67	72	73		212	12,797
Jesper Parnevik	70	70	72		212	12,797
Ted Purdy	70	70	72		212	12,797
Charlie Wi	73	67	72		212	12,797
Brad Fritsch	69	71	73		213	12,328
Pat Perez	70	69	74		213	12,328
Brian Stuard	71	69	73		213	12,328
Tim Herron	70	70	74		214	11,926
Greg Owen	70	70	74		214	11,926
Vijay Singh	71	67	76		214	11,926
Patrick Reed	67	73	76		216	11,658

Crowne Plaza Invitational

Colonial Country Club, Fort Worth, Texas
Par 35-35–70; 7,204 yards

May 23-26
purse, $6,400,000

	SCORES				TOTAL	MONEY
Boo Weekley	67	67	66	66	266	$1,152,000
Matt Kuchar	65	65	69	68	267	691,200
Zach Johnson	69	65	68	66	268	435,200
Scott Stallings	69	65	69	66	269	264,533.34
Matt Every	65	69	66	69	269	264,533.33

	SCORES				TOTAL	MONEY
John Rollins	63	71	67	68	269	264,533.33
Tim Clark	67	69	65	69	270	192,800
Jordan Spieth	65	67	71	67	270	192,800
Chris Stroud	67	66	67	70	270	192,800
Josh Teater	65	67	71	67	270	192,800
Jonas Blixt	67	68	67	69	271	147,200
John Huh	66	68	72	65	271	147,200
Chez Reavie	70	64	70	67	271	147,200
Bud Cauley	67	69	66	70	272	112,000
Franklin Corpening	68	70	72	62	272	112,000
Martin Flores	66	70	65	71	272	112,000
Ryan Palmer	62	72	71	67	272	112,000
Charley Hoffman	66	70	67	70	273	86,400
Jason Kokrak	66	71	68	68	273	86,400
David Lingmerth	72	64	72	65	273	86,400
Ted Potter, Jr.	70	66	68	69	273	86,400
Brendon de Jonge	66	70	68	70	274	64,000
Graham DeLaet	64	67	69	74	274	64,000
Steve Flesch	68	64	69	73	274	64,000
Brian Stuard	67	70	69	68	274	64,000
Hunter Mahan	69	68	68	70	275	47,360
John Merrick	68	70	71	66	275	47,360
John Peterson	64	71	71	69	275	47,360
Scott Piercy	69	69	70	67	275	47,360
Camilo Villegas	70	68	69	68	275	47,360
Angel Cabrera	70	67	70	69	276	38,800
Ken Duke	66	68	73	69	276	38,800
Jim Furyk	69	66	70	71	276	38,800
Bo Van Pelt	70	68	67	71	276	38,800
Brandt Jobe	68	68	75	66	277	30,217.15
Henrik Stenson	68	70	72	67	277	30,217.15
Freddie Jacobson	66	67	69	75	277	30,217.14
Chris Kirk	67	66	70	74	277	30,217.14
Richard Lee	70	68	69	70	277	30,217.14
Carl Pettersson	66	69	73	69	277	30,217.14
Daniel Summerhays	65	73	67	72	277	30,217.14
Brian Davis	67	68	70	73	278	23,040
Bob Estes	67	68	71	72	278	23,040
J.J. Henry	68	68	67	75	278	23,040
Shawn Stefani	69	70	68	71	278	23,040
Stuart Appleby	69	68	75	67	279	16,864
Roberto Castro	67	68	73	71	279	16,864
Jason Dufner	67	71	71	70	279	16,864
Derek Ernst	66	69	73	71	279	16,864
David Frost	69	70	71	69	279	16,864
Marc Leishman	66	68	72	73	279	16,864
Patrick Reed	70	69	67	73	279	16,864
Michael Thompson	67	72	69	71	279	16,864
Kevin Chappell	69	70	69	72	280	14,400
Rickie Fowler	69	69	70	72	280	14,400
Tommy Gainey	65	72	67	76	280	14,400
Martin Laird	70	69	72	69	280	14,400
Dicky Pride	69	70	70	71	280	14,400
Kyle Reifers	68	69	69	74	280	14,400
D.J. Trahan	67	70	73	70	280	14,400
Cameron Tringale	70	69	72	69	280	14,400
Justin Hicks	71	64	75	71	281	13,696
Ben Kohles	67	67	71	76	281	13,696
Seung-Yul Noh	69	69	69	74	281	13,696
Greg Chalmers	67	72	70	73	282	13,248
Luke Guthrie	71	68	69	74	282	13,248
Tim Herron	71	67	72	72	282	13,248
Bryce Molder	67	70	69	76	282	13,248

	SCORES				TOTAL	MONEY
Morgan Hoffmann	64	73	73	73	283	12,928
Ryo Ishikawa	69	69	74	72	284	12,672
Robert Karlsson	69	68	73	74	284	12,672
Vaughn Taylor	71	68	71	74	284	12,672
Erik Compton	68	71	72	74	285	12,288
Henrik Norlander	69	70	75	71	285	12,288
Charlie Wi	69	66	73	77	285	12,288
Sang-Moon Bae	69	70	70	77	286	11,968
Bobby Gates	69	70	70	77	286	11,968

Memorial Tournament

Muirfield Village Golf Club, Dublin, Ohio
Par 36-36–72; 7,265 yards

May 30-June 2
purse, $6,200,000

	SCORES				TOTAL	MONEY
Matt Kuchar	68	70	70	68	276	$1,116,000
Kevin Chappell	71	71	68	68	278	669,600
Kyle Stanley	67	70	73	71	281	421,600
Bill Haas	68	67	76	71	282	272,800
Scott Stallings	70	70	75	67	282	272,800
Russell Henley	67	77	70	69	283	215,450
Matt Jones	69	72	70	72	283	215,450
Brian Davis	75	70	69	70	284	167,400
Pat Perez	72	69	72	71	284	167,400
Justin Rose	70	70	71	73	284	167,400
Charl Schwartzel	65	71	76	72	284	167,400
Michael Thompson	69	76	70	69	284	167,400
James Driscoll	70	75	73	67	285	119,866.67
Ryan Moore	70	72	73	70	285	119,866.67
Adam Scott	73	70	69	73	285	119,866.66
Ken Duke	75	69	72	70	286	93,000
Hunter Mahan	73	68	75	70	286	93,000
Scott Piercy	66	75	71	74	286	93,000
Cameron Tringale	71	71	74	70	286	93,000
Gary Woodland	70	73	70	73	286	93,000
Roberto Castro	71	70	75	71	287	58,202.50
K.J. Choi	72	74	70	71	287	58,202.50
Graham DeLaet	70	72	74	71	287	58,202.50
Luke Donald	73	73	71	70	287	58,202.50
Jim Furyk	75	70	69	73	287	58,202.50
David Hearn	71	71	74	71	287	58,202.50
Charles Howell	72	70	73	72	287	58,202.50
Bo Van Pelt	73	69	72	73	287	58,202.50
Stewart Cink	70	72	76	70	288	40,300
J.J. Henry	72	72	68	76	288	40,300
Davis Love	73	69	72	74	288	40,300
Carl Pettersson	71	71	73	73	288	40,300
Bubba Watson	71	67	75	75	288	40,300
Bud Cauley	71	73	76	69	289	33,480
Robert Karlsson	69	71	76	73	289	33,480
Justin Leonard	70	76	73	70	289	33,480
Ernie Els	73	70	74	73	290	28,520
Rickie Fowler	72	71	76	71	290	28,520
Trevor Immelman	70	72	74	74	290	28,520
William McGirt	73	73	71	73	290	28,520
Ben Curtis	73	70	73	75	291	20,556.45
Richard Lee	73	71	72	75	291	20,556.45
George McNeill	74	71	71	75	291	20,556.45
Henrik Stenson	71	73	75	72	291	20,556.45

	SCORES				TOTAL	MONEY
Jason Day	72	75	72	72	291	20,556.44
Billy Horschel	70	75	76	70	291	20,556.44
Brandt Jobe	70	75	78	68	291	20,556.44
Marc Leishman	74	72	77	68	291	20,556.44
Camilo Villegas	72	71	76	72	291	20,556.44
Keegan Bradley	71	74	75	72	292	15,252
Fred Couples	70	75	70	77	292	15,252
Luke Guthrie	72	74	72	74	292	15,252
Robert Allenby	74	73	72	74	293	14,353
Martin Laird	71	75	71	76	293	14,353
Chris Stroud	69	77	69	78	293	14,353
Mike Weir	75	72	75	71	293	14,353
Derek Ernst	70	73	78	73	294	13,702
Ryo Ishikawa	74	73	74	73	294	13,702
David Lingmerth	75	70	72	77	294	13,702
Rory McIlroy	78	69	75	72	294	13,702
John Senden	71	72	76	75	294	13,702
Josh Teater	67	79	75	73	294	13,702
Charley Hoffman	73	69	72	81	295	13,206
Jordan Spieth	72	73	82	68	295	13,206
George Coetzee	70	75	72	79	296	12,896
Charlie Wi	67	74	77	78	296	12,896
Tiger Woods	71	74	79	72	296	12,896
Gonzalo Fernandez-Castano	72	74	77	74	297	12,648
Tom Gillis	73	70	75	81	299	12,462
Fabian Gomez	76	68	77	78	299	12,462
Zach Johnson	73	72	81	75	301	12,276
Justin Hicks	73	73	81	76	303	12,152
Jimmy Walker	72	75	77	80	304	12,028

FedEx St. Jude Classic

TPC Southwind, Memphis, Tennessee
Par 35-35–70; 7,244 yards

June 6-9
purse, $5,700,000

	SCORES				TOTAL	MONEY
Harris English	66	64	69	69	268	$1,026,000
Phil Mickelson	71	67	65	67	270	501,600
Scott Stallings	67	68	67	68	270	501,600
Ryan Palmer	72	67	65	67	271	273,600
Patrick Reed	69	69	64	70	272	228,000
John Rollins	67	71	67	68	273	205,200
Justin Hicks	67	69	69	69	274	177,650
Rory Sabbatini	69	69	68	68	274	177,650
Shawn Stefani	67	65	66	76	274	177,650
Robert Allenby	71	70	67	67	275	118,275
Jonathan Byrd	70	69	66	70	275	118,275
Glen Day	66	70	70	69	275	118,275
Padraig Harrington	69	70	65	71	275	118,275
Billy Horschel	71	69	68	67	275	118,275
Dustin Johnson	67	70	68	70	275	118,275
Nick O'Hern	68	71	67	69	275	118,275
Camilo Villegas	69	68	69	69	275	118,275
Jason Bohn	67	70	71	68	276	64,600
Roberto Castro	68	69	67	72	276	64,600
Ben Crane	69	68	68	71	276	64,600
David Hearn	69	71	67	69	276	64,600
Doug LaBelle	70	66	70	70	276	64,600
Davis Love	66	70	71	69	276	64,600
Brendon Todd	69	71	66	70	276	64,600

	SCORES				TOTAL	MONEY
Mark Wilson	70	71	66	69	276	64,600
Gary Woodland	69	72	71	64	276	64,600
Russell Henley	68	73	70	66	277	37,940.63
Chez Reavie	69	68	69	71	277	37,940.63
Tag Ridings	70	71	67	69	277	37,940.63
Boo Weekley	68	69	70	70	277	37,940.63
Brandt Jobe	69	71	66	71	277	37,940.62
Billy Mayfair	68	70	68	71	277	37,940.62
Kevin Stadler	69	70	67	71	277	37,940.62
Nicholas Thompson	67	69	66	75	277	37,940.62
Brian Davis	69	71	69	69	278	28,713.75
Paul Haley	67	68	70	73	278	28,713.75
Peter Hanson	67	71	68	72	278	28,713.75
Eric Meierdierks	68	69	66	75	278	28,713.75
Stuart Appleby	66	71	72	70	279	21,660
Scott Brown	69	69	70	71	279	21,660
Brendon de Jonge	70	69	68	72	279	21,660
Brian Gay	70	71	71	67	279	21,660
Charles Howell	71	67	68	73	279	21,660
Robert Karlsson	69	69	70	71	279	21,660
Justin Leonard	69	71	66	73	279	21,660
Robert Streb	72	67	72	68	279	21,660
Joe Affrunti	68	71	70	71	280	15,333
Martin Flores	66	72	68	74	280	15,333
Jim Herman	69	69	68	74	280	15,333
Scott Verplank	74	66	69	71	280	15,333
Tom Gillis	72	69	69	71	281	13,497.60
Luke Guthrie	70	67	73	71	281	13,497.60
J.J. Henry	69	72	69	71	281	13,497.60
Ian Poulter	69	68	68	76	281	13,497.60
Cameron Tringale	71	70	70	70	281	13,497.60
Stephen Ames	70	68	73	71	282	12,654
George Coetzee	71	67	75	69	282	12,654
Steve Flesch	69	72	69	72	282	12,654
Brad Fritsch	68	73	68	73	282	12,654
Jerry Kelly	69	71	68	74	282	12,654
Tim Petrovic	67	72	72	71	282	12,654
David Toms	67	71	70	74	282	12,654
Bob Estes	68	69	69	77	283	12,084
Ben Kohles	71	70	72	70	283	12,084
John Merrick	69	71	66	77	283	12,084
Arjun Atwal	71	68	73	72	284	11,628
Nathan Green	66	75	74	69	284	11,628
Jeff Maggert	69	71	72	72	284	11,628
Vaughn Taylor	72	67	68	77	284	11,628
D.J. Trahan	69	69	75	71	284	11,628
Andres Gonzales	71	68	72	74	285	11,172
Kevin Sutherland	70	71	73	71	285	11,172
Lee Williams	72	69	72	72	285	11,172
Russell Knox	70	68	76	72	286	10,944
Chad Campbell	70	71	73	73	287	10,773
Jeff Overton	69	72	71	75	287	10,773
John Daly	71	69	76	74	290	10,602

U.S. Open Championship

Merion Golf Club, Ardmore, Pennsylvania
Par 36-34–70; 6,996 yards

June 13-16
purse, $8,000,000

	SCORES				TOTAL	MONEY
Justin Rose	71	69	71	70	281	$1,440,000
Jason Day	70	74	68	71	283	696,104
Phil Mickelson	67	72	70	74	283	696,104
Jason Dufner	74	71	73	67	285	291,406
Ernie Els	71	72	73	69	285	291,406
Billy Horschel	72	67	72	74	285	291,406
Hunter Mahan	72	69	69	75	285	291,406
Luke Donald	68	72	71	75	286	210,006
Steve Stricker	71	69	70	76	286	210,006
Hideki Matsuyama	71	75	74	67	287	168,530
Nicolas Colsaerts	69	72	74	72	287	168,530
Gonzalo Fernandez-Castano	71	72	72	72	287	168,530
Rickie Fowler	70	76	67	74	287	168,530
Charl Schwartzel	70	71	69	78	288	144,444
Lee Westwood	70	77	69	73	289	132,453
John Senden	70	71	74	74	289	132,453
John Huh	71	73	75	71	290	115,591
Brandt Snedeker	74	74	70	72	290	115,591
David Lingmerth	74	71	71	74	290	115,591
*Michael Kim	73	70	71	76	290	
Martin Laird	74	73	76	68	291	86,579
David Hearn	78	69	73	71	291	86,579
Padraig Harrington	73	71	75	72	291	86,579
Mathew Goggin	68	74	76	73	291	86,579
Bo Van Pelt	73	71	72	75	291	86,579
Ian Poulter	71	71	73	76	291	86,579
Henrik Stenson	74	68	73	76	291	86,579
Mike Weir	72	76	75	69	292	60,183
John Parry	76	71	72	73	292	60,183
Matt Kuchar	74	73	72	73	292	60,183
Morten Orum Madsen	74	74	70	74	292	60,183
Kevin Chappell	72	76	74	71	293	47,246
Geoff Ogilvy	74	70	77	72	293	47,246
Webb Simpson	71	75	75	72	293	47,246
K.J. Choi	70	76	75	72	293	47,246
Tiger Woods	73	70	76	74	293	47,246
Jamie Donaldson	73	73	73	74	293	47,246
Edward Loar	73	71	73	76	293	47,246
Bubba Watson	71	76	70	76	293	47,246
Paul Lawrie	76	71	69	77	293	47,246
Carl Pettersson	72	75	74	73	294	37,324
Scott Langley	75	70	75	74	294	37,324
Rory McIlroy	73	70	75	76	294	37,324
Jerry Kelly	70	73	75	76	294	37,324
Steven Alker	73	75	75	72	295	28,961
Russell Knox	69	75	77	74	295	28,961
Sergio Garcia	73	73	75	74	295	28,961
Bio Kim	72	75	73	75	295	28,961
Adam Scott	72	75	73	75	295	28,961
*Cheng-Tsung Pan	72	72	75	76	295	
Charley Hoffman	71	73	72	79	295	28,961
Paul Casey	73	72	71	79	295	28,961
Scott Stallings	71	76	76	73	296	23,446
Matt Bettencourt	72	71	76	77	296	23,446
Dustin Johnson	71	77	75	74	297	22,561
Nicholas Thompson	72	76	74	76	298	21,485
Josh Teater	74	74	74	76	298	21,485

	SCORES				TOTAL	MONEY
George Coetzee	71	73	77	77	298	21,485
Shawn Stefani	72	73	85	69	299	20,111
Martin Kaymer	76	72	77	74	299	20,111
Marcel Siem	73	71	77	78	299	20,111
*Kevin Phelan	71	77	78	74	300	
Matt Weibring	75	73	76	76	300	19,406
*Michael Weaver	74	74	78	75	301	
Peter Hedblom	70	78	79	75	302	18,926
David Howell	77	71	77	77	302	18,926
Kevin Sutherland	73	74	84	72	303	17,965
John Peterson	73	75	78	77	303	17,965
Jim Herman	76	72	76	79	303	17,965
Alistair Presnell	73	75	76	79	303	17,965
Robert Karlsson	74	72	86	73	305	17,165
Simon Khan	74	74	82	76	306	16,844
Kyle Stanley	71	74	85	78	308	16,523

Out of Final 36 Holes

Player				Player			
Zach Johnson	74	77	151	Eddie Pepperell	77	77	154
D.A. Points	77	74	151	Jesse Smith	73	81	154
Sang-Moon Bae	77	74	151	Jay Don Blake	74	80	154
*Gavin Hall	74	77	151	Michael Campbell	76	78	154
*Max Homa	73	78	151	Brandt Jobe	74	80	154
Nick Watney	73	78	151	Ryan Palmer	75	79	154
Bill Haas	77	74	151	Darren Clarke	80	75	155
Boo Weekley	75	76	151	Angel Cabrera	74	81	155
Andrew Svoboda	81	70	151	Rikard Karlberg	78	77	155
Ryan Nelson	73	78	151	Wil Collins	76	79	155
Brendan Steele	76	76	152	Harold Varner	76	79	155
David Toms	75	77	152	Jose Maria Olazabal	75	81	156
Marcus Fraser	79	73	152	Jim Furyk	77	79	156
Francesco Molinari	78	74	152	Joe Ogilvie	75	81	156
Luke Guthrie	73	79	152	Lucas Glover	74	82	156
Brandon Brown	75	77	152	Ryan Moore	79	77	156
Keegan Bradley	77	75	152	Russell Henley	77	80	157
Y.E. Yang	77	75	152	Adam Hadwin	81	76	157
Marc Leishman	78	75	153	Thorbjorn Olesen	79	79	158
Graeme McDowell	76	77	153	Yoshinobu Tsukada	78	80	158
Thongchai Jaidee	79	74	153	Zack Fischer	82	76	158
Branden Grace	70	83	153	Matt Harmon	78	81	159
Jordan Spieth	77	76	153	Brandon Crick	81	78	159
Jung-Gon Hwang	75	78	153	Roger Tambellini	80	80	160
Ryan Yip	76	77	153	*Cory McElyea	81	79	160
Mackenzie Hughes	75	78	153	Yui Ueda	78	83	161
Geoffrey Sisk	78	75	153	John Nieporte	78	84	162
Randall Hutchison	74	79	153	Ryan Sullivan	81	82	163
John Hahn	75	78	153	*Grayson Murray	83	81	164
Estanislao Goya	71	83	154	Louis Oosthuizen	75		WD
Scott Piercy	78	76	154	Robert Garrigus	80		WD

(Professionals who did not complete 72 holes received $2,000.)

Travelers Championship

TPC River Highlands, Cromwell, Connecticut
Par 35-35–70; 6,844 yards

June 20-23
purse, $6,100,000

	SCORES				TOTAL	MONEY
Ken Duke	69	68	65	66	268	$1,098,000
Chris Stroud	66	69	66	67	268	658,800
(Duke defeated Stroud on second playoff hole.)						
Graham DeLaet	65	70	65	69	269	414,800
Bubba Watson	63	67	70	70	270	292,800
J.J. Henry	68	67	68	68	271	231,800
Webb Simpson	65	69	72	65	271	231,800
Charley Hoffman	61	73	66	72	272	196,725
Ryan Moore	68	70	66	68	272	196,725
Stuart Appleby	69	67	69	68	273	158,600
Angel Cabrera	67	72	71	63	273	158,600
Morgan Hoffmann	68	71	66	68	273	158,600
Jeff Maggert	70	70	65	68	273	158,600
Ricky Barnes	67	68	71	68	274	111,020
Rickie Fowler	72	68	70	64	274	111,020
Russell Knox	69	67	69	69	274	111,020
Justin Rose	67	68	68	71	274	111,020
Brendan Steele	68	68	72	66	274	111,020
Keegan Bradley	69	65	72	69	275	76,860
Tommy Gainey	66	67	70	72	275	76,860
Jim Herman	69	67	67	72	275	76,860
Nick O'Hern	67	66	68	74	275	76,860
Patrick Reed	66	66	73	70	275	76,860
Kevin Sutherland	69	70	68	68	275	76,860
Gary Christian	71	69	70	66	276	49,410
Jerry Kelly	67	68	71	70	276	49,410
Hunter Mahan	62	71	70	73	276	49,410
Greg Owen	70	69	69	68	276	49,410
Andres Romero	71	68	67	70	276	49,410
Nicholas Thompson	71	66	66	73	276	49,410
Erik Compton	72	66	71	68	277	32,584.17
Freddie Jacobson	69	70	70	68	277	32,584.17
William McGirt	67	68	73	69	277	32,584.17
John Merrick	65	71	71	70	277	32,584.17
Bryce Molder	67	70	73	67	277	32,584.17
Cameron Percy	71	68	71	67	277	32,584.17
Aaron Watkins	69	69	70	69	277	32,584.17
Chris Williams	71	68	69	69	277	32,584.17
Brian Davis	72	67	66	72	277	32,584.16
Richard Lee	66	71	66	74	277	32,584.16
Marc Leishman	66	70	68	73	277	32,584.16
D.J. Trahan	71	68	68	70	277	32,584.16
*Justin Thomas	72	66	66	73	277	
Jonas Blixt	70	67	73	68	278	19,626.75
K.J. Choi	70	68	70	70	278	19,626.75
Harris English	72	67	69	70	278	19,626.75
Ian Poulter	73	66	67	72	278	19,626.75
Chez Reavie	71	69	70	68	278	19,626.75
Tag Ridings	68	65	71	74	278	19,626.75
Vijay Singh	70	68	69	71	278	19,626.75
Bo Van Pelt	67	70	72	69	278	19,626.75
Brad Fritsch	70	69	70	70	279	14,500.57
Brian Gay	68	69	71	71	279	14,500.57
Tom Gillis	69	69	71	70	279	14,500.57
Brian Harman	69	69	69	72	279	14,500.57
D.H. Lee	72	68	70	69	279	14,500.57
Kevin Stadler	68	67	73	71	279	14,500.57

	SCORES				TOTAL	MONEY
Camilo Villegas	65	70	75	69	279	14,500.57
Tim Clark	73	67	66	74	280	13,542
Zach Johnson	65	70	75	70	280	13,542
Chris Kirk	66	72	69	73	280	13,542
Seung-Yul Noh	68	68	72	72	280	13,542
Robert Streb	67	70	70	73	280	13,542
Brendon de Jonge	67	67	75	72	281	12,871
David Mathis	67	71	72	71	281	12,871
Tim Petrovic	69	70	70	72	281	12,871
Dicky Pride	67	71	72	71	281	12,871
Heath Slocum	71	69	70	71	281	12,871
Mark Wilson	70	69	71	71	281	12,871
David Branshaw	67	71	72	72	282	12,444
Chad Campbell	70	69	70	74	283	12,261
Rod Pampling	65	74	71	73	283	12,261
Padraig Harrington	66	66	72	80	284	12,017
Casey Wittenberg	68	69	71	76	284	12,017
Lee Westwood	67	73	69	78	287	11,834
Ben Crane	68	72	71		211	11,651
George McNeill	69	67	75		211	11,651
Joe Affrunti	71	69	72		212	11,407
Stephen Ames	70	69	73		212	11,407
John Huh	66	69	78		213	11,163
John Rollins	67	68	78		213	11,163
Stewart Cink	67	73	74		214	10,919
Billy Mayfair	69	71	74		214	10,919
Henrik Norlander	75	65	75		215	10,736

AT&T National

Congressional Country Club, Bethesda, Maryland
Par 36-35–71; 7,569 yards

June 27-30
purse, $6,500,000

	SCORES				TOTAL	MONEY
Bill Haas	70	68	68	66	272	$1,170,000
Roberto Castro	66	69	71	69	275	702,000
Jason Kokrak	71	66	70	69	276	377,000
D.H. Lee	71	66	75	64	276	377,000
Stewart Cink	70	69	71	67	277	260,000
Jordan Spieth	69	66	74	69	278	234,000
Charlie Wi	72	71	65	71	279	217,750
Brian Davis	70	72	71	67	280	175,500
Graham DeLaet	68	72	71	69	280	175,500
James Driscoll	69	69	68	74	280	175,500
Morgan Hoffmann	73	68	69	70	280	175,500
Brandt Snedeker	69	71	69	71	280	175,500
Angel Cabrera	70	70	72	69	281	125,666.67
Brendon Todd	74	67	68	72	281	125,666.67
Andres Romero	70	66	70	75	281	125,666.66
Chad Campbell	72	70	69	71	282	97,500
Richard Lee	74	68	71	69	282	97,500
Brendan Steele	73	71	66	72	282	97,500
Camilo Villegas	71	70	71	70	282	97,500
Gary Woodland	70	69	72	71	282	97,500
Jason Day	70	73	71	69	283	62,864.29
Martin Flores	73	71	68	71	283	62,864.29
Luke Guthrie	71	74	69	69	283	62,864.29
Chez Reavie	71	71	73	68	283	62,864.29
Nicolas Colsaerts	69	68	73	73	283	62,864.28
Rickie Fowler	71	71	70	71	283	62,864.28

	SCORES				TOTAL	MONEY
Fabian Gomez	69	73	69	72	283	62,864.28
Ricky Barnes	72	71	72	69	284	43,225
Kevin Chappell	70	72	73	69	284	43,225
Charley Hoffman	74	71	70	69	284	43,225
John Huh	71	71	71	71	284	43,225
Chris Stroud	70	74	71	69	284	43,225
Nicholas Thompson	73	69	71	71	284	43,225
Harris English	74	71	71	69	285	30,095
Bob Estes	73	71	70	71	285	30,095
Tom Gillis	70	72	66	77	285	30,095
Russell Henley	69	70	75	71	285	30,095
Ryan Palmer	73	71	72	69	285	30,095
Ted Potter, Jr.	72	70	72	71	285	30,095
Patrick Reed	76	64	74	71	285	30,095
John Rollins	73	72	72	68	285	30,095
Vijay Singh	70	75	69	71	285	30,095
Shawn Stefani	70	74	68	73	285	30,095
Jason Bohn	73	70	71	72	286	18,785
Derek Ernst	73	72	71	70	286	18,785
Jim Furyk	69	74	74	69	286	18,785
David Hearn	73	68	74	71	286	18,785
Steve LeBrun	71	72	72	71	286	18,785
David Mathis	71	70	72	73	286	18,785
George McNeill	71	69	75	71	286	18,785
Cameron Tringale	71	67	75	73	286	18,785
Ken Duke	71	70	70	76	287	15,470
Troy Matteson	72	68	77	70	287	15,470
Erik Compton	73	72	71	72	288	14,950
Martin Laird	71	73	72	72	288	14,950
David Lingmerth	74	65	73	76	288	14,950
Lucas Glover	72	70	74	73	289	14,560
Dicky Pride	72	73	73	71	289	14,560
Adam Scott	73	71	69	76	289	14,560
Brandt Jobe	71	73	72	74	290	14,300
Billy Horschel	68	72	79	72	291	14,040
Bryce Molder	72	71	77	71	291	14,040
Nick Watney	70	75	72	74	291	14,040
Bud Cauley	68	72	80	72	292	13,325
Brad Fritsch	72	72	74	74	292	13,325
Robert Garrigus	72	71	73	76	292	13,325
Matt Jones	72	72	71	77	292	13,325
Sean O'Hair	73	72	71	76	292	13,325
Joe Ogilvie	76	69	73	74	292	13,325
Brian Stuard	74	69	73	76	292	13,325
Y.E. Yang	74	71	70	77	292	13,325
Tommy Gainey	73	71	75	74	293	12,545
Ben Kohles	69	71	79	74	293	12,545
Henrik Norlander	72	72	74	75	293	12,545
John Senden	71	73	76	73	293	12,545
Pat Perez	73	72	77	72	294	12,220
Doug LaBelle	73	71	75	77	296	12,090

Greenbrier Classic

The Old White TPC, White Sulphur Springs, West Virginia
Par 34-36–70; 7,287 yards

July 4-7
purse, $6,300,000

	SCORES				TOTAL	MONEY
Jonas Blixt	66	67	67	67	267	$1,134,000
Steven Bowditch	65	67	69	68	269	415,800

	SCORES				TOTAL	MONEY
Matt Jones	69	66	66	68	269	415,800
Johnson Wagner	62	70	64	73	269	415,800
Jimmy Walker	69	65	64	71	269	415,800
Pat Perez	71	65	66	69	271	211,050
Ted Potter, Jr.	69	66	69	67	271	211,050
Brian Stuard	71	66	67	67	271	211,050
Bill Haas	68	67	67	70	272	140,962.50
D.H. Lee	66	68	68	70	272	140,962.50
David Lingmerth	71	66	67	68	272	140,962.50
Davis Love	67	70	68	67	272	140,962.50
Tim Petrovic	69	68	67	68	272	140,962.50
Tag Ridings	65	69	68	70	272	140,962.50
Rory Sabbatini	70	65	67	70	272	140,962.50
Daniel Summerhays	65	67	73	67	272	140,962.50
Ben Curtis	67	66	71	69	273	85,260
Brendon de Jonge	66	68	73	66	273	85,260
Bill Lunde	66	66	71	70	273	85,260
George McNeill	66	71	68	68	273	85,260
Bryce Molder	71	67	66	69	273	85,260
Louis Oosthuizen	67	68	69	69	273	85,260
K.J. Choi	71	67	68	68	274	53,100
Morgan Hoffmann	69	67	67	71	274	53,100
Greg Owen	67	66	72	69	274	53,100
Jordan Spieth	67	67	67	73	274	53,100
Scott Stallings	70	67	67	70	274	53,100
Cameron Tringale	73	66	67	68	274	53,100
Nick Watney	72	67	65	70	274	53,100
Brian Davis	67	68	70	70	275	36,618.75
Graham DeLaet	69	70	66	70	275	36,618.75
Russell Henley	67	65	72	71	275	36,618.75
Jim Herman	72	67	71	65	275	36,618.75
Billy Horschel	69	70	67	69	275	36,618.75
Cameron Percy	71	68	65	71	275	36,618.75
John Senden	70	68	69	68	275	36,618.75
Bubba Watson	68	69	69	69	275	36,618.75
Matt Every	69	62	74	71	276	28,980
Tom Watson	68	69	72	67	276	28,980
*Michael Kim	70	69	67	70	276	
Robert Streb	69	70	70	68	277	20,121.24
Chad Campbell	69	66	72	70	277	20,121.23
Kevin Chappell	67	68	71	71	277	20,121.23
Brad Fritsch	68	71	66	72	277	20,121.23
Tommy Gainey	62	71	69	75	277	20,121.23
James Hahn	72	67	68	70	277	20,121.23
Jason Kokrak	66	71	68	72	277	20,121.23
Richard Lee	68	70	70	69	277	20,121.23
Troy Matteson	69	70	66	72	277	20,121.23
Kenny Perry	68	67	73	69	277	20,121.23
Andres Romero	68	71	69	69	277	20,121.23
Webb Simpson	64	73	70	70	277	20,121.23
Brendan Steele	66	70	72	69	277	20,121.23
James Driscoll	66	68	71	73	278	14,515.20
Martin Flores	71	65	74	68	278	14,515.20
Andres Gonzales	71	68	70	69	278	14,515.20
D.A. Points	70	65	73	70	278	14,515.20
Charlie Wi	73	65	67	73	278	14,515.20
Luke List	71	67	69	72	279	13,986
Jeff Overton	68	68	72	71	279	13,986
Shawn Stefani	70	69	70	70	279	13,986
Ryan Palmer	68	71	70	71	280	13,608
Chez Reavie	70	69	68	73	280	13,608
Gary Woodland	69	70	64	77	280	13,608
Tom Gillis	67	71	71	72	281	13,230

	SCORES				TOTAL	MONEY
Brian Harman	68	70	70	73	281	13,230
Jin Park	64	73	71	73	281	13,230
Carl Pettersson	69	70	70	73	282	12,978
William McGirt	69	70	71	73	283	12,852
Justin Leonard	68	70	67	82	287	12,726
Scott Brown	66	72	73		211	12,285
Alistair Presnell	68	69	74		211	12,285
Dicky Pride	72	66	73		211	12,285
D.J. Trahan	70	69	72		211	12,285
Neal Lancaster	65	71	76		212	11,970
Gary Christian	71	67	75		213	11,718
Ben Crane	66	70	77		213	11,718
Fabian Gomez	70	69	74		213	11,718
Erik Compton	69	67	79		215	11,466
Brad Adamonis	68	71	77		216	11,340

John Deere Classic

TPC Deere Run, Silvis, Illinois
Par 35-36–71; 7,257 yards

July 11-14
purse, $4,600,000

	SCORES				TOTAL	MONEY
Jordan Spieth	70	65	65	65	265	$828,000
David Hearn	66	66	64	69	265	404,800
Zach Johnson	64	66	67	68	265	404,800
(Spieth defeated Hearn and Johnson on fifth playoff hole.)						
Martin Flores	67	67	69	63	266	190,133.34
Jerry Kelly	68	64	66	68	266	190,133.33
Daniel Summerhays	65	67	62	72	266	190,133.33
Matt Jones	66	65	68	68	267	143,366.67
Patrick Reed	67	63	70	67	267	143,366.67
J.J. Henry	68	65	65	69	267	143,366.66
Jim Herman	66	68	67	67	268	119,600
Steve Stricker	67	66	69	66	268	119,600
Steven Bowditch	69	68	67	65	269	96,600
Kevin Sutherland	70	65	65	69	269	96,600
Nicholas Thompson	69	66	64	70	269	96,600
Chad Campbell	69	67	66	68	270	71,300
Harris English	69	69	65	67	270	71,300
Lucas Glover	68	62	71	69	270	71,300
Morgan Hoffmann	74	64	63	69	270	71,300
Steve LeBrun	67	67	72	64	270	71,300
Chez Reavie	72	61	69	68	270	71,300
*Patrick Rodgers	67	69	65	69	270	
Jason Bohn	69	69	64	69	271	47,840
Scott Brown	71	67	65	68	271	47,840
Chris Kirk	67	66	66	72	271	47,840
Ryan Moore	67	70	65	69	271	47,840
Robert Streb	66	72	65	68	271	47,840
Troy Matteson	68	64	69	71	272	33,350
Bryce Molder	70	66	70	66	272	33,350
Kevin Stadler	70	68	66	68	272	33,350
Nick Watney	67	70	69	66	272	33,350
Boo Weekley	66	69	71	66	272	33,350
Mike Weir	69	69	67	67	272	33,350
Joe Affrunti	69	67	69	68	273	22,874.55
Stuart Appleby	70	68	68	67	273	22,874.55
Jonathan Byrd	69	68	67	69	273	22,874.55
K.J. Choi	67	70	68	68	273	22,874.55
Charles Howell	68	66	71	68	273	22,874.55

	SCORES				TOTAL	MONEY
Lee Williams	67	68	73	65	273	22,874.55
Brian Davis	70	68	66	69	273	22,874.54
Justin Hicks	71	66	66	70	273	22,874.54
Ryo Ishikawa	68	69	66	70	273	22,874.54
Scott Langley	68	67	67	71	273	22,874.54
Joey Snyder	72	64	67	70	273	22,874.54
Erik Compton	72	66	64	72	274	15,640
Andres Romero	71	67	69	67	274	15,640
Heath Slocum	71	67	66	70	274	15,640
Kevin Streelman	66	66	71	71	274	15,640
Ken Duke	69	67	72	67	275	12,162.40
John Kimbell	69	69	66	71	275	12,162.40
Dicky Pride	68	69	68	70	275	12,162.40
Vaughn Taylor	66	71	69	69	275	12,162.40
Gary Woodland	69	68	69	69	275	12,162.40
Y.E. Yang	70	66	69	71	276	11,040
Brendon de Jonge	65	68	74	70	277	10,501.15
David Mathis	70	66	71	70	277	10,501.15
Tom Gillis	67	68	72	70	277	10,501.14
Brandt Jobe	69	67	70	71	277	10,501.14
Rod Pampling	69	69	68	71	277	10,501.14
Tim Petrovic	70	68	69	70	277	10,501.14
Carl Pettersson	70	67	70	70	277	10,501.14
Matt Bettencourt	65	73	70	70	278	9,844
Keegan Bradley	69	69	70	70	278	9,844
Brian Gay	68	69	70	71	278	9,844
Doug LaBelle	69	69	71	69	278	9,844
Michael Letzig	68	69	69	72	278	9,844
Greg Owen	71	67	71	69	278	9,844
Andrew Svoboda	68	69	68	73	278	9,844
Roberto Castro	68	68	72	72	280	9,384
Nick O'Hern	69	69	73	69	280	9,384
Darron Stiles	71	67	72	70	280	9,384
Camilo Villegas	64	73	73	71	281	9,200
Davis Love	67	71	73	73	284	9,108

The Open Championship

See European Tours chapter.

Sanderson Farms Championship

Annandale Golf Club, Madison, Mississippi
Par 36-36–72; 7,199 yards

July 18-21
purse, $3,000,000

	SCORES				TOTAL	MONEY
Woody Austin	69	65	67	67	268	$540,000
Cameron Beckman	72	64	65	67	268	264,000
Daniel Summerhays	63	67	69	69	268	264,000
(Austin defeated Beckman and Summerhays on first playoff hole.)						
Nicholas Thompson	69	65	65	71	270	144,000
Billy Andrade	73	66	67	65	271	114,000
Kyle Reifers	65	69	67	70	271	114,000
Chad Campbell	67	69	65	71	272	96,750
Bill Lunde	67	67	68	70	272	96,750
Jason Bohn	73	68	66	66	273	75,000
Jim Herman	66	69	68	70	273	75,000
Chris Kirk	69	65	70	69	273	75,000
Billy Mayfair	72	62	71	68	273	75,000

	SCORES			TOTAL	MONEY
Chris Stroud	69	70	68	66	273	75,000
Seung-Yul Noh	69	68	67	70	274	54,000
Jonathan Randolph	66	69	70	69	274	54,000
Brendon Todd	72	64	66	72	274	54,000
Stuart Appleby	73	67	69	66	275	36,666.67
Steven Bowditch	67	68	73	67	275	36,666.67
Glen Day	70	69	71	65	275	36,666.67
Russell Knox	69	69	69	68	275	36,666.67
Peter Lonard	67	67	72	69	275	36,666.67
Troy Matteson	67	67	70	71	275	36,666.67
Rory Sabbatini	68	68	67	72	275	36,666.66
Paul Stankowski	66	68	70	71	275	36,666.66
Vaughn Taylor	67	67	68	73	275	36,666.66
Ryan Blaum	70	68	71	67	276	20,416.67
Brandt Jobe	75	65	69	67	276	20,416.67
Scott Langley	70	69	67	70	276	20,416.67
Steve LeBrun	67	71	69	69	276	20,416.67
William McGirt	66	70	70	70	276	20,416.67
Chris Riley	67	68	72	69	276	20,416.67
Martin Flores	71	65	70	70	276	20,416.66
Brad Fritsch	66	69	70	71	276	20,416.66
Charles Howell	72	69	69	66	276	20,416.66
Matt Every	71	67	66	73	277	14,790
Scott Gardiner	71	69	71	66	277	14,790
Fabian Gomez	70	64	71	72	277	14,790
Ken Looper	68	69	69	71	277	14,790
Cameron Percy	71	65	71	70	277	14,790
Michael Bradley	66	70	74	68	278	11,400
Will Claxton	66	71	68	73	278	11,400
Brian Harman	70	68	70	70	278	11,400
Ben Kohles	73	68	68	69	278	11,400
Heath Slocum	69	71	69	69	278	11,400
Lee Williams	69	70	69	70	278	11,400
Brendon de Jonge	75	65	69	70	279	7,905
Davis Love	71	70	72	66	279	7,905
David Mathis	70	67	72	70	279	7,905
Joe Ogilvie	70	67	71	71	279	7,905
Jeff Overton	68	71	72	68	279	7,905
Tag Ridings	74	66	67	72	279	7,905
Andre Stolz	70	69	71	69	279	7,905
Kevin Sutherland	70	69	66	74	279	7,905
Joe Durant	70	71	69	70	280	6,870
Skip Kendall	67	68	74	71	280	6,870
Eric Meierdierks	68	70	70	72	280	6,870
Darron Stiles	73	68	68	71	280	6,870
Greg Chalmers	70	69	67	75	281	6,630
Marco Dawson	72	67	71	71	281	6,630
Kent Jones	72	69	68	72	281	6,630
Michael Letzig	70	71	72	68	281	6,630
Chez Reavie	70	70	72	70	282	6,420
Wes Short, Jr.	71	70	68	73	282	6,420
D.J. Trahan	67	70	74	71	282	6,420
Robert Gamez	72	68	70	73	283	6,180
Bobby Gates	70	70	73	70	283	6,180
Kevin Kisner	65	73	71	74	283	6,180
Dicky Pride	67	72	71	73	283	6,180
Marc Turnesa	69	71	74	69	283	6,180
Chris DiMarco	72	67	76	69	284	5,970
Nathan Green	69	72	67	76	284	5,970
Andrew Johnson	72	69	74	72	287	5,850
Henrik Norlander	72	69	71	75	287	5,850
Frank Lickliter	72	69	73	74	288	5,730
Nick O'Hern	70	69	78	71	288	5,730
Colt Knost	72	69	74	75	290	5,640

RBC Canadian Open

Glen Abbey Golf Club, Oakville, Ontario, Canada

Par 35-37–72; 7,253 yards

July 25-28

purse, $5,600,000

	SCORES				TOTAL	MONEY
Brandt Snedeker	70	69	63	70	272	$1,008,000
Jason Bohn	70	68	66	71	275	369,600
Dustin Johnson	75	67	63	70	275	369,600
Matt Kuchar	66	74	64	71	275	369,600
William McGirt	71	69	67	68	275	369,600
Roberto Castro	69	70	67	70	276	187,600
John Merrick	71	62	72	71	276	187,600
Mark Wilson	70	69	67	70	276	187,600
Aaron Baddeley	68	68	73	68	277	151,200
Jim Furyk	72	67	68	70	277	151,200
Patrick Reed	68	68	70	71	277	151,200
David Lingmerth	67	71	65	75	278	113,400
Greg Owen	70	68	67	73	278	113,400
Rory Sabbatini	69	71	71	67	278	113,400
Kyle Stanley	68	71	66	73	278	113,400
Chad Campbell	71	72	66	70	279	84,000
Fabian Gomez	72	68	67	72	279	84,000
Charley Hoffman	69	69	67	74	279	84,000
Hideki Matsuyama	69	69	71	70	279	84,000
Marcel Siem	71	70	69	69	279	84,000
James Driscoll	69	69	71	71	280	54,160
Ernie Els	71	72	67	70	280	54,160
Trevor Immelman	68	73	66	73	280	54,160
Chris Kirk	68	69	71	72	280	54,160
Luke List	72	69	70	69	280	54,160
Andres Romero	69	70	71	70	280	54,160
Bubba Watson	68	67	72	73	280	54,160
Matt Every	71	71	67	72	281	39,760
Charl Schwartzel	73	70	66	72	281	39,760
Nicholas Thompson	73	70	68	70	281	39,760
Stuart Appleby	69	73	69	71	282	30,426.67
Sang-Moon Bae	71	70	72	69	282	30,426.67
J.J. Henry	73	67	72	70	282	30,426.67
David Mathis	71	69	70	72	282	30,426.67
Ryan Palmer	70	70	72	70	282	30,426.67
Chez Reavie	68	73	68	73	282	30,426.67
Jason Kokrak	72	68	69	73	282	30,426.66
Jeff Maggert	72	67	68	75	282	30,426.66
Vijay Singh	69	73	66	74	282	30,426.66
Greg Chalmers	73	68	67	75	283	22,400
Jeff Gove	71	70	71	71	283	22,400
James Hahn	69	68	69	77	283	22,400
Scott Verplank	72	68	73	70	283	22,400
David Hearn	70	73	68	73	284	17,404.80
Richard Lee	72	69	69	74	284	17,404.80
Justin Leonard	71	72	67	74	284	17,404.80
Cameron Percy	71	70	73	70	284	17,404.80
Cameron Tringale	72	67	73	72	284	17,404.80
Mike Weir	73	67	73	72	285	14,149.34
Alistair Presnell	72	67	68	78	285	14,149.33
Andrew Svoboda	71	72	70	72	285	14,149.33
Bob Estes	73	68	74	71	286	12,805.34
Scott Langley	71	72	71	72	286	12,805.34
Scott Piercy	71	71	73	71	286	12,805.34
Cameron Beckman	70	71	71	74	286	12,805.33
Tommy Gainey	73	64	74	75	286	12,805.33
Morgan Hoffmann	70	70	71	75	286	12,805.33

	SCORES				TOTAL	MONEY
Roger Sloan	71	71	72	72	286	12,805.33
Camilo Villegas	74	65	74	73	286	12,805.33
Casey Wittenberg	71	69	70	76	286	12,805.33
Robert Allenby	72	69	74	72	287	11,984
Scott Brown	66	72	77	72	287	11,984
Will Claxton	69	74	72	72	287	11,984
Scott Gardiner	66	74	75	72	287	11,984
Gary Woodland	69	72	72	74	287	11,984
Justin Hicks	72	71	68	77	288	11,592
Y.E. Yang	75	68	68	77	288	11,592
Kevin Chappell	68	75	69	77	289	11,256
Billy Horschel	71	69	72	77	289	11,256
Tim Petrovic	71	69	73	76	289	11,256
Brendan Steele	65	75	74	75	289	11,256
Steve LeBrun	73	70	71	76	290	10,976
Brian Gay	72	71	72	77	292	10,864
Graeme McDowell	76	65	76		217	10,752
Seung-Yul Noh	70	73	75		218	10,584
Brian Stuard	72	71	75		218	10,584
Ryo Ishikawa	72	71	80		223	10,416

WGC - Bridgestone Invitational

Firestone Country Club, South Course, Akron, Ohio
Par 35-35–70; 7,400 yards

August 1-4
purse, $8,750,000

	SCORES				TOTAL	MONEY
Tiger Woods	66	61	68	70	265	$1,500,000
Keegan Bradley	66	68	71	67	272	692,500
Henrik Stenson	65	70	67	70	272	692,500
Miguel Angel Jimenez	71	69	65	69	274	321,666.67
Zach Johnson	69	70	68	67	274	321,666.67
Jason Dufner	67	69	67	71	274	321,666.66
Bill Haas	67	68	69	71	275	205,000
Chris Wood	66	68	70	71	275	205,000
Luke Donald	67	69	68	72	276	145,750
Jim Furyk	67	69	72	68	276	145,750
Martin Kaymer	74	67	69	66	276	145,750
Richard Sterne	70	68	70	68	276	145,750
Steve Stricker	71	67	70	69	277	114,000
Harris English	70	68	72	68	278	102,666.67
Webb Simpson	64	75	73	66	278	102,666.67
Adam Scott	73	68	66	71	278	102,666.66
Jamie Donaldson	70	69	71	69	279	93,000
Justin Rose	69	72	69	69	279	93,000
John Merrick	72	66	70	72	280	89,000
Ian Poulter	69	72	69	70	280	89,000
Hideki Matsuyama	72	68	70	71	281	81,166.67
Charl Schwartzel	74	74	64	69	281	81,166.67
Michael Thompson	72	71	70	68	281	81,166.67
Bo Van Pelt	71	73	68	69	281	81,166.67
Rickie Fowler	67	71	70	73	281	81,166.66
Phil Mickelson	72	71	67	71	281	81,166.66
Paul Casey	70	70	73	69	282	73,500
Russell Henley	72	69	75	66	282	73,500
Matt Kuchar	72	71	69	70	282	73,500
Paul Lawrie	69	72	71	70	282	73,500
Rory McIlroy	70	71	69	72	282	73,500
Bubba Watson	67	69	72	74	282	73,500
Peter Hanson	70	72	70	71	283	68,000

	SCORES				TOTAL	MONEY
Dustin Johnson	72	69	75	67	283	68,000
Ryan Moore	66	74	70	73	283	68,000
Brandt Snedeker	72	70	71	70	283	68,000
Boo Weekley	73	70	70	70	283	68,000
Angel Cabrera	72	68	70	74	284	64,500
Gonzalo Fernandez-Castano	70	74	68	72	284	64,500
Kiradech Aphibarnrat	69	68	73	75	285	61,500
Sergio Garcia	71	76	70	68	285	61,500
Graeme McDowell	71	71	71	72	285	61,500
Lee Westwood	71	71	71	72	285	61,500
Stephen Gallacher	74	74	67	71	286	57,500
Billy Horschel	74	74	72	66	286	57,500
Francesco Molinari	70	70	72	74	286	57,500
Nick Watney	71	72	70	73	286	57,500
Ernie Els	71	72	70	74	287	53,000
Martin Laird	77	70	71	69	287	53,000
Shane Lowry	72	76	70	69	287	53,000
Thorbjorn Olesen	73	69	72	73	287	53,000
Richie Ramsay	73	69	73	72	287	53,000
Sang-Moon Bae	73	73	70	72	288	48,875
Jason Day	74	72	72	70	288	48,875
David Lynn	71	73	73	71	288	48,875
Matteo Manassero	71	70	74	73	288	48,875
Nicolas Colsaerts	72	70	74	73	289	47,250
Derek Ernst	73	76	71	69	289	47,250
Jonas Blixt	70	75	73	72	290	45,750
Scott Piercy	68	77	75	70	290	45,750
D.A. Points	73	69	75	73	290	45,750
Kevin Streelman	76	73	71	70	290	45,750
Brian Gay	72	70	75	75	292	44,250
Brett Rumford	76	74	72	70	292	44,250
Ken Duke	70	75	73	75	293	42,800
Tommy Gainey	74	71	76	72	293	42,800
Branden Grace	70	75	70	78	293	42,800
Mikko Ilonen	73	73	73	74	293	42,800
Satoshi Kodaira	70	74	76	73	293	42,800
Carl Pettersson	72	73	73	77	295	42,000
Toru Taniguchi	75	73	79	73	300	41,750
Jaco Van Zyl	73	82	78	72	305	41,500
Daniel Popovic	79	77	76	82	314	41,250

Reno-Tahoe Open

Montreux Golf & Country Club, Reno, Nevada
Par 36-36–72; 7,472 yards

August 1-4
purse, $3,000,000

	POINTS				TOTAL	MONEY
Gary Woodland	14	7	16	7	44	$540,000
Jonathan Byrd	2	4	11	18	35	264,000
Andres Romero	8	14	5	8	35	264,000
Brendan Steele	5	8	17	3	33	144,000
David Mathis	10	7	12	3	32	114,000
Dicky Pride	5	6	13	8	32	114,000
Seung-Yul Noh	3	4	14	10	31	96,750
Rory Sabbatini	3	12	8	8	31	96,750
Chris DiMarco	6	8	6	10	30	87,000
Johnson Wagner	4	11	2	12	29	81,000
Brian Harman	5	13	4	6	28	72,000
Charlie Wi	4	15	6	3	28	72,000
Brandt Jobe	8	8	4	7	27	58,000

	POINTS				TOTAL	MONEY
Richard Lee	6	5	7	9	27	58,000
Brendon Todd	7	4	8	8	27	58,000
Stuart Appleby	12	7	2	5	26	46,500
Will Claxton	8	5	9	4	26	46,500
Russell Knox	4	8	10	4	26	46,500
David Toms	2	15	1	8	26	46,500
Brad Fritsch	-1	10	10	6	25	36,200
Scott Langley	4	2	7	12	25	36,200
John Rollins	0	8	10	7	25	36,200
Woody Austin	7	5	3	9	24	28,800
James Hahn	7	5	2	10	24	28,800
Mark Wilson	9	-1	6	10	24	28,800
Michael Bradley	5	8	6	4	23	21,750
Glen Day	-3	12	6	8	23	21,750
Justin Hicks	-2	11	8	6	23	21,750
Robert Karlsson	5	5	10	3	23	21,750
Rod Pampling	2	17	-3	7	23	21,750
Peter Tomasulo	3	8	9	3	23	21,750
Justin Bolli	10	-1	11	2	22	16,980
Ben Kohles	4	5	3	10	22	16,980
Davis Love	2	12	2	6	22	16,980
Ted Potter, Jr.	7	2	0	13	22	16,980
Kevin Stadler	9	4	0	9	22	16,980
Bud Cauley	10	7	4	0	21	14,400
Brian Stuard	1	6	1	13	21	14,400
Greg Chalmers	13	5	0	2	20	11,700
James Driscoll	14	2	5	-1	20	11,700
Robert Gamez	5	2	6	7	20	11,700
Bobby Gates	6	3	1	10	20	11,700
Tom Gillis	6	10	6	-2	20	11,700
Nathan Green	7	4	4	5	20	11,700
Trevor Immelman	10	-2	9	3	20	11,700
Steve LeBrun	6	3	7	3	19	8,740
Robert Streb	7	10	4	-2	19	8,740
Dean Wilson	10	4	2	3	19	8,740
Ben Crane	3	7	4	4	18	7,680
Luke List	0	15	2	1	18	7,680
Thomas Aiken	2	7	10	-2	17	7,104
Matt Bettencourt	6	5	9	-3	17	7,104
Colt Knost	12	6	-1	0	17	7,104
Chris Riley	3	3	9	2	17	7,104
Camilo Villegas	1	6	8	2	17	7,104
Jeff Gove	2	5	7	2	16	6,720
Skip Kendall	7	4	2	3	16	6,720
Josh Teater	15	0	2	-1	16	6,720
Marc Turnesa	-4	13	12	-5	16	6,720
Chris Williams	9	6	-8	9	16	6,720
Vaughn Taylor	3	9	7	-4	15	6,540
Ricky Barnes	9	-1	2	2	12	6,480
Jim Herman	4	5	0	1	10	6,360
Heath Slocum	4	3	-2	5	10	6,360
Joey Snyder	2	10	-3	1	10	6,360
David Duval	1	5	2	1	9	6,210
Tag Ridings	5	7	-6	3	9	6,210
Ryuji Imada	3	4	-1	2	8	6,120
Scott McCarron	8	1	0	-3	6	6,060
Wes Short, Jr.	-2	8	3	-10	-1	6,000

PGA Championship

Oak Hill Country Club, Rochester, New York
Par 35-35–70; 7,163 yards

August 8-11
purse, $8,000,000

	SCORES				TOTAL	MONEY
Jason Dufner	68	63	71	68	270	$1,445,000
Jim Furyk	65	68	68	71	272	865,000
Henrik Stenson	68	66	69	70	273	545,000
Jonas Blixt	68	70	66	70	274	385,000
Scott Piercy	67	71	72	65	275	304,000
Adam Scott	65	68	72	70	275	304,000
David Toms	71	69	69	67	276	259,000
Jason Day	67	71	72	67	277	206,250
Dustin Johnson	72	71	65	69	277	206,250
Zach Johnson	69	70	70	68	277	206,250
Rory McIlroy	69	71	67	70	277	206,250
Roberto Castro	68	69	71	70	278	132,785.71
Marc Leishman	70	70	70	68	278	132,785.71
Graeme McDowell	70	69	73	66	278	132,785.71
Kevin Streelman	70	72	66	70	278	132,785.71
Steve Stricker	68	67	70	73	278	132,785.71
Marc Warren	74	67	68	69	278	132,785.71
Boo Weekley	72	69	70	67	278	132,785.71
Keegan Bradley	69	72	72	66	279	93,166.66
Rickie Fowler	70	68	72	69	279	93,166.66
Hideki Matsuyama	72	68	73	66	279	93,166.66
Matt Kuchar	67	66	76	71	280	75,000
David Lynn	69	69	71	71	280	75,000
Michael Thompson	72	67	72	69	280	75,000
Kiradech Aphibarnrat	68	71	71	71	281	58,750
Robert Garrigus	67	68	74	72	281	58,750
Bill Haas	68	70	71	72	281	58,750
Webb Simpson	72	64	73	72	281	58,750
Rafa Cabrera-Bello	68	75	69	70	282	48,500
Ryo Ishikawa	69	71	70	72	282	48,500
Scott Jamieson	69	72	70	71	282	48,500
Miguel Angel Jimenez	68	72	75	67	282	48,500
Paul Casey	67	72	74	70	283	38,571.42
Brendon de Jonge	71	71	71	70	283	38,571.42
Peter Hanson	72	69	74	68	283	38,571.42
Martin Kaymer	68	68	78	69	283	38,571.42
Francesco Molinari	72	68	70	73	283	38,571.42
Justin Rose	68	66	77	72	283	38,571.42
Lee Westwood	66	73	68	76	283	38,571.42
J.J. Henry	71	71	73	69	284	28,000
Charley Hoffman	69	67	73	75	284	28,000
Matt Jones	72	71	73	68	284	28,000
Thorbjorn Olesen	71	70	74	69	284	28,000
D.A. Points	73	70	72	69	284	28,000
Danny Willett	73	70	72	69	284	28,000
Tiger Woods	71	70	73	70	284	28,000
K.J. Choi	76	65	71	73	285	18,875
Marcus Fraser	67	69	75	74	285	18,875
Luke Guthrie	71	71	69	74	285	18,875
David Hearn	66	76	71	72	285	18,875
Thongchai Jaidee	70	71	75	69	285	18,875
John Merrick	75	68	73	69	285	18,875
Ryan Palmer	73	70	71	71	285	18,875
Josh Teater	71	71	71	72	285	18,875
Ryan Moore	69	71	73	73	286	16,900
Scott Stallings	73	70	73	70	286	16,900
Ken Duke	75	68	70	74	287	16,300

	SCORES				TOTAL	MONEY
Chris Kirk	71	69	73	74	287	16,300
Shane Lowry	71	70	75	71	287	16,300
Hunter Mahan	70	68	78	71	287	16,300
Harris English	74	69	72	73	288	15,700
Tommy Gainey	69	74	73	72	288	15,700
Stephen Gallacher	75	68	76	69	288	15,700
Sergio Garcia	69	68	75	76	288	15,700
Ian Poulter	70	71	77	70	288	15,700
Ben Curtis	73	70	74	72	289	15,350
Brandt Snedeker	70	73	70	76	289	15,350
Tim Clark	69	71	75	75	290	15,150
Vijay Singh	70	72	73	75	290	15,150
Brooks Koepka	71	72	71	77	291	14,950
John Senden	72	70	73	76	291	14,950
Matteo Manassero	72	69	74	77	292	14,750
Phil Mickelson	71	71	78	72	292	14,750
Gary Woodland	73	70	80	70	293	14,600
Darren Clarke	69	73	74	80	296	14,500

Out of Final 36 Holes

Woody Austin	69	75	144	Matt Every	71	77	148
Sang-Moon Bae	75	69	144	Kohki Idoki	72	76	148
Nicolas Colsaerts	71	73	144	Geoff Ogilvy	74	74	148
Branden Grace	71	73	144	Jeff Sorenson	73	75	148
Charles Howell	71	73	144	Jordan Spieth	74	74	148
Martin Laird	71	73	144	JC Anderson	73	76	149
Paul Lawrie	72	72	144	Alexander Noren	76	73	149
Davis Love	74	70	144	George Coetzee	74	76	150
Joost Luiten	71	73	144	Pablo Larrazabal	76	74	150
Charl Schwartzel	71	73	144	David McNabb	74	76	150
Chris Stroud	71	73	144	Ryan Polzin	73	77	150
Bubba Watson	70	74	144	Jaco Van Zyl	74	76	150
Rich Beem	71	74	145	Nick Watney	76	74	150
Luke Donald	71	74	145	Tom Watson	73	77	150
Mikko Ilonen	73	72	145	Chris Wood	75	75	150
David Lingmerth	74	71	145	Daniel Balin	73	78	151
David Muttitt	75	70	145	Thomas Bjorn	70	81	151
Marcel Siem	73	72	145	Kevin Chappell	79	72	151
Jimmy Walker	71	74	145	Caine Fitzgerald	75	76	151
Bernd Wiesberger	70	75	145	Bob Gaus	74	77	151
Charlie Beljan	71	75	146	Rob Labritz	78	73	151
Stewart Cink	75	71	146	Kyle Stanley	73	78	151
Graham DeLaet	70	76	146	Lucas Glover	76	76	152
Ernie Els	74	72	146	Paul McGinley	78	74	152
G. Fernandez-Castano	74	72	146	Shaun Micheel	76	76	152
Russell Henley	76	70	146	Mike Small	76	76	152
John Huh	72	74	146	Freddie Jacobson	76	77	153
Jason Kokrak	74	72	146	Mark Sheftic	75	78	153
Carl Pettersson	74	72	146	Stuart Smith	78	75	153
Richard Sterne	72	74	146	Kirk Hanefeld	76	78	154
Y.E. Yang	72	74	146	Bob Sowards	73	82	155
Scott Brown	73	74	147	Jeff Martin	78	78	156
Hiroyuki Fujita	71	76	147	Rod Perry	78	78	156
Brian Gay	73	74	147	Sonny Skinner	76	80	156
Padraig Harrington	76	71	147	Mark Brown	77	82	159
Billy Horschel	69	78	147	Chip Sullivan	84	76	160
Richie Ramsay	72	75	147	Lee Rhind	81	82	163
Brett Rumford	70	77	147	Angel Cabrera	80		WD
Kevin Stadler	74	73	147	Jamie Donaldson	80		WD
Peter Uihlein	77	70	147	Bo Van Pelt	80		WD
Derek Ernst	72	76	148				

Wyndham Championship

Sedgefield Country Club, Greensboro, North Carolina
Par 35-35–70; 7,130 yards

August 15-18
purse, $5,300,000

	SCORES				TOTAL	MONEY
Patrick Reed	65	64	71	66	266	$954,000
Jordan Spieth	65	66	70	65	266	572,400
(Reed defeated Spieth on second playoff hole.)						
Brian Harman	67	66	69	66	268	307,400
John Huh	68	62	70	68	268	307,400
Matt Every	67	67	68	67	269	193,450
Zach Johnson	67	68	66	68	269	193,450
Matt Jones	65	71	71	62	269	193,450
Bob Estes	67	66	68	69	270	153,700
Andres Gonzales	69	67	70	64	270	153,700
Rory Sabbatini	67	66	72	65	270	153,700
Robert Garrigus	65	69	68	69	271	116,600
Jim Herman	67	66	72	66	271	116,600
Webb Simpson	71	67	70	63	271	116,600
Brendan Steele	71	67	66	67	271	116,600
Hideki Matsuyama	70	65	71	66	272	95,400
Martin Flores	67	72	71	63	273	82,150
Bryce Molder	66	69	71	67	273	82,150
Henrik Norlander	67	68	72	66	273	82,150
David Toms	72	66	73	62	273	82,150
Ricky Barnes	69	69	69	67	274	57,416.67
Ernie Els	71	68	70	65	274	57,416.67
Bill Haas	69	66	71	68	274	57,416.67
Martin Kaymer	70	68	73	63	274	57,416.67
Charlie Beljan	69	67	69	69	274	57,416.66
Jin Park	67	69	70	68	274	57,416.66
Tim Clark	69	70	72	64	275	40,810
Ryo Ishikawa	70	69	69	67	275	40,810
Brendon Todd	68	68	75	64	275	40,810
Steven Bowditch	71	66	72	67	276	32,263.75
Will Claxton	68	67	72	69	276	32,263.75
Sergio Garcia	65	70	70	71	276	32,263.75
Paul Haley	69	68	72	67	276	32,263.75
Jeff Overton	68	71	72	65	276	32,263.75
Alistair Presnell	67	71	67	71	276	32,263.75
John Senden	66	70	72	68	276	32,263.75
Camilo Villegas	69	68	72	67	276	32,263.75
K.J. Choi	69	68	72	68	277	22,260
Trevor Immelman	65	71	70	71	277	22,260
Colt Knost	69	67	72	69	277	22,260
Geoff Ogilvy	67	70	71	69	277	22,260
Robert Streb	68	70	70	69	277	22,260
Chris Stroud	64	72	73	68	277	22,260
Andrew Svoboda	65	69	74	69	277	22,260
Boo Weekley	69	67	73	68	277	22,260
J.J. Henry	68	70	71	69	278	14,855.15
Jerry Kelly	68	71	68	71	278	14,855.15
Stuart Appleby	66	70	76	66	278	14,855.14
Doug LaBelle	67	72	71	68	278	14,855.14
Justin Leonard	69	70	71	68	278	14,855.14
Nick O'Hern	68	71	67	72	278	14,855.14
Shawn Stefani	67	70	70	71	278	14,855.14
Sang-Moon Bae	68	70	72	69	279	12,176.75
Greg Chalmers	69	69	71	70	279	12,176.75
Brendon de Jonge	70	68	70	71	279	12,176.75
Chris DiMarco	70	68	70	71	279	12,176.75
Ross Fisher	64	69	74	72	279	12,176.75

		SCORES			TOTAL	MONEY
Tommy Gainey	68	69	73	69	279	12,176.75
Scott Gardiner	67	72	67	73	279	12,176.75
Jeff Maggert	69	68	70	72	279	12,176.75
Tom Gillis	69	68	73	70	280	11,448
George McNeill	69	68	75	68	280	11,448
Greg Owen	68	69	75	68	280	11,448
Cameron Percy	68	68	74	70	280	11,448
Charlie Wi	68	65	75	72	280	11,448
Morgan Hoffmann	65	69	75	72	281	10,918
Chris Kirk	66	71	72	72	281	10,918
Steve LeBrun	68	70	72	71	281	10,918
David Mathis	71	68	73	69	281	10,918
William McGirt	70	68	73	70	281	10,918
Robert Karlsson	70	66	75	71	282	10,600
Arjun Atwal	69	70	78	66	283	10,494
Nicholas Thompson	70	69	75	70	284	10,388
Kevin Chappell	69	69	75	72	285	10,282

PGA Tour Playoffs for the FedExCup

The Barclays

Liberty National Golf Club, Jersey City, New Jersey
Par 36-35–71; 7,400 yards

August 22-25
purse, $8,000,000

		SCORES			TOTAL	MONEY
Adam Scott	69	66	72	66	273	$1,440,000
Graham DeLaet	67	73	69	65	274	528,000
Justin Rose	68	68	70	68	274	528,000
Gary Woodland	69	64	68	73	274	528,000
Tiger Woods	67	69	69	69	274	528,000
Jim Furyk	70	66	70	69	275	268,000
Phil Mickelson	71	69	70	65	275	268,000
D.A. Points	70	72	66	67	275	268,000
Matt Every	67	72	69	68	276	208,000
Rickie Fowler	71	64	71	70	276	208,000
Jason Kokrak	70	69	70	67	276	208,000
Nick Watney	68	70	69	69	276	208,000
Rory Sabbatini	71	67	71	68	277	160,000
Bubba Watson	68	70	68	71	277	160,000
Kevin Chappell	68	72	62	76	278	132,000
John Huh	73	64	71	70	278	132,000
Webb Simpson	67	66	74	71	278	132,000
Daniel Summerhays	70	69	69	70	278	132,000
Brendon de Jonge	67	69	72	71	279	93,600
Matt Kuchar	66	65	70	78	279	93,600
David Lynn	71	65	69	74	279	93,600
Rory McIlroy	71	65	71	72	279	93,600
Jordan Spieth	70	68	68	73	279	93,600
Kevin Streelman	70	68	68	73	279	93,600
Roberto Castro	70	70	69	71	280	58,500
Jason Day	66	73	71	70	280	58,500
Bill Haas	73	66	71	70	280	58,500

	SCORES				TOTAL	MONEY
Hunter Mahan	69	68	72	71	280	58,500
Bryce Molder	69	69	72	70	280	58,500
Ryan Moore	67	72	69	72	280	58,500
Charl Schwartzel	68	67	74	71	280	58,500
Lee Westwood	73	68	71	68	280	58,500
Keegan Bradley	72	63	74	72	281	44,200
Charles Howell	72	66	73	70	281	44,200
Matt Jones	71	68	72	70	281	44,200
Chris Stroud	73	66	70	72	281	44,200
Greg Chalmers	73	69	66	74	282	36,800
Jason Dufner	71	70	71	70	282	36,800
Sergio Garcia	70	66	71	75	282	36,800
Freddie Jacobson	68	68	74	72	282	36,800
Stuart Appleby	69	71	72	71	283	32,000
Luke Donald	67	72	72	72	283	32,000
Aaron Baddeley	69	72	66	77	284	24,960
Erik Compton	72	70	72	70	284	24,960
Brian Gay	68	72	77	67	284	24,960
George McNeill	71	68	76	69	284	24,960
Scott Piercy	72	70	69	73	284	24,960
Kevin Stadler	64	73	76	71	284	24,960
Henrik Stenson	65	73	75	71	284	24,960
Martin Kaymer	68	70	75	72	285	19,480
John Merrick	69	73	70	73	285	19,480
Kyle Stanley	70	67	76	72	285	19,480
Nicholas Thompson	67	74	72	72	285	19,480
Martin Flores	71	69	77	69	286	18,320
Carl Pettersson	68	73	73	72	286	18,320
Camilo Villegas	65	73	72	76	286	18,320
Jimmy Walker	68	73	72	73	286	18,320
Jonas Blixt	69	67	70	81	287	17,680
Bob Estes	72	68	74	73	287	17,680
Cameron Tringale	74	67	73	73	287	17,680
Boo Weekley	69	72	75	71	287	17,680
Scott Brown	70	70	78	70	288	17,120
Scott Langley	72	69	76	71	288	17,120
John Senden	71	71	71	75	288	17,120
Geoff Ogilvy	68	73	77	71	289	16,800
Jeff Overton	68	74	74	74	290	16,560
Ryan Palmer	65	73	75	77	290	16,560
K.J. Choi	71	71	73	76	291	16,240
Stewart Cink	70	70	79	72	291	16,240
Charley Hoffman	68	71	79	74	292	16,000
Marc Leishman	72	70	75	77	294	15,840
David Hearn	73	68	79	75	295	15,520
Martin Laird	74	68	77	76	295	15,520
Josh Teater	68	72	76	79	295	15,520

Deutsche Bank Championship

TPC Boston, Norton, Massachusetts
Par 36-35–71; 7,214 yards

August 30-September 2
purse, $8,000,000

	SCORES				TOTAL	MONEY
Henrik Stenson	67	63	66	66	262	$1,440,000
Steve Stricker	66	68	63	67	264	864,000
Graham DeLaet	67	68	62	69	266	544,000
Sergio Garcia	65	64	65	73	267	315,000
Matt Kuchar	66	66	69	66	267	315,000
Jordan Spieth	67	66	72	62	267	315,000
Kevin Stadler	64	71	64	68	267	315,000

	SCORES				TOTAL	MONEY
Brian Davis	63	72	66	67	268	248,000
Roberto Castro	65	65	68	71	269	208,000
Brendon de Jonge	69	65	69	66	269	208,000
Jason Dufner	66	66	66	71	269	208,000
Ian Poulter	66	68	66	69	269	208,000
Jason Day	67	67	67	69	270	154,666.67
Scott Piercy	68	66	67	69	270	154,666.67
Hunter Mahan	65	70	66	69	270	154,666.66
Keegan Bradley	69	65	67	70	271	124,000
Chris Kirk	66	71	65	69	271	124,000
Marc Leishman	70	67	64	70	271	124,000
Justin Rose	70	63	69	69	271	124,000
Ernie Els	66	69	68	69	272	100,000
Brendan Steele	67	67	69	69	272	100,000
Kevin Chappell	68	70	64	71	273	76,800
John Huh	66	71	70	66	273	76,800
Charl Schwartzel	67	68	67	71	273	76,800
Daniel Summerhays	68	68	69	68	273	76,800
Nicholas Thompson	66	68	67	72	273	76,800
Stewart Cink	66	69	70	69	274	53,250
Harris English	66	67	72	69	274	53,250
Jim Furyk	70	68	63	73	274	53,250
Brian Gay	67	67	73	67	274	53,250
Charley Hoffman	70	65	66	73	274	53,250
Dustin Johnson	68	69	68	69	274	53,250
Zach Johnson	69	72	67	66	274	53,250
Lee Westwood	66	72	69	67	274	53,250
David Hearn	68	69	67	71	275	38,600
Scott Stallings	68	69	69	69	275	38,600
Chris Stroud	69	70	67	69	275	38,600
Camilo Villegas	71	68	67	69	275	38,600
Nick Watney	69	67	72	67	275	38,600
Boo Weekley	67	69	69	70	275	38,600
K.J. Choi	67	67	68	74	276	28,800
Luke Donald	71	70	67	68	276	28,800
Phil Mickelson	63	71	71	71	276	28,800
Bryce Molder	71	67	67	71	276	28,800
Kevin Streelman	66	71	70	69	276	28,800
Gary Woodland	72	67	66	71	276	28,800
Bob Estes	66	69	70	72	277	20,826.67
Graeme McDowell	72	66	69	70	277	20,826.67
Rory McIlroy	70	71	64	72	277	20,826.67
Brandt Snedeker	68	68	69	72	277	20,826.67
Martin Kaymer	69	72	67	69	277	20,826.66
Justin Leonard	69	70	72	66	277	20,826.66
Charles Howell	71	67	69	71	278	18,097.78
Jerry Kelly	66	72	70	70	278	18,097.78
John Merrick	67	69	67	75	278	18,097.78
Rory Sabbatini	70	71	69	68	278	18,097.78
Adam Scott	73	66	67	72	278	18,097.78
Webb Simpson	73	68	67	70	278	18,097.78
Bo Van Pelt	68	71	69	70	278	18,097.78
Jonas Blixt	66	75	69	68	278	18,097.77
Michael Thompson	71	70	71	66	278	18,097.77
Matt Every	70	67	72	70	279	17,120
Russell Henley	70	70	66	73	279	17,120
Josh Teater	70	67	73	69	279	17,120
Stuart Appleby	74	67	68	71	280	16,720
Tiger Woods	68	67	72	73	280	16,720
Brian Stuard	71	66	71	73	281	16,320
Cameron Tringale	73	67	71	70	281	16,320
Bubba Watson	71	69	70	71	281	16,320
Billy Horschel	72	66	72	72	282	15,840
Pat Perez	68	72	66	76	282	15,840

	SCORES				TOTAL	MONEY
Patrick Reed	68	72	73	69	282	15,840
Jason Kokrak	70	71	70	72	283	15,440
Richard Lee	69	70	68	76	283	15,440
Ryan Moore	66	73	68	77	284	15,200
Angel Cabrera	72	67	72	77	288	15,040

BMW Championship

Conway Farms Golf Club, Lake Forest, Illinois
Par 35-36–71; 7,216 yards
(Event completed on Monday—rain.)

September 12-16
purse, $8,000,000

	SCORES				TOTAL	MONEY
Zach Johnson	64	70	69	65	268	$1,440,000
Nick Watney	67	69	70	64	270	864,000
Jim Furyk	72	59	69	71	271	544,000
Jason Day	71	66	70	66	273	315,000
Luke Donald	70	70	67	66	273	315,000
Hunter Mahan	68	73	65	67	273	315,000
Steve Stricker	66	71	64	72	273	315,000
Matt Jones	69	71	67	67	274	232,000
Charl Schwartzel	66	70	69	69	274	232,000
Brandt Snedeker	63	68	71	72	274	232,000
Ryan Moore	67	69	69	70	275	176,000
Rory Sabbatini	69	71	66	69	275	176,000
Jimmy Walker	72	65	70	68	275	176,000
Tiger Woods	66	72	66	71	275	176,000
Roberto Castro	68	69	71	68	276	144,000
Keegan Bradley	74	67	70	66	277	132,000
Jordan Spieth	71	65	73	68	277	132,000
Brendon de Jonge	71	68	70	70	279	104,320
Sergio Garcia	70	68	69	72	279	104,320
Billy Horschel	73	69	71	66	279	104,320
John Merrick	67	73	69	70	279	104,320
Gary Woodland	68	72	71	68	279	104,320
David Lynn	73	71	68	68	280	83,200
Chris Kirk	75	70	70	66	281	68,200
Matt Kuchar	74	73	61	73	281	68,200
Webb Simpson	72	69	69	71	281	68,200
Bubba Watson	71	71	69	70	281	68,200
Graham DeLaet	70	73	72	67	282	54,400
Bill Haas	72	71	72	67	282	54,400
David Hearn	72	68	71	71	282	54,400
Adam Scott	67	73	75	67	282	54,400
Daniel Summerhays	72	70	68	72	282	54,400
Brian Davis	72	67	74	70	283	42,266.67
Phil Mickelson	70	74	68	71	283	42,266.67
Kevin Stadler	69	74	70	70	283	42,266.67
Kevin Streelman	66	70	74	73	283	42,266.67
Justin Rose	71	71	69	72	283	42,266.66
Henrik Stenson	72	70	67	74	283	42,266.66
Matt Every	79	66	69	70	284	32,800
Rickie Fowler	77	68	68	71	284	32,800
Russell Henley	74	70	70	70	284	32,800
Charles Howell	71	71	71	71	284	32,800
Marc Leishman	73	71	71	69	284	32,800
Angel Cabrera	71	72	73	69	285	24,864
Jason Kokrak	70	73	71	71	285	24,864
Bryce Molder	73	72	72	68	285	24,864
Ian Poulter	73	73	69	70	285	24,864

	SCORES				TOTAL	MONEY
Nicholas Thompson	69	75	65	76	285	24,864
John Huh	72	71	72	71	286	20,800
Harris English	70	74	71	72	287	20,160
Jonas Blixt	72	73	73	70	288	19,253.34
Ernie Els	71	71	74	72	288	19,253.33
Chris Stroud	70	73	72	73	288	19,253.33
Sang-Moon Bae	70	71	75	73	289	18,400
Jason Dufner	71	73	72	73	289	18,400
Boo Weekley	72	76	71	70	289	18,400
Graeme McDowell	70	73	72	75	290	18,000
D.A. Points	71	72	75	72	290	18,000
Rory McIlroy	78	77	68	68	291	17,680
Patrick Reed	72	78	70	71	291	17,680
Brendan Steele	75	68	72	77	292	17,440
Kevin Chappell	77	72	73	71	293	17,120
Dustin Johnson	74	75	72	72	293	17,120
Michael Thompson	70	74	76	73	293	17,120
Ken Duke	73	77	68	76	294	16,720
Brian Gay	70	74	74	76	294	16,720
Lee Westwood	80	73	69	74	296	16,480
Charley Hoffman	78	76	70	73	297	16,320
Scott Piercy	81	73	76	72	302	16,080
Scott Stallings	75	71	73	83	302	16,080

Tour Championship

East Lake Golf Club, Atlanta, Georgia
Par 35-35–70; 7,307 yards

September 19-22
purse, $8,000,000

	SCORES				TOTAL	MONEY
Henrik Stenson	64	66	69	68	267	$1,440,000
Jordan Spieth	68	67	71	64	270	708,000
Steve Stricker	66	71	68	65	270	708,000
Webb Simpson	68	71	69	63	271	384,000
Dustin Johnson	68	68	67	69	272	320,000
Justin Rose	68	68	70	67	273	288,000
Billy Horschel	66	70	70	68	274	264,000
Zach Johnson	69	68	69	68	274	264,000
Roberto Castro	67	71	72	65	275	227,733.34
Jason Dufner	74	70	66	65	275	227,733.33
Sergio Garcia	68	71	69	67	275	227,733.33
Keegan Bradley	72	65	72	67	276	200,000
Phil Mickelson	71	67	70	68	276	200,000
Jason Day	68	74	68	67	277	173,600
Jim Furyk	70	68	73	66	277	173,600
Adam Scott	65	69	74	69	277	173,600
Nick Watney	72	65	70	70	277	173,600
Brendon de Jonge	70	72	71	65	278	158,400
Luke Donald	70	70	67	71	278	158,400
Hunter Mahan	70	69	71	69	279	152,000
Brandt Snedeker	69	75	67	68	279	152,000
Gary Woodland	70	67	71	72	280	145,600
Tiger Woods	73	71	69	67	280	145,600
Bill Haas	70	69	69	74	282	139,200
Kevin Streelman	69	72	74	67	282	139,200
Matt Kuchar	69	74	69	71	283	133,600
D.A. Points	72	67	70	74	283	133,600
Graham DeLaet	68	71	72	73	284	131,200
Charl Schwartzel	68	79	77	66	290	129,600
Boo Weekley	70	75	73	74	292	128,000

Final Standings – PGA Tour Playoffs for the FedExCup

RANK	NAME	FEDEXCUP POINTS	BONUS MONEY
1	Henrik Stenson	4,750	$10,000,000
2	Tiger Woods	2,743	3,000,000
3	Steve Stricker	2,650	2,000,000
4	Adam Scott	2,278	1,500,000
5	Zach Johnson	2,238	1,000,000
6	Matt Kuchar	1,823	800,000
7	Jordan Spieth	1,690	700,000
8	Graham DeLaet	1,415	600,000
9	Phil Mickelson	1,313	550,000
10	Justin Rose	1,300	500,000
11	Webb Simpson	1,050	300,000
12	Brandt Snedeker	853	290,000
13	Dustin Johnson	760	280,000
14	Jim Furyk	758	270,000
15	Nick Watney	738	250,000
16	Billy Horschel	728	245,000
17	Jason Day	698	240,000
18	Keegan Bradley	693	235,000
19	Jason Dufner	685	230,000
20	Hunter Mahan	653	225,000
21	Roberto Castro	645	220,000
22	Sergio Garcia	635	215,000
23	Gary Woodland	603	210,000
24	Bill Haas	573	205,000
25	Kevin Streelman	553	200,000
26	Brendon de Jonge	503	195,000
27	Charl Schwartzel	490	190,000
28	Luke Donald	483	185,000
29	Boo Weekley	455	180,000
30	D.A. Points	453	175,000

The Presidents Cup

Muirfield Village Golf Club, Dublin, Ohio   October 3-6
Par 36-36–72; 7,352 yards

FIRST DAY
Fourball

Jason Day and Graham DeLaet (Int'l) defeated Hunter Mahan and Brandt Snedeker, 1 up.
Bill Haas and Webb Simpson (US) halved with Adam Scott and Hideki Matsuyama.
Louis Oosthuizen and Charl Schwartzel (Int'l) defeated Phil Mickelson and Keegan Bradley, 2 and 1.
Steve Stricker and Jordan Spieth (US) defeated Ernie Els and Brendon de Jonge, 1 up.
Matt Kuchar and Tiger Woods (US) defeated Angel Cabrera and Marc Leishman, 5 and 4.
Zach Johnson and Jason Dufner (US) defeated Branden Grace and Richard Sterne, 5 and 3.

POINTS: United States 4, International 2

SECOND DAY
Foursomes

Mickelson and Bradley (US) defeated Day and DeLaet, 4 and 3.
Els and de Jonge (Int'l) defeated Haas and Mahan, 4 and 3.
Stricker and Spieth (US) defeated Grace and Sterne, 2 and 1.
Cabrera and Leishman (Int'l) defeated Simpson and Snedeker, 2 and 1.
Woods and Kuchar (US) defeated Oosthuizen and Schwartzel, 4 and 2.
Matsuyama and Scott (Int'l) defeated Dufner and Johnson, 2 and 1.

POINTS: United States 6½, International 5½

THIRD DAY
Morning Fourball

Bradley and Mickelson (US) defeated Els and de Jonge, 2 and 1.
Day and DeLaet (Int'l) defeated Stricker and Spieth, 2 up.
Haas and Simpson (US) defeated Cabrera and Grace, 4 and 3.
Snedeker and Mahan (US) defeated Oosthuizen and Schwartzel, 2 up.
Woods and Kuchar (US) defeated Scott and Matsuyama, 1 up.

THIRD DAY
Afternoon Foursomes

Mickelson and Bradley (US) halved with Day and DeLaet.
Dufner and Johnson (US) defeated Sterne and Leishman, 4 and 3.
Haas and Stricker (US) defeated Scott and Matsuyama, 4 and 3.
Els and de Jonge (Int'l) defeated Woods and Kuchar, 1 up.
Simpson and Snedeker (US) defeated Oosthuizen and Schwartzel, 1 up.

POINTS: United States 14, International 8

FINAL DAY
Singles

Els (Int'l) defeated Stricker, 1 up.
Mahan (US) defeated Matsuyama, 3 and 2.
Dufner (US)defeated de Jonge, 4 and 3.
Day (Int'l) defeated Snedeker, 6 and 4.
DeLaet (Int'l) defeated Spieth, 1 up.
Scott (Int'l) defeated Haas, 2 and 1.
Johnson (US) defeated Grace, 4 and 2.
Leishman (Int'l) defeated Kuchar, 1 up.
Woods (US) defeated Sterne, 1 up.
Schwartzel (Int'l) defeated Bradley, 2 and 1.
Oosthuizen (Int'l) halved with Simpson.
Cabrera (Int'l) defeated Mickelson, 1 up.

TOTAL POINTS: United States 18½, International 15½

Frys.com Open

CordeValle Golf Club, San Martin, California
Par 35-36–71; 7,379 yards

October 10-13
purse, $5,000,000

	SCORES				TOTAL	MONEY
Jimmy Walker	70	69	62	66	267	$900,000
Vijay Singh	69	67	65	68	269	540,000
Scott Brown	68	67	71	64	270	240,000
Brooks Koepka	67	64	67	72	270	240,000
Hideki Matsuyama	70	66	68	66	270	240,000
Kevin Na	75	67	64	64	270	240,000
Brian Harman	65	74	67	65	271	161,250
George McNeill	68	70	62	71	271	161,250
Max Homa	69	68	66	69	272	135,000
Billy Hurley	69	66	69	68	272	135,000
Will MacKenzie	69	70	64	69	272	135,000
Robert Garrigus	70	63	68	72	273	101,250
Jason Kokrak	67	65	68	73	273	101,250
Spencer Levin	71	65	68	69	273	101,250
Charlie Wi	67	68	69	69	273	101,250
Andres Gonzales	74	62	69	69	274	75,000
J.J. Henry	67	71	68	68	274	75,000
Justin Hicks	68	68	68	70	274	75,000

	SCORES				TOTAL	MONEY
Ben Martin	69	68	66	71	274	75,000
Jeff Overton	64	72	69	69	274	75,000
James Driscoll	74	67	65	69	275	52,000
David Hearn	73	68	66	68	275	52,000
Trevor Immelman	70	69	68	68	275	52,000
Ryo Ishikawa	69	67	67	72	275	52,000
John Peterson	68	70	68	69	275	52,000
Briny Baird	71	68	65	72	276	35,500
Jason Gore	73	69	68	66	276	35,500
Jim Herman	67	66	70	73	276	35,500
Russell Knox	71	68	69	68	276	35,500
Sean O'Hair	71	70	65	70	276	35,500
Brendon Todd	71	70	69	66	276	35,500
Camilo Villegas	68	66	77	65	276	35,500
Charles Howell	72	70	65	70	277	25,857.15
Danny Lee	73	68	66	70	277	25,857.15
Ricky Barnes	71	69	64	73	277	25,857.14
Brian Davis	70	69	66	72	277	25,857.14
Kevin Kisner	73	69	68	67	277	25,857.14
Kyle Stanley	66	69	72	70	277	25,857.14
Y.E. Yang	71	68	71	67	277	25,857.14
Jason Bohn	70	70	69	69	278	19,000
Luke Guthrie	69	70	68	71	278	19,000
Heath Slocum	71	71	69	67	278	19,000
Daniel Summerhays	72	68	69	69	278	19,000
Kevin Tway	70	65	72	71	278	19,000
Tyrone van Aswegen	69	72	68	69	278	19,000
Charlie Beljan	73	66	71	69	279	13,860
Kevin Chappell	70	69	65	75	279	13,860
Will Claxton	70	72	67	70	279	13,860
Morgan Hoffmann	70	72	67	70	279	13,860
John Rollins	74	68	66	71	279	13,860
Brice Garnett	71	67	70	72	280	11,766.67
Robert Streb	70	70	68	72	280	11,766.67
Josh Teater	71	70	67	72	280	11,766.67
Lee Williams	68	71	68	73	280	11,766.67
Jonas Blixt	69	72	69	70	280	11,766.66
Chez Reavie	73	69	69	69	280	11,766.66
Jerry Kelly	69	72	67	73	281	11,300
Scott Langley	71	68	71	72	282	11,050
Pat Perez	72	70	70	70	282	11,050
Brian Stuard	71	71	70	70	282	11,050
Johnson Wagner	68	73	71	70	282	11,050
Robert Allenby	68	73	71	71	283	10,500
Ben Crane	69	71	68	75	283	10,500
Davis Love	69	69	71	74	283	10,500
Jamie Lovemark	70	71	71	71	283	10,500
Bryce Molder	72	69	69	73	283	10,500
Michael Putnam	67	71	71	74	283	10,500
Mike Weir	72	70	69	72	283	10,500
Mark Hubbard	69	71	72	73	285	10,100
John Huh	70	69	73	75	287	10,000
Bud Cauley	69	69	74	76	288	9,900
Tim Clark	73	67	73		213	9,600
Chad Collins	72	68	73		213	9,600
Chesson Hadley	72	68	73		213	9,600
Geoff Ogilvy	76	66	71		213	9,600
Justin Thomas	72	70	71		213	9,600
Alex Aragon	68	73	73		214	9,250
Stewart Cink	72	69	73		214	9,250
Justin Leonard	70	72	73		215	9,100
Jeff Maggert	73	69	76		218	9,000

Shriners Hospitals for Children Open

TPC Summerlin, Las Vegas, Nevada
Par 35-36–71; 7,223 yards

October 17-20
purse, $6,000,000

	SCORES				TOTAL	MONEY
Webb Simpson	64	63	67	66	260	$1,080,000
Jason Bohn	67	64	69	66	266	528,000
Ryo Ishikawa	67	66	68	65	266	528,000
Charley Hoffman	66	70	67	64	267	288,000
Luke Guthrie	69	64	71	64	268	210,750
Chesson Hadley	65	66	67	70	268	210,750
Charles Howell	67	69	67	65	268	210,750
Troy Matteson	67	69	68	64	268	210,750
Freddie Jacobson	67	67	71	64	269	162,000
Ryan Moore	69	63	69	68	269	162,000
Jeff Overton	63	68	68	70	269	162,000
Carl Pettersson	68	67	69	66	270	126,000
Brendon Todd	67	68	67	68	270	126,000
Jimmy Walker	71	68	64	67	270	126,000
Ricky Barnes	66	71	67	67	271	87,150
Greg Chalmers	67	68	69	67	271	87,150
Ken Duke	73	65	68	65	271	87,150
J.J. Henry	60	71	70	70	271	87,150
Will MacKenzie	70	68	68	65	271	87,150
Sean O'Hair	66	72	63	70	271	87,150
Brian Stuard	68	65	70	68	271	87,150
Andrew Svoboda	68	67	67	69	271	87,150
Stuart Appleby	70	68	65	69	272	53,400
Brian Davis	68	66	71	67	272	53,400
Robert Garrigus	69	70	66	67	272	53,400
Vijay Singh	67	69	70	66	272	53,400
Daniel Summerhays	66	68	68	70	272	53,400
James Driscoll	63	72	71	67	273	43,500
William McGirt	71	66	64	72	273	43,500
Jose Coceres	67	70	67	70	274	36,450
Max Homa	69	70	68	67	274	36,450
John Huh	69	70	69	66	274	36,450
Russell Knox	67	65	69	73	274	36,450
Kevin Stadler	70	65	69	70	274	36,450
Hudson Swafford	68	69	70	67	274	36,450
Briny Baird	70	69	65	71	275	28,875
Chad Campbell	71	66	70	68	275	28,875
Chris Kirk	68	70	70	67	275	28,875
David Toms	68	68	69	70	275	28,875
Harris English	69	67	70	70	276	24,600
Zach Johnson	69	70	70	67	276	24,600
Jhonattan Vegas	68	67	68	73	276	24,600
Justin Hicks	71	65	72	69	277	19,800
Morgan Hoffmann	67	67	71	72	277	19,800
Richard Lee	70	69	67	71	277	19,800
Kevin Penner	71	65	72	69	277	19,800
Cameron Tringale	66	71	69	71	277	19,800
Stephen Ames	65	68	71	74	278	15,264
Ben Curtis	71	68	72	67	278	15,264
Brian Harman	70	67	69	72	278	15,264
Billy Hurley	69	70	66	73	278	15,264
Nick Watney	73	66	66	73	278	15,264
Brice Garnett	67	68	73	71	279	13,890
Spencer Levin	69	69	72	69	279	13,890
John Senden	65	66	71	77	279	13,890
Marc Turnesa	68	69	71	71	279	13,890
Jonathan Byrd	63	72	70	75	280	13,320

	SCORES				TOTAL	MONEY
Jim Herman	70	69	71	70	280	13,320
Seung-Yul Noh	69	65	72	74	280	13,320
Ted Potter, Jr.	69	68	73	70	280	13,320
Brendan Steele	67	67	74	72	280	13,320
Ben Crane	68	68	72	73	281	12,840
Davis Love	69	70	70	72	281	12,840
George McNeill	70	67	71	73	281	12,840
John Merrick	71	67	70	74	282	12,540
Tyrone van Aswegen	70	69	71	72	282	12,540
Bryce Molder	65	73	72	73	283	12,300
Kyle Reifers	69	68	71	75	283	12,300
Geoff Ogilvy	71	67	75	71	284	12,120
Josh Teater	69	69	74	74	286	12,000
Will Claxton	66	73	73	75	287	11,880

CIMB Classic

See Asia/Japan Tours chapter.

WGC - HSBC Champions

See Asia/Japan Tours chapter.

McGladrey Classic

Sea Island Golf Club, Seaside Course, St. Simons Island, Georgia November 7-10
Par 35-35–70; 7,055 yards purse, $5,500,000

	SCORES				TOTAL	MONEY
Chris Kirk	66	66	68	66	266	$990,000
Briny Baird	63	70	67	67	267	484,000
Tim Clark	67	67	71	62	267	484,000
Scott Brown	66	68	68	66	268	227,333.34
Brian Gay	63	72	66	67	268	227,333.33
John Senden	66	67	68	67	268	227,333.33
Matt Every	67	68	69	66	270	171,416.67
Webb Simpson	65	68	71	66	270	171,416.67
Matt Kuchar	68	68	68	66	270	171,416.66
Greg Chalmers	68	68	72	64	272	121,916.67
Brian Harman	67	68	70	67	272	121,916.67
Robert Karlsson	68	68	71	65	272	121,916.67
Daniel Summerhays	69	66	69	68	272	121,916.67
Jason Kokrak	69	65	69	69	272	121,916.66
Kevin Stadler	68	68	65	71	272	121,916.66
Brendon de Jonge	67	71	70	65	273	85,250
Zach Johnson	70	68	68	67	273	85,250
Heath Slocum	67	71	69	66	273	85,250
Brendon Todd	68	67	67	71	273	85,250
Trevor Immelman	67	72	70	65	274	68,750
Kevin Kisner	65	73	70	66	274	68,750
Robert Garrigus	65	74	67	69	275	52,800
Charley Hoffman	66	73	68	68	275	52,800
Scott Langley	66	71	68	70	275	52,800
George McNeill	62	76	68	69	275	52,800
Boo Weekley	67	69	73	66	275	52,800
Harris English	68	70	71	67	276	39,050
Charles Howell	69	70	66	71	276	39,050
Seung-Yul Noh	65	70	73	68	276	39,050
David Toms	68	73	68	67	276	39,050

	SCORES				TOTAL	MONEY
Cameron Tringale	70	69	68	69	276	39,050
Kevin Chappell	65	68	74	70	277	31,831.25
Ben Curtis	68	69	72	68	277	31,831.25
Russell Knox	70	71	69	67	277	31,831.25
John Rollins	65	76	66	70	277	31,831.25
Stuart Appleby	68	70	71	69	278	26,468.75
Chad Campbell	70	70	71	67	278	26,468.75
Brice Garnett	67	72	67	72	278	26,468.75
Ted Potter, Jr.	67	67	72	72	278	26,468.75
Woody Austin	68	73	68	70	279	19,800
Aaron Baddeley	68	71	70	70	279	19,800
Will Claxton	65	71	71	72	279	19,800
Lucas Glover	69	72	68	70	279	19,800
David Hearn	74	66	70	69	279	19,800
Danny Lee	70	71	70	68	279	19,800
Troy Matteson	71	69	70	69	279	19,800
Camilo Villegas	66	74	72	67	279	19,800
Eric Axley	71	70	68	71	280	13,671.43
James Hahn	69	72	73	66	280	13,671.43
J.J. Henry	67	72	72	69	280	13,671.43
Pat Perez	68	71	72	69	280	13,671.43
Michael Putnam	68	73	72	67	280	13,671.43
Mark Wilson	70	71	68	71	280	13,671.43
Josh Broadaway	72	68	75	65	280	13,671.42
Blake Adams	73	68	73	67	281	12,320
Jonathan Byrd	66	69	72	74	281	12,320
Martin Flores	70	68	72	71	281	12,320
Spencer Levin	69	70	71	71	281	12,320
Carl Pettersson	66	74	75	66	281	12,320
Kyle Stanley	68	71	70	72	281	12,320
Mike Weir	70	71	68	72	281	12,320
Steven Bowditch	68	73	68	73	282	11,880
Erik Compton	68	73	76	66	283	11,715
Scott Piercy	67	73	71	72	283	11,715
Darren Clarke	69	70	71	74	284	11,385
Retief Goosen	68	71	69	76	284	11,385
Russell Henley	69	71	71	73	284	11,385
Justin Leonard	71	70	73	70	284	11,385
Andres Romero	70	69	72	74	285	11,110
D.H. Lee	67	70	71	78	286	10,945
Rory Sabbatini	66	73	73	74	286	10,945
Paul Goydos	68	71	76	72	287	10,725
Y.E. Yang	68	71	76	72	287	10,725

OHL Classic at Mayakoba

El Camaleon, Playa del Carmen, Mexico,
Par 36-35-71; 6,987 yards

November 14-17
purse, $6,000,000

	SCORES				TOTAL	MONEY
Harris English	68	62	68	65	263	$1,080,000
Brian Stuard	65	70	65	67	267	648,000
Jason Bohn	67	68	65	68	268	312,000
Rory Sabbatini	68	65	65	70	268	312,000
Chris Stroud	66	68	66	68	268	312,000
Justin Hicks	69	67	66	67	269	194,250
Charles Howell	67	67	66	69	269	194,250
Robert Karlsson	63	67	67	72	269	194,250
Justin Leonard	70	67	65	67	269	194,250
Bob Estes	68	69	65	69	271	156,000

	SCORES				TOTAL	MONEY
Tim Wilkinson	70	63	71	67	271	156,000
Freddie Jacobson	70	69	67	66	272	126,000
Will MacKenzie	69	69	69	65	272	126,000
Kevin Stadler	67	63	68	74	272	126,000
Peter Malnati	69	69	70	65	273	108,000
Robert Allenby	70	68	66	70	274	84,171.43
Jeff Maggert	69	66	69	70	274	84,171.43
Jay McLuen	67	69	69	69	274	84,171.43
Pat Perez	66	68	71	69	274	84,171.43
Alvaro Quiros	67	70	66	71	274	84,171.43
Brendan Steele	70	66	68	70	274	84,171.43
Scott Brown	69	66	67	72	274	84,171.42
Chad Collins	69	67	70	69	275	49,350
Tommy Gainey	71	65	68	71	275	49,350
J.J. Henry	72	65	70	68	275	49,350
John Huh	70	68	71	66	275	49,350
Ryan Moore	67	67	71	70	275	49,350
Jeff Overton	68	70	70	67	275	49,350
Wes Roach	67	70	68	70	275	49,350
Josh Teater	68	73	67	67	275	49,350
James Driscoll	69	68	68	71	276	35,580
Charley Hoffman	73	68	68	67	276	35,580
Matt Jones	69	69	68	70	276	35,580
Russell Knox	67	70	68	71	276	35,580
Ben Martin	69	70	68	69	276	35,580
Matt Every	71	67	68	71	277	25,833.34
Davis Love	69	68	68	72	277	25,833.34
Michael Putnam	69	69	69	70	277	25,833.34
Tim Clark	71	70	63	73	277	25,833.33
Erik Compton	67	69	71	70	277	25,833.33
Scott Gardiner	70	70	69	68	277	25,833.33
Kevin Na	71	70	71	65	277	25,833.33
Tim Petrovic	71	68	70	68	277	25,833.33
Camilo Villegas	70	67	67	73	277	25,833.33
Joe Durant	70	68	71	69	278	18,060
Brian Gay	70	71	67	70	278	18,060
William McGirt	70	68	74	66	278	18,060
Jhonattan Vegas	66	68	71	73	278	18,060
Jose Coceres	68	69	72	70	279	14,660
Oscar Fraustro	72	68	69	70	279	14,660
Morgan Hoffmann	69	71	72	67	279	14,660
Len Mattiace	69	68	69	73	279	14,660
Brendon Todd	71	66	70	72	279	14,660
Tyrone van Aswegen	69	69	71	70	279	14,660
Cameron Beckman	72	67	71	70	280	13,560
Luke Guthrie	71	70	70	69	280	13,560
Spencer Levin	70	68	65	77	280	13,560
Seung-Yul Noh	69	70	71	70	280	13,560
Lee Williams	73	68	67	72	280	13,560
Greg Chalmers	70	70	66	75	281	12,960
Ben Curtis	72	68	70	71	281	12,960
Kevin Kisner	65	75	67	74	281	12,960
Ryan Palmer	70	71	67	73	281	12,960
Kyle Stanley	73	68	67	73	281	12,960
Lucas Glover	70	70	70	72	282	12,420
Billy Hurley	69	69	72	72	282	12,420
Jamie Lovemark	68	69	70	75	282	12,420
John Senden	73	68	72	69	282	12,420
Brian Davis	71	70	71	71	283	12,000
Derek Ernst	69	70	72	72	283	12,000
Tag Ridings	70	69	74	70	283	12,000
Martin Flores	69	71	74	71	285	11,700
Richard Lee	75	65	72	73	285	11,700

	SCORES				TOTAL	MONEY
Y.E. Yang	74	67	70	75	286	11,520
David Duval	67	73	75	73	288	11,340
Mike Weir	72	69	72	75	288	11,340
Darren Clarke	71	68	73	78	290	11,160

Special Events

Tavistock Cup

Isleworth Golf & Country Club, Windermere, Florida
Par 36-36–72; 7,215 yards
(First-round results unofficial.)

March 25-26
purse, $2,170,000

FIRST DAY
(Team fourball–better ball)

Group 1
Paul McGinley and Tom Lewis (Queenwood) defeated Bob Tway and Scott Verplank (Oak Tree National), 67-70.

Group 2
Peter Hanson (Lake Nona) and Webb Simpson (Primland) defeated Brian Davis and D.A. Points (Isleworth), 66-69.

Group 3
Tim Clark (Albany) and Adam Scott (Queenwood) defeated Ross Fisher and Graeme McDowell (Lake Nona), 64-65.

Group 4
Fred Couples and Jay Haas (Primland) defeated Bo Van Pelt and Bubba Watson (Isleworth), 65-66.

SECOND DAY
(Singles stroke play – cumulative team score)

Group 1
Graeme McDowell (Lake Nona), 71
Ian Poulter (Albany), 72
Adam Scott (Queenwood), 74

Group 2
Ross Fisher (Lake Nona), 72
Bill Haas (Primland), 74
D.A. Points (Isleworth), 74

Group 3
Jay Haas (Primland), 74
Paul McGinley (Queenwood), 82
Bob Tway (Oak Tree National), 79

Group 4
Charles Howell (Oak Tree National), 76
Justin Rose (Albany), 77
Bubba Watson (Isleworth), 72

Group 5
Tim Clark (Albany), 73
Henrik Stenson (Lake Nona), 74
Bo Van Pelt (Isleworth), 77

Group 6
Peter Hanson (Lake Nona), 78
Martin Laird (Queenwood), 73
Webb Simpson (Primland), 70

Group 7
Brian Davis (Isleworth), 74
Tom Lewis (Queenwood), 79
Scott Verplank (Oak Tree National), 72

Group 8
Fred Couples (Primland), 78
Rickie Fowler (Oak Tree National), 73
Tiger Woods (Albany), 73

TOTAL: Albany 295, Lake Nona 295, Primland 296, Isleworth 297, Oak Tree National 300, Queenwood 308.
Albany (Woods and Poulter) defeated Lake Nona (McDowell and Stenson) on first playoff hole.)

(Each member of the Albany team received $150,000; each member of the Lake Nona team received $100,000; each member of the Primland team received $75,000; each member of the Isleworth, Oak Tree National and Queenwood teams received $50,000. Simpson received $100,000 and McDowell received $62,500 for the lowest scores on the second day.)

CVS Caremark Charity Classic

Rhode Island Country Club, Barrington, Rhode Island
Par 36-35–71; 6,688 yards

June 24-25
purse $1,500,000

	SCORES		TOTAL	MONEY (Team)
Steve Stricker/Bo Van Pelt	59	58	117	$300,000
Billy Andrade/Bill Haas	60	61	121	200,000
Jay Haas/Morgan Pressel	62	61	123	170,000
Bubba Watson/Rickie Fowler	60	64	124	150,000
Brad Faxon/Jeff Sluman	66	60	126	122,500
Russell Henley/Juli Inkster	64	62	126	122,500
Lexi Thompson/Peter Jacobsen	67	61	128	115,000
Michael Thompson/Fuzzy Zoeller	64	64	128	115,000
Louis Oosthuizen/Nick Price	64	66	130	105,000
Billy Horschel/Annika Sorenstam	67	65	132	100,000

PGA Grand Slam of Golf

Port Royal Golf Course, Southampton Parish, Bermuda
Par 36-35–71; 6,821 yards

October 14-16
purse, $1,350,000

	SCORES		TOTAL	MONEY
Adam Scott	70	64	134	$600,000
Justin Rose	67	69	136	300,000
Jason Dufner	69	70	139	250,000
Padraig Harrington	74	71	145	200,000

ISPS Handa World Cup of Golf

See Australasian Tour chapter.

Callaway Pebble Beach Invitational

Pebble Beach GL: Par 36-36–72; 6,828 yards
Spyglass Hills GC: Par 36-36–72; 6,953 yards
Del Monte GC: Par 36-36–72; 6,365 yards
Pebble Beach, California

November 21-24
purse, $300,000

	SCORES				TOTAL	MONEY
Kevin Kisner	70	67	64	74	275	$60,000
Chesson Hadley	66	73	67	70	276	32,200
Scott Langley	72	70	70	68	280	13,500
William McGirt	70	67	70	73	280	13,500
Mark Brooks	71	72	68	70	281	8,000
Mina Harigae	70	70	70	71	281	8,000
Sam Saunders	70	69	68	74	281	8,000
Tommy Armour	73	74	67	68	282	5,620
Kirk Triplett	69	70	72	71	282	5,620
Andrew Putnam	73	72	65	72	282	5,620
Scott Brown	66	68	73	75	282	5,620
Skip Kendall	70	67	67	78	282	5,620
Robert Streb	69	72	73	69	283	3,785
John Cook	69	70	73	71	283	3,785
Jeff Gove	67	75	70	71	283	3,785
Ryan Palmer	71	71	70	71	283	3,785
Shawn Stefani	73	68	71	71	283	3,785
Kelly Kraft	69	74	67	73	283	3,785
Jason Kokrak	67	68	68	80	283	3,785
Ted Potter, Jr.	66	71	74	73	284	2,800
Brendon Todd	72	67	72	73	284	2,800
Duffy Waldorf	69	71	69	75	284	2,800
Brice Garnett	67	74	72	72	285	2,410
Mark Hubbard	68	69	75	73	285	2,410
Michael Putnam	69	74	69	73	285	2,410
Martin Flores	69	72	66	78	285	2,410
Morgan Hoffmann	65	71	70	79	285	2,410
Luke Guthrie	71	69	75	71	286	2,135
Scott Simpson	68	74	73	71	286	2,135
Arron Oberholser	68	72	71	75	286	2,135
Mike Small	67	71	73	76	286	2,135
Bobby Gates	74	69	72	73	288	2,050
Annika Sorenstam	70	71	72	75	288	2,050
Brian Stuard	70	74	70	75	289	2,000
Andrew Svoboda	73	67	74	75	289	2,000
Luke List	70	69	72	78	289	2,000

	SCORES				TOTAL	MONEY
Vicky Hurst	70	73	71	76	290	1,950
Olin Browne	75	68	69	78	290	1,950
John Mallinger	71	73	71	77	292	1,920
Jason Gore	68	77	69	79	293	1,900
Matt Bettencourt	73	71	70	80	294	1,900
Tommy Masters	71	68	75	80	294	1,900

Northwestern Mutual World Challenge

Sherwood Country Club, Thousand Oaks, California
Par 36-36–72; 7,027 yards

December 5-8
purse, $3,500,000

	SCORES				TOTAL	MONEY
Zach Johnson	67	68	72	68	275	$1,000,000
Tiger Woods	71	62	72	70	275	400,000
(Johnson defeated Woods on first playoff hole.)						
Bubba Watson	70	70	69	70	279	212,500
Matt Kuchar	68	68	76	67	279	212,500
Webb Simpson	73	71	69	68	281	150,000
Graeme McDowell	72	67	75	69	283	145,000
Ian Poulter	76	67	73	69	285	140,000
Jim Furyk	72	69	74	71	286	135,000
Bill Haas	73	68	74	72	287	122,500
Jason Day	76	68	70	73	287	122,500
Rory McIlroy	73	77	68	70	288	115,000
Hunter Mahan	70	80	72	69	291	110,000
Keegan Bradley	75	68	75	74	292	108,500
Jason Dufner	74	71	78	69	292	108,500
Steve Stricker	75	74	74	72	295	107,000
Lee Westwood	74	75	74	74	297	105,500
Jordan Spieth	77	72	77	71	297	105,500
Dustin Johnson	74	79	72	74	299	100,000

Franklin Templeton Shootout

Tiburon Golf Course, Naples, Florida
Par 36-36–72; 7,288 yards

December 13-15
purse, $3,100,000

	SCORES			TOTAL	MONEY (Each)
Harris English/Matt Kuchar	64	60	58	182	$385,000
Retief Goosen/Fredrik Jacobson	67	61	61	189	242,500
Ian Poulter/Lee Westwood	70	61	59	190	145,000
Chris DiMarco/Billy Horschel	68	64	60	192	115,000
Sean O'Hair/Kenny Perry	64	69	60	193	100,000
Rory Sabbatini/Scott Verplank	69	64	61	194	90,000
Charles Howell/Justin Leonard	64	67	64	195	85,000
Jonas Blixt/Greg Norman	72	63	62	197	80,000
Jerry Kelly/Steve Stricker	71	65	61	197	80,000
Graham DeLaet/Mike Weir	73	64	60	197	80,000
Jason Dufner/Dustin Johnson	68	69	61	198	75,000
Mark Calcavecchia/Chad Campbell	72	66	63	201	72,500

PNC Father/Son Challenge

Ritz-Carlton Golf Club, Orlando, Florida
Par 37-35–72; 7,120 yards

December 14-15
purse, $1,085,000

	SCORES		TOTAL	MONEY (Team)
Stewart Cink/Conner Cink	61	61	122	$200,000
Steve Elkington/Sam Elkington	62	63	125	68,625
Vijay Singh/Qass Singh	64	61	125	68,625
Davis Love/Dru Love	64	63	127	50,000
Jack Nicklaus/Gary Nicklaus	63	65	128	48,500
Curtis Strange/Thomas Strange	65	63	128	48,500
Raymond Floyd/Ray Floyd, Jr.	66	63	129	46,500
Hale Irwin/Steve Irwin	64	65	129	46,500
Bernhard Langer/Christina Langer	66	64	130	44,250
Larry Nelson/Drew Nelson	67	63	130	44,250
Mark O'Meara/Shaun O'Meara	68	62	130	44,250
Lanny Wadkins/Tucker Wadkins	65	65	130	44,250
David Duval/Dean Karavites	64	68	132	42,750
Nick Faldo/Matthew Faldo	67	65	132	42,750
Lee Janzen/Connor Janzen	68	65	133	42,000
Sandy Lyle/James Lyle	67	67	134	41,500
Dave Stockton/Dave Stockton, Jr.	68	67	135	41,000
Lee Trevino/Daniel Trevino	70	68	138	40,500
Fuzzy Zoeller/Gretchen Zappo	70	69	139	40,250
Nick Price/Greg Price	72	69	141	40,000

Web.com Tour

Panama Claro Championship

Panama Golf Club, Panama City, Panama
Par 35-35–70; 7,102 yards

February 21-24
purse, $600,000

	SCORES				TOTAL	MONEY
Kevin Foley	66	69	70	67	272	$108,000
Mathew Goggin	69	68	66	70	273	64,800
Scott Brown	68	70	70	66	274	40,800
Scott Dunlap	70	66	72	68	276	24,800
Len Mattiace	70	65	72	69	276	24,800
Roland Thatcher	67	69	69	71	276	24,800
Bobby Gates	70	67	68	72	277	19,350
Jordan Spieth	71	69	71	66	277	19,350
Nick Flanagan	70	72	69	67	278	15,600
Aaron Goldberg	70	69	72	67	278	15,600
Vaughn Taylor	67	69	71	71	278	15,600
Chris Wilson	66	71	70	71	278	15,600
Joseph Bramlett	69	69	71	70	279	9,975
Daniel Chopra	73	69	68	69	279	9,975
Gavin Coles	69	67	75	68	279	9,975
Billy Hurley	68	68	74	69	279	9,975
Randall Hutchison	69	72	72	66	279	9,975
Dae-Hyun Kim	65	68	75	71	279	9,975
Chris Tidland	69	73	68	69	279	9,975
Peter Tomasulo	65	71	71	72	279	9,975
Oscar Fraustro	69	73	70	68	280	5,862.86
Hunter Haas	71	69	73	67	280	5,862.86
Brett Stegmaier	72	68	71	69	280	5,862.86
Matt Weibring	71	70	72	67	280	5,862.86
Steve Wheatcroft	72	69	70	69	280	5,862.86
Todd Hamilton	69	68	73	70	280	5,862.85
Brendon Todd	68	69	69	74	280	5,862.85

Colombia Championship

Country Club de Bogota, Bogota, Colombia
Par 35-36–71; 7,102 yards

February 28-March 3
purse, $700,000

	SCORES				TOTAL	MONEY
Patrick Cantlay	67	68	65	66	266	$126,000
Jim Renner	69	65	66	70	270	75,600
Shane Bertsch	65	70	67	70	272	47,600
Alexandre Rocha	66	70	69	68	273	30,800
Jordan Spieth	67	70	69	67	273	30,800
Bhavik Patel	68	66	69	71	274	25,200
Scott Brown	70	70	67	68	275	21,087.50
Dusty Fielding	70	71	65	69	275	21,087.50
Manuel Villegas	68	69	70	68	275	21,087.50
Steve Wheatcroft	66	69	69	71	275	21,087.50
Alex Cejka	69	68	68	71	276	15,400
Andres Echavarria	73	67	66	70	276	15,400

	SCORES				TOTAL	MONEY
Whee Kim	68	69	72	67	276	15,400
Ron Whittaker	66	71	72	67	276	15,400
Daniel Chopra	71	70	69	67	277	11,550
Andrew Putnam	69	68	70	70	277	11,550
Michael Putnam	68	68	69	72	277	11,550
Roger Sloan	68	68	69	72	277	11,550
Miguel Angel Carballo	71	67	72	68	278	8,484
Marco Dawson	68	71	68	71	278	8,484
Bobby Gates	68	70	70	70	278	8,484
Edward Loar	66	69	70	73	278	8,484
Ryan Spears	70	66	68	74	278	8,484
Oscar Álvarez	68	72	69	70	279	5,640
Joseph Bramlett	67	72	71	69	279	5,640
D.J. Brigman	67	67	74	71	279	5,640
Mathew Goggin	68	72	70	69	279	5,640
Will MacKenzie	68	72	71	68	279	5,640
Martin Piller	71	70	69	69	279	5,640
B.J. Staten	67	67	73	72	279	5,640

Chile Classic

Prince of Wales Country Club, Santiago, Chile
Par 36-36–72; 6,711 yards

March 7-10
purse, $650,000

	SCORES				TOTAL	MONEY
Kevin Kisner	71	67	61	68	267	$117,000
Brice Garnett	66	66	68	68	268	57,200
Edward Loar	65	65	69	69	268	57,200
Benjamin Alvarado	69	64	66	71	270	28,600
Guy Boros	71	67	67	65	270	28,600
Felipe Aguilar	66	68	69	68	271	20,345
Scott Harrington	65	70	68	68	271	20,345
I.J. Jang	70	65	70	66	271	20,345
Danny Lee	67	65	70	69	271	20,345
Troy Merritt	69	69	64	69	271	20,345
Ryan Spears	68	67	70	67	272	16,250
Philip Pettitt, Jr.	66	73	67	67	273	13,162.50
Sam Saunders	68	69	70	66	273	13,162.50
Scott Sterling	69	70	69	65	273	13,162.50
Will Wilcox	69	66	70	68	273	13,162.50
Daniel Chopra	68	67	69	70	274	9,425
Jason Gore	70	66	66	72	274	9,425
Bronson La'Cassie	68	72	67	67	274	9,425
John Peterson	68	67	69	70	274	9,425
Byron Smith	68	65	73	68	274	9,425
Brett Stegmaier	70	66	71	67	274	9,425
Alex Aragon	68	69	71	67	275	6,500
Franklin Corpening	68	72	68	67	275	6,500
Derek Fathauer	69	68	68	70	275	6,500
Aaron Goldberg	68	68	67	72	275	6,500

Chitimacha Louisiana Open

Le Triomphe Country Club, Broussard, Louisiana
Par 36-35–71; 7,004 yards

March 21-24
purse, $550,000

	SCORES				TOTAL	MONEY
Edward Loar	68	66	64	69	267	$99,000
Morgan Hoffmann	69	69	62	69	269	59,400
Brett Wetterich	68	66	71	65	270	37,400
Nick O'Hern	70	68	66	67	271	24,200
Jim Renner	68	69	64	70	271	24,200
Blayne Barber	67	69	65	71	272	17,806.25
Michael Putnam	71	69	64	68	272	17,806.25
Brendon Todd	67	69	67	69	272	17,806.25
Tim Wilkinson	70	68	64	70	272	17,806.25
Gary Christian	69	68	66	70	273	13,750
John Peterson	65	72	65	71	273	13,750
D.J. Trahan	67	72	67	67	273	13,750
Brenden Pappas	69	66	72	67	274	8,861.12
Lee Bedford	67	73	67	67	274	8,861.11
Marco Dawson	68	68	69	69	274	8,861.11
Jason Gore	68	65	71	70	274	8,861.11
Billy Hurley	70	66	67	71	274	8,861.11
Richard Johnson	73	64	64	73	274	8,861.11
Russell Knox	69	68	68	69	274	8,861.11
Byron Smith	69	66	67	72	274	8,861.11
Darron Stiles	67	64	71	72	274	8,861.11
Shane Bertsch	71	66	64	74	275	5,170
Brice Garnett	68	72	63	72	275	5,170
Hunter Haas	70	69	70	66	275	5,170
Ben Martin	66	67	71	71	275	5,170
John Riegger	70	68	69	68	275	5,170
Patrick Sheehan	67	73	62	73	275	5,170

Brasil Classic

Sao Paulo Golf Club, Sao Paulo, Brazil
Par 35-36–71

April 4-7
purse, $675,000

	SCORES				TOTAL	MONEY
Benjamin Alvarado	67	63	66	69	265	$121,500
Dawie Van der Walt	69	66	65	66	266	72,900
Kevin Kim	68	64	67	68	267	45,900
Kevin Tway	67	69	66	66	268	32,400
Wes Roach	71	67	63	68	269	27,000
Scott Dunlap	68	70	68	65	271	21,853.13
Brett Stegmaier	67	70	68	66	271	21,853.13
Brice Garnett	70	68	66	67	271	21,853.12
Richard Johnson	65	65	70	71	271	21,853.12
Oscar Fraustro	69	69	69	65	272	16,200
Danny Lee	65	65	70	72	272	16,200
Michael Putnam	71	65	72	64	272	16,200
Tim Wilkinson	67	67	69	69	272	16,200
Aron Price	70	65	70	68	273	12,825
Ariel Canete	69	69	71	65	274	11,812.50
Philippe Gasnier	67	68	71	68	274	11,812.50
Steven Alker	67	70	72	66	275	8,250
Joseph Bramlett	73	67	66	69	275	8,250
Josh Broadaway	68	72	66	69	275	8,250
Clodomiro Carranza	68	70	67	70	275	8,250

	SCORES				TOTAL	MONEY
Odair De Lima	69	71	69	66	275	8,250
Jonathan Hodge	67	68	67	73	275	8,250
Kent Jones	67	71	67	70	275	8,250
Andy Pope	70	68	69	68	275	8,250
Roland Thatcher	72	68	68	67	275	8,250

WNB Golf Classic

Midland Country Club, Midland, Texas   April 11-14
Par 36-36–72; 7,354 yards   purse, $600,000

	SCORES				TOTAL	MONEY
Alex Aragon	71	69	66	66	272	$108,000
Byron Smith	71	68	64	70	273	64,800
Brice Garnett	70	65	69	71	275	40,800
Nick Flanagan	68	68	66	74	276	24,800
Edward Loar	71	67	63	75	276	24,800
Will MacKenzie	70	69	65	72	276	24,800
Todd Baek	72	68	67	70	277	18,075
Miguel Angel Carballo	70	69	68	70	277	18,075
Danny Lee	68	66	70	73	277	18,075
Rod Pampling	68	67	73	69	277	18,075
Joe Durant	67	71	67	73	278	13,200
Whee Kim	69	66	71	72	278	13,200
Ben Martin	71	68	67	72	278	13,200
Martin Piller	71	68	66	73	278	13,200
Lee Bedford	69	71	67	72	279	9,600
Clodomiro Carranza	68	67	69	75	279	9,600
Russell Knox	71	68	71	69	279	9,600
Brendon Todd	69	70	70	70	279	9,600
Tim Wilkinson	71	67	70	71	279	9,600
Daniel Chopra	66	69	70	75	280	6,500
Gavin Coles	72	69	65	74	280	6,500
Mathew Goggin	70	68	67	75	280	6,500
Adam Hadwin	70	70	68	72	280	6,500
Bhavik Patel	72	68	71	69	280	6,500
Garrett Willis	69	71	73	67	280	6,500

South Georgia Classic

Kinderlou Forest Golf Club, Valdosta, Georgia   April 25-28
Par 36-36–72; 7,781 yards   purse, $650,000

	SCORES				TOTAL	MONEY
Will Wilcox	71	66	63	73	273	$117,000
Zack Sucher	72	70	70	65	277	48,533.34
D.J. Brigman	70	67	70	70	277	48,533.33
Michael Putnam	69	68	70	70	277	48,533.33
Andrew Loupe	69	68	71	70	278	23,725
Alexandre Rocha	68	71	72	67	278	23,725
Ryan Spears	66	73	68	71	278	23,725
Camilo Benedetti	70	72	69	70	281	18,850
Daniel Bowden	72	70	69	70	281	18,850
Tyrone van Aswegen	68	72	71	70	281	18,850
Ariel Canete	68	74	70	70	282	14,300
Ben Martin	69	72	71	70	282	14,300
Bhavik Patel	67	70	74	71	282	14,300

	SCORES				TOTAL	MONEY
Hudson Swafford	69	67	72	74	282	14,300
Miguel Angel Carballo	70	73	71	69	283	10,075
Troy Merritt	67	72	71	73	283	10,075
Adam Mitchell	69	73	74	67	283	10,075
Philip Pettitt, Jr.	67	72	71	73	283	10,075
Andrew Putnam	69	74	69	71	283	10,075
Byron Smith	69	74	69	71	283	10,075
Danny Lee	71	70	74	69	284	7,540
Will MacKenzie	68	73	68	75	284	7,540
Paul Claxton	73	71	73	68	285	5,720
Nick Flanagan	73	71	70	71	285	5,720
Mathew Goggin	69	71	73	72	285	5,720
Adam Hadwin	69	72	71	73	285	5,720
Jamie Lovemark	71	72	71	71	285	5,720
Nick Rousey	69	70	71	75	285	5,720

Stadion Classic

University of Georgia Golf Club, Athens, Georgia   May 2-5
Par 35-36–71; 7,240 yards   purse, $600,000
(Fourth round cancelled—rain.)

	SCORES			TOTAL	MONEY
Brendon Todd	66	70	69	205	$108,000
Tim Wilkinson	67	69	70	206	64,800
Nick Rousey	72	69	66	207	40,800
Alexandre Rocha	68	72	68	208	28,800
Woody Austin	71	68	70	209	21,900
Miguel Angel Carballo	72	66	71	209	21,900
Michael Putnam	67	68	74	209	21,900
Daniel Chopra	68	68	74	210	16,200
Joe Durant	71	66	73	210	16,200
Ryuji Imada	68	70	72	210	16,200
Ben Martin	69	72	69	210	16,200
Wes Roach	69	69	72	210	16,200
Rafael Echenique	66	75	70	211	10,920
Kevin Kisner	71	71	69	211	10,920
Russell Knox	69	66	76	211	10,920
Bhavik Patel	68	69	74	211	10,920
Tim Petrovic	69	70	72	211	10,920
Matt Bettencourt	69	67	76	212	8,100
Richard Johnson	70	73	69	212	8,100
Edward Loar	68	72	72	212	8,100
Corey Nagy	73	67	72	212	8,100
Chad Collins	71	72	70	213	5,808
Mathew Goggin	72	69	72	213	5,808
Brenden Pappas	67	72	74	213	5,808
Patrick Sheehan	72	70	71	213	5,808
Will Wilcox	70	71	72	213	5,808

BMW Charity Pro-Am

Thornblade Club, Greer, South Carolina
Par 35-36–71; 7,024 yards
Greenville Country Club, Greenville, South Carolina
Par 36-36–72; 6,864 yards
Reserve at Lake Keowee, Sunset, South Carolina
Par 36-36–72; 7,112 yards

May 16-19
purse, $650,000

	SCORES				TOTAL	MONEY
Mark Anderson	63	67	64	65	259	$117,000
Tom Hoge	66	63	68	67	264	70,200
Michael Connell	69	66	65	65	265	33,800
Franklin Corpening	62	66	67	70	265	33,800
Chesson Hadley	68	69	65	63	265	33,800
Kevin Foley	67	68	62	69	266	21,775
Edward Loar	71	64	64	67	266	21,775
Tyrone van Aswegen	68	68	65	65	266	21,775
Michael Sims	67	68	70	62	267	18,200
Hudson Swafford	63	70	70	64	267	18,200
Stephan Jaeger	67	67	66	68	268	14,950
Garth Mulroy	68	67	66	67	268	14,950
Tim Wilkinson	72	66	66	64	268	14,950
Hunter Haas	65	72	66	66	269	11,050
Kevin Kisner	67	64	69	69	269	11,050
Danny Lee	70	69	64	66	269	11,050
Will MacKenzie	65	70	70	64	269	11,050
Roland Thatcher	71	61	70	67	269	11,050
Miguel Angel Carballo	65	65	70	70	270	8,157.50
Erik Flores	68	67	67	68	270	8,157.50
Jason Gore	65	72	66	67	270	8,157.50
Bronson La'Cassie	72	66	66	66	270	8,157.50
Guy Boros	66	72	67	66	271	5,720
Rafael Echenique	70	65	68	68	271	5,720
Whee Kim	68	67	68	68	271	5,720
John Peterson	68	67	65	71	271	5,720
Alex Prugh	70	68	67	66	271	5,720
Will Wilcox	70	64	68	69	271	5,720

Mexico Championship

El Bosque Golf Club, Leon, Mexico
Par 36-36–72; 7,696 yards

May 23-26
purse, $700,000

	SCORES				TOTAL	MONEY
Michael Putnam	64	72	73	66	275	$126,000
Whee Kim	72	67	66	72	277	52,266.67
Wes Roach	67	69	71	70	277	52,266.67
Alex Prugh	68	67	70	72	277	52,266.66
Tim Wilkinson	70	70	66	72	278	28,000
Mathew Goggin	66	73	67	73	279	23,450
Chesson Hadley	71	69	70	69	279	23,450
Jose de Jesus Rodriguez	72	69	69	69	279	23,450
D.J. Brigman	73	69	69	69	280	18,900
Andrew Putnam	70	69	72	69	280	18,900
Jim Renner	68	68	73	71	280	18,900
Jason Gore	71	69	67	74	281	14,700
Russell Knox	70	70	70	71	281	14,700
Andrew Svoboda	71	67	72	71	281	14,700
Camilo Benedetti	76	68	67	71	282	11,200

	SCORES				TOTAL	MONEY
Nathan Green	69	73	71	69	282	11,200
Ben Martin	71	72	68	71	282	11,200
Corey Nagy	70	74	69	69	282	11,200
Philip Pettitt, Jr.	71	70	70	71	282	11,200
Alex Aragon	70	73	68	72	283	7,340
Scott Dunlap	72	69	70	72	283	7,340
Sung Kang	72	67	73	71	283	7,340
Jeff Klauk	66	71	70	76	283	7,340
Manuel Merizalde	67	77	71	68	283	7,340
James Nitties	66	75	71	71	283	7,340
Tyrone van Aswegen	70	65	75	73	283	7,340

Mid-Atlantic Championship

TPC Potomac at Avenel Farm, Potomac, Maryland
Par 35-35–70; 7,139 yards

May 30-June 2
purse, $600,000

	SCORES				TOTAL	MONEY
Michael Putnam	71	64	70	68	273	$108,000
Chesson Hadley	66	75	67	67	275	64,800
Daniel Chopra	71	69	67	70	277	31,200
Chad Collins	68	67	70	72	277	31,200
Bronson La'Cassie	67	74	69	67	277	31,200
Scott Dunlap	71	67	70	71	279	19,425
Sung Kang	67	68	71	73	279	19,425
Alex Prugh	69	73	69	68	279	19,425
Peter Tomasulo	70	73	71	65	279	19,425
Tim Wilkinson	73	70	65	72	280	16,200
Jason Gore	71	69	69	72	281	13,200
Si-Woo Kim	65	72	73	71	281	13,200
Will MacKenzie	73	69	71	68	281	13,200
Nick Rousey	73	70	72	66	281	13,200
Mathew Goggin	68	75	66	73	282	9,300
Jim Herman	67	70	71	74	282	9,300
Mike Lavery	74	69	70	69	282	9,300
John Peterson	71	71	69	71	282	9,300
Brendon Todd	71	71	71	69	282	9,300
Brett Wetterich	68	74	73	67	282	9,300
Gary Christian	70	73	72	68	283	6,040
Gavin Coles	66	72	75	70	283	6,040
Adam Crawford	69	67	75	72	283	6,040
Andres Gonzales	67	76	68	72	283	6,040
Jamie Lovemark	73	67	72	71	283	6,040
Steve Wheatcroft	75	66	70	72	283	6,040

Air Capital Classic

Crestview Country Club, Wichita, Kansas
Par 35-36–71; 6,931 yards

June 13-16
purse, $650,000

	SCORES				TOTAL	MONEY
Scott Parel	69	66	67	64	266	$117,000
Alex Aragon	72	67	65	65	269	70,200
Alex Prugh	63	71	70	67	271	44,200
Camilo Benedetti	71	66	67	68	272	26,866.67
Franklin Corpening	71	68	65	68	272	26,866.67
Steve Wheatcroft	67	68	68	69	272	26,866.66

	SCORES				TOTAL	MONEY
Dustin Garza	66	71	68	68	273	19,581.25
Jace Long	71	63	72	67	273	19,581.25
Aron Price	74	67	64	68	273	19,581.25
Chris Thompson	69	71	64	69	273	19,581.25
Bronson La'Cassie	68	70	69	67	274	14,300
Rob Oppenheim	71	69	69	65	274	14,300
Alexandre Rocha	68	73	68	65	274	14,300
Kevin Tway	70	65	70	69	274	14,300
Paul Claxton	70	71	63	71	275	9,750
Matt Hill	68	72	67	68	275	9,750
Billy Hurley	70	69	69	67	275	9,750
Richard Johnson	68	71	70	66	275	9,750
Danny Lee	69	66	73	67	275	9,750
Peter Malnati	68	67	70	70	275	9,750
Nathan Tyler	67	65	74	69	275	9,750
Woody Austin	74	66	68	68	276	6,500
Nathan Green	68	73	66	69	276	6,500
Bhavik Patel	68	67	69	72	276	6,500
Aaron Watkins	71	69	70	66	276	6,500

Rex Hospital Open

TPC Wakefield Plantation, Raleigh, North Carolina
Par 36-35–71; 7,257 yards

June 20-23
purse, $625,000

	SCORES				TOTAL	MONEY
Chesson Hadley	63	69	69	64	265	$112,500
Danny Lee	67	66	63	71	267	67,500
Edward Loar	68	65	67	68	268	42,500
Josh Broadaway	69	68	65	67	269	27,500
Ben Martin	71	67	65	66	269	27,500
Michael Putnam	68	68	65	69	270	22,500
Len Mattiace	71	65	68	67	271	20,156.25
Andrew Putnam	62	72	66	71	271	20,156.25
Cameron Beckman	65	71	68	68	272	16,250
Guy Boros	66	72	65	69	272	16,250
Randall Hutchison	65	74	66	67	272	16,250
Garth Mulroy	68	69	67	68	272	16,250
Matt Davidson	68	72	67	67	274	11,375
Scott Dunlap	69	65	70	70	274	11,375
Bhavik Patel	70	70	68	66	274	11,375
Chase Seiffert	68	69	72	65	274	11,375
Ryan Spears	67	68	68	71	274	11,375
Mathew Goggin	67	68	73	67	275	7,875
Jamie Lovemark	66	71	69	69	275	7,875
Jim Renner	69	68	69	69	275	7,875
Nick Rousey	66	70	72	67	275	7,875
Hudson Swafford	67	69	73	66	275	7,875
Tyrone van Aswegen	66	71	71	67	275	7,875
Oscar Fraustro	71	68	71	66	276	5,166.67
J.J. Killeen	69	70	69	68	276	5,166.67
Peter Malnati	70	70	68	68	276	5,166.67
Brett Stegmaier	68	69	70	69	276	5,166.67
Tom Hoge	72	65	66	73	276	5,166.66
Kent Jones	65	71	71	69	276	5,166.66

United Leasing Championship

Victoria National Golf Club, Newburgh, Indiana
Par 36-36–72; 7,239 yards
(Event completed on Monday—darkness.)

June 27-July 1
purse, $600,000

	SCORES				TOTAL	MONEY
Ben Martin	69	72	69	67	277	$108,000
Joe Affrunti	70	69	68	70	277	44,800
Ashley Hall	71	69	71	66	277	44,800
Billy Hurley	69	68	68	72	277	44,800
(Martin won on first playoff hole.)						
Adam Hadwin	70	71	67	71	279	24,000
Alex Cejka	68	72	69	71	280	21,600
Hunter Haas	69	71	73	68	281	19,350
James Nitties	69	71	71	70	281	19,350
Peter Malnati	69	75	68	70	282	15,000
Jim Renner	76	67	68	71	282	15,000
Jerod Turner	73	68	70	71	282	15,000
Kevin Tway	67	72	71	72	282	15,000
Will Wilcox	72	72	69	69	282	15,000
Joseph Bramlett	70	71	70	73	284	9,900
Adam Crawford	67	73	73	71	284	9,900
Fernando Mechereffe	69	73	71	71	284	9,900
Andrew Putnam	72	73	70	69	284	9,900
Michael Putnam	68	73	70	73	284	9,900
Scott Sterling	72	70	75	67	284	9,900
Joe Durant	71	70	74	70	285	6,990
Sung Kang	68	75	72	70	285	6,990
Wes Roach	72	70	71	72	285	6,990
Roland Thatcher	74	70	70	71	285	6,990

Utah Championship

Willow Creek Country Club, Sandy, Utah
Par 35-36–71; 7,104 yards

July 11-14
purse, $625,000

	SCORES				TOTAL	MONEY
Steven Alker	71	64	61	66	262	$112,500
Ashley Hall	68	62	67	65	262	67,500
(Alker defeated Hall on first playoff hole.)						
Chad Collins	66	60	68	69	263	32,500
Ben Martin	67	63	67	66	263	32,500
Will Wilcox	68	65	71	59	263	32,500
Shane Bertsch	65	67	66	66	264	22,500
Alex Cejka	68	62	68	67	265	18,187.50
Todd Demsey	70	66	65	64	265	18,187.50
Adam Hadwin	64	65	69	67	265	18,187.50
Jamie Lovemark	67	62	70	66	265	18,187.50
Roger Sloan	65	66	67	67	265	18,187.50
Alex Prugh	66	65	67	68	266	12,656.25
Hudson Swafford	66	70	66	64	266	12,656.25
Peter Tomasulo	68	62	68	68	266	12,656.25
Tim Wilkinson	68	67	66	65	266	12,656.25
Derek Fathauer	64	69	67	67	267	10,312.50
Andy Pope	65	70	66	66	267	10,312.50
Daniel Chopra	66	68	70	64	268	8,750
Aaron Goldberg	69	67	66	66	268	8,750
Ryan Spears	69	66	66	67	268	8,750
Richard Johnson	66	69	63	71	269	6,500

	SCORES				TOTAL	MONEY
Fran Quinn	69	67	68	65	269	6,500
Jim Renner	70	65	65	69	269	6,500
Richard Scott	69	66	67	67	269	6,500
Kevin Tway	68	66	69	66	269	6,500

Midwest Classic

Nicklaus Golf Club at LionsGate, Overland Park, Kansas   July 18-21
Par 35-36–71; 7,237 yards   purse, $600,000

	SCORES				TOTAL	MONEY
Jamie Lovemark	67	68	65	66	266	$108,000
Mark Anderson	69	67	66	65	267	64,800
Matt Davidson	68	70	64	66	268	34,800
Chesson Hadley	68	67	63	70	268	34,800
Edward Loar	69	68	68	64	269	24,000
Paul Claxton	68	64	67	71	270	18,780
Adam Crawford	67	72	63	68	270	18,780
Scott Harrington	70	67	66	67	270	18,780
Roger Sloan	70	67	65	68	270	18,780
Brett Stegmaier	69	69	65	67	270	18,780
Matt Hendrix	73	66	68	64	271	13,800
Joey McLister	67	70	69	65	271	13,800
Tyrone van Aswegen	65	68	68	70	271	13,800
Alex Aragon	70	69	64	69	272	10,500
Richard Johnson	67	69	70	66	272	10,500
Ben Martin	65	73	65	69	272	10,500
Chris Smith	65	71	67	69	272	10,500
Brad Adamonis	71	67	67	68	273	6,624
Chad Collins	67	69	68	69	273	6,624
Franklin Corpening	67	66	73	67	273	6,624
Reid Edstrom	67	72	66	68	273	6,624
Mathew Goggin	66	70	71	66	273	6,624
David Gossett	70	68	67	68	273	6,624
Randall Hutchison	70	66	69	68	273	6,624
Troy Merritt	69	69	69	66	273	6,624
John Peterson	70	67	66	70	273	6,624
B.J. Staten	67	71	70	65	273	6,624

Albertsons Boise Open

Hillcrest Country Club, Boise, Idaho   July 25-28
Par 36-35–71; 6,698 yards   purse, $775,000

	SCORES				TOTAL	MONEY
Kevin Tway	65	69	63	64	261	$139,500
Spencer Levin	67	65	66	63	261	83,700
(Tway defeated Levin on first playoff hole.)						
Bronson La'Cassie	66	63	68	65	262	40,300
Philip Pettitt, Jr.	65	67	63	67	262	40,300
Michael Putnam	67	64	68	63	262	40,300
Jason Allred	68	63	67	66	264	23,443.75
Matt Bettencourt	68	64	67	65	264	23,443.75
Hunter Haas	62	67	71	64	264	23,443.75
Jamie Lovemark	67	62	69	66	264	23,443.75
Ben Martin	67	67	67	63	264	23,443.75
Will Wilcox	66	69	62	67	264	23,443.75

	SCORES				TOTAL	MONEY
Michael Connell	68	68	61	68	265	15,190
Russell Knox	69	59	68	69	265	15,190
Will MacKenzie	69	63	65	68	265	15,190
Alex Prugh	64	67	67	67	265	15,190
Tim Wilkinson	63	71	64	67	265	15,190
Mark Anderson	65	65	70	66	266	10,488.34
Edward Loar	66	68	69	63	266	10,488.34
Oscar Fraustro	66	67	67	66	266	10,488.33
Brice Garnett	66	66	68	66	266	10,488.33
Kelly Kraft	65	68	67	66	266	10,488.33
Steve Wheatcroft	67	66	65	68	266	10,488.33
Chad Collins	65	65	67	70	267	7,440
John Peterson	68	66	68	65	267	7,440
Tyrone van Aswegen	70	66	68	63	267	7,440

Mylan Classic

Southpointe Golf Club, Canonsburg, Pennsylvania
Par 35-36–71; 6,951 yards

August 1-4
purse, $675,000

	SCORES				TOTAL	MONEY
Ben Martin	66	67	67	67	267	$121,500
Kelly Kraft	71	68	69	64	272	72,900
Ariel Canete	69	72	66	70	277	28,856.25
Chad Collins	66	72	69	70	277	28,856.25
Brad Elder	68	68	70	71	277	28,856.25
I.J. Jang	68	67	71	71	277	28,856.25
Whee Kim	66	65	73	73	277	28,856.25
Nick Rousey	70	65	73	69	277	28,856.25
Cliff Kresge	67	67	74	70	278	19,575
Chesson Hadley	71	69	68	71	279	15,525
Billy Hurley	66	72	69	72	279	15,525
Peter Malnati	68	70	69	72	279	15,525
Zack Sucher	65	71	77	66	279	15,525
Hudson Swafford	69	71	71	68	279	15,525
Randall Hutchison	72	70	70	68	280	11,475
Kevin Kim	68	67	72	73	280	11,475
John Peterson	73	69	71	67	280	11,475
Camilo Benedetti	71	70	72	68	281	9,450
Will MacKenzie	69	69	73	70	281	9,450
Wes Roach	70	70	69	72	281	9,450
Guy Boros	66	69	75	72	282	6,795
Brice Garnett	70	72	70	70	282	6,795
Adam Hadwin	70	72	69	71	282	6,795
Kevin Kisner	71	70	70	71	282	6,795
Spencer Levin	73	66	72	71	282	6,795
Brett Stegmaier	71	71	73	67	282	6,795

Price Cutter Charity Championship

Highland Springs Country Club, Springfield, Missouri
Par 36-36–72; 7,060 yards

August 8-11
purse, $675,000

	SCORES				TOTAL	MONEY
Andrew Svoboda	64	72	66	64	266	$121,500
Fernando Mechereffe	66	69	67	67	269	72,900
Daniel Chopra	67	69	66	68	270	39,150

	SCORES				TOTAL	MONEY
Matt Davidson	70	66	70	64	270	39,150
Alex Prugh	69	63	68	71	271	27,000
Joe Durant	68	68	71	65	272	24,300
Brian Duncan	68	70	68	67	273	20,334.38
Brice Garnett	70	69	67	67	273	20,334.38
Jason Gore	71	66	66	70	273	20,334.37
Russell Knox	71	66	67	69	273	20,334.37
Kyle Reifers	69	70	67	68	274	15,525
Nate Smith	67	68	70	69	274	15,525
Brett Stegmaier	66	72	66	70	274	15,525
Miguel Angel Carballo	67	65	72	71	275	11,475
Gavin Coles	71	67	68	69	275	11,475
Skip Kendall	66	69	69	71	275	11,475
Peter Malnati	67	68	73	67	275	11,475
James Nitties	66	71	68	70	275	11,475
Steven Alker	67	70	69	70	276	7,155
Alex Aragon	71	65	69	71	276	7,155
Paul Claxton	72	67	67	70	276	7,155
Hunter Haas	67	65	70	74	276	7,155
Randall Hutchison	65	72	67	72	276	7,155
Ryan Nelson	68	69	67	72	276	7,155
Scott Sterling	71	68	68	69	276	7,155
Roland Thatcher	68	70	66	72	276	7,155
Tyrone van Aswegen	69	68	70	69	276	7,155

News Sentinel Open

Fox Den Country Club, Knoxville, Tennessee
Par 35-36–71; 7,110 yards

August 15-18
purse, $550,000

	SCORES				TOTAL	MONEY
Peter Malnati	70	67	66	65	268	$99,000
Blayne Barber	66	67	68	68	269	36,300
Matt Bettencourt	69	67	66	67	269	36,300
Miguel Angel Carballo	69	68	65	67	269	36,300
James White	69	68	66	66	269	36,300
Kevin Kisner	70	65	66	69	270	19,112.50
Tim Wilkinson	65	70	69	66	270	19,112.50
Mark Anderson	68	69	66	68	271	17,050
Richard Scott	67	66	70	69	272	15,950
Spencer Levin	69	67	69	68	273	11,785.72
Ryan Nelson	70	67	70	66	273	11,785.72
Patrick Sheehan	68	71	68	66	273	11,785.72
Franklin Corpening	71	65	67	70	273	11,785.71
Ashley Hall	68	67	68	70	273	11,785.71
Corey Nagy	70	66	67	70	273	11,785.71
Aron Price	69	67	64	73	273	11,785.71
Nick Flanagan	67	68	69	70	274	7,700
Cliff Kresge	68	68	70	68	274	7,700
Andrew Putnam	67	69	71	67	274	7,700
Wes Short, Jr.	70	68	69	67	274	7,700
Michael Sims	69	69	67	69	274	7,700
Reid Edstrom	68	71	67	69	275	5,720
Scott Harrington	69	67	72	67	275	5,720
Roland Thatcher	71	68	68	68	275	5,720
Adam Hadwin	69	68	68	71	276	4,400
Fran Quinn	69	69	69	69	276	4,400
Wes Roach	72	67	70	67	276	4,400
Byron Smith	66	71	70	69	276	4,400
Dawie Van der Walt	73	66	68	69	276	4,400

Cox Classic

Champions Run, Omaha, Nebraska

August 22-25

Par 35-36–71; 7,145 yards

purse, $800,000

	SCORES				TOTAL	MONEY
Bronson La'Cassie	66	65	65	67	263	$144,000
Matt Bettencourt	67	64	65	67	263	86,400
(La'Cassie defeated Bettencourt on third playoff hole.)						
John Peterson	66	65	66	67	264	54,400
D.J. Brigman	67	68	67	64	266	35,200
Kevin Tway	69	66	66	65	266	35,200
Russell Knox	67	65	69	66	267	28,800
Len Mattiace	67	64	70	67	268	25,800
Alex Prugh	66	68	66	68	268	25,800
Oscar Fraustro	66	70	67	66	269	21,600
Peter Lonard	70	68	64	67	269	21,600
Nick O'Hern	65	67	67	70	269	21,600
Camilo Benedetti	66	69	70	65	270	16,200
Miguel Angel Carballo	67	68	65	70	270	16,200
Andrew Loupe	63	68	67	72	270	16,200
Michael Putnam	67	66	65	72	270	16,200
Wes Roach	65	66	70	70	271	12,800
Manuel Villegas	69	63	69	70	271	12,800
Will Wilcox	69	68	64	70	271	12,800
Will MacKenzie	70	67	67	68	272	9,028.58
Brad Elder	66	68	68	70	272	9,028.57
Hunter Haas	66	67	68	71	272	9,028.57
Stephan Jaeger	68	67	67	70	272	9,028.57
Richard Johnson	68	69	69	66	272	9,028.57
Kelly Kraft	66	69	68	69	272	9,028.57
Alexandre Rocha	64	69	68	71	272	9,028.57

Hotel Fitness Championship

Sycamore Hills Golf Club, Fort Wayne, Indiana

August 29-September 1

Par 36-36–72; 7,275 yards

purse, $1,000,000

	SCORES				TOTAL	MONEY
Trevor Immelman	67	66	69	66	268	$180,000
Patrick Cantlay	68	65	64	72	269	108,000
Scott Gardiner	69	67	66	68	270	58,000
Kevin Kisner	68	69	63	70	270	58,000
Bud Cauley	65	69	68	69	271	38,000
John Peterson	72	66	69	64	271	38,000
Will Claxton	67	69	67	69	272	30,125
Bobby Gates	69	69	64	70	272	30,125
Seung-Yul Noh	68	71	64	69	272	30,125
Michael Putnam	70	63	69	70	272	30,125
Adam Crawford	69	72	67	65	273	22,000
Sean O'Hair	70	70	64	69	273	22,000
Alistair Presnell	68	70	66	69	273	22,000
Ryan Spears	72	68	70	63	273	22,000
Brice Garnett	68	70	68	68	274	17,000
Troy Merritt	70	68	66	70	274	17,000
Brendon Todd	70	68	70	66	274	17,000
Russell Knox	69	69	69	68	275	12,600
Danny Lee	72	67	69	67	275	12,600
Arron Oberholser	66	68	68	73	275	12,600
Bhavik Patel	71	66	67	71	275	12,600

	SCORES				TOTAL	MONEY
Alexandre Rocha	69	69	68	69	275	12,600
Lee Williams	69	68	69	69	275	12,600
Hunter Haas	69	68	70	69	276	8,266.67
Peter Malnati	73	68	68	67	276	8,266.67
Henrik Norlander	74	67	66	69	276	8,266.67
Nick O'Hern	69	72	66	69	276	8,266.67
Jeff Klauk	66	72	68	70	276	8,266.66
Tim Wilkinson	69	71	67	69	276	8,266.66

Chiquita Classic

River Run Country Club, Davidson, North Carolina
Par 36-36–72; 7,321 yards

September 5-8
purse, $1,000,000

	SCORES				TOTAL	MONEY
Andrew Svoboda	72	65	69	70	276	$180,000
Will MacKenzie	69	68	72	67	276	108,000
(Svoboda defeated MacKenzie on first playoff hole.)						
Ben Martin	71	69	69	68	277	58,000
John Peterson	71	68	67	71	277	58,000
Ryo Ishikawa	70	72	70	66	278	40,000
Ricky Barnes	72	68	69	70	279	34,750
Troy Matteson	71	69	67	72	279	34,750
Camilo Benedetti	70	67	74	69	280	26,000
Brice Garnett	72	70	68	70	280	26,000
Peter Malnati	70	68	69	73	280	26,000
Greg Owen	70	66	71	73	280	26,000
Heath Slocum	72	71	71	66	280	26,000
Vaughn Taylor	73	66	70	71	280	26,000
Michael Putnam	69	74	69	69	281	18,000
Hudson Swafford	67	71	71	72	281	18,000
Tim Wilkinson	72	67	71	71	281	18,000
Scott Dunlap	73	67	71	71	282	15,500
Troy Merritt	68	72	71	71	282	15,500
Hunter Haas	72	71	69	71	283	12,120
Ben Kohles	67	71	73	72	283	12,120
Tim Petrovic	69	70	72	72	283	12,120
Wes Roach	73	69	73	68	283	12,120
Brendon Todd	71	70	68	74	283	12,120
Chad Collins	71	70	72	71	284	8,700
Edward Loar	67	73	73	71	284	8,700
Aron Price	72	72	72	68	284	8,700
Peter Tomasulo	68	72	72	72	284	8,700

Nationwide Children's Hospital Championship

The OSU Golf Club, Scarlet Course, Columbus, Ohio
Par 36-35–71; 7,141 yards

September 12-15
purse, $1,000,000

	SCORES				TOTAL	MONEY
Seung-Yul Noh	68	65	70	69	272	$180,000
Edward Loar	67	71	74	65	277	108,000
John Peterson	71	71	70	66	278	68,000
Ben Martin	70	69	73	67	279	41,333.34
Chesson Hadley	68	67	73	71	279	41,333.33
Tyrone van Aswegen	65	73	68	73	279	41,333.33
Alex Aragon	69	71	68	72	280	27,071.43

	SCORES				TOTAL	MONEY
Chad Collins	69	72	68	71	280	27,071.43
Ryo Ishikawa	71	72	69	68	280	27,071.43
Bronson La'Cassie	69	71	72	68	280	27,071.43
Spencer Levin	71	68	73	68	280	27,071.43
Hudson Swafford	74	67	68	71	280	27,071.43
Jim Herman	64	75	67	74	280	27,071.42
Will Claxton	71	68	73	69	281	18,000
Troy Matteson	72	71	70	68	281	18,000
Steve Wheatcroft	71	69	72	69	281	18,000
Kris Blanks	70	71	72	69	282	14,000
Sean O'Hair	66	72	71	73	282	14,000
Michael Putnam	73	70	70	69	282	14,000
Heath Slocum	72	70	73	67	282	14,000
Shawn Stefani	71	70	69	72	282	14,000
Billy Hurley	69	75	68	71	283	10,400
Will MacKenzie	70	73	71	69	283	10,400
Rod Pampling	71	70	72	70	283	10,400
Guy Boros	74	67	73	70	284	8,400
Ben Kohles	69	74	69	72	284	8,400
Marcel Siem	69	70	73	72	284	8,400

Web.com Tour Championship

Dye's Valley Course, Ponte Vedra Beach, Florida
Par 35-35–70; 6,864 yards

September 26-29
purse, $1,000,000

	SCORES				TOTAL	MONEY
Chesson Hadley	65	66	70	69	270	$180,000
Brad Fritsch	70	68	68	66	272	66,000
Scott Gardiner	67	68	65	72	272	66,000
John Peterson	66	71	68	67	272	66,000
Brendon Todd	71	67	69	65	272	66,000
Russell Knox	67	69	68	69	273	34,750
Andrew Loupe	68	69	67	69	273	34,750
Billy Hurley	66	70	70	68	274	23,333.34
Danny Lee	71	69	66	68	274	23,333.34
Sean O'Hair	70	70	67	67	274	23,333.34
Joe Durant	66	67	68	73	274	23,333.33
Andres Gonzales	70	68	67	69	274	23,333.33
Ryo Ishikawa	69	68	68	69	274	23,333.33
Jamie Lovemark	70	67	66	71	274	23,333.33
Byron Smith	67	70	69	68	274	23,333.33
Lee Williams	69	67	69	69	274	23,333.33
Bud Cauley	70	69	65	71	275	14,000
Paul Goydos	72	68	68	67	275	14,000
Tom Hoge	68	71	69	67	275	14,000
Tim Petrovic	69	70	68	68	275	14,000
Heath Slocum	68	70	70	67	275	14,000
Robert Karlsson	64	74	69	69	276	10,800
Will MacKenzie	69	67	71	69	276	10,800
Nick O'Hern	71	67	70	69	277	8,480
Rod Pampling	70	66	68	73	277	8,480
Andrew Putnam	68	67	67	75	277	8,480
Hudson Swafford	66	71	69	71	277	8,480
Roland Thatcher	69	69	68	71	277	8,480

PGA Tour Canada

Times Colonist Island Savings Open

Uplands Golf Club, Victoria, British Columbia
Par 35-35–70; 6,420 yards

June 6-9
purse, C$150,000

	SCORES				TOTAL	MONEY
Stephen Gangluff	69	68	66	66	269	C$27,000
Tyler Aldridge	67	68	67	69	271	16,200
Riley Wheeldon	65	72	69	67	273	10,200
Devin Carrey	68	68	70	68	274	5,906.25
Nick Taylor	67	70	67	70	274	5,906.25
Matt Marshall	63	70	69	72	274	5,906.25
David Skinns	65	70	65	74	274	5,906.25
Cory Renfrew	71	70	69	66	276	4,050
Chris Epperson	71	68	70	67	276	4,050
Fergal Rafferty	66	70	72	68	276	4,050
Tyler Weworski	68	70	69	69	276	4,050
J.J. Spaun	69	71	67	69	276	4,050
Wes Homan	69	71	70	67	277	2,900
Adam Cornelson	69	72	67	69	277	2,900
Dan Buchner	70	68	68	71	277	2,900
John Ellis	68	72	69	69	278	2,325
Kent Eger	68	69	70	71	278	2,325
Micah Burke	67	71	69	71	278	2,325
Darren Griff	68	70	68	72	278	2,325
Garrett Sapp	69	72	73	65	279	1,521.67
Clark MacPherson	69	72	72	66	279	1,521.67
Doug McGuigan	73	66	71	69	279	1,521.67
Albin Choi	68	71	71	69	279	1,521.67
Nathan Tyler	70	71	69	69	279	1,521.67
Josh Persons	71	70	69	69	279	1,521.67
Trey Denton	69	70	70	70	279	1,521.67
Steele DeWald	71	70	69	69	279	1,521.67
Joe Panzeri	64	71	71	73	279	1,521.67

Dakota Dunes Open

Dakota Dunes Golf Links, Saskatoon, Saskatchewan
Par 36-36–72; 7,301 yards

July 4-7
purse, C$150,000

	SCORES				TOTAL	MONEY
Wil Collins	66	65	70	66	267	C$27,000
Ryan Yip	71	65	66	66	268	11,200
John Ellis	64	69	68	67	268	11,200
Nick Taylor	67	63	67	71	268	11,200
Joshua Creel	68	65	69	68	270	5,475
Jaco Ahlers	65	63	70	72	270	5,475
Dan Buchner	67	67	67	69	270	5,475
Joel Dahmen	70	62	71	68	271	4,500
Doug McGuigan	66	64	71	70	271	4,500
Chris Epperson	66	69	68	70	273	4,050
Brady Schnell	69	67	72	66	274	3,300

	SCORES				TOTAL	MONEY
Erik Barnes	67	69	70	68	274	3,300
Hugo Leon	72	65	68	69	274	3,300
Matt Hoffman	64	67	73	70	274	3,300
Christopher DeForest	75	62	72	66	275	2,325
Michael Gligic	68	65	74	68	275	2,325
Josh Habig	68	67	71	69	275	2,325
Matt Richardson	68	69	69	69	275	2,325
Russell Surber	67	69	69	70	275	2,325
George Bradford	69	65	68	73	275	2,325

Syncrude Boreal Open

Fort McMurray Golf Club, Ft. McMurray, Alberta   July 11-14
Par 36-36–72; 6,886 yards   purse, C$150,000

	SCORES				TOTAL	MONEY
Riley Wheeldon	66	75	68	66	275	C$27,000
Lucas Lee	70	70	67	69	276	16,200
Cory Renfrew	71	69	70	67	277	10,200
David Dragoo	67	71	70	70	278	6,600
Joel Dahmen	67	73	67	71	278	6,600
John Ellis	69	74	72	64	279	4,856.25
Eugene Wong	71	73	68	67	279	4,856.25
Brock Mackenzie	72	70	69	68	279	4,856.25
Nick Taylor	65	71	73	70	279	4,856.25
Bo Hoag	73	72	68	67	280	3,750
Jason Scrivener	69	72	71	68	280	3,750
Tyler Aldridge	69	70	69	72	280	3,750
Dan Buchner	71	70	72	68	281	3,000
Garrett Sapp	73	71	67	70	281	3,000
Wes Homan	68	74	72	68	282	2,475
Nate McCoy	71	72	69	70	282	2,475
Russell Surber	68	72	69	73	282	2,475
Brett Lederer	70	70	68	74	282	2,475
Trey Denton	69	71	75	68	283	1,768.75
Neil Johnson	70	70	74	69	283	1,768.75
Michael McCabe	72	72	70	69	283	1,768.75
Chris Killmer	69	70	73	71	283	1,768.75
Stuart Anderson	69	68	73	73	283	1,768.75
Wil Collins	71	70	69	73	283	1,768.75

PGA Tour Canada Players Cup

Pine Ridge Golf Club, Winnipeg, Manitoba   July 18-21
Par 37-35–72; 6,641 yards   purse, C$150,000

	SCORES				TOTAL	MONEY
Carlos Sainz, Jr.	65	67	71	68	271	C$27,000
Nathan Tyler	68	64	69	71	272	16,200
Kent Eger	68	71	67	68	274	8,700
Mackenzie Hughes	66	67	70	71	274	8,700
Wil Collins	67	68	73	67	275	5,475
David Skinns	71	68	69	67	275	5,475
Brady Schnell	71	69	68	67	275	5,475
Hugo Leon	69	68	67	72	276	4,650
Derek Gillespie	68	69	71	70	278	4,200
Kyle Stough	67	69	71	71	278	4,200

	SCORES				TOTAL	MONEY
Sean Shahi	67	72	71	70	280	3,450
Cory Renfrew	68	66	74	72	280	3,450
Trevor Murphy	72	68	68	72	280	3,450
Eugene Wong	67	71	76	67	281	2,550
Doug McGuigan	66	69	74	72	281	2,550
Brock Mackenzie	72	71	67	71	281	2,550
Darren Wallace	67	71	69	74	281	2,550
J.J. Spaun	68	68	70	75	281	2,550
Devin Carrey	70	73	73	66	282	1,950
Jon McLean	68	72	71	71	282	1,950
Riley Wheeldon	69	73	69	71	282	1,950

ATB Financial Classic

Country Hills Golf Club, Talons Course, Calgary, Alberta
Par 36-36–72; 7,209 yards

August 6-9
purse, C$150,000

	SCORES				TOTAL	MONEY
Joe Panzeri	68	64	69	70	271	C$27,000
Kevin Tucker	69	66	70	68	273	11,200
Kyle Stough	70	69	66	68	273	11,200
Chris Epperson	66	66	72	69	273	11,200
Tony Finau	71	68	71	64	274	5,700
Beon Yeong Lee	68	69	71	66	274	5,700
Matt Marshall	71	68	69	67	275	4,365
Jon McLean	68	68	70	69	275	4,365
Nick Taylor	68	66	71	70	275	4,365
Lucas Lee	70	68	67	70	275	4,365
Maxwell Scodro	66	69	70	70	275	4,365
Brock Mackenzie	71	68	70	68	277	3,037.50
Doug McGuigan	71	66	70	70	277	3,037.50
Mark Hubbard	67	67	72	71	277	3,037.50
Brad Boyle	71	65	70	71	277	3,037.50
Bo Hoag	73	66	71	68	278	2,250
Wes Homan	69	67	75	67	278	2,250
Ryan Yip	68	68	76	66	278	2,250
Derek Berg	70	68	69	71	278	2,250
Wil Collins	67	68	71	72	278	2,250

Great Waterway Classic

Upper Canada Golf Course, Morrisburg, Ontario
Par 36-36–72; 6,926 yards

August 22-25
purse, C$150,000

	SCORES				TOTAL	MONEY
Hugo Leon	68	64	67	67	266	C$27,000
Brandon Harkins	68	70	67	62	267	16,200
Sean Shahi	67	65	66	70	268	10,200
Will Strickler	66	68	71	65	270	6,200
Josh Anderson	69	67	68	66	270	6,200
Joe Panzeri	67	66	70	67	270	6,200
Andrew Georgiou	70	62	72	67	271	4,675
Chris Epperson	68	65	68	70	271	4,675
Tony Finau	67	68	67	69	271	4,675
Mackenzie Hughes	70	67	69	66	272	3,214.29
Cory Renfrew	67	70	69	66	272	3,214.29
Mark Hubbard	69	68	68	67	272	3,214.29

	SCORES				TOTAL	MONEY
Wil Collins	68	70	67	67	272	3,214.29
Garrett Sapp	71	69	64	68	272	3,214.29
Ryan Blaum	66	66	70	70	272	3,214.29
Darren Wallace	71	67	65	69	272	3,214.29
Andrew Roque	71	65	72	65	273	2,400
Justin Shin	70	68	69	67	274	2,175
Joel Dahmen	70	68	68	68	274	2,175
Brett Lederer	68	73	69	65	275	1,812.50
Jesse Speirs	74	63	69	69	275	1,812.50
Michael McCabe	71	66	68	70	275	1,812.50

Wildfire Invitational

Wildfire Golf Club, Peterborough, Ontario
Par 35-36–71; 6,771 yards

August 29-September 1
purse, C$150,000

	SCORES				TOTAL	MONEY
Mark Hubbard	68	65	65	66	264	C$27,000
Kyle Stough	63	68	69	66	266	13,200
Mackenzie Hughes	65	66	68	67	266	13,200
Jorge Fernandez-Valdes	66	69	66	66	267	7,200
Nick Taylor	66	67	67	68	268	6,000
Brady Schnell	69	66	70	64	269	5,025
Cory Renfrew	65	67	68	69	269	5,025
David Skinns	67	67	66	69	269	5,025
Chris Epperson	69	68	65	68	270	4,350
Carlos Sainz, Jr.	68	71	67	66	272	3,600
Kevin McAlpine	70	68	67	67	272	3,600
T.J. Vogel	70	67	67	68	272	3,600
Michael McCabe	68	70	66	68	272	3,600
Sean Shahi	70	68	69	66	273	2,254.17
Derek Berg	66	67	73	67	273	2,254.17
Danny Sahl	70	69	68	66	273	2,254.17
Sejun Yoon	69	66	71	67	273	2,254.17
Will Strickler	66	70	70	67	273	2,254.17
Nathan Tyler	69	68	69	67	273	2,254.17
Jose Toledo	69	69	68	67	273	2,254.17
Beon Yeong Lee	73	66	67	67	273	2,254.17
Alex Kang	67	71	67	68	273	2,254.17

Cape Breton Celtic Classic

Lakes Golf Club, Ben Eoin, Nova Scotia
Par 36-36–72; 6,904 yards

September 5-8
purse, C$150,000

	SCORES				TOTAL	MONEY
Mackenzie Hughes	68	69	71	66	274	C$27,000
Ryan Williams	69	68	67	71	275	16,200
Wes Homan	64	74	70	69	277	8,700
David Skinns	67	68	67	75	277	8,700
John Ellis	68	70	72	69	279	6,000
Chris Epperson	74	68	68	70	280	5,400
Joel Dahmen	62	69	73	77	281	5,025
Mike Mezei	72	71	71	69	283	4,050
Riley Wheeldon	68	72	73	70	283	4,050
Micah Burke	67	74	71	71	283	4,050
Dan Buchner	68	75	69	71	283	4,050

	SCORES				TOTAL	MONEY
Michael McCabe	68	73	70	72	283	4,050
Hugo Leon	71	66	76	71	284	2,730
Nick Taylor	73	69	71	71	284	2,730
Albin Choi	70	72	70	72	284	2,730
Nathan Tyler	69	72	70	73	284	2,730
James Allenby	70	70	70	74	284	2,730
Joshua Creel	72	72	74	67	285	1,957.50
Kyle Stough	72	68	76	69	285	1,957.50
Brock Mackenzie	69	71	73	72	285	1,957.50
Joe Panzeri	71	67	74	73	285	1,957.50
Kyle Kallan	72	71	68	74	285	1,957.50

Tour Championship of Canada

Sunningdale Golf & Country Club, London, Ontario
Par 36-36–72; 7,089 yards

September 12-15
purse, C$150,000

	SCORES				TOTAL	MONEY
Max Gilbert	69	67	66	66	268	C$27,000
Trevor Murphy	66	66	69	68	269	16,200
Jose Toledo	71	67	70	66	274	8,700
Eugene Wong	70	66	71	67	274	8,700
Alex Kang	71	64	67	73	275	5,700
Nathan Tyler	71	70	66	68	275	5,700
Mark Hubbard	69	67	68	72	276	4,675
Brock Mackenzie	69	68	67	72	276	4,675
Brady Schnell	69	66	72	69	276	4,675
James Allenby	72	71	65	70	278	3,450
Josh Habig	69	72	67	70	278	3,450
Brandon Harkins	72	70	70	66	278	3,450
Lucas Lee	73	66	68	71	278	3,450
J.J. Spaun	70	69	69	70	278	3,450
Kyle Kallan	74	68	67	70	279	2,625
Darren Wallace	69	73	67	70	279	2,625
Micah Burke	70	69	73	68	280	1,967.15
Jorge Fernandez-Valdes	72	70	71	67	280	1,967.15
Stuart Anderson	73	69	67	71	280	1,967.14
Devin Carrey	73	68	70	69	280	1,967.14
Albin Choi	69	73	70	68	280	1,967.14
Chris Epperson	73	66	70	71	280	1,967.14
Tony Finau	69	68	71	72	280	1,967.14

PGA Tour Latinoamerica

Abierto Mexicano de Golf

Club de Golf Mexico, Mexico City, Mexico
Par 36-36–72

March 14-17
purse, US$150,000

	SCORES				TOTAL	MONEY
Ted Purdy	74	69	68	70	281	US$27,000
David Vanegas	70	68	73	71	282	16,200
Benjamin Alvarado	70	70	72	72	284	8,700
Jorge Fernandez-Valdes	70	68	72	74	284	8,700
Oscar Serna	70	72	73	70	285	6,000
Alfredo Adrian	71	71	74	70	286	5,025
Estanislao Guerrero	70	72	72	72	286	5,025
Oscar David Alvarez	72	72	70	72	286	5,025
Daniel Brunson	72	70	77	68	287	3,900
Daniel Miernicki	73	72	73	69	287	3,900
Oscar Fraustro	75	67	74	71	287	3,900
Sebastian Salem	69	75	72	71	287	3,900
Julian Etulain	68	74	75	71	288	3,000
Manuel Inman	71	74	71	72	288	3,000
Jose Toledo	69	77	75	68	289	2,400
Vince India	74	71	75	69	289	2,400
Juan P. Luna	73	74	69	73	289	2,400
Federico Garcia	70	73	71	75	289	2,400
Sebastian Vazquez	76	68	69	76	289	2,400
Ben Briscoe	72	75	73	70	290	1,605
Mike Stern	76	69	73	72	290	1,605
Carlos Franco	72	72	73	73	290	1,605
Denis Meneghini	74	70	72	74	290	1,605
Rafael Campos	71	71	72	76	290	1,605
Michael Buttacavoli	72	71	71	76	290	1,605
Dustin Garza	69	75	69	77	290	1,605

TransAmerican Power Products CRV Open

Atlas Country Club, Guadalajara, Mexico
Par 35-36–71

March 21-24
purse, US$150,000

	SCORES				TOTAL	MONEY
Manuel Villegas	66	69	74	67	276	US$27,000
Jose de Jesus Rodriguez	71	73	67	66	277	16,200
Carlos Franco	70	71	72	68	281	7,800
Jose Octavio Gonzalez	72	70	71	68	281	7,800
Bronson Burgoon	71	74	66	70	281	7,800
Armando Favela	72	73	68	69	282	5,213
Sebastian Vazquez	69	71	72	70	282	5,213
Ted Purdy	69	69	73	72	283	4,650
Fernando Figueroa	75	70	72	67	284	3,750
Horacio Leon	70	73	71	70	284	3,750
Hugo Leon	68	73	72	71	284	3,750
Manuel Inman	71	70	72	71	284	3,750
Estanislao Guerrero	69	72	71	72	284	3,750

	SCORES				TOTAL	MONEY
Juan P. Luna	69	72	74	70	285	2,475
Andres Echavarria	69	74	72	70	285	2,475
Chris Gilman	72	73	70	70	285	2,475
Roberto Diaz	74	69	70	72	285	2,475
Christian Espinoza	71	73	68	73	285	2,475
Oscar Serna	67	73	68	77	285	2,475
Max Scodro	67	74	77	68	286	1,562
Jorge Fernandez-Valdes	69	75	74	68	286	1,562
Austin Graham	71	72	73	70	286	1,562
Jhared Hack	71	71	73	71	286	1,562
Daniel Balin	69	71	74	72	286	1,562
Andrew Parr	71	72	70	73	286	1,562
Willy Pumarol	71	73	69	73	286	1,562
Sebastian Saavedra	70	73	68	75	286	1,562

Abierto OSDE del Centro

Cordoba Golf Club, Cordoba, Argentina
Par 35-36–71; 6,794 yards

April 18-21
purse, US$150,000

	SCORES				TOTAL	MONEY
Angel Cabrera	72	72	76	64	284	US$27,000
Rafael Gomez	68	76	72	68	284	16,200
(Cabrera defeated Gomez on first playoff hole.)						
Andres Echavarria	71	74	76	68	289	8,700
Michael Buttacavoli	76	73	70	70	289	8,700
Santiago Russi	71	76	75	68	290	5,269
Oscar Serna	71	74	75	70	290	5,269
Jorge Fernandez-Valdes	71	74	73	72	290	5,269
Nelson Ledesma	69	74	73	74	290	5,269
Andres Romero	73	73	73	72	291	4,200
Jacobo Pastor	72	75	71	73	291	4,200
Franco Romero	73	72	80	67	292	3,075
Eduardo Romero	69	79	73	71	292	3,075
Santiago Rivas	70	75	75	72	292	3,075
Cody Slover	72	73	74	73	292	3,075
Cesar Monasterio	73	73	72	74	292	3,075
Vince India	73	72	72	75	292	3,075
Timothy O'Neal	72	76	73	72	293	2,100
Nicolas Geyger	76	67	76	74	293	2,100
Mark Murphy	76	71	70	76	293	2,100
Sergio Acevedo	71	72	72	78	293	2,100
Mauricio Azcue	70	71	73	79	293	2,100

Roberto de Vicenzo Invitational Copa NEC

Club de Golf Uruguay, Montevideo, Uruguay
Par 36-36–72

April 25-28
purse, US$150,000

	SCORES				TOTAL	MONEY
Jose de Jesus Rodriguez	71	66	66	68	271	US$27,000
Timothy O'Neal	69	63	67	72	271	13,200
Sebastian Saavedra	67	69	66	69	271	13,200
(Rodriguez defeated Saavedra on first and O'Neal on second playoff hole.)						
Christian Espinoza	67	67	70	68	272	6,600
Sebastian Vazquez	68	67	68	69	272	6,600
Liam Logan	66	68	69	70	273	5,400

	SCORES				TOTAL	MONEY
Alan Wagner	64	72	69	69	274	4,519
Oscar David Alvarez	65	70	69	70	274	4,519
Ryan Blaum	68	69	66	71	274	4,519
Emilio Dominguez	69	67	66	72	274	4,519
Rafael Campos	65	71	72	67	275	3,075
Bronson Burgoon	69	66	71	69	275	3,075
Oscar Serna	69	67	70	69	275	3,075
Pete Campbell	73	66	67	69	275	3,075
David Vanegas	71	66	66	72	275	3,075
Marcelo Rozo	68	65	69	73	275	3,075
Olin Browne, Jr.	72	66	70	68	276	2,250
Samuel Del Val	66	71	70	69	276	2,250
Otto Solis	68	68	70	70	276	2,250
Julian Etulain	68	69	70	70	277	1,653
Andres Echavarria	69	70	68	70	277	1,653
Philippe Gasnier	72	68	67	70	277	1,653
Martin Ureta	69	70	71	67	277	1,653
Kevin Durkin	70	69	72	66	277	1,653
Maximiliano Godoy	67	70	67	73	277	1,653

Arturo Calle Colombian Open

Club Campestre de Pereira, Pereira, Colombia　　　　　　　　　May 2-5
Par 36-35–71　　　　　　　　　　　　　　　　　　　　　purse, US$150,000

	SCORES				TOTAL	MONEY
Timothy O'Neal	68	66	68	66	268	US$27,000
Oscar Serna	68	67	69	66	270	16,200
Jose de Jesus Rodriguez	69	66	69	67	271	10,200
Jose Manuel Garrido	69	68	70	65	272	6,200
Julio Santos	71	65	69	67	272	6,200
Jesus Osmar	65	70	67	70	272	6,200
Liam Logan	67	68	68	70	273	5,025
Manuel Merizalde	68	68	73	65	274	4,200
Jhonathan Perez	67	73	67	67	274	4,200
Jorge Fernandez-Valdes	70	66	68	70	274	4,200
Jhared Hack	71	66	66	71	274	4,200
Alvaro Pinedo	70	65	70	70	275	3,300
Marcelo Rozo	70	64	69	72	275	3,300
Santiago Russi	71	67	71	67	276	2,700
Oscar David Alvarez	70	68	69	69	276	2,700
Roberto Diaz	71	66	68	71	276	2,700
Juan P. Luna	71	67	71	68	277	2,031
Sebastian Fernandez	72	66	72	67	277	2,031
Adam Cornelson	69	66	72	70	277	2,031
Manuel Inman	65	73	69	70	277	2,031
Jesus Amaya	68	67	71	71	277	2,031
Daniel Zuluaga	71	70	64	72	277	2,031

Mundo Maya Open

Yucatan Country Club, Meridia, Mexico
Par 36-36–72; 7,282 yards

May 16-19
purse, US$150,000

	SCORES				TOTAL	MONEY
Jorge Fernandez-Valdes	67	69	68	73	277	US$27,000
Armando Villarreal	69	71	67	71	278	16,200
Gunner Wiebe	73	69	69	68	279	7,800
Jose de Jesus Rodriguez	74	67	68	70	279	7,800
Manuel Villegas	65	71	71	72	279	7,800
Hugo Leon	73	70	69	68	280	5,025
Michael Buttacavoli	69	73	69	69	280	5,025
Rafael Campos	68	69	73	70	280	5,025
Ryan Blaum	71	69	75	66	281	3,471
Derek Gillespie	70	69	73	69	281	3,471
Alejandro Munoz	69	71	71	70	281	3,471
Oscar Serna	73	69	69	70	281	3,471
Maximiliano Godoy	72	67	71	71	281	3,471
Horacio Leon	71	71	68	71	281	3,471
Yoshio Yamamoto	67	71	71	72	281	3,471
Austin Graham	69	71	71	71	282	2,550
Julian Etulain	74	70	67	72	283	2,250
Vince India	69	68	72	74	283	2,250
Liam Logan	70	67	69	77	283	2,250
Corbin Mills	70	70	72	72	284	1,875
Max Scodro	72	67	72	73	284	1,875

Dominican Republic Open

Hard Rock Golf Club at Cana Bay, Punta Cana, Dominican Republic
Par 36-36–72

May 29-June 1
purse, US$150,000

	SCORES				TOTAL	MONEY
Ryan Blaum	74	69	68	68	279	US$27,000
Maximiliano Godoy	69	68	70	74	281	16,200
Nicolas Geyger	68	73	70	71	282	8,700
Santiago Rivas	69	70	70	73	282	8,700
Jorge Fernandez-Valdes	68	73	73	69	283	5,700
Julian Etulain	73	68	68	74	283	5,700
Jose de Jesus Rodriguez	74	70	66	74	284	5,025
Gunner Wiebe	71	70	73	71	285	4,350
Emilio Dominguez	73	71	70	71	285	4,350
Mark Murphy	71	72	70	72	285	4,350
Oscar David Alvarez	73	72	70	71	286	3,600
Alex Ching	72	73	70	71	286	3,600
Bruce McDonald	74	72	69	72	287	2,730
Oscar Serna	71	75	73	68	287	2,730
Mauricio Azcue	69	69	76	73	287	2,730
Daniel Balin	74	72	68	73	287	2,730
Horacio Leon	69	71	71	76	287	2,730
Juan Ignacio Lizarralde	72	71	74	71	288	1,958
Tanner Ervin	75	71	72	70	288	1,958
Timothy O'Neal	73	71	73	71	288	1,958
Philippe Gasnier	72	74	68	74	288	1,958
Chris Evans	72	69	72	75	288	1,958

Puerto Rico Classic

Dorado Beach Resort, East Course, San Juan, Puerto Rico
Par 36-36–72
(Event shortened to 54 holes—lightning.)

October 10-13
purse, US$150,000

	SCORES			TOTAL	MONEY
Ryan Sullivan	74	66	65	205	US$27,000
Samuel Del Val	66	72	68	206	13,200
Armando Favela	66	70	70	206	13,200
Cesar Agustin Costilla	71	71	65	207	6,200
Dustin Garza	72	66	69	207	6,200
Jorge Fernandez-Valdes	67	71	69	207	6,200
Stephen Jaeger	69	72	67	208	4,519
Rafael Campos	68	73	67	208	4,519
Jorge Monroy	69	69	70	208	4,519
Julian Etulain	69	68	71	208	4,519
Steven Fox	73	68	68	209	2,888
Sebastian Saavedra	72	69	68	209	2,888
Horacio Leon	69	72	68	209	2,888
Vince India	68	72	69	209	2,888
Oscar Serna	72	68	69	209	2,888
Craig Hocknull	75	68	66	209	2,888
Tommy Cocha	70	69	70	209	2,888
Manuel Villegas	65	73	71	209	2,888
Andres Echavarria	71	70	69	210	1,769
Rafael Gomez	71	70	69	210	1,769
Sebastian MacLean	73	69	68	210	1,769
Roberto Diaz	74	68	68	210	1,769
Nicolas Geyger	72	68	70	210	1,769
Estanislao Goya	71	72	67	210	1,769

Abierto do Brasil

Gavea Golf Club, Rio de Janeiro, Brazil
Par 33-36–69

October 17-20
purse, US$150,000

	SCORES				TOTAL	MONEY
Ryan Blaum	69	63	67	66	265	US$27,000
Alan Wagner	66	65	68	66	265	16,200
(Blaum defeated Wagner on first playoff hole.)						
Alexandre Rocha	66	71	65	65	267	10,200
Ronaldo Francisco	65	65	72	66	268	7,200
Paulo Pinto	68	63	71	67	269	5,269
Nicolas Geyger	65	69	68	67	269	5,269
Andres Echavarria	69	64	68	68	269	5,269
Gustavo Acosta	68	69	62	70	269	5,269
Manuel Villegas	65	70	68	67	270	4,200
Bronson Burgoon	68	66	67	69	270	4,200
Armando Villarreal	70	67	68	66	271	3,075
Santiago Rivas	67	72	66	66	271	3,075
Julio Zapata	69	67	68	67	271	3,075
Samuel Del Val	69	68	66	68	271	3,075
Mauricio Molina	71	66	66	68	271	3,075
Philippe Gasnier	62	72	68	69	271	3,075
Estanislao Goya	73	68	63	68	272	2,400
Cesar Agustin Costilla	68	68	70	67	273	2,100
Nelson Ledesma	67	70	68	68	273	2,100
Sebastian Saavedra	66	70	67	70	273	2,100

Arturo Calle Colombian Classic

San Andres Golf Club, Bogota, Colombia
Par 35-36–71

October 31-November 3
purse, US$150,000

	SCORES				TOTAL	MONEY
Jose de Jesus Rodriguez	67	73	65	65	270	US$27,000
Manuel Villegas	66	64	70	70	270	16,200
(Rodriguez defeated Villegas on second playoff hole.)						
Jose Manuel Garrido	71	70	66	65	272	7,800
Timothy O'Neal	69	67	69	67	272	7,800
Corbin Mills	66	67	64	75	272	7,800
Omar Beltran	69	71	64	69	273	5,213
Emilio Dominguez	69	66	68	70	273	5,213
Jesus Amaya	69	67	71	67	274	4,350
Andres Echavarria	74	67	65	68	274	4,350
Vince India	66	66	70	72	274	4,350
Ryan Blaum	67	71	68	69	275	3,450
Eric Atsma	70	70	66	69	275	3,450
Sebastian Saavedra	71	66	67	71	275	3,450
Tiago Silva	68	71	70	67	276	2,700
Julian Etulain	69	71	69	67	276	2,700
Sebastian Vazquez	70	66	72	68	276	2,700
Jose Toledo	69	70	71	67	277	2,175
Diego Vanegas	70	66	73	68	277	2,175
Estanislao Goya	73	69	69	66	277	2,175
Nelson Ledesma	70	70	68	69	277	2,175

Lexus Peru Open

Los Inkas Golf Club, Lima, Peru
Par 36-36–72

November 7-10
purse, US$150,000

	SCORES				TOTAL	MONEY
Julian Etulain	68	70	67	70	275	US$27,000
Ryan Blaum	71	70	67	68	276	13,200
Bronson Burgoon	72	68	67	69	276	13,200
Timothy O'Neal	70	67	73	67	277	7,200
Santiago Russi	68	68	74	68	278	5,700
Sebastian Saavedra	68	68	71	71	278	5,700
Jorge Fernandez-Valdes	74	68	69	68	279	5,025
Jhared Hack	75	67	71	67	280	4,200
Ryan Sullivan	72	68	72	68	280	4,200
Emilio Dominguez	69	66	76	69	280	4,200
Francisco Bide	66	72	72	70	280	4,200
Carlos Franco	70	69	72	70	281	2,764
Christian Espinoza	72	68	70	71	281	2,764
Manuel Inman	69	67	73	72	281	2,764
Armando Villarreal	73	67	69	72	281	2,764
Marco Ruiz	70	70	69	72	281	2,764
Marcelo Rozo	71	66	70	74	281	2,764
Rafael Campos	67	70	69	75	281	2,764
Diego Velasquez	73	69	69	71	282	1,884
Derek Gillespie	65	74	70	73	282	1,884
Augusto Nunez	71	69	69	73	282	1,884
Gato Zarlenga	70	63	75	74	282	1,884

Abierto de Chile

Club de Golf Los Leones, Santiago, Chile
Par 36-36–72

November 21-24
purse, US$150,000

	SCORES				TOTAL	MONEY
Timothy O'Neal	66	72	70	67	275	US$27,000
Sebastian Saavedra	71	73	69	62	275	13,200
Ryan Blaum	71	68	68	68	275	13,200
(O'Neal defeated Saavedra and Blaum on first playoff hole.)						
Mario Clemens	67	69	68	73	277	6,600
Miguel Carballo	70	67	67	73	277	6,600
Rafael Echenique	72	67	68	71	278	5,213
Juan Cerda	70	71	64	73	278	5,213
Bronson Burgoon	71	70	71	67	279	4,650
Sebastian MacLean	74	66	68	72	280	3,900
Sebastian Vazquez	72	69	67	72	280	3,900
Daniel Stapff	66	74	67	73	280	3,900
Cesar Agustin Costilla	67	68	70	75	280	3,900
Clodomiro Carranza	75	69	71	66	281	3,000
Juan Ignacio Lizarralde	72	72	68	69	281	3,000
Matias O'Curry	65	71	77	69	282	2,550
Nelson Ledesma	69	71	73	69	282	2,550
Julio Zapata	72	69	67	74	282	2,550
Augusto Nunez	74	70	72	67	283	2,100
Nicolas Geyger	69	73	70	71	283	2,100
Rafael Becker	70	74	66	73	283	2,100

Personal Classic

La Reserva Cardales, Buenos Aires, Argentina
Par 36-36–72

November 28-December 1
purse, US$150,000

	SCORES				TOTAL	MONEY
Fabian Gomez	67	69	66	67	269	US$27,000
Christian Espinoza	72	69	67	63	271	16,200
Bronson Burgoon	67	69	71	65	272	7,200
Matias O'Curry	67	73	67	65	272	7,200
Rafael Echenique	66	70	70	66	272	7,200
Maximiliano Godoy	66	68	69	69	272	7,200
Sebastian Vazquez	63	74	70	66	273	4,838
Rafael Becker	71	67	68	67	273	4,838
Samuel Del Val	67	70	71	66	274	4,050
Gustavo Acosta	72	68	67	67	274	4,050
Rafael Campos	69	67	67	71	274	4,050
Clodomiro Carranza	69	72	69	65	275	3,450
Sebastian MacLean	67	71	73	65	276	2,730
Dudley Hart	69	66	73	68	276	2,730
Cesar Agustin Costilla	73	66	68	69	276	2,730
Ryan Sullivan	71	66	69	70	276	2,730
Julian Etulain	70	69	66	71	276	2,730
Paulo Pinto	68	68	74	67	277	2,025
Nelson Ledesma	68	71	69	69	277	2,025
Mario Clemens	71	70	66	70	277	2,025
Bruce McDonald	67	70	69	71	277	2,025

Visa Open de Argentina

Nordelta Golf Club, Buenos Aires, Argentina
Par 36-36–72

December 5-8
purse, US$150,000

	SCORES				TOTAL	MONEY
Marcelo Rozo	73	64	69	72	278	US$27,000
Jeff Gove	72	72	69	67	280	16,200
Bronson Burgoon	73	68	72	68	281	8,700
Emiliano Grillo	70	71	72	68	281	8,700
Angel Cabrera	71	74	68	69	282	5,700
Ryan Blaum	67	73	72	70	282	5,700
Emilio Dominguez	70	70	73	71	284	4,838
Rafael Echenique	67	70	74	73	284	4,838
Mauricio Molina	74	71	71	71	287	4,350
Ronaldo Francisco	74	75	67	72	288	4,050
Scott Dunlap	71	74	74	70	289	3,450
Manuel Inman	72	75	72	70	289	3,450
Bruce McDonald	72	68	75	74	289	3,450
Sergio Acevedo	70	70	73	77	290	2,850
Santiago Russi	75	74	75	67	291	2,180
Sebastian MacLean	76	71	75	69	291	2,180
Gustavo Acosta	72	74	74	71	291	2,180
Abbie Valentine	77	69	73	72	291	2,180
Max Scodro	76	72	71	72	291	2,180
Russell Surber	71	77	70	73	291	2,180
Julio Santos	73	71	73	74	291	2,180
Jacobo Pastor	72	74	71	74	291	2,180

European Tours

Volvo Golf Champions

Durban Country Club, Durban, South Africa
Par 36-36–72; 6,732 yards

January 10-13
purse, €2,000,000

	SCORES				TOTAL	MONEY
Louis Oosthuizen	68	64	74	66	272	€350,000
Scott Jamieson	69	64	68	72	273	226,300
Thongchai Jaidee	65	68	73	68	274	131,300
Padraig Harrington	70	71	67	68	276	111,300
Julien Quesne	72	67	67	71	277	87,850
Danny Willett	69	70	70	68	277	87,850
Branden Grace	75	67	69	67	278	66,400
Paul Lawrie	69	70	70	69	278	66,400
Thomas Bjorn	69	70	72	68	279	45,357
Rafa Cabrera-Bello	72	69	70	68	279	45,357
Nicolas Colsaerts	73	67	71	68	279	45,357
Shane Lowry	70	69	70	70	279	45,357
Matteo Manassero	75	69	66	69	279	45,357
Francesco Molinari	70	70	68	71	279	45,357
Richie Ramsay	69	73	70	67	279	45,357
Jamie Donaldson	69	72	73	66	280	37,150
Jeev Milkha Singh	69	70	72	69	280	37,150
Paul Casey	74	69	69	69	281	34,950
Ernie Els	68	72	71	70	281	34,950
Gonzalo Fernandez-Castano	75	70	69	68	282	33,550
Retief Goosen	72	70	70	70	282	33,550
Darren Clarke	75	68	71	69	283	32,150
Henrik Stenson	72	70	70	71	283	32,150
Robert Rock	70	74	70	70	284	31,100
Michael Hoey	72	74	66	73	285	30,400
Marcel Siem	74	74	72	66	286	29,700
Bernd Wiesberger	76	71	73	68	288	29,000
Ricardo Santos	76	76	65	72	289	28,300
Darren Fichardt	78	70	75	67	290	27,250
Colin Montgomerie	72	78	70	70	290	27,250
Thorbjorn Olesen	75	72	74	71	292	26,200
Jbe' Kruger	75	73	70	75	293	25,150
Jose Maria Olazabal	74	72	72	75	293	25,150

Abu Dhabi HSBC Golf Championship

Abu Dhabi Golf Club, Abu Dhabi, United Arab Emirates
Par 36-36–72; 7,600 yards

January 17-20
purse, $2,700,000

	SCORES				TOTAL	MONEY
Jamie Donaldson	67	70	69	68	274	€336,726
Thorbjorn Olesen	68	69	69	69	275	175,479
Justin Rose	67	69	68	71	275	175,479
Ricardo Santos	71	72	66	68	277	101,018
Branden Grace	71	69	73	65	278	85,663
David Howell	69	71	68	71	279	60,611
Martin Kaymer	71	69	70	69	279	60,611
Joost Luiten	70	69	73	67	279	60,611

		SCORES			TOTAL	MONEY
Jorge Campillo	74	68	69	69	280	34,902
George Coetzee	69	71	71	69	280	34,902
Jason Dufner	71	69	72	68	280	34,902
Gonzalo Fernandez-Castano	70	67	71	72	280	34,902
Anders Hansen	71	71	69	69	280	34,902
Peter Hanson	73	72	66	69	280	34,902
Thongchai Jaidee	70	71	66	73	280	34,902
Jbe' Kruger	72	69	69	70	280	34,902
Michael Campbell	69	71	69	72	281	25,658
S.S.P. Chowrasia	73	73	65	70	281	25,658
Andrew Dodt	74	70	65	72	281	25,658
Craig Lee	72	70	72	67	281	25,658
Marcus Fraser	75	71	67	69	282	23,133
Bernd Wiesberger	74	71	66	71	282	23,133
Rafa Cabrera-Bello	74	72	69	68	283	19,799
Paul Casey	71	73	70	69	283	19,799
Richard Green	71	75	70	67	283	19,799
Padraig Harrington	72	72	70	69	283	19,799
Peter Lawrie	72	72	69	70	283	19,799
Matteo Manassero	72	68	73	70	283	19,799
Richie Ramsay	73	68	67	75	283	19,799
Henrik Stenson	69	71	76	67	283	19,799
Danny Willett	70	71	71	71	283	19,799
Darren Fichardt	72	70	72	71	285	15,239
Lorenzo Gagli	74	68	70	73	285	15,239
Keith Horne	72	69	73	71	285	15,239
Soren Kjeldsen	70	71	75	69	285	15,239
Alexander Noren	76	70	68	71	285	15,239
Phillip Price	72	74	69	70	285	15,239
Steve Webster	73	72	72	68	285	15,239
Alejandro Canizares	73	69	72	72	286	11,920
Ernie Els	71	73	72	70	286	11,920
Mark Foster	72	72	74	68	286	11,920
Andreas Harto	74	72	68	72	286	11,920
Raphael Jacquelin	72	69	73	72	286	11,920
Pablo Larrazabal	68	74	72	72	286	11,920
Wen-Chong Liang	69	72	74	71	286	11,920
Gareth Maybin	71	71	71	73	286	11,920
Marcel Siem	72	72	72	70	286	11,920
Richard Bland	72	73	72	70	287	9,294
Prom Meesawat	76	69	69	73	287	9,294
Garth Mulroy	71	68	75	73	287	9,294
Peter Whiteford	73	70	73	71	287	9,294
Thomas Bjorn	72	74	71	71	288	7,677
Simon Dyson	75	70	72	71	288	7,677
Ricardo Gonzalez	72	72	70	74	288	7,677
Paul Lawrie	74	71	71	72	288	7,677
Johan Edfors	71	73	68	77	289	6,101
Ignacio Garrido	75	70	73	71	289	6,101
Todd Hamilton	75	69	71	74	289	6,101
Joel Sjoholm	71	70	74	74	289	6,101
Fabrizio Zanotti	76	70	73	70	289	6,101
Gregory Bourdy	72	73	73	72	290	5,253
Michael Hoey	72	73	74	71	290	5,253
Tom Lewis	74	72	71	73	290	5,253
Graeme Storm	72	73	73	73	291	4,748
Romain Wattel	73	69	73	76	291	4,748
Robert Coles	73	70	77	72	292	4,344
Oliver Fisher	73	71	74	74	292	4,344
Andy Sullivan	71	73	76	73	293	4,041
David Horsey	74	72	73	75	294	3,839
Chris Wood	73	71	77	75	296	3,682

Commercial Bank Qatar Masters

Doha Golf Club, Doha, Qatar
Par 36-36–72; 7,400 yards

January 23-26
purse, $2,500,000

	SCORES				TOTAL	MONEY
Chris Wood	67	70	64	69	270	€310,917
George Coetzee	69	67	70	65	271	162,029
Sergio Garcia	69	66	70	66	271	162,029
Alexander Noren	71	67	66	71	275	86,188
Steve Webster	69	71	67	68	275	86,188
Branden Grace	70	68	67	71	276	55,966
Simon Khan	67	73	64	72	276	55,966
Anthony Wall	66	71	70	69	276	55,966
Felipe Aguilar	69	67	73	68	277	33,073
Victor Dubuisson	68	72	68	69	277	33,073
Jason Dufner	71	70	67	69	277	33,073
Mikko Ilonen	71	69	68	69	277	33,073
Thongchai Jaidee	70	69	70	68	277	33,073
Martin Kaymer	68	67	72	70	277	33,073
Andy Sullivan	67	71	74	65	277	33,073
Michael Campbell	68	68	68	74	278	23,786
Gonzalo Fernandez-Castano	69	70	70	69	278	23,786
Gary Lockerbie	67	69	71	71	278	23,786
Prom Meesawat	71	71	68	68	278	23,786
Justin Rose	68	71	71	68	278	23,786
Henrik Stenson	70	69	69	70	278	23,786
Thomas Aiken	71	68	71	69	279	18,002
Rafa Cabrera-Bello	71	72	72	64	279	18,002
Marcus Fraser	68	67	71	73	279	18,002
Lorenzo Gagli	68	71	69	71	279	18,002
Peter Hanson	68	73	68	70	279	18,002
David Howell	69	73	68	69	279	18,002
Jbe' Kruger	70	68	68	73	279	18,002
Matteo Manassero	69	72	71	67	279	18,002
Damien McGrane	68	72	70	69	279	18,002
Thorbjorn Olesen	68	68	70	73	279	18,002
Brett Rumford	67	73	69	70	279	18,002
Ricardo Santos	65	70	76	68	279	18,002
Alexandre Kaleka	66	71	73	70	280	13,991
Louis Oosthuizen	71	69	68	72	280	13,991
Joel Sjoholm	69	72	70	69	280	13,991
Paul Casey	70	68	72	71	281	12,872
Tommy Fleetwood	72	71	68	70	281	12,872
David Horsey	68	72	72	69	281	12,872
Richard Green	68	73	68	73	282	11,939
Garth Mulroy	69	68	71	74	282	11,939
Mark Foster	71	71	72	69	283	10,260
Anders Hansen	68	71	70	74	283	10,260
Michael Hoey	70	69	74	70	283	10,260
Raphael Jacquelin	73	67	69	74	283	10,260
Peter Lawrie	72	71	71	69	283	10,260
Marcel Siem	72	71	72	68	283	10,260
Bernd Wiesberger	70	72	71	70	283	10,260
Richard Bland	71	69	72	72	284	7,108
S.S.P. Chowrasia	70	73	69	72	284	7,108
David Drysdale	72	71	71	70	284	7,108
Estanislao Goya	71	72	70	71	284	7,108
Todd Hamilton	73	69	70	72	284	7,108
Andreas Harto	68	69	71	76	284	7,108
Mikael Lundberg	72	67	72	73	284	7,108
Gareth Maybin	72	71	72	69	284	7,108
Romain Wattel	72	70	69	73	284	7,108

	SCORES				TOTAL	MONEY
Peter Whiteford	66	73	72	73	284	7,108
Thomas Bjorn	72	69	70	74	285	5,037
Robert-Jan Derksen	71	69	73	72	285	5,037
Stephen Gallacher	72	71	69	73	285	5,037
Tom Lewis	70	71	74	70	285	5,037
Fabrizio Zanotti	70	73	73	69	285	5,037
Simon Dyson	71	72	72	71	286	4,291
Jean-Baptiste Gonnet	71	72	71	72	286	4,291
Simon Wakefield	71	72	74	69	286	4,291
Matthew Baldwin	73	70	75	69	287	3,824
Craig Lee	72	69	74	72	287	3,824
Gregory Havret	70	69	74	75	288	3,545
Scott Henry	69	74	72	75	290	3,104
Lee Slattery	70	73	75	72	290	3,104
Chris Doak	72	71	73	75	291	2,795
Ernie Els	72	71	74	76	293	2,792
Paul Waring	73	69	76	77	295	2,789

Omega Dubai Desert Classic

Emirates Golf Club, Dubai, United Arab Emirates
Par 35-37–72; 7,316 yards

January 31-February 3
purse, $2,500,000

	SCORES				TOTAL	MONEY
Stephen Gallacher	63	70	62	71	266	€309,233
Richard Sterne	62	70	66	71	269	206,153
Felipe Aguilar	68	68	66	69	271	104,460
Thorbjorn Olesen	67	66	67	71	271	104,460
Marcus Fraser	67	69	69	67	272	71,805
Lee Westwood	67	71	66	68	272	71,805
Robert Rock	70	68	67	68	273	47,870
Ricardo Santos	66	71	69	67	273	47,870
Steve Webster	69	69	65	70	273	47,870
Tommy Fleetwood	65	68	69	72	274	35,624
Jeev Milkha Singh	68	67	67	72	274	35,624
Matteo Manassero	66	71	70	68	275	30,058
Gareth Maybin	69	67	69	70	275	30,058
Andy Sullivan	69	67	69	70	275	30,058
Lorenzo Gagli	68	71	69	68	276	26,718
Garth Mulroy	71	70	66	69	276	26,718
Fredrik Andersson Hed	67	71	68	71	277	21,812
Rafa Cabrera-Bello	69	69	69	70	277	21,812
Sergio Garcia	68	67	71	71	277	21,812
Ignacio Garrido	69	68	70	70	277	21,812
Andreas Harto	67	67	71	72	277	21,812
Maximilian Kieffer	66	68	69	74	277	21,812
Peter Lawrie	66	70	71	70	277	21,812
Jose Maria Olazabal	70	67	71	69	277	21,812
Marc Warren	67	72	71	67	277	21,812
Scott Jamieson	65	72	70	71	278	17,905
Seung-Yul Noh	66	72	67	73	278	17,905
Henrik Stenson	69	69	71	69	278	17,905
Justin Walters	68	70	67	73	278	17,905
Robert-Jan Derksen	68	72	69	70	279	14,923
Ricardo Gonzalez	71	70	69	69	279	14,923
David Howell	70	68	72	69	279	14,923
Raphael Jacquelin	70	68	68	73	279	14,923
Alexander Noren	68	71	67	73	279	14,923
Anthony Wall	68	72	68	71	279	14,923
Chris Wood	68	68	74	69	279	14,923

	SCORES				TOTAL	MONEY
Paul Casey	66	70	73	71	280	11,875
Robert Coles	73	68	70	69	280	11,875
Jamie Donaldson	67	73	68	72	280	11,875
Gregory Havret	70	67	72	71	280	11,875
Craig Lee	69	70	71	70	280	11,875
Gary Lockerbie	68	70	71	71	280	11,875
Marcel Siem	68	72	68	72	280	11,875
Lee Slattery	69	70	70	71	280	11,875
Gregory Bourdy	67	71	71	72	281	9,648
S.S.P. Chowrasia	69	70	74	68	281	9,648
David Drysdale	69	70	69	73	281	9,648
Simon Khan	68	73	70	70	281	9,648
Jorge Campillo	69	71	69	73	282	8,349
Maarten Lafeber	69	71	71	71	282	8,349
Pablo Larrazabal	71	70	71	70	282	8,349
Chris Doak	65	69	71	78	283	6,520
Simon Dyson	70	71	73	69	283	6,520
Mikko Ilonen	71	70	69	73	283	6,520
Jbe' Kruger	70	66	69	78	283	6,520
Matthew Nixon	69	69	73	72	283	6,520
Alessandro Tadini	70	71	71	71	283	6,520
Romain Wattel	68	67	71	77	283	6,520
Todd Hamilton	70	68	70	76	284	5,010
David Horsey	75	66	70	73	284	5,010
Tom Lewis	69	72	74	69	284	5,010
Mark O'Meara	67	74	71	72	284	5,010
Bernd Wiesberger	71	68	73	72	284	5,010
Jean-Baptiste Gonnet	72	68	73	72	285	4,267
Thongchai Jaidee	68	68	73	76	285	4,267
Damien McGrane	68	72	73	72	285	4,267
Oliver Fisher	69	72	73	73	287	3,896
Keith Horne	68	71	74	75	288	3,543
Thomas Levet	68	70	77	73	288	3,543
Eddie Pepperell	68	70	72	78	288	3,543
Jaco Van Zyl	69	71	73	77	290	2,783

Joburg Open

See African Tours chapter.

Africa Open

See African Tours chapter.

Tshwane Open

See African Tours chapter.

Avantha Masters

See Asia/Japan Tours chapter.

Maybank Malaysian Open

See Asia/Japan Tours chapter.

Trophee Hassan II

Golf du Palais Royal, Agadir, Morocco
Par 36-36-72; 6,844 yards

March 28-31
purse, €1,500,000

	SCORES				TOTAL	MONEY
Marcel Siem	64	68	69	70	271	€250,000
David Horsey	68	67	70	69	274	130,280
Mikko Ilonen	69	66	70	69	274	130,280
Pablo Larrazabal	72	64	69	71	276	75,000
Matthew Baldwin	72	70	68	69	279	53,700
Alvaro Velasco	67	74	69	69	279	53,700
Bernd Wiesberger	72	66	69	72	279	53,700
David Howell	71	70	72	68	281	37,500
Craig Lee	69	69	70	74	282	31,800
Julien Quesne	71	72	71	68	282	31,800
David Drysdale	74	72	67	70	283	25,125
Emiliano Grillo	74	70	69	70	283	25,125
Chris Paisley	73	67	75	68	283	25,125
Steve Webster	74	72	69	68	283	25,125
Oliver Fisher	73	69	70	72	284	18,917
Andreas Harto	71	67	73	73	284	18,917
Gary Lockerbie	69	76	69	70	284	18,917
Joost Luiten	70	69	72	73	284	18,917
Andrew Marshall	73	71	72	68	284	18,917
Francesco Molinari	73	71	70	70	284	18,917
Richie Ramsay	74	69	69	72	284	18,917
Simon Wakefield	68	72	71	73	284	18,917
Paul Waring	71	72	71	70	284	18,917
Jorge Campillo	72	74	72	67	285	15,375
Lorenzo Gagli	74	73	69	69	285	15,375
Richard Green	75	71	68	71	285	15,375
Lee Slattery	74	71	72	68	285	15,375
Chris Lloyd	72	68	75	71	286	13,575
Mikael Lundberg	73	69	68	76	286	13,575
Garth Mulroy	73	67	74	72	286	13,575
Graeme Storm	68	77	73	68	286	13,575
Daniel Brooks	72	70	75	70	287	12,000
Alejandro Canizares	73	73	72	69	287	12,000
Michael Hoey	74	69	74	70	287	12,000
J.B. Hansen	73	73	70	72	288	10,950
Alexander Levy	73	74	70	71	288	10,950
Matthew Southgate	72	75	72	69	288	10,950
Robert Coles	76	70	70	73	289	9,600
Stephen Gallacher	75	68	70	76	289	9,600
Ignacio Garrido	77	69	70	73	289	9,600
Keith Horne	77	69	72	71	289	9,600
John Parry	73	73	70	73	289	9,600
Anthony Snobeck	75	67	72	75	289	9,600
Jamie Elson	77	69	70	74	290	7,950
Mikko Korhonen	76	71	73	70	290	7,950
Bernd Ritthammer	73	73	72	72	290	7,950
Joel Sjoholm	78	69	72	71	290	7,950
Justin Walters	71	71	79	69	290	7,950
Scott Arnold	71	71	70	79	291	6,750
Richard McEvoy	71	70	75	75	291	6,750
Alessandro Tadini	72	74	77	68	291	6,750
Matteo Delpodio	74	70	78	70	292	5,400
Gregory Havret	70	71	77	74	292	5,400
Scott Henry	72	71	80	69	292	5,400
Espen Kofstad	74	73	70	75	292	5,400
Jose Manuel Lara	72	71	74	75	292	5,400
Martin Wiegele	75	69	73	75	292	5,400

	SCORES				TOTAL	MONEY
Stephen Dodd	74	70	77	72	293	4,350
Morten Orum Madsen	78	69	76	70	293	4,350
Daniel Popovic	72	72	71	78	293	4,350
Fredrik Andersson Hed	75	72	73	74	294	3,975
Peter Erofejeff	76	69	72	77	294	3,975
Maarten Lafeber	77	67	74	77	295	3,750
Carlos Del Moral	78	68	74	78	298	3,450
Santiago Luna	72	73	76	77	298	3,450
Edoardo Molinari	81	66	73	78	298	3,450

Open de Espana

Parador de El Saler, Valencia, Spain
Par 36-36—72; 7,052 yards

April 18-21
purse, €1,500,000

	SCORES				TOTAL	MONEY
Raphael Jacquelin	73	66	73	71	283	€250,000
Felipe Aguilar	68	71	74	70	283	130,280
Maximilian Kieffer	75	68	69	71	283	130,280
(Jacquelin defeated Aguilar on third and Kieffer on ninth playoff hole.)						
Magnus A. Carlsson	70	75	68	71	284	59,025
David Horsey	71	74	66	73	284	59,025
Paul Waring	71	71	69	73	284	59,025
Marc Warren	70	70	68	76	284	59,025
Matteo Delpodio	73	69	73	70	285	32,175
Espen Kofstad	71	72	70	72	285	32,175
Eddie Pepperell	70	70	73	72	285	32,175
Peter Uihlein	70	68	74	73	285	32,175
Nacho Elvira	71	72	71	72	286	23,738
Sergio Garcia	72	73	70	71	286	23,738
Lasse Jensen	71	70	74	71	286	23,738
Andrew Marshall	72	74	70	70	286	23,738
Paul Casey	72	70	72	73	287	19,470
Emiliano Grillo	74	72	68	73	287	19,470
Peter Lawrie	71	74	72	70	287	19,470
Matteo Manassero	78	68	72	69	287	19,470
Gareth Maybin	74	71	75	67	287	19,470
Gregory Bourdy	72	73	68	75	288	16,275
Joakim Lagergren	69	76	69	74	288	16,275
Craig Lee	69	71	70	78	288	16,275
Joost Luiten	74	72	70	72	288	16,275
James Morrison	72	73	73	70	288	16,275
Lee Slattery	75	71	70	72	288	16,275
Eduardo De La Riva	72	73	70	74	289	13,125
Rikard Karlberg	72	67	75	75	289	13,125
Moritz Lampert	76	68	71	74	289	13,125
Callum Macaulay	73	71	74	71	289	13,125
Edoardo Molinari	70	73	78	68	289	13,125
Phillip Price	70	74	72	73	289	13,125
Julien Quesne	72	70	73	74	289	13,125
Mark Tullo	71	71	74	73	289	13,125
Robert-Jan Derksen	69	73	77	71	290	10,050
David Drysdale	73	72	68	77	290	10,050
Richard Finch	70	73	76	71	290	10,050
Ignacio Garrido	72	71	77	70	290	10,050
Jean-Baptiste Gonnet	73	73	70	74	290	10,050
Anders Hansen	72	71	74	73	290	10,050
Mikko Korhonen	71	73	72	74	290	10,050
Matthew Nixon	74	72	71	73	290	10,050
Jarmo Sandelin	74	71	72	73	290	10,050

	SCORES				TOTAL	MONEY
Rafa Cabrera-Bello	72	73	75	71	291	7,650
Gonzalo Fernandez-Castano	69	73	74	75	291	7,650
Kenneth Ferrie	72	73	69	77	291	7,650
Ricardo Gonzalez	74	70	72	75	291	7,650
Soren Hansen	74	70	72	75	291	7,650
David Howell	70	71	71	79	291	7,650
Joel Sjoholm	69	76	72	74	291	7,650
Matthew Baldwin	73	68	73	78	292	5,850
Tommy Fleetwood	72	69	74	77	292	5,850
Alastair Forsyth	76	70	74	72	292	5,850
David Higgins	69	75	72	76	292	5,850
Morten Orum Madsen	68	72	74	78	292	5,850
Carlos Aguilar	71	72	80	70	293	4,530
Alejandro Canizares	71	73	73	76	293	4,530
Rhys Davies	73	72	74	74	293	4,530
Andreas Harto	73	67	81	72	293	4,530
Pedro Oriol	71	75	72	75	293	4,530
Seve Benson	74	72	72	76	294	3,675
Daniel Brooks	69	75	76	74	294	3,675
Christian Cevaer	76	70	72	76	294	3,675
Victor Dubuisson	74	70	72	78	294	3,675
Richard Green	73	72	73	76	294	3,675
Alvaro Velasco	71	71	76	76	294	3,675
Sam Little	73	72	74	76	295	3,075
Tjaart van der Walt	73	72	73	77	295	3,075
Shane Lowry	78	66	74	78	296	2,850
Jose Manuel Lara	70	74	80	74	298	2,740
Jordi Garcia Pinto	73	71	82	73	299	2,250
Guillaume Cambis	77	69	76	78	300	2,246
Gary Stal	68	78	83	71	300	2,246

Ballantine's Championship

See Asia/Japan Tours chapter.

Volvo China Open

See Asia/Japan Tours chapter.

Volvo World Match Play Championship

Thracian Cliffs Golf & Beach Resort, Kavarna, Bulgaria
Par 35-37–72; 7,291 yards

May 16-19
purse, €3,000,000

FIRST ROUND

Gonzalo Fernandez-Castano defeated Jamie Donaldson, 1 up.
Carl Pettersson defeated Thorbjorn Olesen, 4 and 3.
Francesco Molinari defeated Henrik Stenson, 2 and 1.
Branden Grace defeated Nicolas Colsaerts, 4 and 3.
Bo Van Pelt halved with Richard Sterne.
Peter Hanson defeated George Coetzee, 2 and 1.
Thongchai Jaidee defeated Ian Poulter, 3 and 2.
Graeme McDowell defeated Chris Wood, 5 and 3.

SECOND ROUND

Brett Rumford defeated Jamie Donaldson, 5 and 3.
Scott Jamieson defeated Carl Pettersson, 1 up.
Francesco Molinari defeated Felipe Aguilar, 4 and 3.

Nicolas Colsaerts defeated Kiradech Aphibarnrat, 3 and 2.
Richard Sterne defeated Geoff Ogilvy, 5 and 4.
George Coetzee defeated Shane Lowry, 3 and 2.
Thongchai Jaidee defeated Thomas Aiken, 1 up.
Chris Wood defeated Stephen Gallacher, 2 and 1.

THIRD ROUND

Fernandez-Castano defeated Rumford, 3 and 2.
Jamieson defeated Olesen, 5 and 3.
Aguilar defeated Stenson, 3 and 1.
Grace halved with Aphibarnrat.
Van Pelt halved with Ogilvy.
Lowry defeated Hanson
Aiken defeated Poulter, 1 up.
McDowell defeated Gallacher, 4 and 2.

(Each eliminated player received €50,000)

ROUND OF TOP 16

Grace defeated Rumford, 4 and 3.
Wood defeated Sterne, 5 and 3.
Molinari defeated Pettersson, 6 and 4.
Aiken defeated Lowry, 19 holes.
Jamieson defeated Aguilar, 1 up.
Jaidee defeated Hanson, 21 holes.
Colsaerts defeated Fernandez-Castano, 2 up.
McDowell defeated Van Pelt, 1 up.

(Each losing player received €75,000.)

QUARTER-FINALS

Grace defeated Wood, 2 and 1.
Aiken defeated Molinari, 3 and 2.
Jaidee defeated Jamieson, 4 and 3.
McDowell defeated Colsaerts, 2 and 1.

(Each losing player received €100,000.)

SEMI-FINALS

Jaidee defeated Aiken, 3 and 2.
McDowell defeated Grace, 3 and 2.

(Each losing player received €200,000.)

FINAL

McDowell defeated Jaidee, 2 and 1.

(McDowell received €800,000; Jaidee received €400,000.)

Madeira Islands Open - Portugal - BPI

Clube de Golf do Santo da Serra, Santo Antonio da Serra,
Madeira, Portugal
Par 36-36–72; 6,826 yards

May 16-19
purse, €600,000

	SCORES				TOTAL	MONEY
Peter Uihlein	72	64	69	68	273	€100,000
Morten Orum Madsen	72	69	67	67	275	52,110
Mark Tullo	67	69	68	71	275	52,110
Craig Lee	67	68	70	71	276	30,000
Seve Benson	74	69	69	67	279	19,860
Richard Bland	66	75	70	68	279	19,860
Rhys Davies	74	68	70	67	279	19,860
Roope Kakko	70	70	71	68	279	19,860
Christophe Brazillier	70	68	74	68	280	12,160
Jamie Elson	72	71	70	67	280	12,160
Jose-Filipe Lima	73	71	66	70	280	12,160
Daniel Im	72	71	67	71	281	9,990
Jarmo Sandelin	69	69	70	73	281	9,990
John Parry	70	72	75	65	282	9,180
Markus Brier	72	73	68	70	283	8,280
Jamie Howarth	72	70	70	71	283	8,280
Dodge Kemmer	72	70	71	70	283	8,280
Chris Paisley	71	72	68	72	283	8,280
Robert-Jan Derksen	72	69	72	71	284	6,996
Chris Doak	73	70	70	71	284	6,996
Mikko Korhonen	72	71	71	70	284	6,996
Ricardo Santos	76	70	69	69	284	6,996
Tim Sluiter	71	72	72	69	284	6,996
Jens Dantorp	70	72	71	72	285	5,970
Simon Dyson	75	70	71	69	285	5,970
Soren Hansen	70	68	74	73	285	5,970
Brooks Koepka	72	73	68	72	285	5,970
Steven Tiley	71	73	69	72	285	5,970
Peter Whiteford	70	74	70	71	285	5,970
H.P. Bacher	73	70	70	73	286	4,900
David Dixon	70	74	73	69	286	4,900
Joakim Lagergren	67	75	72	72	286	4,900
Raul Quiros	73	71	70	72	286	4,900
Raymond Russell	73	72	71	70	286	4,900
Sam Walker	77	68	71	70	286	4,900
Niclas Fasth	75	68	69	75	287	4,080
Oscar Floren	72	72	73	70	287	4,080
Tyrrell Hatton	71	74	72	70	287	4,080
David Higgins	75	69	69	74	287	4,080
Lloyd Saltman	64	75	74	74	287	4,080
Alessandro Tadini	71	72	70	74	287	4,080
Matteo Delpodio	72	74	75	67	288	3,480
Damien McGrane	71	71	73	73	288	3,480
Nicolo Ravano	73	73	74	68	288	3,480
Victor Riu	70	72	72	74	288	3,480
Thomas Haylock	71	73	69	76	289	2,880
Peter Hedblom	71	73	72	73	289	2,880
Rikard Karlberg	72	68	71	78	289	2,880
Andrea Pavan	73	70	72	74	289	2,880
Niccolo Quintarelli	71	73	75	70	289	2,880
James Ruth	71	75	71	72	289	2,880
Scott Arnold	72	74	72	72	290	2,340
Klas Eriksson	73	69	75	73	290	2,340
Thomas Levet	70	67	75	78	290	2,340
*Goncalo Pinto	73	70	75	72	290	
Pelle Edberg	70	76	72	73	291	1,980

	SCORES				TOTAL	MONEY
Mikael Lundberg	70	72	73	76	291	1,980
Robert Rock	74	72	73	72	291	1,980
Adam Gee	71	75	73	73	292	1,740
Nuno Henriques	71	73	74	74	292	1,740
Anthony Snobeck	72	74	71	75	292	1,740
Andrew Marshall	75	71	73	74	293	1,590
Andrea Perrino	70	73	77	73	293	1,590
Carlos Del Moral	71	72	77	74	294	1,500
Sam Hutsby	74	70	77	74	295	1,410
Ross McGowan	68	77	75	75	295	1,410
*Joao Carlota	72	74	76	74	296	
Antonio Rosado	73	73	80	74	300	1,260
Graeme Storm	73	73	80	74	300	1,260
Alvaro Velasco	75	71	75	79	300	1,260

BMW PGA Championship

Wentworth Club, Virginia Water, Surrey, England
Par 35-37–72; 7,302 yards

May 23-26
purse, €4,750,000

	SCORES				TOTAL	MONEY
Matteo Manassero	69	71	69	69	278	€791,660
Simon Khan	69	72	71	66	278	412,560
Marc Warren	69	70	70	69	278	412,560
(Manassero defeated Warren on first and Khan on fourth playoff hole.)						
Alejandro Canizares	69	70	68	72	279	219,450
Miguel Angel Jimenez	76	69	67	67	279	219,450
Ernie Els	72	69	72	67	280	142,500
James Kingston	66	77	69	68	280	142,500
Eddie Pepperell	71	69	71	69	280	142,500
Francesco Molinari	70	68	73	70	281	96,267
Richie Ramsay	71	75	66	69	281	96,267
Lee Westwood	70	71	67	73	281	96,267
Gregory Bourdy	71	73	70	68	282	70,436
Niclas Fasth	70	71	72	69	282	70,436
Mikko Ilonen	67	76	70	69	282	70,436
Pablo Larrazabal	71	73	67	71	282	70,436
Shane Lowry	70	71	69	72	282	70,436
Peter Uihlein	72	73	68	69	282	70,436
Bernd Wiesberger	73	71	70	68	282	70,436
Richard Bland	71	71	69	72	283	55,385
David Drysdale	71	73	69	70	283	55,385
Sergio Garcia	72	71	68	72	283	55,385
Gregory Havret	70	71	71	71	283	55,385
Edoardo Molinari	71	71	69	72	283	55,385
George Coetzee	69	70	75	70	284	45,838
Nicolas Colsaerts	72	70	73	69	284	45,838
Tommy Fleetwood	71	74	68	71	284	45,838
Mark Foster	70	69	72	73	284	45,838
Branden Grace	71	73	71	69	284	45,838
Raphael Jacquelin	71	71	73	69	284	45,838
Phillip Price	73	69	70	72	284	45,838
Fabrizio Zanotti	71	75	70	68	284	45,838
Darren Clarke	74	70	72	69	285	36,860
Ross Fisher	72	73	68	72	285	36,860
Alexander Noren	74	71	71	69	285	36,860
Alvaro Quiros	70	73	69	73	285	36,860
Danny Willett	73	72	73	67	285	36,860
Jamie Donaldson	71	75	73	67	286	32,775
Anders Hansen	70	74	73	69	286	32,775

	SCORES			TOTAL	MONEY
Lee Slattery	71	71	69	75	286	32,775
Thomas Bjorn	69	74	75	69	287	28,975
Chris Doak	74	71	72	70	287	28,975
Thongchai Jaidee	74	71	72	70	287	28,975
Marcel Siem	75	71	71	70	287	28,975
Graeme Storm	73	71	69	74	287	28,975
Oliver Fisher	70	75	73	70	288	24,225
Soren Kjeldsen	74	72	70	72	288	24,225
Colin Montgomerie	71	75	72	70	288	24,225
Garth Mulroy	74	71	72	71	288	24,225
Jaco Van Zyl	75	69	73	71	288	24,225
Martin Kaymer	70	74	73	72	289	18,525
Jbe' Kruger	71	74	72	72	289	18,525
Thomas Levet	71	75	70	73	289	18,525
Wen-Chong Liang	75	68	72	74	289	18,525
Paul McGinley	71	75	70	73	289	18,525
Justin Rose	72	74	69	74	289	18,525
Ricardo Santos	73	72	76	68	289	18,525
Peter Lawrie	74	72	72	72	290	14,488
Richard Sterne	71	74	71	74	290	14,488
Gary Lockerbie	71	74	73	73	291	13,300
Damien McGrane	72	73	72	74	291	13,300
Jarmo Sandelin	76	69	74	72	291	13,300
Gonzalo Fernandez-Castano	68	75	74	75	292	11,638
Greig Hutcheon	72	74	67	79	292	11,638
Brett Rumford	75	71	72	74	292	11,638
Alessandro Tadini	73	71	74	74	292	11,638
Jason Levermore	72	70	73	78	293	10,450
Andrew Dodt	75	71	73	75	294	9,975
Julien Quesne	71	75	78	71	295	9,500
Robert Coles	75	71	75	75	296	8,273
Scott Drummond	70	75	75	76	296	8,273
Jose Maria Olazabal	75	71	78	72	296	8,273

Nordea Masters

Bro Hof Slott Golf Club, Stockholm, Sweden
Par 36-36–72; 7,607 yards

May 30-June 2
purse, €1,500,000

	SCORES			TOTAL	MONEY
Mikko Ilonen	70	63	65	69	267	€250,000
Jonas Blixt	70	66	66	68	270	166,660
Bernd Wiesberger	69	72	64	66	271	93,900
Thomas Bjorn	70	67	68	67	272	59,025
Rikard Karlberg	69	68	67	68	272	59,025
Matteo Manassero	66	65	71	70	272	59,025
Alexander Noren	67	69	64	72	272	59,025
Ross Fisher	72	67	70	64	273	37,500
Felipe Aguilar	71	67	70	66	274	31,800
Julien Quesne	73	67	66	68	274	31,800
Jamie Donaldson	67	70	72	66	275	25,850
Joost Luiten	68	67	70	70	275	25,850
Henrik Norlander	73	67	67	68	275	25,850
Gregory Havret	69	70	70	67	276	20,725
Miguel Angel Jimenez	72	67	68	69	276	20,725
Soren Kjeldsen	70	69	69	68	276	20,725
Pablo Larrazabal	66	70	70	70	276	20,725
Damien McGrane	73	67	68	68	276	20,725
Peter Whiteford	71	63	73	69	276	20,725
Emiliano Grillo	69	71	70	67	277	18,000

	SCORES			TOTAL	MONEY
Rhys Davies	69	70	68	71	278	16,275
Richard S. Johnson	72	66	71	69	278	16,275
Paul Lawrie	70	71	68	69	278	16,275
Francesco Molinari	70	67	73	68	278	16,275
Jose Maria Olazabal	72	68	71	67	278	16,275
Peter Uihlein	71	70	68	69	278	16,275
Alejandro Canizares	68	72	70	69	279	14,250
David Drysdale	71	68	71	69	279	14,250
Maximilian Kieffer	71	69	69	70	279	14,250
Kiradech Aphibarnrat	73	69	70	68	280	12,064
Simon Dyson	70	70	71	69	280	12,064
J.B. Hansen	69	73	67	71	280	12,064
Peter Hanson	69	69	73	69	280	12,064
Roope Kakko	71	68	70	71	280	12,064
Chris Lloyd	67	73	73	67	280	12,064
Alvaro Quiros	71	68	70	71	280	12,064
Seve Benson	70	71	68	72	281	9,750
Richard Bland	72	70	70	69	281	9,750
Chris Doak	72	68	71	70	281	9,750
Tommy Fleetwood	72	70	72	67	281	9,750
Ricardo Gonzalez	71	71	71	68	281	9,750
Lee Slattery	72	69	71	69	281	9,750
Simon Wakefield	67	73	72	69	281	9,750
Fredrik Andersson Hed	67	72	72	71	282	7,950
Eduardo De La Riva	71	70	71	70	282	7,950
Andrew Dodt	77	65	67	73	282	7,950
Mark Foster	73	68	73	68	282	7,950
Craig Lee	72	70	67	73	282	7,950
Andy Sullivan	71	70	70	72	283	7,050
Magnus A. Carlsson	70	71	71	72	284	6,600
Estanislao Goya	73	68	71	72	284	6,600
Paul Casey	74	68	77	66	285	5,700
S.S.P. Chowrasia	71	69	74	71	285	5,700
Soren Hansen	71	70	69	75	285	5,700
Joel Sjoholm	69	73	71	72	285	5,700
Matthew Baldwin	71	69	73	73	286	4,700
Joakim Lagergren	70	72	73	71	286	4,700
Sam Little	73	69	75	69	286	4,700
Gregory Bourdy	70	71	71	75	287	4,050
Jorge Campillo	72	68	72	75	287	4,050
Richard Green	70	72	76	69	287	4,050
Lasse Jensen	71	68	72	76	287	4,050
Gary Orr	68	71	72	76	287	4,050
Richie Ramsay	70	70	72	76	288	3,600
John Parry	68	73	73	75	289	3,450
Alan Dunbar	72	69	75	74	290	3,300
Andreas Harto	72	68	74	77	291	3,150
Peter Erofejeff	70	71	76	75	292	2,863
Matthew Southgate	70	71	73	78	292	2,863
Mark Tullo	70	71	77	74	292	2,863
Pablo Martin Benavides	69	72	71	81	293	2,248
Fabrizio Zanotti	72	66	76	79	293	2,248
Johan Edfors	71	70	76	79	296	2,244
Michael Campbell	75	67	75	80	297	2,241

Lyoness Open

Diamond Country Club, Atzenbrugg, Austria
Par 36-36–72; 7,386 yards

June 6-9
purse, €1,000,000

	SCORES				TOTAL	MONEY
Joost Luiten	65	68	67	71	271	€166,660
Thomas Bjorn	71	70	64	68	273	111,110
Wen-Chong Liang	67	72	69	66	274	56,300
Romain Wattel	68	68	69	69	274	56,300
Jorge Campillo	70	67	66	72	275	38,700
Paul Waring	67	67	72	69	275	38,700
Eduardo De La Riva	69	65	69	73	276	30,000
Gregory Bourdy	70	68	70	69	277	25,000
Lee Slattery	71	68	70	69	278	22,400
Lorenzo Gagli	72	67	68	72	279	17,925
Shiv Kapur	68	72	71	68	279	17,925
Alexander Levy	66	75	68	70	279	17,925
Graeme Storm	66	74	71	68	279	17,925
Craig Lee	70	73	68	69	280	14,400
Damien McGrane	69	72	70	69	280	14,400
Hennie Otto	71	65	71	73	280	14,400
*Matthias Schwab	67	74	70	69	280	
Bernd Wiesberger	68	71	72	69	280	14,400
Fredrik Andersson Hed	74	67	70	70	281	11,867
Magnus A. Carlsson	69	72	70	70	281	11,867
Soren Hansen	70	72	68	71	281	11,867
Tyrrell Hatton	74	69	66	72	281	11,867
Miguel Angel Jimenez	67	70	69	75	281	11,867
Simon Wakefield	75	65	70	71	281	11,867
Matthew Baldwin	71	66	71	74	282	10,100
Simon Dyson	66	74	69	73	282	10,100
Sam Little	69	73	66	74	282	10,100
Tjaart van der Walt	72	66	70	74	282	10,100
Steve Webster	68	71	71	72	282	10,100
Alastair Forsyth	70	68	70	75	283	8,450
Emiliano Grillo	72	67	71	73	283	8,450
Moritz Lampert	69	72	69	73	283	8,450
Thomas Levet	73	70	70	70	283	8,450
Tom Lewis	63	74	71	75	283	8,450
Chris Paisley	69	72	70	72	283	8,450
Richard Bland	72	70	73	69	284	6,900
David Drysdale	71	66	72	75	284	6,900
Gareth Maybin	72	68	74	70	284	6,900
Anthony Snobeck	70	71	72	71	284	6,900
Andy Sullivan	67	71	71	75	284	6,900
Mark Tullo	69	70	73	72	284	6,900
Martin Wiegele	73	71	67	73	284	6,900
Bradley Dredge	71	69	72	73	285	6,000
Lukas Nemecz	71	69	76	69	285	6,000
Gaganjeet Bhullar	72	67	72	75	286	5,600
Mikko Korhonen	72	72	71	71	286	5,600
Robert-Jan Derksen	74	70	72	71	287	4,900
Peter Gustafsson	71	73	67	76	287	4,900
J.B. Hansen	69	73	75	70	287	4,900
David Higgins	71	72	74	70	287	4,900
Richard McEvoy	66	74	73	74	287	4,900
Stephen Dodd	72	71	75	70	288	3,800
Peter Hedblom	70	72	74	72	288	3,800
James Kingston	72	69	72	75	288	3,800
Matthew Nixon	69	71	74	74	288	3,800
Matthew Southgate	73	70	69	76	288	3,800
Gary Stal	73	71	71	73	288	3,800

	SCORES				TOTAL	MONEY
Jason Barnes	68	72	76	73	289	3,050
Oscar Floren	71	69	74	75	289	3,050
Mikael Lundberg	71	73	73	73	290	2,800
Callum Macaulay	68	66	75	81	290	2,800
Ricardo Santos	72	71	74	73	290	2,800
Trevor Fisher, Jr.	72	70	73	76	291	2,500
Ignacio Garrido	69	74	77	71	291	2,500
Scott Henry	75	66	77	73	291	2,500
Leonhard Ástl	71	71	72	78	292	2,200
Daniel Gaunt	70	74	71	77	292	2,200
Jacob Glennemo	70	68	77	77	292	2,200
Christian Cevaer	74	68	79	72	293	2,000
Andreas Harto	73	71	75	76	295	1,900
Niclas Fasth	75	68	74	79	296	1,830

Najeti Hotels et Golfs Open

Aa St. Omer Golf Club, St. Omer, France
Par 36-35–71; 6,799 yards

June 13-16
purse, €500,000

	SCORES				TOTAL	MONEY
Simon Thornton	74	70	65	70	279	€83,330
Tjaart van der Walt	67	71	71	70	279	55,550
(Thornton defeated van der Walt on first playoff hole.)						
Seve Benson	75	65	70	70	280	31,300
Robert Dinwiddie	72	66	74	70	282	25,000
Pelle Edberg	74	69	69	71	283	19,350
Chris Lloyd	73	68	70	72	283	19,350
Agustin Domingo	74	71	68	71	284	12,900
Jeppe Huldahl	73	67	73	71	284	12,900
Victor Riu	68	71	72	73	284	12,900
Jamie Elson	75	69	68	73	285	8,700
Daniel Gaunt	70	70	75	70	285	8,700
Max Glauert	77	65	69	74	285	8,700
Brooks Koepka	75	70	68	72	285	8,700
Gary Orr	73	71	74	67	285	8,700
Francois Calmels	73	71	71	71	286	6,514
Baptiste Chapellan	72	68	69	77	286	6,514
Scott Henry	72	69	74	71	286	6,514
Sihwan Kim	73	71	73	69	286	6,514
Mikael Lundberg	73	71	71	71	286	6,514
Gareth Shaw	76	69	70	71	286	6,514
Daniel Vancsik	73	67	75	71	286	6,514
Daniel Brooks	69	71	76	71	287	5,275
Rhys Davies	77	67	71	72	287	5,275
Alexandre Kaleka	73	71	71	72	287	5,275
Thomas Norret	75	69	74	69	287	5,275
Andrea Pavan	74	70	70	73	287	5,275
Justin Walters	71	69	75	72	287	5,275
Christophe Brazillier	75	70	73	70	288	4,675
Anthony Snobeck	76	69	72	71	288	4,675
Luke Goddard	75	67	76	71	289	4,300
Roope Kakko	72	71	77	69	289	4,300
Simon Wakefield	71	68	77	73	289	4,300
Gary Boyd	76	68	75	71	290	3,556
Paul Dwyer	73	70	78	69	290	3,556
Tyrrell Hatton	75	67	74	74	290	3,556
Michael Jonzon	74	70	70	76	290	3,556
Jose-Filipe Lima	74	71	72	73	290	3,556
Richard McEvoy	71	71	74	74	290	3,556

	SCORES			TOTAL	MONEY
Charles-Edouard Russo	73	72	73 72	290	3,556
Gary Stal	75	68	76 71	290	3,556
Alessandro Tadini	73	71	75 71	290	3,556
*Mathieu Decottignies-Lafon	75	69	75 72	291	
Chris Hanson	71	68	77 75	291	2,800
Daniel Im	73	72	69 77	291	2,800
Sam Little	74	70	78 69	291	2,800
Andrew Marshall	74	68	76 73	291	2,800
Jamie McLeary	75	70	76 70	291	2,800
Taco Remkes	75	70	76 70	291	2,800
Alastair Forsyth	73	70	76 73	292	2,250
Jordi Garcia Pinto	73	68	78 73	292	2,250
Mikko Korhonen	74	70	74 74	292	2,250
Jerome Lando Casanova	73	72	72 75	292	2,250
Florian Praegant	73	70	75 74	292	2,250
Jens Dantorp	73	70	76 74	293	1,850
Garry Houston	74	70	76 73	293	1,850
Damien Perrier	77	66	76 74	293	1,850
Edouard Dubois	71	74	71 78	294	1,567
Benjamin Hebert	74	68	77 75	294	1,567
Ake Nilsson	71	74	73 76	294	1,567
Marco Crespi	75	68	82 70	295	1,425
Carl Suneson	72	71	75 77	295	1,425
Thomas Fournier	71	71	79 75	296	1,300
Tom Murray	75	70	78 73	296	1,300
Terry Pilkadaris	71	72	76 77	296	1,300
Paul Maddy	72	72	78 75	297	1,175
Raul Quiros	75	70	76 76	297	1,175
Oscar Floren	72	71	77 78	298	1,100
Lionel Weber	75	70	80 78	303	1,050

BMW International Open

Golfclub Munchen Eichenried, Munich, Germany
Par 36-36–72; 7,157 yards

June 20-23
purse, €2,000,000

	SCORES			TOTAL	MONEY
Ernie Els	63	69	69 69	270	€333,330
Thomas Bjorn	68	69	65 69	271	222,220
Alexander Levy	65	68	68 71	272	125,200
Martin Kaymer	64	71	69 69	273	84,933
Alexander Noren	64	71	66 72	273	84,933
Bernd Wiesberger	66	68	71 68	273	84,933
Darren Fichardt	70	66	69 69	274	51,600
Sergio Garcia	71	69	65 69	274	51,600
Wen-Yi Huang	71	69	69 65	274	51,600
Robert-Jan Derksen	64	72	70 69	275	32,325
Joost Luiten	69	68	67 71	275	32,325
John Parry	67	72	67 69	275	32,325
Marcel Siem	67	68	69 71	275	32,325
Henrik Stenson	68	69	71 67	275	32,325
Brandon Stone	66	71	67 71	275	32,325
Peter Uihlein	70	66	67 72	275	32,325
Paul Waring	66	73	67 69	275	32,325
Matthew Baldwin	64	69	69 74	276	24,450
Ross Fisher	68	69	69 70	276	24,450
Dustin Johnson	66	71	73 66	276	24,450
Danny Willett	69	65	70 72	276	24,450
Shane Lowry	69	69	74 65	277	21,700
Matteo Manassero	68	69	71 69	277	21,700

	SCORES				TOTAL	MONEY
Matthew Nixon	65	71	70	71	277	21,700
Bernd Ritthammer	68	70	69	70	277	21,700
Rafa Cabrera-Bello	67	70	71	70	278	19,600
Tommy Fleetwood	66	69	72	71	278	19,600
Miguel Angel Jimenez	68	67	72	71	278	19,600
Oscar Floren	68	70	70	71	279	16,900
Peter Fowler	67	71	70	71	279	16,900
David Higgins	67	71	70	71	279	16,900
Peter Lawrie	67	69	72	71	279	16,900
Tjaart van der Walt	70	68	69	72	279	16,900
Justin Walters	67	73	74	65	279	16,900
Oliver Fisher	69	69	72	70	280	14,000
Maximilian Kieffer	68	73	70	69	280	14,000
Callum Macaulay	69	68	74	69	280	14,000
James Morrison	68	70	70	72	280	14,000
Brett Rumford	70	68	74	68	280	14,000
Jaco Van Zyl	75	65	72	68	280	14,000
Felipe Aguilar	70	69	71	71	281	11,800
Andreas Harto	68	73	69	71	281	11,800
Thongchai Jaidee	66	74	69	72	281	11,800
Richard McEvoy	68	72	71	70	281	11,800
Dawie Van der Walt	70	71	68	72	281	11,800
Seve Benson	71	67	76	68	282	9,400
Raphael Jacquelin	73	67	68	74	282	9,400
Alexandre Kaleka	72	68	70	72	282	9,400
Robert Rock	73	68	76	65	282	9,400
Anthony Snobeck	70	71	72	69	282	9,400
Gary Stal	68	68	74	72	282	9,400
Mark Tullo	68	69	73	72	282	9,400
Paul Casey	71	70	72	70	283	7,000
Victor Dubuisson	68	69	73	73	283	7,000
Ricardo Gonzalez	72	69	70	72	283	7,000
Shiv Kapur	69	68	75	71	283	7,000
Martin Wiegele	69	69	74	71	283	7,000
Gregory Bourdy	68	73	70	73	284	5,700
David Horsey	68	73	73	70	284	5,700
Scott Jamieson	68	70	74	72	284	5,700
Morten Orum Madsen	74	65	75	70	284	5,700
Jorge Campillo	66	70	77	72	285	4,700
Magnus A. Carlsson	69	71	72	73	285	4,700
Chris Doak	72	69	72	72	285	4,700
David Drysdale	68	72	72	73	285	4,700
Lorenzo Gagli	69	71	74	71	285	4,700
Maarten Lafeber	70	71	73	71	285	4,700
Soren Kjeldsen	69	72	72	73	286	3,612
Mikko Korhonen	71	69	74	72	286	3,612
Romain Wattel	67	72	75	72	286	3,612
Pontus Widegren	71	70	72	73	286	3,612
Marco Crespi	69	72	72	74	287	2,996
Gary Orr	73	68	73	73	287	2,996
Estanislao Goya	66	74	74	74	288	2,988
Joakim Lagergren	66	73	75	74	288	2,988
Chris Paisley	69	72	74	73	288	2,988
Kristoffer Broberg	70	71	77	73	291	2,980
Marc Warren	72	68	76	75	291	2,980

Irish Open

Carton House Golf Club, Maynooth, Co. Kildare,
Republic of Ireland
Par 36-36–72; 7,301 yards

June 27-30
purse, €2,000,000

	SCORES				TOTAL	MONEY
Paul Casey	68	72	67	67	274	€333,330
Joost Luiten	67	70	66	74	277	173,710
Robert Rock	69	66	71	71	277	173,710
Pablo Larrazabal	69	69	66	75	279	100,000
Rafa Cabrera-Bello	69	70	70	71	280	61,920
Shane Lowry	67	70	74	69	280	61,920
Jose Maria Olazabal	68	69	71	72	280	61,920
Alvaro Quiros	72	68	68	72	280	61,920
Gareth Shaw	73	68	70	69	280	61,920
Alejandro Canizares	71	69	69	72	281	34,800
Jamie Donaldson	69	71	69	72	281	34,800
Peter Lawrie	72	71	67	71	281	34,800
Peter Whiteford	71	68	69	73	281	34,800
Danny Willett	73	68	71	69	281	34,800
Gregory Havret	74	70	68	70	282	28,200
Jose Manuel Lara	71	70	70	71	282	28,200
Ricardo Santos	71	66	71	74	282	28,200
Thomas Bjorn	68	71	70	74	283	24,450
Soren Kjeldsen	71	70	72	70	283	24,450
Simon Thornton	69	73	70	71	283	24,450
Marc Warren	69	75	67	72	283	24,450
Ross Fisher	73	70	70	71	284	20,500
Anders Hansen	69	70	71	74	284	20,500
Scott Henry	74	64	69	77	284	20,500
Raphael Jacquelin	69	69	70	76	284	20,500
Eddie Pepperell	71	69	74	70	284	20,500
Brett Rumford	72	71	69	72	284	20,500
Richard Sterne	73	70	67	74	284	20,500
Andy Sullivan	72	72	67	73	284	20,500
Richard Bland	71	72	70	72	285	17,500
Oscar Floren	66	71	71	77	285	17,500
Fredrik Andersson Hed	70	71	68	77	286	14,460
Jorge Campillo	72	68	72	74	286	14,460
Eduardo De La Riva	73	71	74	68	286	14,460
Alan Dunbar	70	72	69	75	286	14,460
Daniel Gaunt	71	68	72	75	286	14,460
Michael Hoey	67	76	72	71	286	14,460
Mikko Ilonen	70	73	70	73	286	14,460
Francesco Molinari	73	67	76	70	286	14,460
Graeme Storm	69	73	74	70	286	14,460
Peter Uihlein	67	68	74	77	286	14,460
Seve Benson	73	71	70	73	287	11,400
Alexandre Kaleka	72	68	71	76	287	11,400
James Morrison	73	70	73	71	287	11,400
Garth Mulroy	69	75	69	74	287	11,400
Anthony Snobeck	71	71	71	74	287	11,400
Andrew Dodt	68	74	69	77	288	9,200
David Drysdale	72	71	72	73	288	9,200
Oliver Fisher	71	70	73	74	288	9,200
Stephen Gallacher	72	70	73	73	288	9,200
Paul Lawrie	71	70	73	74	288	9,200
Patrik Sjoland	73	70	72	73	288	9,200
Richard Finch	71	71	78	69	289	7,000
Emiliano Grillo	73	67	74	75	289	7,000
Andreas Harto	70	72	73	74	289	7,000
Callum Macaulay	73	71	76	69	289	7,000

	SCORES				TOTAL	MONEY
Justin Walters	72	69	70	78	289	7,000
Stephen Dodd	71	70	73	76	290	5,800
Lasse Jensen	72	71	72	75	290	5,800
Sam Little	71	72	74	73	290	5,800
Carlos Del Moral	72	72	75	72	291	5,300
Robert-Jan Derksen	73	71	73	74	291	5,300
Seamus Power	69	75	71	77	292	4,900
Romain Wattel	74	70	74	74	292	4,900
Matthew Baldwin	71	73	75	74	293	4,300
Jean-Baptiste Gonnet	67	75	75	76	293	4,300
Wen-Yi Huang	77	67	74	75	293	4,300
Chris Paisley	69	72	74	78	293	4,300
Chris Lloyd	72	71	76	75	294	3,800
Damian Mooney	74	68	76	77	295	3,650
David Howell	70	72	77	78	297	2,998
Maximilian Kieffer	70	73	75	79	297	2,998

Alstom Open de France

Le Golf National, Paris, France
Par 36-35–71; 7,331 yards

July 4-7
purse, €3,000,000

	SCORES				TOTAL	MONEY
Graeme McDowell	69	69	70	67	275	€500,000
Richard Sterne	68	69	71	71	279	333,330
Eduardo De La Riva	72	67	72	69	280	168,900
Graeme Storm	70	68	73	69	280	168,900
Simon Dyson	70	68	72	71	281	127,200
Jamie Donaldson	70	70	71	71	282	97,500
Richard Green	69	70	70	73	282	97,500
Thomas Bjorn	68	69	74	72	283	61,800
Stephen Gallacher	68	70	75	70	283	61,800
David Howell	69	71	69	74	283	61,800
Soren Kjeldsen	69	68	73	73	283	61,800
Gareth Maybin	71	73	71	68	283	61,800
Martin Kaymer	68	76	69	71	284	44,220
Hennie Otto	71	71	69	73	284	44,220
Gareth Shaw	72	69	74	69	284	44,220
Marc Warren	69	72	70	73	284	44,220
Bernd Wiesberger	70	71	68	75	284	44,220
Felipe Aguilar	68	72	74	71	285	35,100
Seve Benson	71	72	73	69	285	35,100
Jorge Campillo	74	69	68	74	285	35,100
Victor Dubuisson	68	75	76	66	285	35,100
Simon Khan	71	73	68	73	285	35,100
Damien McGrane	70	72	74	69	285	35,100
Francesco Molinari	71	74	67	73	285	35,100
Kristoffer Broberg	72	69	73	72	286	29,850
Matteo Manassero	73	69	73	71	286	29,850
Ian Poulter	73	71	69	73	286	29,850
Lee Slattery	71	70	70	75	286	29,850
Rafa Cabrera-Bello	70	72	72	73	287	25,800
Robert-Jan Derksen	72	70	73	72	287	25,800
Scott Henry	73	68	74	72	287	25,800
Thomas Pieters	70	72	75	70	287	25,800
Romain Wattel	67	75	74	71	287	25,800
Gregory Bourdy	69	73	70	76	288	22,200
Alan Dunbar	70	75	72	71	288	22,200
Richard Finch	75	70	74	69	288	22,200
Ross Fisher	70	73	71	74	288	22,200

	SCORES				TOTAL	MONEY
Gonzalo Fernandez-Castano	74	71	72	72	289	19,800
Anders Hansen	66	78	75	70	289	19,800
Morten Orum Madsen	71	71	77	70	289	19,800
Matthew Nixon	68	73	74	74	289	19,800
Alejandro Canizares	71	69	80	70	290	16,500
Chris Doak	71	70	72	77	290	16,500
Luke Donald	71	73	71	75	290	16,500
David Drysdale	70	74	69	77	290	16,500
Chris Lloyd	70	73	73	74	290	16,500
Mikael Lundberg	71	74	72	73	290	16,500
Fabrizio Zanotti	68	68	78	76	290	16,500
Soren Hansen	75	67	74	75	291	13,500
Matt Kuchar	70	75	73	73	291	13,500
Joost Luiten	71	71	73	76	291	13,500
Estanislao Goya	68	76	77	71	292	10,800
Maarten Lafeber	76	69	74	73	292	10,800
Alexander Levy	69	76	75	72	292	10,800
James Morrison	69	72	75	76	292	10,800
John Parry	74	70	70	78	292	10,800
Anthony Snobeck	76	69	73	74	292	10,800
Miguel Angel Jimenez	69	76	68	80	293	9,000
Thomas Aiken	71	74	74	75	294	8,400
Ignacio Garrido	75	70	68	81	294	8,400
Scott Jamieson	69	70	80	75	294	8,400
Richie Ramsay	69	71	73	82	295	7,800
Lorenzo Gagli	73	72	75	76	296	7,350
Michael Hoey	69	74	74	79	296	7,350
S.S.P. Chowrasia	76	67	82	74	299	6,900

Aberdeen Asset Management Scottish Open

Castle Stuart Golf Links, Inverness, Scotland
Par 36-36–72; 7,193 yards

July 11-14
purse, £3,000,000

	SCORES				TOTAL	MONEY
Phil Mickelson	66	70	66	69	271	€579,080
Branden Grace	71	65	66	69	271	386,049
(Mickelson defeated Grace on first playoff hole.)						
J.B. Hansen	68	65	69	71	273	195,613
Henrik Stenson	70	64	66	73	273	195,613
Martin Laird	68	69	69	68	274	124,386
Gareth Maybin	69	70	64	71	274	124,386
John Parry	64	72	66	72	274	124,386
Nicolas Colsaerts	70	68	68	69	275	82,345
Raphael Jacquelin	68	70	65	72	275	82,345
Marcel Siem	67	69	72	69	277	66,710
Peter Uihlein	67	66	70	74	277	66,710
Chris Doak	66	66	73	73	278	53,785
Simon Dyson	70	69	69	70	278	53,785
Brooks Koepka	70	68	68	72	278	53,785
Hennie Otto	70	70	66	72	278	53,785
Eddie Pepperell	69	69	68	72	278	53,785
Seve Benson	69	69	71	70	279	42,041
Victor Dubuisson	68	66	74	71	279	42,041
Tommy Fleetwood	70	67	68	74	279	42,041
Lorenzo Gagli	67	67	70	75	279	42,041
Ricardo Gonzalez	70	68	68	73	279	42,041
Simon Khan	65	69	70	75	279	42,041
David Lynn	69	70	68	72	279	42,041
Paul Casey	70	67	68	75	280	34,050

	SCORES				TOTAL	MONEY
Ross Fisher	68	65	73	74	280	34,050
David Horsey	69	67	71	73	280	34,050
Joakim Lagergren	71	67	72	70	280	34,050
Morten Orum Madsen	70	67	70	73	280	34,050
Paul McGinley	67	72	70	71	280	34,050
Alvaro Quiros	68	71	68	73	280	34,050
Richard Bland	71	69	69	72	281	27,051
Mikko Ilonen	66	71	70	74	281	27,051
Soren Kjeldsen	69	69	70	73	281	27,051
Shane Lowry	66	73	70	72	281	27,051
Chris Paisley	70	65	71	75	281	27,051
Richard Sterne	67	69	71	74	281	27,051
Bernd Wiesberger	68	70	71	72	281	27,051
Kiradech Aphibarnrat	66	73	68	75	282	22,932
Matteo Delpodio	67	73	69	73	282	22,932
Garth Mulroy	69	67	71	75	282	22,932
Marc Warren	71	68	72	71	282	22,932
Jorge Campillo	72	67	72	72	283	19,110
Robert-Jan Derksen	67	69	72	75	283	19,110
David Howell	68	71	73	71	283	19,110
Greig Hutcheon	69	71	69	74	283	19,110
Chris Lloyd	68	69	72	74	283	19,110
Damien McGrane	67	69	72	75	283	19,110
Francesco Molinari	69	66	72	76	283	19,110
Matthew Baldwin	69	71	71	73	284	13,898
Gregory Bourdy	68	70	74	72	284	13,898
David Drysdale	70	69	70	75	284	13,898
Johan Edfors	69	71	73	71	284	13,898
Keith Horne	67	73	67	77	284	13,898
Paul Lawrie	69	71	73	71	284	13,898
Sam Little	68	71	74	71	284	13,898
James Morrison	66	68	75	75	284	13,898
Alejandro Canizares	70	69	68	78	285	9,381
Niclas Fasth	70	66	71	78	285	9,381
Darren Fichardt	70	70	73	72	285	9,381
Richard Green	70	69	74	72	285	9,381
Scott Henry	69	69	73	74	285	9,381
Matteo Manassero	69	70	70	76	285	9,381
Matthew Southgate	69	64	71	81	285	9,381
Jaco Van Zyl	68	69	71	77	285	9,381
Chris Wood	68	70	71	76	285	9,381
Thongchai Jaidee	66	71	73	76	286	7,644
Thorbjorn Olesen	67	69	78	73	287	7,296
Craig Lee	68	69	77	76	290	6,949
Lee Slattery	71	66	80	74	291	6,602

The Open Championship

Muirfield, Gullane, East Lothian, Scotland
Par 36-35–71; 7,192 yards

July 18-21
purse, £5,250,000

	SCORES				TOTAL	MONEY
Phil Mickelson	69	74	72	66	281	£945,000
Henrik Stenson	70	70	74	70	284	545,000
Ian Poulter	72	71	75	67	285	280,833
Adam Scott	71	72	70	72	285	280,833
Lee Westwood	72	68	70	75	285	280,833
Hideki Matsuyama	71	73	72	70	286	163,333
Zach Johnson	66	75	73	72	286	163,333
Tiger Woods	69	71	72	74	286	163,333

	SCORES				TOTAL	MONEY
Francesco Molinari	69	74	72	72	287	115,000
Hunter Mahan	72	72	68	75	287	115,000
Brandt Snedeker	68	79	69	72	288	93,500
Angel Cabrera	69	72	73	74	288	93,500
Justin Leonard	74	70	74	71	289	79,500
Miguel Angel Jimenez	68	71	77	73	289	79,500
Eduardo De La Riva	73	73	75	69	290	62,250
Harris English	74	71	75	70	290	62,250
Charl Schwartzel	75	68	76	71	290	62,250
Daniel Willett	75	72	72	71	290	62,250
Matt Kuchar	74	73	72	71	290	62,250
Keegan Bradley	75	74	70	71	290	62,250
Stephen Gallacher	76	70	76	69	291	47,300
Darren Clarke	72	71	76	72	291	47,300
Richard Sterne	75	75	68	73	291	47,300
Rafa Cabrera-Bello	67	74	76	74	291	47,300
Sergio Garcia	75	73	68	75	291	47,300
Jason Dufner	72	77	76	67	292	37,250
Stewart Cink	72	75	76	69	292	37,250
Jonas Blixt	72	78	73	69	292	37,250
Steven Tiley	72	75	73	72	292	37,250
Paul Lawrie	81	69	70	72	292	37,250
Ernie Els	74	74	70	74	292	37,250
Oliver Fisher	70	78	77	68	293	25,708
Shane Lowry	74	74	75	70	293	25,708
Fred Couples	75	74	73	71	293	25,708
Y.E. Yang	78	70	73	72	293	25,708
Thongchai Jaidee	79	71	71	72	293	25,708
Bubba Watson	70	73	77	73	293	25,708
Bud Cauley	74	75	71	73	293	25,708
Martin Kaymer	72	74	72	75	293	25,708
Dustin Johnson	68	72	76	77	293	25,708
Jason Day	73	71	72	77	293	25,708
Jamie Donaldson	74	71	71	77	293	25,708
Ryan Moore	72	70	72	79	293	25,708
Bo Van Pelt	76	73	77	68	294	16,139
Tim Clark	72	76	76	70	294	16,139
Martin Laird	70	71	81	72	294	16,139
Freddie Jacobson	72	75	75	72	294	16,139
*Matthew Fitzpatrick	73	76	73	72	294	
Geoff Ogilvy	75	75	72	72	294	16,139
Mark Brown	77	73	72	72	294	16,139
K.J. Choi	76	74	71	73	294	16,139
Jordan Spieth	69	74	76	75	294	16,139
Shingo Katayama	73	77	69	75	294	16,139
Padraig Harrington	73	75	77	70	295	13,725
Marcus Fraser	73	74	76	72	295	13,725
Gonzalo Fernandez-Castano	70	79	73	73	295	13,725
Carl Pettersson	74	76	70	75	295	13,725
Mark O'Meara	67	78	77	74	296	13,150
Richie Ramsay	76	74	72	74	296	13,150
Boo Weekley	74	76	71	75	296	13,150
Tom Lehman	68	77	75	76	296	13,150
Graeme McDowell	75	71	73	77	296	13,150
Johnson Wagner	73	72	73	78	296	13,150
Ben Curtis	74	71	80	72	297	12,500
Chris Wood	75	75	75	72	297	12,500
Branden Grace	74	71	77	75	297	12,500
Webb Simpson	73	70	77	77	297	12,500
Bernd Wiesberger	71	74	75	77	297	12,500
Gregory Bourdy	76	70	74	77	297	12,500
Ken Duke	70	77	73	77	297	12,500
Gareth Wright	71	78	75	74	298	12,050

	SCORES				TOTAL	MONEY
George Coetzee	76	71	75	76	298	12,050
Shiv Kapur	68	77	83	71	299	11,700
K.T. Kim	73	76	77	73	299	11,700
Russell Henley	78	71	75	75	299	11,700
*Jimmy Mullen	71	78	75	75	299	
Todd Hamilton	69	81	70	79	299	11,700
Thomas Bjorn	73	74	72	80	299	11,700
Kevin Streelman	74	71	82	73	300	11,300
Mikko Ilonen	72	78	76	74	300	11,300
Peter Senior	74	76	73	77	300	11,300
Josh Teater	72	77	75	77	301	11,100
Graham DeLaet	76	72	76	79	303	11,000
Sandy Lyle	76	72	80	79	307	10,900

Out of Final 36 Holes

	SCORES		TOTAL	MONEY
Oscar Floren	74	77	151	3,700
Mark Leishman	76	75	151	3,700
Alvaro Quiros	77	74	151	3,700
Kyle Stanley	82	69	151	3,700
Michael Thompson	72	79	151	3,700
Bill Haas	77	74	151	3,700
Marcel Siem	75	76	151	3,700
George Murray	76	75	151	3,700
Thomas Aiken	71	80	151	3,700
Jimmy Walker	72	79	151	3,700
Nicolas Colsaerts	75	76	151	3,700
Camilo Villegas	72	79	151	3,700
Niclas Fasth	77	75	152	3,000
Jim Furyk	78	74	152	3,000
Luke Donald	80	72	152	3,000
Hiroyuki Fujita	78	74	152	3,000
Justin Harding	78	74	152	3,000
Stephen Dartnall	80	72	152	3,000
Marc Warren	72	80	152	3,000
Justin Rose	75	77	152	3,000
Nick Watney	75	77	152	3,000
Mark Calcavecchia	72	80	152	3,000
Hyung-Sung Kim	76	76	152	3,000
Toru Taniguchi	78	75	153	3,000
D.A. Points	78	75	153	3,000
*Ben Stow	76	77	153	
Ashun Wu	76	77	153	3,000
Robert Garrigus	78	75	153	3,000
John Senden	77	76	153	3,000
*Garrick Porteous	76	77	153	
Tom Watson	75	78	153	3,000
Vijay Singh	77	77	154	3,000
Thorbjorn Olesen	78	76	154	3,000
Rickie Fowler	78	76	154	3,000
Gareth Maybin	78	76	154	3,000
Robert Karlsson	77	77	154	3,000
Scott Stallings	76	78	154	3,000
David Lynn	79	75	154	3,000
Billy Horschel	74	80	154	3,000
Rory McIlroy	79	75	154	3,000
John Huh	74	80	154	3,000
Kenichi Kuboya	76	79	155	2,500
Darryn Lloyd	79	76	155	2,500
David Duval	76	79	155	2,500
Richard McEvoy	73	82	155	2,500
Steven Jeffress	76	79	155	2,500
John Wade	74	81	155	2,500

	SCORES				TOTAL	MONEY
Thaworn Wiratchant	79	77			156	2,500
Lucas Glover	80	76			156	2,500
Brett Rumford	79	77			156	2,500
Scott Jamieson	80	76			156	2,500
Lloyd Saltman	79	77			156	2,500
Brooks Koepka	76	80			156	2,500
Estanislao Goya	75	81			156	2,500
Brendan Jones	78	78			156	2,500
*Steven Fox	78	79			157	
Matteo Manassero	76	81			157	2,500
Daisuke Maruyama	78	79			157	2,500
Kiradech Aphibarnrat	72	85			157	2,500
Brian Davis	80	77			157	2,500
Sir Nick Faldo	79	78			157	2,500
Luke Guthrie	78	80			158	2,500
*Grant Forrest	73	86			159	
Makoto Inoue	83	76			159	2,500
Scott Brown	79	81			160	2,500
*Rhys Pugh	84	77			161	
Satoshi Kodaira	80	81			161	2,500
Tyrrell Hatton	82	79			161	2,500
Scott Piercy	74	88			162	2,500
Alexander Noren	83				WD	
Peter Hanson					WD	
Louis Oosthuizen					WD	

M2M Russian Open

Tseleevo Golf & Polo Club, Moscow, Russia
Par 36-36–72; 7,491 yards

July 25-28
purse, €1,000,000

	SCORES				TOTAL	MONEY
Michael Hoey	70	67	65	70	272	€166,660
Alexandre Kaleka	70	67	71	68	276	86,855
Matthew Nixon	69	70	68	69	276	86,855
J.B. Hansen	72	70	67	68	277	50,000
Mark Foster	69	69	72	68	278	33,100
Gregory Havret	72	70	70	66	278	33,100
Wen-Chong Liang	67	70	75	66	278	33,100
James Morrison	68	71	70	69	278	33,100
Simon Dyson	67	74	71	68	280	22,400
Matthew Baldwin	68	69	73	72	282	18,533
Mikko Korhonen	69	70	70	73	282	18,533
Alexander Levy	72	72	71	67	282	18,533
Magnus A. Carlsson	71	72	69	71	283	15,050
Jean-Baptiste Gonnet	70	71	70	72	283	15,050
Andreas Harto	70	71	76	66	283	15,050
Rikard Karlberg	67	68	72	76	283	15,050
Matteo Delpodio	69	74	69	72	284	12,100
Richard Finch	73	74	69	68	284	12,100
David Horsey	70	72	71	71	284	12,100
Joakim Lagergren	74	74	68	68	284	12,100
Sam Little	69	72	74	69	284	12,100
Richard McEvoy	74	71	69	70	284	12,100
Chris Paisley	72	71	68	73	284	12,100
Michael Campbell	70	73	72	70	285	9,950
Jorge Campillo	72	71	67	75	285	9,950
Oscar Floren	76	69	66	74	285	9,950
Maarten Lafeber	69	73	71	72	285	9,950
Terry Pilkadaris	71	71	70	73	285	9,950

	SCORES				TOTAL	MONEY
Joel Sjoholm	78	69	70	68	285	9,950
Soren Hansen	77	67	70	72	286	8,750
Scott Hend	70	69	74	73	286	8,750
S.S.P. Chowrasia	72	72	72	71	287	7,650
Peter Hedblom	73	74	70	70	287	7,650
Gary Lockerbie	72	70	69	76	287	7,650
Jake Roos	70	71	74	72	287	7,650
Alessandro Tadini	68	73	73	73	287	7,650
Romain Wattel	72	72	72	71	287	7,650
James Kingston	71	69	68	80	288	6,600
Espen Kofstad	74	73	70	71	288	6,600
Prom Meesawat	71	74	73	70	288	6,600
Anthony Snobeck	70	73	73	72	288	6,600
Tom Lewis	71	74	75	69	289	6,000
Jeev Milkha Singh	71	71	72	75	289	6,000
Jamie Elson	71	71	72	76	290	5,100
Alastair Forsyth	74	73	73	70	290	5,100
Daniel Gaunt	70	72	73	75	290	5,100
Scott Henry	73	73	73	71	290	5,100
Haydn Porteous	71	76	70	73	290	5,100
Mark Tullo	74	69	71	76	290	5,100
Simon Wakefield	73	68	74	75	290	5,100
David Higgins	71	71	76	73	291	4,000
Chris Lloyd	71	73	72	75	291	4,000
Pablo Martin Benavides	70	77	75	69	291	4,000
Gareth Shaw	71	77	70	73	291	4,000
Nils Floren	71	75	68	78	292	3,300
Anirban Lahiri	78	70	76	68	292	3,300
Tjaart van der Walt	73	71	76	72	292	3,300
Gaganjeet Bhullar	74	73	69	77	293	2,950
Martin Wiegele	72	72	74	75	293	2,950
Jurgen Maurer	71	74	75	74	294	2,800
*Jack Singh Brar	77	66	81	70	294	
Oliver Bekker	74	71	74	76	295	2,600
Daniel Brooks	77	71	75	72	295	2,600
Javier Colomo	68	79	76	72	295	2,600
Tommy Fleetwood	72	76	76	75	299	2,350
Matthew Southgate	73	74	75	77	299	2,350
Callum Macaulay	72	76	77	76	301	2,200
Sebi Garcia	75	71	81	76	303	2,100

Johnnie Walker Championship

Gleneagles Hotel, Auchterarder, Perthshire, Scotland
Par 36-36–72; 7,296 yards

August 22-25
purse, £1,400,000

	SCORES				TOTAL	MONEY
Tommy Fleetwood	68	65	67	70	270	€272,273
Stephen Gallacher	71	68	64	67	270	141,889
Ricardo Gonzalez	65	65	70	70	270	141,889
(Fleetwood defeated Gallacher and Gonzalez on first playoff hole.)						
Scott Henry	72	65	67	67	271	75,475
Bernd Wiesberger	65	66	72	68	271	75,475
Emiliano Grillo	71	66	69	66	272	49,010
Brett Rumford	66	69	69	68	272	49,010
Paul Waring	75	63	67	67	272	49,010
Thorbjorn Olesen	71	68	66	68	273	36,594
David Drysdale	71	67	68	68	274	29,283
Mikko Korhonen	71	69	67	67	274	29,283
Shane Lowry	68	70	67	69	274	29,283

	SCORES				TOTAL	MONEY
Richie Ramsay	69	68	69	68	274	29,283
David Horsey	70	68	69	68	275	24,015
Craig Lee	69	67	71	68	275	24,015
Morten Orum Madsen	70	70	67	68	275	24,015
Gary Boyd	71	69	68	68	276	20,067
Ross Fisher	66	72	66	72	276	20,067
Anders Hansen	70	69	68	69	276	20,067
David Howell	71	70	67	68	276	20,067
Thongchai Jaidee	66	69	73	68	276	20,067
Tom Lewis	67	71	67	71	276	20,067
Fredrik Andersson Hed	68	67	66	76	277	16,990
Gregory Bourdy	68	71	70	68	277	16,990
Richard Finch	73	67	68	69	277	16,990
Espen Kofstad	71	70	68	68	277	16,990
John Parry	71	66	70	70	277	16,990
Matthew Baldwin	70	70	66	72	278	14,049
Simon Dyson	72	67	71	68	278	14,049
Mark Foster	66	67	73	72	278	14,049
Michael Hoey	68	72	70	68	278	14,049
Brooks Koepka	68	66	75	69	278	14,049
Paul Lawrie	70	67	71	70	278	14,049
Eddie Pepperell	72	66	72	68	278	14,049
Rafa Cabrera-Bello	71	69	71	68	279	11,272
Gregory Havret	67	69	70	73	279	11,272
Matthew Nixon	68	71	71	69	279	11,272
Alvaro Quiros	70	67	68	74	279	11,272
Ricardo Santos	69	72	71	67	279	11,272
Joel Sjoholm	68	71	71	69	279	11,272
Mark Tullo	69	71	70	69	279	11,272
Darren Fichardt	69	70	72	69	280	8,985
Alexander Levy	70	71	67	72	280	8,985
Francesco Molinari	69	67	73	71	280	8,985
Anthony Snobeck	72	69	69	70	280	8,985
Matthew Southgate	72	68	69	71	280	8,985
Gary Stal	69	71	71	69	280	8,985
Simon Wakefield	70	71	68	71	280	8,985
Eduardo De La Riva	68	72	71	70	281	7,351
Joakim Lagergren	68	71	70	72	281	7,351
Andy Sullivan	67	73	73	68	281	7,351
Jorge Campillo	69	71	67	75	282	6,045
Chris Doak	69	69	69	75	282	6,045
Oliver Fisher	66	70	69	77	282	6,045
Soren Hansen	69	71	74	68	282	6,045
Gareth Wright	69	72	70	71	282	6,045
James Morrison	72	69	70	72	283	5,064
Ignacio Garrido	66	73	72	73	284	4,574
Raphael Jacquelin	69	71	75	69	284	4,574
Peter Lawrie	71	67	75	71	284	4,574
Thomas Levet	71	70	71	72	284	4,574
Simon Thornton	74	67	69	74	284	4,574
Gareth Maybin	68	70	70	77	285	3,921
Paul McGinley	68	71	71	75	285	3,921
Danny Willett	72	69	68	76	285	3,921
Lasse Jensen	70	71	69	76	286	3,431
Michael Jonzon	71	70	72	73	286	3,431
Mikael Lundberg	70	69	75	72	286	3,431
Marcus Both	69	70	72	76	287	3,046
Martin Wiegele	69	70	74	74	287	3,046
Neil Fenwick	75	66	74	76	291	2,450
Jose Maria Olazabal	73	68	76	75	292	2,447

ISPS Handa Wales Open

Celtic Manor Resort, City of Newport, Wales
Par 36-35–71; 7,352 yards

August 29-September 1
purse, £1,800,000

	SCORES				TOTAL	MONEY
Gregory Bourdy	67	72	70	67	276	€348,660
Peter Uihlein	69	70	67	72	278	232,440
Soren Kjeldsen	69	74	70	66	279	130,957
Joost Luiten	73	68	69	71	281	96,649
John Parry	71	69	73	68	281	96,649
Damien McGrane	70	71	70	71	282	67,989
Graeme Storm	72	67	72	71	282	67,989
Seve Benson	76	70	69	68	283	40,166
Gonzalo Fernandez-Castano	70	75	69	69	283	40,166
Anders Hansen	71	71	70	71	283	40,166
Mikko Korhonen	71	70	70	72	283	40,166
Paul McGinley	70	69	77	67	283	40,166
Brett Rumford	72	69	72	70	283	40,166
Simon Wakefield	70	74	70	69	283	40,166
Rafa Cabrera-Bello	71	68	71	74	284	29,497
Eduardo De La Riva	71	70	71	72	284	29,497
Robert Rock	68	73	73	70	284	29,497
Matthew Baldwin	74	72	70	69	285	24,136
Simon Dyson	76	69	72	68	285	24,136
Johan Edfors	72	69	74	70	285	24,136
Emiliano Grillo	68	76	70	71	285	24,136
Brooks Koepka	72	71	73	69	285	24,136
Alexander Levy	71	69	77	68	285	24,136
Tjaart van der Walt	67	71	74	73	285	24,136
Paul Waring	72	70	71	72	285	24,136
Peter Hedblom	72	72	66	76	286	19,874
David Higgins	74	70	71	71	286	19,874
Thongchai Jaidee	71	74	72	69	286	19,874
Thomas Levet	75	67	67	77	286	19,874
Justin Walters	71	71	69	75	286	19,874
S.S.P. Chowrasia	72	70	75	70	287	16,056
Chris Doak	72	70	76	69	287	16,056
David Drysdale	70	73	72	72	287	16,056
Oliver Fisher	71	72	72	72	287	16,056
Mark Foster	67	75	71	74	287	16,056
Craig Lee	77	67	70	73	287	16,056
Matthew Nixon	72	71	68	76	287	16,056
Chris Paisley	74	69	70	74	287	16,056
Felipe Aguilar	72	72	71	73	288	13,389
Richard Green	66	76	70	76	288	13,389
Alessandro Tadini	70	72	75	71	288	13,389
Chris Wood	66	75	73	74	288	13,389
Richard Bland	75	71	71	72	289	10,878
Liam Bond	69	68	78	74	289	10,878
Jorge Campillo	71	73	72	73	289	10,878
Andreas Harto	72	72	72	73	289	10,878
Scott Jamieson	74	72	74	69	289	10,878
Alexandre Kaleka	71	72	70	76	289	10,878
Jose Manuel Lara	73	70	75	71	289	10,878
Mark Tullo	74	70	71	74	289	10,878
Mikko Ilonen	69	74	75	72	290	8,995
Rhys Enoch	73	70	73	75	291	7,531
Soren Hansen	72	73	70	76	291	7,531
Maximilian Kieffer	69	75	74	73	291	7,531
Gareth Maybin	71	75	73	72	291	7,531
Anthony Snobeck	73	71	71	76	291	7,531
Romain Wattel	72	74	73	72	291	7,531

	SCORES				TOTAL	MONEY
Thomas Bjorn	72	73	74	73	292	5,962
Joakim Lagergren	74	72	72	74	292	5,962
Andrew Marshall	71	72	81	68	292	5,962
Julien Quesne	73	69	77	73	292	5,962
Ross Fisher	71	71	74	77	293	5,334
Espen Kofstad	64	74	76	79	293	5,334
Scott Arnold	72	74	69	79	294	4,812
Robert Coles	69	73	79	73	294	4,812
Ricardo Santos	70	76	73	75	294	4,812
Magnus A. Carlsson	72	74	68	81	295	4,393
Christian Cevaer	70	72	80	74	296	3,990
Raphael Jacquelin	70	71	80	75	296	3,990
Eddie Pepperell	77	69	71	79	296	3,990
Peter Erofejeff	71	74	76	76	297	3,138
Michael Jonzon	71	74	74	79	298	3,135
Andrew Dodt	71	75	74	80	300	3,132

Omega European Masters

Crans-sur-Sierre Golf Club, Crans Montana, Switzerland
Par 36-35–71; 6,881 yards

September 5-8
purse, €2,200,000

	SCORES				TOTAL	MONEY
Thomas Bjorn	66	66	67	65	264	€366,660
Craig Lee	71	65	61	67	264	244,440
(Bjorn defeated Lee on first playoff hole.)						
Victor Dubuisson	68	65	66	66	265	137,720
Alejandro Canizares	69	65	65	67	266	110,000
Ross Fisher	71	69	63	66	269	85,140
Miguel Angel Jimenez	65	68	69	67	269	85,140
Gregory Havret	68	69	70	63	270	60,500
Brooks Koepka	68	66	69	67	270	60,500
Tommy Fleetwood	65	68	69	70	272	44,587
Stephen Gallacher	67	65	72	68	272	44,587
Thongchai Jaidee	68	69	70	65	272	44,587
Paul Lawrie	68	70	70	65	273	37,840
Maximilian Kieffer	68	69	69	68	274	34,540
Richard Sterne	69	66	71	68	274	34,540
Paul Casey	65	69	71	70	275	29,744
Andrew Dodt	69	72	66	68	275	29,744
Rikard Karlberg	69	69	71	66	275	29,744
Tom Lewis	71	70	67	67	275	29,744
Brett Rumford	68	68	70	69	275	29,744
Marcus Fraser	69	71	68	68	276	25,960
Mark Tullo	68	66	73	69	276	25,960
Simon Dyson	71	69	68	69	277	23,870
Gareth Maybin	70	69	70	68	277	23,870
Angelo Que	70	70	68	69	277	23,870
Jaco Van Zyl	68	68	73	68	277	23,870
Seve Benson	70	68	70	70	278	19,910
Stephen Dodd	69	72	67	70	278	19,910
Richard Finch	67	66	73	72	278	19,910
Soren Hansen	69	71	70	68	278	19,910
Scott Hend	69	70	68	71	278	19,910
David Howell	70	67	72	69	278	19,910
Shiv Kapur	70	69	70	69	278	19,910
Danny Willett	69	64	72	73	278	19,910
Scott Henry	70	70	72	67	279	15,620
Berry Henson	67	72	70	70	279	15,620
Keith Horne	69	69	70	71	279	15,620

	SCORES				TOTAL	MONEY
Pariya Junhasavasdikul	67	72	71	69	279	15,620
Mikko Korhonen	72	69	68	70	279	15,620
Matteo Manassero	70	69	72	68	279	15,620
Jose Maria Olazabal	67	71	72	69	279	15,620
Jorge Campillo	71	70	73	66	280	13,420
Padraig Harrington	70	65	72	73	280	13,420
Julien Quesne	72	69	66	73	280	13,420
Kiradech Aphibarnrat	71	68	74	68	281	11,660
Gregory Bourdy	69	71	69	72	281	11,660
Joost Luiten	70	71	69	71	281	11,660
Chapchai Nirat	71	70	70	70	281	11,660
Anthony Wall	70	71	70	70	281	11,660
Robert Coles	69	71	73	69	282	9,460
Gonzalo Fernandez-Castano	70	67	72	73	282	9,460
Oliver Fisher	77	64	76	65	282	9,460
Michael Hoey	67	73	75	67	282	9,460
Damian Ulrich	71	69	66	76	282	9,460
Kristoffer Broberg	70	68	75	70	283	7,700
Soren Kjeldsen	70	71	77	65	283	7,700
Hao-Tong Li	68	69	72	74	283	7,700
Eduardo De La Riva	68	71	73	72	284	6,600
Anirban Lahiri	63	71	75	75	284	6,600
Simon Wakefield	72	69	68	75	284	6,600
Christian Cevaer	70	71	74	70	285	6,050
Jean-Baptiste Gonnet	72	69	72	72	285	6,050
*Edouard Amacher	72	69	73	72	286	
Scott Barr	69	72	74	71	286	5,610
Gaganjeet Bhullar	68	71	70	77	286	5,610
Thomas Levet	68	72	78	69	287	5,170
Alessandro Tadini	68	73	74	72	287	5,170
Kieran Pratt	71	69	77	73	290	4,840
Jonathan Moore	69	72	77	75	293	4,620

KLM Open

Kennemer Golf & Country Club, Zandvoort, The Netherlands
Par 36-34–70; 6,057 yards

September 12-15
purse, €1,800,000

	SCORES				TOTAL	MONEY
Joost Luiten	69	65	66	68	268	€300,000
Miguel Angel Jimenez	64	67	70	67	268	200,000
(Luiten defeated Jimenez on first playoff hole.)						
Simon Dyson	69	63	71	68	271	85,500
Ross Fisher	69	68	68	66	271	85,500
Gregory Havret	67	70	68	66	271	85,500
Damien McGrane	65	70	67	69	271	85,500
Julien Quesne	67	65	70	70	272	54,000
Soren Kjeldsen	68	67	72	66	273	45,000
David Horsey	71	66	70	67	274	38,160
Pablo Larrazabal	65	66	77	66	274	38,160
Robert Allenby	65	71	68	71	275	29,412
Magnus A. Carlsson	68	69	69	69	275	29,412
Oliver Fisher	67	65	71	72	275	29,412
Emiliano Grillo	72	66	69	68	275	29,412
Michael Jonzon	70	65	73	67	275	29,412
Thomas Aiken	72	64	74	66	276	22,950
Eduardo De La Riva	68	71	71	66	276	22,950
Darren Fichardt	70	68	68	70	276	22,950
Marcus Fraser	67	71	72	66	276	22,950
Matthew Nixon	69	65	73	69	276	22,950

	SCORES			TOTAL	MONEY
Paul Waring	70	68	69 69	276	22,950
Brooks Koepka	70	66	71 70	277	19,530
Espen Kofstad	69	66	73 69	277	19,530
Alvaro Quiros	72	64	71 70	277	19,530
Richie Ramsay	70	68	75 64	277	19,530
Mikko Korhonen	71	67	74 66	278	17,370
Shane Lowry	69	68	68 73	278	17,370
Matteo Manassero	70	68	74 66	278	17,370
Hennie Otto	68	67	69 74	278	17,370
David Drysdale	69	64	74 72	279	13,664
Tommy Fleetwood	70	68	74 67	279	13,664
Oscar Floren	66	73	67 73	279	13,664
Mark Foster	68	70	71 70	279	13,664
Richard Green	70	66	73 70	279	13,664
Alexander Levy	73	65	72 69	279	13,664
Paul McGinley	68	67	73 71	279	13,664
Chris Paisley	68	68	73 70	279	13,664
Thomas Pieters	68	70	71 70	279	13,664
Simon Wakefield	68	67	73 71	279	13,664
Fabrizio Zanotti	65	73	71 70	279	13,664
Richard Bland	67	71	68 74	280	10,620
Paul Casey	68	71	68 73	280	10,620
David Howell	65	70	74 71	280	10,620
Lasse Jensen	72	66	71 71	280	10,620
Rikard Karlberg	70	67	72 71	280	10,620
Rafa Cabrera-Bello	69	67	72 73	281	9,000
Mikko Ilonen	71	66	69 75	281	9,000
Jose Maria Olazabal	69	68	76 68	281	9,000
Ashun Wu	69	68	69 75	281	9,000
Seve Benson	69	70	76 67	282	7,200
Wil Besseling	67	71	71 73	282	7,200
Scott Henry	69	69	73 71	282	7,200
Jin Jeong	67	71	71 73	282	7,200
Andrew Marshall	69	67	74 72	282	7,200
Gary Orr	65	70	75 72	282	7,200
Matthew Baldwin	69	70	74 70	283	5,760
Anthony Snobeck	68	66	73 76	283	5,760
Felipe Aguilar	69	68	73 74	284	5,040
Jorge Campillo	71	63	79 71	284	5,040
Christian Cevaer	70	69	74 71	284	5,040
David Higgins	72	67	74 71	284	5,040
Prom Meesawat	67	70	73 74	284	5,040
*Rowin Caron	73	65	73 74	285	
Robert Coles	69	70	75 71	285	4,320
Richard Finch	69	69	73 74	285	4,320
Simon Thornton	70	68	75 72	285	4,320
Bjorn Akesson	71	67	71 77	286	3,457
Alejandro Canizares	69	68	76 73	286	3,457
Lorenzo Gagli	70	69	76 71	286	3,457
Peter Hedblom	71	66	74 75	286	3,457
Scott Jamieson	69	68	74 75	286	3,457
Kevin Phelan	71	68	73 74	286	3,457
Joakim Lagergren	73	65	75 74	287	2,696
Ricardo Santos	70	69	77 71	287	2,696
Matteo Delpodio	68	71	77 72	288	2,688
Robert Rock	69	69	78 72	288	2,688
Alessandro Tadini	72	67	74 75	288	2,688
Chris Lloyd	69	69	79 72	289	2,682

Open d'Italia Lindt

Golf Club Torino, Turin, Italy
Par 36-36–72; 7,208 yards

September 19-22
purse, €1,500,000

	SCORES				TOTAL	MONEY
Julien Quesne	70	68	71	67	276	€250,000
David Higgins	67	69	73	68	277	130,280
Steve Webster	67	69	73	68	277	130,280
Felipe Aguilar	69	66	72	71	278	59,025
Fredrik Andersson Hed	73	67	71	67	278	59,025
Nicolas Colsaerts	65	71	70	72	278	59,025
Emiliano Grillo	70	72	68	68	278	59,025
Seve Benson	68	70	72	69	279	29,775
Robert-Jan Derksen	71	69	71	68	279	29,775
Marcus Fraser	66	71	68	74	279	29,775
Hennie Otto	71	67	70	71	279	29,775
Alvaro Quiros	71	67	73	68	279	29,775
Romain Wattel	71	72	66	70	279	29,775
Maximilian Kieffer	65	72	72	71	280	22,500
Espen Kofstad	70	69	73	68	280	22,500
Mark Foster	74	65	71	71	281	18,814
David Horsey	72	70	73	66	281	18,814
Morten Orum Madsen	72	71	70	68	281	18,814
Francesco Molinari	68	67	71	75	281	18,814
Simon Thornton	68	67	72	74	281	18,814
Jaco Van Zyl	70	69	71	71	281	18,814
Fabrizio Zanotti	71	70	69	71	281	18,814
Matthew Baldwin	71	68	72	71	282	14,700
Jorge Campillo	68	73	70	71	282	14,700
Chris Doak	74	67	69	72	282	14,700
David Drysdale	69	72	71	70	282	14,700
Scott Hend	72	71	66	73	282	14,700
Scott Jamieson	72	69	70	71	282	14,700
Joakim Lagergren	72	67	67	76	282	14,700
Mark Tullo	70	70	74	68	282	14,700
Bernd Wiesberger	69	72	68	73	282	14,700
Robert Allenby	71	72	70	70	283	11,475
Magnus A. Carlsson	72	71	68	72	283	11,475
Oscar Floren	71	72	71	69	283	11,475
Ricardo Gonzalez	65	73	70	75	283	11,475
Mikko Korhonen	70	70	73	70	283	11,475
Simon Wakefield	70	73	68	72	283	11,475
Thomas Aiken	69	71	74	70	284	10,050
Alejandro Canizares	71	67	72	74	284	10,050
Gonzalo Fernandez-Castano	71	70	73	70	284	10,050
*Renato Paratore	72	66	71	75	284	
Gregory Bourdy	71	72	73	69	285	8,850
Alexander Levy	70	72	72	71	285	8,850
Matteo Manassero	70	70	69	76	285	8,850
Matthew Nixon	70	69	74	72	285	8,850
Gary Orr	73	68	72	72	285	8,850
Bjorn Akesson	72	69	75	70	286	7,200
Simon Dyson	69	74	72	71	286	7,200
Johan Edfors	69	70	71	76	286	7,200
Richard Finch	68	74	69	75	286	7,200
James Kingston	68	71	75	72	286	7,200
James Ruth	69	72	73	72	286	7,200
Kristoffer Broberg	70	73	70	74	287	5,400
J.B. Hansen	68	74	70	75	287	5,400
David Howell	71	72	72	72	287	5,400
Simon Khan	73	70	71	73	287	5,400
Garth Mulroy	71	72	72	72	287	5,400

	SCORES				TOTAL	MONEY
Alessandro Tadini	72	71	71	73	287	5,400
Gary Boyd	74	69	74	71	288	4,050
Andreas Harto	69	74	71	74	288	4,050
Tom Lewis	70	72	75	71	288	4,050
Jean-Francois Lucquin	71	72	74	71	288	4,050
Damien McGrane	71	69	76	72	288	4,050
Richie Ramsay	75	68	70	75	288	4,050
Lee Slattery	70	73	71	74	288	4,050
Retief Goosen	70	72	74	73	289	3,225
Mathias Gronberg	71	70	73	75	289	3,225
Justin Walters	70	73	71	75	289	3,225
Peter Whiteford	73	68	74	74	289	3,225
Jose Maria Olazabal	71	68	74	77	290	2,850
Richard McEvoy	73	70	73	75	291	2,740
Estanislao Goya	69	72	80	71	292	2,250
Graeme Storm	70	71	73	79	293	2,247
*Edoardo Raffaele Lipparelli	69	73	78	74	294	
Peter Erofejeff	74	69	77	79	299	2,244

Alfred Dunhill Links Championship

St. Andrews Old Course: Par 36-36–72; 7,279 yards
Carnoustie Championship Course: Par 36-36–72; 7,412 yards
Kingsbarns Golf Links: Par 36-36–72; 7,150 yards
St. Andrews & Fife, Scotland

September 26-29
purse, US$5,000,000

	SCORES				TOTAL	MONEY
David Howell	67	68	63	67	265	€589,562
Peter Uihlein	71	60	65	69	265	393,039
(Howell defeated Uihlein on second playoff hole.)						
Tom Lewis	64	65	73	64	266	199,154
Shane Lowry	68	66	64	68	266	199,154
Tommy Fleetwood	65	66	69	67	267	149,985
Garth Mulroy	66	69	65	68	268	123,808
Ricardo Gonzalez	67	69	63	70	269	81,926
Martin Kaymer	69	66	63	71	269	81,926
Thomas Levet	68	64	68	69	269	81,926
Charl Schwartzel	68	68	66	67	269	81,926
Chris Wood	66	69	69	65	269	81,926
Darren Clarke	69	66	66	69	270	54,759
Morten Orum Madsen	66	74	66	64	270	54,759
Hennie Otto	68	63	69	70	270	54,759
Chris Paisley	72	62	66	70	270	54,759
Bernd Wiesberger	70	65	67	68	270	54,759
Ernie Els	69	65	64	73	271	45,750
Scott Jamieson	71	65	67	68	271	45,750
Pablo Larrazabal	70	68	63	70	271	45,750
Chris Doak	70	67	63	72	272	40,591
David Horsey	66	70	65	71	272	40,591
Paul McGinley	70	68	67	67	272	40,591
Julien Quesne	69	66	67	70	272	40,591
Alejandro Canizares	69	65	70	69	273	37,319
Joost Luiten	67	63	68	75	273	37,319
Matthew Baldwin	65	70	70	69	274	32,544
Jamie Donaldson	65	67	71	71	274	32,544
Michael Hoey	68	66	67	73	274	32,544
Soren Kjeldsen	66	66	72	70	274	32,544
Richard McEvoy	64	67	67	76	274	32,544
Eddie Pepperell	66	67	69	72	274	32,544
Justin Walters	68	69	70	67	274	32,544

		SCORES			TOTAL	MONEY
Gary Lockerbie	69	67	71	68	275	27,768
Richie Ramsay	69	70	68	68	275	27,768
Magnus A. Carlsson	69	69	68	70	276	25,115
Alexandre Kaleka	64	70	73	69	276	25,115
Graeme Storm	67	69	70	70	276	25,115
Alessandro Tadini	66	70	70	70	276	25,115
Marc Warren	70	66	66	74	276	25,115
Jorge Campillo	68	71	67	71	277	19,809
Greg Chalmers	68	72	66	71	277	19,809
Eduardo De La Riva	67	69	71	70	277	19,809
Anders Hansen	71	68	67	71	277	19,809
Padraig Harrington	76	66	64	71	277	19,809
Gregory Havret	69	66	71	71	277	19,809
Mikko Ilonen	68	67	70	72	277	19,809
George Murray	65	69	70	73	277	19,809
Alexander Noren	67	72	66	72	277	19,809
Romain Wattel	70	70	67	70	277	19,809
Gregory Bourdy	70	71	63	74	278	14,503
Paul Casey	74	67	62	75	278	14,503
Simon Khan	69	71	66	72	278	14,503
Brooks Koepka	69	66	70	73	278	14,503
Richard Sterne	72	70	65	71	278	14,503
Richard Finch	68	71	68	72	279	11,408
Mark Foster	65	66	74	74	279	11,408
J.B. Hansen	69	69	68	73	279	11,408
Maarten Lafeber	71	70	66	72	279	11,408
Branden Grace	70	69	68	73	280	10,082
Oliver Wilson	64	67	73	76	280	10,082
Robert Coles	72	69	65	75	281	9,374
Soren Hansen	69	69	66	77	281	9,374
Felipe Aguilar	68	71	68	75	282	8,313
Bjorn Akesson	69	68	68	77	282	8,313
Matteo Delpodio	68	67	71	76	282	8,313
Retief Goosen	70	68	68	76	282	8,313
James Kingston	72	69	66	76	283	7,428
Anthony Wall	68	67	72	77	284	7,075

Seve Trophy

Saint-Nom-La-Breteche, Paris, France
Par 35-36-71; 6,983 yards

October 3-6
€1,750,000

FIRST DAY
Fourballs

Paul Lawrie and Stephen Gallacher (GB&I) defeated Thomas Bjorn and Miguel Angel Jimenez, 3 and 2.
Mikko Ilonen and Thorbjorn Olesen (Europe) defeated Tommy Fleetwood and Chris Wood, 1 up.
Paul Casey and Simon Khan (GB&I) halved with Francesco Molinari and Matteo Manassero.
Joost Luiten and Gregory Bourdy (Europe) defeated Jamie Donaldson and David Lynn, 2 and 1.
Nicolas Colsaerts and Gonzalo Fernandez-Castano (Europe) defeated Marc Warren and Scott Jamieson, 5 and 3.

POINTS: Continental Europe 3½, Great Britain & Ireland 1½

SECOND DAY
Fourballs

Casey and Khan (GB&I) defeated Ilonen and Olesen, 3 and 2.
Lynn and Jamieson (GB&I) defeated Molinari and Manassero, 1 up.
Donaldson and Warren (GB&I) defeated Bjorn and Jimenez, 4 and 2.
Luiten and Bourdy (Europe) defeated Fleetwood and Wood, 1 up.
Colsaerts and Fernandez-Castano (Europe) defeated Lawrie and Gallacher, 6 and 5.

POINTS: Continental Europe 5½, Great Britain & Ireland 4½

THIRD DAY
Morning Foursomes

Colsaerts and Fernandez-Castano (Europe) halved with Gallacher and Lawrie.
Luiten and Bourdy (Europe) defeated Donaldson and Warren, 2 and 1.
Wood and Jamieson (GB&I) defeated Olesen and Molinari, 2 and 1.
Jimenez and Manassero (Europe) defeated Casey and Fleetwood, 1 up.

POINTS: Continental Europe 8, Great Britain & Ireland 6

THIRD DAY
Afternoon Foursomes

Lawrie and Gallacher (GB&I) defeated Colsaerts and Fernandez-Castano, 2 and 1.
Donaldson and Warren (GB&I) defeated Bjorn and Ilonen, 2 and 1.
Luiten and Bourdy (Europe) defeated Wood and Jamieson, 2 up.
Casey and Lynn (GB&I) defeated Jimenez and Manassero, 1 up.

POINTS: Continental Europe 9, Great Britain & Ireland 9

FOURTH DAY
Singles

Fernandez-Castano (Europe) halved with Donaldson.
Colsaerts (Europe) defeated Casey, 1 up.
Fleetwood (GB&I) defeated Luiten, 3 and 2.
Bjorn (Europe) halved with Khan.
Bourdy (Europe) defeated Jamieson, 4 and 3.
Warren (GB&I) defeated Olesen, 4 and 3.
Manassero (Europe) defeated Gallacher, 3 and 2.
Lawrie (GB&I) defeated Ilonen, 2 and 1.
Jimenez (Europe) defeated Lynn, 6 and 4.
Molinari (Europe) defeated Wood, 3 and 2.

TOTAL POINTS: Continental Europe 15, Great Britain & Ireland 13

Portugal Masters

Oceanico Victoria Golf Course, Algarve, Portugal
Par 35-36–71; 7,192 yards

October 10-13
purse, €2,000,000

	SCORES				TOTAL	MONEY
David Lynn	65	65	73	63	266	€333,330
Justin Walters	69	63	69	66	267	222,220
Stephen Gallacher	70	67	65	66	268	103,333
Paul Waring	67	63	67	71	268	103,333
Bernd Wiesberger	66	65	70	67	268	103,333
Jamie Donaldson	65	68	66	70	269	65,000
Hennie Otto	66	64	69	70	269	65,000
Robert-Jan Derksen	69	68	67	66	270	41,200
Chris Doak	67	64	69	70	270	41,200

	SCORES				TOTAL	MONEY
Ross Fisher	67	66	71	66	270	41,200
Pablo Larrazabal	69	67	64	70	270	41,200
Simon Thornton	65	69	65	71	270	41,200
Scott Jamieson	66	73	60	72	271	31,400
Martin Kaymer	68	68	68	67	271	31,400
Matthew Baldwin	67	66	69	70	272	28,800
Nicolas Colsaerts	68	67	67	70	272	28,800
Victor Dubuisson	67	67	72	67	273	24,960
Richard Green	71	69	68	65	273	24,960
Francesco Molinari	68	72	63	70	273	24,960
Marcel Siem	66	72	69	66	273	24,960
Anthony Wall	68	68	69	68	273	24,960
Fredrik Andersson Hed	67	71	68	68	274	21,700
Soren Hansen	66	72	70	66	274	21,700
Alvaro Quiros	65	67	68	74	274	21,700
Lee Slattery	71	66	70	67	274	21,700
Seve Benson	67	72	70	66	275	17,000
Richard Bland	69	71	70	65	275	17,000
Jorge Campillo	69	68	69	69	275	17,000
Robert Coles	67	71	64	73	275	17,000
Eduardo De La Riva	69	71	66	69	275	17,000
Tommy Fleetwood	67	69	71	68	275	17,000
Alexandre Kaleka	72	65	68	70	275	17,000
Maximilian Kieffer	65	71	72	67	275	17,000
Eddie Pepperell	67	72	72	64	275	17,000
Robert Rock	71	68	72	64	275	17,000
Romain Wattel	71	67	67	70	275	17,000
Chris Wood	66	71	67	71	275	17,000
Felipe Aguilar	65	70	70	71	276	12,400
Thomas Aiken	71	69	70	66	276	12,400
Rafa Cabrera-Bello	71	66	69	70	276	12,400
Ricardo Gonzalez	72	68	65	71	276	12,400
Jose Manuel Lara	67	69	66	74	276	12,400
Paul Lawrie	69	66	73	68	276	12,400
Tom Lewis	70	67	68	71	276	12,400
Mark Tullo	66	70	71	69	276	12,400
Soren Kjeldsen	69	65	71	72	277	9,800
Garth Mulroy	70	69	68	70	277	9,800
Alexander Noren	70	68	69	70	277	9,800
Julien Quesne	66	69	71	71	277	9,800
Andy Sullivan	66	74	66	71	277	9,800
David Horsey	67	69	73	69	278	7,600
David Howell	69	68	71	70	278	7,600
Joost Luiten	68	69	73	68	278	7,600
Morten Orum Madsen	71	68	67	72	278	7,600
Paul McGinley	71	66	71	70	278	7,600
Jaco Van Zyl	69	67	74	68	278	7,600
Thomas Bjorn	74	63	72	70	279	5,700
David Drysdale	71	68	69	71	279	5,700
Gonzalo Fernandez-Castano	69	67	71	72	279	5,700
David Higgins	71	68	69	71	279	5,700
Miguel Angel Jimenez	71	69	69	70	279	5,700
Graeme Storm	65	72	72	70	279	5,700
Alejandro Canizares	67	68	71	74	280	4,600
Andrew Dodt	72	66	69	73	280	4,600
Raphael Jacquelin	71	66	67	76	280	4,600
Espen Kofstad	72	67	70	71	280	4,600
Danny Willett	69	67	69	75	280	4,600
Andreas Harto	69	71	71	70	281	3,900
Joel Sjoholm	71	67	75	68	281	3,900
Gregory Havret	70	70	69	73	282	3,325
Richie Ramsay	70	70	70	72	282	3,325
Chris Paisley	71	69	71	76	287	2,997

ISPS Handa Perth International
See Australasian Tour chapter.

The Final Series

BMW Masters

Lake Malaren Golf Club, Shanghai, China
Par 36-36–72; 7,607 yards

October 24-27
purse, US$7,000,000

	SCORES				TOTAL	MONEY
Gonzalo Fernandez-Castano	71	71	67	68	277	€851,346
Thongchai Jaidee	70	70	72	66	278	445,158
Francesco Molinari	72	71	71	64	278	445,158
Luke Guthrie	65	71	72	71	279	255,491
Thomas Bjorn	73	72	69	66	280	183,269
Pablo Larrazabal	70	73	69	68	280	183,269
Peter Uihlein	69	75	69	67	280	183,269
Rafa Cabrera-Bello	73	68	67	73	281	110,560
Paul Casey	70	70	71	70	281	110,560
Peter Hanson	79	68	71	63	281	110,560
Scott Jamieson	72	68	71	70	281	110,560
Marcus Fraser	73	70	70	69	282	88,375
Gregory Bourdy	70	73	67	73	283	79,982
Martin Kaymer	75	71	70	67	283	79,982
Ian Poulter	74	69	72	69	284	72,502
Brett Rumford	73	69	75	67	284	72,502
Eduardo De La Riva	75	72	70	68	285	63,250
Ricardo Gonzalez	73	67	74	71	285	63,250
David Horsey	72	72	72	69	285	63,250
Soren Kjeldsen	76	71	67	71	285	63,250
Craig Lee	70	70	71	74	285	63,250
Garth Mulroy	74	72	71	68	285	63,250
Bernd Wiesberger	75	69	69	72	285	63,250
Darren Fichardt	74	75	72	65	286	54,076
Shane Lowry	78	71	70	67	286	54,076
Lee Westwood	72	71	70	73	286	54,076
Padraig Harrington	72	72	70	73	287	48,894
Rory McIlroy	71	72	71	73	287	48,894
Danny Willett	74	72	70	71	287	48,894
Maximilian Kieffer	72	72	70	74	288	45,537
Luke Donald	75	72	71	71	289	42,399
Thorbjorn Olesen	75	70	72	72	289	42,399
Richard Sterne	74	72	71	72	289	42,399
Jamie Donaldson	79	70	71	70	290	35,138
Ross Fisher	75	70	72	73	290	35,138
Tommy Fleetwood	72	77	71	70	290	35,138
Paul Lawrie	74	73	72	71	290	35,138
Julien Quesne	73	77	72	68	290	35,138
Ricardo Santos	77	76	73	64	290	35,138
Marcel Siem	81	71	71	67	290	35,138
Henrik Stenson	72	74	79	65	290	35,138
Hao-Tong Li	78	72	75	66	291	29,264
Paul McGinley	77	71	70	73	291	29,264
Alejandro Canizares	75	75	73	69	292	26,126

	SCORES				TOTAL	MONEY
Nicolas Colsaerts	74	76	72	70	292	26,126
Victor Dubuisson	78	75	72	67	292	26,126
Matthew Griffin	74	72	74	72	292	26,126
John Daly	68	74	78	73	293	21,528
Mikko Ilonen	80	70	70	73	293	21,528
Raphael Jacquelin	76	72	72	73	293	21,528
Steve Webster	79	73	70	71	293	21,528
Ashun Wu	73	76	75	69	293	21,528
Stephen Gallacher	77	71	74	72	294	16,985
Wen-Chong Liang	75	75	74	70	294	16,985
Graeme McDowell	70	74	76	74	294	16,985
Alexander Noren	74	76	75	69	294	16,985
Felipe Aguilar	77	72	74	72	295	14,121
George Coetzee	78	74	74	69	295	14,121
Louis Oosthuizen	74	77	70	75	296	12,698
Miguel Angel Jimenez	74	75	75	73	297	11,749
Thomas Aiken	80	70	75	74	299	9,943
Branden Grace	79	69	75	76	299	9,943
David Howell	76	74	79	70	299	9,943
Lian-Wei Zhang	78	74	75	72	299	9,943
Simon Khan	77	76	73	74	300	8,684
Dong Su	76	75	74	77	302	8,246
Mu Hu	75	73	75	80	303	7,663
Ming-Jie Huang	81	75	72	75	303	7,663
Marc Warren	73	77	76	77	303	7,663
Xin-Yang Li	77	77	76	75	305	6,933
Xin-Jun Zhang	76	77	76	76	305	6,933
Shao-Cai He	83	73	78	72	306	6,349
Wen-Yi Huang	71	79	78	78	306	6,349
*Yan-Wei Liu	78	77	76	77	308	
Chris Wood	79	83	74	73	309	5,911
Xuen-Cheng Li	85	78	78	77	318	5,765

WGC - HSBC Champions

See Asia/Japan Tours chapter.

Turkish Airlines Open

Montgomerie Maxx Royal, Antalya, Turkey
Par 35-37–72; 7,100 yards

November 7-10
purse, US$7,000,000

	SCORES				TOTAL	MONEY
Victor Dubuisson	67	65	63	69	264	€848,930
Jamie Donaldson	68	67	68	63	266	567,603
Justin Rose	70	66	67	65	268	287,567
Tiger Woods	70	63	68	67	268	287,567
Raphael Jacquelin	67	72	62	68	269	197,624
Ian Poulter	66	66	68	69	269	197,624
Henrik Stenson	64	68	69	69	270	132,562
Marc Warren	69	70	66	65	270	132,562
Bernd Wiesberger	68	72	66	64	270	132,562
Ross Fisher	68	68	70	65	271	98,421
Justin Walters	66	66	70	69	271	98,421
Paul Casey	66	73	67	66	272	82,618
George Coetzee	66	71	68	67	272	82,618
Julien Quesne	67	69	68	68	272	82,618
Thomas Aiken	71	67	66	69	273	71,217
Darren Fichardt	64	73	71	65	273	71,217

	SCORES				TOTAL	MONEY
Chris Wood	69	70	65	69	273	71,217
Thomas Bjorn	64	72	71	67	274	61,272
Alejandro Canizares	67	68	66	73	274	61,272
Robert-Jan Derksen	67	69	69	69	274	61,272
Maximilian Kieffer	66	73	68	67	274	61,272
Joost Luiten	72	70	65	67	274	61,272
Garth Mulroy	70	69	66	69	274	61,272
Richie Ramsay	70	69	71	64	274	61,272
Stephen Gallacher	68	71	68	68	275	51,375
Martin Kaymer	69	68	68	70	275	51,375
Francesco Molinari	69	68	71	67	275	51,375
Paul Waring	68	68	71	68	275	51,375
Jonas Blixt	68	74	66	68	276	42,445
Marcus Fraser	67	71	71	67	276	42,445
Branden Grace	69	69	67	71	276	42,445
Thongchai Jaidee	69	68	70	69	276	42,445
Thorbjorn Olesen	66	72	71	67	276	42,445
Charl Schwartzel	68	70	68	70	276	42,445
Lee Westwood	70	66	73	67	276	42,445
Rafa Cabrera-Bello	67	73	69	68	277	34,493
Tommy Fleetwood	69	71	69	68	277	34,493
Craig Lee	69	68	69	71	277	34,493
David Lynn	68	68	68	73	277	34,493
Richard Sterne	69	65	71	72	277	34,493
Felipe Aguilar	69	68	70	71	278	29,836
J.B. Hansen	72	71	69	66	278	29,836
Marcel Siem	69	71	72	66	278	29,836
Gregory Bourdy	69	72	66	72	279	25,106
David Howell	70	72	67	70	279	25,106
Paul Lawrie	74	70	66	69	279	25,106
Wen-Chong Liang	71	66	70	72	279	25,106
Shane Lowry	72	75	65	67	279	25,106
Matteo Manassero	70	70	70	69	279	25,106
Nicolas Colsaerts	73	68	72	67	280	20,521
Padraig Harrington	68	70	71	71	280	20,521
Eddie Pepperell	69	74	65	72	280	20,521
Pablo Larrazabal	68	70	72	71	281	18,483
Kiradech Aphibarnrat	66	73	72	71	282	16,519
Ricardo Gonzalez	66	75	71	70	282	16,519
Gregory Havret	72	69	68	73	282	16,519
John Parry	78	67	72	67	284	14,154
Peter Uihlein	67	72	71	74	284	14,154
Eduardo De La Riva	70	73	70	72	285	12,262
Steve Webster	65	75	75	70	285	12,262
David Horsey	69	71	73	73	286	10,552
Ricardo Santos	68	75	71	72	286	10,552
David Drysdale	70	73	71	73	287	8,969
Morten Orum Madsen	73	71	72	71	287	8,969
Colin Montgomerie	72	72	74	69	287	8,969
Danny Willett	75	71	74	67	287	8,969
Louis Oosthuizen	72	74	69	73	288	7,859
Graeme Storm	70	79	72	67	288	7,859
Scott Jamieson	74	69	78	68	289	7,423
Miguel Angel Jimenez	73	71	73	73	290	6,986
Damien McGrane	70	73	72	75	290	6,986
Brett Rumford	72	71	78	70	291	6,549
Simon Khan	73	73	72	76	294	6,258
Soren Kjeldsen	69	77	76	74	296	5,967
*Ediz Kemaloglu	76	74	74	73	297	
Hamza Sayin	75	79	76	70	300	5,822
*Ali Altuntas	80	77	79	75	311	
Alexander Noren	73	70			WD	

DP World Tour Championship

Jumeirah Golf Estates, Dubai, United Arab Emirates
Par 36-36–72; 7,675 yards

November 14-17
purse, US$8,000,000

	SCORES				TOTAL	MONEY
Henrik Stenson	68	64	67	64	263	€985,476
Ian Poulter	69	68	66	66	269	657,009
Victor Dubuisson	70	66	64	71	271	384,345
Joost Luiten	73	68	65	66	272	295,650
Luke Donald	73	66	67	67	273	200,106
Rory McIlroy	71	67	68	67	273	200,106
Lee Westwood	70	70	65	68	273	200,106
Jamie Donaldson	68	72	67	67	274	153,738
Miguel Angel Jimenez	72	66	66	70	274	153,738
Peter Hanson	70	68	70	67	275	130,086
Justin Rose	70	67	68	70	275	130,086
Jonas Blixt	72	65	71	68	276	118,260
Francesco Molinari	70	68	70	69	277	112,347
Rafa Cabrera-Bello	68	71	68	71	278	100,521
Alejandro Canizares	66	67	70	75	278	100,521
Richard Sterne	70	70	70	68	278	100,521
Graeme McDowell	72	68	68	71	279	85,739
Thorbjorn Olesen	69	70	71	69	279	85,739
Mikko Ilonen	72	68	69	71	280	73,913
Martin Kaymer	70	69	72	69	280	73,913
Thomas Bjorn	71	74	69	67	281	65,043
Gregory Bourdy	76	70	66	69	281	65,043
Darren Fichardt	71	71	67	72	281	65,043
Marcus Fraser	67	69	72	73	281	65,043
Matteo Manassero	71	72	68	70	281	65,043
Ross Fisher	75	64	72	71	282	57,947
Scott Jamieson	73	70	70	69	282	57,947
Pablo Larrazabal	72	66	72	72	282	57,947
Kiradech Aphibarnrat	67	70	70	76	283	52,626
David Horsey	72	72	68	71	283	52,626
Chris Wood	73	66	71	73	283	52,626
George Coetzee	74	67	69	74	284	48,191
Louis Oosthuizen	73	70	71	70	284	48,191
Stephen Gallacher	77	71	71	66	285	44,348
David Howell	75	66	70	74	285	44,348
Bernd Wiesberger	72	73	66	74	285	44,348
Gonzalo Fernandez-Castano	71	74	67	74	286	41,391
Tommy Fleetwood	72	76	70	68	286	41,391
Simon Khan	72	72	74	69	287	38,435
Shane Lowry	71	71	74	71	287	38,435
Marcel Siem	75	67	70	75	287	38,435
Nicolas Colsaerts	71	75	71	71	288	35,478
David Lynn	71	72	73	72	288	35,478
Eduardo De La Riva	71	71	72	75	289	32,522
Raphael Jacquelin	77	66	72	74	289	32,522
Craig Lee	73	70	71	75	289	32,522
Felipe Aguilar	79	66	73	72	290	28,382
Thongchai Jaidee	69	70	74	77	290	28,382
Julien Quesne	74	73	69	74	290	28,382
Brett Rumford	71	72	74	73	290	28,382
Peter Uihlein	72	72	76	71	291	25,426
Branden Grace	76	70	71	75	292	23,652
Marc Warren	74	71	73	74	292	23,652
Paul Casey	75	68	73	77	293	21,878
Thomas Aiken	76	74	73	74	297	20,696
Garth Mulroy	76	75	74	78	303	19,513

South African Open Championship
See African Tours chapter.

Alfred Dunhill Championship
See African Tours chapter.

Nedbank Golf Challenge
See African Tours chapter.

Hong Kong Open
See Asia/Japan Tours chapter.

Nelson Mandela Championship
See African Tours chapter.

Challenge Tour

Gujarat Kensville Challenge

Kensville Golf & Country Club, Ahmedabad, India
Par 36-36–72; 7,224 yards

January 31-February 3
purse, €200,000

	SCORES				TOTAL	MONEY
Shiv Kapur	67	71	65	71	274	€32,000
Andrew McArthur	67	69	71	69	276	22,000
Phillip Archer	73	69	66	69	277	14,000
Daniel Im	73	68	70	69	280	12,000
Mukesh Kumar	73	71	68	69	281	9,000
Tim Sluiter	70	69	70	72	281	9,000
Mithun Perera	69	77	67	69	282	6,400
Gaganjeet Bhullar	71	70	73	70	284	4,700
Rhys Enoch	71	72	70	71	284	4,700
Rahil Gangjee	72	69	74	69	284	4,700
Victor Riu	68	72	73	71	284	4,700
Byeong-Hun An	73	69	72	71	285	3,600
Agustin Domingo	66	73	72	74	285	3,600
George Murray	69	73	72	71	285	3,600
Rich Beem	73	73	73	67	286	3,000
Terry Pilkadaris	71	71	73	71	286	3,000
Daniel Vancsik	72	72	67	75	286	3,000
Jason Barnes	73	72	70	72	287	2,252
Kunal Bhasin	76	70	70	71	287	2,252
Tyrrell Hatton	73	71	73	70	287	2,252
Lasse Jensen	71	75	70	71	287	2,252
Peter Uihlein	71	72	69	75	287	2,252

	SCORES				TOTAL	MONEY
Shankar Das	73	71	72	72	288	1,900
Himmat Rai	71	74	68	75	288	1,900
Raju Ali Mollah	76	70	69	74	289	1,760
Jacob Glennemo	68	75	74	72	289	1,760
Andrea Pavan	69	71	78	71	289	1,760
Digvijay Singh	73	73	73	70	289	1,760
Steven Tiley	70	73	72	74	289	1,760

Barclays Kenya Open

Karen Country Club, Nairobi, Kenya
Par 35-35–71; 6,969 yards

February 14-17
purse, €195,000

	SCORES				TOTAL	MONEY
Jordi Garcia Pinto	69	66	68	69	272	€31,200
Tim Sluiter	69	65	69	70	273	21,450
George Murray	68	67	71	69	275	13,650
Jose-Filipe Lima	70	68	73	65	276	11,700
Edouard Dubois	71	69	69	68	277	8,775
Brooks Koepka	70	68	68	71	277	8,775
Christophe Brazillier	69	71	69	69	278	5,168
Dylan Frittelli	71	70	68	69	278	5,168
Bernd Ritthammer	73	71	66	68	278	5,168
Raymond Russell	67	69	72	70	278	5,168
Andrew McArthur	68	73	67	71	279	3,802
Steven Tiley	74	68	70	67	279	3,802
Byeong-Hun An	69	72	73	66	280	3,510
Phillip Archer	69	69	76	67	281	2,828
Jens Dantorp	74	69	67	71	281	2,828
Sebastian Garcia Rodriguez	72	71	67	71	281	2,828
Sam Hutsby	68	70	70	73	281	2,828
Adrian Otaegui	67	72	68	74	281	2,828
Martin Sell	73	71	70	67	281	2,828
Matt Ford	68	73	75	66	282	2,096
Pedro Oriol	70	70	70	72	282	2,096
H.P. Bacher	66	76	71	70	283	1,696
Jason Barnes	71	69	76	67	283	1,696
Lucas Bjerregaard	70	72	68	73	283	1,696
Wallace Booth	75	67	71	70	283	1,696
Thomas Fournier	72	68	71	72	283	1,696
Tyrrell Hatton	69	69	73	72	283	1,696
Dodge Kemmer	70	72	71	70	283	1,696
David Law	68	69	71	75	283	1,696
Jamie Moul	71	73	71	68	283	1,696
Andrea Pavan	70	67	75	71	283	1,696
Carl Suneson	74	70	70	69	283	1,696
Peter Uihlein	69	71	74	69	283	1,696

Challenge de Madrid

El Encin Golf Hotel, Alcala de Henares, Madrid, Spain
Par 36-36–72; 7,561 yards

April 24-27
purse, €160,000

	SCORES				TOTAL	MONEY
Francois Calmels	63	69	72	67	271	€25,600
Tapio Pulkkanen	72	67	68	71	278	17,600
Thomas Norret	67	71	67	74	279	11,200

	SCORES				TOTAL	MONEY
Jens Dantorp	66	69	71	74	280	8,000
Edouard Dubois	69	70	68	73	280	8,000
Sam Walker	71	69	71	69	280	8,000
Christophe Brazillier	69	70	69	73	281	4,240
Sam Hutsby	66	70	72	73	281	4,240
Roope Kakko	67	74	69	71	281	4,240
Moritz Lampert	70	72	67	72	281	4,240
Phillip Archer	67	67	72	76	282	2,960
Mikko Korhonen	69	72	68	73	282	2,960
Sam Little	68	75	65	74	282	2,960
Terry Pilkadaris	69	72	69	72	282	2,960
Byeong-Hun An	70	71	68	74	283	2,400
Carlos Garcia Simarro	67	72	69	75	283	2,400
Alvaro Velasco	71	65	71	76	283	2,400
Simon Thornton	67	74	70	73	284	2,080
Carlos Aguilar	67	70	72	76	285	1,787
Dylan Frittelli	68	73	72	72	285	1,787
Benjamin Hebert	71	70	68	76	285	1,787
Jason Barnes	67	72	70	77	286	1,472
Filippo Bergamaschi	70	73	68	75	286	1,472
Wil Besseling	70	74	70	72	286	1,472
Marco Crespi	72	71	67	76	286	1,472
Sebastian Garcia Rodriguez	69	68	71	78	286	1,472
Eirik Tage Johansen	69	73	69	75	286	1,472
Matthew Zions	68	72	69	77	286	1,472

Montecchia Golf Open

Golf Club della Montecchia, Padova, Italy　　　　　　　　　　May 2-5
Par 35-36–71; 6,886 yards　　　　　　　　　　　　　　　　purse, €160,000

	SCORES				TOTAL	MONEY
Brooks Koepka	66	67	62	66	261	€25,600
Agustin Domingo	68	68	64	68	268	17,600
Andrea Rota	66	67	70	68	271	11,200
Stuart Manley	70	68	68	67	273	9,600
Pelle Edberg	68	70	66	70	274	7,200
Julien Guerrier	68	65	70	71	274	7,200
Seve Benson	71	64	70	70	275	3,726
Gary Boyd	68	68	70	69	275	3,726
Federico Colombo	68	70	66	71	275	3,726
Edouard Espana	65	68	67	75	275	3,726
Ross McGowan	69	69	68	69	275	3,726
Jamie Moul	65	67	72	71	275	3,726
Pedro Oriol	69	68	71	67	275	3,726
Nacho Elvira	70	67	69	70	276	2,400
Eirik Tage Johansen	68	69	68	71	276	2,400
Niccolo Quintarelli	68	70	67	71	276	2,400
Charles-Edouard Russo	64	69	72	71	276	2,400
Reinier Saxton	70	67	68	71	276	2,400
Jens Dantorp	67	72	68	70	277	1,732
David Dixon	68	71	68	70	277	1,732
Thomas Norret	68	69	69	71	277	1,732
Gary Stal	69	70	71	67	277	1,732
Oliver Bekker	69	68	73	68	278	1,424
Lucas Bjerregaard	65	72	68	73	278	1,424
Jordi Garcia Pinto	69	70	69	70	278	1,424
Benjamin Hebert	69	69	74	66	278	1,424
Alexander Levy	66	69	69	74	278	1,424
Jose-Filipe Lima	70	67	73	68	278	1,424

	SCORES				TOTAL	MONEY
Sam Little	68	69	66	75	278	1,424
Andrea Romano	71	68	70	69	278	1,424

Madeira Islands Open - Portugal - BPI

See European Tour section.

Telenet Trophy

Royal Waterloo Golf Club, Lasne, Belgium
Par 36-35–71; 6,664 yards

May 23-26
purse, €160,000

	SCORES				TOTAL	MONEY
Daniel Gaunt	69	66	69	69	273	€25,600
Wil Besseling	69	68	71	65	273	17,600
(Gaunt defeated Besseling on first playoff hole.)						
Jose-Filipe Lima	72	65	68	69	274	9,600
Stuart Manley	67	70	67	70	274	9,600
Daniel Vancsik	66	71	69	68	274	9,600
Carlos Aguilar	71	66	71	67	275	5,333
Sihwan Kim	69	69	70	67	275	5,333
Brooks Koepka	68	70	68	69	275	5,333
Roope Kakko	65	68	73	70	276	3,520
Dodge Kemmer	67	68	72	69	276	3,520
Steven Tiley	71	69	68	68	276	3,520
Wallace Booth	70	68	71	68	277	2,720
Robert Dinwiddie	68	65	71	73	277	2,720
Paul Maddy	72	66	70	69	277	2,720
Ross McGowan	72	68	67	70	277	2,720
Adrian Otaegui	67	70	69	71	277	2,720
Tyrrell Hatton	71	68	66	73	278	2,000
Ben Parker	70	70	75	63	278	2,000
Gareth Shaw	70	70	65	73	278	2,000
Damian Ulrich	74	65	69	70	278	2,000
Jacob Glennemo	69	72	72	66	279	1,498
Luke Goddard	64	71	72	72	279	1,498
Julien Guerrier	68	70	72	69	279	1,498
Antonio Hortal	71	69	69	70	279	1,498
Victor Riu	68	69	72	70	279	1,498
Raymond Russell	70	70	70	69	279	1,498
James Ruth	67	71	72	69	279	1,498
Tim Sluiter	68	67	73	71	279	1,498

Fred Olsen Challenge de Espana

Tecina Golf, La Gomera, Canary Islands, Spain
Par 36-35–71; 6,937 yards

May 30-June 2
purse, €160,000

	SCORES				TOTAL	MONEY
Brooks Koepka	64	66	64	66	260	€25,600
Luis Claverie	69	66	69	66	270	12,800
Edouard Dubois	63	67	68	72	270	12,800
Bernd Ritthammer	67	70	65	68	270	12,800
Alfredo Garcia-Heredia	70	65	68	68	271	6,507
Julien Guerrier	64	70	71	66	271	6,507
Daniel Im	74	65	66	66	271	6,507

	SCORES				TOTAL	MONEY
Daniel Brooks	69	66	70	67	272	3,947
Terry Pilkadaris	67	69	68	68	272	3,947
Roland Steiner	69	67	68	68	272	3,947
Sihwan Kim	69	68	67	69	273	3,040
Andrea Pavan	70	68	68	67	273	3,040
Pierre Relecom	67	68	68	70	273	3,040
Byeong-Hun An	70	69	66	69	274	2,400
Lucas Bjerregaard	67	74	67	66	274	2,400
Sebastian Garcia Rodriguez	69	71	69	65	274	2,400
Jamie McLeary	72	68	72	62	274	2,400
Daniel Wuensche	70	65	70	69	274	2,400
Mark F. Haastrup	71	66	72	66	275	1,661
Sam Hutsby	68	71	69	67	275	1,661
Nicolas Meitinger	64	72	67	72	275	1,661
Marcos Pastor	67	69	71	68	275	1,661
Duncan Stewart	68	73	63	71	275	1,661
Damian Ulrich	67	68	72	68	275	1,661
Adrien Bernadet	69	72	67	68	276	1,424
Chris Devlin	69	68	67	72	276	1,424
Stuart Manley	71	69	68	68	276	1,424
Charles-Edouard Russo	70	71	65	70	276	1,424

D+D Real Czech Challenge Open

Golf & Spa Kuneticka Hora, Dritec, Czech Republic
Par 36-36–72; 7,337 yards

June 6-9
purse, €160,000

	SCORES				TOTAL	MONEY
Francois Calmels	67	69	65	65	266	€25,600
Robert Dinwiddie	68	64	72	65	269	12,800
Adam Gee	66	66	66	71	269	12,800
Sam Walker	71	65	67	66	269	12,800
Adrian Otaegui	64	68	68	70	270	8,000
Andrea Pavan	68	64	68	71	271	6,400
Carlos Aguilar	65	67	70	70	272	4,480
Agustin Domingo	66	67	70	69	272	4,480
Brooks Koepka	70	71	69	62	272	4,480
Chris Hanson	71	68	64	71	274	3,253
Jose-Filipe Lima	69	72	67	66	274	3,253
Raymond Russell	67	67	71	69	274	3,253
Byeong-Hun An	68	72	68	67	275	2,800
Lloyd Kennedy	69	65	68	73	275	2,800
Marco Crespi	70	68	68	70	276	2,240
Oliver Farr	67	70	70	69	276	2,240
Matt Ford	66	73	63	74	276	2,240
Dylan Frittelli	67	69	72	68	276	2,240
Jerome Lando Casanova	68	67	69	72	276	2,240
Filippo Bergamaschi	72	68	69	68	277	1,669
Wil Besseling	71	70	68	68	277	1,669
Stuart Davis	71	69	70	67	277	1,669
Julien Guerrier	67	69	71	71	278	1,504
Benjamin Hebert	68	67	72	71	278	1,504
Nicolo Ravano	66	70	71	71	278	1,504

Najeti Hotels et Golfs Open

See European Tour section.

Scottish Hydro Challenge

Macdonald Spey Valley Golf Club, Aviemore, Scotland
Par 35-36–71; 7,100 yards

June 20-23
purse, €220,000

	SCORES				TOTAL	MONEY
Brooks Koepka	70	66	62	68	266	€35,200
Byeong-Hun An	62	70	65	72	269	15,950
Andrea Pavan	65	67	66	71	269	15,950
Steven Tiley	67	67	63	72	269	15,950
Sam Walker	67	65	68	69	269	15,950
Johan Carlsson	66	68	67	71	272	6,820
Sebi Garcia	63	70	70	69	272	6,820
Paul Maddy	68	68	68	68	272	6,820
Duncan Stewart	65	67	68	72	272	6,820
Jack Doherty	66	66	68	73	273	4,473
Tyrrell Hatton	65	69	67	72	273	4,473
Tom Murray	67	65	70	71	273	4,473
Guillaume Cambis	66	66	69	73	274	3,630
Dylan Frittelli	65	68	67	74	274	3,630
Greig Hutcheon	68	69	64	73	274	3,630
Chris Kelly	68	71	65	70	274	3,630
Edouard Dubois	66	67	68	74	275	2,662
Julien Guerrier	68	70	69	68	275	2,662
Lloyd Kennedy	67	71	67	70	275	2,662
Sihwan Kim	69	69	68	69	275	2,662
Tim Sluiter	71	65	70	69	275	2,662
Jordi Garcia Pinto	70	69	68	69	276	2,112
Manuel Trappel	68	69	65	74	276	2,112
Alvaro Velasco	66	69	65	76	276	2,112
Domenico Geminiani	71	67	68	71	277	1,980
Jeppe Huldahl	68	67	71	71	277	1,980
Nick McCarthy	69	69	66	73	277	1,980

Karnten Golf Open

Jacques Lemans Golf Club, St. Veit-Langsee, Austria
Par 36-35–71; 7,073 yards

June 27-30
purse, €160,000

	SCORES				TOTAL	MONEY
Dylan Frittelli	67	64	65	71	267	€25,600
Filippo Bergamaschi	69	65	68	68	270	14,400
Daan Huizing	68	69	67	66	270	14,400
Andrew McArthur	70	70	65	66	271	9,600
Mark F. Haastrup	65	69	69	69	272	5,568
Andrea Pavan	69	65	70	68	272	5,568
Andrea Rota	69	67	70	66	272	5,568
Lloyd Saltman	63	69	69	71	272	5,568
Sam Walker	68	67	67	70	272	5,568
Francois Calmels	68	69	66	70	273	3,360
Manuel Trappel	66	73	70	64	273	3,360
Edouard Dubois	66	67	71	70	274	2,800
Billy Hemstock	66	67	67	74	274	2,800
Niall Kearney	69	65	69	71	274	2,800
Zane Scotland	67	69	67	71	274	2,800
Rhys Enoch	70	70	67	68	275	2,080
Jens Fahrbring	69	68	68	70	275	2,080
Adam Gee	68	70	69	68	275	2,080
Peter O'Keeffe	66	67	69	73	275	2,080
Victor Riu	68	72	66	69	275	2,080

	SCORES			TOTAL	MONEY
Oliver Farr	70	68	67	71	276	1,624
Pierre Relecom	67	70	71	68	276	1,624
Matt Ford	70	68	69	70	277	1,488
James Frazer	70	65	72	70	277	1,488
George Murray	70	69	68	70	277	1,488
Thomas Pieters	72	68	70	67	277	1,488

Bad Griesbach Challenge

Hartl Resort, Bad Griesbach, Germany
Par 36-36–72; 7,322 yards

July 4-7
purse, €170,000

	SCORES			TOTAL	MONEY
Andrea Pavan	68	67	66	68	269	€27,200
Marco Crespi	69	69	66	66	270	18,700
Knut Borsheim	67	72	67	68	274	11,050
Victor Riu	63	69	70	72	274	11,050
Edouard Dubois	69	67	68	71	275	5,916
Daan Huizing	66	68	69	72	275	5,916
Jeppe Huldahl	68	68	71	68	275	5,916
Lloyd Kennedy	70	67	69	69	275	5,916
Sihwan Kim	72	69	69	65	275	5,916
Jens Dantorp	69	69	71	67	276	3,570
Robin Kind	66	71	71	68	276	3,570
Byeong-Hun An	68	69	71	69	277	3,060
Lucas Bjerregaard	68	71	69	69	277	3,060
Eirik Tage Johansen	68	66	70	73	277	3,060
Lionel Weber	68	69	71	70	278	2,720
Carlos Aguilar	69	70	69	71	279	2,210
Kenneth Ferrie	67	74	65	73	279	2,210
Luke Goddard	70	72	67	70	279	2,210
Terry Pilkadaris	68	68	70	73	279	2,210
Duncan Stewart	69	68	74	68	279	2,210
Wil Besseling	72	69	72	67	280	1,610
Jordi Garcia Pinto	72	68	70	70	280	1,610
Adam Gee	67	73	69	71	280	1,610
Chris Hanson	65	74	68	73	280	1,610
Sebastian Heisele	68	72	71	69	280	1,610
David Palm	67	68	74	71	280	1,610
Pierre Relecom	65	72	70	73	280	1,610

Swiss Challenge

Golf Sempachersee, Lucerne, Switzerland
Par 36-35–71; 7,147 yards

July 11-14
purse, €160,000

	SCORES			TOTAL	MONEY
Victor Riu	69	64	62	70	265	€25,600
Adam Gee	66	69	66	67	268	14,400
Brinson Paolini	70	69	64	65	268	14,400
Sihwan Kim	67	66	70	66	269	8,000
Jamie McLeary	70	64	65	70	269	8,000
Pedro Oriol	70	69	66	64	269	8,000
Johan Carlsson	69	66	67	68	270	4,480
Roope Kakko	72	68	67	63	270	4,480
Andrea Perrino	71	64	65	70	270	4,480
Marco Crespi	68	68	66	69	271	3,360

	SCORES				TOTAL	MONEY
Thomas Norret	67	69	68	67	271	3,360
Wallace Booth	69	69	65	69	272	3,040
Pelle Edberg	69	66	67	71	273	2,480
Chris Hanson	68	68	69	68	273	2,480
Andrea Pavan	65	71	69	68	273	2,480
Nicolo Ravano	69	69	66	69	273	2,480
Bernd Ritthammer	69	70	67	67	273	2,480
Martin Rominger	66	73	69	65	273	2,480
Daan Huizing	69	66	69	70	274	1,787
Steven Tiley	68	65	70	71	274	1,787
Alvaro Velasco	69	70	68	67	274	1,787
Jose-Filipe Lima	69	69	70	67	275	1,568
Dylan Frittelli	73	67	73	63	276	1,504
Jurgen Maurer	72	67	69	68	276	1,504
Zane Scotland	73	66	67	70	276	1,504

Mugello Tuscany Open

UNA Poggio dei Medici Golf Club, Scarperia, Florence, Italy
Par 35-36–71; 7,119 yards

July 18-21
purse, €160,000

	SCORES				TOTAL	MONEY
Marco Crespi	72	64	66	65	267	€25,600
Knut Borsheim	62	65	71	70	268	14,400
Jose-Filipe Lima	70	68	66	64	268	14,400
Lloyd Kennedy	69	67	65	70	271	8,800
Adrian Otaegui	66	69	69	67	271	8,800
Phillip Archer	66	68	69	69	272	5,760
Jerome Lando Casanova	70	67	68	67	272	5,760
Roope Kakko	67	68	72	66	273	4,480
Jin Jeong	65	70	63	76	274	3,400
Niklas Lemke	73	66	68	67	274	3,400
Gary Stal	70	66	71	67	274	3,400
Roland Steiner	71	67	68	68	274	3,400
Floris De Vries	66	64	73	72	275	2,640
Kenneth Ferrie	68	70	66	71	275	2,640
Luke Goddard	71	69	64	71	275	2,640
Jamie McLeary	66	68	70	71	275	2,640
Filippo Bergamaschi	71	69	67	69	276	2,160
Andrew McArthur	66	71	65	74	276	2,160
Baptiste Chapellan	72	68	69	68	277	1,661
Julien Guerrier	67	71	69	70	277	1,661
Sihwan Kim	72	65	73	67	277	1,661
David Palm	69	69	72	67	277	1,661
Raymond Russell	74	68	65	70	277	1,661
Sam Walker	69	68	71	69	277	1,661
Brinson Paolini	68	71	69	70	278	1,456
Martin Rominger	70	67	73	68	278	1,456

Le Vaudreuil Golf Challenge

Golf PGA France du Vaudreuil, Le Vaudreuil, France
Par 35-37–72; 6,814 yards

July 25-28
purse, €180,000

	SCORES				TOTAL	MONEY
Brinson Paolini	69	66	66	68	269	€28,800
Sihwan Kim	65	64	67	74	270	16,200
Adrian Otaegui	68	65	67	70	270	16,200
Phillip Archer	70	67	67	67	271	8,190
Dylan Frittelli	64	66	73	68	271	8,190
Daan Huizing	61	72	70	68	271	8,190
Duncan Stewart	66	66	71	68	271	8,190
Jamie McLeary	68	69	71	64	272	4,680
Alvaro Velasco	66	71	69	66	272	4,680
Jason Barnes	63	71	69	70	273	3,456
Edouard Espana	64	66	71	72	273	3,456
Andrew Johnston	64	69	70	70	273	3,456
Lloyd Kennedy	68	68	69	68	273	3,456
Chan Kim	67	65	73	68	273	3,456
Scott Fallon	69	70	66	69	274	2,520
Jordan Gibb	71	65	68	70	274	2,520
Mark F. Haastrup	71	68	66	69	274	2,520
Jose-Filipe Lima	65	69	72	68	274	2,520
Paul Maddy	67	70	67	70	274	2,520
Francois Calmels	64	72	69	70	275	1,739
Guillaume Cambis	71	69	68	67	275	1,739
Johan Carlsson	68	67	68	72	275	1,739
Jens Fahrbring	66	70	69	70	275	1,739
Hugues Joannes	67	70	69	69	275	1,739
*Clement Sordet	70	69	71	65	275	
Gary Stal	70	70	65	70	275	1,739
Steven Tiley	71	68	70	66	275	1,739
Lionel Weber	64	70	67	74	275	1,739

Finnish Challenge

Kytaga Golf, Hyvinkaa, Finland
Par 36-36–72; 7,201 yards

August 1-4
purse, €170,000

	SCORES				TOTAL	MONEY
Stuart Manley	65	69	64	69	267	€27,200
Jose-Filipe Lima	68	68	66	67	269	18,700
Jamie Elson	67	67	70	68	272	11,050
Jens Fahrbring	65	69	66	72	272	11,050
Francois Calmels	68	71	66	68	273	5,916
Daan Huizing	67	71	64	71	273	5,916
Andrew Johnston	68	68	68	69	273	5,916
Niklas Lemke	64	68	70	71	273	5,916
Jamie McLeary	69	69	67	68	273	5,916
*Erik Myllymaki	66	70	70	68	274	
Lucas Bjerregaard	69	69	69	68	275	3,358
Roope Kakko	66	68	71	70	275	3,358
Lloyd Kennedy	67	65	73	70	275	3,358
Duncan Stewart	65	68	70	72	275	3,358
Wil Besseling	66	70	71	69	276	2,720
Bernd Ritthammer	68	70	69	69	276	2,720
Brandon Stone	65	66	69	76	276	2,720
Guillaume Cambis	69	72	68	68	277	1,992
Domenico Geminiani	68	72	69	68	277	1,992

	SCORES				TOTAL	MONEY
Shiv Kapur	70	71	71	65	277	1,992
Mikko Korhonen	71	71	67	68	277	1,992
Mark Tullo	66	76	66	69	277	1,992
Pontus Widegren	70	71	69	67	277	1,992
Edouard Espana	70	70	69	69	278	1,581
Tyrrell Hatton	65	70	69	74	278	1,581
Sam Hutsby	69	66	69	74	278	1,581
Daniel Im	70	72	66	70	278	1,581

Norwegian Challenge

Losby Golf & Country Club, Finstadjordet, Oslo, Norway
Par 35-37–72; 7,047 yards

August 8-11
purse, €175,000

	SCORES				TOTAL	MONEY
Jens Fahrbring	69	72	62	66	269	€28,000
Daniel Im	73	68	64	67	272	15,750
Pontus Widegren	70	66	68	68	272	15,750
Johan Carlsson	71	69	68	65	273	10,500
Jason Barnes	65	70	72	68	275	7,875
Matt Ford	71	67	69	68	275	7,875
Scott Arnold	71	67	69	69	276	4,410
Knut Borsheim	70	67	70	69	276	4,410
Nacho Elvira	68	71	69	68	276	4,410
Tim Sluiter	69	70	69	68	276	4,410
Alvaro Velasco	72	65	68	71	276	4,410
Phillip Archer	64	71	69	73	277	2,975
Oliver Bekker	69	69	68	71	277	2,975
James Heath	68	70	70	69	277	2,975
Eirik Tage Johansen	70	67	72	68	277	2,975
Gareth Shaw	71	69	69	68	277	2,975
Lloyd Kennedy	70	66	72	70	278	2,188
Andrew McArthur	72	69	67	70	278	2,188
Nicolo Ravano	72	68	70	68	278	2,188
Taco Remkes	68	73	68	69	278	2,188
Laurie Canter	72	67	74	66	279	1,698
Edouard Dubois	70	68	69	72	279	1,698
Damien Perrier	69	70	71	69	279	1,698
Charles-Edouard Russo	71	67	72	69	279	1,698
Daniel Vancsik	69	71	70	69	279	1,698

Rolex Trophy

Golf Club de Geneve, Geneva, Switzerland
Par 36-36–72; 6,727 yards

August 21-24
purse, €228,000

	SCORES				TOTAL	MONEY
Jens Dantorp	67	67	66	70	270	€26,000
Adrian Otaegui	65	70	66	70	271	19,000
Jordi Garcia Pinto	69	67	70	66	272	11,650
Jose-Filipe Lima	69	65	66	72	272	11,650
Damian Ulrich	69	69	65	70	273	9,000
Victor Riu	66	70	69	69	274	8,000
Thomas Norret	66	69	69	71	275	7,000
Francois Calmels	68	71	69	68	276	6,300
Daniel Gaunt	63	72	70	72	277	5,200
Sihwan Kim	69	69	73	66	277	5,200

	SCORES				TOTAL	MONEY
Tim Sluiter	69	69	69	70	277	5,200
Marco Crespi	70	72	69	68	279	4,125
Robert Dinwiddie	67	67	71	74	279	4,125
Agustin Domingo	65	72	70	72	279	4,125
Lloyd Kennedy	68	68	72	71	279	4,125
Byeong-Hun An	69	70	70	71	280	3,500
Jeppe Huldahl	68	72	67	73	280	3,500
Jamie Elson	68	71	68	74	281	3,033
Daan Huizing	74	66	68	73	281	3,033
Stuart Manley	73	67	66	75	281	3,033
Johan Carlsson	72	68	71	71	282	2,700
Brinson Paolini	65	70	74	73	282	2,700
Andrea Pavan	70	68	71	73	282	2,700
Pelle Edberg	71	69	74	69	283	2,500
Jens Fahrbring	70	70	70	73	283	2,500
Shiv Kapur	73	73	66	71	283	2,500
Andrew McArthur	67	72	73	71	283	2,500

Northern Ireland Open Challenge

Galgorm Castle Golf Club & Estates, Ballymena,
County Antrim, Northern Ireland
Par 35-36–71; 6,930 yards

August 29-September 1
purse, €170,000

	SCORES				TOTAL	MONEY
Daan Huizing	65	66	66	74	271	€27,200
Oliver Wilson	66	70	68	67	271	18,700
(Huizing defeated Wilson on first playoff hole.)						
James Heath	67	71	65	69	272	11,050
Jamie McLeary	66	75	65	66	272	11,050
Bernd Ritthammer	64	71	68	70	273	8,500
Jens Dantorp	65	69	69	72	275	6,120
Andrew Johnston	66	73	69	67	275	6,120
Marcus Armitage	70	65	71	70	276	4,760
Jonathan Caldwell	68	69	71	70	278	3,303
Johan Carlsson	68	69	72	69	278	3,303
Matt Ford	71	69	68	70	278	3,303
Niklas Lemke	70	69	67	72	278	3,303
*Dermot McElroy	67	70	74	67	278	
Terry Pilkadaris	66	71	72	69	278	3,303
Duncan Stewart	70	66	72	70	278	3,303
Daniel Vancsik	69	70	69	70	278	3,303
Marco Crespi	67	69	72	71	279	2,295
Garry Houston	67	69	72	71	279	2,295
Roope Kakko	70	70	69	70	279	2,295
Mark Murphy	72	69	69	69	279	2,295
Jason Barnes	68	73	68	71	280	1,710
Tyrrell Hatton	67	72	70	71	280	1,710
Benjamin Hebert	67	69	75	69	280	1,710
Ross McGowan	65	69	76	70	280	1,710
Thomas Norret	66	75	68	71	280	1,710

Open Blue Green Cotes d'Armor Bretagne

Golf Blue Green de Pleneuf Val Andre, Pleneuf, France
Par 35-35–70; 6,447 yards

September 5-8
purse, €180,000

	SCORES				TOTAL	MONEY
Andrea Pavan	64	65	68	72	269	€28,800
Rhys Davies	73	67	67	66	273	16,200
Robert Dinwiddie	74	66	66	67	273	16,200
Alan Dunbar	66	67	70	72	275	8,190
Matt Haines	70	67	72	66	275	8,190
Sam Hutsby	72	65	68	70	275	8,190
Adrien Saddier	69	65	72	69	275	8,190
Daniel Gaunt	70	67	69	70	276	4,680
Jerome Lando Casanova	72	65	74	65	276	4,680
Tyrrell Hatton	70	70	69	68	277	3,960
Byeong-Hun An	67	68	73	70	278	3,150
Lucas Bjerregaard	67	68	69	74	278	3,150
Agustin Domingo	67	69	72	70	278	3,150
Paul Dwyer	67	71	72	68	278	3,150
Mark F. Haastrup	72	65	72	69	278	3,150
Jamie McLeary	66	67	73	72	278	3,150
Domenico Geminiani	71	64	72	72	279	2,340
Moritz Lampert	66	70	73	70	279	2,340
Nicolo Ravano	71	67	70	71	279	2,340
Nacho Elvira	71	68	69	72	280	1,761
James Frazer	71	71	68	70	280	1,761
Thomas Haylock	69	72	69	70	280	1,761
George Murray	71	64	75	70	280	1,761
Brinson Paolini	67	70	71	72	280	1,761
Victor Riu	67	71	73	69	280	1,761
Roland Steiner	72	69	70	69	280	1,761

Kharkov Superior Cup

Superior Golf & Spa Resort, Kharkov, Ukraine
Par 36-36–72; 6,892 yards

September 12-15
purse, €200,000

	SCORES				TOTAL	MONEY
Daan Huizing	70	69	67	67	273	€32,000
Sihwan Kim	66	64	75	70	275	22,000
Daniel Brooks	73	68	67	68	276	14,000
Andrea Pavan	70	69	68	70	277	12,000
Nacho Elvira	70	71	69	68	278	7,500
Mark F. Haastrup	68	69	71	70	278	7,500
Adrian Otaegui	70	72	67	69	278	7,500
Damian Ulrich	71	67	69	71	278	7,500
Agustin Domingo	69	69	70	71	279	4,120
Edouard Dubois	71	71	67	70	279	4,120
Lloyd Kennedy	70	66	70	73	279	4,120
Andrew McArthur	72	72	67	68	279	4,120
Bernd Ritthammer	69	68	75	67	279	4,120
Jason Barnes	71	68	69	72	280	3,200
Pedro Figueiredo	72	71	67	70	280	3,200
Terry Pilkadaris	68	74	68	70	280	3,200
Byeong-Hun An	69	69	75	68	281	2,420
Rhys Davies	71	67	70	73	281	2,420
Victor Riu	64	73	70	74	281	2,420
Andrea Rota	73	70	69	69	281	2,420
Charles-Edouard Russo	68	70	71	72	281	2,420

	SCORES				TOTAL	MONEY
Jamie Elson	72	68	71	71	282	1,920
Jose-Filipe Lima	74	67	73	68	282	1,920
Steven Tiley	68	69	73	72	282	1,920
Phillip Archer	67	75	70	71	283	1,780
Marco Crespi	68	74	70	71	283	1,780
Stuart Manley	69	76	71	67	283	1,780
Thomas Norret	71	72	74	66	283	1,780

Kazakhstan Open

Nurtau Golf Club, Almaty, Kazakhstan
Par 36-36–72; 7,336 yards

September 19-22
purse, €400,000

	SCORES				TOTAL	MONEY
Johan Carlsson	69	67	67	67	270	€64,000
Tyrrell Hatton	68	72	65	72	277	32,000
Adrian Otaegui	67	70	69	71	277	32,000
Duncan Stewart	70	70	65	72	277	32,000
Robert Dinwiddie	71	68	70	69	278	18,000
Oliver Wilson	70	66	75	67	278	18,000
Roope Kakko	72	71	70	66	279	12,000
Andrea Pavan	70	71	69	69	279	12,000
Nacho Elvira	69	73	68	70	280	8,240
Jeppe Huldahl	63	72	73	72	280	8,240
Sihwan Kim	69	69	75	67	280	8,240
Niklas Lemke	73	68	72	67	280	8,240
Florian Praegant	71	69	69	71	280	8,240
Shiv Kapur	71	71	69	70	281	6,400
Chan Kim	65	74	73	69	281	6,400
Pedro Oriol	71	71	74	65	281	6,400
Daniel Brooks	71	69	73	69	282	5,200
Carlos Del Moral	71	71	72	68	282	5,200
Andrea Rota	74	70	70	68	282	5,200
Scott Arnold	67	67	74	75	283	4,024
Charlie Ford	72	70	72	69	283	4,024
Paul Maddy	69	69	71	74	283	4,024
Bernd Ritthammer	69	70	74	70	283	4,024
Victor Riu	73	64	73	73	283	4,024
Byeong-Hun An	70	68	73	73	284	3,640
Markus Brier	70	73	71	70	284	3,640

Foshan Open

Foshan Golf Club, Shishan, Foshan, China
Par 36-36–72; 7,148 yards

October 17-20
purse, US$350,000

	SCORES				TOTAL	MONEY
Nacho Elvira	68	68	66	72	274	€41,234
Tyrrell Hatton	66	69	70	70	275	20,617
Shiv Kapur	70	68	68	69	275	20,617
Sam Walker	66	69	70	70	275	20,617
Phillip Archer	71	69	68	69	277	12,886
Scott Arnold	65	72	72	69	278	9,278
Niklas Lemke	68	76	67	67	278	9,278
Wil Besseling	68	69	70	72	279	7,216
Jamie Elson	70	71	73	66	280	5,927
Julien Guerrier	69	69	74	68	280	5,927

	SCORES				TOTAL	MONEY
Marco Crespi	71	70	69	71	281	5,154
Daniel Im	72	68	69	73	282	4,510
Roope Kakko	72	71	68	71	282	4,510
Gary Stal	72	68	72	70	282	4,510
Duncan Stewart	68	71	74	69	282	4,510
Rhys Davies	65	73	70	75	283	3,243
Robert Dinwiddie	72	69	71	71	283	3,243
Jens Fahrbring	73	70	68	72	283	3,243
Terry Pilkadaris	73	70	71	69	283	3,243
Raymond Russell	68	70	73	72	283	3,243
Steven Tiley	69	71	71	72	283	3,243
Stuart Manley	70	71	71	72	284	2,474
Brinson Paolini	71	68	72	73	284	2,474
Kang-Chun Wu	71	70	70	73	284	2,474
Byeong-Hun An	73	66	76	70	285	2,294
Do Eun An	70	74	71	70	285	2,294
George Murray	75	70	72	68	285	2,294
Andrea Pavan	70	73	72	70	285	2,294

National Bank of Oman Golf Classic

Almouj Golf, The Wave, Muscat, Oman
Par 36-36–72; 7,310 yards

October 24-27
purse, US$300,000

	SCORES				TOTAL	MONEY
Roope Kakko	70	69	66	69	274	€35,029
Lucas Bjerregaard	76	68	65	67	276	24,082
Daniel Im	69	69	68	72	278	15,325
Matt Ford	72	74	68	67	281	12,041
Brandon Stone	71	68	74	68	281	12,041
Byeong-Hun An	79	68	71	65	283	7,298
Johan Carlsson	72	72	70	69	283	7,298
Jeppe Huldahl	76	67	66	74	283	7,298
Guillaume Cambis	76	66	73	69	284	4,132
Marco Crespi	72	67	69	76	284	4,132
Nacho Elvira	74	70	73	67	284	4,132
Luke Goddard	78	67	69	70	284	4,132
Sihwan Kim	71	74	68	71	284	4,132
Andrew McArthur	71	74	69	70	284	4,132
Terry Pilkadaris	71	69	72	72	284	4,132
Nicolo Ravano	68	72	75	69	284	4,132
Scott Arnold	71	71	72	71	285	3,065
Wil Besseling	74	72	70	70	286	2,465
Jamie Elson	74	73	72	67	286	2,465
*Nathan Kimsey	71	72	74	69	286	
George Murray	74	72	66	74	286	2,465
Raymond Russell	75	70	68	73	286	2,465
Gary Stal	74	72	68	72	286	2,465
Ross McGowan	72	72	75	68	287	2,080
Sam Walker	74	73	73	67	287	2,080

Dubai Festival City Challenge Tour Grand Final

Al Badia Golf Club, Dubai, United Arab Emirates
Par 36-36–72; 7,333 yards

October 31-November 3
purse, €330,000

	SCORES				TOTAL	MONEY
Shiv Kapur	69	66	67	70	272	€56,650
Jose-Filipe Lima	70	66	71	69	276	29,425
Jamie McLeary	68	70	69	69	276	29,425
Rhys Davies	69	69	70	69	277	15,730
Andrea Pavan	66	66	75	70	277	15,730
Edouard Dubois	68	72	73	65	278	12,210
Tyrrell Hatton	69	67	74	68	278	12,210
Stuart Manley	73	67	68	70	278	12,210
Johan Carlsson	68	70	72	69	279	9,955
Nacho Elvira	70	68	75	66	279	9,955
Wil Besseling	70	68	68	74	280	8,030
Niklas Lemke	70	73	69	68	280	8,030
Andrew McArthur	70	69	68	73	280	8,030
Byeong-Hun An	74	71	70	66	281	5,638
Adam Gee	73	69	70	69	281	5,638
Julien Guerrier	69	69	71	72	281	5,638
Brinson Paolini	66	77	67	71	281	5,638
Lucas Bjerregaard	73	77	67	65	282	4,400
Jens Fahrbring	73	71	71	68	283	3,677
Jordi Garcia Pinto	71	70	71	71	283	3,677
Jeppe Huldahl	73	72	66	72	283	3,677
Thomas Norret	71	69	69	74	283	3,677
Bernd Ritthammer	74	69	73	67	283	3,677
Steven Tiley	73	65	73	72	283	3,677
Oliver Wilson	71	67	71	74	283	3,677

Asian Tour

Zaykabar Myanmar Open

Royal Mingalardon Golf & Country Club, Yangon, Myanmar
Par 36-36–72; 7,218 yards

February 21-24
purse, US$300,000

	SCORES				TOTAL	MONEY
Chawalit Plaphol	67	66	68	69	270	US$54,000
Mithun Perera	71	68	67	65	271	33,000
Kiradech Aphibarnrat	64	67	71	70	272	18,900
In-Choon Hwang	66	70	70	67	273	12,430
Darren Beck	66	69	69	69	273	12,430
Angelo Que	69	68	66	70	273	12,430
Quincy Quek	71	69	67	67	274	7,440
Lionel Weber	67	69	70	68	274	7,440
Rahil Gangjee	71	66	67	70	274	7,440
Chien-Yao Hung	67	67	71	70	275	5,280
Arnond Vongvanij	68	67	69	71	275	5,280
Chapchai Nirat	64	72	67	72	275	5,280
Rikard Karlberg	67	71	71	67	276	4,070
Antonio Lascuna	67	73	69	67	276	4,070
Himmat Rai	70	71	67	68	276	4,070
Thanyakon Khrongpha	66	67	74	69	276	4,070
Danny Chia	68	70	68	70	276	4,070
Thammanoon Sriroj	69	70	66	71	276	4,070
Prom Meesawat	65	72	71	69	277	3,360
Tim Stewart	71	70	67	69	277	3,360
Seuk-Hyun Baek	67	68	72	70	277	3,360
Berry Henson	70	68	68	72	278	3,135
Young Nam	66	73	67	72	278	3,135
Anthony Kang	70	70	73	66	279	2,730
Sujjan Singh	71	70	71	67	279	2,730
Ajeetesh Sandhu	70	68	73	68	279	2,730
Yuta Ikeda	68	71	71	69	279	2,730
Carlos Pigem	67	72	70	70	279	2,730
Frankie Minoza	74	66	69	70	279	2,730
Mardan Mamat	67	69	69	74	279	2,730

SAIL-SBI Open

Delhi Golf Club, New Delhi, India
Par 36-36–72; 6,963 yards

March 6-9
purse, US$300,000

	SCORES				TOTAL	MONEY
Anirban Lahiri	71	68	66	68	273	US$54,000
Rashid Khan	72	64	71	66	273	33,000
(Lahiri defeated Khan on first playoff hole.)						
Siddikur	68	68	68	73	277	18,900
Shiv Kapur	69	70	69	70	278	15,000
Pawin Ingkhapradit	70	69	71	69	279	11,145
Matthew Stieger	70	71	68	70	279	11,145
Namchok Tantipokhakul	69	75	68	68	280	8,550
Boonchu Ruangkit	72	69	70	70	281	6,500
Chan Kim	67	68	74	72	281	6,500
Chapchai Nirat	66	75	67	73	281	6,500

	SCORES				TOTAL	MONEY
Jake Higginbottom	70	70	73	69	282	4,747.50
Seuk-Hyun Baek	71	69	72	70	282	4,747.50
Antonio Lascuna	71	73	67	71	282	4,747.50
Khalin Joshi	66	69	71	76	282	4,747.50
Shankar Das	73	72	71	67	283	3,725
Sattaya Supupramai	70	71	72	70	283	3,725
Jason Knutzon	69	74	70	70	283	3,725
Vinod Kumar	73	73	66	71	283	3,725
Ajeetesh Sandhu	70	70	71	72	283	3,725
Adam Groom	71	71	69	72	283	3,725
Carlos Pigem	69	74	72	69	284	3,135
Sam Brazel	70	74	71	69	284	3,135
Scott Barr	74	71	71	68	284	3,135
Chiragh Kumar	68	70	73	73	284	3,135
Daisuke Kataoka	73	71	72	69	285	2,648.57
Sung Lee	74	69	72	70	285	2,648.57
Mardan Mamat	72	73	71	69	285	2,648.57
Rattanon Wannasrichan	71	71	72	71	285	2,648.57
Gaganjeet Bhullar	75	70	73	67	285	2,648.57
Chris Rodgers	73	69	72	71	285	2,648.57
Lam Chih Bing	73	67	71	74	285	2,648.57

Avantha Masters

Jaypee Greens Golf & Spa Resort, Noida, India
Par 36-36–72; 7,347 yards

March 14-17
purse, €1,800,000

	SCORES				TOTAL	MONEY
Thomas Aiken	67	69	62	67	265	US$390,000
Gaganjeet Bhullar	68	69	67	64	268	260,000
Wen-Chong Liang	66	66	69	69	270	146,484
Kiradech Aphibarnrat	68	68	66	69	271	117,000
Seuk-Hyun Baek	68	68	70	66	272	99,216
David Horsey	72	68	66	67	273	70,200
Scott Hend	67	68	68	70	273	70,200
David Drysdale	67	67	68	71	273	70,200
Himmat Rai	70	71	68	65	274	45,630
Victor Dubuisson	69	68	70	67	274	45,630
Julien Quesne	69	66	69	70	274	45,630
Tommy Fleetwood	69	65	69	71	274	45,630
Emilliano Grillo	68	71	71	65	275	35,217
Magnus A. Carlsson	66	73	67	69	275	35,217
Gi-Whan Kim	71	70	65	69	275	35,217
Joonas Granberg	67	67	69	72	275	35,217
Peter Whiteford	68	69	71	68	276	28,743
Adilson Da Silva	70	65	72	69	276	28,743
Pablo Larrazabal	68	68	71	69	276	28,743
Berry Henson	69	71	67	69	276	28,743
David Howell	68	72	65	71	276	28,743
Chapchai Nirat	66	66	72	72	276	28,743
Ricardo Gonzalez	69	72	70	66	277	23,985
Andy Sullivan	71	68	69	69	277	23,985
Chinnarat Phadungsil	61	74	72	70	277	23,985
Maximilian Kieffer	68	68	70	71	277	23,985
Jeev Milkha Singh	69	68	69	71	277	23,985
Rikard Karlberg	67	69	69	72	277	23,985
Matthew Baldwin	69	70	69	70	278	20,124
Jyoti Randhawa	70	70	68	70	278	20,124
Rahil Gangjee	69	66	72	71	278	20,124
Anirban Lahiri	68	69	70	71	278	20,124

	SCORES				TOTAL	MONEY
Prom Meesawat	68	73	64	73	278	20,124
Rashid Khan	67	73	73	66	279	16,146
Mark Foster	70	67	74	68	279	16,146
Kieran Pratt	71	70	70	68	279	16,146
Chawalit Plaphol	66	68	76	69	279	16,146
Soren Kjeldsen	72	67	71	69	279	16,146
Mithun Perera	70	70	69	70	279	16,146
Raphael Jacquelin	69	71	69	70	279	16,146
Kristoffer Broberg	69	71	65	74	279	16,146
Boonchu Ruangkit	70	70	65	74	279	16,146
Darren Beck	69	71	71	69	280	12,870
Thongchai Jaidee	70	71	70	69	280	12,870
Manav Jaini	70	71	69	70	280	12,870
Marc Warren	71	69	69	71	280	12,870
Jaakko Makitalo	67	68	69	76	280	12,870
Scott Barr	67	72	74	68	281	9,828
Jason Knutzon	71	70	72	68	281	9,828
Mardan Mamat	68	71	72	70	281	9,828
Martin Wiegele	72	67	72	70	281	9,828
Robert Coles	68	73	70	70	281	9,828
Abhijit Chadha	66	69	74	72	281	9,828
Siddikur	73	67	68	73	281	9,828
Lee Slattery	72	67	68	74	281	9,828
Craig Lee	70	71	71	70	282	7,066.80
Kwanchai Tannin	72	68	71	71	282	7,066.80
Ashok Kumar	68	71	70	73	282	7,066.80
Alvaro Quiros	70	70	69	73	282	7,066.80
Paul Waring	70	68	69	75	282	7,066.80
Vikrant Chopra	72	69	74	68	283	6,084
Bernd Wiesberger	70	71	74	68	283	6,084
Maarten Lafeber	73	66	70	74	283	6,084
Robert Derksen	72	69	72	71	284	5,499
Sung Lee	70	70	72	72	284	5,499
Oliver Fisher	69	71	71	74	285	5,148
Ajeetesh Sandhu	72	69	74	71	286	4,576
S.S.P. Chowrasia	68	72	74	72	286	4,576
Mukesh Kumar	72	69	72	73	286	4,576
Marcus Both	72	69	70	75	286	4,576
Brett Rumford	68	69	77	73	287	3,508.05
Angelo Que	71	70	72	74	287	3,508.05
Anura Rohana	72	69	73	74	288	3,502.20
Hyun-Bin Park	71	70	77	77	295	3,498.30

Maybank Malaysian Open

Kuala Lumpur Golf & Country Club, Kuala Lumpur, Malaysia
Par 36-36–72; 6,967 yards
(Event reduced to 54 holes—thunderstorm.)

March 21-24
purse, US$2,750,000

	SCORES			TOTAL	MONEY
Kiradech Aphibarnrat	65	68	70	203	US$458,330
Edoardo Molinari	66	71	67	204	305,550
Anders Hansen	66	73	66	205	172,150
Victor Dubuisson	67	69	70	206	127,050
Charl Schwartzel	67	68	71	206	127,050
Pablo Larrazabal	69	70	68	207	72,820
Mark Foster	69	69	69	207	72,820
Alexander Noren	69	68	70	207	72,820
David Howell	69	68	70	207	72,820
Padraig Harrington	69	68	70	207	72,820

	SCORES			TOTAL	MONEY
Thomas Aiken	71	71	66	208	43,908.33
Joonas Granberg	71	68	69	208	43,908.33
Peter Lawrie	68	69	71	208	43,908.33
Tommy Fleetwood	70	66	72	208	43,908.33
Gregory Bourdy	66	69	73	208	43,908.33
Ashun Wu	67	68	73	208	43,908.33
Jeev Milkha Singh	71	70	68	209	34,320
Mikko Ilonen	70	70	69	209	34,320
Matteo Manassero	69	71	69	209	34,320
Lee Slattery	68	70	71	209	34,320
Scott Jamieson	66	72	71	209	34,320
*Gavin Green	73	68	69	210	
Joost Luiten	69	71	70	210	29,425
Shiv Kapur	72	71	67	210	29,425
Rafa Cabrera-Bello	72	67	71	210	29,425
Wen-Chong Liang	70	68	72	210	29,425
Stephen Gallacher	71	73	66	210	29,425
Ignacio Garrido	70	71	70	211	25,300
Álvaro Quiros	75	67	69	211	25,300
Alastair Forsyth	69	70	72	211	25,300
Prom Meesawat	68	71	72	211	25,300
Jbe' Kruger	73	71	67	211	25,300
Chinnarat Phadungsil	70	71	71	212	21,037.50
Berry Henson	71	71	70	212	21,037.50
Raphael Jacquelin	70	70	72	212	21,037.50
Bernd Wiesberger	71	69	72	212	21,037.50
Thongchai Jaidee	70	74	68	212	21,037.50
Wade Ormsby	70	65	77	212	21,037.50
Scott Barr	75	69	69	213	18,975
Adilson Da Silva	68	74	72	214	15,675
Mardan Mamat	70	72	72	214	15,675
Jean Gonnet	70	70	74	214	15,675
Angelo Que	70	72	72	214	15,675
Robert Derksen	72	70	72	214	15,675
Jorge Campillo	73	70	71	214	15,675
Sung Lee	68	70	76	214	15,675
Gi-Whan Kim	70	73	71	214	15,675
Oliver Fisher	69	75	70	214	15,675
Thaworn Wiratchant	73	71	70	214	15,675
Seuk-Hyun Baek	72	72	70	214	15,675
Andrew Dodt	69	72	74	215	11,550
Masanori Kobayashi	72	70	73	215	11,550
Danny Chia	71	71	73	215	11,550
Thomas Levet	73	71	71	215	11,550
Fredrik Andersson Hed	68	73	75	216	8,277.50
Gunn Charoenkul	71	70	75	216	8,277.50
Prayad Marksaeng	69	72	75	216	8,277.50
Simon Khan	71	68	77	216	8,277.50
Joong-Kyung Mo	71	72	73	216	8,277.50
Julien Quesne	72	71	73	216	8,277.50
Alejandro Canizares	72	71	73	216	8,277.50
James Morrison	76	68	72	216	8,277.50
Soren Kjeldsen	71	73	72	216	8,277.50
Romain Wattel	75	69	72	216	8,277.50
Phillip Price	72	71	74	217	6,187.50
S. Murthy	67	70	80	217	6,187.50
Steve Webster	71	73	73	217	6,187.50
Richard Green	74	70	73	217	6,187.50
Marcus Fraser	69	75	74	218	5,500
Siddikur	71	72	78	221	4,790.12
In-Woo Lee	71	73	77	221	4,790.12
Johan Edfors	76	68	77	221	4,790.12
Thitiphun Chuayprakong	72	71	79	222	4,121.44

Chiangmai Golf Classic

Alpine Golf Resort, Chiangmai, Thailand
Par 36-36–72; 7,471 yards

March 28-31
purse, US$750,000

	SCORES				TOTAL	MONEY
Scott Hend	68	69	67	64	268	US$135,000
Bryce Easton	68	67	72	64	271	82,500
Prayad Marksaeng	65	67	66	74	272	47,250
Mu Hu	66	69	70	68	273	37,500
Jbe' Kruger	71	69	70	64	274	22,305
Seuk-Hyun Baek	69	69	68	68	274	22,305
Siddikur	69	67	69	69	274	22,305
Kiradech Aphibarnrat	71	67	66	70	274	22,305
Matthew Stieger	68	67	68	71	274	22,305
Joong-Kyung Mo	70	67	71	67	275	12,741
Thitiphun Chuayprakong	68	70	68	69	275	12,741
Digvijay Singh	67	67	70	71	275	12,741
Thongchai Jaidee	69	65	69	72	275	12,741
Gi-Whan Kim	71	70	69	66	276	9,725.50
Chris Rodgers	72	66	71	67	276	9,725.50
Anirban Lahiri	71	69	68	68	276	9,725.50
Jake Higginbottom	70	68	69	69	276	9,725.50
Jaakko Makitalo	72	66	69	69	276	9,725.50
Ernie Els	69	71	66	70	276	9,725.50
Tetsuji Hiratsuka	70	68	71	68	277	7,831.33
Mithun Perera	70	66	71	70	277	7,831.33
Wade Ormsby	70	70	67	70	277	7,831.33
Jason Knutzon	67	69	70	71	277	7,831.33
Y.E. Yang	69	68	67	73	277	7,831.33
Anton Haig	72	66	66	73	277	7,831.33

Panasonic Open India

Delhi Golf Club, New Delhi, India
Par 36-36–72; 6,963 yards

April 4-7
purse, US$300,000

	SCORES				TOTAL	MONEY
Wade Ormsby	67	67	74	71	279	US$54,000
Boonchu Ruangkit	70	68	73	69	280	33,000
Lam Chih Bing	67	69	73	72	281	18,900
Shiv Kapur	71	68	72	71	282	15,000
S.S.P. Chowrasia	69	69	77	68	283	10,280
Anura Rohana	71	72	71	69	283	10,280
Digvijay Singh	71	71	71	70	283	10,280
Richard T. Lee	72	68	77	67	284	6,885
Shamim Khan	73	75	67	69	284	6,885
Rahil Gangjee	73	73	71	68	285	5,280
Siddikur	71	71	74	69	285	5,280
Manav Jaini	75	70	68	72	285	5,280
Pawin Ingkhapradit	78	68	70	70	286	4,440
Jyoti Randhawa	73	72	67	74	286	4,440
Adam Groom	70	74	75	68	287	4,065
Chia-Jen Hsu	73	72	73	69	287	4,065
Sattaya Supupramai	80	68	69	71	288	3,705
Amardip Malik	71	71	72	74	288	3,705
Elias Bertheussen	75	71	74	69	289	3,315
James Byrne	73	74	73	69	289	3,315
Namchok Tantipokhakul	74	73	72	70	289	3,315
Jeev Milkha Singh	72	73	73	71	289	3,315

	SCORES				TOTAL	MONEY
Pariya Junhasavasdikul	71	78	74	67	290	2,736.67
Abhinav Lohan	73	74	73	70	290	2,736.67
Anirban Lahiri	71	72	76	71	290	2,736.67
Kieran Pratt	67	77	75	71	290	2,736.67
Gaurav Ghei	73	75	71	71	290	2,736.67
Mars Pucay	73	74	71	72	290	2,736.67
Jay Bayron	70	72	74	74	290	2,736.67
Shankar Das	72	73	71	74	290	2,736.67
Matthew Stieger	71	74	70	75	290	2,736.67

Solaire Open

Wack Wack Golf & Country Club, Manila, Philippines — April 11-14
Par 36-36–72; 7,222 yards — purse, US$300,000

	SCORES				TOTAL	MONEY
Wen-Tang Lin	69	73	70	73	285	US$54,000
Richard T. Lee	72	71	74	69	286	25,950
Thammanoon Sriroj	73	69	71	73	286	25,950
Jeung-Hun Wang	72	76	70	69	287	15,000
Elmer Salvador	74	69	71	74	288	12,300
Mars Pucay	69	76	73	71	289	8,077.50
Miguel Tabuena	73	72	72	72	289	8,077.50
Gunn Charoenkul	73	71	72	73	289	8,077.50
Unho Park	73	71	72	73	289	8,077.50
Mong-Nan Hsu	74	72	71	73	290	5,280
Dodge Kemmer	66	79	71	74	290	5,280
Pawin Ingkhapradit	68	75	71	76	290	5,280
Sam Brazel	73	75	73	70	291	4,161
Yih-Shin Chan	75	72	73	71	291	4,161
Daisuke Kataoka	70	75	73	73	291	4,161
Jake Higginbottom	74	71	73	73	291	4,161
Sam Cyr	76	70	69	76	291	4,161
Jay Bayron	74	72	74	72	292	3,615
Chawalit Plaphol	72	75	77	69	293	3,225
Antonio Lascuna	73	77	74	69	293	3,225
Himmat Rai	75	76	72	70	293	3,225
Carl Santos-Ocampo	72	72	76	73	293	3,225
Matt Jager	70	72	76	75	293	3,225
Panuwat Muenlek	74	70	73	76	293	3,225
Yoshinobu Tsukada	72	73	79	70	294	2,538
Jesper Kennegard	73	77	74	70	294	2,538
Panuphol Pittayarat	75	72	76	71	294	2,538
Abhinav Lohan	76	71	74	73	294	2,538
Zaw Moe	74	74	73	73	294	2,538
Marvin Dumandan	77	72	72	73	294	2,538
Zanie Boy Gialon	74	77	69	74	294	2,538
Arnond Vongvanij	75	74	70	75	294	2,538
Kwanchai Tannin	71	71	76	76	294	2,538
Chinnarat Phadungsil	75	71	72	76	294	2,538

Ballantine's Championship

Blackstone Resort, Seoul, South Korea
Par 36-36–72; 7,302 yards

April 25-28
purse, US$2,800,000

	SCORES				TOTAL	MONEY
Brett Rumford	73	67	69	68	277	US$478,499.70
Marcus Fraser	70	70	69	68	277	249,362.15
Peter Whiteford	70	69	69	69	277	249,362.15
(Rumford defeated Fraser and Whiteford on first playoff hole.)						
Romain Wattel	70	69	71	69	279	143,549.91
Louis Oosthuizen	69	71	71	69	280	121,730.32
Hyung-Sung Kim	71	69	74	67	281	76,024.03
Thongchai Jaidee	71	72	73	65	281	76,024.03
Stephen Gallacher	70	68	75	68	281	76,024.03
Pablo Larrazabal	70	70	68	73	281	76,024.03
Alexander Noren	71	67	69	74	281	76,024.03
Soon-Sang Hong	71	71	73	67	282	45,840.27
Gi-Whan Kim	67	72	75	68	282	45,840.27
S.S.P. Chowrasia	71	70	73	68	282	45,840.27
K.T. Kim	74	68	71	69	282	45,840.27
Kiradech Aphibarnrat	71	66	75	70	282	45,840.27
Jose Manuel Lara	71	67	72	72	282	45,840.27
Jason Knutzon	72	70	73	68	283	35,265.43
Heung-Chol Joo	70	70	74	69	283	35,265.43
Kieran Pratt	67	77	69	70	283	35,265.43
Jyoti Randhawa	72	69	72	70	283	35,265.43
Sang-Hyun Park	74	69	69	71	283	35,265.43
Wade Ormsby	70	67	74	72	283	35,265.43
Jung-Gon Hwang	70	74	71	69	284	30,719.68
Ashun Wu	75	65	73	71	284	30,719.68
Gregory Havret	71	70	72	71	284	30,719.68
Siddikur	74	69	71	71	285	27,274.48
Johan Edfors	67	75	74	69	285	27,274.48
Rikard Karlberg	69	73	74	69	285	27,274.48
Arnond Vongvanij	68	69	76	72	285	27,274.48
Berry Henson	70	70	77	68	285	27,274.48
Peter Lawrie	68	73	74	71	286	21,723.89
Joel Sjoholm	73	71	70	72	286	21,723.89
Shiv Kapur	71	71	74	70	286	21,723.89
Bernd Wiesberger	71	69	74	72	286	21,723.89
Scott Hend	76	66	72	72	286	21,723.89
Magnus A. Carlsson	71	69	73	73	286	21,723.89
Tommy Fleetwood	68	71	73	74	286	21,723.89
Paul McGinley	73	70	75	68	286	21,723.89
David Howell	69	73	76	68	286	21,723.89
Mu Hu	72	69	74	72	287	16,364.69
Matteo Delpodio	71	69	76	71	287	16,364.69
Marc Warren	70	73	71	73	287	16,364.69
Lee Slattery	70	71	75	71	287	16,364.69
James Morrison	72	66	75	74	287	16,364.69
Jbe' Kruger	71	67	79	70	287	16,364.69
Felipe Aguilar	74	70	74	69	287	16,364.69
Damien McGrane	71	72	70	74	287	16,364.69
Simon Dyson	71	72	69	75	287	16,364.69
Rafa Cabrera-Bello	72	70	73	73	288	12,058.19
Paul Lawrie	75	67	73	73	288	12,058.19
Richie Ramsay	71	70	76	71	288	12,058.19
Ricardo Gonzalez	69	73	75	71	288	12,058.19
Adilson Da Silva	71	72	75	70	288	12,058.19
Y.E. Yang	70	72	79	67	288	12,058.19
Kyung-Nam Kang	72	68	75	74	289	9,474.29
Wen-Chong Liang	76	68	73	72	289	9,474.29
Jean-Baptiste Gonnet	67	76	75	71	289	9,474.29

	SCORES				TOTAL	MONEY
Hyun-Woo Ryu	69	73	73	75	290	8,182.34
Matthew Baldwin	67	73	76	74	290	8,182.34
Eddie Pepperell	72	69	71	78	290	8,182.34
Seng-Yong Kim	74	70	76	70	290	8,182.34
Min-Kyu Han	71	69	75	76	291	7,177.50
Alejandro Canizares	69	75	75	72	291	7,177.50
Darren Beck	74	70	76	71	291	7,177.50
Yong-Jin Shin	71	71	74	76	292	6,316.20
Sang-Hee Lee	73	71	76	72	292	6,316.20
Peter Uihlein	75	68	78	71	292	6,316.20
Ho-Sung Choi	73	70	75	75	293	5,598.45
Fabrizio Zanotti	69	73	78	73	293	5,598.45
Javi Colomo	69	75	74	76	294	4,768.73
Dong-Seop Maeng	74	69	78	73	294	4,768.73
Hyun-Bin Park	73	70	74	80	297	4,301.94

CIMB Niaga Indonesian Masters

Royale Jakarta Golf Club, Jakarta, Indonesia
Par 36-36–72; 7,322 yards

May 2-5
purse, US$750,000

	SCORES				TOTAL	MONEY
Bernd Wiesberger	67	72	67	67	273	US$135,000
Ernie Els	68	70	68	68	274	82,500
Daisuke Kataoka	70	69	66	70	275	47,250
Thongchai Jaidee	69	65	75	69	278	37,500
Angelo Que	70	70	70	70	280	25,700
Ryan McCarthy	70	70	70	70	280	25,700
Joong-Kyung Mo	72	69	68	71	280	25,700
Unho Park	68	72	70	71	281	15,459.50
In-Choon Hwang	66	74	70	71	281	15,459.50
Jake Higginbottom	69	69	71	72	281	15,459.50
Rahil Gangjee	71	69	69	72	281	15,459.50
Anthony Kang	73	71	69	69	282	10,463
Scott Barr	68	68	75	71	282	10,463
Gunn Charoenkul	69	72	70	71	282	10,463
Jason Knutzon	68	74	69	71	282	10,463
Wade Ormsby	69	68	73	72	282	10,463
Chien-Yao Hung	70	68	70	74	282	10,463
Richard T. Lee	72	68	67	75	282	10,463
Rikard Karlberg	73	71	70	69	283	8,287.75
Iain Steel	70	73	70	70	283	8,287.75
Kodai Ichihara	73	70	69	71	283	8,287.75
Arnond Vongvanij	68	74	69	72	283	8,287.75
Adilson Da Silva	68	73	72	71	284	7,275
Chapchai Nirat	71	68	72	73	284	7,275
Simon Dyson	69	74	68	73	284	7,275
David Lutterus	68	73	69	74	284	7,275
Shiv Kapur	70	69	70	75	284	7,275

Queen's Cup

Santiburi Samui Country Club, Samui, Thailand
Par 36-35–71; 6,832 yards

June 13-16
purse, US$312,000

	SCORES				TOTAL	MONEY
Prayad Marksaeng	71	64	68	67	270	US$56,142.90
Arnond Vongvanij	69	67	68	69	273	34,309.55

	SCORES				TOTAL	MONEY
Daisuke Kataoka	65	68	74	68	275	19,650.02
Panuphol Pittayarat	70	72	72	64	278	11,914.77
Tetsuji Hiratsuka	71	67	70	70	278	11,914.77
Mong-Nan Hsu	70	70	68	70	278	11,914.77
Jazz Janewattananond	68	68	70	72	278	11,914.77
Chien-Yao Hung	69	70	72	68	279	7,158.22
Siddikur	66	69	67	77	279	7,158.22
Wade Ormsby	72	71	68	69	280	5,700.07
Anirban Lahiri	71	67	67	75	280	5,700.07
Hyun-Bin Park	73	73	69	66	281	4,655.18
Quincy Quek	71	67	71	72	281	4,655.18
Mardan Mamat	71	68	70	72	281	4,655.18
Nicholas Fung	72	64	71	74	281	4,655.18
Antonio Lascuna	74	69	70	69	282	4,039.17
Berry Henson	72	67	71	72	282	4,039.17
Richard T. Lee	72	71	72	69	284	3,559.62
David Lutterus	70	69	74	71	284	3,559.62
Udorn Duangdecha	72	70	69	73	284	3,559.62
Chawalit Plaphol	69	70	70	75	284	3,559.62
Lam Chih Bing	73	72	69	71	285	3,165.84
Chase Wright	71	71	70	73	285	3,165.84
Martin Rominger	69	69	70	77	285	3,165.84
Chapchai Nirat	71	68	69	77	285	3,165.84

Worldwide Holdings Selangor Masters

Seri Selangor Golf Club, Petaling Jaya, Selangor, Malaysia
Par 36-35–71

June 20-23
purse, US$400,000

	SCORES				TOTAL	MONEY
Pariya Junhasavasdikul	66	68	71	70	275	US$68,954.44
Anirban Lahiri	73	68	67	68	276	42,138.83
Namchok Tantipokhakul	72	74	66	65	277	21,644.04
Seuk-Hyun Baek	67	68	71	71	277	21,644.04
Wen-The Lu	70	72	70	67	279	15,706.29
Scott Hend	70	73	70	67	280	11,019.94
Peter Richardson	69	73	69	69	280	11,019.94
Wade Ormsby	68	70	72	70	280	11,019.94
*Gavin Green	68	69	70	73	280	
Marcus Both	73	69	70	69	281	8,197.92
Adilson Da Silva	74	70	70	68	282	7,316.83
Javi Colomo	74	68	71	70	283	6,237.82
Steve Lewton	73	70	68	72	283	6,237.82
Thanyakon Khrongpha	75	67	67	74	283	6,237.82
Sam Brazel	71	71	73	69	284	4,967.28
Wen-Tang Lin	68	77	69	70	284	4,967.28
Gi-Whan Kim	75	70	68	71	284	4,967.28
Berry Henson	74	68	70	72	284	4,967.28
Anthony Kang	73	68	70	73	284	4,967.28
Konosuke Nakazato	71	73	67	73	284	4,967.28
Elias Bertheussen	69	75	71	70	285	4,223.46
Chawalit Plaphol	70	71	72	72	285	4,223.46
Jonathan Moore	73	71	71	71	286	3,945.73
Jazz Janewattananond	69	77	71	69	286	3,945.73
Richard T. Lee	71	72	69	74	286	3,945.73

Omega European Masters

See European Tours chapter.

Yeangder Tournament Players Championship

Linkou International Golf & Country Club, Chinese Taipei
Par 36-36—72; 7,125 yards

September 12-15
purse, US$500,000

	SCORES				TOTAL	MONEY
Thaworn Wiratchant	69	67	71	68	275	US$90,000
Chan Kim	70	68	68	70	276	55,000
Angelo Que	74	72	67	66	279	31,500
Shih-Chang Chan	71	71	71	67	280	25,000
Chien Soon Lu	72	72	68	69	281	14,870
Chiragh Kumar	68	69	74	70	281	14,870
Seuk-Hyun Baek	73	69	69	70	281	14,870
Mong-Nan Hsu	69	68	71	73	281	14,870
Wei-Tze Yeh	73	67	67	74	281	14,870
Matthew Stieger	69	73	72	68	282	9,137.50
Berry Henson	71	70	71	70	282	9,137.50
Rory Hie	72	72	72	68	284	7,850
Gunn Charoenkul	72	75	67	70	284	7,850
Prayad Marksaeng	73	74	70	68	285	7,225
Jake Higginbottom	69	73	76	68	286	6,625
Lam Chih Bing	72	70	72	72	286	6,625
Jaakko Makitalo	73	73	65	75	286	6,625
Yih-Shin Chan	75	72	70	70	287	5,791.67
Rattanon Wannasrichan	70	75	72	70	287	5,791.67
Mao-Chang Sung	70	74	71	72	287	5,791.67
Michael Tran	78	67	76	67	288	5,075
Steve Lewton	74	74	70	70	288	5,075
Kieran Pratt	71	75	70	72	288	5,075
Adam Groom	69	72	74	73	288	5,075
Richard T. Lee	74	68	73	73	288	5,075
Thitiphun Chuayprakong	66	76	72	74	288	5,075

Asia-Pacific Panasonic Open

See Japan Tour section.

Mercuries Taiwan Masters

Taiwan Golf & Country Club, Chinese Taipei
Par 36-36—72; 6,923 yards

October 3-6
purse, US$600,000

	SCORES				TOTAL	MONEY
Scott Hend	69	72	70	74	285	US$120,000
Sam Cyr	70	69	73	77	289	72,000
Arnond Vongvanij	75	73	70	73	291	36,000
Siddikur	72	71	71	77	291	36,000
Panuphol Pittayarat	72	70	72	79	293	24,000
Wen-The Lu	73	75	72	74	294	19,500
Seuk-Hyun Baek	73	70	74	77	294	19,500
Matthew Stieger	74	71	74	76	295	13,500
Antonio Lascuna	72	76	70	77	295	13,500
Thaworn Wiratchant	72	75	78	71	296	10,500
Chawalit Plaphol	76	70	73	77	296	10,500
Elmer Salvador	73	74	76	74	297	8,700
Prayad Marksaeng	71	78	74	74	297	8,700
Jazz Janewattananond	75	72	75	75	297	8,700
Gunn Charoenkul	75	73	73	76	297	8,700
Sam Brazel	73	71	81	73	298	6,677.14

	SCORES				TOTAL	MONEY
Carlos Pigem	74	74	75	75	298	6,677.14
Thanyakon Khrongpha	73	76	74	75	298	6,677.14
Wade Ormsby	74	75	74	75	298	6,677.14
Hyun-Bin Park	76	73	73	76	298	6,677.14
Kodai Ichihara	72	74	75	77	298	6,677.14
Ryan McCarthy	75	73	72	78	298	6,677.14
Chapchai Nirat	72	75	77	75	299	5,700
Marcus Both	72	74	75	78	299	5,700
David Lutterus	70	76	75	78	299	5,700
Jake Higginbottom	78	70	73	78	299	5,700

CJ Invitational

Haesley Nine Bridges Golf Club, Seoul, South Korea
Par 36-36–72; 7,152 yards

October 10-13
purse, US$750,000

	SCORES				TOTAL	MONEY
Sung Kang	68	69	69	70	276	US$135,000
Jyoti Randhawa	67	74	73	67	281	64,875
Tae-Hoon Kim	66	69	74	72	281	64,875
Jason Knutzon	72	71	70	69	282	31,075
Seuk-Hyun Baek	70	73	70	69	282	31,075
Kiradech Aphibarnrat	66	71	72	73	282	31,075
Gi-Whan Kim	69	72	72	70	283	19,875
Dong-Seop Maeng	69	70	70	74	283	19,875
Panuphol Pittayarat	70	77	69	68	284	15,187.50
Zaw Moe	70	74	71	69	284	15,187.50
Kyoung-Hoon Lee	69	77	71	68	285	12,638
Rikard Karlberg	69	68	71	77	285	12,638
Berry Henson	69	74	75	68	286	10,631.75
Ju-Hyuk Park	74	68	72	72	286	10,631.75
Unho Park	70	76	68	72	286	10,631.75
Jbe' Kruger	71	72	70	73	286	10,631.75
Wook-Soon Kang	75	72	71	69	287	8,888
Hyung-Tae Kim	70	76	71	70	287	8,888
In-Choon Hwang	72	73	70	72	287	8,888
Anirban Lahiri	69	76	69	73	287	8,888
Meen-Whee Kim	71	74	76	67	288	7,725
Hyun-Woo Ryu	68	78	75	67	288	7,725
Sung-Kug Park	70	72	73	73	288	7,725
Matthew Stieger	67	77	71	73	288	7,725
K.J. Choi	71	74	70	73	288	7,725

Venetian Macau Open

Macau Golf & Country Club, Macau
Par 35-36–71; 6,624 yards

October 17-20
purse, US$800,000

	SCORES				TOTAL	MONEY
Scott Hend	74	64	63	67	268	US$144,000
Anirban Lahiri	73	68	68	62	271	88,000
Elmer Salvador	70	66	70	66	272	45,200
Ernie Els	71	65	69	67	272	45,200
Antonio Lascuna	71	68	71	65	275	29,720
Daisuke Kataoka	71	66	69	69	275	29,720
Adam Groom	70	69	71	66	276	21,200
Siddikur	69	66	70	71	276	21,200

	SCORES				TOTAL	MONEY
Steve Lewton	72	67	72	66	277	16,200
Seuk-Hyun Baek	71	65	70	71	277	16,200
Wen-Chong Liang	71	72	66	69	278	13,480
Rahil Gangjee	73	67	66	72	278	13,480
Arjun Atwal	72	69	68	70	279	11,586.67
Chien-Yao Hung	70	71	68	70	279	11,586.67
Kalle Samooja	68	71	69	71	279	11,586.67
Thongchai Jaidee	73	67	71	69	280	10,600
Prom Meesawat	69	71	75	66	281	9,328
Dodge Kemmer	75	67	69	70	281	9,328
Javi Colomo	75	66	69	71	281	9,328
Lian-Wei Zhang	69	74	67	71	281	9,328
Scott Barr	68	69	70	74	281	9,328
Gaganjeet Bhullar	73	70	72	67	282	7,760
Wen-Tang Lin	73	70	70	69	282	7,760
S.S.P. Chowrasia	72	72	69	69	282	7,760
Mithun Perera	71	70	71	70	282	7,760
Chiragh Kumar	73	69	68	72	282	7,760
Jay Bayron	70	67	71	74	282	7,760
Jason Knutzon	69	71	68	74	282	7,760

CIMB Classic

Kuala Lumpur Golf & Country Club, Kuala Lumpur, Malaysia
Par 36-36–72; 6,951 yards
(Playoff held on Monday — darkness.)

October 24-28
purse, US$7,000,000

	SCORES				TOTAL	MONEY
Ryan Moore	63	72	69	70	274	$1,260,000
Gary Woodland	68	70	67	69	274	756,000
(Moore defeated Woodland on first playoff hole.)						
Kiradech Aphibarnrat	67	69	69	70	275	406,000
Chris Stroud	67	69	68	71	275	406,000
Aaron Baddeley	73	67	70	66	276	280,000
Jimmy Walker	74	68	67	68	277	252,000
Charles Howell	69	72	69	68	278	218,166.67
Harris English	71	67	71	69	278	218,166.67
Graham DeLaet	72	67	68	71	278	218,166.67
Keegan Bradley	65	66	76	72	279	189,000
Billy Horschel	72	69	72	67	280	161,000
Sergio Garcia	66	71	71	72	280	161,000
Stewart Cink	70	68	69	73	280	161,000
K.J. Choi	68	71	70	72	281	129,500
Bryce Molder	73	69	67	72	281	129,500
Jeff Overton	73	67	72	70	282	112,000
Bill Haas	72	67	71	72	282	112,000
Shiv Kapur	69	70	71	72	282	112,000
Rickie Fowler	71	72	73	67	283	81,900
Kevin Stadler	71	69	73	70	283	81,900
Bo Van Pelt	72	77	69	65	283	81,900
Phil Mickelson	71	70	68	74	283	81,900
Kyle Stanley	73	67	68	75	283	81,900
Jerry Kelly	71	69	66	77	283	81,900
Siddikur	75	70	69	70	284	53,433.33
Brendan Steele	74	70	72	68	284	53,433.33
Kevin Chappell	73	71	72	68	284	53,433.33
Chris Kirk	67	71	72	74	284	53,433.33
Hideki Matsuyama	70	68	72	74	284	53,433.33
Jonas Blixt	72	70	68	74	284	53,433.33
Bubba Watson	78	69	65	73	285	44,450

	SCORES				TOTAL	MONEY
Tim Clark	72	69	70	74	285	44,450
Boo Weekley	67	74	72	73	286	40,425
Gaganjeet Bhullar	72	70	71	73	286	40,425
Michael Thompson	75	71	68	73	287	34,510
Richard H. Lee	70	73	72	72	287	34,510
Roberto Castro	74	70	70	73	287	34,510
Nick Watney	75	69	70	73	287	34,510
Anirban Lahiri	74	70	75	68	287	34,510
Matt Jones	73	71	71	73	288	28,000
Nicholas Thompson	69	71	76	72	288	28,000
Patrick Reed	74	71	72	71	288	28,000
Scott Hend	74	72	71	71	288	28,000
Marc Leishman	72	65	77	75	289	23,100
Camilo Villegas	70	71	73	75	289	23,100
Prayad Marksaeng	74	71	71	73	289	23,100
Retief Goosen	72	74	69	75	290	18,223.33
Ernie Els	76	71	69	74	290	18,223.33
Berry Henson	74	71	72	73	290	18,223.33
Matt Every	72	77	68	73	290	18,223.33
Brian Gay	72	72	74	72	290	18,223.33
Scott Stallings	73	70	78	69	290	18,223.33
John Huh	71	74	69	77	291	15,907.50
Charley Hoffman	69	72	74	76	291	15,907.50
Ryan Palmer	76	68	71	76	291	15,907.50
Brendon de Jonge	72	71	73	75	291	15,907.50
Rory Sabbatini	67	74	75	75	291	15,907.50
Kevin Streelman	72	73	71	75	291	15,907.50
Josh Teater	74	66	72	79	291	15,907.50
Daniel Summerhays	75	69	73	74	291	15,907.50
Martin Laird	68	70	76	78	292	15,190
Russell Henley	71	74	72	75	292	15,190
Nicholas Fung	74	78	71	70	293	14,980
David Lynn	75	70	71	79	295	14,630
Lucas Glover	71	75	75	74	295	14,630
John Merrick	77	75	69	74	295	14,630
David Lingmerth	73	78	73	71	295	14,630
David Hearn	72	70	73	81	296	14,070
Wade Ormsby	70	69	74	83	296	14,070
D.A. Points	71	76	73	76	296	14,070
Sang-Moon Bae	80	71	74	71	296	14,070
Scott Brown	77	72	75	74	298	13,720
Cameron Tringale	79	77	71	75	302	13,580
Martin Flores	73	79	74	78	304	13,440
Brian Davis	79	75	74	78	306	13,230
Rashid Ismail	73	76	80	77	306	13,230
John Rollins	74	76	77	82	309	12,950
Seuk-Hyun Baek	80	72	82	75	309	12,950

WGC - HSBC Champions

Sheshan International Golf Club, Shanghai, China
Par 36-36–72; 7,266 yards

October 31-November 3
purse, US$8,500,000

	SCORES				TOTAL	MONEY
Dustin Johnson	69	63	66	66	264	$1,400,000
Ian Poulter	71	67	63	66	267	850,000
Graeme McDowell	69	69	64	66	268	480,000
Sergio Garcia	70	68	69	63	270	365,000
Justin Rose	68	71	65	68	272	300,000
Graham DeLaet	71	68	65	69	273	231,500

	SCORES			TOTAL	MONEY
Rory McIlroy	65	72	67	69	273	231,500
Jamie Donaldson	67	74	66	67	274	161,666.67
Bubba Watson	68	69	69	68	274	161,666.67
Martin Kaymer	70	74	62	68	274	161,666.66
Keegan Bradley	71	68	68	68	275	116,666.67
Ernie Els	69	69	71	66	275	116,666.67
Boo Weekley	70	67	69	69	275	116,666.66
Phil Mickelson	71	68	72	65	276	100,000
Wen-Chong Liang	72	67	72	66	277	93,500
Louis Oosthuizen	70	70	70	67	277	93,500
Jordan Spieth	68	71	70	69	278	90,000
Tommy Fleetwood	68	70	69	72	279	87,000
Jin Jeong	70	69	71	69	279	87,000
Paul Casey	69	73	69	69	280	84,000
Gregory Bourdy	75	68	67	71	281	75,100
Bill Haas	72	72	69	68	281	75,100
Peter Hanson	70	73	70	68	281	75,100
Scott Hend	69	74	66	72	281	75,100
Mikko Ilonen	72	69	72	68	281	75,100
Matteo Manassero	72	70	70	69	281	75,100
Francesco Molinari	72	69	70	70	281	75,100
Scott Piercy	72	73	68	68	281	75,100
Bo Van Pelt	77	67	66	71	281	75,100
Jaco Van Zyl	72	73	68	68	281	75,100
Luke Donald	70	71	70	71	282	68,000
Henrik Stenson	74	76	67	65	282	68,000
Nick Watney	75	74	67	66	282	68,000
Mark Brown	72	68	72	71	283	64,000
Jason Dufner	73	67	71	72	283	64,000
Billy Horschel	71	69	72	71	283	64,000
Wen-Yi Huang	70	74	69	70	283	64,000
Kevin Streelman	70	73	72	68	283	64,000
Thomas Bjorn	74	72	70	68	284	58,000
Gonzalo Fernandez-Castano	67	71	70	76	284	58,000
Branden Grace	77	71	67	69	284	58,000
Hao-Tong Li	72	71	74	67	284	58,000
David Lynn	74	70	69	71	284	58,000
Richard Sterne	74	73	74	63	284	58,000
Chris Wood	71	71	73	69	284	58,000
Ken Duke	70	72	73	70	285	52,500
Brian Gay	71	72	72	70	285	52,500
Thongchai Jaidee	76	68	68	73	285	52,500
Jimmy Walker	73	73	69	70	285	52,500
Hiroyuki Fujita	75	70	68	73	286	49,000
Michael Hendry	72	73	73	68	286	49,000
Masahiro Kawamura	73	72	70	71	286	49,000
Ryan Moore	70	74	69	73	286	49,000
Michael Thompson	74	72	68	72	286	49,000
Kiradech Aphibarnrat	69	78	68	72	287	46,250
Rickie Fowler	74	70	70	73	287	46,250
John Merrick	72	75	69	71	287	46,250
Brandt Snedeker	73	74	70	70	287	46,250
Peter Uihlein	71	73	73	70	287	46,250
Lee Westwood	71	73	68	75	287	46,250
Derek Ernst	71	72	73	72	288	44,250
Darren Fichardt	70	74	75	69	288	44,250
Gaganjeet Bhullar	69	71	75	74	289	43,500
Jonas Blixt	70	75	74	70	289	43,500
Stephen Gallacher	73	73	72	71	289	43,500
Ryo Ishikawa	81	72	68	69	290	42,875
Daniel Popovic	77	71	69	73	290	42,875
D.A. Points	72	74	70	75	291	42,375
Ashun Wu	74	75	70	72	291	42,375

	SCORES				TOTAL	MONEY
David Howell	72	75	73	72	292	42,000
Seuk-Hyun Baek	81	68	69	75	293	41,750
Miguel Angel Jimenez	75	76	70	74	295	41,500
Raphael Jacquelin	81	70	71	74	296	41,250
George Coetzee	75	77	74	71	297	41,000
Mu Hu	76	75	73	75	299	40,750
Brett Rumford	75	77	79	72	303	40,500
Ming-Jie Huang	83	77	80	83	323	40,250
Hideki Matsuyama	71				WD	

Hero Indian Open

Delhi Golf Club, New Delhi, India
Par 36-36–72; 6,963 yards

November 7-10
purse, US$1,250,000

	SCORES				TOTAL	MONEY
Siddikur	66	66	67	75	274	US$225,000
Anirban Lahiri	71	67	67	70	275	108,125
S.S.P. Chowrasia	69	68	66	72	275	108,125
Seuk-Hyun Baek	69	69	70	68	276	47,750
Chiragh Kumar	69	70	69	68	276	47,750
Angelo Que	69	68	67	72	276	47,750
Rashid Khan	69	70	65	72	276	47,750
Unho Park	68	73	65	71	277	30,625
Chapchai Nirat	66	68	77	67	278	25,312.50
Mithun Perera	70	72	68	68	278	25,312.50
Namchok Tantipokhakul	73	70	69	67	279	21,063
Sanjay Kumar	70	68	72	69	279	21,063
Shiv Kapur	75	66	71	68	280	17,719.25
Mardan Mamat	66	73	72	69	280	17,719.25
Antonio Lascuna	71	70	68	71	280	17,719.25
Adam Groom	69	67	70	74	280	17,719.25
Scott Barr	71	70	69	71	281	15,438
Rahil Gangjee	66	69	73	73	281	15,438
Carlos Pigem	66	77	70	69	282	13,625.20
Chawalit Plaphol	70	68	73	71	282	13,625.20
Shankar Das	67	70	73	72	282	13,625.20
Lee Sung	70	70	70	72	282	13,625.20
Jake Higginbottom	72	70	68	72	282	13,625.20
Abhinav Lohan	70	72	72	69	283	12,312.50
Daniel Chopra	74	71	70	68	283	12,312.50

Resorts World Manila Masters

Manila Southwoods Golf & Country Club, Manila, Philippines
Par 36-36–72

November 14-17
purse, US$750,000

	SCORES				TOTAL	MONEY
Wen-Chong Liang	67	69	67	69	272	US$135,000
Prom Meesawat	67	67	73	65	272	82,500
(Liang defeated Meesawat on first playoff hole.)						
Richard T. Lee	65	68	76	64	273	42,375
Carlos Pigem	68	66	74	65	273	42,375
Steve Lewton	70	66	71	67	274	23,868.75
Sutijet Kooratanapisan	67	71	68	68	274	23,868.75
Jazz Janewattananond	64	69	72	69	274	23,868.75
Nicholas Fung	70	64	70	70	274	23,868.75

	SCORES				TOTAL	MONEY
Charles Hong	66	70	75	65	276	14,487.67
Mithun Perera	69	67	71	69	276	14,487.67
David Lipsky	66	69	69	72	276	14,487.67
Jeung-Hun Wang	67	74	68	68	277	12,188
Carlos Sainz, Jr.	66	71	74	67	278	9,959.43
Jyoti Randhawa	72	69	71	66	278	9,959.43
Chris Rodgers	68	66	75	69	278	9,959.43
Thaworn Wiratchant	69	68	71	70	278	9,959.43
Adilson Da Silva	68	67	72	71	278	9,959.43
Chien-Yao Hung	68	68	71	71	278	9,959.43
David Lutterus	68	70	69	71	278	9,959.43
Quincy Quek	69	70	71	69	279	7,942.60
Pariya Junhasavasdikul	68	70	70	71	279	7,942.60
Javi Colomo	71	71	71	66	279	7,942.60
S.S.P. Chowrasia	71	66	69	73	279	7,942.60
Himmat Rai	68	69	68	74	279	7,942.60
Chapchai Nirat	71	70	69	70	280	6,937.50
Anthony Kang	67	71	70	72	280	6,937.50
Joong-Kyung Mo	71	68	69	72	280	6,937.50
Angelo Que	67	66	74	73	280	6,937.50

Indonesia Open

Pantai Indah Kapuk, Jakarta, Indonesia
Par 35-36–71

November 28-December 1
purse, US$750,000

	SCORES				TOTAL	MONEY
Gaganjeet Bhullar	64	67	69	68	268	US$135,000
Nicholas Fung	66	67	72	66	271	64,875
Chapchai Nirat	67	67	71	66	271	64,875
Siddikur	71	65	69	67	272	37,500
Jyoti Randhawa	69	70	65	69	273	30,750
Antonio Lascuna	74	65	67	68	274	20,193.75
Anirban Lahiri	71	68	67	68	274	20,193.75
Thaworn Wiratchant	70	64	69	71	274	20,193.75
Jazz Janewattananond	66	66	68	74	274	20,193.75
Prom Meesawat	67	66	71	71	275	13,706.50
Thongchai Jaidee	67	67	68	73	275	13,706.50
Sutijet Kooratanapisan	70	71	71	64	276	11,775.50
Steve Lewton	71	68	71	66	276	11,775.50
Sam Brazel	67	72	71	67	277	10,388
Daniel Chopra	71	69	68	69	277	10,388
Rattanon Wannasrichan	72	68	67	70	277	10,388
David Lutterus	69	69	72	68	278	8,612.83
Panuphol Pittayarat	70	68	72	68	278	8,612.83
Lee Sung	70	72	67	69	278	8,612.83
David Lipsky	67	71	71	69	278	8,612.83
Chan Kim	68	72	69	69	278	8,612.83
Namchok Tantipokhakul	69	68	69	72	278	8,612.83
Andrew Dodt	71	71	71	66	279	7,162.50
Joong-Kyung Mo	66	74	72	67	279	7,162.50
Shiv Kapur	72	69	70	68	279	7,162.50
Chiragh Kumar	74	67	70	68	279	7,162.50
S.S.P. Chowrasia	72	66	72	69	279	7,162.50
Gi-Whan Kim	68	68	72	71	279	7,162.50

Hong Kong Open

Hong Kong Golf Club, Fanling, Hong Kong
Par 34-36–70; 6,699 yards

December 5-8
purse, US$1,300,000

	SCORES				TOTAL	MONEY
Miguel Angel Jimenez	70	67	65	66	268	US$216,660
Prom Meesawat	66	70	67	65	268	112,910
Stuart Manley	67	67	66	68	268	112,910
(Jimenez defeated Meesawat and Manley on first playoff hole.)						
Robert-Jan Derksen	69	67	68	65	269	65,000
Javi Colomo	72	66	68	66	272	46,540
Angelo Que	69	67	68	68	272	46,540
Jose Manuel Lara	69	68	65	70	272	46,540
Andrea Pavan	65	72	68	68	273	27,885
Richard Finch	70	67	68	68	273	27,885
Joel Sjoholm	68	70	65	70	273	27,885
Wade Ormsby	67	68	66	72	273	27,885
Chawalit Plaphol	69	70	69	66	274	19,695
Oliver Fisher	68	70	67	69	274	19,695
Anirban Lahiri	68	70	67	69	274	19,695
David Lipsky	69	68	67	70	274	19,695
Alex Cejka	68	67	68	71	274	19,695
Shiv Kapur	69	66	66	73	274	19,695
Byeong-Hun An	69	69	71	66	275	15,426.67
Seve Benson	66	72	69	68	275	15,426.67
Panuphol Pittayarat	69	70	68	68	275	15,426.67
Johan Carlsson	70	70	66	69	275	15,426.67
Gregory Havret	71	70	65	69	275	15,426.67
Unho Park	71	66	67	71	275	15,426.67
Lucas Bjerregaard	70	67	73	66	276	12,935
Rikard Karlberg	69	68	72	67	276	12,935
Jorge Campillo	73	65	69	69	276	12,935
Jbe' Kruger	67	66	73	70	276	12,935
Espen Kofstad	68	68	70	70	276	12,935
Roope Kakko	71	66	69	70	276	12,935
David Higgins	64	74	71	68	277	10,154.44
Wen-Yi Huang	72	69	68	68	277	10,154.44
Gi-Whan Kim	70	69	69	69	277	10,154.44
Adilson Da Silva	71	70	67	69	277	10,154.44
Chinnarat Phadungsil	68	71	68	70	277	10,154.44
Boonchu Ruangkit	69	67	70	71	277	10,154.44
Jyoti Randhawa	72	67	66	72	277	10,154.44
Jaakko Makitalo	67	71	66	73	277	10,154.44
Steve Webster	71	66	65	75	277	10,154.44
David Drysdale	72	68	71	67	278	7,800
Chris Paisley	71	70	70	67	278	7,800
Jason Knutzon	70	71	69	68	278	7,800
Chris Doak	68	68	73	69	278	7,800
Anthony Wall	71	70	68	69	278	7,800
Daniel Im	71	66	71	70	278	7,800
Nacho Elvira	67	72	67	72	278	7,800
Daisuke Kataoka	68	68	69	73	278	7,800
Alexander Levy	70	70	72	67	279	5,460
Chapchai Nirat	71	70	71	67	279	5,460
John Hahn	70	68	73	68	279	5,460
Scott Henry	68	72	71	68	279	5,460
Lee Sung	70	70	71	68	279	5,460
Wei-Chih Lu	69	72	70	68	279	5,460
Marcus Fraser	68	69	72	70	279	5,460
Edoardo Molinari	72	69	68	70	279	5,460
Andrew Dodt	66	70	72	71	279	5,460
James Morrison	71	67	69	72	279	5,460

	SCORES				TOTAL	MONEY
Antonio Lascuna	72	69	70	69	280	3,900
Thitiphun Chuayprakong	69	72	70	69	280	3,900
Himmat Rai	72	67	68	73	280	3,900
Gary Stal	70	71	73	67	281	3,380
Alastair Forsyth	68	72	71	70	281	3,380
Pariya Junhasavasdikul	73	68	70	70	281	3,380
Thorbjorn Olesen	69	71	70	71	281	3,380
Rafa Cabrera-Bello	70	71	69	71	281	3,380
Juvic Pagunsan	71	70	73	68	282	2,795
Sujjan Singh	66	73	73	70	282	2,795
Lam Chih Bing	66	72	72	72	282	2,795
S.S.P. Chowrasia	68	69	70	75	282	2,795
Mo Joong Kyung	70	70	76	69	285	2,425
Brinson Paolini	70	68	70	77	285	2,425
Wen-Tang Lin	74	64	75	73	286	1,948.49
Andy Sullivan	70	71	70	75	286	1,948.49
Daniel Brooks	69	71	77	71	288	1,942.35
Scott Hend	70	70	75	74	289	1,936.23
Timothy Tang	71	70	72	76	289	1,936.23

Thailand Golf Championship

Amata Spring Country Club, Chonburi, Thailand
Par 36-36–72; 7,453 yards

December 12-15
purse, US$1,000,000

	SCORES				TOTAL	MONEY
Sergio Garcia	68	65	65	68	266	US$180,000
Henrik Stenson	70	67	65	68	270	110,000
Alexander Levy	70	65	70	69	274	63,000
Charl Schwartzel	68	73	67	67	275	38,200
Yuki Kono	72	69	65	69	275	38,200
Justin Rose	65	68	70	72	275	38,200
Anirban Lahiri	71	64	67	73	275	38,200
Chapchai Nirat	72	69	67	69	277	22,950
Rickie Fowler	70	66	71	70	277	22,950
Thongchai Jaidee	71	71	68	68	278	17,600
Marcus Fraser	69	73	67	69	278	17,600
Gaganjeet Bhullar	66	73	69	70	278	17,600
Hunter Mahan	71	72	68	68	279	14,800
Chinnarat Phadungsil	74	68	65	72	279	14,800
Seuk-Hyun Baek	72	71	68	69	280	13,250
Ryo Ishikawa	74	68	68	70	280	13,250
Berry Henson	72	71	66	71	280	13,250
Prayad Marksaeng	72	72	71	66	281	10,781.25
Masahiro Kawamura	69	70	72	70	281	10,781.25
Masanori Kobayashi	75	68	67	71	281	10,781.25
Alex Cejka	64	71	73	73	281	10,781.25
Kiradech Aphibarnrat	69	68	71	73	281	10,781.25
D.A. Points	73	69	66	73	281	10,781.25
Panuphol Pittayarat	71	68	67	75	281	10,781.25
Gi-Whan Kim	74	68	64	75	281	10,781.25

OneAsia Tour

Thailand Open

Thana City Golf & Sports Club, Bangkok, Thailand
Par 36-36—72; 6,930 yards

March 14-17
purse, US$1,000,000

	SCORES				TOTAL	MONEY
Prayad Marksaeng	68	67	65	64	264	US$180,000
Scott Strange	66	65	68	67	266	105,000
Nick Cullen	69	67	66	65	267	70,000
Jung-Gon Hwang	65	68	72	63	268	37,033.33
Min-Gyu Cho	65	68	69	66	268	37,033.33
David McKenzie	65	68	68	67	268	37,033.33
Simon Yates	66	69	64	69	268	37,033.33
Chris Wood	67	66	65	70	268	37,033.33
Mu Hu	67	67	64	70	268	37,033.33
Hideto Tanihara	67	67	70	65	269	24,600
Terry Pilkadaris	68	64	68	69	269	24,600
Do-Hoon Kim	70	68	69	63	270	15,975
Brad Kennedy	69	70	66	65	270	15,975
Thaworn Wiratchant	70	68	69	63	270	15,975
Daisuke Maruyama	70	67	66	67	270	15,975
Kyoung-Hoon Lee	67	66	69	68	270	15,975
Kazuhiro Yamashita	70	66	66	68	270	15,975
David Smail	69	66	66	69	270	15,975
Lucas Lee	65	67	65	73	270	15,975
John Young Kim	65	68	72	66	271	10,760
Matthew Griffin	65	71	71	64	271	10,760
Thanyakon Khrongpha	70	63	70	68	271	10,760
Juvic Pagunsan	67	69	66	69	271	10,760
Yoshinori Fujimoto	67	67	67	70	271	10,760
Stephen Dartnall	69	68	69	66	272	9,000
Jason Kang	71	68	67	66	272	9,000
Brad Shilton	73	66	64	69	272	9,000

Enjoy Jakarta Indonesia PGA Championship

Emeralda Golf Club, Jakarta, Indonesia
Par 36-36—72; 7,198 yards

March 28-31
purse, US$1,000,000

	SCORES				TOTAL	MONEY
Ho-Sung Choi	67	70	65	67	269	US$180,000
Juvie Pagunsan	69	71	65	66	271	75,000
Young-Han Song	65	66	72	68	271	75,000
Kaname Yokoo	68	66	67	70	271	75,000
Hideto Tanihara	66	68	70	68	272	39,900
Toshinori Muto	67	65	70	70	272	39,900
Thaworn Wiratchant	71	68	66	68	273	29,650
Wen-Chong Liang	66	69	69	69	273	29,650
Scott Strange	68	67	67	71	273	29,650
Yuta Ikeda	67	68	67	71	273	29,650
Simon Dyson	69	70	68	67	274	20,200
Azuma Yano	67	69	67	71	274	20,200

	SCORES				TOTAL	MONEY
Aaron Townsend	69	63	70	72	274	20,200
Kyoung-Hoon Lee	65	71	66	72	274	20,200
Shingo Katayama	65	69	71	70	275	15,900
Ashun Wu	70	68	67	70	275	15,900
K.T. Kim	68	70	69	69	276	13,600
Tae-Hee Lee	69	70	70	68	277	11,000
Matthew Griffin	69	70	69	69	277	11,000
Koichiro Kawano	69	71	69	68	277	11,000
Mark Brown	69	72	68	68	277	11,000
Sang-Hyun Park	67	69	73	68	277	11,000
Richard T. Lee	65	71	70	71	277	11,000
Sang-Hee Lee	70	70	65	72	277	11,000
Yoshinori Fujimoto	66	66	71	74	277	11,000

Volvo China Open

Binhai Lake Golf Club, Tianjin, China
Par 36-36–72; 7,667 yards

May 2-5
purse, RMB20,000,000

	SCORES				TOTAL	MONEY
Brett Rumford	68	67	69	68	272	US$534,120.73
Mikko Ilonen	69	63	73	71	276	356,080.49
Victor Dubuisson	71	72	66	68	277	200,615.95
Robert-Jan Derksen	66	70	73	69	278	160,236.38
Ricardo Santos	70	72	68	69	279	124,022.96
Pablo Larrazabal	71	66	69	73	279	124,022.96
Andreas Harto	72	71	70	67	280	96,141.83
Felipe Aguilar	71	73	68	69	281	68,741.41
Paul Casey	71	68	72	70	281	68,741.41
Thomas Bjorn	70	73	68	70	281	68,741.41
Joost Luiten	73	67	68	73	281	68,741.41
Ricardo Gonzalez	73	71	67	71	282	53,358.71
Kiradech Aphibarnrat	68	67	72	75	282	53,358.71
Raphael Jacquelin	68	72	75	68	283	43,446.95
Jeev Milkha Singh	72	69	73	69	283	43,446.95
Andy Sullivan	74	68	72	69	283	43,446.95
Aaron Townsend	69	70	74	70	283	43,446.95
Gregory Havret	72	70	71	70	283	43,446.95
Lee Slattery	69	68	74	72	283	43,446.95
Paul Lawrie	69	72	70	72	283	43,446.95
Emiliano Grillo	73	71	70	70	284	36,213.42
Paul Waring	72	68	73	71	284	36,213.42
Steve Webster	73	67	71	73	284	36,213.42
Johan Edfors	73	69	73	70	285	32,367.75
Mark Foster	70	69	75	71	285	32,367.75
Stephen Gallacher	70	71	71	73	285	32,367.75
Matthew Baldwin	70	71	70	74	285	32,367.75
Sang-Hyun Park	69	70	71	75	285	32,367.75
Tommy Fleetwood	71	70	72	73	286	28,041.37
Soren Hansen	72	69	72	73	286	28,041.37
Richie Ramsay	71	68	73	74	286	28,041.37
Damien McGrane	73	66	73	74	286	28,041.37
Byeong-Hun An	73	68	74	72	287	23,440.29
Markus Brier	71	71	73	72	287	23,440.29
Moritz Lampert	72	72	71	72	287	23,440.29
Matthew Griffin	70	68	76	73	287	23,440.29
Soren Kjeldsen	72	68	74	73	287	23,440.29
*Ze-Cheng Dou	70	72	72	73	287	
Branden Grace	74	67	72	74	287	23,440.29
Graeme Storm	70	68	74	75	287	23,440.29

	SCORES				TOTAL	MONEY
Nick Cullen	72	69	78	69	288	18,587.42
Eddie Pepperell	75	68	75	70	288	18,587.42
Richard Bland	72	71	75	70	288	18,587.42
Estanislao Goya	70	74	74	70	288	18,587.42
Kristoffer Broberg	74	67	75	72	288	18,587.42
Edoardo Molinari	75	68	73	72	288	18,587.42
Gaganjeet Bhullar	74	69	72	73	288	18,587.42
Alexander Noren	70	73	71	74	288	18,587.42
Andrew Dodt	72	71	77	69	289	15,382.70
Magnus A. Carlsson	71	73	72	73	289	15,382.70
Prom Meesawat	76	68	76	70	290	13,459.86
Wen-Chong Liang	74	70	75	71	290	13,459.86
Fabrizio Zanotti	71	69	77	73	290	13,459.86
Rafa Cabrera-Bello	72	70	72	76	290	13,459.86
Michael Hendry	74	67	75	75	291	10,896.08
Richard Finch	71	70	75	75	291	10,896.08
Terry Pilkadaris	69	73	74	75	291	10,896.08
J.B. Hansen	73	69	71	78	291	10,896.08
Niclas Fasth	73	68	78	73	292	9,453.95
Garrett Sapp	70	74	74	74	292	9,453.95
Joel Sjoholm	74	65	76	78	293	8,813.00
Peter Whiteford	73	69	73	78	293	8,813.00
Phillip Price	76	68	73	77	294	8,332.29
Hyung-Joon Lee	70	70	75	80	295	8,011.82
Chris Lloyd	71	72	73	80	296	7,691.35
Scott Jamieson	73	71	77	83	304	7,370.87
Wen-Yi Huang	74	69	80	82	305	7,050.40

GS Caltex Maekyung Open

Nam Seoul Golf & Country Club, Seoul, South Korea
Par 36-36–72; 6,964 yards

May 9-12
purse, KRW1,000,000,000

	SCORES				TOTAL	MONEY
Hyun-Woo Ryu	72	65	67	70	274	US$177,803.07
Do-Hoon Kim	67	70	70	68	275	83,567.44
Hyung-Sung Kim	67	67	71	70	275	83,567.44
Kyoung-Hoon Lee	67	71	69	71	278	42,672.74
Dae-Sub Kim	70	66	71	71	278	42,672.74
Kyung-Nam Kang	68	71	68	72	279	29,337.51
Tae-Hee Lee	69	72	68	72	281	26,670.46
Jake Higginbottom	69	71	74	68	282	18,615.98
Ho-Sung Choi	70	68	75	69	282	18,615.98
Ju-Hyuk Park	68	70	73	71	282	18,615.98
Il-Hwan Park	68	72	71	71	282	18,615.98
Young-Han Song	68	70	73	71	282	18,615.98
Joong-Kyung Mo	70	68	74	71	283	11,557.20
Do-Yeob Mun	70	72	69	72	283	11,557.20
Rory Hie	71	73	72	68	284	9,530.24
Matthew Griffin	67	73	73	71	284	9,530.24
Jung-Ho Yoon	72	67	74	71	284	9,530.24
Bio Kim	72	71	70	71	284	9,530.24
Jin-Jae Byun	71	68	71	74	284	9,530.24
Seng-Yong Kim	68	75	72	70	285	7,885.57
Jae-Kyung Park	68	75	72	70	285	7,885.57
Stephen Dartnall	73	69	72	71	285	7,885.57
Min-Gyu Cho	64	73	75	73	285	7,885.57
Soon-Sang Hong	71	70	71	73	285	7,885.57
Hui-Soo Kim	70	69	71	75	285	7,885.57

SK Telecom Open

Pinx Golf Club, Jeju-do, South Korea
Par 36-36–72; 7,363 yards
(Final round cancelled—fog.)

May 16-19
purse, KRW1,000,000,000

	SCORES			TOTAL	MONEY
Matthew Griffin	64	67	72	203	US$179,484.88
Wook-Soon Kang	65	72	67	204	89,742.44
Ki-Sang Lee	67	68	72	207	44,272.94
Do-Kyu Park	67	66	74	207	44,272.94
Mu Hu	66	68	73	207	44,272.94
David Oh	66	72	70	208	26,115.05
Jae-Hyun An	71	69	68	208	26,115.05
Hyung-Tae Kim	67	69	72	208	26,115.05
Kyong-Jun Moon	67	69	72	208	26,115.05
Michael Long	66	72	71	209	17,230.55
*Soo-Min Lee	70	72	67	209	
Do-Hoon Kim	66	70	73	209	17,230.55
K.J. Choi	69	67	73	209	17,230.55
Chang-Yoon Kim	68	62	79	209	17,230.55
Jason Norris	66	66	77	209	17,230.55
Andre Stolz	69	70	71	210	12,204.97
Bio Kim	68	70	72	210	12,204.97
David McKenzie	68	70	72	210	12,204.97
Sang-Hyun Park	68	68	74	210	12,204.97
Jin Jeong	68	67	75	210	12,204.97
Andrew Kelly	70	69	72	211	8,615.27
Sang-Hee Lee	69	70	72	211	8,615.27
In-Choon Hwang	69	70	72	211	8,615.27
Jung-Ho Yoon	71	68	72	211	8,615.27
Joshua Younger	71	69	71	211	8,615.27
Ryan Haller	70	70	71	211	8,615.27
Jake Higginbottom	68	69	74	211	8,615.27
Ryan Fox	70	71	70	211	8,615.27
Kyung-Nam Kang	66	75	70	211	8,615.27

Nanshan China Masters

Nanshan International Golf Club, Nanshan, China
Par 36-36–72; 7,379 yards

October 10-13
purse, US$1,000,000

	SCORES				TOTAL	MONEY
Charl Schwartzel	71	72	68	68	279	US$180,000
Wen-Chong Liang	74	64	70	72	280	87,500
Darren Clarke	72	68	68	72	280	87,500
Rhein Gibson	74	69	70	69	282	38,760
Rory Hie	75	65	72	70	282	38,760
Mark Brown	71	72	69	70	282	38,760
Scott Strange	72	69	69	72	282	38,760
Sung-Yeol Kwon	73	70	67	72	282	38,760
Ryan Haller	72	72	73	67	284	24,650
Il-Hwan Park	73	70	71	70	284	24,650
Scott Laycock	70	73	69	72	284	24,650
Xin-Jun Zhang	71	67	72	74	284	24,650
Thanyakon Khrongpha	72	70	71	72	285	19,000
Lian-Wei Zhang	75	72	69	70	286	17,800
Nick Cullen	75	71	69	72	287	15,900
Gareth Paddison	69	69	73	76	287	15,900
Jason Norris	72	72	72	72	288	13,200

	SCORES				TOTAL	MONEY
Ted Oh	69	74	71	74	288	13,200
Ryan Carter	75	73	73	68	289	11,200
Hyun-Seok Lim	74	75	72	68	289	11,200
Geon-Ha Kim	74	72	72	71	289	11,200
Terry Pilkadaris	71	70	70	78	289	11,200
Se-Jun Yoon	75	73	70	72	290	9,850
Brad Shilton	73	69	75	73	290	9,850
Lucas Lee	69	74	72	75	290	9,850
Sung-Ho Lee	73	71	71	75	290	9,850

Kolon Korea Open

Woo Jeong Hills Country Club, Cheonan, South Korea
Par 36-35–71; 7,210 yards

October 17-20
purse, KRW1,000,000,000

	SCORES				TOTAL	MONEY
Sung Kang	68	70	73	69	280	US$277,628.68
Rory McIlroy	70	69	75	67	281	53,674.88
Sang-Hee Lee	72	69	72	68	281	53,674.88
*Chang-Woo Lee	73	71	68	69	281	
Joong-Kyung Mo	72	69	68	72	281	53,674.88
Hyung-Tae Kim	72	66	66	77	281	53,674.88
*Jeong-Woo Ham	69	74	72	67	282	
Hyun-Woo Ryu	69	72	70	71	282	27,762.87
I.J. Jang	67	72	76	68	283	22,210.30
Dong-Seop Maeng	70	70	71	72	283	22,210.30
Il-Hwan Park	77	68	66	72	283	22,210.30
Ji-Man Kang	71	71	69	72	283	22,210.30
Woo-Hyun Kim	77	69	72	66	284	14,899.41
Jae-Kyung Park	71	72	70	71	284	14,899.41
Soon-Sang Hong	69	68	71	76	284	14,899.41
Sang-Hyun Park	74	73	70	68	285	10,642.44
Seung-Hyuk Kim	70	74	72	69	285	10,642.44
Kyung-Nam Kang	73	75	70	68	286	9,485.65
Joon-Woo Choi	72	71	72	71	286	9,485.65
Jung-Ho Yoon	68	73	75	71	287	8,791.57
*Soo-Min Lee	72	70	75	71	288	
In-Choon Hwang	70	68	77	73	288	8,513.95
Geon-Ha Kim	74	68	73	73	288	8,513.95
Richard T. Lee	71	74	72	72	289	8,236.32
Ju-Hyuk Park	70	74	75	71	290	7,607.03
Min-Kyu Han	68	74	75	73	290	7,607.03
Ryan Yip	69	74	73	74	290	7,607.03
Simon Yates	70	75	71	74	290	7,607.03
Gyoung-Yoon Yu	71	68	75	76	290	7,607.03

Australian PGA Championship

See Australasian Tour chapter.

Emirates Australian Open

See Australasian Tour chapter.

Dongfeng Nissan Cup

CTS Tycoon Golf Club, Shenzhen, China   December 13-15

FIRST DAY
Fourball

Scott Laycock and Michael Long (Asia-Pacific) defeated Ashun Wu and Kangchun Wu, 7 and 6.
Lian-Wei Zhang and Wen-Yi Huang (China) defeated Tze-Huang Choo and Eric Mina, 2 and 1.
Rory Hie and Thaworn Wiratchant (AP) defeated Guan-Ming Yang and Bin Yan, 1 up.
Dae-Sub Kim and Ho-Sung Choi (AP) defeated Chao Li and Ming-Jie Huang, 4 and 2.
Masamichi Uehira and Kazuhiro Yamashita (AP) defeated Min-Gao Wang and Xin-Yang Li, 4 and 3.
Dong Su and Zecheng Dou (C) halved with Matthew Griffin and Gareth Paddison.

POINTS: China 1½, Asia-Pacific 4½

SECOND DAY
Foursomes

Zhang and Wen-Yi Huang (C) defeated Long and Laycock, 5 and 4.
Yang and Yan (C) defeated Mina and Choo, 2 and 1.
Wiratchant and Hie (AP) defeated Ming-Jie Huang and Kangchun Wu, 3 and 2.
Su and Dou (C) defeated Kim and Choi, 3 and 1.
Ashun Wu and Wang (C) defeated Uehira and Yamashita, 1 up.
Paddison and Griffin (AP) defeated Chao Li and Xin-Yang Li, 3 and 2.

POINTS: China 4, Asia-Pacific 2

FINAL DAY
Singles

Uehira (AP) defeated Wang, 3 and 1.
Ashun Wu (C) defeated Long, 4 and 3.
Wen-Yi Huang (C) halved with Choi.
Yang (C) defeated Kim, 1 up.
Yan (C) defeated Mina, 4 and 3.
Dou (C) defeated Wiratchant, 4 and 3.
Yamashita (AP) defeated Xin-Yang Li, 2 and 1.
Kangchun Wu (C) halved with Choo.
Ming-Jie Huang (C) halved with Hie.
Zhang (C) halved with Griffin.
Su (C) defeated Laycock, 1 up.
Paddison (AP) defeated Chao Li, 2 and 1.

POINTS: China 7, Asia-Pacific 5

TOTAL POINTS: China 12½, Asia-Pacific 11½

Japan Tour

Thailand Open

See OneAsia Tour section.

Enjoy Jakarta Indonesia PGA Championship

See OneAsia Tour section.

Token Homemate Cup

Token Tado Country Club, Nagoya, Mie
Par 35-36–71; 7,081 yards

April 18-21
purse, ¥130,000,000

	SCORES				TOTAL	MONEY
Yoshinobu Tsukada	72	71	63	69	275	¥26,000,000
Koumei Oda	66	73	69	71	279	10,920,000
Kunihiro Kamii	71	72	62	74	279	10,920,000
Hiroyuki Fujita	71	73	69	67	280	5,373,333
Toru Taniguchi	68	76	68	68	280	5,373,333
I.J. Jang	70	73	65	72	280	5,373,333
Brendan Jones	69	77	67	68	281	3,973,666
S.K. Ho	71	74	68	68	281	3,973,666
Sung-Joon Park	67	72	69	73	281	3,973,666
Hideki Matsuyama	67	75	74	66	282	3,146,000
Sang-Hee Lee	68	73	71	70	282	3,146,000
Hiroo Kawai	69	76	65	72	282	3,146,000
Satoshi Kodaira	69	75	70	69	283	2,496,000
Tomohiro Kondo	70	74	65	74	283	2,496,000
Steven Conran	66	75	73	70	284	2,106,000
Hideto Tanihara	69	74	69	72	284	2,106,000
Atomu Shigenaga	66	74	69	75	284	2,106,000
Satoshi Tomiyama	69	75	70	71	285	1,794,000
Keisuke Sato	72	72	69	72	285	1,794,000
Taichi Teshima	71	75	68	72	286	1,348,285
Chi-Hsien Hsieh	71	75	68	72	286	1,348,285
Masanori Kobayashi	71	73	70	72	286	1,348,285
Han Lee	70	74	71	71	286	1,348,285
Brad Kennedy	73	71	74	68	286	1,348,285
Norio Shinozaki	69	74	74	69	286	1,348,285
Kiyoshi Murota	67	72	68	79	286	1,348,285

Tsuruya Open

Yamanohara Golf Club, Kawanishi, Hyogo
Par 35-36–71; 6,793 yards

April 25-28
purse, ¥120,000,000

	SCORES				TOTAL	MONEY
Hideki Matsuyama	69	63	68	66	266	¥24,000,000
David Oh	68	69	64	66	267	12,000,000
Kunihiro Kamii	69	68	64	69	270	8,160,000
Hideto Tanihara	70	66	70	65	271	4,960,000

	SCORES				TOTAL	MONEY
Brendan Jones	66	71	68	66	271	4,960,000
Juvic Pagunsan	66	68	66	71	271	4,960,000
Tomohiro Kondo	67	71	67	67	272	3,668,000
Seong-Ho Lee	66	68	68	70	272	3,668,000
Tae-Hee Lee	66	65	67	74	272	3,668,000
Masahiro Kawamura	66	72	67	68	273	2,784,000
Eric Chun	70	68	66	69	273	2,784,000
Keiichiro Fukabori	69	69	66	69	273	2,784,000
Yosuke Asaji	69	68	65	71	273	2,784,000
Toru Taniguchi	66	70	69	69	274	2,064,000
Koumei Oda	67	70	68	69	274	2,064,000
Hiroshi Iwata	69	64	69	72	274	2,064,000
Daisuke Kataoka	72	69	67	67	275	1,564,000
I.J. Jang	66	69	73	67	275	1,564,000
Akio Sadakata	69	71	67	68	275	1,564,000
Michio Matsumura	65	74	67	69	275	1,564,000
Sung-Joon Park	72	69	64	70	275	1,564,000
Kodai Ichihara	65	70	65	75	275	1,564,000
Tadahiro Takayama	69	70	67	70	276	1,176,000
Yoshinori Fujimoto	65	71	68	72	276	1,176,000
Richard Tate	70	70	68	69	277	984,000
David Smail	67	71	70	69	277	984,000
Jay Choi	71	69	69	68	277	984,000
Atomu Shigenaga	67	74	69	67	277	984,000
Dong-Kyu Jang	70	70	71	66	277	984,000

The Crowns

Nagoya Golf Club, Wago Course, Togo, Aichi
Par 35-35–70; 6,545 yards

May 2-5
purse, ¥120,000,000

	SCORES				TOTAL	MONEY
Michio Matsumura	71	71	69	67	278	¥24,000,000
Hideki Matsuyama	72	67	73	67	279	12,000,000
Shingo Katayama	72	68	69	73	282	6,960,000
Steven Conran	70	74	68	70	282	6,960,000
Toshinori Muto	73	73	70	67	283	4,560,000
Kazuhiro Yamashita	75	70	69	69	283	4,560,000
Tomohiro Kondo	69	75	72	68	284	3,810,000
S.K. Ho	72	69	73	70	284	3,810,000
Min-Gyu Cho	74	72	71	68	285	3,144,000
Kyoung-Hoon Lee	79	67	72	67	285	3,144,000
Katsumasa Miyamoto	72	73	73	67	285	3,144,000
Kenichi Kuboya	74	69	76	67	286	2,544,000
Yuki Kono	75	72	70	69	286	2,544,000
Toru Suzuki	78	70	71	68	287	1,834,285
Tetsuya Haraguchi	72	74	72	69	287	1,834,285
Ryuichi Kondo	78	72	68	69	287	1,834,285
I.J. Jang	72	71	74	70	287	1,834,285
Ryota Kojima	75	71	71	70	287	1,834,285
Yoshikazu Haku	75	72	70	70	287	1,834,285
Kunihiro Kamii	72	71	71	73	287	1,834,285
Juvic Pagunsan	77	73	72	66	288	1,140,000
Yuta Ikeda	75	71	75	67	288	1,140,000
Eun-Shin Park	76	71	73	68	288	1,140,000
Yui Ueda	72	72	73	71	288	1,140,000
Akio Sadakata	71	72	74	71	288	1,140,000
J.B. Park	73	75	69	71	288	1,140,000
Hiroo Kawai	74	72	70	72	288	1,140,000
Hirofumi Miyase	76	70	69	73	288	1,140,000

Japan PGA Championship

Sobu Country Club, Sobu, Chiba
Par 35-36–71; 7,327 yards

May 16-19
purse, ¥150,000,000

	SCORES				TOTAL	MONEY
Hyung-Sung Kim	69	70	75	65	279	¥30,000,000
Yoshinori Fujimoto	69	65	78	68	280	10,800,000
Hiroyuki Fujita	72	72	67	69	280	10,800,000
Hideki Matsuyama	67	71	67	75	280	10,800,000
Satoshi Kodaira	67	69	74	72	282	6,000,000
Yusaku Miyazato	68	70	77	68	283	5,175,000
Toru Taniguchi	74	69	69	71	283	5,175,000
Sung-Yoon Kim	70	70	73	71	284	4,245,000
Prayad Marksaeng	69	72	72	71	284	4,245,000
Yuki Kono	69	71	69	75	284	4,245,000
Hiroshi Iwata	72	71	73	69	285	3,180,000
Dinesh Chand	72	68	72	73	285	3,180,000
Yoshikazu Haku	73	70	69	73	285	3,180,000
Tetsuji Hiratsuka	70	73	69	73	285	3,180,000
Scott Strange	72	68	75	71	286	2,355,000
Brendan Jones	72	72	71	71	286	2,355,000
I.J. Jang	69	74	71	72	286	2,355,000
Paul Sheehan	72	69	72	73	286	2,355,000
Akira Endo	73	72	71	71	287	1,830,000
Kazuhiro Yamashita	79	67	70	71	287	1,830,000
Tadahiro Takayama	71	75	70	71	287	1,830,000
Han Lee	71	72	70	74	287	1,830,000
J.B. Park	74	71	71	72	288	1,362,000
Shingo Katayama	73	73	69	73	288	1,362,000
Keiichiro Fukabori	67	71	76	74	288	1,362,000
Ashun Wu	66	70	77	75	288	1,362,000
Yasuharu Imano	71	71	71	75	288	1,362,000

Diamond Cup

Oarai Golf Club Japan, Oarai, Ibaraki
Par 36-36–72; 7,190 yards

May 30-June 2
purse, ¥120,000,000

	SCORES				TOTAL	MONEY
Hideki Matsuyama	71	69	68	71	279	¥24,000,000
Hyung-Sung Kim	69	74	67	71	281	8,640,000
Brad Kennedy	68	72	70	71	281	8,640,000
Sung-Joon Park	71	70	68	72	281	8,640,000
Toru Taniguchi	72	69	70	71	282	4,800,000
Shingo Katayama	71	70	70	72	283	3,980,000
Satoshi Kodaira	71	67	71	74	283	3,980,000
Tommy Nakajima	74	68	66	75	283	3,980,000
Kyoung-Hoon Lee	70	68	76	70	284	3,264,000
I.J. Jang	69	69	73	73	284	3,264,000
Akio Sadakata	69	71	73	72	285	2,664,000
Katsumasa Miyamoto	69	73	71	72	285	2,664,000
Hideto Tanihara	73	71	67	74	285	2,664,000
David Oh	70	75	70	71	286	2,184,000
Yusaku Miyazato	73	71	72	71	287	1,828,800
Dong-Kyu Jang	69	72	73	73	287	1,828,800
Ryan Haller	71	71	72	73	287	1,828,800
Shintaro Kai	71	71	70	75	287	1,828,800
Daisuke Maruyama	67	71	72	77	287	1,828,800
Makoto Inoue	68	73	74	73	288	1,416,000

	SCORES			TOTAL	MONEY
Daisuke Kataoka	68	71	75 74	288	1,416,000
Hiroo Kawai	72	71	71 74	288	1,416,000
Masanori Kobayashi	73	70	74 72	289	1,116,000
Brendan Jones	72	72	71 74	289	1,116,000
Yoshikazu Haku	68	74	72 75	289	1,116,000
Kazuhiro Yamashita	69	71	73 76	289	1,116,000

Japan Golf Tour Championship

Shishido Hills Country Club, West Course, Kasama, Ibaraki   June 20-23
Par 36-36–72; 7,402 yards   purse, ¥150,000,000

	SCORES				TOTAL	MONEY
Satoshi Kodaira	70	64	70	70	274	¥30,000,000
S.K. Ho	67	68	70	70	275	12,600,000
Kiradech Aphibarnrat	71	67	67	70	275	12,600,000
Sung-Joon Park	69	67	72	68	276	7,200,000
David Oh	70	69	70	68	277	5,700,000
Hiroshi Iwata	78	65	66	68	277	5,700,000
Hideki Matsuyama	67	72	72	67	278	4,585,000
I.J. Jang	74	65	70	69	278	4,585,000
In-Hoi Hur	74	68	64	72	278	4,585,000
Daisuke Maruyama	68	72	71	68	279	3,630,000
Steven Conran	70	71	68	70	279	3,630,000
Eun-Shin Park	69	64	75	71	279	3,630,000
Brad Kennedy	69	72	71	68	280	2,455,714
Yusaku Miyazato	69	70	72	69	280	2,455,714
Koichiro Kawano	70	68	72	70	280	2,455,714
Shingo Katayama	70	69	71	70	280	2,455,714
Tadahiro Takayama	69	71	69	71	280	2,455,714
Jay Choi	77	66	66	71	280	2,455,714
Toshinori Muto	73	65	70	72	280	2,455,714
Jung-Gon Hwang	70	70	70	71	281	1,830,000
David Smail	73	68	67	73	281	1,830,000
Hidemasa Hoshino	72	71	70	69	282	1,485,000
Hyung-Sung Kim	69	72	71	70	282	1,485,000
Toru Taniguchi	69	70	71	72	282	1,485,000
Hiroyuki Fujita	69	67	69	77	282	1,485,000

Gateway to the Open Mizuno Open

JFE Setonaikai Golf Club, Kasaoka, Okayama   June 27-30
Par 36-36–72; 7,404 yards   purse, ¥110,000,000

	SCORES				TOTAL	MONEY
Brendan Jones	67	66	68	68	269	¥22,000,000
K.T. Kim	67	69	67	69	272	11,000,000
Makoto Inoue	70	69	68	68	275	7,480,000
Tetsuji Hiratsuka	72	69	68	68	277	4,840,000
Shingo Katayama	67	67	71	72	277	4,840,000
Jung-Gon Hwang	74	66	70	68	278	3,265,166
Ji-Ho Yang	68	68	73	69	278	3,265,166
Dong-Kyu Jang	71	70	68	69	278	3,265,166
Michael Hendry	70	68	70	70	278	3,265,166
Daisuke Kataoka	73	66	67	72	278	3,265,166
Hidemasa Hoshino	68	71	65	74	278	3,265,166
Do-Hoon Kim	68	68	73	70	279	2,442,000

	SCORES				TOTAL	MONEY
Tadahiro Takayama	68	71	70	71	280	2,112,000
Yusaku Miyazato	69	68	71	72	280	2,112,000
Sung-Joon Park	70	67	74	70	281	1,727,000
Yasuharu Imano	66	76	69	70	281	1,727,000
Yui Ueda	71	72	71	67	281	1,727,000
Kyoung-Hoon Lee	70	69	68	74	281	1,727,000
Kenichi Kuboya	74	68	71	69	282	1,254,000
Taichi Teshima	68	73	70	71	282	1,254,000
David Oh	73	68	69	72	282	1,254,000
Hyung-Sung Kim	70	68	71	73	282	1,254,000
S.K. Ho	69	67	72	74	282	1,254,000
Hiroshi Iwata	67	71	69	75	282	1,254,000
Koichiro Kawano	68	69	75	71	283	880,000
Ashun Wu	68	68	76	71	283	880,000
Hiroo Kawai	70	70	71	72	283	880,000
Shigeru Nonaka	72	67	71	73	283	880,000
Ho-Sung Choi	72	71	71	69	283	880,000
Seung-Hyuk Kim	73	61	71	78	283	880,000

Nagashima Shigeo Invitational

North Country Golf Club, Chitose, Hokkaido
Par 36-36–72; 7,096 yards

July 4-7
purse, ¥150,000,000

	SCORES				TOTAL	MONEY
Shunsuke Sonoda	69	71	61	67	268	¥30,000,000
Tomohiro Kondo	71	68	67	65	271	12,600,000
Yuki Kono	68	68	69	66	271	12,600,000
Hideki Matsuyama	71	67	68	66	272	6,200,000
S.K. Ho	69	71	66	66	272	6,200,000
Hideto Tanihara	72	68	65	67	272	6,200,000
Hiroyuki Fujita	64	71	68	70	273	4,762,500
Yusaku Miyazato	71	66	67	69	273	4,762,500
Wen-Chong Liang	70	67	69	68	274	3,780,000
Daisuke Kataoka	71	69	66	68	274	3,780,000
Makoto Inoue	67	69	69	69	274	3,780,000
Satoshi Kodaira	68	71	66	69	274	3,780,000
Seung-Hyuk Kim	70	70	68	67	275	2,455,714
Katsumasa Miyamoto	68	69	70	68	275	2,455,714
Jay Choi	69	71	67	68	275	2,455,714
Kyoung-Hoon Lee	70	69	67	69	275	2,455,714
Sung-Yoon Kim	71	71	64	69	275	2,455,714
Shingo Katayama	67	69	69	70	275	2,455,714
Hyung-Sung Kim	66	70	69	70	275	2,455,714
Brad Kennedy	74	68	66	68	276	1,890,000
Atomu Shigenaga	71	72	69	65	277	1,710,000
Shintaro Kai	70	68	69	70	277	1,710,000
Ryan Haller	72	70	69	67	278	1,330,000
Kazuhiro Yamashita	70	73	67	68	278	1,330,000
Ryutaro Nagano	72	69	68	69	278	1,330,000
Ryuko Tokimatsu	71	68	69	70	278	1,330,000
Takashi Kanemoto	68	71	68	71	278	1,330,000
Hiroo Kawai	70	71	73	64	278	1,330,000

Kansai Open

Olympic Golf Club, Hyogo
Par 36-36–72; 7,298 yards
(Event shortened to 54 holes—rain.)

August 22-25
purse, ¥60,000,000

	SCORES			TOTAL	MONEY
Brad Kennedy	69	70	67	206	¥9,000,000
Sung-Joon Park	68	71	68	207	4,500,000
Azuma Yano	76	65	67	208	3,060,000
Aaron Townsend	73	70	66	209	2,160,000
Ryuko Tokimatsu	73	70	67	210	1,569,375
Thaworn Wiratchant	71	68	71	210	1,569,375
Kyoung-Hoon Lee	69	70	71	210	1,569,375
Yuta Ikeda	70	68	72	210	1,569,375
Yoshiharu Tomotsugu	72	71	68	211	1,179,000
Yuki Kono	72	72	67	211	1,179,000
Min-Gyu Cho	73	71	67	211	1,179,000
*Yujiro Ohori	69	68	74	211	
Tetsuji Hiratsuka	73	70	69	212	725,400
Shigeru Nonaka	69	74	69	212	725,400
Kazuhiro Yamashita	72	71	69	212	725,400
Hideto Tanihara	70	74	68	212	725,400
Kiyoshi Murota	71	70	71	212	725,400
Norio Shinozaki	71	70	71	212	725,400
Michio Matsumura	70	71	71	212	725,400
Eric Chun	70	70	72	212	725,400
Genki Yanase	72	68	72	212	725,400
Masahiro Kawamura	69	70	73	212	725,400
Yosuke Asaji	73	70	70	213	445,500
Michael Hendry	69	75	69	213	445,500
Han Lee	72	70	71	213	445,500
Hidemasa Hoshino	73	68	72	213	445,500

Vana H Cup KBC Augusta

Keya Golf Club, Shima, Fukuoka
Par 36-36–72; 7,150 yards
(Event shortened to 54 holes—rain.)

August 29-September 1
purse, ¥110,000,000

	SCORES			TOTAL	MONEY
Sung-Joon Park	67	68	69	204	¥16,500,000
Jung-Gon Hwang	68	69	69	206	8,250,000
Azuma Yano	71	70	66	207	4,290,000
Shigeru Nonaka	71	67	69	207	4,290,000
Yoshinori Fujimoto	68	67	72	207	4,290,000
Yuta Ikeda	73	65	70	208	2,970,000
Tadahiro Takayama	70	72	67	209	2,521,750
Toshinori Muto	68	73	68	209	2,521,750
Satoshi Tomiyama	68	67	74	209	2,521,750
Kazuhiro Yamashita	74	68	68	210	1,914,000
Taichi Teshima	71	71	68	210	1,914,000
Hyun-Woo Ryu	74	70	66	210	1,914,000
Michael Hendry	70	69	71	210	1,914,000
Daisuke Yasumoto	71	71	69	211	1,377,750
Young-Han Song	74	67	70	211	1,377,750
Masahiro Kawamura	69	70	72	211	1,377,750
K.T. Kim	70	68	73	211	1,377,750
Tetsuya Haraguchi	72	71	69	212	1,039,500
Yoshinobu Tsukada	70	70	72	212	1,039,500

	SCORES			TOTAL	MONEY
Kiyoshi Murota	70	71	71	212	1,039,500
Tetsuji Hiratsuka	70	70	72	212	1,039,500
Yusaku Miyazato	73	67	72	212	1,039,500
Yosuke Tsukada	71	72	70	213	648,750
Ju-Hyuk Park	73	69	71	213	648,750
Taichiro Kiyota	74	69	70	213	648,750
Ho-Sung Choi	68	72	73	213	648,750
Hyung-Joon Lee	68	72	73	213	648,750
Hyung-Sung Kim	73	67	73	213	648,750
Dong-Kyu Jang	72	72	69	213	648,750
Tatsunori Nukaga	73	70	70	213	648,750
Shingo Katayama	70	69	74	213	648,750
Daisuke Maruyama	74	65	74	213	648,750
Hideto Tanihara	73	71	69	213	648,750

Fujisankei Classic

Fujizakura Country Club, Fujikawaguchiko, Yamanashi
Par 35-36–71; 7,437 yards

September 5-8
purse, ¥110,000,000

	SCORES				TOTAL	MONEY
Hideki Matsuyama	66	70	66	73	275	22,000,000
Hideto Tanihara	66	70	70	69	275	9,240,000
Sung-Joon Park	72	66	68	69	275	9,240,000
(Matsuyama defeated Tanihara and Park on second playoff hole.)						
Hyung-Joon Lee	68	68	70	70	276	4,840,000
Shingo Katayama	71	66	69	70	276	4,840,000
Michio Matsumura	69	69	71	68	277	3,795,000
Kaname Yokoo	67	69	70	71	277	3,795,000
Hyung-Sung Kim	68	73	70	67	278	3,355,000
J.B. Park	69	70	71	69	279	2,882,000
K.T. Kim	72	69	68	70	279	2,882,000
Masahiro Kawamura	69	69	69	72	279	2,882,000
Yosuke Tsukada	69	73	72	66	280	2,068,000
Shigeru Nonaka	70	69	73	68	280	2,068,000
Do-Hoon Kim	74	68	70	68	280	2,068,000
Hiroshi Iwata	68	70	70	72	280	2,068,000
Kiyoshi Murota	68	73	68	71	280	2,068,000
Brendan Jones	72	68	74	67	281	1,569,333
Koumei Oda	66	71	74	70	281	1,569,333
Masamichi Uehira	74	67	67	73	281	1,569,333
Hiroyuki Fujita	71	73	70	68	282	1,210,000
Michael Hendry	70	70	72	70	282	1,210,000
David Smail	75	69	67	71	282	1,210,000
Daisuke Kataoka	71	68	70	73	282	1,210,000
Kyoung-Hoon Lee	71	70	68	73	282	1,210,000
Hiroo Kawai	70	70	73	70	283	817,666
Sung-Yoon Kim	72	70	71	70	283	817,666
Yoshinobu Tsukada	70	70	72	71	283	817,666
Sang-Hee Lee	71	69	72	71	283	817,666
Young-Han Song	72	71	69	71	283	817,666
Kazuhiro Yamashita	69	70	73	71	283	817,666
S.K. Ho	71	71	70	71	283	817,666
Yuta Ikeda	73	68	69	73	283	817,666
Masao Nakajima	70	68	69	76	283	817,666

ANA Open

Sapporo Golf Club, Wattsu Course, Kitahiroshima, Hokkaido
Par 36-36–72; 7,063 yards

September 19-22
purse, ¥110,000,000

	SCORES				TOTAL	MONEY
Koumei Oda	66	68	71	68	273	¥22,000,000
Kyoung-Hoon Lee	69	70	70	68	277	9,240,000
Shingo Katayama	65	70	73	69	277	9,240,000
Daisuke Kataoka	68	69	72	69	278	4,125,000
Taichi Teshima	69	69	71	69	278	4,125,000
Yasuharu Imano	73	69	67	69	278	4,125,000
Wen-Chong Liang	68	71	69	70	278	4,125,000
Hyung-Sung Kim	68	69	70	71	278	4,125,000
Tomohiro Kondo	67	75	68	69	279	2,992,000
Young-Han Song	71	71	66	71	279	2,992,000
Satoshi Kodaira	70	74	69	67	280	2,332,000
Toshinori Muto	70	71	69	70	280	2,332,000
Ashun Wu	69	71	69	71	280	2,332,000
Hiroyuki Fujita	67	69	70	74	280	2,332,000
Hideto Tanihara	71	70	70	70	281	1,782,000
Satoshi Tomiyama	71	70	70	70	281	1,782,000
Michio Matsumura	71	71	68	71	281	1,782,000
Masahiro Kawamura	69	70	74	69	282	1,386,000
Tetsuji Hiratsuka	72	67	73	70	282	1,386,000
K.T. Kim	73	70	69	70	282	1,386,000
David Smail	70	68	72	72	282	1,386,000
Hideki Matsuyama	70	69	71	72	282	1,386,000
Hiroo Kawai	69	73	70	71	283	1,122,000
Yusaku Miyazato	71	73	69	71	284	924,000
Azuma Yano	70	74	69	71	284	924,000
Kazuhiro Yamashita	70	74	68	72	284	924,000
Kurt Barnes	72	67	72	73	284	924,000
Ryuko Tokimatsu	70	71	70	73	284	924,000
Seung-Hyuk Kim	70	72	68	74	284	924,000

Asia-Pacific Panasonic Open

Ibaraki Country Club, West Course, Ibaraki, Osaka
Par 35-36–71; 7,328 yards

September 26-29
purse, ¥150,000,000

	SCORES				TOTAL	MONEY
Masahiro Kawamura	69	68	71	67	275	¥30,000,000
Sung-Joon Park	71	67	68	70	276	16,500,000
Y.E. Yang	71	68	69	69	277	11,550,000
Wen-Chong Liang	73	71	67	68	279	6,350,000
Brad Kennedy	72	66	71	70	279	6,350,000
Akio Sadakata	75	65	68	71	279	6,350,000
Wade Ormsby	72	67	71	71	281	4,200,000
Kazuhiro Yamashita	73	67	70	71	281	4,200,000
Kyoung-Hoon Lee	70	73	69	70	282	3,300,000
Gunn Charoenkul	72	69	74	68	283	2,737,500
Joonas Granberg	73	72	72	66	283	2,737,500
Han Lee	71	72	72	69	284	2,021,250
Prayad Marksaeng	70	73	71	70	284	2,021,250
Wei-Chih Lu	72	71	71	70	284	2,021,250
Tetsuji Hiratsuka	71	66	71	76	284	2,021,250
S.K. Ho	71	70	74	70	285	1,467,500
Masanori Kobayashi	74	67	75	69	285	1,467,500
Katsumasa Miyamoto	73	69	73	70	285	1,467,500
Rory Hie	69	69	74	73	285	1,467,500

	SCORES				TOTAL	MONEY
David Oh	75	67	69	74	285	1,467,500
Young-Han Song	69	69	71	76	285	1,467,500
Hideto Tanihara	75	68	73	70	286	1,200,000
Juvic Pagunsan	73	70	73	70	286	1,200,000
Sung-Yoon Kim	70	71	73	72	286	1,200,000
Yoshikazu Haku	72	66	73	75	286	1,200,000
Pariya Junhasavasdikul	65	70	74	77	286	1,200,000

Coca-Cola Tokai Classic

Miyoshi Country Club, West Course, Miyoshi, Aichi
Par 36-36–72; 7,315 yards

October 3-6
purse, ¥120,000,000

	SCORES				TOTAL	MONEY
Shingo Katayama	74	76	64	67	281	¥24,000,000
Hidemasa Hoshino	70	74	70	67	281	10,080,000
Satoshi Tomiyama	73	70	69	69	281	10,080,000
(Katayama defeated Hoshino and Tomiyama on first playoff hole.)						
Kunihiro Kamii	74	74	70	66	284	5,760,000
Shunsuke Sonoda	75	71	69	71	286	4,560,000
Toshinori Muto	69	72	69	76	286	4,560,000
Peter Uihlein	73	71	75	68	287	3,668,000
Masanori Kobayashi	75	70	73	69	287	3,668,000
Masamichi Uehira	75	72	67	73	287	3,668,000
Hyung-Sung Kim	75	71	72	70	288	2,904,000
Ho-Sung Choi	76	67	72	73	288	2,904,000
Tetsuji Hiratsuka	72	71	70	75	288	2,904,000
Yoshinori Fujimoto	72	75	72	70	289	2,024,000
Ashun Wu	72	69	77	71	289	2,024,000
Koumei Oda	70	73	73	73	289	2,024,000
Yoshinobu Tsukada	74	74	68	73	289	2,024,000
Tomohiro Kondo	73	70	70	76	289	2,024,000
Yusaku Miyazato	68	72	72	77	289	2,024,000
Sung-Joon Park	75	72	72	71	290	1,512,000
Kazuhiro Yamashita	72	71	74	73	290	1,512,000
Azuma Yano	74	70	71	75	290	1,512,000
Tae-Hee Lee	75	75	69	72	291	1,156,800
Hyun-Woo Ryu	75	76	67	73	291	1,156,800
David Smail	70	75	73	73	291	1,156,800
Hiroyuki Fujita	75	69	71	76	291	1,156,800
Yosuke Tsukada	70	71	73	77	291	1,156,800

Toshin Golf Tournament

Toshin Golf Club, Central Course, Gifu
Par 36-36–72; 7,008 yards

October 10-13
purse, ¥90,000,000

	SCORES				TOTAL	MONEY
Yoshinori Fujimoto	63	64	70	67	264	¥18,000,000
Koumei Oda	64	65	70	69	268	9,000,000
Ashun Wu	62	69	75	63	269	5,220,000
Yosuke Tsukada	69	65	68	67	269	5,220,000
Masahiro Kawamura	68	64	72	66	270	3,420,000
Shunsuke Sonoda	68	66	70	66	270	3,420,000
Yasuharu Imano	67	70	68	66	271	2,751,000
K.T. Kim	67	69	68	67	271	2,751,000
Yuki Kono	69	69	65	68	271	2,751,000
Yuta Ikeda	70	67	67	68	272	2,268,000

	SCORES				TOTAL	MONEY
Tetsuji Hiratsuka	71	66	66	69	272	2,268,000
I.J. Jang	70	68	71	65	274	1,586,571
Jay Choi	69	68	71	66	274	1,586,571
Shigeru Nonaka	66	67	74	67	274	1,586,571
Sang-Hee Lee	64	69	71	70	274	1,586,571
Masamichi Uehira	65	69	70	70	274	1,586,571
Michio Matsumura	65	71	67	71	274	1,586,571
Kurt Barnes	66	66	70	72	274	1,586,571
David Smail	71	64	74	66	275	967,500
Eun-Shin Park	66	73	70	66	275	967,500
Kazuhiro Yamashita	71	67	70	67	275	967,500
Young-Han Song	69	67	71	68	275	967,500
Eric Chun	67	70	69	69	275	967,500
Tomohiro Kondo	70	69	67	69	275	967,500
In-Hoi Hur	68	67	68	72	275	967,500
Akio Sadakata	65	69	68	73	275	967,500

Japan Open

Ibaraki Golf Club, East Course, Tsukubamiraishi, Ibaraki   October 17-21
Par 35-36–71; 7,320 yards   purse, ¥200,000,000
(Event completed on Monday—rain.)

	SCORES				TOTAL	MONEY
Masanori Kobayashi	69	69	69	67	274	¥40,000,000
Koumei Oda	69	68	67	73	277	22,000,000
Juvic Pagunsan	71	69	71	68	279	10,200,000
Hyung-Sung Kim	66	72	72	69	279	10,200,000
Shingo Katayama	66	71	72	70	279	10,200,000
K.T. Kim	69	69	71	70	279	10,200,000
Shunsuke Sonoda	68	70	72	70	280	5,200,000
Hidemasa Hoshino	70	69	70	71	280	5,200,000
Scott Strange	73	68	67	72	280	5,200,000
Jung-Gon Hwang	73	69	71	68	281	3,650,000
Shigeru Nonaka	69	66	75	71	281	3,650,000
Prayad Marksaeng	73	73	69	67	282	2,806,666
Shintaro Kai	66	70	75	71	282	2,806,666
Azuma Yano	70	69	71	72	282	2,806,666
Kyoung-Hoon Lee	72	70	73	68	283	2,280,000
Yusaku Miyazato	71	74	69	69	283	2,280,000
Ryutaro Nagano	70	71	71	72	284	2,050,000
Katsumasa Miyamoto	68	72	70	74	284	2,050,000
Sung-Joon Park	75	70	72	68	285	1,850,000
Do-Hoon Kim	73	69	69	74	285	1,850,000
Hiroyuki Fujita	72	74	71	69	286	1,644,000
Ho-Sung Choi	69	72	74	71	286	1,644,000
Ashun Wu	69	74	71	72	286	1,644,000
Kunihiro Kamii	73	71	70	72	286	1,644,000
Brad Kennedy	69	71	73	73	286	1,644,000

Bridgestone Open

Sodegaura Country Club, Chiba   October 24-27
Par 35-36–71; 7,119 yards   purse, ¥150,000,000
(Third round cancelled—rain.)

	SCORES			TOTAL	MONEY
Daisuke Maruyama	68	67	68	203	¥22,500,000
I.J. Jang	69	71	66	206	11,250,000

	SCORES			TOTAL	MONEY
Koumei Oda	71	69	67	207	5,400,000
Yoshinobu Tsukada	72	68	67	207	5,400,000
Tetsuji Hiratsuka	70	68	69	207	5,400,000
Kurt Barnes	72	66	69	207	5,400,000
Jay Choi	71	70	67	208	3,315,937
Sung-Joon Park	70	68	70	208	3,315,937
Sung-Yoon Kim	67	71	70	208	3,315,937
Toru Taniguchi	67	68	73	208	3,315,937
Katsumasa Miyamoto	69	71	69	209	2,295,000
Yuta Ikeda	72	68	69	209	2,295,000
David Oh	70	69	70	209	2,295,000
Ryutaro Nagano	72	68	69	209	2,295,000
Yuki Kono	71	68	70	209	2,295,000
Tomohiro Kondo	70	71	69	210	1,611,000
Masamichi Uehira	71	69	70	210	1,611,000
Keiichiro Fukabori	72	71	67	210	1,611,000
Yoshinori Fujimoto	70	69	71	210	1,611,000
Eun-Shin Park	71	64	75	210	1,611,000
Brad Kennedy	71	70	70	211	992,045
Young-Han Song	70	71	70	211	992,045
Shingo Katayama	74	66	71	211	992,045
K.T. Kim	71	71	69	211	992,045
Juvic Pagunsan	71	68	72	211	992,045
Mamo Osanai	74	69	68	211	992,045
Satoshi Tomiyama	72	67	72	211	992,045
J.B. Park	72	67	72	211	992,045
S.K. Ho	73	71	67	211	992,045
Masahiro Kawamura	74	70	67	211	992,045
Yosuke Tsukada	74	70	67	211	992,045

Mynavi ABC Championship

ABC Golf Club, Kato, Hyogo
Par 35-36–71; 7,130 yards

October 31-November 3
purse, ¥150,000,000

	SCORES				TOTAL	MONEY
Yuta Ikeda	63	69	70	67	269	¥30,000,000
S.K. Ho	67	66	68	68	269	15,000,000
(Ikeda defeated Ho on first playoff hole.)						
Yoshinori Fujimoto	69	64	69	68	270	10,200,000
Shingo Katayama	70	66	70	67	273	7,200,000
Hyung-Sung Kim	68	67	70	69	274	6,000,000
Sang-Hee Lee	71	70	67	67	275	5,175,000
Keiichiro Fukabori	64	69	71	71	275	5,175,000
Prayad Marksaeng	69	65	73	69	276	4,575,000
Hideto Tanihara	66	76	67	68	277	3,780,000
Satoshi Tomiyama	70	70	68	69	277	3,780,000
Hiroo Kawai	67	66	74	70	277	3,780,000
K.T. Kim	67	70	68	72	277	3,780,000
Kunihiro Kamii	69	69	72	68	278	2,780,000
David Smail	72	71	67	68	278	2,780,000
Tadahiro Takayama	73	69	67	69	278	2,780,000
Katsumasa Miyamoto	74	68	70	67	279	2,085,000
Kiyoshi Miyazato	75	70	67	67	279	2,085,000
Kyoung-Hoon Lee	70	70	70	69	279	2,085,000
Toru Taniguchi	71	71	69	68	279	2,085,000
Ryuko Tokimatsu	70	71	68	70	279	2,085,000
Ryutaro Nagano	69	67	70	73	279	2,085,000
Sung-Joon Park	72	71	68	69	280	1,590,000
Min-Gyu Cho	70	74	65	71	280	1,590,000

	SCORES				TOTAL	MONEY
Dong-Kyu Jang	69	73	73	66	281	1,350,000
Sushi Ishigaki	71	72	75	63	281	1,350,000
Tetsuji Hiratsuka	69	69	69	74	281	1,350,000

Heiwa PGM Championship

Miho Golf Club, Kasumigaura, Ibaraki
Par 36-35–71; 6,953 yards

November 7-10
purse, ¥200,000,000

	SCORES				TOTAL	MONEY
Ashun Wu	67	66	65	75	273	¥40,000,000
Hyung-Sung Kim	69	66	67	72	274	20,000,000
Kazuhiro Yamashita	67	70	68	72	277	10,400,000
Han Lee	67	68	70	72	277	10,400,000
Kyoung-Hoon Lee	66	68	70	73	277	10,400,000
Brad Kennedy	70	67	69	72	278	6,900,000
Koumei Oda	70	65	67	76	278	6,900,000
David Smail	67	67	74	71	279	5,252,000
Shingo Katayama	72	68	68	71	279	5,252,000
Yasuharu Imano	68	66	73	72	279	5,252,000
Yoshinori Fujimoto	69	66	70	74	279	5,252,000
Katsunori Kuwabara	67	66	71	75	279	5,252,000
Yuta Ikeda	65	70	69	76	280	3,706,666
Hideto Tanihara	70	69	66	75	280	3,706,666
Hiroyuki Fujita	68	68	68	76	280	3,706,666
Prayad Marksaeng	70	71	68	72	281	3,140,000
Yusaku Miyazato	69	66	68	78	281	3,140,000
K.T. Kim	68	68	72	74	282	2,600,000
Kurt Barnes	67	71	70	74	282	2,600,000
Ryo Ishikawa	71	68	69	74	282	2,600,000
Tetsuya Haraguchi	72	68	67	75	282	2,600,000
Toru Taniguchi	71	72	70	70	283	1,980,000
Daisuke Kataoka	72	72	68	71	283	1,980,000
Tadahiro Takayama	67	71	72	73	283	1,980,000
Yuji Igarashi	73	68	69	73	283	1,980,000

Mitsui Sumitomo Visa Taiheiyo Masters

Taiheiyo Club, Gotemba Course, Gotemba, Shizuoka
Par 36-36–72; 7,246 yards

November 14-17
purse, ¥150,000,000

	SCORES				TOTAL	MONEY
Hideto Tanihara	66	69	67	73	275	¥30,000,000
Tomohiro Kondo	66	71	70	69	276	10,800,000
Ryo Ishikawa	67	70	70	69	276	10,800,000
Masahiro Kawamura	66	70	68	72	276	10,800,000
Tetsuji Hiratsuka	72	67	69	69	277	6,000,000
Hyung-Sung Kim	71	70	70	67	278	5,175,000
Koumei Oda	66	67	73	72	278	5,175,000
Yuta Ikeda	73	66	73	67	279	4,402,500
Satoshi Tomiyama	69	69	69	72	279	4,402,500
Tadahiro Takayama	69	69	70	72	280	3,780,000
Shingo Katayama	67	68	72	73	280	3,780,000
Ho-Sung Choi	71	72	73	65	281	3,030,000
Prayad Marksaeng	70	71	69	71	281	3,030,000
Kazuhiro Yamashita	68	68	71	74	281	3,030,000
Azuma Yano	69	73	72	68	282	2,430,000

	SCORES				TOTAL	MONEY
Kyoung-Hoon Lee	72	72	68	70	282	2,430,000
Hyun-Woo Ryu	68	70	70	74	282	2,430,000
Do-Hoon Kim	72	73	69	69	283	2,010,000
Yoshikazu Haku	70	71	71	71	283	2,010,000
Kiyoshi Miyazato	70	74	73	66	283	2,010,000
I.J. Jang	68	72	75	69	284	1,461,428
Yoshinori Fujimoto	69	71	75	69	284	1,461,428
Brad Kennedy	70	68	75	71	284	1,461,428
Daisuke Maruyama	71	72	73	68	284	1,461,428
Keiichiro Fukabori	73	69	71	71	284	1,461,428
Toshinori Muto	70	72	71	71	284	1,461,428
Hiroyuki Fujita	72	72	67	73	284	1,461,428

Dunlop Phoenix

Phoenix Country Club, Miyazaki
Par 36-35–71; 7,027 yards

November 21-24
purse, ¥200,000,000

	SCORES				TOTAL	MONEY
Luke Donald	73	66	65	66	270	¥40,000,000
Hyung-Sung Kim	69	70	67	70	276	20,000,000
Shingo Katayama	69	74	69	65	277	13,600,000
Gonzalo Fernandez-Castano	73	69	71	67	280	8,800,000
Shunsuke Sonoda	70	73	68	69	280	8,800,000
Kyoung-Hoon Lee	73	70	72	66	281	6,633,333
Hideki Matsuyama	71	71	69	70	281	6,633,333
Brad Kennedy	71	72	67	71	281	6,633,333
Han Lee	75	67	68	72	282	5,640,000
Yoshinori Fujimoto	74	70	73	66	283	4,640,000
Yoshinobu Tsukada	68	71	75	69	283	4,640,000
K.T. Kim	72	71	70	70	283	4,640,000
Hiroshi Iwata	73	69	68	73	283	4,640,000
Billy Horschel	71	76	71	66	284	3,240,000
Yosuke Tsukada	71	74	74	65	284	3,240,000
Toshinori Muto	74	72	69	69	284	3,240,000
Kazuhiko Hosokawa	73	69	71	71	284	3,240,000
Koumei Oda	69	74	68	73	284	3,240,000
Yusaku Miyazato	70	72	73	70	285	2,520,000
Kunihiro Kamii	74	68	70	73	285	2,520,000
Sung-Joon Park	71	68	71	75	285	2,520,000
Kurt Barnes	74	70	72	70	286	1,928,000
Ho-Sung Choi	71	72	71	72	286	1,928,000
Kazuhiro Yamashita	67	74	73	72	286	1,928,000
Tomohiro Kondo	72	72	70	72	286	1,928,000
Keiichiro Fukabori	71	74	69	72	286	1,928,000
Yuta Ikeda	76	72	70	69	287	1,520,000
Akio Sadakata	71	72	72	72	287	1,520,000
Kiyoshi Miyazato	72	70	77	68	287	1,520,000
Ryuichi Oda	72	68	74	73	287	1,520,000

Casio World Open

Kochi Kuroshio Country Club, Geisei, Kochi
Par 36-36–72; 7,316 yards

November 28-December 1
purse, ¥200,000,000

	SCORES				TOTAL	MONEY
Hideki Matsuyama	72	66	68	70	276	¥40,000,000
Yuta Ikeda	73	67	68	69	277	20,000,000

	SCORES				TOTAL	MONEY
Koumei Oda	72	66	70	71	279	13,600,000
Sung-Joon Park	72	73	67	69	281	8,800,000
Kazuhiro Yamashita	71	71	69	70	281	8,800,000
Hideto Tanihara	76	70	68	68	282	7,200,000
Ryuji Imada	72	72	71	68	283	5,684,000
Hyung-Sung Kim	71	70	74	68	283	5,684,000
Yusaku Miyazato	74	72	69	68	283	5,684,000
Masahiro Kawamura	75	68	70	70	283	5,684,000
Ashun Wu	70	74	69	70	283	5,684,000
David Oh	70	77	69	69	285	3,760,000
Tomohiro Kondo	73	71	71	70	285	3,760,000
Satoshi Kodaira	72	71	71	71	285	3,760,000
Toshinori Muto	74	66	72	73	285	3,760,000
Ryutaro Nagano	70	73	69	73	285	3,760,000
Min-Gyu Cho	70	73	74	69	286	2,853,333
Kenichi Kuboya	72	73	70	71	286	2,853,333
Jung-Gon Hwang	72	70	72	72	286	2,853,333
Shingo Katayama	73	72	73	69	287	2,440,000
Prayad Marksaeng	73	71	71	72	287	2,440,000
Masamichi Uehira	74	72	72	70	288	1,980,000
Tadahiro Takayama	74	74	70	70	288	1,980,000
K.T. Kim	72	75	70	71	288	1,980,000
Kurt Barnes	69	76	69	74	288	1,980,000

Golf Nippon Series JT Cup

Tokyo Yomiuri Country Club, Tokyo
Par 35-35–70; 7,023 yards

December 5-8
purse, ¥130,000,000

	SCORES				TOTAL	MONEY
Yusaku Miyazato	66	66	64	71	267	¥40,000,000
Ashun Wu	67	67	68	68	270	15,000,000
Hideto Tanihara	67	68	64	72	271	10,000,000
Kazuhiro Yamashita	67	71	61	74	273	6,211,593
Kyoung-Hoon Lee	67	64	71	73	275	5,171,593
Yoshinori Fujimoto	66	73	69	68	276	4,456,593
Koumei Oda	68	70	67	71	276	4,456,593
Hiroyuki Fujita	75	67	66	69	277	3,936,593
Masanori Kobayashi	70	71	68	69	278	3,377,593
Satoshi Kodaira	69	67	70	72	278	3,377,593
Kiradech Aphibarnrat	69	68	69	72	278	3,377,593
Tomohiro Kondo	66	71	71	71	279	2,857,593
Shingo Katayama	69	65	75	72	281	2,467,593
Masahiro Kawamura	70	70	69	72	281	2,467,593
Sang-Moon Bae	73	71	68	70	282	2,012,593
Daisuke Maruyama	69	69	71	73	282	2,012,593
Hyung-Sung Kim	71	68	67	76	282	2,012,593
Prayad Marksaeng	70	69	67	76	282	2,012,593
Sung-Joon Park	73	71	70	69	283	1,661,592
Ho-Sung Choi	70	74	68	71	283	1,661,592
Michio Matsumura	73	72	68	71	284	1,349,592
Shunsuke Sonoda	69	71	71	73	284	1,349,592
Tetsuji Hiratsuka	69	74	67	74	284	1,349,592
Yuta Ikeda	70	70	69	75	284	1,349,592
Brad Kennedy	74	71	68	73	286	1,115,592
K.T. Kim	72	70	70	74	286	1,115,592

Australasian Tour

Turner Plumbing Victorian PGA Championship

Forest Resort, Creswick, Victoria
Par 36-36-72; 6,890 yards

January 17-20
purse, A$130,000

	SCORES				TOTAL	MONEY
David McKenzie	71	69	65	70	275	A$19,500
Scott Laycock	70	68	71	68	277	12,350
Stephen Dartnall	72	65	74	69	280	9,100
Matthew Griffin	73	70	66	72	281	6,500
John Wade	72	68	74	68	282	5,330
Matthew Millar	71	71	73	68	283	4,322.50
Daniel Nisbet	72	70	73	68	283	4,322.50
Michael Foster	70	70	73	71	284	3,412.50
Andre Stolz	69	71	71	73	284	3,412.50
Rohan Blizard	71	68	75	71	285	2,860
Michael Choi	71	73	69	73	286	2,340
Josh Younger	69	72	71	74	286	2,340
Anthony Summers	72	70	70	74	286	2,340
Aaron Townsend	70	74	71	72	287	1,820
Paul Gow	73	69	72	73	287	1,820
Ashley Hall	70	72	71	74	287	1,820
Gareth Paddison	77	66	74	71	288	1,560
Michael Long	71	75	67	75	288	1,560
Chris Gaunt	77	69	73	70	289	1,443
Michael Wright	70	71	75	73	289	1,443
Anthony Brown	74	70	71	74	289	1,443
*Nathan Holman	66	71	77	75	289	
Marcus Cain	72	69	78	71	290	1,339
Bradley Lamb	75	72	71	72	290	1,339
Jason Norris	73	71	73	73	290	1,339
Tom Bond	71	74	71	74	290	1,339

Lexus of Blackburn Heritage Classic

Heritage Golf & Country Club, Chirnside Park, Victoria
Par 36-36-72; 7,294 yards

January 24-27
purse, A$130,000

	SCORES				TOTAL	MONEY
David Bransdon	64	68	71	71	274	A$19,500
Max McCardle	70	68	69	67	274	12,350
*Lucas Herbert	70	69	67	68	274	
(Bransdon defeated McCardle and Herbert on first playoff hole.)					274	
Michael Hendry	67	71	64	73	275	9,100
Matt Giles	73	67	68	70	278	6,500
*Nathan Holman	69	73	66	70	278	
Matthew Millar	73	66	71	70	280	4,403.75
Paul Spargo	71	69	70	70	280	4,403.75
Gareth Paddison	69	67	72	72	280	4,403.75
Kurt Barnes	69	74	65	72	280	4,403.75
Jason Norris	69	73	70	69	281	2,881.66
Daniel Nisbet	70	73	68	70	281	2,881.66
Steven Jeffress	70	71	68	72	281	2,881.66

	SCORES				TOTAL	MONEY
Scott Laycock	73	70	69	70	282	2,047.50
Jason Scrivener	75	67	72	68	282	2,047.50
Rohan Blizard	69	73	69	71	282	2,047.50
Sven Puymbroeck	73	68	66	75	282	2,047.50
Hao-Tong Li	75	68	71	69	283	1,547
Anthony Summers	72	69	69	73	283	1,547
Josh Geary	69	70	70	74	283	1,547
Bradley Hughes	67	68	73	75	283	1,547
Ryan Lynch	67	72	69	75	283	1,547
Peter O'Malley	71	68	74	71	284	1,339
Clint Rice	69	73	70	72	284	1,339
Leigh Deagan	69	67	75	73	284	1,339
Brent McCullough	68	72	74	70	284	1,339
Ryan Haller	72	71	66	75	284	1,339
Gavin Fairfax	72	70	75	67	284	1,339

Coca-Cola Queensland PGA Championship

City Golf Club, Toowoomba, Queensland
Par 33-35-68; 6,348 yards

February 14-17
purse, A$115,000

	SCORES				TOTAL	MONEY
Brad Kennedy	64	62	65	63	254	A$17,250
Michael Hendry	62	66	62	66	256	10,925
Anthony Summers	67	64	62	65	258	8,050
*Cameron Smith	66	60	68	65	259	
Ryan McCarthy	62	66	68	64	260	4,528.12
Gareth Paddison	65	64	66	65	260	4,528.12
Scott Laycock	65	65	65	65	260	4,528.12
Rohan Blizard	64	64	64	68	260	4,528.12
David Bransdon	64	63	68	66	261	2,855.83
Anthony Brown	66	64	65	66	261	2,855.83
Tom Bond	65	67	62	67	261	2,855.83
Brent McCullough	65	65	67	65	262	2,300
Adam Bland	65	68	61	69	263	1,878.33
Matt Giles	64	63	66	70	263	1,878.33
David McKendrick	68	61	62	72	263	1,878.33
Steven Jeffress	71	63	66	64	264	1,502.66
Daniel Fox	67	64	64	69	264	1,502.66
Ryan Haywood	65	69	67	63	264	1,502.66
Nick Cullen	65	69	65	66	265	1,281.10
Pieter Zwart	67	66	63	69	265	1,281.10
Brad Shilton	62	67	66	70	265	1,281.10
Andrew Martin	66	67	68	64	265	1,281.10
Kevin Conlong	67	64	71	63	265	1,281.10
Matt Jager	66	66	67	67	266	1,161.50
Terry Pilkadaris	67	63	68	68	266	1,161.50
Josh Younger	69	62	68	67	266	1,161.50
*Kevin Marques	62	64	71	69	266	
*Taylor MacDonald	68	65	66	67	266	
Matthew Millar	64	69	68	65	266	1,161.50

Victorian Open

13th Beach Golf Links, Barwon Heads, Victoria
Par 36-36–72

February 21-24
purse, A$150,000

	SCORES				TOTAL	MONEY
Matthew Giles	69	71	68	67	275	A$22,500
Ryan Lynch	70	70	68	68	276	14,250
*Nathan Holman	71	69	66	70	276	
Stephen Dartnall	71	68	72	66	277	9,000
Neven Basic	73	71	67	66	277	9,000
Aaron Townsend	71	72	69	66	278	5,081.25
Leigh McKechnie	71	70	67	70	278	5,081.25
Steven Jones	67	72	68	71	278	5,081.25
Bradley Hughes	73	67	67	71	278	5,081.25
Terry Pilkadaris	70	72	70	67	279	3,168.75
Peter O'Malley	72	71	69	67	279	3,168.75
Kurt Carlson	73	72	68	66	279	3,168.75
Craig Parry	70	70	68	71	279	3,168.75
Richard Green	69	74	73	64	280	2,001.42
Matthew Griffin	71	69	75	65	280	2,001.42
Anthony Brown	69	72	71	68	280	2,001.42
Marcus Cain	71	70	69	70	280	2,001.42
David Bransdon	73	69	68	70	280	2,001.42
Michael Wright	74	69	66	71	280	2,001.42
Michael Long	77	67	70	66	280	2,001.42
Tarquin MacManus	72	71	72	66	281	1,642.50
Peter Wilson	73	72	69	67	281	1,642.50
*Cameron Smith	73	67	69	72	281	
Jin Jeong	73	71	71	67	282	1,560
*Brett Drewitt	74	71	70	67	282	
David McKendrick	71	71	71	69	282	1,560
Nick Cullen	74	71	69	68	282	1,560

New Zealand PGA Championship

The Hills Golf Course, Queenstown, New Zealand
Par 36-36–72

February 28-March 3
purse, NZ$550,000

	SCORES				TOTAL	MONEY
Michael Hendry	67	67	68	67	269	A$79,789.68
Scott Strange	69	65	69	66	269	45,214.15
(Hendry defeated Strange on first playoff hole.)						
Josh Geary	69	68	70	66	273	25,599.19
Gareth Paddison	69	66	70	68	273	25,599.19
Michael Tran	70	68	68	68	274	15,957.93
Hao-Tong Li	74	65	66	69	274	15,957.93
Rohan Blizard	67	68	66	73	274	15,957.93
Steven Alker	71	69	70	66	276	10,416.98
Matthew Stieger	72	69	68	67	276	10,416.98
Jared Pender	70	69	68	69	276	10,416.98
Daniel Nisbet	73	67	66	70	276	10,416.98
Toshinori Muto	68	69	69	70	276	10,416.98
Leigh Deagan	67	69	68	72	276	10,416.98
Steven Jeffress	68	70	69	70	277	6,693.46
Peter Cooke	70	69	68	70	277	6,693.46
Jake Higginbottom	69	69	68	71	277	6,693.46
Greg Turner	71	68	67	71	277	6,693.46
Michael Long	68	67	72	71	278	5,031.18
David Bransdon	70	73	64	71	278	5,031.18

	SCORES				TOTAL	MONEY
Aaron Townsend	66	68	72	72	278	5,031.18
Mark Brown	72	67	72	68	279	4,454.92
Hong Soon Sang	70	68	73	68	279	4,454.92
Richard Lee	72	68	70	69	279	4,454.92
Craig Palmer	71	69	68	71	279	4,454.92
Kurt Carlson	73	69	71	67	280	3,989.48

Isuzu Queensland Open

Brookwater Golf & Country Club, Ipswich, Queensland
Par 36-36-72; 7,114 yards

August 22-25
purse, A$110,000

	SCORES				TOTAL	MONEY
Nick Cullen	73	72	65	69	279	A$16,500
Peter O'Malley	71	71	69	73	284	10,450
David McKenzie	75	71	72	68	286	7,700
Jake Higginbottom	76	68	74	69	287	5,500
Scott Laycock	71	76	72	69	288	3,923.33
Jason Scrivener	71	73	73	71	288	3,923.33
Ryan Fox	69	74	69	76	288	3,923.33
David Bransdon	75	72	71	71	289	2,887.50
Josh Younger	67	75	75	72	289	2,887.50
Christopher Campbell	71	73	74	72	290	2,200
Marcus Cain	70	72	75	73	290	2,200
Ryan Lynch	71	73	72	74	290	2,200
Jun Seok Lee	72	70	77	72	291	1,650
Adam Bland	74	73	70	74	291	1,650
Cameron Smith	72	72	72	75	291	1,650
Jamie Arnold	77	72	74	69	292	1,356.67
Andre Stolz	73	72	70	77	292	1,356.67
Clint Rice	71	73	70	78	292	1,356.67
Chris Gaunt	74	75	73	71	293	1,207.25
Leigh McKechnie	73	76	74	70	293	1,207.25
*Ryan Ruffels	72	76	73	72	293	
Rika Batibasaga	73	72	74	74	293	1,207.25
Jason Norris	76	74	75	68	293	1,207.25
Leigh Deagan	73	73	76	72	294	1,122
Anthony Brown	76	73	72	73	294	1,122
*Cameron Davis	70	78	76	70	294	
Adam Groom	72	74	72	76	294	1,122

South Pacific Open Championship

Tina Golf Club, Noumea, New Caledonia
Par 36-35-71; 6,442 yards

September 18-21
purse, A$130,000

	SCORES				TOTAL	MONEY
Andre Stolz	67	66	69	66	268	A$19,500
Michael Wright	62	70	67	69	268	12,350
(Stolz defeated Wright on fifth playoff hole.)						
Matthew Griffin	67	65	69	69	270	9,100
Christopher Campbell	68	67	70	66	271	6,500
Clint Rice	70	71	63	68	272	4,940
Brett Rankin	69	65	69	69	272	4,940
Rohan Blizard	68	67	68	71	274	3,835
Theodore Coroneo	62	68	72	72	274	3,835
Nick Cullen	70	69	70	66	275	3,185

	SCORES				TOTAL	MONEY
Jason Scrivener	70	68	72	66	276	2,600
Andrew Martin	68	69	70	69	276	2,600
Adam Bland	71	67	69	69	276	2,600
Kalem Richardson	69	72	68	68	277	1,950
Paul Spargo	70	64	74	69	277	1,950
Nick Gillespie	67	73	67	70	277	1,950
Christopher Wood	71	68	70	69	278	1,638
Scott Laycock	65	71	70	72	278	1,638
*Taylor MacDonald	73	72	68	66	279	
Neven Basic	74	70	68	67	279	1,486.33
Josh Younger	69	70	69	71	279	1,486.33
Daniel Nisbet	68	67	65	79	279	1,486.33
Kevin Conlong	72	70	72	67	281	1,313
Ian Esson	71	68	73	69	281	1,313
Marcus Cain	67	73	71	70	281	1,313
Edward Stedman	72	69	70	70	281	1,313
Ryan Fox	71	74	66	70	281	1,313
Matthew Guyatt	74	67	69	71	281	1,313
Matt Jager	69	70	70	72	281	1,313
Kurt Carlson	68	71	68	74	281	1,313

Western Australia Goldfields PGA Championship

Kalgoorlie Golf Course, Kalgoorlie, Western Australia   October 3-6
Par 36-36–72; 7,399 yards   purse, A$110,000

	SCORES				TOTAL	MONEY
Jack Wilson	67	68	71	72	278	A$16,500
Nick Gillespie	69	67	73	69	278	10,450
(Wilson defeated Gillespie on first playoff hole.)						
Adam Bland	68	69	72	70	279	6,600
James Nitties	73	68	68	70	279	6,600
Jordan Sherratt	73	69	70	69	281	4,510
Scott Laycock	71	71	73	67	282	3,630
Max McCardle	71	70	69	72	282	3,630
Tarquin MacManus	70	70	69	74	283	3,080
Aaron Pike	70	73	67	74	284	2,695
Andrew Kelly	74	71	69	72	286	2,200
Brett Drewitt	70	73	71	72	286	2,200
Leigh McKechnie	68	72	73	73	286	2,200
Ryan Lynch	70	72	76	69	287	1,595
Kieran Muir	71	73	73	70	287	1,595
Lincoln Tighe	68	72	75	72	287	1,595
Matthew Ballard	73	68	74	72	287	1,595
Rohan Blizard	70	71	78	69	288	1,342
Chris Gaunt	68	74	75	72	289	1,276
Steven Jeffress	72	71	70	76	289	1,276
Paul Fenton	68	75	74	73	290	1,145.57
Timothy Wood	71	75	71	73	290	1,145.57
Ben Pisani	70	72	73	75	290	1,145.57
Nathan Holman	70	73	72	75	290	1,145.57
Mahal Pearce	72	73	70	75	290	1,145.57
Terry Pilkadaris	72	74	74	70	290	1,145.57
Josh Geary	72	72	70	76	290	1,145.57

John Hughes/Nexus Risk Services WA Open

Mt. Lawley Golf Course, Perth, Western Australia
Par 36-36–72; 6,818 yards

October 10-13
purse, A$110,000

	SCORES				TOTAL	MONEY
Josh Geary	73	68	67	65	273	A$16,500
Kristopher Mueck	65	73	69	71	278	10,450
Nathan Holman	69	72	70	68	279	7,700
Kim Felton	69	77	66	68	280	4,620
Peter O'Malley	67	75	70	68	280	4,620
Steven Jones	68	69	74	69	280	4,620
Adam Bland	67	74	75	65	281	3,061.67
Brett Drewitt	71	69	72	69	281	3,061.67
David Bransdon	69	69	72	71	281	3,061.67
Troy Cox	66	74	72	70	282	2,420
Nick O'Hern	68	74	72	69	283	1,980
Grant Thomas	67	77	69	70	283	1,980
Matthew Guyatt	72	68	70	73	283	1,980
Matthew Millar	72	74	68	70	284	1,419
Chris Gaunt	72	68	73	71	284	1,419
Rory Bourke	73	71	69	71	284	1,419
Michael Hansen	71	68	73	72	284	1,419
Marcus Cain	68	72	72	72	284	1,419
Lincoln Tighe	74	69	67	74	284	1,419
Theodore Coroneo	71	75	71	68	285	1,191.67
Clint Rice	69	75	72	69	285	1,191.67
John Wade	71	73	72	69	285	1,191.67
Sven Puymbroeck	74	71	71	70	286	1,089
Ashley Hall	71	74	72	69	286	1,089
Peter Lonard	72	73	71	70	286	1,089
Matt Jager	66	78	68	74	286	1,089
Jason Scrivener	69	73	69	75	286	1,089
Kieran Muir	74	70	66	76	286	1,089

ISPS Handa Perth International

Lake Karrinyup Country Club, Perth, Western Australia
Par 36-36–72; 7,143 yards

October 17-20
purse, US$2,000,000

	SCORES				TOTAL	MONEY
Jin Jeong	68	72	69	69	278	A$329,927.07
Ross Fisher	72	67	71	68	278	219,952.07
(Jeong defeated Fisher on first playoff hole.)						
Dimitrios Papadatos	69	71	72	68	280	102,278.25
Danny Willett	72	71	68	69	280	102,278.25
Brody Ninyette	72	69	67	72	280	102,278.25
Brett Rumford	71	73	65	72	281	69,285.27
Joel Sjoholm	71	73	67	71	282	51,073.14
Richard Finch	72	69	69	72	282	51,073.14
J.B. Hansen	70	73	66	73	282	51,073.14
Peter Hedblom	68	69	75	71	283	38,007.92
Fredrik Andersson Hed	69	73	68	73	283	38,007.92
Espen Kofstad	71	73	72	68	284	29,990.62
Ryan Haller	72	70	74	68	284	29,990.62
Josh Younger	70	70	73	71	284	29,990.62
Dustin Johnson	69	74	75	66	284	29,990.62
Soren Hansen	71	69	72	72	284	29,990.62
James Nitties	68	73	69	74	284	29,990.62
Daniel Popovic	72	74	69	70	285	22,210.88

	SCORES				TOTAL	MONEY
Peter Lawrie	73	70	72	70	285	22,210.88
Fabrizio Zanotti	75	68	72	70	285	22,210.88
David McKenzie	75	68	71	71	285	22,210.88
Gareth Paddison	74	69	71	71	285	22,210.88
Marcus Fraser	72	70	71	72	285	22,210.88
Justin Walters	76	69	73	67	285	22,210.88
Oliver Fisher	72	72	69	72	285	22,210.88
Bo Van Pelt	70	71	71	73	285	22,210.88
Michael Hoey	73	69	69	74	285	22,210.88
Craig Lee	73	71	72	70	286	17,321.32
Wade Ormsby	73	72	71	70	286	17,321.32
Alexandre Kaleka	74	69	72	71	286	17,321.32
Nick O'Hern	69	73	72	72	286	17,321.32
Nick Cullen	69	73	71	73	286	17,321.32
Jason Scrivener	75	67	68	76	286	17,321.32
Rohan Blizard	70	74	72	71	287	15,044.80
Adam Bland	72	72	73	70	287	15,044.80
Mark Brown	70	72	74	72	288	13,263.18
Scott Henry	74	72	70	72	288	13,263.18
Christopher Campbell	71	71	73	73	288	13,263.18
Chris Doak	72	73	72	71	288	13,263.18
Richard Bland	75	71	72	70	288	13,263.18
Gregory Havret	73	73	73	69	288	13,263.18
Richard McEvoy	76	70	73	69	288	13,263.18
Paul Spargo	72	71	73	73	289	10,491.77
Branden Grace	73	73	69	74	289	10,491.77
Soren Kjeldsen	76	68	73	72	289	10,491.77
Troy Cox	75	70	72	72	289	10,491.77
Steven Jones	74	72	71	72	289	10,491.77
Tom Bond	71	73	74	71	289	10,491.77
James Morrison	73	72	73	71	289	10,491.77
Stephen Dartnall	74	71	72	73	290	8,908.11
Mikko Korhonen	73	71	72	75	291	7,720.36
James McLean	76	68	73	74	291	7,720.36
David Bransdon	71	73	74	73	291	7,720.36
John Wade	76	70	74	71	291	7,720.36
Mark Tullo	75	71	75	70	291	7,720.36
Clint Rice	68	72	75	77	292	5,872.75
Sam Little	69	75	71	77	292	5,872.75
David Higgins	73	72	74	73	292	5,872.75
Craig Parry	72	74	74	72	292	5,872.75
Anthony Brown	70	75	76	71	292	5,872.75
David Drysdale	72	74	75	71	292	5,872.75
Ross McGowan	71	72	74	76	293	5,047.93
Bjorn Akesson	69	77	77	70	293	5,047.93
Steven Jeffress	76	70	74	74	294	4,750.99
Peter Wilson	72	71	73	79	295	4,454.05
Simon Wakefield	72	74	68	81	295	4,454.05
Leigh McKechnie	74	72	72	78	296	4,058.14
Peter Cooke	72	73	74	77	296	4,058.14
Neven Basic	72	74	78	78	302	3,761.20

Australian PGA Championship

RACV Royal Pines Resort, Gold Coast, Queensland
Par 35-36-71; 6,747 yards

November 7-10
purse, A$1,250,000

	SCORES				TOTAL	MONEY
Adam Scott	65	67	71	67	270	A$225,000
Rickie Fowler	63	72	71	68	274	127,500
Jack Wilson	68	71	69	68	276	84,375
Cameron Percy	69	73	67	68	277	60,000
Michael Wright	69	70	68	71	278	50,000
Jason Norris	67	74	71	67	279	37,250
Ji-Man Kang	72	68	70	69	279	37,250
Gareth Paddison	68	67	73	71	279	37,250
Nathan Green	66	69	73	71	279	37,250
Ashley Hall	68	69	71	71	279	37,250
Stephen Leaney	68	73	69	70	280	25,000
Marc Leishman	69	71	68	72	280	25,000
David McKenzie	65	69	72	74	280	25,000
Jason Scrivener	70	67	76	68	281	16,382.81
David Klein	72	69	72	68	281	16,382.81
Mathew Goggin	73	70	69	69	281	16,382.81
Scott Hend	72	68	71	70	281	16,382.81
Peter Cooke	70	74	67	70	281	16,382.81
Nathan Holman	69	71	70	71	281	16,382.81
Nick Flanagan	75	68	67	71	281	16,382.81
Steven Jeffress	68	68	71	74	281	16,382.81
James McLean	70	73	72	67	282	11,479.17
Scott Strange	75	69	70	68	282	11,479.17
Adam Bland	69	70	73	70	282	11,479.17
Aron Price	72	71	69	70	282	11,479.17
Matthew Griffin	69	69	73	71	282	11,479.17
Nick Cullen	71	72	68	71	282	11,479.17

Talisker Masters

Royal Melbourne Golf Club, Melbourne, Victoria
Par 35-36–71; 7,046 yards

November 14-17
purse, A$1,000,000

	SCORES				TOTAL	MONEY
Adam Scott	67	66	66	71	270	A$186,120
Matt Kuchar	71	66	67	68	272	105,468
Vijay Singh	72	68	63	71	274	69,795
Nick Cullen	65	69	69	72	275	49,632
Ryan Fox	68	71	66	73	278	39,292
Matthew Griffin	69	65	69	75	278	39,292
Marc Leishman	71	71	72	65	279	26,711.67
Aron Price	73	71	67	68	279	26,711.67
Jason Scrivener	69	71	70	69	279	26,711.67
Geoff Ogilvy	71	72	67	69	279	26,711.67
Mathew Goggin	72	71	67	69	279	26,711.67
Brendon de Jonge	68	70	68	73	279	26,711.67
Matthew Millar	69	70	71	70	280	18,095
Gaganjeet Bhullar	69	72	69	70	280	18,095
Nathan Holman	68	65	70	78	281	16,544
Gareth Paddison	74	69	72	67	282	13,093.03
Peter Senior	74	68	71	69	282	13,093.03
Michael Hendry	72	69	71	70	282	13,093.03
Maximilian Kieffer	67	72	72	71	282	13,093.03
Peter Fowler	73	71	71	68	283	10,960.40

	SCORES				TOTAL	MONEY
Scott Strange	73	71	68	71	283	10,960.40
Anthony Brown	68	73	75	68	284	9,232.14
Jin Jeong	73	70	71	70	284	9,232.14
Peter O'Malley	68	71	74	71	284	9,232.14
Michael Long	75	69	69	71	284	9,232.14
Mark Brown	71	70	71	72	284	9,232.14
Stephen Leaney	68	74	70	72	284	9,232.14
Jason Norris	69	69	73	73	284	9,232.14

ISPS Handa World Cup of Golf

Royal Melbourne Golf Club, Melbourne, Victoria
Par 35-36–71; 6,985 yards

November 21-24
purse, US$8,000,000

	SCORES				TOTAL	MONEY
Jason Day	68	70	66	70	274	$1,200,000
Thomas Bjorn	66	68	71	71	276	760,000
Adam Scott	75	68	68	66	277	490,000
Matt Kuchar	71	68	68	71	278	340,000
Ryo Ishikawa	71	71	70	69	281	270,000
Kiradech Aphibarnrat	71	70	70	70	281	270,000
Hideto Tanihara	72	67	71	72	282	240,000
David Hearn	70	71	71	71	283	197,500
Stuart Manley	67	72	72	72	283	197,500
Kevin Streelman	66	69	74	74	283	197,500
Francesco Molinari	75	67	66	75	283	197,500
Brendon de Jonge	74	72	70	68	284	145,000
Maximilian Kieffer	73	71	70	70	284	145,000
Bernd Wiesberger	71	72	69	72	284	145,000
Roope Kakko	72	72	70	71	285	100,000
Gregory Bourdy	72	69	72	72	285	100,000
K.J. Choi	67	74	71	73	285	100,000
Ricardo Santos	69	69	73	74	285	100,000
Graeme McDowell	72	71	67	75	285	100,000
George Coetzee	74	71	73	68	286	68,000
Branden Grace	73	70	72	71	286	68,000
Martin Laird	67	72	74	73	286	68,000
Miguel Angel Jimenez	73	69	71	73	286	68,000
Oscar Fraustro	74	67	71	74	286	68,000
Thorbjorn Olesen	71	72	76	68	287	56,000
Vijay Singh	73	69	75	70	287	56,000
Nicolas Colsaerts	70	76	70	71	287	56,000
Anirban Lahiri	72	70	73	72	287	56,000
Brad Fritsch	71	73	70	73	287	56,000
Jonas Blixt	76	72	74	66	288	49,500
Victor Dubuisson	73	71	73	71	288	49,500
Fabian Gomez	72	75	72	70	289	45,500
Chris Wood	75	70	72	72	289	45,500
Mark Tullo	74	72	71	72	289	45,500
Peter Hanson	72	71	73	73	289	45,500
Marcel Siem	71	74	69	75	289	45,500
Danny Willett	69	73	71	76	289	45,500
Ashun Wu	77	69	75	69	290	40,500
Michael Hendry	75	73	71	71	290	40,500
Robert-Jan Derksen	74	75	70	71	290	40,500
Stephen Gallacher	74	71	72	73	290	40,500
Tim Sluiter	76	72	69	74	291	37,500
Adilson Da Silva	72	71	71	77	291	37,500
Shane Lowry	75	72	71	74	292	35,500
Alexandre Rocha	72	72	70	78	292	35,500

	SCORES				TOTAL	MONEY
Emilliano Grillo	77	71	74	71	293	32,500
Tim Wilkinson	79	71	70	73	293	32,500
Mikko Korhonen	70	75	74	74	293	32,500
Angelo Que	74	72	70	77	293	32,500
Antonio Lascuna	70	71	77	76	294	29,500
Prayad Marksaeng	72	72	73	77	294	29,500
Sang-Moon Bae	74	74	73	74	295	28,000
Rafa Cabrera-Bello	75	75	70	76	296	27,000
Jose-Filipe Lima	71	73	73	80	297	26,000
Siddikur	73	75	77	73	298	24,500
Wen-Chong Liang	75	76	73	74	298	24,500
Felipe Aguilar	75	72	74	78	299	23,000
Matteo Manassero	76	74	76	74	300	22,000
Espen Kofstad	72	75	74	82	303	21,000
Gaganjeet Bhullar	82	77	76	71	306	20,000

Gloria Jean's NSW Open

Castle Hill Country Club, Sydney, New South Wales
Par 36-36–72; 6,767 yards

November 21-24
purse, A$110,000

	SCORES				TOTAL	MONEY
Aron Price	66	66	67	70	269	A$16,500
Adam Bland	72	67	67	67	273	7,883.33
Aaron Townsend	68	65	72	68	273	7,883.33
Jack Wilson	71	67	67	68	273	7,883.33
Jun Seok Lee	67	76	63	68	274	4,180
Bryden Macpherson	70	68	68	68	274	4,180
Ryan Fox	67	72	68	68	275	3,061.67
Ashley Hall	67	68	70	70	275	3,061.67
*Callan O'Reilly	70	70	65	70	275	
Steven Bowditch	70	65	64	76	275	3,061.67
Nick Gillespie	74	67	70	65	276	2,310
Bradley Hughes	68	70	71	67	276	2,310
Stephen Dartnall	70	70	71	66	277	1,796.67
Hamish Robertson	71	70	69	67	277	1,796.67
Edward Stedman	68	71	67	71	277	1,796.67
Matthew Millar	72	68	68	70	278	1,485
*Ben Eccles	69	74	73	62	278	
Jason Scrivener	72	68	66	72	278	1,485
Max McCardle	69	73	69	68	279	1,278.75
Pieter Zwart	68	74	69	68	279	1,278.75
Mark Brown	72	68	70	69	279	1,278.75
Scott Laycock	70	70	69	70	279	1,278.75
*Cameron Davis	72	68	67	72	279	
Josh Geary	69	73	68	70	280	1,155
Paul Spargo	72	63	72	73	280	1,155
Nathan Holman	70	69	68	73	280	1,155
Brett Rankin	69	67	70	74	280	1,155

Emirates Australian Open

Royal Sydney Golf Club, Sydney, New South Wales
Par 36-36–72; 6,939 yards

November 28-December 1
purse, A$1,250,000

	SCORES				TOTAL	MONEY
Rory McIlroy	69	65	70	66	270	A$225,000
Adam Scott	62	70	68	71	271	127,500
John Senden	73	68	70	66	277	84,375
Bryden Macpherson	71	70	69	69	279	55,000
Rhein Gibson	71	70	69	69	279	55,000
Mark Brown	75	70	66	69	280	40,416.67
Jason Day	70	74	66	70	280	40,416.67
Matthew Jones	68	68	72	72	280	40,416.67
Nathan Holman	69	72	68	72	281	33,750
Adam Bland	69	72	70	71	282	26,562.50
Ashley Hall	71	71	68	72	282	26,562.50
Leigh McKechnie	73	65	71	73	282	26,562.50
Max McCardle	68	71	69	74	282	26,562.50
James Nitties	70	71	74	68	283	18,100
Alistair Presnell	67	71	74	71	283	18,100
David McKenzie	66	75	71	71	283	18,100
Nick O'Hern	70	72	70	71	283	18,100
*Brady Watt	68	70	73	72	283	
Stuart Appleby	75	67	67	74	283	18,100
Jamie Arnold	72	68	74	70	284	13,328.13
Mahal Pearce	72	71	71	70	284	13,328.13
Rod Pampling	75	68	69	72	284	13,328.13
Richard Green	69	66	73	76	284	13,328.13
Adam Crawford	71	73	72	69	285	12,250
Matthew Griffin	73	72	70	70	285	12,250
*Ryan Ruffels	77	67	68	73	285	

African Tours

Telkom PGA Pro-Am

Century Country Club, Tshwane, South Africa
Par 36-36–72; 7,328 yards

January 23-25
purse, R600,000

	SCORES			TOTAL	MONEY
Oliver Bekker	66	64	66	196	R95,100
Ryan Strauss	68	66	64	198	58,500
P.H. McIntyre	66	64	68	198	58,500
M.J. Daffue	70	67	65	202	29,600
Shaun Norris	68	67	67	202	29,600
Matthew Carvell	64	69	69	202	29,600
Ryan Tipping	67	72	64	203	18,900
Tyrone Ferreira	69	67	68	204	14,900
Desvonde Botes	70	62	72	204	14,900
Steven Ferreira	65	67	72	204	14,900
Ulrich van den Berg	72	67	66	205	11,140
Toto Thimba	69	69	67	205	11,140
Jean Hugo	69	68	68	205	11,140
Teboho Sefatsa	71	66	68	205	11,140
Martin du Toit	71	66	68	205	11,140
Ross McGowan	64	70	71	205	11,140
Johan Bekker	66	73	67	206	9,000
Louis de Jager	68	70	68	206	9,000
James Kingston	68	68	70	206	9,000
Theunis Spangenberg	71	69	67	207	8,040
Jared Harvey	68	69	70	207	8,040
Tjaart van der Walt	69	67	71	207	8,040
Ryan Cairns	71	68	69	208	7,160
Dawie Van der Walt	66	72	70	208	7,160
J.J. Senekal	67	71	70	208	7,160

Joburg Open

Royal Johannesburg & Kensington Golf Club,
Johannesburg, South Africa
Par 37-35–72; 7,650 yards

February 7-10
purse, €1,300,000

	SCORES				TOTAL	MONEY
Richard Sterne	63	65	68	64	260	R2,493,205
Charl Schwartzel	68	65	68	66	267	1,808,950
Ricardo Santos	70	65	69	64	268	836,836
George Coetzee	67	64	70	67	268	836,836
Felipe Aguilar	67	66	68	67	268	836,836
Keith Horne	67	66	71	65	269	469,278.33
Thomas Aiken	67	70	66	66	269	469,278.33
Trevor Fisher, Jr.	66	62	68	73	269	469,278.33
Lorenzo Gagli	67	68	68	67	270	324,038
Garth Mulroy	70	68	65	67	270	324,038
Brandon Pieters	69	69	67	66	271	263,739.66
David Drysdale	68	67	68	68	271	263,739.66
Jaco Van Zyl	66	68	67	70	271	263,739.66
Bryce Easton	65	70	70	67	272	227,298.50
Tommy Fleetwood	68	66	69	69	272	227,298.50

	SCORES				TOTAL	MONEY
James Kingston	66	70	70	67	273	207,636
Justin Walters	71	67	67	68	273	207,636
Paul Waring	71	67	67	68	273	207,636
Tyrone Ferreira	66	70	71	67	274	177,749
Ricardo Gonzalez	70	66	70	68	274	177,749
Hennie Otto	70	67	69	68	274	177,749
Lee Slattery	67	72	67	68	274	177,749
Danie van Tonder	68	70	67	69	274	177,749
Peter Uihlein	65	69	68	72	274	177,749
Tyrone Mordt	65	70	71	69	275	153,367.50
Darren Fichardt	67	69	70	69	275	153,367.50
Adilson Da Silva	66	72	70	67	275	153,367.50
Robert-Jan Derksen	69	70	67	69	275	153,367.50
Steve Webster	71	67	69	69	276	134,019.60
Maximilian Kieffer	63	72	72	69	276	134,019.60
George Murray	71	66	69	70	276	134,019.60
Jacques Blaauw	70	67	71	68	276	134,019.60
James Kamte	70	67	68	71	276	134,019.60
Allan Versfeld	66	73	69	69	277	119,548
Jake Redman	66	71	72	68	277	119,548
Bjorn Akesson	69	67	73	68	277	119,548
Dean Burmester	67	68	69	73	277	119,548
Richard Finch	67	68	71	72	278	99,099
Jose Manuel Lara	69	65	73	71	278	99,099
Oliver Fisher	68	68	70	72	278	99,099
Jaco Ahlers	71	68	69	70	278	99,099
Justin Harding	69	70	70	69	278	99,099
Tjaart van der Walt	67	69	69	73	278	99,099
Tom Lewis	72	65	67	74	278	99,099
David Horsey	66	72	72	68	278	99,099
Lasse Jensen	68	70	73	67	278	99,099
M.J. Daffue	65	70	71	73	279	80,223
P.H. McIntyre	72	67	72	68	279	80,223
Jbe' Kruger	68	70	74	67	279	80,223
Phillip Price	68	71	69	72	280	67,639
Espen Kofstad	66	71	72	71	280	67,639
Alexandre Kaleka	66	73	71	70	280	67,639
Scott Henry	69	70	71	70	280	67,639
Merrick Bremner	68	69	73	70	280	67,639
Ulrich van den Berg	71	68	68	74	281	52,852.80
Gary Boyd	67	71	69	74	281	52,852.80
Ryan Cairns	67	70	70	74	281	52,852.80
Joakim Lagergren	65	71	73	72	281	52,852.80
Peter Hedblom	72	67	72	70	281	52,852.80
Bradford Vaughan	69	70	71	72	282	45,617
Andy Sullivan	68	70	72	72	282	45,617
Graeme Storm	76	62	73	71	282	45,617
Ockie Strydom	66	71	73	73	283	41,684.50
Gregory Havret	70	69	74	70	283	41,684.50
Alessandro Tadini	67	71	69	77	284	37,752
Oliver Bekker	68	68	73	75	284	37,752
Gary Lockerbie	70	69	75	70	284	37,752
Michael Hollick	70	69	71	78	288	34,606
Joshua Cunliffe	67	70	82	71	290	33,033

Africa Open

East London Golf Club, East London,
Eastern Cape, South Africa
Par 37-36–73; 6,632 yards

February 14-17
purse, €1,000,000

	SCORES				TOTAL	MONEY
Darren Fichardt	69	67	65	71	272	R1,886,150
Gregory Bourdy	70	67	67	70	274	1,095,990
Jaco Van Zyl	66	67	68	73	274	1,095,990
Garth Mulroy	72	67	69	67	275	584,290
Andy Sullivan	70	70	69	68	277	389,130
Desvonde Botes	74	67	66	70	277	389,130
Mark Tullo	69	69	68	71	277	389,130
Tjaart van der Walt	70	68	68	71	277	389,130
Andrew Curlewis	69	73	69	67	278	234,430
Ricardo Santos	71	66	70	71	278	234,430
Emiliano Grillo	70	71	64	73	278	234,430
Thomas Aiken	74	70	66	69	279	186,830
Brett Rumford	71	70	68	70	279	186,830
Adilson Da Silva	62	68	73	76	279	186,830
Seve Benson	71	71	68	70	280	166,005
James Kingston	69	71	69	71	280	166,005
Lorenzo Gagli	73	69	66	73	281	151,130
John Parry	68	66	73	74	281	151,130
David Higgins	70	68	69	74	281	151,130
Morten Orum Madsen	71	69	67	75	282	138,040
Jorge Campillo	73	70	63	76	282	138,040
Lyle Rowe	74	67	71	71	283	124,950
Chris Paisley	73	70	69	71	283	124,950
Bjorn Akesson	70	70	71	72	283	124,950
Eddie Pepperell	77	67	67	72	283	124,950
Oliver Bekker	69	67	72	75	283	124,950
David Drysdale	74	67	71	72	284	107,338
Matthew Nixon	77	67	67	73	284	107,338
Trevor Fisher, Jr.	72	69	69	74	284	107,338
Lee Slattery	74	68	68	74	284	107,338
Maximilian Kieffer	71	72	67	74	284	107,338
Wallie Coetsee	69	73	75	68	285	90,440
Jake Roos	72	72	72	69	285	90,440
James Morrison	72	72	69	72	285	90,440
Danie van Tonder	73	71	68	73	285	90,440
John Moore	76	67	68	74	285	90,440
Niclas Fasth	72	71	67	75	285	90,440
Keith Horne	76	68	66	75	285	90,440
Phillip Price	69	74	66	76	285	90,440
Vaughn Groenewald	71	73	71	71	286	78,540
Merrick Bremner	72	71	70	73	286	78,540
Magnus A. Carlsson	73	70	74	70	287	67,830
Brandon Pieters	76	68	70	73	287	67,830
Derik Ferreira	69	70	74	74	287	67,830
Doug McGuigan	78	66	69	74	287	67,830
Alexandre Kaleka	72	67	73	75	287	67,830
Charl Coetzee	73	70	67	77	287	67,830
Mikko Korhonen	70	73	66	78	287	67,830
Michael Jonzon	69	74	73	72	288	47,719
Christiaan Basson	72	68	75	73	288	47,719
Andreas Harto	72	72	71	73	288	47,719
Joost Luiten	74	67	73	74	288	47,719
Louis de Jager	72	71	70	75	288	47,719
Simon Wakefield	70	73	69	76	288	47,719
Robert-Jan Derksen	72	72	68	76	288	47,719
Ulrich van den Berg	71	68	72	77	288	47,719

	SCORES				TOTAL	MONEY
Ignacio Garrido	69	72	70	77	288	47,719
Tommy Fleetwood	69	72	69	78	288	47,719
Anthony Snobeck	72	71	73	73	289	32,725
Jbe' Kruger	73	71	71	74	289	32,725
Andrew Marshall	75	66	73	75	289	32,725
Peter Erofejeff	73	68	73	75	289	32,725
Lasse Jensen	72	69	72	76	289	32,725
Ross McGowan	73	69	71	76	289	32,725
Warren Abery	73	71	69	76	289	32,725
Tyrone Mordt	71	69	71	78	289	32,725
Christian Cevaer	74	70	76	70	290	25,585
Alessandro Tadini	71	73	72	74	290	25,585
Daniel Greene	70	74	71	75	290	25,585
Matthew Baldwin	74	70	68	78	290	25,585
Matteo Delpodio	72	68	74	77	291	17,814.30
Christopher Doak	74	67	71	79	291	17,814.30
Alexander Levy	73	66	72	80	291	17,814.30
Justin Walters	72	71	69	80	292	17,742.90
Ryan Strauss	71	71	73	78	293	17,689.35
Titch Moore	74	70	69	80	293	17,689.35
Jaco Ahlers	71	73	75	75	294	17,635.80
Mark Williams	73	71	81	73	298	17,600.10

Dimension Data Pro-Am

Fancourt, George, South Africa
Par 36-36–72; 7,342 yards

February 21-24
purse, R4,000,000

	SCORES				TOTAL	MONEY
Jaco Van Zyl	68	64	70	70	272	R594,375
Daniel Brooks	68	67	68	70	273	431,250
Dean Burmester	68	67	72	68	275	182,812.50
Wallie Coetsee	72	64	72	67	275	182,812.50
Trevor Fisher, Jr.	69	67	69	70	275	182,812.50
Hennie Otto	66	66	70	73	275	182,812.50
Darren Fichardt	68	72	69	67	276	101,437.50
Jaco Ahlers	67	69	70	70	276	101,437.50
Alexander Levy	71	71	70	65	277	64,500
Jake Roos	70	68	73	66	277	64,500
Jean Hugo	67	71	71	68	277	64,500
Mark Tullo	69	69	70	69	277	64,500
Jared Harvey	68	69	71	69	277	64,500
Simon Dyson	66	67	73	71	277	64,500
Andrew Marshall	69	67	70	71	277	64,500
Martin Rominger	69	72	68	69	278	49,500
Ockie Strydom	68	69	71	70	278	49,500
Garth Mulroy	69	71	69	69	278	49,500
Desvonde Botes	67	72	70	70	279	45,750
Danie van Tonder	71	68	74	67	280	42,281.25
James Kingston	67	71	75	67	280	42,281.25
Alexandre Kaleka	74	69	68	69	280	42,281.25
Vaughn Groenewald	74	68	66	72	280	42,281.25
Thabo Maseko	74	68	73	66	281	36,562.50
Doug McGuigan	72	71	69	69	281	36,562.50
Ulrich van den Berg	72	69	69	71	281	36,562.50
Seve Benson	74	66	70	71	281	36,562.50
Dawie Van der Walt	67	68	75	71	281	36,562.50
Ruan de Smidt	70	69	69	73	281	36,562.50

Tshwane Open

Els Club, Copperleaf Golf & Country Estate,
Centurion, South Africa
Par 36-36–72; 7,791 yards

February 28-March 3
purse, €1,500,000

	SCORES				TOTAL	MONEY
Dawie Van der Walt	68	65	67	67	267	R2,781,675
Darren Fichardt	65	71	64	69	269	2,018,250
Louis de Jager	71	65	65	69	270	1,214,460
Peter Uihlein	68	66	68	69	271	861,705
Bjorn Akesson	66	75	66	65	272	621,270
Danny Willett	68	68	70	66	272	621,270
Charl Coetzee	67	65	68	72	272	621,270
Morten Orum Madsen	70	67	69	67	273	405,405
Graham van der Merwe	70	66	68	69	273	405,405
Desvonde Botes	69	70	71	64	274	288,990
Vaughn Groenewald	68	70	70	66	274	288,990
Romain Wattel	70	66	71	67	274	288,990
Hennie Otto	71	68	68	67	274	288,990
Jake Roos	69	67	69	69	274	288,990
David Howell	67	69	67	71	274	288,990
James Kingston	70	72	68	65	275	223,236
James Kamte	69	70	71	65	275	223,236
Ross McGowan	73	68	68	66	275	223,236
Justin Walters	71	71	66	67	275	223,236
Garth Mulroy	69	70	69	67	275	223,236
Ruan de Smidt	69	70	70	67	276	186,907.50
Jean Hugo	67	71	70	68	276	186,907.50
Soren Kjeldsen	70	69	68	69	276	186,907.50
Joel Sjoholm	68	68	70	70	276	186,907.50
Graeme Storm	70	68	67	71	276	186,907.50
Oliver Bekker	71	67	67	71	276	186,907.50
Maximilian Kieffer	72	69	69	67	277	152,246.25
Jbe' Kruger	71	70	67	69	277	152,246.25
Damien McGrane	68	71	69	69	277	152,246.25
Christiaan Basson	70	66	71	70	277	152,246.25
Joost Luiten	69	69	69	70	277	152,246.25
Matthew Baldwin	70	68	69	70	277	152,246.25
Andrew Curlewis	73	68	65	71	277	152,246.25
Mark Tullo	67	66	67	77	277	152,246.25
Keith Horne	68	70	72	68	278	126,360
Peter Whiteford	71	69	68	70	278	126,360
Jaco Ahlers	68	72	68	70	278	126,360
Gary Lockerbie	67	71	69	71	278	126,360
Kristoffer Broberg	72	67	67	72	278	126,360
Richard Finch	70	66	69	73	278	126,360
Dean Burmester	68	70	74	67	279	103,545
Ryan Cairns	70	71	70	68	279	103,545
Gary Stal	72	69	69	69	279	103,545
Dylan Frittelli	71	68	71	69	279	103,545
Justin Harding	68	70	71	70	279	103,545
Merrick Bremner	68	70	71	70	279	103,545
Adilson Da Silva	69	70	69	71	279	103,545
Mikko Korhonen	68	72	69	71	280	82,485
Matteo Delpodio	71	68	70	71	280	82,485
Colin Nel	69	70	70	71	280	82,485
Robert Rock	71	69	68	72	280	82,485
Paul Waring	74	65	69	72	280	82,485
Neil Schietekat	75	67	71	68	281	64,935
Matthew Southgate	71	71	70	69	281	64,935
Doug McGuigan	71	67	72	71	281	64,935
Lasse Jensen	73	67	70	71	281	64,935

	SCORES				TOTAL	MONEY
Scott Henry	72	69	67	73	281	64,935
Tjaart van der Walt	71	70	73	68	282	52,650
Danie van Tonder	73	69	71	69	282	52,650
Jorge Campillo	69	73	71	69	282	52,650
Thabo Maseko	70	69	74	69	282	52,650
Eddie Pepperell	70	72	68	72	282	52,650
Darren Clarke	69	73	72	69	283	45,630
Chris Paisley	71	70	72	70	283	45,630
Magnus A. Carlsson	76	65	71	71	283	45,630
David Horsey	68	74	74	68	284	40,365
Shaun Smith	68	73	72	71	284	40,365
Oscar Floren	73	69	69	73	284	40,365
Scott Arnold	68	72	78	68	286	31,142.47
Marc Warren	70	72	74	70	286	31,142.47
Mark Williams	69	70	73	74	286	31,142.47
Matthew Nixon	70	69	68	79	286	31,142.47
Simon Wakefield	68	74	71	74	287	26,254.80
Chris Lloyd	71	70	69	78	288	26,219.70
Daniel Gaunt	72	69	73	76	290	26,184.60
Grant Muller	70	72	75	74	291	26,131.95
Jose Maria Olazabal	76	66	74	75	291	26,131.95

Telkom PGA Championship

The Country Club, Johannesburg, South Africa
Par 36-36–72; 7,546 yards

March 14-17
purse, R3,750,000

	SCORES				TOTAL	MONEY
Jaco Van Zyl	67	65	67	69	268	R594,375
Dylan Frittelli	67	65	70	67	269	431,250
Chris Swanepoel	65	71	63	71	270	259,500
Jean Hugo	67	67	66	71	271	184,125
Ulrich van den Berg	64	72	67	69	272	154,875
Trevor Fisher, Jr.	69	69	69	68	275	104,156.25
Merrick Bremner	68	65	72	70	275	104,156.25
Steve Surry	66	68	69	72	275	104,156.25
Brandon Pieters	69	68	64	74	275	104,156.25
Hennie Otto	68	70	68	70	276	58,921.87
Louis de Jager	68	68	69	71	276	58,921.87
Thabo Maseko	67	69	69	71	276	58,921.87
Bryce Easton	68	71	66	71	276	58,921.87
Danie van Tonder	70	64	70	72	276	58,921.87
Vaughn Groenewald	69	67	68	72	276	58,921.87
Matthew Carvell	69	70	65	72	276	58,921.87
Oliver Bekker	68	70	65	73	276	58,921.87
Le Roux Ferreira	65	72	73	67	277	46,687.50
Justin Harding	70	71	65	71	277	46,687.50
Grant Muller	68	72	70	68	278	41,700
Charl Coetzee	67	68	74	69	278	41,700
Tjaart van der Walt	68	69	71	70	278	41,700
Andrew Georgiou	68	72	67	71	278	41,700
Jeff Inglis	68	68	68	74	278	41,700
Johan Bekker	67	71	72	69	279	37,125
Christiaan Basson	67	73	69	70	279	37,125
Jean-Paul Strydom	64	70	73	72	279	37,125

Investec Cup

Lost City Golf Club, Sun City, South Africa
Par 36-36–72; 7,310 yards

March 21-24
purse, R1,000,000

	SCORES				TOTAL	MONEY
Jaco Van Zyl	66	64	69	68	267	R163,400
Hennie Otto	69	67	69	62	267	117,700
(Van Zyl defeated Otto on first playoff hole.)						
Justin Walters	64	70	68	67	269	69,200
Trevor Fisher, Jr.	74	66	66	66	272	50,700
Jean Hugo	65	70	69	70	274	39,500
Garth Mulroy	66	69	67	72	274	39,500
Keith Horne	69	71	68	67	275	34,500
Richard Sterne	72	70	68	68	278	30,500
Ulrich van den Berg	70	70	67	71	278	30,500
Jake Roos	68	72	67	71	278	30,500
Vaughn Groenewald	70	70	70	69	279	26,033.33
Chris Swanepoel	72	69	69	69	279	26,033.33
Colin Nel	71	65	71	72	279	26,033.33
Dean Burmester	72	69	70	69	280	23,500
Doug McGuigan	71	70	71	69	281	21,400
Desvonde Botes	73	71	68	69	281	21,400
Merrick Bremner	72	68	70	71	281	21,400
Oliver Bekker	76	72	71	64	283	19,175
P.H. McIntyre	72	71	73	67	283	19,175
Ruan de Smidt	75	67	73	68	283	19,175
Danie van Tonder	73	71	66	73	283	19,175
Jaco Ahlers	77	72	64	71	284	18,100
Louis de Jager	71	72	70	72	285	17,700
Matthew Carvell	75	73	71	67	286	16,966.67
Tyrone Ferreira	74	68	74	70	286	16,966.67
James Kingston	71	69	69	77	286	16,966.67

Golden Pilsener Zimbabwe Open

Royal Harare Golf Club, Harare, Zimbabwe
Par 36-36–72; 7,166 yards

April 18-21
purse, R1,650,000

	SCORES				TOTAL	MONEY
Jake Roos	69	67	71	67	274	R261,525
Darren Fichardt	66	69	68	72	275	151,965
Francesco Laporta	74	66	63	72	275	151,965
Doug McGuigan	70	71	69	66	276	74,580
Lindani Ndwandwe	70	68	68	70	276	74,580
Jaco Ahlers	70	70	69	68	277	58,410
Desvonde Botes	69	69	75	65	278	39,311.25
Ryan Cairns	71	70	69	68	278	39,311.25
Charl Coetzee	68	70	71	69	278	39,311.25
Titch Moore	68	72	69	69	278	39,311.25
Andrew Georgiou	72	72	70	66	280	28,545
P.H. McIntyre	71	73	67	69	280	28,545
Jared Harvey	68	72	73	68	281	24,530
Dean Burmester	72	67	72	70	281	24,530
Christiaan Basson	72	69	70	70	281	24,530
Martin du Toit	73	71	71	67	282	21,367.50
Grant Veenstra	73	69	71	69	282	21,367.50
Bryce Easton	73	66	70	73	282	21,367.50
Ulrich van den Berg	70	67	71	74	282	21,367.50
Merrick Bremner	73	69	71	70	283	19,470

	SCORES				TOTAL	MONEY
Divan van den Heever	68	73	72	71	284	18,067.50
Darryn Lloyd	66	71	74	73	284	18,067.50
Theunis Spangenberg	69	69	73	73	284	18,067.50
Louis de Jager	71	66	71	76	284	18,067.50
Brett Liddle	73	73	70	69	285	16,335
Justin Harding	70	70	75	70	285	16,335
Neil Schietekat	73	69	71	72	285	16,335

Investec Royal Swazi Open

Royal Swazi Sun Country Club, Mbabane, Swaziland May 1-4
Par 36-36–72; 6,715 yards purse, R1,000,000

	POINTS				TOTAL	MONEY
James Kingston	10	9	17	9	45	R158,500
Ruan de Smidt	14	7	13	11	45	115,000
(Kingston defeated de Smidt on second playoff hole.)						
Darryn Lloyd	10	5	14	15	44	60,950
Mark Williams	14	10	9	11	44	60,950
James Kamte	6	15	13	7	41	39,350
Michael Hollick	16	7	17	1	41	39,350
P.H. McIntyre	8	13	5	14	40	27,650
Jaco Ahlers	11	12	9	8	40	27,650
Jacques Blaauw	7	9	13	10	39	20,950
Jake Redman	15	8	8	8	39	20,950
Wallie Coetsee	12	12	8	6	38	18,606
Charl Coetzee	6	5	8	18	37	15,931
Justin Harding	4	14	7	12	37	15,931
Andrew Curlewis	7	8	11	11	37	15,931
Bradford Vaughan	9	8	14	6	37	15,931
Ulrich van den Berg	7	14	8	7	36	13,806
Shaun Norris	1	12	9	14	36	13,806
Jean Hugo	10	10	17	-1	36	13,806
Jake Roos	7	10	11	7	35	12,706
Michiel Bothma	4	9	14	8	35	12,706
Warren Abery	4	13	8	9	34	11,956
Ryan Cairns	13	4	10	7	34	11,956
Martin du Toit	10	6	9	8	33	11,356
Lyle Rowe	5	8	13	7	34	11,956
Brandon Pieters	8	7	5	11	31	10,756
Brandon Detweiler	11	8	8	4	31	10,756

Zambia Sugar Open

Lusaka Golf Club, Lusaka, Zambia May 16-19
Par 35-38–73; 7,225 yards purse, R1,200,000

	SCORES				TOTAL	MONEY
Adilson Da Silva	67	72	69	73	281	R190,200
Alex Haindl	69	74	69	70	282	110,520
Martin du Toit	66	70	74	72	282	110,520
Anthony Michael	72	72	72	67	283	43,176
Ryan Cairns	71	71	72	69	283	43,176
Titch Moore	71	72	69	71	283	43,176
Desne van den Bergh	67	70	73	73	283	43,176
Doug McGuigan	69	69	71	74	283	43,176
Jacques Blaauw	69	72	71	72	284	24,720

	SCORES				TOTAL	MONEY
Ulrich van den Berg	69	70	72	73	284	24,720
Mark Williams	72	73	69	71	285	20,760
Vaughn Groenewald	73	67	70	75	285	20,760
Des Terblanche	72	72	72	70	286	18,240
Matthew Carvell	72	69	68	77	286	18,240
Justin Harding	73	71	73	70	287	16,140
Micky Hough	70	72	71	74	287	16,140
Desvonde Botes	71	68	73	75	287	16,140
Hendrik Buhrmann	70	71	70	76	287	16,140
Madalitso Muthiya	73	68	74	73	288	14,400
Steven Ferreira	73	70	72	73	288	14,400
Sipho Bujela	71	65	76	77	289	13,500
Neil Schietekat	72	67	73	77	289	13,500
Andrew Georgiou	74	69	71	76	290	12,960
Ryan Thompson	72	74	72	73	291	11,880
Jared Harvey	77	66	74	74	291	11,880
Allan Versfeld	75	70	72	74	291	11,880
Jake Roos	75	68	73	75	291	11,880
Theunis Spangenberg	76	71	75	69	291	11,880

Lombard Insurance Classic

Royal Swazi Sun Country Club, Mbabane, Swaziland
Par 36-36–72; 6,715 yards

May 31-June 2
purse, R900,000

	SCORES			TOTAL	MONEY
Merrick Bremner	63	65	71	199	R142,650
P.H. McIntyre	68	66	67	201	103,500
Jean Hugo	69	63	71	203	64,260
Justin Harding	72	67	65	204	45,450
Jacques Blaauw	69	69	67	205	35,415
Toto Thimba	65	68	72	205	35,415
Jacques Kruyswijk	69	69	68	206	23,190
Danie van Tonder	69	68	69	206	23,190
Warren Abery	66	68	72	206	23,190
Alex Haindl	68	70	69	207	17,327.50
Ulrich van den Berg	69	67	71	207	17,327.50
James Kingston	69	70	69	208	14,337.50
Oliver Bekker	71	70	67	208	14,337.50
Jake Roos	74	64	70	208	14,337.50
Dean Burmester	69	65	74	208	14,337.50
Callie Swart	70	70	69	209	12,425
Drikus Bruyns	70	71	68	209	12,425
Adilson Da Silva	71	66	72	209	12,425
Jake Redman	70	70	70	210	10,949
Desne van den Bergh	67	74	69	210	10,949
Charl Coetzee	67	71	72	210	10,949
Bradford Vaughan	72	69	69	210	10,949
Grant Muller	68	68	74	210	10,949
Lyle Rowe	73	67	71	211	9,045
Morne Buys	69	71	71	211	9,045
Chris Erasmus	70	69	72	211	9,045
Peter Karmis	70	70	71	211	9,045
Andrew Curlewis	67	73	71	211	9,045
Ruan de Smidt	67	71	73	211	9,045
Wynand Dingle	73	68	70	211	9,045
Graham van der Merwe	68	73	70	211	9,045
Brandon Pieters	67	69	75	211	9,045

Vodacom Origins of Golf - Simola

Simola Golf & Country Estate, Eastern Cape, South Africa
Par 36-36–72; 7,003 yards

June 5-7
purse, R600,000

	SCORES			TOTAL	MONEY
Jacques Blaauw	68	67	69	204	R95,100
P.H. McIntyre	69	71	65	205	51,600
Danie van Tonder	73	65	67	205	51,600
Neil Schietekat	67	69	69	205	51,600
Desvonde Botes	73	66	67	206	25,500
Bradford Vaughan	72	67	67	206	25,500
Jake Redman	65	75	67	207	17,700
Tyrone Mordt	69	69	69	207	17,700
Ulrich van den Berg	73	68	67	208	14,700
Bryce Easton	72	71	66	209	12,700
Justin Harding	72	67	70	209	12,700
Ruan de Smidt	69	69	71	209	12,700
Merrick Bremner	72	69	69	210	11,400
Vaughn Groenewald	70	71	70	211	10,530
James Kamte	72	68	71	211	10,530
Michael Hollick	70	73	69	212	8,860
Ockie Strydom	72	70	70	212	8,860
Jean Hugo	72	69	71	212	8,860
Grant Veenstra	73	72	67	212	8,860
Ryan Cairns	70	71	71	212	8,860
C.J. du Plessis	69	71	72	212	8,860
Derick Petersen	73	70	70	213	7,176
Andrew Curlewis	74	68	71	213	7,176
Allan Versfeld	72	70	71	213	7,176
Pieter Moolman	71	70	72	213	7,176
Mark Murless	71	68	74	213	7,176

Polokwane Classic

Polokwane Golf Club, Limpopo, South Africa
Par 36-36–72; 7,051 yards

June 13-15
purse, R550,000

	SCORES			TOTAL	MONEY
Dean Burmester	69	67	68	204	R87,175
Merrick Bremner	72	69	67	208	53,625
Justin Harding	69	67	72	208	53,625
Titch Moore	65	67	77	209	34,650
Mark Murless	74	69	67	210	23,375
Heinrich Bruiners	66	73	71	210	23,375
J.J. Senekal	71	70	70	211	15,308.33
Ryan Cairns	69	70	72	211	15,308.33
Pieter Moolman	71	68	72	211	15,308.33
Andrew Curlewis	71	73	68	212	11,641.67
Graham van der Merwe	70	71	71	212	11,641.67
Beyers Smith	68	73	71	212	11,641.67
Peter Karmis	71	73	69	213	9,258.33
Chris Erasmus	74	69	70	213	9,258.33
Keith Horne	73	69	71	213	9,258.33
Thabo Maseko	72	70	71	213	9,258.33
Jacques Kruyswijk	71	71	71	213	9,258.33
Stefan Engell Andersen	71	70	72	213	9,258.33
Mark Williams	73	72	69	214	7,370
Erik van Rooyen	69	75	70	214	7,370
Henk Alberts	76	68	70	214	7,370

	SCORES			TOTAL	MONEY
Derik Ferreira	71	72	71	214	7,370
Divan Gerber	73	67	74	214	7,370
Martin du Toit	71	74	70	215	6,105
P.H. McIntyre	73	71	71	215	6,105
Ulrich van den Berg	77	66	72	215	6,105
Jacques van Tonder	68	73	74	215	6,105
Toto Thimba	70	69	76	215	6,105

Vodacom Origins of Golf - Selborne

Selborne Park Golf Club, KwaZulu-Natal, South Africa   June 26-28
Par 36-36–72; 6,509 yards   purse, R600,000

	SCORES			TOTAL	MONEY
Jacques Blaauw	67	67	64	198	R95,100
Danie van Tonder	70	63	66	199	58,500
Adilson Da Silva	65	68	66	199	58,500
Merrick Bremner	63	68	70	201	37,800
Ulrich van den Berg	67	69	66	202	25,500
Ross Wellington	69	65	68	202	25,500
Grant Muller	70	68	65	203	17,700
Musiwalo Nethunzwi	67	68	68	203	17,700
Alex Haindl	69	68	68	205	14,700
Steven Ferreira	69	70	67	206	12,060
Ruan de Smidt	68	71	67	206	12,060
Gert Myburgh	66	73	67	206	12,060
Derik Ferreira	70	68	68	206	12,060
Trevor Fisher, Jr.	70	67	69	206	12,060
Jared Harvey	70	70	67	207	9,800
Dean Burmester	68	69	70	207	9,800
Wallie Coetsee	68	69	70	207	9,800
Charl Coetzee	72	68	68	208	8,820
Titch Moore	69	71	68	208	8,820
Warren Abery	70	69	70	209	7,740
Andrew Curlewis	70	69	70	209	7,740
Justin Harding	73	68	68	209	7,740
Ryan Cairns	72	66	71	209	7,740
Tyrone Mordt	68	69	72	209	7,740
Lindani Ndwandwe	71	69	70	210	6,205.71
Jean Hugo	67	72	71	210	6,205.71
Christiaan Basson	69	70	71	210	6,205.71
Neil Schietekat	66	72	72	210	6,205.71
Theunis Spangenberg	68	70	72	210	6,205.71
Jake Roos	70	68	72	210	6,205.71
Drikus van der Walt	70	66	74	210	6,205.71

Sun City Challenge

Lost City Golf Club, Sun City, South Africa   July 3-5
Par 36-36–72; 7,310 yards   purse, R600,000

	SCORES			TOTAL	MONEY
Adilson Da Silva	67	70	70	207	R95,100
Jared Harvey	68	73	67	208	69,000
Merrick Bremner	70	71	71	212	42,900
Vaughn Groenewald	68	71	73	212	42,900
Ruan de Smidt	71	72	70	213	25,500

	SCORES			TOTAL	MONEY
Andrew Curlewis	73	69	71	213	25,500
Jean Hugo	71	70	73	214	18,900
Alex Haindl	69	74	72	215	15,600
Grant Muller	72	70	73	215	15,600
Mark Murless	73	69	74	216	12,700
Ryan Tipping	67	73	76	216	12,700
Jake Roos	66	74	76	216	12,700
Anthony Michael	72	73	72	217	10,820
Bradley Sinnett	74	71	72	217	10,820
Attie Schwartzel	67	73	77	217	10,820
Ulrich van den Berg	71	75	72	218	9,024
Charl Coetzee	74	72	72	218	9,024
Daniel Greene	70	73	75	218	9,024
Sipho Bujela	71	70	77	218	9,024
Jacques Blaauw	68	73	77	218	9,024
Bradford Vaughan	72	73	74	219	7,590
Jeff Inglis	70	73	76	219	7,590
Ockie Strydom	72	71	76	219	7,590
Dion Fourie	72	71	76	219	7,590
Danie van Tonder	71	75	74	220	6,310
Wallie Coetsee	73	72	75	220	6,310
Ryan Cairns	71	73	76	220	6,310
Matthew Carvell	70	74	76	220	6,310
Neil Cheetham	70	72	78	220	6,310
Lindani Ndwandwe	73	68	79	220	6,310

Vodacom Origins of Golf - Euphoria

Euphoria Golf Estate, Naboomspruit, Limpopo, South Africa
Par 36-36–72; 7,699 yards

August 7-9
purse, R600,000

	SCORES			TOTAL	MONEY
Heinrich Bruiners	68	69	71	208	R95,100
Jake Roos	74	70	69	213	58,500
Adilson Da Silva	74	69	70	213	58,500
Allan Versfeld	73	70	71	214	33,000
Desvonde Botes	70	71	73	214	33,000
Neil Schietekat	71	72	72	215	19,400
Peter Karmis	73	70	72	215	19,400
Jake Redman	72	70	73	215	19,400
Mark Williams	73	72	71	216	13,200
Danie van Tonder	75	70	71	216	13,200
Ulrich van den Berg	70	73	73	216	13,200
Tjaart van der Walt	73	69	74	216	13,200
Ruan de Smidt	73	74	70	217	11,100
Anthony Michael	72	72	73	217	11,100
Darren Fichardt	76	71	71	218	10,020
Jacques Blaauw	72	73	73	218	10,020
Andrew Curlewis	72	73	74	219	9,180
James Kamte	71	71	77	219	9,180
Daniel Hammond	74	72	74	220	8,490
Dion Fourie	74	72	74	220	8,490
Jean Hugo	78	71	72	221	7,890
Jbe' Kruger	73	73	75	221	7,890
Titch Moore	74	74	74	222	6,790
Tyrone Mordt	71	77	74	222	6,790
Keith Horne	74	75	73	222	6,790
Chris Swanepoel	72	74	76	222	6,790
Theunis Spangenberg	74	71	77	222	6,790
Bryce Easton	75	69	78	222	6,790

Vodacom Origins of Golf - Langebaan

Langebaan Country Estate, Western Cape, South Africa
Par 36-36–72; 6,952 yards

August 21-23
purse, R600,000

	SCORES			TOTAL	MONEY
Jean Hugo	72	63	67	202	R95,100
Merrick Bremner	76	66	67	209	51,600
Jbe' Kruger	71	69	69	209	51,600
Andrew Curlewis	71	68	70	209	51,600
Steven Ferreira	72	69	69	210	25,500
Titch Moore	70	70	70	210	25,500
Vaughn Groenewald	72	70	69	211	15,900
Mark Murless	71	70	70	211	15,900
Heinrich Bruiners	70	69	72	211	15,900
Attie Schwartzel	69	67	75	211	15,900
Keenan Davidse	73	70	69	212	12,600
Jared Harvey	71	73	69	213	11,400
Lyle Rowe	72	71	70	213	11,400
Oliver Bekker	73	68	72	213	11,400
Jake Roos	76	70	68	214	10,020
Christiaan Basson	77	68	69	214	10,020
Martin du Toit	75	70	70	215	9,180
Charl Coetzee	74	70	71	215	9,180
Bryce Easton	76	70	70	216	8,340
Theunis Spangenberg	74	71	71	216	8,340
Erik van Rooyen	77	70	69	216	8,340
Neil Schietekat	75	71	71	217	7,050
Shaun Smith	77	69	71	217	7,050
Wallie Coetsee	75	70	72	217	7,050
Alan Michell	74	73	70	217	7,050
Dean Burmester	73	72	72	217	7,050
Ulrich van den Berg	71	70	76	217	7,050

Wild Waves Golf Challenge

Wild Coast Sun Country Club, KwaZulu-Natal, South Africa
Par 35-35–70; 6,351 yards

August 27-29
purse, R600,000

	SCORES			TOTAL	MONEY
Andrew Curlewis	66	63	65	194	R95,100
Desvonde Botes	65	65	65	195	58,500
Titch Moore	65	63	67	195	58,500
Christiaan Basson	64	69	66	199	33,000
Ulrich van den Berg	67	66	66	199	33,000
J.J. Senekal	68	65	68	201	20,850
Oliver Bekker	64	69	68	201	20,850
Ruan de Smidt	64	72	66	202	13,860
Merrick Bremner	66	69	67	202	13,860
Alex Haindl	69	65	68	202	13,860
Wallie Coetsee	66	68	68	202	13,860
Stuart Smith	67	67	68	202	13,860
Shaun Norris	70	68	65	203	10,560
Adilson Da Silva	66	68	69	203	10,560
Jeff Inglis	65	67	71	203	10,560
Trevor Fisher, Jr.	70	62	71	203	10,560
Jaco Ahlers	66	73	65	204	9,000
Jacques Blaauw	66	71	67	204	9,000
Doug McGuigan	66	68	70	204	9,000
Danie van Tonder	67	69	69	205	8,040

	SCORES			TOTAL	MONEY
Daniel Greene	65	71	69	205	8,040
Lyle Rowe	67	67	71	205	8,040
Neil Schietekat	67	72	67	206	6,790
Clifford Howes	73	66	67	206	6,790
Andre Cruse	66	72	68	206	6,790
Ryan Strauss	69	69	68	206	6,790
Jared Harvey	69	68	69	206	6,790
Mark Williams	68	68	70	206	6,790

Vodacom Origins of Golf - Parys

Parys Golf & Country Estate, Parys, South Africa   September 11-13
Par 36-36–72; 7,500 yards   purse, R600,000

	SCORES			TOTAL	MONEY
Andrew Curlewis	72	69	68	209	R95,100
Lyle Rowe	72	65	72	209	69,000
(Curlewis defeated Rowe on first playoff hole.)					
Daniel Greene	69	72	70	211	42,900
Ulrich van den Berg	71	69	71	211	42,900
Michael Hollick	70	71	71	212	28,200
Wallie Coetsee	71	71	71	213	20,850
Dean Burmester	69	69	75	213	20,850
Anthony Michael	66	72	76	214	16,500
Jean Hugo	72	71	72	215	14,100
Doug McGuigan	68	73	74	215	14,100
Toto Thimba	74	70	72	216	12,600
Jacques Blaauw	77	70	71	218	11,115
Mark Murless	73	73	72	218	11,115
Jake Roos	72	72	74	218	11,115
Titch Moore	71	72	75	218	11,115
Ryan Cairns	73	74	72	219	8,860
Trevor Fisher, Jr.	74	72	73	219	8,860
Derik Ferreira	74	70	75	219	8,860
Drikus Bruyns	73	71	75	219	8,860
P.H. McIntyre	69	73	77	219	8,860
Colin Nel	70	71	78	219	8,860
Justin Harding	72	74	74	220	7,050
James Kamte	74	72	74	220	7,050
Vaughn Groenewald	70	75	75	220	7,050
Desvonde Botes	69	75	76	220	7,050
Jaco Ahlers	71	71	78	220	7,050
Attie Schwartzel	67	71	82	220	7,050

Platinum Classic

Mooinooi Golf Club, Rustenburg, South Africa   September 19-21
Par 36-36–72; 6,948 yards   purse, R500,000

	SCORES			TOTAL	MONEY
Neil Schietekat	65	68	68	201	R79,250
Jaco Ahlers	65	70	69	204	57,500
James Kamte	68	67	70	205	40,000
Vaughn Groenewald	66	69	71	206	31,500
Michael Hollick	64	70	73	207	21,250
Jacques Kruyswijk	67	65	75	207	21,250
Ockie Strydom	70	69	69	208	13,250

	SCORES			TOTAL	MONEY
Louis de Jager	67	68	73	208	13,250
Riekus Nortje	70	65	73	208	13,250
Ryan Cairns	70	65	73	208	13,250
Christiaan Basson	70	71	68	209	9,071.43
Attie Schwartzel	69	69	71	209	9,071.43
Morne Buys	67	71	71	209	9,071.43
Bradford Vaughan	69	68	72	209	9,071.43
Teboho Sefatsa	69	66	74	209	9,071.43
Danie van Tonder	69	66	74	209	9,071.43
Doug McGuigan	65	69	75	209	9,071.43
Mark Williams	74	67	71	212	7,216.67
Dean O'Riley	73	64	75	212	7,216.67
Tyrone Ferreira	66	71	75	212	7,216.67
Dean Burmester	68	71	74	213	6,450
P.H. McIntyre	71	67	75	213	6,450
Jean Hugo	66	69	78	213	6,450
Allan Versfeld	69	71	74	214	5,850
Ulrich van den Berg	68	67	79	214	5,850

Vodacom Origins of Golf Final

St. Francis Links, Eastern Cape, South Africa
Par 36-36–72; 7,283 yards

October 9-11
purse, R600,000

	SCORES			TOTAL	MONEY
J.J. Senekal	70	70	72	212	R95,100
Titch Moore	72	68	72	212	69,000
(Senekal defeated Moore on second playoff hole.)					
Lyle Rowe	72	69	73	214	48,000
Charl Coetzee	76	67	72	215	29,600
Jean Hugo	73	69	73	215	29,600
Riekus Nortje	71	68	76	215	29,600
Drikus Bruyns	69	77	70	216	16,700
Heinrich Bruiners	70	76	70	216	16,700
Oliver Bekker	73	70	73	216	16,700
Ulrich van den Berg	75	71	71	217	12,375
C.J. du Plessis	71	72	74	217	12,375
Merrick Bremner	72	69	76	217	12,375
Jake Roos	69	71	77	217	12,375
Louis Calitz	71	75	72	218	10,530
Wallie Coetsee	79	70	69	218	10,530
Johan du Buisson	76	70	73	219	9,195
Alex Haindl	68	78	73	219	9,195
Tyrone Mordt	80	69	70	219	9,195
Daniel Greene	75	70	74	219	9,195
Christiaan Basson	73	73	74	220	7,890
Daniel Hammond	72	75	73	220	7,890
Steven Ferreira	73	73	74	220	7,890
Erik van Rooyen	75	71	74	220	7,890
Dean Burmester	72	74	75	221	6,900
Attie Schwartzel	74	75	72	221	6,900
Michael Hollick	75	70	76	221	6,900

BMG Classic

Glendower Golf Club, Johannesburg, South Africa
Par 36-36–72; 7,564 yards

October 18-20
purse, R600,000

	SCORES			TOTAL	MONEY
Ulrich van den Berg	65	69	67	201	R95,100
Titch Moore	69	67	70	206	58,500
Hennie Otto	65	68	73	206	58,500
Colin Nel	68	70	70	208	33,000
Merrick Bremner	68	68	72	208	33,000
Warren Abery	67	70	72	209	22,800
C.J. du Plessis	67	69	74	210	18,900
Andrew Curlewis	71	70	70	211	13,860
Jean-Paul Strydom	72	69	70	211	13,860
Jbe' Kruger	70	70	71	211	13,860
Johan du Buisson	66	73	72	211	13,860
Anton Haig	69	74	68	211	13,860
Shaun Smith	71	71	70	212	10,320
Drikus van der Walt	68	72	72	212	10,320
Desvonde Botes	74	69	69	212	10,320
Dean Burmester	67	71	74	212	10,320
Lyle Rowe	67	68	77	212	10,320
Wallie Coetsee	71	70	72	213	8,820
Neil Schietekat	69	74	70	213	8,820
Grant Veenstra	70	72	72	214	7,335
Jake Roos	69	73	72	214	7,335
Brett Liddle	68	70	76	214	7,335
Oliver Bekker	67	70	77	214	7,335
Vaughn Groenewald	70	73	71	214	7,335
Jared Harvey	69	74	71	214	7,335
Ryan Cairns	72	71	71	214	7,335
Allan Versfeld	75	68	71	214	7,335

Lion of Africa Cape Town Open

Royal Cape Golf Club, Western Cape, South Africa
Par 36-36–72; 6,818 yards

October 31-November 3
purse, R2,000,000

	SCORES				TOTAL	MONEY
Tjaart van der Walt	69	69	65	71	274	R237,750
Michael Hollick	69	72	71	68	280	172,500
Hennie Otto	66	68	71	76	281	103,800
Jared Harvey	70	70	68	74	282	73,650
Trevor Fisher, Jr.	71	71	71	70	283	57,525
Doug McGuigan	70	71	69	73	283	57,525
Anthony Michael	68	73	72	71	284	40,575
Alan Michell	72	73	68	71	284	40,575
Desvonde Botes	69	71	74	71	285	28,425
Charl Coetzee	71	71	71	72	285	28,425
Mark Murless	73	71	69	72	285	28,425
Andrew Curlewis	70	73	69	73	285	28,425
Ryan Cairns	73	70	74	69	286	20,657.14
Ruan de Smidt	77	68	70	71	286	20,657.14
Bradford Vaughan	70	71	73	72	286	20,657.14
Jbe' Kruger	69	72	73	72	286	20,657.14
Danie van Tonder	70	76	68	72	286	20,657.14
J.J. Senekal	71	70	71	74	286	20,657.14
Justin Walters	69	73	70	74	286	20,657.14
Peter Wilson	69	75	74	69	287	15,993.75

	SCORES			TOTAL	MONEY
Shaun Smith	71	75	72	69	287	15,993.75
Matthew Carvell	73	73	70	71	287	15,993.75
Warren Abery	71	74	70	72	287	15,993.75
Wynand Dingle	70	72	71	74	287	15,993.75
Ulrich van den Berg	74	68	71	74	287	15,993.75
Jean Hugo	72	74	67	74	287	15,993.75
Allan Versfeld	70	70	71	76	287	15,993.75

Nedbank Affinity Cup

Lost City Golf Club, Sun City, South Africa
Par 36-36–72; 7,310 yards

November 5-7
purse, R700,000

	SCORES			TOTAL	MONEY
Jacques Blaauw	64	69	68	201	R110,950
Ulrich van den Berg	67	68	67	202	68,250
Steve Surry	64	70	68	202	68,250
Ross Wellington	71	67	65	203	44,100
Justin Harding	71	66	68	205	32,900
Ruan de Smidt	70	68	68	206	22,633.33
Neil Schietekat	67	69	70	206	22,633.33
Michael Hollick	65	69	72	206	22,633.33
Warren Abery	69	69	69	207	17,150
James Kingston	71	71	66	208	14,816.67
Jared Harvey	67	72	69	208	14,816.67
Stuart Smith	64	70	74	208	14,816.67
Attie Schwartzel	69	69	71	209	13,300
Danie van Tonder	67	75	68	210	12,285
Andrew Curlewis	70	70	70	210	12,285
Theunis Spangenberg	72	71	68	211	10,528
Alan McLean	69	73	69	211	10,528
Chris Swanepoel	70	70	71	211	10,528
Daniel Greene	72	67	72	211	10,528
Dean Burmester	69	69	73	211	10,528
Mark Murless	73	69	70	212	8,694
Shaun Smith	70	71	71	212	8,694
Grant Muller	68	73	71	212	8,694
Christiaan Basson	69	72	71	212	8,694
Allan Versfeld	68	73	71	212	8,694

South African Open Championship

Glendower Golf Club, Ekurhuleni, Gauteng, South Africa
Par 36-36–72; 7,564 yards

November 21-24
purse, €1,100,000

	SCORES				TOTAL	MONEY
Morten Orum Madsen	67	66	69	67	269	R2,388,595
Jbe' Kruger	65	70	71	65	271	1,387,947
Hennie Otto	72	66	65	68	271	1,387,947
Marco Crespi	65	67	70	70	272	681,164
Charl Schwartzel	67	65	69	71	272	681,164
Alejandro Canizares	69	67	69	68	273	533,478
Trevor Fisher, Jr.	70	67	73	64	274	407,643.50
Johan Carlsson	69	70	68	67	274	407,643.50
Warren Abery	68	71	68	68	275	325,512
Garth Mulroy	70	67	70	69	276	282,562.50
Christiaan Basson	66	68	71	71	276	282,562.50

	SCORES				TOTAL	MONEY
Jean Hugo	71	67	70	69	277	226,050
Martin du Toit	70	70	68	69	277	226,050
Peter Karmis	69	72	67	69	277	226,050
Andy Sullivan	71	68	68	70	277	226,050
Jaco Van Zyl	71	70	66	70	277	226,050
Daan Huizing	68	69	73	68	278	184,758.20
Thomas Levet	69	70	70	69	278	184,758.20
Peter Whiteford	71	68	70	69	278	184,758.20
Merrick Bremner	73	69	67	69	278	184,758.20
Thomas Aiken	70	67	71	70	278	184,758.20
Michael Hollick	75	67	68	69	279	153,714
James Morrison	69	66	74	70	279	153,714
Tom Lewis	68	68	72	71	279	153,714
Ross Fisher	71	69	68	71	279	153,714
Jorge Campillo	72	70	66	71	279	153,714
Ulrich van den Berg	70	66	71	72	279	153,714
Retief Goosen	66	71	70	72	279	153,714
Jared Harvey	71	69	70	71	281	128,396.40
Anthony Wall	70	70	70	71	281	128,396.40
P.H. McIntyre	73	68	69	71	281	128,396.40
Seve Benson	72	70	68	71	281	128,396.40
Sihwan Kim	72	70	66	73	281	128,396.40
Alastair Forsyth	72	66	71	73	282	116,039
Oliver Bekker	70	69	70	73	282	116,039
Matthew Nixon	64	72	72	74	282	116,039
Vaughn Groenewald	70	70	74	69	283	105,490
Christopher Doak	71	68	74	70	283	105,490
Darren Fichardt	77	65	69	72	283	105,490
Andrea Pavan	67	70	68	78	283	105,490
Danie van Tonder	68	70	75	71	284	91,927
Attie Schwartzel	67	71	73	73	284	91,927
Heinrich Bruiners	69	72	70	73	284	91,927
Keenan Davidse	70	72	68	74	284	91,927
Magnus A. Carlsson	72	68	66	78	284	91,927
Allan Versfeld	71	68	74	72	285	78,364
Neil Schietekat	69	68	74	74	285	78,364
Alexander Levy	69	72	69	75	285	78,364
Adam Gee	73	69	67	76	285	78,364
Kristoffer Broberg	73	67	75	71	286	69,322
Bennie van der Merwe	69	70	75	72	286	69,322
Charl Coetzee	70	71	75	71	287	57,266
Justin Walters	72	70	71	74	287	57,266
James Heath	75	66	71	75	287	57,266
Edoardo Molinari	72	69	70	76	287	57,266
Simon Dyson	68	74	68	77	287	57,266
James Kamte	69	67	70	81	287	57,266
Jamie McLeary	74	68	75	71	288	48,224
Doug McGuigan	71	70	78	70	289	44,456.50
David Drysdale	71	71	75	72	289	44,456.50
Simon Thornton	70	72	75	72	289	44,456.50
*Louis Taylor	70	70	78	71	289	
Steve Surry	68	73	70	78	289	44,456.50
Chris Swanepoel	70	71	78	71	290	39,935.50
J.J. Senekal	71	70	70	79	290	39,935.50
Lucas Bjerregaard	73	69	76	74	292	37,675

Alfred Dunhill Championship

Leopard Creek Golf Club, Mpumalanga, South Africa
Par 35-37-72; 7,287 yards

November 28-December 1
purse, €1,500,000

	SCORES				TOTAL	MONEY
Charl Schwartzel	68	68	67	68	271	R3,209,625
Richard Finch	68	70	67	70	275	2,328,750
Simon Dyson	72	69	70	67	278	1,077,300
Ross Fisher	72	65	72	69	278	1,077,300
Romain Wattel	70	69	68	71	278	1,077,300
Soren Hansen	72	65	71	71	279	716,850
Magnus A. Carlsson	70	72	72	66	280	547,762.50
Simon Wakefield	74	68	70	68	280	547,762.50
Warren Abery	73	71	69	68	281	417,150
Danny Willett	69	70	73	69	281	417,150
Andrea Pavan	72	71	74	65	282	339,525
David Drysdale	68	72	72	70	282	339,525
Victor Riu	68	71	67	76	282	339,525
*Garrick Porteous	71	69	74	69	283	
Andy Sullivan	71	72	70	70	283	297,675
Morten Orum Madsen	65	71	79	69	284	258,042.86
James Kingston	69	74	70	71	284	258,042.86
Ricardo Santos	66	74	72	72	284	258,042.86
Allan Versfeld	66	77	69	72	284	258,042.86
Lucas Bjerregaard	72	72	67	73	284	258,042.86
Tyrone van Aswegen	70	68	72	74	284	258,042.86
Brendon de Jonge	73	69	68	74	284	258,042.86
Alejandro Canizares	74	69	68	74	285	224,775
Steve Webster	71	73	73	69	286	206,550
Hendrik Buhrmann	72	72	72	70	286	206,550
Brinson Paolini	73	71	69	73	286	206,550
Kevin Phelan	70	74	68	74	286	206,550
Hennie Otto	69	71	69	77	286	206,550
Daniel Brooks	70	74	73	70	287	170,859.38
Jaco Van Zyl	70	72	73	72	287	170,859.38
Adrien Saddier	72	71	72	72	287	170,859.38
Alex Haindl	71	73	70	73	287	170,859.38
Sihwan Kim	70	69	74	74	287	170,859.38
Titch Moore	71	69	73	74	287	170,859.38
Niclas Fasth	72	68	73	74	287	170,859.38
Carlos Del Moral	73	71	66	77	287	170,859.38
Johan Carlsson	73	70	79	66	288	139,725
Tjaart van der Walt	70	74	74	70	288	139,725
Francois Calmels	74	68	75	71	288	139,725
Robert Rock	75	69	73	71	288	139,725
Ruan de Smidt	69	74	73	72	288	139,725
Oliver Fisher	71	73	72	72	288	139,725
Matthew Nixon	72	71	71	74	288	139,725
Haydn Porteous	72	69	78	70	289	109,350
Graeme Storm	72	68	77	72	289	109,350
Ryan Cairns	70	71	76	72	289	109,350
John Parry	70	73	74	72	289	109,350
Yubin Jung	73	70	73	73	289	109,350
Jorge Campillo	70	70	75	74	289	109,350
Michael Hollick	69	70	74	76	289	109,350
Garth Mulroy	76	67	68	78	289	109,350
J.J. Senekal	72	72	80	66	290	83,025
Jbe' Kruger	74	68	81	67	290	83,025
Lee Slattery	73	71	75	71	290	83,025
Alexander Levy	73	68	74	75	290	83,025
Gareth Maybin	69	75	71	75	290	83,025
Chris Doak	69	73	76	74	292	68,850

	SCORES				TOTAL	MONEY
Damien McGrane	72	72	74	74	292	68,850
Andrew Curlewis	70	73	72	78	293	64,800
Jens Dantorp	70	71	75	78	294	62,775
Jaco Ahlers	71	71	79	74	295	60,750
Justin Walters	76	68	79	74	297	57,712.50
Jacques Blaauw	76	68	73	80	297	57,712.50
J.G. Claassen	70	73	76	79	298	53,662.50
Charl Coetzee	70	72	71	85	298	53,662.50
Tyrone Ferreira	72	70	81	76	299	50,625
Mark Williams	76	68	87	71	302	48,600

Nedbank Golf Challenge

Gary Player Country Club, Sun City, South Africa
Par 36-36–72; 7,831 yards

December 5-8
purse, US$6,500,000

	SCORES				TOTAL	MONEY
Thomas Bjorn	67	70	66	65	268	R12,875,000
Sergio Garcia	66	73	66	65	270	6,221,200
Jamie Donaldson	67	66	67	70	270	6,221,200
Henrik Stenson	69	67	69	67	272	3,584,400
Brendon de Jonge	70	68	69	66	273	3,038,500
Charl Schwartzel	68	70	71	66	275	2,523,500
Justin Rose	73	67	69	67	276	1,905,500
Ryan Moore	71	65	67	73	276	1,905,500
Thongchai Jaidee	69	70	66	72	277	1,668,600
Peter Uihlein	70	69	70	70	279	1,627,400
Gonzalo Fernandez-Castano	67	72	72	69	280	1,586,200
Francesco Molinari	76	70	69	67	282	1,524,400
Darren Fichardt	71	68	69	74	282	1,524,400
Richard Sterne	73	73	71	66	283	1,442,000
Louis Oosthuizen	74	69	67	73	283	1,442,000
Joost Luiten	74	68	75	69	286	1,359,600
Martin Kaymer	71	66	74	75	286	1,359,600
D.A. Points	71	67	70	78	286	1,359,600
Luke Donald	68	71	74	74	287	1,297,800
Victor Dubuisson	73	72	71	72	288	1,251,450
Branden Grace	75	71	69	73	288	1,251,450
Gary Woodland	74	73	75	68	290	1,192,225
Matteo Manassero	72	74	72	72	290	1,192,225
Dawie Van der Walt	77	72	73	69	291	1,153,600
David Lynn	73	71	75	74	293	1,102,100
Thaworn Wiratchant	71	76	70	76	293	1,102,100
Morten Orum Madsen	76	71	68	78	293	1,102,100
Kevin Streelman	75	71	77	72	295	1,060,900
Ernie Els	75	71	77	77	300	1,045,450
Peter Senior	80	68	75	81	304	1,030,000

Nelson Mandela Championship

Mount Edgecombe Country Club, Durban, South Africa
Par 34-36–70; 6,612 yards
(Event shortened to 54 holes — rain.)

December 11-14
purse, €1,000,000

	SCORES			TOTAL	MONEY
Dawie Van der Walt	67	62	66	195	R2,250,700
Matthew Baldwin	67	62	68	197	1,307,820
Jorge Campillo	70	59	68	197	1,307,820
Romain Wattel	64	67	67	198	697,220
Oliver Bekker	64	66	69	199	586,460
John Hahn	69	66	65	200	394,405
Jaco Ahlers	66	68	66	200	394,405
Adrien Saddier	66	67	67	200	394,405
Branden Grace	64	66	70	200	394,405
Merrick Bremner	68	66	67	201	278,320
Joel Sjoholm	65	70	67	202	215,231.43
Jbe' Kruger	67	67	68	202	215,231.43
Titch Moore	69	64	69	202	215,231.43
Fredrik Andersson Hed	68	65	69	202	215,231.43
Jacques Blaauw	68	64	70	202	215,231.43
David Higgins	68	64	70	202	215,231.43
Daniel Brooks	62	64	76	202	215,231.43
Julien Guerrier	68	69	66	203	168,128
Estanislao Goya	66	71	66	203	168,128
Oliver Fisher	70	66	67	203	168,128
Andrew Johnston	68	67	68	203	168,128
Jose-Filipe Lima	70	64	69	203	168,128
Jeppe Huldahl	72	65	67	204	144,840
Scott Jamieson	73	65	66	204	144,840
Alastair Forsyth	68	67	69	204	144,840
Jake Roos	68	70	66	204	144,840
Francois Calmels	63	70	71	204	144,840
Shiv Kapur	71	65	69	205	121,308.57
Victor Riu	66	70	69	205	121,308.57
Anthony Wall	71	66	68	205	121,308.57
Keenan Davidse	67	70	68	205	121,308.57
Daniel Gaunt	68	70	67	205	121,308.57
Adilson Da Silva	67	68	70	205	121,308.57
Tjaart van der Walt	67	67	71	205	121,308.57
Jens Dantorp	69	67	70	206	103,660
Brandon Stone	68	69	69	206	103,660
Thomas Pieters	73	66	67	206	103,660
Lee Slattery	73	66	67	206	103,660
Thomas Aiken	70	69	67	206	103,660
Oliver Wilson	70	67	70	207	82,360
Phillip Archer	67	69	71	207	82,360
Lyle Rowe	71	66	70	207	82,360
Bjorn Akesson	69	67	71	207	82,360
Colin Nel	77	59	71	207	82,360
Andrew McArthur	66	72	69	207	82,360
Charl Coetzee	67	68	72	207	82,360
Jens Fahrbring	68	70	69	207	82,360
Jaco Van Zyl	74	65	68	207	82,360
Robert Rock	72	67	68	207	82,360
Gary Stal	70	67	71	208	56,800
Darren Fichardt	66	70	72	208	56,800
Keith Horne	69	67	72	208	56,800
Soren Hansen	71	67	70	208	56,800
Bradford Vaughan	67	71	70	208	56,800
Matthew Carvell	67	67	74	208	56,800
Michael Hoey	65	69	74	208	56,800

	SCORES			TOTAL	MONEY
Damien McGrane	71	68	69	208	56,800
Carlos Del Moral	69	67	73	209	41,890
Matthew Nixon	69	69	71	209	41,890
Daniel Im	70	68	71	209	41,890
Simon Wakefield	70	69	70	209	41,890
Pablo Martin Benavides	70	69	70	209	41,890
Vaughn Groenewald	68	71	70	209	41,890
Byeong-Hun An	67	69	74	210	34,080
Chris Hanson	72	66	72	210	34,080
Niklas Lemke	73	66	71	210	34,080
Garth Mulroy	69	70	71	210	34,080
Stuart Manley	71	68	71	210	34,080
Edouard Dubois	64	71	76	211	26,506.67
Alex Haindl	68	71	72	211	26,506.67
Dean Burmester	70	69	72	211	26,506.67
James Kamte	70	67	75	212	21,214.80
James Kingston	67	71	74	212	21,214.80
Christiaan Basson	68	71	73	212	21,214.80
Duncan Stewart	68	70	75	213	21,129.60

Women's Tours

ISPS Handa Women's Australian Open
See Australian Ladies Tour section.

Honda LPGA Thailand

Siam Country Club, Pattaya Old Course, Chonburi, Thailand
Par 36-36–72; 6,469 yards

February 21-24
purse, $1,500,000

	SCORES				TOTAL	MONEY
Inbee Park	67	71	71	67	276	$225,000
Ariya Jutanugarn	69	66	70	72	277	140,305
Stacy Lewis	63	69	76	70	278	73,935
Beatriz Recari	68	68	72	70	278	73,935
So Yeon Ryu	68	68	74	68	278	73,935
Yani Tseng	75	68	72	63	278	73,935
Na Yeon Choi	73	71	67	68	279	43,401
Lizette Salas	68	69	73	70	280	36,104
Shanshan Feng	71	72	68	69	280	36,104
I.K. Kim	70	72	72	67	281	29,958
Gerina Piller	67	74	70	70	281	29,958
Lexi Thompson	71	70	72	69	282	26,040
Amy Yang	67	75	70	70	282	26,040
Catriona Matthew	67	69	76	71	283	21,739
Nicole Castrale	74	68	71	70	283	21,739
Jiyai Shin	70	73	70	70	283	21,739
*Lydia Ko	69	71	74	69	283	
Jessica Korda	73	67	74	69	283	21,739
Se Ri Pak	69	68	71	76	284	18,666
Danielle Kang	76	70	71	67	284	18,666
Suzann Pettersen	71	70	74	70	285	16,746
Ai Miyazato	69	71	74	71	285	16,746
Azahara Munoz	70	73	73	69	285	16,746
Caroline Hedwall	69	75	72	69	285	16,746
Angela Stanford	69	73	71	73	286	14,672
Katie Futcher	74	72	72	68	286	14,672
Hee-Won Han	72	72	71	71	286	14,672
Karrie Webb	69	71	77	70	287	13,059
Sandra Gal	71	72	76	68	287	13,059
Ayako Uehara	70	71	72	74	287	13,059

HSBC Women's Champions

Sentosa Golf Club, Serapong Course, Singapore
Par 36-36–72; 6,600 yards

February 28-March 3
purse, $1,400,000

	SCORES				TOTAL	MONEY
Stacy Lewis	67	66	69	71	273	$210,000
Na Yeon Choi	69	66	67	72	274	134,116
Paula Creamer	68	67	69	71	275	97,292
Ariya Jutanugarn	69	66	72	71	278	75,263
Candie Kung	69	71	69	70	279	50,543
Jessica Korda	72	68	68	71	279	50,543

	SCORES				TOTAL	MONEY
Danielle Kang	68	69	70	72	279	50,543
Lexi Thompson	73	68	69	70	280	34,511
Chella Choi	68	67	74	71	280	34,511
Catriona Matthew	70	69	72	70	281	27,657
Pornanong Phatlum	67	71	72	71	281	27,657
Morgan Pressel	70	71	69	71	281	27,657
Lizette Salas	67	74	70	71	282	24,084
Moriya Jutanugarn	73	68	71	71	283	20,780
Jenny Shin	71	72	70	70	283	20,780
Nicole Castrale	69	71	69	74	283	20,780
Sun Young Yoo	67	68	72	76	283	20,780
Jiyai Shin	71	69	70	74	284	16,619
Brittany Lincicome	69	73	72	70	284	16,619
Azahara Munoz	65	70	72	77	284	16,619
Jodi Ewart Shadoff	69	71	74	70	284	16,619
Hee-Won Han	72	71	71	70	284	16,619
Karrie Webb	71	71	73	69	284	16,619
Ilhee Lee	70	74	72	69	285	13,768
Beatriz Recari	71	72	69	73	285	13,768
Hee Kyung Seo	71	69	74	71	285	13,768
Anna Nordqvist	72	71	70	72	285	13,768
Chie Arimura	69	72	72	73	286	11,993
Karine Icher	70	71	68	77	286	11,993
Yani Tseng	68	73	71	74	286	11,993

RR Donnelley LPGA Founders Cup

Wildfire Golf Club at JW Marriott Phoenix Desert Ridge
Resort & Spa, Phoenix, Arizona
Par 36-36–72; 6,583 yards

March 14-17
purse, $1,500,000

	SCORES				TOTAL	MONEY
Stacy Lewis	68	65	68	64	265	$225,000
Ai Miyazato	63	67	67	71	268	138,527
Angela Stanford	68	70	65	68	271	100,492
Jee Young Lee	65	64	72	71	272	58,588
Giulia Sergas	69	69	66	68	272	58,588
Jessica Korda	70	67	69	66	272	58,588
Lizette Salas	69	68	66	69	272	58,588
Gerina Piller	66	69	68	70	273	31,399
Candie Kung	66	69	71	67	273	31,399
Sydnee Michaels	70	67	67	69	273	31,399
Nicole Castrale	71	67	66	69	273	31,399
Lindsey Wright	68	67	72	66	273	31,399
Paula Creamer	69	70	69	66	274	22,146
Jiyai Shin	67	70	71	66	274	22,146
I.K. Kim	69	67	69	69	274	22,146
Pernilla Lindberg	72	66	69	67	274	22,146
Jimin Kang	68	69	67	70	274	22,146
Caroline Hedwall	70	70	68	67	275	16,859
Mina Harigae	70	68	69	68	275	16,859
Thidapa Suwannapura	69	68	68	70	275	16,859
Juli Inkster	68	70	69	68	275	16,859
Karrie Webb	70	69	66	70	275	16,859
Sandra Gal	67	69	70	69	275	16,859
Amy Yang	68	67	71	69	275	16,859
Jacqui Concolino	70	70	70	66	276	13,690
Austin Ernst	70	72	66	68	276	13,690
Stacy Prammanasudh	69	72	67	68	276	13,690
Inbee Park	69	71	64	72	276	13,690

	SCORES			TOTAL	MONEY
Daniela Iacobelli	71	65	70	71	277	11,680
So Yeon Ryu	72	70	66	69	277	11,680
Cristie Kerr	71	65	72	69	277	11,680
Na Yeon Choi	69	72	68	68	277	11,680

Kia Classic

Aviara Golf Club, Carlsbad, California
Par 36-36–72; 6,593 yards

March 21-24
purse, $1,700,000

	SCORES			TOTAL	MONEY
Beatriz Recari	69	67	69	74	279	$255,000
I.K. Kim	71	67	70	71	279	156,616
(Recari defeated Kim on second playoff hole.)					
Cristie Kerr	70	68	71	71	280	90,748
Mo Martin	69	71	71	69	280	90,748
Pornanong Phatlum	75	68	69	68	280	90,748
Jane Park	66	72	72	71	281	49,590
Karrie Webb	67	70	70	74	281	49,590
Lizette Salas	69	70	70	72	281	49,590
Giulia Sergas	68	74	72	68	282	33,762
Haeji Kang	69	69	76	68	282	33,762
Stacy Lewis	70	70	69	73	282	33,762
Azahara Munoz	72	70	69	71	282	33,762
Na Yeon Choi	72	71	68	72	283	26,467
Suzann Pettersen	71	71	69	72	283	26,467
Ha-Neul Kim	73	72	68	70	283	26,467
Jodi Ewart Shadoff	69	74	72	69	284	23,494
Inbee Park	69	69	72	75	285	20,922
Paula Creamer	69	68	71	77	285	20,922
Chella Choi	71	70	71	73	285	20,922
Jacqui Concolino	70	72	71	72	285	20,922
Carlota Ciganda	70	72	74	70	286	18,350
Sandra Gal	70	72	71	73	286	18,350
Caroline Hedwall	67	72	75	72	286	18,350
Amy Yang	73	73	68	73	287	14,634
Catriona Matthew	75	72	71	69	287	14,634
Moriya Jutanugarn	71	73	72	71	287	14,634
Stacy Prammanasudh	71	70	74	72	287	14,634
Jee Young Lee	72	69	74	72	287	14,634
Vicky Hurst	74	71	72	70	287	14,634
Gerina Piller	74	70	74	69	287	14,634
Jeong Jang	72	68	72	75	287	14,634
Ai Miyazato	72	72	72	71	287	14,634

Kraft Nabisco Championship

Mission Hills Country Club, Dinah Shore Course,
Rancho Mirage, California
Par 36-36–72; 6,738 yards

April 4-7
purse, $2,000,000

	SCORES			TOTAL	MONEY
Inbee Park	70	67	67	69	273	$300,000
So Yeon Ryu	73	71	68	65	277	187,073
Suzann Pettersen	68	75	67	69	279	120,345
Caroline Hedwall	71	68	72	68	279	120,345
Haeji Kang	72	69	73	68	282	76,816

	SCORES				TOTAL	MONEY
Karrie Webb	72	71	67	72	282	76,816
Giulia Sergas	70	69	76	68	283	44,980
Jiyai Shin	70	71	71	71	283	44,980
Hee Young Park	70	70	72	71	283	44,980
Anna Nordqvist	69	72	72	70	283	44,980
Catriona Matthew	72	73	70	68	283	44,980
Jodi Ewart Shadoff	68	72	74	69	283	44,980
Caroline Masson	70	73	71	70	284	29,156
Moriya Jutanugarn	70	72	72	70	284	29,156
Jennifer Johnson	72	71	73	68	284	29,156
Paula Creamer	74	68	69	73	284	29,156
Pornanong Phatlum	71	69	70	74	284	29,156
Hee Kyung Seo	72	70	71	71	284	29,156
Se Ri Pak	72	69	75	69	285	22,328
Angela Stanford	70	74	66	75	285	22,328
Karine Icher	72	70	68	75	285	22,328
Ayako Uehara	72	72	70	71	285	22,328
Cristie Kerr	71	71	72	71	285	22,328
Jane Park	70	73	73	69	285	22,328
*Lydia Ko	72	74	71	69	286	
Beatriz Recari	75	70	71	70	286	17,787
Jacqui Concolino	70	73	73	70	286	17,787
Shanshan Feng	78	71	70	67	286	17,787
Lizette Salas	70	68	69	79	286	17,787
Alison Walshe	71	74	72	69	286	17,787
Jessica Korda	70	72	68	76	286	17,787
Sarah Jane Smith	72	72	69	74	287	13,178
Jee Young Lee	76	70	72	69	287	13,178
Mariajo Uribe	72	76	69	70	287	13,178
Stacy Lewis	73	71	71	72	287	13,178
Chella Choi	75	72	69	71	287	13,178
Natalie Gulbis	74	72	72	69	287	13,178
Na Yeon Choi	68	75	72	72	287	13,178
Amy Yang	69	73	73	72	287	13,178
Mina Harigae	72	74	71	70	287	13,178
Momoko Ueda	74	71	71	72	288	9,645
Belen Mozo	74	72	69	73	288	9,645
Michelle Wie	72	70	73	73	288	9,645
Julieta Granada	77	69	73	69	288	9,645
Gerina Piller	73	71	73	71	288	9,645
Christel Boeljon	74	73	71	70	288	9,645
*Stephanie Meadow	73	73	71	72	289	
Eun-Hee Ji	73	71	72	74	290	8,091
Lexi Thompson	76	72	71	71	290	8,091
*Ashlan Ramsey	71	75	73	71	290	
Yani Tseng	72	75	69	74	290	8,091
Karin Sjodin	72	74	73	73	292	7,204
Ha-Neul Kim	73	75	73	71	292	7,204
Morgan Pressel	72	75	72	73	292	7,204
Vicky Hurst	75	74	71	73	293	6,248
Jenny Shin	75	74	71	73	293	6,248
Ai Miyazato	74	68	75	76	293	6,248
Karen Stupples	73	72	75	73	293	6,248
I.K. Kim	75	73	74	71	293	6,248
Pernilla Lindberg	72	75	74	72	293	6,248
*Angel Yin	73	75	74	71	293	
Hee-Won Han	74	75	73	72	294	5,530
Sophie Gustafson	74	72	74	75	295	5,156
Paige Mackenzie	72	75	76	72	295	5,156
Mika Miyazato	76	72	76	71	295	5,156
Mo Martin	78	71	71	76	296	4,865
Carlota Ciganda	76	72	70	78	296	4,865
Cindy LaCrosse	72	73	74	78	297	4,712

	SCORES				TOTAL	MONEY
Maria Hjorth	75	74	75	74	298	4,507
Meena Lee	76	72	75	75	298	4,507
Candie Kung	75	72	77	74	298	4,507
*Camilla Hedberg	72	72	79	78	301	
Lindsey Wright	74	75	76	79	304	4,301

LPGA LOTTE Championship

Ko Olina Golf Club, Kapolei, Oahu, Hawaii   April 17-20
Par 36-36–72; 6,383 yards   purse, $1,700,000

	SCORES				TOTAL	MONEY
Suzann Pettersen	65	69	68	67	269	$255,000
Lizette Salas	69	71	67	62	269	155,874
(Pettersen defeated Salas on first playoff hole.)						
Ariya Jutanugarn	64	75	68	66	273	113,075
Inbee Park	70	71	67	67	275	78,939
I.K. Kim	70	70	70	65	275	78,939
Jessica Korda	72	70	66	69	277	49,355
Na Yeon Choi	70	74	67	66	277	49,355
Ai Miyazato	67	68	70	72	277	49,355
Hyo Joo Kim	66	71	69	72	278	32,480
*Lydia Ko	71	71	70	66	278	
Hee Kyung Seo	65	72	66	75	278	32,480
Shanshan Feng	70	70	73	65	278	32,480
Caroline Hedwall	69	72	70	67	278	32,480
Stacy Lewis	67	71	69	71	278	32,480
Haeji Kang	68	71	74	66	279	25,516
Karine Icher	70	71	72	66	279	25,516
Karrie Webb	69	74	70	67	280	21,762
Paula Creamer	71	72	71	66	280	21,762
Vicky Hurst	69	72	72	67	280	21,762
Beatriz Recari	67	70	72	71	280	21,762
Jodi Ewart Shadoff	72	68	68	73	281	19,287
Azahara Munoz	72	73	70	66	281	19,287
Paola Moreno	72	70	69	71	282	16,949
Mo Martin	70	75	71	66	282	16,949
Meena Lee	72	71	69	70	282	16,949
Hee Young Park	69	72	69	72	282	16,949
Pornanong Phatlum	70	70	73	69	282	16,949
Danah Bordner	70	76	68	69	283	13,961
Danielle Kang	66	76	69	72	283	13,961
Giulia Sergas	72	71	70	70	283	13,961
Se Ri Pak	70	69	71	73	283	13,961
Michelle Wie	70	76	69	68	283	13,961

North Texas LPGA Shootout

Las Colinas Country Club, Irving, Texas   April 25-28
Par 36-35–71; 6,410 yards   purse, $1,300,000

	SCORES				TOTAL	MONEY
Inbee Park	67	70	67	67	271	$195,000
Carlota Ciganda	66	70	66	70	272	118,649
Suzann Pettersen	70	70	68	66	274	86,072
Hee Young Park	68	70	73	64	275	60,088
So Yeon Ryu	71	68	68	68	275	60,088

	SCORES				TOTAL	MONEY
I.K. Kim	70	71	67	68	276	43,848
Karine Icher	71	69	67	70	277	31,019
Stacy Lewis	72	70	69	66	277	31,019
Shanshan Feng	71	67	70	69	277	31,019
Na Yeon Choi	70	69	66	72	277	31,019
Paula Creamer	73	69	69	67	278	22,102
Dewi Claire Schreefel	75	70	65	68	278	22,102
Christina Kim	68	72	67	71	278	22,102
Cristie Kerr	70	73	67	68	278	22,102
Giulia Sergas	73	68	72	66	279	17,842
Caroline Masson	64	71	69	75	279	17,842
Mo Martin	67	74	70	68	279	17,842
Julieta Granada	70	70	71	69	280	15,233
Lexi Thompson	71	71	68	70	280	15,233
Jane Park	72	69	73	66	280	15,233
Chella Choi	71	69	70	70	280	15,233
Angela Stanford	69	70	72	70	281	12,667
Haeji Kang	69	72	69	71	281	12,667
Jiyai Shin	70	71	73	67	281	12,667
Jennifer Johnson	71	69	70	71	281	12,667
Kathleen Ekey	70	67	73	71	281	12,667
Lizette Salas	71	70	72	68	281	12,667
Azahara Munoz	69	75	70	68	282	9,448
Christel Boeljon	71	71	71	69	282	9,448
Mindy Kim	72	69	69	72	282	9,448
Moira Dunn	69	71	70	72	282	9,448
Brittany Lincicome	70	68	71	73	282	9,448
Rebecca Lee-Bentham	72	68	73	69	282	9,448
Moriya Jutanugarn	71	66	72	73	282	9,448
Jodi Ewart Shadoff	72	69	72	69	282	9,448
Yani Tseng	69	69	71	73	282	9,448

Kingsmill Championship

Kingsmill Resort, Williamsburg, Virginia
Par 36-35–71; 6,379 yards

May 2-5
purse, $1,300,000

	SCORES				TOTAL	MONEY
Cristie Kerr	66	71	66	69	272	$195,000
Suzann Pettersen	68	69	68	67	272	118,649
(Kerr defeated Pettersen on second playoff hole.)						
Ilhee Lee	69	69	69	67	274	76,327
Ariya Jutanugarn	64	71	73	66	274	76,327
Stacy Lewis	68	68	69	70	275	48,720
Angela Stanford	68	68	70	69	275	48,720
Inbee Park	68	72	69	67	276	36,702
So Yeon Ryu	67	71	73	68	279	32,156
Gerina Piller	72	71	71	66	280	26,525
Sandra Gal	68	69	73	70	280	26,525
Anna Nordqvist	70	72	70	68	280	26,525
Paula Creamer	69	70	74	68	281	20,137
Katie Burnett	68	70	71	72	281	20,137
Caroline Hedwall	68	73	70	70	281	20,137
Na Yeon Choi	69	73	70	69	281	20,137
Amy Yang	69	72	71	69	281	20,137
Chella Choi	70	73	68	71	282	16,154
Alison Walshe	69	70	74	69	282	16,154
Lizette Salas	72	71	65	74	282	16,154
Giulia Sergas	74	68	70	71	283	14,161
Jane Park	68	71	72	72	283	14,161

	SCORES				TOTAL	MONEY
Hee Kyung Seo	71	71	74	67	283	14,161
Shanshan Feng	69	69	73	72	283	14,161
Julia Boland	73	71	70	70	284	12,180
Yani Tseng	69	72	71	72	284	12,180
Mo Martin	68	72	70	74	284	12,180
Karrie Webb	70	71	70	73	284	12,180
Jenny Shin	71	72	68	74	285	10,410
Jee Young Lee	68	74	74	69	285	10,410
Brittany Lincicome	75	69	71	70	285	10,410
Sun Young Yoo	71	73	69	72	285	10,410

Mobile Bay LPGA Classic

Robert Trent Jones Golf Trail, Magnolia Grove May 16-19
Crossings Course, Mobile, Alabama purse, $1,200,000
Par 36-36–72; 6,521 yards

	SCORES				TOTAL	MONEY
Jennifer Johnson	67	70	65	65	267	$180,000
Pornanong Phatlum	69	65	71	63	268	94,065
Jessica Korda	66	65	69	68	268	94,065
Jiyai Shin	72	66	68	63	269	42,802
Karrie Webb	69	63	69	68	269	42,802
Anna Nordqvist	73	66	61	69	269	42,802
Ariya Jutanugarn	69	66	69	65	269	42,802
Chella Choi	67	66	66	70	269	42,802
Stacy Lewis	70	70	63	67	270	26,565
Lexi Thompson	65	70	69	67	271	23,281
Hee Kyung Seo	68	68	70	65	271	23,281
Beatriz Recari	68	70	68	66	272	20,893
Azahara Munoz	71	64	73	66	274	16,993
Mariajo Uribe	70	67	68	69	274	16,993
Eun-Hee Ji	65	72	67	70	274	16,993
Thidapa Suwannapura	67	67	72	68	274	16,993
Sydnee Michaels	72	62	69	71	274	16,993
Mo Martin	70	69	71	64	274	16,993
Lisa McCloskey	69	68	71	67	275	14,208
Julieta Granada	69	70	67	70	276	13,491
Nicole Castrale	67	69	68	72	276	13,491
Angela Stanford	71	68	71	67	277	11,215
Meena Lee	70	71	65	71	277	11,215
Hee Young Park	67	71	68	71	277	11,215
Karine Icher	73	68	68	68	277	11,215
Chie Arimura	72	72	65	68	277	11,215
Katie Burnett	73	68	67	69	277	11,215
Mina Harigae	67	68	73	69	277	11,215
Sun Young Yoo	73	69	68	67	277	11,215
Katherine Hull-Kirk	69	69	69	71	278	8,835
Alison Walshe	69	72	66	71	278	8,835
Jane Park	73	69	66	70	278	8,835
Tiffany Joh	72	72	67	67	278	8,835

Pure Silk-Bahamas LPGA Classic

Ocean Club Golf Course, Paradise Island, Bahamas
Par 22-25–47; 6,644 yards
(Course shorted to 12-hole layout due to heavy rain.)

May 24-26
purse, $1,300,000

	SCORES			TOTAL	MONEY
Ilhee Lee	41	43	42	126	$195,000
Irene Cho	45	43	40	128	120,353
Anna Nordqvist	40	44	45	129	87,308
Mindy Kim	39	46	45	130	47,245
Karine Icher	41	44	45	130	47,245
Paula Creamer	43	42	45	130	47,245
Cristie Kerr	44	40	46	130	47,245
Mika Miyazato	42	43	45	130	47,245
Julieta Granada	41	42	48	131	25,945
Giulia Sergas	46	42	43	131	25,945
Katie Futcher	42	43	46	131	25,945
Heather Bowie Young	39	45	47	131	25,945
Ai Miyazato	43	43	46	132	15,960
Alena Sharp	41	50	41	132	15,960
Brittany Lang	41	46	45	132	15,960
Lexi Thompson	45	41	46	132	15,960
So Yeon Ryu	42	46	44	132	15,960
Caroline Masson	45	43	44	132	15,960
Paola Moreno	40	41	51	132	15,960
Natalie Gulbis	45	42	45	132	15,960
Morgan Pressel	43	42	47	132	15,960
Sun Young Yoo	42	44	46	132	15,960
Sandra Gal	44	43	45	132	15,960
Lindsey Wright	44	38	50	132	15,960
Jennifer Rosales	46	43	43	132	15,960
Jennifer Johnson	42	46	44	132	15,960
Stacy Lewis	44	42	47	133	10,780
Hee Young Park	41	43	49	133	10,780
Mina Harigae	42	42	49	133	10,780
I.K. Kim	44	45	44	133	10,780
Caroline Hedwall	44	42	47	133	10,780

ShopRite LPGA Classic

Stockton Seaview Hotel & Golf Club, Galloway, New Jersey
Par 37-34–71; 6,155 yards

May 31-June 2
purse, $1,500,000

	SCORES			TOTAL	MONEY
Karrie Webb	72	69	68	209	$225,000
Shanshan Feng	69	67	75	211	138,191
Hee Young Park	69	72	71	212	100,248
Jenny Shin	70	73	70	213	77,549
I.K. Kim	72	70	72	214	48,422
Chie Arimura	73	67	74	214	48,422
Jeong Jang	73	71	70	214	48,422
Gerina Piller	70	75	69	214	48,422
Caroline Hedwall	73	72	70	215	29,790
Ayako Uehara	75	69	71	215	29,790
Michelle Wie	68	73	74	215	29,790
Julieta Granada	71	73	71	215	29,790
Mika Miyazato	72	70	74	216	22,092
Cristie Kerr	73	75	68	216	22,092
Anna Nordqvist	72	68	76	216	22,092

	SCORES			TOTAL	MONEY
Paula Creamer	74	74	68	216	22,092
Amanda Blumenherst	66	75	75	216	22,092
Christina Kim	71	74	72	217	15,949
Alison Walshe	77	71	69	217	15,949
Hee Kyung Seo	75	72	70	217	15,949
Na Yeon Choi	74	71	72	217	15,949
Nicole Castrale	74	72	71	217	15,949
Moriya Jutanugarn	66	73	78	217	15,949
Ai Miyazato	70	74	73	217	15,949
Beatriz Recari	69	73	75	217	15,949
Jiyai Shin	71	76	70	217	15,949
Jennifer Rosales	72	75	70	217	15,949
Jodi Ewart Shadoff	76	70	72	218	10,796
Lindsey Wright	71	74	73	218	10,796
Lizette Salas	72	76	70	218	10,796
Meena Lee	73	72	73	218	10,796
Karine Icher	74	67	77	218	10,796
Marcy Hart	78	69	71	218	10,796
Becky Morgan	72	73	73	218	10,796
Pat Hurst	75	73	70	218	10,796
Mi Hyang Lee	70	77	71	218	10,796
Moira Dunn	72	74	72	218	10,796

Wegmans LPGA Championship

Locust Hill Country Club, Pittsford, New York
Par 35-37–72; 6,534 yards

June 6-9
purse, $2,250,000

	SCORES				TOTAL	MONEY
Inbee Park	72	68	68	75	283	$337,500
Catriona Matthew	71	71	73	68	283	206,304
(Park defeated Matthew on third playoff hole.)						
Suzann Pettersen	72	73	74	65	284	132,716
Morgan Pressel	68	70	71	75	284	132,716
Jiyai Shin	68	73	69	75	285	72,288
Chella Choi	67	73	73	72	285	72,288
Amy Yang	71	70	74	70	285	72,288
Sun Young Yoo	73	69	70	73	285	72,288
Michelle Wie	76	68	71	71	286	46,121
Shanshan Feng	74	70	72	70	286	46,121
Na Yeon Choi	72	70	70	74	286	46,121
Caroline Masson	74	69	71	73	287	37,122
Anna Nordqvist	71	74	73	69	287	37,122
Cristie Kerr	75	72	70	70	287	37,122
Ai Miyazato	74	75	66	73	288	31,851
Kristy McPherson	73	72	69	74	288	31,851
*Lydia Ko	77	70	73	69	289	
Brittany Lincicome	69	73	77	70	289	29,367
Beatriz Recari	74	71	73	72	290	26,957
Jennifer Rosales	76	71	70	73	290	26,957
Yani Tseng	72	74	71	73	290	26,957
Eun-Hee Ji	72	72	74	73	291	22,873
Jenny Shin	78	70	70	73	291	22,873
Danielle Kang	75	72	72	72	291	22,873
Mina Harigae	75	74	73	69	291	22,873
I.K. Kim	75	74	73	69	291	22,873
Mika Miyazato	77	71	71	72	291	22,873
Lexi Thompson	71	73	73	75	292	18,478
Se Ri Pak	70	74	76	72	292	18,478
Angela Stanford	71	71	75	75	292	18,478

	SCORES				TOTAL	MONEY
Stacy Lewis	74	72	76	70	292	18,478
Pernilla Lindberg	73	71	71	77	292	18,478
Haeji Kang	73	74	71	75	293	15,389
Chie Arimura	71	72	73	77	293	15,389
Danah Bordner	73	71	73	76	293	15,389
Karrie Webb	76	72	75	70	293	15,389
Ji Young Oh	75	72	71	76	294	12,296
M.J. Hur	71	74	76	73	294	12,296
Moira Dunn	75	71	75	73	294	12,296
Carlota Ciganda	75	71	71	77	294	12,296
Paige Mackenzie	76	74	71	73	294	12,296
Mo Martin	77	73	71	73	294	12,296
Caroline Hedwall	77	71	70	76	294	12,296
Candie Kung	75	75	71	74	295	9,623
Pornanong Phatlum	72	74	73	76	295	9,623
Vicky Hurst	73	72	77	73	295	9,623
Giulia Sergas	76	72	73	74	295	9,623
Ayako Uehara	76	73	73	73	295	9,623
Jessica Korda	70	74	76	76	296	8,414
Lisa Ferrero	78	71	71	76	296	8,414
Hee Young Park	75	71	75	76	297	7,794
Paola Moreno	74	74	73	76	297	7,794
Sarah Jane Smith	72	69	76	81	298	7,003
Ilhee Lee	71	74	74	79	298	7,003
Laura Diaz	75	73	73	77	298	7,003
Mariajo Uribe	76	74	74	74	298	7,003
Nicole Castrale	73	72	77	76	298	7,003
Paula Creamer	76	71	76	76	299	5,987
Lorie Kane	74	74	74	77	299	5,987
Belen Mozo	77	71	74	77	299	5,987
Breanna Elliott	75	74	77	73	299	5,987
Jacqui Concolino	78	70	77	75	300	5,478
Lisa McCloskey	74	72	76	78	300	5,478
Marcy Hart	78	71	75	78	302	5,026
Laura Davies	71	73	80	78	302	5,026
Melissa Reid	76	74	76	76	302	5,026
Moriya Jutanugarn	74	74	72	82	302	5,026
Jane Park	74	74	78	76	302	5,026
Mi Hyang Lee	75	71	78	78	302	5,026
Alison Walshe	75	74	77	77	303	4,631
Amelia Lewis	74	74	78	78	304	4,519
Brittany Lang	75	71	80	79	305	4,405
Sue Kim	75	74	81	75	305	4,405
Tiffany Joh	77	72	78	78	305	4,405
Kathleen Ekey	76	74	79	78	307	4,292
Lauren Doughtie	75	75	81	80	311	4,240

Walmart NW Arkansas Championship

Pinnacle Country Club, Rogers, Arkansas
Par 36-35–71; 6,389 yards

June 21-23
purse, $2,000,000

	SCORES			TOTAL	MONEY
Inbee Park	69	65	67	201	$300,000
So Yeon Ryu	66	66	69	201	184,703
(Park defeated Ryu on first playoff hole.)					
Mika Miyazato	65	70	67	202	133,989
Stacy Lewis	67	65	71	203	93,539
*Lydia Ko	69	66	68	203	
I.K. Kim	70	64	69	203	93,539

	SCORES			TOTAL	MONEY
Beatriz Recari	67	65	72	204	55,113
Suzann Pettersen	67	70	67	204	55,113
Paula Creamer	68	68	68	204	55,113
Chie Arimura	67	65	72	204	55,113
Ai Miyazato	73	64	68	205	39,438
Haeji Kang	72	66	67	205	39,438
Brittany Lang	70	67	69	206	32,258
Juli Inkster	71	65	70	206	32,258
Shanshan Feng	71	67	68	206	32,258
Brooke Pancake	69	67	70	206	32,258
Jenny Shin	71	69	67	207	24,809
Sarah Kemp	67	69	71	207	24,809
Moriya Jutanugarn	69	67	71	207	24,809
Mina Harigae	67	69	71	207	24,809
Na Yeon Choi	71	70	66	207	24,809
Amy Yang	70	68	69	207	24,809
Lisa McCloskey	67	71	70	208	21,236
Alison Walshe	71	67	70	208	21,236
Christel Boeljon	67	69	73	209	16,938
Karine Icher	70	68	71	209	16,938
Julieta Granada	70	72	67	209	16,938
Becky Morgan	73	68	68	209	16,938
Ayako Uehara	71	71	67	209	16,938
Caroline Hedwall	72	68	69	209	16,938
Morgan Pressel	68	69	72	209	16,938
Lizette Salas	71	69	69	209	16,938
Mo Martin	72	69	68	209	16,938
Hee-Won Han	70	71	68	209	16,938

U.S. Women's Open

Sebonack Golf Club, Southampton, New York
Par 35-37–72; 6,821 yards

June 27-30
purse, $3,250,000

	SCORES				TOTAL	MONEY
Inbee Park	67	68	71	74	280	$585,000
I.K. Kim	68	69	73	74	284	350,000
So Yeon Ryu	73	69	73	72	287	217,958
Angela Stanford	73	68	74	74	289	127,972
Paula Creamer	72	73	72	72	289	127,972
Jodi Ewart Shadoff	70	69	74	76	289	127,972
Brittany Lang	76	69	73	72	290	94,357
Jessica Korda	70	71	76	73	290	94,357
Shanshan Feng	71	75	75	70	291	79,711
Brittany Lincicome	72	72	74	73	291	79,711
Ai Miyazato	76	70	72	74	292	69,432
Anna Nordqvist	68	74	77	73	292	69,432
Lexi Thompson	75	69	76	73	293	61,477
Karrie Webb	73	73	73	74	293	61,477
Catriona Matthew	70	75	74	75	294	54,755
Lindy Duncan	71	73	75	75	294	54,755
Haeji Kang	71	73	77	74	295	47,784
Na Yeon Choi	71	77	72	75	295	47,784
Mariajo Uribe	70	76	76	73	295	47,784
Karine Icher	70	72	77	77	296	37,920
Lizette Salas	68	72	82	74	296	37,920
Cristie Kerr	72	72	74	78	296	37,920
Morgan Pressel	73	74	75	74	296	37,920
Jennifer Rosales	70	76	76	74	296	37,920
Ha-Neul Kim	66	77	78	76	297	27,548

	SCORES				TOTAL	MONEY
*Casie Cathrea	75	73	79	70	297	
Julieta Granada	74	76	73	74	297	27,548
Hee Kyung Seo	75	74	75	73	297	27,548
Chella Choi	73	75	76	73	297	27,548
M.J. Hur	75	71	75	76	297	27,548
Meena Lee	71	79	77	71	298	21,434
Mika Miyazato	72	77	74	75	298	21,434
Caroline Hedwall	68	75	79	76	298	21,434
Christina Kim	75	75	74	74	298	21,434
Gerina Piller	73	76	76	73	298	21,434
Dewi Claire Schreefel	76	71	77	75	299	18,263
*Lydia Ko	72	76	79	72	299	
Kristy McPherson	74	75	72	78	299	18,263
Thidapa Suwannapura	75	74	73	77	299	18,263
Ayako Uehara	75	75	73	76	299	18,263
Soo-Jin Yang	72	72	79	76	299	18,263
Ryann O'Toole	72	73	78	77	300	15,430
Stacy Lewis	71	76	75	78	300	15,430
Mo Martin	74	74	77	75	300	15,430
Jane Park	73	76	76	75	300	15,430
Pornanong Phatlum	71	77	76	77	301	13,544
Sarah Jane Smith	71	76	76	78	301	13,544
Azahara Munoz	73	74	73	82	302	12,287
Austin Ernst	75	74	82	71	302	12,287
Maude-Aimee Leblanc	69	77	77	80	303	10,715
*Doris Chen	74	74	79	76	303	
Amy Yang	74	72	78	79	303	10,715
Laura Diaz	76	74	76	77	303	10,715
Jenny Shin	78	71	78	77	304	9,693
Caroline Masson	71	74	81	78	304	9,693
*Yueer Cindy Feng	72	77	79	76	304	
Carlota Ciganda	76	72	82	75	305	9,211
Amy Meier	74	72	82	77	305	9,211
*Brooke Mackenzie Henderson	71	76	83	77	307	
Caroline Westrup	74	76	78	79	307	8,875
Eun-Hee Ji	73	77	83	75	308	8,574
Natalie Gulbis	70	78	76	84	308	8,574
Cindy LaCrosse	74	74	82	79	309	8,313
Becky Morgan	75	73	79	83	310	8,089
*Nelly Korda	73	77	79	81	310	
Moira Dunn	78	72	77	83	310	8,089
Danah Bordner	73	74	82	83	312	7,890
Jackie Barenborg Stoelting	75	74	82	82	313	7,746

Manulife Financial LPGA Classic

Grey Silo Golf Course, Waterloo, Ontario, Canada
Par 36-35–71; 6,330 yards

July 11-14
purse, $1,300,000

	SCORES				TOTAL	MONEY
Hee Young Park	65	67	61	65	258	$195,000
Angela Stanford	63	67	64	64	258	120,353
(Park defeated Stanford on third playoff hole.)						
Catriona Matthew	63	64	68	66	261	87,308
Meena Lee	65	66	65	68	264	67,539
Karine Icher	67	66	69	63	265	54,362
Gerina Piller	70	67	62	67	266	31,158
Na Yeon Choi	69	68	67	62	266	31,158
Amy Yang	66	67	66	67	266	31,158
Austin Ernst	68	64	67	67	266	31,158

	SCORES				TOTAL	MONEY
Stacy Lewis	68	67	67	64	266	31,158
Suzann Pettersen	68	64	68	66	266	31,158
Haeji Kang	70	67	67	62	266	31,158
Hanna Kang	69	70	64	64	267	21,612
Inbee Park	65	67	68	68	268	19,702
Jessica Korda	68	66	69	65	268	19,702
Chella Choi	66	65	70	68	269	16,803
Jennifer Johnson	67	68	68	66	269	16,803
Michelle Wie	69	67	67	66	269	16,803
Irene Cho	65	72	67	65	269	16,803
Christina Kim	71	65	66	68	270	13,849
Sun Young Yoo	68	67	68	67	270	13,849
I.K. Kim	68	66	70	66	270	13,849
So Yeon Ryu	71	67	68	64	270	13,849
Dewi Claire Schreefel	69	67	69	65	270	13,849
Ryann O'Toole	66	65	71	68	270	13,849
Morgan Pressel	68	70	69	64	271	11,894
Anna Nordqvist	67	64	67	73	271	11,894
Lizette Salas	70	67	67	68	272	10,971
Lisa McCloskey	68	69	67	68	272	10,971
Mariajo Uribe	70	68	67	68	273	9,554
Belen Mozo	65	66	73	69	273	9,554
Alena Sharp	68	71	69	65	273	9,554
Jee Young Lee	68	68	68	69	273	9,554
Katie Burnett	72	66	69	66	273	9,554

Marathon Classic

Highland Meadows Golf Club, Sylvania, Ohio
Par 34-37–71; 6,428 yards

July 18-21
purse, $1,300,000

	SCORES				TOTAL	MONEY
Beatriz Recari	69	65	67	66	267	$195,000
Paula Creamer	66	68	67	67	268	120,655
Jodi Ewart Shadoff	69	68	68	66	271	77,618
Lexi Thompson	66	71	67	67	271	77,618
Angela Stanford	71	72	64	67	274	49,544
Jacqui Concolino	67	68	69	70	274	49,544
Jennifer Johnson	73	66	66	70	275	31,543
Stacy Lewis	70	72	69	64	275	31,543
Meena Lee	70	73	70	62	275	31,543
Chie Arimura	69	67	68	71	275	31,543
*Lydia Ko	69	67	71	68	275	
Brittany Lang	68	72	68	68	276	22,476
Haeji Kang	67	71	71	67	276	22,476
So Yeon Ryu	68	69	70	69	276	22,476
Se Ri Pak	69	74	67	66	276	22,476
Chella Choi	68	71	66	72	277	18,144
Mo Martin	68	70	68	71	277	18,144
I.K. Kim	70	69	70	68	277	18,144
Amelia Lewis	74	68	68	68	278	15,220
Ayako Uehara	68	72	68	70	278	15,220
Hee Young Park	71	68	67	72	278	15,220
Dewi Claire Schreefel	69	71	67	71	278	15,220
Danah Bordner	73	70	66	69	278	15,220
Heather Bowie Young	70	69	68	72	279	13,102
Cindy LaCrosse	71	68	69	71	279	13,102
Kristy McPherson	73	71	68	67	279	13,102
Gerina Piller	67	72	68	73	280	11,032
Brooke Pancake	71	72	66	71	280	11,032

	SCORES				TOTAL	MONEY
Moira Dunn	73	67	72	68	280	11,032
Mika Miyazato	70	70	72	68	280	11,032
Candie Kung	71	69	70	70	280	11,032
Eun-Hee Ji	68	72	67	73	280	11,032

Ricoh Women's British Open

See Ladies European Tour section.

The Solheim Cup

Colorado Golf Club, Parker, Colorado   August 16-18
Par 36-36–72; 7,604 yards

FIRST DAY
Morning Foursomes

Anna Nordqvist and Caroline Hedwall (Europe) defeated Stacy Lewis and Lizette Salas, 4 and 2.
Suzann Pettersen and Beatriz Recari (Europe) defeated Brittany Lang and Angela Stanford, 2 and 1.
Morgan Pressel and Jessica Korda (US) defeated Catriona Matthew and Jodi Ewart Shadoff, 3 and 2.
Azahara Munoz and Karine Icher (Europe) defeated Cristie Kerr and Paula Creamer, 2 and 1.

POINTS: Europe 3, United States 1

Afternoon Fourball

Pettersen and Carlota Ciganda (Europe) defeated Lewis and Lexi Thompson, 1 up.
Hedwall and Caroline Masson (Europe) defeated Stanford and Gerina Piller 2 and 1.
Brittany Lincicome and Lang (US) defeated Nordqvist and Giulia Sergas, 4 and 3.
Kerr and Michelle Wie (US) defeated Matthew and Charley Hull, 2 and 1.

POINTS: Europe 5, United States 3

SECOND DAY
Morning Foursomes

Nordqvist and Hedwall (Europe) defeated Pressel and Korda, 2 and 1.
Lewis and Creamer (US) defeated Munoz and Icher, 1 up.
Matthew and Masson (Europe) halved with Lincicome and Salas.
Wie and Lang (US) defeated Pettersen and Recari, 2 and 1.

POINTS: Europe 6½, United States 5½

Afternoon Fourball

Ewart Shadoff and Hull (Europe) defeated Creamer and Thompson, 2 up.
Munoz and Ciganda (Europe) defeated Piller and Stanford, 1 up.
Hedwall and Masson (Europe) defeated Wie and Korda, 2 and 1.
Recari and Icher (Europe) defeated Kerr and Pressel, 1 up.

POINTS: Europe 10½, United States 5½

THIRD DAY
Singles

Nordqvist (Europe) halved with Lewis.
Hull (Europe) defeated Creamer, 5 and 4
Lang (US) defeated Munoz, 2 and 1
Ciganda (Europe) defeated Pressel, 4 and 2
Hedwall (Europe) defeated Wie, 1 up.
Matthew (Europe) halved with Piller.
Pettersen (Europe) halved with Salas.
Sergas (Europe) halved with Korda.
Lexi Thompson (US) defeated Caroline Masson, 4 and 3.
Ewart Shadoff (Europe) defeated Lincicome, 3 and 2.
Recari (Europe) defeated Stanford, 2 and 1.
Icher (Europe) halved with Kerr.

TOTAL POINTS: Europe 18, United States 10

CN Canadian Women's Open

Royal Mayfair Golf Club, Edmonton, Alberta, Canada
Par 35-35–70; 6,403 yards

August 22-25
purse, $2,000,000

	SCORES				TOTAL	MONEY
*Lydia Ko	65	69	67	64	265	
Karine Icher	67	66	70	67	270	$300,000
Brittany Lincicome	68	68	66	69	271	159,346
Caroline Hedwall	68	68	64	71	271	159,346
Stacy Prammanasudh	68	67	69	68	272	93,539
I.K. Kim	71	66	65	70	272	93,539
Suzann Pettersen	69	67	65	72	273	62,697
Caroline Masson	70	67	67	69	273	62,697
Gerina Piller	70	66	67	71	274	50,057
Paula Creamer	66	68	69	72	275	41,292
Jessica Korda	70	66	68	71	275	41,292
Jodi Ewart Shadoff	71	66	67	71	275	41,292
Brittany Lang	70	67	68	71	276	32,258
Angela Stanford	65	68	73	70	276	32,258
Inbee Park	67	65	74	70	276	32,258
Mika Miyazato	70	67	70	69	276	32,258
Charley Hull	69	66	71	71	277	26,359
Na Yeon Choi	67	71	70	69	277	26,359
Catriona Matthew	70	66	71	70	277	26,359
Lexi Thompson	71	65	69	73	278	22,854
Ai Miyazato	70	68	71	69	278	22,854
Cristie Kerr	66	66	75	71	278	22,854
Anna Nordqvist	70	70	70	68	278	22,854
Danielle Kang	71	67	69	72	279	19,335
Juli Inkster	69	72	69	69	279	19,335
Jiyai Shin	74	66	67	72	279	19,335
Yani Tseng	72	68	66	73	279	19,335
Pernilla Lindberg	70	69	72	68	279	19,335
Mina Harigae	73	69	69	69	280	15,896
Christel Boeljon	65	72	71	72	280	15,896
Haeji Kang	72	68	70	70	280	15,896
Sandra Gal	72	68	69	71	280	15,896
Chella Choi	69	70	69	72	280	15,896

Safeway Classic

Columbia Edgewater Country Club, Portland, Oregon
Par 36-36–72; 6,465 yards

August 29-September 1
purse, $1,300,000

	SCORES				TOTAL	MONEY
Suzann Pettersen	68	63	70	67	268	$195,000
Stacy Lewis	67	70	65	68	270	117,114
Lizette Salas	66	68	68	69	271	84,958
Cristie Kerr	66	68	69	69	272	65,722
Caroline Masson	69	64	70	70	273	52,899
Sandra Gal	66	66	73	69	274	39,754
Gerina Piller	67	72	69	66	274	39,754
Karrie Webb	69	67	67	72	275	31,739
Lexi Thompson	65	70	71	70	276	23,628
Pornanong Phatlum	64	66	71	75	276	23,628
Sandra Changkija	68	66	69	73	276	23,628
Dewi Claire Schreefel	70	70	69	67	276	23,628
Austin Ernst	67	75	62	72	276	23,628
Yani Tseng	67	68	63	78	276	23,628
Beatriz Recari	71	66	69	71	277	15,837
Jiyai Shin	68	68	71	70	277	15,837
Angela Stanford	71	67	67	72	277	15,837
Ai Miyazato	67	70	73	67	277	15,837
Heather Bowie Young	67	69	71	70	277	15,837
Na Yeon Choi	70	66	70	71	277	15,837
Anna Nordqvist	69	70	63	75	277	15,837
Sun Young Yoo	68	70	71	68	277	15,837
Brittany Lang	68	68	68	74	278	12,717
Paige Mackenzie	71	68	70	69	278	12,717
Morgan Pressel	69	68	65	76	278	12,717
Michelle Wie	67	73	72	67	279	11,125
Hee-Won Han	71	65	72	71	279	11,125
Pernilla Lindberg	68	74	67	70	279	11,125
Natalie Gulbis	68	68	70	73	279	11,125
*Soo-Bin Kim	73	69	68	70	280	
Jacqui Concolino	73	68	72	67	280	8,940
Maria Hjorth	70	70	64	76	280	8,940
Min Seo Kwak	69	67	71	73	280	8,940
Jodi Ewart Shadoff	69	70	68	73	280	8,940
Brooke Pancake	70	72	68	70	280	8,940
Dori Carter	68	70	70	72	280	8,940
Carlota Ciganda	73	68	69	70	280	8,940

Evian Championship

See Ladies European Tour section.

Reignwood LPGA Classic

Pine Valley Golf Club, Beijing, China
Par 36-37–731; 6,596 yards

October 3-6
purse, $1,800,000

	SCORES				TOTAL	MONEY
Shanshan Feng	70	64	64	68	266	$270,000
Stacy Lewis	68	66	65	68	267	165,043
Inbee Park	69	68	66	68	271	119,727
Karrie Webb	71	68	66	67	272	92,618
Na Yeon Choi	64	71	72	69	276	74,547

	SCORES				TOTAL	MONEY
Yani Tseng	72	70	70	66	278	60,993
Pornanong Phatlum	70	70	69	71	280	45,331
Beatriz Recari	73	68	71	68	280	45,331
Christel Boeljon	70	71	70	69	280	45,331
So Yeon Ryu	71	69	70	71	281	31,915
Sun Young Yoo	72	70	72	67	281	31,915
Amy Yang	69	71	73	68	281	31,915
Caroline Hedwall	71	68	72	70	281	31,915
Chella Choi	73	70	68	70	281	31,915
Hee Young Park	68	73	74	67	282	24,216
Anna Nordqvist	69	72	72	69	282	24,216
Jessica Korda	64	68	76	74	282	24,216
Sandra Gal	72	73	66	71	282	24,216
Li-Ying Ye	69	74	68	72	283	21,144
Carlota Ciganda	69	73	72	69	283	21,144
Brittany Lang	71	70	71	72	284	19,699
Paola Moreno	69	71	72	72	284	19,699
Lisa McCloskey	74	72	73	66	285	16,958
Xi Yu Lin	72	66	71	76	285	16,958
Morgan Pressel	72	73	70	70	285	16,958
Mo Martin	70	68	75	72	285	16,958
Karine Icher	71	73	73	68	285	16,958
Vicky Hurst	73	67	75	70	285	16,958
Azahara Munoz	71	70	73	72	286	13,915
Moriya Jutanugarn	72	73	70	71	286	13,915
Caroline Masson	70	73	73	70	286	13,915
Ilhee Lee	71	71	73	71	286	13,915
*Simin Feng	72	75	68	71	286	

Sime Darby LPGA Malaysia

Kuala Lumpur Golf & Country Club, Kuala Lumpur, Malaysia October 10-13
Par 35-36–71; 6,246 yards purse, $2,000,000

	SCORES				TOTAL	MONEY
Lexi Thompson	67	63	66	69	265	$300,000
Shanshan Feng	67	65	70	67	269	186,577
Suzann Pettersen	67	68	67	70	272	120,026
Ilhee Lee	64	65	70	73	272	120,026
Amy Yang	72	62	74	66	274	84,274
Sandra Gal	69	70	71	66	276	50,394
Karine Icher	70	66	68	72	276	50,394
Chella Choi	72	66	71	67	276	50,394
Stacy Lewis	69	68	70	69	276	50,394
Beatriz Recari	66	71	70	69	276	50,394
Alison Walshe	67	71	69	69	276	50,394
Morgan Pressel	68	72	70	67	277	33,573
Michelle Wie	71	66	71	69	277	33,573
Hee Young Park	69	67	70	71	277	33,573
Paula Creamer	66	67	75	70	278	26,763
Na Yeon Choi	76	68	68	66	278	26,763
So Yeon Ryu	70	65	70	73	278	26,763
Anna Nordqvist	68	71	65	74	278	26,763
Pornanong Phatlum	71	66	68	73	278	26,763
Jodi Ewart Shadoff	66	70	69	74	279	22,677
I.K. Kim	67	66	72	74	279	22,677
Caroline Hedwall	68	69	72	70	279	22,677
Gerina Piller	70	66	71	74	281	20,260
Carlota Ciganda	71	69	71	70	281	20,260
Sun Young Yoo	70	68	71	72	281	20,260

	SCORES				TOTAL	MONEY
Jane Park	69	69	73	71	282	17,059
Jennifer Johnson	71	70	68	73	282	17,059
Jessica Korda	68	70	76	68	282	17,059
Jiyai Shin	71	66	75	70	282	17,059
Brittany Lang	65	71	70	76	282	17,059
Azahara Munoz	72	68	69	73	282	17,059

LPGA KEB - HanaBank Championship

Sky 72 Golf Club, Ocean Course, Incheon, South Korea   October 18-20
Par 36-36–72; 6,364 yards   purse, $1,900,000

	SCORES			TOTAL	MONEY
Amy Yang	67	71	69	207	$285,000
Hee Kyung Seo	71	68	68	207	173,411
(Yang defeated Seo on first playoff hole.)					
Michelle Wie	69	73	66	208	100,479
Sei Young Kim	71	68	69	208	100,479
Suzann Pettersen	69	69	70	208	100,479
Ha-Neul Kim	69	70	71	210	64,085
Brittany Lincicome	71	71	69	211	53,642
Jane Park	70	72	70	212	40,825
Se Ri Pak	73	68	71	212	40,825
Jiyai Shin	69	71	72	212	40,825
Anna Nordqvist	67	70	75	212	40,825
Jodi Ewart Shadoff	71	72	70	213	29,431
Eun-Hee Ji	71	72	70	213	29,431
Caroline Hedwall	68	74	71	213	29,431
Chella Choi	73	68	72	213	29,431
Ju Young Park	67	71	75	213	29,431
Alison Walshe	71	68	75	214	22,748
Ha Na Jang	74	71	69	214	22,748
Sun Young Yoo	72	73	69	214	22,748
Na Yeon Choi	71	72	71	214	22,748
Haeji Kang	72	69	73	214	22,748
Sandra Gal	76	72	67	215	18,514
Soo Jin Yang	73	74	68	215	18,514
Lexi Thompson	71	74	70	215	18,514
Carlota Ciganda	69	76	70	215	18,514
So Yeon Ryu	70	72	73	215	18,514
Hyo Joo Kim	71	70	74	215	18,514
In Gee Chun	77	71	68	216	15,214
Cristie Kerr	73	72	71	216	15,214
Jenny Shin	69	75	72	216	15,214
Inbee Park	70	73	73	216	15,214

Sunrise LPGA Taiwan Championship

Sunrise Golf & Country Club, Yang Mei, Taoyuan, Taiwan   October 24-27
Par 36-36–72; 6,390 yards   purse, $2,000,000

	SCORES				TOTAL	MONEY
Suzann Pettersen	68	69	73	69	279	$300,000
Azahara Munoz	73	72	69	70	284	186,096
Caroline Hedwall	71	73	72	70	286	135,000
Eun-Hee Ji	72	76	69	70	287	104,433
Mina Harigae	74	71	75	68	288	70,132

	SCORES				TOTAL	MONEY
Se Ri Pak	76	72	69	71	288	70,132
Irene Cho	71	74	72	71	288	70,132
M.J. Hur	75	71	72	71	289	45,680
Beatriz Recari	72	71	73	73	289	45,680
Sun Young Yoo	73	69	72	75	289	45,680
Moriya Jutanugarn	76	75	72	68	291	30,986
Candie Kung	73	73	74	71	291	30,986
Chella Choi	72	72	76	71	291	30,986
Anna Nordqvist	77	71	71	72	291	30,986
Paula Creamer	72	74	73	72	291	30,986
Hee Kyung Seo	74	70	74	73	291	30,986
Na Yeon Choi	74	72	71	74	291	30,986
Carlota Ciganda	72	70	72	77	291	30,986
Mika Miyazato	75	75	70	72	292	23,841
Lexi Thompson	74	74	70	74	292	23,841
Ilhee Lee	73	75	71	74	293	21,804
Pernilla Lindberg	75	71	72	75	293	21,804
Alison Walshe	71	73	79	70	293	21,804
Michelle Wie	74	77	72	71	294	19,817
Catriona Matthew	75	72	74	73	294	19,817
Juli Inkster	75	74	72	74	295	18,391
Katherine Hull-Kirk	73	70	77	75	295	18,391
Hee-Won Han	77	76	72	71	296	15,399
Haeji Kang	77	73	73	73	296	15,399
Rebecca Lee-Bentham	73	78	71	74	296	15,399
Ai Miyazato	74	76	72	74	296	15,399
Julieta Granada	74	76	70	76	296	15,399
Gerina Piller	74	74	72	76	296	15,399
Belen Mozo	72	77	70	77	296	15,399

Mizuno Classic

See Japan LPGA Tour section.

Lorena Ochoa Invitational

Guadalajara Country Club, Guadalajara, Mexico
Par 36-36–72; 6,626 yards

November 14-17
purse, $1,000,000

	SCORES				TOTAL	MONEY
Lexi Thompson	72	64	67	69	272	$200,000
Stacy Lewis	72	66	67	68	273	103,449
So Yeon Ryu	68	67	71	69	275	75,045
Inbee Park	68	68	72	69	277	58,053
Pornanong Phatlum	66	69	72	71	278	42,479
Suzann Pettersen	70	68	70	70	278	42,479
I.K. Kim	70	67	67	75	279	25,884
Michelle Wie	69	73	67	70	279	25,884
Azahara Munoz	71	69	69	70	279	25,884
Amy Yang	67	73	70	69	279	25,884
Lizette Salas	70	67	71	71	279	25,884
Anna Nordqvist	68	67	72	73	280	19,200
Chella Choi	74	68	72	66	280	19,200
Karine Icher	70	68	72	71	281	16,462
Ilhee Lee	74	66	73	68	281	16,462
Jenny Shin	69	69	75	68	281	16,462
Gerina Piller	71	65	74	72	282	14,386
Mo Martin	73	69	70	70	282	14,386
Caroline Hedwall	73	73	69	68	283	13,253

	SCORES				TOTAL	MONEY
Carlota Ciganda	72	69	69	73	283	13,253
Jessica Korda	72	68	74	71	285	11,894
Angela Stanford	75	72	71	67	285	11,894
Ai Miyazato	70	72	72	71	285	11,894
Cristie Kerr	77	67	72	69	285	11,894
Jodi Ewart Shadoff	75	67	72	72	286	10,620
Brittany Lincicome	76	67	69	74	286	10,620
Morgan Pressel	73	66	74	74	287	10,024
Paula Creamer	74	67	77	70	288	9,628
Catriona Matthew	74	71	71	73	289	9,232
Sandra Gal	72	74	74	70	290	8,892

CME Group Titleholders

Tiburon Golf Club, Naples, Florida
Par 36-36–72; 6,949 yards

November 21-24
purse, $2,000,000

	SCORES				TOTAL	MONEY
Shanshan Feng	66	74	67	66	273	$700,000
Gerina Piller	71	67	67	69	274	139,713
Pornanong Phatlum	70	68	67	70	275	101,352
Sandra Gal	64	69	74	69	276	78,404
Inbee Park	68	72	69	68	277	63,106
Stacy Lewis	71	73	63	71	278	44,238
Cristie Kerr	69	69	71	69	278	44,238
Sun Young Yoo	68	68	73	69	278	44,238
Jennifer Johnson	71	69	70	69	279	32,509
So Yeon Ryu	70	71	69	69	279	32,509
Michelle Wie	72	70	66	72	280	26,848
Ilhee Lee	69	77	69	65	280	26,848
Amy Yang	73	68	69	70	280	26,848
Azahara Munoz	72	68	69	73	282	22,871
Angela Stanford	74	69	69	70	282	22,871
Hee Young Park	69	70	72	72	283	19,123
Meena Lee	69	72	70	72	283	19,123
Morgan Pressel	71	68	74	70	283	19,123
Brittany Lang	68	76	70	69	283	19,123
Lexi Thompson	66	74	67	76	283	19,123
Catriona Matthew	70	73	75	66	284	16,063
Sandra Changkija	67	74	70	73	284	16,063
Lydia Ko	71	71	72	70	284	16,063
Anna Nordqvist	66	73	75	70	284	16,063
Jane Park	68	77	69	71	285	13,807
Karrie Webb	70	73	69	73	285	13,807
Chella Choi	71	70	71	73	285	13,807
Ayako Uehara	69	72	71	73	285	13,807
Mika Miyazato	70	73	68	76	287	11,780
Suzann Pettersen	72	72	71	72	287	11,780
Mo Martin	69	72	74	72	287	11,780
Natalie Gulbis	70	70	65	82	287	11,780

Ladies European Tour

Volvik RACV Ladies Masters

See Australian Ladies Tour section.

ISPS Handa New Zealand Women's Open

See Australian Ladies Tour section.

ISPS Handa Women's Australian Open

See Australian Ladies Tour section.

Mission Hills World Ladies Championship

Mission Hills, Sandbelt Trails Course, Haikou, Hainan, China
Par 36-36–72; 6,296 yards

March 7-10
purse, US$500,000

	SCORES				TOTAL	MONEY
Suzann Pettersen	70	67	67	66	270	€57,560.40
Inbee Park	68	65	69	69	271	38,949.20
Shanshan Feng	70	69	72	66	277	26,861.52
Soo Jin Yang	69	69	68	72	278	18,496.08
Bo-Mi Suh	68	69	72	69	278	18,496.08
Veronica Zorzi	70	67	72	70	279	13,430.76
Dewi Claire Schreefel	71	71	68	70	280	11,512.08
Xi Yu Lin	72	67	71	71	281	8,269.51
Carlota Ciganda	71	63	74	73	281	8,269.51
Hyo-Joo Kim	68	70	71	72	281	8,269.51
Gwladys Nocera	67	74	69	71	281	8,269.51
Beth Allen	72	73	67	70	282	6,341.24
Bree Arthur	70	74	69	69	282	6,341.24
Trish Johnson	70	69	74	69	282	6,341.24
Ariya Jutanugarn	69	71	69	73	282	6,341.24
Karen Lunn	72	71	70	71	284	5,679.29
Kristie Smith	69	70	75	70	284	5,679.29
Nikki Campbell	72	72	73	68	285	5,372.30
Stefania Croce	70	75	67	73	285	5,372.30
Sophie Walker	67	75	70	74	286	5,026.94

Lalla Meryem Cup

Golf de l'Ocean, Agadir, Morocco
Par 35-36–71; 6,282 yards

March 28-31
purse, €325,000

	SCORES				TOTAL	MONEY
Ariya Jutanugarn	69	67	67	67	270	€48,750
Beth Allen	70	68	67	68	273	27,868.75
Charley Hull	68	70	64	71	273	27,868.75
Katie Burnett	70	70	65	69	274	17,550
Mikaela Parmlid	73	66	69	68	276	13,780

	SCORES				TOTAL	MONEY
Sarah Kemp	72	68	69	69	278	10,562.50
Marianne Skarpnord	66	76	70	66	278	10,562.50
Klara Spilkova	72	70	71	66	279	6,971.25
Laura Davies	71	68	69	71	279	6,971.25
Lee-Anne Pace	70	68	67	74	279	6,971.25
Melissa Reid	69	71	70	69	279	6,971.25
Cheyenne Woods	72	73	69	66	280	5,167.50
Celine Palomar	72	68	74	66	280	5,167.50
Emma Cabrera-Bello	70	76	68	66	280	5,167.50
Mallory Fraiche	70	68	72	70	280	5,167.50
Nikki Campbell	71	70	71	69	281	4,680
Marta Silva Zamora	75	67	73	67	282	4,550
Linda Wessberg	73	70	72	68	283	4,249.38
Karen Lunn	72	73	70	68	283	4,249.38
Elizabeth Bennett	72	69	72	70	283	4,249.38
Line Vedel	71	71	73	68	283	4,249.38

South African Women's Open

Southbroom Golf Club, Hibiscus Coast, South Africa
Par 36-36–72; 5,785 yards
(Event shortened to 18 holes—rain and wind.)

April 19-21
purse, €290,000

	SCORES	TOTAL	MONEY
Marianne Skarpnord	69	69	€43,500
Stacy Lee Bregman	70	70	14,827.29
Charley Hull	70	70	14,827.29
Minea Blomqvist	70	70	14,827.29
Ashleigh Simon	70	70	14,827.29
Nina Holleder	70	70	14,827.29
Camilla Lennarth	70	70	14,827.29
Katie Burnett	70	70	14,827.29
Valentine Derrey	71	71	5,153.71
Miriam Nagl	71	71	5,153.71
Cathryn Bristow	71	71	5,153.71
Emily Taylor	71	71	5,153.71
Rebecca Hudson	71	71	5,153.71
Line Vedel	71	71	5,153.71
Mallory Fraiche	71	71	5,153.71
Sarah King	72	72	3,714.90
Becky Brewerton	72	72	3,714.90
Ursula Wikstrom	72	72	3,714.90
*Kim Williams	72	72	
Melissa Eaton	72	72	3,714.90
Katy McNicoll	72	72	3,714.90
Nontaya Srisawang	72	72	3,714.90
Trish Johnson	72	72	3,714.90
Nicola Eaton	72	72	3,714.90
Lee-Anne Pace	72	72	3,714.90
Celine Palomar	72	72	3,714.90

Turkish Airlines Ladies Open

National Golf Club, Belek, Antalya, Turkey
Par 36-37–73; 6,194 yards

May 9-12
purse, €250,000

	SCORES				TOTAL	MONEY
Lee-Anne Pace	70	77	70	72	289	€37,500
Minea Blomqvist	75	75	70	70	290	18,791.67
Charley Hull	75	71	69	75	290	18,791.67
Carlota Ciganda	69	74	72	75	290	18,791.67
Christel Boeljon	71	78	67	75	291	10,600
Holly Clyburn	74	71	75	72	292	7,025
Florentyna Parker	74	71	72	75	292	7,025
Eleanor Givens	72	73	74	73	292	7,025
Trish Johnson	71	71	75	75	292	7,025
Vikki Laing	77	73	68	75	293	4,800
Linda Wessberg	72	77	70	74	293	4,800
Gwladys Nocera	81	71	70	72	294	3,975
Line Vedel	76	76	71	71	294	3,975
Laura Davies	72	70	78	74	294	3,975
Sarah Kemp	70	79	71	74	294	3,975
Carmen Alonso	70	72	79	75	296	3,600
Klara Spilkova	76	72	76	73	297	3,158.33
Caroline Afonso	76	69	76	76	297	3,158.33
Bree Arthur	75	77	72	73	297	3,158.33
Margarita Ramos	75	72	73	77	297	3,158.33
Sharmila Nicollet	74	75	76	72	297	3,158.33
Valentine Derrey	74	74	74	75	297	3,158.33
Mireia Prat	73	75	75	74	297	3,158.33
Ann-Kathrin Lindner	72	77	74	74	297	3,158.33
Miriam Nagl	72	75	74	76	297	3,158.33

Deloitte Ladies Open

The International, Amsterdam, Netherlands
Par 37-36–73; 6,404 yards

May 24-26
purse, €250,000

	SCORES			TOTAL	MONEY
Holly Clyburn	71	69	71	211	€37,500
Charley Hull	72	73	69	214	25,375
Carin Koch	73	71	71	215	17,500
Carlota Ciganda	71	71	74	216	10,950
Bree Arthur	70	75	71	216	10,950
Camilla Lennarth	66	73	77	216	10,950
Florentyna Parker	74	72	71	217	6,450
Pamela Pretswell	71	73	73	217	6,450
Melissa Reid	70	72	75	217	6,450
Stacey Keating	72	74	72	218	4,800
Hannah Burke	71	74	73	218	4,800
Hannah Jun	72	74	73	219	4,162.50
Christel Boeljon	70	72	77	219	4,162.50
Mikaela Parmlid	76	73	71	220	3,468.75
Tania Elosegui	74	69	77	220	3,468.75
Veronica Zorzi	73	77	70	220	3,468.75
Vikki Laing	73	74	73	220	3,468.75
Nikki Campbell	71	76	73	220	3,468.75
Emily Taylor	71	74	75	220	3,468.75
Line Vedel	70	75	75	220	3,468.75
Miriam Nagl	70	74	76	220	3,468.75

UniCredit Ladies German Open

Golfpark Gut Hausern, Munich, Germany
Par 36-36–72; 6,204 yards
(Event shortened to 27 holes—rain.)

May 30-June 2
purse, €350,000

	SCORES		TOTAL	MONEY
Carlota Ciganda	68	33	101	€52,500
Charley Hull	67	34	101	35,525
(Ciganda defeated Hull on first playoff hole.)				
Rebecca Hudson	68	34	102	24,500
Marjet van der Graaff	69	34	103	14,112.50
Nontaya Srisawang	68	35	103	14,112.50
Stefanie Michl	67	36	103	14,122.50
Linda Wessberg	69	34	103	14,112.50
Bree Arthur	70	34	104	8,750
Line Vedel	67	38	105	5,614.58
Sophie Walker	70	35	105	5,614.58
Valentine Derrey	70	35	105	5,614.58
Lee-Anne Pace	69	36	105	5,614.58
Jade Schaeffer	68	37	105	5,614.58
Holly Clyburn	70	35	105	5,614.58
Nikki Campbell	70	35	105	5,614.58
Cassandra Kirkland	70	35	105	5,614.58
Marion Ricordeau	70	35	105	5,614.58
Ursula Wikstrom	70	35	105	5,614.58
Hannah Jun	71	34	105	5,614.58
Maria Hernandez	71	34	105	5,614.58
*Sophia Popov	72	33	105	

Allianz Ladies Slovak Open

Golf Resort Tale, Brezno, Tale, Slovakia
Par 35-37–72; 6,242 yards

June 20-23
purse, €250,000

	SCORES				TOTAL	MONEY
Gwladys Nocera	70	68	71	70	279	€37,500
Lee-Anne Pace	71	70	70	72	283	25,375
Whitney Hillier	75	70	69	70	284	17,500
Liz Young	73	74	65	73	285	12,050
Mikaela Parmlid	72	70	73	70	285	12,050
Noora Tamminen	73	71	70	72	286	8,750
Hannah Burke	72	70	70	75	287	6,450
Klara Spilkova	71	72	70	74	287	6,450
Nikki Campbell	67	78	69	73	287	6,450
Malene Jorgensen	75	71	68	74	288	4,800
Trish Johnson	69	72	75	72	288	4,800
Nontaya Srisawang	74	68	74	73	289	3,975
Veronica Zorzi	73	70	76	70	289	3,975
Laura Davies	70	76	72	71	289	3,975
Daniela Holmqvist	70	72	78	69	289	3,975
Mireia Prat	75	71	69	75	290	3,450
Linda Wessberg	71	70	74	75	290	3,450
Louise Larsson	70	72	74	74	290	3,450
Florentyna Parker	69	76	76	69	290	3,450
Margherita Rigon	73	71	73	74	291	3,187.50
Diana Luna	71	75	72	73	291	3,187.50

Open de Espana Femenino

Club de Campo Villa de Madrid, Madrid, Spain
Par 37-35–72; 6,411 yards

July 18-21
purse, €350,000

	SCORES				TOTAL	MONEY
Lee-Anne Pace	67	69	68	71	275	€52,500
Mikaela Parmlid	69	71	66	70	276	35,525
Joanna Klatten	69	71	67	72	279	24,500
Celine Herbin	68	68	68	76	280	18,900
Ashleigh Simon	70	71	71	69	281	13,545
Gwladys Nocera	69	72	69	71	281	13,545
Minea Blomqvist	74	72	67	69	282	8,106
Carlota Ciganda	74	71	66	71	282	8,106
Linda Wessberg	74	67	72	69	282	8,106
Titiya Plucksataporn	72	75	68	67	282	8,106
Marta Silva Zamora	70	74	69	69	282	8,106
Viva Schlasberg	73	68	72	70	283	5,565
Laura Cabanillas	71	72	72	68	283	5,565
Melissa Reid	70	69	72	72	283	5,565
Beth Allen	69	72	69	73	283	5,565
Margherita Rigon	74	67	73	70	284	4,650
Ann-Kathrin Lindner	73	70	71	70	284	4,650
Veronica Zorzi	73	70	69	72	284	4,650
Nontaya Srisawang	73	69	69	73	284	4,650
Rebecca Artis	72	72	69	71	284	4,650
Eleanor Givens	72	70	71	71	284	4,650
Valentine Derrey	70	69	73	72	284	4,650

ISPS Handa Ladies European Masters

Buckinghamshire Golf Club, Denham, Buckinghamshire, England
Par 36-36–72; 6,401 yards

July 26-28
purse, €400,000

	SCORES			TOTAL	MONEY
Karrie Webb	68	67	65	200	€60,000
Ashleigh Simon	63	69	69	201	40,600
Caroline Masson	63	69	70	202	28,000
Sandra Gal	68	68	67	203	19,280
Christina Kim	68	67	68	203	19,280
Line Vedel	68	71	66	205	13,000
Klara Spilkova	66	66	73	205	13,000
Nontaya Srisawang	71	66	69	206	10,000
Charley Hull	68	66	74	208	8,480
Rebecca Artis	66	72	70	208	8,480
Camilla Lennarth	70	67	72	209	7,360
Nikki Campbell	75	67	68	210	6,360
Pernilla Lindberg	70	69	71	210	6,360
Trish Johnson	70	68	72	210	6,360
Pamela Pretswell	68	69	73	210	6,360
Lee-Anne Pace	76	68	67	211	5,448
Julie Greciet	72	70	69	211	5,448
Becky Morgan	70	66	75	211	5,448
Diana Luna	67	73	71	211	5,448
Cheyenne Woods	67	71	73	211	5,448

Ricoh Women's British Open

St. Andrews Old Course, St. Andrews, Fife, Scotland   August 1-4
Par 36-36–72; 6,672 yards   purse, US$2,500,000

	SCORES				TOTAL	MONEY
Stacy Lewis	67	72	69	72	280	€302,982.14
Hee Young Park	70	69	70	73	282	161,437.96
Na Yeon Choi	67	67	75	73	282	161,437.96
Suzann Pettersen	70	67	72	74	283	94,495.41
Morgan Pressel	66	70	71	76	283	94,495.41
Lizette Salas	68	72	72	73	285	74,203.77
Mamiko Higa	70	69	72	75	286	63,759.54
Miki Saiki	69	66	74	77	286	63,759.54
Natalie Gulbis	71	72	74	70	287	52,420.09
Nicole Castrale	67	70	76	74	287	52,420.09
Meena Lee	71	69	70	78	288	38,235.83
Anna Nordqvist	70	74	72	72	288	38,235.83
Catriona Matthew	68	74	68	78	288	38,235.83
Pernilla Lindberg	68	73	73	74	288	38,235.83
Paula Creamer	68	72	72	76	288	38,235.83
Cristie Kerr	71	74	75	69	289	29,840.66
Xi Yu Lin	72	68	73	77	290	25,861.90
Ayako Uehara	69	74	70	77	290	25,861.90
Jenny Shin	69	71	74	76	290	25,861.90
Angela Stanford	69	70	76	75	290	25,861.90
So Yeon Ryu	69	70	73	78	290	25,861.90
Karine Icher	70	74	75	72	291	21,750.52
Katherine Hull-Kirk	69	73	75	74	291	21,750.52
Mariajo Uribe	69	73	72	77	291	21,750.52
Jessica Korda	72	71	73	76	292	16,710.77
Candie Kung	72	70	73	77	292	16,710.77
Sun Young Yoo	71	71	72	78	292	16,710.77
Lee-Anne Pace	70	71	72	79	292	16,710.77
Shanshan Feng	69	76	76	71	292	16,710.77
Hee-Kyung Seo	69	76	76	71	292	16,710.77
Sandra Gal	69	74	75	74	292	16,710.77
Malene Jorgensen	69	74	75	74	292	16,710.77
Dori Carter	68	72	72	80	292	16,710.77
Eun Hee Ji	67	75	72	78	292	16,710.77
Ryann O'Toole	67	73	73	79	292	16,710.77
Gerina Piller	74	69	77	73	293	12,433.61
Jiyai Shin	71	72	77	73	293	12,433.61
Holly Clyburn	70	73	75	75	293	12,433.61
Jee Young Lee	70	67	77	79	293	12,433.61
Marianne Skarpnord	69	74	75	75	293	12,433.61
Mikaela Parmlid	69	69	75	80	293	12,433.61
*Lydia Ko	69	76	75	74	294	
Florentyna Parker	69	74	76	75	294	10,411.07
Inbee Park	69	73	74	78	294	10,411.07
Danielle Kang	68	75	75	76	294	10,411.07
*Georgia Hall	68	75	74	77	294	
Christel Boeljon	72	71	77	75	295	8,594.11
Minea Blomqvist	71	74	76	74	295	8,594.11
Se Ri Pak	71	73	75	76	295	8,594.11
Ashleigh Simon	71	72	75	77	295	8,594.11
I.K. Kim	70	73	75	77	295	8,594.11
Moriya Jutanugarn	72	73	79	72	296	6,564.94
M.J. Hur	72	72	78	74	296	6,564.94
Brittany Lincicome	70	73	81	72	296	6,564.94
Sydnee Michaels	67	75	79	75	296	6,564.94
Michelle Wie	74	70	78	75	297	5,172.38
Dewi Claire Schreefel	73	71	80	73	297	5,172.38

	SCORES				TOTAL	MONEY
*Celine Boutier	72	72	81	72	297	
Mika Miyazato	74	71	80	74	299	4,575.57
Lindsey Wright	70	74	79	76	299	4,575.57
Linda Wessberg	70	73	78	78	299	4,575.57
Line Vedel	72	71	80	77	300	4,177.69
Gwladys Nocera	74	71	78	78	301	3,879.29
Liz Young	68	75	77	81	301	3,879.29
Rikako Morita	70	75	86	71	302	3,580.88
Thidapa Suwannapura	71	74	83	75	303	3,282.47
Emily Taylor	70	74	82	77	303	3,282.47
Sarah Kemp	73	71	78	86	308	2,065.78
Moira Dunn	71	74	81	82	308	2,065.78

Honma Pilsen Golf Masters

Golf Park Plzen–Dysina, Prague, Czech Republic   August 9-11
Par 36-35–71; 5,817 yards   purse, €250,000

	SCORES			TOTAL	MONEY
Ann-Kathrin Lindner	66	67	68	201	€37,500
Alexandra Vilatte	70	69	63	202	21,437.50
Diana Luna	66	69	67	202	21,437.50
Katie Burnett	71	68	64	203	12,050
Maria Balikoeva	67	66	70	203	12,050
Veronica Zorzi	69	67	68	204	6,620
Stacey Keating	68	66	70	204	6,620
Lee-Anne Pace	67	68	69	204	6,620
Alison Whitaker	64	71	69	204	6,620
Jade Schaeffer	64	69	71	204	6,620
Liz Young	70	67	68	205	3,942.86
Sarah Kemp	69	67	69	205	3,942.86
Henni Zuel	68	68	69	205	3,942.86
Malene Jorgensen	68	67	70	205	3,942.86
Melissa Reid	67	69	69	205	3,942.86
Line Vedel	67	66	72	205	3,942.86
Ai Miyazato	65	71	69	205	3,942.86
Camilla Lennarth	72	68	66	206	3,230
Isabella Ramsay	69	68	69	206	3,230
Cheyenne Woods	68	70	68	206	3,230
Maria Hernandez	66	71	69	206	3,230
Laura Cabanillas	62	74	70	206	3,230

The Solheim Cup

See LPGA Tour section.

Aberdeen Asset Management Ladies Scottish Open

Archerfield Links, East Lothian, Scotland   August 30-September 1
Par 36-36–72; 6,322 yards   purse, €220,000

	SCORES			TOTAL	MONEY
Catriona Matthew	71	67	70	208	€31,536.90
Hannah Burke	71	71	68	210	21,339.97
Holly Clyburn	74	73	71	218	14,717.22
Pamela Pretswell	74	71	74	219	10,133.86

	SCORES	TOTAL	MONEY
Carly Booth	73 73 73	219	10,133.86
Stacy Lee Bregman	77 73 70	220	5,298.20
Stephanie Na	73 70 77	220	5,298.20
Rebecca Artis	72 76 72	220	5,298.20
Camilla Lennarth	71 73 76	220	5,298.20
Heather Macrae	70 80 70	220	5,298.20
Anne-Lise Caudal	69 72 79	220	5,298.20
Stacey Keating	75 73 73	221	3,474.32
Liz Young	73 68 80	221	3,474.32
Ann-Kathrin Lindner	72 70 79	221	3,474.32
Klara Spilkova	70 74 77	221	3,474.32
Minea Blomqvist	74 74 74	222	2,972.88
Rebecca Hudson	74 72 76	222	2,972.88
Maria Hernandez	74 69 79	222	2,972.88
Beth Allen	73 73 76	222	2,972.88
Emily Taylor	70 76 76	222	2,972.88

Helsingborg Open

Vasatorp Golf Club, Helsingborg, Skane, Sweden
Par 36-36–72; 6,318 yards

September 5-8
purse, €250,000

	SCORES	TOTAL	MONEY
Rebecca Artis	69 71 71 69	280	€37,500
Caroline Hedwall	69 70 67 75	281	25,375
Valentine Derrey	68 68 74 73	283	17,500
Lee-Anne Pace	69 68 73 75	285	13,500
Laura Davies	73 72 72 69	286	10,600
Caroline Afonso	72 71 71 73	287	8,750
Anna Nordqvist	70 71 73 74	288	6,450
Malene Jorgensen	70 70 71 77	288	6,450
Pernilla Lindberg	66 73 75 74	288	6,450
Linda Wessberg	70 72 70 77	289	4,633.33
Nontaya Srisawang	68 74 72 75	289	4,633.33
I.K. Kim	65 72 75 77	289	4,633.33
Trish Johnson	73 70 73 74	290	3,683.33
Stacy Lee Bregman	70 74 73 73	290	3,683.33
Nikki Garrett	68 78 70 74	290	3,683.33
Maria Hjorth	68 76 72 74	290	3,683.33
Liz Young	68 74 75 73	290	3,683.33
Camilla Lennarth	68 70 77 75	290	3,683.33
Marianne Skarpnord	73 73 73 72	291	3,075
Pamela Pretswell	72 76 73 70	291	3,075
Celine Herbin	72 73 75 71	291	3,075
Stephanie Na	70 72 77 72	291	3,075
Ashleigh Simon	70 72 74 75	291	3,075
Joanna Klatten	69 79 72 71	291	3,075
Gwladys Nocera	68 73 75 75	291	3,075

Evian Championship

Evian Golf Club, Evians-les-Bains, France
Par 35-36–71; 6,427 yards
(Event shortened to 54 holes—rain.)

September 12-15
purse, €2,496,170

	SCORES			TOTAL	MONEY
Suzann Pettersen	66	69	68	203	€366,393
*Lydia Ko	68	67	70	205	
Lexi Thompson	72	67	68	207	223,963.83
So Yeon Ryu	71	66	71	208	144,065.73
Se Ri Pak	66	71	71	208	144,065.73
Chella Choi	70	67	72	209	84,408.81
Angela Stanford	69	71	69	209	84,408.81
Stacy Lewis	69	67	73	209	84,408.81
Jennifer Johnson	70	70	70	210	57,633.62
Beatriz Recari	69	69	72	210	57,633.62
Rebecca Lee-Bentham	75	66	70	211	44,693.84
Shanshan Feng	70	72	69	211	44,693.84
Lizette Salas	70	71	70	211	44,693.84
Ilhee Lee	70	71	70	211	44,693.84
Ai Miyazato	75	68	69	212	34,697.42
Cindy Lacrosse	73	70	69	212	34,697.42
Katherine Hull-Kirk	71	71	70	212	34,697.42
Karrie Webb	68	72	72	212	34,697.42
Caroline Hedwall	74	68	71	213	26,777.22
Mi Hyang Lee	73	70	70	213	26,777.22
Hee Young Park	72	74	67	213	26,777.22
Azahara Munoz	70	71	72	213	26,777.22
Paula Creamer	70	69	74	213	26,777.22
I.K. Kim	69	69	75	213	26,777.22
Sandra Gal	66	74	73	213	26,777.22
Mika Miyazato	65	69	79	213	26,777.22
Mina Harigae	71	73	70	214	21,275.22
Holly Clyburn	71	70	73	214	21,275.22
Momoko Ueda	70	70	74	214	21,275.22
Ayako Uehara	69	73	72	214	21,275.22
Danielle Kang	72	73	70	215	17,436.24
Jenny Shin	71	73	71	215	17,436.24
Meena Lee	71	72	72	215	17,436.24
Morgan Pressel	70	72	73	215	17,436.24
Hee-Won Han	69	72	74	215	17,436.24
Christina Kim	67	73	75	215	17,436.24
Jessica Korda	75	70	71	216	13,343.68
Belen Mozo	75	70	71	216	13,343.68
Juli Inkster	74	68	74	216	13,343.68
Eun-Hee Ji	72	74	70	216	13,343.68
Sydnee Michaels	71	72	73	216	13,343.68
Caroline Masson	70	72	74	216	13,343.68
Michelle Wie	68	72	76	216	13,343.68
Jodi Ewart Shadoff	77	68	72	217	9,886.50
Brittany Lincicome	75	71	71	217	9,886.50
Anna Nordqvist	74	68	75	217	9,886.50
Jiyai Shin	73	71	73	217	9,886.50
Haeji Kang	72	72	73	217	9,886.50
Vicky Hurst	71	68	78	217	9,886.50
Ji Young Oh	69	74	74	217	9,886.50
Na Yeon Choi	69	73	75	217	9,886.50
Carlota Ciganda	78	68	72	218	7,840.81
Natalie Gulbis	75	69	74	218	7,840.81
Candie Kung	73	73	72	218	7,840.81
Pornanong Phatlum	72	71	75	218	7,840.81
Lindsey Wright	68	70	80	218	7,840.81

	SCORES			TOTAL	MONEY
Thidapa Suwannapura	76	70	73	219	6,427.58
Paige Mackenzie	75	71	73	219	6,427.58
Brittany Lang	74	71	74	219	6,427.58
Mo Martin	73	72	74	219	6,427.58
Kris Tamulis	73	71	75	219	6,427.58
Julieta Granada	73	71	75	219	6,427.58
Lee-Anne Pace	69	74	76	219	6,427.58
Catriona Matthew	73	73	74	220	5,642.45
Pernilla Lindberg	72	73	75	220	5,642.45
Hee Kyung Seo	70	76	74	220	5,642.45
Jane Park	75	70	76	221	5,056.22
Gwladys Nocera	74	72	75	221	5,056.22
Inbee Park	74	71	76	221	5,056.22
Giulia Sergas	73	70	78	221	5,056.22
Amy Yang	72	73	76	221	5,056.22
Gerina Piller	72	72	77	221	5,056.22
Mariajo Uribe	70	76	75	221	5,056.22
Amanda Blumenherst	75	71	76	222	4,714.26
Lisa McCloskey	70	76	77	223	4,665.40
Danah Bordner	69	73	82	224	4,592.13
Sarah Kemp	73	72	81	226	4,543.27

Lacoste Ladies Open de France

Chantaco Golf Club, Saint-Jean-de-Luz, Aquitaine, France
Par 35-35–70; 5,965 yards

September 26-29
purse, €250,000

	SCORES				TOTAL	MONEY
Azahara Munoz	68	65	68	65	266	€37,500
Valentine Derrey	68	65	67	67	267	21,437.50
Gwladys Nocera	67	63	70	67	267	21,437.50
Joanna Klatten	64	66	70	68	268	13,500
Karine Icher	67	69	70	64	270	9,675
Lee-Anne Pace	67	65	70	68	270	9,675
Rebecca Artis	69	67	71	64	271	7,500
Bree Arthur	71	66	69	66	272	5,925
Carlota Ciganda	66	70	66	70	272	5,925
Sahra Hassan	70	68	67	68	273	4,850
Charley Hull	65	68	69	71	273	4,850
Holly Clyburn	72	68	67	67	274	4,216.67
Liz Young	72	66	65	71	274	4,216.67
Diana Luna	66	70	69	69	274	4,216.67
Anne-Lise Caudal	66	73	70	66	275	3,812.50
Hannah Burke	64	71	70	70	275	3,812.50
Holly Aitchison	68	68	70	70	276	3,600
Lindsey Wright	67	70	71	68	276	3,600
Sarah Kemp	72	67	65	73	277	3,450
Mallory Fraiche	73	68	72	66	279	3,125
Rebecca Hudson	71	69	70	69	279	3,125
Maha Haddioui	67	72	73	67	279	3,125
Stacy Lee Bregman	65	71	69	74	279	3,125

Sanya Ladies Open

Yalong Bay Golf Club, Sanya, China
Par 36-36–72; 6,461 yards

October 25-27
purse, €300,000

	SCORES			TOTAL	MONEY
Lee-Anne Pace	67	66	70	203	€45,000
Yu Yang Zhang	69	69	65	203	30,450
(Pace defeated Zhang on first playoff hole.)					
Ye Na Chung	64	68	72	204	21,000
Linda Wessberg	67	68	70	205	16,200
*Yu Ting Shi	67	67	71	205	
Jia Yun Li	71	73	63	207	11,610
Xi Yu Lin	67	73	67	207	11,610
Trish Johnson	70	67	72	209	9,000
Nikki Campbell	63	78	69	210	7,500
Kusuma Meechai	72	69	70	211	5,331.43
Sophie Giquel-Bettan	69	74	68	211	5,331.43
Patcharajutar Kongkrapan	69	73	69	211	5,331.43
Valentine Derrey	69	73	69	211	5,331.43
Felicity Johnson	69	72	70	211	5,331.43
Kristie Smith	69	69	73	211	5,331.43
Beth Allen	68	73	70	211	5,331.43
Maria Hernandez	72	69	71	212	4,086
Joanna Klatten	71	70	71	212	4,086
Gwladys Nocera	69	69	74	212	4,086
Laura Davies	68	71	73	212	4,086
Alison Whitaker	68	69	75	212	4,086

China Suzhou Taihu Open

Suzhou Taihu International Golf Club, Suzhou, China
Par 36-36–72; 6,320 yards

November 1-3
purse, €400,000

	SCORES			TOTAL	MONEY
Gwladys Nocera	69	67	65	201	€60,000
Carlota Ciganda	67	68	68	203	40,600
*Jing Yan	67	70	67	204	
Joanna Klatten	72	69	64	205	28,000
Charley Hull	70	66	70	206	19,280
Patcharajutar Kongkrapan	67	71	68	206	19,280
Anne-Lise Caudal	70	65	72	207	13,000
Ashleigh Simon	65	70	72	207	13,000
Lee-Anne Pace	71	67	70	208	8,986.67
Stacy Lee Bregman	68	71	69	208	8,986.67
Veronica Zorzi	65	68	75	208	8,986.67
Line Vedel	67	72	70	209	7,360
Julie Greciet	73	67	70	210	5,940
Lindsey Wright	72	69	69	210	5,940
Sarah Kemp	70	69	71	210	5,940
Beth Allen	70	66	74	210	5,940
Bree Arthur	69	70	71	210	5,940
Na Zhang	69	67	74	210	5,940
Nontaya Srisawang	69	67	74	210	5,940
Kristie Smith	68	70	72	210	5,940

Hero Women's Indian Open

Delhi Golf Club, New Delhi, India
Par 36-36–72; 6,235 yards

November 28-30
purse, US$300,000

	SCORES			TOTAL	MONEY
Thidapa Suwannapura	66	74	68	208	€33,113.10
Valentine Derrey	66	75	70	211	22,406.53
Hannah Burke	73	71	68	212	13,686.75
Saraporn Chamchoi	73	70	69	212	13,686.75
Beth Allen	74	73	66	213	8,543.18
*Gauri Monga	73	70	70	213	
Charley Hull	69	72	72	213	8,543.18
Ye Na Chung	73	72	70	215	6,070.74
Elina Nummenpaa	72	73	70	215	6,070.74
Pennapa Pulsawath	73	72	71	216	4,944.89
Klara Spilkova	78	68	71	217	4,091.31
Maria Balikoeva	73	74	70	217	4,091.31
Bo-Mi Suh	70	75	72	217	4,091.31
Gwladys Nocera	75	72	71	218	3,476.88
Rungthiwa Pangjan	75	70	73	218	3,476.88
Tanaporn Kongkiatkrai	76	74	69	219	3,094.97
Mallory Fraiche	73	76	70	219	3,094.97
Camilla Lennarth	73	73	73	219	3,094.97
Nanthikarn Rakasachat	73	72	74	219	3,094.97
Hannah Jun	68	76	75	219	3,094.97

Omega Dubai Ladies Masters

Emirates Golf Club, Dubai, United Arab Emirates
Par 35-37–72; 6,425 yards

December 4-7
purse, €500,000

	SCORES				TOTAL	MONEY
Pornanong Phatlum	68	70	69	66	273	€75,000
Stacy Lewis	70	65	70	69	274	50,000
Carlota Ciganda	67	70	73	71	281	35,000
Diana Luna	73	68	69	73	283	27,000
Shanshan Feng	76	67	71	71	285	17,900
Louise Larsson	72	71	68	74	285	17,900
Laura Davies	70	71	71	73	285	17,900
*Jing Yan	75	72	68	71	286	
Vikki Laing	71	70	69	76	286	11,850
Charley Hull	70	72	73	71	286	11,850
Nontaya Srisawang	73	72	71	71	287	9,600
Pernilla Lindberg	67	69	75	76	287	9,600
Anne-Lise Caudal	72	73	70	73	288	8,116.67
Sarah Kemp	70	72	72	74	288	8,116.67
Caroline Masson	69	72	78	69	288	8,116.67
Klara Spilkova	74	73	73	69	289	6,916.67
Margherita Rigon	73	76	72	68	289	6,916.67
Sophie Gustafson	73	72	71	73	289	6,916.67
Cindy Lacrosse	73	70	73	73	289	6,916.67
Gwladys Nocera	71	73	71	74	289	6,916.67
Patcharajutar Kongkraphan	70	78	73	68	289	6,916.67

Japan LPGA Tour

Daikin Orchid Ladies

Ryukyu Golf Club, Nanjo, Okinawa
Par 36-36–72; 6,435 yards

March 8-10
purse, ¥80,000,000

	SCORES			TOTAL	MONEY
Rikako Morita	68	67	68	203	¥14,400,000
Sakura Yokomine	70	67	66	203	7,040,000
(Morita defeated Yokomine on first playoff hole.)					
Onnarin Sattayabanphot	67	72	67	206	4,080,000
Ritsuko Ryu	70	69	67	206	4,080,000
Soo-Yun Kang	71	67	68	206	4,080,000
Junko Omote	69	68	69	206	4,080,000
Megumi Kido	68	66	72	206	4,080,000
Eun-Bi Jang	69	72	66	207	1,874,000
Harukyo Nomura	69	70	68	207	1,874,000
Erika Kikuchi	69	70	68	207	1,874,000
Phoebe Yao	70	69	68	207	1,874,000
Esther Lee	72	70	66	208	1,216,000
Asuka Tsujimura	73	69	66	208	1,216,000
Shiho Oyama	72	69	67	208	1,216,000
Mika Miyazato	70	70	68	208	1,216,000
Ji-Hee Lee	69	68	71	208	1,216,000
Na-Ri Kim	69	68	71	208	1,216,000
Saki Okamura	72	69	68	209	856,000
Young Kim	71	69	69	209	856,000
Hiromi Mogi	67	70	72	209	856,000

Yokohama Tire PRGR Ladies Cup

Tosa Country Club, Kanan, Kochi
Par 36-36–72; 6,232 yards

March 15-17
purse, ¥80,000,000

	SCORES			TOTAL	MONEY
Mi-Jeong Jeon	68	70	69	207	¥14,400,000
Young Kim	73	65	69	207	7,040,000
(Jeon defeated Kim on first playoff hole.)					
Rikako Morita	72	69	67	208	5,600,000
Erika Kikuchi	69	74	66	209	2,785,000
Lala Anai	69	73	67	209	2,785,000
Kaori Nakamura	71	70	68	209	2,785,000
Bo-Mee Lee	71	70	68	209	2,785,000
Da-Ye Na	69	70	70	209	2,785,000
Yun-Jye Wei	68	70	71	209	2,785,000
Ji-Hee Lee	69	69	71	209	2,785,000
Erina Hara	71	66	72	209	2,785,000
Sun-Ju Ahn	74	70	66	210	1,280,000
Hiromi Mogi	70	71	69	210	1,280,000
Yuri Fudoh	70	70	70	210	1,280,000
Yukari Baba	70	69	71	210	1,280,000
Sakura Yokomine	72	71	68	211	1,040,000
Harukyo Nomura	72	70	69	211	1,040,000

	SCORES			TOTAL	MONEY
Akane Iijima	75	68	69	212	771,428
Eun-Bi Jang	72	71	69	212	771,428
Airi Saitoh	70	72	70	212	771,428
Yuko Fukuda	71	71	70	212	771,428
Onnarin Sattayabanphot	72	70	70	212	771,428
Miki Saiki	70	71	71	212	771,428
Esther Lee	69	67	76	212	771,428

T-Point Ladies

Takamaki Country Club, Kamo, Kagoshima
Par 36-36–72; 6,346 yards

March 22-24
purse, ¥70,000,000

	SCORES			TOTAL	MONEY
Yuki Ichinose	68	64	70	202	¥12,600,000
Rikako Morita	69	66	68	203	6,160,000
Mi-Jeong Jeon	70	67	67	204	4,900,000
Ritsuko Ryu	70	71	65	206	3,010,000
Teresa Lu	70	69	67	206	3,010,000
Na-Ri Lee	74	65	67	206	3,010,000
Erika Kikuchi	66	71	69	206	3,010,000
Yukari Baba	66	71	69	206	3,010,000
Maiko Wakabayashi	70	68	69	207	1,750,000
Asako Fujimoto	72	70	66	208	1,361,500
Yun-Jye Wei	67	71	70	208	1,361,500
Da-Ye Na	71	70	68	209	1,148,000
Mami Fukuda	74	67	68	209	1,148,000
Sakura Yokomine	70	70	69	209	1,148,000
Hiromi Mogi	71	69	69	209	1,148,000
Sun-Ju Ahn	75	69	67	211	787,000
Phoebe Yao	72	71	68	211	787,000
Rui Kitada	72	71	68	211	787,000
Harukyo Nomura	69	72	70	211	787,000
Lala Anai	76	65	70	211	787,000
So-Hee Kim	69	71	71	211	787,000
Miki Saiki	71	68	72	211	787,000

AXA Ladies

UMK Country Club, Miyazaki
Par 36-36–72; 6,470 yards

March 29-31
purse, ¥80,000,000

	SCORES			TOTAL	MONEY
Natsuka Hori	69	64	69	202	¥14,400,000
Harukyo Nomura	68	69	68	205	7,040,000
Rikako Morita	68	70	68	206	5,200,000
Shiho Oyama	67	69	70	206	5,200,000
Mikiko Nishi	70	70	69	209	3,600,000
Erika Kikuchi	68	70	71	209	3,600,000
Ritsuko Ryu	70	72	68	210	2,400,000
Miki Saiki	69	72	69	210	2,400,000
Megumi Kido	67	72	71	210	2,400,000
Nachiyo Ohtani	69	72	70	211	1,366,666
Yumiko Yoshida	70	71	70	211	1,366,666
Na-Ri Lee	71	73	67	211	1,366,666
Erina Hara	71	70	70	211	1,366,666
Ah-Reum Hwang	70	70	71	211	1,366,666

	SCORES			TOTAL	MONEY
Onnarin Sattayabanphot	67	71	73	211	1,366,666
Mi-Jeong Jeon	69	73	70	212	960,000
Teresa Lu	71	71	70	212	960,000
Bo-Mee Lee	74	69	69	212	960,000
*Asuka Kashiwabara	72	70	70	212	
Sakura Yokomine	72	70	70	212	960,000

Yamaha Ladies Open

Katsuragi Golf Club, Fukuroi, Shizuoka
Par 36-36–72; 6,549 yards

April 4-7
purse, ¥100,000,000

	SCORES				TOTAL	MONEY
Mamiko Higa	69	74	71	70	284	¥18,000,000
Kaori Ohe	71	72	71	70	284	7,900,000
Teresa Lu	70	74	69	71	284	7,900,000
(Higa defeated Ohe and Lu on second playoff hole.)						
Yukari Baba	68	70	77	70	285	5,500,000
Miki Saiki	73	70	69	73	285	5,500,000
Li-Ying Ye	77	70	70	69	286	2,608,571
Hiromi Mogi	69	73	74	70	286	2,608,571
Ritsuko Ryu	68	72	75	71	286	2,608,571
Yumiko Yoshida	73	73	69	71	286	2,608,571
Rikako Morita	68	72	74	72	286	2,608,571
Esther Lee	68	70	74	74	286	2,608,571
Sakura Yokomine	72	69	71	74	286	2,608,571
Mayu Hattori	74	69	71	73	287	1,330,000
Onnarin Sattayabanphot	66	71	76	74	287	1,330,000
Shiho Oyama	67	71	73	76	287	1,330,000
Bo-Mee Lee	68	70	71	78	287	1,330,000
Da-Ye Na	70	70	73	75	288	1,080,000
Mami Fukuda	71	74	73	71	289	794,285
Rui Kitada	69	73	74	73	289	794,285
Na-Ri Lee	71	74	71	73	289	794,285
Hyo-Joo Kim	71	67	77	74	289	794,285
Mi-Jeong Jeon	70	72	72	75	289	794,285
Yan-Hong Pan	71	67	75	76	289	794,285
Soo-Yun Kang	70	70	73	76	289	794,285

Studio Alice Ladies Open

Hanayashiki Golf Club, Yokawa Course, Miki, Hyogo
Par 36-36–72; 6,444 yards

April 12-14
purse, ¥60,000,000

	SCORES			TOTAL	MONEY
Na-Ri Kim	70	72	70	212	¥10,800,000
Yuki Sakurai	73	70	70	213	5,280,000
Miki Saiki	71	75	68	214	3,600,000
Megumi Shimokawa	73	72	69	214	3,600,000
Miki Sakai	74	67	73	214	3,600,000
Lala Anai	71	73	71	215	2,250,000
Mayu Hattori	71	71	73	215	2,250,000
Megumi Kido	74	73	69	216	1,402,500
Teresa Lu	71	72	73	216	1,402,500
Rui Kitada	71	72	73	216	1,402,500
Da-Ye Na	75	68	73	216	1,402,500
*Minami Katsu	73	73	71	217	

	SCORES			TOTAL	MONEY
Ji-Hee Lee	75	71	72	218	1,020,000
Bo-Bae Song	71	73	74	218	1,020,000
Ikue Asama	71	75	73	219	840,000
Rikako Morita	73	72	74	219	840,000
Natsuka Hori	73	69	77	219	840,000
Ah-Reum Hwang	73	68	78	219	840,000
Jessica Speechley	74	73	73	220	570,000
Yuko Saitoh	73	73	74	220	570,000
Serena Aoki	75	70	75	220	570,000
Hiromi Kamata	75	70	75	220	570,000
Junko Omote	76	69	75	220	570,000
Chie Sakai	72	77	71	220	570,000
Erina Hara	76	68	76	220	570,000
Yumiko Yoshida	74	76	70	220	570,000
*Nozomi Uetake	74	68	78	220	

Vantelin Ladies Open KKT Cup

Kumamoto Kuko Country Club, Kikuyo, Kumamoto
Par 36-36–72; 6,455 yards

April 19-21
purse, ¥60,000,000

	SCORES			TOTAL	MONEY
Miki Saiki	73	68	71	212	¥10,800,000
Ritsuko Ryu	72	71	70	213	5,280,000
Miki Sakai	71	72	71	214	4,200,000
Yumiko Yoshida	73	73	69	215	3,000,000
Yukari Baba	71	73	71	215	3,000,000
Natsuka Hori	73	70	72	215	3,000,000
Bo-Mee Lee	74	72	70	216	1,950,000
Kumiko Kaneda	71	73	72	216	1,950,000
Yeo-Jin Kang	74	70	73	217	1,350,000
Junko Omote	75	69	73	217	1,350,000
Na-Ri Kim	74	74	70	218	972,000
Eun-Bi Jang	72	74	72	218	972,000
Asako Fujimoto	74	75	69	218	972,000
Rui Kitada	73	71	74	218	972,000
Esther Lee	69	74	75	218	972,000
Yuki Ichinose	70	72	76	218	972,000
Ji-Hee Lee	76	72	71	219	672,000
Lala Anai	76	70	73	219	672,000
Sun-Ju Ahn	74	75	70	219	672,000
Sakura Yokomine	71	71	77	219	672,000
Hyun-Ju Shin	74	73	73	220	546,000

Fujisankei Ladies Classic

Kawana Hotel Golf Club, Fuji Course, Ito, Shizuoka
Par 36-36–72; 6,367 yards

April 26-28
purse, ¥80,000,000

	SCORES			TOTAL	MONEY
Miki Saiki	69	66	67	202	¥14,400,000
Sakura Yokomine	70	68	67	205	7,040,000
Soo-Yun Kang	68	71	67	206	5,600,000
Junko Omote	69	68	71	208	4,400,000
Teresa Lu	68	68	72	208	4,400,000
Yuki Ichinose	72	73	64	209	2,800,000
Na-Ri Lee	68	71	70	209	2,800,000

	SCORES			TOTAL	MONEY
Sun-Ju Ahn	70	67	72	209	2,800,000
Ji-Woo Lee	72	69	70	211	1,800,000
Miki Sakai	70	66	75	211	1,800,000
Satsuki Oshiro	70	72	70	212	1,224,000
Bo-Mee Lee	71	71	70	212	1,224,000
Yuko Fukuda	72	70	70	212	1,224,000
Yumiko Yoshida	74	68	70	212	1,224,000
Na-Ri Kim	71	70	71	212	1,224,000
Erina Yamato	72	69	71	212	1,224,000
Akane Iijima	73	67	72	212	1,224,000
Misuzu Narita	71	74	68	213	782,400
Yukari Baba	69	74	70	213	782,400
Jin-Joo Hong	73	70	70	213	782,400
Orie Fujino	70	71	72	213	782,400
Shiho Oyama	71	67	75	213	782,400

Cyber Agent Ladies

Tsurumai Country Club, Ichihara, Chiba
Par 36-36–72; 6,445 yards

May 3-5
purse, ¥70,000,000

	SCORES			TOTAL	MONEY
Sakura Yokomine	68	68	70	206	¥12,600,000
Natsuka Hori	69	72	67	208	4,690,000
Yuki Sakurai	68	71	69	208	4,690,000
Maiko Wakabayashi	69	69	70	208	4,690,000
Mi-Jeong Jeon	69	65	74	208	4,690,000
Ayako Uehara	70	70	70	210	2,450,000
Na-Ri Lee	72	67	71	210	2,450,000
Hiromi Mogi	70	68	72	210	2,450,000
Kaori Ohe	72	70	69	211	1,488,666
Jin-Joo Hong	72	68	71	211	1,488,666
Rui Kitada	70	69	72	211	1,488,666
Harukyo Nomura	73	69	70	212	1,211,000
Erina Hara	68	68	76	212	1,211,000
Kumiko Kaneda	74	71	68	213	1,036,000
Rikako Morita	69	73	71	213	1,036,000
Mamiko Higa	70	72	71	213	1,036,000
Yumiko Yoshida	69	73	72	214	896,000
Mayu Hattori	74	70	71	215	719,600
Mihoko Iseri	74	70	71	215	719,600
Ji-Woo Lee	73	70	72	215	719,600
Mami Fukuda	73	69	73	215	719,600
Ah-Reum Hwang	70	71	74	215	719,600

World Ladies Championship Salonpas Cup

Ibaraki Golf Club, West Course, Tsukubamirai, Ibaraki
Par 36-36–72; 6,669 yards

May 9-12
purse, ¥120,000,000

	SCORES				TOTAL	MONEY
Hiromi Mogi	71	70	70	68	279	¥24,000,000
Miki Saiki	69	70	72	70	281	12,000,000
Rikako Morita	71	70	68	73	282	9,000,000
*Lydia Ko	72	70	73	68	283	
Ji-Woo Lee	72	74	66	71	283	6,600,000
So Yeon Ryu	68	71	72	72	283	6,600,000

	SCORES				TOTAL	MONEY
Sakura Yokomine	73	70	70	71	284	4,800,000
Yuri Fudoh	72	70	73	70	285	2,940,000
Sun-Ju Ahn	73	69	73	70	285	2,940,000
Shanshan Feng	72	69	73	71	285	2,940,000
Saiki Fujita	68	69	75	73	285	2,940,000
Mayu Hattori	74	73	69	70	286	2,040,000
Junko Omote	73	72	71	70	286	2,040,000
Miki Sakai	71	74	71	71	287	1,800,000
Yuko Saitoh	70	73	71	73	287	1,800,000
So-Hee Kim	74	70	77	67	288	1,476,000
Morgan Pressel	70	73	75	70	288	1,476,000
Li-Ying Ye	72	71	75	70	288	1,476,000
Ah-Reum Hwang	74	72	74	69	289	1,041,600
Bo-Mee Lee	73	71	75	70	289	1,041,600
Yuki Ichinose	73	69	75	72	289	1,041,600
Misuzu Narita	72	72	73	72	289	1,041,600
Ayako Uehara	73	72	72	72	289	1,041,600

Hoken no Madoguchi Ladies

Fukuoka Country Club, Wajiro Course, Asakura, Fukuoka
Par 36-36–72; 6,304 yards

May 17-19
purse, ¥120,000,000

	SCORES			TOTAL	MONEY
Onnarin Sattayabanphot	70	68	72	210	¥21,600,000
Kumiko Kaneda	69	71	71	211	9,480,000
Maiko Wakabayashi	71	68	72	211	9,480,000
Rui Kitada	70	70	72	212	7,200,000
Phoebe Yao	74	70	69	213	6,000,000
Shinobu Moromizato	69	73	72	214	3,600,000
Yukari Baba	74	68	72	214	3,600,000
Erina Hara	68	72	74	214	3,600,000
Shiho Oyama	72	68	74	214	3,600,000
Ritsuko Ryu	73	66	75	214	3,600,000
Satsuki Oshiro	76	68	71	215	2,016,000
Eun-Bi Jang	72	70	73	215	2,016,000
Bo-Bae Song	68	73	74	215	2,016,000
Soo-Yun Kang	71	70	74	215	2,016,000
Yuki Ichinose	68	71	76	215	2,016,000
Sun-Ju Ahn	70	73	73	216	1,596,000
Mayu Hattori	72	71	73	216	1,596,000
Miki Saiki	74	72	71	217	1,212,000
Hiromi Mogi	71	73	73	217	1,212,000
Ayako Uehara	72	72	73	217	1,212,000
Ji-Hee Lee	71	72	74	217	1,212,000
Sakura Yokomine	72	70	75	217	1,212,000
Na-Ri Kim	74	68	75	217	1,212,000

Chukyo TV Bridgestone Ladies Open

Chukyo Golf Club, Ishino Course, Toyota, Aichi
Par 36-36–72; 6,519 yards

May 24-26
purse, ¥70,000,000

	SCORES			TOTAL	MONEY
Rikako Morita	67	67	74	208	¥12,600,000
Mi-Jeong Jeon	72	69	68	209	6,160,000
Natsuka Hori	73	67	70	210	4,900,000

	SCORES			TOTAL	MONEY
Momoko Ueda	72	69	70	211	3,850,000
Shiho Oyama	66	70	75	211	3,850,000
Yuki Ichinose	70	75	67	212	2,450,000
Esther Lee	73	72	67	212	2,450,000
Shiho Toyonaga	70	69	73	212	2,450,000
Da-Ye Na	71	70	72	213	1,575,000
Miki Saiki	71	70	72	213	1,575,000
Bo-Mee Lee	75	70	69	214	1,204,000
Kumiko Kaneda	72	73	69	214	1,204,000
Na-Ri Kim	72	71	71	214	1,204,000
Akane Iijima	73	70	71	214	1,204,000
Yuki Sakurai	70	74	71	215	924,000
Yukari Baba	74	69	72	215	924,000
Mihoko Iseri	70	71	74	215	924,000
Sakura Yokomine	72	69	74	215	924,000
Mayu Hattori	73	74	69	216	676,200
Ji-Woo Lee	74	70	72	216	676,200
Harukyo Nomura	72	71	73	216	676,200
Ji-Hee Lee	71	71	74	216	676,200
Miki Sakai	70	71	75	216	676,200

Resort Trust Ladies

Kansai Country Club, Miki, Hyogo
Par 36-36–72; 6,522 yards

May 31-June 2
purse, ¥70,000,000

	SCORES			TOTAL	MONEY
Mamiko Higa	70	67	70	207	¥12,600,000
Mayu Hattori	69	71	68	208	6,160,000
Rikako Morita	74	66	70	210	4,900,000
Yukari Baba	71	72	68	211	2,432,500
Sakura Yokomine	73	69	69	211	2,432,500
Junko Omote	70	70	71	211	2,432,500
Yumiko Yoshida	70	70	71	211	2,432,500
Maiko Wakabayashi	66	73	72	211	2,432,500
Yayoi Arasaki	68	71	72	211	2,432,500
Phoebe Yao	70	68	73	211	2,432,500
Megumi Kido	68	69	74	211	2,432,500
Da-Ye Na	72	72	68	212	910,000
Yuko Mitsuka	72	71	69	212	910,000
Akane Iijima	69	73	70	212	910,000
Ikue Asama	69	73	70	212	910,000
Na-Ri Lee	70	72	70	212	910,000
Hyun-Ju Shin	71	71	70	212	910,000
Satsuki Oshiro	75	66	71	212	910,000
Miki Sakai	71	70	71	212	910,000
Yuki Ichinose	67	73	72	212	910,000

Yonex Ladies

Yonex Country Club, Nagaoka, Niigata
Par 36-36–72; 6,336 yards

June 7-9
purse, ¥60,000,000

	SCORES			TOTAL	MONEY
Junko Omote	67	69	70	206	¥10,800,000
Rikako Morita	72	71	65	208	5,280,000
Ritsuko Ryu	70	70	69	209	4,200,000

	SCORES			TOTAL	MONEY
Shiho Oyama	70	70	70	210	3,600,000
Mayu Hattori	69	70	72	211	2,700,000
Li-Ying Ye	68	68	75	211	2,700,000
Miki Saiki	68	71	73	212	1,800,000
Yukari Baba	69	70	73	212	1,800,000
Natsuka Hori	70	68	74	212	1,800,000
Hiroko Fukushima	70	71	72	213	1,056,000
Teresa Lu	69	71	73	213	1,056,000
Mi-Jeong Jeon	69	70	74	213	1,056,000
Yuko Fukuda	68	68	77	213	1,056,000
Tamie Durdin	69	67	77	213	1,056,000
Miki Sakai	71	70	73	214	840,000
Ah-Reum Hwang	72	69	73	214	840,000
Kaori Ohe	71	73	71	215	660,000
Hiromi Mogi	73	70	72	215	660,000
Rino Kotake	69	72	74	215	660,000
Yuki Ichinose	68	71	76	215	660,000

Suntory Ladies Open

Rokko Kokusai Golf Club, Kobe, Hyogo
Par 36-36–72; 6,537 yards

June 13-16
purse, ¥100,000,000

	SCORES				TOTAL	MONEY
Rikako Morita	73	66	72	67	278	¥18,000,000
Mamiko Higa	67	70	73	69	279	7,266,666
Yumiko Yoshida	70	74	66	69	279	7,266,666
Kumiko Kaneda	68	71	69	71	279	7,266,666
Ritsuko Ryu	70	70	74	66	280	4,500,000
Yuri Fudoh	73	69	68	70	280	4,500,000
Ji-Hee Lee	70	71	72	69	282	3,000,000
Kaori Nakamura	70	70	71	71	282	3,000,000
Esther Lee	66	71	72	73	282	3,000,000
Sun-Ju Ahn	66	74	71	72	283	2,000,000
Yuki Ichinose	71	73	71	69	284	1,690,000
Asako Fujimoto	73	71	70	70	284	1,690,000
Yun-Jye Wei	70	70	73	71	284	1,690,000
Misuzu Narita	64	75	75	71	285	1,440,000
*Haruka Morita	71	74	69	71	285	
Megumi Kido	71	70	72	72	285	1,440,000
Kaori Ohe	71	74	72	69	286	1,053,333
Yayoi Arasaki	68	71	76	71	286	1,053,333
Ah-Reum Hwang	70	70	75	71	286	1,053,333
Shinobu Moromizato	74	70	71	71	286	1,053,333
Ikue Asama	70	72	71	73	286	1,053,333
Sakura Yokomine	73	73	67	73	286	1,053,333

Nichirei Ladies

Sodegaura Country Club, Shinsode Course, Chiba
Par 36-36–72; 6,584 yards

June 21-23
purse, ¥80,000,000

	SCORES			TOTAL	MONEY
Yumiko Yoshida	68	67	70	205	¥14,400,000
Kaori Aoyama	69	70	68	207	5,813,333
Kaori Ohe	69	70	68	207	5,813,333
Na-Ri Lee	70	66	71	207	5,813,333

	SCORES			TOTAL	MONEY
Misuzu Narita	70	69	69	208	4,000,000
Mamiko Higa	72	70	67	209	3,000,000
Rie Tsuji	67	73	69	209	3,000,000
Yuri Fudoh	70	70	70	210	1,880,000
Nachiyo Ohtani	72	68	70	210	1,880,000
Kaori Nakamura	73	66	71	210	1,880,000
Megumi Kido	68	70	72	210	1,880,000
Erika Kikuchi	76	69	66	211	1,320,000
Mayu Hattori	74	70	67	211	1,320,000
Sakura Yokomine	70	72	69	211	1,320,000
Yun-Jye Wei	70	67	74	211	1,320,000
Yuko Fukuda	70	73	69	212	1,000,000
Riho Fujisaki	72	71	69	212	1,000,000
Yukari Baba	71	69	72	212	1,000,000
Phoebe Yao	69	68	75	212	1,000,000
Kumiko Kaneda	67	76	70	213	744,000
Soo-Yun Kang	69	74	70	213	744,000
Miki Uehara	76	67	70	213	744,000
Megumi Shimokawa	72	71	70	213	744,000
Kaori Yamamoto	72	69	72	213	744,000
Hiroko Azuma	72	69	72	213	744,000
Na-Ri Kim	73	68	72	213	744,000
Erina Hara	71	68	74	213	744,000

Earth Mondahmin Cup

Camellia Hills Country Club, Sodegaura, Chiba
Par 36-36–72; 6,516 yards

June 27-30
purse, ¥140,000,000

	SCORES				TOTAL	MONEY
Natsuka Hori	69	67	64	67	267	¥25,200,000
Mi-Jeong Jeon	68	64	70	73	275	12,320,000
Asako Fujimoto	68	73	67	68	276	9,100,000
Bo-Mee Lee	72	66	68	70	276	9,100,000
Misuzu Narita	70	67	71	69	277	6,300,000
Hiroko Azuma	71	69	66	71	277	6,300,000
Sun-Ju Ahn	69	69	71	69	278	4,200,000
Teresa Lu	69	66	73	70	278	4,200,000
Kumiko Kaneda	71	69	68	70	278	4,200,000
Kaori Nakamura	71	67	70	71	279	2,800,000
So-Hee Kim	70	69	72	69	280	2,268,000
Yuri Fudoh	72	69	70	69	280	2,268,000
Yuki Ichinose	69	73	69	69	280	2,268,000
Esther Lee	73	67	73	68	281	1,512,000
Rikako Morita	72	69	70	70	281	1,512,000
Lala Anai	73	66	71	71	281	1,512,000
Erina Hara	70	69	71	71	281	1,512,000
Ji-Hee Lee	70	71	69	71	281	1,512,000
Akane Iijima	70	66	72	73	281	1,512,000
Maiko Wakabayashi	70	70	68	73	281	1,512,000
Eun-Bi Jang	69	69	69	74	281	1,512,000

Nichi-Iko Ladies Open

Yatsuo Country Club, Toyama
Par 36-36–72; 6,476 yards

July 5-7
purse, ¥60,000,000

	SCORES			TOTAL	MONEY
Young Kim	67	67	69	203	¥10,800,000
Mayumi Shimomura	70	66	68	204	5,280,000
Erika Kikuchi	69	68	68	205	3,900,000
Eun-Bi Jang	69	67	69	205	3,900,000
Misuzu Narita	70	69	67	206	2,325,000
Bo-Mee Lee	70	68	68	206	2,325,000
Na-Ri Lee	71	66	69	206	2,325,000
Mi-Jeong Jeon	69	66	71	206	2,325,000
Sae Yamamura	68	69	70	207	1,500,000
Yuko Fukuda	68	70	70	208	1,128,000
Teresa Lu	70	67	71	208	1,128,000
Megumi Kido	67	69	72	208	1,128,000
Ji-Hee Lee	69	70	70	209	882,000
Mina Nakayama	72	67	70	209	882,000
Kumiko Kaneda	70	68	71	209	882,000
Saiki Fujita	68	69	72	209	882,000
Junko Omote	68	68	73	209	882,000
Sakura Yokomine	69	71	70	210	672,000
Akane Iijima	73	66	71	210	672,000
Yumiko Yoshida	72	69	70	211	552,000
Yuki Ichinose	71	69	71	211	552,000
Yuko Mitsuka	71	70	70	211	552,000
Rikako Morita	70	69	72	211	552,000
Ayaka Watanabe	67	74	70	211	552,000
Yukari Baba	71	65	75	211	552,000

Samantha Thavasa Girls Collection Ladies

Eagle Point Golf Club, Ami, Ibaraki
Par 36-36–72; 6,474 yards

July 19-21
purse, ¥60,000,000

	SCORES			TOTAL	MONEY
Yumiko Yoshida	66	67	67	200	¥10,800,000
Junko Omote	63	65	72	200	5,280,000
(Yoshida defeated Omote on second playoff hole.)					
Kumiko Kaneda	68	70	65	203	3,900,000
Sun-Ju Ahn	71	67	65	203	3,900,000
Kaori Nakamura	67	68	69	204	2,500,000
Rui Kitada	68	67	69	204	2,500,000
Mamiko Higa	69	66	69	204	2,500,000
Ji-Hee Lee	67	72	66	205	1,500,000
Chiharu Tsunekawa	69	68	68	205	1,500,000
Akane Iijima	68	67	70	205	1,500,000
Hyo-Joo Kim	71	68	67	206	924,000
Harukyo Nomura	69	69	68	206	924,000
So-Hee Kim	70	68	68	206	924,000
Saiki Fujita	66	71	69	206	924,000
Mi-Jeong Jeon	69	68	69	206	924,000
Hyun-Ju Shin	67	67	72	206	924,000
Yoshimi Koda	69	71	67	207	624,000
Yun-Jye Wei	72	67	68	207	624,000
Mayumi Nakajima	71	67	69	207	624,000
Ritsuko Ryu	67	69	71	207	624,000

Meiji Cup

Sapporo International Country Club, Kitahiroshima, Hokkaido
Par 36-36–72; 6,498 yards

August 9-11
purse, ¥90,000,000

	SCORES			TOTAL	MONEY
Da-Ye Na	67	70	67	204	¥16,200,000
Yuki Ichinose	69	71	65	205	7,920,000
Shanshan Feng	68	71	67	206	6,300,000
Soo-Yun Kang	71	69	68	208	4,950,000
Teresa Lu	71	68	69	208	4,950,000
Bo-Mee Lee	74	68	67	209	2,925,000
Kaori Aoyama	70	70	69	209	2,925,000
Jiyai Shin	71	69	69	209	2,925,000
Nachiyo Ohtani	71	69	69	209	2,925,000
Esther Lee	73	69	68	210	1,800,000
Yuri Fudoh	72	72	67	211	1,449,000
Hiroko Fukushima	72	71	68	211	1,449,000
Lala Anai	71	71	69	211	1,449,000
Yukari Baba	72	70	69	211	1,449,000
Mayu Hattori	73	68	70	211	1,449,000
Erina Hara	69	71	71	211	1,449,000
Risa Ogusu	69	75	68	212	925,714
Sun-Ju Ahn	72	72	68	212	925,714
Young Kim	72	70	70	212	925,714
Mi-Jeong Jeon	73	69	70	212	925,714
Saiki Fujita	70	71	71	212	925,714
Misuzu Narita	73	68	71	212	925,714
Harukyo Nomura	70	67	75	212	925,714

NEC Karuizawa 72

Karuizawa 72 Golf Club, Karuizawa, Nagano
Par 36-36–72; 6,555 yards

August 16-18
purse, ¥70,000,000

	SCORES			TOTAL	MONEY
Misuzu Narita	72	65	65	202	¥12,600,000
Esther Lee	67	64	71	202	6,160,000
(Narita defeated Lee on second playoff hole.)					
Ritsuko Ryu	69	67	67	203	4,900,000
Yuri Fudoh	69	65	70	204	4,200,000
Yumiko Yoshida	70	67	68	205	3,500,000
Da-Ye Na	69	72	65	206	2,275,000
Na-Ri Lee	69	70	67	206	2,275,000
Akane Iijima	70	67	69	206	2,275,000
Asako Fujimoto	71	66	69	206	2,275,000
Ji-Hee Lee	71	67	69	207	1,316,000
Onnarin Sattayabanphot	68	69	70	207	1,316,000
Shanshan Feng	68	68	71	207	1,316,000
Harukyo Nomura	68	71	69	208	1,134,000
Shiho Toyonaga	66	71	71	208	1,134,000
Miki Sakai	75	67	67	209	827,000
Bo-Mee Lee	70	71	68	209	827,000
Hyun-Ju Shin	71	69	69	209	827,000
Ayako Uehara	71	69	69	209	827,000
Ayaka Watanabe	67	72	70	209	827,000
Eun-Bi Jang	70	69	70	209	827,000
Teresa Lu	70	67	72	209	827,000

CAT Ladies

Daihakone Country Club, Hakone, Kanagawa
Par 36-37–73; 6,655 yards

August 23-25
purse, ¥60,000,000

	SCORES			TOTAL	MONEY
Sun-Ju Ahn	70	68	66	204	¥10,800,000
Ritsuko Ryu	68	70	69	207	5,280,000
Yumiko Yoshida	70	68	70	208	4,200,000
Sakura Yokomine	69	71	72	212	3,300,000
Na-Ri Kim	68	67	77	212	3,300,000
Megumi Kido	71	69	73	213	2,250,000
Da-Ye Na	66	71	76	213	2,250,000
Junko Omote	72	73	69	214	1,287,000
Asako Fujimoto	75	68	71	214	1,287,000
Mayu Hattori	73	70	71	214	1,287,000
Rino Kotake	70	70	74	214	1,287,000
Ji-Hee Lee	72	67	75	214	1,287,000
Miki Saiki	66	69	79	214	1,287,000
Yuko Mitsuka	72	72	71	215	864,000
Eun-Bi Jang	73	71	71	215	864,000
Teresa Lu	71	70	74	215	864,000
Yukari Baba	69	71	75	215	864,000
Esther Lee	73	73	70	216	684,000
Rie Tsuji	68	70	78	216	684,000
Mamiko Higa	71	71	75	217	588,000
Shiho Toyonaga	74	68	75	217	588,000

Nitori Ladies

Katsura Golf Club, Tomakomai, Hokkaido
Par 36-36–72; 6,480 yards

August 30-September 1
purse, ¥100,000,000

	SCORES			TOTAL	MONEY
Sun-Ju Ahn	70	70	65	205	¥18,000,000
Teresa Lu	71	71	65	207	8,800,000
Yuko Fukuda	68	74	67	209	7,000,000
Ayako Uehara	72	70	68	210	5,500,000
Mi-Jeong Jeon	71	70	69	210	5,500,000
Yeo-Jin Kang	71	73	67	211	4,000,000
Saiki Fujita	70	76	66	212	2,413,333
Ritsuko Ryu	71	73	68	212	2,413,333
Asako Fujimoto	70	73	69	212	2,413,333
Miki Sakai	70	73	69	212	2,413,333
Bo-Mee Lee	69	71	72	212	2,413,333
Lala Anai	66	72	74	212	2,413,333
Yumiko Yoshida	72	74	67	213	1,540,000
Misuzu Narita	71	70	72	213	1,540,000
Jessica Speechley	72	73	69	214	1,290,000
Li-Ying Ye	74	71	69	214	1,290,000
Esther Lee	70	70	74	214	1,290,000
Na-Ri Lee	72	73	70	215	938,000
Mami Fukuda	71	73	71	215	938,000
Akane Iijima	70	73	72	215	938,000
Kaori Ohe	72	71	72	215	938,000
Rui Kitada	72	69	74	215	938,000

Golf 5 Ladies

Alpen Golf Club, Bibai Course, Hokkaido
Par 36-36–72; 6,364 yards

September 6-8
purse, ¥60,000,000

	SCORES			TOTAL	MONEY
Yumiko Yoshida	69	68	67	204	¥10,800,000
Miki Saiki	67	70	67	204	5,280,000
(Yoshida defeated Saiki on fourth playoff hole.)					
Shiho Oyama	71	67	68	206	3,900,000
Sun-Ju Ahn	67	70	69	206	3,900,000
Yun-Jye Wei	67	72	68	207	2,700,000
Yuko Mitsuka	72	66	69	207	2,700,000
Sakura Yokomine	71	69	68	208	2,100,000
Yukari Baba	68	73	68	209	1,650,000
Bo-Bae Song	73	68	68	209	1,650,000
Yuki Sakurai	74	71	65	210	1,167,000
Miki Sakai	71	67	72	210	1,167,000
Asako Fujimoto	69	74	68	211	834,000
Bo-Mee Lee	73	70	68	211	834,000
Phoebe Yao	67	75	69	211	834,000
Rie Tsuji	70	72	69	211	834,000
Ritsuko Ryu	73	69	69	211	834,000
Onnarin Sattayabanphot	68	73	70	211	834,000
Mamiko Higa	73	68	70	211	834,000
Kaori Nakamura	73	67	71	211	834,000
Na-Ri Lee	67	72	72	211	834,000

Japan LPGA Championship

Eniwa Country Club, Eniwa, Hokkaido
Par 36-36–72; 6,682 yards
(Final round cancelled—rain.)

September 12-15
purse, ¥140,000,000

	SCORES			TOTAL	MONEY
Bo-Mee Lee	68	69	68	205	¥18,900,000
Mamiko Higa	69	68	68	205	9,240,000
(Lee defeated Higa on sixth playoff hole.)					
Yuri Fudoh	71	70	68	209	7,350,000
Erina Hara	69	70	71	210	6,300,000
Rui Kitada	71	71	70	212	5,250,000
Na-Ri Kim	72	72	69	213	3,412,500
Sakura Yokomine	70	74	69	213	3,412,500
Onnarin Sattayabanphot	73	71	69	213	3,412,500
Mami Fukuda	70	72	71	213	3,412,500
Yuki Ichinose	68	74	72	214	1,963,500
Miki Sakai	66	73	75	214	1,963,500
Yukari Baba	76	71	68	215	1,669,500
Kumiko Kaneda	72	72	71	215	1,669,500
Ji-Hee Lee	73	73	70	216	1,249,500
Esther Lee	70	76	70	216	1,249,500
Sun-Ju Ahn	72	72	72	216	1,249,500
Hiroko Fukushima	72	72	72	216	1,249,500
Yumiko Yoshida	68	76	72	216	1,249,500
Teresa Lu	71	69	76	216	1,249,500

Munsingwear Ladies Tokai Classic

Shin Minami Aichi Country Club, Mihama, Aichi
Par 36-36–72; 6,399 yards

September 20-22
purse, ¥80,000,000

	SCORES			TOTAL	MONEY
Sakura Yokomine	68	66	67	201	¥14,400,000
Ji-Hee Lee	69	69	65	203	5,813,333
Da-Ye Na	70	65	68	203	5,813,333
Asako Fujimoto	70	65	68	203	5,813,333
Kaori Aoyama	68	70	66	204	3,333,333
Rui Kitada	70	68	66	204	3,333,333
Erika Kikuchi	69	65	70	204	3,333,333
Bo-Mee Lee	67	70	68	205	2,000,000
Jiyai Shin	69	68	68	205	2,000,000
Na-Ri Lee	65	70	70	205	2,000,000
Yuki Ichinose	72	70	64	206	1,504,000
Misuzu Narita	69	71	67	207	1,304,000
Onnarin Sattayabanphot	69	70	68	207	1,304,000
Rikako Morita	71	67	69	207	1,304,000
Erina Hara	71	66	70	207	1,304,000
Akane Iijima	68	74	66	208	1,024,000
Yayoi Arasaki	73	67	68	208	1,024,000
Mami Fukuda	71	68	69	208	1,024,000
Kaori Yamamoto	71	71	67	209	780,800
Satsuki Oshiro	69	71	69	209	780,800
Sun-Ju Ahn	70	70	69	209	780,800
Shanshan Feng	72	67	70	209	780,800
Lala Anai	69	69	71	209	780,800

Miyagi TV Cup Dunlop Ladies Open

Rifu Golf Club, Rifu, Miyagi
Par 36-36–72; 6,498 yards

September 27-29
purse, ¥70,000,000

	SCORES			TOTAL	MONEY
Na-Ri Lee	71	70	70	211	¥12,600,000
Ai Miyazato	69	75	68	212	5,530,000
Teresa Lu	69	72	71	212	5,530,000
Yukari Baba	72	72	69	213	3,850,000
Lala Anai	73	70	70	213	3,850,000
Esther Lee	76	66	72	214	2,800,000
Mamiko Higa	71	78	66	215	2,100,000
Erika Kikuchi	78	68	69	215	2,100,000
Miki Saiki	72	73	70	215	2,100,000
Shiho Oyama	72	74	70	216	1,354,500
Junko Omote	72	73	71	216	1,354,500
Akane Iijima	73	74	70	217	1,134,000
Erina Hara	71	75	71	217	1,134,000
Mami Fukuda	74	72	71	217	1,134,000
Saiki Fujita	74	69	74	217	1,134,000
Ayako Uehara	74	74	70	218	924,000
Miki Sakai	74	73	71	218	924,000
Miho Mori	74	75	70	219	700,000
Maiko Wakabayashi	76	73	70	219	700,000
Momoko Ueda	73	73	73	219	700,000
Rikako Morita	73	73	73	219	700,000
Ji-Woo Lee	71	74	74	219	700,000
Mayu Hattori	72	73	74	219	700,000

Japan Women's Open

Sagamihara Golf Club, East Course, Sagamihara, Kanagawa
Par 36-36–72; 6,652 yards

October 3-6
purse, ¥140,000,000

	SCORES				TOTAL	MONEY
Mika Miyazato	70	70	73	75	288	¥28,000,000
Miki Saiki	70	76	74	69	289	13,090,000
Erika Kikuchi	73	73	72	71	289	13,090,000
Rikako Morita	74	72	76	68	290	5,495,000
Harukyo Nomura	73	72	76	69	290	5,495,000
Teresa Lu	70	77	74	69	290	5,495,000
Jiyai Shin	76	69	74	71	290	5,495,000
Sun-Ju Ahn	75	71	76	69	291	3,126,666
Sakura Yokomine	73	72	76	70	291	3,126,666
Bo-Mee Lee	74	72	73	72	291	3,126,666
Shiho Oyama	74	69	77	72	292	2,450,000
Natsuka Hori	73	75	76	69	293	2,212,000
I.K. Kim	76	73	75	70	294	1,668,800
Esther Lee	74	76	73	71	294	1,668,800
Na-Ri Lee	73	76	73	72	294	1,668,800
Soo-Yun Kang	74	71	74	75	294	1,668,800
Asako Fujimoto	73	73	73	75	294	1,668,800
Yuri Fudoh	71	74	81	69	295	1,302,000
Miki Sakai	74	72	78	71	295	1,302,000
Ji-Hee Lee	74	73	76	72	295	1,302,000
*Yumi Matsubara	74	71	78	72	295	
Mihoko Iseri	70	75	77	73	295	1,302,000

Stanley Ladies

Tomei Country Club, Susono, Shizuoka
Par 36-36–72; 6,540 yards

October 11-13
purse, ¥90,000,000

	SCORES			TOTAL	MONEY
Soo-Yun Kang	68	70	66	204	¥16,200,000
Harukyo Nomura	71	67	69	207	7,110,000
Sakura Yokomine	69	68	70	207	7,110,000
Ah-Reum Hwang	72	69	67	208	4,500,000
Rikako Morita	69	70	69	208	4,500,000
Mayu Hattori	65	71	72	208	4,500,000
Rie Tsuji	70	71	68	209	2,202,000
Kaori Ohe	71	70	68	209	2,202,000
Na-Ri Lee	68	72	69	209	2,202,000
Saki Okamura	68	71	70	209	2,202,000
Keiko Sasaki	69	70	70	209	2,202,000
Teresa Lu	69	69	71	209	2,202,000
Ji-Hee Lee	72	72	66	210	1,431,000
Akane Iijima	70	71	69	210	1,431,000
Satsuki Oshiro	66	72	72	210	1,431,000
Li-Ying Ye	69	73	69	211	1,116,000
Esther Lee	73	69	69	211	1,116,000
Saiki Fujita	71	70	70	211	1,116,000
Yumiko Yoshida	68	70	73	211	1,116,000
Lala Anai	73	71	68	212	882,000
*Yumi Matsubara	72	71	69	212	
Ritsuko Ryu	71	69	72	212	882,000

Fujitsu Ladies

Tokyu Seven Hundred Club, West Course, Chiba
Par 36-36–72; 6,635 yards
(Event shortened to 36 holes — rain.)

October 18-20
purse, ¥80,000,000

	SCORES		TOTAL	MONEY
Na-Ri Lee	71	67	138	¥10,800,000
Ayaka Watanabe	70	69	139	5,280,000
Esther Lee	72	68	140	3,600,000
Miki Sakai	72	68	140	3,600,000
*Megumi Takahashi	71	69	140	
Teresa Lu	70	70	140	3,600,000
Harukyo Nomura	72	69	141	1,800,000
Ah-Reum Hwang	72	69	141	1,800,000
Sun-Ju Ahn	71	70	141	1,800,000
Eun-Bi Jang	70	71	141	1,800,000
Yukari Baba	67	74	141	1,800,000
Erika Kikuchi	72	70	142	1,044,000
Akane Iijima	72	70	142	1,044,000
Satsuki Oshiro	71	71	142	1,044,000
Onnarin Sattayabanphot	73	70	143	804,000
Na-Ri Kim	71	72	143	804,000
Megumi Kido	71	72	143	804,000
Ritsuko Ryu	68	75	143	804,000
Mihoko Iseri	67	76	143	804,000
Yuki Ichinose	74	70	144	580,000
Misuzu Narita	75	69	144	580,000
Kaori Nakamura	72	72	144	580,000

Nobuta Group Masters Golf Club Ladies

Masters Golf Club, Miki, Hyogo
Par 36-36–72; 6,445 yards
(Event shortened to 54 holes — rain.)

October 24-27
purse, ¥140,000,000

	SCORES			TOTAL	MONEY
Sakura Yokomine	70	63	71	204	¥18,900,000
Sun-Ju Ahn	69	69	69	207	9,240,000
Momoko Ueda	69	70	69	208	6,825,000
Shanshan Feng	70	68	70	208	6,825,000
Misuzu Narita	72	71	67	210	4,725,000
Shiho Oyama	70	69	71	210	4,725,000
Hiroko Fukushima	74	68	69	211	3,412,500
Bo-Mee Lee	73	68	70	211	3,412,500
Maiko Wakabayashi	73	71	68	212	2,236,500
Yuko Saitoh	71	72	69	212	2,236,500
Phoebe Yao	69	69	74	212	2,236,500
Ah-Reum Hwang	74	70	69	213	1,722,000
Shiho Toyonaga	76	70	67	213	1,722,000
Harukyo Nomura	74	72	67	213	1,722,000
Ayako Uehara	70	72	71	213	1,722,000
Yukari Baba	71	74	69	214	1,249,500
Yuko Fukuda	72	72	70	214	1,249,500
Airi Sugimoto	72	71	71	214	1,249,500
Ji-Hee Lee	69	74	71	214	1,249,500
Da-Ye Na	69	73	72	214	1,249,500

Hisako Higuchi Morinaga Weider Ladies

Morinaga Takataki Country Club, Ichihara, Chiba
Par 36-36–72; 6,652 yards

November 1-3
purse, ¥70,000,000

	SCORES			TOTAL	MONEY
Bo-Mee Lee	70	66	65	201	¥12,600,000
Sun-Ju Ahn	69	68	69	206	6,300,000
Shanshan Feng	67	71	69	207	4,900,000
Yuko Fukuda	72	71	65	208	3,500,000
Ayaka Watanabe	68	71	69	208	3,500,000
Jiyai Shin	70	69	69	208	3,500,000
Lala Anai	72	69	68	209	2,275,000
Mayu Hattori	69	68	72	209	2,275,000
Asako Fujimoto	67	72	71	210	1,575,000
Na-Ri Kim	70	68	72	210	1,575,000
Yukari Baba	72	70	69	211	1,197,000
Yumiko Yoshida	72	70	69	211	1,197,000
Erina Hara	68	72	71	211	1,197,000
Yuki Ichinose	70	70	71	211	1,197,000
Soo-Yun Kang	69	69	73	211	1,197,000
Ah-Reum Hwang	69	73	70	212	882,000
Miki Saiki	69	73	70	212	882,000
*Shoko Sasaki	71	70	71	212	
Mina Nakayama	73	68	71	212	882,000
Mi-Jeong Jeon	72	69	71	212	882,000

Mizuno Classic

Kintetsu Kashikojima Country Club, Shima, Mie
Par 36-36–72; 6,506 yards

November 8-10
purse, US$1,200,000

	SCORES			TOTAL	MONEY
Teresa Lu	70	68	64	202	¥17,634,600
Chella Choi	69	69	66	204	10,754,460
Mamiko Higa	70	66	70	206	6,918,347
Yuki Ichinose	70	66	70	206	6,918,347
Yumiko Yoshida	74	65	68	207	4,415,997
Shiho Oyama	68	68	71	207	4,415,997
Asako Fujimoto	70	67	71	208	3,326,767
Eun-Bi Jang	69	69	71	209	2,639,801
Stacy Lewis	71	68	70	209	2,639,801
Shanshan Feng	72	71	66	209	2,639,801
Jiyai Shin	69	72	69	210	2,134,374
Kaori Nakamura	69	73	68	210	2,134,374
Harukyo Nomura	72	69	70	211	1,766,399
Catriona Matthew	71	71	69	211	1,766,399
Esther Lee	70	72	69	211	1,766,399
Ah-Reum Hwang	71	68	72	211	1,766,399
Mina Harigae	73	69	70	212	1,290,068
Julieta Granada	71	68	73	212	1,290,068
Brittany Lang	70	70	72	212	1,290,068
Sakura Yokomine	72	71	69	212	1,290,068
Jenny Shin	72	71	69	212	1,290,068
Mayu Hattori	76	68	68	212	1,290,068
Miki Saiki	73	66	73	212	1,290,068
Erina Hara	71	73	68	212	1,290,068
Hee-Won Han	69	71	72	212	1,290,068
Junko Omote	69	69	74	212	1,290,068
Yuri Fudoh	73	69	71	213	1,000,959

	SCORES			TOTAL	MONEY
So Yeon Ryu	71	71	71	213	1,000,959
Rui Kitada	71	70	72	213	1,000,959
Kumiko Kaneda	71	70	73	214	889,077
Moriya Jutanugarn	75	70	69	214	889,077
Brittany Lincicome	69	68	77	214	889,077

Itoen Ladies

Great Island Club, Chonan, Chiba
Par 36-36–72; 6,639 yards

November 15-17
purse, ¥90,000,000

	SCORES			TOTAL	MONEY
Sakura Yokomine	70	68	68	206	¥16,200,000
Yumiko Yoshida	69	70	68	207	7,920,000
Da-Ye Na	70	73	65	208	4,950,000
Mayu Hattori	69	70	69	208	4,950,000
Na-Ri Kim	67	71	70	208	4,950,000
Shiho Oyama	69	68	71	208	4,950,000
Yayoi Arasaki	68	72	69	209	2,700,000
Kumiko Kaneda	67	72	70	209	2,700,000
Ayaka Watanabe	69	68	72	209	2,700,000
Rikako Morita	69	72	69	210	1,741,500
Phoebe Yao	70	69	71	210	1,741,500
Miki Sakai	72	71	68	211	1,548,000
Akane Yoshino	65	73	73	211	1,548,000
Kaori Nakamura	73	71	69	213	1,188,000
Sun-Ju Ahn	70	73	70	213	1,188,000
Ji-Hee Lee	72	71	70	213	1,188,000
Ritsuko Ryu	73	72	68	213	1,188,000
Mamiko Higa	73	69	71	213	1,188,000
*Mayu Hosaka	69	72	72	213	
Miki Saiki	69	68	76	213	1,188,000

Daio Paper Elleair Ladies Open

Elleair Golf Club, Matsuyama, Ehime
Par 36-36–72; 6,442 yards

November 21-24
purse, ¥100,000,000

	SCORES				TOTAL	MONEY
Rikako Morita	70	70	64	69	273	¥18,000,000
Asako Fujimoto	70	70	68	66	274	8,800,000
Mamiko Higa	71	71	68	66	276	5,500,000
Yukari Baba	68	68	73	67	276	5,500,000
Ji-Hee Lee	68	72	67	69	276	5,500,000
Momoko Ueda	69	68	69	70	276	5,500,000
Sakura Yokomine	73	67	68	69	277	3,500,000
Yuki Ichinose	68	73	71	66	278	2,500,000
Bo-Mee Lee	69	73	69	67	278	2,500,000
Yuri Fudoh	69	68	70	71	278	2,500,000
Erina Hara	75	68	68	68	279	1,790,000
Shiho Oyama	67	73	70	69	279	1,790,000
Sun-Ju Ahn	70	68	71	70	279	1,790,000
Na-Ri Kim	73	68	70	70	281	1,540,000
Onnarin Sattayabanphot	71	69	69	72	281	1,540,000
Yumiko Yoshida	72	72	73	65	282	1,240,000
Kumiko Kaneda	73	72	68	69	282	1,240,000
Mihoko Iseri	71	70	71	70	282	1,240,000

	SCORES				TOTAL	MONEY
Aoi Nagata	70	73	69	70	282	1,240,000
Hiroko Azuma	68	74	72	69	283	970,000
Teresa Lu	72	69	71	71	283	970,000
Ritsuko Ryu	72	71	66	74	283	970,000

Japan LPGA Tour Championship Ricoh Cup

Miyazaki Country Club, Miyazaki
Par 36-36-72; 6,451 yards

November 28-December 1
purse, ¥100,000,000

	SCORES				TOTAL	MONEY
Shiho Oyama	69	71	73	66	279	¥25,000,000
Teresa Lu	72	70	70	71	283	14,500,000
Sun-Ju Ahn	69	72	72	71	284	10,000,000
Bo-Mee Lee	71	70	71	75	287	8,000,000
Jiyai Shin	73	74	72	70	289	6,140,000
Na-Ri Lee	69	72	73	75	289	6,140,000
Sakura Yokomine	74	76	71	70	291	2,864,000
Esther Lee	71	77	71	72	291	2,864,000
Yukari Baba	73	73	72	73	291	2,864,000
Yumiko Yoshida	69	73	75	74	291	2,864,000
Junko Omote	74	74	68	75	291	2,864,000
Rikako Morita	74	73	72	73	292	1,360,000
Onnarin Sattayabanphot	75	70	72	76	293	1,160,000
Asako Fujimoto	77	75	75	68	295	846,666
Miki Saiki	74	74	76	71	295	846,666
Mi-Jeong Jeon	72	72	72	79	295	846,666
Yuki Ichinose	71	76	74	75	296	640,000
Mamiko Higa	74	70	75	78	297	550,000
Kumiko Kaneda	76	78	73	71	298	500,000
Misuzu Narita	76	75	73	74	298	500,000
Erika Kikuchi	73	77	73	75	298	500,000
Da-Ye Na	76	76	74	73	299	465,000
Na-Ri Kim	75	77	72	75	299	465,000
Ritsuko Ryu	71	77	75	76	299	465,000
Soo-Yun Kang	75	70	77	77	299	465,000
Young Kim	77	74	72	78	301	440,000
Natsuka Hori	74	75	79	76	304	425,000
Mayu Hattori	75	77	73	79	304	425,000

Australian Ladies Tour

Vintage Golf Club Pro-Am

Vintage Golf Club, Hunter Valley, New South Wales
Par 71; 6,058 yards

January 14-15
purse, A$30,000

	SCORES		TOTAL	MONEY
Stacey Keating	69	70	139	A$4,500
Whitney Hillier	74	67	141	3,300
Emma De Groot	72	70	142	2,000
Sarah Kemp	72	70	142	2,000
Stephanie Na	76	66	142	2,000
Holly Aitchison	75	68	143	1,275
Julia Boland	75	68	143	1,275
Nikki Garrett	73	71	144	1,050
Tamara Johns	75	70	145	900
Lee Park	69	77	146	810
Kristie Smith	78	68	146	810
Caroline Bon	73	74	147	630
Mallory Fraiche	77	70	147	630
Aimee Neff	74	73	147	630
Sarah Jane Smith	72	75	147	630
Rebecca Artis	76	72	148	480
Sophie Walker	76	73	149	450
Inhong Lim	76	74	150	360
Courtney Massey	77	73	150	360
Katelyn Must	75	75	150	360
Elisa Serramia	76	74	150	360
Jana Welsford	74	76	150	360

Mount Broughton Classic

Mount Broughton Golf Club, Sutton Forest, New South Wales
Par 72; 6,200 yards

January 19-20
purse, A$30,000

	SCORES		TOTAL	MONEY
Caroline Hedwall	67	65	132	A$4,500
Emma De Groot	66	70	136	3,300
Whitney Hillier	67	70	137	2,550
Joanna Klatten	67	72	139	1,950
Beth Allen	67	73	140	1,425
Ashlee Dewhurst	74	66	140	1,425
Hannah Burke	71	70	141	1,050
Stacey Keating	70	71	141	1,050
Marnie McGuire	73	68	141	1,050
Lacey Agnew	71	71	142	780
Bree Arthur	71	71	142	780
Sarah King	71	71	142	780
Corie Hou	71	72	143	600
Tamara Johns	69	74	143	600
Aimee Neff	72	71	143	600
Nancy Harvey	73	71	144	450
Inhong Lim	74	70	144	450

	SCORES			TOTAL	MONEY
Kristie Smith	74	70		144	450
Antonella Cvitan	73	72		145	333
Laura Davies	75	70		145	333
Karen Lunn	73	72		145	333
Stephanie Na	71	74		145	333
Shani Waugh	74	71		145	333

Bing Lee Samsung NSW Open

Oatlands Golf Club, Sydney, New South Wales
Par 36-36–72; 6,008 yards

January 25-27
purse, A$125,000

	SCORES			TOTAL	MONEY
Caroline Hedwall	66	69	68	203	A$18,750
*Lydia Ko	67	69	69	205	
*Minjee Lee	66	69	71	206	
Bree Arthur	66	73	68	207	12,500
Stacey Keating	66	73	69	208	8,500
Emma De Groot	72	71	66	209	5,375
Joanna Klatten	73	67	69	209	5,375
Kristie Smith	68	70	71	209	5,375
Jessica Speechley	71	70	69	210	4,187.50
Stephanie Na	68	71	72	211	3,531.25
Sarah Jane Smith	68	70	73	211	3,531.25
Whitney Hillier	68	72	72	212	3,062.50
Laura Davies	68	72	73	213	2,750
Elizabeth Bennett	70	70	74	214	2,245.83
Julia Boland	73	72	69	214	2,245.83
Vicky Thomas	72	74	68	214	2,245.83
Caroline Bon	73	70	72	215	1,708.33
Cathryn Bristow	70	72	73	215	1,708.33
Lynnette Brooky	71	70	74	215	1,708.33
*Cathleen Santoso	72	70	73	215	

Volvik RACV Ladies Masters

RACV Royal Pines Resort, Ashmore, Queensland
Par 36-36–72; 6,511 yards

February 1-3
purse, A$250,000

	SCORES			TOTAL	MONEY
Karrie Webb	70	66	67	203	A$39,000
Chella Choi	69	67	69	205	21,840
Ariya Jutanugarn	69	65	71	205	21,840
*Su-Hyun Oh	70	64	71	205	
Jessica Korda	67	68	71	206	12,740
Stacey Keating	68	67	72	207	10,400
Dori Carter	68	69	72	209	9,360
Pernilla Lindberg	70	67	72	209	9,360
So Yeon Ryu	71	70	69	210	7,800
Alison Walshe	66	71	74	211	7,020
Hannah Burke	72	71	69	212	5,590
Nontaya Srisawang	68	70	74	212	5,590
Sara Maude Juneau	72	73	68	213	4,229.33
Sarah Kemp	71	70	72	213	4,229.33
Amelia Lewis	71	69	73	213	4,229.33
Carlota Ciganda	75	69	70	214	3,354
Joanna Klatten	70	73	71	214	3,354

	SCORES			TOTAL	MONEY
Jee Young Lee	71	73	70	214	3,354
*Minjee Lee	71	70	73	214	
Belen Mozo	68	71	75	214	3,354

ISPS Handa New Zealand Women's Open

Clearwater Golf Club, Christchurch, New Zealand
Par 36-36–72; 6,343 yards

February 8-10
purse, A$260,000

	SCORES			TOTAL	MONEY
*Lydia Ko	70	68	68	206	
Amelia Lewis	73	68	66	207	A$36,040.68
Stacey Keating	73	68	67	208	24,387.53
Seonwoo Bae	74	64	71	209	16,818.98
Elizabeth Bennett	74	71	65	210	10,523.88
Nikki Campbell	69	71	70	210	10,523.88
Sarah Jane Smith	71	71	68	210	10,523.88
Giulia Sergas	71	68	72	211	7,208.14
Pernilla Lindberg	76	69	67	212	5,177.84
*Su-Hyun Oh	74	69	69	212	
Beatriz Recari	73	71	68	212	5,177.84
Emily Taylor	74	69	69	212	5,177.84
Alison Walshe	70	75	67	212	5,177.84
Connie Chen	73	70	70	213	3,970.48
Sarah Kemp	73	69	71	213	3,970.48
Min-Sun Kim	73	68	72	213	3,970.48
Joanna Klatten	75	71	67	213	3,970.48
*Jing Yan	74	73	66	213	
Rebecca Artis	74	68	72	214	3,335.77
Dori Carter	73	70	71	214	3,335.77
Lydia Hall	74	70	70	214	3,335.77
Christina Kim	76	70	68	214	3,335.77
Caroline Masson	73	73	68	214	3,335.77
Marion Ricordeau	72	73	69	214	3,335.77

ISPS Handa Women's Australian Open

Royal Canberra Golf Club, Canberra, ACT
Par 37-36–73; 6,664 yards

February 14-17
purse, US$1,200,000

	SCORES				TOTAL	MONEY
Jiyai Shin	65	67	70	72	274	US$180,000
Yani Tseng	68	71	71	66	276	109,560
*Lydia Ko	63	69	70	76	278	
Moriya Jutanugarn	70	70	70	69	279	70,440
Beatriz Recari	68	69	71	71	279	70,440
Carlota Ciganda	71	70	69	70	280	44,940
Gwladys Nocera	74	71	65	70	280	44,940
Katherine Hull-Kirk	68	73	71	69	281	28,590
Catriona Matthew	69	75	70	67	281	28,590
Thidapa Suwannapura	71	72	71	67	281	28,590
Mariajo Uribe	64	67	79	71	281	28,590
Anna Nordqvist	72	70	69	71	282	21,720
Florentyna Parker	71	71	72	68	282	21,720
Dewi Claire Schreefel	70	72	69	72	283	19,680
Christel Boeljon	72	68	74	70	284	17,440
Stacy Lewis	69	74	69	72	284	17,440

	SCORES				TOTAL	MONEY
Sarah Jane Smith	68	70	73	73	284	17,440
Rebecca Artis	72	67	73	73	285	13,140
Whitney Hillier	74	69	69	73	285	13,140
Jessica Korda	70	69	77	69	285	13,140
Rebecca Lee-Bentham	66	74	76	69	285	13,140
Brittany Lincicome	71	70	72	72	285	13,140
Gerina Piller	72	67	73	73	285	13,140
Stacy Prammanasudh	70	71	70	74	285	13,140
Giulia Sergas	67	72	73	73	285	13,140
Jenny Shin	71	69	73	72	285	13,140
Jennifer Song	71	74	69	71	285	13,140
Ashlee Dewhurst	73	70	69	74	286	9,394.29
Austin Ernst	69	74	70	73	286	9,394.29
Stacey Keating	74	71	71	70	286	9,394.29
Cindy Lacrosse	71	71	74	70	286	9,394.29
Belen Mozo	71	71	71	73	286	9,394.29
*Su-Hyun Oh	75	70	71	70	286	
Lee-Anne Pace	74	71	70	71	286	9,394.29
Angela Stanford	68	75	71	72	286	9,394.29

Women's Victorian Open

13th Beach Golf Links, Bellarine Peninsula, Victoria
Par 37-37–74; 6,398 yards

February 21-24
purse, A$150,000

	SCORES				TOTAL	MONEY
Stacey Keating	71	68	68	71	278	A$22,500
Hannah Burke	73	70	71	66	280	12,562.50
Kristie Smith	66	74	72	68	280	12,562.50
Nikki Campbell	70	72	71	68	281	7,725
Bree Arthur	76	71	68	67	282	5,700
Mireia Prat	74	70	71	67	282	5,700
Rebecca Artis	73	71	71	68	283	4,650
Laura Davies	67	75	71	70	283	4,650
Tamie Durdin	71	71	72	70	284	3,810
Jessica Speechley	70	70	74	70	284	3,810
Beth Allen	69	74	74	68	285	3,067.50
Valentine Derrey	73	72	73	67	285	3,067.50
*Grace Lennon	69	71	71	74	285	
Lacey Agnew	72	69	73	72	286	2,531.25
Heather Bowie Young	70	71	72	73	286	2,531.25
Emma De Groot	73	72	73	69	287	2,025
Ashlee Dewhurst	71	74	72	70	287	2,025
*Su-Hyun Oh	70	74	73	70	287	
Sarah Jane Smith	65	73	75	74	287	2,025
Lee-Anne Pace	68	75	74	71	288	1,770

Senior Tours

Mitsubishi Electric Championship

Hualalai Golf Course, Ka'upulehu-Kona, Hawaii
Par 36-36–72; 7,053 yards

January 18-20
purse, $1,800,000

	SCORES			TOTAL	MONEY
John Cook	66	66	67	199	$309,000
David Frost	65	65	69	199	187,000
(Cook defeated Frost on second playoff hole.)					
Bernhard Langer	68	68	64	200	133,000
Fred Couples	66	69	67	202	111,500
Kenny Perry	67	72	64	203	86,500
Kirk Triplett	66	68	69	203	86,500
Russ Cochran	67	70	69	206	71,500
Tom Lehman	66	71	70	207	62,500
Corey Pavin	68	71	69	208	46,150
Hale Irwin	70	68	70	208	46,150
Jay Haas	68	69	71	208	46,150
Steve Elkington	68	69	71	208	46,150
Tom Kite	66	69	73	208	46,150
Joe Daley	69	72	68	209	32,175
Mark O'Meara	70	70	69	209	32,175
Willie Wood	66	72	71	209	32,175
Larry Nelson	69	70	70	209	32,175
Fred Funk	69	69	71	209	32,175
Mark Wiebe	70	73	67	210	26,125
Jeff Sluman	69	72	70	211	24,125
Jim Thorpe	71	73	68	212	22,625
Loren Roberts	72	69	71	212	22,625
Tom Watson	69	74	70	213	20,125
Jay Don Blake	71	72	70	213	20,125
Craig Stadler	70	71	72	213	20,125
Olin Browne	73	71	70	214	17,083
Roger Chapman	70	73	71	214	17,083
Mike Reid	73	70	71	214	17,083
John Huston	67	75	73	215	15,250
Mark Calcavecchia	71	70	74	215	15,250

Allianz Championship

Old Course at Broken Sound, Boca Raton, Florida
Par 36-36–72; 6,807 yards

February 8-10
purse, $1,800,000

	SCORES			TOTAL	MONEY
Rocco Mediate	67	61	71	199	$270,000
Bernhard Langer	66	67	68	201	144,000
Tom Pernice, Jr.	66	65	70	201	144,000
Mark O'Meara	69	67	69	205	96,300
Corey Pavin	67	69	69	205	96,300
Fred Funk	67	69	71	207	64,800
Tom Lehman	68	73	66	207	64,800
Duffy Waldorf	74	66	67	207	64,800
John Cook	68	70	70	208	45,000
David Frost	70	65	73	208	45,000

	SCORES			TOTAL	MONEY
John Huston	68	69	71	208	45,000
Larry Mize	69	67	72	208	45,000
Jay Don Blake	72	66	71	209	31,500
Andrew Magee	70	71	68	209	31,500
Mark McNulty	70	70	69	209	31,500
Peter Senior	69	69	71	209	31,500
Esteban Toledo	70	70	69	209	31,500
Kirk Triplett	69	70	70	209	31,500
Michael Allen	68	70	72	210	20,700
Olin Browne	71	69	70	210	20,700
Brad Faxon	69	72	69	210	20,700
Jay Haas	73	68	69	210	20,700
Mark Mouland	68	73	69	210	20,700
Kenny Perry	70	71	69	210	20,700
Scott Simpson	67	73	70	210	20,700
Jim Thorpe	71	69	70	210	20,700
Roger Chapman	67	75	69	211	14,610
Russ Cochran	70	70	71	211	14,610
Jim Gallagher, Jr.	68	71	72	211	14,610
Steve Jones	70	69	72	211	14,610
Lee Rinker	75	67	69	211	14,610
Bob Tway	71	67	73	211	14,610

ACE Group Classic

TwinEagles Golf Club, Talon Course, Naples, Florida
Par 36-36–72; 7,300 yards

February 15-17
purse, $1,600,000

	SCORES			TOTAL	MONEY
Bernhard Langer	62	70	72	204	$240,000
Jay Don Blake	66	71	68	205	140,800
John Cook	71	68	68	207	105,200
Tom Pernice, Jr.	66	69	72	207	105,200
David Frost	68	72	68	208	70,000
Rocco Mediate	72	67	69	208	70,000
Jeff Freeman	68	70	71	209	51,200
Mark Mouland	70	71	68	209	51,200
Mark O'Meara	67	69	73	209	51,200
Bill Glasson	71	69	70	210	36,800
John Huston	66	71	73	210	36,800
Chien Soon Lu	67	68	75	210	36,800
Kenny Perry	68	73	69	210	36,800
Bart Bryant	72	70	69	211	28,000
Mike Goodes	68	73	70	211	28,000
Gene Sauers	71	67	73	211	28,000
Mark Wiebe	67	70	74	211	28,000
Fred Funk	67	71	74	212	23,200
Peter Jacobsen	71	70	71	212	23,200
Olin Browne	69	73	71	213	18,266.67
Roger Chapman	68	73	72	213	18,266.67
Russ Cochran	72	71	70	213	18,266.67
Jim Rutledge	71	73	69	213	18,266.67
Steve Elkington	69	70	74	213	18,266.66
Scott Hoch	73	68	72	213	18,266.66
Tom Lehman	73	72	69	214	14,560
Andrew Magee	71	71	72	214	14,560
Gil Morgan	68	73	73	214	14,560
Brad Faxon	68	75	72	215	11,588.58
Tommy Armour	74	69	72	215	11,588.57
Jay Haas	72	72	71	215	11,588.57

	SCORES			TOTAL	MONEY
Gary Hallberg	73	72	70	215	11,588.57
Mark McNulty	71	74	70	215	11,588.57
David Peoples	72	75	68	215	11,588.57
Duffy Waldorf	69	74	72	215	11,588.57

Toshiba Classic

Newport Beach Country Club, Newport Beach, California
Par 35-36–71; 6,591 yards

March 15-17
purse, $1,750,000

	SCORES			TOTAL	MONEY
David Frost	63	66	65	194	$262,500
Fred Couples	64	66	69	199	154,000
Jay Haas	69	66	67	202	115,062.50
Peter Senior	68	68	66	202	115,062.50
Tom Watson	70	67	66	203	83,125
Rocco Mediate	70	68	66	204	66,500
Esteban Toledo	68	68	68	204	66,500
Steve Elkington	70	70	65	205	44,333.34
Jim Rutledge	72	71	62	205	44,333.34
Michael Allen	70	68	67	205	44,333.33
Dan Forsman	68	68	69	205	44,333.33
Jim Gallagher, Jr.	66	68	71	205	44,333.33
Scott Simpson	71	69	65	205	44,333.33
Fred Funk	70	67	69	206	31,500
Jeff Sluman	73	68	65	206	31,500
Bob Tway	68	67	71	206	31,500
Mark Brooks	68	71	68	207	26,250
Chien Soon Lu	67	72	68	207	26,250
D.A. Weibring	67	68	72	207	26,250
Tommy Armour	68	70	70	208	19,979.17
Mark McNulty	73	68	67	208	19,979.17
Steve Pate	71	68	69	208	19,979.17
Corey Pavin	71	68	69	208	19,979.17
Scott Hoch	71	64	73	208	19,979.16
Bernhard Langer	67	70	71	208	19,979.16
Jay Don Blake	70	68	71	209	14,875
Russ Cochran	70	72	67	209	14,875
Jeff Freeman	68	70	71	209	14,875
Barry Lane	67	71	71	209	14,875
Andrew Magee	76	67	66	209	14,875
Mark O'Meara	75	69	65	209	14,875

Mississippi Gulf Resort Classic

Fallen Oak Golf Club, Biloxi, Mississippi
Par 36-36–72; 7,054 yards

March 22-24
purse, $1,600,000

	SCORES			TOTAL	MONEY
Michael Allen	70	68	67	205	$240,000
Bernhard Langer	71	65	70	206	140,800
Russ Cochran	74	67	67	208	95,466.67
Gene Sauers	71	66	71	208	95,466.67
Tom Pernice, Jr.	72	65	71	208	95,466.66
David Frost	70	71	69	210	54,400
Rocco Mediate	73	70	67	210	54,400
Mark O'Meara	70	70	70	210	54,400

	SCORES			TOTAL	MONEY
Peter Senior	71	67	72	210	54,400
Roger Chapman	69	67	75	211	40,000
Steve Elkington	69	71	71	211	40,000
Jay Don Blake	74	66	72	212	29,866.67
Olin Browne	70	69	73	212	29,866.67
John Cook	73	72	67	212	29,866.67
Scott Hoch	72	70	70	212	29,866.67
Fred Couples	72	66	74	212	29,866.66
Duffy Waldorf	71	67	74	212	29,866.66
Jay Haas	72	73	68	213	19,022.23
Gene Jones	72	70	71	213	19,022.23
Joe Daley	70	66	77	213	19,022.22
David Eger	71	69	73	213	19,022.22
Neal Lancaster	71	70	72	213	19,022.22
Chien Soon Lu	71	68	74	213	19,022.22
Andrew Magee	71	68	74	213	19,022.22
Hal Sutton	69	72	72	213	19,022.22
Esteban Toledo	72	65	76	213	19,022.22
Dan Forsman	72	68	74	214	13,280
John Huston	74	72	68	214	13,280
Corey Pavin	69	67	78	214	13,280
Jim Rutledge	73	71	70	214	13,280
Jeff Sluman	71	70	73	214	13,280

Greater Gwinnett Championship

TPC Sugarloaf, Duluth, Georgia
Par 36-36–72; 7,259 yards

April 19-21
purse, $1,800,000

	SCORES			TOTAL	MONEY
Bernhard Langer	73	66	67	206	$270,000
Tom Lehman	71	71	67	209	144,000
Tom Pernice, Jr.	71	68	70	209	144,000
Chien Soon Lu	71	71	69	211	107,100
Mark Calcavecchia	68	71	73	212	78,750
Duffy Waldorf	69	73	70	212	78,750
Bart Bryant	68	73	72	213	50,400
Fred Funk	69	73	71	213	50,400
Wayne Levi	72	72	69	213	50,400
Steve Pate	75	69	69	213	50,400
Jeff Sluman	76	66	71	213	50,400
Esteban Toledo	68	70	75	213	50,400
Michael Allen	67	73	74	214	35,100
Roger Chapman	71	68	75	214	35,100
Neal Lancaster	69	75	71	215	31,500
Andrew Magee	70	71	74	215	31,500
Mike Goodes	71	72	73	216	26,145
Gary Hallberg	72	70	74	216	26,145
Gene Sauers	72	68	76	216	26,145
Tom Watson	69	75	72	216	26,145
Bill Glasson	73	74	70	217	20,940
Jay Haas	73	70	74	217	20,940
Rod Spittle	72	73	72	217	20,940
Rocco Mediate	75	69	74	218	18,450
Larry Mize	72	75	71	218	18,450
Jay Don Blake	76	71	72	219	16,020
John Cook	71	73	75	219	16,020
Chie-Hsiang Lin	72	77	70	219	16,020
Jim Rutledge	73	77	69	219	16,020
Chip Beck	72	79	69	220	12,720

	SCORES			TOTAL	MONEY
Brad Faxon	69	82	69	220	12,720
Dan Forsman	71	75	74	220	12,720
Mark McNulty	76	73	71	220	12,720
Mark O'Meara	68	78	74	220	12,720
Bob Tway	71	72	77	220	12,720

Liberty Mutual Insurance Legends of Golf

Savannah Harbor Golf Resort, Savannah, Georgia
Par 36-36–72; 7,087 yards

April 26-28
purse, $2,700,000

	SCORES			TOTAL	MONEY (Each)
Brad Faxon/Jeff Sluman	62	66	65	193	$230,000
Fred Funk/Mike Goodes	66	65	63	194	123,000
Gene Sauers/Kenny Perry	66	66	62	194	123,000
Larry Mize/Hal Sutton	65	65	65	195	57,125
Brad Bryant/Tom Purtzer	66	65	64	195	57,125
Fred Couples/Jay Haas	66	64	65	195	57,125
Michael Allen/David Frost	67	62	66	195	57,125
Mark Calcavecchia/Peter Senior	65	64	66	195	57,125
Mark O'Meara/Esteban Toledo	66	63	66	195	57,125
Craig Stadler/Kirk Triplett	64	64	67	195	57,125
Andy North/Tom Watson	64	64	67	195	57,125
Steve Elkington/Rocco Mediate	65	65	66	196	32,500
David Eger/Mark McNulty	66	63	67	196	32,500
Bernhard Langer/Tom Lehman	63	65	69	197	28,250
Scott Hoch/Jim Gallagher, Jr.	67	61	69	197	28,250
Tom Pernice, Jr./Bob Tway	67	63	68	198	22,250
Tom Kite/Gil Morgan	64	67	67	198	22,250
Morris Hatalsky/Don Pooley	68	64	66	198	22,250
Larry Nelson/Wayne Levi	67	66	65	198	22,250
Dan Forsman/Scott Simpson	70	63	65	198	22,250
Jay Don Blake/Roger Chapman	66	61	71	198	22,250
Bill Glasson/Steve Pate	65	65	69	199	17,500
Peter Jacobsen/D.A. Weibring	66	64	70	200	15,500
Sandy Lyle/Ian Woosnam	65	69	66	200	15,500
John Cook/Corey Pavin	69	65	66	200	15,500
Bob Gilder/Bobby Wadkins	66	67	68	201	14,000
Gary Hallberg/Jim Rutledge	66	69	68	203	13,250
Joe Daley/Steve Jones	68	68	67	203	13,250
John Jacobs/Fuzzy Zoeller	69	66	69	204	12,000
Loren Roberts/Mark Wiebe	69	67	68	204	12,000
Allen Doyle/Bruce Vaughan	68	69	67	204	12,000
Andy Bean/Chien Soon Lu	69	68	69	206	11,000
Mark Brooks/Willie Wood	70	69	70	209	10,500

Insperity Championship

The Woodlands Country Club, The Woodlands, Texas
Par 36-36–72; 7,018 yards

May 3-5
purse, $1,800,000

	SCORES			TOTAL	MONEY
Esteban Toledo	72	71	67	210	$270,000
Mike Goodes	69	69	72	210	144,000
Gene Sauers	70	66	74	210	144,000
(Toledo defeated Sauers on second and Goodes on third playoff hole.)					
Mark Calcavecchia	75	69	69	213	96,300

	SCORES			TOTAL	MONEY
Loren Roberts	72	69	72	213	96,300
Jay Haas	73	75	67	215	68,400
Barry Lane	77	67	71	215	68,400
John Cook	73	72	71	216	45,600
David Eger	75	70	71	216	45,600
Dan Forsman	76	71	69	216	45,600
Tom Kite	76	70	70	216	45,600
Mark O'Meara	73	71	72	216	45,600
Jeff Sluman	72	76	68	216	45,600
Chien Soon Lu	75	71	71	217	33,300
Hal Sutton	71	74	72	217	33,300
Michael Allen	71	74	73	218	27,900
Jay Don Blake	75	71	72	218	27,900
Bart Bryant	75	74	69	218	27,900
Steve Elkington	73	74	71	218	27,900
David Frost	80	69	70	219	21,600
Steve Jones	72	72	75	219	21,600
Peter Senior	73	70	76	219	21,600
Bob Tway	73	74	72	219	21,600
Jim Rutledge	73	75	72	220	18,900
Fred Funk	75	76	70	221	16,050
Bill Glasson	79	74	68	221	16,050
Bernhard Langer	77	72	72	221	16,050
Blaine McCallister	73	72	76	221	16,050
Kenny Perry	74	75	72	221	16,050
Tom Purtzer	76	72	73	221	16,050

Senior PGA Championship

Bellerive Country Club, St. Louis, Missouri
Par 36-35–71; 6,959 yards

May 23-26
purse, $2,000,000

	SCORES				TOTAL	MONEY
Kohki Idoki	71	69	68	65	273	$378,000
Kenny Perry	69	66	68	72	275	185,000
Jay Haas	66	72	67	70	275	185,000
Mark O'Meara	73	70	68	65	276	100,000
Kiyoshi Murota	67	70	73	67	277	80,000
Jim Rutledge	75	67	72	64	278	59,600
Kirk Triplett	70	71	69	68	278	59,600
Duffy Waldorf	66	72	71	69	278	59,600
Russ Cochran	69	66	71	72	278	59,600
Rod Spittle	69	71	67	71	278	59,600
Dan Forsman	69	71	70	69	279	45,000
Peter Senior	68	71	69	71	279	45,000
Bart Bryant	73	69	71	67	280	33,000
Bernhard Langer	79	67	67	67	280	33,000
Joel Edwards	72	69	69	70	280	33,000
Tommy Armour	72	70	68	70	280	33,000
Steve Pate	73	68	68	71	280	33,000
Fred Funk	69	71	69	71	280	33,000
Joe Ozaki	71	74	67	69	281	25,000
Neal Lancaster	73	71	71	67	282	20,200
Bill Glasson	69	73	72	68	282	20,200
Rocco Mediate	69	74	71	68	282	20,200
Michael Allen	73	70	71	68	282	20,200
Brian Henninger	73	68	71	70	282	20,200
Gene Sauers	70	71	72	70	283	16,000
Chien Soon Lu	68	72	72	71	283	16,000
Tom Pernice, Jr.	72	71	69	71	283	16,000

	SCORES				TOTAL	MONEY
Jeff Hart	72	72	71	69	284	12,829
Tom Kite	72	71	70	71	284	12,829
Mark McNulty	71	74	68	71	284	12,829
Tom Watson	69	71	72	72	284	12,829
Jeff Coston	71	69	72	72	284	12,829
Jim Carter	70	72	70	72	284	12,829
Mark Mielke	69	71	71	73	284	12,829
Dick Mast	70	72	74	69	285	9,600
Jerry Pate	73	71	71	70	285	9,600
Gary Rusnak	72	69	73	71	285	9,600
Don Berry	72	69	73	71	285	9,600
Peter Jacobsen	75	69	69	72	285	9,600
Sonny Skinner	67	73	71	74	285	9,600
Tom Byrum	72	71	68	74	285	9,600
Brad Bryant	73	71	73	69	286	7,260
Andrew Oldcorn	69	74	73	70	286	7,260
Gil Morgan	69	72	74	71	286	7,260
Sandy Lyle	71	74	70	71	286	7,260
Bruce Vaughan	70	71	70	75	286	7,260
Boonchu Ruangkit	75	70	71	71	287	5,617
Jeff Sluman	75	71	70	71	287	5,617
Mike Hulbert	73	70	71	73	287	5,617
Loren Roberts	70	68	75	74	287	5,617
Jay Don Blake	71	69	71	76	287	5,617
Willie Wood	74	68	73	72	287	5,617
Scott Hoch	76	67	73	72	288	4,900
Morris Hatalsky	75	70	71	72	288	4,900
Kazuhiro Takami	76	70	70	72	288	4,900
Greg Turner	74	70	73	72	289	4,600
Hale Irwin	70	73	73	73	289	4,600
Philip Golding	73	72	70	74	289	4,600
Mark Mouland	73	72	75	70	290	4,350
Mark Wiebe	70	71	77	72	290	4,350
Bob Gaus	71	74	72	73	290	4,350
Ian Woosnam	75	71	71	73	290	4,350
Frankie Minoza	71	70	75	74	290	4,350
Bob Tway	76	67	78	70	291	4,115
Hal Sutton	72	74	75	70	291	4,115
Barry Lane	75	71	72	73	291	4,115
Peter Fowler	72	72	72	75	291	4,115
Roger Chapman	72	74	66	79	291	4,115
Jim Gallagher, Jr.	73	68	78	73	292	3,975
Jay Delsing	70	76	73	73	292	3,975
Gene Jones	70	74	75	73	292	3,975
Des Smyth	73	72	71	76	292	3,975
Mike Goodes	69	77	69	77	292	3,975
Wayne Levi	71	75	71	76	293	3,900
John Jacobs	73	73	74	74	294	3,875
Jeff Freeman	70	74	76	75	295	3,850
Terry Price	71	72	73	80	296	3,825
D.A. Weibring	73	72	76	77	298	3,800
Tom Purtzer	76	70	75	78	299	3,763
Lanny Wadkins	71	75	73	80	299	3,763

Principal Charity Classic

Wakonda Club, Des Moines, Iowa
Par 36-36–72; 6,959 yards

May 31-June 2
purse, $1,750,000

	SCORES			TOTAL	MONEY
Russ Cochran	71	67	67	205	$262,500
Jay Don Blake	71	66	69	206	154,000
Mark Calcavecchia	70	70	67	207	104,416.67
Kirk Triplett	72	68	67	207	104,416.67
Duffy Waldorf	69	67	71	207	104,416.66
Peter Senior	74	65	69	208	70,000
Michael Allen	72	67	70	209	45,281.25
Bart Bryant	73	64	72	209	45,281.25
Joel Edwards	71	72	66	209	45,281.25
David Eger	71	68	70	209	45,281.25
Doug Garwood	70	71	68	209	45,281.25
Jay Haas	71	70	68	209	45,281.25
Tom Lehman	69	70	70	209	45,281.25
Ian Woosnam	73	69	67	209	45,281.25
Roger Chapman	74	68	68	210	30,625
Loren Roberts	70	69	71	210	30,625
Kirk Hanefeld	72	70	69	211	28,000
Steve Pate	75	69	68	212	24,558.34
Hale Irwin	70	71	71	212	24,558.33
Corey Pavin	70	71	71	212	24,558.33
Dan Forsman	69	75	69	213	20,912.50
Dick Mast	72	70	71	213	20,912.50
John Cook	74	70	70	214	17,937.50
Scott Hoch	69	72	73	214	17,937.50
Mark O'Meara	74	68	72	214	17,937.50
Gene Sauers	71	70	73	214	17,937.50
Tommy Armour	73	73	69	215	14,875
Jim Gallagher, Jr.	74	68	73	215	14,875
Rocco Mediate	72	71	72	215	14,875
Jeff Sluman	70	72	73	215	14,875

Regions Tradition

Shoal Creek, Shoal Creek, Alabama
Par 36-36–72; 7,197 yards

June 6-9
purse, $2,200,000

	SCORES				TOTAL	MONEY
David Frost	68	70	66	68	272	$330,000
Fred Couples	66	71	68	68	273	193,600
John Cook	70	68	71	66	275	144,650
Esteban Toledo	70	69	69	67	275	144,650
Michael Allen	68	69	69	70	276	90,566.67
Russ Cochran	71	68	70	67	276	90,566.67
Duffy Waldorf	67	68	71	70	276	90,566.66
Morris Hatalsky	71	68	67	71	277	66,000
Jeff Sluman	65	71	72	69	277	66,000
Bernhard Langer	71	73	71	63	278	55,000
Kirk Triplett	71	70	69	68	278	55,000
Fred Funk	72	67	72	68	279	44,733.34
Mark Calcavecchia	68	69	73	69	279	44,733.33
Peter Senior	67	71	73	68	279	44,733.33
Bart Bryant	69	69	70	72	280	36,300
Scott Hoch	72	67	69	72	280	36,300
Kenny Perry	69	73	67	71	280	36,300

	SCORES				TOTAL	MONEY
Gene Sauers	72	69	70	69	280	36,300
Steve Elkington	71	70	72	68	281	28,893.34
Barry Lane	70	71	71	69	281	28,893.33
Corey Pavin	68	74	68	71	281	28,893.33
Bill Glasson	72	73	69	68	282	22,623.34
Tom Pernice, Jr.	70	75	71	66	282	22,623.34
Tom Jenkins	69	72	71	70	282	22,623.33
Tom Lehman	69	71	69	73	282	22,623.33
Loren Roberts	69	69	70	74	282	22,623.33
Rod Spittle	71	66	73	72	282	22,623.33
David Eger	69	70	70	74	283	18,260
Jim Thorpe	72	68	72	71	283	18,260
Willie Wood	71	70	73	69	283	18,260
Jay Haas	71	71	71	71	284	15,840
Larry Mize	72	70	69	73	284	15,840
Bruce Vaughan	71	72	72	69	284	15,840
Craig Stadler	71	75	70	69	285	14,520
Rocco Mediate	72	71	71	72	286	13,860
Mike Goodes	70	68	71	78	287	12,144
Chien Soon Lu	70	74	72	71	287	12,144
Mark O'Meara	73	70	71	73	287	12,144
Steve Pate	72	71	74	70	287	12,144
Scott Simpson	71	72	76	68	287	12,144
Mark Brooks	70	73	71	74	288	10,340
Roger Chapman	70	76	69	73	288	10,340
Bob Tway	69	71	73	75	288	10,340
Jay Don Blake	71	71	71	76	289	8,360
Dan Forsman	71	73	74	71	289	8,360
Jim Gallagher, Jr.	70	73	72	74	289	8,360
Jeff Hart	73	69	70	77	289	8,360
Mark McNulty	69	74	71	75	289	8,360
Mark Mouland	70	73	72	74	289	8,360
Chip Beck	72	75	68	75	290	6,160
Bruce Fleisher	73	73	73	71	290	6,160
Blaine McCallister	72	73	74	71	290	6,160
Mike Reid	72	71	75	72	290	6,160
Hale Irwin	71	76	71	73	291	5,060
Jerry Pate	74	71	74	72	291	5,060
Jim Rutledge	75	73	72	71	291	5,060
Joe Daley	71	72	76	73	292	4,400
Gary Hallberg	80	70	69	73	292	4,400
Larry Nelson	78	71	70	73	292	4,400
Tom Kite	74	72	71	76	293	3,630
Neal Lancaster	75	67	71	80	293	3,630
Andrew Magee	73	74	70	76	293	3,630
Hal Sutton	73	72	71	77	293	3,630
Gene Jones	71	76	74	74	295	2,970
Dick Mast	69	76	75	75	295	2,970
Bobby Clampett	74	75	74	73	296	2,420
Joel Edwards	74	75	72	75	296	2,420
Don Pooley	73	71	76	76	296	2,420
Brad Faxon	77	74	71	75	297	1,870
Bob Gilder	69	81	73	74	297	1,870
Wayne Levi	73	71	76	77	297	1,870
Sandy Lyle	78	72	74	73	297	1,870
Tom Purtzer	74	77	75	74	300	1,540
Dana Quigley	74	80	75	72	301	1,408
Bobby Wadkins	71	77	76	77	301	1,408
Gil Morgan	74	78	72	80	304	1,276
Mark Wiebe	69	77	74	87	307	1,188
Jeff Freeman	79	81	75	75	310	1,100

Encompass Championship

North Shore Country Club, Glenview, Illinois
Par 36-36–72; 7,103 yards

June 21-23
purse, $1,800,000

	SCORES			TOTAL	MONEY
Craig Stadler	67	65	71	203	$270,000
Fred Couples	70	68	66	204	158,400
David Frost	68	67	70	205	81,000
Bernhard Langer	67	69	69	205	81,000
Tom Lehman	70	66	69	205	81,000
Mark O'Meara	70	67	68	205	81,000
Tom Pernice, Jr.	70	68	67	205	81,000
Kenny Perry	69	69	67	205	81,000
Jeff Sluman	68	66	71	205	81,000
Mark Calcavecchia	67	69	71	207	45,000
Bob Tway	69	65	73	207	45,000
Bart Bryant	69	68	71	208	36,600
Steve Pate	70	66	72	208	36,600
Rod Spittle	71	67	70	208	36,600
Jay Haas	71	68	70	209	28,800
Jeff Hart	68	71	70	209	28,800
Corey Pavin	69	69	71	209	28,800
Peter Senior	70	68	71	209	28,800
Esteban Toledo	67	73	69	209	28,800
Mike Goodes	69	69	72	210	23,580
Gary Hallberg	68	72	71	211	19,944
Scott Hoch	68	75	68	211	19,944
Chien Soon Lu	69	68	74	211	19,944
Kirk Triplett	70	72	69	211	19,944
Duffy Waldorf	67	72	72	211	19,944
John Riegger	70	68	74	212	16,740
Loren Roberts	72	72	68	212	16,740
Michael Allen	75	71	67	213	14,580
Jay Don Blake	72	70	71	213	14,580
Mark Brooks	69	73	71	213	14,580
Fred Funk	70	73	70	213	14,580

Constellation Senior Players Championship

Fox Chapel Golf Club, Pittsburgh, Pennsylvania
Par 35-35–70; 6,710 yards

June 27-30
purse, $2,700,000

	SCORES				TOTAL	MONEY
Kenny Perry	71	63	63	64	261	$405,000
Fred Couples	66	62	67	68	263	216,000
Duffy Waldorf	66	67	66	64	263	216,000
Michael Allen	67	68	68	65	268	144,450
John Huston	65	67	68	68	268	144,450
Jeff Hart	68	65	70	67	270	102,600
Morris Hatalsky	70	67	66	67	270	102,600
Bernhard Langer	72	69	63	67	271	86,400
Mark Calcavecchia	68	68	66	70	272	64,800
Bill Glasson	69	67	70	66	272	64,800
Colin Montgomerie	69	70	68	65	272	64,800
Corey Pavin	71	65	67	69	272	64,800
Peter Senior	69	69	68	66	272	64,800
Mike Goodes	67	68	65	73	273	49,950
Tom Pernice, Jr.	67	71	71	64	273	49,950
Tom Lehman	68	68	69	69	274	44,550

	SCORES				TOTAL	MONEY
Jeff Sluman	72	69	67	66	274	44,550
Roger Chapman	69	69	69	68	275	36,720
Fred Funk	66	69	69	71	275	36,720
Chien Soon Lu	72	66	70	67	275	36,720
Rod Spittle	69	68	70	68	275	36,720
Sandy Lyle	70	69	71	66	276	30,510
Rocco Mediate	70	69	68	69	276	30,510
Steve Elkington	68	69	70	70	277	27,000
Larry Mize	68	71	71	67	277	27,000
Hal Sutton	69	71	67	70	277	27,000
David Frost	68	68	73	69	278	21,445.72
Tom Kite	74	68	67	69	278	21,445.72
Tom Watson	72	69	71	66	278	21,445.72
Jay Haas	69	72	68	69	278	21,445.71
Jim Rutledge	74	71	68	65	278	21,445.71
Esteban Toledo	75	69	69	65	278	21,445.71
Bruce Vaughan	71	66	71	70	278	21,445.71
Chip Beck	68	72	69	70	279	17,415
Joe Daley	71	69	69	70	279	17,415
Jay Don Blake	73	67	73	67	280	15,795
John Cook	70	69	70	71	280	15,795
Bart Bryant	70	67	72	72	281	14,850
Mark Brooks	71	68	69	74	282	12,420
Joel Edwards	67	70	72	73	282	12,420
Scott Hoch	68	74	69	71	282	12,420
Peter Jacobsen	69	71	69	73	282	12,420
Dick Mast	72	72	68	70	282	12,420
Mark Mouland	70	71	76	65	282	12,420
Mark O'Meara	68	66	75	73	282	12,420
Bob Tway	70	71	70	71	282	12,420
David Eger	70	70	68	75	283	8,910
Jim Gallagher, Jr.	67	74	72	70	283	8,910
Steve Lowery	71	71	68	73	283	8,910
Gene Sauers	69	69	73	72	283	8,910
Willie Wood	70	70	74	69	283	8,910
Brad Faxon	71	74	70	69	284	6,682.50
Dan Forsman	70	73	70	71	284	6,682.50
Steve Jones	70	68	71	75	284	6,682.50
Mark McNulty	73	70	74	67	284	6,682.50
Loren Roberts	73	71	75	66	285	5,940
Tom Byrum	70	75	71	70	286	5,400
Steve Pate	70	74	72	70	286	5,400
Scott Simpson	73	72	67	74	286	5,400
Jeff Freeman	71	71	74	71	287	3,915
Barry Lane	77	67	72	71	287	3,915
Andrew Magee	71	73	71	72	287	3,915
Gil Morgan	71	75	69	72	287	3,915
Larry Nelson	76	68	73	70	287	3,915
Mike Reid	71	73	72	71	287	3,915
Kirk Triplett	74	68	73	72	287	3,915
Mark Wiebe	71	75	72	69	287	3,915
Hale Irwin	72	71	76	69	288	2,538
Tom Jenkins	77	72	68	71	288	2,538
David Peoples	72	74	73	69	288	2,538
Bobby Clampett	68	73	74	74	289	2,052
Bob Gilder	72	72	69	76	289	2,052
Gary Hallberg	72	74	73	70	289	2,052
Kohki Idoki	75	72	70	73	290	1,674
Nick Price	72	70	75	73	290	1,674
Tom Purtzer	73	73	74	70	290	1,674
Craig Stadler	70	69	76	76	291	1,458
Wayne Levi	76	71	76	70	293	1,350
Joey Sindelar	72	77	71	74	294	1,242

	SCORES				TOTAL	MONEY
Ben Crenshaw	74	80	77	74	305	1,161
Russ Cochran	66	69			WD	

U.S. Senior Open

Omaha Country Club, Omaha, Nebraska
Par 35-35–70; 6,657 yards

July 11-14
purse, $2,600,000

	SCORES				TOTAL	MONEY
Kenny Perry	67	73	64	63	267	$500,000
Fred Funk	67	70	67	68	272	295,000
Rocco Mediate	68	67	72	66	273	155,503
Corey Pavin	69	73	64	67	273	155,503
Michael Allen	67	63	72	72	274	103,416
Steve Elkington	70	70	71	65	276	83,461
Chien Soon Lu	68	75	65	68	276	83,461
Jeff Sluman	69	67	72	68	276	83,461
Bart Bryant	72	69	67	70	278	60,800
Tom Lehman	67	71	70	70	278	60,800
Kirk Triplett	70	72	71	65	278	60,800
Duffy Waldorf	70	69	72	67	278	60,800
Chris Williams	70	72	66	70	278	60,800
Fred Couples	71	69	70	69	279	44,989
Jeff Hart	71	74	69	65	279	44,989
Bernhard Langer	68	74	68	69	279	44,989
Loren Roberts	76	67	68	68	279	44,989
Peter Senior	68	73	70	68	279	44,989
Mark O'Meara	67	71	70	72	280	37,890
Joe Daley	72	70	68	71	281	33,779
David Frost	72	70	67	72	281	33,779
Steve Pate	72	69	67	73	281	33,779
Jeff Brehaut	69	68	72	73	282	24,845
Gary Hallberg	67	74	69	72	282	24,845
Kohki Idoki	69	74	70	69	282	24,845
Barry Lane	73	71	68	70	282	24,845
Tom Pernice, Jr.	74	69	65	74	282	24,845
John Riegger	72	69	67	74	282	24,845
Tom Watson	70	70	73	69	282	24,845
Jeff Freeman	73	68	72	70	283	18,023
John Huston	77	68	69	69	283	18,023
Larry Mize	71	72	68	72	283	18,023
Colin Montgomerie	69	73	72	69	283	18,023
Esteban Toledo	71	69	71	72	283	18,023
Jay Don Blake	67	74	73	70	284	14,827
John Cook	72	70	69	73	284	14,827
Joel Edwards	73	71	72	68	284	14,827
Peter Fowler	70	70	68	76	284	14,827
Jay Haas	73	72	69	70	284	14,827
Gene Sauers	73	70	68	73	284	14,827
Willie Wood	75	68	71	70	284	14,827
Mark McNulty	72	72	68	73	285	12,446
Gil Morgan	73	70	68	74	285	12,446
Tom Kite	70	75	69	72	286	11,124
Gary Koch	71	68	72	75	286	11,124
Larry Nelson	73	72	68	73	286	11,124
David Eger	70	71	75	71	287	9,538
Don Pooley	74	69	69	75	287	9,538
Gary Wolstenholme	72	72	76	67	287	9,538
Dan Forsman	70	74	72	72	288	8,156
George Forster	70	73	75	70	288	8,156

	SCORES				TOTAL	MONEY
Steve Lowery	69	72	73	74	288	8,156
Andy Morse	74	70	70	74	288	8,156
Mark Calcavecchia	72	73	74	70	289	7,556
Joe Ozaki	71	72	77	69	289	7,556
Brian Henninger	71	72	70	77	290	7,067
Hale Irwin	74	69	73	74	290	7,067
Gene Jones	73	72	71	74	290	7,067
Stan Utley	70	74	70	76	290	7,067
*Douglas Hanzel	74	70	73	73	290	
Eduardo Romero	69	73	76	73	291	6,635
Lance Ten Broeck	74	71	73	73	291	6,635
Tim Thelen	74	71	75	71	291	6,635
Walt Chapman	69	73	79	75	296	6,417

The Senior Open Championship presented by Rolex

See European Senior Tour section.

3M Championship

TPC Twin Cities, Blaine, Minnesota
Par 36-36–72; 7,100 yards

August 2-4
purse, $1,750,000

	SCORES			TOTAL	MONEY
Tom Pernice, Jr.	66	65	68	199	$262,500
Corey Pavin	65	69	66	200	140,000
Jeff Sluman	69	69	62	200	140,000
Bart Bryant	66	69	67	202	85,750
Jay Haas	69	68	65	202	85,750
Rod Spittle	68	66	68	202	85,750
Colin Montgomerie	67	69	67	203	53,375
Kenny Perry	65	71	67	203	53,375
Craig Stadler	72	66	65	203	53,375
Kirk Triplett	71	64	68	203	53,375
John Cook	68	69	67	204	38,500
Gene Sauers	70	66	68	204	38,500
Peter Senior	66	72	66	204	38,500
Fred Funk	71	68	66	205	29,750
Tom Kite	68	65	72	205	29,750
Rocco Mediate	68	69	68	205	29,750
John Riegger	66	69	70	205	29,750
Mark Wiebe	64	71	70	205	29,750
Jay Don Blake	68	66	72	206	20,625
Jeff Brehaut	66	70	70	206	20,625
Mark Bucek	68	71	67	206	20,625
David Eger	72	66	68	206	20,625
Jeff Hart	72	67	67	206	20,625
Larry Mize	71	69	66	206	20,625
Loren Roberts	69	69	68	206	20,625
Mark Calcavecchia	69	70	68	207	15,925
Mike Goodes	68	69	70	207	15,925
Jim Thorpe	71	70	66	207	15,925
Bobby Clampett	70	67	71	208	13,518.75
Tom Lehman	69	69	70	208	13,518.75
Mark McNulty	71	66	71	208	13,518.75
Larry Nelson	71	67	70	208	13,518.75

Dick's Sporting Goods Open

En-Joie Golf Course, Endicott, New York
Par 37-35–72; 6,974 yards

August 16-18
purse, $1,800,000

	SCORES			TOTAL	MONEY
Bart Bryant	66	62	72	200	$270,000
Russ Cochran	67	67	67	201	144,000
Corey Pavin	68	64	69	201	144,000
Gene Sauers	69	66	67	202	96,300
Duffy Waldorf	68	65	69	202	96,300
Chien Soon Lu	72	66	65	203	72,000
John Cook	70	69	65	204	57,600
Kenny Perry	65	71	68	204	57,600
Rod Spittle	69	66	69	204	57,600
Fred Funk	71	67	67	205	39,960
Scott Hoch	73	63	69	205	39,960
Bernhard Langer	73	66	66	205	39,960
Peter Senior	68	69	68	205	39,960
Esteban Toledo	67	68	70	205	39,960
Tom Pernice, Jr.	69	71	66	206	32,400
Joel Edwards	66	71	70	207	27,036
Rick Fehr	67	67	73	207	27,036
Jeff Freeman	67	70	70	207	27,036
David Frost	70	66	71	207	27,036
Larry Nelson	68	70	69	207	27,036
Joe Daley	68	69	71	208	19,470
Mike Goodes	70	69	69	208	19,470
Jeff Hart	68	70	70	208	19,470
Peter Jacobsen	72	70	66	208	19,470
Gil Morgan	70	70	68	208	19,470
Jeff Sluman	70	69	69	208	19,470
Mark Brooks	74	66	69	209	15,660
Brad Bryant	66	72	71	209	15,660
Dan Forsman	70	71	68	209	15,660
Steve Elkington	72	68	70	210	12,996
John Huston	70	71	69	210	12,996
Steve Jones	68	72	70	210	12,996
Joey Sindelar	70	70	70	210	12,996
Craig Stadler	73	69	68	210	12,996

Boeing Classic

TPC Snoqualmie Ridge, Snoqualmie, Washington
Par 36-36–72; 7,264 yards

August 23-25
purse, $2,000,000

	SCORES			TOTAL	MONEY
John Riegger	69	64	68	201	$300,000
John Cook	69	68	66	203	176,000
Fred Couples	69	70	66	205	144,000
John Huston	70	68	68	206	76,857.15
Gene Sauers	72	67	67	206	76,857.15
Bobby Clampett	67	69	70	206	76,857.14
Bernhard Langer	68	68	70	206	76,857.14
Tom Lehman	69	67	70	206	76,857.14
Tom Pernice, Jr.	70	68	68	206	76,857.14
Duffy Waldorf	67	71	68	206	76,857.14
Joel Edwards	71	68	68	207	48,000
Bart Bryant	66	75	67	208	42,000
Kirk Triplett	68	68	72	208	42,000

	SCORES			TOTAL	MONEY
Brian Henninger	70	71	68	209	38,000
Jay Don Blake	72	67	71	210	33,000
David Frost	72	68	70	210	33,000
Dick Mast	68	71	71	210	33,000
Rocco Mediate	70	69	71	210	33,000
Russ Cochran	73	69	69	211	28,000
Steve Lowery	72	71	69	212	24,666.67
Mark McNulty	70	70	72	212	24,666.67
Kenny Perry	70	69	73	212	24,666.66
Tom Byrum	71	70	72	213	20,040
Dan Forsman	73	72	68	213	20,040
Mike Goodes	70	72	71	213	20,040
Gary Hallberg	72	69	72	213	20,040
Esteban Toledo	72	69	72	213	20,040
Jeff Brehaut	71	70	73	214	15,500
David Eger	72	70	72	214	15,500
Jim Gallagher, Jr.	74	70	70	214	15,500
Peter Jacobsen	70	72	72	214	15,500
Gene Jones	72	69	73	214	15,500
James Mason	75	67	72	214	15,500

Shaw Charity Classic

Canyon Meadows Golf & Country Club, Calgary,
Alberta, Canada
Par 35-36–71; 7,158 yards

August 30-September 1
purse, $2,000,000

	SCORES			TOTAL	MONEY
Rocco Mediate	63	64	64	191	$300,000
Tom Byrum	66	68	64	198	176,000
Kirk Triplett	66	66	67	199	131,500
Duffy Waldorf	67	67	65	199	131,500
Michael Allen	65	66	69	200	73,400
Bobby Clampett	64	65	71	200	73,400
Jeff Freeman	67	68	65	200	73,400
Scott Hoch	65	70	65	200	73,400
Tom Pernice, Jr.	67	64	69	200	73,400
Jay Don Blake	66	66	69	201	44,400
Bart Bryant	64	68	69	201	44,400
Fred Couples	69	65	67	201	44,400
David Frost	65	66	70	201	44,400
Bill Glasson	67	72	62	201	44,400
Russ Cochran	67	68	67	202	33,000
Joe Daley	70	64	68	202	33,000
Mike Goodes	70	63	69	202	33,000
Jeff Sluman	64	68	70	202	33,000
R.W. Eaks	68	70	65	203	26,266.67
Peter Senior	67	71	65	203	26,266.67
Olin Browne	68	70	65	203	26,266.66
John Cook	70	68	66	204	20,114.29
Joel Edwards	66	72	66	204	20,114.29
Mark O'Meara	67	69	68	204	20,114.29
Esteban Toledo	67	68	69	204	20,114.29
Roger Chapman	69	65	70	204	20,114.28
Fred Funk	68	66	70	204	20,114.28
Steve Lowery	69	64	71	204	20,114.28
Mark Brooks	66	67	72	205	15,450
Rod Spittle	64	73	68	205	15,450
Craig Stadler	65	68	72	205	15,450
Mark Wiebe	70	70	65	205	15,450

Montreal Championship

Vallee du Richelieu Rouville, Sainte-Julie, Quebec, Canada
Par 36-36–72; 7,092 yards

September 6-8
purse, $1,600,000

	SCORES			TOTAL	MONEY
Esteban Toledo	73	69	69	211	$240,000
Kenny Perry	70	71	70	211	140,800
(Toledo defeated Perry on third playoff hole.)					
Duffy Waldorf	72	70	70	212	115,200
Michael Allen	74	68	71	213	73,200
Anders Forsbrand	72	69	72	213	73,200
David Frost	71	72	70	213	73,200
Bernhard Langer	71	67	75	213	73,200
Loren Roberts	72	72	70	214	51,200
Russ Cochran	73	72	70	215	34,800
Bill Glasson	72	69	74	215	34,800
Scott Hoch	76	69	70	215	34,800
Dick Mast	69	75	71	215	34,800
Tom Pernice, Jr.	71	72	72	215	34,800
Rod Spittle	72	72	71	215	34,800
Kirk Triplett	77	67	71	215	34,800
Willie Wood	73	68	74	215	34,800
Jim Carter	72	71	73	216	24,000
Dan Forsman	76	68	72	216	24,000
Sandy Lyle	76	71	69	216	24,000
Andrew Magee	74	73	70	217	17,828.58
Olin Browne	77	67	73	217	17,828.57
Brad Faxon	77	69	71	217	17,828.57
Jim Gallagher, Jr.	74	69	74	217	17,828.57
Rocco Mediate	75	68	74	217	17,828.57
Peter Senior	72	71	74	217	17,828.57
Jeff Sluman	73	72	72	217	17,828.57
David Eger	76	70	72	218	13,600
Gary Hallberg	73	70	75	218	13,600
Chien Soon Lu	73	68	77	218	13,600
Steve Pate	74	71	73	218	13,600

Pacific Links Hawai'i Championship

Kapolei Golf Course, Kapolei, Hawaii
Par 36-36–72; 7,001 yards

September 20-22
purse, $1,800,000

	SCORES			TOTAL	MONEY
Mark Wiebe	64	69	72	205	$270,000
Corey Pavin	68	68	69	205	158,400
(Wiebe defeated Pavin on second playoff hole.)					
Bernhard Langer	69	69	68	206	129,600
John Cook	66	71	70	207	96,300
Esteban Toledo	71	70	66	207	96,300
Fred Couples	71	71	66	208	55,800
David Frost	69	69	70	208	55,800
Brian Henninger	67	69	72	208	55,800
Gene Sauers	69	69	70	208	55,800
Vijay Singh	69	66	73	208	55,800
Kirk Triplett	69	70	69	208	55,800
Sandy Lyle	70	67	72	209	39,600
Mark Calcavecchia	66	72	72	210	35,100
Rocco Mediate	69	71	70	210	35,100
Mark Mouland	72	72	67	211	32,400

	SCORES			TOTAL	MONEY
Bart Bryant	68	70	74	212	27,900
Dan Forsman	73	69	70	212	27,900
Mark O'Meara	70	73	69	212	27,900
Duffy Waldorf	71	69	72	212	27,900
Joel Edwards	70	72	71	213	21,600
Bill Glasson	74	68	71	213	21,600
Dick Mast	72	69	72	213	21,600
Willie Wood	69	75	69	213	21,600
Jay Don Blake	71	72	71	214	16,087.50
Steve Elkington	71	74	69	214	16,087.50
Brad Faxon	68	73	73	214	16,087.50
Doug Garwood	71	75	68	214	16,087.50
Jeff Hart	71	69	74	214	16,087.50
Larry Mize	71	72	71	214	16,087.50
Scott Simpson	70	71	73	214	16,087.50
Bob Tway	73	71	70	214	16,087.50

Nature Valley First Tee Open

Pebble Beach Golf Links: Par 36-36–72; 6,822 yards
Del Monte Golf Course: Par 36-36–72; 6,357 yards
Monterey Peninsula, California

September 27-29
purse, $1,800,000

	SCORES			TOTAL	MONEY
Kirk Triplett	67	70	68	205	$270,000
Dan Forsman	68	70	69	207	144,000
Doug Garwood	67	71	69	207	144,000
Tom Lehman	67	67	74	208	107,100
Russ Cochran	68	67	74	209	85,500
John Cook	70	68	72	210	68,400
Willie Wood	72	69	69	210	68,400
Bernhard Langer	63	74	74	211	57,600
Olin Browne	69	72	71	212	45,000
Craig Stadler	70	69	73	212	45,000
Esteban Toledo	69	72	71	212	45,000
Duffy Waldorf	72	68	72	212	45,000
Scott Hoch	70	69	74	213	36,000
Chien Soon Lu	71	67	76	214	31,500
Mark McNulty	67	74	73	214	31,500
Tom Pernice Jr.	71	70	73	214	31,500
Loren Roberts	70	72	72	214	31,500
Fred Couples	68	71	76	215	23,760
David Frost	73	72	70	215	23,760
John Inman	73	66	76	215	23,760
Tom Kite	72	72	71	215	23,760
Ted Schulz	73	67	75	215	23,760
Mark Brooks	77	66	73	216	17,640
Tom Byrum	72	68	76	216	17,640
Mark Calcavecchia	68	72	76	216	17,640
Bill Glasson	71	68	77	216	17,640
Dick Mast	72	70	74	216	17,640
Mark O'Meara	79	67	70	216	17,640
Joel Edwards	71	69	77	217	13,905
Mike Goodes	70	72	75	217	13,905
Jeff Sluman	75	67	75	217	13,905
Rod Spittle	70	72	75	217	13,905

SAS Championship

Prestonwood Country Club, Cary, North Carolina   October 11-13
Par 35-37–72; 7,137 yards   purse, $2,100,000

	SCORES			TOTAL	MONEY
Russ Cochran	66	66	67	199	$315,000
David Frost	67	67	66	200	184,800
Kirk Triplett	67	67	68	202	151,200
Gary Hallberg	68	69	66	203	124,950
Michael Allen	67	68	70	205	91,875
Anders Forsbrand	69	67	69	205	91,875
Tom Byrum	69	69	68	206	75,600
Joe Daley	68	69	70	207	60,200
Bernhard Langer	67	67	73	207	60,200
Peter Senior	69	69	69	207	60,200
Olin Browne	70	66	72	208	40,800
Bobby Clampett	69	70	69	208	40,800
Doug Garwood	68	71	69	208	40,800
Bill Glasson	69	69	70	208	40,800
Tom Kite	68	69	71	208	40,800
Mark O'Meara	73	70	65	208	40,800
Kenny Perry	68	68	72	208	40,800
Tommy Armour	70	73	66	209	28,560
Colin Montgomerie	71	69	69	209	28,560
Larry Nelson	66	75	68	209	28,560
Craig Stadler	68	68	73	209	28,560
Brad Faxon	71	68	71	210	22,092
Brian Henninger	71	68	71	210	22,092
Scott Hoch	72	69	69	210	22,092
Gene Jones	73	69	68	210	22,092
Steve Jones	71	70	69	210	22,092
Chip Beck	71	69	71	211	17,045
Steve Elkington	70	71	70	211	17,045
Andrew Magee	72	66	73	211	17,045
Steve Pate	71	73	67	211	17,045
Bob Tway	73	69	69	211	17,045
Duffy Waldorf	68	69	74	211	17,045

Greater Hickory Kia Classic

Rock Barn Golf & Spa, Conover, North Carolina   October 18-20
Par 34-36–70; 6,871 yards   purse, $1,600,000

	SCORES			TOTAL	MONEY
Michael Allen	67	65	65	197	$240,000
Olin Browne	65	68	64	197	140,800
(Allen defeated Browne on first playoff hole.)					
Bernhard Langer	64	66	69	199	115,200
Brad Bryant	66	66	69	201	95,200
John Riegger	65	67	70	202	76,000
Anders Forsbrand	64	70	69	203	57,600
Tom Kite	69	67	67	203	57,600
Chien Soon Lu	70	67	66	203	57,600
Jim Gallagher, Jr.	68	66	70	204	38,400
Bill Glasson	73	70	61	204	38,400
John Inman	67	68	69	204	38,400
Tom Pernice, Jr.	67	70	67	204	38,400
Bruce Vaughan	71	62	71	204	38,400
Steve Elkington	68	69	68	205	26,400

	SCORES			TOTAL	MONEY
Jay Haas	69	69	67	205	26,400
Brian Henninger	71	67	67	205	26,400
Dick Mast	64	73	68	205	26,400
Bob Tway	67	71	67	205	26,400
Willie Wood	67	69	69	205	26,400
Mark Brooks	67	68	71	206	18,266.67
David Frost	67	69	70	206	18,266.67
Kenny Perry	68	69	69	206	18,266.67
Jeff Sluman	72	68	66	206	18,266.67
Russ Cochran	67	67	72	206	18,266.66
Jay Delsing	70	66	70	206	18,266.66
Mike Goodes	66	70	71	207	14,880
Jim Rutledge	71	72	64	207	14,880
Tom Byrum	69	69	70	208	12,672
Joel Edwards	67	72	69	208	12,672
Gil Morgan	68	69	71	208	12,672
Craig Stadler	73	68	67	208	12,672
Duffy Waldorf	71	69	68	208	12,672

AT&T Championship

TPC San Antonio, AT&T Canyons Course, San Antonio, Texas
Par 36-36–72; 6,932 yards

October 25-27
purse, $1,900,000

	SCORES			TOTAL	MONEY
Kenny Perry	65	71	67	203	$285,000
Bernhard Langer	67	69	67	203	167,200
(Perry defeated Langer on first playoff hole.)					
Fred Funk	69	69	67	205	113,366.67
Kirk Triplett	70	67	68	205	113,366.67
Colin Montgomerie	68	68	69	205	113,366.66
Russ Cochran	68	70	69	207	68,400
Anders Forsbrand	67	69	71	207	68,400
John Riegger	70	70	67	207	68,400
Tom Kite	73	67	68	208	49,400
Mark O'Meara	70	68	70	208	49,400
Tom Pernice, Jr.	66	73	69	208	49,400
John Cook	69	73	67	209	38,633.34
Michael Allen	73	67	69	209	38,633.33
Jeff Hart	72	70	67	209	38,633.33
Scott Dunlap	69	68	73	210	32,300
Peter Senior	72	70	68	210	32,300
Rod Spittle	69	70	71	210	32,300
Bobby Clampett	70	68	73	211	25,840
Joe Daley	70	72	69	211	25,840
Mike Goodes	73	63	75	211	25,840
Dick Mast	69	71	71	211	25,840
Mark Brooks	73	68	71	212	18,691.25
Bart Bryant	73	71	68	212	18,691.25
David Frost	77	69	66	212	18,691.25
Bob Gilder	70	71	71	212	18,691.25
Brian Henninger	71	71	70	212	18,691.25
Steve Lowery	69	77	66	212	18,691.25
Rocco Mediate	72	68	72	212	18,691.25
Steve Pate	69	73	70	212	18,691.25
Olin Browne	72	68	73	213	12,331
Fred Couples	75	70	68	213	12,331
Bill Glasson	77	69	67	213	12,331
Gary Hallberg	69	72	72	213	12,331
John Inman	73	71	69	213	12,331

	SCORES			TOTAL	MONEY
Mark McNulty	73	70	70	213	12,331
Larry Mize	70	74	69	213	12,331
Corey Pavin	69	70	74	213	12,331
Jim Thorpe	70	70	73	213	12,331
Willie Wood	73	67	73	213	12,331

Charles Schwab Cup Championship

TPC Harding Park, San Francisco, California
Par 36-35–71; 6,889 yards

October 31-November 3
purse, $2,500,000

	SCORES				TOTAL	MONEY
Fred Couples	65	65	68	69	267	$440,000
Bernhard Langer	67	68	71	67	273	214,333.34
Mark O'Meara	66	70	67	70	273	214,333.33
Peter Senior	63	69	72	69	273	214,333.33
Bart Bryant	68	66	70	70	274	113,750
Mark Calcavecchia	70	71	68	65	274	113,750
Rocco Mediate	70	70	66	68	274	113,750
Kenny Perry	68	71	67	68	274	113,750
Jay Don Blake	69	69	71	66	275	76,000
Fred Funk	70	70	71	64	275	76,000
Tom Lehman	69	70	65	71	275	76,000
Mike Goodes	68	68	69	71	276	64,000
David Frost	64	73	71	69	277	59,000
Russ Cochran	68	68	73	70	279	52,000
Tom Pernice, Jr.	71	73	69	66	279	52,000
Duffy Waldorf	67	71	74	67	279	52,000
Gene Sauers	68	71	72	69	280	43,166.67
Esteban Toledo	70	71	69	70	280	43,166.67
Jay Haas	70	69	70	71	280	43,166.66
John Cook	69	71	71	70	281	37,000
Jeff Sluman	71	69	69	72	281	37,000
Michael Allen	68	72	71	71	282	34,000
Chien Soon Lu	72	68	73	70	283	32,000
John Riegger	72	70	68	75	285	30,000
Steve Elkington	67	77	72	70	286	29,000
Kirk Triplett	71	69	70	77	287	26,500
Mark Wiebe	75	72	68	72	287	26,500
Corey Pavin	70	74	72	72	288	25,000
Dan Forsman	74	73	69	76	292	24,500
Craig Stadler	74	76	75	77	302	24,000

European Senior Tour

U.S. Senior PGA Championship

See Champions Tour section.

ISPS Handa PGA Seniors Championship

De Vere Mottram Hall, Mottram St. Andrew,
Cheshire, England
Par 36-37–73; 6,940 yards

June 6-9
purse, £260,000

	SCORES				TOTAL	MONEY
Paul Wesselingh	68	70	70	64	272	€48,687
Angel Franco	70	70	70	66	276	34,081
Ian Woosnam	72	69	71	65	277	22,822
Mike Cunning	71	68	70	71	280	16,730
Steen Tinning	71	72	67	70	280	16,730
Gordon J. Brand	67	78	69	67	281	10,529
Jose Manuel Carriles	71	67	72	71	281	10,529
Andrew Oldcorn	72	70	73	67	282	7,806
Des Smyth	67	69	73	73	282	7,806
Philip Golding	70	72	70	72	284	6,250
Sam Torrance	69	73	73	69	284	6,250
David J. Russell	71	67	71	76	285	5,648
Philip Walton	70	70	75	71	286	5,368
Angel Fernandez	75	74	71	67	287	4,182
Nick Job	72	75	73	67	287	4,182
Pedro Linhart	71	74	67	75	287	4,182
Carl Mason	72	73	71	71	287	4,182
Peter Mitchell	72	71	73	71	287	4,182
Kevin Spurgeon	75	73	69	70	287	4,182
Jim Woodward	74	70	71	72	287	4,182

Speedy Services Wales Senior Open

Royal Porthcawl Golf Club, Bridgend, Wales
Par 35-36–71; 7,071 yards

June 14-16
purse, £250,000

	SCORES			TOTAL	MONEY
Philip Golding	66	79	66	211	€44,004
David J. Russell	69	73	71	213	29,336
Barry Lane	67	77	70	214	16,643
Andrew Oldcorn	66	77	71	214	16,643
Ian Woosnam	65	74	75	214	16,643
Mike Cunning	71	72	73	216	9,974
Denis O'Sullivan	68	72	76	216	9,974
Terry Price	69	72	75	216	9,974
Tim Thelen	70	75	71	216	9,974
Miguel Angel Martin	70	75	72	217	7,334
Andrew Sherborne	70	73	74	217	7,334
Angel Franco	70	78	70	218	6,161

	SCORES			TOTAL	MONEY
Mark James	69	71	78	218	6,161
Eamonn Darcy	74	79	66	219	4,987
Phil Jonas	70	78	71	219	4,987
Juan Quiros	70	76	73	219	4,987
Des Smyth	74	71	74	219	4,987
Steen Tinning	74	74	71	219	4,987
Gordon Manson	71	79	70	220	4,004
Jose Rivero	72	73	75	220	4,004

Bad Ragaz PGA Seniors Open

Golf Club Bad Ragaz, Bad Ragaz, Switzerland
Par 35-35–70; 6,157 yards

July 5-7
purse, €280,000

	SCORES			TOTAL	MONEY
Paul Wesselingh	71	66	64	201	€42,000
Kevin Spurgeon	68	68	65	201	28,000
(Wesselingh defeated Spurgeon on third playoff hole.)					
Pedro Linhart	67	69	68	204	17,500
Carl Mason	67	70	67	204	17,500
Bob Cameron	67	68	70	205	11,312
Juan Quiros	67	68	70	205	11,312
Gary Wolstenholme	64	68	73	205	11,312
Steve Cipa	69	72	65	206	8,027
Phil Jonas	66	69	71	206	8,027
Santiago Luna	64	68	74	206	8,027
Jerry Bruner	70	71	66	207	5,768
Luis Carbonetti	70	74	63	207	5,768
Philip Golding	66	70	71	207	5,768
Gordon Manson	67	70	70	207	5,768
George Ryall	66	72	69	207	5,768
Andrew Murray	71	70	67	208	4,347
Jose Rivero	73	70	65	208	4,347
David J. Russell	70	65	73	208	4,347
Andrew Sherborne	70	70	68	208	4,347
Gordon Brand, Jr.	70	68	71	209	2,920
Anders Forsbrand	68	73	68	209	2,920
Peter Fowler	70	69	70	209	2,920
John Gould	75	66	68	209	2,920
Stephen McAllister	72	70	67	209	2,920
Peter Mitchell	73	67	69	209	2,920
Noel Ratcliffe	69	68	72	209	2,920
Tim Thelen	70	72	67	209	2,920
Steen Tinning	73	69	67	209	2,920
Chris Williams	67	73	69	209	2,920

U.S. Senior Open Championship

See Champions Tour section.

The Senior Open Championship presented by Rolex

Royal Birkdale, Southport, Merseyside, England
Par 34-36—70; 7,082 yards
(Playoff completed on Monday—darkness.)

July 25-28
purse, US$2,000,000

	SCORES				TOTAL	MONEY
Mark Wiebe	70	65	70	66	271	€240,000
Bernhard Langer	68	67	66	70	271	160,076
(Wiebe defeated Langer on fifth playoff hole.)						
David Frost	68	68	68	70	274	74,383
Corey Pavin	69	71	69	65	274	74,383
Peter Senior	68	71	69	66	274	74,383
Peter Fowler	69	68	70	69	276	50,403
Sandy Lyle	70	68	69	70	277	43,194
Jeff Hart	69	69	73	67	278	34,122
Tom Pernice, Jr.	70	72	70	66	278	34,122
Gene Sauers	67	70	70	72	279	28,760
Steve Elkington	72	68	71	69	280	25,589
Gary Wolstenholme	70	72	68	70	280	25,589
Kohki Idoki	71	68	73	69	281	23,057
Russ Cochran	71	73	70	68	282	20,700
Tom Kite	70	72	71	69	282	20,700
Des Smyth	76	69	69	68	282	20,700
Jamie Spence	75	69	70	68	282	20,700
Rocco Mediate	70	68	75	70	283	18,281
Steve Pate	70	72	68	73	283	18,281
Greg Turner	70	69	75	70	284	17,460
Fred Couples	74	72	68	71	285	16,000
Steve Jones	73	70	70	72	285	16,000
Barry Lane	72	68	74	71	285	16,000
Larry Mize	71	73	70	71	285	16,000
Colin Montgomerie	72	71	69	73	285	16,000
Michael Allen	75	70	72	69	286	13,154
Tom Lehman	72	72	70	72	286	13,154
Mark McNulty	70	67	76	73	286	13,154
Mark O'Meara	74	68	72	72	286	13,154
Rod Spittle	71	72	70	73	286	13,154
Steen Tinning	71	74	71	70	286	13,154
Katsuyoshi Tomori	71	72	73	70	286	13,154
Brad Faxon	74	69	74	70	287	11,138
Gary Hallberg	69	75	73	70	287	11,138
Pedro Linhart	73	72	72	70	287	11,138
Kirk Hanefeld	73	75	70	70	288	10,061
David J. Russell	72	73	72	71	288	10,061
Bob Tway	74	72	69	73	288	10,061
Tom Watson	73	71	73	71	288	10,061
John Inman	71	76	70	72	289	8,821
Peter Mitchell	75	72	68	74	289	8,821
Seiki Okuda	73	72	73	71	289	8,821
Duffy Waldorf	76	72	70	71	289	8,821
Paul Wesselingh	70	76	74	69	289	8,821
Miguel Angel Martin	72	75	65	78	290	7,863
Willie Wood	75	71	72	72	290	7,863
Mark James	74	73	71	73	291	7,452
Mike Goodes	71	74	73	74	292	6,494
Chien Soon Lu	71	77	71	73	292	6,494
Santiago Luna	72	74	72	74	292	6,494
*Chip Lutz	71	71	75	75	292	
Dick Mast	72	73	73	74	292	6,494
Eduardo Romero	75	70	72	75	292	6,494
Boonchu Ruangkit	73	73	73	73	292	6,494
Philip Golding	74	74	71	74	293	5,407

	SCORES				TOTAL	MONEY
Bruce Vaughan	73	74	72	74	293	5,407
Mark Brooks	74	73	73	74	294	4,684
Anders Forsbrand	73	70	73	78	294	4,684
Jeff Sluman	71	75	72	76	294	4,684
Esteban Toledo	74	72	74	74	294	4,684
John Cook	69	79	73	74	295	3,901
Massy Kuramoto	70	77	74	74	295	3,901
Carl Mason	74	70	73	78	295	3,901
Frankie Minoza	68	78	72	77	295	3,901
Hendrik Buhrmann	76	72	75	73	296	3,281
Mark Calcavecchia	75	72	73	76	296	3,281
Joe Daley	75	73	73	75	296	3,281
Philip Walton	70	76	75	75	296	3,281
Fred Funk	75	71	78	73	297	2,867
Bill Longmuir	73	69	77	78	297	2,867
Peter Dahlberg	76	72	73	77	298	2,593
Andrew Oldcorn	74	72	75	77	298	2,593
Phil Gresswell	74	71	79	77	301	2,388
Mitch Kierstenson	74	72	77	81	304	2,251

Berenberg Masters

Golf-und-Land-Club Koln, Refrath, Germany
Par 36-36–72; 6,783 yards

August 2-4
purse, €400,000

	SCORES			TOTAL	MONEY
Steen Tinning	68	70	69	207	€60,000
Bernhard Langer	67	73	68	208	40,000
Nick Job	69	69	71	209	28,000
Miguel Angel Martin	72	67	71	210	22,000
Barry Lane	67	75	69	211	16,160
Boonchu Ruangkit	72	68	71	211	16,160
Greg Turner	65	74	72	211	16,160
Mike Cunning	73	69	70	212	12,000
Ian Woosnam	67	72	73	212	12,000
Rick Gibson	75	71	67	213	9,200
Philip Golding	69	74	70	213	9,200
Tim Thelen	70	72	71	213	9,200
Gary Wolstenholme	73	69	71	213	9,200
John Gould	70	73	71	214	7,000
David J. Russell	70	76	68	214	7,000
Des Smyth	71	73	70	214	7,000
Philip Walton	70	75	69	214	7,000
Jerry Bruner	71	73	71	215	5,470
Anders Forsbrand	72	71	72	215	5,470
Bill Longmuir	72	73	70	215	5,470
Paul Wesselingh	70	71	74	215	5,470

SSE Scottish Senior Open

Fairmont St. Andrews, Torrance Championship Course,
St. Andrews, Fife, Scotland
Par 35-37–72; 6,804 yards

August 16-18
purse, £250,000

	SCORES			TOTAL	MONEY
Santiago Luna	69	71	71	211	€43,485
Denis O'Sullivan	68	72	72	212	24,642
Sam Torrance	70	72	70	212	24,642
Peter Fowler	73	66	74	213	13,548
Philip Golding	73	70	70	213	13,548
Peter Mitchell	70	70	73	213	13,548
Miguel Angel Martin	68	73	73	214	10,436
Angel Franco	71	73	71	215	8,697
Nick Job	73	70	72	215	8,697
Barry Lane	73	74	69	216	6,668
Bill Longmuir	70	73	73	216	6,668
Steen Tinning	71	70	75	216	6,668
Chris Williams	72	73	71	216	6,668
Rick Gibson	72	70	75	217	4,928
Des Smyth	71	75	71	217	4,928
Jamie Spence	68	78	71	217	4,928
Kevin Spurgeon	69	74	74	217	4,928
Paul Wesselingh	71	72	74	217	4,928
Bob Cameron	73	72	73	218	3,517
Ross Drummond	73	72	73	218	3,517
Marc Farry	72	73	73	218	3,517
George Ryall	74	70	74	218	3,517
Philip Walton	71	69	78	218	3,517
Gary Wolstenholme	73	71	74	218	3,517

Travis Perkins plc Senior Masters

Woburn Golf Club, Duke's Course, Woburn, England
Par 35-37–72; 6,904 yards

August 30-September 1
purse, £300,000

	SCORES			TOTAL	MONEY
Colin Montgomerie	68	68	70	206	€52,299
Miguel Angel Martin	71	70	71	212	29,636
Paul Wesselingh	74	72	66	212	29,636
Ross Drummond	70	70	73	213	17,468
Carl Mason	70	69	74	213	17,468
Angel Franco	73	74	67	214	13,249
Jamie Spence	70	74	70	214	13,249
Gary Wolstenholme	74	72	69	215	11,157
Luis Carbonetti	67	74	75	216	9,065
Andrew Oldcorn	71	74	71	216	9,065
Ian Woosnam	72	72	72	216	9,065
Rick Gibson	70	73	74	217	6,886
Andrew Murray	77	70	70	217	6,886
Andrew Sherborne	69	77	71	217	6,886
Steen Tinning	73	71	73	217	6,886
Bob Cameron	73	73	72	218	5,251
Mark James	69	75	74	218	5,251
Pedro Linhart	72	71	75	218	5,251
Robert Thompson	74	71	73	218	5,251
Steve Van Vuuren	68	77	73	218	5,251

WINSTONgolf Senior Open

WINSTONopen Course, Vorbeck, Germany
Par 36-36–72; 6,833 yards

September 6-8
purse, €400,000

	SCORES			TOTAL	MONEY
Gordon Brand, Jr.	68	68	68	204	€60,000
Angel Franco	67	69	69	205	30,000
Andrew Oldcorn	73	71	61	205	30,000
David J. Russell	67	71	67	205	30,000
Paul Eales	72	67	67	206	15,320
Peter Fowler	67	73	66	206	15,320
Philip Golding	70	67	69	206	15,320
Steen Tinning	66	72	68	206	15,320
Bob Cameron	71	63	73	207	10,800
Tony Johnstone	71	67	69	207	10,800
Hendrik Buhrmann	67	73	69	209	8,500
Phil Jonas	65	71	73	209	8,500
Boonchu Ruangkit	67	72	70	209	8,500
Ian Woosnam	65	75	69	209	8,500
Simon P. Brown	74	69	67	210	6,800
Nick Job	73	67	70	210	6,800
Tim Thelen	71	70	69	210	6,800
Rick Gibson	73	71	67	211	6,000
Mike Harwood	72	70	70	212	5,130
Santiago Luna	70	71	71	212	5,130
Miguel Angel Martin	71	70	71	212	5,130
Mike McLean	70	70	72	212	5,130

Russian Open

Moscow Country Club, Moscow, Russia
Par 36-36–72; 6,877 yards

September 13-15
purse, US$850,000

	SCORES			TOTAL	MONEY
Simon P. Brown	66	68	70	204	€97,306
Mike Harwood	67	71	68	206	55,140
Carl Mason	70	68	68	206	55,140
Miguel Angel Martin	66	69	72	207	30,316
Colin Montgomerie	69	67	71	207	30,316
Steen Tinning	67	68	72	207	30,316
Andrew Oldcorn	70	68	70	208	22,056
David J. Russell	72	68	68	208	22,056
Massy Kuramoto	69	71	69	209	16,218
Barry Lane	68	69	72	209	16,218
Boonchu Ruangkit	68	71	70	209	16,218
Paul Wesselingh	69	68	72	209	16,218
Paul Eales	70	71	69	210	12,650
Greg Turner	71	70	69	210	12,650
Bob Cameron	71	71	69	211	11,352
Tim Thelen	71	68	72	211	11,352
Jean Laforce	72	69	71	212	9,752
Bill Longmuir	68	75	69	212	9,752
George Ryall	71	71	70	212	9,752
Gordon Brand, Jr.	71	68	74	213	7,247
Peter Fowler	68	72	73	213	7,247
Angel Franco	69	72	72	213	7,247
Philip Golding	73	67	73	213	7,247
Gordon Manson	73	67	73	213	7,247
Mike McLean	68	77	68	213	7,247
Robert Thompson	72	72	69	213	7,247

French Riviera Masters

Terre Blanche Hotel Spa Golf Resort, Tourrettes,
Provence, France
Par 36-36–72; 6,955 yards

September 20-22
purse, €400,000

	SCORES			TOTAL	MONEY
Peter Fowler	68	71	66	205	€60,000
Santiago Luna	73	69	66	208	34,000
Andrew Oldcorn	67	68	73	208	34,000
Katsuyoshi Tomori	70	74	65	209	22,000
Philip Golding	68	72	70	210	16,160
Greg Turner	72	69	69	210	16,160
Ian Woosnam	72	71	67	210	16,160
Paul Wesselingh	72	68	71	211	12,000
Chris Williams	70	69	72	211	12,000
Bob Cameron	71	71	70	212	8,880
Jose Manuel Carriles	72	71	69	212	8,880
Angel Franco	70	70	72	212	8,880
Gordon Manson	73	71	68	212	8,880
Miguel Angel Martin	68	73	71	212	8,880
Massy Kuramoto	72	72	69	213	7,200
Jerry Pate	73	71	70	214	6,800
Simon P. Brown	73	69	73	215	5,830
Jerry Bruner	71	72	72	215	5,830
Tim Elliott	70	72	73	215	5,830
Steve Van Vuuren	72	75	68	215	5,830

English Senior Open

Rockliffe Hall, County Durham, England
Par 36-36–72; 6,949 yards

October 4-6
purse, £200,000

	SCORES			TOTAL	MONEY
Steen Tinning	69	63	67	199	€35,898
Santiago Luna	67	67	66	200	23,932
Paul Eales	70	67	66	203	16,752
Miguel Angel Martin	70	66	70	206	13,163
Gordon Manson	70	67	70	207	9,166
Andrew Oldcorn	70	68	69	207	9,166
David J. Russell	68	69	70	207	9,166
Paul Wesselingh	70	70	67	207	9,166
Gary Emerson	70	72	67	209	6,462
Chris Williams	69	70	70	209	6,462
Jose Manuel Carriles	67	69	74	210	5,265
Mike Cunning	70	71	69	210	5,265
Juan Quiros	69	73	68	210	5,265
Philip Golding	70	68	73	211	4,547
Peter Fowler	75	69	68	212	4,308
Ross Drummond	71	70	72	213	3,949
Wraith Grant	69	73	71	213	3,949
Gordon Brand, Jr.	72	72	70	214	3,002
Marc Farry	72	73	69	214	3,002
Rick Gibson	72	71	71	214	3,002
Mark James	70	73	71	214	3,002
Barry Lane	71	72	71	214	3,002
Peter Mitchell	66	76	72	214	3,002
Gerry Norquist	70	72	72	214	3,002

Dutch Senior Open

The International, Amsterdam, The Netherlands
Par 37-36–73; 6,966 yards
(Third round cancelled—rain.)

October 11-13
purse, €200,000

	SCORES		TOTAL	MONEY
Simon P. Brown	72	71	143	€30,475
Ross Drummond	76	69	145	20,316
Jose Manuel Carriles	75	71	146	11,526
Paul Eales	74	72	146	11,526
Marc Farry	72	74	146	11,526
Philip Golding	73	74	147	6,582
Phil Jonas	75	72	147	6,582
Gordon Manson	78	69	147	6,582
Miguel Angel Martin	75	72	147	6,582
Paul Wesselingh	77	70	147	6,582
Gary Emerson	76	72	148	4,673
Nick Job	72	76	148	4,673
Hendrik Buhrmann	74	75	149	3,657
Mike Harwood	78	71	149	3,657
Santiago Luna	75	74	149	3,657
Peter Mitchell	75	74	149	3,657
Denis O'Sullivan	73	76	149	3,657
Bob Cameron	78	72	150	2,693
Peter Fowler	78	72	150	2,693
Terry Price	76	74	150	2,693
Des Smyth	77	73	150	2,693
Steen Tinning	73	77	150	2,693

Australian PGA Seniors Championship

Richmond Golf Club, Richmond, Australia
Par 72

October 31-November 3
purse, A$70,000

	SCORES			TOTAL	MONEY
Darryl Purchase	69	74	67	210	A$12,707.10
Kym Olsen	70	68	74	212	7,341.88
Russell Swanson	72	69	72	213	4,066.27
David Merriman	72	69	72	213	4,066.27
Wayne Grady	69	77	68	214	2,614.37
Graeme Cheshire	72	72	70	214	2,614.37
Terry Price	70	71	73	214	2,614.37
Michael Clayton	69	70	76	215	2,068.43
Michael Harwood	71	73	72	216	1,736.64
Mike Zilko	72	72	72	216	1,736.64
Tim Elliott	72	70	74	216	1,736.64
Gregory Hohnen	73	71	73	217	1,383.67
Rodger Davis	71	73	73	217	1,383.67
Garry Merrick	76	72	70	218	1,136.58
Michael Sprengel	76	72	70	218	1,136.58
Chris Fox	72	75	72	219	969.50
Mus Deboub	72	75	72	219	969.50
Roger Stephens	74	71	74	219	969.50
Gregory Carroll	74	74	72	220	780.08
Bruce McLean	72	75	73	220	780.08
Geoffrey Nicholas	75	69	76	220	780.08
Paul Powell	71	77	72	220	780.08

Fubon Senior Open

Miramar Golf & Country Club, Taipei, Taiwan
Par 36-36–72; 6,706 yards

November 15-17
purse, US$450,000

	SCORES			TOTAL	MONEY
Paul Wesselingh	69	68	70	207	€59,869
Wen-Teh Lu	70	66	72	208	33,926
Bob Cameron	69	71	72	212	22,455
Simon P. Brown	71	72	72	215	13,748
Paul Eales	71	71	73	215	13,748
Chin-Sheng Hsieh	72	72	71	215	13,748
Chien Soon Lu	76	71	69	216	9,756
Tim Thelen	73	71	72	216	9,756
Katsuyoshi Tomori	73	69	74	216	9,756
David Ishii	72	71	74	217	7,428
Phil Jonas	72	74	71	217	7,428
Ter-Chang Wang	71	71	75	217	7,428
Andre Bossert	68	76	74	218	5,987
Jong-Duck Kim	76	71	72	219	5,488
*Wei-Hou Liu	75	70	74	219	
Gary Wolstenholme	72	75	72	219	5,488
T.C. Chen	73	73	74	220	4,089
Rick Gibson	74	72	74	220	4,089
Wraith Grant	72	74	74	220	4,089
Gordon Manson	73	68	79	220	4,089
Boonchu Ruangkit	74	74	72	220	4,089

MCB Tour Championship

Constance Belle Mare Plage, Poste de Flacq, Mauritius
Par 36-36–72; 6,614 yards

December 13-15
purse, €400,000

	SCORES			TOTAL	MONEY
Paul Wesselingh	67	66	69	202	€62,814
David Frost	70	71	66	207	35,595
Miguel Angel Martin	66	74	67	207	35,595
Roger Chapman	67	72	69	208	20,980
Pedro Linhart	72	68	68	208	20,980
Colin Montgomerie	70	66	74	210	16,750
Simon P. Brown	72	73	66	211	14,238
Mike Cunning	72	73	66	211	14,238
Ross Drummond	71	70	71	212	10,469
Marc Farry	71	69	72	212	10,469
Philip Golding	72	72	68	212	10,469
Chris Williams	72	72	68	212	10,469
Mike McLean	69	71	73	213	8,166
Andrew Sherborne	68	72	73	213	8,166
Jose Manuel Carriles	74	68	72	214	6,709
Peter Fowler	72	69	73	214	6,709
Costantino Rocca	73	72	69	214	6,709
George Ryall	68	75	71	214	6,709
Robert Thompson	70	71	73	214	6,709
Paul Eales	72	70	73	215	5,193
Barry Lane	74	73	68	215	5,193
Steen Tinning	71	71	73	215	5,193

Japan PGA Senior Tour

Kanehide Senior Okinawa Open

Kise Country Club, Okinawa
Par 36-36–72; 6,881 yards

April 19-20
purse, ¥20,000,000

	SCORES		TOTAL	MONEY
Takeshi Sakiyama	66	70	136	¥3,600,000
Akihiro Ito	69	70	139	1,333,333
Kohki Idoki	68	71	139	1,333,333
Katsunari Takahashi	65	74	139	1,333,333
Katsuyoshi Tomori	70	70	140	786,666
Gregory Meyer	69	71	140	786,666
Norikazu Kawakami	69	71	140	786,666
Yoichi Shimizu	71	70	141	580,000
Nobumasa Nakanishi	70	71	141	580,000
Peter Fowler	73	69	142	344,444
Jyunji Kawase	71	71	142	344,444
Hideki Kase	71	71	142	344,444
Hiroyuki Iwabuchi	71	71	142	344,444
Joe Ozaki	70	72	142	344,444
Anthony Gilligan	70	72	142	344,444
Atsushi Takamatsu	70	72	142	344,444
Kiyoshi Maita	70	72	142	344,444
Frankie Minoza	69	73	142	344,444

ISPS Handa Cup Satsukibare Senior Masters

Kyusyu Golf Club, Yahata Course, Fukuoka
Par 36-36–72; 6,935 yards

May 31-June 1
purse, ¥20,000,000

	SCORES		TOTAL	MONEY
Boonchu Ruangkit	71	70	141	¥3,600,000
Kiyoshi Maita	70	71	141	1,800,000
(Ruangkit defeated Maita on first playoff hole.)				
Masami Ito	70	72	142	1,100,000
Seiki Okuda	69	73	142	1,100,000
Gregory Meyer	75	68	143	618,000
Naonori Nakamura	73	70	143	618,000
Shinji Ikeuchi	71	72	143	618,000
Yuji Takagi	70	73	143	618,000
Kohki Idoki	68	75	143	618,000
Akihiro Ito	75	69	144	310,000
David Ishii	74	70	144	310,000
Seiji Ebihara	72	72	144	310,000
Anthony Gilligan	72	72	144	310,000
Ikuo Shirahama	71	73	144	310,000
Takashi Miyoshi	70	74	144	310,000
Tatsuya Shiraishi	69	75	144	310,000
Satoshi Higashi	74	71	145	215,142
Tatsuya Kaneko	74	71	145	215,142
Hirokazu Hagiwara	74	71	145	215,142
Yutaka Hagawa	73	72	145	215,142

	SCORES			TOTAL	MONEY
Kazuhiro Takami	73	72		145	215,142
Katsunari Takahashi	67	78		145	215,142
Jamniana Chitprasong	69	76		145	215,142

Kyoraku More Surprise Cup

Ryosen Golf Club, Mie
Par 36-36–72; 7,036 yards

June 7-9
purse, ¥65,000,000

	SCORES			TOTAL	MONEY
Kiyoshi Murota	67	66	71	204	¥13,000,000
Seiki Okuda	71	68	65	204	6,175,000
(Murota defeated Okuda on first playoff hole.)					
Gregory Meyer	67	69	69	205	4,225,000
Massy Kuramoto	68	69	69	206	2,704,000
Kiyoshi Maita	70	67	69	206	2,704,000
Kazuhiro Takami	68	72	67	207	2,015,000
Yoichi Shimizu	69	71	67	207	2,015,000
Tommy Nakajima	70	71	67	208	1,625,000
Minoru Hatsumi	67	73	69	209	1,478,750
Satoshi Higashi	69	71	69	209	1,478,750
Ikuo Shirahama	69	70	71	210	1,283,750
Hideki Kase	71	69	70	210	1,283,750
Atsushi Takamatsu	71	75	65	211	1,118,000
Boonchu Ruangkit	69	73	69	211	1,118,000
Yoshinori Mizumaki	69	78	65	212	1,001,000
Takeshi Sakiyama	73	71	69	213	806,000
Nobumitsu Yuhara	73	71	69	213	806,000
Kohki Idoki	74	68	71	213	806,000
Masami Ito	72	70	71	213	806,000
Yutaka Hagawa	69	72	72	213	806,000
Motomasa Aoki	70	69	74	213	806,000

Starts Senior

Kasama Golf Club, Ibaraki
Par 36-36–72; 6,936 yards

June 14-16
purse, ¥56,500,000

	SCORES			TOTAL	MONEY
Tommy Nakajima	69	65	64	198	¥14,000,000
Kiyoshi Murota	66	68	65	199	6,800,000
Katsunari Takahashi	70	64	68	202	3,285,000
Satoshi Higashi	65	68	69	202	3,285,000
Tsukasa Watanabe	70	67	66	203	1,900,000
Massy Kuramoto	69	68	67	204	1,420,750
Frankie Minoza	69	67	68	204	1,420,750
Boonchu Ruangkit	68	68	68	204	1,420,750
Yoshinori Mizumaki	71	65	68	204	1,420,750
Yoichi Shimizu	67	72	66	205	1,045,000
Hajime Meshiai	71	68	66	205	1,045,000
Kohki Idoki	61	71	73	205	1,045,000
Katsuyoshi Tomori	69	68	69	206	901,000
Ikuo Shirahama	67	69	70	206	901,000
Takeshi Sakiyama	72	68	67	207	743,000
Minoru Hatsumi	72	68	67	207	743,000
Kazuhiro Takami	71	69	67	207	743,000
Joe Ozaki	69	68	70	207	743,000

Women's Tours

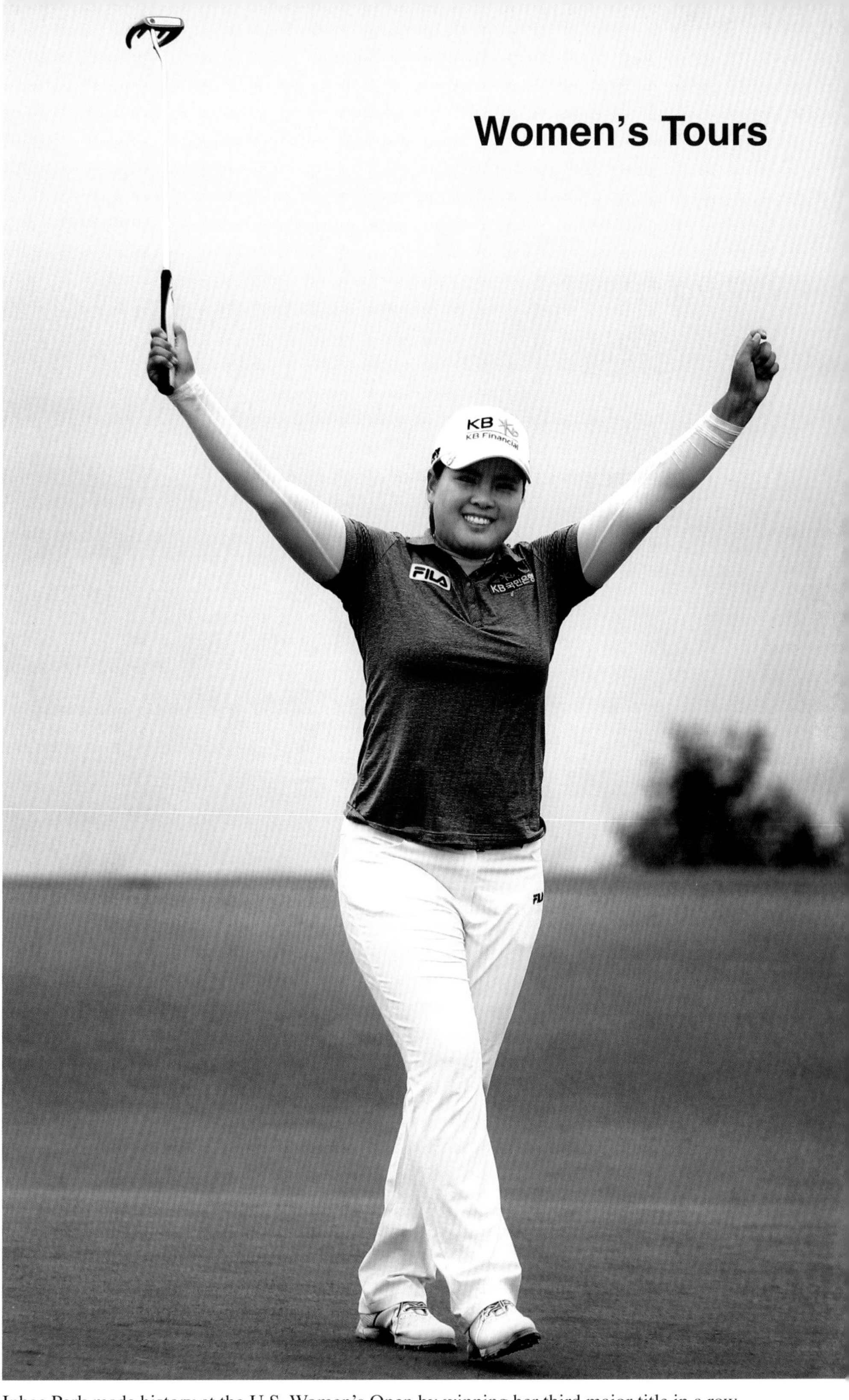

Al Bello/Getty Images

Inbee Park made history at the U.S. Women's Open by winning her third major title in a row.

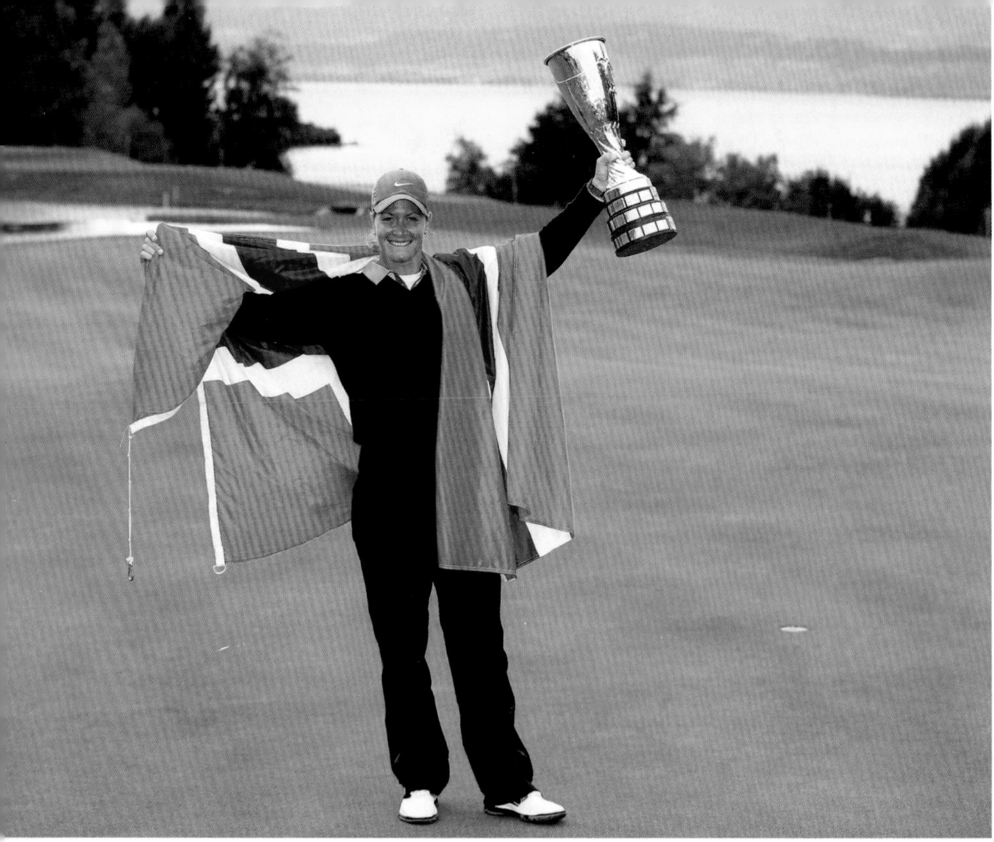

Richard Heathcote/Getty Images

Suzann Pettersen won the inaugural, but rain-shortened, Evian Championship.

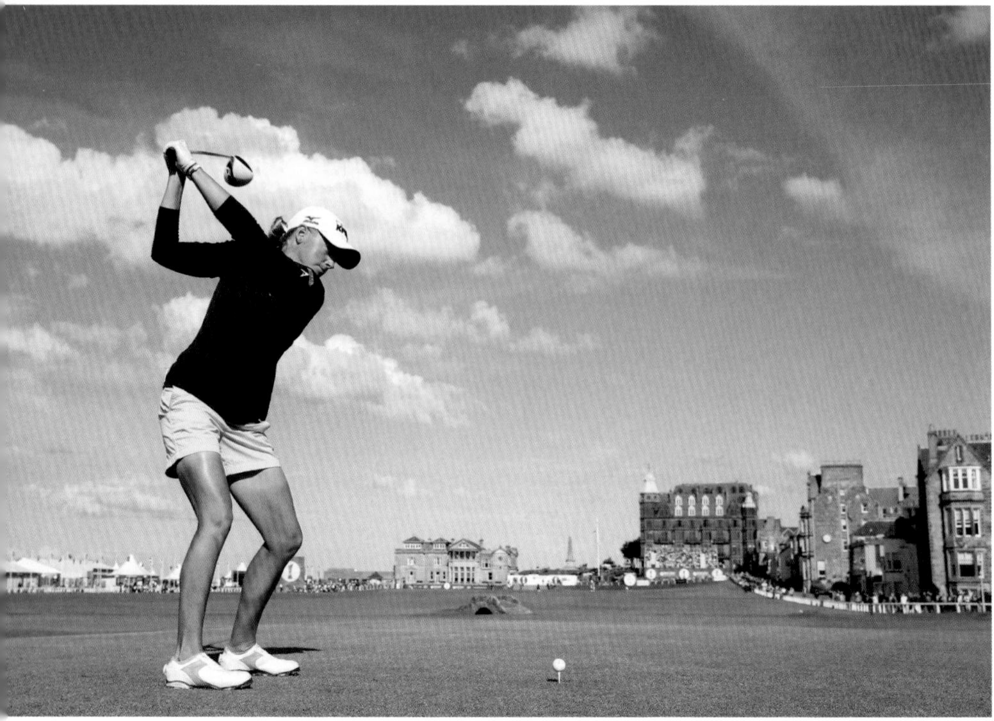

Warren Little/Getty Images

Stacy Lewis birdied the last two holes to win the Ricoh Women's British Open at St. Andrews.

Amateur Lydia Ko retained the Canadian Open.

Karrie Webb won the European Masters.

Shanshan Feng took the CME Titleholders.

So Yeon Ryu was runner-up at Kraft Nabisco.

Teenager Lexi Thompson won twice.

I.K. Kim was second at U.S. Women's Open.

Paula Creamer had six top-10 finishes.

Angela Stanford was 12th on LPGA list.

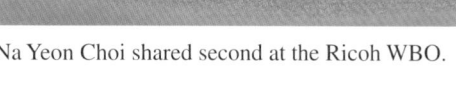

Lee-Anne Pace won three times on LET.

Na Yeon Choi shared second at the Ricoh WBO.

Azahara Munoz won once in France.

Beatriz Recari won twice in America.

Sakura Yokomine matched Morita's four wins.

Rikako Morita topped the JLPGA money list.

Yumiko Yoshida, Japan LPGA champion.

Senior Tours

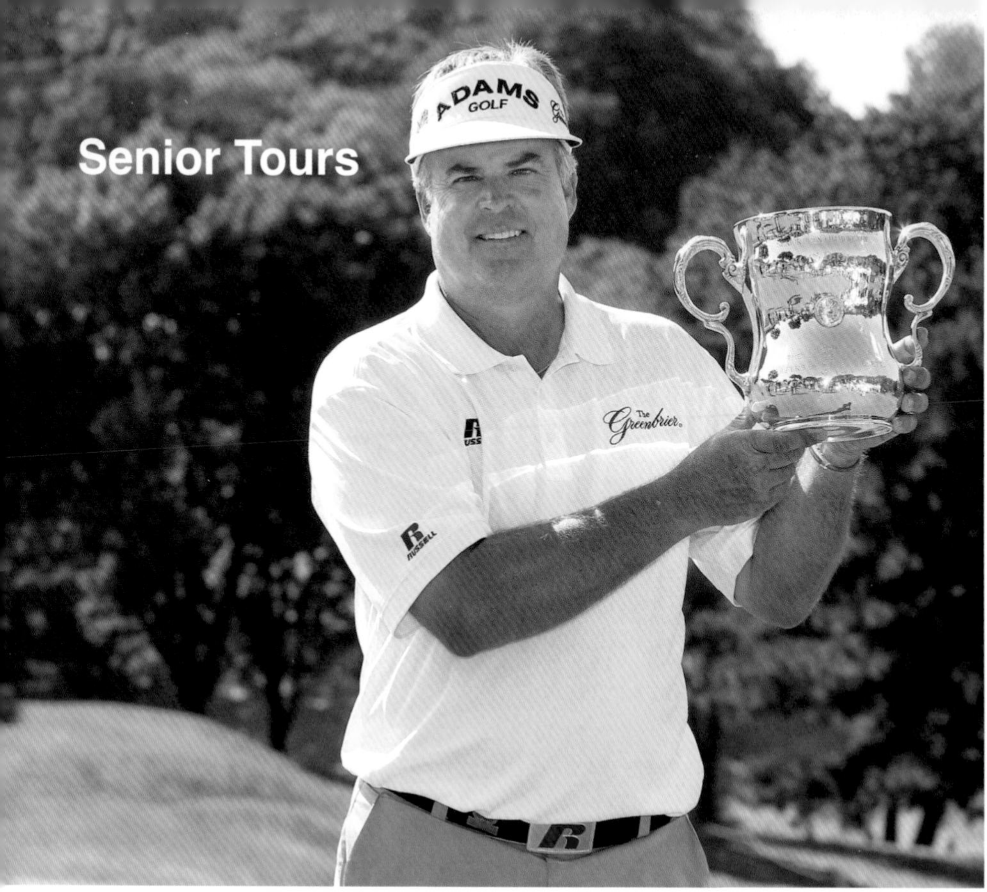

Scott Halleran/Getty Images

Kenny Perry won both the Senior Players title and the U.S. Senior Open.

Christian Petersen/Getty Images

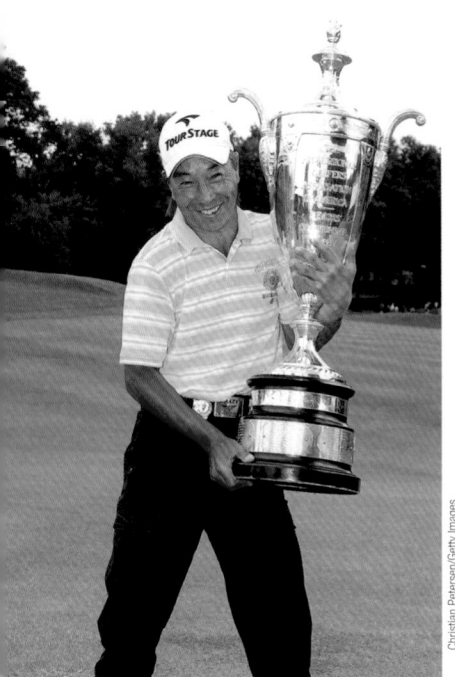

Kohki Idoki, Senior PGA champion.

Phil Inglis/Getty Images

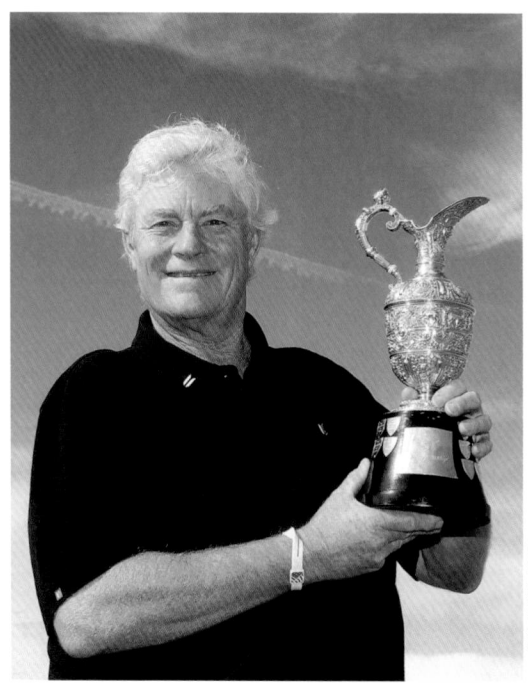

Mark Wiebe, Senior Open champion.

David Frost's two wins included the Tradition.

Fred Couples was the Schwab Cup champion.

Duffy Waldorf was second at the Senior Players.

Michael Allen won twice on the Champions Tour.

Bernhard Langer, No. 1 on the money list.

Paul Wesselingh was No. 1 in Europe.

Kirk Triplett claimed victory at Pebble Beach.

English Senior Open champion Steen Tinning.

Russ Cochran, SAS champion.

Simon P. Brown won the Russian Open.

	SCORES			TOTAL	MONEY
Seiji Ebihara	68	71	69	208	619,500
Seiki Okuda	66	70	72	208	619,500

ISPS Handa Cup Philanthropy Senior

Hakone Kohan Golf Club, Kanagawa
Par 71; 6,478 yards

July 11-12
purse, ¥20,000,000

	SCORES		TOTAL	MONEY
Satoshi Higashi	65	65	130	¥3,600,000
Nobumitsu Yuhara	68	65	133	1,800,000
Yoichi Sugawara	72	63	135	1,100,000
Kazuhiro Takami	68	67	135	1,100,000
Kazunari Matsunaga	67	69	136	840,000
Gohei Sato	70	67	137	603,333
Takeshi Sakiyama	70	67	137	603,333
Gregory Meyer	66	71	137	603,333
Tsukasa Watanabe	70	68	138	337,142
Seiji Ebihara	70	68	138	337,142
Tatsuya Shiraishi	70	68	138	337,142
Hiroshi Ueda	68	70	138	337,142
Kiyoshi Maita	68	70	138	337,142
Yutaka Hagawa	67	71	138	337,142
Takaaki Fukuzawa	67	71	138	337,142
Hiroyuki Iwabuchi	73	66	139	214,000
Norikazu Kawakami	71	68	139	214,000
Takashi Miyoshi	70	69	139	214,000
Shinji Ikeuchi	70	69	139	214,000
Yuji Takagi	69	70	139	214,000
Hatsuo Nakane	70	69	139	214,000
Tommy Nakajima	69	70	139	214,000
Kiyoshi Murota	68	71	139	214,000
Toshiaki Nakagawa	64	75	139	214,000
David Ishii	65	74	139	214,000

Fancl Classic

Susono Country Club, Susono, Shizuoka
Par 36-36–72; 6,865 yards

August 16-18
purse, ¥62,000,000

	SCORES			TOTAL	MONEY
Yutaka Hagawa	73	73	62	208	¥15,000,000
Kohki Idoki	71	69	68	208	6,900,000
(Hagawa defeated Idoki on first playoff hole.)					
Joe Ozaki	71	71	67	209	3,300,000
Gregory Meyer	67	70	72	209	3,300,000
Satoshi Higashi	69	72	69	210	2,400,000
Junji Kawase	68	73	70	211	1,680,000
Frankie Minoza	70	70	71	211	1,680,000
Hideki Kase	69	70	72	211	1,680,000
Jong-Duck Kim	71	66	74	211	1,680,000
Tsukasa Watanabe	67	72	73	212	1,149,000
Boonchu Ruangkit	66	72	74	212	1,149,000
Kazuhiro Takami	70	76	67	213	990,000
Ikuo Shirahama	70	72	71	213	990,000
Masami Ito	72	70	72	214	851,000
Norikazu Kawakami	68	73	73	214	851,000

	SCORES			TOTAL	MONEY
Kiyoshi Murota	75	66	73	214	851,000
Atsushi Takamatsu	73	74	68	215	720,000
Yoshinori Mizumaki	74	71	70	215	720,000
Seiki Okuda	74	69	72	215	720,000
Hiroshi Ueda	71	70	74	215	720,000
Takaaki Fukuzawa	72	69	74	215	720,000

ISPS Handa Cup Akibare-no Senior Masters

Hokkaido Brooks Country Club, Hokkaido
Par 36-36–72; 6,959 yards

August 30-31
purse, ¥20,000,000

	SCORES		TOTAL	MONEY
Frankie Minoza	69	70	139	¥3,600,000
Ikuo Shirahama	70	70	140	1,800,000
Seiji Ebihara	68	74	142	1,200,000
Seiki Okuda	72	71	143	920,000
Tsukasa Watanabe	71	72	143	920,000
Hideki Kase	72	72	144	530,000
Satoshi Higashi	71	73	144	530,000
Yoichi Shimizu	70	74	144	530,000
Tatsuya Shiraishi	70	74	144	530,000
Takeshi Sakiyama	68	76	144	530,000
Yasumasa Oikubo	75	70	145	326,666
Jong-Duck Kim	72	73	145	326,666
Ahmad Bateman	70	75	145	326,666
Yuji Takagi	75	71	146	246,666
Tatsuya Kaneko	75	71	146	246,666
Yoshio Fumiyama	71	75	146	246,666
Yoshitaka Yamamoto	71	75	146	246,666
Katsunari Takahashi	70	76	146	246,666
Hajime Meshiai	70	76	146	246,666
Masao Suzuki	74	73	147	194,666
Hiroshi Makino	73	74	147	194,666
Satoshi Oide	73	74	147	194,666
Hatsuo Nakane	72	75	147	194,666
Tamiya Aoki	74	73	147	194,666
Masanori Ushiyama	71	76	147	194,666
Hitoshi Kato	71	76	147	194,666
T.C. Chen	69	78	147	194,666
Masami Ito	69	78	147	194,666

Komatsu Open

Komatsu Country Club, Komatsu, Ishikawa
Par 36-36–72; 6,932 yards

September 12-14
purse, ¥60,000,000

	SCORES			TOTAL	MONEY
Kiyoshi Maita	67	69	68	204	¥12,000,000
Kazuhiro Takami	68	69	68	205	4,860,000
Seiki Okuda	71	65	69	205	4,860,000
Tsukasa Watanabe	72	71	63	206	2,535,000
Yutaka Hagawa	67	71	68	206	2,535,000
Satoshi Higashi	70	69	68	207	2,010,000
Kiyoshi Murota	72	67	69	208	1,559,000
Hideki Kase	68	69	71	208	1,559,000
Yoshinori Mizumaki	66	70	72	208	1,559,000

	SCORES			TOTAL	MONEY
Gregory Meyer	71	72	66	209	1,305,000
Frankie Minoza	72	71	66	209	1,305,000
Shinji Ikeuchi	71	67	72	210	1,179,000
Yuji Takagi	70	74	67	211	878,250
Takeshi Sakiyama	74	70	67	211	878,250
Yoichi Shimizu	66	76	69	211	878,250
Joe Ozaki	71	71	69	211	878,250
Anthony Gilligan	71	71	69	211	878,250
Norikazu Kawakami	70	70	71	211	878,250
Katsunari Takahashi	69	71	71	211	878,250
Ikuo Shirahama	66	73	72	211	878,250

Japan PGA Senior Championship

Summit Golf Club, Ibaraki
Par 36-36–72; 6,921 yards

October 10-13
purse, ¥50,000,000

	SCORES				TOTAL	MONEY
Tsukasa Watanabe	70	64	70	73	277	¥10,000,000
Kiyoshi Murota	69	69	74	65	277	5,000,000
(Watanabe defeated Murota on first playoff hole.)						
Boonchu Ruangkit	71	66	74	67	278	3,500,000
Frankie Minoza	70	73	68	71	282	2,500,000
Yoshinori Mizumaki	73	73	68	69	283	1,750,000
Gregory Meyer	68	72	69	74	283	1,750,000
Tatsuya Shiraishi	68	76	74	66	284	1,200,000
Seiki Okuda	72	73	71	68	284	1,200,000
Hideki Kase	72	71	71	70	284	1,200,000
Katsumi Nanjo	66	70	74	74	284	1,200,000
Hiroshi Ueda	71	75	68	71	285	1,000,000
Nobumasa Nakanishi	74	70	69	73	286	950,000
Joe Ozaki	71	73	72	71	287	850,000
Atsushi Takamatsu	74	69	71	73	287	850,000
Katsumi Kubo	70	71	73	73	287	850,000
Hitoshi Iwata	76	72	72	68	288	680,000
Masanori Ushiyama	75	70	73	70	288	680,000
Yasuaki Takashima	74	71	72	71	288	680,000
Massy Kuramoto	71	72	73	72	288	680,000
Ikuo Shirahama	72	72	74	71	289	536,000
Kiyoshi Maita	71	72	74	72	289	536,000
Nobumitsu Yuhara	71	73	72	73	289	536,000
Takeshi Sakiyama	71	73	72	73	289	536,000
David Ishii	71	72	72	74	289	536,000

Japan Senior Open Championship

Aso Iizuka Golf Club, Fukuoka
Par 36-36–72; 6,726 yards

October 31-November 3
purse, ¥80,000,000

	SCORES				TOTAL	MONEY
Kiyoshi Murota	66	73	67	73	279	¥16,000,000
Satoshi Higashi	69	74	72	67	282	8,800,000
Paul Wesselingh	71	67	74	71	283	5,080,000
Yoshinori Mizumaki	66	73	69	75	283	5,080,000
Barry Lane	68	73	68	75	284	3,080,000
Hideki Kase	68	75	68	73	284	3,080,000
Massy Kuramoto	71	73	75	67	286	2,400,000

	SCORES				TOTAL	MONEY
Ikuo Shirahama	73	75	71	68	287	1,690,000
Joe Ozaki	68	76	72	71	287	1,690,000
Tsukasa Watanabe	69	75	71	72	287	1,690,000
Katsunari Takahashi	71	75	69	72	287	1,690,000
Gregory Meyer	72	76	69	71	288	1,180,000
Masami Ito	73	70	69	76	288	1,180,000
Boonchu Ruangkit	72	73	72	72	289	944,000
Yutaka Hagawa	71	71	73	74	289	944,000
Jong-Duck Kim	74	71	70	74	289	944,000
Ahmad Bateman	72	73	73	73	291	840,000
Anthony Gilligan	73	73	71	75	292	800,000
Yoichi Sugawara	75	73	71	74	293	740,000
Shinji Ikeuchi	74	71	72	76	293	740,000

Fuji Film Senior Championship

The Country Club of Japan, Chiba
Par 36-36–72; 6,947 yards

November 7-9
purse, ¥70,000,000

	SCORES			TOTAL	MONEY
Seiki Okuda	67	69	68	204	¥14,000,000
Kiyoshi Murota	70	69	67	206	6,650,000
Nobuo Serizawa	70	68	69	207	4,900,000
Ahmad Bateman	69	73	68	210	3,500,000
Yoichi Shimizu	73	72	66	211	2,146,666
Yutaka Hagawa	69	75	67	211	2,146,666
Massy Kuramoto	69	72	70	211	2,146,666
Nobumitsu Yuhara	71	71	70	212	1,540,000
Shinji Ikeuchi	73	67	72	212	1,540,000
Frankie Minoza	72	69	72	213	1,330,000
Yoshinori Mizumaki	71	69	73	213	1,330,000
Takeshi Sakiyama	74	71	69	214	1,155,000
Nobumasa Nakanishi	72	72	70	214	1,155,000
Yuji Takagi	69	75	70	214	1,155,000
Barry Lane	71	72	71	214	1,155,000
Kiyoshi Maita	77	69	69	215	834,750
Anthony Gilligan	75	71	69	215	834,750
Tim Thelen	71	75	69	215	834,750
Ikuo Shirahama	74	70	71	215	834,750
Gregory Meyer	71	73	71	215	834,750
Jamniana Chitprasong	76	68	71	215	834,750
Masanori Ushiyama	74	68	73	215	834,750
Joe Ozaki	72	70	73	215	834,750

Iwasaki Shiratsuyu Senior

Ibusuki Golf Club, Kaimon Course, Kagoshima
Par 36-36–72; 6,923 yards

November 22-24
purse, ¥60,000,000

	SCORES			TOTAL	MONEY
Kiyoshi Murota	67	68	65	200	¥12,000,000
Tsukasa Watanabe	69	66	67	202	5,700,000
Jong-Duck Kim	70	66	67	203	3,900,000
Kohki Idoki	68	67	70	205	2,700,000
Gregory Meyer	71	72	65	208	2,280,000
Takeshi Sakiyama	71	72	66	209	1,700,000
Kiyoshi Maita	70	71	68	209	1,700,000

	SCORES			TOTAL	MONEY
Hideki Kase	71	70	68	209	1,700,000
Massy Kuramoto	70	70	70	210	1,335,000
Frankie Minoza	71	69	70	210	1,335,000
Satoshi Higashi	73	69	69	211	1,200,000
Yoichi Shimizu	73	70	69	212	1,140,000
Yutaka Hagawa	71	74	68	213	1,020,000
Ikuo Shirahama	70	72	71	213	1,020,000
Nobuo Serizawa	68	68	77	213	1,020,000
Hajime Meshiai	74	69	71	214	900,000
Hiroshi Makino	74	72	69	215	780,000
Minoru Hatsumi	71	73	71	215	780,000
Ahmad Bateman	70	70	75	215	780,000
Yuji Takagi	73	73	70	216	589,000
Yoshinori Mizumaki	71	74	71	216	589,000
Hiroshi Ueda	72	72	72	216	589,000
Boonchu Ruangkit	72	72	72	216	589,000
Joe Ozaki	72	71	73	216	589,000
Hatsuo Nakane	73	70	73	216	589,000